W9-BNI-948

THE OFFICIAL®
PRICE GUIDE TO

Records

THE OFFICIAL® PRICE GUIDE TO

Records

EIGHTH EDITION

JERRY OSBORNE

THE HOUSE OF COLLECTIBLES
New York, New York 10022

All of the information, including valuations, in this book has been compiled from the most reliable sources, and every effort has been made to eliminate errors and questionable data. Nevertheless the possibility of error, in a work of such immense scope, always exists. The publisher will not be held responsible for losses which may occur in the purchase, sale, or other transaction of items because of information contained herein. Readers who feel they have discovered errors are invited to *write* and inform us, so they may be corrected in subsequent editions. Those seeking further information on the topics covered in this book are advised to refer to the complete line of *Official Price Guides* published by The House of Collectibles.

CONTENTS

ACKNOWLEDGMENTS

The single, most important element in the updating and revision of a price and reference guide is reader input.

From dealers and collectors, based in every state and in nearly every country around the globe, we receive suggestions, additions, and corrections. Every single piece of data we acquire from readers is carefully reviewed, with all appropriate and usable information utilized in the next edition of this guide.

As enthusiastically as we encourage your contribution, let us equally encourage that when you write, you'll either type or print your name clearly. It's as frustrating for us to receive a mailing of useful information, and not be able to credit the sender, as it probably is for the sender to not see his or her name in the Acknowledgments section.

A vital reference source, which we regularly consult when editing record guides, is the "Record Research" series of books. For more information, write: Record Research, P.O. Box 200, Menomonee Falls, WI 53051.

In compiling this edition, information supplied by the people whose names appear below was of great importance. To these good folks, our deepest gratitude is extended. The amount of data and investment of time, of course, varied, but without each and every one of them this book would have been something less than it is.

Here then, alphabetically listed, is the board of advisors to this edition:

David Abbott
Joan Alk
Brian Barabe
David Block
Ed Broderick
Patricia L. Brown
Denise M. Brown
Bud Buschardt
Roger Bush

Michael Cain
Frank G. Castillo
Dennis Chiesa
Don Chiesa
Tom Christopher
Tom Clark
Robert B. Clere
Ron Cornelius
Perry Cox

Don Crawford
Dorothy R. Crouch
Tony Dee
Michael Devich
Jack Dey
Aeiko Doornbosch
Judy Ebner
Larry Finn
Rob Friedman
Arnie Ganem
Steve Goddard
Ed Godin
Gary Griffin
Bruce Hamilton
Dorothy Harris
Michael Harris
Kiersten Hartman
Lannie Hartman
Mike Haston
Nick Hatch
Dennis V. Hickey
Fred & Sally Huff
B.J. Hunter
Rick Hyman
Jon E. Johnson
George H. Kane
Norm Katuna
Gary Keltner
W. Frank Kramer
Milt Krantz
Gladys Lambert
George J. Lapata
Al La Soya
Warren Leech
Dottie Leesekamp
Craig Lewis
Joe Lindsay
Larry J. Linn
Steven R. Lounsbury
Sharon Maher

Paul F. Martens
Jim Martin
Tony Mastrianni
Dee Mc Vicker
Robert Miller
Tom Morley
Don Muller
Robert Overstreet
Bill Owens, Jr.
John Pacheco
Gareth Pawlowski
Richard Pearce
Victor Pearlin
John Andrew Pollock
Steve C. Plucker
Gilbert Quintero
Peter A. Rafter
Walker Reddick
Bob Rice
E.M. Rohner
Mrs. Richard K. Ross
Fred & Jenny Rozakis
William Sabath
John Sanidad
Frederick Schmid
Scrappy
Vicki Shaver
Pat Smith
Seth Strongin
Howard A. Sweet
Rod Sweetland
Dan Trebik
Vicki Trimble
Stan Vitek
Mike Waston
Bruce Wemett
Kurt L. White
Robert B. Williams
Mike Wolstein

THE OFFICIAL®
PRICE GUIDE TO

Records

INTRODUCTION

In determining what should be included in the revised edition of *The Official Price Guide to Records,* we tried to take into account factors that would make this guide applicable to the needs and interests of not only avid record connoisseurs and collectors, but also of individuals curious to get some idea of the value of all those records that they have bought over the years just because they liked them.

As an author and publisher team, we have put together some 35 record guides and reference books over the past 13 years, and as the result of our experience, we developed some basic criteria that provided the foundation for this guide. The first thing was to establish what records most people would own. The solution we came up with was to include those records made by *charted artists.* We began with the national pop/rock charts, published by *Billboard, Cash Box,* and other trade publications, but there has been so much crossover since the development of Rock & Roll in the early fifties, particularly between "black music" charts and the national surveys, that we have included these as well. Thus, whether it appeared on the national surveys as a *single,* an *extended play,* or a *long-playing* record (regardless of the format), and regardless of whether it was charted in the "race," "rhythm and blues," "soul," "disco and dance music," or even the "sepia" surveys, you'll find that record priced here.

Performers who regularly appear on other charts—such as "Jazz," "Adult Contemporary," "Country," "Gospel," "Classical," and so on—do occasionally cross over to the pop/rock and black charts, and all who have done so will be found here. However, these music forms are intrinsically diverse enough to deserve separate publications.

1

The second decision we made was to restrict the material covered to records made from 1950 through 1985—though there is some overlap here as well. Some records released prior to 1950 remained in the charts well into that year, just as some records made in 1985 stayed on the charts into 1986.

This time frame works well from an historical standpoint, because it was during this time that the single (45rpm) and long-playing record (33rpm) were becoming the rule of the industry, while the old 78rpm records were becoming a thing of the past. So, while there are some exceptions, which we'll talk about later, we do not include 78rpm records in this guide.

These guidelines are important to recognize from the start, for the country music fan, for example, might find it hard to understand why Hank Thompson is contained in this book while Mel Tillis is not. Similarly, the jazz buff might be bewildered by the fact that he will find Stan Getz here but not Dizzy Gillespie. And the reason is that while both Gillespie and Tillis have had numerous hits on their respective charts, they have not made it onto the charts we've covered. Hank Thompson and Stan Getz, on the other hand, did.

But just because we're listing all of the aforementioned charted artists, however, does not mean we are listing only the charted records made by those artists. Once an artist is included in the guide, we list and price *every known release* by that performer. Using Hank Thompson as an example, let's show just how comprehensive the coverage in this guide really is.

Despite his prominence in the country and western field, Hank had only one song appear on the pop and rock top 100 chart (1950 to present). In fact, that one 45rpm single only managed to reach #99, and stayed on the chart for only one week. Nevertheless, having qualified for this guide with just that one charted appearance, every known single, extended play, and long-playing album by Hank Thompson is documented and priced in this edition. The reason behind the extensiveness of this coverage is that if people like a performer well enough to put one of his records on the charts, they may own other records made by that artist, even if they didn't reach the pop hits survey.

So, *anyone* who made either pop/rock or "black music" surveys between 1950 and 1985 is included here, with not only the charted records, but their *entire* catalog. This should effectively cover most of the records to be found in the library of the average person.

If you are looking for information on any other recordings not covered in this book, just write the author (the address is featured later in the introduction). We'll even provide you with information on upcoming titles now in various stages of production!

RECORD COLLECTING GUIDELINES

HOW THE RECORD PRICES ARE DETERMINED

Record values featured in this edition were derived and averaged from a number of sources:

- The most important is a proven review program, to which many of the world's most active dealers and collectors regularly contribute additional listings and corrections to existing data. Price changes, in either direction, are often brought to our attention by these reviewers.
- Because of the expansive range of material covered in this guide, we consulted authorities in such diverse fields as rhythm and blues, jazz, big bands, soundtracks, original casts, non-rock, specific labels and time periods, certain artists, and an assortment of other specialists.
- As is the case with most types of collectibles, record prices can vary drastically from one region of the country to another. Having reviewers and annotators in every state, as well as around the world, enables us to present a realistic average of the highest and lowest current asking prices for an identically graded copy of a record.
- Other sources include: set sale lists, auction results, record convention trading, conversations with private collectors and retail locations around the country, and many hours on the telephone with our key advisors.

Another but more intangible thing we took into account in the price-averaging procedure was the availability of collectible records *beyond* the circle of collectors active in that particular field. For example, there are hundreds of records by artists like Frank Sinatra, Dean Martin, and Kay Starr that interested collectors would trade for at a certain level—for the purpose of this example, say $10.

Yet because so many of these records were sold, the very same discs might easily be found with dealers not interested in that area for, say, $2. This is quite a common occurrence. Our position in evaluating such records is to value them slightly above the lower value but significantly below the higher—in the case cited here, we would opt for a price range of $3 to $5, which reflects the ease with which a copy can be found and the seriousness of collectors who might buy or sell for prices even higher than the ones we've shown.

What it comes down to is knowing the various sources for collectible merchandise and, of course, shopping around. For instance, the best prices for the country, jazz, or non-rock records you're looking for may be at a shop specializing in rock & roll and rhythm and blues.

An important thing to note is that while the prices cited here were accurate at press time, the market can change drastically. At any time, there may be a major bulk discovery, quantity dumps, an artist's death, and "overnight success"—these all can affect availability, scarcity, and demand.

Since compiling record guides is a full-time occupation with this author, it is a continuous process of keeping track of the changes and discoveries that take place in the fascinating world of record collecting. Every tidbit of newly discovered information that affects the market will be reported in future editions of this guide. Obviously, then, we can never hear enough from interested collectors nor can we have too many reviewers. We wholeheartedly encourage readers to submit whatever information they feel would be useful in building a better guide or otherwise updating the present one. We have learned that there is simply no such thing as too much or too little information. So, please submit any suggested additions and/or corrections to:

Jerry Osborne
P.O. Box 255
Port Townsend, WA 98363

If writing is inconvenient, you may call the GUIDELINE: (206) 385-3029. During non-office hours, an answering machine will joyfully record whatever you have to say. *Collect calls will not be accepted.*

RECORD GRADING AND THE PRICE RANGE

The pricing shown in this edition represents the price range for *near-mint* condition copies of the records listed. Collectors and dealers agree that this is a tremendous improvement over the older method of listing an absolute value for "good," "very good," and "near-mint" records. It seems that people seldom looked at any price other than what was shown in the "near-mint" category in the first place, even if the record was only in "good" condition. So, while the range we offer is for "near-mint" records, it also allows for the countless variables that affect record pricing, of which condition is only one.

The standardized system of record grading endorsed by the House of Collectibles and used by sellers and buyers worldwide is as follows:

MINT: A "mint" item must be perfect—nothing less will do. Even brand-new purchases can easily be flawed in some manner and not qualify as "mint." To allow for tiny blemishes, the highest grade used in our record series is *near-mint.* An absolutely pristine mint item may carry a slight premium above the near-mint range shown in this guide.

NEAR MINT: These are generally the highest quality records in which record collectors deal. Neither the records nor the covers will be flawed except with the lightest scuff (even the scuffing a record might undergo as it is being put into the sleeve at the factory, while it won't affect its playability, can turn mint into near-mint). Naturally, because this tends to be the highest grade available, both the record and the cover should be without scratches, handwriting (such as a previous owner's name on the label or the jacket), or similar flaws.

VERY GOOD: Records in "very good" condition should have a minimum of visual or audible imperfections, which should not detract much from your enjoyment of owning them. Scuffs and scratches on either the record, the cover, or both should be slight.

GOOD: Practically speaking, the grade of "good" means that the item is good enough to fill a gap in your collection until a better copy comes along. Good condition merchandise will show definite signs of wear-and-tear, indicating that no protective care was given the record. Even so, records in good condition should play all the way through without skipping.

There are other, lesser scales of quality *(fair* and *poor),* but these apply to recordings that are generally undesirable, and so are not even considered here.

Naturally, most older records are going to be in something less than near-mint condition. It is very important to realize, then, that the "near-mint" price range listed in this guide is really a starting point in record appraising. Be honest about the actual condition. Apply the same standards to the records you trade or sell as you would to the records you buy. The following formula is a good rule of thumb in determining the value of lesser-quality records:

- For "very good" condition, figure the price to be 50% to 70% of the near-mint price.
- For "good" condition, figure about 10% to 20% of the near-mint price.

But remember that all the price guides in the world—no matter how authoritative—won't change the fact that true value is nothing more than what one person is willing to accept and another is willing to pay. In the end, it's always a matter of *scarcity and demand.* A recording, or anything else for that matter, can be 50 or 100 years old, but if no one wants it, the actual value will be minimal. Just because something is old does not necessarily mean that it is valuable. On the other hand, a recent release, perhaps just weeks old, can have exceptionally high value if it has already become scarce and is by an artist who is very much in demand. Old or new, the point here is that someone has to want it!

DEFINITION OF RECORD TYPE

We have already mentioned in passing the basic formats in which recordings are presented—the 45rpm single, the EP or "extended play" and the LP. The record companies have been particularly inconsistent in describing what constitutes an EP or an LP. For example, some labels call a 10-inch LP an "EP" if it has something less than the prescribed number of tracks found on their LPs. Others call an EP a "Little LP." A few companies have even created special names, associated only with their own labels, for the basic record formats. It can end up being extremely confusing.

For the purposes of this volume, we have adopted the following classifications of record formats:

- *"Singles:* 78rpm" are those that play at 78rpm! 78s are almost always 10-inch discs, but there have been some 7-inch 78rpm singles (none are listed in this edition). There are only a few 78rpm singles included here because they were vital to the documentation of an artist, and so would be conspicuous by their absence. Several (and of the over 100,000 records priced in this guide, we mean "several") 8-track tapes and cassettes appear for the same reasons.

- *"Singles:* 7-inch" can be *either* 45rpm or 33⅓ (always referred to simply as 33) rpm singles. If a 7-inch disc has more than one track on either side, then it's an EP. Singles are priced strictly as a disc, though there is a separate section devoted to picture sleeves (which are often traded separately). If we know that picture sleeves apply to a given artist's work, a separate grouping will appear for the label, price, and year of release. (Should the reader know of picture sleeves for performers that should have been in this edition but were overlooked, please advise us accordingly.)

- *"EPs:* 7-inch 33/45rpm" are 7-inch discs that have more than one track on one or both sides. Even if labeled an "EP" by the manufacturer, if it's pressed on a 10- or 12-inch disc, then it's an LP in our book. Unless otherwise noted, EPs are presumed to be accompanied by a standard, cardboard stock cover. Exceptions, such as EPs with paper sleeves or no sleeves at all, are designated as such when known.

- *"LPs:* 10/12-inch 33rpm" is self-explanatory. The only possible confusion that might exist here is with 12-inch singles. If it's 10 or 12 inches in diameter, and labeled, priced, and marketed as a 12-inch single ("maxi-single," etc.), then that's how you'll find it in our guide, regardless of its speed. Often, 12-inch singles will have a 12-inch die-cut cardboard sleeve or jacket, but many have covers that are exactly like LP jackets, with photos of the artist, etc. Unless otherwise noted, all LPs are presumed to be accompanied by their original covers, in a condition about equal to the disc. An appropriate adjustment in value should be made if the disc and the cover are not in equivalent condition.

All of the other record type headings used in this edition are self-explanatory.

CROSS-REFERENCING AND MULTIPLE ARTISTS

The cross-referencing in this edition is intended to provide the easiest possible method of discovering other artists with whom a particular performer has worked in any capacity. We've also tried to minimize in this edition the unnecessary duplication of cross-references. It is not necessary, for example, to list every group that Eric Clapton has played with under each and every one of those artists' entries. What we've done is simply indicate "Also see Eric Clapton," where you *will* find listed a complete reference to all the other entries in which he appears.

In future editions, we plan to provide brief explanatory notes describing why an artist is cross-referenced with another. Boots Randolph, for example, is cross-referenced to Elvis Presley because he was the saxophone player on many of Presley's recordings. Such bits of information may prove of interest to readers.

Some artists are featured in several entries, one right after the other, because they were involved in different duets and/or compilation releases. In such cases, the primary artist (whose section begins first) is cross-referenced *not* after each and every subsequent section but only after the last section in which the artist is involved. Thus, if you don't find the listing you're searching for right away, remember to check the sections that follow, as the artist may have been joined by someone else on that recording, leading us to list it in a separate section.

There are two formats for such listings in this guide. For example:

LEWIS, Jerry Lee, Carl Perkins & Johnny Cash

This type of heading refers to those recordings where the artists perform together on the same songs. Often, these releases will include solo tracks by one or all of the performers as well as those on which they collaborate.

LEWIS, Jerry Lee / Carl Perkins / Johnny Cash

This heading, with the names separated by the slash, indicates a release on which the artists perform, but *not* together—in other words, they perform by themselves on the same release. The maximum number of performers listed in this kind of heading here is four. Compilations containing five or more individual performers are, for the purposes of this edition, classified as "Various Artists" issues, and will be more closely documented in a separate guide in the future.

But whenever more than one act is featured on a record, cross-references appear for all of the artists on the disc, *provided* they were charted, and thus have their own entries in this guide. If you're interested in a record with a different artist on each side and you can't find it under one artist's name, be sure to look for it under the other artist's name.

PROMOTIONAL ISSUES

The separate documenting and pricing of promotional issues is, for the most part, unnecessary. Because most of the records released during the 35 years covered in this guide were simultaneously pressed for promotional purposes, a separate listing of them would potentially double the size of an already large book. We've chosen instead to list promotional copies separately when we know that a different price is consistently asked for them. Promos of everyday releases will fall into the same range given for store stock copies. Slight premiums may be asked for promos with different versions of the material (longer, shorter, differently mixed, and so on), even though the artist may not be particularly hot in the collectors' marketplace.

When identifying a "Promotional issue," we are usually describing a record with a special promotional label or sleeve (marked "Not For Sale," "Dee Jay Copy," etc.) and not a "designate promo." Designate promos are identical with commercial releases, except that they have been rubber- or mechanically stamped, stickered, written on by hand, or in some way altered to accommodate their use for promotional purposes. There are very few designate promos listed here, and those that are (such as in the Presley section) are clearly identified as such.

COLORED VINYL PRESSINGS

Records that we know exist on both black vinyl as well as on colored vinyl (the phrase used regardless of whether it's vinyl or polystyrene) are listed separately, since there is usually a value difference to be dealt with. However, some colored vinyl releases were never pressed on black vinyl, and there is no way, other than colored vinyl, to have the record. Therefore, it may not be specifically noted as being on colored vinyl.

FOREIGN RELEASES

This edition, by design, lists only U.S. releases. There is, however, an occasional exception. A handful of records that were widely distributed in the United States or sold via widespread U.S. advertising, even though manufactured outside of this country, are included.

The millions of releases from Canada, Europe, and elsewhere certainly have collector value to both fans in those countries as well as to many stateside collectors. Unfortunately, the tremendous volume of material and the variances in pricing make it impossible to consider documenting such foreign products.

BOOTLEG AND COUNTERFEIT RECORDS

Bootleg and counterfeit records are not intended to be listed in this guide, though an occasional pirate release may have slipped by us.

For the record, a bootleg recording is one illegally manufactured, usually containing material that has not previously appeared in a legitimate form. Often a bootlegger, with the serious collector in mind, will package previously issued tracks that have achieved some degree of value or scarcity. If the material is easily and legally available, the bootlegger would otherwise have nothing to gain.

The counterfeit record is one manufactured as close as possible in sound and appearance to the source disc from which it was taken. Not all counterfeits were created to fool an unsuspecting buyer, but some were. Many were designated in some way—usually a slight marking or variance—so as to distinguish them from the original. Such a fake record will only fill the gap in the collection until the real thing comes along.

With both bootleg and counterfeit records, the appropriate and deserving recipients of royalties are, of course, denied remuneration for their works.

Since most of the world's valuable records have been counterfeited, it is always a good idea to consult with an expert when there is any doubt. The trained eye can usually spot a fake.

This does not mean that "unauthorized" releases do not appear in this guide. There are many legitimate releases that are unauthorized by one entity or another. But these are not necessarily bootlegs or counterfeits; "unauthorized" does not mean illegal.

GROUP NAMES AND PERSONNEL

One chronic problem that we'll probably never cure completely is the many instances in which groups using the exact same name are lumped together with other groups, even though they are completely different and share none of the same personnel.

The listing sequence for artists using the same name is chronological. Thus, the ABC recording group, Silk, who had a release in 1969, is listed before the Philadelphia International group of the same name who first recorded in 1979.

As for the changes of personnel within a single group, we've tried, whenever possible, to list the original line-up first, with the lead singer coming at the top of the list. But still, it might be confusing for the reader to see 12 different members making up The Five Satins.

If you can fill in the members' names on any groups where we don't list that information, we'll see that it gets into our next edition.

As more and more groups are named in future editions, there will be added cross-referencing to reflect the constant shuffle of performers from one group to another.

PARENTHETICAL NOTES

These notes include:

1. Complete artist and group or artist and band names. Some artists were shown as being with one group on a few releases and with another on other issues. We've tried to present the information as it appeared on the record label.
2. Variations of spelling or names for the same artist. With some, it's convenient to have everything in one section. However, when it is illogical to combine listings, perhaps because the performer was popular under more than one name (for example, Johnny Cymbal and Derek), you'll find individual sections for each name, complete with cross-references. When you see "Kenneth Rogers" in parentheses, we are certainly not trying to tell you that Kenneth is Kenny Rogers' real name! Rather, we're letting you know that on some releases he was shown as Kenneth instead of Kenny Rogers.
3. Names of guest performers who may or may not have been credited on the actual label, but who we feel you should know about, will be found in parentheses.
4. Real names of artists, but only when we feel they need to be given. We have no desire to give the real names of everyone who has recorded under a pseudonym, but there are times when you do need this information, particularly when they have also recorded under their real name or when more than one person has recorded under the same pseudonym. To help sort things, we will, when known, give the real name of someone who has recorded under a nom de guerre, such as Guitar Slim (Johnny Winter).

OLDIES LABELS AND REISSUES

An effort has been made to include "oldies" or reissue records in the guide. Admittedly, most of the reissues of this type are of no value beyond their current retail cost, but some are. Look at the early RCA Victor Gold Standard Series Elvis releases, for example. Once in a blue moon, a tune will turn up in true stereo on a reissue label that previously was hard to find in stereo (such as "I Ran All the Way Home," on Collectables). Otherwise, it's just our desire to report comprehensively on all artists that prompted the listing of reissues. You may be surprised to find out just how much stuff is available in reissue form. The one thing we were not able to devote much time to in this edition (because of the endless numbering systems used by the different labels) was reissues of records by the same label that had the original release. We felt that this was the least important area of reissues at this time, since almost all labels clearly identify their oldies series in some manner so as to eliminate any possibility of confusing them with originals.

If there are reissues that are issued and numbered as part of a label's standard release series that are not documented in this edition, please tell us about them.

ABOUT THE NEW FORMAT

This new record price guide format is one that was carefully devised to allow for an enormous amount of record pricing information. In this edition, you'll find documentation and pricing information on over 100,000 records by over 7,700 artists. This arrangement was introduced and tested a few years ago in an earlier Osborne record guide and has been developed into a successful means of presenting a great deal of information in convenient, easy-to-carry format.

The headings are alphabetical, by *artist,* and then are broken down still further by *label.* Because of the number of recordings we're dealing with here, the reader may be confused by the fact that we generally do not refer to recordings by name; indeed, you may find that sometimes we don't even refer to a specific catalog number. To economize on space, we generally refer to an artist's recordings in *catalog series.* Since these typically (though not always) occur in chronological order of appearance, with the earliest release in the series having the lowest catalog number, we also include the *years of issue* together. And because these releases, grouped together by format (in the main, 45rpm, EP, or LP), tend to be of equivalent value, the last entry involves *price range.*

It might seem confusing, but once you get used to the format, you'll find it easy and functional, particularly when using the guide along with an artist or label discography. Let's look at a condensed entry to see what kinds of information *may* be found.

MIRACLES, The{1} (Smokey Robinson & The Miracles; The Miracles Featuring Bill Smokey Robinson){2}

Singles: 7-inch {3}

CHESS{4} (119; "Bad Girl"){5}: *84*{6} . . . . **1–3**{7}

CHESS (1768; "All I Want"): *60* **8–10**

END: *59* **275–300**

(. . .)

LPs: 10/12-Inch 33rpm

COLUMBIA: *77–78* **8–10**

TAMLA (220; "Hi! We're the Miracles"): *61* **45–50**

TAMLA (267 through 297): *65–69* **15–20**

Members: William "Smokey" Robinson; Pete Moore; Bobby Rogers; Ron White; Claudette Rogers{8}

Also see ROBINSON, Smokey{9}

Also see RON & BILL

{1} Refers to the section heading, {2} alternate or variation of name(s) for the artist. {3} Indicates the format of the releases. {4} Indicates the label. {5} Indicates either the catalog reference or a specific title. {6} Denotes the year/s of release for the recording/s, while {7} gives the price range for near-mint copies. {8} Refers to the membership of the group (when known) and {9} provides the cross-references. It's important to remember that a single line of information may refer to more than one release (for instance, "TAMLA (267 through 297) 65–69 15–20" refers to all The Miracles' albums released on Tamla between 1965 and 1969).

One facet of our approach that was of great concern was the artist who had one or more records of a value indicated for a particular label or series, but who also had one release (or more) that is a notable exception. Every effort has been to document such exceptions separately; however, the sheer bulk of information contained in this guide makes us suspicious that there may be some we have missed. If you know of any, let us know about them.

USING THIS GUIDE—ADDITIONAL POINTS

The alphabetization used makes finding any artist or label easy, but a few guidelines may speed the process along for you:

- Names that are simply letters (and are not intended to be pronounced as a word) are found at the beginning of the listings under each letter of the alphabet (i.e., ABC, AC-DC, GQ, SSQ, etc.). The same rule applies to acronyms and to initials (G.T.O., MFSB, etc.). When known, we'll parenthetically tell you what the abbreviation represents.
- Names are listed in the alphabetical order of the first word. This means you'll find "Rock Squad" before "Rocket." Hyphenated words are looked upon as whole words (i.e., Mello-Kings is treated the same as Mellokings). Proper nouns that are divided (i.e., McCartney, De Vorzon, El Dorados, etc.) are alphabetically treated as if they were a one-word name.
- Possessive names precede similarly spelled names that are not possessive. For example, Knight's would be found before Knights.
- With record labels, the listings appear in alpha/ numeric/ chronological order. Prefixes are generally not used (they make it more difficult to scan the numbers) unless it is necessary for identification. With some artists (Beatles, Elvis, etc.) it is essential at times because of the constant reissues of their work.
- Some sections make use of the label prefixes to sort things out, but most use a number series. If the numbers are duplicated by the label, or if any of a variety of confusing similarities exist, we resort to the prefixes for clarity.
- Any time we find that the monaural or the stereo issue of a particular record is in need of a separate listing (because there is a price difference for one that is outside the boundaries of the price range of the other), we provide it. If there is only one listing, this means that we have no reason to believe there is that much difference between the two forms. Of course, a little application of the known variables will help in this area. For example, if the range is $20 to $30 for a 1963 LP and you know that the stereo issue is in true stereo (and *not* "reprocessed for stereo, electronic stereo, or stereo-enhanced") it's safe to place the mono at the lower end of the range ($20 to $25) and the stereo at the high end ($25 to $30). The calculation may be reversed for the late sixties and for most electronically reprocessed issues.

The year or years of release given are believed to be accurate. In some cases, the record may have been released in one year and debuted on the nation's music charts the following year. This is particularly common for December issues.

When multiple years are indicated, such as "64–66," it means the records described on that line spanned the years 1964 through 1966. They may have had one issue in 1964 and another in 1966, or may have had eight releases during those years. It *does not* mean that we believe the release came out sometime between 1964 and 1966.

As for the photographs of performers interspersed throughout the guide, the captions provided include the following information: the artist's name, number of charted singles (years spanned), and number of charted LPs (years spanned). Charted records here include those that reached either the pop/rock or the black music charts.

WHAT TO EXPECT WHEN SELLING YOUR RECORDS TO A DEALER

As nearly everyone in the hobby knows, there is a notable difference between the prices reported in this guide and the prices that one can expect a dealer to pay when buying records for resale.

Unless a dealer is buying for a personal collection and without thoughts of resale, he or she is simply not in a position to pay full price. Dealers work on a percentage basis, largely determined by the total dollar investment, quality, and quantity of material offered, as well as the general financial condition and inventory of the dealer at the time.

Another very important consideration is the length of time it will take the dealer to recover at least the amount of the original investment. The quicker the demand for the stock and the better the condition, the quicker the return and, therefore, the greater the percentage that can be paid. Our experience has shown that, day in and day out, most dealers will pay from 25% to 50% of "guide" prices. And that's assuming they are planning to resell at "guide" prices. If they traditionally sell below guide, that will be reflected in what they can pay for stock.

If you have records to sell, it would be wise to check with several shops. In doing so, you'll begin to get a good idea of the value of your collection to a dealer.

Consult the Buyer-Seller Directory in this edition for the names of many dealers who not only might be interested in buying, but from whom many collectible records are available for purchase.

CONCLUDING THOUGHTS

The purpose of this guide is to report as accurately as possible the most recent prices asked and paid for records within the area of its coverage. There are two key words here that deserve emphasis: *guide* and *report.*

We cannot stress enough that this book is only a guide! There always have and always will be instances of records selling well above and well below the prices shown within these pages. These extremes are recognized in the final averaging process, but it's still important to understand that just because we've reported a 30-year-old record as having a $25–$50 near-mint value, it doesn't mean that a collector of that material should be hesitant to pay $75 for it. How badly he or she wants it and how often it's possible to purchase it *at any price* should be the prime factors to consider, not the fact that we last reported it at a lower price. Of course, we'd like to know about sales of this sort so that the next edition can reflect the new pricing information.

We also encourage record companies, artist management organizations, talent agencies, and performers to make certain that we are on the active mailing list for new release information, press releases, bios, publicity photos, and anything pertaining to recordings.

There is an avalanche of helpful information in this guide to aid the collector in determining what is valuable and what may not be worth fooling with, but the wise fan will also keep abreast of current trends and news through the pages of fanzines and publications devoted to their favorite forms of music.

BUYERS-SELLERS DIRECTORY

After you have learned the current value of your records, you may wish to offer them for sale. Just as likely, you may decide you would like to purchase out-of-print records for your collection.

Either way, I recommend you do two things:

First, request a free sample copy of DISCoveries, the record collector's tabloid publication where buyers and sellers get together each month. From the pages of DISCoveries, you'll get an idea of what's being traded and the prices being asked for records and other music collectibles. (DISCoveries, P.O. Box 58, Annandale, MN 55302.)

Second, listed below is a random sampling of well-known collectors and dealers, any one of which may be just the right contact to assist you. In addition, a handful of names offering other services to the record hobby are provided. For your convenience, at least one source in nearly every state is included.

Ace-High Records
5708 Winona Ave.
Des Moines, IA 50312

Amber's Records
N. 21 Skipworth
Spokane, WA 99206
(509) 926–0113

Arc Promotions
(317) 747–7360

Not a record dealer, but responsible for many record conventions. Could give you the dates and times of a convention near you.

Aural Fixations
130 Glen Ave.
Berlin, NH 03570

Bagatelle Records
140 E. Third St.
Long Beach, CA 90802
(213) 432–7534

Leon Bjella
1918 16th St.
South Fargo, ND 58103
(701) 235–1410

Bluesland Oldies Record Shop
P.O. Box 1247
Daphne, AL 36526
(205) 626–0272

Bob's Record Rack
P.O. Box 500
Ozark, MO 65721
(417) 485–7186

John Bosco
P.O. Box 361
Levittown, NY 11756

Michael Briggs
P.O. Box 5544
Mill Valley, CA 94942

The Collector's Sound
P.O. Box 48154
Los Angeles, CA 90048
(818) 990–1847

Colleen's Collectables
1482 Oakland Park
Columbus, OH 43224
(614) 261–1585

Connoisseur's Groovy Originals
1815 B East Park Row
Arlington, TX 76010

Disc Collector
P.O. Box 315
Cheswold, DE 19936

DISCoveries
P.O. Box 58
Annandale, MN 55302
Monthly publication for record buyers
and sellers.

Ellis Audiotics
247 Garfield–3A
Brooklyn, NY 11215
(718) 662–0923

Elvis Specialties
P.O. Box 504
Pasadena, MD 21122
(301) 437–2278

Frank G. Castillo
1182 Rancho Ave.
Colton, CA 92324
(714) 824–2292

Frank Cavaliere
Forest Haven 5/3A
Carmel, NY 10512
(914) 225–4453

Terry Gesten
16386 Drake Rd.
Strongsville, OH 44136

Grassroot Record Exchanger
2717 N. 24th St.
Phoenix, AZ 85034

Bernie Greene
P.O. Box 14084
Portland, OR 97214
(503) 232–5964

P.D. Hamlin
P.O. Box 1981
Susanville, CA 96130
(916) 257–0596

Paul Hollister
P.O. Box 19952
San Diego, CA 92119
(619) 463–3978

Hula Rock Records
840 Kawaiahao
Honolulu, HI 96813

Igloo Graffiti
P.O. Box 73678
Fairbanks, AK 99707
(907) 456–3227

JLO West
P.O. Box 8892
Universal City, CA 91608

Jellyroll Productions
P.O. Box 255
Port Townsend, WA 98363
(206) 385-3029
Offering an assortment of publications
for the record collector.

LP Larry
P.O. Box 349
Bay Ridge Station
Brooklyn, NY 11220

Garry Larson
1147 E. Broadway–Ste. 136
Glendale, CA 91205

Memory Lane Out-of-Print Records
1940 E. University Dr.
Tempe, AZ 85281
(602) 968-1512

Midnight Records
P.O. Box 390
Old Chelsea Station
New York, NY 10011
(212) 675-2768

Mighty John's
9 Birchwood Blvd.
Brewer, ME 04412
(207) 989-3635

Mr. Doug Rockin' Records
P.O. Box 44011
Omaha, NE 68144

Craig Moerer
P.O. Box 19231
Portland, OR 97219

Mole's CDX
2497 E. Main St.
Columbus, OH 43209
(614) 231-1701

Moskal Records
P.O. Box 442
Holyoke, MA 01041

Bob Murret
3612 Lyndell Dr.
Chalmette, LA 70043

National Record Collectors
P.O. Box 1058
Florence, AL 35631

Richard Ochoa
1206 N. 15th St.
Coeur d'Alene, ID 83814
(208) 664-4549

Victor Pearlin
P.O. Box 199, Greendale Station
Worcester, MA 01606

Bob Pegg
8420 S. 16th St.
Tacoma, WA 98465
(206) 564-2846

Pellett Records
42 Park Pl.
Morristown, NJ
(201) 540-0188

Prestige Records
2634 Linwood Dr.
Smyrna, GA 30080

Randy's Record Shop
157 E. 900 South
Salt Lake City, UT 84111
(801) 532-4413

Rare Records
3145 Poplar Ave.
Memphis, TN 38111
(901) 327-RARE

Record Castle
336 Loney St.
Philadelphia, PA 19111
(215) 745-4151

Record Exchange
5840 Hampton
St. Louis, MO 63109

Record Junction
9717 Chatfield
Houston, TX 77025

Record Showcase
228 Redbank Rd.
Goose Creek, SC 29445
(803) 553–1991

Record Stop
13 E. Hartsdale Ave.
Hartsdale, NY 10530

Roanoke's Record Room
P.O. Box 2445
Roanoke, VA 24010
(703) 343–9570

Cliff Robnett
7804 NW 27th
Bethany, OK 73008
(405) 787–6703

Rockaway Records
2506 N. Glendale Blvd.
Los Angeles, CA 90039
(213) 664–2135

Salty's Record Attic
1326 9th St.
Modesto, CA 95354
(209) 527–4010

Set Sail Records
3331 Foxridge Dr.
Tampa, FL 33618
(813) 969–2299

Sidestreet Records
P.O. Box 7028
Burbank, CA 91510
(213) 874–9319

Specialty Records
3452 Park Ave.
Memphis, TN 38111
(901) 324–1757

Joe Thomas
2530 Harry Wurzbach–28D
San Antonio, TX 78209

Tracks in Wax Records
4741 N. Central Ave.
Phoenix, AZ 85012
(602) 274–2660

Very English & Rolling Stone
P.O. Box 7061
Lancaster, PA 17604

Stan Vitek
180 Manchester Ave.
Youngstown, OH 44509

Wild Records
906 Baltier St.
St. Paul, MN 55117

Worldwide Records
P.O. Box 2905
Southfield, MI 48037
(313) 626–0216

Wreckords
P.O. Box 3164
Burnsville, MN 55337

RECORD LISTINGS

A

**A FLOCK OF SEAGULLS: see
FLOCK OF SEAGULLS, A**

**A TASTE OF HONEY: see TASTE
OF HONEY, A**

A's, The   *Price Range*
   Singles: 7-Inch
ARISTA: *79* **$1–3**
   LPs: 10/12-Inch 33rpm
ARISTA: *79–81*. **5–8**
 Members: Richard Bush; Rick DiFonzo; Michael Snyder; Terry Bortman; Rocco Nolte.

A.B. SKHY
   Singles: 7-Inch
MGM: *69–70*. **2–4**
   LPs: 10/12-Inch 33rpm
MGM: *69–70*. **10–12**

ABC
   Singles: 12-Inch 33/45rpm
MERCURY: *83–85*. **4–6**
   Singles: 7-Inch
MERCURY: *82–85*. **1–3**
   LPs: 10/12-Inch 33rpm
MERCURY: *82–85*. **5–8**

AC-DC   *Price Range*
   Singles: 7-Inch
ATCO: *77* **$2–4**
ATLANTIC: *77–85* **1–3**
   Picture Sleeves
ATLANTIC: *81* . . . . **INC**
   LPs: 10/12-Inch 33rpm
ATCO: *76–77*. **8–12**
ATLANTIC: *77–85* **5–10**
 Members: Bonn Scott; Angus Young; Malcomb Young; Phil Rudd; Cliff Williams; Brian Johnson.

ADC BAND, The
   Singles: 7-Inch
COTILLION: *78–82*. **1–3**
   LPs: 10/12-Inch 33rpm
COTILLION: *78–82*. **5–8**
 Members: Michael Judkins; Arwell Mathew, Jr; Audrey Mathew; Mark Patterson.

AM-FM
   Singles: 7-Inch
DAKAR: *82* **1–3**

APB
   Singles: 12-Inch 33/45rpm
IMPORT: *83*. **4–6**
SLEEPING BAG: *84*. **4–6**
   Singles: 7-Inch
IMPORT: *83*. **1–3**
   LPs: 10/12-Inch 33rpm
MCA: *83* **5–8**

Price Range

AWB: see AVERAGE WHITE BAND, The

AALON
Singles: 7-Inch
ARISTA: 77 .... $1–3
LPs: 10/12-Inch 33rpm
ARISTA: 77 5–8

ABACO DREAM
Singles: 7-Inch
A&M: 69–70 2–4

ABBA
Singles: 12-Inch 33/45rpm
ATLANTIC: 77–79 4–6
Singles: 7-Inch
ATLANTIC: 75–82 2–4
Picture Sleeves
ATLANTIC: 77–81 2–4
LPs: 10/12-Inch 33rpm
ATLANTIC: 74–82 8–10
  Members: Anni-frid Lyngstad; Bjorn Ulvaeus;
  Benny Andersson; Agnetha Faltskog.
  Also see FALTSKOG, Agnetha
  Also see FRIDA

ABBA / Spinners / Firefall / England Dan & John Ford Coley
EPs: 7-Inch 33/45rpm
WARNER SPECIAL
  PRODUCTS: 78 5–10
  (Coca-Cola/Burger King promotional issue. Is-
  sued with paper sleeve.)
  Also see ABBA
  Also see ENGLAND DAN & JOHN FORD
  COLEY
  Also see FIREFALL
  Also see SPINNERS, The

ABBEY TAVERN SINGERS, The
Singles: 7-Inch
HBR: 66 2–4

ABBOTT, Billy, & The Jewels
Singles: 7-Inch
PARKWAY: 63–64 3–5

ABRAMS, Colonel
Singles: 12-Inch 33/45rpm
MCA: 85 4–6
STREETWISE: 84 4–6

Price Range

Singles: 7-Inch
MCA: 85 .... $1–3
STREETWISE: 84 1–3

ABRAMS, Miss, & The Strawberry Point School Third Grade Class
Singles: 7-Inch
REPRISE: 70 1–3
Picture Sleeves
REPRISE: 70 1–3

ACCENTS, The (Featuring Robert Draper, Jr.)
Singles: 7-Inch
BRUNSWICK (55100;
  "Wiggle Wiggle"): 58 5–8
BRUNSWICK (55123;
  "Ching A Ling"): 58–59 8–10
CORAL: 59 8–10
JUBILEE: 59 4–6

ACCEPT
LPs: 10/12-Inch 33rpm
PVC: 83 5–8
PASSPORT: 81 6–10
PORTRAIT: 84–85 5–8

ACE
Singles: 7-Inch
ABC: 76–78 1–3
ANCHOR: 75–77 2–4
LPs: 10/12-Inch 33rpm
ANCHOR: 75–77 8–10
  Members: Paul Carrack; Fran Byrne; Tex
  Comer; Phil Harris; Bam King; Jon Woodhead.
  Also see CARRACK, Paul

ACE, Buddy
Singles: 7-Inch
DUKE: 60–69 3–5
FIDELITY: 59 4–6
PAULA: 70–72 2–4

ACE, Johnny (Johnny Ace & The Beale Streeters)
Singles: 7-Inch
ABC: 73 1–3
DUKE: 52–55 6–10
FLAIR: 53 30–35
MCA: 84 1–3

Price Range

Price Range

EPs: 7-Inch 33/45rpm
DUKE (71; "Memorial
  Album"): *63* **$12–15**
  (Jukebox issue only.)
DUKE (80; "Memorial
  Album"): *55* **25–30**
DUKE (81; "Tribute
  Album"): *55* **25–30**

LPs: 10/12-Inch 33rpm
DUKE (70; "Memorial
  Album"): *55* **125–175**
  (10-Inch LP.)
DUKE (71; "Memorial
  Album"): *56* **60–75**
  (No playing card shown on cover.)
DUKE (71; "Memorial
  Album"): *61* **30–35**
  (Playing card shown on cover.)
DUKE (71; "Memorial
  Album"): *74* **8–10**
  (With an "X" prefix.)
MCA: *83* **4–6**

ACE SPECTRUM
Singles: 7-Inch
ATLANTIC: *74–76* **2–4**

LPs: 10/12-Inch 33rpm
ATLANTIC: *74–76* **8–10**

ACKLES, David
Singles: 7-Inch
ELEKTRA: *68–72* **2–4**

LPs: 10/12-Inch 33rpm
COLUMBIA: *73* **5–10**
ELEKTRA: *69–72* **8–12**

ACKLIN, Barbara
Singles: 7-Inch
BRUNSWICK: *67–73* **2–4**
CAPITOL: *74–75* **2–3**
ERIC: *83* **1–3**

Picture Sleeves
BRUNSWICK: *68* **2–4**

LPs: 10/12-Inch 33rpm
BRUNSWICK: *68–71* **8–12**
CAPITOL: *75* **5–8**
  Also see CHANDLER, Gene, & Barbara Ac-
  klin

ACT I
Singles: 7-Inch
SPRING: *73–74* **$2–4**
LPs: 10/12-Inch 33rpm
SPRING: *74* **5–8**

AD LIBS, The
Singles: 7-Inch
A.G.P: *66* **3–5**
BLUE CAT: *65* **4–6**
CAPITOL: *70* **2–4**
KAREN: *66* **3–5**
PHILIPS: *67* **3–5**
SHARE: *69* **2–4**

ADAM & THE ANTS
Singles: 12-Inch 33/45rpm
EPIC: *81* **4–6**
Singles: 7-Inch
EPIC: *81* **1–3**
LPs: 10/12-Inch 33rpm
EDITIONS EG: *82* **5–8**
EPIC: *81–82* **8–10**
  Members: Adam Ant; Johnny Bivouac; Andy
  Watson; Dave Barb.
  Also see ANT, Adam
  Also see BOW WOW WOW

ADAMS, Bobby
Singles: 7-Inch
BATTLE: *63* **3–5**
HOME-TOWN: *70* **2–4**
PET: *58* **12–15**
PURDY: *64* **3–5**

ADAMS, Bryan
Singles: 12-Inch 33/45rpm
A&M: *82* **4–6**
Singles: 7-Inch
A&M: *80–85* **1–3**
LPs: 10/12-Inch 33rpm
A&M: *80–85* **5–8**

ADAMS, Faye
Singles: 7-Inch
ABC: *73* **1–3**
ATLANTIC: *52–53* **10–15**
COLLECTABLES: *82* **1–3**
HERALD (Black vinyl):
  53–57 . . . . **5–10**

Price Range

Price Range

HERALD (Colored vinyl):
53 .... $10–20
IMPERIAL: 55................. 8–10
LIDO: 59–60..................... 4–6
SAVOY: 61 3–5
WARWICK: 61.................. 3–5

LPs: 10/12-Inch 33rpm
SAVOY: 76 5–8
WARWICK: 61.................. 30–35
   Also see MORRIS, Joe, & His Orchestra

ADAMS, Gayle
Singles: 7-Inch
PRELUDE: 80–81................. 1–3

LPs: 10/12-Inch 33rpm
PRELUDE: 82.................... 5–8

ADAMS, Johnny
Singles: 7-Inch
ARIOLA AMERICAN: 78.......... 1–3
ATLANTIC: 71–72 2–4
J.B: 76 2–3
MODERN: 67.................... 3–5
PAID: 84........................ 1–3
RIC: 59–62 5–8
RON: 64–65..................... 3–5
SSS INT'L: 68–74................. 2–4
WATCH: 63 3–5

LPs: 10/12-Inch 33rpm
ARIOLA AMERICAN: 78.......... 5–8
CHELSEA: 77.................... 8–10
SSS INT'L: 70................... 8–10

ADAMS, Johnny, & The Gondoliers
Singles: 7-Inch
RIC: 59 10–15
   Also see ADAMS, Johnny

ADAMS, Marie (Marie Adams With Three Tons Of Joy)
Singles: 7-Inch
PEACOCK: 51–54 8–10
VANTAGE: 73.................... 2–4
   Also see OTIS, Johnny

ADDEO, Leo, & His Orchestra
LPs: 10/12-Inch 33rpm
CAMDEN: 59–68................. 4–8
RCA VICTOR: 61–64 4–8

ADDERLEY, Julian "Cannonball"
Singles: 7-Inch
BLUE NOTE: 59 .... $2–4
CAPITOL: 61–73 2–4
RIVERSIDE: 61–64 2–4

EPs: 7-Inch 33/45rpm
EMARCY: 55 10–15

LPs: 10/12-Inch 33rpm
BLUE NOTE: 58 15–25
   (Label reads "Blue Note Records Inc. - New York, U.S.A.")
BLUE NOTE: 66 10–20
   (Label reads "Blue Note Records - A Division Of Liberty Records Inc.")
CAPITOL (Except 2200 & 2300 series): 66–80 6–15
CAPITOL (2200 & 2300 series): 64–65 10–20
DOBRE: 77...................... 5–8
EMARCY (400 series): 76.......... 8–12
EMARCY (36000 series): 55–58 20–25
EVEREST: 71 5–10
FANTASY: 73–75................. 6–10
LIMELIGHT: 66 8–15
MERCURY (1000 series): 81 5–8
MERCURY (20000 & 60000 series): 61–62 12–18
MILESTONE: 73–82 6–12
PACIFIC JAZZ: 73 10–20
RIVERSIDE (032 through 142): 82–85..................... 5–8
RIVERSIDE (200 through 400 series): 58–63 12–25
RIVERSIDE (1100 series): 59–60 12–25
RIVERSIDE (3000 series): 68 6–12
RIVERSIDE (9000 series): 60–63 10–20
SAVOY (2200 series): 76.......... 8–12
SAVOY (12000 series): 55 25–35
TRIP: 75 5–8
VSP: 65 10–15
WING: 68 6–12
   Also see WILSON, Nancy, & Cannonball Adderley

Price Range

Price Range

ADDERLEY, Julian "Cannonball," & John Coltrane
LPs: 10/12-Inch 33rpm
LIMELIGHT: 65 .... **$10–15**
MERCURY: 61.................. **12–18**
Also see Coltrane, John

ADDERLEY, Julian "Cannonball," & Sergio Mendes
LPs: 10/12-Inch 33rpm
CAPITOL: 68–71 .... **8–12**
EVEREST: 73 .... **5–8**
Also see ADDERLEY, Julian "Cannonball"
Also see Mendes, Sergio

ADDRISI BROTHERS, The
Singles: 7-Inch
BELL: 74........................ **2–4**
BRAD: 58 .... **5–8**
BUDDAH: 77..................... **2–3**
COLUMBIA: 72–73 .... **2–4**
DEL-FI: 59 .... **5–8**
ELEKTRA: 81 .... **1–3**
IMPERIAL: 60.................... **4–6**
POM POM: 62 .... **4–6**
PRIVATE STOCK: 75.............. **2–3**
SCOTTI BROTHERS: 79 .... **2–3**
VALIANT: 64–65.................. **3–5**
WARNER BROS: 62–68 .... **3–5**

LPs: 10/12-Inch 33rpm
BUDDAH: 77.................... **5–10**
COLUMBIA: 72 .... **5–10**
Members: Dick Addrisi; Don Addrisi.

ADE, King Sunny (King Sunny Ade & His African Beats)
Singles: 12-Inch 33/45rpm
MANGO: 83 .... **4–6**

Singles: 7-Inch
MANGO: 83 .... **1–3**

LPs: 10/12-Inch 33rpm
MANGO: 83 .... **5–8**

ADVANCE
Singles: 12-Inch 33/45rpm
POLYDOR: 83 .... **4–6**
Singles: 7-Inch
POLYDOR: 83 .... **1–3**

AEROSMITH
Singles: 7-Inch
COLUMBIA: 73–80 .... **$2–4**
LPs: 10/12-Inch 33rpm
COLUMBIA (Except
KC-32005 with orange
cover): 73–82 .... **6–10**
COLUMBIA (KC-32005;
"Aerosmith" with orange
cover): 73 .... **20–25**
(This issue incorrectly shows "Walking The Dog" as "Walking The Dig.")
GEFFEN: 85..................... **5–8**
Promotional LPs
COLUMBIA (187; "Pure
Gold"): 76 .... **50–55**
(Boxed set of the group's first three LPs.)
Members: Steve Tyler; Tom Hamilton; Joey Kramer; Joe Perry; Brad Whitford.
Also see PERRY, Joe, Project

AFRIKA BAMBAATAA & JAMES BROWN
Singles: 7-Inch
TOMMY BOY: 82–83 .... **1–3**
LPs: 10/12-Inch 33rpm
TOMMY BOY: 83–84 .... **5–8**
Also see BROWN, James

AFRIKA BAMBAATAA & THE SOUL SONIC FORCE
Singles: 12-Inch 33/45rpm
TOMMY BOY: 83 .... **4–6**
Also see AFRIKA BAMBAATAA & JAMES BROWN
Also see SHANGO

AFRIQUE
Singles: 7-Inch
MAINSTREAM: 73................ **2–4**
LPs: 10/12-Inch 33rpm
MAINSTREAM: 73.............. **8–12**

AFRO CUBAN BAND, The
Singles: 7-Inch
ARISTA: 78 .... **1–3**
LPs: 10/12-Inch 33rpm
ARISTA: 78 .... **5–8**

AFTER THE FIRE
Singles: 12-Inch 33/45rpm
EPIC: 83 .... **4–6**

Price Range

Singles: 7-Inch
EPIC: *83–84* **$1–3**
LPs: 10/12-Inch 33rpm
EPIC: *82* **5–8**
Members: Peter Banks; Iver Piercy; Tim Haywell; Nick Battle.
Also see BANKS, Peter

AFTERBACH
Singles: 7-Inch
COLUMBIA/ARC: *81*............. **1–3**
LPs: 10/12-Inch 33rpm
COLUMBIA/ARC: *81*............. **5–8**

AFTERNOON DELIGHTS, The
Singles: 12-Inch 33/45rpm
MCA: *81* **4–6**
Singles: 7-Inch
MCA: *81* **1–3**
LPs: 10/12-Inch 33rpm
MCA: *81* **5–8**

A-HA (Featuring Morten Harket)
Singles: 7-Inch
REPRISE: *85–86*.................. **1–3**
LPs: 10/12-Inch 33rpm
REPRISE: *85–86*.................. **5–8**

AIDA
Singles: 12-Inch 33/45rpm
VANGUARD: *84*................... **4–6**
Singles: 7-Inch
VANGUARD: *84*.................. **1–3**

AIR SUPPLY
Singles: 7-Inch
ARISTA: *80–85*................... **1–3**
FLASHBACK: *82*.................. **1–3**
Picture Sleeves
ARISTA: *80–82*................... **INC**
LPs: 10/12-Inch 33rpm
ARISTA: *80–85*................... **5–8**
COLUMBIA: *77*................ **10–15**
Members: Graham Russell; Russell Hitchcock.

AIRWAVES
Singles: 7-Inch
A&M: *78–79* **1–3**
LPs: 10/12-Inch 33rpm
A&M: *78–79* **5–8**

Price Range

Members: John David; Dave Charles; Ray Martinez.

AKENS, Jewel
Singles: 7-Inch
AMERICAN INT'L
  ARTISTS: *75*.................. **$2–4**
CAPEHART: *61*................... **3–5**
COLGEMS: *67*................... **3–5**
ERA: *65*.......................... **3–5**
MINASA: *65*...................... **3–5**
RTV: *72*.......................... **2–4**
LPs: 10/12-Inch 33rpm
ERA: *65*....................... **15–25**

AKKERMAN, Jan (Jan Akkerman & Kaz Lux)
Singles: 7-Inch
ATLANTIC: *77–79* **1–3**
LPs: 10/12-Inch 33rpm
ATCO: *73* **10–12**
ATLANTIC: *76–79* **5–10**
SIRE: *73* **10–15**
Also see FOCUS

ALABAMA
Singles: 7-Inch
GRT: *77*......................... **2–4**
MDJ: *79–80*...................... **2–4**
RCA VICTOR: *80–85* **1–3**
Picture Sleeves
RCA VICTOR: *80–85* .... **INC**
LPs: 10/12-Inch 33rpm
ALABAMA RECORDS:
  78 .... **60–75**
PLANTATION: *81*............... **40–50**
RCA VICTOR: *80–85* **5–8**
Members: Randy Owen; Jeff Cook; Teddy Gentry; Mark Herndon.

ALAIMO, Chuck (The Chuck Alaimo Quartet)
Singles: 7-Inch
KEN: *57*......................... **8–12**
MGM: *57*........................ **6–10**

ALAIMO, Steve (Steve Alaimo & The Redcoats)
Singles: 7-Inch
ABC: *66–67*...................... **2–4**

Price Range

ABC-PARAMOUNT:
64–66 . . . . $3–5
ATCO: *67–71.* 3–5
CHECKER: *61–63* 3–5
DADE: *59* 4–6
DICKSON: *60.* 6–10
ENTRANCE: *71–72.* 2–4
ERIC: *83* 1–3
IMPERIAL: *60–63* 3–6
LIFETIME: *58* 15–20
MARLIN (Except 6064):
59 8–10
MARLIN (6064; "I Want
You To Love Me"): *59.* 10–15

EPs: 7-Inch 33/45rpm
ABC-PARAMOUNT (531;
"Where The Action Is"):
65 8–15
(Jukebox issue only.)

LPs: 10/12-Inch 33rpm
ABC-PARAMOUNT:
65–66 15–20
CHECKER: *61–63* 20–30
CROWN: *63* 10–12

ALAIMO, Steve, & Betty Wright
Singles: 7-Inch
ATCO: *69* 2–4
Also see ALAIMO, Steve
Also see WRIGHT, Betty

ALARM
Singles: 7-Inch
I.R.S: *83–85* 1–3
LPs: 10/12-Inch 33rpm
I.R.S: *83–85* 5–8

ALBERT, Eddie
Singles: 7-Inch
COLUMBIA: *68* 2–3
HICKORY: *64–65* 2–3
KAPP: *54–56.* 2–4
LPs: 10/12-Inch 33rpm
HAMILTON: *59.* 5–15

ALBERT, Eddie, & Sondra Lee
Singles: 7-Inch
KAPP: *56* 2–4
Also see ALBERT, Eddie

Price Range

ALBERT, Morris
Singles: 7-Inch
RCA VICTOR: *75–76* $2–3
LPs: 10/12-Inch 33rpm
RCA VICTOR: *75–76* 5–8

ALBERTI, Willy
Singles: 7-Inch
EPIC: *59* 2–4
LONDON: *59* 2–4
LPs: 10/12-Inch 33rpm
LONDON: *59* 5–10

ALCATRAZZ (Featuring Graham Bonnet)
Singles: 7-Inch
ROCSHIRE: *83.* 1–3
LPs: 10/12-Inch 33rpm
CAPITOL: *85* 5–8
ROCSHIRE: *83–84.* 5–8
Also see RAINBOW
Also see SCHENKER, Michael

ALDO NOVA: see NOVA, Aldo

ALDRICH, Ronnie
Singles: 7-Inch
LONDON: *60–62* 1–3
LPs: 10/12-Inch 33rpm
LONDON: *61–76* 4–8
RICHMOND: *59* 5–10

ALEEMS
Singles: 12-Inch 33/45rpm
NIA: *85* 4–6
Singles: 7-Inch
NIA: *84* 1–3

ALEXANDER, Arthur
Singles: 7-Inch
BUDDAH: *75–76* 2–4
DOT: *62–64.* 3–5
MONUMENT: *68.* 2–4
MUSIC MILL: *77.* 2–4
SOUND STAGE 7: *65–71* 3–5
WARNER BROS: *72–73* 2–4
EPs: 7-Inch 33/45rpm
DOT: *62.* 15–20
LPs: 10/12-Inch 33rpm
DOT: *62.* 20–30
WARNER BROS: *72* 5–8

Price Range   *Price Range*

ALEXANDER, Goldie
Singles: 7-Inch
ARISTA: *82* $1–3

ALEXANDER, Margie
Singles: 12-Inch 33/45rpm
CHI-SOUND: *77.* 4–6
Singles: 7-Inch
ATLANTIC: *71* 2–4
CHI-SOUND: *76–77.* 2–3
FUTURE STARS: *74.* 2–4

ALFIE: see SILAS, Alfie

ALFONZO (Alfonzo Jones)
Singles: 12-Inch 33/45rpm
JOE-WES: *83.* 4–6
Singles: 7-Inch
JOE-WES: *82.* 1–3
LARC: *82* 1–3
LPs: 10/12-Inch 33rpm
LARC: *83* 5–8

ALI, Muhammed: see CLAY, Cassius

ALICE COOPER: see COOPER, Alice

ALICE WONDER-LAND
Singles: 7-Inch
BARDELL: *63* 3–5

ALISHA
Singles: 12-Inch 33/45rpm
VANGUARD: *84–85* 4–6
Singles: 7-Inch
VANGUARD: *84.* 1–3

ALIVE 'N KICKING
Singles: 7-Inch
ROULETTE: *70–71* 2–4
LPs: 10/12-Inch 33rpm
ROULETTE: *70* 12–15

ALL POINTS BULLETIN BAND, The
Singles: 7-Inch
LITTLE CITY: *75–79* 2–3

ALL SPORTS BAND, The
Singles: 7-Inch
RADIO: *81–82* $1–3
LPs: 10/12-Inch 33rpm
RADIO: *81* 5–8

ALLAN, Davie (Davie Allan & The Arrows)
Singles: 7-Inch
A.O.A: *76* 2–4
CUDE: *63* 10–12
MARC: *63.* 4–6
MGM: *71–73.* 2–4
MRC: *84* 1–3
PRIVATE STOCK: *74.* 2–4
SIDEWALK: *64* 5–10
TOWER: *65–68.* 3–5
WHAT: *82.* 1–3
LPs: 10/12-Inch 33rpm
ALKOR: *84.* 5–8
ARROW DYNAMICS: *85* 5–8
TOWER: *65–68.* 15–20
WHAT: *83.* 5–8
Also see DALE, Dick

ALLEN, Annisteen (Annisteen Allen & Her Home Town Boys)
Singles: 7-Inch
CAPITOL: *55* 5–8
DECCA: *56–57.* 5–8
KING (4600 series): *53–54* 10–12
TRUE SOUND.................... 3–5
WIG: *59.* 3–5

ALLEN, Dayton
LPs: 10/12-Inch 33rpm
GRAND AWARD: *60.* 6–12

ALLEN, Jonelle
Singles: 7-Inch
ALEXANDER STREET:
78 1–3

ALLEN, Lee
Singles: 7-Inch
ALADDIN: *56* 8–10
COLLECTABLES: *82* 1–3
EMBER: *58–59.* 3–5
EPs: 7-Inch 33/45rpm
EMBER: *58.* 20–25

Price Range

LPs: 10/12-Inch 33rpm
EMBER (Red label): *58* **$75–100**
EMBER ("Logs" label): *58* **60–75**
(On this label, the name Ember is formed with logs.)
EMBER (Black label): *60*. **25–30**

ALLEN, Peter
Singles: 12-Inch 33/45rpm
A&M: *79* **4–6**
Singles: 7-Inch
A&M: *74–82* **1–3**
ARISTA: *83–84*. **1–3**
METROMEDIA: *71–73*. **2–4**
LPs: 10/12-Inch 33rpm
A&M: *74–82* **5–8**
ARISTA: *83–84*. **5–8**
METROMEDIA: *71–72*. **10–12**

ALLEN, Rance, Group
Singles: 7-Inch
CAPITOL: *77–79* **1–3**
GOSPEL TRUTH: *72–73* **2–4**
STAX: *78–81*. **1–3**
TRUTH: *74–75* **2–3**
LPs: 10/12-Inch 33rpm
CAPITOL: *77–79* **5–8**
GOSPEL TRUTH: *72–74* **8–12**
MYRRH: *84* **5–8**
STAX: *78–81*. **5–8**
TRUTH: *75*. **8–10**
Members: Rance Allen; Thomas Allen; Steven Allen.

ALLEN, Rex
Singles: 7-Inch
BUENA VISTA: *59* **2–4**
DECCA (Except 28000 &
29000 series): *56–72* **2–4**
DECCA (28000 & 29000
series): *52–56* **3–5**
JMI: *73*. **1–3**
MERCURY: *53–62*. **2–4**
WILDCAT **3–5**
EPs: 7-Inch 33/45rpm
DECCA: *56* **6–10**
MERCURY: *53–56*. **8–10**
LPs: 10/12-Inch 33rpm
BUENA VISTA: *61* **18–22**
COLLECTOR'S
CLASSICS. **5–8**

CORAL: *73* **$4–6**
DECCA (5000 series):
68–70 . . . . **10–12**
(Decca LP numbers in this series preceded by a "7" or a "DL-7" are stereo issues.)
DECCA (8000 series):
56–58 . . . . **20–25**
DESIGN: *62* **10–12**
DISNEYLAND: *70* **6–10**
HACIENDA **20–22**
JMI. **5–8**
MCA. **4–6**
MERCURY: *62*. **12–15**
PICKWICK/HILLTOP:
65 . . . . **10–12**
VOCALION: *70* **6–10**
WING: *64–66* **10–12**

ALLEN, Richie (Richie Allen & The Pacific Surfers)
Singles: 7-Inch
ERA: *61*. **3–5**
IMPERIAL: *60–63* **3–5**
TOWER: *66*. **3–5**
LPs: 10/12-Inch 33rpm
IMPERIAL: *63* **20–25**

ALLEN, Steve
Singles: 7-Inch
BRUNSWICK: *53*. **3–5**
CORAL: *55–56* **2–5**
DOT: *59–66*. **2–4**
DUNHILL: *67–68*. **1–3**
SIGNATURE: *59–60* **2–4**
EPs: 7-Inch 33/45rpm
BRUNSWICK: *53*. **10–15**
CORAL: *55–56* **10–15**
DECCA: *55* **15–20**
LPs: 10/12-Inch 33rpm
CORAL (100; "Jazz
Story"): *59* **25–35**
(Narration by Steve Allen, music by various artists.)
CORAL (57000 series,
except 57099): *55–56*. **15–20**
CORAL (57099; "The
James Dean Story"): *56* **35–50**
(With Bill Randle.)
CORAL (57400 series): *63*. **10–15**
(Coral LP numbers in this series preceded by a "7" are stereo issues.)

Price Range

DECCA: *55* **$20–25**
DOT (Except 3472 &
  3517): *59–66* **8–12**
DOT (3472; "Steve Allen's
  Funny Fone Calls"): *63* **15–20**
DOT (3517; "More Funny
  Fone Calls"): *63* **15–20**
DUNHILL: *67* **8–10**
EMARCY: *58* **15–20**
HAMILTON: *59–64* **10–15**
HANOVER: *59* **10–15**
MERCURY: *61* **10–15**
PETE: *69* **5–10**
ROULETTE: *59* **15–20**
SIGNATURE (Except
  1004): *59* **15–20**
SIGNATURE (1004; "Man
  On The Street"): *59* **30–40**
  (With Louis Nye, Tom Poston & Don Knotts.)

ALLEN, Vee
Singles: 7-Inch
LION: *73* **2–4**
MCA: *83* **1–3**

LPs: 10/12-Inch 33rpm
MCA: *83* **5–8**

ALLEN, Woody
LPs: 10/12-Inch 33rpm
BELL: *67* **10–15**
CAPITOL: *68* **8–12**
COLPIX: *64–65* **15–20**
UNITED ARTISTS (800
  series): *77* **6–10**
UNITED ARTISTS (9900
  series): *72* **8–12**

ALLEY CATS, The
Singles: 7-Inch
PHILLES: *62* **8–10**

ALLISON, Gene
Singles: 7-Inch
CALVERT: *56* **8–10**
CHAMPION: *59* **4–6**
DECCA: *57* **5–8**
MONUMENT: *65* **3–5**
VALDOT: *62* **3–5**
VEE JAY: *57–60* **5–8**

Price Range

LPs: 10/12-Inch 33rpm
VEE JAY (Maroon label):
  59 . . . . **$40–50**
VEE JAY (Black label): *61* **20–25**

ALLISONS, The
Singles: 7-Inch
TIP: *63* **5–8**

ALLMAN, Duane
LPs: 10/12-Inch 33rpm
CAPRICORN: *72–74* **10–12**
Also see DEREK & THE DOMINOS

ALLMAN, Duane & Gregg
Singles: 7-Inch
BOLD: *73* **4–6**

LPs: 10/12-Inch 33rpm
BOLD (301; "Duane &
  Gregg Allman"): *72* **20–25**
  (With gatefold cover.)
BOLD (301; "Duane &
  Gregg Allman"): *73* **8–10**
  (With standard cover.)
SPRINGBOARD: *75* **8–10**
  Also see ALLMAN, Duane
  Also see ALLMAN, Gregg
  Also see ALLMAN BROTHERS BAND, The
  Also see ALLMAN JOYS, The

ALLMAN, Gregg (The Gregg Allman Band)
Singles: 7-Inch
CAPRICORN: *73–77* **2–4**

LPs: 10/12-Inch 33rpm
CAPRICORN: *73–77* **8–12**
  Also see ALLMAN, Duane & Gregg
  Also see ALLMAN & WOMAN
  Also see ALLMAN BROTHERS BAND, The
  Also see ALLMAN JOYS, The

ALLMAN & WOMAN
Singles: 7-Inch
WARNER BROS: *77* **2–3**

LPs: 10/12-Inch 33rpm
WARNER BROS: *77* **8–10**
  Members: Gregg Allman; Cher.
  Also see ALLMAN, Gregg
  Also see CHER

Price Range

ALLMAN BROTHERS BAND, The
Singles: 7-Inch
ARISTA: *80–81.*................... $1–3
CAPRICORN: *71–79*.............. 2–4
Picture Sleeves
ARISTA: *81* .... INC
EPs: 7-Inch 33/45rpm
ATLANTIC: *73* 10–12
(Jukebox issue only.)
CAPRICORN: *73*............... 10–12
(Jukebox issue only.)
LPs: 10/12-Inch 33rpm
ARISTA: *80–81.*................... 5–8
ATCO: *69–73.*.................. 15–20
CAPRICORN (Except
802): *72–79.*.................... 8–12
CAPRICORN (802; "The
Allman Brothers Band
At The Fillmore East"):
71 15–18
K-TEL 5–8
POLYDOR: *81* 5–8
Members: Duane Allman; Gregg Allman;
Dicky Betts; Les Dudek; David Goldflies; Paul
Hornsby; Berry Oakley; Dan Toler; Johnny
Sandlin; Butch Trucks; Johnny Johanson.
Also see ALLMAN, Duane & Gregg
Also see BETTS, Richard
Also see HOUR GLASS
Also see DUDEK, Les
Also see SEA LEVEL

ALLMAN JOYS, The
Singles: 7-Inch
DIAL: *66*...................... 20–25
LPs: 10/12-Inch 33rpm
DIAL: *73*...................... 10–12
Members: Duane Allman; Gregg Allman;
Ralph Balinger; Ronnie Wilkin; Tommy
Amato; Jack Jackson; Bobby Dennis.
Also see ALLMAN, Duane & Gregg

ALMEIDA, Laurindo (Laurindo Almeida & The Modern Jazz Quartet)
Singles: 7-Inch
ATLANTIC: *64* 2–3
CAPITOL: *55–65* 2–4
PACIFIC JAZZ: *55* 3–5
EPs: 7-Inch 33/45rpm
CAPITOL: *56–59* 5–10
CORAL: *54–56*.................. 2–4

Price Range

PACIFIC JAZZ: *54* $10–15
LPs: 10/12-Inch 33rpm
ATLANTIC: *64* 10–15
CAPITOL (Except 8000
series): *59–65*................ 10–15
CAPITOL (8000 series):
56–58 15–25
CORAL: *54–56*................. 15–25
CRYSTAL CLEAR: *80*............ 5–8
DAYBREAK: *73* 5–8
DOBRE: *76–77*.................. 5–8
INNER CITY: *79*................ 5–8
PACIFIC JAZZ: *54* 25–35
(10-Inch LPs.)
SURREY: *65*.................... 8–12
WORLD PACIFIC: *56–62* 10–20
Also see BYRD, Charlie, & Laurindo Almeida
Also see DAVIS, Sammy, Jr., & Laurindo Al-
meida
Also see SOMMERS, Joanie, & Laurindo Al-
meida

ALMEIDA, Laurindo / Chico Hamilton
LPs: 10/12-Inch 33rpm
JAZZTONE: *64*................. 12–18
Also see ALMEIDA, Laurindo
Also see HAMILTON, Chico

ALPACA PHASE III
Singles: 7-Inch
ATLANTIC: *74* 2–4

ALPERT, Herb (Herb Alpert & The Tijuana Brass; Herbie Alpert)
Singles: 12-Inch 33/45rpm
A&M: *79–84* 4–6
Singles: 7-Inch
A&M: *62–85* 1–3
ANDEX: *59* 2–4
CAROL: *59*..................... 2–4
Picture Sleeves
A&M: *65–81* 1–3
EPs: 7-Inch 33/45rpm
A&M: *65–66* 3–6
(Jukebox issues only.)
LPs: 10/12-Inch 33rpm
A&M (Except 100 series):
66–85 5–8
A&M (100 series): *62–66* 5–15

Price Range

ALPERT, Herb, & Hugh Masekela
Singles: 7-Inch
A&M/HORIZON: 78.............. $1–3
LPs: 10/12-Inch 33rpm
A&M/HORIZON: 78.............. 5–8
Also see ALPERT, Herb
Also see MASEKELA, Hugh

ALPHAVILLE
Singles: 12-Inch 33/45rpm
ATLANTIC: 84–85 4–6
Singles: 7-Inch
ATLANTIC: 84–85 1–3
LPs: 10/12-Inch 33rpm
ATLANTIC: 84 5–8

ALWAYS, Billy
Singles: 7-Inch
WAYLO: 82 1–3

ALVIN LEE: see LEE, Alvin

AMAZING RHYTHM ACES, The
Singles: 7-Inch
ABC: 75–79..................... 2–3
COLUMBIA: 79.................. 2–3
WARNER BROS: 80.............. 1–3
LPs: 10/12-Inch 33rpm
ABC: 75–78..................... 8–10
COLUMBIA: 79.................. 5–8
WARNER BROS: 80.............. 5–8
Members: Russell Smith; James Brown, Jr;
Byrd Burton; Stick Davis; Billy Earhart III;
James Hooker; Butch McDade.

AMBASSADORS, The
Singles: 7-Inch
ARCTIC: 68–69 2–4
ATLANTIC: 67–68 3–5
SOUND STAGE 7: 67–68.......... 3–5
TIME......................... 3–5
LPs: 10/12-Inch 33rpm
ARCTIC: 69 10–12

AMBOY DUKES, The
Singles: 7-Inch
MAINSTREAM: 67–69............ 5–10
LPs: 10/12-Inch 33rpm
MAINSTREAM (Except
801): 68–69.................... 20–25

Price Range

MAINSTREAM (801;
"Journeys &
Migrations"): 74 .... $10–12
POLYDOR: 70 10–12
Members: Ted Nugent; Greg Arama; Rusty
Day; John Drake; Steve Farmer; Dave Palmer;
Andy Solomon.
Also see NUGENT, Ted

AMBROSIA
Singles: 7-Inch
20TH CENTURY-FOX:
74–78 2–3
WARNER BROS: 78–82........... 1–3
LPs: 10/12-Inch 33rpm
20TH CENTURY-FOX:
74–78 8–10
WARNER BROS: 78–82........... 5–8
Members: Burleigh Drummond; Joe Puerta;
David Pack; Christopher North.

AMECHE, Don, & Frances Langford
(As The Bickersons)
LPs: 10/12-Inch 33rpm
COLUMBIA (Except
30000 series): 61–62 15–20
COLUMBIA (30000
series): 71..................... 8–12

AMERICA
Singles: 7-Inch
AMERICAN INT'L: 79 2–3
CAPITOL: 80–85 1–3
WARNER BROS: 72–77........... 2–4
Picture Sleeves
AMERICAN INT'L: 79 2–3
WARNER BROS: 72–74........... 2–4
LPs: 10/12-Inch 33rpm
CAPITOL: 80–85 5–8
WARNER BROS. (Except
2576): 72–77................... 8–10
WARNER BROS. (2576;
"America"): 71 15–20
(For copies that do NOT include "A Horse
With No Name.")
WARNER BROS. (2576;
"America"): 72 8–10
(For copies that DO include "A Horse With No
Name.")
Members: Gerry Beckley; Dan Peek; Dewey
Bunnell.
Also see PEEK, Dan

Price Range

AMERICAN BREED, The
Singles: 7-Inch
ABC: 75 . . . . **$1–3**
ACTA: 67–69. . . . . **3–5**
MCA: 84 . . . . **1–3**
PARAMOUNT: 70. . . . . **2–4**
Picture Sleeves
ACTA: 68 . . . . **3–5**
LPs: 10/12-Inch 33rpm
ACTA: 67–68. . . . . **15–25**
Members: Gary Loizzo; Al Ciner; Chuck Colbert; Lee Graziano; Kevin Murphy.
Also see RUFUS

AMERICAN COMEDY
NETWORK, The
LPs: 10/12-Inch 33rpm
CRITIQUE: 84 . . . . **5–8**

AMERICAN DREAM
Singles: 7-Inch
AMPEX: 70. . . . . **2–4**
DEMIK: 68 . . . . **3–5**
LPs: 10/12-Inch 33rpm
AMPEX: 70. **15–18**
Members: Nick Jameson; Dooley Van Winkle; Nicky Indelicato; Don Ferris; Mickey Brook.

AMERICAN FLYER
Singles: 7-Inch
UNITED ARTISTS: 76–77 . . . . **2–4**
LPs: 10/12-Inch 33rpm
UNITED ARTISTS: 76–77 . . . . **8–10**
Members: Eric Kaz; Steve Katz; Craig Fuller; Doug Yule.
Also see PURE PRAIRIE LEAGUE
Also see VELVET UNDERGROUND, The

AMES, Ed
Singles: 7-Inch
RCA VICTOR: 63–73 . . . . **2–3**
Picture Sleeves
RCA VICTOR: 67 . . . . **2–3**
LPs: 10/12-Inch 33rpm
CAMDEN: 72–73 . . . . **4–8**
RCA VICTOR: 64–77 . . . . **5–15**
Also see AMES BROTHERS, The

AMES, Nancy
Singles: 7-Inch
ABC: 68 . . . . **1–3**
EPIC: 66–68 . . . . **2–3**

Price Range

LIBERTY: 61–65 . . . . **$2–3**
SC: 68 . . . . **1–3**
LPs: 10/12-Inch 33rpm
EPIC: 66–68 . . . . **5–10**
LIBERTY: 61–65 . . . . **5–12**

AMES BROTHERS, The
Singles: 7-Inch
CORAL: 50–53 . . . . **2–5**
EPIC: 62–63 . . . . **2–3**
RCA VICTOR: 53–62 . . . . **2–5**
Picture Sleeves
EPIC: 62 . . . . **2–3**
RCA VICTOR: 60 . . . . **2–4**
EPs: 7-Inch 33/45rpm
CORAL: 50–53 . . . . **5–10**
RCA VICTOR: 53–61 . . . . **5–10**
LPs: 10/12-Inch 33rpm
CORAL: 53–62 . . . . **10–20**
EPIC: 63 . . . . **10–15**
RCA VICTOR (1200
through 2200 series):
55–61 . . . . **10–20**
RCA VICTOR (2800
series): 64 . . . . **8–12**
RCA VICTOR (6000
series): 72 . . . . **5–10**
Also see AMES, Ed

AMESBURY, Bill
Singles: 7-Inch
CASABLANCA: 74–75 . . . . **2–4**
LPs: 10/12-Inch 33rpm
CAPITOL: 76 . . . . **5–8**
CASABLANCA: 74 . . . . **8–10**

AMMONS, Gene
Singles: 7-Inch
ARGO: 62 . . . . **2–4**
DECCA: 54 . . . . **3–5**
MERCURY: 50–53 . . . . **3–6**
PRESTIGE (100 through
400 series): 60–68 . . . . **2–4**
PRESTIGE (700 series):
69–73 . . . . **2–3**
(This "700" series can easily be distinguished from the early fifties "700" series that follows. The address of the company, shown on the label, is in New Jersey, whereas in the fifties the company was in New York.)

Price Range

Price Range

PRESTIGE (713 through
921.): *51–57* **$3–5**
(Black vinyl.)
PRESTIGE (713 through
921.): *51–57* **8–10**
(Colored vinyl.)
SAVOY: *60* **2–4**
UNITED: *53–54* **3–5**

EPs: 7-Inch 33/45rpm

EMARCY: *54* **15–20**
PRESTIGE: *51* **20–25**

LPs: 10/12-Inch 33rpm

ARGO: *62* **15–20**
CHESS: *59* **15–20**
EMARCY (400 series): *76* **8–12**
EMARCY (26000 series):
54 . . . . **40–50**
(10-Inch LPs.)
ENJA: *81* **5–8**
MERCURY: *60–63* **15–20**
OLYMPIC: *74* **5–8**
PRESTIGE (014 through
192): *82–85* **5–8**
PRESTIGE (7010 through
7132): *55–58* **20–30**
(The following LPs in this series were reissued
using the original catalog number but a differ-
ent title: Prestige 7050, "All Star Jam Session,"
was reissued as "Woofin' & Tweetin;" Prestige
7039, "Hi-Fi Jam Session," was reissued as
"Happy Blues" & Prestige 7060, "Jammin'
With Gene," was reissued as "Not Really The
Blues." These three 1960 reissues are valued in
the $15-$20 range.)
PRESTIGE (7146 through
7287): *58–64* **15–20**
PRESTIGE (7300 & 7400
series): *65–68* **10–15**
PRESTIGE (7500 through
7800 series): *68–70* **5–10**
PRESTIGE (10000 series):
71–74 . . . . **5–10**
PRESTIGE (24000 series):
73–81 . . . . **8–12**
ROOTS: *76* **5–8**
SAVOY: *61* **15–20**
TRIP: *73–75* **5–8**
VEE JAY: *60* **15–20**
WING: *60–63* **12–15**
Also see MC DUFF, Brother Jack, & Gene
Ammons

AMMONS, Gene, & Richard "Groove" Holmes
LPs: 10/12-Inch 33rpm
PACIFIC JAZZ (32;
"Groovin' With Jug"):
61 . . . . **$15–20**
Also see HOLMES, Richard "Groove"

AMMONS, Gene, & James Moody
LPs: 10/12-Inch 33rpm
PRESTIGE (10000 series):
73 . . . . **5–10**

AMMONS, Gene, & Sonny Stitt
Singles: 7-Inch
PRESTIGE (700 series):
50–51 . . . . **3–5**
(Black vinyl.)
PRESTIGE (700 series):
50–51 . . . . **8–10**
(Colored vinyl.)
LPs: 10/12-Inch 33rpm
ARGO: *63* **12–15**
CADET: *67* **10–15**
CHESS: *60* **15–20**
PRESTIGE (100 series):
51–54 . . . . **50–75**
(10-Inch LPs.)
PRESTIGE (7600 series):
69 . . . . **6–10**
PRESTIGE (10000 series):
76 . . . . **5–8**
VERVE (8400 series):
61–62 . . . . **15–20**
(Reads "MGM Records - A Division Of Metro-
Goldwyn-Mayer, Inc." at bottom of label.)
VERVE (8800 series): *72* **8–12**
(Reads "Manufactured By MGM Record
Corp.," or mentions either Polydor or Poly-
gram at bottom of label.)
Also see AMMONS, Gene
Also see STITT, Sonny

AMUZEMENT PARK (Featuring Paul Richmond; Amusement Park Band)
Singles: 7-Inch
ATLANTIC: *84–85* **1–3**
OUR GANG: *82–83* **1–3**
LPs: 10/12-Inch 33rpm
ATLANTIC: *84* **5–8**

Price Range

Price Range

ANACOSTIA
Singles: 7-Inch
COLUMBIA: *72–75* **$2–4**
MCA: *77* **2–3**
ROULETTE: *84* **1–3**
TABU: *78–79.* **1–3**
LPs: 10/12-Inch 33rpm
MCA: *77* **5–8**
TABU: *78* **5–8**

ANDERSEN, Eric
Singles: 7-Inch
ARISTA: *75–77.* **1–3**
COLUMBIA: *72* **2–4**
WARNER BROS: *68–71* **2–4**
LPs: 10/12-Inch 33rpm
ARISTA: *75–77.* **5–8**
COLUMBIA: *72* **8–10**
VANGUARD: *65–70* **15–20**
WARNER BROS: *68–70* **10–12**

ANDERSON, Bill
Singles: 7-Inch
DECCA (30000 & 31000
  series): *58–66* **3–5**
DECCA (32000 & 33000
  series): *67–72* **2–4**
MCA: *73–81* **1–3**
SOUTHERN TRACKS:
  82–84 .... **1–3**
SWANEE: *85.* **1–3**
TNT: *59* **4–6**
Picture Sleeves
DECCA: *63–69* **2–3**
EPs: 7-Inch 33/45rpm
DECCA: *63–65* **5–8**
LPs: 10/12-Inch 33rpm
CORAL: *73* **4–6**
DECCA (4192 through
  4686): *62–65* **15–20**
DECCA (4771 through
  5344): *66–72* **10–15**
(Decca LP numbers in this series preceded by
a "7" or a "DL-7" are stereo issues.)
DECCA (7100 series): *69* **15–20**
DECCA (7200 series): *72* **10–12**
EPIC: *82–85* **5–8**
MCA: *73–80* **5–10**
SOUTHERN TRACKS: *84* **5–8**
VOCALION: *68–71* **8–12**
Also see COE, David Allan, & Bill Anderson

ANDERSON, Carl
Singles: 12-Inch 33/45rpm
EPIC: *82–85* **$4–6**
Singles: 7-Inch
EPIC: *82–85* **1–3**
LPs: 10/12-Inch 33rpm
EPIC: *82–85* **5–8**

ANDERSON, Elton
Singles: 7-Inch
CAPITOL: *62* **3–5**
LANOR: *63.* **3–5**
MERCURY: *59–61.* **8–10**
VIN: *59* **10–15**

ANDERSON, Ernestine
Singles: 7-Inch
MERCURY: *60–62.* **2–4**
SUE: *63–64* **2–4**
LPs: 10/12-Inch 33rpm
MERCURY: *58–60.* **15–25**
OMEGA DISK: *59.* **10–15**
SUE: *63* **10–15**
WING: *64* **10–15**

ANDERSON, Jesse
Singles: 7-Inch
CADET: *67–68* **3–5**
JEWEL: *72* **2–4**
THOMAS: *70* **2–4**

ANDERSON, John
Singles: 7-Inch
WARNER BROS: *77–85* **1–3**
LPs: 10/12-Inch 33rpm
WARNER BROS: *80–85* **5–8**

ANDERSON, Jon
Singles: 7-Inch
ATLANTIC: *76–82* **1–3**
LPs: 10/12-Inch 33rpm
ATLANTIC: *76–82* **5–8**
ELEKTRA: *85* **5–8**
Also see JON & VANGELIS
Also see YES

ANDERSON, Lale
Singles: 7-Inch
KING: *61–62.* **2–4**
LPs: 10/12-Inch 33rpm
UNIVERSE: *61.* **5–10**

Price Range

ANDERSON, Laurie
Singles: 12-Inch 33/45rpm
WARNER BROS: *81* $4–6
Singles: 7-Inch
WARNER BROS: *81* 1–3
EPs: 7-Inch 33/45rpm
WARNER BROS: *81* 3–5
LPs: 10/12-Inch 33rpm
WARNER BROS (Except
25192): *82–85*. 5–8
WARNER BROS (25192;
"United States Live"): *85* 30–40
(A 5-LP set.)

ANDERSON, Leroy
Singles: 7-Inch
DECCA: *51–62* 2–4
EPs: 7-Inch 33/45rpm
DECCA: *51–58* 4–8
LPs: 10/12-Inch 33rpm
DECCA: *51–63* 5–15

ANDERSON, Lynn
Singles: 7-Inch
CHART: *66–71*. 2–4
COLUMBIA: *70–80* 1–3
PERMIAN: *83* 1–3
RCA VICTOR: *68* 2–4
LPs: 10/12-Inch 33rpm
ALBUM GLOBE: *76* 5–8
CHART (Except 1050):
67–71 8–12
CHART (1050; "Lynn
Anderson"): *72* 10–18
COLUMBIA: *70–80* 6–10
HARMONY: *71–73* 5–10
PERMIAN: *83* 5–8
PICKWICK 5–10
TIME-LIFE: *81*. 5–8
Also see ANDERSON, Liz, & Lynn

ANDERSON, Lynn, & Gary Morris
Singles: 7-Inch
PERMIAN: *83* 1–3
Also see MORRIS, Gary

ANDERSON, Roshell
Singles: 7-Inch
EXCELLO: *71*. 2–4
SUNBURST: *73–74* 2–4

Price Range

ANDERSON, Vicki (Vikki Anderson; Vickie Anderson)
Singles: 7-Inch
BROWNSTONE: *71–72*. $2–4
DELUXE: *66*. 3–5
FONTANA: *64* 3–5
KING: *66–70*. 3–5
SMASH: *65* 3–5
TUFF: *67*. 3–5
Also see BROWN, James, & Vickie Anderson

ANDREA TRUE CONNECTION, The: see TRUE, Andrea

ANDREWS, Chris
Singles: 7-Inch
ATCO: *66* 3–5
RCA VICTOR: *69* 2–4

ANDREWS, Inez (Inez Andrews & The Andrewettes)
Singles: 7-Inch
MCA: *84* 1–3
SONG BIRD: *64–73*. 2–4
LPs: 10/12-Inch 33rpm
MCA: *84* 5–8
SAVOY: *80–81* 5–8

ANDREWS, Julie
Singles: 7-Inch
BUENA VISTA: *65* 2–3
COLUMBIA: *67*. 2–3
DECCA: *67*. 2–3
LONDON: *60* 2–4
RCA VICTOR: *70* 2–3
EPs: 7-Inch 33/45rpm
RCA VICTOR: *56* 8–12
LPs: 10/12-Inch 33rpm
ANGEL: *58*. 15–20
COLUMBIA (1700 & 8500
series): *62*. 15–20
COLUMBIA (31000
series): *72*. 8–12
HARMONY: *70–72* 8–10
RCA VICTOR (1000
series): *70*. 8–12
RCA VICTOR (1400
through 1600 series):
56–58 20–25

Price Range

RCA VICTOR (3800
  series): *67* **$8–12**
20TH CENTURY-FOX:
  68 . . . . **8–12**

ANDREWS, Julie, & Carol Burnett
LPs: 10/12-Inch 33rpm
COLUMBIA (2200 & 5800
  series): *62* **15–20**
COLUMBIA (31000
  series): *72* **8–12**
  Also see ANDREWS, Julie
  Also see BURNETT, Carol

ANDREWS, Lee (Lee Andrews & The Hearts)
Singles: 7-Inch
ARGO: *57* **10–15**
CASINO: *58–59* **15–20**
CHESS: *57* **4–6**
COLLECTABLES: *82* **1–3**
CRIMSON: *67–68* **3–5**
GOTHAM: *56* **40–50**
GOWEN: *61* **4–6**
GRAND: *62* **3–5**
JORDAN: *60* **10–15**
LOST NITE: *65* **3–5**
MAIN LINE (Green
  label): *57* **75–90**
MAIN LINE (Black label):
  62 . . . . **5–8**
PARKWAY: *62–63* **3–5**
RAINBOW (Except
  colored vinyl & 256): *54* **75–100**
RAINBOW (Colored
  vinyl): *54* **125–150**
RAINBOW (256; "White
  Cliffs Of Dover"): *54* **150–175**
RCA VICTOR: *66* **3–5**
SWAN: *61* **3–5**
UNITED ARTISTS (100
  series): *58–59* **5–8**
UNITED ARTISTS (500
  series): *63* **3–5**

LPs: 10/12-Inch 33rpm
LOST-NITE (1 & 2): *81* **5–8**
  (Colored vinyl 10-Inch LPs.)
LOST-NITE (100 series):
  63 . . . . **10–15**
POST **10–12**

Price Range

Members: Lee Andrews & The Hearts; Arthur
Thompson; Roy Calhoun; Wendell Calhoun;
Butch Curry; Ted Weems.

ANDREWS, Patty
Singles: 7-Inch
CAPITOL: *55–56* **$2–4**
DECCA: *50–54* **3–5**
  Also see ANDREWS SISTERS, The

ANDREWS, Ruby
Singles: 7-Inch
ABC: *76–77* **2–3**
ZODIAC: *67–71* **2–4**
LPs: 10/12-Inch 33rpm
ABC: *77* **8–10**
ZODIAC: *72* **10–12**
  Also see STAEKHOUSE, Ruby

ANDREWS SISTERS, The
Singles: 7-Inch
ABC: *74* **1–3**
DECCA: *50–54* **3–5**
DOT: *64* **2–3**
KAPP: *59* **2–3**
PARAMOUNT: *73* **1–3**
EPs: 7-Inch 33/45rpm
DECCA: *51–58* **5–10**
LPs: 10/12-Inch 33rpm
ABC: *74* **5–8**
CAPITOL: *64* **5–10**
DECCA (4000 series): *67* **8–12**
  (Decca LP numbers in this series preceded by
  a "7" or a "DL-7" are stereo issues.)
DECCA (5000 series):
  51–54 . . . . **15–25**
  (10-Inch LPs.)
DECCA (8000 series):
  55–58 . . . . **10–20**
DOT: *61–67* **5–10**
HAMILTON: *64–65* **4–6**
PARAMOUNT: *73* **6–10**
  Members: Patty Andrews; Maxene Andrews;
  Lavern Andrews.
  Also see ANDREWS, Patty
  Also see CROSBY, Bing

ANGEL
Singles: 7-Inch
CASABLANCA: *75–80* **1–3**
LPs: 10/12-Inch 33rpm
CASABLANCA: *75–80* **6–10**

Price Range

Members: Barry Brandt; Frank Dimino; Greg
Giuffria; Mickey Jones; Punky Meadows; Felix
Robinson.
Also see GIUFFRIA, Greg

ANGEL, Johnny T: see JOHNNY T.
ANGEL

ANGEL CITY
Singles: 7-Inch
EPIC: *80–82* **$1–3**
LPs: 10/12-Inch 33rpm
EPIC: *80–82* **5–8**
MCA: *85* **5–8**
Members: Doc Neeson; Rick Brewster; John
Brewster.

ANGELS, The
Singles: 7-Inch
ASCOT: *63* **3–5**
CAPRICE: *61–62* **4–6**
COLLECTABLES: *82* **1–3**
ERIC: *74* **2–3**
POLYDOR: *74* **2–4**
RCA VICTOR: *67–68* **4–6**
SMASH: *63–64* **3–5**
Picture Sleeves
SMASH: *63* **4–6**
LPs: 10/12-Inch 33rpm
ASCOT: *64* **15–20**
CAPRICE: *62* **40–45**
SMASH: *63–64* **20–25**
Members: Linda Jansen; Barbara Allbut; Phylis
"Jiggs" Allbut; Peggy Santaglia.

ANIMALS, The (Eric Burdon & The
Animals; The Original Animals)
Singles: 7-Inch
ABKCO: *75* **2–3**
COLLECTABLES: *82* **1–3**
I.R.S: *83* **1–3**
JET: *77* **2–3**
MGM: *64–71* **4–6**
Picture Sleeves
MGM (Except 13264):
64–67 .... **4–6**
MGM (13264; "House Of
The Rising Sun"): *64* **6–10**
LPs: 10/12-Inch 33rpm
ABKCO: *73–76* **8–12**
ACCORD: *82* **5–8**

Price Range

I.R.S: *83–85* **$5–8**
MGM (Except 4264):
65–69 .... **10–15**
MGM (4264; "The
Animals"): *64* **15–20**
PICKWICK: *71* **5–8**
SCEPTER/CITATION: *76* **5–8**
SPRINGBOARD: *72* **5–8**
UNITED ARTISTS: *77* **5–8**
WAND: *70* **8–12**
Members: Eric Burdon; Alan Price; Hilton Val-
entine; Chas Chandler; John Steel.
Also see BURDON, Eric
Also see PRICE, Alan

ANIMOTION
Singles: 12-Inch 33/45rpm
MERCURY: *85* **4–6**
Singles: 7-Inch
MERCURY: *84–85* **1–3**
LPs: 10/12-Inch 33rpm
MERCURY: *84–85* **5–8**

ANITA & THE SO-AND-SOs (The
Anita Kerr Singers)
Singles: 7-Inch
RCA VICTOR: *62* **4–6**
Also see KERR, Anita

ANKA, Paul
Singles: 12-Inch 33/45rpm
COLUMBIA: *83* **4–6**
Singles: 7-Inch
ABC-PARAMOUNT
(Except stereo singles):
57–62 .... **4–6**
ABC-PARAMOUNT
(Stereo singles): *58–60* **10–15**
BARNABY: *71* **1–3**
BUDDAH: *72–78* **2–3**
COLUMBIA: *83–85* **1–3**
ERIC: *74* **2–3**
FAME: *73* **2–4**
RCA VICTOR (Except
8000 & 10000 series):
67–79 .... **2–4**
RCA VICTOR (8000
series): *62–66* **3–5**
RCA VICTOR (10000
series): *78–81* **1–3**
RPM: *56* **20–25**

Price Range

UNITED ARTISTS: 75–77 . . . . $2–3

Promotional Singles
ABC-PARAMOUNT (104;
"Share Your Love") 10–12
(Special issue for fan club members.)

Picture Sleeves
ABC-PARAMOUNT:
56–61 10–15
RCA VICTOR (Except
11000 series): 62–65 6–10
RCA VICTOR (11000
series): 78 2–3
UNITED ARTISTS: 75 2–3

EPs: 7-Inch 33/45rpm
ABC 12–15
(Jukebox issue only.)
ABC-PARAMOUNT: 59 20–25
SIRE: 74 10–12
(Jukebox issue only.)

LPs: 10/12-Inch 33rpm
ABC-PARAMOUNT (200
series): 58–59 20–25
(With an "ABC" prefix. Monaural.)
ABC-PARAMOUNT (200
series): 58–59 35–40
(With an "ABCS" prefix. Stereo.)
ABC-PARAMOUNT (300
& 400 series, except
ABCS-323): 60–61 20–25
ABC-PARAMOUNT
(ABCS-323; "Paul Anka
Sings His Big 15"): 60 35–40
(Stereo issue.)
ACCORD: 81 5–8
BUDDAH: 71–76 6–10
CAMDEN: 74 6–10
COLUMBIA: 83–85 5–8
LIBERTY: 81–83 5–8
PICKWICK: 75 5–8
RCA VICTOR (Except
"LPM" & "LSP" series):
75–80 5–8
RCA VICTOR (With an
"LPM" or "LSP"
prefix): 62–70 10–15
RANWOOD: 81 5–8
RIVERA (0047; "Paul
Anka & Others"): 63 20–25
(Contains two tracks by Paul Anka, with the
remaining songs by other artists.)
RHINO: 86 5–8

Price Range

SIRE: 74–78 . . . . $10–12
UNITED ARTISTS: 74–78 5–8
Also see JACKS, The
Also see MARLO, Micki

ANKA, Paul, & Odia Coates
Singles: 12-Inch 33/45rpm
EPIC: 77 4–6

Singles: 7-Inch
EPIC: 76 2–3
UNITED ARTISTS: 74–75 2–3
Also see COATES, Odia

ANKA, Paul / Sam Cooke / Neil Sedaka
LPs: 10/12-Inch 33rpm
RCA VICTOR: 64 15–20
Also see COOKE, Sam
Also see SEDAKA, Neil

ANKA, Paul, George Hamilton IV & Johnny Nash
Singles: 7-Inch
ABC-PARAMOUNT: 58 5–8
Also see ANKA, Paul
Also see HAMILTON, George
Also see NASH, Johnny

ANNETTE (Annette Funicello; Annette & The Afterbeats; Annette & The Upbeats)
Singles: 7-Inch
BUENA VISTA (Except
336 & 440): 59–65 5–8
BUENA VISTA (336,
"Jo-Jo The Dog Faced
Boy"/"Lonely Guitar"):
59 10-15
BUENA VISTA (336,
"Jo-Jo The Dog Faced
Boy"/"Love Me
Forever"): 59 5–8
(Note different flip side on each of the above.)
BUENA VISTA (440;
"The Monkey's Uncle"):
65 10–12
(With The Beach Boys.)
DISNEYLAND: 57–58 8–10
EPIC: 65 4–6
STARVIEW: 83 1–3
TOWER: 67 4–6

Price Range

Picture Sleeves
BUENA VISTA: *60–65* $10–20
DISNEYLAND: *58* 20–25
EPs: 7-Inch 33/45rpm
BUENA VISTA: *59* 25–30
DISNEYLAND: *58* 25–30
LPs: 10/12-Inch 33rpm
BUENA VISTA: *59–65* 25–35
RHINO (Except picture
  discs): *84* 5–8
RHINO (Picture Discs): *84* 10–12
SILHOUETTE. 8–10
STARVIEW: *84* 5–8
  Also see BEACH BOYS, The

ANNETTE & HALEY MILLS
LPs: 10/12-Inch 33rpm
BUENA VISTA: *62* 25–35
  Also see MILLS, Haley

ANNETTE & TOMMY SANDS
Singles: 7-Inch
BUENA VISTA: *61* 5–8
Picture Sleeves
BUENA VISTA: *61* 8–12
  Also see ANNETTE
  Also see SANDS, Tommy

ANNIE G.
Singles: 12-Inch 33/45rpm
MCA: *84* 4–6
Singles: 7-Inch
MCA: *84* 1–3

ANN-MARGRET (Ann-Margret & The Ja-Da Quartet)
Singles: 12-Inch 33/45rpm
OCEAN/ARIOLA
  AMERICA: *79* 4–8
Singles: 7-Inch
LHI: *68* 2–4
MCA: *80* 1–3
OCEAN/ARIOLA
  AMERICA: *79* 1–3
RCA VICTOR: *61–62* 8–15
  (With a "37" prefix. Compact 33 Singles.)
RCA VICTOR: *61–66* 3–6
  (With a "47" prefix.)
WARNER BROS: *59* 5–10
Picture Sleeves
RCA VICTOR: *61–63* 6–10

Price Range

EPs: 7-Inch 33/45rpm
RCA VICTOR: *63* $15–20
LPs: 10/12-Inch 33rpm
LHI: *68–69* 12–15
MCA: *80* 5–8
RCA VICTOR (Except
  2399): *61–66*. 15–25
RCA VICTOR (2399;
  "And Here She Is"): *61* 25–30
WARNER BROS: *59* 30–40

ANN-MARGRET & JOHN GARY
LPs: 10/12-Inch 33rpm
RCA VICTOR: *64* 10–20
  Also see GARY, John

ANN-MARGRET & LEE HAZLEWOOD
Singles: 7-Inch
LHI: *69* 2–4
LPs: 10/12-Inch 33rpm
LHI: *69* 12–15
  Also see HAZLEWOOD, Lee

ANN-MARGRET & AL HIRT
LPs: 10/12-Inch 33rpm
RCA VICTOR: *64* 10–20
  Also see HIRT, Al

ANN-MARGRET / Kitty Kalen / Della Reese
LPs: 10/12-Inch 33rpm
RCA VICTOR: *63* 15–20
  Also see ANN-MARGRET
  Also see KALEN, Kitty
  Also see REESE, Della

ANT, Adam
Singles: 12-Inch 33/45rpm
EPIC: *82–85* 4–6
Singles: 7-Inch
EPIC: *82–85* 1–3
LPs: 10/12-Inch 33rpm
EPIC: *82–85* 5–8
  Also see ADAM & THE ANTS

ANTELL, Peter
Singles: 7-Inch
BOUNTY: *65*. 4–6
CAMEO: *62–63*. 3–5
  Also see WILD ONES, The

Price Range

ANTHONY, Alan
Singles: 7-Inch
CHALET: *82*.................... **$1–3**

ANTHONY, Ray, & His Orchestra
Singles: 7-Inch
CAPITOL: *50–62* **2–4**
EPs: 7-Inch 33/45rpm
CAPITOL: *52–59* **4–8**
LPs: 10/12-Inch 33rpm
CAPITOL: *52–62* **5–15**
Also see BEACH BOYS, The
Also see SINATRA, Frank

ANTHONY & THE IMPERIALS: see LITTLE ANTHONY & THE IMPERIALS

ANTHRAX
LPs: 10/12-Inch 33rpm
ISLAND: *85* **5–8**

ANTON, Susan
Singles: 7-Inch
COLUMBIA: *78*.................. **1–3**
Also see KNOBLOCK, Fred, & Susan Anton

AORTA
Singles: 7-Inch
ATLANTIC: *68* **3–5**
COLUMBIA: *69*.................. **2–4**
LPs: 10/12-Inch 33rpm
COLUMBIA (9000 series):
69 .... **15–20**
(With a "CS" prefix.)
COLUMBIA (38000 series) **5–8**
HAPPY TIGER: *70*............. **12–15**

APOLLO 100
Singles: 7-Inch
MEGA: *71–72*................... **1–3**
LPs: 10/12-Inch 33rpm
MEGA: *72*..................... **5–10**

APOLLONIA 6
Singles: 12-Inch 33/45rpm
WARNER BROS: *84–85*........... **4–6**
Singles: 7-Inch
WARNER BROS: *84–85*........... **1–3**

Price Range

LPs: 10/12-Inch 33rpm
WARNER BROS: *84–85*.......... **$5–8**
Also see VANITY 6

APPALACHIANS, The
Singles: 7-Inch
ABC-PARAMOUNT:
62–63 .... **3–5**

APPALOOSA (Robin Batteaux)
LPs: 10/12-Inch 33rpm
COLUMBIA: *69*................ **10–15**
WHITE GOLD: *82*................ **5–8**

APPLEJACKS, The (Featuring Dave Appell)
Singles: 7-Inch
CAMEO (Except 100
series): *61–64*.................. **3–5**
CAMEO (100 series):
57–60 .... **4–6**
DECCA: *54*...................... **5–8**
PRESIDENT: *56*................. **5–6**
TONE-CRAFT: *55*................ **4–6**

APRIL WINE
Singles: 7-Inch
BIG TREE: *72–75* **2–4**
CAPITOL: *78–84* **1–3**
LONDON: *76–78* **2–3**
Picture Sleeves
CAPITOL (Except 4975):
81 .... **INC**
CAPITOL (4975; "Just
Between You & Me"):
81 .... **2–3**
(Sleeve opens to become a 22x15 poster.)
CAPITOL (4975; "Just
Between You & Me"):
81 .... **INC**
(Standard sleeve. Does not open to become
poster.)
LPs: 10/12-Inch 33rpm
AQUARIUS **5–8**
ATLANTIC: *81* **5–8**
BIG TREE: *72–75* **10–15**
CAPITOL: *78–84* **5–8**
LONDON: *76–77* **10–12**
Members: Steve Lang; Jerry Mercer; Myles
Goodwyn; Brian Greenway; Gary Moffet.

Price Range

AQUARIAN DREAM
Singles: 7-Inch
BUDDAH: *76–77* **$2–4**
ELEKTRA: *78* **1–3**
LPs: 10/12-Inch 33rpm
BUDDAH: *76* **8–10**
ELEKTRA: *78–79* **5–8**
Members: Claude Bartee; Pete Bartee; Jacques Burvick; Mike Fowler; Valerie Horn; Gloria Jones; Pat Shannon.
Also see CONNORS, Norman

AQUARIANS, The
Singles: 7-Inch
UNI: *69* **2–4**
LPs: 10/12-Inch 33rpm
UNI: *69* **12–15**

AQUATONES, The (Featuring Barbara Lee)
Singles: 7-Inch
FARGO: *58–61* **4–6**
LPs: 10/12-Inch 33rpm
FARGO: *64* **100–125**

ARBORS, The
Singles: 7-Inch
COLUMBIA: *73* **2–4**
DATE: *66–70.* **2–5**
MERCURY: *65.* **3–5**
LPs: 10/12-Inch 33rpm
DATE: *68* **12–15**
VANGUARD: *62* **15–18**

ARCADIA
Singles: 12-Inch 33/45rpm
CAPITOL: *85* **4–6**
Singles: 7-Inch
CAPITOL: *85* **1–3**
LPs: 10/12-Inch 33rpm
CAPITOL: *85* **5–8**
Members: Roger Taylor; Simon LeBon.
Also see DURAN DURAN
Also see TAYLOR, Roger

ARCHIBALD (Archibald With Dave Bartholomew's Band)
Singles: 7-Inch
IMPERIAL (Except 5212):
52–57 .... **10–15**

Price Range

IMPERIAL (5212; "Early
Morning Blues"): *52* **$40–45**

ARCHIES, The
Singles: 7-Inch
CALENDAR: *68–69* **2–4**
ERIC: *81* **1–3**
KIRSHNER: *69–72* **2–4**
Picture Sleeves
CALENDAR: *68* **2–4**
LPs: 10/12-Inch 33rpm
ACCORD: *81* **5–8**
BACK-TRAC: *85* **5–8**
CALENDAR: *68–70* **10–12**
51 WEST: *79* **5–8**
KIRSHNER: *69–71* **8–10**
Promotional LPs
RCA VICTOR (0221;
"The Archies"): *70* **15–20**
Members: Ron Dante; Jeff Barry; Toni Wine. Cross-referenced below are some other performers who have appeared on Archies' recordings.
Also see GREENWICH, Ellie
Also see KIM, Andy
Also see STEVENS, Ray
Also see TEMPO, Nino

ARDEN, Toni
Singles: 7-Inch
COLUMBIA: *50–54* **2–5**
DECCA: *57–59* **2–4**
RCA VICTOR: *55–56* **2–4**
EPs: 7-Inch 33/45rpm
DECCA: *58* **4–6**
COLUMBIA: *56* **4–6**
LPs: 10/12-Inch 33rpm
DECCA: *57–59* **5–10**

AREA CODE 615
Singles: 7-Inch
POLYDOR: *69–70* **2–4**
LPs: 10/12-Inch 33rpm
POLYDOR: *69–70* **8–10**

ARENA BRASS, The
LPs: 10/12-Inch 33rpm
EPIC: *62* **4–6**

ARGENT
Singles: 7-Inch
DATE: *70* **3–5**

Price Range

EPIC: *69–74* $2–4
  LPs: 10/12-Inch 33rpm
EPIC: *69–75* 10–15
UNITED ARTISTS: *76* 5–8
  Members: Rod Argent; Russ Ballard; Robert
  Henrit; Jim Rodford; John Verity.
  Also see BALLARD, Russ
  Also see ZOMBIES, The

ARKADE
  Singles: 7-Inch
DUNHILL: *70–71*. 2–4

ARLEN, Harold, With "Friend"
  LPs: 10/12-Inch 33rpm
COLUMBIA (2920;
  "Harold Sings Arlen") 5–8
  (With a "CSP" prefix.)
COLUMBIA (2920;
  "Harold Sings Arlen"):
  66 20–30
  (With an "OS" prefix. Stereo issue.)
COLUMBIA (6520;
  "Harold Sings Arlen"):
  66 20–30
  (With an "OL" prefix. Monaural issue.)
  Members: Harold Arlen; Barbra Streisand.
  Also see STREISAND, Barbra

ARMADA ORCHESTRA, The
  LPs: 10/12-Inch 33rpm
SCEPTER: *75* 4–6

ARMAGEDDON
  Singles: 7-Inch
CAPITOL: *71–72* 3–5
CREATIVE SOUND: *71* 3–5
  LPs: 10/12-Inch 33rpm
A&M: *75* 8–10
AMOS: *70* 15–18
  Members: Keith Relf; Louis Cennamo; Martin
  Pugh.
  Also see RENAISSANCE
  Also see YARDBIRDS, The

ARMATRADING, Joan
  Singles: 12-Inch 33/45rpm
A&M: *83* 4–6
  Singles: 7-Inch
A&M: *74–85* 1–3
  LPs: 10/12-Inch 33rpm
A&M: *73–85* 8–12

Price Range

ARMEN, Kay
  Singles: 7-Inch
DECCA: *57–59*. $2–3
LONDON: *50–51* 2–4
MGM: *55–56*. 2–3
RCA VICTOR: *53* 2–4
20TH CENTURY-FOX:
  61 2–3
  LPs: 10/12-Inch 33rpm
DECCA: *59*. 4–8
MGM: *54–56*. 4–8
VARSITY: *53* 5–12

ARMENIAN JAZZ SEXTET, The
  Singles: 7-Inch
KAPP: *57–58*. 2–4

ARMENTA
  Singles: 12-Inch 33/45rpm
SAVIOR FAIRE: *83* 4–6

ARMORED SAINT
  LPs: 10/12-Inch 33rpm
CHRYSALIS: *84–85*. 5–8

ARMS, Russell
  Singles: 7-Inch
EPIC: *54–56* 2–4
ERA: *56–57*. 2–4
  LPs: 10/12-Inch 33rpm
ERA: *57*. 8–12

ARMSTEAD, Joshie "Jo"
  Singles: 7-Inch
DE LEX: *62* 4–6
GIANT: *67–69* 2–3
TRUTH: *74*. 2–3

ARMSTRONG, Chuck
  Singles: 7-Inch
R&R: *76*. 2–3

ARMSTRONG, Louis (Louis Armstrong & The All Stars)
  Singles: 7-Inch
ABC: *67–73* 1–3
AMSTERDAM: *71*. 1–3
AUDIO FIDELITY: *71*. 1–3
AVCO EMBASSY: *71* 1–3
BRUNSWICK: *67–68*. 2–3

Price Range

BUENA VISTA: *68* $2–3
CAPITOL: *56* 2–4
COLUMBIA: *56–66* 2–4
CONTINENTAL: *71* 2–3
DECCA (25000 series):
   61–64 2–3
DECCA (27000 through
   29000 series): *50–56* 3–5
DECCA (30000 through
   31000 series): *56–59* 2–4
DOT: *59* 2–4
EPIC: *69* 2–3
KAPP: *64–69* 2–4
MGM: *59–60* 2–4
MERCURY: *64–66* 2–4
RCA VICTOR: *56* 2–4
UNITED ARTISTS: *68–69* 2–3
VERVE: *59–60* 2–4

Picture Sleeves

BUENA VISTA: *68* 2–3
CONTINENTAL: *71* 2–3
KAPP: *64* 2–4
MERCURY: *64* 2–4

EPs: 7-Inch 33/45rpm

COLUMBIA: *55–59* 5–10
DECCA: *55–57* 5–10
RCA VICTOR: *53–59* 5–10

LPs: 10/12-Inch 33rpm

ABC: *68–76* 5–10
AMSTERDAM: *70* 5–8
AUDIO FIDELITY: *60* 15–20
BIOGRAPH: *73* 5–8
BRUNSWICK: *68–71* 6–10
BUENA VISTA: *68* 8–12
CHIAROSCURO: *77* 5–8
COLUMBIA (700 through
   900 series): *55–57* 20–30
COLUMBIA (2600 series):
   67 8–12
COLUMBIA (9400 series):
   67 8–12
COLUMBIA (30000
   series): *71–80* 8–12
CORAL: *73* 5–8
DECCA (100 series): *65–66* 15–20
DECCA (4000 series):
   61–63 10–15
DECCA (5000 series):
   51–54 25–35
   (10-Inch LPs.)

Price Range

DECCA (8000 series):
   55–59 . . . . $15–20
DECCA (9000 series): *67* 8–12
   (Decca LP numbers in this series preceded by
   a "7" or a "DL-7" are stereo issues.)
EVEREST: *71–76* 5–8
GNP/CRESCENDO: *77* 8–12
HARMONY: *69* 5–10
JAZZ HERITAGE: *80* 5–8
MCA: *73–82* 6–10
MERCURY: *66* 10–12
METRO: *65* 10–12
MILESTONE: *74–75* 5–8
OLYMPIC: *74* 5–8
PAUSA: *83* 5–8
RCA VICTOR (1300 &
   1400 series): *53–56* 20–30
RCA VICTOR (2300
   through 2900 series):
   61–64 10–15
   (With an "LPM" or "LSP" prefix.)
RCA VICTOR (2600
   series): *77* 5–8
   (With a "CPL1" prefix.)
RCA VICTOR (5500
   series): *77* 8–12
RCA VICTOR (6000
   series): *71* 8–12
SAGA: *72* 5–8
STORYVILLE: *80* 5–8
TRIP: *72* 5–8
UNITED ARTISTS: *68–69* 2–3
VANGUARD: *76* 8–12
VERVE: *60–64* 15–20
VOCALION: *68–69* 5–10
   Also see BARRY, John
   Also see BRUBECK, Dave, & Louis Armstrong
   Also see CROSBY, Bing, & Louis Armstrong
   Also see FITZGERALD, Ella, & Louis Armstrong
   Also see JENKINS, Gordon, & His Orchestra
   Also see KAYE, Danny, & Louis Armstrong
   Also see MILLS BROTHERS, The, & Louis Armstrong

ARMSTRONG, Louis, & Duke Ellington

Singles: 7-Inch

ROULETTE: *63* 2–4

LPs: 10/12-Inch 33rpm
ROULETTE (100 series):
71 . . . . **$8–12**
ROULETTE (52000
series): *63* **15–20**
   Also see ELLINGTON, Duke

ARMSTRONG, Louis, & Guy Lombardo
Singles: 7-Inch
CAPITOL: *66* **2–3**
   Also see LOMBARDO, Guy

ARMSTRONG, Louis, & Oscar Peterson
Singles: 7-Inch
VERVE: *59* **2–4**
LPs: 10/12-Inch 33rpm
VERVE: *59* **15–20**
   Also see ARMSTRONG, Louis
   Also see PETERSON, Oscar

ARNELL, Ginny
Singles: 7-Inch
DECCA: *60* **3–5**
MGM: *63–65* **3–5**
WARWICK: *61* **3–5**
LPs: 10/12-Inch 33rpm
MGM: *64* **10–20**
   Also see JAMIE & JANE

ARNO, Audrey
Singles: 7-Inch
DECCA: *61* **3–5**

ARNOLD, Calvin
Singles: 7-Inch
IX CHAINS: *75* **2–4**
VENTURE: *67–68* **3–5**

ARNOLD, Eddy
Singles: 7-Inch
MGM: *73–76* **1–3**
RCA VICTOR (0100
through 0400 series):
50–51 . . . . **4–6**
   (Black or turquoise labels.)
RCA VICTOR (0500
through 0700 series):
71–72 . . . . **1–3**
   (Orange labels.)

RCA VICTOR (4000
through 6000 series):
51–57 . . . . **$3–5**
RCA VICTOR (7000
through 9000 series):
57–71 . . . . **2–4**
RCA VICTOR (10000
through 13000 series):
76–83 . . . . **1–3**

Picture Sleeves
RCA VICTOR: *56–66* **2–5**

EPs: 7-Inch 33/45rpm
RCA VICTOR (100 series):
61 . . . . **10–12**
   (With an "LPC" prefix. Compact 33 Double.)
RCA VICTOR (200
through 900 series):
52–56 . . . . **10–15**
   (With an "EPA" prefix.)
RCA VICTOR (1100 &
1200 series): *55–56* **15–20**
   (With an "EPB" prefix.)
RCA VICTOR (1400 &
1500 series): *57* **8–12**
   (With an "EPA" prefix.)
RCA VICTOR (3000
series): *52–54* **20–25**
   (With an "EPB" prefix.)
RCA VICTOR (4000 &
5000 series): *57–59* **6–12**
   (With an "EPA" prefix.)

LPs: 10/12-Inch 33rpm
CAMDEN: *72–74* **5–10**
   (With an "ACL1" prefix.)
CAMDEN (CAL & CAS
series): *60–72* **8–15**
   (With a "CAL," "CAS" or "CXS" prefix.)
GREEN VALLEY: *76* **8–10**
K-TEL: *74* **8–10**
MGM: *74–76* **8–12**
RCA VICTOR (AHL1,
ANL1, APL1, & AYL1
series): *73–81* **5–10**
RCA VICTOR (CPL1
series): *83* **8–12**
RCA VICTOR (1100
through 2200 series):
55–60 . . . . **20–30**
   (Monaural issues. With an "LPM" prefix.)

Price Range

RCA VICTOR (2300
through 2900 series):
60–64 . . . . **$12–20**
(Monaural issues. With an "LPM" prefix.)
RCA VICTOR (3000
series): *52–54* **45–55**
(10-Inch LPs. With an "LPM" prefix.)
RCA VICTOR (3000
series): *64–68* **8–12**
(12-Inch LPs. With an "LPM" prefix.)
RCA VICTOR (1900
through 3400 series):
60–65 . . . . **15–25**
(Stereo issues. With an "LSP" prefix. "LSP"
numbers below 1900 were reprocessed stereo
issues of fifties' LPs. They were issued in the
sixties and are in the $10-$15 range.)
RCA VICTOR (3500
through 4800 series):
68–73 . . . . **10–15**
RCA VICTOR (6000
series): *70* **8–12**
SUNRISE: *79*. **5–8**
TIME-LIFE: *81*. **5–8**

ARRINGTON, Steve (Steve Arrington's Hall Of Fame)
Singles: 12-Inch 33/45rpm
ATLANTIC: *83* **4–6**

Singles: 7-Inch
ATLANTIC: *83–85* **1–3**
KONGLATHER: *82* **1–3**

LPs: 10/12-Inch 33rpm
ATLANTIC: *83–85* **5–8**
Also see SLAVE

ART ATTACK
Singles: 12-Inch 33/45rpm
B.M.O: *83* **4–6**

Singles: 7-Inch
B.M.O: *83* **1–3**

LPs: 10/12-Inch 33rpm
B.M.O: *83* **5–8**

ART IN AMERICA
Singles: 7-Inch
PAVILLION: *83*. **1–3**

LPs: 10/12-Inch 33rpm
PAVILLION: *83*. **5–8**

Price Range

ART OF NOISE, The
Singles: 12-Inch 33/45rpm
ISLAND: *83–84* **$4–6**
Singles: 7-Inch
ISLAND: *83–84* **1–3**
LPs: 10/12-Inch 33rpm
ISLAND: *84–85* **5–8**

ARTISTICS, The
Singles: 7-Inch
BRUNSWICK: *66–73*. **2–4**
OKEH: *63–66* **3–5**
LPs: 10/12-Inch 33rpm
BRUNSWICK: *67–73*. **10–12**
OKEH: *67* **12–18**
Members: Jesse Bolian; Daniel Reed; Bernard
Reed; Larry Johnson; Tommy Green.

ARTISTS UNITED AGAINST APARTHEID
Singles: 12-Inch 33/45rpm
MANHATTAN: *85* **4–6**
Singles: 7-Inch
MANHATTAN: *85* **1–3**
LPs: 10/12-Inch 33rpm
MANHATTAN: *85* **5–8**

ARVON, Bobby
Singles: 7-Inch
ARIOLA AMERICAN: *76*. **2–3**
FIRST ARTISTS: *77–78* **1–3**
LPs: 10/12-Inch 33rpm
FIRST ARTISTS: *78* **5–8**

ASHE, Clarence
Singles: 7-Inch
ABC-PARAMOUNT: *65*. **3–5**
CHESS: *64*. **3–5**
J&S: *64*. **3–5**

ASHFORD, Nick
Singles: 7-Inch
ABC: *70*. **2–4**
VERVE: *66–68* **3–5**
Also see ASHFORD & SIMPSON

ASHFORD & SIMPSON
Singles: 12-Inch 33/45rpm
CAPITOL: *82–85* **4–6**
WARNER BROS: *79* **4–6**

Price Range

Singles: 7-Inch
CAPITOL: *82–85* **$1–3**
EMI AMERICA: *84–85*............ **1–3**
WARNER BROS: *73–79*........... **1–3**
Picture Sleeves
CAPITOL: *80–82* .... **INC**
LPs: 10/12-Inch 33rpm
CAPITOL: *82–85* **5–8**
WARNER BROS (Except
HS series): *73–81*............... **5–10**
WARNER BROS (HS
series): *79–80* **15–18**
(Half-speed mastered LPs.)
Members: Nick Ashford; Valerie Simpson.
Also see ASHFORD, Nick
Also see JONES, Quincy
Also see SIMPSON, Valerie
Also see VALERIE & NICK

ASHLEY, Del (David Gates)
Singles: 7-Inch
PLANETARY: *65* **8–15**
Also see GATES, David

ASHLEY, Tyrone (Tyrone Ashley & The Funky Music Machine)
Singles: 7-Inch
PHIL-L.A. OF SOUL:
70–71 .... **2–4**
UNITED ARTISTS: *78*............ **1–3**
LPs: 10/12-Inch 33rpm
UNITED ARTISTS: *78*............ **5–8**

ASHTON, GARDNER & DYKE
Singles: 7-Inch
CAPITOL: *70–72* **2–4**
LPs: 10/12-Inch 33rpm
CAPITOL: *70–72* **8–10**
Members: Tony Ashton; Kim Gardner; Roy Dyke.
Also see BADGER

ASIA
Singles: 7-Inch
GEFFEN: *82–85*.................. **1–3**
Picture Sleeves
GEFFEN: *81*..................... **INC**
LPs: 10/12-Inch 33rpm
GEFFEN: *82–85*.................. **5–8**
Members: Steve Howe; Carl Palmer; John Wetton; Geoff Downes; Mandy Mayer.
Also see EMERSON, LAKE & PALMER

Price Range

Also see HOWE, Steve, Band

ASLEEP AT THE WHEEL (Featuring Ray Benson)
Singles: 7-Inch
CAPITOL: *75–79* **$1–3**
EPIC: *74* **2–3**
LPs: 10/12-Inch 33rpm
CAPITOL: *75–79* **5–8**
EPIC (33000 series): *75* **12–15**
(With a "BG" prefix.)
EPIC (33000 series).............. **10–12**
(With an "EG" prefix.)
EPIC (33000 series): *74* **8–10**
(With a "KE" prefix.)
EPIC (33000 series)................ **5–8**
(With a "PE" prefix.)
MCA: *80–84* **5–8**
UNITED ARTISTS: *73*............ **8–12**

ASPHALT JUNGLE
Singles: 7-Inch
TEC: *80* **1–3**

ASSEMBLED MULTITUDE, The
Singles: 7-Inch
ATLANTIC: *70–72* **2–4**
ERIC: *81* **1–3**
LPs: 10/12-Inch 33rpm
ATLANTIC: *70* **8–10**

ASSOCIATION, The
Singles: 7-Inch
COLUMBIA: *72*.................. **2–4**
ELEKTRA: *81* **1–3**
JUBILEE: *65*..................... **4–6**
MUMS: *73*....................... **2–4**
RCA VICTOR: *75* **2–4**
VALIANT: *66*.................... **2–5**
WARNER BROS: *67–71*........... **2–4**
Picture Sleeves
VALIANT: *66*.................... **2–5**
LPs: 10/12-Inch 33rpm
COLUMBIA: *72*.................. **8–10**
VALIANT: *66*................... **12–15**
WARNER BROS: *67–70*.......... **10–12**
Members: Gary Alexander; Ted Bluechel, Jr; Brian Cole; Russ Giguere; Terry Kirkman; Cliff Nivison; Larry Ramos; Richard Thompson; Jim Yester.

Price Range

Price Range

ASTORS, The
Singles: 7-Inch
STAX: 65–67 . . . . $3–5

ASTRONAUTS, The
Singles: 7-Inch
PALLADIUM: 61 50–60
RCA VICTOR: 63–65 4–6
Picture Sleeves
RCA VICTOR: 63 15–20
EPs: 7-Inch 33/45rpm
RCA VICTOR: 63 20–22
RCA VICTOR
WURLITZER
DISCOTHEQUE: 64 25–30
(Promotional issue only.)
LPs: 10/12-Inch 33rpm
RCA VICTOR: 64–67 20–30

ASYLUM CHOIR, The
Singles: 7-Inch
SHELTER: 71 2–4
SMASH: 69 2–4
LPs: 10/12-Inch 33rpm
SHELTER (2000 series):
74 8–10
SHELTER (8000 series):
71 12–15
SHELTER (52000 series):
75 5–8
SMASH (67107; "Look
Inside"): 68 25–30
(With toilet tissue cover.)
SMASH (67107; "Look
Inside"): 68 10–15
(With photo cover.)
Members: Leon Russell; Marc Benno.
Also see BENNO, Marc
Also see RUSSELL, Leon

ATILLA (With Billy Joel)
LPs: 10/12-Inch 33rpm
BACK-TRAC: 85 5–8
EPIC: 70 40–45
Also see JOEL, Billy

ATKINS
Singles: 7-Inch
WARNER BROS: 82 1–3
LPs: 10/12-Inch 33rpm
WARNER BROS: 82 5–8

ATKINS, Chet
Singles: 7-Inch
RCA VICTOR (0100
through 0400 series):
50–51 . . . . $4–6
(Black or turquoise labels.)
RCA VICTOR (0100
through 0700 series):
71–74 1–3
(Orange labels.)
RCA VICTOR (4000
through 6000 series):
51–57 3–5
RCA VICTOR (7000
through 9000 series):
57–71 2–4
RCA VICTOR (10000
through 13000 series):
75–83 1–3

Picture Sleeves
RCA VICTOR: 61–67 2–4

EPs: 7-Inch 33/45rpm
RCA VICTOR (100 series):
61 8–12
(With an "LPC" prefix. Compact 33 Double.)
RCA VICTOR (500
through 900 series):
55–56 8–12
(With an "EPA" prefix.)
RCA VICTOR (1100 &
1200 series): 55–56 8–12
(With an "EPB" prefix.)
RCA VICTOR (1300
through 1500 series):
56–57 8–12
(With an "EPA" prefix.)
RCA VICTOR (3000
series): 52–54 15–20
(With an "EPB" prefix.)
RCA VICTOR (4000 &
5000 series): 58–60 5–10
SESAC (13; "Mr. Atkins If
You Please"): 59 20–30
(Promotional issue only.)

LPs: 10/12-Inch 33rpm
CAMDEN: 61–72 8–12
COLUMBIA: 83–85 5–8
DOLTON: 67 15–20
PICKWICK/CAMDEN:
75 8–10

Price Range

RCA VICTOR (AHL1,
ANL1, APL1, & AYL1
series): *73–83* **$5–10**
RCA VICTOR (CPL1
series): *77* **8–12**
RCA VICTOR (1000
series): *54* **25–35**
  (With an "LPM" prefix.)
RCA VICTOR (1100
through 2200 series,
except 1236): *55–60* **15–25**
  (With an "LPM" prefix.)
RCA VICTOR (1236:
"Stringin' Along With
Chet Atkins"): *55* **30–40**
  (With an "LPM" prefix.)
RCA VICTOR (2300
through 2900 series):
60–64 . . . . **10–15**
  (With an "LPM" prefix.)
RCA VICTOR (3000
series): *53* **45–55**
  (10-Inch LPs. With an "LPM" prefix.)
RCA VICTOR (3000
series): *64–68* **8–12**
  (12-Inch LPs. With an "LPM" prefix.)
RCA VICTOR (2000 &
3000 series): *66–69* **10–15**
  (With an "LSC" prefix.)
RCA VICTOR (1900
through 3400 series):
60–65 . . . . **10–20**
  (Stereo issues. With an "LSP" prefix. "LSP"
  numbers below 1900 were reprocessed stereo
  issues of fifties' LPs. They were issued in the
  sixties and are in the $10-$15 range.)
RCA VICTOR (3500
through 4800 series):
68–73 . . . . **8–12**
RCA VICTOR (6000
series): *70–72* **8–12**
TIME-LIFE: *81* **5–8**
  Also see ATKINS STRING COMPANY, The
  Also see CHARLES, Ray, George Jones &
  Chet Atkins
  Also see COUNTRY HAMS, The
  Also see KERR, Anita
  Also see REED, Jerry, & Chet Atkins
  Also see SNOW, Hank, & Chet Atkins

ATKINS, Chet, & Les Paul
Singles: 7-Inch
RCA VICTOR: *78* **1–3**

Price Range

LPs: 10/12-Inch 33rpm
RCA VICTOR: *78* **$5–8**
  Also see PAUL, Les

ATKINS, Chet, & Doc Watson
LPs: 10/12-Inch 33rpm
RCA VICTOR: *80* **5–8**
  Also see WATSON, Doc

ATKINS, Chet / Faron Young
EPs: 7-Inch 33/45rpm
SESAC (48; "No Greater
Love"): *59* **20–30**
  (Promotional issue only.)
  Also see ATKINS, Chet
  Also see YOUNG, Faron

ATKINS, Christopher
Singles: 7-Inch
POLYDOR: *82* **1–3**

ATKINS STRING COMPANY, The
Singles: 7-Inch
RCA VICTOR: *75* **1–3**
  Also see ATKINS, Chet

ATLANTA
Singles: 7-Inch
MCA: *84–85* **1–3**
MDJ: *83* **1–3**
LPs: 10/12-Inch 33rpm
MCA: *84* **5–8**

ATLANTA DISCO BAND, The
Singles: 7-Inch
ARIOLA AMERICA: *76* **1–3**
LPs: 10/12-Inch 33rpm
ARIOLA AMERICA: *76* **5–8**

**ATLANTA RHYTHM SECTION,
The**
Singles: 7-Inch
COLUMBIA: *81* **1–3**
DECCA: *72* **2–4**
MCA: *73* **2–3**
POLYDOR: *74–80* **1–3**
LPs: 10/12-Inch 33rpm
COLUMBIA: *81* **5–8**
DECCA: *72* **12–15**
MCA: *77* **5–10**
POLYDOR: *74–80* **5–8**

Price Range

Members: Ronnie Hammond; Rodney Justo; Robert Nix; Barry Bailey; J.R. Cobb; Dean Daughtry; Paul Goddard.
Also see CANDYMEN, The
Also see CLASSICS IV, The

ATLANTIC STARR (Featuring Sharon Bryant)

Singles: 12-Inch 33/45rpm
A&M: 79–85 . . . . $4–6
Singles: 7-Inch
A&M: 78–85 1–3
LPs: 10/12-Inch 33rpm
A&M: 78–84 5–8

ATOMIC ROOSTER

Singles: 7-Inch
ELEKTRA: 71–72 2–4
LPs: 10/12-Inch 33rpm
ELEKTRA: 71–73 12–15
PVC: 83 5–8
Members: Chris Farlowe; Pete French; Steve Bolton; John Cann; Vincent Crane; Paul Hammond; Carl Palmer; Johnny Mandala; Rick Parnell.
Also see BROWN, Arthur

ATTACK, Art: see ART ATTACK

ATTITUDE

Singles: 12-Inch 33/45rpm
ATLANTIC: 83 4–6
Singles: 7-Inch
ATLANTIC: 83 1–3
LPs: 10/12-Inch 33rpm
ATLANTIC: 83 5–8

ATTITUDES, The

Singles: 7-Inch
DARK HORSE: 75–76 2–4
LPs: 10/12-Inch 33rpm
DARK HORSE: 76–77 5–8
Members: Danny Kortchmar; David Foster; Jim Keltner; Paul Stallworth.

AUDIENCE

Singles: 7-Inch
ELEKTRA: 71–72 2–4
LPs: 10/12-Inch 33rpm
AUDIENCE: 71–72 10–15

Price Range

Members: Trevor Williams; Howard Werth; Pat Neubergh; Nick Judd; Tony Connor; Keith Gemmell.

AUDREY

Singles: 7-Inch
PLUS (104; "Dear Elvis"):
56 . . . . $20–25
(Break-in novelty. Contains excerpts of Elvis' recordings.)
Also see PRESLEY, Elvis

AUGER, Brian (Brian Auger & The Trinity; Brian Auger's Oblivion Express)

Singles: 7-Inch
ATCO: 68–69. 3–5
RCA VICTOR: 70–74 2–4
LPs: 10/12-Inch 33rpm
ATCO: 69 12–15
CAPITOL: 69 10–12
POLYDOR: 74 5–8
RCA VICTOR: 70–77 6–10
WARNER BROS: 77. 5–8
Also see PAGE, Jimmy, Sonny Boy Williamson & Brian Auger

AUGUST, Jan

Singles: 7-Inch
MERCURY: 50–62. 2–4
EPs: 7-Inch 33/45rpm
MERCURY: 50–56. 3–6
LPs: 10/12-Inch 33rpm
MERCURY: 50–62. 5–10
WING: 59 4–8
Also see HAYMAN, Richard, Orchestra

AURRA

Singles: 12-Inch 33/45rpm
SALSOUL: 82 4–6
Singles: 7-Inch
DREAM: 80 1–3
SALSOUL: 81–83 1–3
LPs: 10/12-Inch 33rpm
DREAM: 80 5–8
SALSOUL: 81–83 5–8
Members: Curt Jones; Starleana Young.

AUSTIN, Gene

Singles: 7-Inch
COLUMBIA: 54–56 2–4
DECCA: 56 2–4

Price Range

EPs: 7-Inch 33/45rpm
RCA VICTOR: 53 .... **$5–10**
LPs: 10/12-Inch 33rpm
RCA VICTOR: 53–57 .... **8–18**
X: 54 .... **8–18**

AUSTIN, Patti
Singles: 12-Inch 33/45rpm
QWEST: 84–85 .... **4–6**
Singles: 7-Inch
ABC: 68 .... **2–3**
CTI: 76–80 .... **1–3**
COLUMBIA: 71–73 .... **2–3**
CORAL: 65–68 .... **3–5**
QWEST: 81–85 .... **1–3**
UNITED ARTISTS: 69–70 .... **2–4**
LPs: 10/12-Inch 33rpm
CTI: 77–80 .... **5–8**
QWEST: 81–85 .... **5–8**
Also see JONES, Quincy
Also see YUTAKA

AUSTIN, Patti, & Jerry Butler
Singles: 7-Inch
CTI: 83 .... **1–3**
Also see BUTLER, Jerry

AUSTIN, Patti, & James Ingram
Singles: 7-Inch
QWEST: 82–84 .... **1–3**
Also see AUSTIN, Patti
Also see INGRAM, James

AUSTIN, Sil (Sil Austin & Red Prysock)
Singles: 7-Inch
JUBILEE: 54–55 .... **5–8**
MERCURY: 56–65 .... **3–5**
SSS INT'L: 70 .... **1–3**
SEW CITY: 66 .... **2–4**
EPs: 7-Inch 33/45rpm
MERCURY: 56–57 .... **10–15**
LPs: 10/12-Inch 33rpm
MERCURY: 59–67 .... **10–20**
SSS INT'L: 69–82 .... **8–10**
WING: 63–68 .... **10–12**

AUTOGRAPH (Featuring Steve Plunkett)
Singles: 7-Inch
RCA VICTOR: 84–85 .... **1–3**

LPs: 10/12-Inch 33rpm
RCA VICTOR: 84–85 .... **$5–8**

AUTOMATIC MAN
Singles: 7-Inch
ISLAND: 76–77 .... **2–3**
LPs: 10/12-Inch 33rpm
ISLAND: 76–77 .... **5–8**
Members: Michael Schrieve; Todd Cochran;
Doni Harvey; Pat Thrall.

AUTRY, Gene
Singles: 7-Inch
COLUMBIA (20700
through 21500 series):
50–56 .... **3–5**
COLUMBIA (38700
through 40500 series):
50–55 .... **3–5**
COLUMBIA (44000
series): 68 .... **1–3**
MISTLETOE: 74 .... **1–3**
REPUBLIC: 69–76 .... **1–3**
EPs: 7-Inch 33/45rpm
COLUMBIA: 51–56 .... **40–50**
LPs: 10/12-Inch 33rpm
BIRCHMOUNT **8–12**
CHALLENGE: 58 .... **25–30**
COLUMBIA (55 through
154): 51–55 .... **80–100**
(10-Inch LPs.)
COLUMBIA (600 series):
55 .... **80–100**
COLUMBIA (1000 series):
70–82 .... **8–10**
COLUMBIA (1500 series):
61 .... **20–25**
COLUMBIA (2500 series):
55 .... **80–100**
(10-Inch LPs.)
COLUMBIA (6000 series):
51 .... **40–60**
(10-Inch LPs.)
COLUMBIA (8000 series) **80–100**
COLUMBIA (9000 series) **40–60**
(10-Inch LPs.)
COLUMBIA (15000
series): 81 .... **8–10**
COLUMBIA (37000
series): 82 .... **5–8**
DESIGN **8–10**

GENE AUTRY

Price Range

ENCORE: *80.* $6–10
GRT: *77.* 10–15
GRAND PRIX 8–10
HALLMARK 8–12
HARMONY (7100
    through 7300 series):
    56–65 20–30
HARMONY (9000 series):
    59–64 20–25
HARMONY (11000
    series): *64–66* 10–15
HURRAH 5–8
MELODY RANCH: *65* 20–25
MISTLETOE: *74.* 8–12
MURRAY HILL (897296;
    "Melody Ranch Radio
    Show") 45–55
    (A 4-LP set.)
RCA VICTOR (2600
    series): *62* 25–30
RADIOLA: *75.* 5–8
REPUBLIC (1900 series) 5–15
    (2-LP sets.)
REPUBLIC (6000 series):
    76–78 5–15
STARDAY: *78* 6–10

AVALANCHE '77
Singles: 7-Inch
ABC: *77.* 1–3
BOBLO: *77* 2–3

Price Range

LPs: 10/12-Inch 33rpm
ABC: *77* $5–8

AVALON, Frankie
Singles: 7-Inch
ABC: *74* 1–3
AMOS: *69* 2–4
BOBCAT: *83* 1–3
CHANCELLOR (1; "Shy
    Guy") 8–10
    (Acnecare promotional special products issue.)
CHANCELLOR (1004;
    "Cupid"): *57* 8–12
CHANCELLOR (1011
    through 1139): *57–63* 4–6
    (Monaural singles.)
CHANCELLOR (Stereo
    singles): *59–60* 10–15
COLLECTABLES: *81* 1–3
DE LITE: *76–78* 2–3
ERIC: *73* 1–3
LIBERTY: *82* 5–8
MCA: *84* 1–3
METROMEDIA: *70.* 2–4
REGAILA: *72.* 2–4
REPRISE: *68–69.* 2–4
UNITED ARTISTS: *64–65* 3–5
X: *54.* 10–15

Picture Sleeves
CHANCELLOR (1026
    through 1045): *58–59* 10–15
CHANCELLOR (1048
    through 1125): *60–63* 6–10
DE LITE: *78* 2–3
UNITED ARTISTS: *64* 2–4

EPs: 7-Inch 33/45rpm
CHANCELLOR: *58–60* 15–20
X: *55* 20–25

Promotional EPs
CHANCELLOR (303;
    "Ballad Of The Alamo"):
    60 35–40
    (With complete publicity kit.)
CHANCELLOR (303;
    "Ballad Of The Alamo"):
    60 20–25
    (Without publicity kit.)
CHANCELLOR (5004;
    "Swingin On A
    Rainbow"): *59* 20–25

Price Range

Price Range

(White label. Includes paper sleeve with note from Frankie, thanking dee jays for their support.)

LPs: 10/12-Inch 33rpm
ABC: *73* **$5–8**
CHANCELLOR: *58–63* **20–30**
DE-LITE: *76–78* **5–8**
EVEREST: *82* **5–8**
MCA: *85* **5–8**
METROMEDIA: *70.* **5–8**
SUNSET: *69* **8–10**
TRIP: *77* **5–8**
UNITED ARTISTS: *64* **12–15**
(With a "UAL" or "UAS" prefix.)
UNITED ARTISTS: *75* **5–8**
(With a "UA-LA" prefix.)
Also see FABIAN / Frankie Avalon

AVANT-GARDE, The
Singles: 7-Inch
COLUMBIA: *67–68* **3–5**

AVERAGE, Johnny, Band: see JOHNNY AVERAGE BAND, The

AVERAGE WHITE BAND, The (AWB)
Singles: 7-Inch
ARISTA: *80* **1–3**
ATLANTIC: *74–80* **1–3**
MCA: *73–74* **2–4**
LPs: 10/12-Inch 33rpm
ATLANTIC (Except 19000
    series): *74–76* **8–12**
ATLANTIC (19000 series):
    77–80 .... **5–8**
MCA (Except 345): *73–75* **8–10**
MCA (345; "Show Your
    Hand"): *73* **15–18**
    (With "Jack-in-the-box" cover.)
MCA (345; "Show Your
    Hand"): *73* **8–10**
    (With standard cover.)
    Members: Roger Ball; Malcolm Duncan; Steve Ferrone; Alan Garrie; Robbie McIntosh; Owen McIntyre.
    Also see FOREVER MORE
    Also see KING, Ben E., & The Average White Band

AXE (Featuring Bobby Barth)
Singles: 7-Inch
ATCO: *82–84.* **1–3**

MCA: *79–80* **$1–3**
LPs: 10/12-Inch 33rpm
ATCO: *82–84.* **5–8**
MCA: *79–80* **5–8**

AXTON, Hoyt (Hoyt Axton & The Sherwood Singers)
Singles: 7-Inch
A&M: *73–76* **1–3**
BRIAR: *61* **3–5**
CAPITOL: *71–72* **1–3**
COLGEMS: *67* **2–4**
COLUMBIA: *69* **2–3**
ELEKTRA: *81* **1–3**
HORIZON: *62–63.* **3–5**
JEREMIAH: *79–83.* **1–3**
MCA: *77–78* **1–3**
20TH CENTURY-FOX:
    66 .... **2–4**
VEE JAY: *64–65.* **2–4**

LPs: 10/12-Inch 33rpm
A&M: *73–77* **5–8**
ACCORD: *82* **5–8**
ALLEGIANCE: *84.* **5–8**
BRYLEN: *82.* **5–8**
CAPITOL: *71* **8–10**
COLUMBIA: *69* **8–10**
EXODUS: *66.* **10–15**
HORIZON: *62–63.* **15–20**
JEREMIAH: *79–82.* **8–10**
LAKE SHORE: *81* **5–8**
MCA: *77–78* **5–8**
SURREY: *65* **15–18**
VEE JAY: *64–65.* **10–15**
VEE JAY
    INTERNATIONAL
    (Except 1000 series):
    74–77 .... **5–8**
VEE JAY
    INTERNATIONAL
    (1000 series): *74.* **10–12**

AXTON, Hoyt, & The Chambers Brothers
Singles: 7-Inch
HORIZON: *62.* **3–5**

LPs: 10/12-Inch 33rpm
HORIZON: *63.* **15–20**
    Also see AXTON, Hoyt
    Also see CHAMBERS BROTHERS, The

Price Range

AYERS, Roy (Roy Ayers' Ubiquity)
Singles: 12-Inch 33/45rpm
COLUMBIA: *84–85* $4–6
POLYDOR: *79* 4–6
Singles: 7-Inch
COLUMBIA: *84–85* 1–3
POLYDOR: *77* 2–3
LPs: 10/12-Inch 33rpm
ATLANTIC: *68–76* 8–12
COLUMBIA: *84–85* 5–8
ELEKTRA: *78* 5–8
POLYDOR: *70–81* 6–10
Also see DUNLAP, Gene
Also see UBIQUITY

AYERS, Roy, & Wayne Henderson
Singles: 7-Inch
POLYDOR: *79–80* 1–3
LPs: 10/12-Inch 33rpm
POLYDOR: *80* 5–8
Also see AYERS, Roy
Also see HENDERSON, Wayne

AZTEC CAMERA
Singles: 12-Inch 33/45rpm
SIRE: *84* 4–6
Singles: 7-Inch
SIRE: *83–85* 1–3
LPs: 10/12-Inch 33rpm
SIRE: *83–85* 5–8

AZTEC TWO STEP
Singles: 7-Inch
ELEKTRA: *72–73* 2–4
RCA VICTOR: *76–78* 2–3
LPs: 10/12-Inch 33rpm
ELEKTRA: *72* 10–12
RCA VICTOR: *76–80* 5–8
WATERHOUSE: *80* 5–8
Members: Rex Fowler; Alan Schwartzberg; Neal Schulman.

AZTECA
Singles: 7-Inch
COLUMBIA: *72–73* 2–4
LPs: 10/12-Inch 33rpm
COLUMBIA: *72–73* 10–12
Members: Coke Escovedo; Tony Smith.
Also see ESCOVEDO, Coke
Also see MALO
Also see SANTANA

B

Price Range

B.B.C.S. & A.
Singles: 7-Inch
SAM: *82* $1–3

B.B. & Q. BAND, The (The Brooklyn, Bronx & Queens Band)
Singles: 12-Inch 33/45rpm
CAPITOL: *81–83* 4–6
Singles: 7-Inch
CAPITOL: *81–83* 1–3
LPs: 10/12-Inch 33rpm
CAPITOL: *81–83* 5–8

B. BEAT GIRLS, The
Singles: 12-Inch 33/45rpm
25 WEST: *83* 4–6
Singles: 7-Inch
25 WEST: *83* 1–3

B. BUMBLE & THE STINGERS
Singles: 7-Inch
MERCURY: *66* 3–5
RENDEZVOUS: *61–63* 4–6
Members: Billy Brumble; Ron Brady; Fred Richard.

B-52s, The
Singles: 7-Inch
DB-52: *78* 5–8
WARNER BROS: *79–84* 1–3
Picture Sleeves
WARNER BROS: *80–82* . . . . INC
LPs: 10/12-Inch 33rpm
WARNER BROS: *79–84* 5–8

B-H-Y
Singles: 7-Inch
SALSOUL: *79* 1–3
LPs: 10/12-Inch 33rpm
SALSOUL: *79* 5–8

B.T. EXPRESS
Singles: 12-Inch 33/45rpm
COAST TO COAST: *81* 4–6
COLUMBIA: *81* 4–6
Singles: 7-Inch
COAST TO COAST: *82* 1–3
COLUMBIA: *76–80* 1–3

EARTHTONE: *84* **$1–3**
ROADSHOW: *75* **2–4**
SCEPTER: *74* **2–4**
LPs: 10/12-Inch 33rpm
COAST TO COAST: *82* **5–8**
COLUMBIA: *76–80* **5–8**
ROADSHOW: *75–76* **10–12**
SCEPTER: *74* **8–10**

BTO: see BACHMAN-TURNER OVERDRIVE

BABE RUTH
Singles: 7-Inch
CAPITOL: *76* **1–3**
HARVEST: *73–76* **2–4**
LPs: 10/12-Inch 33rpm
HARVEST: *73–76* **5–8**
Members: Ellie Hope; Steve Gurl; Jenny Haan;
Dave Hewitt; Ray Knott; Bernie Marsden;
Alan Shacklock; Ed Spevock.

BABY JANE & THE ROCK-A-BYES
Singles: 7-Inch
SPOKANE: *63* **6–10**
UNITED ARTISTS: *62* **5–8**

BABY RAY (Ray Eddlemon)
Singles: 7-Inch
IMPERIAL: *66–67* **3–5**
LPs: 10/12-Inch 33rpm
IMPERIAL: *67* **10–15**

BABY RAY & THE FERNS (Frank Zappa)
Singles: 7-Inch
DONNA: *63* **20–25**
Also see ZAPPA, Frank

BABYS, The
Singles: 7-Inch
CHRYSALIS: *77–81* **1–3**
Picture Sleeves
CHRYSALIS: *79* **1–3**
LPs: 10/12-Inch 33rpm
CHRYSALIS: *77–81* **5–8**
Members: Mike Corby; John Waite; Tony
Brock; Wally Stocker.
Also see WAITE, John

BACHARACH, Burt
Singles: 7-Inch
A&M: *69–74* **$1–3**
KAPP: *63–65* **2–4**
LIBERTY: *66* **1–3**
UNITED ARTISTS: *67* **1–3**
Picture Sleeves
A&M: *71* **1–3**
LPs: 10/12-Inch 33rpm
A&M: *67–74* **5–10**
KAPP: *65* **8–15**
MCA: *73* **5–8**

BACHELORS, The
Singles: 7-Inch
LONDON: *63–72* **3–5**
Picture Sleeves
LONDON: *64–65* **3–5**
LPs: 10/12-Inch 33rpm
LONDON: *64–72* **10–15**
Members: Con Cluskey; Declan Stokes; John
Stokes.

BACHMAN, Randy
Singles: 7-Inch
POLYDOR: *78* **1–3**
LPs: 10/12-Inch 33rpm
POLYDOR: *78* **5–8**
RCA VICTOR (1100
series): *75* **5–8**
RCA VICTOR (4300
series): *70* **10–12**
Also see BACHMAN-TURNER-BACHMAN
Also see BACHMAN-TURNER OVER-DRIVE
Also see GUESS WHO, The
Also see IRONHORSE

BACHMAN-TURNER-BACHMAN
LPs: 10/12-Inch 33rpm
REPRISE: *75* **8–10**
Members: Randy Bachman; C.F. Turner;
Robin Bachman.
Also see BRAVE BELT

BACHMAN-TURNER OVERDRIVE
Singles: 7-Inch
COMPLEAT: *84–85* **1–3**
MERCURY: *73–79* **2–4**
Picture Sleeves
MERCURY: *74–75* **2–4**

Price Range

LPs: 10/12-Inch 33rpm
COMPLEAT: *84–85* **$5–8**
MERCURY: *73–78* **8–12**
  Members: Randy Bachman; C.F. Turner;
  Robin Bachman; Tim Bachman; Jim Clench;
  Norman Durkee; Blair Thornton.
  Also see BACHMAN, Randy

BACK STREET CRAWLER
(Crawler)
Singles: 7-Inch
EPIC: *77–78* **2–3**
LPs: 10/12-Inch 33rpm
ATCO: *75–76* **10–12**
EPIC (Except picture
  discs): *77–78* **5–8**
EPIC (Picture discs): *78* **25–30**
  Members: Tony Braunagel; John Bundrick;
  Paul Kossoff; Mike Montgomery; Geoff White-
  horn; Terry Wilson Slesser.
  Also see FREE
  Also see KOSSOFF, Paul

BACKTRACK (Featuring John Hunt)
Singles: 7-Inch
GOLDMINE: *85* **1–3**

BACKUS, Jim (Jim Backus & Friend)
Singles: 7-Inch
JUBILEE: *58–59* **3–5**
LPs: 10/12-Inch 33rpm
DORE: *74* **6–10**

BAD BOYS FEATURING K LOVE, The
Singles: 12-Inch 33/45rpm
STARLITE: *85* **4–6**

BAD COMPANY
Singles: 7-Inch
SWAN SONG: *74–84* **2–4**
Picture Sleeves
SWAN SONG: *79* **1–3**
LPs: 10/12-Inch 33rpm
SWAN SONG: *74–84* **6–10**
  Members: Paul Rodgers; Boz Burrell; Simon
  Kirke; Mick Ralphs; Mick Jones; Brian Howe.
  Also see FIRM, The
  Also see FOREIGNER
  Also see FREE
  Also see KING CRIMSON

Price Range

Also see NUGENT, Ted
Also see RODGERS, Paul

BAD GIRLS, The
Singles: 7-Inch
BC: *81* **$1–3**

BAD HABITS, The
Singles: 7-Inch
PAULA: *70–72* **2–4**
  Members: Delaney Bramlett; Bonnie Bramlett.
  Also see DELANEY & BONNIE

BADFINGER
Singles: 7-Inch
APPLE: *70–73* **4–6**
ATLANTIC: *81* **1–3**
ELEKTRA: *79* **2–3**
RADIO: *81* **1–3**
WARNER BROS: *74* **2–4**
Picture Sleeves
SWAN SONG: *72* **4–6**
LPs: 10/12-Inch 33rpm
APPLE (Except 3387):
  70–73 . . . . **10–20**
APPLE (3387; "Straight
  Up"): *71* **35–50**
ELEKTRA: *79* **5–8**
RADIO: *81* **5–8**
WARNER BROS: *74* **8–10**
  Members: Tom Evans; Mike Gibbons; Pete
  Ham; Joey Molland; Peter Clarke; Tony Kaye.
  Also see IVEYS, The

BADGER
LPs: 10/12-Inch 33rpm
ATCO: *73* **10–12**
EPIC: *74* **8–10**
  Members: Roy Dyke; Kim Gardner; Dave Fos-
  ter; Tony Kaye; Jackie Lomax; Brian Parrish;
  Paul Pilnick.
  Also see ASHTON, GARDNER & DYKE
  Also see LOMAX, Jackie

BAEZ, Joan
Singles: 7-Inch
A&M: *72–77* **2–4**
PORTRAIT: *77–79* **2–3**
VANGUARD (35000
  series): *63–69* **3–5**
VANGUARD (35100
  series): *70–71* **2–4**

Price Range

Picture Sleeves
A&M: *72* **$2–4**
PORTRAIT: *79*.................... **1–3**
VANGUARD: *65–67*.............. **4–6**

LPs: 10/12-Inch 33rpm
A&M (Except 8375): *72–77*........ **6–10**
A&M (8375; "Joan Baez
  Radio Airplay Album"):
  76 .... **10–15**
  (Promotional issue only.)
EMUS........................... **8–12**
FANTASY **10–15**
PORTRAIT: *77–79*................. **5–8**
SQUIRE: *63* **15–20**
VANGUARD (41/42;
  "Ballad Book"): *72* **10–12**
VANGUARD (077
  through 123): *60–63* **15–20**
VANGUARD (160
  through 306): *64–69* **10–15**
VANGUARD (308
  through 332): *69–73* **6–10**
VANGUARD (400 series)........... **5–8**
  (Vanguard numbers 077 through 446 may be
  preceeded by a "2," indicating mono, or a "9"
  or "79" for stereo issues.)
VANGUARD (6500
  series): *70–71* **10–12**

BAGBY, Doc
Singles: 7-Inch
END: *60*........................ **3–5**
KAISER: *59* **3–5**
OKEH: *57*....................... **4–6**
TALLY HO: *61*................... **3–5**
VIM: *57*........................ **4–6**
LPs: 10/12-Inch 33rpm
KING: *59* **20–25**
Also see TERRY, Sonny

BAILEY, Arthur
Singles: 12-Inch 33/45rpm
ATLANTIC: *84* **4–6**
Singles: 7-Inch
ATLANTIC: *84* **1–3**

BAILEY, J.R.
Singles: 7-Inch
CALLA: *68*...................... **3–5**
MAM: *74*........................ **2–4**
MIDLAND INT'L: *75*.............. **2–4**

Price Range

RCA VICTOR: *76* **$2–4**
SPRING: *84* **1–3**
TOY: *72–73*..................... **2–4**
UNITED ARTISTS: *78*............ **1–3**
LPs: 10/12-Inch 33rpm
MAM: *74*....................... **8–10**
UNITED ARTISTS: *78*............ **5–8**

BAILEY, Pearl
Singles: 7-Inch
COLUMBIA (38000
  series): *50*..................... **3–5**
COLUMBIA (43000
  series): *66*..................... **2–4**
CORAL: *52–55*................... **3–5**
DECCA: *64*...................... **2–4**
MERCURY: *56*................... **3–5**
PROJECT 3: *68–70*................ **1–3**
RCA VICTOR (500 series):
  71 .... **1–3**
RCA VICTOR (9400
  series): *67*..................... **1–3**
ROULETTE: *59–68* **1–3**
SUNSET: *56* **3–5**
VERVE: *56*...................... **3–5**

EPs: 7-Inch 33/45rpm
COLUMBIA: *52–56*.............. **5–10**
CORAL: *54*..................... **5–10**

LPs: 10/12-Inch 33rpm
ACCORD: *83* **5–8**
COLUMBIA (900 series):
  57 .... **15–25**
COLUMBIA (2600 series):
  56 .... **20–25**
  (10-Inch LPs.)
COLUMBIA (6000 series):
  50 .... **20–30**
CORAL (56000 series): *54*........ **20–30**
  (10-Inch LPs.)
CORAL (57000 series): *57*........ **15–25**
CO-STAR: *58* **15–20**
MERCURY (Except 100
  series): *56–58*................. **15–25**
MERCURY (100 series):
  69 .... **8–12**
PROJECT 3: *70*................... **5–10**
RCA VICTOR (4500
  series): *71*.................... **5–10**
ROULETTE (100 series):
  71 .... **8–12**

Price Range

ROULETTE (25000 &
25100 series): *57–63* **$15–20**
ROULETTE (25200 &
25300 series): *64–65* **10–15**
VOCALION: *58* **15–20**
WING: *59–63* **15–20**

BAILEY, Pearl, & Mike Douglas
Singles: 7-Inch
PROJECT 3: *68*. **1–3**
Also see BAILEY, Pearl
Also see DOUGLAS, Mike

BAILEY, Philip
Singles: 12-Inch 33/45rpm
COLUMBIA: *83–85* **4–6**
Singles: 7-Inch
COLUMBIA: *83–85* **1–3**
LPs: 10/12-Inch 33rpm
COLUMBIA: *84–85* **5–8**
Also see EARTH, WIND & FIRE

BAILEY, Philip, & Phil Collins
Singles: 12-Inch 33/45rpm
COLUMBIA: *84* **4–6**
Singles: 7-Inch
COLUMBIA: *84* **1–3**
Also see BAILEY, Philip
Also see COLLINS, Phil

BAILEY, Razzy (Razzie Bailey)
Singles: 7-Inch
ABC-PARAMOUNT: *67*. **4–6**
B&K: *59*. **6–10**
CAPRICORN: *75*. **2–4**
ERASTUS: *76*. **2–4**
MCA: *85* **1–3**
1-2-3: *69*. **2–4**
PEACH: *66* **3–5**
RCA VICTOR: *77–84* **1–3**
Picture Sleeves
RCA VICTOR: *80–81* .... **INC**
LPs: 10/12-Inch 33rpm
MCA: *85* **5–8**
RCA VICTOR: *79–84* **5–8**

BAIO, Scott
Singles: 7-Inch
RCA VICTOR: *82–83* **1–3**
LPs: 10/12-Inch 33rpm
RCA VICTOR: *82–83* **5–8**

Price Range

BAJA MARIMBA BAND, The (Featuring Julius Wechter)
Singles: 7-Inch
A&M: *66–67* **$2–3**
ALMO: *63–66*. **2–4**
BELL: *73*. **1–3**
SHOUT: *81* **1–3**
Picture Sleeves
A&M: *66–68* **1–3**
LPs: 10/12-Inch 33rpm
A&M: *64–70* **5–10**
BELL: *73*. **5–8**
Also see DENNY, Martin

BAKER, Anita
Singles: 7-Inch
BEVERLY GLEN: *83–84* **1–3**
LPs: 10/12-Inch 33rpm
BEVERLY GLEN: *83* **5–8**
Also see CHAPTER 8

BAKER, George (The George Baker Selection)
Singles: 7-Inch
COLOSSUS: *70*. **2–4**
WARNER BROS: *75–76*. **2–4**
Picture Sleeves
COLOSSUS: *70*. **2–4**
LPs: 10/12-Inch 33rpm
COLOSSUS: *70*. **15–20**
WARNER BROS: *76*. **10–12**

BAKER, Ginger (Ginger Baker's Air Force)
Singles: 7-Inch
ATCO: *70* **2–4**
LPs: 10/12-Inch 33rpm
ATCO: *70–72*. **12–15**
SIRE: *77* **5–8**
POLYDOR: *72–79* **8–10**
Also see BAKER-GURVITZ ARMY, The
Also see BLIND FAITH
Also see CREAM
Also see WINWOOD, Steve

BAKER, LaVern (LaVern Baker & The Gliders)
Singles: 7-Inch
ATLANTIC (1000 series,
except 1004): *55–58*. **5–8**

Price Range

ATLANTIC (1004; "Soul
On Fire"): *53–54* $10–12
ATLANTIC (2000 series):
59–65 3–6
BRUNSWICK: *66.* 3–5
KING: *55* 10–15

EPs: 7-Inch 33/45rpm
ATLANTIC: *56–58* 20–25

LPs: 10/12-Inch 33rpm
ATCO: *71* 8–10
ATLANTIC (Except 8002,
8007 & 8030): *59–63* 15–20
ATLANTIC (8002;
"Lavern"): *56–59.* 35–40
   (Black label.)
ATLANTIC (8002;
"Lavern"): *56–59.* 15–20
   (Red label.)
ATLANTIC (8007;
"Lavern Baker"): *57* 30–35
ATLANTIC (8030; "Blues
Ballads"): *59.* 30–35
   (Black label.)
ATLANTIC (8030; "Blues
Ballads"): *59.* 15–20
   (Red label.)
BRUNSWICK: *70.* 10–12
   Also see KING, Ben E., & LaVern Baker
   Also see RHODES, Todd
   Also see WILSON, Jackie, & LaVern Baker

BAKER-GURVITZ ARMY, The
Singles: 7-Inch
ATCO: *74–76.* 2–4
JANUS: *75* 2–4

LPs: 10/12-Inch 33rpm
ATCO: *75–76.* 8–10
JANUS: *75* 10–12
   Members: Ginger Baker; Adrian Gurvitz; Paul
   Gurvitz; Peter Lemer; John Norman; Snips.
   Also see BAKER, Ginger
   Also see GURVITZ, Adrian

BALANCE
Singles: 7-Inch
PORTRAIT: *81–82.* 1–3

LPs: 10/12-Inch 33rpm
PORTRAIT: *81–82.* 5–8
   Also see BLUES MAGOOS, The

Price Range

BALDRY, Long John (Long John Baldry & The Hootchie Cootchie Men)
Singles: 7-Inch
A&M: *68* $3–5
ASCOT: *66–67.* 4–6
EMI AMERICA: *79.* 1–3
WARNER BROS: *68–72.* 2–4

LPs: 10/12-Inch 33rpm
ASCOT: *65* 15–20
CASABLANCA: *75–76* 5–8
EMI AMERICA: *79–80.* 5–8
UNITED ARTISTS: *71* 8–10
WARNER BROS: *71–72* 8–10

BALDRY, Long John, & Kathi McDonald
Singles: 7-Inch
EMI AMERICA: *79.* 1–3
   Also see BALDRY, Long John
   Also see McDONALD, Kathi

BALIN, Marty
Singles: 7-Inch
CHALLENGE: *62* 15–20
EMI AMERICA: *81–84.* 1–3

LPs: 10/12-Inch 33rpm
EMI AMERICA: *81–82.* 8–10
   Also see JEFFERSON AIRPLANE, The
   Also see JEFFERSON STARSHIP, The

BALL, Kenny (Kenny Ball & His Jazzmen)
Singles: 7-Inch
DECCA: *67.* 1–3
GUYDEN: *61* 2–4
KAPP: *62–64.* 2–4

LPs: 10/12-Inch 33rpm
JAZZOLOGY: *79.* 5–8
KAPP: *62–64.* 10–20

BALLADS, The
Singles: 7-Inch
VENTURE: *68* 3–5

BALLARD, Hank (Hank Ballard & The Midnight Lighters; Hank Ballard & The Dapps)
Singles: 7-Inch
KING: *68* 2–4

Price Range

PEOPLE: *72* $2–4
POLYDOR: *72* 2–4
SILVER FOX: *70* 2–4
LPs: 10/12-Inch 33rpm
KING (1000 series): *69* 10–12
Also see SUGAR PIE & HANK

BALLARD, Hank, & The Midnighters
Singles: 7-Inch
GUSTO: *78* 1–3
KING (5100 through 5500
series): *59–62* 3–5
LE JOINT: *79* 1–3
Picture Sleeves
KING: *61* 3–5
EPs: 7-Inch 33/45rpm
FEDERAL: *54* 45–55
KING: *58–63* 20–25
LPs: 10/12-Inch 33rpm
FEDERAL (90; "Their
Greatest Hits"): *54* 250–275
(10-Inch LP.)
FEDERAL (541; "Their
Greatest Hits"): *56* 100–125
FEDERAL (581;
"Midnighters, Vol. 2"):
57 75–90
KING (500 through 800
series, except KS-740):
58–64 25–35
KING (KS-740; "Spotlight
On Hank Ballard"): *61* 75–100
(Stereo issue.)
KING (900 series): *65–68* 15–20
KING (5000 series): *77* 8–10
Also see BALLARD, Hank
Also see MIDNIGHTERS, The
Also see ROYALS, The

BALLARD, Russ
Singles: 7-Inch
EMI AMERICA: *84*................ 1–3
EPIC: *74–80* 1–3
LPs: 10/12-Inch 33rpm
EPIC: *74–80* 8–10
Also see ARGENT
Also see UNIT 4 + 2, The

BALLIN' JACK
Singles: 7-Inch
COLUMBIA: *71*.................. 2–4

Price Range

MERCURY: *73*.................. $2–4
LPs: 10/12-Inch 33rpm
COLUMBIA: *70–72*.............. 10–12
MERCURY: *73–74*............... 8–10

BALLOON FARM, The
Singles: 7-Inch
LAURIE: *68* 3–5

BALTIMORE & OHIO MARCHING BAND, The
Singles: 7-Inch
JUBILEE: *67*..................... 2–4

BAMA
Singles: 7-Inch
FREE FLIGHT: *79* 1–3
LPs: 10/12-Inch 33rpm
FREE FLIGHT: *79* 5–8

BAMBAATAA, Afrika: see AFRIKA BAMBAATAA

BANANA SPLITS, The
Singles: 7-Inch
DECCA: *68–69*.................... 3–5
Picture Sleeves
DECCA: *69–70*................... 4–6
EPs: 7-Inch 33/45rpm
KELLOGG: *69*.................... 5–8

BANANARAMA
Singles: 12-Inch 33/45rpm
LONDON: *83* 4–6
Singles: 7-Inch
LONDON: *82–85* 1–3
LPs: 10/12-Inch 33rpm
LONDON: *83–84* 5–8
Also see BAND AID

BAND, The
Singles: 7-Inch
CAPITOL (Except 2000
series): *71–77*................... 2–4
CAPITOL (2000 series):
67–70 3–5
WARNER BROS: *78*............... 1–3
Picture Sleeves
CAPITOL: *70* 2–4

Price Range

LPs: 10/12-Inch 33rpm
CAPITOL (Except 2955):
69–85 .... **$8–12**
CAPITOL (2955; "Music
From Big Pink"): *68* **12–15**
WARNER BROS (737;
"The Last Waltz"): *78* **15–18**
(Promotional issue only.)
WARNER BROS (3146;
"The Last Waltz"): *78* **15–18**
Members: Levon Helm; Rick Danko; Garth
Hudson; Richard Manuel; Robbie Robertson;
Jimmy Wieder.
Also see DANKO, Rick
Also see DYLAN, Bob
Also see HAWKINS, Ronnie
Also see HELM, Levon
Also see LEVON & THE HAWKS
Also see MILLER, Steve / The Band / Quick-
silver Messinger Service

BAND AID
Singles: 7-Inch
COLUMBIA (04749; "Do
They Know It's
Christmas"): *84* **1–3**
(Performed by an accumulation of the artists
and members of the groups listed below.)
Also see BANANARAMA
Also see BOOMTOWN RATS
Also see COLLINS, Phil
Also see CULTURE CLUB
Also see DURAN DURAN
Also see HEAVEN 17
Also see KOOL & THE GANG
Also see SPANDAU BALLET
Also see STATUS QUO
Also see STING
Also see STYLE COUNCIL
Also see U2
Also see ULTRAVOX
Also see YOUNG, Paul
Also see WHAM

BAND OF GOLD
Singles: 7-Inch
VIK: *85* **1–3**

BAND OF THE BLACK WATCH
Singles: 7-Inch
PRIVATE STOCK: *75–76* **1–3**
LPs: 10/12-Inch 33rpm
PRIVATE STOCK: *76* **5–8**

Price Range

BANDIT
Singles: 7-Inch
ABC: *75* **$1–3**
ARISTA: *77* **1–3**
LPs: 10/12-Inch 33rpm
ABC: *75* **8–10**
ARISTA: *77* **6–10**
Members: Jim Diamond; Danny McIntosh;
James Litherland; Cliff Williams; Graham
Broad.

BANDOLERO
Singles: 12-Inch 33/45rpm
SIRE: *84* **4–6**
Singles: 7-Inch
SIRE: *84* **1–3**
LPs: 10/12-Inch 33rpm
ECLIPSE: *75* **8–10**

BANDWAGON
Singles: 7-Inch
EPIC: *68* **2–4**

BANG
Singles: 7-Inch
CAPITOL: *72–74* **2–4**
LPs: 10/12-Inch 33rpm
CAPITOL: *72–73* **8–12**

BANGLES, The
Singles: 12-Inch 33/45rpm
COLUMBIA: *85* **4–6**
Singles: 7-Inch
COLUMBIA: *84–85* **1–3**
Picture Sleeves
COLUMBIA: *84–85* .... **INC**
LPs: 10/12-Inch 33rpm
COLUMBIA: *84–85* **5–8**
I.R.S.: *83* **6–10**
Members: Vicki Peterson; Debbi Peterson;
Susanna Hoffs; Michael Steele.

BANGOR FLYING CIRCUS, The
Singles: 7-Inch
DUNHILL: *70*. **2–4**
LPs: 10/12-Inch 33rpm
DUNHILL: *69*. **12–15**
Members: Michael Tegza; David Wolinski;
Alan DeCarlo.

Price Range

BANKS, Darrell
Singles: 7-Inch
ATCO: 67 .... $3–5
REVILOT: 66 3–5
SOULTOWN: 66 3–5
LPs: 10/12-Inch 33rpm
ATCO: 67 15–18
VOLT: 69 10–12

BANKS, Peter
Singles: 7-Inch
CAPITOL: 73 2–4
LPs: 10/12-Inch 33rpm
CAPITOL: 73 10–12
Also see AFTER THE FIRE
Also see BLODWYN PIG
Also see FLASH
Also see YES

BANKS, Ron
Singles: 12-Inch 33/45rpm
CBS ASSOCIATED: 83 4–6
Singles: 7-Inch
ABC: 75 2–3
CBS ASSOCIATED: 83 1–3
LPs: 10/12-Inch 33rpm
CBS ASSOCIATED: 83 5–8
Also see DRAMATICS, The

BANKS, Rose
Singles: 7-Inch
MOTOWN: 76 2–3
SOURCE: 80 1–3
LPs: 10/12-Inch 33rpm
MOTOWN: 76 8–10
Also see SLY & THE FAMILY STONE

BANKS, Tony
Singles: 7-Inch
ATLANTIC: 83 1–3
CHARISMA: 79 2–3
LPs: 10/12-Inch 33rpm
ATLANTIC: 83 5–8
CHARISMA: 79 5–10
Also see GENESIS

BANKS & HAMPTON
Singles: 7-Inch
WARNER BROS: 76–77 2–4
LPs: 10/12-Inch 33rpm
WARNER BROS: 77 5–8

Price Range

BANZAII
Singles: 7-Inch
SCEPTER: 75 .... $2–4

BARBARA & THE BROWNS
Singles: 7-Inch
SOUND OF MEMPHIS:
72 2–4
STAX: 64 3–5

BARBARA & THE UNIQUES
(Featuring Barbara Blake)
Singles: 7-Inch
ABBOTT: 72 2–4
ARDEN: 70 2–4
NEW CHICAGO
SOUND: 70 2–4
20TH CENTURY-FOX:
74 2–4

BARBARA LYNN: see LYNN, Barbara

BARBARIANS, The
Singles: 7-Inch
JOY: 64 8–10
LAURIE: 65–66 5–8
LPs: 10/12-Inch 33rpm
LAURIE: 66 40–50
RHINO: 79 5–8
Also see ELEGANTS, The

BARBER, Chris (Chris Barber's Jazz Band)
Singles: 7-Inch
ATLANTIC: 59 2–4
LAURIE: 58–63 2–4
LONDON: 62 2–4
Picture Sleeves
LAURIE: 59 2–4
LPs: 10/12-Inch 33rpm
ARCHIVE OF FOLK
MUSIC: 68 8–12
ATLANTIC: 59 10–15
COLPIX: 59 10–15
LAURIE: 59–62 10–15

BARBER, Frank
Singles: 7-Inch
VICTORY: 82 1–3

Price Range

LPs: 10/12-Inch 33rpm
VICTORY: 82 . . . . $5–8

BARBIERI, Gato
Singles: 7-Inch
A&M: 76–79 1–3
UNITED ARTISTS: 73 1–3

LPs: 10/12-Inch 33rpm
A&M: 76–79 5–10
ARISTA: 75 8–10
FLYING DUTCHMAN:
70–80 5–10
IMPULSE: 73–75 8–10
UNITED ARTISTS: 73 5–10

BARBOUR, Dave
Singles: 7-Inch
ARWIN: 59 2–4
CAPITOL: 50–51 3–5

EPs: 7-Inch 33/45rpm
CAPITOL: 54 5–8
DECCA: 53 5–8

LPs: 10/12-Inch 33rpm
DECCA: 53 10–20

BARBOUR, Keith
Singles: 7-Inch
BARNABY: 71 2–4
EPIC: 69–70 2–4

LPs: 10/12-Inch 33rpm
EPIC: 69 12–18

BARCLAY, Eddie
Singles: 7-Inch
TICO: 55 3–5

BARCLAY JAMES HARVEST
Singles: 7-Inch
HARVEST: 73 2–4
MCA: 76–77 2–4
POLYDOR: 75–79 1–3

LPs: 10/12-Inch 33rpm
HARVEST: 73 8–10
MCA: 77 5–8
POLYDOR: 74–80 8–10
SIRE: 70–71 12–15
Members: Les Holroyd; John Lees; John
Pritchard; Wolly Wolstenholme.

Price Range

BARE, Bobby (Bobby Bare & The All American Boys; Bobby Bare & The Hillsiders; Bobby Bare & Bobby Bare, Jr; Bobby Bare & The Family; Bobby & Jeannie Bare)
Singles: 7-Inch
CAPITOL: 57 . . . . $5–8
COLUMBIA: 78–85 1–3
EMI AMERICA: 85 1–3
FRATERNITY (835
through 878): 58–61 5–8
FRATERNITY (885
through 892): 61 3–5
MERCURY: 70–72 1–3
RCA VICTOR (Except
8000 & 9000 series):
69–77 1–3
RCA VICTOR (8000 &
9000 series): 62–68 2–4
RICE: 73–74 1–3
Picture Sleeves
RCA VICTOR: 62–65 4–6
LPs: 10/12-Inch 33rpm
CAMDEN: 68–73 8–12
COLUMBIA: 78–85 5–10
MERCURY: 70–72 10–15
PICKWICK: 75–80 5–10
PICKWICK/HILLTOP:
65 10–15
RCA VICTOR (ANL1 &
APL1 series): 73–77 8–12
RCA VICTOR (AYL1
series): 81 5–8
RCA VICTOR (2776
through 3994): 63–69 15–20
(With an "LPM" or "LSP" prefix.)
RCA VICTOR (4000
series): 69–71 10–15
(With an "LSP" prefix.)
RCA VICTOR (6000
series): 73 10–15
SUN (136; "Bobby Bare's
Greatest Hits"): 74 15–25
UNITED ARTISTS: 75–76 8–12
Also see ORBISON, Roy / Bobby Bare / Joey
Powers
Also see PARSONS, Bill

BARE, Bobby, & Rosanne Cash
Singles: 7-Inch
COLUMBIA: 79 1–3
Also see CASH, Rosanne

Price Range

BARE, Bobby, & Skeeter Davis
Singles: 7-Inch
RCA VICTOR (8000 &
  9000 series): 65–70 . . . . $2–4

LPs: 10/12-Inch 33rpm
RCA VICTOR: 65–70 10–15
Also see DAVIS, Skeeter

BARE, Bobby, / Donna Fargo / Jerry Wallace
LPs: 10/12-Inch 33rpm
OUT OF TOWN DIST: 82 5–8
Also see BARE, Bobby
Also see FARGO, Donna
Also see WALLACE, Jerry

BAR-KAYS, The
Singles: 12-Inch 33/45rpm
MERCURY: 79–85 4–6

Singles: 7-Inch
MERCURY: 76–84 1–3
STAX: 78–81 1–3
VOLT: 67–74 2–4

LPs: 10/12-Inch 33rpm
MERCURY: 76–84 5–8
STAX: 78–81 5–8
VOLT: 67–74 10–12
Members: Jimmy King; Phalin Jones; Carl
Cunningham; Ron Caldwell; Larry Dodson;
James Alexander; Charles Allen; Vernon
Burch; Ben Cauley; Donnelle Hagan; Harvey
Henderson; Winston Stewart.
Also see REDDING, Otis

BARKLEY, Tyrone
Singles: 7-Inch
MIDSONG INT'L: 79 1–3

BARNES, Cheryl
Singles: 7-Inch
MILLENNIUM: 77 2–3
POLYDOR: 80 1–3
RCA VICTOR: 79 1–3

BARNES, J.J.
Singles: 7-Inch
GROOVESVILLE: 67 3–5
PERCEPTION: 74 2–4
RIC-TIC: 66 3–5

Price Range

BARNES, J.J., & Steve Mancha
LPs: 10/12-Inch 33rpm
VOLT: 69 . . . . $10–12
Also see BARNES, J.J.
Also see MANCHA, Steve

BARNES, Jimmy
Singles: 7-Inch
GIBRALTAR: 59 4–6

BARNUM, H.B.
Singles: 7-Inch
CAPITOL: 65–68 3–5
DECCA: 71 2–4
ELDO: 60–61 3–5
IMPERIAL: 64 3–5
MUN RAB: 59 3–5
RCA VICTOR: 61–63 3–5
ULTRA SONIC: 60 3–5
UNITED ARTISTS: 73 1–3
Picture Sleeves
RCA VICTOR: 62 . . . . INC
LPs: 10/12-Inch 33rpm
CAPITOL: 65 12–15
RCA VICTOR: 62 15–20
TROPIC ISLE: 59 15–20
Also see ROBINS, The

BARRABAS
Singles: 7-Inch
ATCO: 75–76 2–4
LPs: 10/12-Inch 33rpm
ATCO: 75–76 5–8
RCA VICTOR: 72–73 8–10
Members: Jo Tejada; Ricky Morales; Miquel
Morales; Juan Videl; Daniel Louis; Ernest
Duarte.

BARRACUDA
Singles: 12-Inch 33/45rpm
EPIC: 83 4–6
Singles: 7-Inch
RCA VICTOR: 68 3–5
20TH CENTURY-FOX:
  73 2–4

BARRETT, Richard (Richie Barrett; Richard Barrett & The Chantels; Richard Barrett & The Sevilles)
Singles: 7-Inch
ATLANTIC: 62 4–6

Price Range

GONE: *59* **$8–10**
MGM: *58* **10–12**
METRO **4–6**
SEVILLE: *60* **4–6**
Also see CHANTELS, The

BARRETT, Syd
LPs: 10/12-Inch 33rpm
HARVEST: *74* **10–12**
Also see PINK FLOYD

BARRETTO, Ray
Singles: 7-Inch
ASCOT: *66* **1–3**
ATLANTIC: *77–78* **2–3**
FANIA: *68–72* **2–4**
RIVERSIDE: *61* **2–4**
ROULETTE **1–3**
TICO: *63* **3–5**
UNITED ARTISTS: *65–67* **2–3**
LPs: 10/12-Inch 33rpm
ATLANTIC: *76–78* **5–10**
CTI: *81* **5–8**
FANIA: *68–73* **5–10**
FANTASY: *73* **8–10**
RIVERSIDE: *61–66* **10–15**
TICO: *62–63* **10–15**
UNITED ARTISTS: *65–67* **8–15**
Also see LYTLE, Johnny, & Ray Barretto

BARRON, Blue
Singles: 7-Inch
MGM: *50–55* **2–4**
EPs: 7-Inch 33/45rpm
MGM: *54–55* **3–6**
LPs: 10/12-Inch 33rpm
MGM: *54* **8–12**

BARRON KNIGHTS, The
Singles: 7-Inch
DECCA: *67* **5–8**
EPIC (Except 9835): *79* **1–3**
EPIC (9835; "Pop Go The
 Workers"): *65* **5–8**
MERCURY: *72* **2–4**
Members: Barron Anthony; Peanut Langford;
Butch Baker; Dave Ballinger; Duke D'mond.

BARROW, Keith
Singles: 12-Inch 33/45rpm
COLUMBIA: *79* **4–6**

Price Range

Singles: 7-Inch
CAPITOL: *80* **$1–3**
COLUMBIA: *76–79* **2–3**
JEWEL: *73* **2–4**
LPs: 10/12-Inch 33rpm
CAPITOL: *80* **5–8**
COLUMBIA: *77* **5–8**
JEWEL: *73* **8–10**

BARRY, Claudja
Singles: 12-Inch 33/45rpm
CHRYSALIS: *79* **4–6**
PERSONAL: *83* **4–6**
TSR: *85* **4–6**
Singles: 7-Inch
CHRYSALIS: *79–84* **1–3**
MIRAGE: *82* **1–3**
PERSONAL: *83* **1–3**
SALSOUL: *77–78* **2–3**
LPs: 10/12-Inch 33rpm
CHRYSALIS: *79–84* **5–8**
HANDSHAKE: *82* **5–8**
SALSOUL: *77* **5–8**

BARRY, Jan: see BERRY, Jan

BARRY, Joe
Singles: 7-Inch
ABC/DOT: *77* **2–3**
JIN: *61* **5–8**
NUGGET **3–5**
SMASH: *61–62* **3–5**
Picture Sleeves
SMASH: *61* **3–5**
LPs: 10/12-Inch 33rpm
ABC/DOT: *77* **5–10**

BARRY, John, Orchestra
Singles: 7-Inch
A&M: *83* **1–3**
CAPITOL (4200 series): *59* **2–4**
CAPITOL (5400 series): *86* **1–3**
COLUMBIA: *65–70* **2–3**
EPIC: *72* **1–3**
KING: *61* **2–4**
MCA: *85* **1–3**
MGM: *66* **2–3**
MERCURY: *64* **2–4**
20TH CENTURY-FOX:
 64 . . . . **2–4**

Price Range

UNITED ARTISTS: *63–65* **$2–3**
WARNER BROS: *68* **2–3**

Picture Sleeves
UNITED ARTISTS: *65* **2–4**

LPs: 10/12-Inch 33rpm
ABC (852; "The Dove"):
  74 . . . . **15–20**
  (Soundtrack.)
BUENA VISTA (5008;
  "The Black Hole"): *80* **5–10**
  (Soundtrack.)
CAPITOL (2500 series): *66* **10–15**
CAPITOL (12413; "A
  View To Kill"): *86* **5–8**
  (Soundtrack.)
COLUMBIA (1003;
  "Ready When You Are
  Mr. J.B."): *70*. **8–12**
COLUMBIA (2493; "Great
  Movie Themes"): *66* **10–15**
COLUMBIA (2708; "You
  Only Live Twice"): *67* **8–12**
  (Soundtrack.)
COLUMBIA (2710;
  "Sophia Loren In
  Rome"): *64*. **20–30**
  (Soundtrack.)
COLUMBIA (2960; "The
  Chase"): *66*. **35–40**
  (Soundtrack.)
COLUMBIA (3250; "The
  Lion In Winter"): *68*. **12–15**
  (Soundtrack.)
COLUMBIA (6310;
  "Sophia Loren In
  Rome"): *64*. **50–60**
  (Soundtrack.)
COLUMBIA (6560; "The
  Chase"): *66*. **40–45**
  (Soundtrack.)
COLUMBIA (9293; "Great
  Movie Themes"): *66* **10–15**
COLUMBIA (9508; "You
  Only Live Twice"): *67* **10–12**
  (Soundtrack.)
DECCA (9124; "The
  Ipcress File"): *65*. **15–20**
  (Soundtrack.)
DUNHILL (50102; "The
  Last Valley"): *71*. **20–25**
  (Soundtrack.)

Price Range

GEFFEN (24062; "The
  Cotton Club"): *85* **$5–8**
  (Soundtrack.)
LIBERTY: *85* **4–6**
LONDON (912; "The Day
  Of The Locust"): *75* **10–15**
  (Soundtrack.)
MCA (5154; "Somewhere
  In Time"): *80*. **5–8**
  (Soundtrack.)
MGM (4368; "Born
  Free"): *66*. **10–12**
  (Soundtrack.)
MAINSTREAM (6061;
  "King Rat"): *65*. **25–30**
  (Soundtrack.)
MAINSTREAM (56061;
  "King Rat"): *65*. **20–25**
  (Soundtrack.)
MAINSTREAM (6088;
  "The Wrong Box"): *66*. **35–40**
  (Soundtrack.)
MAINSTREAM (56088;
  "The Wrong Box"): *66*. **30–35**
  (Soundtrack.)
REPRISE (2260; "King
  Kong"): *76*. **8–12**
  (Soundtrack.)
ROULETTE (805; "Four
  In The Morning"): *66*. **25–35**
  (Soundtrack.)
20TH CENTURY-FOX
  (3128; "Man In The
  Middle"): *64*. **20–25**
  (Soundtrack.)
20TH CENTURY-FOX
  (4128; "Man In The
  Middle"): *64*. **25–30**
  (Soundtrack.)
UNITED ARTISTS (91;
  "James Bond Tenth
  Anniversary"): *72* **8–12**
UNITED ARTISTS (270;
  "The Knack"): *74*. **8–12**
  (Soundtrack.)
UNITED ARTISTS (289;
  "You Only Live Twice"):
  74 . . . . **8–10**
  (Soundtrack.)
UNITED ARTISTS (299;
  "On Her Majesty's
  Secret Service"): *74*. **8–12**
  (Soundtrack.)

Price Range

UNITED ARTISTS (301;
"Diamonds Are
Forever"): *74* **$8–10**
(Soundtrack.)
UNITED ARTISTS (3424;
"Goldfinger & Other
Favorites"): *65* **8–12**
UNITED ARTISTS (4114;
"From Russia With
Love"): *64* **10–15**
(Soundtrack.)
UNITED ARTISTS (4117;
"Goldfinger"): *64* **10–15**
(Soundtrack.)
UNITED ARTISTS (4129;
"The Knack"): *65* **20–25**
(Soundtrack.)
UNITED ARTISTS (4132;
"Thunderball"): *65* **15–20**
(Soundtrack.)
UNITED ARTISTS (4155;
"You Only Live Twice"):
67 . . . . **10–15**
(Soundtrack.)
UNITED ARTISTS (4161;
"The Whisperers"): *67* **15–18**
(Soundtrack.)
UNITED ARTISTS (5114;
"From Russia With
Love"): *64* **15–20**
(Soundtrack.)
UNITED ARTISTS (5117;
"Goldfinger"): *64* **15–20**
(Soundtrack.)
UNITED ARTISTS (5129;
"The Knack"): *65* **25–30**
(Soundtrack.)
UNITED ARTISTS (5132;
"Thunderball"): *65* **20–25**
(Soundtrack.)
UNITED ARTISTS (5155;
"You Only Live Twice"):
67 . . . . **15–20**
(Soundtrack.)
UNITED ARTISTS (5161;
"The Whisperers"): *67* **18–20**
(Soundtrack.)
UNITED ARTISTS (5204;
"On Her Majesty's
Secret Service"): *69* **12–18**
(Soundtrack.)

Price Range

UNITED ARTISTS (5220;
"Diamonds Are
Forever"): *71* **$10–15**
(Soundtrack.)
UNITED ARTISTS (6424;
"Goldfinger & Other
Favorites"): *65* **10–12**
WARNER BROS (1755;
"Petulia"): *68* **15–20**
(Soundtrack.)
WARNER BROS (2671;
"Alice's Adventures In
Wonderland"): *72* **15–20**
(Soundtrack.)
Also see ARMSTRONG, Louis
Also see BASIE, Count
Also see BASSEY, Shirley
Also see JONES, Tom
Also see MONRO, Matt
Also see SINATRA, Nancy

BARRY, Len
Singles: 7-Inch
AMY: *68–69* **3–5**
BUDDAH: *72* **2–4**
CAMEO: *64* **3–5**
DECCA: *65–66* **3–5**
MCA: *83* **1–3**
MERCURY: *64* **3–5**
PARAMOUNT: *73* **2–4**
PARKWAY: *65* **3–5**
RCA VICTOR: *67–68* **3–5**
SCEPTER: *69–70* **2–4**

EPs: 7-Inch 33/45rpm
DECCA (74720; "1-2-3"):
65 . . . . **8–15**
(Jukebox issue only.)

LPs: 10/12-Inch 33rpm
BUDDAH: *72* **10–12**
CAMEO: *64* **20–25**
DECCA: *65* **20–25**
RCA VICTOR: *67* **15–18**
Also see DOVELLS, The

BARRY & THE TAMERLANES
Singles: 7-Inch
VALIANT: *63–65* **4–6**

LPs: 10/12-Inch 33rpm
VALIANT: *63* **35–40**
Members: Barry DeVorzon; Terry Smith;
Bodie Chandler.
Also see DE VORZON, Barry

Price Range

BARTLEY, Chris
Singles: 7-Inch
VANDO: 67 . . . . $3–5
LPs: 10/12-Inch 33rpm
VANDO: 67 10–15

BARTON, Eileen
Singles: 7-Inch
CORAL: 51–56 3–5
CREST: 62 2–4
MGM: 59 2–4
MERCURY: 53 3–5
20TH CENTURY-FOX:
    63 2–3
UNITED ARTISTS: 59 2–4
EPs: 7-Inch 33/45rpm
CORAL: 54 5–10
LPs: 10/12-Inch 33rpm
CORAL: 54 15–20

BARTON, Lou Ann
Singles: 7-Inch
ASYLUM: 82 1–3
LPs: 10/12-Inch 33rpm
ASYLUM: 82 5–8

BARTZ, Gary (Gary Bartz Ntu Troop)
Singles: 7-Inch
ARISTA: 80 1–3
CAPITOL: 77–78 2–3
LPs: 10/12-Inch 33rpm
ARISTA: 80 5–8
CAPITOL: 77–78 5–10
CATALYST: 76 5–10
MILESTONE: 68–69 8–12
PRESTIGE: 73–75 6–10
VEE JAY: 78 5–8

BASIE, Count
Singles: 7-Inch
ABC-PARAMOUNT: 66 2–3
BRUNSWICK: 67 2–3
CLEF: 52–56 3–5
COLUMBIA (33000
    series): 76 1–3
COLUMBIA (38000 &
    39000 series): 50–51 3–5
COMMAND: 67 2–3
DECCA: 53 3–5

Price Range

HAPPY TIGER: 70 . . . . $1–3
MERCURY: 52–53 3–5
OKEH: 52 3–5
REPRISE: 63 2–3
ROULETTE: 58–63 2–4
UNITED ARTISTS: 66 2–3
VERVE: 60–67 2–4
EPs: 7-Inch 33/45rpm
BRUNSWICK: 54 10–15
CAMDEN: 58 8–12
CLEF: 52–55 10–15
COLUMBIA: 50 10–15
CORAL 10–15
DECCA: 53 10–15
EPIC: 55 10–15
RCA VICTOR (Except
    5000 series): 54 10–15
RCA VICTOR (5000
    series): 59 6–10
ROULETTE: 58–60 8–12
VERVE: 56 8–12
LPs: 10/12-Inch 33rpm
ABC: 76 5–8
ABC-PARAMOUNT: 66 10–15
ACCORD: 82–83 5–8
AMERICAN: 57 15–25
BRIGHT ORANGE: 73 5–8
BRUNSWICK (54000
    series): 63–67 10–20
BRUNSWICK (58000
    series): 54 25–35
    (10-Inch LPs.)
CAMDEN: 58–60 10–20
CIRCLE: 54 40–50
CLEF (100 series): 52 40–60
    (10-Inch LPs.)
CLEF (600 series): 53–55 25–35
CLEF (700 series): 56 20–30
COLISEUM: 67 8–12
COLUMBIA (700 & 900
    series): 56–57 20–30
COLUMBIA (6000 series):
    50 25–35
    (10-Inch LPs.)
COLUMBIA (31000
    series): 72 10–12
COMMAND: 66–71 10–15
DAYBREAK: 71 6–10
DECCA (100 series): 64 15–25
DECCA (5000 series):
    50–53 25–35
    (10-Inch LPs.)

Price Range

DECCA (8000 series): *65* **$10–15**
DOCTOR JAZZ: *85–86* **5–8**
DOT: *68* **8–12**
EMARCY (26000 series):
   54 .... **30–45**
   (10-Inch LPs.)
EPIC (1000 & 1100 series):
   54 .... **25–35**
   (10-Inch LPs.)
EPIC: *55* **25–35**
FLYING DUTCHMAN:
   71 .... **6–10**
HAPPY TIGER: *70* **8–12**
HARMONY (7000 series):
   60 .... **10–20**
HARMONY (11000
   series): *67–69* **5–10**
IMPULSE: *62* **10–20**
JAZZ PANORAMA: *52* **50–75**
MCA: *77–82* **8–12**
MGM: *70* **6–10**
MPS: *72* **10–12**
MERCURY (25000 series):
   50–51 .... **25–35**
   (10-Inch LPs.)
METRO: *65–66* **6–10**
OLYMPIC: *74* **5–10**
PABLO: *74–83* **5–10**
PAUSA: *83* **5–8**
PRESTIGE: *82* **5–8**
RCA VICTOR (500 series):
   65 .... **10–15**
RCA VICTOR (1100
   series): *54* **25–35**
REPRISE: *63–65* **10–15**
ROULETTE (100 series):
   71 .... **12–18**
ROULETTE (52003
   through 52106): *58–64* **15–20**
ROULETTE
   (52111/12/13; "The
   World Of Count Basie"):
   64 .... **30–40**
   (A 3-LP set.)
SCEPTER: *74* **5–10**
SOLID STATE: *68* **8–12**
TRIP: *75* **5–10**
UNITED ARTISTS: *66* **10–15**
VSP: *66* **10–15**
VANGUARD: *57* **15–25**

Price Range

VERVE: *73–84* **$5–10**
   (Reads "Manufactured By MGM Record
   Corp.," or mentions either Polydor or Poly-
   gram at bottom of label.)
VERVE (2000 series): *56* **20–30**
   (Reads "Verve Records, Inc." at bottom of
   label.)
VERVE (2500 series):
   77–82 .... **8–12**
VERVE (2600 series): *82* **5–8**
VERVE (6000 series): *56* **20–30**
   (Reads "Verve Records, Inc." at bottom of
   label.)
VERVE (8000 & 8100
   series): *56–57* **15–25**
   (Reads "Verve Records, Inc." at bottom of
   label.)
VERVE (8200 through
   8400): *58–61* **15–20**
   (Reads "Verve Records, Inc." at bottom of
   label.)
VERVE (8500 through
   8600 series): *62–67* **10–15**
   (Reads "MGM Records - A Division Of Metro-
   Goldwyn-Mayer, Inc." at bottom of label.)
VERVE (8700 series): *69* **6–10**
   (Reads "MGM Records - A Division Of Metro-
   Goldwyn-Mayer, Inc." at bottom of label.)
VERVE (68000 series):
   63–65 .... **10–20**
   (Reads "MGM Records - A Division Of Metro-
   Goldwyn-Mayer, Inc." at bottom of label.)
   Also see BARRY, John
   Also see BREWER, Teresa, & Count Basie
   Also see CROSBY, Bing, & Count Basie
   Also see DAVIS, Sammy, Jr., & Count Basie
   Also see FITZGERALD, Ella, & Count Basie
   Also see MILLS BROTHERS, The, & Count
   Basie
   Also see PRYSOCK, Arthur, & Count Basie
   Also see SINATRA, Frank, & Count Basie
   Also see STARR, Kay, & Count Basie
   Also see WILSON, Jackie, & Count Basie

BASIE, Count, & Tony Bennett
   EPs: 7-Inch 33/45rpm
ROULETTE: *59* **6–10**
   LPs: 10/12-Inch 33rpm
ROULETTE: *59–63* **10–20**
   Also see BENNETT, Tony

BASIE, Count, & Billy Eckstine
   LPs: 10/12-Inch 33rpm
ROULETTE: *59* **15–20**
   Also see ECKSTINE, Billy

Price Range

Price Range

BASIE, Count, & Duke Ellington
Singles: 7-Inch
COLUMBIA: 62 . . . . **$2–4**

LPs: 10/12-Inch 33rpm
ACCORD: 82 . . . . **5–8**
COLUMBIA: 62 . . . . **15–20**
Also see ELLINGTON, Duke

BASIE, Count, & Maynard Ferguson
LPs: 10/12-Inch 33rpm
ROULETTE: 65 . . . . **10–15**
Also see FERGUSON, Maynard

BASIE, Count, & Benny Goodman
LPs: 10/12-Inch 33rpm
ABC: 73 . . . . **10–12**
VANGUARD: 59 . . . . **15–20**
Also see GOODMAN, Benny

BASIE, Count, & Oscar Peterson
LPs: 10/12-Inch 33rpm
PABLO: 75–83 . . . . **5–10**
VERVE: 59 . . . . **15–20**
Also see PETERSON, Oscar

BASIE, Count, & Sarah Vaughan
LPs: 10/12-Inch 33rpm
ROULETTE: 61 . . . . **15–20**

BASIE, Count, Sarah Vaughan & Joe Williams
Singles: 7-Inch
ROULETTE: 60 . . . . **2–4**

LPs: 10/12-Inch 33rpm
ROULETTE: 60 . . . . **15–20**
Note: Joe Williams is a featured vocalist on
many of the recordings included in the section
of listings for Count Basie.
Also see BASIE, Count
Also see VAUGHAN, Sarah

BASIL, Toni
Singles: 12-Inch 33/45rpm
CHRYSALIS: 82–85 . . . . **4–6**

Singles: 7-Inch
A&M: 66 . . . . **3–5**
CHRYSALIS: 82–85 . . . . **1–3**

Picture Sleeves
CHRYSALIS: 82 . . . . **INC**

LPs: 10/12-Inch 33rpm
CHRYSALIS: 82–84 . . . . **$5–8**

BASKERVILLE HOUNDS, The
Singles: 7-Inch
AVCO EMBASSY: 69 . . . . **2–4**
DOT: 67 . . . . **2–4**
TEMA: 67 . . . . **4–6**

LPs: 10/12-Inch 33rpm
DOT: 67 . . . . **15–20**

BASS, Fontella
Singles: 7-Inch
ABC: 74 . . . . **1–3**
BOBBIN: 61 . . . . **4–6**
CHECKER: 65–66 . . . . **3–5**
CHESS: 75–85 . . . . **1–3**
ERIC: 73 . . . . **1–3**
MCA: 83 . . . . **1–3**
PAULA: 74 . . . . **2–4**
SONJA: 62 . . . . **4–6**

LPs: 10/12-Inch 33rpm
CHECKER: 66 . . . . **15–20**
PAULA: 71 . . . . **5–8**

BASS, Fontella, & Bobby McClure
Singles: 7-Inch
CHECKER: 65–66 . . . . **3–5**
Also see BASS, Fontella
Also see MC CLURE, Bobby

BASSEY, Shirley
Singles: 12-Inch 33/45rpm
UNITED ARTISTS: 79 . . . . **4–6**
Singles: 7-Inch
EPIC: 59 . . . . **2–5**
MGM: 60 . . . . **2–4**
UNITED ARTISTS: 61–79 . . . . **1–3**
LPs: 10/12-Inch 33rpm
EPIC: 62 . . . . **10–20**
LIBERTY: 81–82 . . . . **4–6**
MGM: 60 . . . . **12–20**
PHILIPS: 65 . . . . **10–15**
SPRINGBOARD: 75 . . . . **5–10**
UNITED ARTISTS: 80 . . . . **4–6**
(With an "LM" prefix.)
UNITED ARTISTS: 62–72 . . . . **10–15**
(With a "UAL" or "UAS" prefix.)
UNITED ARTISTS: 73–79 . . . . **5–10**
(With a "UA-LA" prefix.)
Also see BARRY, John

Price Range

BATAAN, Joe (Joe Bataan & The Mestizo Band)
Singles: 7-Inch
SALSOUL: 80................... **$1–3**
LPs: 10/12-Inch 33rpm
SALSOUL: 80–81................. **5–8**

BATDORF & RODNEY
Singles: 7-Inch
ARISTA: 75...................... **1–3**
ASYLUM: 72..................... **2–4**
ATLANTIC: 71–72................ **2–4**
LPs: 10/12-Inch 33rpm
ATLANTIC: 71.................. **8–12**
ARISTA: 75.................... **6–10**
ASYLUM: 72.................... **8–10**
Members: John Batdorf: Mark Rodney.
Also see SILVER

BAUMANN, Peter
Singles: 12-Inch 33/45rpm
PORTRAIT: 82–83................. **4–6**
Singles: 7-Inch
PORTRAIT: 83................... **1–3**
LPs: 10/12-Inch 33rpm
PORTRAIT: 82–83................. **5–8**
VIRGIN: 77..................... **8–10**
Also see TANGERINE DREAM

BAXTER, Duke
Singles: 7-Inch
MERCURY: 70................... **2–4**
VMC: 69....................... **2–4**
LPs: 10/12-Inch 33rpm
VMC: 69.................... **12–15**

BAXTER, Les (Les Baxter & His Orchestra & Chorus; The Les Baxter Balladeers)
Singles: 7-Inch
A/S: 70........................ **1–3**
CAPITOL: 50–61................. **2–4**
GNP/CRESCENDO:
64–69....................... **2–3**
LINK: 64...................... **2–4**
REPRISE: 62–63................. **2–3**
EPs: 7-Inch 33/45rpm
CAPITOL: 51–56................. **4–8**
GNP/CRESCENDO:
67–69....................... **5–10**
RCA VICTOR: 52................ **5–10**

Price Range

LPs: 10/12-Inch 33rpm
ALSHIRE: 70–85................. **$5–8**
AMERICAN INTERNATIONAL
(1028; "Dunwich Horror"): 70.................. **15–20**
(Soundtrack.)
CAPITOL (200 through 900 series): 51–58............... **8–18**
CAPITOL (1000 through 1800 series): 58–63.............. **4–10**
CAPITOL (11000 series):
77–79......................... **4–6**
GNP/CRESCENDO: 69........... **5–10**
RCA VICTOR: 52.............. **15–20**
REPRISE: 62–63................. **10–15**

BAY CITY ROLLERS, The
Singles: 7-Inch
ARISTA: 75–78................... **2–3**
BELL: 72–76.................... **2–4**
FLASHBACK: 80................. **1–3**
Picture Sleeves
ARISTA: 75–78................... **1–3**
LPs: 10/12-Inch 33rpm
ARISTA: 75–79.................. **5–8**
Members: Les McKeowen; Eric Faulkner; Stuart Wood; Alan Longmuir; Derek Longmuir; Billy Lyall; Pat McGlynn; Ian Mitchell.
Also see ROLLERS, The

BAYER, Carole: see SAGER, Carole Bayer

BAZUKA (Tony Camillo's Bazuka)
Singles: 7-Inch
A&M: 75....................... **2–4**
VENTURE: 79................... **1–3**
LPs: 10/12-Inch 33rpm
A&M: 75....................... **5–8**

BEACH BOYS, The
Singles: 12-Inch 33/45rpm
CARIBOU (9028; "Here Comes The Night"): 79........... **4–6**
CARIBOU (9028; "Here Comes The Night"): 79......... **20–25**
(Promotional issue only.)
Singles: 7-Inch
BROTHER: 67................... **5–8**
CANDIX (301; "Surfin"):
61........................... **50–60**

Price Range

Price Range

(Label reads "Distributed by Era Record Sales Inc.")

CANDIX (301; "Surfin"):
61 .... **$75–90**
(Label does NOT say "Distributed by Era Record Sales Inc.")

CANDIX (331; "Surfin"):
62 .... **60–75**

CAPITOL (2000 series
except 2765): *67–69.* **5–8**

CAPITOL (2765;
"Cottonfields"): *70* **12–15**

CAPITOL (4000 series
Except 4880): *62–63* **8–10**

CAPITOL (4880; "Ten
Little Indians"): *62* **15–20**

CAPITOL (5000 series,
except 5096 & 5312):
63–66 .... **5–8**
(Orange/yellow labels.)

CAPITOL (5096; "Little
Saint Nick"): *63.* **12–15**

CAPITOL (5312; "The
Man With All The
Toys"): *63* **12–15**

CAPITOL (5000 series):
81–86 .... **2–4**
(Purple labels.)

CAPITOL (6000 series):
67–68 .... **5–8**

CARIBOU: *79–85.* **3–5**

ODE '70: *71* **12–15**

REPRISE (0894; "Add
Some Music To Your
Day"): *70* **5–10**

REPRISE (0929; "Slip On
Through"): *70* **5–10**

REPRISE (0957; "Tears In
The Morning"): *70* **12–15**

REPRISE (0998; "Cool,
Cool Water"): *71.* **60–75**

REPRISE (1015; "Long
Promised Road"): *71* **20–25**

REPRISE (1047; "Long
Promised Road"): *71* **20–25**

REPRISE (1058; "Surf's
Up"): *71.* **45–50**

REPRISE (1091; "Cuddle
Up"): *72.* **25–30**

REPRISE (1101;
"Marcella"): *72* **25–30**

REPRISE (1138; "Sail On
Sailor"): *73.* **$10–12**

REPRISE (1156;
"California Saga"): *73.* **5–10**

REPRISE (1310; "I Can
Hear Music"): *74.* **3–5**

REPRISE (1321; "Child Of
Winter"): *74.* **20–30**

REPRISE (1325; "Sail On
Sailor"): *75.* **5–8**

REPRISE (1336;
"Wouldn't It Be Nice"):
75 .... **5–8**

REPRISE (1354 through
1394): *76–78.* **3–5**

X: *61.* **100–125**

Promotional Singles

CAPITOL (2360;
"Bluebirds Over The
Mountain"): *69* **15–20**

CAPITOL (2936/7; "Salt
Lake City"): *65* **175–200**

CAPITOL CUSTOM
("Spirit Of America"):
63 .... **125–150**

CARIBOU (557; "Here
Comes The Night"): *79* **10–12**
(Blue vinyl.)

CARIBOU (557; "Here
Comes The Night"): *79* **50–60**
(Special Edition autographed copies. Blue vinyl.)

CARIBOU (9026; "Here
Comes The Night"): *79* **10–15**

ODE '70 (66016;
"Wouldn't It Be
Nice-Live Version"): *71* **35–40**

REPRISE (557-2; "Sail On
Sailor"): *73.* **75–100**

REPRISE (0998; "Cool,
Cool Water"): *71.* **45–50**

WHAT'S IT ALL ABOUT
(449/450 & 507/508) **20–22**
(Public service radio station issues. Program disc 449/450 has The Beach Boys on one side and Dr. Hook on the flip. 507/508 features The Beach Boys on one side and The Rolling Stones on the other.)

Picture Sleeves
BROTHER: *67* **15–18**

Price Range

CAPITOL (4777; "Surfin'
Safari"): *62*................... **$18–20**
CAPITOL (4880; "Ten
Little Indians"): *62*............. **50–60**
CAPITOL (5000 series
except 5561): *63–66*............. **10–15**
CAPITOL (5561; "Barbara
Ann"): *65*..................... **40–45**

EPs: 7-Inch 33/45rpm

BROTHER (1; "Radio
Spot Backing Tracks"):
73 .... **225–250**
(Promotional issue only.)
CAPITOL (189; "Best Of
The Beach Boys"): *66*........... **15–20**
(With an "LLP" prefix. Jukebox issue only.)
CAPITOL (1981; "Surfer
Girl"): *63* **45–55**
CAPITOL (2186; "10
Little Indians"): *64*........... **300–325**
(One side of this EP contains selections by Ray
Anthony.)
CAPITOL (2027; "Shut
Down, Vol. 2"): *64*............. **45–55**
CAPITOL (2269; "The
Beach Boys Today"): *65*........ **50–75**
(Jukebox issue only.)
CAPITOL (2293/94;
"Beach Boys' Party"): *65*...... **125–150**
(Jukebox issue only.)
CAPITOL (2545; "Best Of
The Beach Boys"): *66*........... **50–75**
(With a "DU" prefix. Jukebox issue only.)
CAPITOL (2545; "Best Of
The Beach Boys"): *66*........... **15–20**
CAPITOL (2754/55;
"Brian Wilson
Introduces Selections"):
64 .... **350–375**
(Promotional issue only. Includes selections
from "Beach Boys Concert" & "Beach Boys
Songbook.")
CAPITOL (5267; "4 By
The Beach Boys"): *66*........... **35–45**
REPRISE (2118; "Mount
Vernon & Fairway"): *73*......... **8–10**
(Originally packaged with Reprise LP 2118,
"Holland.")
ROCK SHOPPE ("The
Beach Years"): *75*............. **75–100**

Price Range

(Demo disc for "A Six Hour Radio Special."
Also contains excerpts by Jan & Dean, Dick
Dale & The Surfaris, narrated by Roger Chris-
tian. Promotional issue, pressed in a quantity of
200 copies.)
WARNER BROS (422;
"Sunflower Promo
Spots"): *70*................. **$100–125**
WARNER BROS (534;
"Vote '72"): *72* **35–45**
(Promotional issue only.)
WHAT'S IT ALL ABOUT........ **20–25**
(Promotional issue only.)

LPs: 10/12-Inch 33rpm

ACCORD: *83* **5–8**
BROTHER: *67* **12–15**
CAPITOL (133; "20/20"):
69 .... **10–12**
CAPITOL (133; 20/20): *69*....... **30–35**
(With an "SKAO-8" prefix. Capitol Record
Club issue.)
CAPITOL (253; "Close
Up"): *69*..................... **35–40**
CAPITOL (442; "Good
Vibrations"): *70*............... **20–25**
CAPITOL (500; "All
Summer Long/California
Girls"): *70* **8–10**
CAPITOL (701; "Dance,
Dance, Dance/Fun, Fun,
Fun"): *71* **8–10**
CAPITOL (1808 through
1998): *63–67*................... **8–15**
(With a "DT" prefix.)
CAPITOL (1808 through
1998): *75–78*................... **5–8**
(With an "SM" prefix.)
CAPITOL (1808 through
1998): *62–63*.................. **15–20**
(With a "T" or "ST" prefix.)
CAPITOL (2027; "Shut
Down, Volume 2"): *63* **8–15**
(With a "DT" prefix.)
CAPITOL (2027; "Shut
Down, Volume 2"): *75*............ **5–8**
(With an "SM" prefix.)
CAPITOL (2027; "Shut
Down, Volume 2"): *63* **15–20**
(With a "T" or ST" prefix.)
CAPITOL (2110; "All
Summer Long"): *64*............. **25–30**

Price Range   *Price Range*

(With "Don't Break Down." The track "Don't
Back Down" was incorrectly shown as "Don't
Break Down" on these pressings.)

CAPITOL (2110; "All
Summer Long"): *64*. **$15–20**
(With "Don't Back Down" shown correctly.)

CAPITOL (2164; "Beach
Boys' Christmas
Album"): *75*. **5–8**
(With an "SM" prefix.)

CAPITOL (2164; "Beach
Boys' Christmas
Album"): *64*. **20–35**
(With a "T" or "ST" prefix.)

CAPITOL (2198; "Beach
Boys Concert"): *64* **10–15**

CAPITOL (2269; "The
Beach Boys Today"): *65*. **15–20**
(With a "T" or DT" prefix.)

CAPITOL (2354; "Summer
Days & Summer
Nights"): *65*. **15–20**
(With a "T" or DT" prefix.)

CAPITOL (2398; "Beach
Boys Party"): *65* **30–35**
(With an "SMAS" prefix. Price includes 15
bonus photos. Deduct $5-$8 if these photos are
missing.)

CAPITOL (2398; "Beach
Boys Party"): *65* **20–30**
(With a "DMAS" prefix. Price includes 15
bonus photos. Deduct $5-$8 if these photos are
missing.)

CAPITOL (2458; "Pet
Sounds"): *66*. **15–20**
(With a "T" or DT" prefix.)

CAPITOL (2545; "Best Of
The Beach Boys"): *66*. **10–15**
(With a "T" or DT" prefix.)

CAPITOL (2706; "Best Of
The Beach Boys, Volume
2"): *67* **10–15**
(With a "T" or DT" prefix.)

CAPITOL (2813; "Beach
Boys Deluxe Set"): *67*. **100–125**
(With a "TCL" prefix.)

CAPITOL (2813; "Beach
Boys Deluxe Set"): *67*. **35–40**
(With a "DTCL" prefix.)

CAPITOL (2859; "Wild
Honey"): *67*. **10–15**
(With a "T" or DT" prefix.)

CAPITOL (ST-8-2891;
"Smiley Smile"): *69*. **$60–75**
(With an "ST-8" prefix. Capitol Record Club
issue.)

CAPITOL (2893;
"Stack-o-Tracks"): *68* **100–125**
(With music-lyrics booklet.)

CAPITOL (2893;
"Stack-o-Tracks"): *68* **50–60**
(Without music-lyrics booklet.)

CAPITOL (2893;
"Stack-o-Tracks"): *69* **100–125**
(With an "ST-8" prefix. Capitol Record Club
issue.)

CAPITOL (2895;
"Friends"): *68* **10–15**

CAPITOL (2945; "Best Of
The Beach Boys, Volume
3"): *68* **35–40**

CAPITOL (3352;
"Sunflower"): *70* **30–35**
(With an "SKAO-9" prefix. Capitol Record
Club issue.)

CAPITOL (6994; "Golden
Years Of The Beach
Boys"): *75* **25–30**
(TV mail-order offer.)

CAPITOL (10000 series):
78–85 . . . . **5–8**

CAPITOL (153477;
"Rarities"): *75* **20–25**
(RCA Record Club issue.)

CAPITOL (233593;
"American Summer"):
75 . . . . **20–25**
(RCA Record Club issue.)

CARIBOU: *78–85*. **5–8**

ERA: *69*. **12–15**

EVEREST: *81* **5–8**

PICKWICK: *72–75* **8–12**

REPRISE (Except 2118 &
6453): *70–78*. **8–12**

REPRISE (2118;
"Holland"): *73*. **15–18**
(With "Mount Vernon & Fairway" EP.)

REPRISE (2118;
"Holland"): *73*. **8–12**
(Without "Mount Vernon & Fairway" EP.)

REPRISE (6453; "Surf's
Up"): *71* **15–20**
(Capitol Record Club issue.)

RONCO: *78* **8–10**

SEARS: *70*. **90–100**
(Sold only at Sears retail stores.)

Price Range

SESSIONS: *80* **$15–20**
SPRINGBOARD: *72* **5–8**

Promotional LPs

CAPITOL (1; "Open
House"): *78* **175–200**
CAPITOL (2754/5; "Beach
Boys' Concert"): *64* **300–350**
CAPITOL (3123; "Silver
Platter Service"): *64* **75–100**
(With selections by The Hollyridge Strings.)
CAPITOL (3133; "Silver
Platter Service"): *64* **125–150**
("Beach Boys Christmas Special.")
CAPITOL (3266; "Silver
Platter Service"): *67* **75–100**
CARIBOU (1024; "Keepin'
The Summer Alive"): *80* **45–50**
CRAWDADDY ("Brian
Wilson Interview"): *77* **90–100**
MORE MUSIC (03-179-72;
"Good Vibrations From
London") **50-60**
MUTUAL RADIO ("Dick
Clark Presents The
Beach Boys"): *81* **150–175**
(A 3-LP boxed set.)
REPRISE ("Radio Spot
Backing Tracks For
Beach Boys In
Concert"): *73* **225-250**
Members: Brian Wilson; Carl Wilson; Dennis
Wilson; Mike Love; Al Jardine.
Note: Promos NOT listed separately are priced
in the same range as commercial issues.
Also see ANNETTE
Also see ANTHONY, Ray
Also see BEATLES, The / The Beach Boys /
Buddy Holly
Also see CALIFORNIA MUSIC
Also see CAMPBELL, Glen
Also see CELEBRATION
Also see CHICAGO
Also see CLAYTON, Merry
Also see DALE, Dick
Also see DR. HOOK
Also see FLAME
Also see HONDELLS, The
Also see JAN & DEAN
Also see KENNY & THE CADETS
Also see PETERSEN, Paul
Also see ROTH, David Lee
Also see SURFARIS, The
Also see SURVIVORS, The

Price Range

Also see WILSON, Brian
Also see WILSON, Brian, & Mike Love
Also see WILSON, Carl
Also see WILSON, Dennis

BEACH BOYS, The / Tony & Joe
Singles: 7-Inch
ERA: *70* **$2–4**
Also see BEACH BOYS, The
Also see TONY & JOE

BEACH BUMS, The
Singles: 7-Inch
ARE YOU KIDDING
ME?: *66* **15–20**
Also see SEGER, Bob

BEACON STREET UNION
Singles: 7-Inch
JANUS: *70* **2–4**
MGM: *67–69* **3–5**
RTP: *69* **2–4**
LPs: 10/12-Inch 33rpm
MGM: *68* **12–15**
Members: Robert Rhodes; Paul Tartachny;
Wayne Ulaky; Richard Weisburg; John Wright.

**BEAR, Edward: see EDWARD
BEAR**

**BEAR ESSENCE STARRING
MARIANNA**
Singles: 12-Inch 33/45rpm
MOBY DICK: *84* **4–6**

BEAST
LPs: 10/12-Inch 33rpm
COTILLION: *69* **10–12**
EVOLUTION: *70* **8–10**

BEAT, B: see B. BEAT GIRLS, The

BEAT FARMERS, The
LPs: 10/12-Inch 33rpm
RHINO: *85* **5–8**

BEATLES, The
Singles: 7-Inch
APPLE: *71–75* **3–5**
ATCO (6302; "Sweet
Georgia Brown"): *64* **25–35**

Price Range

(Shown as by "The Beatles With Tony Sheridan.")

ATCO (6308; "Ain't She
Sweet"): *64*. **$8–12**
(Shown as by "The Beatles - Vocal By John Lennon.")

ATLANTIC: *83* **1–3**

CAPITOL (Orange, black
or purple label): *75–85* **2–3**
(Includes reissues of 1964-1975 material and original pressings of 1975-1985 releases.)

CAPITOL (2056; "Hello
Goodbye"): *67*. **4–6**
(Orange/yellow "swirl" label.)

CAPITOL (2056; "Hello
Goodbye"): *68*. **8–10**
(Red/orange "target" label.)

CAPITOL (2138; "Lady
Madonna"): *68*. **4–6**
(Orange/yellow "swirl" label.)

CAPITOL (2138; "Lady
Madonna"): *68*. **8–10**
(Red/orange "target" label.)

CAPITOL (5100; "Movie
Medley"/"Fab Four On
Film"): *81* **60–70**
(First issued with "Movie Medley" backed with "Fab Four On Film," which was The Beatles talking about the film "A Hard Day's Night." With a "B" prefix.)

CAPITOL (5100; "Movie
Medley"/"I'm Happy
Just To Dance With
You"): *81* **2-3**
(With a "B" prefix.)

CAPITOL (5107; "Movie
Medley"): *82* **2–3**
(With a "B" prefix.)

CAPITOL (5189; "Love
Me Do"): *82*. **2–3**
(With a "B" prefix.) This recent Capitol 5000 series differs from the 1964 5000 series by its use of the "B" prefix.)

CAPITOL (5112 through
5964): *64–67*. **8–12**
(Price range here is for orange/yellow swirl label issues.)

CAPITOL (5112; "I Want
To Hold Your Hand"):
84 . . . . **2–3**

Price Range

("I Want To Hold Your Hand," was reissued on STEREO single in 1984. Even though the reissue is on the orange/yellow label, it has black print around the border of the label. 1964 issues have this print in white letters.

CAPITOL (5112 through
5964): *68* **$12–15**
(Price range here is for red/orange target label issues.)

CAPITOL (5555; "We Can
Work It Out" - red &
white label): *68* **450–500**
(Issued on this "Starline" label due to an error in production.)

CAPITOL (6061 through
6066): *65* **25–35**
(Price range here is for the green label "Starline" series.)

CAPITOL (6278 through
6300): *81* **2–3**
(Price range here is for the blue label "Starline" series.)

CAPITOL (72144; "All
My Loving"): *72* **80–100**
(An error in production created a U.S. pressing of the Canadian release, "All My Loving"/"This Boy.")

COLLECTABLES: *82* **2–3**

DECCA (31382; "My
Bonnie"): *62*. **2000–2500**
(Shown as by Tony Sheridan And The Beat Brothers. Note: this price is for a COMMERCIAL copy and NOT a promotional issue! Commercial copies are on Decca's black label with silver print and a multi-color stripe across the center of the label. Black & silver, 1950s' style, Decca labels without the other colors are bootleg copies of this release.)

IBC (0082; "Murray The
'K' & The Beatles As It
Happened"): *76*. **4–6**

MGM (13213; "My
Bonnie"): *64*. **10–15**
(Shown as by The Beatles With Tony Sheridan.)

MGM (13227; "Why"): *64*. **15–20**
(Shown as by The Beatles With Tony Sheridan.)

MURRAY THE "K" &
THE BEATLES (33
Single): *64* **20–25**
Note: Reissued in 1976 as IBC 0082.

OLDIES 45: *64*. **5–8**

SWAN (4152; "She Loves
You"): *63* **150–200**

Price Range

(White label, with red print. Titles are in quotes. Does NOT have "Don't Drop Out" on label.)

SWAN (4152; "She Loves
You"): *63* **$125–175**
(White label, with red print. Does NOT have "Don't Drop Out" on label.)

SWAN (4152; "She Loves
You"): *63* **100–150**
(White label, with red print. No quotes on titles. Says "Don't Drop Out" on label.)

SWAN (4152; "She Loves
You"): *63* **100–150**
(White label, with blue print. No quotes on titles. Says "Don't Drop Out" on label.)

SWAN (4152; "She Loves
You"): *64* **10–20**
(Black label.)

SWAN (4182; "Sie Liebt
Dich"): *64* **35–45**
(With–She Loves You" following "Sie Liebt Dich" on the same line. White label with red print.)

SWAN (4182; "Sie Liebt
Dich"): *64* **30–40**
(With "She Loves You" under "Sie Liebt Dich" on a separate line. White label with orange print.)

SWAN (4182; "Sie Liebt
Dich"): *64* **25–35**
(With "She Loves You" under "Sie Liebt Dich" on a separate line. White label with red print.)

TOLLIE: *64*.................. **15–25**
(Black label.)

TOLLIE: *64*.................. **25–30**
(Yellow label with blue print.)

TOLLIE: *64*.................. **30–40**
(Yellow label with black print. Label name in brackets.)

TOLLIE: *64*.................. **12–18**
(Yellow label with black print. Label name is either in a box or is by itself, with no lines, box or brackets.)

TOLLIE: *64*.................. **20–25**
(Yellow label with green print. Label name is all upper case.)

TOLLIE: *64*.................. **15–18**
(Yellow label with green print. Label name is all lower case.)

VEE JAY (498; "Please
Please Me"): *63*............. **500–600**
(Showing group as The "BEATTLES." With thin lettering & oval label logo.)

VEE JAY (498; "Please
Please Me"): *63*............. **350–400**

(Showing group as The "BEATTLES." With bold lettering & oval label logo.)

VEE JAY (498; "Please
Please Me"): *63*............. **$500–600**
(Showing group as The "BEATTLES." With 'brackets' label logo.)

VEE JAY (498; "Please
Please Me"): *63*............. **350–400**
(Showing group as The "BEATTLES." With thin lettering & oval label logo.)

VEE JAY (498; "Please
Please Me"): *63*............. **400–500**
(Showing group as The "BEATTLES." With 'brackets' label logo.)

VEE JAY (498; "Please
Please Me"): *63*............. **600–700**
(Showing group as The "BEATTLES." With thin lettering & oval label logo. Catalog number, at bottom of label, is preceded by the number symbol: "#498.")

VEE JAY (522; "From Me
To You"): *63*............. **125–150**
(Black label with horizontal silver lines.)

VEE JAY (522; "From Me
To You"): *63*............. **75–100**
(Black label. With rainbow circle.)

VEE JAY (581; "Please
Please Me"): *64*............. **100–125**
(Purple label.)

VEE JAY (581; "Please
Please Me"): *64*............. **50–75**
(White label.)

VEE JAY (581; "Please
Please Me"): *64*............. **30–40**
(Yellow label.)

VEE JAY (581; "Please
Please Me"): *64*............. **15–20**
(Black label with horizontal silver lines.)

VEE JAY (581; "Please
Please Me"): *64*............. **12–15**
(Black label. No rainbow circle.)

VEE JAY (581; "Please
Please Me"): *64*............. **20–25**
(Black label with rainbow circle.)

VEE JAY (587; "Do You
Want To Know A
Secret"): *64*.................. **30–40**
(Yellow label.)

VEE JAY (587; "Do You
Want To Know A
Secret"): *64*.................. **15–20**
(Black label with horizontal silver lines.)

Price Range   *Price Range*

VEE JAY (587; "Do You
Want To Know A
Secret"): *64*. **$25–30**
(Black label. No rainbow circle. Brackets Vee
Jay logo.)

VEE JAY (587; "Do You
Want To Know A
Secret"): *64*. **15–20**
(Black label. No rainbow circle. Oval Vee Jay
logo.)

VEE JAY (587; "Do You
Want To Know A
Secret"): *64*. **12–16**
(Black label with rainbow circle.)

Promotional Singles

APPLE ("Let It Be"): *70*. **20–25**
(Identified as "Beatles Promo 1970." A one-
sided promo issue.)

ATCO (6302; "Sweet
Georgia Brown"): *64*. **75–125**

ATCO (6308; "Ain't She
Sweet"): *64*. **90–100**

BACKSTAGE (1100 series,
except 1112): *83*. **8–10**
(Picture discs.)

BACKSTAGE (1112; "Oui
Presents The Silver
Beatles"): *82*. **5–8**
(Oui Magazine promotional giveaway. Features
a "Like Dreamers Do" - "Love Of The Loved"
montage. Mailing also included Oui News Release and subscription form. This is not a picture disc single, as the other Backstage 1100
singles are.)

CAPITOL (2056; "Hello
Goodbye"): *67*. **60–80**

CAPITOL (2138; "Lady
Madonna"): *68*. **50–75**

CAPITOL (4274; "Got To
Get You Into My Life"):
76 . . . . **20–25**

CAPITOL (4347; "Helter
Skelter"): *76*. **20–25**

CAPITOL (4347;
"Ob-La-Di, Ob-La-Da"):
76 . . . . **20–25**

CAPITOL (4506; "Girl"):
78 . . . . **75–90**

CAPITOL (4612; "Sgt.
Pepper's Lonely Hearts
Club Band"/"With A
Little Help From My
Friends"): *78* **12-15**

CAPITOL (5100; "Movie
Medley"/"Fab Four On
Film"): *81* **$15–20**
(First issued with "Movie Medley" backed with
"Fab Four On Film," which was The Beatles
talking about the film "A Hard Day's Night."
Later issues had "I'm Happy Just To Dance
With You" on the flip side.)

CAPITOL (5112; "I Want
To Hold Your Hand"):
84 . . . . **8–10**
(The promo of this single is actually numbered
9076, but we have it listed both ways for your
convenience.)

CAPITOL (PB-5189;
"Love Me Do"): *82*. **10–12**
(With a "PB" prefix. Promo copies of this issue
were on commercial stock labels, but are
quickly identified by the printing of an "Intro"
time of :13 on the right side of the label. Also,
store stock copies were B-5189, not PB-
5189.)

CAPITOL (5810; "Penny
Lane"): *67* **90–100**

CAPITOL (5964; "All You
Need Is Love"): *67* **70–85**
(This promo, as well as many Capitol issues by
other artists, was shipped in a "Rush" paper
sleeve. It's possible a slight premium may be
placed on these sleeves, although they were
NOT identified in any way as a Beatles
item.)

CAPITOL (9076; "I Want
To Hold Your Hand"):
84 . . . . **8–10**

CAPITOL (9758; "Movie
Medley"): *81* **30–35**
(With an "SPRO" prefix.)

CAPITOL CUSTOM
(2637; "Music City
KFWBeatles"): *64*. **200–250**
(Radio KFWB & Wallichs Music City promo
disc, "The Beatles Talking"/"You Can't Do
That.")

DECCA (31382; "My
Bonnie"): *62*. **500–600**
(Shown as by Tony Sheridan And The Beat
Brothers. Pink label with black lettering.)

MGM (13213; "My
Bonnie"): *64*. **90–100**
(Shown as by The Beatles With Tony Sheridan.)

Price Range

MGM (13227; "Why"): *64*. **$75–125**
(Shown as by The Beatles With Tony Sheridan.)
SWAN (4152; "She Loves
You"): *63*. **150–200**
SWAN (4152; "I'll Get
You"): *64*. **175–225**
(One-sided pressing. Flip side has blank
grooves.)
SWAN (4182; "Sie Liebt
Dich"): *64*. **125–150**
TOLLIE: *64*. **100–125**
UNITED ARTISTS
(42370; "Let It Be"): *70*. **500–700**
(Contains three radio advertisements for the
film.)
VEE JAY (8;
"Anna"/"Ask Me
Why"): *64* **2500–3000**
VEE JAY (498; "Please
Please Me"): *63*. **350–450**
VEE JAY (522; "From Me
To You"): *63*. **100–150**
VEE JAY (581; "Please
Please Me" - purple
label): *64*. **100–150**
VEE JAY (581; "Please
Please Me" - white
label): *64*. **100–125**
VEE JAY (587; "Do You
Want To Know A
Secret"): *64*. **100–125**
WHAT'S IT ALL ABOUT **15–20**

Plastic Soundsheets/Flexi-Discs
AMERICOM: *69*. **350–450**
(4-inch "Pocket Discs.")
EVA-TONE (8464; "All
My Loving"): *82* **5–8**
(Back side reads either "Compliments Of Mu-
sicland" or "Compliments Of Discount.")
EVA-TONE (8464; "All
My Loving"): *82* **15–20**
(Back side reads "Compliments Of Sam
Goody.")
EVA-TONE (830771; "Till
There Was You"): *83* **3–5**
EVA-TONE (420826; "All
My Loving"): *82* **5–8**
(Back side reads either "Compliments Of Mu-
sicland" or "Compliments Of Discount.")
EVA-TONE (420826; "All
My Loving"): *82* **15–20**

Price Range

(Back side reads "Compliments Of Sam
Goody.")
EVA-TONE (420827;
"Magical Mystery
Tour"): *82* **$5–8**
(Back side reads either "Compliments Of Mu-
sicland" or "Compliments Of Discount.")
EVA-TONE (420827;
"Magical Mystery
Tour"): *82* **15–20**
(Back side reads "Compliments Of Sam
Goody.")
EVA-TONE (420828;
"Rocky Raccoon"): *82* **5–8**
(Back side reads either "Compliments Of Mu-
sicland" or "Compliments Of Discount.")
EVA-TONE (420828;
"Rocky Raccoon"): *82* **15–20**
(Back side reads "Compliments Of Sam
Goody.")
EVA-TONE (1214825;
"The Beatles German
Medley): *83* **30–40**
OFFICIAL BEATLES
FAN CLUB
("1964-Season's
Greetings From The
Beatles"): *64*. **175-200**
OFFICIAL BEATLES
FAN CLUB
("1965-Beatles Christmas
Record"): *65*. **100–125**
OFFICIAL BEATLES
FAN CLUB
("1966-Season's
Greetings From The
Beatles"): *66*. **100-125**
OFFICIAL BEATLES
FAN CLUB
("1967-Christmas Time
Is Here Again"): *67* **100-125**
OFFICIAL BEATLES
FAN CLUB
("1968-Beatles Christmas
Record"): *68*. **50–75**
OFFICIAL BEATLES
FAN CLUB
("1969-Happy
Christmas"): *69* **40–50**
SILHOUETTE: *86* **6–10**

Price Range

Price Range

Picture Sleeves

APPLE (Except 2531):
68–70 .... **$12–18**

APPLE (2531; "Ballad Of
John & Yoko"): *69* **18–22**

ATCO (6308; "Ain't She
Sweet"): *64*................. **100–125**

CAPITOL/HOLIDAY
INN SLEEVE: *64*............ **250–300**
(Promotional sleeve, pictures the four Beatles
on front and their first three Capitol LPs on the
back. Not known to have been issued containing any particular single.)

CAPITOL (2056; "Hello
Goodbye"): *67*................. **18–20**

CAPITOL (2138; "Lady
Madonna"): *68*................. **12–18**

CAPITOL (4000 series,
except 4506): *76*................. **4–6**

CAPITOL (4506; "Girl"):
78 .... **10–15**

CAPITOL (5100; "Movie
Medley"/"Fab Four On
Film"): *81* **12–15**
(With a "B" prefix.)

CAPITOL (5107; "Movie
Medley"/"I'm Happy
Just To Dance With
You"): *81*..................... **2–3**
(With a "B" prefix.)

CAPITOL (B-5189; "Love
Me Do"): *82*.................... **2–3**
(With a "B" prefix. This recent Capitol 5000
series differs from the 1964 5000 series by its use
of the "B" prefix.)

CAPITOL (5112; "I Want
To Hold Your Hand"):
64 .... **20–30**

CAPITOL (5112; WMCA
radio promotional
sleeve): *64*.................... **650–750**
(Back side of this sleeve pictures WMCA dee
jays. Front side is identical to standard commercial issue.)

CAPITOL (5112; "I Want
To Hold Your Hand"):
84 .... **2–3**
(This reissue sleeve is clearly dated "1984" in
lower left corner.)

CAPITOL (5150; "Can't
Buy Me Love"): *64*.......... **250–300**

CAPITOL CUSTOM
("Music City
KFWBeatles"): *64*.......... **$550–600**
(Promotional sleeve for the "Souvenir Record"
from KFWB & Wallichs Music City.)

CAPITOL (5222; "A Hard
Day's Night"): *64* **20–25**

CAPITOL (5234; "I'll Cry
Instead"): *64* **35–45**

CAPITOL (5235; "And I
Love Her"): *64*................ **30–35**

CAPITOL (5255; "Slow
Down"): *64*................... **35–40**

CAPITOL (5327; "I Feel
Fine"): *64*.................... **12–15**

CAPITOL (5371; "Eight
Days A Week"): *65*........... **10–12**

CAPITOL (5407; "Ticket
To Ride"): *65*................. **35–50**

CAPITOL (5439; "Leave
My Kitten Alone"): *85*....... **450–500**

CAPITOL (5476; "Help"):
65 .... **15–20**

CAPITOL (5498;
"Yesterday"): *65* **12–18**

CAPITOL (5555; "We Can
Work It Out"): *65*............. **15–20**

CAPITOL (5587;
"Nowhere Man"): *66* **12–18**

CAPITOL (5651;
"Paperback Writer"): *66*........ **12–18**

CAPITOL (5715; "Yellow
Submarine"): *66*............... **12–18**

CAPITOL (5810; "Penny
Lane"): *67* **25–30**

CAPITOL (5964; "All You
Need Is Love"): *67*............. **8–12**

COLLECTABLES: *82* **2–3**

IBC (0082; "Murray The
'K' & The Beatles As It
Happened"): *76*................. **4–6**

MGM (13213; "My
Bonnie"): *64*................. **35–40**

MGM (13227; "Why"): *64*....... **75–100**

MURRAY THE "K" &
THE BEATLES: *64* **60–75**
Note: Reissued in 1976 as IBC 0082.

SWAN: *63* **30–35**

TOLLIE: *64*.................... **35–40**

Price Range

VEE JAY SPECIAL
CHRISTMAS SLEEVE:
64 .... **$30–40**
(Standard center-cut paper sleeve printed with
the Beatles' faces and "We Wish You A Merry
Christmas And A Happy New Year." Issued
with assorted Vee Jay singles during the holiday
season.)
VEE JAY (581; "Please
Please Me" commercial
issue): *64* **100–125**
(Pictures the four Beatles.)
VEE JAY (581; "Please
Please Me" promotional
issue): *64* **500–600**
(Reads "The Record That Started Beatle-
mania" across the top. Does not picture the
group.)
VEE JAY (587; "Do You
Want To Know A
Secret"): *64*. **35–40**

EPs: 7-Inch 33/45rpm
CAPITOL (EAP 1-3121;
"Four By The Beatles"):
64 .... **100–150**
CAPITOL (R-5365; "4-By
The Beatles"): *65*. **100–125**
VEE JAY (VJEP 1-903;
"Souvenir Of Their Visit
To America"): *64* **65-80**
(Solid black label with either oval or block style
Vee Jay logo.)
VEE JAY (VJEP 1-903;
"Souvenir Of Their Visit
To America"): *64* **80-100**
(Solid black label with brackets Vee Jay logo.)
VEE JAY (VJEP 1-903;
"Souvenir Of Their Visit
To America"): *64* **45-50**
(Black label with rainbow color-band. All four
song titles in same size type.)
VEE JAY (VJEP 1-903;
"Souvenir Of Their Visit
To America"): *64* **60-75**
(Black label with rainbow color-band. Has
"Ask Me Why" in much larger type size than
other titles.)

Promotional EPs
CAPITOL 33 COMPACT
(2047; "Meet The
Beatles"): *64*. **175–225**
(Jukebox issue only.)

Price Range

CAPITOL 33 COMPACT
(2080; "Beatles Second
Album"): *64*. **$175-225**
(Jukebox issue only.)
CAPITOL 33 COMPACT
(2108; "Something
New"): *64* **250–300**
(Jukebox issue only.)
CAPITOL 33 COMPACT
(2548/49; "Open-End
Interview"): *64*. **550-600**
(Issued with a paper sleeve and script, which
represents about $300-$400 of the value.)
CAPITOL 33 COMPACT
(2598/99 "Second
Open-End Interview"):
64 .... **500-600**
(Issued with a paper sleeve and script, which
represents about $300-$400 of the value.)
CAPITOL (2720/21; "The
Beatles Introduce New
Songs"): *64*. **500–600**
(A 45rpm EP with John Lennon about Cilla
Black's "It's For You," and Paul talking about
Peter & Gordon's "I Don't Want To See You
Again.")
CAPITOL 33 COMPACT
(2905/06; "The Capitol
Souvenir Record"): *64* **250-300**
(Issued with a paper sleeve and script, which
represents about $100-$125 of the value. Con-
tains excerpts of 15 different songs by 15 artists,
including The Beatles.)
VEE JAY (903; "Souvenir
Of Their Visit To
America"): *64* **100–150**

Price Range

(White label with blue print. Price is for disc only.)

VEE JAY (903; "Souvenir
Of Their Visit To
America"): *64* **$1500–2000**
(Special sleeve in which some copies of the EP were supplied to radio stations.)

LPs: 10/12-Inch 33rpm

ALBUM GLOBE (8146;
"Happy Michaelmas"):
81 . . . . **8–12**

APPLE (101; "The
Beatles"): *68*. **25–30**
(With Capitol logo at bottom of label.)

APPLE (101; "The
Beatles"): *71*. **20–25**
(Without Capitol logo at bottom of label.)

APPLE (153; "Yellow
Submarine"): *69*. **12–18**
(With Capitol logo at bottom of label.)

APPLE (153; "Yellow
Submarine"): *71*. **10–12**
(Without Capitol logo at bottom of label.)

APPLE (383; "Abbey
Road"): *69*. **12–18**
(With Capitol logo at bottom of label.)

APPLE (383; "Abbey
Road"): *71*. **10–12**
(Without Capitol logo at bottom of label.)

APPLE (385; "Hey Jude"):
70 . . . . **15–25**
(With Capitol logo at bottom of label.)

APPLE (385; "Hey Jude"):
71 . . . . **10–12**
(Without Capitol logo at bottom of label.)

APPLE (ST-2047; "Meet
The Beatles"): *71*. **12–18**
(With Capitol logo at bottom of label.)

APPLE (ST-2047; "Meet
The Beatles"): *71*. **10–12**
(Without Capitol logo at bottom of label.)

APPLE (ST-2080; "The
Beatles' Second Album"):
71 . . . . **12–18**
(With Capitol logo at bottom of label.)

APPLE (ST-2080; "The
Beatles' Second Album"):
71 . . . . **10–12**
(Without Capitol logo at bottom of label.)

APPLE (ST-2108;
"Something New"): *71* **12–18**
(With Capitol logo at bottom of label.)

Price Range

APPLE (ST-2108;
"Something New"): *71* **$10–12**
(Without Capitol logo at bottom of label.)

APPLE (ST-2222; "The
Beatles' Story"): *71* **12–18**
(With Capitol logo at bottom of label.)

APPLE (ST-2228; "The
Beatles' Story"): *71* **10–12**
(Without Capitol logo at bottom of label.)

APPLE (ST-2228; "Beatles
'65"): *71* **12–18**
(With Capitol logo at bottom of label.)

APPLE (ST-2228; "Beatles
'65"): *71* **10–12**
(Without Capitol logo at bottom of label.)

APPLE (ST-2309; "The
Early Beatles"): *71* **12–18**
(With Capitol logo at bottom of label.)

APPLE (ST-2309; "The
Early Beatles"): *71* **10–12**
(Without Capitol logo at bottom of label.)

APPLE (ST-2358; "Beatles
VI"): *71* **12–18**
(With Capitol logo at bottom of label.)

APPLE (ST-2358; "Beatles
VI"): *71* **10–12**
(Without Capitol logo at bottom of label.)

APPLE (ST-2386; "Help"):
71 . . . . **12–18**
(With Capitol logo at bottom of label.)

APPLE (ST-2386; "Help"):
71 . . . . **10–12**
(Without Capitol logo at bottom of label.)

APPLE (ST-2442; "Rubber
Soul"): *71*. **12–18**
(With Capitol logo at bottom of label.)

APPLE (ST-2442; "Rubber
Soul"): *71*. **10–12**
(Without Capitol logo at bottom of label.)

APPLE (ST-2576;
"Revolver"): *71* **12–18**
(With Capitol logo at bottom of label.)

APPLE (ST-2576;
"Revolver"): *71* **10–12**
(Without Capitol logo at bottom of label.)

APPLE (SMAS-2653; "Sgt.
Pepper's Lonely Hearts
Club Band"): *71* **12–18**
(With Capitol logo at bottom of label.)

APPLE (SMAS-2653; "Sgt.
Pepper's Lonely Hearts
Club Band"): *71* **10–12**
(Without Capitol logo at bottom of label.)

APPLE (SMAL-2835;
"Magical Mystery
Tour"): *71* **$12–18**
(With Capitol logo at bottom of label.)
APPLE (SMAL-2835;
"Magical Mystery
Tour"): *71* **10–12**
(Without Capitol logo at bottom of label.)
APPLE (3403; "The
Beatles/1962-1966"): *73* **15–20**
APPLE (3404; "The
Beatles/1967-1970"): *73* **15–20**
APPLE (34001; "Let It
Be"): *70* **10–15**
ATCO (169; "Ain't She
Sweet"): *64*. **75–100**
(Monaural issue. Also contains selections by
The Swallows.)
ATCO (169; "Ain't She
Sweet"): *64–69*. **100–150**
(Stereo issue. Also contains selections by The
Swallows.)
AUDIO FIDELITY (339;
"First Movement" -
picture disc): *82*. **8–12**
AUDIO RARITIES (2452;
"The Complete Silver
Beatles): *82*. **6–10**
AUDIO RARITIES
(30003; "The Silver
Beatles): *82*. **15–20**
(Picture disc.)
BACKSTAGE (Except
1111): *82–83*. **10–15**
BACKSTAGE (1111;
"Like Dreamers Do"):
82 .... **20–25**
(A 3-LP set. Contains two picture discs and a
white vinyl LP.)
BACKSTAGE (1111;
"Like Dreamers Do"):
82 .... **30–45**
(A 3-LP set. Contains two picture discs and a
gray vinyl LP.)
BACKSTAGE (1111;
"Like Dreamers Do"):
82 .... **30–40**
(A 3-LP set. Includes any of the custom issues,
which had various logos printed on the reverse
side of the picture discs.)

BACKSTAGE (1111;
"Like Dreamers Do"):
82 .... **$15–18**
(A 3-LP set. No custom artwork on picture
disc. With gatefold cover.)
BACKSTAGE (1111;
"Like Dreamers Do"):
82 .... **12–15**
(A 2-LP set. With standard cover.)
CAPITOL (101; "The
Beatles"): *76*. **10–12**
(Orange label.)
CAPITOL (101; "The
Beatles"): *78*. **8–12**
(Purple label.)
CAPITOL (101; "The
Beatles"): *84*. **6–10**
(Black label.)
CAPITOL (153; "Yellow
Submarine"): *76*. **8–10**
(Orange label.)
CAPITOL (153; "Yellow
Submarine"): *78*. **6–10**
(Purple label.)
CAPITOL (153; "Yellow
Submarine"): *84*. **5–8**
(Black label.)
CAPITOL (383; "Abbey
Road"): *76*. **8–10**
(Orange label.)
CAPITOL (383; "Abbey
Road"): *78* **6–10**
(Purple label.)
CAPITOL (383; "Abbey
Road"): *84* **5–8**
(Black label.)
CAPITOL (385; "Hey
Jude"): *76*. **8–10**
(Orange label.)
CAPITOL (385; "Hey
Jude"): *78*. **6–10**
(Purple label.)
CAPITOL (385; "Hey
Jude"): *84*. **5–8**
(Black label.)
CAPITOL (T-2047; "Meet
The Beatles"): *64*. **25–30**
(Monaural issue.)
CAPITOL (ST-2047;
"Meet The Beatles"): *64*. **20–25**
(Stereo issue. Black label with white print
around border.)

Price Range

Price Range

CAPITOL (ST-2047;
"Meet The Beatles"): *69* **$20–25**
(Green label.)
CAPITOL (ST-2047;
"Meet The Beatles"): *76* **8–12**
(Orange label.)
CAPITOL (ST-2047;
"Meet The Beatles"): *78* **6–10**
(Purple label.)
CAPITOL (ST-2047;
"Meet The Beatles"): *84* **5–8**
(Black label with black print around border.)
CAPITOL (ST-8-2047;
"Meet The Beatles"):
64–69 . . . . **25–30**
(Capitol Record Club issue.)
CAPITOL (T-2080; "The
Beatles' Second Album"):
64 . . . . **25–30**
(Monaural issue.)
CAPITOL (ST-2080; "The
Beatles' Second Album"):
64 . . . . **20–25**
(Stereo issue. Black label with white print
around border.)
CAPITOL (ST-2080; "The
Beatles' Second Album"):
69 . . . . **20–25**
(Green label.)
CAPITOL (ST-2080; "The
Beatles' Second Album"):
76 . . . . **8–12**
(Orange label.)
CAPITOL (ST-2080; "The
Beatles' Second Album"):
78 . . . . **6–10**
(Purple label.)
CAPITOL (ST-2080; "The
Beatles' Second Album"):
84 . . . . **5–8**
(Black label with black print around border.)
CAPITOL (ST-8-2080;
"The Beatles' Second
Album"): *64–69* **25–30**
(Capitol Record Club issue.)
CAPITOL (T-2108;
"Something New"): *64* **25–30**
(Monaural issue.)
CAPITOL (ST-2108;
"Something New"): *64* **20–25**
(Stereo issue. Black label with white print
around border.)

CAPITOL (ST-2108;
"Something New"): *69* **$20–25**
(Green label.)
CAPITOL (ST-2108;
"Something New"): *76* **8–12**
(Orange label.)
CAPITOL (ST-2108;
"Something New"): *78* **6–10**
(Purple label.)
CAPITOL (ST-2108;
"Something New"): *84* **5–8**
(Black label with black print around border.)
CAPITOL (ST-8-2108;
"Something New"):
64–69 . . . . **25–30**
(Capitol Record Club issue.)
CAPITOL (TBO-2222;
"The Beatles' Story"): *64* **30–35**
(Monaural issue.)
CAPITOL (STBO-2222;
"The Beatles' Story"): *64* **30–35**
(Stereo issue. Black label with white print
around border.)
CAPITOL (STBO-2222;
"The Beatles' Story"): *69* **20–25**
(Green label.)
CAPITOL (STBO-2222;
"The Beatles' Story"): *76* **8–12**
(Orange label.)
CAPITOL (STBO-2222;
"The Beatles' Story"): *78* **8–10**
(Purple label.)
CAPITOL (STBO-2222;
"The Beatles' Story"): *84* **6–10**
(Black label with black print around border.)
CAPITOL (T-2228;
"Beatles '65"): *65* **25–30**
(Monaural issue.)
CAPITOL (ST-2228;
"Beatles '65"): *65* **20–25**
(Stereo issue. Black label with white print
around border.)
CAPITOL (ST-2228;
"Beatles '65"): *69* **20–25**
(Green label.)
CAPITOL (ST-2228;
"Beatles '65"): *76* **8–12**
(Orange label.)
CAPITOL (ST-2228;
"Beatles '65"): *78* **6–10**
(Purple label.)
CAPITOL (ST-2228;
"Beatles '65"): *84* **5–8**
(Black label with black print around border.)

Price Range

Price Range

CAPITOL (T-2309; "The
Early Beatles"): *65* **$25–30**
(Monaural issue.)

CAPITOL (ST-2309; "The
Early Beatles"): *65* **20–25**
(Stereo issue. Black label with white print
around border.)

CAPITOL (ST-2309; "The
Early Beatles"): *69* **20–25**
(Green label.)

CAPITOL (ST-2309; "The
Early Beatles"): *76* **8–12**
(Orange label.)

CAPITOL (ST-2309; "The
Early Beatles"): *78* **6–10**
(Purple label.)

CAPITOL (ST-2309; "The
Early Beatles"): *84* **5–8**
(Black label with black print around border.)

CAPITOL (T-2358;
"Beatles VI"): *65* **25–30**
(Monaural issue.)

CAPITOL (ST-2358;
"Beatles VI"): *65* **20–25**
(Stereo issue. Black label with white print
around border.)

CAPITOL (ST-2358;
"Beatles VI"): *69* **20–25**
(Green label.)

CAPITOL (ST-2358;
"Beatles VI"): *76* **8–12**
(Orange label.)

CAPITOL (ST-2358;
"Beatles VI"): *78* **6–10**
(Purple label.)

CAPITOL (ST-2358;
"Beatles VI"): *84* **5–8**
(Black label with black print around border.)

CAPITOL (MAS-2386;
"Help"): *65.* **25–30**
(Monaural issue.)

CAPITOL (SMAS-2386;
"Help"): *65.* **20–25**
(Stereo issue. Black label with white print
around border.)

CAPITOL (SMAS-2386;
"Help"): *69.* **20–25**
(Green label.)

CAPITOL (SMAS-2386;
"Help"): *76.* **8–12**
(Orange label.)

CAPITOL (SMAS-2386;
"Help"): *78.* **$6–10**
(Purple label.)

CAPITOL (SMAS-2386;
"Help"): *84.* **5–8**
(Black label with black print around border.)

CAPITOL (SMAS-8-2386;
"Help"): *65–69.* **25–30**
(Capitol Record Club issue.)

CAPITOL (T-2442;
"Rubber Soul"): *65* **25–30**
(Monaural issue.)

CAPITOL (ST-2442;
"Rubber Soul"): *65* **20–25**
(Stereo issue. Black label with white print
around border.)

CAPITOL (ST-2442;
"Rubber Soul"): *69* **20–25**
(Green label.)

CAPITOL (ST-2442;
"Rubber Soul"): *76* **8–12**
(Orange label.)

CAPITOL (ST-2442;
"Rubber Soul"): *78* **6–10**
(Purple label.)

CAPITOL (ST-2442;
"Rubber Soul"): *84* **5–8**
(Black label with black print around border.)

CAPITOL (ST-8-2442;
"Rubber Soul"): *65–69* **25–30**
(Capitol Record Club issue.)

CAPITOL (T-2553;
"Yesterday And
Today"): *66* **700–900**
(Monaural issues. FIRST STATE "Butcher
cover" issues.)

CAPITOL (ST-2553;
"Yesterday And
Today"): *66* **1500–2000**
(Stereo issues. FIRST STATE "Butcher
Cover" issues.)

CAPITOL (T-2553;
"Yesterday And
Today"): *66* **250–350**
(Monaural issues. PASTE OVER or PEELED
"Butcher cover" copies.)

CAPITOL (ST-2553;
"Yesterday And
Today"): *66* **350–450**
(Stereo issues. PASTE OVER or PEELED
"Butcher cover" copies.)

Note: The wide range of values exists here due to varied opinions on the practice of peeling the "Trunk cover" from the "Butcher cover"; the expertise used in the peeling is also a major factor affecting the value of these LPs.

CAPITOL (T-2553;
"Yesterday And
Today"): *66* **$25–30**
(Monaural issue. "Trunk cover.")

CAPITOL (ST-2553;
"Yesterday And
Today"): *66* **20–25**
(Stereo issue. Black label with white print around border. "Trunk cover.")

CAPITOL (ST-2553;
"Yesterday And
Today"): *69* **20–25**
(Green label.)

CAPITOL (ST-2553;
"Yesterday And
Today"): *76* **8–12**
(Orange label.)

CAPITOL (ST-2553;
"Yesterday And
Today"): *78* **6–10**
(Purple label.)

CAPITOL (ST-2553;
"Yesterday And
Today"): *84* **5–8**
(Black label with black print around border.)

CAPITOL (ST-8-2553;
"Yesterday And
Today"): *66–69* **25–30**
(Capitol Record Club issue.)

CAPITOL (T-2576;
"Revolver"): *66* **$25–30**
(Monaural issue.)

CAPITOL (ST-2576;
"Revolver"): *66* **20–25**
(Stereo issue. Black label with white print around border.)

CAPITOL (ST-2576;
"Revolver"): *69* **20–25**
(Green label.)

CAPITOL (ST-2576;
"Revolver"): *76* **8–12**
(Orange label.)

CAPITOL (ST-2576;
"Revolver"): *78* **6–10**
(Purple label.)

CAPITOL (ST-2576;
"Revolver"): *84* **5–8**
(Black label with black print around border.)

CAPITOL (ST-8-2576;
"Revolver"): *66–69* **25–30**
(Capitol Record Club issue.)

CAPITOL (MAS-2653;
"Sgt. Pepper's Lonely
Hearts Club Band"): *67* **35–45**
(Monaural issue.)

CAPITOL (SMAS-2653;
"Sgt. Pepper's Lonely
Hearts Club Band"): *67* **20–25**
(Stereo issue. Black label with white print around border.)

CAPITOL (SMAS-2653;
"Sgt. Pepper's Lonely
Hearts Club Band"): *69* **18–22**
(Green label.)

CAPITOL (SMAS-2653;
"Sgt. Pepper's Lonely
Hearts Club Band"): *76* **8–12**
(Orange label.)

CAPITOL (SMAS-2653;
"Sgt. Pepper's Lonely
Hearts Club Band"): *78* **6–10**
(Purple label.)

CAPITOL (SMAS-2653;
"Sgt. Pepper's Lonely
Hearts Club Band"): *84* **5–8**
(Black label with black print around border.)

CAPITOL (MAL-2835;
"Magical Mystery
Tour"): *67* **35–45**
(Monaural issue.)

Price Range

CAPITOL (SMAL-2835;
"Magical Mystery
Tour"): *67* **$20–25**
(Stereo issue. Black label with white print around border.)

CAPITOL (SMAL-2835;
"Magical Mystery
Tour"): *69* **18–22**
(Green label.)

CAPITOL (SMAL-2835;
"Magical Mystery
Tour"): *76* **8–12**
(Orange label.)

CAPITOL (SMAL-2835;
"Magical Mystery
Tour"): *78* **6–10**
(Purple label.)

CAPITOL (SMAL-2835;
"Magical Mystery
Tour"): *84* **5–8**
(Black label with black print around border.)

CAPITOL (3403; "The
Beatles/1962-1966"): *78* **8–12**

CAPITOL (3404; "The
Beatles/1967-1970"): *78* **8–12**

CAPITOL (11537; "Rock
'N' Roll Music"): *76* **12–18**

CAPITOL (11638; "Beatles
At The Hollywood
Bowl"): *77* **5-8**

CAPITOL (11711; "Love
Songs"): *77* **6–10**

CAPITOL (11840; " "Sgt.
Pepper's Lonely Hearts
Club Band"): *78* **15–20**
(Picture disc.)

CAPITOL (11841; "Abbey
Road"): *78* **20–30**
(Colored vinyl.)

CAPITOL (11842; "The
Beatles/1962-1966"): *78* **20–25**

CAPITOL (11843; "The
Beatles/1967-1970"): *78* **20–25**

CAPITOL (11900; "Abbey
Road" - picture disc): *78* **20–30**

CAPITOL (11921; "A
Hard Day's Night"): *79* **8–10**
(Purple label.)

CAPITOL (11921; "A
Hard Day's Night"): *84* **5–8**
(Black label with black print around border.)

Price Range

CAPITOL (11922; "Let It
Be"): *79* **$8–10**
(Purple label.)

CAPITOL (11922; "Let It
Be"): *84* **5–8**
(Black label with black print around border.)

CAPITOL (12009;
"Rarities"): *78* **40–60**

CAPITOL (12060; "The
Beatles Rarities"): *80* **6–10**

CAPITOL (12199; "Reel
Music"): *82* **6–10**

CAPITOL (12245; "The
Beatles 20 Greatest
Hits"): *82* **8–12**
(Purple label.)

CAPITOL (12245; "The
Beatles 20 Greatest
Hits"): *84* **5–8**
(Black label.)

CAPITOL (16020; "Rock
'N' Roll Music, Volume
I"): *80* **5–8**

CAPITOL (16021; "Rock
'N' Roll Music, Volume
II"): *80* **5–8**

CAPITOL/APPLE: *68–75* **10–12**
(The "Capitol/Apple" label is simply the Apple label with the Capitol logo near the bottom of the label.)

CAPITOL RECORD
CLUB ISSUES (Except
ST-8-2553) **25–30**

CAPITOL RECORD
CLUB (ST-8-2553;
"Yesterday And
Today"): *66* **40–45**

CHARLY: *84* **5–8**

CICADELIC: *85–86*.............. **5–8**

CLARION (601; "The
Amazing Beatles &
Other Great English
Sounds"): *66*................... **60-75**
(Stereo issue. Back cover lists song titles. Also contains selections by The Swallows.)

CLARION (601; "The
Amazing Beatles &
Other Great English
Sounds"): *66* **75-100**
(Stereo issue. Back cover does NOT list song titles. Also contains selections by The Swallows.)

Price Range

CLARION (601; "The
   Amazing Beatles &
   Other Great English
   Sounds"): *66*. **$50-75**
   (Monaural issue. Also contains selections by
   The Swallows.)
GREAT NORTHWEST
   MUSIC CO: *78* **5–8**
H.S.R.D: *82* **8–12**
HALL OF MUSIC: *81* **12–18**
HERITAGE SOUND: *82* **8–10**
I-N-S RADIO NEWS
   ("American Tour With
   Ed Rudy #2"): *80* **12–18**
LINGASONG: *77*. **10–12**
LLOYDS ("The Great
   American Tour-1965
   Live Beatlemania
   Concert"): *65* **125-175**
   (With selections by The Liverpool Lads.)
MFSL ("The Beatles-The
   Collection"): *82* **375–425**
MFSL (023; "Abbey
   Road"): *79* **20–25**
MFSL (047; "Magical
   Mystery Tour"): *81* **20–25**
MFSL (072; "The
   Beatles"): *82*. **20–25**
MFSL (100; "Sgt. Pepper's
   Lonely Hearts Club
   Band"): *82* **125–175**
   (Silver label. Reads "UHQR" near top of label.)
MFSL (100; "Sgt. Pepper's
   Lonely Hearts Club
   Band"): *85* **15–20**
   (White label. No "UHQR" on label.)
MFSL (105; "Help"): *79* **20–25**
MGM (E-4215; "The
   Beatles With Tony
   Sheridan & Guests"): *64*. **45–55**
   (Monaural issue. With selections by Tony
   Sheridan & by The Titans.)
MGM (SE-4215; "The
   Beatles With Tony
   Sheridan & Guests"): *64*. **75–100**
   (Stereo issue. With selections by Tony Sheridan
   & by The Titans.)
METRO (M-563; "This Is
   Where It Started"): *66* **40–50**
   (Also contains selections by Tony Sheridan &
   by The Titans.)

Price Range

METRO (MS-563; "This Is
   Where It Started"): *66* **$50–75**
   (Also contains selections by Tony Sheridan &
   by The Titans.)
PAC: *81* **15–20**
PBR INT'L: *78* **20–30**
PHOENIX 10: *82* **5–8**
PHOENIX 20: *83* **5–8**
PICKWICK (Except
   90071): *78–79* **8–12**
PICKWICK (90071;
   "Recorded Live In
   Hamburg, 1962, Volume
   3"): *78* **15–20**
POLYDOR (4504; "In The
   Beginning - Circa
   1960"): *70* **12–15**
   (With gatefold cover.)
POLYDOR (4504; "In The
   Beginning - Circa
   1960"): *81–84*. **5–8**
   (With standard cover.)
POLYDOR (93199; "In
   The Beginning - Circa
   1960"): *70* **15–18**
   (Capitol Record Club issue.)
RPN (RADIO
   PULSEBEAT NEWS)
   "American Tour With
   Ed Rudy #2"): *64* **40-50**
   (This LP was occasionally issued with a "Teen
   Talk" booklet. The value of the booklet is ap-
   proximately the same as for the LP. This edition
   has NO pictures of The Beatles on the LP
   cover.)
RPN (RADIO
   PULSEBEAT NEWS)
   ("1965 Talk Album, Ed
   Rudy With New U.S.
   Tour"): *65* **50-75**
RAVEN: *81* **5–8**
SAVAGE (69; "The Savage
   Young Beatles"): *68* **75–100**
   (Label is yellow. Cover is orange.)
SAVAGE (69; "The Savage
   Young Beatles"): *68* **40–50**
   (Label is orange. Cover is yellow.)
SILHOUETTE: *81–84* **8–12**
STERLING
   PRODUCTIONS (6481;
   "I Apologize"): *66*. **70–80**

Price Range

Price Range

(Price includes bonus 8x10 photo, which represents $5-$15 of the value.)

UNITED ARTISTS
(UAL-3366; "A Hard
Day's Night"): *64* **$25–30**
(Monaural issue.)

UNITED ARTISTS
(UAS-6366; "A Hard
Day's Night"): *64* **25–30**
(Stereo issue. Black label.)

UNITED ARTISTS
(UAS-6366; "A Hard
Day's Night"): *68–70* **20–25**
(Stereo issue. Pink & orange or black & orange label.)

UNITED ARTISTS
(UAS-6366; "A Hard
Day's Night"): *71* **10–15**
(Stereo issue. Tan label.)

UNITED ARTISTS
(UAS-6366; "A Hard
Day's Night"): *77* **8–12**
(Stereo issue. Orange & yellow label.)

UNITED ARTISTS
(90828; "A Hard Day's
Night"): *65* **40–50**
(Capitol Record Club issue.)

VEE JAY (202; "Hear The
Beatles Tell All"): *64* **50–60**
(Monaural issue. Black label with rainbow color-band.)

VEE JAY (202; "Hear The
Beatles Tell All"): *79* **5–8**
(Stereo issue.)

VEE JAY (1062;
"Introducing The
Beatles"): *63* **600–700**
(Stereo Issue. With "Love Me Do" & "P.S. I Love You." Back cover pictures 25 other Vee Jay albums.)

VEE JAY (1062;
"Introducing The
Beatles"): *63* **325–375**
(Monaural issue. With "Love Me Do" & "P.S. I Love You." Back cover pictures 25 other Vee Jay albums.)

VEE JAY (1062;
"Introducing The
Beatles"): *63–64* **250–300**
(Monaural issue. With "Love Me Do" & "P.S. I Love You." Back cover is blank. May be regarded as a promotional issue, however nothing on the LP supports that theory.)

VEE JAY (1062;
"Introducing The
Beatles"): *63–64* **$500–600**
(Stereo issue. With "Love Me Do" & "P.S. I Love You." Back cover is blank. May be regarded as a promotional issue, however nothing on the LP supports that theory.)

VEE JAY (1062;
"Introducing The
Beatles"): *64* **75–100**
(Monaural issue. With "Love Me Do" & "P.S. I Love You." Back cover lists contents. Has brackets style label logo.)

VEE JAY (1062;
"Introducing The
Beatles"): *64* **60–75**
(Monaural issue. With "Love Me Do" & "P.S. I Love You." Back cover lists contents. Oval style label logo.)

VEE JAY (1062;
"Introducing The
Beatles"): *64* **150–200**
(Stereo issue. With "Ask Me Why" & "Please Please Me." Covers either label style or design.)

VEE JAY (1062;
"Introducing The
Beatles"): *64* **40–60**
(Monaural issue, rainbow color-band label. With "Ask Me Why" & "Please Please Me.")

VEE JAY (1062;
"Introducing The
Beatles"): *64* **65–80**
(Monaural issue, black label, no color-band. With "Ask Me Why" & "Please Please Me." Has brackets style label logo.)

VEE JAY (1062;
"Introducing The
Beatles"): *64* **35–45**
(Monaural issue, black label, no color-band. With "Ask Me Why" & "Please Please Me." Label logo has neither oval nor brackets.)

VEE JAY (1092; "Songs,
Pictures And Stories"):
64 . . . . **50–75**
(Monaural issue.)

VEE JAY (1092; "Songs,
Pictures And Stories"):
64 . . . . **150–200**
(Stereo issue.)

Promotional LPs

ABC/WATERMARK
("Ringo's Yellow
Submarine"): *84* **700–800**

Price Range

Price Range

(A set of 24 LPs, in eight boxed sets, featuring Ringo Starr telling the story of The Beatles. Issued to radio stations only.)

APPLE (SBC-100; "The
Beatles' Christmas
Album"): 70. . . . . **$90–100**
(Special issue for Beatles fan club members.)

APPLE FILMS (004; The
Yellow Submarine"): 69 . . . . **400–450**
(Contains the advertisements used on radio stations to promote the film.)

ATCO (33-169; "Ain't She
Sweet"): 64. . . . . **300–350**
(Also contains selections by The Swallows.)

BACKSTAGE (Colored
vinyl): 82 . . . . **20–30**

CAPITOL ("The Platinum
Beatles Collection"): 84 . . . . **475–500**
(An 18-LP boxed set.)

CAPITOL (SPRO-8969;
"Rarities"): 78. . . . . **35–40**

CAPITOL (SMAS-11638;
"Beatles At The
Hollywood Bowl"): 77 . . . . **90–100**

CAPITOL (12199; "Reel
Music"): 82 . . . . **45–55**
(Colored vinyl.)

CAPITOL/EMI (BC-13;
"The Beatles
Collection"): 78 . . . . **250–300**
(A 14-LP boxed set.)

I-N-S RADIO NEWS (1;
"Beatlemania Tour
Coverage"): 64. . . . . **150–200**
(An open-end interview. Includes a script.)

LINGASONG (7001;
"Live! At The
Star-Club"): 77. . . . . **90–100**
(Blue vinyl.)

LINGASONG (7001;
"Live! At The
Star-Club"): 77. . . . . **75–90**
(Red vinyl.)

LINGASONG (7001;
"Live! At The
Star-Club"): 77. . . . . **30–40**
(Black vinyl.)

ORANGE (12880; "The
Silver Beatles"): 85 . . . . **35–45**

RAVEN: 81. **15–20**

UNITED ARTISTS
(UA-HELP; "United
Artists Presents
'Help!' "): 65. . . . . **$400–450**
(Contains the advertisements used on radio stations to promote the film.)

UNITED ARTISTS
(UA-HELP INT;
"Special Open-End
Interview"): 65. . . . . **500–550**
(Price includes script and programming information, which represents about $50-$75 of the value.)

UNITED ARTISTS
(2359/60; "Special
Beatles Half Hour Open
End Interview"): 64 . . . . **500–550**
(Price includes 12-pages of script and programming information, which represents about $50-$75 of the value.)

UNITED ARTISTS
(2362/63; "United
Artists Presents 'A Hard
Day's Night' "): 64 . . . . **400–450**
(Contains the advertisements used on radio stations to promote the film.)

UNITED ARTISTS
(UAL-6366; "A Hard
Day's Night"): 64 . . . . **300–350**
(White label.)
Members: John Lennon; Paul McCartney; George Harrison; Ringo Starr; Pete Best.
Also see BEST, Pete
Also see HARRISON, George
Also see LENNON, John
Also see MARTIN, George
Also see McCARTNEY, Paul
Also see PRESLEY, Elvis / The Beatles
Also see PRESTON, Billy
Also see STARR, Ringo

**BEATLES, The / The Beach Boys /
Buddy Holly**
LPs: 10/12-Inch 33rpm

CREATIVE RADIO
SHOWS (Demo of
"Specials"): 79. . . . . **75–100**
(Promotional issue only.)
Also see HOLLY, Buddy

Price Range

BEATLES, The / The Beach Boys / The Kingston Trio
Plastic Soundsheets/Flexi-Discs:
EVA-TONE (8464; "A
Surprise Gift From The
Beatles, The Beach Boys
And The Kingston
Trio"): *64* **$300-350**
(Plastic soundsheet.)
EVA-TONE (8464; "A
Surprise Gift From The
Beatles, The Beach Boys
And The Kingston
Trio"): *64* **200-250**
(A 5-inch edition of the above plastic sound-
sheet.)
Also see BEACH BOYS, The
Also see KINGSTON TRIO, The

BEATLES, The / The 4 Seasons
LPs: 10/12-Inch 33rpm
VEE JAY (DX-30;
"Beatles Vs. The Four
Seasons"): *64* **250–275**
(Monaural issue.)
VEE JAY (DXS-30;
"Beatles Vs. The Four
Seasons"): *64* **450–500**
(Stereo issue.)
Note: Price ranges include a bonus Beatles
poster, which represents $80-$100 of the value.
Also see 4 SEASONS, The

BEATLES, The / Frank Ifield
LPs: 10/12-Inch 33rpm
VEE JAY (1085; "The
Beatles & Frank Ifield"):
64 . . . . **550–650**
(Monaural issue. Pictures the Beatles on cover.)
VEE JAY (1085; "The
Beatles & Frank Ifield"):
64 . . . . **1000–1200**
(Stereo issue. Pictures the Beatles on cover.)
VEE JAY (1085; "Jolly
What! The Beatles &
Frank Ifield"): *64* **75–90**
(Monaural issue. Pictures an Englishman on
cover.)
VEE JAY (1085; "Jolly
What! The Beatles &
Frank Ifield"): *64* **150–200**

Price Range

(Stereo issue. Pictures an Englishman on
cover.)
Also see BEATLES, The
Also see IFIELD, Frank

BEATMASTER
Singles: 7-Inch
TOMMY BOY: *84* **$1–3**

BEATTY, E.C
Singles: 7-Inch
CAMPBELL: *64* **3–5**
COLONIAL: *59–61* **3–5**

BEAU, Toby: see TOBY BEAU

BEAU BRUMMELS, The
Singles: 7-Inch
AUTUMN: *64–65* **4–6**
WARNER BROS: *66–75* **3–5**
LPs: 10/12-Inch 33rpm
ACCORD: *82* **5–8**
AUTUMN: *65* **35–40**
JAS **8–10**
POST **8–10**
RHINO: *81–82* **5–8**
VAULT (114; "Best Of
The Beau Brummels"):
67 . . . . **25–30**
VAULT (121; "Beau
Brummels, Vol. 44"): *68* **15–18**
WARNER BROS. (Except
1644): *67–75* **20–25**
WARNER BROS. (1644;
"Beau Brummels '66"):
66 . . . . **30–35**
Members: Sal Valentino; Ron Elliott; Ron
Meagher; Dee Mulligan; John Petersen.

BEAU-MARKS, The
Singles: 7-Inch
MAINSTREAM: *68* **3–5**
PORT: *62* **4–6**
RUST: *61* **4–6**
SHAD: *60* **5–8**
TIME: *59* **12–15**

**BEAUMONT, Jimmy (Jimmy
Beaumont & The Skyliners)**
Singles: 7-Inch
BANG: *66* **4–6**

Price Range

CAPITOL: *74* **$2–4**
COLPIX: *61* **4–6**
DRIVE: *76* **2–4**
GALLANT **4–6**
MAY: *61–63* **4–6**
   Also see SKYLINERS, The

BE-BOP DELUXE
Singles: 7-Inch
HARVEST: *75–78*. **1–3**
LPs: 10/12-Inch 33rpm
HARVEST (Black vinyl):
   76–78 . . . . **5–8**
HARVEST (Colored vinyl):
   77–78 . . . . **15–20**
Promotional LPs
HARVEST (8531; "Be
   Bop's Biggest"): *75* **25–30**
   Members: Richard Brown; Robert Bryan;
   Nicholas Chatterton-Dew; Andrew Clarke;
   Simon Fox; Paul Jeffreys; Milton R. James; Bill
   Nelson; Ian Parkin; Charles Tumahai.

BECK, BOGERT & APPICE
Singles: 7-Inch
EPIC: *73* **2–4**
LPs: 10/12-Inch 33rpm
EPIC: *73* **10–12**
   Members: Jeff Beck; Tim Bogert; Carmine Appice.
   Also see BECK, Jeff
   Also see CACTUS
   Also see SCOTT, Neal
   Also see VANILLA FUDGE

BECK, Jeff (The Jeff Beck Group)
Singles: 7-Inch
EPIC (10000 series): *67–69* **4–6**
EPIC (50000 series): *75–76* **3–5**
LPs: 10/12-Inch 33rpm
ACCORD: *81* **5–8**
EPIC (Except 43000
   series): *69–85* **8–12**
EPIC (43000 series): *80–82* **12–15**
   (Half-speed mastered LPs.)
MFP **8–10**
SPRINGBOARD: *75* **5–8**
Promotional LPs
EPIC (151; "Everything
   You Always Wanted To
   Hear"): *76* **15–20**
   Also see BECK, BOGERT & APPICE

Also see DONOVAN
Also see HAMMER, Jan
Also see HONEYDRIPPERS, The
Also see LORD SUTCH
Also see POWELL, Cozy
Also see YARDBIRDS, The
Also see WOOD, Ron

BECK, Jeff, & Rod Stewart
Singles: 7-Inch
EPIC: *85* **$1–3**
   Also see BECK, Jeff
   Also see STEWART, Rod

BECK, Jimmy
Singles: 7-Inch
CHAMPION: *59*. **4–6**

BECK, Joe
Singles: 7-Inch
POLYDOR: *77* **1–3**
LPs: 10/12-Inch 33rpm
KUDU: *75*. **8–10**
POLYDOR: *77* **5–8**
VERVE/FORECAST: *69* **10–12**
   Also see PHILLIPS, Esther, & Joe Beck

BECK FAMILY, The
Singles: 7-Inch
LE JOINT: *79*. **1–3**

BECKHAM, Bob
Singles: 7-Inch
DECCA: *59–63* **2–4**
MONUMENT: *67*. **1–3**
SMASH: *65* **1–3**
Picture Sleeves
DECCA: *59–60* **2–4**
LPs: 10/12-Inch 33rpm
DECCA: *59* **12–15**

BECKMEIER BROTHERS, The
Singles: 7-Inch
CASABLANCA: *79* **1–3**
LPs: 10/12-Inch 33rpm
CASABLANCA: *79* **5–8**
   Members: Fred Beckmeier; Steve Beckmeier.

BEE, Celi: see CELI BEE

BEE, Jimmy (Jimmy Bee With Ernie Fields Jr.'s Orchestra)
Singles: 7-Inch
ALA: *73* $2–4
CALLA: *76* 1–3
KENT: *70* 2–4
20TH CENTURY-FOX:
  66–67 3–5
UNITED ARTISTS: *71* 2–4

BEE GEES, The
Singles: 7-Inch
ATCO: *67–72.* 3–5
RSO: *73–84* 1–3
EPs: 7-Inch 33/45rpm
ATCO (37264; "Rare,
  Precious & Beautiful"):
  69 8–15
  (Promotional issue only.)
LPs: 10/12-Inch 33rpm
ATCO (Except
  TL-ST-142): *67–72* 15–25
ATCO (TL-ST-142;
  "Odessa"): *69.* 40–50
  (Promotional issue only.)
RSO (Except 1): *73–84.* 5–8
RSO (1; "Words &
  Music") 50–60
  (Promotional issue only.)
  Members: Barry Gibb; Maurice Gibb; Robin
  Gibb; Vince Melouney; Colin Petersen.
  Also see GIBB, Andy
  Also see GIBB, Barry
  Also see GIBB, Maurice
  Also see GIBB, Robin
  Also see SANG, Samantha

BEECHER, Johnny, & His Buckingham Road Quintet
Singles: 7-Inch
CHARTER: *63* 3–5
WARNER BROS: *63* 2–4
LPs: 10/12-Inch 33rpm
CHARTER: *63* 10–20

BEEFEATERS, The
Singles: 7-Inch
ELEKTRA: *64* 35–40
  Members: David Crosby; Gene Clark; Jim
  McGuinn.
  Also see BYRDS, The

Also see McGUINN, CLARK & HILLMAN

BEEFHEART, Captain: see CAPTAIN BEEFHEART

BEGINNING OF THE END, The
Singles: 7-Inch
ALSTON: *71–72* $2–4
LPs: 10/12-Inch 33rpm
ALSTON: *71–76* 10–12

BELAFONTE, Harry
Singles: 7-Inch
COLUMBIA: *81* 1–3
JUBILEE: *54* 5–8
RCA VICTOR (0300
  series): *57* 2–4
RCA VICTOR (0400
  through 0600 series):
  71–72 1–3
RCA VICTOR (4000 &
  5000 series): *52–55* 3–6
RCA VICTOR (6000 &
  7000 series): *55–62* 2–5
RCA VICTOR (8000 &
  9000 series): *62–67* 2–4
Picture Sleeves
RCA VICTOR: *55–67* 2–5
EPs: 7-Inch 33/45rpm
RCA VICTOR: *55–60* 6–12
LPs: 10/12-Inch 33rpm
CAMDEN: *73–74* 5–10
COLUMBIA: *81* 5–8
RCA VICTOR (0000
  through 0900 series): *73* 5–10
RCA VICTOR (1000
  through 1900 series):
  56–59 15–25
  (With an "LPM" or "LSP" prefix.)
RCA VICTOR (2400
  series): *78–81* 5–8
  (With an "AYL1" or "CPL1" prefix.)
RCA VICTOR (2000 &
  3000 series, except 2449):
  60–67 10–20
  (With an "LPM" or "LSP" prefix.)
RCA VICTOR (2449;
  "The Midnight Special"):
  62 20–30
  (With Bob Dylan playing harmonica on the title
  track, his first appearance on record.)

Price Range

RCA VICTOR (4000
   series): *68–71* **$10–15**
RCA VICTOR (6000
   series): *59–72* **15–25**
   Also see DYLAN, Bob

BELAFONTE, Harry, & Miriam Makeba
LPs: 10/12-Inch 33rpm
RCA VICTOR: *65* **10–15**
   Also see BELAFONTE, Harry
   Also see MAKEBA, Miriam

BELEW, Adrian
LPs: 10/12-Inch 33rpm
ISLAND: *82–83* **5–8**

BELL, Archie (Archie Bell & The Drells)
Singles: 12-Inch 33/45rpm
PHILADELPHIA INT'L:
   79 .... **4–6**
PLAYHOUSE: *84*................... **4–6**
Singles: 7-Inch
ATLANTIC: *68–72* **2–4**
BECKETT: *81–84*................. **1–3**
GLADES: *73*..................... **2–4**
PHILADELPHIA INT'L:
   76–79 .... **1–3**
TSOP: *75–76* **2–3**
LPs: 10/12-Inch 33rpm
ATLANTIC: *68–69* **10–12**
BECKETT: *81–84*................. **5–8**
PHILADELPHIA INT'L:
   75–79 .... **8–10**

Price Range

Also see PHILADELPHIA INTERNA-
TIONAL ALL STARS, The

BELL, Benny
Singles: 7-Inch
ENTERPRISE: *62* **$3–5**
VANGUARD: *75*.................. **2–4**

BELL, Jerry
Singles: 7-Inch
MCA: *80* **1–3**

BELL, Madeline
Singles: 7-Inch
ASCOT: *64–65*.................... **3–5**
BRUT: *73* **2–4**
MOD: *67* **3–5**
PHILIPS: *67–68* **2–4**
PYE: *76* **2–3**
LPs: 10/12-Inch 33rpm
PHILIPS: *68* **15–18**
PYE: *76*......................... **8–10**
   Also see BLUE MINK
   Also see WATERS, Roger

BELL, Maggie
Singles: 7-Inch
ATLANTIC: *73–74* **2–4**
SWAN SONG: *76*.................. **2–3**
LPs: 10/12-Inch 33rpm
ATLANTIC: *74* **10–12**
SWAN SONG: *75*.................. **8–10**

BELL, Maggie, & Bobby Whitlock
Singles: 7-Inch
SWAN SONG: *83–84*............... **1–3**
   Also see BELL, Maggie
   Also see WHITLOCK, Bobby

BELL, Randy
Singles: 7-Inch
EPIC: *84* **1–3**

BELL, Rueben
Singles: 7-Inch
ALARM: *75–77*.................... **2–3**
DELUXE: *72–73*................... **2–4**
MURCO: *68* **3–5**
SILVER FOX: *69*................. **2–4**

Price Range

BELL, Trudy
Singles: 7-Inch
PHILIPS: *62–63* **$3–5**

BELL, Vincent (Vinnie Bell & The Bell Men)
Singles: 7-Inch
DECCA: *67–70* **2–3**
MUSICOR: *64.* **2–4**
VERVE: *63* **3–5**
LPs: 10/12-Inch 33rpm
DECCA: *67–70* **8–12**
INDEPENDENT: *60* **12–18**
MUSICOR: *64.* **10–12**
VERVE: *64* **10–12**

BELL, William
Singles: 7-Inch
KAT FAMILY: *83–84.* **1–3**
MERCURY: *76–77.* **2–3**
STAX (Except 100 series):
67–74 .... **2–4**
STAX (100 series): *61–67.* **3–5**
LPs: 10/12-Inch 33rpm
KAT FAMILY: *83–84.* **5–8**
MERCURY: *77.* **8–10**
STAX: *67–74.* **10–12**

BELL, William, & Judy Clay
Singles: 7-Inch
STAX: *68.* **2–4**
Also see CLAY, Judy

BELL, William, & Mavis Staples
Singles: 7-Inch
STAX: *69.* **2–4**
Also see STAPLES, Mavis

BELL, William, & Carla Thomas
Singles: 7-Inch
STAX: *69–70.* **2–4**
Also see BELL, William
Also see THOMAS, Carla

BELL & JAMES
Singles: 12-Inch 33/45rpm
A&M: *79* **4–6**
LORIMAR: *80* **4–6**
Singles: 7-Inch
A&M: *78–84* **2–3**
LORIMAR: *80* **2–3**

Price Range

LPs: 10/12-Inch 33rpm
A&M: *79–84* **$5–8**
Members: Leroy Bell; Casey James.

BELL NOTES, The
Singles: 7-Inch
AUTOGRAPH: *60.* **4–6**
ERIC: *73* **1–3**
MADISON: *60* **4–6**
TIME (Blue label): *59* **5–8**
TIME (Red label): *59–60.* **3–5**

EPs: 7-Inch 33/45rpm
TIME: *59.* **20–25**
Members: Carl Bonura; Ray Ceroni; Lenny
Giambalvo; Pete Kane; John Casey.

BELL SISTERS, The
Singles: 7-Inch
RCA VICTOR: *50–53* **2–4**
Also see RENE, Henri, & His Orchestra

BELLAMY, David
Singles: 7-Inch
WARNER BROS: *75.* **2–3**
Also see BELLAMY BROTHERS, The

BELLAMY BROTHERS, The
Singles: 7-Inch
CURB: *84* **1–3**
ELEKTRA: *83* **1–3**
WARNER BROS: *76–83.* **2–3**

LPs: 10/12-Inch 33rpm
ELEKTRA: *83* **5–8**
MCA: *84* **5–8**
WARNER BROS: *76–83.* **8–10**
Members: David Bellamy; Howard Bellamy.
Also see BELLAMY, David

BELLE EPOQUE
Singles: 7-Inch
BIG TREE: *78* **2–3**

BELLE STARS, The
Singles: 12-Inch 33/45rpm
WARNER BROS: *83–84.* **4–6**

Singles: 7-Inch
WARNER BROS: *83–84.* **1–3**

LPs: 10/12-Inch 33rpm
WARNER BROS: *83–84.* **5–8**

Price Range   *Price Range*

BELLS, The
Singles: 7-Inch
MGM: *73* $2–4
POLYDOR: *70–73* 2–4

LPs: 10/12-Inch 33rpm
POLYDOR: *71–72* 10–12
Members: Jacki Ralph; Cliff Edwards; Frank Mills.
Also see MILLS, Frank

BELLUS, Tony
Singles: 7-Inch
ABC: *73* 1–3
COLLECTABLES: *81* 1–3
KING: *65* 3–5
NRC: *59–60* 5–8

Picture Sleeves
NRC: *60* 6–10

LPs: 10/12-Inch 33rpm
NRC: *60* 35–45

BELMONTS, The (The Belmonts With Dion)
Singles: 7-Inch
COLLECTABLES: *81* 1–3
CRYSTAL BALL: *79*. 2–3
DOT: *68* 8–10
LAURIE: *75* 2–4
MOHAWK: *57* 20–25
ROULETTE 1–3
SABINA (Except 521):
 61–64 8–12
SABINA (521 "Nothing In
 Return"): *64*. 15–20
SABRINA: *61* 10–15
(The Sabrina label changed its name to Sabina in 1961.)
STRAWBERRY: *76*. 2–4
SURPRISE: *61* 25–30
UNITED ARTISTS (800
 & 900 series): *65* 5–8
UNITED ARTISTS (50000
 series): *66* 10–12

LPs: 10/12-Inch 33rpm
BUDDAH: *72* 12–15
DOT: *69* 20–25
SABINA: *62* 45–50
STRAWBERRY: *78*. 8–10
Also see DION & THE BELMONTS
Also see SOUL, Jimmy / The Belmonts

BELMONTS, The, Freddy Cannon & Bo Diddley
Singles: 12-Inch 33/45rpm
ROCK & ROLL
 TRAVELLING SHOW $2–4
Also see BELMONTS, The
Also see CANNON, Freddy
Also see DIDDLEY, Bo

BELOUIS SOME
Singles: 12-Inch 33/45rpm
CAPITOL: *85* 4–6

Singles: 7-Inch
CAPITOL: *85* 1–3

LPs: 10/12-Inch 33rpm
CAPITOL: *85* 5–8

BELOYD
Singles: 7-Inch
20TH CENTURY-FOX:
 77 1–3

BELUSHI, John
Singles: 7-Inch
MCA: *78* 2–3
Also see BLUES BROTHERS, The
Also see NATIONAL LAMPOON

BELVIN, Jesse (Jesse Belvin & The Sharptones; Jesse Belvin With Three Dots & A Dash)
Singles: 7-Inch
ALADDIN: *58* 10–12
CASH: *56*. 25–30
CLASS: *60*. 3–5
COLLECTABLES: *81* 1–3
ERIC: *73* 1–3
HOLLYWOOD: *56*. 35–40
IMPACT: *62* 4–6
IMPERIAL: *51*. 60–75
JAMIE: *59*. 4–6
KENT: *59* 4–6
KNIGHT: *59*. 4–6
MODERN: *56*. 5–8
RCA VICTOR (7000
 series): *58–60* 3–5
(With a "47" prefix.)
RCA VICTOR (7000
 series): *59–60* 8–10
(With a "61" prefix. Stereo singles.)

Price Range   *Price Range*

SPECIALTY (400 series):
52 . . . . **$30–40**
SPECIALTY (500 series):
54–55 . . . . **12–15**
TENDER: *59.* **15–20**
EPs: 7-Inch 33/45rpm
RCA VICTOR: *59–60* **20–25**
LPs: 10/12-Inch 33rpm
CAMDEN: *66* **12–15**
CROWN: *60–63* **15–20**
RCA VICTOR (0900
series): *75* **8–10**
RCA VICTOR (2000 &
2100 series): *59–60* **25–30**
UNITED **10–12**
Also see BENTON, Brook / Jesse Belvin
Also see CHARGERS, The
Also see CLIQUES, The
Also see JESSE & MARVIN

BENATAR, Pat
Singles: 12-Inch 33/45rpm
CHRYSALIS: *79–85.* **4–6**
Singles: 7-Inch
CHRYSALIS: *79–86.* **1–3**
Picture Sleeves
CHRYSALIS: *79–85.* **1–3**
LPs: 10/12-Inch 33rpm
CHRYSALIS: *79–85.* **5–8**

**BENNETT, Boyd (Boyd Bennett &
The Rockets; Boyd Bennett & The
Southlanders)**
Singles: 7-Inch
KING (1400 series): *54–55* **12–15**
(Maroon labels.)
KING (1400 series): *56* **8–10**
(Blue labels.)
KING (4000 series): *56–58* **5–8**
KING (5000 series): *58–63* **3–5**
MERCURY: *59–61.* **4–6**
EPs: 7-Inch 33/45rpm
KING: *57* **45–55**
LPs: 10/12-Inch 33rpm
KING (594; "Boyd
Bennett"): *57* **400–500**

BENNETT, Joe, & The Sparkletones
Singles: 7-Inch
ABC: *73* **1–3**

ABC-PARAMOUNT:
57–58 . . . . **$5–8**
PARIS: *59–60* **4–6**
LPs: 10/12-Inch 33rpm
MCA: *83* **5–8**

BENNETT, Tony
Singles: 7-Inch
COLUMBIA (06000
series): *86* **1–3**
COLUMBIA (38000
through 41000 series):
50–61 . . . . **2–4**
COLUMBIA (42000
through 45000 series):
61–70 . . . . **2–3**
IMPROV: *75–77.* **1–3**
MGM: *73.* **1–3**
VERVE: *72–73* **1–3**
Picture Sleeves
COLUMBIA (40000 &
41000 series): *53–61* **4–6**
COLUMBIA (42000
through 44000 series):
61–67 . . . . **2–3**
LPs: 10/12-Inch 33rpm
COLUMBIA (Except 600
through 1200 series):
59–75 . . . . **6–12**
COLUMBIA (600 through
1200 series): *55–59* **10–20**
HARMONY: *69–73* **5–8**
IMPROV: *75–78.* **5–8**
MGM: *73.* **6–10**
MGM/VERVE: *72* **6–10**
Also see GETZ, Stan

BENNETT, Tony, & Count Basie
EPs: 7-Inch 33/45rpm
COLUMBIA: *59* **6–10**
LPs: 10/12-Inch 33rpm
COLUMBIA: *59* **10–20**
Also see BASIE, Count
Also see BENNETT, Tony

BENNO, Marc
Singles: 7-Inch
A&M: *71–79* **2–4**
LPs: 10/12-Inch 33rpm
A&M: *70–79* **8–10**
MCA. **5–8**
Also see ASYLUM CHOIR, The

Price Range

Price Range

BENSON, George
Singles: 12-Inch 33/45rpm
WARNER BROS: 80–83 . . . . **$4–6**

Singles: 7-Inch
A&M: 68–70 . . . . **2–4**
ARISTA: 77 . . . . **2–3**
CTI: 75–78. . . . . **2–3**
COLUMBIA: 66–67 . . . . **3–5**
GROOVE: 54. . . . . **10–15**
PRESTIGE: 64 . . . . **3–5**
WARNER BROS: 76–85 . . . . **1–3**

Picture Sleeves
WARNER BROS: 78–85 . . . . **INC**

LPs: 10/12-Inch 33rpm
A&M: 68–70 . . . . **8–12**
CTI: 71–78. . . . . **8–10**
COLUMBIA: 66–67 . . . . **8–10**
    (With a "CL" or "CS" prefix.)
COLUMBIA: 76. . . . . **5–8**
    (With a "CG" or "PC" prefix.)
POLYDOR: 76 . . . . **5–8**
VERVE: 69 . . . . **10–12**
WARNER BROS: 75–85 . . . . **5–8**
    Also see FRANKLIN, Aretha, & George Benson
    Also see McDUFF, Brother Jack

BENT FABRIC: see FABRIC, Bent

BENTLEY, Erlene
Singles: 12-Inch 33/45rpm
MEGATONE: 83 . . . . **4–6**
TVI: 84. . . . . **4–6**

Singles: 7-Inch
MEGATONE: 83 . . . . **1–3**

BENTON, Brook
Singles: 7-Inch
ALL PLATINUM: 76 . . . . **2–3**
BRUT: 73 . . . . **2–4**
COTILLION: 68–72. . . . . **2–4**
EPIC: 56 . . . . **5–10**
MGM: 72. . . . . **2–4**
MERCURY: 59–65. . . . . **3–5**
MUSICOR: 77. **2–3**
OKEH: 55 . . . . **5–10**
OLDE WORLD: 77–78 . . . . **2–3**
RCA VICTOR: 65–67 . . . . **3–5**
REPRISE: 67–68. . . . . **2–4**

STAX: 74. . . . . **$2–3**
VIK: 57–58 . . . . **5–8**

Picture Sleeves
MERCURY: 60–62. . . . . **3–5**
RCA VICTOR: 65 . . . . **3–5**

EPs: 7-Inch 33/45rpm
MERCURY: 59–61. . . . . **10–15**

LPs: 10/12-Inch 33rpm
ALL PLATINUM: 76 . . . . **8–10**
CAMDEN (Except 564):
    70 . . . . **8–10**
CAMDEN (564; "Brook
    Benton"): 60. . . . . **15–20**
    (With a "CAL" prefix.)
COTILLION: 70–72. . . . . **8–10**
EPIC: 59 . . . . **15–20**
HARMONY: 65 . . . . **8–12**
MGM: 73. . . . . **8–10**
MERCURY (MG & SR
    series): 59–65. . . . . **12–18**
    (With an "MG" or "SR" prefix.)
MERCURY: 84. **5–8**
    (With an "822" prefix.)
MUSICOR: 77. **8–10**
OLDE WORLD: 77. . . . . **5–8**
RCA VICTOR (APL1
    series): 75 . . . . **8–10**
    (With an "APL1" prefix.)
RCA VICTOR (LPM/LSP
    series): 66 . . . . **10–12**
    (With an "LPM" or "LSP" prefix.)
WING: 66 . . . . **8–10**

BENTON, Brook / Jesse Belvin
LPs: 10/12-Inch 33rpm
CROWN: 63 . . . . **12–15**
    Also see BELVIN, Jesse

BENTON, Brook, & Damita Jo
Singles: 7-Inch
MERCURY: 63. **3–5**
    Also see DAMITA JO

**BENTON, Brook, & Dinah
Washington**
Singles: 7-Inch
MERCURY: 60. **3–5**
Picture Sleeves
MERCURY: 60. **3–5**
EPs: 7-Inch 33/45rpm
MERCURY: 60. . . . . **10–15**

Price Range

LPs: 10/12-Inch 33rpm
MERCURY: *60.* **$15–25**
Also see BENTON, Brook
Also see WASHINGTON, Dinah

BERG, Gertrude
LPs: 10/12-Inch 33rpm
AMY: *65* **6–12**

BERGEN, Polly
Singles: 7-Inch
COLUMBIA: *57–61* **2–4**
RCA VICTOR: *50–51* **2–5**

EPs: 7-Inch 33/45rpm
JUBILEE: *56.* **6–10**

LPs: 10/12-Inch 33rpm
CAMDEN: *56* **10–15**
COLUMBIA: *57–61* **10–15**
HARMONY: *60* **8–12**
JUBILEE: *56.* **10–20**
PHILLIPS: *63* **8–12**

LPs: 10/12-Inch 33rpm
RKO: *59* **8–15**

BERLIN
Singles: 12-Inch 33/45rpm
GEFFEN: *83–84* **4–6**
Singles: 7-Inch
GEFFEN: *82–84* **1–3**
I.R.S.: *80* **1–3**
LPs: 10/12-Inch 33rpm
GEFFEN: *82–84* **5–8**

BERLIN PHILHARMONIC, The (With Karl Boehm)
Singles: 7-Inch
POLYDOR: *69* **2–3**

BERMAN, Shelley
LPs: 10/12-Inch 33rpm
METRO: *65.* **8–12**
VERVE (15000 series):
 59–64 .... **10–20**

BERMUDAS, The (Featuring Rickie Page)
Singles: 7-Inch
ERA: *64.* **4–6**

Price Range

BERNARD, Chuck
Singles: 7-Inch
LAWRENCE: *67* **$3–5**
SATELLITE: *65* **3–5**
ZODIAC: *70–71* **2–4**

BERNARD, Rod (Rod Bernard & The Twisters)
Singles: 7-Inch
ABC: *74.* **1–3**
ARBEE: *65–66* **3–5**
ARGO: *59* **4–6**
COLLECTABLES: *81* **1–3**
COPYRIGHT: *68.* **2–4**
CRAZY CAJUN: *78* **2–3**
HALL: *61–64.* **3–5**
HALLWAY: *61–64.* **3–5**
JIN (105; "This Should Go
 On Forever"): *59.* **25–30**
JIN (200 series): *74–76.* **2–3**
MERCURY: *59–61.* **3–5**
TEARDROP: *64–65.* **3–5**
LPs: 10/12-Inch 33rpm
JIN **50–60**
Also see SHONDELLS, The / Rod Bernard / Warren Storm / Skip Stewart

BERNSTEIN, Elmer, & His Orchestra
Singles: 7-Inch
AVA: *62–65.* **2–3**
CAPITOL: *59–60* **2–3**
CHOREO: *62.* **2–3**
COLUMBIA: *65* **2–3**
DECCA: *56* **2–4**
DOT: *66.* **2–4**
UNITED ARTISTS: *65–68* **2–3**
EPs: 7-Inch 33/45rpm
CAPITOL: *59* **3–6**
LPs: 10/12-Inch 33rpm
AVA (4; "Walk On The
 Wild Side"): *62* **25–35**
 (Soundtrack.)
AVA (20; "To Kill A
 Mockingbird"): *63* **25–40**
 (Soundtrack.)
AVA (31; "The
 Caretakers"): *63.* **25–35**
 (Soundtrack.)
AVA (45; "The
 Carpetbaggers"): *64.* **25–35**
 (Soundtrack.)

Price Range

AVA (53; "Baby, The Rain
  Must Fall"): 65 . . . . $30–35
  (Soundtrack.)
CAPITOL: 59–60 4–8
CHOREO (4; "Walk On
  The Wild Side"): 62 25–35
  (Soundtrack.)
CHOREO (11; "Movie &
  TV Themes"): 62 10–15
  (Soundtrack.)
COLUMBIA: 60 5–15
DOT: 59 5–10
HAMILTON: 59 4–8
MAINSTREAM (6056;
  "Baby, The Rain Must
  Fall"): 65 30–35
  (Soundtrack.)
MAINSTREAM (6083;
  "Walk On The Wild
  Side"): 67 20–30
  (Soundtrack.)
MAINSTREAM (6094; "A
  Man & His Movies"): 67 8–15
RCA VICTOR (1120;
  "The Silencers"): 66 15–25
  (Soundtrack.)
UNITED ARTISTS (304;
  "The Ten
  Commandments"): 74 5–10
  (Soundtrack.)
UNITED ARTISTS (3495;
  "The Ten
  Commandments"): 66 15–25
  (Soundtrack. Monaural.)
UNITED ARTISTS (4127;
  "The Hallelujah Trail"):
  65 25–30
  (Soundtrack. Monaural.)
UNITED ARTISTS (4138;
  "Cast A Giant
  Shadow"): 66 20–25
  (Soundtrack. Monaural.)
UNITED ARTISTS (4143;
  "Hawaii"): 66 15–20
  (Soundtrack. Monaural.)
UNITED ARTISTS (4146;
  "Return Of The Seven"):
  66 10–20
  (Soundtrack. Monaural.)
UNITED ARTISTS (4176;
  "The Scalphunters"): 68 15–20

Price Range

  (Soundtrack. Monaural.)
UNITED ARTISTS (5127;
  "The Hallelujah Trail"):
  65 . . . . $30–35
  (Soundtrack. Stereo.)
UNITED ARTISTS (5138;
  "Cast A Giant
  Shadow"): 66 25–30
  (Soundtrack. Stereo.)
UNITED ARTISTS (5143;
  "Hawaii"): 66 15–25
  (Soundtrack. Stereo.)
UNITED ARTISTS (5146;
  "Return Of The Seven"):
  66 10–20
  (Soundtrack. Stereo.)
UNITED ARTISTS (5176;
  "The Scalphunters"): 68 20–30
  (Soundtrack. Stereo.)
UNITED ARTISTS (6495;
  "The Ten
  Commandments"): 66 15–25
  (Soundtrack. Stereo.)

BERNSTEIN, Leonard, & His Orchestra
  LPs: 10/12-Inch 33rpm
CAMDEN: 55–56 8–15
COLUMBIA ("What Is
  Jazz"): 56 20–40

BERRY, Chuck
  Singles: 7-Inch
ATCO: 79 1–3
CHESS (1604 through
  1615): 55–56 10–15
CHESS (1626 through
  1645): 56 8–10
CHESS (1653 through
  1729): 57–59 4–6
CHESS (1737 through
  1963): 59–69 3–5
CHESS (2000 & 9000
  series): 70–73 2–4
ERIC: 73 1–3
MERCURY: 66–72 3–5

  Picture Sleeves
CHESS: 64–65 5–10

  EPs: 7-Inch 33/45rpm
CHESS: 57–59 30–35

Price Range

Price Range

LPs: 10/12-Inch 33rpm
ACCORD: *82* **$5–8**
ATCO: *79* **5–8**
BROOKVILLE: *73* **12–15**
CHESS (Except 1400 &
  9000 series): *66–76* **10–15**
CHESS (1426; "After
  School Session"): *57* **30–40**
CHESS (1432; "One Dozen
  Berrys"): *58* **30–40**
CHESS (1435; "Chuck
  Berry's On Top"): *59* **30–40**
CHESS (1448; "Rockin' At
  The Hops"): *59* **30–40**
CHESS (1456; "Chuck
  Berry's New Jukebox
  Hits"): *61* **25–35**
CHESS (1465; "More
  Chuck Berry"): *63* **25–30**
CHESS (1466; "Chuck
  Berry Twist"): *62* **20–25**
CHESS (1480; "Chuck
  Berry On Stage"): *63* **20–25**
CHESS (1485; "Chuck
  Berry's Greatest Hits"):
  64 . . . . **25–30**
CHESS (1488; "St. Louis
  To Liverpool"): *64* **20–25**
CHESS (1495; "Chuck
  Berry In London"): *65* **25–30**
CHESS (1498; "Fresh
  Berrys"): *65* **20–25**
CHESS (9000 series): *85* **5–8**
EVEREST: *76* **8–10**
GUSTO: *78* **5–8**
MCA: *86* **8–12**
MAGNUM: *69* **10–12**
MERCURY: *67–72* **10–15**
PICKWICK: *72* **8–10**
TRIP: *78* **8–10**
UPFRONT: *79* **5–8**

BERRY, Chuck, & Bo Diddley
Singles: 7-Inch
CHECKER: *64* **3–5**

LPs: 10/12-Inch 33rpm
CHECKER: *64* **20–25**
Also see DIDDLEY, Bo

BERRY, Chuck, & Howlin' Wolf
LPs: 10/12-Inch 33rpm
CHESS: *69* **$15–18**
Also see BERRY, Chuck
Also see HOWLIN' WOLF

BERRY, Jan (Jan; Jan Barry)
Singles: 7-Inch
A&M: *77–78* **3–5**
LIBERTY: *66* **4–6**
ODE '70 (Except 66034):
  72–77 . . . . **12–15**
ODE '70 (66034 "Don't
  You Just Know It"): *73* **30–35**
  (With Brian Wilson.)
RIPPLE: *61* **25–30**
Also see JAN & ARNIE
Also see JAN & DEAN
Also see WILSON, Brian

BERTEI, Adele
Singles: 12-Inch 33/45rpm
GEFFEN: *83* **4–6**

Singles: 7-Inch
GEFFEN: *83* **1–3**

BEST, Peter
Singles: 7-Inch
CAMEO: *66* **15–20**
CAPITOL: *67* **15–20**
HAPPENING: *66* **30–40**
MR. MAESTRO: *65* **30–40**
ORIGINAL BEATLES
  DRUMMER: *64* **30–40**

Picture Sleeves
CAMEO: *66* **40–50**

LPs: 10/12-Inch 33rpm
BEST FAN CLUB: *66* **25–30**
PHOENIX 10: *82* **8–10**
SAVAGE: *65* **50–75**
Also see BEATLES, The

BETH, Karen
Singles: 7-Inch
BUDDAH: *75* **2–4**

LPs: 10/12-Inch 33rpm
BUDDAH: *75* **8–10**

Price Range

BETHEA, Harmon (Bethea; Bethea With The Maskman & The Agents)
Singles: 7-Inch
DYNAMO: *69–71* **$2–4**
MUSICOR: *70–74* **1–3**

BETTERS, Harold
Singles: 7-Inch
GATEWAY: *63–65* **3–5**
REPRISE: *66–67* **3–5**
LPs: 10/12-Inch 33rpm
GATEWAY: *64–66* **12–15**
REPRISE: *65–67* **12–15**

BETTS, Richard (Dickey Betts & Great Southern)
Singles: 7-Inch
ARISTA: *77–78* **2–3**
CAPRICORN: *74–76* **2–4**
LPs: 10/12-Inch 33rpm
ARISTA: *78* **5–8**
CAPRICORN: *74* **8–10**
Also see ALLMAN BROTHERS BAND, The

BEVEL, Charles "Mississippi"
Singles: 7-Inch
A&M: *73–74* **2–4**

BEVERLY & DUANE
Singles: 7-Inch
ARIOLA AMERICA:
78–79 .... **1–3**
Members: Beverly Wheeler; Duane Williams.

BEVERLY SISTERS, The
Singles: 7-Inch
MERCURY: *60* **3–5**
LPs: 10/12-Inch 33rpm
CAPITOL: *61* **10–12**

BICKERSONS, The: see AMECHE, Don, & Frances Langford

BIDDU (Biddu & Orchestra)
Singles: 7-Inch
COLOSSUS: *70* **2–4**
EPIC: *76–77* **2–3**
LPs: 10/12-Inch 33rpm
EPIC: *76–77* **5–8**

Price Range

BIG AUDIO DYNAMITE (With Mick Jones)
Singles: 12-Inch 33/45rpm
COLUMBIA: *85–86* **$4–6**
Singles: 7-Inch
COLUMBIA: *85–86* **1–3**
LPs: 10/12-Inch 33rpm
COLUMBIA: *85–86* **5–8**
Also see CLASH

BIG BOPPER, The
Singles: 7-Inch
D: *58* **45–50**
MERCURY (71300 series):
58 .... **4–6**
(Black vinyl.)
MERCURY (71300 series):
58 .... **20–25**
(Colored vinyl.)
MERCURY (71400)
series): *59* **8–10**
LPs: 10/12-Inch 33rpm
MERCURY: *59* **60–75**
(Black label.)
MERCURY: *81* **5–8**
(Chicago "skyline" label.)
PICKWICK: *73* **8–10**
Also see PRESTON, Johnny
Also see RICHARDSON, Jape

BIG BROTHER & THE HOLDING COMPANY (Featuring Janis Joplin)
Singles: 7-Inch
COLUMBIA: *68–71* **3–5**
MAINSTREAM: *67–68* **5–8**
Picture Sleeves
COLUMBIA: *68* **3–5**
LPs: 10/12-Inch 33rpm
COLUMBIA: *68–71* **10–12**
MADE TO LAST: *84* **5–8**
MAINSTREAM: *67* **20–25**
Also see JOPLIN, Janis

BIG COUNTRY
Singles: 12-Inch 33/45rpm
MERCURY: *83–85* **4–6**
Singles: 7-Inch
MERCURY: *83–85* **1–3**
LPs: 10/12-Inch 33rpm
MERCURY: *83–84* **5–8**

Price Range

BIG MAYBELLE
Singles: 7-Inch
BRUNSWICK: *63.* $3–5
CHESS: *66* 3–5
OKEH: *53–56* 6–10
PARAMOUNT: *73.* 2–4
PORT: *65* 3–5
ROJAC: *64–69.* 3–5
SAVOY: *56–61* 4–6

EPs: 7-Inch 33/45rpm
EPIC: *57* 15–20

LPs: 10/12-Inch 33rpm
BRUNSWICK: *62–68.* 12–15
ENCORE: *67.* 10–12
EPIC: *83* 8–10
PARAMOUNT: *73.* 8–10
ROJAC: *67–69.* 10–12
SAVOY (14000 series):
    58–61 25–30
SCEPTER: *64* 12–15
UPFRONT: *73* 8–10

BIG RIC
Singles: 7-Inch
ROCK 'N' ROLL: *83.* 1–3
SCOTTI BROTHERS: *83* 1–3

LPs: 10/12-Inch 33rpm
SCOTTI BROTHERS:
    83–84 5–8

BIG SAMBO (Big Sambo & The House Wreckers; Big Sam & The House Wreckers)
Singles: 7-Inch
ERIC: *62* 3–5

BIG THREE, The
Singles: 7-Inch
FM: *63* 4–6
ROULETTE: *66* 3–5
TOLLIE: *64.* 4–6

LPs: 10/12-Inch 33rpm
ACCORD: *82* 5–8
FM: *63–64* 15–20
ROULETTE: *67* 10–12
    Members: Cass Elliott; Tim Rose; Denny
    Dougherty.
    Also see ELLIOTT, Cass
    Also see MAMAS & THE PAPAS, The

STRANGER ON THE SHORE
MR. ACKER BILK STEREO
WITH THE LEON YOUNG STRING CHORALE

Price Range

BILK, Mr. Acker
Singles: 7-Inch
ATCO: *61–66.* $2–4
REPRISE: *62.* 2–4

LPs: 10/12-Inch 33rpm
ASCOT: *62* 8–12
ATCO: *62–66.* 8–12

BILK, Mr. Acker, & Bent Fabric
LPs: 10/12-Inch 33rpm
ATCO: *65* 8–12
    Also see BILK, Mr. Acker
    Also see FABRIC, Bent

BILL & TAFFY
Singles: 7-Inch
RCA VICTOR: *74* 3–5

LPs: 10/12-Inch 33rpm
RCA VICTOR: *73–74* 10–12
    Members: Bill Danoff; Taffy Danoff.
    Also see STARLAND VOCAL BAND, The

BILL BLACK'S COMBO: see BLACK, Bill

BILLION DOLLAR BABIES, The
Singles: 7-Inch
POLYDOR (Except
    14406): *77* 3–5

Price Range

POLYDOR (14406; "Too
Young"): 77 . . . . $8–10
(Promotional issue only.)

LPs: 10/12-Inch 33rpm
POLYDOR (Except 022):
77 12–15
POLYDOR (022; "Battle
Axe"): 77 20–25
(Promotional issue only.)
Also see COOPER, Alice

**BILLY ALWAYS: see ALWAYS,
Billy**

BILLY & BABY GAP
Singles: 7-Inch
TOTAL EXPERIENCE:
85 1–3

**BILLY & LILLIE (Billy & Lillie &
The Thunderbirds)**
Singles: 7-Inch
ABC: 73 1–3
ABC-PARAMOUNT: 63 4–6
CAMEO: 66 3–5
COLLECTABLES: 81 1–3
SWAN: 57–61 4–6
Members: Billy Ford; Lillie Bryant.
Also see BRYANT, Lillie

BILLY & SUE
Singles: 7-Inch
CREW: 70 3–5
Members: William Oliver Swofford; Lesley
Gore.
Also see GORE, Lesley
Also see OLIVER

**BILLY & THE BEATERS
(Featuring Billy Vera)**
Singles: 7-Inch
ALFA: 81 1–3
LPs: 10/12-Inch 33rpm
ALFA: 81 5–8
Also see VERA, Bill

**BILLY JOE & THE
CHECKMATES (Billy Joe Hunter)**
Singles: 7-Inch
DORE: 61–66 3–5

Price Range

BILLY SATELLITE
Singles: 7-Inch
CAPITOL: 84 . . . . $1–3
LPs: 10/12-Inch 33rpm
CAPITOL: 84 5–8

BIMBO JET
Singles: 7-Inch
SCEPTER: 75 2–3

**BIONIC BOOGIE (With Gregg
Diamond)**
Singles: 7-Inch
POLYDOR: 77–78 1–3
LPs: 10/12-Inch 33rpm
POLYDOR: 78 5–8

BIRD, J.
Singles: 12-Inch 33/45rpm
WARRIOR: 84 4–6

BIRDLEGS & PAULINE
Singles: 7-Inch
VEE JAY: 63 3–5

BIRDSONG, Edwin
Singles: 12-Inch 33/45rpm
PHILADELPHIA INT'L:
78–79 4–6
SALSOUL: 81–84 4–6
Singles: 7-Inch
PHILADELPHIA INT'L:
78 1–3
POLYDOR: 71–72 2–4
SALSOUL: 81–84 1–3
LPs: 10/12-Inch 33rpm
PHILADELPHIA INT'L:
78 5–8
POLYDOR: 71–73 8–10

BIRKIN, Jane, & Serge Gainsbourg
Singles: 7-Inch
FONTANA: 69 2–3
LPs: 10/12-Inch 33rpm
FONTANA: 70 5–10

Price Range

BISHOP, Elvin (The Elvin Bishop Group; Elvin Bishop & Crabshaw Rising)
Singles: 7-Inch
CAPRICORN: *74–79* $2–3
EPIC: *72–75* 2–4
FILLMORE: *70–71* 2–4
WARNER BROS: *72* 2–4
LPs: 10/12-Inch 33rpm
CAPRICORN: *74–78* 5–8
EPIC: *72–75* 8–10
FILLMORE: *69–72* 10–12
Also see BUTTERFIELD, Paul

BISHOP, Stephen
Singles: 7-Inch
ABC: *76–78* 2–3
WARNER BROS: *80–83* 1–3
Picture Sleeves
ABC: *78* 2–3
LPs: 10/12-Inch 33rpm
ABC: *76–78* 5–8
MCA: *80* 5–8
WARNER BROS: *80* 5–8
Also see NEWMAN, Randy

BISHOP, Stephen, & Yvonne Elliman
Singles: 7-Inch
WARNER BROS: *80* 1–3
Also see BISHOP, Stephen
Also see ELLIMAN, Yvonne

BITS & PIECES
Singles: 7-Inch
MANGO: *81* 1–3
NASCO: *73–74* 2–4
PARAMOUNT: *74* 2–4

BLACK, Bill (Bill Black's Combo)
Singles: 7-Inch
COLUMBIA: *70* 2–4
ECHO: *72* 2–4
GUSTO: *83* 1–3
HI (Except 2000 series):
67–76 2–4
HI (2000 series): *59–66* 3–5
LONDON: *84* 1–3
MEGA: *71–74* 2–4
MOTOWN: *83* 1–3

Price Range

Picture Sleeves
HI: *60–62* $3–5
LPs: 10/12-Inch 33rpm
COLUMBIA: *69–70* 8–10
51 WEST: *84* 5–8
HI (6000 & 8000 series):
77–78 5–8
HI (12001 through 12005):
60–62 15–30
HI (12006 through 12041):
62–68 8–18
HI (32000 through 32010):
61–63 15–30
HI (32011 through 32110):
63–77 8–18
MEGA: *71–74* 5–8
ZODIAC: *77* 5–8
Also see PRESLEY, Elvis

BLACK, Cilla
Singles: 7-Inch
BELL: *68* 3–4
CAPITOL: *64–66* 3–5
DJM: *68–70* 2–4
EMI AMERICA: *74* 2–4
PRIVATE STOCK: *75–76* 2–3
LPs: 10/12-Inch 33rpm
CAPITOL: *65* 20–25

BLACK, Jay
Singles: 7-Inch
ATLANTIC: *75* 2–4
MIDSONG: *80* 1–3
MIGRATION: *75* 2–4
MILLENNIUM: *78* 1–3
PRIVATE STOCK: *76* 2–3
ROULETTE: *76* 2–4
UNITED ARTISTS: *67* 3–5
Picture Sleeves
UNITED ARTISTS: *67* 3–5
Also see JAY & THE AMERICANS

BLACK, Jeanne
Singles: 7-Inch
CAPITOL: *60–62* 2–4
LPs: 10/12-Inch 33rpm
CAPITOL: *60* 15–20

BLACK, Marion
Singles: 7-Inch
AVCO EMBASSY: *71* 2–4

Price Range   *Price Range*

SHAKAT: *74*..................... **$2–3**

BLACK, Oscar
Singles: 7-Inch
ATLANTIC: *51* **15–20**
GROOVE: *54–55*................. **8–10**
SAVOY: *61* **3–5**

BLACK, Shelly
Singles: 7-Inch
VIGOR: *76–77*.................... **1–3**

BLACK, Stanley
Singles: 7-Inch
LONDON: *50–58* **2–4**
EPs: 7-Inch 33/45rpm
LONDON: *55* **3–6**
LPs: 10/12-Inch 33rpm
LONDON: *51–65* **4–8**

BLACK, Terry
Singles: 7-Inch
DUNHILL: *65–66*................. **3–5**
KAMA SUTRA: *72* **2–4**
TOLLIE: *64–65*................... **3–6**
Picture Sleeves
TOLLIE: *65*...................... **3–5**

BLACK & BLUE
Singles: 7-Inch
GEFFEN: *84* **1–3**
MERCURY: *70*................... **2–4**
LPs: 10/12-Inch 33rpm
GEFFEN: *84*..................... **5–8**

BLACK BLOOD
Singles: 7-Inch
CHRYSALIS: *77*.................. **2–3**
MAINSTREAM: *75*............... **2–4**
LPs: 10/12-Inch 33rpm
CHRYSALIS: *77*.................. **5–8**
MAINSTREAM: *75*.............. **8–10**

BLACK HEAT
Singles: 7-Inch
ATLANTIC: *72–74* **2–4**
LPs: 10/12-Inch 33rpm
ATLANTIC: *72–75* **8–10**

BLACK ICE
Singles: 7-Inch
AMHERST: *76* **$2–4**
HDM: *77*......................... **2–3**
MONTAGE: *81–84*................ **1–3**
LPs: 10/12-Inch 33rpm
AMHERST: *76*................... **8–10**
MONTAGE: *82*................... **5–8**

BLACK IVORY
Singles: 7-Inch
BUDDAH: *75–84*................. **1–3**
KWANZA: *74*..................... **2–4**
PANORAMIC: *85* **1–3**
PERCEPTION: *72* **2–4**
TODAY: *71–73*................... **2–4**
LPs: 10/12-Inch 33rpm
BUDDAH: *75–84*................. **5–8**
TODAY: *72*..................... **10–12**

BLACK MAMBA
Singles: 12-Inch 33/45rpm
GARAGE: *84* **4–6**

BLACK OAK ARKANSAS (Black Oak)
Singles: 7-Inch
ATCO: *71–75*..................... **2–4**
CAPRICORN: *77–78*............... **2–3**
ENTERPRISE: *70* **2–4**
MCA: *75–77* **1–3**
LPs: 10/12-Inch 33rpm
ATCO: *71–84*.................... **10–12**
CAPRICORN: *77–78*.............. **5–8**
MCA: *75–77* **8–10**
STAX: *74*....................... **10–12**
Members: Jim Mangrum; Ruby Starr; Rickie Reynolds; Stanley Knight; Harvey Jett; Jimmy Henderson; Pat Daugherty; Tom Aldridge.

BLACK OAK ARKANSAS / THE COOPER BROTHERS
LPs: 10/12-Inch 33rpm
CAPRICORN (0005; "I'd Rather Be Sailing"): *78*......... **10–15**
(Promotional issue only.)
Also see BLACK OAK ARKANSAS
Also see COOPER BROTHERS, The

BLACK PEARL
Singles: 7-Inch
ATLANTIC: *69* $2–4
PROPHESY: *70* 2–4
LPs: 10/12-Inch 33rpm
ATLANTIC: *69* 12–15
PROPHESY: *70* 15–20

BLACK SABBATH
Singles: 7-Inch
WARNER BROS: *70–76* 2–3
LPs: 10/12-Inch 33rpm
WARNER BROS (Except
1000 & 2000 series):
76–84 6–10
WARNER BROS (1000 &
2000 series): *70–76* 10–12
Members: Ozzy Osbourne; Tony Iommi; Kip
Treavor; Bill Ward; Ronnie Dio; Terry
"Geezer" Butler.
Also see OSBOURNE, Ozzy

BLACK SATIN (Featuring Fred Parris)
Singles: 7-Inch
BUDDAH: *75* 2–4
LPs: 10/12-Inch 33rpm
BUDDAH: *76* 8–10
Also see FIVE SATINS, The

BLACK UHURU
LPs: 10/12-Inch 33rpm
ISLAND: *84* 5–8
MANGO: *80–85* 5–8

BLACKBYRDS, The
Singles: 7-Inch
FANTASY: *74–84*. 1–3
LPs: 10/12-Inch 33rpm
FPM: *75*. 10–12
FANTASY: *74–84*. 10–12
Members: Gary Hart; Joe Hall, III; Stephe
Johnson; Keith Killgo; Orville Saunders; Kevin
Toney.
Also see BYRD, Donald

BLACKFOOT
Singles: 7-Inch
ATCO: *79–84*. 1–3
LPs: 10/12-Inch 33rpm
ANTILLES: *78* 5–8
ATCO: *79–84*. 5–8

EPIC: *76* $8–10
ISLAND: *75* 10–12
Members: Rick Medlocke; Jackson Spires;
Charlie Hargrett; Greg Walker.

BLACKFOOT, J.
Singles: 7-Inch
SOUND TOWN: *83–84* 1–3
LPs: 10/12-Inch 33rpm
SOUND TOWN: *84* 5–8

BLACKJACK
Singles: 7-Inch
POLYDOR: *79–84* 1–3
20TH CENTURY-FOX:
76 2–4
LPs: 10/12-Inch 33rpm
POLYDOR: *79–80* 5–8
Also see BOLTON, Michael

BLACKMORE, Ritchie
Singles: 7-Inch
POLYDOR: *75* 2–4
LPs: 10/12-Inch 33rpm
POLYDOR: *75* 8–10
Also see BLACKMORE'S RAINBOW
Also see LORD SUTCH

BLACKMORE'S RAINBOW
Singles: 7-Inch
OYSTER: *76* 2–4
POLYDOR: *75–79* 2–3
LPs: 10/12-Inch 33rpm
OYSTER: *76* 8–10
Members: Ritchie Blackmore; Roger Glover;
Ronnie Dio.
Also see BLACKMORE, Ritchie
Also see DEEP PURPLE
Also see RAINBOW

BLACKSMOKE
Singles: 7-Inch
CHOCOLATE CITY: *76* 2–3

BLACKWELL
Singles: 7-Inch
ASTRO: *69–70* 2–4
BUTTERFLY: *78* 2–3
LPs: 10/12-Inch 33rpm
ASTRO: *69* 8–10
BUTTERFLY: *78* 5–8

Price Range

BLACKWELL, Charlie
Singles: 7-Inch
WARNER BROS: *59* $3–5

BLADES OF GRASS, The
Singles: 7-Inch
JUBILEE: *67–68* 3–5
LPs: 10/12-Inch 33rpm
JUBILEE: *67* 12–15
Members: Bruce Ames; Marc Black; Frank Di-Chiara; Dave Gordon.

BLANC, Mel
Singles: 7-Inch
CAPITOL: *50–54* 5–10
WARNER BROS: *60* 2–5
EPs: 7-Inch 33/45rpm
CAPITOL: *51–53* 15–20
LPs: 10/12-Inch 33rpm
CAPITOL (400 series): *53* 20–30
(10-Inch LPs.)
CAPITOL (3200 series):
61–63 10–20
GOLDEN: *61* 10–15

BLANCHARD, Jack, & Misty Morgan
Singles: 7-Inch
EPIC: *73–75* 1–3
MEGA: *71–73* 2–3
WAYSIDE: *69–70* 2–4
LPs: 10/12-Inch 33rpm
MEGA: *72* 8–12
WAYSIDE: *70* 10–15

BLANC, De: see DE BLANC

BLANCMANGE
Singles: 12-Inch 33/45rpm
ISLAND: *83–84* 4–6
SIRE: *84–85* 4–6
Singles: 7-Inch
ISLAND: *83–84* 1–3
SIRE: *84–85* 1–3
LPs: 10/12-Inch 33rpm
ISLAND: *82–84* 5–8
SIRE: *84–85* 5–8

BLAND, Billy
Singles: 7-Inch
ATLANTIC: *84* 1–3

Price Range

COLLECTABLES: *81* $1–3
TIP TOP: *58* 4–6
OLD TOWN (1016
through 1035): *55–57* 6–10
OLD TOWN (1076
through 1143): *60–63* 3–5

BLAND, Bobby (Bobby "Blue" Bland)
Singles: 7-Inch
ABC: *73–78* 1–3
DUKE (105; "I.O.U.
Blues"): *54* 35–40
DUKE (115; "No Blow No
Show"): *54* 30–35
DUKE (141; "It's My Life,
Baby"): *56* 18–22
DUKE (146 through 196):
57–58 4–6
DUKE (300 series): *60–66* 3–5
DUKE (400 series): *66–72* 2–4
DUNHILL: *74* 2–3
MCA: *79–84* 1–3
LPs: 10/12-Inch 33rpm
ABC: *75–78* 5–8
ABC/DUKE: *73* 5–8
BLUESWAY: *73* 5–8
DUKE (74 through 78):
62–64 20–25
DUKE (79 through 89):
66–69 15–20
DUKE (90 through 92):
70–74 10–15
DUNHILL: *73–74* 8–10
MCA: *79–84* 5–8

BLAND, Bobby, & B.B. King
Singles: 7-Inch
ABC: *78* 1–3
IMPULSE: *76* 2–3
LPs: 10/12-Inch 33rpm
DUNHILL: *74* 10–12
IMPULSE: *76* 8–10
MCA: *82* 5–8
Also see KING, B.B.

BLAND, Bobby / Little Junior Parker
LPs: 10/12-Inch 33rpm
DUKE: *74* 8–10
Also see PARKER, Little Junior

BLAND, Bobby, & Ike Turner
Singles: 7-Inch
KENT: *62* **$3–5**
Also see TURNER, Ike, & Tina

BLAND, Bobby / Johnny Guitar Watson
LPs: 10/12-Inch 33rpm
CROWN: *63* **15–20**
Also see BLAND, Bobby
Also see WATSON, Johnny

BLANE, Marcie
Singles: 7-Inch
LONDON: *84* **1–3**
SEVILLE: *62–65* **3–5**

BLAST, C.L.
Singles: 7-Inch
ATLANTIC: *69* **2–4**
COTILLION: *80* **1–3**
PARK PLACE: *85* **1–3**
STAX: *67* **3–5**
UNITED: *70–71* **2–4**
LPs: 10/12-Inch 33rpm
COTILLION: *80* **5–8**

BLASTERS, The
Singles: 7-Inch
MCA: *84* **1–3**
SLASH: *82–85* **1–3**
LPs: 10/12-Inch 33rpm
ROLLIN' ROCK: *80* **8–10**
SLASH: *81–85* **5–8**

BLAZE
Singles: 7-Inch
EPIC: *76–77* **2–3**
FRATERNITY: *76* **2–4**

BLEND
Singles: 7-Inch
MCA: *78–79* **1–3**
LPs: 10/12-Inch 33rpm
MCA: *78–79* **5–8**

BLENDELLS, The
Singles: 7-Inch
COLLECTABLES: *81* **1–3**
COTILLION: *68* **3–5**
ERA: *73* **2–4**

RAMPART: *64* **$5–8**
REPRISE: *64–65* **3–5**

BLENDERS, The
Singles: 7-Inch
CORTLAND: *62* **3–5**
MAR-V-LOUS: *66* **3–5**
VISION: *62* **3–5**
WITCH: *63* **3–6**

BLESSING, Michael (Michael Nesmith)
Singles: 7-Inch
COLPIX: *65* **8–10**
Also see NESMITH, Michael

BLEYER, Archie
Singles: 7-Inch
CADENCE: *54–57* **3–5**
LPs: 10/12-Inch 33rpm
CADENCE: *62* **8–18**
Also see CHORDETTES, The

BLIND FAITH
Singles: 7-Inch
RSO: *77* **2–3**
LPs: 10/12-Inch 33rpm
ATCO (304A; "Blind
Faith"): *69* **20–30**
(Front cover pictures nude girl.)
ATCO (304B; "Blind
Faith"): *69* **10–12**
(Front cover pictures the group.)
RSO: *76* **5–8**
(Reissue. Pictures the nude girl.)
Members: Eric Clapton; Ginger Baker; Steve
Winwood; Rick Gretch.
Also see BAKER, Ginger
Also see CLAPTON, Eric
Also see WINWOOD, Steve

BLODWYN PIG
Singles: 7-Inch
A&M: *69–70* **2–4**
LPs: 10/12-Inch 33rpm
A&M (3000 series): *82* **5–8**
A&M (4000 series): *69–70* **10–15**
Members: Blodwyn; Mick Abrahams; Peter
Banks; Ron Berg; Clive Bunker; Jack Lancaster; Andy Pyle.
Also see BANKS, Peter

Price Range

BLONDIE
Singles: 12-Inch 33/45rpm
CHRYSALIS: 78–84............... $5–8
Singles: 7-Inch
CHRYSALIS: 77–84................ 1–3
PRIVATE STOCK: 76–77.......... 6–10
Picture Sleeves
CHRYSALIS: 79–81................ 1–3
LPs: 10/12-Inch 33rpm
CHRYSALIS (Except
picture discs): 76–84............. 6–10
CHRYSALIS (Picture
discs): 78 15–20
PRIVATE STOCK: 75............. 15–20
Members: Deborah Harry; Clem Burke; Jimmy
Destri; Chris Stein; Gary Valentine; Fred
Smith.
Also see HARRY, Debbie
Also see WIND IN THE WILLOWS

BLOOD, SWEAT & TEARS
(Featuring David Clayton-Thomas)
Singles: 7-Inch
ABC: 78.......................... 1–3
COLUMBIA: 69–77................ 2–4
Picture Sleeves
COLUMBIA: 70–72................ 2–4
LPs: 10/12-Inch 33rpm
ABC: 77.......................... 5–8
COLUMBIA (Except 9619
& 49000 series): 69–76.......... 10–12
COLUMBIA (9619; "Child
Is Father To The Man"):
68 15–20
COLUMBIA (49000
series): 81.................... 12–15
(Half-speed mastered LPs.)
LAX (1865; "Nuclear
Blues"): 80..................... 5–8
(Black vinyl.)
LAX (1865; "Nuclear
Blues"): 80.................... 10–12
(Colored vinyl. Promotional issue only.)
Also see CLAYTON-THOMAS, David
Also see KOOPER, Al

BLOODROCK
Singles: 7-Inch
CAPITOL: 69–75.................. 2–4
LPs: 10/12-Inch 33rpm
CAPITOL: 69–75............... 10–15

Price Range

Members: Rick Cobb; Eddie Grundy; Steve
Hill; Lee Pickens; Nick Taylor; Warren Ham.

BLOODSTONE
Singles: 12-Inch 33/45rpm
MOTOWN: 79.................... $4–6
T-NECK: 82–85 4–6
Singles: 7-Inch
EPIC: 82 1–3
LONDON: 73–75 2–3
MOTOWN: 79.................... 1–3
T-NECK: 82–85 1–3
Picture Sleeves
LONDON: 74–75 2–3
LPs: 10/12-Inch 33rpm
LONDON: 73–74 8–10
MOTOWN: 78.................... 5–8
T-NECK: 82 5–8
Members: Harry Williams; Charles McCor-
mick; Charles Love; Steve Ferrone; Roger Lee
Durham; Willis Draffen.

BLOOM, Bobby
Singles: 7-Inch
EARTH: 69....................... 2–4
KAMA SUTRA: 67................ 3–5
L&R: 70......................... 2–4
MGM: 70–73..................... 2–4
ROULETTE: 70 2–4
WHITE WHALE: 69.............. 2–4
LPs: 10/12-Inch 33rpm
BUDDAH: 71.................... 8–10
L&R: 70....................... 10–12
Also see MANN, Bobby
Also see MUSIC EXPLOSION, The

BLOOMFIELD, Mike
LPs: 10/12-Inch 33rpm
CLOUDS: 78...................... 5–8
COLUMBIA (9000 series):
69 12–15
COLUMBIA (37000
series): 81–83 6–10
GUITAR PLAYER: 77............. 8–10
HARMONY: 71 8–10
TAKOMA: 77–81................. 5–8
WATERHOUSE: 81............... 5–8

BLOOMFIELD, Mike, Dr. John &
John Paul Hammond
LPs: 10/12-Inch 33rpm
COLUMBIA: 73.................. 8–10

Price Range

Also see DR. JOHN
Also see HAMMOND, John

BLOOMFIELD, Mike, & Nick Graventes
LPs: 10/12-Inch 33rpm
COLUMBIA: 69 . . . . **$10–12**
Also see ELECTRIC FLAG, The

BLOOMFIELD, Mike, & Al Kooper
LPs: 10/12-Inch 33rpm
COLUMBIA: 68 . . . . **12–15**
Also see KOOPER, Al
Also see MOBY GRAPE

BLOOMFIELD, Mike, Al Kooper & Steve Stills
Singles: 7-Inch
COLUMBIA: 68 . . . . **2–4**

LPs: 10/12-Inch 33rpm
COLUMBIA: 68 . . . . **10–12**
Also see BLOOMFIELD, Mike
Also see STILLS, Stephen

BLOSSOMS, The
Singles: 7-Inch
BELL: 69–70 . . . . **4–6**
CAPITOL: 57–58 . . . . **4–6**
CHALLENGE: 61–62 . . . . **5–8**
EEOC (8472; "Things Are
  Changing"): 65 . . . . **45–50**
  (Promotional issue only.)
EPIC: 77 . . . . **2–3**
LION: 72 . . . . **2–4**
MGM: 68 . . . . **3–5**
ODE: 67–69 . . . . **3–5**
OKEH: 62–63 . . . . **4–6**
REPRISE: 65–67 . . . . **3–5**

Picture Sleeves
EEOC (8472; "Things Are
  Changing"): 65 . . . . **55–60**
  (Promotional issue only.)

LPs: 10/12-Inch 33rpm
LION: 72 . . . . **8–10**
  Members: Darlene Love; Gloria Jones; Fanita
  Barrett; Annette Williams; Nanette Jackson.
  Also see BOB B. SOXX & THE BLUE JEANS
  Also see EDDY, Duane
  Also see LOVE, Darlene
  Also see PRESLEY, Elvis

Price Range

BLOW, Kurtis
Singles: 12-Inch 33/45rpm
MERCURY: 80–85 . . . . **$4–6**
Singles: 7-Inch
MERCURY: 80–85 . . . . **1–3**
POLYDOR: 85 . . . . **1–3**
LPs: 10/12-Inch 33rpm
MERCURY: 80–85 . . . . **5–8**
  Also see KRUSH GROVE ALL STARS, The

BLOWFLY
Singles: 7-Inch
WEIRD WORLD: 80 . . . . **1–3**
LPs: 10/12-Inch 33rpm
WEIRD WORLD: 80 . . . . **8–10**

BLUE
Singles: 7-Inch
IRIS **1–3**
MCA/PIG: 77 . . . . **3–5**
  (Colored vinyl. Promotional issue only.)
RSO: 73–75 . . . . **2–4**
ROCKET: 77 . . . . **1–3**
LPs: 10/12-Inch 33rpm
RSO: 73 . . . . **8–10**
ROCKET: 77 . . . . **5–8**
  Members: Tim Donald; Ian MacMillan; Jimmy
  McCullough; Hugh Nicholson.
  Also see MARMALADE

BLUE, David (David Cohen)
Singles: 7-Inch
ASYLUM: 73 . . . . **2–3**
REPRISE: 69 . . . . **2–4**
LPs: 10/12-Inch 33rpm
ASYLUM: 73–76 . . . . **8–10**
ELEKTRA: 66 . . . . **12–15**
REPRISE: 68 . . . . **12–15**

BLUE BARRON: see BARRON, Blue

BLUE CHEER
Singles: 7-Inch
MERCURY: 76 . . . . **2–4**
PHILIPS: 68–70 . . . . **3–5**
Picture Sleeves
PHILIPS: 68 . . . . **6–10**
LPs: 10/12-Inch 33rpm
PHILIPS (9000 series): 80 . . . . **5–8**

Price Range

PHILIPS (600000 series):
68–71 .... **$15–20**
Members: Leigh Stephens; Paul Whaley; Dick
Peterson; Randy Holden; Tony Rainer; Bruce
Stephens; Ralph Kellogg; Gary Yoder.

BLUE DIAMONDS, The (With Ernie Kador)
Singles: 7-Inch
SAVOY: 54 .... **10–15**
Also see K-DOE, Ernie

BLUE HAZE
Singles: 7-Inch
A&M: 72–74 .... **2–4**

BLUE JAYS, The (Featuring Leon Peels)
Singles: 7-Inch
COLLECTABLES: 81 .... **1–3**
ERA: 72.......................... **1–3**
MILESTONE: 61–62 .... **5–8**

BLUE JAYS, The / Little Caesar & The Romans
LPs: 10/12-Inch 33rpm
MILESTONE: 62 .... **35–40**
Also see BLUE JAYS, The
Also see LITTLE CAESAR & THE RO-
MANS

BLUE MAGIC
Singles: 12-Inch 33/45rpm
MIRAGE: 83..................... **4–6**
Singles: 7-Inch
ATCO: 73–76..................... **2–4**
CAPITOL: 81 .... **1–3**
LIBERTY: 69 .... **2–4**
LPs: 10/12-Inch 33rpm
ATCO: 74–77.................... **8–10**
ATLANTIC: 83 .... **5–8**
CAPITOL: 81 .... **5–8**
MIRAGE: 83..................... **5–8**
Members: Ted Mills; Margie Joseph; Vernon
Sawyer; Wendell Sawyer; Richard Pratt; Keath
Beaton.
Also see JOSEPH, Margie

BLUE MINK
Singles: 7-Inch
BELL: 71–72..................... **2–4**
MCA: 73–74 .... **1–3**

Price Range

PHILIPS: 69–70 .... **$3–5**
Picture Sleeves
PHILIPS: 70 .... **3–5**
LPs: 10/12-Inch 33rpm
MCA: 73 .... **8–10**
PHILIPS: 69–70 .... **12–15**
Members: Madeline Bell; Roger Cook; Barry
Morgan; Herbie Flowers; Alan Parker; Ann
Odell; Roger Coulan; Ray Cooper.
Also see BELL, Madeline

BLUE NOTES, The (With Harold Melvin)
Singles: 7-Inch
COLLECTABLES: 81 .... **1–3**
3 SONS: 62 .... **5–8**
VAL-UE: 60 .... **5–8**
Also see MELVIN, Harold, & The Blue Notes

BLUE OYSTER CULT
Singles: 7-Inch
COLUMBIA: 72–84............... **1–3**
LPs: 10/12-Inch 33rpm
COLUMBIA (Except
31000 through 33000
series): 76–84 .... **5–8**
COLUMBIA (31000
through 33000 series):
72–75 .... **10–15**
Members: Al Bouchard; Joe Bouchard; Eric
Bloom; Alan Lanier; Donald "Buck Dharma"
Roeser.

BLUE PRINT
Singles: 7-Inch
FANTASY: 83.................... **1–3**

BLUE RIDGE RANGERS, The (John Fogerty)
Singles: 7-Inch
FANTASY: 72–73................. **2–4**
LPs: 10/12-Inch 33rpm
FANTASY: 73................... **10–12**
Also see FOGERTY, John

BLUE STARS, The
Singles: 7-Inch
MERCURY: 55–56................. **2–4**

BLUE SWEDE
Singles: 7-Inch
EMI AMERICA: 73–75............. **2–4**

Price Range

Picture Sleeves
EMI AMERICA: *73–74* **$2–4**

LPs: 10/12-Inch 33rpm
EMI AMERICA: *74–75* **8–10**
  Members: Bjorn Skifs; Jan Guldback; Bosse
  Liljedahl; Michael Areklew; Ladislau Balaz;
  Tommy Berglund; Hinke Ekestubble.

BLUE-BELLES, The (With Patti Labelle)
Singles: 7-Inch
NEWTOWN: *62* **4–6**
  Also see LABELLE, Patti

BLUENOTES, The
Singles: 7-Inch
BROOKE: *59–60.* **4–6**

BLUES BROTHERS, The
Singles: 7-Inch
ATLANTIC: *78–81* **1–3**
Picture Sleeves
ATLANTIC: *80* **2–4**
LPs: 10/12-Inch 33rpm
ATLANTIC: *78–81* **6–10**
  Members: Dan Aykroyd; John Belushi.
  Also see BELUSHI, John

BLUES IMAGE
Singles: 7-Inch
ATCO: *69–71.* **3–5**
LPs: 10/12-Inch 33rpm
ATCO: *69–70.* **10–12**
  Members: Mike Pinera; Joe Lala; Frank Konte;
  Malcolm Jones; Manuel Bertematti.
  Also see PINERA, Mike

BLUES MAGOOS
Singles: 7-Inch
ABC: *68–70.* **3–5**
GANIM: *69.* **15–20**
MERCURY (30000 series):
  76 . . . . **2–4**
MERCURY (70000 series):
  66–68 . . . . **5–8**
VERVE/FOLKWAYS
  (5006; "So I'm Wrong"):
  66 . . . . **15–20**
VERVE/FOLKWAYS
  (5044; "So I'm Wrong"):
  67 . . . . **10–15**

Price Range

Picture Sleeves
MERCURY: *67.* **$6–10**
LPs: 10/12-Inch 33rpm
ABC: *69–70.* **8–10**
MERCURY: *66–68.* **20–25**
  (Red label.)
MERCURY: *81.* **5–8**
  (Chicago "skyline" label.)
  Members: Geoff Daking; Mike Esposito; Ron
  Gilbert; Ralph Scala; Emil Thielhelm.
  Also see BALANCE

BLUES PROJECT, The
Singles: 7-Inch
CAPITOL: *72* **4–6**
MCA: *73* **1–3**
VERVE/FOLKWAYS:
  66–67 . . . . **8–10**
LPs: 10/12-Inch 33rpm
CAPITOL: *72* **10–12**
ELEKTRA: *80* **5–8**
MCA: *73* **8–10**
MGM: *70–74.* **8–12**
VERVE/FOLKWAYS: *66.* **15–18**
VERVE/FORECAST:
  67–70 . . . . **12–15**
  Members: Al Kooper; Roy Blumenfeld; David
  Cohen; Tommy Flanders; Richard Green; John
  Gregory; Don Gretmar; Danny Kalb; Steve
  Katz; Andy Kulbert; Bill Lussenden; Chicken
  Hirsch.
  Also see KOOPER, Al
  Also see SEATRAIN

BO, Eddie
Singles: 7-Inch
ACE: *57–59* **5–8**
APOLLO: *55–56.* **8–10**
AT LAST: *63.* **3–5**
BLUE JAY: *64* **3–5**
BO-SOUND: *71.* **2–4**
CAPITOL: *61* **3–5**
CHECKER: *58* **5–8**
CHESS (Except 1600
  series): *62* **3–5**
CHESS (1600 series): *58.* **5–8**
CINDERELLA: *63.* **3–5**
RIC: *59–62* **4–6**
SEVEN B: *66–68.* **3–5**
SCRAM: *69.* **2–4**
SWAN: *62* **3–5**
  Also see BO, Little
  Also see PARKER, Robert

Price Range   *Price Range*

BO DIDDLEY: see DIDDLEY, Bo

BOB & EARL
Singles: 7-Inch
CLASS: *59* $4–6
    Members: Earl Nelson; Bobby Byrd.
    Also see BYRD, Bobby
    Also see LEE, Jackie

BOB & EARL
Singles: 7-Inch
ABC: *73* 1–3
CHENE: *64* 3–5
COLLECTABLES: *81* 1–3
CRESTVIEW: *69* 2–4
MARC: *63–64* 3–5
MIRWOOD: *66* 3–5
TEMPE: *62* 3–5
UNI: *70* 2–4
WHITE WHALE: *69* 2–4

LPs: 10/12-Inch 33rpm
CRESTVIEW: *69* 15–18
TIP: *64* 20–25
UPFRONT 10–15
    Members: Earl Nelson; Bobby Relf.
    Also see BYRD, Bobby
    Also see WHITE, Barry

BOB B. SOXX & THE BLUE JEANS
Singles: 7-Inch
PHILLES: *62–63* 5–8

LPs: 10/12-Inch 33rpm
PHILLES: *63* 50–60
    Members: Bobby Sheen; Darlene Love; Fanita
    Barrett-James.
    Also see BLOSSOMS, The
    Also see LOVE, Darlene
    Also see RONETTES, The / The Crystals /
    Darlene Love / Bob B. Soxx & The
    Blue Jeans
    Also see SHEEN, Bobby

BOBBETTES, The
Singles: 7-Inch
ATLANTIC: *57–60* 5–8
DIAMOND: *62–65* 3–5
END: *61* 3–5
GALLIANT: *60* 4–6
GONE: *61* 3–5

JUBILEE: *62* $3–5
KING: *61–62* 3–5
MAYHEW: *72–74* 2–4
RCA VICTOR: *66* 3–5
TRIPLE-X: *60* 4–6
    Members: Emma Pought; Jan Pought; Laura
    Webb; Helen Gathers.

BOBBY & THE MIDNITES
(Featuring Bobby Weir)
Singles: 7-Inch
ARISTA: *81* 1–3
COLUMBIA: *84* 1–3

LPs: 10/12-Inch 33rpm
ARISTA: *81* 5–8
COLUMBIA: *84* 5–8
    Also see WEIR, Bobby

BOBBY LEE: see LEE, Bobby

BOBO, Willie (Bobo)
Singles: 7-Inch
BLUE NOTE: *77* 1–3
CAPITOL: *76* 2–3
JUPITER JAZZ: *75* 2–3
VERVE: *65–69* 2–4

LPs: 10/12-Inch 33rpm
BLUE NOTE: *77* 5–8
ROULETTE: *63–64* 10–15
VERVE: *65–69* 8–12
    Also see HANCOCK, Herbie, & Willie Bobo

BOFILL, Angela
Singles: 12-Inch 33/45rpm
ARISTA: *81–85* 4–6

Singles: 7-Inch
ARISTA: *81–85* 1–3
GRP: *79* 2–3

LPs: 10/12-Inch 33rpm
ARISTA: *81–85* 5–8
GRP: *78* 5–10

BOHANNON (Hamilton Bohannon)
Singles: 12-Inch 33/45rpm
COMPLEAT: *84–85* 4–6
MERCURY: *77–80* 4–6
MCA: *84* 4–6
PHASE 2: *80–83* 4–6

Price Range

Singles: 7-Inch
DAKAR: *73–75* $2–4
MERCURY: *77–80*. 1–3
PHASE 2: *80–83* 1–3
LPs: 10/12-Inch 33rpm
DAKAR: *73–75* 10–12
MERCURY: *77–80*. 8–10
PHASE 2: *80–83* 5–8

BOHN, Rudi, & His Band
EPs: 7-Inch 33/45rpm
LONDON: *59* 3–6
LPs: 10/12-Inch 33rpm
LONDON: *59–61* 5–10

BOILING POINT
Singles: 7-Inch
BULLET: *78* 1–3

BOLGER, Ray
Singles: 7-Inch
ARMOUR: *63*. 2–4
DECCA: *50–51* 3–5
LPs: 10/12-Inch 33rpm
DISNEYLAND: *65* 6–10

BOLIN, Tommy
Singles: 7-Inch
NEMPEROR: *76* 2–4
LPs: 10/12-Inch 33rpm
COLUMBIA: *76*. 8–10
NEMPEROR: *75* 10–12
(With an "NZ" prefix.)
NEMPEROR: *81* 5–8
(With a "PZ" prefix.)
Also see JAMES GANG, The
Also see ZEPHYR

BOLTON, Michael
Singles: 7-Inch
COLUMBIA: *83* 1–3
RCA VICTOR: *75–76* 2–4
LPs: 10/12-Inch 33rpm
COLUMBIA: *83–85* 5–8
RCA VICTOR: *75–76* 8–10
Also see BLACKJACK

BOMBERS, The
Singles: 7-Inch
WEST END: *79* 1–3

Price Range

LPs: 10/12-Inch 33rpm
WEST END: *79* $10–12

BON JOVI
Singles: 7-Inch
MERCURY: *84–86*. 1–3
LPs: 10/12-Inch 33rpm
MERCURY: *85–86*. 5–8
Members: Jon Bon Jovi; Richie Sambora;
David Bryan; Alec John Such; Tico Torres.

BON ROCK (With Keith Rogers)
Singles: 12-Inch 33/45rpm
EARTHTONE: *84* 4–6
LPs: 10/12-Inch 33rpm
EARTHTONE: *84* 5–8

BOND, Angelo
Singles: 7-Inch
ABC: *75–76*. 2–3
LPs: 10/12-Inch 33rpm
ABC: *75–77*. 8–10

BOND, Johnny
Singles: 7-Inch
COLUMBIA (Except
21521): *50–56*. 3–6
COLUMBIA (21521;
"Little Rock & Roll"):
· *56* 8–12
DITTO: *59*. 3–5
LAMB & LION: *74* 1–3
MGM: *73*. 1–3
REPUBLIC: *60*. 3–5
SMASH: *62* 2–4
STARDAY (600 through
900 series): *63–72* 2–4
STARDAY (8000 series):
72 1–3
EPs: 7-Inch 33/45rpm
COLUMBIA: *58* 10–15
REPUBLIC: *60*. 10–15
LPs: 10/12-Inch 33rpm
CMH: *77* 5–8
HARMONY: *64–65* 10–20
LAMB & LION: *74* 5–8
NASHVILLE: *71* 5–8
SHASTA 10–15
STARDAY (100 & 200
series): *61–64* 20–25

Price Range

STARDAY (300 series,
except 354): *65–66*. **$15–20**
STARDAY (354; "Famous
Hot Rodders I Have
Known"): *65* **25–30**
STARDAY (400 series):
67–71 . . . . **10–15**
STARDAY (900 series): *74* **6–10**

BONDS, Gary "U.S." (U.S. Bonds)
Singles: 7-Inch
ABC: *73*. **1–3**
ATCO: *69* **2–4**
BLUFF CITY: *74*. **2–4**
BOTANIC: *68*. **3–5**
COLLECTABLES: *81* **1–3**
EMI AMERICA: *81–82*. **1–3**
LEGRAND: *60–65*. **4–6**
MCA: *84* **1–3**
PRODIGAL: *75* **2–3**
SUE: *70* **2–4**
Picture Sleeves
EMI AMERICA: *81–82*. **1–3**
LEGRAND: *61*. **6–10**
LPs: 10/12-Inch 33rpm
EMI AMERICA: *81–82*. **5–8**
LEGRAND (1000 series):
86 . . . . **5–8**
LEGRAND (3000 series):
61–62 . . . . **25–30**
PHOENIX: *84*. **5–8**
RHINO: *84* **5–8**
Also see CHECKER, Chubby / Gary U.S.
Bonds
Also see GREENWICH, Ellie
Also see JACKSON, Chuck
Also see KING, Ben E.
Also see SPRINGSTEEN, Bruce

BONE SYMPHONY
Singles: 12-Inch 33/45rpm
CAPITOL: *83* **4–6**
Singles: 7-Inch
CAPITOL: *83* **1–3**
LPs: 10/12-Inch 33rpm
CAPITOL: *83* **5–8**

BONES
Singles: 7-Inch
MCA: *73* **2–4**
SIGNPOST: *72* **3–5**

Price Range

LPs: 10/12-Inch 33rpm
MCA: *73* **$8–10**
SIGNPOST: *72* **10–12**

BONES, Elbow: see ELBOW BONES

BONEY M
Singles: 12-Inch 33/45rpm
CARRERE: *85* **4–6**
SIRE: *79* **4–6**
Singles: 7-Inch
ATCO: *76–77*. **2–4**
ATLANTIC: *77* **2–3**
SIRE: *78–79* **1–3**
Picture Sleeves
SIRE: *79* **1–3**
LPs: 10/12-Inch 33rpm
ATCO: *76* **10–12**
ATLANTIC: *77* **8–10**
SIRE: *77–79* **5–8**
Members: Marcia Barrett; Bobby Farrell; Liz
Mitchell; Maizie Williams.

BONNIE & THE TREASURES
(Featuring Charlott O'Hara)
Singles: 7-Inch
PHI DAN: *65* **20–25**

BONNIE SISTERS, The
Singles: 7-Inch
RAINBOW: *56*. **8–10**

BONO, Sonny: see SONNY

BONOFF, Karla
Singles: 7-Inch
COLUMBIA: *77–84* **1–3**
LPs: 10/12-Inch 33rpm
COLUMBIA: *77–82* **5–8**

BONZO DOG BAND, The
Singles: 7-Inch
IMPERIAL: *69*. **2–4**
LIBERTY: *68* **3–5**
UNITED ARTISTS: *71–72* **2–4**
LPs: 10/12-Inch 33rpm
IMPERIAL: *68–70*. **15–18**
LIBERTY: *83* **5–8**
UNITED ARTISTS: *71–74* **10–12**

Members: The Bonzo Dog Doo-Dah Band; Vivian Stanshall; Neil Innes; Roger Ruskin Spear; Hughie Flint; Tony Kaye; Dave Richards; Andy Roberts.
Also see RUTLES, The

BONZO GOES TO WASHINGTON
Singles: 12-Inch 33/45rpm
SLEEPING BAG: *84* **$4–6**

BOOGIE BOYS, The (Featuring William Stroman)
Singles: 12-Inch 33/45rpm
CAPITOL: *84* **4–6**
Singles: 7-Inch
CAPITOL: *84* **1–3**
LPs: 10/12-Inch 33rpm
CAPITOL: *85* **5–8**

BOOGIE MAN ORCHESTRA, The
Singles: 7-Inch
BOOGIE MAN: *75.* **2–3**

BOOK OF LOVE
Singles: 12-Inch 33/45rpm
SIRE: *84–85* **4–6**

BOOKER, James
Singles: 7-Inch
PEACOCK: *60–64* **3–5**
LPs: 10/12-Inch 33rpm
ROUNDER: *84.* **5–8**
Also see LITTLE BOOKER

BOOKER T. & PRISCILLA
Singles: 7-Inch
A&M: *71–73* **2–4**
LPs: 10/12-Inch 33rpm
A&M: *71–73* **8–10**
Members: Booker T. Jones; Priscilla Coolidge-Jones.

BOOKER T. & THE MGs (Booker T. Jones)
Singles: 12-Inch 33/45rpm
A&M: *82–84* **4–6**
Singles: 7-Inch
A&M: *81–82* **1–3**
ASYLUM: *77.* **2–3**
EPIC: *75* **2–3**
STAX (Except 100 series):
67–71 . . . . **2–4**

STAX (100 series): *62–66* **$3–5**
LPs: 10/12-Inch 33rpm
A&M: *72–81* **8–10**
ASYLUM: *77.* **5–8**
ATLANTIC: *68* **10–12**
EPIC: *74* **8–10**
STAX (700 series, except
701): *65–68* **12–15**
STAX (701; "Green
Onions"): *62.* **15–18**
STAX (2000 series): *68–71* **10–12**
STAX (8000 series): *81–84* **5–8**
Also see BOOKER T. & PRISCILLA
Also see MGs, The
Also see MAR-KEYS, The / Booker T. & The MGs
Also see SANTANA

BOOM, Taka
Singles: 7-Inch
ARIOLA: *79* **1–3**
LPs: 10/12-Inch 33rpm
ARIOLA: *79* **5–8**

BOOMTOWN RATS, The
Singles: 7-Inch
COLUMBIA: *79–80* **1–3**
LPs: 10/12-Inch 33rpm
COLUMBIA: *79–85* **5–8**
MERCURY: *77.* **8–12**
Members: Bob Geldof; Pete Briquette; Gerry Cott; Simon Crowe; Johnny Fingers; Garry Roberts.
Also see BAND AID

BOONE, Daniel
Singles: 7-Inch
EPIC: *72* **2–4**
MERCURY: *72–74.* **2–4**
PYE: *75* **2–3**
LPs: 10/12-Inch 33rpm
MERCURY: *72.* **10–12**

BOONE, Debbie
Singles: 7-Inch
WARNER BROS: *77–80* **1–3**
Picture Sleeves
WARNER BROS: *78* **1–3**
LPs: 10/12-Inch 33rpm
LAMB & LION: *80–84* **5–8**
WARNER BROS: *77–80* **5–8**
Also see BOONE, Pat, & The Boone Girls
Also see BOONE GIRLS, The

Price Range

BOONE, Pat
Singles: 7-Inch
ABC: *74–75* $1–3
BUENA VISTA: *73* 2–3
CAPITOL: *70* 2–4
DOT: *55–57* 4–6
  (Maroon labels.)
DOT (15000 & 16000
  series): *57–66* 3–5
  (Black labels.)
DOT (200 series): *59–60* 6–10
  (Stereo singles.)
DOT (17000 series): *66–75* 2–4
HITSVILLE: *76–77* 2–3
LION: *72* 2–3
MC: *77* 2–3
MCA: *84* 1–3
MGM: *71–73* 2–3
MELODYLAND: *74–76* 2–3
REPUBLIC: *54* 6–10
TETRAGRAMMATON:
  69 2–4
WARNER BROS: *80–81* 1–3

Picture Sleeves
DOT: *57–62* 3–5

EPs: 7-Inch 33/45rpm
DOT: *57–60* 8–12

LPs: 10/12-Inch 33rpm
ABC: *74* 5–8
BIBLE VOICE: *70* 5–8
CANDLELITE 6–10
  (A mail-order LP offer.)
DOT (3000 series, except
  maroon labels): *57–68* 12–15
  (Monaural issues.)
DOT (Maroon label):
  55–56 15–25
DOT (25000 series): *58–68* 12–15
  (Stereo issues.)
HAMILTON: *65* 10–12
HITSVILLE: *76* 8–10
LAMB & LION: *73–81* 5–8
MCA: *82* 5–8
MGM: *73* 5–8
PARAMOUNT: *74* 5–8
PICKWICK 5–8
SUPREME: *70* 6–10
TETRAGRAMMATON:
  69 10–12

Price Range

WORD: *75–84* $5–8
  Also see JENKINS, Gordon, & His Orchestra

BOONE, Pat & Shirley (The Pat Boone Family)
Singles: 7-Inch
DOT: *62–64* 2–4
MGM: *72* 2–3
MELODYLAND: *75* 2–3
MOTOWN: *74* 2–3
WARNER BROS: *79* 1–3
EPs: 7-Inch 33/45rpm
DOT: *59* 5–8
LPs: 10/12-Inch 33rpm
LION: *72* 5–8
MC: *77* 5–8
WORD: *71* 5–8

BOONE, Pat, & The Boone Girls
Singles: 7-Inch
LION: *72* 2–3
  Also see BOONE, Pat & Shirley
  Also see BOONE GIRLS, The

BOONE FAMILY, The: see BOONE, Pat & Shirley

BOONE GIRLS, The (The Boones)
Singles: 7-Inch
LAMB & LION: *77* 1–3
LION: *72* 2–3
MGM: *71–73* 2–4
MOTOWN: *75* 2–3
WARNER BROS: *77* 1–3
LPs: 10/12-Inch 33rpm
LAMB & LION: *77–83* 5–8
  Also see BOONE, Debbie
  Also see BOONE, Pat, & The Boone Girls

BOOTEE, Duke
Singles: 7-Inch
MERCURY: *84* 1–3

BOOTSY'S RUBBER BAND (William "Bootsy" Collins)
Singles: 12-Inch 33/45rpm
WARNER BROS: *79–82* 4–6
Singles: 7-Inch
WARNER BROS: *75–82* 1–3
LPs: 10/12-Inch 33rpm
WARNER BROS: *76–82* 5–8

Also see PARLIAMENT
Also see SWEAT BAND
Also see ZAPP

BOOTY PEOPLE, The
Singles: 7-Inch
CALLA: 76 . . . . **$2–3**
LPs: 10/12-Inch 33rpm
ABC: 77 . . . . **5–8**

BOSTIC, Earl
Singles: 7-Inch
KING (4000 series): 52–56 . . . . **8–10**
(Colored vinyl.)
KING (4000 series, except
4491): 50–57 . . . . **4–6**
(Black vinyl.)
KING (4491; "I Got
Loaded"): 52 . . . . **8–10**
KING (5000 series): 57–65 . . . . **3–5**
KING (6000 series): 65–69 . . . . **1–3**
KING (15000 series): 72 . . . . **1–3**
EPs: 7-Inch 33/45rpm
KING: 52–62 . . . . **5–10**
LPs: 10/12-Inch 33rpm
KING (70 through 103):
52–55 . . . . **15–20**
(10-Inch LPs.)
KING (500 series): 54–58 . . . . **10–15**
KING (600 through 1000
series): 59–70 . . . . **6–12**
PHILLIPS: 68 . . . . **8–12**

BOSTIC, Earl, & Bill Doggett
Singles: 7-Inch
KING: 56 . . . . **3–5**
Also see BOSTIC, Earl
Also see DOGGETT, Bill

BOSTIC, Sam
Singles: 7-Inch
ATLANTIC: 85 . . . . **1–3**

BOSTON
Singles: 7-Inch
EPIC: 76–79 . . . . **2–3**
MCA: 85–86 . . . . **1–3**
LPs: 10/12-Inch 33rpm
EPIC (34188; "Boston"):
78 . . . . **15–25**
(With an "E99" prefix. Picture disc.)

EPIC (34188; "Boston"):
80 . . . . **$12–15**
(With an "HE" prefix. Half-speed mastered.)
EPIC (34188; "Boston"):
76 . . . . **15–25**
(With a "PE" prefix.)
EPIC (35000 series): 78 . . . . **10–12**
EPIC (45000 series): 81 . . . . **12–15**
(With an "HE" prefix. Half-speed mastered.)
MCA: 85–86 . . . . **5–8**
Members: Brad Delp; Tom Scholz; Barry Goudreau; Sib Hashian; Fran Sheehan.
Also see GOUDREAU, Barry
Also see ORION THE HUNTER

BOSTON POPS ORCHESTRA, The
(Conducted by Arthur Fiedler)
Singles: 7-Inch
RCA VICTOR: 50–65 . . . . **2–4**
EPs: 7-Inch 33/45rpm
RCA VICTOR: 50–61 . . . . **4–8**
LPs: 10/12-Inch 33rpm
DEUTSCHE
GRAMMOPHON: 78 . . . . **4–8**
MIDSONG INT'L: 79 . . . . **4–8**
POLYDOR: 71–72 . . . . **5–10**
RCA VICTOR: 50–69 . . . . **8–18**

BOSTON POPS ORCHESTRA, The
(Conducted by John Williams)
LPs: 10/12-Inch 33rpm
PHILIPS: 80 . . . . **5–8**
Also see WILLIAMS, John

BOSWELL, Connie
Singles: 7-Inch
CHARLES: 62 . . . . **2–4**
DECCA: 50–56 . . . . **2–5**

BOTTOM COMPANY
Singles: 7-Inch
MOTOWN: 74–75 . . . . **2–4**
LPs: 10/12-Inch 33rpm
GORDY: 76 . . . . **8–10**

BOTTOM LINE
Singles: 7-Inch
GREEDY: 76 . . . . **2–3**
LPs: 10/12-Inch 33rpm
GREEDY: 76 . . . . **8–10**

BOW WOW WOW
Singles: 12-Inch 33/45rpm
RCA VICTOR: *83* **$4–6**
Singles: 7-Inch
RCA VICTOR: *81–84* **1–3**
Picture Sleeves
RCA VICTOR: *82* .... **INC**
LPs: 10/12-Inch 33rpm
HARVEST: *82.* **5–8**
RCA VICTOR: *81–84* **5–8**
Also see ADAM & THE ANTS

BOWEN, Jimmy
Singles: 7-Inch
CAPEHART: *61–62.* **3–5**
CREST: *61.* **3–5**
REPRISE: *64–66.* **3–5**
ROULETTE: *57–60* **4–6**
Picture Sleeves
CAPEHART: *61.* **6–10**
EPs: 7-Inch 33/45rpm
ROULETTE: *57* **25–30**
LPs: 10/12-Inch 33rpm
REPRISE: *66.* **15–20**
ROULETTE: *57* **60–80**
Also see KNOX, Buddy / Jimmy Bowen

BOWIE, David
Singles: 12-Inch 33/45rpm
EMI AMERICA: *82–85.* **4–8**
RCA VICTOR: *79–80* **8–15**
Promotional 12-Inch Singles
EMI AMERICA: *82–85.* **5–10**
RCA VICTOR: *79–80* **10–20**
Singles: 7-Inch
BACKSTREET: *82.* **2–3**
DERAM: *67* **15–20**
LONDON: *74* **5–8**
MERCURY: *69–71.* **20–25**
RCA VICTOR: *71–84* **2–4**
WARNER BROS: *66.* **35–40**
Picture Sleeves
RCA VICTOR: *72–85* **3–6**
EPs: 7-Inch 33/45rpm
RCA VICTOR. **20–25**
(Promotional issues only.)
LPs: 10/12-Inch 33rpm
DERAM: *67* **40–45**
EMI AMERICA: *83–85.* **5–8**
LONDON: *73–85* **8–12**
MFSL: *83.* **12–15**

MERCURY (61246; "Man
Of Words/Man Of
Music"): *69* **$60–70**
MERCURY (61246;
"Space Oddity"): *72* **10–12**
MERCURY (61325; "The
Man Who Sold The
World"): *71* **20–25**
RCA VICTOR (0291;
"Bowie Pin Ups"): *73.* **8–12**
RCA VICTOR (0576,
"Diamond Dogs"): *74.* **250–350**
(With "Dog Genitals" cover.)
RCA VICTOR (0576,
"Diamond Dogs"): *74.* **6–10**
(With dog's genitals covered.)
RCA VICTOR (0700
through 1300 series):
74–76 .... **8–15**
RCA VICTOR (1732;
"Changesone Bowie"): *76.* **60–75**
(With the alternate take of "John, I'm Only
Dancing.")
RCA VICTOR (1732;
"Changesone Bowie"): *76.* **6–10**
(With the commonly issued take of "John, I'm
Only Dancing.")
RCA VICTOR (2000
through 2500: *77.* **6–10**
RCA VICTOR (2743;
"Peter & The Wolf"): *78* **6–10**
(Black vinyl.)
RCA VICTOR (2743;
"Peter & The Wolf"): *78* **20–30**
(Colored vinyl.)
RCA VICTOR (2900
through 4200 series):
79–82 .... **5–10**
RCA VICTOR (4600
through 4800 series):
71–73 .... **8–15**
(With an "LSP" prefix.)
RCA VICTOR (4700
through 4900 series,
except 4862): *83–84.* **5–10**
(With an "AFL" or "CPL" prefix.)
RCA VICTOR 4862;
"Ziggy Stardust"): *83* **5–10**
(Black vinyl.)
RCA VICTOR 4862;
"Ziggy Stardust"): *83* **10–20**
(Clear vinyl.)

Price Range

Price Range

Promotional LPs
DERAM: *67* **$75–90**
EMI AMERICA (9960;
  "Let's Talk"): *83* **30–40**
MERCURY (61246; "Man
  Of Words/Man Of
  Music"): *69* **70–80**
RCA VICTOR (0200
  through 4800 series):
  71–73 .... **15–20**
  (With programmer's strip on front cover.)
RCA VICTOR (2697;
  "Bowie Now"): *78*. **25–30**
RCA VICTOR (3016; "An
  Evening With David
  Bowie"): *78* **60–75**
RCA VICTOR (3545;
  "Bowie 1980"): *80*. **30–40**
RCA VICTOR (3829;
  "RCA Special Radio
  Series"): *80*. **20–25**
RCA VICTOR (3840;
  "David Bowie
  Interview"): *80*. **35–40**
RCA VICTOR (11306;
  "Peter & The Wolf"): *78* **25–30**
  Also see HOUSTON, Cissy
  Also see KHAN, Chaka
  Also see QUEEN & DAVID BOWIE
  Also see SPIDERS FROM MARS
  Also see TURNER, Tina
  Also see VANDROSS, Luther

BOWIE, David / Joe Cocker / The Youngbloods
  LPs: 10/12-Inch 33rpm
MERCURY (SRD-2-29;
  "Zig Zag Festival"): *70*. **35–40**
  (Promotional issue only.)
  Also see COCKER, Joe
  Also see YOUNGBLOODS, The

BOWIE, David, & Mick Jagger
  Singles: 12-Inch 33/45rpm
EMI AMERICA (19200;
  "Dancing In The
  Streets"): *85*. **5–8**
  Also see JAGGER, Mick

BOWIE, David, & The Pat Metheny Group
  Singles: 12-Inch 33/45rpm
EMI AMERICA: *85*. **$4–6**
  LPs: 10/12-Inch 33rpm
EMI AMERICA: *85*. **5–8**
  Also see METHENY, Pat

BOWIE, David / Iggy Pop
  Singles: 12-Inch 33/45rpm
RCA VICTOR: *77* **25–30**
  (Promotional issue only.)
  Also see BOWIE, David
  Also see POP, Iggy

BOWLES, Rick
  Singles: 7-Inch
POLYDOR: *82* **1–3**
  LPs: 10/12-Inch 33rpm
POLYDOR: *82* **5–8**

BOX OF FROGS
  Singles: 7-Inch
EPIC: *84* **1–3**
  LPs: 10/12-Inch 33rpm
EPIC: *84* **5–8**
  Members: Chris Dreja; Jim McCarty; Jeff Beck.
  Also see YARDBIRDS, The

BOX TOPS, The
  Singles: 7-Inch
BELL: *70–71* **2–4**
GUSTO: *84* **1–3**
HI: *71*. **2–4**
MALA: *67–69* **3–5**
SPHERE SOUND: *67* **3–5**
STAX: *74*. **2–4**
  LPs: 10/12-Inch 33rpm
BELL: *67–69* **12–15**
COTILLION: *71*. **10–12**
KORY: *77*. **5–8**
RHINO: *82* **5–8**
  Members: Alex Chilton; Rick Allen; Tom Boggs; Harold Cloud; Bill Cunningham; John Evans; Swain Scharfar; Gary Talley; Danny Smythe.

BOY MEETS GIRL
  Singles: 7-Inch
A&M: *85* **1–3**
  LPs: 10/12-Inch 33rpm
A&M: *85* **5–8**

Price Range

Members: George Merrill; Shannon Rubicam.

BOYCE, Tommy
Singles: 7-Inch

A&M (Except 826): *66* $2–4
A&M (826; "In Case The
   Wind Should Blow"): *66* 8–12
CAPITOL: *71* 2–4
COLPIX: *66* 5–8
DOT: *60* 8–10
MGM: *65* 5–8
RCA VICTOR (7000
   series): *61* 8–10
RCA VICTOR (8000
   series): *62–63* 5–8
R-DELL: *58* 8–10
WOW: *61* 5–8
LPs: 10/12-Inch 33rpm
CAMDEN: *68* 10–15
   Also see CLOUD, Christopher

BOYCE, Tommy, & Bobby Hart
(Boyce & Hart)
Singles: 7-Inch

A&M: *67–69* 3–5
AQUARIAN: *68* 3–5
Picture Sleeves
A&M: *67–69* 3–5
AQUARIAN: *68* 4–6
LPs: 10/12-Inch 33rpm
A&M: *67–69* 10–12
   Also see BOYCE, Tommy
   Also see DOLENZ, JONES, BOYCE & HART

BOYD, Eddie (Eddie Boyd & His
Chess Men; The Eddie Boyd Blues
Combo; Little Eddie Boyd & His
Boogie Band)
Singles: 7-Inch

ART TONE: *62* 3–5
BEA & BABY: *59* 4–6
CHESS (1500 & 1600
   series): *54* 50–60
   (Colored vinyl.)
CHESS (1500 & 1600
   series, except 1523):
   52–56 8–12
   (Black vinyl.)
CHESS (1523; "Cool Kind
   Treatment"): *52* 25–30
HERALD: *52* 60–75

Price Range

J.O.B: *52–58* $25–30
LA SALLE: *61* 3–5
MOJO 3–5
ORIOLE: *58* 12–15
PALOS: *63–64* 3–5
PUSH: *62* 3–5
RCA VICTOR (50-0000
   series): *50* 35–40
EPs: 7-Inch 33/45rpm
ESQUIRE: *60* 12–15
LPs: 10/12-Inch 33rpm
EPIC: *69* 18–20
LONDON: *69* 15–20
   Also see GREEN, Peter

BOYD, Jimmy (Little Jimmy Boyd)
Singles: 7-Inch

CAPITOL: *63* 2–4
COLUMBIA (21571;
   "Rockin' Down The
   Mississippi"): *56* 15–20
COLUMBIA (39000 &
   40000 series): *52–56* 6–10
IMPERIAL: *66–67* 3–5
MGM (12788; "Cream
   Puff"): *59* 25–35
TAKE TEN: *63* 3–5
VEE JAY: *65* 2–4
   Also see LAINE, Frankie, & Jimmy Boyd

BOYD, Jimmy, & Rosemary Clooney
Singles: 7-Inch

COLUMBIA (39000
   series): *53* 5–8
COLUMBIA (41000
   series): *60* 3–5
   Also see BOYD, Jimmy
   Also see CLOONEY, Rosemary

BOYD, Little Eddie: see BOYD,
Eddie

BOYER, Bonnie
Singles: 12-Inch 33/45rpm
COLUMBIA: *79* 4–6
Singles: 7-Inch
COLUMBIA: *79* 1–3
LPs: 10/12-Inch 33rpm
COLUMBIA: *79* 5–8

Price Range

BOYER, Charles
Singles: 7-Inch
VALIANT: 65 . . . . $2–4
LPs: 10/12-Inch 33rpm
VALIANT: 65 10–15

BOYLAN, Terence
Singles: 7-Inch
ASYLUM: 77–80 1–3
LPs: 10/12-Inch 33rpm
ASYLUM: 77–80 5–8
VERVE/FORECAST: 69 12–15

BOYS BAND, The
Singles: 7-Inch
ELEKTRA: 82 1–3
LPs: 10/12-Inch 33rpm
ASYLUM: 82 5–8

BOYS IN THE BAND, The
Singles: 7-Inch
SPRING: 70 2–4

BOZE, Calvin
Singles: 7-Inch
ALADDIN (Except 3055
& 3065): 51–52 15–20
ALADDIN (3055;
"Safronia B."): 50 20–25
ALADDIN (3065; "Lizzie
Lou"): 51 35–40
IMPERIAL: 62 3–5

BRADLEY, James (James Bradley & The Bill Smith Combo)
Singles: 7-Inch
CHESS: 60 4–6
MALACO: 79–84 1–3
MANCO: 61 3–5
LPs: 10/12-Inch 33rpm
MALACO: 84 5–8

BRADLEY, Jan
Singles: 7-Inch
CHESS: 62–68 3–5
ERIC: 73 1–3
FORMAL: 62 10–15
HOOTENANNY: 63 3–5
NIGHT OWL: 63 3–5
SOUND SPECTRUM 3–5

Price Range

BRADLEY, Owen (The Owen Bradley Quintet)
Singles: 7-Inch
CORAL: 50 . . . . $3–5
DECCA: 54–61 2–4
EPs: 7-Inch 33/45rpm
CORAL: 54 8–12
DECCA: 58 6–12
LPs: 10/12-Inch 33rpm
CORAL: 53–55 15–20
DECCA: 58–60 15–25

BRADSHAW, Terry
Singles: 7-Inch
BENSON: 80 1–3
MERCURY: 76 2–4
Picture Sleeves
BENSON: 80 . . . . INC
LPs: 10/12-Inch 33rpm
BENSON: 80 5–8
HEARTWARMING: 82 5–8
MERCURY: 76 6–12

BRADSHAW, Tiny
Singles: 7-Inch
GUSTO: 80–83 1–3
KING (4300 through 4500
series): 50–53 10–15
(Black vinyl.)
KING (4300 through 4500
series): 50–53 25–30
(Colored vinyl.)
KING (4600 through 4800
series): 54–55 5–8
EPs: 7-Inch 33/45rpm
KING: 50–57 15–25
LPs: 10/12-Inch 33rpm
KING: 55–57 20–30

BRAINSTORM
Singles: 12-Inch 33/45rpm
TABU: 77–79 4–6
Singles: 7-Inch
RCA VICTOR: 82 1–3
TABU: 76–79 1–3
LPs: 10/12-Inch 33rpm
RCA VICTOR: 82 5–8
TABU: 77–79 5–8

Price Range

BRAM TCHAIKOVSKY: see TCHAIKOVSKY, Bram

BRAMLETT, Bonnie
Singles: 7-Inch
CAPRICORN: 75–78 . . . . $2–3
COLUMBIA: 72–73 2–4
REFUGE: 81 1–3
LPs: 10/12-Inch 33rpm
CAPRICORN: 75–78 8–10
COLUMBIA: 72–73 10–12
Also see DELANEY & BONNIE

BRAMLETT, Delaney (Delaney & Bekka Bramlett; Delaney Bramlett & Blue Diamond)
Singles: 7-Inch
CREAM: 81 1–3
GNP/CRESCENDO:
64–66 3–5
INDEPENDENCE: 67 3–5
LPs: 10/12-Inch 33rpm
COLUMBIA: 72–73 8–10
MGM: 75 8–10
PRODIGAL: 77 8–10
Also see DELANEY & BONNIE

BRAND X
Singles: 7-Inch
PASSPORT: 78 1–3
LPs: 10/12-Inch 33rpm
PASSPORT: 76–84 5–8
Members: Phil Collins; John Goodsall; Percy Jones; Robin Lumley; Morris Pert.
Also see COLLINS, Phil

BRANDON, Bill
Singles: 7-Inch
MOONSONG: 72–73 2–4
PIEDMONT: 76 2–3
PRELUDE: 77–78 1–3
SOUTH CAMP: 67 3–5
TOWER: 68 2–4

BRANIGAN, Laura
Singles: 12-Inch 33/45rpm
ATLANTIC: 82–85 4–6
Singles: 7-Inch
ATLANTIC: 80–85 1–3
EMI AMERICA: 84 1–3

Price Range

LPs: 10/12-Inch 33rpm
ATLANTIC: 82–85 . . . . $5–8
EMI AMERICA: 84 5–8

BRASS CONSTRUCTION
Singles: 12-Inch 33/45rpm
CAPITOL: 83 4–6
LIBERTY: 82 4–6
Singles: 7-Inch
CAPITOL: 83 1–3
LIBERTY: 82 1–3
UNITED ARTISTS: 75–80 1–3
LPs: 10/12-Inch 33rpm
CAPITOL: 83 5–8
UNITED ARTISTS: 75–80 5–10
LIBERTY: 82 5–8

BRASS FEVER
Singles: 7-Inch
IMPULSE: 76–77 2–3
LPs: 10/12-Inch 33rpm
IMPULSE: 76 8–10

BRASS RING (Featuring Phil Bodner)
Singles: 7-Inch
ABC: 70 1–3
DUNHILL: 66–69 2–4
ITCO: 69 1–3
LPs: 10/12-Inch 33rpm
DUNHILL: 66–73 8–12
ITCO: 70 6–10
PROJECT 3: 72 6–10

BRAUN, Bob
Singles: 7-Inch
AUDIO FIDELITY: 65 2–4
DECCA: 62 2–4
FRATERNITY: 64–66 2–4
KING: 59 2–4
UNITED ARTISTS: 67 2–3
Picture Sleeves
DECCA: 62 2–4
EPs: 7-Inch 33/45rpm
DECCA: 63 4–6
LPs: 10/12-Inch 33rpm
AUDIO FIDELITY: 65 6–10
UNITED ARTISTS: 67 6–10
WRAYCO: 71 5–8

Price Range

BRAVE BELT
Singles: 7-Inch
REPRISE: *71–72*................. **$2–4**
LPs: 10/12-Inch 33rpm
REPRISE: *71–75*................. **15–18**
Members: Chad Allan; Randy Bachman; Robert Bachman; C.F. Turner.
Also see BACHMAN-TURNER-BACHMAN

BRAVOS, Los: see LOS BRAVOS

BRAZOS VALLEY BOYS, The
LPs: 10/12-Inch 33rpm
WARNER BROS: *67*............. **10–15**
Also see THOMPSON, Hank

BREAD
Singles: 7-Inch
ELEKTRA (Except
45668): *70–77*.................. **2–4**
ELEKTRA (45668; "Could
I"): *69*........................ **3–5**
Picture Sleeves
ELEKTRA: *70–72* **2–4**
LPs: 10/12-Inch 33rpm
ELEKTRA: *69–84* **8–12**
Members: David Gates & Bread; David Gates; James Griffin; Mike Botts; Larry Knechtel; Robb Royer.
Also see GATES, David

BREAK MACHINE
Singles: 12-Inch 33/45rpm
SIRE: *84* **4–6**
Singles: 7-Inch
SIRE: *84* **1–3**

BREAKWATER
Singles: 7-Inch
ARISTA: *79–80*.................. **1–3**
LPs: 10/12-Inch 33rpm
ARISTA: *79–80*.................. **5–8**

BREATHLESS
Singles: 7-Inch
EMI AMERICA: *79*.............. **1–3**
LPs: 10/12-Inch 33rpm
EMI AMERICA: *79–80*............ **5–8**

BRECKER BROTHERS, The
Singles: 7-Inch
ARISTA: *75–80*.................. **1–3**

Price Range

LPs: 10/12-Inch 33rpm
ARISTA: *75–81*.................. **$5–8**
Members: Mike Brecker; Randy Brecker; Dave Sanborn.
Also see DREAMS

BREMERS, Beverly
Singles: 7-Inch
COLUMBIA: *75–77*............... **2–3**
ERIC: *83* **1–3**
SCEPTER: *71–75* **2–4**
Picture Sleeves
SCEPTER: *72*.................... **2–4**
LPs: 10/12-Inch 33rpm
SCEPTER: *72* **8–10**

BRENDA & HERB
Singles: 7-Inch
H&L: *78*........................ **2–3**
Members: Brenda Reid; Herb Rooney.
Also see EXCITERS, The

BRENDA & THE TABULATIONS
Singles: 12-Inch 33/45rpm
CHOCOLATE CITY: *77*........... **4–6**
Singles: 7-Inch
CHOCOLATE CITY:
76–77 .... **2–3**
DIONN: *67–69* **3–5**
EPIC: *72–75* **2–4**
TOP & BOTTOM: *69–71*........... **2–4**
LPs: 10/12-Inch 33rpm
CHOCOLATE CITY: *77*........... **5–8**
DIONN: *67*..................... **20–25**
TOP & BOTTOM: *70*............. **12–15**

BRENDA LEE: see LEE, Brenda

BRENNAN, Walter
Singles: 7-Inch
DOT: *60*........................ **2–4**
KAPP: *71* **1–3**
LIBERTY: *62–64* **2–4**
RPC: *61*........................ **2–4**
Picture Sleeves
DOT: *60*........................ **2–4**
LIBERTY: *62–63* **2–4**
LPs: 10/12-Inch 33rpm
DOT: *60*....................... **10–15**
EVEREST: *60*................... **10–15**
HAMILTON: *65*.................. **8–10**

Price Range

LIBERTY: *62* **$10–15**
LONDON: *70* **6–10**
RPC: *62* **10–15**
SUNSET: *66* **8–10**
UNITED ARTISTS: *75* **5–8**

BRENSTEN, Jackie
Singles: 7-Inch
CHESS: *51–52* **35–40**
FEDERAL: *56–57* **8–12**
SUE: *61* **3–5**

BREWER, Teresa (Teresa Brewer & The Lancers)
Singles: 7-Inch
ABC: *67* **2–3**
AMSTERDAM: *72–73* **2–3**
CORAL (60000 & 61000
 series): *52–58* **4–6**
CORAL (62000 & 65000
 series): *58–64* **3–5**
DOCTOR JAZZ: *83* **1–3**
FLYING DUTCHMAN:
 72 .... **1–3**
LONDON: *50–52* **4–6**
PHILIPS: *63–67* **2–4**
PROJECT 3: *82.* **1–3**
SSS INT'L: *68* **2–3**
SIGNATURE: *74–83* **1–3**
Picture Sleeves
CORAL: *58–60* **4–6**
SIGNATURE: *80* .... **INC**
EPs: 7-Inch 33/45rpm
CORAL: *55–60* **8–12**
LONDON: *52* **12–15**
LPs: 10/12-Inch 33rpm
AMSTERDAM: *73–74* **6–10**
COLUMBIA: *81* **5–8**
CORAL (7; "Best Of
 Teresa Brewer"): *65* **12–15**
CORAL (56072 through
 57297): *56–59.* **15–20**
CORAL (57315 through
 57351): *60–65.* **10–15**
DOCTOR JAZZ: *79–83* **5–8**
FLYING DUTCHMAN:
 73–74 .... **6–10**
IMAGE: *78* **5–8**
LONDON: *52* **20–30**
MCA: *83* **5–8**

Price Range

PHILIPS: *63–67* **$8–12**
PROJECT 3: *82.* **5–8**
SIGNATURE: *74–75* **5–8**
VOCALION: *69* **8–10**
WING: *66* **8–10**

BREWER, Teresa, & Count Basie
LPs: 10/12-Inch 33rpm
DOCTOR JAZZ: *84* **5–8**
 Also see BASIE, Count

BREWER, Teresa, & Duke Ellington
LPs: 10/12-Inch 33rpm
COLUMBIA: *81* **5–8**
FLYING DUTCHMAN:
 74 .... **6–10**
 Also see BREWER, Teresa
 Also see ELLINGTON, Duke

BREWER & SHIPLEY
Singles: 7-Inch
A&M: *68–69* **3–5**
BUDDAH: *70* **2–4**
CAPITOL: *74–75* **2–3**
KAMA SUTRA: *70–73* **2–4**
Picture Sleeves
KAMA SUTRA: *72* **2–4**
LPs: 10/12-Inch 33rpm
A&M: *68* **12–15**
ACCORD: *83* **5–8**
CAPITOL: *75* **8–10**
KAMA SUTRA: *70–76* **10–12**
 Members: Mike Brewer; Tom Shipley.

BRIAN & BRENDA
Singles: 7-Inch
ROCKET: *76–78.* **1–3**
 Members: Brian Russell; Brenda Russell.

BRICK
Singles: 12-Inch 33/45rpm
BANG: *79–82* **4–6**
Singles: 7-Inch
BANG: *76–82* **1–3**
MAINSTREET: *76.* **2–3**
STREET: *76* **2–3**
LPs: 10/12-Inch 33rpm
BANG: *76–82* **5–8**
 Members: Jimmy Brown; Regi Harris; Eddie
 Irons; Ray Ransom; Don Nevins.

Price Range

BRIDES OF FUNKENSTEIN, The
Singles: 7-Inch
ATLANTIC: 78–80 . . . . $1–3
LPs: 10/12-Inch 33rpm
ATLANTIC: 78–80 5–8
Members: Lynn Mabry; Dawn Silva.
Also see PARLIAMENT

BRIDGES, Alicia
Singles: 12-Inch 33/45rpm
SECOND WAVE: 84 4–6
POLYDOR: 78–79 4–6
Singles: 7-Inch
A.V.I.: 82 1–3
MEGA: 72 2–3
POLYDOR: 78–79 1–3
SECOND WAVE: 84 1–3
ZODIAC: 73 2–4
LPs: 10/12-Inch 33rpm
POLYDOR: 78–79 5–8

BRIDGEWATER, Dee Dee
Singles: 12-Inch 33/45rpm
ELEKTRA: 79–80 4–6
Singles: 7-Inch
ELEKTRA: 78–79 1–3
LPs: 10/12-Inch 33rpm
ATLANTIC: 76 8–10
ELEKTRA: 78–80 5–8

BRIEF ENCOUNTER
Singles: 7-Inch
CAPITOL: 76–77 1–3
SEVENTY SEVEN: 72–73 2–4

BRIGGS, Lillian
Singles: 7-Inch
ABC-PARAMOUNT: 61 3–5
CORAL: 59–60 3–5
EPIC: 56 4–6

BRIGHT, Larry
Singles: 7-Inch
BRIGHT: 65 3–5
DEL-FI: 63 3–5
DOT: 66 3–5
EDIT: 62 3–5
HIGHLAND: 61 4–6
ORIGINAL SOUND 2–3
RENDEZVOUS: 60 3–5
TIDE: 60–67 4–6

Price Range

BRIGHTER SIDE OF DARKNESS
Singles: 7-Inch
20TH CENTURY-FOX:
72–75 . . . . $2–4
LPs: 10/12-Inch 33rpm
20TH CENTURY-FOX:
73 8–10

BRILEY, Martin
Singles: 7-Inch
EMI AMERICA: 84 1–3
MERCURY: 81–84 1–3
LPs: 10/12-Inch 33rpm
MERCURY: 81–85 5–8

BRILL, Marty, & Larry Foster
LPs: 10/12-Inch 33rpm
COLPIX: 65 10–15
LAURIE: 62 15–20

BRIMMER, Charles
Singles: 7-Inch
CHELSEA: 75–76 2–3
LPs: 10/12-Inch 33rpm
CHELSEA: 76–77 8–10

BRINKLEY, Charles
Singles: 7-Inch
MUSIC MACHINE: 75 2–3

BRINKLEY & PARKER
Singles: 7-Inch
DARNEL: 74 2–4

BRISCOE, Jimmy, & The Little Beavers
Singles: 7-Inch
ATLANTIC: 71 2–4
J-CITY: 72 2–4
PI KAPPA: 73–75 2–4
SALSOUL: 79 1–3
WANDERICK: 77 2–3
LPs: 10/12-Inch 33rpm
PI KAPPA: 74 10–12
WANDERICK: 77 8–10

BRISTOL, Johnny
Singles: 7-Inch
ATLANTIC: 76–78 2–3
HANDSHAKE: 80–81 1–3

Price Range

MGM: 74–75 .... $2–4
LPs: 10/12-Inch 33rpm
ATLANTIC: 76–78 5–8
HANDSHAKE: 81 5–8
MGM: 74–75 8–10
Also see STEWART, Amii, & Johnny Bristol

BRISTOL, Johnny, & Alton McClain
Singles: 7-Inch
POLYDOR: 80 1–3
Also see ALTON & JOHNNY
Also see McCLAIN, Alton, & Destiny

BRISTOL, Johnny, & Spyder Turner
Singles: 7-Inch
POLYDOR: 83 1–3
Also see BRISTOL, Johnny
Also see TURNER, Spyder

BRITISH LIONS, The
Singles: 7-Inch
RSO: 78 2–3
LPs: 10/12-Inch 33rpm
RSO: 78 5–8
Members: John Fiddler; Dale Griffin; Overend
Watts; Ray Major; Morgan Fisher.
Also see MOTT THE HOOPLE

BRITT, Tina
Singles: 7-Inch
EASTERN: 65 3–5
MINIT: 69 2–4
VEEP: 68–69 2–4
LPs: 10/12-Inch 33rpm
MINIT: 69 12–15

BROADWAY
Singles: 7-Inch
GRANITE: 76 2–3
HILLTAK: 78 1–3
LPs: 10/12-Inch 33rpm
HILLTAK: 79 8–10

BROMBERG, David
Singles: 7-Inch
COLUMBIA: 72–73 2–4
FANTASY: 77–79 2–3
LPs: 10/12-Inch 33rpm
ATLANTIC: 80 5–8
COLUMBIA: 72–77 8–10
FANTASY: 76–80 8–12
Also see HARRISON, George

Price Range

Also see LOGGINS & MESSINA / David
Bromberg
Also see SAHM, Doug

BRONNER BROTHERS, The
Singles: 7-Inch
NEIGHBOR: 84 .... $1–3

BRONSKI BEAT (With Steve Bronski)
Singles: 12-Inch 33/45rpm
MCA: 84–85 4–6
Singles: 7-Inch
MCA: 84–85 1–3
LPs: 10/12-Inch 33rpm
MCA: 85 5–8

BROOD, Herman (Herman Brood & Wild Romance)
Singles: 7-Inch
ARIOLA AMERICA: 79 1–3
LPs: 10/12-Inch 33rpm
ARIOLA AMERICA:
79–80 8–10
TOWNHOUSE: 82 5–8

BROOKLYN BRIDGE, The
Singles: 7-Inch
BUDDAH: 68–72 3–5
ERIC: 78 1–3
LPs: 10/12-Inch 33rpm
BUDDAH: 69–72 20–25
COLLECTABLES 5–8
Members: Johnny Maestro; Fred Ferrara; Les
Cauchi; Mike Gregorio; Tom Sullivan; Carolyn
Wood; Jimmy Rosica; Richie Macioce; Artie
Cantanzarita; Shelly Davis; Joe Ruvio.
Also see ESPOSITO, Joe "Bean"
Also see MAESTRO, Johnny

BROOKLYN DREAMS
Singles: 12-Inch 33/45rpm
CASABLANCA: 79 4–6
MILLENNIUM: 78 4–6
Singles: 7-Inch
CASABLANCA: 79–80 1–3
MILLENNIUM: 77–78 2–3
LPs: 10/12-Inch 33rpm
CASABLANCA: 79–80 5–8
MILLENNIUM: 77 8–10
Members: Joe Esposito; Eddie Hokenson;
Bruce Sudano.
Also see SUMMER, Donna

Price Range

BROOKS, Donnie
Singles: 7-Inch
CHALLENGE: *66* $3–5
COLLECTABLES: *81* 1–3
DJ: *65*. 3–5
ERA: *59–68*. 3–5
HAPPY TIGER: *70–71* 2–4
REPRISE: *64*. 3–5
YARDBIRD: *68*. 2–4
Picture Sleeves
ERA: *60–61*. 4–6
LPs: 10/12-Inch 33rpm
ERA: *61*. 25–30

BROOKS, Louis (Louis Brooks & His Hi-Toppers)
Singles: 7-Inch
EXCELLO (2000 series):
  52–53 10–15
EXCELLO (2100 series):
  57–59 4–6

BROOKS, Mel: see REINER, Carl, & Mel Brooks

BROOKS, Nancy
Singles: 7-Inch
ARISTA: *79* 1–3

BROOKS, Ramona
Singles: 7-Inch
MANHATTAN: *77* 2–3
UNITED ARTISTS: *77*. 2–3
LPs: 10/12-Inch 33rpm
MANHATTAN: *78* 8–10

BROOM, Bobby
Singles: 7-Inch
ARISTA: *81–84*. 1–3
GRP: *81*. 1–3
LPs: 10/12-Inch 33rpm
GRP: *81*. 5–8

BROTHER TO BROTHER
Singles: 7-Inch
TURBO: *74–77*. 2–3
LPs: 10/12-Inch 33rpm
SUGAR HILL: *81* 5–8

Price Range

TURBO: *74–77* $10–12

BROTHERHOOD
Singles: 7-Inch
COLUMBIA: *70*. 2–4
DIAL: *69*. 2–5
MCA: *78* 2–3
RCA VICTOR: *69* 2–3
Picture Sleeves
RCA VICTOR: *69* 2–3
LPs: 10/12-Inch 33rpm
MCA: *78* 5–8
RCA VICTOR: *69* 12–15
  Members: Drake Levin; Michael Smith; Phil
  Volk; Ron Collins.
  Also see REVERE, Paul, & The Raiders
  Also see WOMACK, Bobby

BROTHERHOOD OF MAN, The
Singles: 7-Inch
BELL: *74*. 2–3
DERAM: *70–72* 2–4
PRIVATE STOCK: *77*. 2–3
PYE: *75–76*. 2–3
LPs: 10/12-Inch 33rpm
DERAM: *70* 10–12
PYE: *76*. 8–10

BROTHERLY LOVE
Singles: 7-Inch
MUSIC MERCHANT: *72*. 2–4

BROTHERS BY CHOICE
Singles: 7-Inch
ALA: *78–80*. 1–3
FRETONE: *75*. 2–3

BROTHERS FOUR, The
Singles: 7-Inch
COLUMBIA: *59–69*. 2–4
FANTASY: *70*. 1–3
Picture Sleeves
COLUMBIA: *60–63* 2–4
LPs: 10/12-Inch 33rpm
COLUMBIA: *59–69* 10–20
FANTASY: *70*. 8–12
FIRST AMERICAN: *81* 5–8
HARMONY: *69–72* 6–10
  Members: Bob Flick; Dick Foley; John Paine;
  Mike Kirkland.

Price Range

BROTHERS GUIDING LIGHT, The
Singles: 7-Inch
MERCURY: 73.................. $2–4

BROTHERS JOHNSON, The
Singles: 12-Inch 33/45rpm
A&M (Black vinyl): 78–85........... 4–6
A&M (Colored vinyl):
78–85 5–8
Singles: 7-Inch
A&M: 76–85 1–3
Picture Sleeves
A&M: 76–85 .... INC
LPs: 10/12-Inch 33rpm
A&M: 76–85 5–8
(With an "SP" prefix.)
A&M: 79 15–25
(With a "PR" prefix. Picture discs.)
Members: Louis Johnson; George Johnson.
Also see JONES, Quincy

BROTHERS OF SOUL, The
Singles: 7-Inch
BOO: 68–70...................... 2–4

BROWN, Al, & His Tunetoppers (Al Brown's Tunetoppers)
Singles: 7-Inch
AMY: 60–61 3–6
LPs: 10/12-Inch 33rpm
AMY: 60 45–50

BROWN, Alex
Singles: 12-Inch 33/45rpm
MERCURY: 85................... 4–6
Singles: 7-Inch
MERCURY: 85................... 1–3
ROXBURY: 76................... 2–3

BROWN, Arthur (The Crazy World Of Arthur Brown; Arthur Brown's Kingdom Come)
Singles: 7-Inch
ATLANTIC: 68 2–4
TRACK: 68–69.................. 2–4
LPs: 10/12-Inch 33rpm
ATLANTIC: 68 12–15
GULL: 75 8–10
PASSPORT: 74.................. 10–12
Also see ATOMIC ROOSTER

Price Range

BROWN, Boots (Boots Brown & His Blockbusters; Boots Brown & The Pelugelpipers; Boots Brown & Dan Drew)
Singles: 7-Inch
DOT: 68........................ $2–4
RCA VICTOR: 53–60 4–8
EPs: 7-Inch 33/45rpm
RCA VICTOR: 58 15–20
LPs: 10/12-Inch 33rpm
GROOVE...................... 50–60
RCA VICTOR: 58 25–30

BROWN, Buster
Singles: 7-Inch
ABC: 73........................ 1–3
CHECKER: 63 4–6
FIRE: 59–62 4–6
GWENN: 62 3–5
RCA VICTOR: 74 2–4
ROULETTE: 72 1–3
SEROCK: 63.................... 3–5
LPs: 10/12-Inch 33rpm
FIRE: 60 60–70
SOUFFLE: 73 10–12

BROWN, Charles (Charles Brown With Johnny Moore's Three Blazers)
Singles: 7-Inch
ACE: 59........................ 4–6
ALADDIN (3076; "Black
Night"): 51.................... 25–30
ALADDIN (3091 through
3138): 51–52.................. 12–15
ALADDIN (3157; "Rollin'
Like A Pebble In The
Sand"): 52 20–25
ALADDIN (3163 "Hard
Times"): 52................... 12–15
ALADDIN (3176 through
3191): 53 20–25
ALADDIN (3200 & 3300
series): 53–58................. 5–8
CASH: 57...................... 6–10
EAST-WEST: 58................. 5–8
HOLLYWOOD: 54.............. 10–15
IMPERIAL: 62–63............... 3–5
JEWEL: 71–74.................. 2–4
KING: 60–64................... 3–5
LIBERTY: 84 1–3

Price Range

LILLY: *62* **$3–5**
MAINSTREAM: *65* **3–5**
NOLA: *63* **3–5**
STARDAY: *69* **2–4**
SWING TIME: *52* **35–45**
    LPs: 10/12-Inch 33rpm
ALADDIN (Except 700
  series): *56* **75–90**
ALADDIN (700 series): *54* **100–125**
  (10-Inch LPs. Black vinyl.)
ALADDIN (700 series): *54* **200–250**
  (10-Inch LPs. Colored vinyl.)
BIG TOWN: *77–78* **8–10**
BLUESWAY: *70* **8–10**
IMPERIAL: *61* **35–40**
JEWEL: *72* **8–10**
KING (700 & 800 series):
  61–63 . . . . **20–25**
KING (5000 series). **5–8**
MAINSTREAM (300
  series): *72* **8–10**
MAINSTREAM
  (6000/56000 series): *65* **10–12**
SCORE: *57* **50–60**
  Also see MOORE, Johnny

BROWN, Charles, & Jimmy
McCracklin
    LPs: 10/12-Inch 33rpm
IMPERIAL: *64* **15–20**
  Also see MC CRACKLIN, Jimmy

BROWN, Charles, & Amos Milburn
    Singles: 7-Inch
ACE: *59* **4–6**
KING: *61* **3–5**
    LPs: 10/12-Inch 33rpm
GRAND PRIX **10–12**
  Also see BROWN, Charles
  Also see MILBURN, Amos

BROWN, Chuck
    Singles: 7-Inch
EXCELLO: *62* **3–5**

BROWN, Chuck, & The Soul
Searchers
    Singles: 12-Inch 33/45rpm
SOURCE: *78–79* **4–6**
    Singles: 7-Inch
D.E.T.T: *84* **1–3**

Price Range

SOUL SEARCHERS: *84* **$1–3**
SOURCE: *78–80* **1–3**
    LPs: 10/12-Inch 33rpm
SOURCE: *79* **5–8**

BROWN, Clyde
    Singles: 7-Inch
ATLANTIC: *73–74* **2–4**

BROWN, Danny Joe, & The Danny
Joe Brown Band
    Singles: 7-Inch
EPIC: *81* **1–3**
    LPs: 10/12-Inch 33rpm
EPIC: *81* **5–8**
  Also see MOLLY HATCHET

BROWN, Dee, & Lola Grant
    Singles: 7-Inch
SURFINE: *66* **3–5**

BROWN, Dennis
    Singles: 12-Inch 33/45rpm
A&M: *82* **4–6**
    Singles: 7-Inch
A&M: *81–82* **1–3**
    LPs: 10/12-Inch 33rpm
A&M: *81–82* **5–8**

BROWN, Don
    Singles: 7-Inch
FIRST AMERICAN:
  77–78 . . . . **1–3**

BROWN, James (James Brown &
His Famous Flames; James Brown &
The J.B.s)
    Singles: 12-Inch 33/45rpm
CHURCHILL: *83* **4–6**
POLYDOR: *78* **4–6**
    Singles: 7-Inch
AUGUSTA: *83* **1–3**
BACKSTREET: *83* **1–3**
BETHLEHEM: *70* **2–4**
CHURCHILL: *83* **1–3**
FEDERAL (Except stereo
  singles): *56–60* **4–6**
FEDERAL (Stereo singles):
  59 . . . . **8–10**
KING (5000 series): *60–65* **3–5**

Price Range

KING (6000 series): *65–71* $2–4
PEOPLE: *71–76* 2–4
POLYDOR: *71–84* 1–3
SCOTTI BROTHERS: *86* 1–3
SMASH: *64–66* 3–5
T.K: *80–81* 1–3
Picture Sleeves
KING (5000 series): *60–65* 3–5
KING (6000 series): *65–71* 2–4
POLYDOR: *71–84* 1–3
SCOTTI BROTHERS: *86* .... INC
SMASH: *64* 3–5
EPs: 7-Inch 33/45rpm
KING: *59–63* 15–20
SMASH: *65–66* 12–15
(Jukebox issues only.)
LPs: 10/12-Inch 33rpm
CHURCHILL: *83* 5–8
HRB: *73* 8–10
KING (600 series): *59–60* 30–35
KING (700 & 800 series):
61–64 25–30
KING (900 series): *65–66* 15–20
KING (1000 & 1100 series;
except 1038): *67–71* 10–15
KING (1038; "Thinking
About Little Willie
John"): *68* 30–35
POLYDOR: *71–84* 5–8
SMASH: *64–68* 12–15
SOLID SMOKE: *80–81* 5–8
T.K: *80* 5–8
Also see AFRIKA BAMBAATAA & JAMES
BROWN
Also see BROWN, James, Band
Also see BYRD, Bobby, & James Brown
Also see J.B.s, The

BROWN, James, & Vicki Anderson
Singles: 7-Inch
KING: *67–70* 2–4
Also see ANDERSON, Vicki
Also see BROWN, James

BROWN, James, Band
Singles: 7-Inch
KING: *61* 3–5
Also see WESLEY, Fred, & The Horny Horns

BROWN, James, & Lyn Collins
Singles: 7-Inch
POLYDOR: *72* 2–4

Price Range

Also see COLLINS, Lyn

BROWN, James, & Marva Whitney
Singles: 7-Inch
KING: *69* $2–4
Also see WHITNEY, Marva

**BROWN, Jim Edward (Jim Edward
Brown & Helen Cornelius)**
Singles: 7-Inch
RCA VICTOR (Except
8000 & 9000 series):
69–81 1–3
RCA VICTOR (8000 &
9000 series): *65–68* 2–4
LPs: 10/12-Inch 33rpm
RCA VICTOR (Except
3000 & 4000 series):
73–81 5–10
RCA VICTOR (3000 &
4000 series): *66–72* 8–12
(With an "LPM" or "LSP" prefix.)
Also see BROWNS, The

BROWN, Jocelyn
Singles: 12-Inch 33/45rpm
VINYL DREAMS: *84* 4–6

BROWN, Julie
Singles: 7-Inch
RHINO: *84* 1–3
LPs: 10/12-Inch 33rpm
RHINO: *85* 5–8

**BROWN, Les, & His Band Of
Renown**
Singles: 7-Inch
CAPITOL: *56–59* 2–4
COLUMBIA: *50–60* 2–5
CORAL: *59* 2–3
SIGNATURE: *60* 2–3
EPs: 7-Inch 33/45rpm
CAPITOL: *56–58* 4–8
COLUMBIA: *54–56* 5–10
CORAL: *53–56* 5–10
LPs: 10/12-Inch 33rpm
CAPITOL: *56–59* 5–15
COLUMBIA: *50–61* 5–15
CORAL: *59–60* 5–12
HARMONY: *59* 4–8
KAPP: *59* 4–8

Price Range

MEDALLION: *61* **$4–8**

BROWN, Louise
Singles: 7-Inch
WITCH: *61* **3–5**

BROWN, Maxine
Singles: 7-Inch
ABC: *75* **1–3**
ABC-PARAMOUNT:
61–62 .... **3–5**
AVCO EMBASSY: *71* **2–4**
COLLECTABLES: *81* **1–3**
COMMONWEALTH
UNITED: *69–70* **2–4**
ERIC: *83* **1–3**
NORMAR: *61* **3–5**
WAND: *63–66* **3–5**
WHAM **3–5**
Picture Sleeves
WAND: *63* **3–5**
WHAM **5–8**
LPs: 10/12-Inch 33rpm
COMMONWEALTH
UNITED: *69* **10–12**
GUEST STAR **10–12**
WAND: *63–67* **15–20**
Also see JACKSON, Chuck, & Maxine Brown

BROWN, Maxine / Irma Thomas
LPs: 10/12-Inch 33rpm
GRAND PRIX: *64* **12–15**
Also see BROWN, Maxine
Also see THOMAS, Irma

BROWN, Miquel
Singles: 12-Inch 33/45rpm
TSR: *83* **4–6**
Singles: 7-Inch
POLYDOR: *79* **1–3**
TSR: *83* **1–3**
LPs: 10/12-Inch 33rpm
POLYDOR: *78* **5–8**
TSR: *85* **5–8**

BROWN, Nappy (Nappy Brown &
The Gibralters; Nappy Brown & The
Southern Sisters)
Singles: 7-Inch
SAVOY (1100 series): *55* **4–6**

Price Range

SAVOY (1500 series):
57–60 .... **$4–6**
SAVOY (1600 series):
61–63 .... **3–5**
LPs: 10/12-Inch 33rpm
SAVOY (14000 series):
58–60 .... **35–40**
SAVOY (14400 series): *77* **8–10**

BROWN, Odell (Odell Brown & The
Organ-izers)
Singles: 7-Inch
CADET: *67–68* **2–4**
LPs: 10/12-Inch 33rpm
CADET: *67–69* **12–15**
PAULA: *74* **8–10**

BROWN, Oscar, Jr.
Singles: 7-Inch
ATLANTIC: *74* **2–3**
COLUMBIA: *60–62* **3–5**
FONTANA: *65–66* **3–5**
MAD: *59* **5–8**
LPs: 10/12-Inch 33rpm
ATLANTIC **5–8**
COLUMBIA: *61–63* **15–20**
FONTANA: *66* **10–12**

BROWN, Peter
Singles: 12-Inch 33/45rpm
COLUMBIA: *84* **4–6**
RCA VICTOR: *83* **4–6**
Singles: 7-Inch
COLUMBIA: *84* **1–3**
DRIVE: *77–80* **2–3**
RCA VICTOR: *83* **1–3**
LPs: 10/12-Inch 33rpm
COLUMBIA: *84* **5–8**
DRIVE: *78* **5–8**
RCA VICTOR: *82–83* **5–8**

BROWN, Peter, & Betty Wright
Singles: 7-Inch
DRIVE: *78* **2–3**
Also see BROWN, Peter
Also see WRIGHT, Betty

BROWN, Polly
Singles: 7-Inch
ARIOLA AMERICA:
75–76 .... **2–3**

Price Range

BEL: *73* **$2–4**
GTO: *74* **2–4**
Also see PICKETTYWITCH

BROWN, Randy (Randy Brown & Company)
Singles: 12-Inch 33/45rpm
MILLENNIUM: *78* **4–6**
Singles: 7-Inch
CHOCOLATE CITY:
80–81 . . . . **1–3**
IX CHAINS: *75* **2–3**
PARACHUTE: *78–79* **1–3**
STAX: *80* **1–3**
TRUTH: *74–75* **2–4**
LPs: 10/12-Inch 33rpm
CHOCOLATE CITY:
80–81 . . . . **5–8**
PARACHUTE: *78–79* **5–8**
STAX: *80–81* **5–8**

BROWN, Ray, & The Whispers
Singles: 7-Inch
GNP/CRESCENDO: *65* **3–5**

BROWN, Roy
Singles: 7-Inch
BLUESWAY: *67* **3–5**
DELUXE (3319; "Bar
Room Blues"): *51* **50–60**
(Black vinyl.)
DELUXE (3319; "Bar
Room Blues"): *51* **90–100**
(Colored vinyl.)
DELUXE (3323; "I've Got
The Last Laugh Now"):
51 . . . . **30–35**
(Black vinyl.)
DELUXE (3323; "I've Got
The Last Laugh Now" -
colored vinyl): *51* **55–60**
(Colored vinyl.)
GUSTO: *83* **1–3**
HOME OF THE BLUES:
60–61 . . . . **3–5**
IMPERIAL: *57* **8–10**
KING (4000 series): *52–56* **15–20**
KING (5247 through
5333): *59–60* **4–6**
MERCURY: *71* **2–3**

Price Range

EPs: 7-Inch 33/45rpm
KING **$35–40**
LPs: 10/12-Inch 33rpm
BLUESWAY: *68–73* **10–12**
EPIC: *71* **10–12**
INTERMEDIA: *84* **5–8**
KING (900 series): *66* **30–35**
KING (1100 series): *71* **10–12**
KING (5000 series): *79* **8–10**
Also see HARRIS, Wynonie / Roy Brown

BROWN, Ruth (Ruth Brown & The Rhythmakers)
Singles: 7-Inch
ATLANTIC (919;
"Teardrops From My
Eyes"): *50* **200–250**
ATLANTIC (948; "Shine
On"): *51* **15–20**
ATLANTIC (962 through
993): *52–53* **10–15**
ATLANTIC (1005 through
1091): *53–56* **6–10**
ATLANTIC (1100 series):
57–58 . . . . **4–6**
ATLANTIC (2000 series):
59–60 . . . . **3–5**
DECCA: *64* **3–5**
NOSLEN: *64* **3–5**
PHILIPS: *62* **3–5**
SYKE: *69* **2–4**
EPs: 7-Inch 33/45rpm
ATLANTIC: *54–57* **20–25**
PHILIPS: *62* **12–15**
LPs: 10/12-Inch 33rpm
ATLANTIC (1308; "Last
Date With Ruth
Brown"): *59* **25–30**
ATLANTIC (8004; "Ruth
Brown"): *57* **45–50**
(Black label.)
ATLANTIC (8004; "Ruth
Brown"): *57* **20–25**
(Red label.)
ATLANTIC (8026; "Miss
Rhythm"): *59* **30–35**
(Black label.)
ATLANTIC (8026; "Miss
Rhythm"): *59* **15–20**
(Red label.)

Price Range

ATLANTIC (8080; "Best
  Of Ruth Brown"): *63* **$15–20**
COBBLESTONE: *72* **8–10**
DOBRE: *78* **5–8**
MAINSTREAM (300
  series): *72* **8–10**
MAINSTREAM (6000
  series): *65* **12–15**
PHILIPS: *62* **12–15**
SKYE: *70*. **10–12**

BROWN, Savoy: see SAVOY BROWN

BROWN, Sawyer: see SAWYER BROWN

BROWN, Sharon
Singles: 12-Inch 33/45rpm
PROFILE: *83* **4–6**
Singles: 7-Inch
PROFILE: *82–83* **1–3**

BROWN, Shawn
Singles: 12-Inch 33/45rpm
JWP: *85* **4–6**

BROWN, Sheree
Singles: 12-Inch 33/45rpm
CAPITOL: *81* **4–6**
Singles: 7-Inch
CAPITOL: *81–82* **1–3**
LPs: 10/12-Inch 33rpm
CAPITOL: *81–82* **5–8**

BROWN, Shirley
Singles: 12-Inch 33/45rpm
MERCURY: *83*. **4–6**
Singles: 7-Inch
ABET: *71* **2–4**
ARISTA: *77–78*. **2–3**
SOUND TOWN: *84* **1–3**
STAX: *79*. **1–3**
TRUTH: *74–76* **2–3**
20TH CENTURY-FOX:
  80 . . . . **1–3**
LPs: 10/12-Inch 33rpm
ARISTA: *77* **5–8**
COLUMBIA: *68–72* **10–12**
SOUND TRACK: *85* **5–8**

Price Range

STAX: *77–79*. **$5–8**
TRUTH: *75* **8–10**

BROWN, Veda
Singles: 7-Inch
RAKEN: *75* **2–3**
STAX: *73–74*. **2–4**

BROWN, Wini (Wini Brown & The Boyfriends)
Singles: 7-Inch
JARO: *60*. **5–8**
MERCURY: *52*. **40–50**
  Members: Wini Brown; Joe Van Loan; Percy
  Green; Fred Francis; Warren Suttles.
LPs: 10/12-Inch 33rpm
JARO: *60*. **20–25**

BROWN SUGAR (With Clydie King)
Singles: 7-Inch
ABKCO: *72*. **2–4**
CAPITOL: *76* **1–3**
CHELSEA: *73–74*. **2–3**

BROWNE, Duncan
Singles: 7-Inch
IMMEDIATE: *69*. **2–4**
RAK: *72* **2–4**
SIRE: *79* **1–3**
LPs: 10/12-Inch 33rpm
IMMEDIATE: *68*. **10–12**
SIRE: *79* **5–8**

BROWNE, Jackson
Singles: 12-Inch 33/45rpm
ASYLUM: *81–82*. **4–6**
Singles: 7-Inch
ASYLUM: *72–84*. **1–3**
ELEKTRA: *80* **1–3**
Picture Sleeves
ASYLUM: *82–84*. **2–3**
ELEKTRA: *80* **1–3**
LPs: 10/12-Inch 33rpm
ASYLUM (Except 5051):
  72–84 . . . . **6–10**
ASYLUM (5051; "Jackson
  Browne"): *72* **10–15**
  (With burlap cover.)
ASYLUM (5051; "Jackson
  Browne"): *72* **6–10**
  (With standard cover.)

Price Range

ELEKTRA ("Jackson
Browne's First Album"):
67 .... **$20–30**
(Promotional issue only.)
Also see CLEMONS, Clarence
Also see LINDLEY, David

BROWNE, Tom
Singles: 12-Inch 33/45rpm
ARISTA: 83 .... **4–6**
Singles: 7-Inch
ARISTA: 83–84.................... **1–3**
GRP: 79–82....................... **1–3**
LPs: 10/12-Inch 33rpm
ARISTA: 83–84.................... **5–8**
GRP: 79–82....................... **5–8**

BROWNS, The
Singles: 7-Inch
COLUMBIA: 62 .... **2–4**
FABOR: 54–55 .... **4–6**
RCA VICTOR: 56–61 .... **3–5**
EPs: 7-Inch 33/45rpm
RCA VICTOR: 57–60 .... **5–10**
LPs: 10/12-Inch 33rpm
CAMDEN: 65–68 .... **8–12**
RCA VICTOR (1000
through 3000 series):
75–81 .... **5–8**
(With an "ANL1" or "AYL1" prefix.)
RCA VICTOR (1400
series): 57..................... **30–40**
(With an "LPM" prefix.)
RCA VICTOR (2000
series): 59–65 .... **15–25**
(With an "LPM" or "LSP" prefix.)
RCA VICTOR (3000
series): 65–67 .... **12–15**
(With an "LPM" or "LSP" prefix.)
Members: Jim Edward Brown; Maxine Brown;
Bonnie Brown.
Also see BROWN, Jim Edward
Also see COOKE, Sam / Rod Lauren / Neil
Sedaka / The Browns

BROWNSVILLE STATION
Singles: 7-Inch
BIG TREE: 72–75 .... **2–4**
HIDEOUT: 69..................... **3–5**
PALLADIUM: 70.................. **2–4**
POLYDOR: 70 .... **2–4**
PRIVATE STOCK: 77.............. **2–3**

Price Range

WARNER BROS: 71.............. **$2–4**
LPs: 10/12-Inch 33rpm
BIG TREE: 72–74 .... **10–12**
PALLADIUM: 70................ **12–15**
PRIVATE STOCK: 77............. **8–10**
WARNER BROS: 70............. **12–15**
Members: Tony Driggins; Cub Koda; Michael
Lutz; Henry Weck.

BRUBECK, Dave, Quartet
Singles: 7-Inch
COLUMBIA (Except
40000 & 41000 series):
61 .... **1–3**
COLUMBIA (40700
through 41300 series):
56–59 .... **3–5**
COLUMBIA (41400
through 41900 series):
50–61 .... **2–4**
FANTASY (500 series):
52–55 .... **4–6**
FANTASY (4000 series):
56 .... **4–6**
Picture Sleeves
COLUMBIA: 61–63 .... **2–4**
EPs: 7-Inch 33/45rpm
COLUMBIA: 55–59.............. **10–15**
FANTASY: 51–57............... **10–20**
LPs: 10/12-Inch 33rpm
COLUMBIA (600 through
900 series): 54–57 .... **35–45**
COLUMBIA (1000
through 1200 series):
57–59 .... **15–25**
COLUMBIA (1300
through 2300 series):
59–65 .... **10–20**
COLUMBIA (6000 series):
54 .... **35–45**
COLUMBIA (8000 series):
57–59 .... **20–30**
COLUMBIA (8100
through 9100 series):
59–65 .... **10–20**
CROWN: 62–64 .... **10–15**
FANTASY (1 through 16):
51–54 .... **40–50**
(10-Inch LPs.)
FANTASY (200 series):
56–57 .... **20–30**

(Numbers in the 200 series may be preceded by a "3.")
FANTASY (3300 series) **$15–25**
Also see ARMSTRONG, Louis, & Dave Brubeck
Also see TJADER, Cal

BRUBECK, Dave, & Paul Desmond
LPs: 10/12-Inch 33rpm
HORIZON: 75................... **6–10**
Also see DESMOND, Paul

BRUBECK, Dave, & Gerry Mulligan
Singles: 7-Inch
COLUMBIA: 68.................. **2–3**
LPs: 10/12-Inch 33rpm
COLUMBIA: 68–73.............. **8–15**
VERVE: 73.................... **8–12**
Also see BRUBECK, Dave
Also see MULLIGAN, Gerry

BRUCE, Jack (The Jack Bruce Band; Jack Bruce & Friends)
Singles: 7-Inch
RSO: 75....................... **2–3**
LPs: 10/12-Inch 33rpm
ATCO: 69–71................... **10–12**
EPIC: 80 .... **5–8**
POLYDOR: 72.................. **8–10**
RSO: 77 .... **5–8**
Also see CREAM
Also see MAYALL, John
Also see WEST, BRUCE & LAING

BRUCE, Jack, & Robin Trower
LPs: 10/12-Inch 33rpm
CHRYSALIS: 82................. **5–8**
Also see BRUCE, Jack
Also see TROWER, Robin

BRUCE, Lenny
LPs: 10/12-Inch 33rpm
CAPITOL (2630; "Why Did Lenny Bruce Die"):
66 .... **15–20**
DOUGLAS: 68–71 .... **12–18**
FANTASY (1; "Lenny Bruce")..................... **30–40**
FANTASY (7001; "Lenny Bruce's Interviews Of Our Times"): 59 .... **25–30**
(Pressed on THICK red vinyl.)

FANTASY (7001; "Lenny Bruce's Interviews Of Our Times")................. **$12–18**
(Pressed on black vinyl.)
FANTASY (7001; "Lenny Bruce's Interviews Of Our Times").................. **6–10**
(Pressed on THIN red vinyl.)
FANTASY (7003; "The Sick Humor Of Lenny Bruce"): 59................... **25–30**
(Pressed on THICK red vinyl.)
FANTASY (7003; "The Sick Humor Of Lenny Bruce")..................... **12–18**
(Pressed on black vinyl.)
FANTASY (7003; "The Sick Humor Of Lenny Bruce")..................... **6–10**
(Pressed on THIN red vinyl.)
FANTASY (7007; "I Am Not A Nut, Elect Me"):
60 .... **25–30**
(Pressed on THICK red vinyl.)
FANTASY (7007; "I Am Not A Nut, Elect Me") **12–18**
(Pressed on black vinyl.)
FANTASY (7007; "I Am Not A Nut, Elect Me") **6–10**
(Pressed on THIN red vinyl.)
FANTASY (7011; "Lenny Bruce - American"): 62 .... **25–30**
(Pressed on THICK red vinyl.)
FANTASY (7011; "Lenny Bruce - American")............. **12–18**
(Pressed on black vinyl.)
FANTASY (7011; "Lenny Bruce - American")............. **6–10**
(Pressed on THIN red vinyl.)
FANTASY (7012; "The Best Of Lenny Bruce"):
63 .... **25–30**
(Pressed on THICK red vinyl.)
FANTASY (7012; "The Best Of Lenny Bruce").......... **12–18**
(Pressed on black vinyl.)
FANTASY (7012; "The Best Of Lenny Bruce")........... **6–10**
(Pressed on THIN red vinyl.)
FANTASY (7017; "Thank You Masked Man"): 72 .... **10–15**

Price Range

FANTASY (34201; "Lenny
   Bruce Live At The
   Curran Theatre"): *72* **$10–15**
FANTASY (79003; "The
   Real Lenny Bruce"): *75* **6–10**
LENNY BRUCE
   RECORDS ("Recordings
   Submitted As Evidence
   In The San Francisco
   Obscenity Trial In
   March, 1962"): *62* **50-75**
PHILLES (4010; "Lenny
   Bruce Is Out Again"): *66* **30–40**
REPRISE (6329; "The
   Berkeley Concert"): *69* **10–12**
UNITED ARTISTS (3580;
   "Midnight Concert"): *67* **12–18**
UNITED ARTISTS (9800;
   "Lenny Bruce At
   Carnegie Hall"): *71* **12–18**
WARNER BROS. (9101;
   "The Law, Language &
   Lenny Bruce") **10–15**
   (Promotional issue only.)

BRUCE & TERRY
Singles: 7-Inch
COLUMBIA: *64–66* **3–5**
   Members: Bruce Johnston; Terry Melcher.
   Also see CALIFORNIA MUSIC
   Also see NEWTON, Wayne
   Also see RIP CHORDS, The
   Also see SAGITTARIUS

BRUNSON, Tyrone "Tystick"
Singles: 12-Inch 33/45rpm
BELIEVE IN A DREAM:
   82–84 .... **4–6**

Singles: 7-Inch
BELIEVE IN A DREAM:
   82–84 .... **1–3**

LPs: 10/12-Inch 33rpm
BELIEVE IN A DREAM:
   82–84 .... **5–8**

BRYAN, Billy (Gene Pitney)
Singles: 7-Inch
BLAZE: *59* **10–15**
   Also see PITNEY, Gene

Price Range

BRYANT, Anita
Singles: 7-Inch
CARLTON: *58–61* **$2–4**
COLUMBIA: *61–67* **2–3**
DISNEYLAND **2–3**

Picture Sleeves
COLUMBIA: *61–67* **2–3**
DISNEYLAND **2–3**

LPs: 10/12-Inch 33rpm
CARLTON: *59–61* **10–15**
COLUMBIA: *62–64* **8–12**

BRYANT, Lillie
Singles: 7-Inch
CAMEO: *58* **3–5**
SWAN: *59* **3–5**
   Also see BILLY & LILLIE

BRYANT, Ray, Combo
Singles: 7-Inch
COLUMBIA: *60–64* **2–4**

Picture Sleeves
COLUMBIA: *60* **2–4**

LPs: 10/12-Inch 33rpm
COLUMBIA: *60–62* **15–20**
EPIC: *56* **30–40**
PRESTIGE/NEW JAZZ:
   62 .... **15–20**
SIGNATURE: *60* **15–20**
SUE: *63–64* **10–15**

BRYSON, Peabo
Singles: 7-Inch
BULLET: *76–77* **2–3**
CAPITOL: *77–82* **1–3**
ELEKTRA: *84–85* **1–3**
MCA: *84* **1–3**
SHOUT: *75* **2–4**

Picture Sleeves
CAPITOL: *81* .... **INC**

LPs: 10/12-Inch 33rpm
BULLET: *76* **8–10**
CAPITOL: *78–84* **5–8**
ELEKTRA: *84–85* **5–8**
   Also see MANCHESTER, Melissa, & Peabo
   Bryson
   Also see ZAGER, Michael, Moon Band, &
   Peabo Bryson

BRYSON, Peabo, & Natalie Cole
Singles: 7-Inch
CAPITOL: 79 .... $1–3
LPs: 10/12-Inch 33rpm
CAPITOL: 79 5–8
Also see COLE, Natalie

BRYSON, Peabo, & Roberta Flack
Singles: 7-Inch
ATLANTIC: 80 1–3
CAPITOL: 83 1–3
LPs: 10/12-Inch 33rpm
ATLANTIC: 80 5–8
CAPITOL: 83 5–8
Also see BRYSON, Peabo
Also see FLACK, Roberta

BUBBLE PUPPY, The
Singles: 7-Inch
INTERNATIONAL
  ARTISTS: 69–70............... 8–10
LPs: 10/12-Inch 33rpm
INTERNATIONAL
  ARTISTS: 69................. 50–60
Members: Red Prince; Todd Potter; Rory Cox;
M. Taylor; Dave Fore.

BUCHANAN, Bill
Singles: 7-Inch
GONE: 58 10–15
UNITED ARTISTS: 62 4–6
Also see BUCHANAN & ANCELL
Also see BUCHANAN & CELLA
Also see BUCHANAN & GOODMAN
Also see BUCHANAN & GREENFIELD

BUCHANAN, Roy
Singles: 7-Inch
ATLANTIC: 76–78 2–3
BOMARC: 61 5–8
POLYDOR: 72–75 2–4
LPs: 10/12-Inch 33rpm
ALLIGATOR: 85................. 5–8
ATLANTIC: 76–77 5–8
BIOYA: 71 15–20
POLYDOR: 72–75 8–10
WATERHOUSE: 81............... 5–8

BUCHANAN & ANCELL
Singles: 7-Inch
FLYING SAUCER: 57 10–12
Members: Bill Buchanan; Bob Ancell.

BUCHANAN & CELLA
Singles: 7-Inch
ABC-PARAMOUNT: 59.......... $8–10
Member: Bill Buchanan.

BUCHANAN & GOODMAN
Singles: 7-Inch
COMIC: 59 8–10
LUNIVERSE (Except
  101X): 56–58................. 10–15
LUNIVERSE (101X;
  "Back To Earth"): 56........... 50–60
NOVELTY: 59 8–10
RADIOACTIVE................. 12–15
Members: Bill Buchanan; Dickie Goodman.
Also see GOODMAN, Dickie

BUCHANAN & GREENFIELD
Singles: 7-Inch
NOVEL (Red label): 64 8–10
NOVEL (Red & white
  label): 72..................... 2–4
Members: Bill Buchanan; Howard Greenfield.
Also see BUCHANAN, Bill

BUCHANAN BROTHERS, The
Singles: 7-Inch
EVENT: 69–71 2–4
LPs: 10/12-Inch 33rpm
EVENT: 69 15–18
Members: Terry Cashman; Gene Pistilli;
Tommy West.
Also see CASHMAN & WEST

BUCK
Singles: 7-Inch
PLAYBOY: 75 2–3

BUCKEYE
Singles: 7-Inch
POLYDOR: 79 1–3
LPs: 10/12-Inch 33rpm
POLYDOR: 79 5–8

BUCKINGHAM, Lindsey
Singles: 7-Inch
ASYLUM: 81.................... 1–3
ELEKTRA: 84 1–3
WARNER BROS: 83.............. 1–3
Picture Sleeves
ASYLUM: 81..................... INC

Price Range

LPs: 10/12-Inch 33rpm
ASYLUM: 81 .... **$5–8**
ELEKTRA: 84 .... **5–8**
Also see BUCKINGHAM NICKS
Also see EGAN, Walter
Also see FLEETWOOD MAC
Also see STEWART, John

BUCKINGHAM NICKS
Singles: 7-Inch
POLYDOR: 76–79 .... **1–3**
LPs: 10/12-Inch 33rpm
POLYDOR: 73 .... **8–10**
Members: Lindsey Buckingham; Stevie Nicks.
Also see BUCKINGHAM, Lindsey
Also see FLEETWOOD MAC
Also see NICKS, Stevie

BUCKINGHAMS, The
Singles: 7-Inch
COLUMBIA: 67–70 .... **3–5**
RED LABEL: 85 .... **1–3**
SPECTRA-SOUND: 67 .... **10–12**
U.S.A: 66–67 .... **5–8**
Picture Sleeves
COLUMBIA: 67–68 .... **5–8**
LPs: 10/12-Inch 33rpm
COLUMBIA: 67–75 .... **15–20**
RED LABEL: 85 .... **5–8**
U.S.A. (107; "Kind Of A
  Drag"): 67 .... **30–35**
  (With 13 tracks.)
U.S.A. (107; "Kind Of A
  Drag"): 67 .... **15–20**
  (With 12 tracks.)
Members: Dennis Tufano; Carl Giammerese;
Nick Fortune; Marty Grebb; Dennis Miccoli;
Jon-Jon Poulos.
Also see CENTURIES, The
Also see FALLING PEBBLES, The
Also see TUFANO & GIAMMERESE

BUCKLEY, Tim
Singles: 7-Inch
DISC REET: 73–74 .... **2–4**
ELEKTRA: 66–67 .... **3–5**
LPs: 10/12-Inch 33rpm
DISC REET: 73–74 .... **8–10**
ELEKTRA: 66–70 .... **12–15**
RHINO: 83 .... **5–8**
STRAIGHT: 66–69 .... **15–18**
WARNER BROS: 70–72 .... **10–12**

Price Range

BUCKNER & GARCIA
Singles: 12-Inch 33/45rpm
COLUMBIA: 82 .... **$4–6**
Singles: 7-Inch
BGO: 81 .... **3–5**
COLUMBIA: 82 .... **1–3**
LPs: 10/12-Inch 33rpm
COLUMBIA: 82 .... **5–8**
Members: Jerry Buckner; Gary Garcia.
Also see WILLIS "THE GUARD" & VIGOR-ISH

BUCKWHEAT
Singles: 7-Inch
LONDON: 71–73 .... **2–4**
LPs: 10/12-Inch 33rpm
LONDON: 71–73 .... **10–12**

BUD & TRAVIS
Singles: 7-Inch
LIBERTY: 59–64 .... **2–4**
LPs: 10/12-Inch 33rpm
LIBERTY: 59–64 .... **10–15**
LONDON: 71–72 .... **6–10**
SUNSET: 67 .... **8–12**
Members: Bud Dashiel; Travis Edmonson.

BUENA VISTAS, The
Singles: 7-Inch
MARQUEE: 68 .... **3–5**
SWAN: 66 .... **3–5**

BUFFALO REBELS, The
Singles: 7-Inch
MAR-LEE: 60–61 .... **5–8**
Also see REBELS
Also see ROCKIN' REBELS, The

BUFFALO SPRINGFIELD, The
Singles: 7-Inch
ATCO: 67–68 .... **4–6**
LPs: 10/12-Inch 33rpm
ATCO (105;
  "Retrospective"): 75 .... **5–8**
ATCO (200; "Buffalo
  Springfield"): 66 .... **35–40**
  (With the track "Baby Don't Scold Me.")
ATCO (200; "Buffalo
  Springfield"): 67 .... **15–20**
  (With "Baby Don't Scold Me" replaced by
  "For What It's Worth.")

Price Range

ATCO (226 through 283):
  67–69 .... **$15–25**
ATCO (806; "Buffalo
  Springfield"): 73. .... **15–20**
  Members: Stephen Stills; Neil Young; Jim Messina; Richie Furay; Jim Fielder; Doug Hastings; Dewey Martin.
  Also see FURAY, Richie
  Also see MESSINA, Jim
  Also see POCO
  Also see STILLS, Stephen
  Also see YOUNG, Neil

BUFFETT, Jimmy
Singles: 7-Inch
ABC: 75–78 .... **2–3**
ASYLUM: 80. .... **1–3**
BARNABY: 70–72 .... **2–4**
DUNHILL: 73–75. .... **2–4**
FULL MOON: 80. .... **1–3**
MCA: 79–84 .... **1–3**
LPs: 10/12-Inch 33rpm
ABC: 76–78 .... **8–10**
BARNABY: 70–77 .... **10–12**
DUNHILL: 73–74. .... **10–12**
MCA: 79–84 .... **5–8**
UNITED ARTISTS: 75 .... **8–10**

BUFFETT, Mary
Singles: 12-Inch 33/45rpm
MOBY DICK: 84 .... **4–6**
Singles: 7-Inch
MOBY DICK: 84 .... **1–3**

BUGGLES, The
Singles: 7-Inch
CARRERE: 82 .... **1–3**
ISLAND: 79–83 .... **1–3**
LPs: 10/12-Inch 33rpm
CARRERE: 82 .... **5–8**
ISLAND: 80 .... **5–8**
  Members: Trevor Horn; Geoff Downes.
  Also see YES

BULAWAYO SWEET RHYTHM BOYS, The
Singles: 7-Inch
LONDON: 54 .... **2–4**

BULL & THE MATADORS
Singles: 7-Inch
TODDLIN' TOWN: 68–69 .... **2–4**

Price Range

BULLDOG
Singles: 7-Inch
BUDDAH: 72–74 .... **$2–4**
DECCA: 72 .... **2–4**
GUYDEN: 71 .... **2–4**
MCA: 73 .... **2–3**
LPs: 10/12-Inch 33rpm
BUDDAH: 74 .... **8–10**
DECCA: 72 .... **12–15**
  Members: Gene Cornish; Dino Danelli; Billy Hocher; Eric Thorngren; John Turi.
  Also see FOTOMAKER
  Also see RASCALS, The

BULLENS, Cindy
Singles: 7-Inch
CASABLANCA: 79–80 .... **1–3**
UNITED ARTISTS: 78–79 .... **2–3**
LPs: 10/12-Inch 33rpm
CASABLANCA: 79 .... **5–8**
UNITED ARTISTS: 78 .... **5–8**

BUMBLE, B: see B. BUMBLE & THE STINGERS

BUMBLE BEE UNLIMITED
Singles: 7-Inch
MERCURY: 76–77 .... **2–3**
LPs: 10/12-Inch 33rpm
RCA VICTOR: 79 .... **5–8**

BUNN, Allen (Alden Bunn)
Singles: 7-Inch
APOLLO: 52 .... **60–75**
  Also see TARHEEL SLIM

BUONO, Victor
Singles: 7-Inch
DORE: 71 .... **2–4**
FAMILY: 71 .... **2–4**
LPs: 10/12-Inch 33rpm
DORE: 71 .... **5–8**

BUOYS, The
Singles: 7-Inch
POLYDOR: 73 .... **2–4**
SCEPTER: 69–71 .... **2–4**
Picture Sleeves
SCEPTER: 71 .... **2–4**
LPs: 10/12-Inch 33rpm
SCEPTER: 71 .... **8–10**

Price Range

BURCH, Ray
LPs: 10/12-Inch 33rpm
YELLOWSTONE: 72 . . . . $8–10

BURCH, Vernon
Singles: 12-Inch 33/45rpm
CHOCOLATE CITY:
79–80 4–6
SPECTOR: 81 4–6
Singles: 7-Inch
CHOCOLATE CITY:
78–80 1–3
COLUMBIA: 77–78 1–3
SPECTOR: 81–84 1–3
UNITED ARTISTS: 75 2–3
LPs: 10/12-Inch 33rpm
CHOCOLATE CITY:
79–80 5–8
COLUMBIA: 77–78 8–10
SPECTOR: 81–84 5–8
UNITED ARTISTS: 74–76 8–10

BURDON, Eric (The Eric Burdon Band)
Singles: 7-Inch
CAPITOL: 74 2–4
LPs: 10/12-Inch 33rpm
CAPITOL: 74–75 8–10
LAX: 81–84 5–8
VERVE: 72 10–12
Also see ANIMALS, The

BURDON, Eric, & War
Singles: 7-Inch
ABC: 77 1–3
CAPITOL: 74–75 2–4
MGM: 70 2–4
Picture Sleeves
MGM: 70 2–4
LPs: 10/12-Inch 33rpm
ABC: 77 8–10
MGM (Except 4710): 70 10–12
MGM (4710; "Black Man's
Burdon"): 70 20–25
(Promotional issue only.)
Also see WAR

BURDON, Eric, & Jimmy Witherspoon
Singles: 7-Inch
MGM: 71 2–4

Price Range

LPs: 10/12-Inch 33rpm
MGM: 71 . . . . $10–12
Also see BURDON, Eric
Also see WITHERSPOON, Jimmy

BURGESS, Richard James
Singles: 12-Inch 33/45rpm
CAPITOL: 84 4–6
Singles: 7-Inch
CAPITOL: 84 1–3
LPs: 10/12-Inch 33rpm
CAPITOL: 84 5–8

BURKE, Keni
Singles: 7-Inch
DARK HORSE: 77–78 2–3
RCA VICTOR: 81–82 1–3
LPs: 10/12-Inch 33rpm
DARK HORSE: 77 8–10
RCA VICTOR: 81–82 5–8

BURKE, Solomon
Singles: 12-Inch 33/45rpm
SAVOY: 84 4–6
Singles: 7-Inch
ABC/DUNHILL: 74 2–3
AMHERST: 78 2–3
APOLLO: 56–58 8–12
ATLANTIC: 61–68 3–5
BELL: 69–70 2–4
CHESS: 75–77 2–3
DUNHILL: 74 2–4
INFINITY: 79 2–3
MGM: 70–73 2–4
PRIDE: 72–73 2–4
SINGULAR: 60 3–5
LPs: 10/12-Inch 33rpm
ABC/DUNHILL: 74 10–12
APOLLO: 62 50–60
ATLANTIC (8000 series):
62–64 15–20
ATLANTIC (8100 series):
65–68 12–15
BELL: 69 12–15
CHESS: 75–76 8–10
CLARION: 64 12–15
INFINITY: 79 5–8
KENWOOD: 64 12–15
MGM: 71–72 10–12
PRIDE: 73 8–10
ROUNDER: 84 5–8

Price Range

SAVOY: *81–83* **$5–8**
   Also see SOUL CLAN, The

BURNETT, Carol
LPs: 10/12-Inch 33rpm
DECCA: *61–64* **15–20**
COLUMBIA: *71* **8–12**
RCA VICTOR: *67* **10–15**
TETRAGRAMMATON:
   69 .... **8–12**
VOCALION: *68* **8–12**
   Also see ANDREWS, Julie, & Carol Burnett

BURNETT, T-Bone
Singles: 7-Inch
WARNER BROS: *83* **1–3**
LPs: 10/12-Inch 33rpm
TAKOMA: *80* **5–8**
WARNER BROS: *82–83* **5–8**

BURNETTE, Billy (Billy Burnette & Jawbone)
Singles: 7-Inch
A&M: *76* **2–3**
COLUMBIA: *80–81* **1–3**
POLYDOR: *79* **1–3**
WARNER BROS: *69* **2–4**
LPs: 10/12-Inch 33rpm
COLUMBIA: *80–81* **5–8**
ENTRANCE: *72* **10–12**
POLYDOR: *79* **5–8**

BURNETTE, Dorsey
Singles: 7-Inch
ABBOTT: *55* **10–15**
CALLIOPE: *77* **2–3**
CAPITOL: *71–74* **2–4**
CEE-JAM: *57* **10–12**
COLLECTABLES: *81* **1–3**
CONDOR: *70* **2–4**
DOT: *61* **4–6**
ELEKTRA: *79–80* **2–3**
ERA: *60–69* **3–5**
HAPPY TIGER: *70* **2–4**
HICKORY: *67* **3–5**
IMPERIAL: *59–63* **10–12**
LIBERTY: *69* **2–4**
MC: *77* **2–3**
MEL-O-DY: *64* **3–5**
MELODYLAND: *75–76* **2–4**
MERRI: *60* **4–6**

Price Range

MUSIC FACTORY: *68* **$2–4**
REPRISE: *62–63* **3–5**
SMASH: *66* **3–5**
U.S. NAVY ("Be A Navy
   Man") **8–10**
   (U.S. Navy recruiting promotional issue.)

Picture Sleeves
ERA: *61* **8–10**
REPRISE: *63* **4–6**
U.S. NAVY ("Be A Navy
   Man") **15–20**
   (U.S. Navy recruiting promotional issue.)

LPs: 10/12-Inch 33rpm
CALLIOPE: *77* **8–10**
CAPITOL: *72–73* **10–12**
DOT: *63* **15–20**
ERA (100 series): *60* **25–30**
ERA (800 series): *69* **15–18**
GUSTO **5–8**
TRIP: *74* **8–10**
   Also see BURNETTE, Johnny & Dorsey

BURNETTE, Johnny
Singles: 7-Inch
CAPITOL: *63–64* **4–6**
CHANCELLOR: *62* **8–10**
CORAL: *57* **40–50**
FREEDOM: *59* **12–18**
LIBERTY: *60–62* **4–6**
MAGIC LAMP: *64* **4–6**
SAHARA: *64* **4–6**
UNITED ARTISTS: *84* **1–3**
VON: *54* **150–175**

Picture Sleeves
LIBERTY: *60–61* **8–12**

EPs: 7-Inch 33/45rpm
LIBERTY: *60–61* **25–30**

LPs: 10/12-Inch 33rpm
LIBERTY (7100 & 7200
   series): *60–62* **35–40**
LIBERTY (7300 series): *63* **25–30**
LIBERTY (10000 series):
   81 .... **5–8**
SUNSET: *67* **15–18**
UNITED ARTISTS: *75* **8–10**
   Also see BURNETTE, Johnny, & The Rock'n
   Roll Trio

Price Range

Price Range

BURNETTE, Johnny & Dorsey (The Burnette Brothers)
Singles: 7-Inch
CORAL: *60* $20–25
IMPERIAL: *58* 15–18
REPRISE: *63* 4–6
   Also see BURNETTE, Johnny, & The Rock'n
   Roll Trio
   Also see TEXANS, The

BURNETTE, Johnny, & The Rock'n Roll Trio
Singles: 7-Inch
CORAL (61000 series): *56* 30–50
CORAL (62000 series): *60* 20–25
LPs: 10/12-Inch 33rpm
CORAL (57080; "Johnny
  Burnette And The
  Rock'n Roll Trio"): *56* 550–600
MCA: *82* 5–8
SOLID SMOKE (Black
  vinyl): *78–80.* 5–8
SOLID SMOKE (Colored
  vinyl): *78* 8–12
   Members: Johnny Burnette; Dorsey Burnette;
   Paul Burlison.
   Also see BURNETTE, Dorsey
   Also see BURNETTE, Johnny

BURNETTE, Rocky (Rocky Burnette & The Rock 'N Roll Trio)
Singles: 7-Inch
EMI AMERICA: *80.* 1–3
LPs: 10/12-Inch 33rpm
EMI AMERICA: *80–82.* 5–8
GOODS: *82* 5–8
KYD: *83* 5–8

BURNING SENSATIONS
Singles: 7-Inch
CAPITOL: *83* 1–3
LPs: 10/12-Inch 33rpm
CAPITOL: *83* 5–8

BURNS, George
Singles: 7-Inch
MERCURY: *80–81.* 1–3
Picture Sleeves
MERCURY: *80.* 1–3
LPs: 10/12-Inch 33rpm
BUDDAH: *72* 6–10

MERCURY: *80.* $5–8
PRIDE 5–8

BURRAGE, Harold (Harold Barrage)
Singles: 7-Inch
ALADDIN: *50* 20–25
COBRA: *56* 10–15
M-PAC: *62–65.* 3–5
PASO: *61* 3–5
STATES (Black vinyl): *50* 15–20
STATES (Colored vinyl):
  50 35–40
VEE JAY: *60.* 3–5
VIVID: *64* 3–5

BURRELL, Kenny
Singles: 7-Inch
BLUE NOTE: *62* 2–4
LPs: 10/12-Inch 33rpm
ARGO: *60* 15–25
BLUE NOTE: *56–57* 20–40
   (Label gives New York street address for Blue
   Note Records.)
BLUE NOTE: *58–63* 15–25
   (Label reads "Blue Note Records Inc. - New
   York, U.S.A.")
BLUE NOTE: *66* 10–20
   (Label shows Blue Note Records as a division
   of either Liberty or United Artists.)
COLUMBIA: *61* 15–20
KAPP: *62* 12–18
MOODSVILLE: *63.* 15–20
NEW JAZZ: *58.* 20–25
PRESTIGE (Except 7308):
  57–58 20–30
   (Yellow label.)
PRESTIGE (7308; "Blue
  Moods"): *64.* 10–15
   (Yellow label.)
VERVE: *63–65* 12–20

BURRELL, Kenny, & Jack McDuff
LPs: 10/12-Inch 33rpm
PRESTIGE: *64* 10–15
   Also see BURRELL, Kenny
   Also see McDUFF, Brother Jack

BURRITO BROTHERS, The
Singles: 7-Inch
CURB: *81–84.* 1–3
EPIC: *81* 1–3

Price Range

LPs: 10/12-Inch 33rpm
A&M: 80 . . . . $6–10
CURB: 81–82 5–8
Also see FLYING BURRITO BROTHERS,
The

BURROWS, Tony
Singles: 7-Inch
BELL: 70–72 2–4

BURTON, Jenny
Singles: 12-Inch 33/45rpm
ATLANTIC: 83–85 4–6
Singles: 7-Inch
ATLANTIC: 83–85 1–3
LPs: 10/12-Inch 33rpm
ATLANTIC: 83–85 5–8

BURTON, Richard
Singles: 7-Inch
MGM: 65 2–4

BUS BOYS, The
Singles: 7-Inch
ARISTA: 80–84 1–3
LPs: 10/12-Inch 33rpm
ARISTA: 80–82 5–8
Members: Gus Loundermon; Brian O'Neal;
Kevin O'Neal; Michael Jones; Victor Johnson;
Steve Felix.

BUSCH, Lou, Orchestra
Singles: 7-Inch
CAPITOL: 55–56 2–4
Also see CARR, Joe "Fingers"

BUSH, Kate
Singles: 12-Inch 33/45rpm
EMI AMERICA: 85 4–6
Singles: 7-Inch
EMI AMERICA: 78–85 1–3
LPs: 10/12-Inch 33rpm
EMI AMERICA: 78–85 5–8
HARVEST: 78 5–8

BUSHKIN, Joe
EPs: 7-Inch 33/45rpm
CAPITOL: 56 3–6
COLUMBIA: 51 4–8
SAVOY: 55 4–8
LPs: 10/12-Inch 33rpm
CAPITOL: 56–59 5–15

Price Range

COLUMBIA: 51–52 . . . . $8–18
EPIC: 56 5–15
MGM: 50–55 8–18
RONDO: 59 4–8

BUSTERS, The
Singles: 7-Inch
ARLEN: 63–64 5–8

BUTANES, The
Singles: 7-Inch
ENRICA: 61 3–5

BUTCHER, John, Axis
Singles: 7-Inch
POLYDOR: 83 1–3
LPs: 10/12-Inch 33rpm
CAPITOL: 85 5–8
POLYDOR: 83 5–8

BUTLER, Billy (Billy Butler & Infinity; Billy Butler & The Chanters; Billy Butler & The Enchanters)
Singles: 7-Inch
BRUNSWICK: 66–68 3–5
CURTOM: 76 2–3
OKEH: 63–66 3–5
MEMPHIS: 71 2–4
PRIDE: 72–73 2–4
LPs: 10/12-Inch 33rpm
EDSEL: 86 5–8
OKEH: 66 15–18
PRESTIGE: 69–70 10–12
PRIDE: 73 10–12
Also see INFINITY

BUTLER, Carl
Singles: 7-Inch
COLUMBIA: 61–63 2–4
LPs: 10/12-Inch 33rpm
COLUMBIA: 63 12–15
HARMONY: 66–71 8–12

BUTLER, Carl & Pearl
Singles: 7-Inch
COLUMBIA: 63–69 2–4
LPs: 10/12-Inch 33rpm
CMH: 80 5–8
COLUMBIA: 64–70 10–15
HARMONY: 72 8–12

Price Range

PEDACA........................ **$5–8**
   Also see BUTLER, Carl

BUTLER, Champ
   Singles: 7-Inch
COLUMBIA: *50–54*................ **3–5**
CORAL: *55–56*.................. **2–4**
   EPs: 7-Inch 33/45rpm
COLUMBIA: *53*.................. **5–8**

BUTLER, Jerry (Jerry Butler & The Impressions)
   Singles: 7-Inch
ABNER: *58–60*................... **5–8**
COLLECTABLES: *81* **1–3**
ERIC: *73*....................... **1–3**
FALCON: *58*.................... **10–15**
FOUNTAIN: *82*.................. **1–3**
MCA: *83* **1–3**
MERCURY: *67–74*................ **3–5**
MISTLETOE: *75*................. **2–4**
MOTOWN: *76–77*................. **2–3**
PHILADELPHIA INT'L:
   78–81 .... **1–3**
VEE JAY (280; "For Your
   Precious Love"): *58*.......... **125–175**
VEE JAY (300 through
   700 series): *60–66* **3–5**
   Picture Sleeves
VEE JAY: *61–64*................. **3–5**
   LPs: 10/12-Inch 33rpm
ABNER: *59*..................... **50–60**
BUDDAH: *69*.................. **12–15**
EXODUS........................ **5–8**
FOUNTAIN: *82* **5–8**
DYNASTY **12–15**
KENT: *68* **10–12**
LOST-NITE: *81*................. **8–10**
MERCURY: *67–84*.............. **10–12**
MOTOWN: *76–77*................ **5–8**
PHILADELPHIA INT'L:
   78–81 .... **5–8**
POST **5–8**
PRIDE: *72*..................... **8–10**
UPFRONT **8–10**
SCEPTER **8–10**
SUNSET: *68* **10–12**
TRIP: *71–78* **10–12**
UNITED ARTISTS: *75*........... **8–10**
VEE JAY (1000 series):
   60–64 .... **20–25**

Price Range

VEE JAY (1100 series):
   64–65 .... **$15–18**
   Also see AUSTIN, Patti, & Jerry Butler
   Also see CHANDLER, Gene, & Jerry Butler
   Also see IMPRESSIONS, The

BUTLER, Jerry, & Brenda Lee Eager
   Singles: 7-Inch
MERCURY: *71–73*................ **2–4**
   LPs: 10/12-Inch 33rpm
MERCURY: *73*.................. **8–10**
   Also see EAGER, Brenda Lee

BUTLER, Jerry, & Betty Everett
   Singles: 7-Inch
ABC: *73*........................ **1–3**
VEE JAY: *64*.................... **3–5**
   LPs: 10/12-Inch 33rpm
BUDDAH: *69*................... **10–12**
TRADITION: *82* **5–8**
VEE JAY: *64*.................... **15–20**
   Also see DELLS, The
   Also see EVERETT, Betty

BUTLER, Jerry, & Debra Henry
   Singles: 7-Inch
PHILADELPHIA INT'L:
   80 .... **1–3**
   Also see SILK

BUTLER, Jerry, & Stix Hooper
   Singles: 7-Inch
MCA: *83* **1–3**
   Also see HOOPER, Stix

BUTLER, Jerry, & Thelma Houston
   Singles: 7-Inch
MOTOWN: *77*.................... **2–3**
   LPs: 10/12-Inch 33rpm
MOTOWN: *77*.................... **5–8**
   Also see BUTLER, Jerry
   Also see HOUSTON, Thelma

BUTTERFIELD, Paul (The Butterfield Blues Band)
   Singles: 7-Inch
BEARSVILLE: *73–81* **2–4**
ELEKTRA: *67–69*................ **4–6**
   LPs: 10/12-Inch 33rpm
BEARSVILLE: *73–81* **8–10**
ELEKTRA: *65–76* **8–12**

Price Range

RED LIGHTNIN': 72 . . . . **$25–30**
  Also see BISHOP, Elvin

BUTTERFLYS, The
  Singles: 7-Inch
RED BIRD: 64 . . . . **4–6**

BUTTONS, Red
  Singles: 7-Inch
COLUMBIA: 53 . . . . **3–5**

BUZZARD, Dr.: see DR. BUZZARD

BUZZCOCKS, The
  Singles: 7-Inch
I.R.S.: 79–80 . . . . **1–3**
  LPs: 10/12-Inch 33rpm
I.R.S.: 79 . . . . **5–8**
  Members: Pete Shelley; Steve Diggle; Howard
  Devoto; Steve Garvey; John Maher.
  Also see SHELLEY, Pete

BYRD, Bobby (Robert Byrd & His
Birdies; Bobby Day)
  Singles: 7-Inch
CASH: 56. . . . . **25–30**
JAMIE: 57. . . . . **8–10**
SAGE & SAND: 55 . . . . **10–15**
SPARK **15–20**
  Also see BOB & EARL
  Also see DAY, Bobby
  Also see HOLLYWOOD FLAMES, The
  Also see NUNN, Bobby

BYRD, Bobby (Bobby Byrd & The
Byrds)
  Singles: 7-Inch
BROWNSTONE: 71–72. . . . . **2–4**
FEDERAL: 63 . . . . **3–5**
INTERNATIONAL
  BROTHERS: 75 . . . . **2–3**
KING: 67–71. **2–4**
KWANZA: 73. **2–3**
SMASH: 64–65 . . . . **3–5**
  LPs: 10/12-Inch 33rpm
KING: 70 . . . . **10–12**
  Also see KING, Anna, & Bobby Byrd

BYRD, Bobby, & James Brown
  Singles: 7-Inch
KING: 68 . . . . **2–4**
  Also see BROWN, James

Price Range

Also see BYRD, Bobby

BYRD, Charlie
  Singles: 7-Inch
RIVERSIDE: 62–63 . . . . **$2–3**

  LPs: 10/12-Inch 33rpm
OFFBEAT: 59–60. . . . . **20–30**
RIVERSIDE: 62–82 . . . . **15–25**
SAVOY: 58 . . . . **25–35**
  Also see ALMEIDA, Laurindo
  Also see GETZ, Stan, & Charlie Byrd

BYRD, Charlie, & Woody Herman
  LPs: 10/12-Inch 33rpm
EVEREST: 63 . . . . **10–15**
PICKWICK: 66 . . . . **6–12**
  Also see BYRD, Charlie
  Also see HERMAN, Woody

BYRD, Donald (Donald Byrd &
125th Street, N.Y.C.)
  Singles: 7-Inch
BLUE NOTE: 75–77 . . . . **1–3**
ELEKTRA: 78–82 . . . . **1–3**

  LPs: 10/12-Inch 33rpm
BETHLEHEM: 60 . . . . **15–25**
BLUE NOTE: 59–65 . . . . **15–25**
  (Label reads "Blue Note Records Inc. - New
  York, U.S.A.")
BLUE NOTE: 66 . . . . **10–20**
  (Label reads "Blue Note Records - A Division
  Of Liberty Records Inc.")
COLUMBIA: 57–58 . . . . **20–30**
ELEKTRA: 78–82 . . . . **5–8**
JUBILEE: 57. . . . . **20–30**
PRESTIGE: 56 . . . . **40–55**
  (Yellow label.)
REGENT: 57. . . . . **20–30**
SAVOY: 55 . . . . **20–30**
TRANSITION: 56 . . . . **35–50**
VERVE: 58 . . . . **15–20**
  Also see BLACKBYRDS, The

BYRD, Donald, & Stanley Turrentine
  LPs: 10/12-Inch 33rpm
VERVE: 64 . . . . **15–20**
  Also see BYRD, Donald
  Also see TURRENTINE, Stanley

Price Range

BYRD, Gary (Gary Byrd & The G.B. Experience)
Singles: 12-Inch 33/45rpm
WONDIRECTION: *83* $4–6

Singles: 7-Inch
RCA VICTOR: *73* 2–3

BYRD, Jerry
Singles: 7-Inch
MONUMENT: *60–62*............... 2–4

EPs: 7-Inch 33/45rpm
DECCA: *58*..................... 6–10
MERCURY: *53–55*.............. 10–15

LPs: 10/12-Inch 33rpm
DECCA: *58*................... 15–20
LEHUA 8–10
MERCURY (Except 25000
   series): *58–64* 12–18
MERCURY (25000 series):
   53–54 18–25
   (10-Inch LPs.)
MONUMENT: *61–63*............ 10–20
WING: *60–66* 10–15

BYRD, Russell
Singles: 7-Inch
SYMBOL: *62*..................... 3–5
WAND: *61* 3–5

BYRDS, The
Singles: 7-Inch
ASYLUM: *73*.................... 2–4
COLUMBIA: *65–71* 4–8
   (Black vinyl.)
COLUMBIA: *65*................. 25–30
   (Colored vinyl. Promotional issues only.)
SCHOLASTIC: *66* 5–8

Picture Sleeves
COLUMBIA (Except
   43271): *65–71*................. 10–15
COLUMBIA (43271; "Mr.
   Tambourine Man"): *65*......... 60–75
   (Promotional issue only.)

EPs: 7-Inch 33/45rpm
COLUMBIA (10287; "The
   Byrds"): *66*.................. 25–30
   (Columbia Special Products issue for the Scho-
   lastic Book Services.)

Price Range

COLUMBIA (116003/4;
   "Fifth Dimension
   Open-End Interview"):
   66 .... $40–50
   (Promotional issue only.)
LPs: 10/12-Inch 33rpm
ASYLUM: *73*.................... 8–10
COLUMBIA (2000 series):
   65–67 20–25
COLUMBIA (9000 series):
   65–69 15–25
COLUMBIA (30000
   through 33000 series):
   70–75 8–12
COLUMBIA (34000
   through 37000 series):
   75–84 5–8
TOGETHER: *69*................. 15–20
Promotional LPs
BROADCAST ("Byrds
   Live"): *81*.................. 35–40
COLUMBIA (2000 series):
   65–67 40–50
   (White label.)
COLUMBIA (9000 series):
   65–69 35–45
   (White label.)
COLUMBIA (116003/4;
   "Fifth Dimension"
   Interview Album): *66* 60–75
   Members: David Crosby; Gene Clark; Chris
   Hillman; Roger McGuinn; Mike Clark; Skip
   Battin; John Guerin; Kevin Kelley.
   Also see BEEFEATERS, The
   Also see CLARK, Gene
   Also see CROSBY, David
   Also see HILLMAN, Chris
   Also see McGUINN, Roger
   Also see PARSONS, Gram

BYRNE, David
Singles: 12-Inch 33/45rpm
SIRE: *82* 4–6
LPs: 10/12-Inch 33rpm
SIRE: *81* 5–8
   Also see TALKING HEADS, The

BYRNES, Edd "Kookie," With Joanie Sommers & The Mary Kaye Trio
Singles: 7-Inch
WARNER BROS: *59*.............. 3–5

Price Range

Price Range

Picture Sleeves
WARNER BROS: *59* **$5–8**
Also see KAYE, Mary
Also see SOMMERS, Joanie

BYRNES, Edward (Edd "Kookie" Byrnes; Edd Byrnes With Connie Stevens; Edd Byrnes With Friend; Edd Byrnes & The Mary Kaye Trio.)
Singles: 7-Inch
WARNER BROS (Except
stereo singles): *59*. **3–5**
WARNER BROS (Stereo
singles): *59* **8–10**
Picture Sleeves
WARNER BROS: *59* **4–6**
LPs: 10/12-Inch 33rpm
WARNER BROS: *59* **20–25**
Also see BYRNES, Edd "Kookie," With Joanie
Sommers & The Mary Kaye Trio
Also see STEVENS, Connie

BYRON, D.L.
Singles: 7-Inch
ARISTA: *80* **1–3**
LPs: 10/12-Inch 33rpm
ARISTA: *80* **5–8**

C

C., Fantastic Johnny: see FANTASTIC JOHNNY C., The

C & THE SHELLS
Singles: 7-Inch
COTILLION: *69–70*. **2–4**
ZANZEE: *72* **2–4**

C.C. & COMPANY
Singles: 7-Inch
SUSSEX: *75*. **2–3**
20TH CENTURY/
WESTBOUND: *75* **2–3**

C.C.S.
Singles: 7-Inch
BELL: *73* **2–4**
RAK: *71* **2–4**
LPs: 10/12-Inch 33rpm
RAK: *71–72* **8–10**

C.J. & CO.
Singles: 7-Inch
WESTBOUND: *77–78* **$2–3**
LPs: 10/12-Inch 33rpm
WESTBOUND: *77–78* **5–8**

C.L. BLAST: see BLAST, C.L.

C.O.D.s, The
Singles: 7-Inch
ERIC: *74* **2–3**
KELLMAC: *65–66*. **3–5**

C.Q.D.
Singles: 12-Inch 33/45rpm
EMERGENCY: *83*. **4–6**

CABOOSE
Singles: 7-Inch
ENTERPRISE: *70* **2–4**
LPs: 10/12-Inch 33rpm
ENTERPRISE: *71* **10–12**

CACTUS
Singles: 7-Inch
ATCO: *70–72*. **3–5**
LPs: 10/12-Inch 33rpm
ATCO: *70–72*. **20–25**
Members: Carmine Appice; Tim Bogert; Pete
French; Werner Fritzschings; Duane Hitch-
ings; Jerry Norris; Mike Pinera; Roland Robin-
son; Rusty Day; Jim McCarty.
Also see BECK, BOGERT & APPICE
Also see NEW CACTUS BAND, The
Also see PINERA, Mike
Also see YARDBIRDS, The

CADETS, The
Singles: 7-Inch
COLLECTABLES: *81* **1–3**
MODERN (Except 971):
55–57 .... **10–12**
MODERN (971: "If It Is
Wrong"): *55*. **45–50**
SHERWOOD: *60* **3–5**
LPs: 10/12-Inch 33rpm
CROWN (370; "The
Cadets"): *63* **15–18**
CROWN (5015; "Rockin'
'N Reelin' "): *57* **45–55**
RELIC **10–12**

Price Range

Members: Ted Taylor; Aaron Collins; Will Jones; Willie Davis; Lloyd McCraw; Prentice Moreland; Tom Fox; Randolph Jones.
Also see FLARES, The
Also see JACKS, The
Also see TAYLOR, Ted

CADILLAC, Flash: see FLASH
CADILLAC & THE CONTINENTAL KIDS

CADILLACS, The
Singles: 7-Inch
ABC: 73 .... $1–3
CAPITOL: 62 3–5
JOSIE (765; "Gloria"): 54 100–125
JOSIE (769; "Wishing Well"): 54 100–125
JOSIE (773; "No Chance"): 55 30–35
JOSIE (778; "Down The Road"): 55 25–30
JOSIE (785 through 798): 56 10–15
JOSIE (800 series except 820): 56–60.................. 4–8
JOSIE (820; "My Girl Friend"): 57.................. 20–25
JOSIE (900 series): 63............... 3–5
MERCURY: 61.................... 3–5
SMASH: 61 3–5
VIRGO: 72–73................... 1–3
LPs: 10/12-Inch 33rpm
CADAVER 5–8
HARLEM HITPARADE 10–12
JUBILEE (1045; "The Fabulous Cadillacs"): 57........ 80–100
  (Blue label.)
JUBILEE (1045; "The Fabulous Cadillacs"): 59......... 50–75
  (Flat black label.)
JUBILEE (1045; "The Fabulous Cadillacs"): 60......... 25–35
  (Glossy black label.)
JUBILEE (1089; "The Crazy Cadillacs"): 59 60–75
  (Flat black label.)
JUBILEE (1089; "The Crazy Cadillacs"): 60 25–35
  (Glossy black label.)
JUBILEE (5009; "Twistin' With The Cadillacs"): 62 25–30

Price Range

MURRAY HILL (5-LP boxed set)..................... **$30–35**
  Members: Earl "Speedo" Carroll; Jim Clark; Gus Willingham; Bobby Phillips; Laverne Drake; Charles Brooks; James Bailey; Earl Wade.
  Also see ORIGINAL CADILLACS, The
  Also see SCHOOLBOYS, The
  Also see SPEEDO & THE CADILLACS

CADILLACS, The / The Orioles
LPs: 10/12-Inch 33rpm
JUBILEE (1117; "The Cadillacs Meet The Orioles"): 61................... 40–45
  Also see CADILLACS, The
  Also see ORIOLES, The

CAESAR, Shirley (Shirley Caesar & The Caesar Singers)
Singles: 7-Inch
HOB/SCEPTER: 73–75............. 1–3
ROADSHOW: 77–78 1–3
LPs: 10/12-Inch 33rpm
HOB: 70–75...................... 6–10
ROADSHOW: 77.................. 5–8
TRIP: 77 5–8

CAESAR & CLEO
Singles: 7-Inch
REPRISE: 64–65.................. 5–8
VAULT: 63 10–12
Picture Sleeves
REPRISE (0419; "Let The Good Times Roll"): 65.......... 10–15
  Members: Salvatore "Sonny" Bono; Cher La-Piere.
  Also see SONNY & CHER

CAESARS, The
Singles: 7-Inch
LANIE: 67....................... 3–5

CAFFERTY, John (John Cafferty & The Beaver Brown Band)
Singles: 7-Inch
SCOTTI BROTHERS: 83–85 1–3
LPs: 10/12-Inch 33rpm
SCOTTI BROTHERS: 84–85 5–8

CAIN, Joe, & The Red Parrot Orchestra
Singles: 7-Inch
ZOO YORK: *83* **$1–3**

CAIN, Jonathan (The Jonathan Cain Band)
Singles: 7-Inch
BEARSVILLE: *76* **1–3**
OCTOBER: *75–76*. **2–4**
LPs: 10/12-Inch 33rpm
BEARSVILLE: *77* **5–8**
Also see CAIN, Tane
Also see JOURNEY

CAIN, Tane
Singles: 7-Inch
RCA VICTOR: *82–83* **1–3**
LPs: 10/12-Inch 33rpm
RCA VICTOR: *82* **5–8**
Also see CAIN, Jonathan

CAINE, General
Singles: 12-Inch 33/45rpm
CAPITOL: *84* **4–6**
TABU: *82–84*. **4–6**
Singles: 7-Inch
CAPITOL: *84* **1–3**
TABU: *82–84*. **1–3**
LPs: 10/12-Inch 33rpm
TABU: *82–84*. **5–8**

CAIOLA, Al
Singles: 7-Inch
AVLANCHE: *73*. **1–3**
PREFERRED: *59–60*. **2–4**
RCA VICTOR: *53–55* **3–5**
REGENCY: *56* **3–5**
UNITED ARTISTS: *60–68* **2–4**
EPs: 7-Inch 33/45rpm
RCA VICTOR: *53* **5–10**
LPs: 10/12-Inch 33rpm
ATCO: *60* **10–15**
CAMDEN: *62*. **8–12**
CHANCELLOR: *60*. **10–15**
RCA VICTOR: *59* **10–15**
ROULETTE: *60* **10–15**
SAVOY: *56* **15–25**
TIME: *60–61* **10–15**
TWO WORLDS: *72*. **8–10**
UNART: *67*. **8–12**

UNITED ARTISTS: *60–69* **$10–15**

CALDERA
Singles: 7-Inch
CAPITOL: *76* **2–3**
LPs: 10/12-Inch 33rpm
CAPITOL: *76–79* **8–10**

CALDWELL, Bobby
Singles: 12-Inch 33/45rpm
MCA: *84–85* **4–6**
Singles: 7-Inch
CLOUDS: *78–80*. **1–3**
PBR INT'L: *76*. **1–3**
POLYDOR: *82–83* **1–3**
MCA: *84–85* **1–3**
LPs: 10/12-Inch 33rpm
CLOUDS: *78–80*. **5–8**
MCA: *84* **5–8**
POLYDOR: *82* **5–8**
Also see CAPTAIN BEYOND

CALDWELL, Rue
Singles: 12-Inch 33/45rpm
CRITIQUE: *83* **4–6**
Singles: 7-Inch
CRITIQUE: *83* **1–3**

CALE, J.J.
Singles: 7-Inch
LIBERTY: *66* **3–5**
MERCURY: *83–84*. **1–3**
SHELTER: *71–81*. **2–4**
LPs: 10/12-Inch 33rpm
MCA: *81* **5–8**
MERCURY: *82–85*. **5–8**
SHELTER: *71–79*. **8–12**

CALE, John
Singles: 7-Inch
A&M: *81* **1–3**
COLUMBIA: *70*. **2–4**
I.R.S.: *79–80* **1–3**
REPRISE: *72*. **2–4**
Picture Sleeves
I.R.S.: *79–80* **1–3**
LPs: 10/12-Inch 33rpm
A&M: *81* **5–8**
COLUMBIA: *70–71* **12–15**
I.R.S.: *79* **5–8**
ISLAND: *75–77* **8–10**

Price Range

PASSPORT: *84* **$5–8**
REPRISE: *72–73* **10–12**
ZE: *83* **5–8**
   Also see VELVET UNDERGROUND, The

CALEN, Frankie
Singles: 7-Inch
BEAR: *62* **3–5**
EPIC: *63–64* **3–5**
NRC: *59* **3–5**
SPARK: *61* **3–5**
UNITED ARTISTS: *62* **3–5**

CALHOON
Singles: 7-Inch
WARNER/SPECTOR:
  75–76 . . . . **2–3**

CALIFORNIA MUSIC
Singles: 7-Inch
RCA/EQUINOX: *74–76* **8–10**
  Members: Brian Wilson; Bruce Johnston; Terry
  Melcher.
  Also see WILSON, Brian
  Also see BRUCE & TERRY

CALL
Singles: 7-Inch
MERCURY: *83* **1–3**
LPs: 10/12-Inch 33rpm
MERCURY: *82–83* **5–8**

CALLENDER, Bobby
Singles: 7-Inch
CORAL: *67* **3–5**
ROULETTE: *63* **3–5**
LPs: 10/12-Inch 33rpm
MGM: *68* **10–12**

CALLIER, Terry
Singles: 12-Inch 33/45rpm
ERECT: *82* **4–6**
Singles: 7-Inch
CADET: *68–73* **2–4**
ELEKTRA: *78–79* **1–3**
LPs: 10/12-Inch 33rpm
CADET: *72–73* **10–12**
CHESS: *71* **10–12**
ELEKTRA: *78–79* **8–10**

Price Range

CALLOWAY, Cab
Singles: 7-Inch
ABC-PARAMOUNT: *56* **$3–5**
BELL: *54* **4–6**
BOOM: *66* **2–4**
CORAL: *61–62* **2–4**
P.I.P.: *68* **2–3**
RCA VICTOR: *78* **1–3**
LPs: 10/12-Inch 33rpm
COLUMBIA: *74* **8–10**
CORAL: *62* **10–15**
P.I.P.: *68* **10–12**
RCA VICTOR: *60* **10–15**
VOCALION: *68* **8–12**

CALVERT, Eddie
Singles: 7-Inch
ABC-PARAMOUNT:
  60–61 . . . . **2–3**
CAPITOL: *56* **2–4**
ESSEX: *53–54* **2–4**
LPs: 10/12-Inch 33rpm
ABC-PARAMOUNT:
  60–62 . . . . **10–12**

CAMBRIDGE, Godfrey
LPs: 10/12-Inch 33rpm
EPIC: *64–68* **10–15**

CAMBRIDGE STRINGS & SINGERS, The
Singles: 7-Inch
LONDON: *61* **1–3**

CAMEL
Singles: 7-Inch
JANUS: *74–77* **2–4**
LPs: 10/12-Inch 33rpm
ARISTA: *79* **5–8**
JANUS: *74–77* **8–10**
PASSPORT: *81* **5–8**
  Members: Peter Bardens; Doug Ferguson;
  Andy Latimer; Andy Ward.

CAMEO
Singles: 12-Inch 33/45rpm
ATLANTA ARTISTS:
  83–85 . . . . **4–6**
CHOCOLATE CITY:
  78–80 . . . . **4–6**

Price Range

Price Range

Singles: 7-Inch
ATLANTA ARTISTS:
83–85 .... $1–3
CHOCOLATE CITY:
75–82 1–3

LPs: 10/12-Inch 33rpm
ATLANTA ARTISTS:
83–85 .... **5–8**
CHOCOLATE CITY:
77–82 .... **5–8**
  Members: Tomi Jenkins; Larry Blackmon; Nathan Leftenant.
  Also see SINGLETON, Charlie

CAMERON (Rafael Cameron)
Singles: 7-Inch
SALSOUL: 80–82 1–3

LPs: 10/12-Inch 33rpm
SALSOUL: 80–82 .... **5–8**

CAMERON, G.C.
Singles: 7-Inch
MALACO: 83 1–3
MOTOWN: 73–77. 1–3
MOWEST: 71–73 2–4

LPs: 10/12-Inch 33rpm
MOTOWN: 74–77. .... **5–8**

CAMERON, Rafael: see CAMERON

CAMP, Hamilton (Hamid Hamilton Camp & The Skymonters)
Singles: 7-Inch
AMERICAN INT'L: 71 1–3
WARNER BROS: 68 2–4

LPs: 10/12-Inch 33rpm
ELEKTRA (200 series): 64 .... **12–15**
ELEKTRA (75000 series):
73 .... **8–10**
MOUNTAIN RAILROAD. **5–8**
WARNER BROS: 67–69 .... **10–12**

CAMPBELL, Debbie
Singles: 7-Inch
PLAYBOY: 75 2–4

CAMPBELL, Glen (Glen Campbell With The Glen-Aires; Glen Campbell & The Green River Boys)
Singles: 7-Inch
ATLANTIC AMERICA:
82–83 .... $1–3
CAPEHART: 61 .... **8–10**
CAPITOL (2000 & 3000
series): 68–74 1–3
CAPITOL (4000 series):
75–81 1–3
  (Orange or purple labels.)
CAPITOL (4783 through
5360): 61–65. 3–5
  (Orange/yellow swirl labels.)
CAPITOL (5441; "Guess
I'm Dumb"): 65. .... **18–20**
  (With Brian Wilson.)
CAPITOL (5504 through
5939): 65–67. 2–4
CENECO. **6–10**
CREST: 61–62. .... **6–10**
EVEREST: 69 1–3
STARDAY: 68 3–5
WARNER BROS: 80. 1–3

Picture Sleeves
CAPITOL (Except 4856):
68–74 1–3
CAPITOL (4856; "Long
Black Limousine"): 62 3–5

EPs: 7-Inch 33/45rpm
CAPITOL: 68–69 .... **5–10**
  (Jukebox issues only.)
MCA: 84 2–3
MIRAGE: 81. 2–3

LPs: 10/12-Inch 33rpm
ATLANTIC AMERICA:
82–84 .... **5–8**
BUCKBOARD **8–10**
CAPITOL (103 through
733): 68–71. .... **8–12**
CAPITOL (1810; "Big
Bluegrass Special"): 62 .... **60–75**
  (Shown as by The Green River Boys Featuring Glen Campbell.)
CAPITOL (1881 through
2392): 63–65. .... **20–25**
  (With a "T" or "ST" prefix.)
CAPITOL (2809 through
2928): 67–68. .... **8–12**
  (With a "T" or "ST" prefix.)

Price Range

CAPITOL (2000 series): *78* **$5–8**
(With an "SM" prefix.)
CAPITOL (11000 through
16000 series): *72–82* **5–8**
CUSTOM TONE **15–20**
PICKWICK: *68–73* **8–10**
STARDAY: *68–69* **15–20**
    Also see BEACH BOYS, The
    Also see CHAMPS, The
    Also see FOLKSWINGERS, The
    Also see FORD, Tennessee Ernie, & Glen
    Campbell
    Also see SAGITTARIUS
    Also see WILSON, Brian

CAMPBELL, Glen, & Rita Coolidge
Singles: 7-Inch
CAPITOL: *80* **1–3**
    Also see COOLIDGE, Rita

CAMPBELL, Glen, & Bobbie Gentry
Singles: 7-Inch
CAPITOL: *68–70* **2–3**
EPs: 7-Inch 33/45rpm
CAPITOL: *68* **8–10**
(Jukebox issue only.)
LPs: 10/12-Inch 33rpm
CAPITOL: *68* **8–10**
    Also see GENTRY, Bobbie

CAMPBELL, Glen, & Anne Murray
Singles: 7-Inch
CAPITOL: *71–72* **1–3**
LPs: 10/12-Inch 33rpm
CAPITOL: *71–80* **6–10**

Price Range

Also see MURRAY, Anne

CAMPBELL, Glen, & Billy Strange
LPs: 10/12-Inch 33rpm
SURREY: *65* **$12–15**
    Also see STRANGE, Billy

CAMPBELL, Glen, & Tanya Tucker
Singles: 7-Inch
CAPITOL: *81* **1–3**
    Also see CAMPBELL, Glen
    Also see TUCKER, Tanya

CAMPBELL, Jim
Singles: 7-Inch
LAURIE: *69–70* **2–4**

CAMPBELL, Jo Ann
Singles: 7-Inch
ABC-PARAMOUNT
(Except stereo singles):
60–62 .... **4–6**
ABC-PARAMOUNT
(Stereo singles): *60*. **15–20**
CAMEO: *62–63*. **3–5**
ELDORADO: *57* **8–10**
GONE: *59* **5–8**
RORI **4–6**
LPs: 10/12-Inch 33rpm
ABC-PARAMOUNT: *62*. **50–60**
CAMEO: *62* **25–30**
CORONET **25–30**
END: *59*. **40–45**
    Also see JO ANN & TROY

CANDELA
Singles: 12-Inch 33/45rpm
ARISTA: *83* **4–6**
Singles: 7-Inch
ARISTA: *82–83*. **1–3**

CANDY & THE KISSES
Singles: 7-Inch
CAMEO: *64* **4–6**
COLLECTABLES: *81* **1–3**
DECCA: *68*. **3–5**
R&L: *63*. **4–6**
SCEPTER: *65–66* **3–5**

CANDYMEN, The
Singles: 7-Inch
ABC: *67–69*. **3–5**

Price Range

LIBERTY: *70* **$2–4**
LPs: 10/12-Inch 33rpm
ABC: *67–68* **15–18**
Members: Rodney Justo; Barry Bailey; Dean
Daughtry; Billy Gilmore; Paul Goddard; John
Adkins; Bob Nix.
Also see ATLANTA RHYTHM SECTION,
The
Also see CLASSICS IV, The
Also see ORBISON, Roy

CANE, Gary (Gary Cane & His Friends)
Singles: 7-Inch
SHELL: *60–61* **3–5**

CANNED HEAT
Singles: 7-Inch
ATLANTIC: *74* **2–3**
LIBERTY: *68–71* **2–4**
UNITED ARTISTS: *71–73* **2–4**
Picture Sleeves
LIBERTY: *67–69* **2–4**
LPs: 10/12-Inch 33rpm
ACCORD: *81* **5–8**
ATLANTIC: *73–74* **10–12**
JANUS: *69* **12–15**
LIBERTY (1000 series): *80* **5–8**
LIBERTY (7000 series):
67–69 . . . . **10–15**
LIBERTY (10000 series):
81 . . . . **5–8**
LIBERTY (11000 series):
69–70 . . . . **10–15**
SCEPTER **10–12**
SUNSET: *71* **10–12**
UNITED ARTISTS: *71–75* **10–12**
WAND: *70* **15–20**
Members: Bob Hite; Joel Scott Hill; Harvey
Mandel; Mark Andex; Ed Bayer; Frank Cook;
Richard Hite; Chris Morgan; James Shane;
Gene Taylor; Larry Taylor; Henry Vestine;
Alan Wilson; Nolfo De LaParra.
Also see HOOKER, John Lee, & Canned Heat
Also see LITTLE RICHARD
Also see MANDEL, Harvey

CANNED HEAT & THE CHIPMUNKS
Singles: 7-Inch
LIBERTY: *68–70* **15–20**
Also see CANNED HEAT

Price Range

Also see CHIPMUNKS, The

CANNIBAL & THE HEADHUNTERS
Singles: 7-Inch
AIRES: *68* **$3–5**
CAPITOL: *69* **3–5**
COLLECTABLES: *81* **1–3**
DATE: *66* **3–5**
ERA: *73* **2–4**
RAMPART: *65–66* **4–6**
LPs: 10/12-Inch 33rpm
DATE: *66* **20–25**
RAMPART: *65* **25–30**
Members: Frankie "Cannibal" Garcia; Robert
Jaramillo; Joe Jaramillo; Richard Lopez.

CANNON, Ace (Johnny "Ace" Cannon)
Singles: 7-Inch
FERNWOOD: *63–64* **3–5**
HI (2000 series): *61–66* **3–5**
HI (2100-2300 series):
66–76 . . . . **2–4**
MOTOWN: *82* **1–3**
SANTO: *62* **3–5**
Picture Sleeves
HI: *62–63* **2–4**
LPs: 10/12-Inch 33rpm
ALLEGIANCE: *84* **5–8**
GUSTO: *80* **5–8**
HI (007 through 040):
62–67 . . . . **10–15**
(Hi numbers in this series were preceeded by a
"12" for mono or a "35" for stereo issues.)
HI (043 through 090):
68–75 . . . . **6–10**
(All numbers in this series were preceeded by a
35, indicating stereo.)
HI (6000 & 8000 series):
77–79 . . . . **8–10**
MOTOWN: *83* **5–8**

CANNON, Dean
Singles: 7-Inch
VALIANT: *63* **3–5**

CANNON, Freddy (Freddie Cannon)
Singles: 7-Inch
BUDDAH: *71* **2–4**
CLARIDGE: *74–76* **2–3**

Price Range

ERIC: *78* **$1–3**
MCA: *74* **2–3**
METROMEDIA: *72*............... **2–4**
ROYAL AMERICAN:
  69–70 .... **2–4**
SIRE: *69* **2–4**
SWAN: *59–64* **4–6**
WARNER BROS: *64–67*........... **3–5**
WE MAKE ROCK &
  ROLL RECORDS: *68* **2–4**
    Picture Sleeves
SWAN: *59–62*.................. **10–15**
WARNER BROS: *64–65*.......... **8–10**
    LPs: 10/12-Inch 33rpm
RHINO: *82* **5–8**
SWAN: *60–63* **35–45**
WARNER BROS: *64–66*......... **30–35**
  Also see DANNY & THE JUNIORS
  Also see G-CLEFS, The

CANNON, Freddy, & The Belmonts
Singles: 7-Inch
MIA SOUND: *81* **2–3**
  Also see BELMONTS, The, Freddy Cannon &
  Bo Diddley
  Also see CANNON, Freddy

CANO, Eddie
Singles: 7-Inch
DUNHILL: *66–67*................. **2–3**
GNP/CRESCENDO: *62* **2–4**
REPRISE: *62–65*................. **2–3**
    LPs: 10/12-Inch 33rpm
GNP/CRESCENDO:
  61–62 .... **8–15**
RCA VICTOR: *62* **8–15**
REPRISE: *62–65*............... **8–15**

CANTINA BAND, The (Featuring Lou Christie)
Singles: 7-Inch
MILLENNIUM: *81* **1–3**
  Also see CHRISTIE, Lou

CANTRELL, Lana
Singles: 7-Inch
EAST COAST: *74*................. **1–3**
POLYDOR: *74–75* **1–3**
RCA VICTOR: *66–69* **2–3**
    LPs: 10/12-Inch 33rpm
RCA VICTOR: *67–69* **8–12**

Price Range

CANYON
Singles: 7-Inch
MAGNA-GLIDE: *75*.............. **$2–4**

CAPALDI, Jim
Singles: 12-Inch 33/45rpm
RSO: *79*......................... **4–6**
    Singles: 7-Inch
ATLANTIC: *83* **1–3**
ISLAND: *72–76* **2–4**
RSO: *78*......................... **1–3**
    LPs: 10/12-Inch 33rpm
ATLANTIC: *83* **5–8**
CAPITOL: *72* **8–10**
ISLAND: *74–75* **10–12**
RSO: *78–79* **5–8**
  Also see TRAFFIC

CAPITOLS, The
Singles: 7-Inch
COLLECTABLES: *81* **1–3**
KAREN: *66–68*................... **3–5**
    LPs: 10/12-Inch 33rpm
ATCO: *66* **15–20**
SOLID SMOKE: *85*............... **5–8**

CAPRELLS, The
Singles: 7-Inch
ARIOLA AMERICA: *76* **1–3**

CAPRIS, The
Singles: 7-Inch
AMBIENT SOUND: *82* **2–3**
COLLECTABLES: *81* **1–3**
LOST NITE (Pink label):
  60 .... **15–20**
MR. PEEKE: *63*.................. **4–6**
OLD TOWN: *60–61*.............. **8–10**
PLANET: *60*................... **75–90**
TROMMERS: *60* **20–25**
    LPs: 10/12-Inch 33rpm
AMBIENT SOUND: *82* **5–8**
  Members: Nick "Santos" Santamaria; Mike
  Mitchell; Vince Narcardo; John Apostol; Frank
  Reina.

CAPTAIN & TENNILLE, The
Singles: 7-Inch
A&M: *75–78* **2–3**
BUTTERSCOTCH
  CASTLE: *73* **40–50**

Price Range

JOYCE: *74*..................... **$15–20**
CASABLANCA: *79–80*............. **1–3**
Picture Sleeves
A&M: *75–78*...................... **1–3**
LPs: 10/12-Inch 33rpm
A&M: *75–79*..................... **8–10**
CAASABLANCA: *79*.............. **5–8**
Members: Daryl Dragon; Toni Tennille.
Also see TENNILLE, Toni

CAPTAIN BEEFHEART
Singles: 7-Inch
A&M: *66*......................... **4–6**
BUDDAH: *68*..................... **3–5**
MERCURY: *74*.................... **2–4**
REPRISE: *72*..................... **2–4**
VIRGIN: *82*..................... **1–3**
LPs: 10/12-Inch 33rpm
A&M: *84*......................... **5–8**
ACCORD: *83*..................... **5–8**
BIZARRE: *72*................... **10–12**
BLUE THUMB (Black
label): *68*..................... **15–20**
BLUE THUMB (Tan
label): *69*...................... **8–12**
BUDDAH (1001; "Safe As
Milk"): *67*.................... **25–35**
(Monaural. With bumper sticker.)
BUDDAH (5001; "Safe As
Milk"): *67*.................... **25–30**
(Stereo. With bumper sticker.)
BUDDAH (1001/5001;
"Safe As Milk"): *67*............ **15–20**
(Mono or stereo. Without bumper sticker.)
BUDDAH (5077; "Mirror
Man"): *71*.................... **12–15**
BUDDAH (5063; "Safe As
Milk"): *72*.................... **8–10**
EPIC: *82*........................ **5–8**
MERCURY (709;
"Unconditionally
Guaranteed"): *74*.............. **10–12**
MERCURY (1018;
"Bluejeans &
Moonbeams"): *74*.............. **8–10**
REPRISE (Except 447):
70–73....................... **12–15**
REPRISE (447; "Interview
LP"): *70*..................... **40–50**
(Promotional issue only.)
REPRISE/STRAIGHT: *70*........ **12–15**

Price Range

STRAIGHT (1053; "Trout
Mask Replica"): *68*........... **$30–40**
(With lyrics.)
STRAIGHT (1053; "Trout
Mask Replica"): *68*............. **20–25**
(Without lyrics.)
VIRGIN: *80–82*.................. **5–8**
WARNER BROS: *78*.............. **5–8**
Members: Captain Beefheart & His Magic
Band; Don "Captain Beefheart" Van Vliet;
Mark Boston; Ry Cooder; Roy Estrada; Elliot
Ingber; Bill Harkleroad; Ed Marimba; Alex St.
Claire; Herb Bermann.
Also see COODER, Ry
Also see MALLARD
Also see MOTHERS OF INVENTION, The

CAPTAIN BEYOND
Singles: 7-Inch
CAPRICORN: *73*................. **2–4**
LPs: 10/12-Inch 33rpm
CAPRICORN (Except
0105): *72–73*................... **8–12**
CAPRICORN (0105;
"Captain Beyond"): *72*......... **30–40**
(With 3-D cover.)
CAPRICORN (0105;
"Captain Beyond"): *72*.......... **8–12**
(With standard cover.)
WARNER BROS: *77*............. **8–10**
Members: Bobby Caldwell; Rod Evans; Willie
Daffern; Lee Dorman; Larry Reinhardt.
Also see CALDWELL, Bobby
Also see DEEP PURPLE

CAPTAIN RAPP
Singles: 12-Inch 33/45rpm
BECKET: *83*..................... **4–6**
Singles: 7-Inch
BECKET: *83*..................... **1–3**

CAPTAIN SKY (Daryl Cameron)
Singles: 12-Inch 33/45rpm
WMOT: *81*...................... **4–6**
Singles: 7-Inch
A.V.I.: *79–82*.................... **1–3**
TEC: *80*......................... **1–3**
WMOT: *81*...................... **1–3**
LPs: 10/12-Inch 33rpm
A.V.I.: *78–82*.................... **5–8**
TEC: *80*......................... **5–8**

Price Range

Price Range

CARA, Irene
Singles: 12-Inch 33/45rpm
CASABLANCA: *83* **$4–6**
GEFFEN: *83* **4–6**

Singles: 7-Inch
CASABLANCA: *83* **1–3**
GEFFEN: *83–85* **1–3**
NETWORK: *81*. **1–3**
RSO: *80* **1–3**

LPs: 10/12-Inch 33rpm
GEFFEN: *83–85* **5–8**
NETWORK: *82*. **5–8**
RSO: *80* **5–8**

CARAVAN
Singles: 7-Inch
BTM: *75*. **2–3**
DK: *83* **1–3**
LONDON: *71* **2–4**

LPs: 10/12-Inch 33rpm
ARISTA: *76* **5–8**
BTM: *75*. **5–8**
LONDON: *71–75* **12–15**
VERVE/FORECAST: *69* **15–20**
Members: Steve Miller; Richard Coughlan; Pye
Hastings; John Perry; Geoff Richards; Jan
Schelhaas; Dave Sinclair; Richard Sinclair;
Mike Wedgewood.

CARAVELLES, The
Singles: 7-Inch
SMASH: *63–65* **3–5**

LPs: 10/12-Inch 33rpm
SMASH: *63* **20–25**
Members: Lois Wilkinson; Andrea Simpson.

CARDINALS, The
Singles: 7-Inch
ATLANTIC (952 through
995): *51–53*. **35–40**
ATLANTIC (1000 series,
except 1025): *54–56*. **8–12**
ATLANTIC (1025; "Under
A Blanket Of Blue"): *54*. **30–35**
ATLANTIC (1100 series):
57 . . . . **5–8**
Members: Ernie Warren; Meredith Brothers;
Leon Tree; Don Johnson; Sam Aydelotte; Lu-
ther MacArthur; James Brown; Lee Tarver.

CAREFREES, The
Singles: 7-Inch
LONDON INT'L (Except
10614): *64* **$4–6**
LONDON INT'L (10614;
"We Love You Beatles"):
64 . . . . **8–10**
Picture Sleeves
LONDON INT'L (10614;
"We Love You Beatles"):
64 . . . . **10–15**
LPs: 10/12-Inch 33rpm
LONDON: *64* **35–40**

CAREY, Tony
Singles: 7-Inch
MCA: *84* **1–3**
ROCSHIRE: *83*. **1–3**
LPs: 10/12-Inch 33rpm
MCA: *84* **5–8**
ROCSHIRE: *83*. **5–8**
Also see PLANET P PROJECT
Also see RAINBOW

CARGILL, Henson
Singles: 7-Inch
ARCO: *67* **2–4**
ATLANTIC: *73–74* **1–3**
COPPER MOUNTAIN:
79–80 . . . . **1–3**
ELEKTRA: *75* **1–3**
MEGA: *71–73* **2–3**
MONUMENT: *67–70*. **2–3**
TOWER: *68*. **2–4**
LPs: 10/12-Inch 33rpm
ATLANTIC: *73* **6–10**
HARMONY: *72* **6–10**
MEGA: *72*. **6–10**
MONUMENT: *68–70*. **8–12**

CARLA & RUFUS: see RUFUS & CARLA

CARLIN, George
Singles: 7-Inch
LITTLE DAVID: *72–75* **2–3**
RCA VICTOR: *67* **3–5**
LPs: 10/12-Inch 33rpm
ATLANTIC: *81* **5–8**
CAMDEN: *72*. **8–10**
EARDRUM: *84* **5–8**

Price Range

ERA: *72* **$8–12**
LITTLE DAVID: *72–85* **5–10**
RCA VICTOR: *67* **10–15**

CARLISLE, Steve
Singles: 7-Inch
MCA: *81–82* **1–3**
LPs: 10/12-Inch 33rpm
MCA: *82* **5–8**

CARLOS, Walter
LPs: 10/12-Inch 33rpm
COLUMBIA: *69–72* **5–10**

CARLTON, Carl (Little Carl Carlton)
Singles: 12-Inch 33/45rpm
20TH CENTURY-FOX:
80 .... **4–6**
Singles: 7-Inch
ABC: *73–75* **2–3**
BACK BEAT: *68–75* **2–4**
GOLDEN WORLD: *65* **3–5**
LANDO: *65* **3–5**
MCA: *84* **1–3**
MERCURY: *77* **2–3**
RCA VICTOR: *82* **1–3**
20TH CENTURY-FOX:
81–82 .... **1–3**
LPs: 10/12-Inch 33rpm
ABC **10–12**
BACK BEAT: *73* **12–15**
RCA VICTOR: *82* **5–8**
20TH CENTURY-FOX:
81 .... **5–8**

CARLTON, Larry
Singles: 7-Inch
UNI: *68–69* **2–4**
WARNER BROS: *78–83* **1–3**
LPs: 10/12-Inch 33rpm
ATLANTIC: *84* **5–8**
BLUE THUMB: *73* **10–12**
UNI: *68* **12–15**
WARNER BROS: *78–83* **5–8**

CARMEN, Eric
Singles: 12-Inch 33/45rpm
GEFFEN: *85* **4–6**
Singles: 7-Inch
ARISTA: *75–80* **1–3**
COOL: *86* **2–4**

Price Range

EPIC: *70* **$3–5**
GEFFEN: *85* **1–3**
Picture Sleeves
ARISTA: *77* **1–3**
LPs: 10/12-Inch 33rpm
ARISTA: *75–80* **6–10**
GEFFEN: *85* **5–8**
Also see CHOIR, The
Also see QUICK, The
Also see RASPBERRIES, The

CARN, Jean
Singles: 7-Inch
MOTOWN: *82* **1–3**
PHILADELPHIA INT'L:
77–80 .... **1–3**
TSOP: *81* **1–3**
LPs: 10/12-Inch 33rpm
PHILADELPHIA INT'L:
76–80 .... **5–8**
MOTOWN: *82* **5–8**
TSOP: *81* **5–8**
Also see JOHNSON, Al, & Jean Carn
Also see MILITELLO, Bobby

CARNES, Kim
Singles: 12-Inch 33/45rpm
EMI AMERICA: *80–85* **4–6**
Singles: 7-Inch
A&M: *75–82* **1–3**
AMOS: *71–72* **2–4**
EMI AMERICA: *79–85* **1–3**
ELEKTRA: *84* **1–3**
Picture Sleeves
EMI AMERICA: *80–85* .... **INC**
LPs: 10/12-Inch 33rpm
A&M (3000 series): *82* **5–8**
A&M (4000 series): *75–77* **8–10**
AMOS: *71* **12–15**
EMI AMERICA: *79–85* **5–8**
MCA: *84* **5–8**
Also see COTTON, Gene, & Kim Carnes
Also see ROGERS, Kenny, & Kim Carnes
Also see STREISAND, Barbra, & Kim Carnes

CARNIVAL (Featuring Terry Fisher)
Singles: 7-Inch
UNITED ARTISTS: *71* **2–4**
WORLD PACIFIC: *69* **3–5**
LPs: 10/12-Inch 33rpm
WORLD PACIFIC: *69* **10–12**

Price Range

CAROSONE, Renato
Singles: 7-Inch
CAPITOL: 58 . . . . $2–4

CARPENTER, Carleton, & Debbie Reynolds
Singles: 7-Inch
MGM: 51 3–5
EPs: 7-Inch 33/45rpm
MGM: 51 6–10
Also see REYNOLDS, Debbie

CARPENTER, Thelma
Singles: 7-Inch
COLUMBIA: 50 3–5
CORAL: 60–62 3–5
LPs: 10/12-Inch 33rpm
CORAL: 63 10–15

CARPENTERS, The
Singles: 7-Inch
A&M: 69–82 1–3
Picture Sleeves
A&M: 70–81 1–2
LPs: 10/12-Inch 33rpm
A&M: 70–85 6–10
Members: Karen Carpenter; Richard Carpenter; Tony Peluso.

CARR, Cathy
Singles: 7-Inch
ABC: 73 1–3
COLLECTABLES: 81 1–3
CORAL: 53–56 4–6
FRATERNITY: 55–56 4–6
LAURIE: 62–63 3–5
ROULETTE: 59–61 3–5
SMASH: 61 3–5
LPs: 10/12-Inch 33rpm
DOT: 66 15–18
FRATERNITY: 56 25–40
ROULETTE: 59 25–30

CARR, James
Singles: 7-Inch
ATLANTIC: 71 2–4
GOLDWAX: 65–69 3–5
LPs: 10/12-Inch 33rpm
GOLDWAX: 67–68 12–15

Price Range

CARR, Jerry
Singles: 7-Inch
CHERIE: 81 . . . . $1–3

CARR, Joe "Fingers" (Lou Busch)
Singles: 7-Inch
CAPITOL: 50–59 2–4
CORAL: 63 2–3
DOT: 66 1–3
WARNER BROS: 60–62 2–3
EPs: 7-Inch 33/45rpm
CAPITOL: 51–57 5–10
LPs: 10/12-Inch 33rpm
CAPITOL (Except 2000
  series): 51–61 10–20
CAPITOL (2000 series): 64 8–12
CORAL: 63 8–12
DOT: 66 8–12
WARNER BROS: 60–62 8–12
Also see BUSCH, Lou
Also see FRAZIER, Dallas, & Joe "Fingers" Carr
Also see PROVINE, Dorothy, & Joe "Fingers" Carr

CARR, Valerie
Singles: 7-Inch
ATLAS: 64 4–6
ROULETTE: 58–61 3–5
LPs: 10/12-Inch 33rpm
ROULETTE: 59 25–30

CARR, Vikki
Singles: 7-Inch
COLUMBIA: 71–75 1–3
LIBERTY: 62–69 2–4
Picture Sleeves
COLUMBIA: 74 1–3
LIBERTY: 67 2–4
LPs: 10/12-Inch 33rpm
COLUMBIA: 71–75 6–10
LIBERTY (Except 10000
  series): 63–70 10–15
LIBERTY (10000 series):
  81 5–8
UNITED ARTISTS: 71–80 5–10

CARRACK, Paul
Singles: 7-Inch
EPIC: 82 1–3

Price Range

LPs: 10/12-Inch 33rpm
EPIC: *81* $5–8
Also see ACE
Also see SQUEEZE

CARRADINE, Keith
Singles: 7-Inch
ABC: *75* 2–3
ASYLUM: *78.* 1–3
VALA: *83* 1–3
LPs: 10/12-Inch 33rpm
ASYLUM: *77.* 8–10

CARROLL, Andrea
Singles: 7-Inch
BIG TOP: *63.* 3–5
EPIC: *61–62* 3–5
RCA VICTOR: *65* 3–5
UNITED ARTISTS: *66* 3–5

CARROLL, Bernadette
Singles: 7-Inch
COLLECTABLES: *81* 1–3
JULIA: *62* 3–5
LAURIE: *63–64* 3–5

CARROLL, Bob
Singles: 7-Inch
BALLY: *56–57* 3–5
DERBY: *53* 3–5
DOT: *66.* 2–4
MGM: *55.* 3–5
MURBO: *67* 2–4
UNART: *59.* 3–5
UNITED ARTISTS: *59–59* 2–4
Picture Sleeves
UNITED ARTISTS: *58* 2–4

CARROLL, Cathy
Singles: 7-Inch
CHEER: *63–64* 3–5
DOT: *66.* 3–5
MUSICOR: *65.* 3–5
PHILIPS: *63* 3–5
TRIODEX: *61.* 3–5
WARNER BROS: *62–63* 3–5

CARROLL, David, Orchestra
Singles: 7-Inch
MERCURY: *53–62.* 2–4

Price Range

EPs: 7-Inch 33/45rpm
MERCURY: *54–59.* $3–6
LPs: 10/12-Inch 33rpm
MERCURY: *53–62.* 5–12
WING: *59* 4–8

CARROLL, Jim (The Jim Carroll Band)
Singles: 7-Inch
A&M: *72* 2–4
ATCO: *80–81.* 1–3
LPs: 10/12-Inch 33rpm
A&M: *71* 10–12
ATCO: *80–82.* 5–8
ATLANTIC: *83* 5–8

CARROLL, Ronnie
Singles: 7-Inch
PHILIPS: *63–66* 3–5

CARROLL BROTHERS, The
Singles: 7-Inch
CAMEO (100 series): *58* 20–25
CAMEO (200 series): *62* 3–5
FELSTED: *59* 4–6
LPs: 10/12-Inch 33rpm
CAMEO: *62* 20–25

CARS, The
Singles: 7-Inch
ELEKTRA: *78–85* 1–3
Picture Sleeves
ELEKTRA: *78–85* 1–3
LPs: 10/12-Inch 33rpm
ELEKTRA (Except picture
discs): *78–85.* 5–8
ELEKTRA ("Shake It
Up"): *81* 12–15
(Picture disc. Promotional issue only.)
ELEKTRA ("Since You're
Gone"): *82* 10–15
(Picture disc. Promotional issue only.)
Members: Ric Ocasek; Elliot Easton; Greg
Hawkes; Benjamin Orr; Dave Robinson.
Also see EASTON, Elliot
Also see OCASEK, Ric

CARSON, Kit
Singles: 7-Inch
CAPITOL: *55* 3–5

Price Range

CARSON, Mindy
Singles: 7-Inch
COLUMBIA: *52–56* **$3–5**
JOY: *60* **2–4**
RCA VICTOR: *50–52* **3–5**
Also see MITCHELL, Guy, & Mindy Carson

CARTEE, Wayne
Singles: 7-Inch
GROOVY: *77* **1–3**

CARTER, Carlene
Singles: 7-Inch
WARNER BROS: *78–80* **1–3**
LPs: 10/12-Inch 33rpm
WARNER BROS: *78–80* **5–8**
Also see EDMUNDS, Dave, & Carlene Carter
Also see ORRALL, Robert Ellis

CARTER, Clarence
Singles: 7-Inch
ABC: *75–76* **1–3**
ATLANTIC: *68–72* **2–4**
FAME (Except 1000
    series): *72–73* **2–4**
FAME (1000 series): *67* **3–5**
RONN: *77* **1–3**
VENTURE: *80–81* **1–3**
LPs: 10/12-Inch 33rpm
ABC: *74–76* **8–10**
ATLANTIC: *68–71* **10–15**
BIG C: *83* **5–8**
BRYLEN: *84* **5–8**
FAME: *73* **10–12**
VENTURE: *80–81* **5–8**

CARTER, Mel
Singles: 7-Inch
ABKCO: *84* **1–3**
AMOS: *69–70* **2–4**
ARWIN: *60* **4–6**
BELL: *68–69* **2–4**
CREAM: *81* **1–3**
DERBY: *63* **4–6**
IMPERIAL: *64–66* **3–5**
LIBERTY: *67–68* **2–4**
MERCURY: *62* **3–5**
PHILLIPS: *62* **3–5**
ROMAR: *73–74* **2–4**
LPs: 10/12-Inch 33rpm
AMOS: *70* **10–12**

Price Range

DERBY: *63* **$30–35**
IMPERIAL: *65–66* **15–18**
LIBERTY: *67* **12–15**
SUNSET: *68–70* **10–12**

CARTER, Ralph
Singles: 7-Inch
MERCURY: *75–76* **2–3**

CARTER, Ron
LPs: 10/12-Inch 33rpm
MILESTONE: *77–78* **5–8**
NEW JAZZ: *61* **15–20**

CARTER, Valerie
Singles: 7-Inch
COLUMBIA: *77–79* **1–3**
LPs: 10/12-Inch 33rpm
COLUMBIA: *77–78* **8–10**
Also see MONEY, Eddie, & Valerie Carter

CARTER BROTHERS, The
Singles: 7-Inch
COLEMAN: *64* **5–8**
JEWEL: *65–67* **3–5**
Members: Jerry Carter; Al Carter; Roman Carter.

CARTRELL, Delia
Singles: 7-Inch
RIGHT ON: *71–72* **2–4**

CARTRIDGE, Flip
Singles: 7-Inch
PARROT: *66–67* **3–5**

CARUSO, Marian
Singles: 7-Inch
DECCA: *54–55* **2–4**
DEVON: *52* **3–5**

CASCADES, The
Singles: 7-Inch
ABC: *73* **1–3**
ARWIN: *66* **3–5**
CANBASE: *72* **2–4**
CHARTER: *64* **3–5**
COLLECTABLES: *81* **1–3**
LIBERTY: *65* **3–5**
PROBE: *68* **2–4**
RCA VICTOR: *63–64* **3–5**

Price Range

SMASH: *67* **$3–5**
UNI: *69–70* **2–4**
VALIANT: *62–63* **3–5**

Picture Sleeves
PROBE: *68* **2–4**
RCA VICTOR: *63* **4–6**

LPs: 10/12-Inch 33rpm
CASCADES **10–12**
UNI: *69* **15–18**
VALIANT: *63* **35–40**
   Also see LIND, Bob
   Also see YOUNG, Neil

CASEY, Al (The Al Casey Combo; Al Casey & The K-C Ettes)
Singles: 7-Inch
CHALLENGE: *60* **3–5**
GREGMARK (5;
  "Caravan"): *61*. **4–6**
   (This release was shown as by Al Casey, but was
   actually Duane Eddy.)
HIGHLAND (Except
  1002): *60* **10–15**
HIGHLAND (1002; "Got
  The Teenage Blues"): *60* **20–25**
LIBERTY: *58* **8–10**
MCI: *55* **8–10**
STACY: *62–64*. **4–6**
UNITED ARTISTS: *59*. **4–6**

LPs: 10/12-Inch 33rpm
PRESTIGE: *60–61* **15–20**
STACY (Black vinyl): *63* **25–30**
STACY (Colored vinyl.):
  63 .... **45–50**
   Also see CLARK, Sanford
   Also see EDDY, Duane
   Also see EXOTIC GUITARS, The
   Also see REYNOLDS, Jody

CASH, Alvin (Alvin Cash & The Crawlers; Alvin Cash & The Registers)
Singles: 7-Inch
CHESS: *70*. **2–4**
COLLECTABLES: *81* **1–3**
DAKAR: *76* **2–3**
ERIC: *73* **2–3**
MAR-V-LUS: *65*. **3–5**
SEVENTY SEVEN: *72* **2–4**
TODDLIN' TOWN: *68–69* **2–4**

LPs: 10/12-Inch 33rpm
MAR-V-LUS: *65*. **$15–20**
SOUND STAGE 7: *73*. **10–12**

CASH, Johnny (Johnny Cash & The Tennessee Two; Johnny Cash & The Tennessee Three)
Singles: 7-Inch
CACHET: *80*. **1–3**
COLUMBIA (Except
  41000 through 43000
  series): *67–85* **1–3**
COLUMBIA (41000 &
  42000 series): *60–62* **6–10**
   (With a "3" prefix. Compact 33 singles)
COLUMBIA (41000 &
  42000 series): *58–64* **3–5**
   (With a "4" prefix.)
COLUMBIA (43000
  series): *64–66* **2–4**
SSS/SUN: *69–70*. **1–3**
SCOTTI BROS: *82* **1–3**
SUN (200 series): *55–58*. **5–8**
SUN (300 series): *58–62*. **3–5**

EPs: 7-Inch 33/45rpm
COLUMBIA (Except
  jukebox EPs): *58–60* **10–15**
COLUMBIA (Stereo
  jukebox EPs): *69* **25–30**
SUN: *58* **10–15**

Picture Sleeves
COLUMBIA (Except
  41000 & 42000 series):
  67–85 .... **1–3**
COLUMBIA (41000
  series): *58–61* **5–8**
COLUMBIA (42000
  series): *61–64* **3–5**
SUN: *58* **8–10**

LPs: 10/12-Inch 33rpm
COLUMBIA (29; "The
  World Of Johnny
  Cash"): *70* **8–10**
COLUMBIA (1200
  through 1799): *58–61* **15–25**
   (With a "CL" prefix. Monaural series.)
COLUMBIA (8100
  through 8599): *58–61* **20–30**
   (With a "CS" prefix. Stereo series.)
COLUMBIA (1800
  through 2650): *62–68* **10–15**
   (With a "CL" prefix. Monaural series.)

Price Range

COLUMBIA (8600
through 9450): *62–68* **$10–15**
(With a "CS" prefix. Stereo series.)
COLUMBIA (9700
through 9943): *69–70* **8–10**
(With a "CS" prefix.)
COLUMBIA (10000
series): *73* **5–10**
COLUMBIA (30000
through 38000 series):
70–82 .... **5–15**
COLUMBIA/SUFFOLK
MARKETING: *79* **6–10**
OUT OF TOWN DIST: *82* **5–8**
PRIORITY: *81–82* **5–8**
SSS/SUN: *69–84* **5–8**
SUN (100 series): *56–64* **20–30**
TRIP: *74* **8–10**
UNITED ARTISTS: *68* **10–12**
Also see RICH, Charlie
Also see ROBBINS, Marty / Johnny Cash /
Ray Price

CASH, Johnny, & June Carter
(Johnny Cash & June Carter Cash)
Singles: 7-Inch
COLUMBIA: *67–83* **1–3**
LPs: 10/12-Inch 33rpm
COLUMBIA (9500 series):
64–67 .... **10–12**
COLUMBIA (32000
series): *73* **5–10**
HARMONY: *72* **6–10**

CASH, Johnny / Billy Grammer /
The Wilburn Brothers
LPs: 10/12-Inch 33rpm
PICKWICK/HILLTOP:
65 .... **10–15**
Also see GRAMMER, Billy

CASH, Johnny, & Levon Helm
Singles: 7-Inch
A&M: *80* **1–3**
Also see HELM, Levon

CASH, Johnny, & Waylon Jennings
Singles: 7-Inch
COLUMBIA: *78* **1–3**
EPIC: *80* **1–3**
Also see JENNINGS, Waylon

Price Range

CASH, Johnny, Carl Perkins & Jerry
Lee Lewis
LPs: 10/12-Inch 33rpm
COLUMBIA: *82* **$5–8**
Also see LEWIS, Jerry Lee
Also see PERKINS, Carl, Jerry Lee Lewis, Roy
Orbison & Johnny Cash

CASH, Johnny / Tammy Wynette
LPs: 10/12-Inch 33rpm
COLUMBIA (5418; "The
King & Queen") **10–15**
(Columbia Musical Treasury issue.)
Also see CASH, Johnny
Also see WYNETTE, Tammy

CASH, Rosanne
Singles: 7-Inch
COLUMBIA: *80–85* **1–3**
LPs: 10/12-Inch 33rpm
COLUMBIA: *79–85* **6–10**
Also see BARE, Bobby, & Rosanne Cash

CASH, Tommy
Singles: 7-Inch
AUDIOGRAPH: *83* **1–3**
ELEKTRA: *75* **2–3**
EPIC: *68–73* **2–3**
MONUMENT: *77–79* **1–3**
MUSICOR: *65* **2–4**
20TH CENTURY-FOX:
76 .... **2–3**
UNITED ARTISTS: *66–68* **2–4**
LPs: 10/12-Inch 33rpm
EPIC: *69–72* **8–12**
MONUMENT: *78* **5–8**
UNITED ARTISTS: *68* **10–12**

CASHMAN, Terry
Singles: 7-Inch
BOOM: *66* **3–5**
LIFESONG: *76–82* **1–3**
LPs: 10/12-Inch 33rpm
LIFESONG: *76–77* **5–8**

CASHMAN & WEST
Singles: 7-Inch
ABC: *74* **2–3**
DUNHILL: *72–74* **2–4**
LIFESONG: *75* **2–3**

Price Range

LPs: 10/12-Inch 33rpm
ABC: *74* **$8–10**
DUNHILL: *72–74* **8–10**
Members: Terry Cashman; Tommy West.
Also see BUCHANAN BROTHERS, The
Also see CASHMAN, Terry
Also see GENE & TOMMY
Also see MORNING MIST

CASHMAN, PISTILLI & WEST
Singles: 7-Inch
ABC: *68* **2–4**
CAPITOL: *69–71* **2–4**

LPs: 10/12-Inch 33rpm
ABC: *68* **12–15**
CAPITOL: *69–71* **12–15**
Members: Terry Cashman; Gene Pistilli;
Tommy West.
Also see CASHMAN & WEST

CASHMERE
Singles: 12-Inch 33/45rpm
PHILLY WORLD: *83* **4–6**
TNT: *84* **4–6**

Singles: 7-Inch
PHILLY WORLD: *83* **1–3**

LPs: 10/12-Inch 33rpm
PHILLY WORLD: *83–85* **5–8**

CASINOS, The (Gene Hughes & The Casinos)
Singles: 7-Inch
ABC: *73* **2–3**
AIRTOWN: *67* **3–5**
CERTRON: *70* **2–4**
COLLECTABLES: *81* **1–3**
FRATERNITY: *65–71* **3–5**
MILLION: *72* **2–4**
TERRY: *64* **5–8**
UNITED ARTISTS: *68* **2–4**

LPs: 10/12-Inch 33rpm
FRATERNITY: *67* **25–30**

CASLONS, The
Singles: 7-Inch
AMY: *61–62* **4–6**
SEECO: *61* **4–6**

Price Range

CASON, Rich, & The Galactic Orchestra
Singles: 12-Inch 33/45rpm
PRIVATE I: *84* **$4–6**
Singles: 7-Inch
LARC: *83* **1–3**
PRIVATE I: *84* **1–3**

CASPER
Singles: 7-Inch
SUNFLOWER: *71* **2–4**

CASPER
Singles: 7-Inch
A.V.I.: *84* **1–3**
ATLANTIC: *83* **1–3**
LPs: 10/12-Inch 33rpm
A.V.I.: *84* **5–8**
ATLANTIC: *83* **5–8**

CASSIDY, David
Singles: 7-Inch
BELL: *71–73* **2–4**
FLASHBACK: *73* **1–3**
MCA: *79* **1–3**
RCA VICTOR: *75–77* **2–3**
Picture Sleeves
BELL: *71–73* **2–4**
LPs: 10/12-Inch 33rpm
BELL: *72–74* **10–12**
RCA VICTOR: *74–76* **8–10**
Also see PARTRIDGE FAMILY, The

CASSIDY, Shaun
Singles: 7-Inch
WARNER BROS: *77–80* **1–3**
Picture Sleeves
WARNER BROS: *77–80* **1–3**
LPs: 10/12-Inch 33rpm
WARNER BROS: *77–80* **8–10**

CASSIDY, Shaun, & Todd Rundgren's Utopia
Singles: 7-Inch
WARNER BROS: *80* **1–3**
Also see CASSIDY, Shaun
Also see UTOPIA

CASTAWAYS, The
Singles: 7-Inch
COLLECTABLES: *81* **1–3**

Price Range

ERA: *72* $2–3
ERIC: *78* 1–3
FONTANA: *68* 3–5
LANA 2–4
SOMA: *65* 4–6
    Members: Richard Robey; Robert Folschon;
    Ron Hensley; James Donna; Dennis Caswell.

CASTELLS, The
Singles: 7-Inch
COLLECTABLES: *80* 1–3
DECCA: *65–66* 3–5
ERA: *61–63* 3–5
LAURIE: *68* 3–5
UNITED ARTISTS: *68* 3–5
WARNER BROS (Except
    5421): *64* 3–5
WARNER BROS (5421;
    "I Do"): *64* 20–25
LPs: 10/12-Inch 33rpm
COLLECTABLES: *80* 5–8
ERA: *62* 30–40

CASTER, Jimmy: see CASTOR, Jimmy

CASTLE, David
Singles: 7-Inch
PARACHUTE: *77–79* 1–3
LPs: 10/12-Inch 33rpm
PARACHUTE: *77–79* 8–10

CASTLE SISTERS, The
Singles: 7-Inch
ROULETTE: *59–60* 3–5
TERRACE: *62–63* 2–4
TRIODEX: *61* 3–5
Picture Sleeves
TERRACE: *62* 2–4

CASTLEMAN, Boomer
Singles: 7-Inch
MUMS: *75* 2–3

CASTOR, Jimmy (The Jimmy Castor Bunch; The Jimmy Caster Quintet)
Singles: 12-Inch 33/45rpm
SALSOUL: *83* 4–6
Singles: 7-Inch
ATLANTIC: *74–77* 2–4
CAPITOL: *68–69* 2–4

Price Range

CLOWN: *62* $3–5
COMPASS: *68* 2–4
COTILLION: *79* 1–3
DECCA: *66* 3–5
DRIVE: *78* 1–3
JET SET: *65* 4–6
KINETIC: *70* 2–4
LONG DISTANCE: *81* 1–3
RCA VICTOR: *71–73* 2–4
SALSOUL: *82* 1–3
SMASH: *66–67* 3–5
LPs: 10/12-Inch 33rpm
ATLANTIC: *74–77* 8–10
COTILLION: *79* 5–8
DREAM: *83* 5–8
DRIVE: *78* 5–8
LONG DISTANCE: *80* 5–8
RCA VICTOR: *72–75* 10–12
SMASH: *67* 15–18
    Also see CLINTONIAN CUBS, The

CASTOR, Jimmy, & The Juniors
Singles: 7-Inch
ATOMIC: *57* 60–75
WING: *56* 25–30
    Also see CASTOR, Jimmy

CASWELL, Johnny
Singles: 7-Inch
DECCA: *66* 3–5
LUV: *67* 3–5
SMASH: *63–64* 3–5
    Also see CRYSTAL MANSION

CAT MOTHER (Cat Mother & The All Night News Boys)
Singles: 7-Inch
POLYDOR: *69–72* 2–4
LPs: 10/12-Inch 33rpm
POLYDOR: *69–73* 10–12

CATCH
Singles: 12-Inch 33/45rpm
COLUMBIA: *84–85* 4–6
Singles: 7-Inch
COLUMBIA: *84–85* 1–3

CATE BROTHERS, The (The Cates Gang)
Singles: 7-Inch
ASYLUM: *76–78* 2–3

Price Range

ELEKTRA: 77 .... $2–3
METROMEDIA: 70. 2–4
  LPs: 10/12-Inch 33rpm
ASYLUM: 75–77. 5–8
ATLANTIC: 79 5–8
METROMEDIA: 70–73. 10–12
  Members: Earl Cate; Ernie Cate.

CATES, George
  Singles: 7-Inch
CORAL: 51–57 2–4
DOT: 62. 2–3
SIGNATURE: 59–60 2–3
  EPs: 7-Inch 33/45rpm
CORAL: 54–57 3–6
  LPs: 10/12-Inch 33rpm
CORAL: 54–57 5–12

CATHY & JOE
  Singles: 7-Inch
SMASH: 64–65 3–5

CATHY JEAN (Cathy Jean & The Roomates)
  Singles: 7-Inch
ERIC: 73 1–3
PHILIPS (Except 40014):
  63 3–5
PHILIPS (40014; "Believe
  Me"): 62. 5–8
VALMOR: 61–62 3–5
  LPs: 10/12-Inch 33rpm
VALMOR: 61 60–75
  Also see ROOMATES, The

CAVALLARO, Carmen
  Singles: 7-Inch
DECCA: 50–61 2–4
  EPs: 7-Inch 33/45rpm
DECCA: 50–59 4–8
  LPs: 10/12-Inch 33rpm
DECCA (Except "The
  Eddy Duchin Story"):
  50–61 5–15
DECCA (8289; "The Eddy
  Duchin Story"): 54 30–40
  (With a "DL" prefix. Soundtrack.)
DECCA (8289; "The Eddy
  Duchin Story"): 59 20–30
  (With a "DL-7" prefix. Soundtrack.)

Price Range

DECCA (8396; "The Eddy
  Duchin Story"): 56 .... $55–65
  (Soundtrack.)
DECCA (9121; "The Eddy
  Duchin Story"): 65 12–18
VOCALION: 59 4–8

CAVALIERE, Felix
  Singles: 7-Inch
BEARSVILLE: 74–75 2–4
EPIC: 80 1–3
  LPs: 10/12-Inch 33rpm
BEARSVILLE: 74–75 10–12
EPIC: 80 5–8
  Also see RASCALS, The
  Also see 3 GIRLS

CAZZ
  Singles: 7-Inch
NUMBER: 78 1–3

CELEBRATION
  Singles: 7-Inch
MCA: 78 2–3
PACIFIC ARTS: 79. 5–8
  LPs: 10/12-Inch 33rpm
MCA (3037; "Almost
  Summer"): 78. 8–10
  (Soundtrack.)
MOWEST: 72 10–15
PACIFIC ARTS: 79. 8–10
  Members: Mike Love; Charles Lloyd.
  Also see BEACH BOYS, The

CELI BEE & THE BUZZY BUNCH
  Singles: 7-Inch
APA: 77–78. 1–3
  LPs: 10/12-Inch 33rpm
APA: 77–79. 5–8

CELLOS, The
  Singles: 7-Inch
APOLLO: 57–58 10–15
  Members: Cliff Williams; Ken Levinson; Alvin
  Campbell; Bill Montgomery; Alton Thomas.

CENTRAL LINE
  Singles: 12-Inch 33/45rpm
MERCURY: 84–85. 4–6
  Singles: 7-Inch
MERCURY: 81–85. 1–3

Price Range

LPs: 10/12-Inch 33rpm
MERCURY: 82–85................ $5–8

CENTURIES, The
Singles: 7-Inch
SPECTRA-SOUND 10–15
Also see BUCKINGHAMS, The

CERRONE
Singles: 12-Inch 33/45rpm
PAVILLION: 82.................. 4–6
Singles: 7-Inch
ATLANTIC: 79 1–3
COTILLION: 77–78............... 2–3
PAVILLION: 82.................. 1–3
LPs: 10/12-Inch 33rpm
ATLANTIC: 79 5–8
COTILLION: 77–79.............. 5–8
PAVILLION: 82.................. 5–8

CETERA, Peter
Singles: 7-Inch
FULL MOON: 82................. 1–3
LPs: 10/12-Inch 33rpm
FULL MOON: 81................. 5–8

CHABUKOS
Singles: 7-Inch
MAINSTREAM: 73............... 2–3

CHACKSFIELD, Frank, Orchestra
Singles: 7-Inch
LONDON: 53–61 2–3
EPs: 7-Inch 33/45rpm
LONDON: 53–61 3–6
LPs: 10/12-Inch 33rpm
LONDON: 53–61 5–10
RICHMOND: 59–62 4–8

CHAD & JEREMY
Singles: 7-Inch
COLLECTABLES: 81 1–3
COLUMBIA (Black vinyl):
   65–68 3–5
COLUMBIA (Colored
   vinyl): 65 5–8
   (Promotional issues only.)
ERIC: 73 1–3
ROCSHIRE: 84.................. 1–3
WORLD ARTISTS: 64–65 3–5

Price Range

Picture Sleeves
COLUMBIA: 65–66.............. $3–5
WORLD ARTISTS: 64–65 4–6
LPs: 10/12-Inch 33rpm
CAPITOL (2000 series): 66........ 15–20
CAPITOL (12000 & 16000
   series): 80...................... 5–8
COLUMBIA: 65–68.............. 20–25
FIDU......................... 10–12
HARMONY: 69................. 12–15
ROCSHIRE: 84................. 5–8
SIDEWALK: 69................. 12–15
TRADITION REST.............. 10–12
WORLD ARTISTS: 64–65 35–40
Members: Chad Stuart; Jeremy Clyde.

CHAIN REACTION
Singles: 7-Inch
ARIOLA AMERICA: 76 2–3
DATE: 66 3–5
DELICKS: 69.................. 2–4
DIAL: 68...................... 3–5
VERVE: 68 3–5

CHAIRMEN OF THE BOARD, The
Singles: 7-Inch
INVICTUS: 70–76 2–3
Picture Sleeves
INVICTUS: 70–72 2–3
LPs: 10/12-Inch 33rpm
INVICTUS: 70–74 10–12
Members: General Johnson; Eddie Curtis; Harrison Kennedy; Danny Woods.
Also see JOHNSON, General

CHAKA KHAN: see KHAN, Chaka

CHAKACHAS
Singles: 7-Inch
AVCO EMBASSY: 72.............. 2–3
JANUS: 74 2–3
POLYDOR: 71–75 2–3
LPs: 10/12-Inch 33rpm
AVCO EMBASSY: 72............. 8–10
POLYDOR: 72.................. 8–10

CHAKIRIS, George
Singles: 7-Inch
CAPITOL: 62–65 2–4
HORIZON: 62................... 2–4

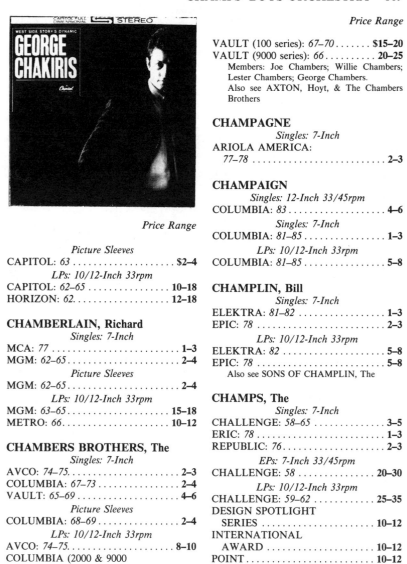

Price Range

Price Range

Price Range   *Price Range*

CHANDLER, Gene
Singles: 12-Inch 33/45rpm
20TH CENTURY-FOX:
79 .... $4–6

Singles: 7-Inch
BRUNSWICK: 67–68. 3–5
CHECKER: 66–69 3–5
CHI-SOUND: 79–82. 1–3
COLLECTABLES: 81 1–3
CONSTELLATION: 63–66. 3–5
CURTOM: 72–73 2–3
ERIC: 73 1–3
MCA: 84 1–3
MARSEL: 76. 2–3
MERCURY: 70. 2–3
SALSOUL: 83 1–3
SOLID SMOKE: 84 1–3
20TH CENTURY-FOX:
78–79 2–3
VEE JAY: 61–63. 3–5

LPs: 10/12-Inch 33rpm
BRUNSWICK: 67–69. 12–15
CHECKER: 67 12–15
CHI-SOUND/20TH
CENTURY-FOX: 78–79 5–8
CONSTELLATION: 64–66. 15–18
KENT: 86 5–8
MERCURY: 70. 10–12
SOLID SMOKE: 84 5–8
20TH CENTURY-FOX:
78–81 5–8
UPFRONT 8–10
VEE JAY: 62. 25–30
Also see DUKAYS, The
Also see DUKE OF EARL, The

CHANDLER, Gene, & Barbara Acklin
Singles: 7-Inch
BRUNSWICK: 68–69. 3–5
Also see ACKLIN, Barbara

CHANDLER, Gene, & Jerry Butler (Gene & Jerry)
Singles: 7-Inch
MERCURY: 70. 2–4
Also see BUTLER, Jerry
Also see CHANDLER, Gene

CHANDLER, Karen
Singles: 7-Inch
CARLTON: 60 .... $2–3
CORAL: 52–55. 3–5
DECCA: 56. 3–5
DOT: 67–68. 2–3
MOHAWK: 62 2–3
STRAND: 61. 2–3
SUNBEAM: 59 2–4
TIVOLI: 65 2–3

EPs: 7-Inch 33/45rpm
CORAL: 52 6–10

LPs: 10/12-Inch 33rpm
STRAND: 61. 10–15

CHANDLER, Karen, & Jimmy Wakely
Singles: 7-Inch
DECCA: 56. 3–5
Also see CHANDLER, Karen
Also see WAKELY, Jimmy

CHANDLER, Kenny
Singles: 7-Inch
AMY: 63 3–5
COLLECTABLES: 81 1–3
CORAL: 62. 3–5
EPIC: 65–66 3–5
LAURIE: 62–63 3–5
TOWER: 67–68. 3–5
UNITED ARTISTS: 61 3–5

CHANGE
Singles: 12-Inch 33/45rpm
ATLANTIC: 84 4–6
RFC: 83 4–6

Singles: 7-Inch
ATLANTIC: 81–85 1–3
WARNER BROS: 80. 1–3

LPs: 10/12-Inch 33rpm
ATLANTIC: 81–85 5–8
RFC: 80 5–8
WARNER BROS: 80. 5–8

CHANGIN' TIMES, The
Singles: 7-Inch
BELL: 67. 3–5
PHILIPS: 65–66 4–6

Price Range

CHANNEL, Bruce
Singles: 7-Inch
CHARAY: *68* **$2–4**
COLLECTABLES: *81* **1–3**
ELEKTRA: *80* **1–3**
KING: *59–60*. **3–5**
LE CAM (100 series): *64* **3–5**
LE CAM (953; "Hey
  Baby"): *62* **8–12**
LE CAM (1100 & 7200
  series): *77*. **2–3**
MALA: *67–68*. **2–4**
MANCO: *62* **3–5**
MEL-O-DY: *64*. **3–5**
SHAH: *64* **3–5**
SMASH: *62–63* **3–5**
TEEN AGER: *59* **10–15**

Picture Sleeves
SMASH: *62–63* **4–6**

LPs: 10/12-Inch 33rpm
SMASH: *62* **20–25**

CHANNEL, Bruce / Paul & Paula
Singles: 7-Inch
ERA **1–3**
  Also see CHANNEL, Bruce
  Also see PAUL & PAULA

CHANSON
Singles: 7-Inch
ARIOLA AMERICA:
  78–79 . . . . **1–3**

LPs: 10/12-Inch 33rpm
ARIOLA AMERICA: *78* **5–8**

CHANTAYS, The
Singles: 7-Inch
ABC: *74* **1–3**
COLLECTABLES: *81* **1–3**
DOT: *63* **3–5**
DOWNEY (104;
  "Pipeline"): *63* **12–15**
DOWNEY (108;
  "Monsoon"): *63* **12–15**
DOWNEY (116 through
  130): *63–65* **8–10**
MCA: *84* **1–3**

Price Range

LPs: 10/12-Inch 33rpm
DOT: *63–66* **$25–30**
DOWNEY: *63* **50–60**
  Members: Bob Marshall; Bob Welsh; Bob Spic-
  kard; Brian Carmen; Warren Waters.

CHANTELS, The
Singles: 7-Inch
ABC: *73* **1–3**
CARLTON: *61* **3–5**
END (Black label): *57* **8–12**
END (White or gray label):
  58–59 . . . . **5–8**
END (Multi-color label):
  58–61 . . . . **4–6**
ERIC: *73* **1–3**
LUDIX: *63* **3–5**
RCA VICTOR: *70* **2–4**
ROULETTE: *69–71* **2–4**
TCF: *65* **3–5**
VERVE: *66* **3–5**

EPs: 7-Inch 33/45rpm
END: *58*. **40–50**

LPs: 10/12-Inch 33rpm
CARLTON: *62* **30–40**
END (301; "We're The
  Chantels"): *58* **200–250**
  (Pictures the group on front cover.)
END (301; "The
  Chantels"): *59* **40–50**
  (Pictures a juke box on front cover.)
END (312; "There's Our
  Song Again"): *62*. **25–30**
FORUM. **20–25**
ROULETTE **5–8**
  Members: Arlene Smith; Lois Harris; Renee
  Minus; Sonia Gorring; Jackie Landry.
  Also see BARRETT, Richard

CHANTERS, The
Singles: 7-Inch
DE LUXE (6100 series):
  58–61 . . . . **8–10**
DE LUXE (6200 series): *63* **3–5**
GUSTO: *77* **1–3**
  Members: Bud Johnson; Larry Pendegrass;
  Fred Paige; Bobby Thompson; Elliot Green.

Harry Chapin, seven charted singles (1972–80), 11 charted LPs (1972–80).

Price Range

CHAPIN, Harry
Singles: 7-Inch
BOARDWALK: *80–81* $1–3
ELEKTRA: *72–79* 2–3

LPs: 10/12-Inch 33rpm
BOARDWALK: *80* 5–8
ELEKTRA: *72–79* 8–10

CHAPLAIN, Paul (Paul Chaplain & His Emeralds)
Singles: 7-Inch
HARPER: *60–61*. 5–8

CHAPTER 8
Singles: 12-Inch 33/45rpm
ARIOLA AMERICA: *79* 4–6

Singles: 7-Inch
ARIOLA AMERICA:
  79–80 1–3

LPs: 10/12-Inch 33rpm
ARIOLA AMERICA: *79* 5–8
Also see BAKER, Anita

CHARADE (Featuring Jessica)
Singles: 12-Inch 33/45rpm
PROFILE: *83* 4–6

Price Range

CHARGERS, The (Featuring Jesse Belvin)
Singles: 7-Inch
RCA VICTOR: *58* $5–8
Also see BELVIN, Jesse

CHARLENE (Charlene Duncan)
Singles: 7-Inch
MOTOWN: *80–85*. 1–3
PRODIGAL: *76* 1–3
LPs: 10/12-Inch 33rpm
MOTOWN: *82–85*. 5–8
PRODIGAL: *76* 8–10

CHARLENE & STEVIE WONDER
Singles: 7-Inch
MOTOWN: *82*. 1–3
Also see CHARLENE
Also see WONDER, Stevie

CHARLES, Jimmy (Jimmy Charles & The Revelletts)
Singles: 7-Inch
ABC: *73*. 1–3
COLLECTABLES: *81* 1–3
ERIC: *79* 1–3
MCA: *84* 1–3
PROMO: *60* 4–6
ROULETTE: *71* 1–3
Picture Sleeves
PROMO: *61* 5–8

CHARLES, Lee
Singles: 7-Inch
BAMBOO: *70–71* 2–3
BRUNSWICK: *69*. 2–4
HOT WAX: *73* 2–3
INVICTUS: *74* 2–3
REVUE: *68* 2–4

CHARLES, Ray (Ray Charles & The Raelettes)
Singles: 7-Inch
ABC: *66–73* 2–4
ABC-PARAMOUNT:
  60–66 3–5
ATLANTIC (900 series):
  52–53 20–25
ATLANTIC (1008 through
  1076): *53–55*. 8–12

Price Range

	Price Range
ATLANTIC (1085 through 1199): *56–57*	**$5–8**
ATLANTIC (2000 through 2470): *58–68*	**3–5**
ATLANTIC (3000 series): *77–79*	**2–3**
BARONET: *62*	**3–5**
COLUMBIA: *82–84*	**1–3**
CROSSOVER: *73–78*	**2–3**
IMPULSE: *61*	**3–5**
RCA VICTOR: *76*	**2–3**
ROCKIN': *53*	**30–35**
SWING TIME: *50–53*	**35–40**
TANGERINE: *71*	**2–3**
TIME: *62*	**3–5**

Picture Sleeves

ABC: *68–70*	**2–4**

EPs: 7-Inch 33/45rpm

ABC-PARAMOUNT: *60–62*	**10–15**
ATLANTIC: *56–59*	**20–25**

LPs: 10/12-Inch 33rpm

ABC (Except 590): *66–73*	**10–12**
ABC (590; "A Man And His Soul"): *67*	**20–25**
ABC-PARAMOUNT (300 & 400 series): *60–64*	**15–25**
ABC-PARAMOUNT (400 & 500 series): *65–66*	**12–15**
ATLANTIC (500 series): *73*	**10–12**
ATLANTIC (900 series): *62*	**25–30**
ATLANTIC (1200 series): *57–58*	**25–35**
ATLANTIC (1300 series): *59–62*	**15–20**
ATLANTIC (1500 series): *70*	**8–10**
ATLANTIC (3700 series): *82*	**20–22**
ATLANTIC (7000 series): *64*	**12–15**
ATLANTIC (8006 through 8039): *57–61* (Black label.)	**25–35**
ATLANTIC (8006 through 8039): *59–61* (Red label.)	**12–15**
ATLANTIC (8063 through 8094): *62–64*	**20–22**

	Price Range
ATLANTIC (19000 series): *77–80*	**$5–8**
BARONET: *62*	**15–20**
BLUESWAY: *73*	**8–10**
BULLDOG: *84*	**5–8**
COLUMBIA: *83–85*	**5–8**
CORONET	**8–10**
CROSSOVER: *73–76*	**8–10**
DESIGN	**8–10**
EVEREST: *70–82*	**8–10**
HOLLYWOOD: *59*	**75–90**
IMPULSE: *61*	**15–20**
INTERMEDIA: *84*	**5–8**
KING: *77*	**8–10**
STRAND	**10–12**
TANGERINE: *70–73*	**10–12**
UPFRONT	**8–10**

Also see RAELETTES, The
Also see THOMAS, B.J., & Ray Charles
Also see U.S.A. FOR AFRICA

CHARLES, Ray, & Clint Eastwood
Singles: 7-Inch

WARNER BROS: *80*	**1–3**

Also see EASTWOOD, Clint

CHARLES, Ray, & Mickey Gilley
Singles: 7-Inch

COLUMBIA: *85*	**1–3**

Also see GILLEY, Mickey

CHARLES, Ray / Ivory Joe Hunter / Jimmy Rushing
LPs: 10/12-Inch 33rpm

DESIGN	**8–10**

Also see HUNTER, Ivory Joe

CHARLES, Ray, George Jones & Chet Atkins
Singles: 7-Inch

COLUMBIA: *83*	**1–3**

Also see ATKINS, Chet
Also see JONES, George

CHARLES, Ray, & Cleo Laine
LPs: 10/12-Inch 33rpm

RCA VICTOR: *76*	**10–12**

Also see LAINE, Cleo

CHARLES, Ray & Jimmy Lewis
Singles: 7-Inch

ABC: *69*	**2–3**

Price Range

TANGERINE: *68*. **$2–4**

CHARLES, Ray, & Willie Nelson
Singles: 7-Inch
COLUMBIA: *84*. **1–3**
   Also see NELSON, Willie

CHARLES, Ray, & Hank Williams, Jr.
Singles: 7-Inch
COLUMBIA: *85*. **1–3**
   Also see CHARLES, Ray
   Also see WILLIAMS, Hank, Jr.

CHARLES, Ray, Singers (Ray Charles "Without Singers")
Singles: 7-Inch
COMMAND: *64–70*. **2–4**
DECCA: *58–59*. **2–3**
JUBILEE: *54*. **2–4**
MGM: *51–56*. **2–4**

EPs: 7-Inch 33/45rpm
DECCA: *59*. **4–6**
MGM: *55–57*. **5–8**

LPs: 10/12-Inch 33rpm
ABC: *73*. **5–8**
ALSHIRE: *70*. **5–8**
ATCO: *68*. **8–12**
CAMDEN: *67*. **6–10**
COMMAND: *62–71*. **8–12**
DECCA: *58–60*. **8–12**
MCA: *82*. **4–6**
MGM (100 series): *71*. **5–10**
MGM (3000 series): *55–60*. **10–12**
MGM (4000 series): *63–66*. **8–12**
METRO: *65*. **6–10**
VOCALION: *66*. **6–10**

CHARLES, Ronnie
Singles: 7-Inch
20TH CENTURY-FOX:
   75. . . . . **2–3**

LPs: 10/12-Inch 33rpm
20TH CENTURY-FOX:
   75. . . . . **5–8**

CHARLES, Roosevelt
LPs: 10/12-Inch 33rpm
VANGUARD: *64*. **10–15**

CHARLES, Sonny (Sonny Charles & Checkmates Ltd.)
Singles: 7-Inch
A&M: *68–73*. **$3–5**
CAPITOL: *66–67*. **3–5**
FRATERNITY: *64*. **4–6**
HIGHRISE: *82*. **1–3**
RCA VICTOR: *72*. **2–3**
LPs: 10/12-Inch 33rpm
HIGHRISE: *82*. **5–8**
A&M: *69*. **15–20**
   Also see CHECKMATES LTD.

CHARLES, Tommy
Singles: 7-Inch
DECCA: *56*. **4–6**
WILLETT: *57*. **15–20**

CHARLESTON CITY ALL-STARS, The
LPs: 10/12-Inch 33rpm
GRAND AWARD: *57–59*. **5–12**

CHARLIE
Singles: 7-Inch
ARISTA: *79*. **1–3**
JANUS: *77–78*. **2–3**
MIRAGE: *83*. **1–3**
RCA VICTOR: *81*. **1–3**
LPs: 10/12-Inch 33rpm
ARISTA: *79*. **5–8**
COLUMBIA: *76*. **8–10**
JANUS: *77–78*. **8–10**
MIRAGE: *83*. **5–8**
RCA VICTOR: *81*. **5–8**

CHARME
Singles: 7-Inch
RCA VICTOR: *79–85*. **1–3**
LPs: 10/12-Inch 33rpm
RCA VICTOR: *79–85*. **5–8**

CHARMETTES, The
Singles: 7-Inch
FEDERAL: *59*. **4–6**
HI: *59*. **4–6**
KAPP: *63–64*. **3–5**
MALA: *64*. **3–5**
MARLIN: *62*. **3–5**
MELOMEGA: *62*. **3–5**

Price Range

MONA: *60.* **$3–5**
WORLD ARTISTS: *65* **3–5**

CHARMS, The (Otis Williams & The Charms)
Singles: 7-Inch
CHART: *55–56.* **10–15**
DELUXE (6000 through
6034): *53–54.* **50–60**
DELUXE (6050; "Quiet
Please"): *54* **25–30**
DELUXE (6056; "My
Baby Dearest Darling"):
54 . . . . **25–30**
DELUXE (6062 through
6098): *54–56.* **6–10**
DELUXE (6100 series):
57–59 . . . . **4–6**
(Monaural singles.)
DELUXE (6100 series): *59* **8–10**
(Stereo singles.)
GUSTO: *77.* **1–3**
KING: *60–63.* **3–5**
OKEH: *65–66* **2–4**
ROCKIN': *53* **75–90**
EPs: 7-Inch 33/45rpm
KING: *57* **35–50**
LPs: 10/12-Inch 33rpm
DELUXE (570; "All Their
Hits"): *57.* **125–150**
KING (614; "This Is Otis
Williams & The
Charms"): *59.* **50–60**
Members: Otis Williams & The Charms; Otis
Williams; Ron Bradley; Don Peark; Joe Renn;
Richard Parker.
Also see WILLIAMS, Otis

CHARO (Charo With The Salsoul Orchestra)
Singles: 7-Inch
CAPITOL: *76* **1–3**
SALSOUL: *77–78.* **1–3**
LPs: 10/12-Inch 33rpm
SALSOUL: *77–78.* **5–8**
Also see SALSOUL ORCHESTRA, The

CHARTBUSTERS, The
Singles: 7-Inch
BELL: *67.* **3–5**
CRUSADER: *65.* **4–6**

Price Range

MUTUAL: *64–65* **$3–5**

CHARTS, The
Singles: 7-Inch
ABC: *73.* **1–3**
EVERLAST (5001;
"Desiree"): *57* **8–12**
EVERLAST (5002 through
5010): *57* **15–20**
EVERLAST (5026;
"Desiree"): *63* **5–8**
GUYDEN: *59.* **4–6**
WAND (1112; "Desiree"):
66 . . . . **4–6**
WAND (1124; "Livin' The
Nightlife"): *66* **3–5**
LPs: 10/12-Inch 33rpm
LOST-NITE: *81.* **8–10**
Members: Joe Grier; Steve Brown; Ross Bu-
ford; Glen Jackson; Leroy Binns.

CHASE
Singles: 7-Inch
EPIC: *71–76* **2–3**
LPs: 10/12-Inch 33rpm
EPIC: *71–76* **10–12**
Members: Bill Chase; Jerry Van Blair; Jay Bur-
rid; Dennis Johnson; Ted Piercefield: Phil Por-
ter; Terry Richards; Angel South; Alan Ware.

CHASE, Ellison
Singles: 7-Inch
BIG TREE: *76–77* **2–3**
COLUMBIA: *82.* **1–3**
MAGNA-GLIDE: *75.* **2–3**
LPs: 10/12-Inch 33rpm
COLUMBIA/ARC: *82.* **5–8**

CHATER, Kerry
Singles: 7-Inch
WARNER BROS: *76–78.* **2–3**
LPs: 10/12-Inch 33rpm
WARNER BROS: *77.* **5–8**

CHAZ
Singles: 7-Inch
PROMISE: *82.* **1–3**

CHEAP TRICK
Singles: 12-Inch 33/45rpm
EPIC: *83* **4–6**

Price Range

Singles: 7-Inch
ASYLUM: *81.* $1–3
EPIC: *77–85* 2–3
PASHA: *84* 1–3
LPs: 10/12-Inch 33rpm
EPIC: *76–85* 5–8
EPIC/NU-DISC: *80* 5–8
PASHA: *84* 5–8
Members: Robert Zander; Tom Petersson; Rick
Nielson; Bun E. Carlos.

CHEATHAM, Oliver
Singles: 7-Inch
MCA: *83* 1–3
LPs: 10/12-Inch 33rpm
MCA: *83* 5–8

CHECKER, Chubby
Singles: 7-Inch
ABKCO: *72*. 2–3
AMHERST: *76* 2–3
BUDDAH: *69* 2–4
MCA: *82* 2–3
PARKWAY (006; "The
　Jet") 3–5
PARKWAY (804 through
　810): *59–60.* 8–10
PARKWAY (811; "The
　Twist"/"Toot"): *60* 5–8
　(White label.)
PARKWAY (811; "The
　Twist"/"Twistin'
　U.S.A."): *61* 3–5
　(Yellow/orange label.)
PARKWAY (811; "The
　Twist"): *61* 10–15
　(Colored vinyl.)
PARKWAY (813 through
　989): *60–66.* 3–5
Picture Sleeves
PARKWAY: *61–65* 4–6
EPs: 7-Inch 33/45rpm
PARKWAY: *61* 15–20
20TH CENTURY-FOX:
　73–74 2–3
LPs: 10/12-Inch 33rpm
ABKCO: *72*. 8–10
EVEREST: *81* 5–8
51 WEST: *84*. 5–8
MCA: *82* 8–10
PARKWAY: *60–66* 15–20

Price Range

Also see DREAMLOVERS, The

CHECKER, Chubby / Gary U.S. Bonds
LPs: 10/12-Inch 33rpm
EXACT: *80* $5–8
Also see BONDS, Gary "U.S."

CHECKER, Chubby, & Bobby Rydell
Singles: 7-Inch
CAMEO (12; "Your Hits
　And Mine"): *61* 8–10
　(Promotional issue only.)
CAMEO (200 series):
　61–62 3–5
Picture Sleeves
CAMEO: *61* 4–6
LPs: 10/12-Inch 33rpm
CAMEO: *61–63*. 15–18
Also see RYDELL, Bobby

CHECKER, Chubby, & Dee Dee Sharp
LPs: 10/12-Inch 33rpm
CAMEO: *62* 15–20
Also see CHECKER, Chubby
Also see SHARP, Dee Dee

CHECKMATES LTD.
Singles: 7-Inch
A&M: *69* 3–5
CAPITOL: *66–67* 3–5
FANTASY: *77–78*. 2–3
GREEDY: *77*. 2–3

Price Range

RUSTIC: *74*. $2–4

LPs: 10/12-Inch 33rpm
A&M: *69* **15–20**
CAPITOL: *67* **15–20**
FANTASY: *77*. **8–10**
IKON. **5–8**
POLYDOR: *76* **8–10**
RUSTIC: *74*. **8–10**
   Members: Sonny Charles; Bill Van Buskirk;
   Marvin Smith; Bobby Stevens; Harvey Trees.
   Also see CHARLES, Sonny

CHEE CHEE & PEPPY
Singles: 7-Inch
BUDDAH: *71* 2–4

LPs: 10/12-Inch 33rpm
BUDDAH: *72* **10–12**

CHEECH & CHONG
Singles: 7-Inch
MCA: *85* 1–3
ODE: *71–77*. 2–4
WARNER BROS: *78* 1–3

Picture Sleeves
ODE: *73–77*. 2–4
WARNER BROS: *78*. 1–3

LPs: 10/12-Inch 33rpm
EPIC/ODE: *77* 5–8
ODE: *71–76*. **8–12**
WARNER BROS: *78–80* **6–10**
   Members: Richard Marin; Thomas Chong.

CHEEKS, Judy
Singles: 7-Inch
DREAM: *80* 1–3
SALSOUL: *78*. 1–3
UNITED ARTISTS: *73* 2–3

LPs: 10/12-Inch 33rpm
SALSOUL: *78*. 5–8
UNITED ARTISTS: *73* **8–10**

CHEERS, The (With Bert Convy)
Singles: 7-Inch
CAPITOL: *54–56* 5–8
MERCURY: *57*. 4–6

EPs: 7-Inch 33/45rpm
CAPITOL: *55* **30–35**

Price Range

CHEMAY, Joe (The Joe Chemay Band)
Singles: 7-Inch
UNICORN: *81* $1–3

LPs: 10/12-Inch 33rpm
UNICORN: *81* 5–8

CHEQUERED PAST
Singles: 7-Inch
EMI AMERICA: *84*. 1–3

LPs: 10/12-Inch 33rpm
EMI AMERICA: *84*. 5–8

CHER (Cher Bono; Cher Allman)
Singles: 12-Inch 33/45rpm
CASABLANCA: *79–82* 4–6

Singles: 7-Inch
ATCO: *69–72*. 2–4
ATLANTIC: *69* 2–4
CASABLANCA: *79* 2–3
COLUMBIA: *82*. 1–3
IMPERIAL: *64–68*. 3–5
KAPP: *71–72*. 2–3
LIBERTY: *82* 1–3
MCA: *73–75* 2–3
UNITED ARTISTS: *71–72* 2–3
WARNER BROS: *75–77* 2–3
WARNER
   BROS/SPECTOR: *74*. 2–4

LPs: 10/12-Inch 33rpm
ATCO: *69* **12–15**
CASABLANCA (Except
   picture discs): *79* 5–8
CASABLANCA (Picture
   discs): *79* **20–25**
COLUMBIA: *82*. 5–8
IMPERIAL: *65–68* **15–20**
KAPP: *71–72*. **10–15**
LIBERTY: *81* 5–8
MCA: *73–74* **8–10**
SPRINGBOARD: *72* **8–10**
SUNSET: *70* **8–10**
UNITED ARTISTS: *71–75* **8–10**
WARNER BROS: *75–77* **8–10**
   Also see ALLMAN & WOMAN
   Also see CHERILYN
   Also see MASON, Bonnie Jo
   Also see SONNY & CHER

Price Range

Price Range

CHER & NILSSON
Singles: 7-Inch
SPECTOR: 75 . . . . $2–4
Also see CHER
Also see NILSSON

CHERI
Singles: 12-Inch 33/45rpm
21: 83 4–6
Singles: 7-Inch
21: 83 1–3
VENTURE: 82 1–3

CHERILYN (Cher Bono)/
Cherilyn's Group
Singles: 7-Inch
IMPERIAL: 64 10–15
Also see CHER

CHERRELLE
Singles: 12-Inch 33/45rpm
TABU: 84 4–6
Singles: 7-Inch
TABU: 84 1–3
LPs: 10/12-Inch 33rpm
TABU: 84 5–8

CHERRY, Ava
Singles: 12-Inch 33/45rpm
CAPITOL: 82 4–6
Singles: 7-Inch
CAPITOL: 82 1–3
CURTOM: 80 1–3
RSO: 80 1–3
LPs: 10/12-Inch 33rpm
RSO: 80 5–8

CHERRY, Don
Singles: 7-Inch
COLUMBIA: 55–59 3–5
DECCA: 50–56 3–5
MONUMENT: 65–78 1–3
STRAND: 59 2–3
VERVE: 62 2–3
WARWICK: 60 2–3
EPs: 7-Inch 33/45rpm
COLUMBIA: 56 6–10
LPs: 10/12-Inch 33rpm
COLUMBIA: 56 15–20
HARMONY: 59 10–12
MONUMENT: 66–73 8–10

Also see DAY, Doris, & Don Cherry

CHERRY PEOPLE, The
Singles: 7-Inch
HERITAGE: 68–69 . . . . $2–4
Picture Sleeves
HERITAGE: 68 3–5
LPs: 10/12-Inch 33rpm
HERITAGE: 68 15–18

CHERYL LYNN: see LYNN, Cheryl

CHEYNE
Singles: 12-Inch 33/45rpm
MCA: 85 4–6

CHIC
Singles: 12-Inch 33/45
ATLANTIC: 78–83 4–6
Singles: 7-Inch
ATLANTIC: 77–83 1–3
MIRAGE: 82 1–3
Picture Sleeves
ATLANTIC: 78–80 1–3
LPs: 10/12-Inch 33rpm
ATLANTIC: 77–82 5–8
Also see HONEYDRIPPERS, The
Also see NORMA JEAN
Also see RODGERS, Nile

CHIC / Leif Garrett / Roberta Flack
/ Genesis
EPs: 7-Inch 33/45rpm
WARNER SPECIAL
    PRODUCTS: 78 5–10
(Coca-Cola/Burger King promotional issue. Issued with paper sleeve.)
Also see CHIC
Also see FLACK, Roberta
Also see GARRETT, Leif
Also see GENESIS

CHICAGO
Singles: 12-Inch 33/45
COLUMBIA: 80 4–6
Singles: 7-Inch
COLUMBIA: 69–80 1–3
FULL MOON: 82–85 1–3
Picture Sleeves
COLUMBIA: 70–80 1–3
EPs: 7-Inch 33/45rpm
COLUMBIA: 70–73 10–15
(Jukebox issues only.)

Price Range

LPs: 10/12-Inch 33rpm
ACCORD: *81* **$5–8**
COLUMBIA: *69–82* **8–12**
FULL MOON: *82–84*. **5–8**
MAGNUM: *78* **10–12**
Also see BEACH BOYS, The

CHICAGO GANGSTERS
Singles: 7-Inch
GOLD PLATE: *75–76*. **2–3**
RCA VICTOR: *78* **1–3**
RED COACH: *74–75*. **2–3**

LPs: 10/12-Inch 33rpm
GOLD PLATE: *75–76* **10–12**

CHICAGO LOOP, The
Singles: 7-Inch
DYNO VOICE: *66–67* **3–5**
MERCURY: *67–68*. **3–5**

CHICANO, El: see EL CHICANO

CHICORY
Singles: 7-Inch
EPIC: *72* **2–4**
LPs: 10/12-Inch 33rpm
EPIC: *72* **10–12**

CHIEFTAINS, The
Singles: 7-Inch
ISLAND: *76* **2–3**
LPs: 10/12-Inch 33rpm
COLUMBIA: *78–80* **5–8**
ISLAND: *75–78* **8–10**

CHIFFONS, The (Featuring Judy Craig)
Singles: 7-Inch
B.T. PUPPY: *70* **2–4**
BIG DEAL: *60* **15–20**
BUDDAH: *71* **2–4**
LAURIE: *63–76* **4–6**
REPRISE: *62*. **4–6**
WILDCAT **5–8**
LPs: 10/12-Inch 33rpm
B.T. PUPPY: *70* **20–30**
LAURIE (2000 series):
63–66 .... **20–30**
LAURIE (4000 series): *75* **10–15**

Also see COASTERS, The / The Crew-Cuts / The Chiffons
Also see FOUR PENNIES, The
Also see ISLEY BROTHERS, The / The Chiffons

CHILD, Desmond, & Rouge
Singles: 12-Inch 33/45rpm
CAPITOL: *79* **$4–6**
Singles: 7-Inch
CAPITOL (Black vinyl):
79–82 .... **1–3**
CAPITOL (Colored vinyl):
79 .... **3–5**
LPs: 10/12-Inch 33rpm
CAPITOL (Black vinyl):
79 .... **5–8**
CAPITOL (Colored vinyl):
79 .... **15–18**
Also see VIDAL, Maria

CHI-LITES, The
Singles: 12-Inch 33/45rpm
LARC: *83* **4–6**
PRIVATE 1: *84*. **4–6**
Singles: 7-Inch
BLUE ROCK: *65* **3–5**
BRUNSWICK: *69–78*. **2–3**
ERIC: *83* **1–3**
INPHASION: *79*. **1–3**
LARC: *83* **1–3**
MERCURY: *76–77*. **2–3**
O'RETTA: *70* **2–4**
PRIVATE 1: *84*. **1–3**
REVUE: *67–68* **3–5**
20TH CENTURY-FOX:
81 .... **1–3**
LPs: 10/12-Inch 33rpm
BRUNSWICK: *69–74*. **10–12**
EPIC: *83–84* **5–8**
LARC: *83* **5–8**
MERCURY: *77*. **5–8**
20TH CENTURY FOX:
80–81 .... **5–8**
Members: Eugene Record; Creadel Jones; Robert Lester; Marshall Thompson.
Also see RECORD, Eugene
Also see WILSON, Jackie, & The Chi-Lites

CHILLIWACK
Singles: 7-Inch
A&M: *72* **2–4**
MILLENNIUM: *81–83* **1–3**

Price Range

MUSHROOM: *76–80* **$1–3**
PARROT: *71* **2–4**
SIRE: *74–76* **2–3**
LPs: 10/12-Inch 33rpm
A&M: *71–73* **12–15**
MILLENNIUM: *81–82* **5–8**
MUSHROOM: *77–80* **8–10**
PARROT: *70* **15–18**
SIRE: *75* **10–12**
  Members: Bill Henderson; Howard Froese;
  Claire Lawrence; Glen Miller; Ross Turney.

CHILLTOWN
Singles: 12-Inch 33/45rpm
A&M: *83* **4–6**

CHIMES, The
Singles: 7-Inch
ABC: *75* **1–3**
COLLECTABLES: *81* **1–3**
LAURIE: *60* **5–8**
LIMELIGHT: *57* **5–8**
METRO INT'L: *63* **4–6**
RESERVE: *57* **4–6**
TAG: *60–62* **4–6**

CHINA CRISIS
Singles: 12-Inch 33/45rpm
VIRGIN: *82* **4–6**
WARNER BROS: *83* **4–6**
Singles: 7-Inch
VIRGIN: *82* **1–3**
WARNER BROS: *84* **1–3**
LPs: 10/12-Inch 33rpm
WARNER BROS: *84* **5–8**

CHIP E. INC.
Singles: 12-Inch 33/45rpm
D.J. INT'L: *85* **4–6**

CHIPMUNKS, The (Starring Alvin, Theodore, & Simon; Featuring David Seville)
Singles: 7-Inch
LIBERTY (Except 77000
  series): *58–74* **2–5**
LIBERTY (77000 series):
  59 . . . . **8–10**
  (Stereo singles.)
SUNSET: *68* **2–3**
UNITED ARTISTS: *74* **1–3**

Price Range

Picture Sleeves
LIBERTY: *59–65* **$3–5**
EPs: 7-Inch 33/45rpm
LIBERTY: *59–63* **10–15**
MISTLETOE: *75* **2–3**
LPs: 10/12-Inch 33rpm
LIBERTY (Except 100
  series & LN series):
  61–65 . . . . **10–15**
LIBERTY (100 & 10000
  series): *59–60* **20–25**
  (Black vinyl. With covers picturing the Chip-
  munks as animals.)
LIBERTY (100 series) **12–15**
  (Black vinyl. With covers picturing the Chip-
  munks as cartoon characters.)
LIBERTY (100 series): *59* **35–45**
  (Colored vinyl.)
  Note: Liberty 100 series numbers were pre-
  ceeded by a "3" for mono or a "7" for stereo
  issues.
LIBERTY (10000 series):
  82 . . . . **5–8**
PICKWICK: *80* **5–8**
SUNSET: *68–69* **10–12**
UNITED ARTISTS: *74–76* **8–10**
  Also see CANNED HEAT & THE CHIP-
  MUNKS
  Also see SEVILLE, David

CHIPMUNKS, The (Starring Alvin, Theodore, & Simon; Featuring David Seville, Jr.)
Singles: 7-Inch
EXCELSIOR: *80* **1–3**
RCA VICTOR: *81–82* **1–3**

ZORRO

Price Range

CHRISTIE, Lou, & Leslie Gore
Singles: 7-Inch
EMI AMERICA: *86*................ $2–3
Also see CHRISTIE, Lou
Also see GORE, Leslie

CHIRSTIE, Susan
Singles: 7-Inch
COLUMBIA: *66–67*................ 3–5

CHRISTMAS SPIRIT
Singles: 7-Inch
WHITE WHALE: *69*.............. 45–55
Members: Mark Volman; Howard Kaylan; Linda Ronstadt.
Also see RONSTADT, Linda
Also see TURTLES, The

CHRISTOPHER, Gavin
Singles: 7-Inch
ISLAND: *76*...................... 2–3
RSO: *79*......................... 1–3
LPs: 10/12-Inch 33rpm
ISLAND: *76*..................... 8–10
RSO: *79*......................... 5–8

CHRISTOPHER, Paul & Shawn
Singles: 7-Inch
CASABLANCA: *75*................ 2–3

CHRISTY, Chic
Singles: 7-Inch
HAC: *62*....................... 10–15
Members: Lou Christie; Kay Chick; Susan Christie.
Also see CHRISTIE, Lou

CHRISTY, Don (Sonny Bono)
Singles: 7-Inch
FIDELITY: *60*.................... 5–8
GO: *60*.......................... 5–8
NAME: *60*....................... 5–8
SPECIALTY: *59*.................. 5–8
Also see SONNY

CHRISTY, June
Singles: 7-Inch
CAPITOL (1800 through
3900 series): *51–58* 3–5
CAPITOL (4000 through
4800 series): *59–62* 2–4

Price Range

EPs: 7-Inch 33/4rpm
CAPITOL: *53–55*................ $5–10
LPs: 10/12-Inch 33rpm
CAPITOL (516;
"Something Cool"): *54*.......... 20–30
(With an "H" prefix. 10-Inch LP.)
CAPITOL (516;
"Something Cool"): *55*.......... 15–20
(Green label. With a "T" prefix.)
CAPITOL (516;
"Something Cool"): *60*.......... 10–12
(Black label. With a "T" or "ST" prefix.)
CAPITOL (516;
"Something Cool"): *75*........... 5–8
(With an "SM" prefix.)
CAPITOL (600 through
900 series): *55–57* 12–18
(Green label.)
CAPITOL (600 through
900 series): *60* 10–12
(Black label.)
CAPITOL (1000 through
2400 series): *60–65* 10–15
CAPITOL (11000 series):
79 5–8
DISCOVERY: *82* 5–8
SEABREEZE: *80* 5–8
Also see JONES, Jonah
Also see KENTON, Stan, & His Orchestra

CHUCKLES, The (Featuring Teddy Randazzo)
Singles: 7-Inch
ABC-PARAMOUNT: *61*............ 3–5
Also see RANDAZZO, Teddy

Price Range

Also see THREE CHUCKLES, The

CHUNG, Wang: see WANG CHUNG

CHURCH, Eugene (Eugene Church & The Fellows)
Singles: 7-Inch
CLASS: *58–60* **$4–6**
COLLECTABLES: *81* **1–3**
KING: *61–63*...................... **3–5**
RENDEZVOUS: *60* **3–5**
SPECIALTY: *57*................... **5–8**
WORLD PACIFIC: *67* **3–5**
Also see CLIQUES, The

CHURCHILL, Savannah
Singles: 7-Inch
ARGO: *56*........................ **3–5**
DECCA: *53–55*.................... **3–5**
JAMIE: *60*........................ **2–4**
RCA VICTOR: *51–52* **4–6**

EPs: 7-Inch 33/4rpm
CAMDEN: *53* **10–15**

CINDY & ROY
Singles: 12-Inch 33/45rpm
CASABLANCA: *79* **4–6**

Singles: 7-Inch
CASABLANCA: *79* **1–3**

LPs: 10/12-Inch 33rpm
CASABLANCA: *79* **5–8**

CIRCUS
Singles: 7-Inch
METROMEDIA: *72–73*............. **2–3**

LPs: 10/12-Inch 33rpm
HEMISPHERE: *74*............... **10–12**
METROMEDIA: *73*.............. **10–12**

CIRCUT
Singles: 12-Inch 33/45rpm
4TH & BROADWAY:
   84–85 .... **4–6**

CISSEL, Chuck
Singles: 7-Inch
ARISTA: *79–82*................... **1–3**

Price Range

LPs: 10/12-Inch 33rpm
ARISTA: *80* **$5–8**

CITY BOY
Singles: 7-Inch
AIRBOY: *77*...................... **2–3**
ATLANTIC: *79–81* **1–3**
MERCURY: *76–78*................. **2–3**
LPs: 10/12-Inch 33rpm
MERCURY: *76–78*............... **8–10**
Members: Steve Broughton; Lol Mason.

CLANCY BROTHERS, The (The Clancy Brothers & Lou Killen; The Clancy Brothers & Robbie O'Connell)
LPs: 10/12-Inch 33rpm
AUDIO FIDELITY: *71–73*........ **8–12**
COLUMBIA: *70*................. **8–12**
VANGUARD: *74–83*............. **8–12**

CLANCY BROTHERS & TOMMY MAKEM, The
Singles: 7-Inch
COLUMBIA: *62–69*............... **2–4**
LPs: 10/12-Inch 33rpm
COLUMBIA: *62–69*............. **10–15**
HARMONY: *71–72*.............. **6–10**
TRADITION: *67–69*............ **10–12**
Also see CLANCY BROTHERS, The

CLANTON, Ike
Singles: 7-Inch
ACE: *59–60*...................... **3–5**
MERCURY: *62–63*................. **3–5**

CLANTON, Jimmy (Jimmie Clanton)
Singles: 7-Inch
ABC: *73*......................... **1–3**
ACE (Except stereo
   singles): *57–63* **4–6**
ACE (Stereo singles): *59*........ **10–15**
COLLECTABLES: *81* **1–3**
ERIC: *73* **1–3**
IMPERIAL: *67–68*................. **3–5**
LAURIE: *69* **2–4**
MALA: *65*........................ **3–5**
PHILIPS: *63–64* **3–5**
SPIRAL: *71*...................... **2–4**
STARCREST: *76* **2–3**
STARFIRE: *78*.................... **2–4**
VIN: *62* **3–5**

Price Range

Price Range

Picture Sleeves
ACE (Except 51860):
  59–63 .... **$5–10**
ACE (51860; "The Slave"):
  60 .... **10–20**
  (Promotional issue only. A mail-order bonus offer to buyers of the "Jimmy's Happy/Jimmy's Blue" LP. All copies of this sleeve were autographed by Clanton.)
PHILIPS: *64* **4–6**

Promotional Singles
ACE (644; "Venus In Blue
  Jeans"): *62* **10–15**
ACE (51860; "The Slave"):
  60 .... **5–10**
  (Promotional issue only. A bonus disc with the "Jimmy's Happy/Jimmy's Blue" LP.)
UNITED ARTISTS
  ("Teenage Millionaire"):
  62 .... **5–8**
  (5-inch cardboard flexi-disc.)

EPs: 7-Inch 33/45rpm
ACE: *59–61* **15–25**

LPs: 10/12-Inch 33rpm
ACE: *59–62* **30–40**
DESIGN **10–15**
PHILLIPS: *64* **15–20**
  Also see DALE, Jimmy

CLAPTON, Eric
Singles: 7-Inch
ATCO: *70–71* **2–4**
DUCK: *83–85* **1–3**
POLYDOR: *72–73* **2–3**
RSO: *74–82* **1–3**

Picture Sleeves
RSO: *80–81* **1–3**

LPs: 10/12-Inch 33rpm
ATCO: *70–72* **15–18**
DUCK: *83–85* **5–8**
POLYDOR: *72–73* **10–12**
RSO: *73–82* **6–10**
  Also see BLIND FAITH
  Also see CREAM
  Also see DELANEY & BONNIE
  Also see DEREK & THE DOMINOES
  Also see LOMAX, Jackie
  Also see MAYALL, John
  Also see STARR, Ringo
  Also see TOWNSHEND, Pete, & Ronnie Lane
  Also see WATERS, Roger
  Also see YARDBIRDS, The

CLARK, Chris
Singles: 7-Inch
MOTOWN: *67–68* **$3–5**
V.I.P.: *65–67* **3–5**

LPs: 10/12-Inch 33rpm
MOTOWN: *67* **12–15**
WEED **10–12**

CLARK, Claudine (Claudine Clark & The Spinners)
Singles: 7-Inch
CHANCELLOR: *62–63* **3–5**
COLLECTABLES: *81* **1–3**
ERIC: *73* **1–3**
HERALD: *58* **10–12**
JAMIE: *64* **3–5**

LPs: 10/12-Inch 33rpm
CHANCELLOR: *62* **30–35**

CLARK, Dave, Five (Dave Clark & Friends)
Singles: 7-Inch
CONGRESS: *64* **4–6**
EPIC (9656 through
  10265): *64–67* **3–5**
  (Black vinyl.)
EPIC (9700 & 9800 series):
  65 .... **8–10**
  (Colored vinyl. Promotional issues only.)
EPIC (10325 through
  10894): *68–72* **6–10**
JUBILEE: *64* **10–12**
LAURIE: *63* **15–18**
RUST: *64* **20–30**

Picture Sleeves
CONGRESS (212; "I
  Knew It All The Time"):
  64 .... **10–15**
EPIC: *64–70* **5–10**

EPs: 7-Inch 33/45rpm
COLUMBIA: *64–65* **20–30**
EPIC: *66* **15–20**
  (Jukebox issues only.)

LPs: 10/12-Inch 33rpm
CORTLEIGH **15–20**
CROWN: *65* **20–25**
CUSTOM **15–20**
EPIC (Except 77238):
  64–75 .... **15–25**

THE DAVE CLARK FIVE
"I KNEW IT ALL THE TIME"
B/W "THAT'S WHAT I SAID"   CG 212

Price Range

Note: Monaural Epic LPs are valued near the higher end of the price range, whereas reprocessed stereo issues usually bring prices toward the lower end.

EPIC (77238; "The Dave
Clark Interviews"): *65* **$40–45**
(Promotional issue only.)
I-N-S RADIO NEWS: *64* **60–80**
Members: Dave Clark; Mike Smith; Lenny Davidson; Denny Payton; Rick Huxley.

CLARK, Dave, Five / Lulu
Singles: 7-Inch
EPIC (10260/65;
"Everybody
Knows"/"Best Of Both
Worlds"): *67*. **10–15**
(Promotional issue only.)
Also see CLARK, Dave, Five
Also see LULU

CLARK, Dee
Singles: 7-Inch
ABC: *73* **1–3**
ABNER (Except stereo
singles): *58–60* **4–6**
ABNER (Stereo singles):
59–60 .... **8–12**
CHELSEA: *75*. **2–3**
COLLECTABLES: *83* **1–3**
ERIC: *73* **1–3**
COLUMBIA: *67*. **3–5**
CONSTELLATION: *63–65*. **3–5**
FALCON: *58*. **8–12**
LIBERTY: *70* **2–3**
MCA: *84* **1–3**

Price Range

VEE JAY (Except stereo
singles): *60–63* **$4–6**
VEE JAY (Stereo singles):
60–63 .... **8–10**
UNITED ARTISTS: *71* **2–3**
WAND: *68* **3–5**
WARNER BROS: *73* **2–3**
Picture Sleeves
ABNER: *59*. **8–12**
EPs: 7-Inch 33/45rpm
ABNER: *61*. **35–40**
VEE JAY: *61*. **25–30**
LPs: 10/12-Inch 33rpm
ABNER: *59–60*. **30–35**
SOLID SMOKE: *84* **5–8**
SUNSET: *68* **10–12**
VEE JAY: *60–64*. **20–25**

CLARK, Gene (Gene Clark & The Gosdin Brothers)
Singles: 7-Inch
ASYLUM: *74*. **2–3**
COLUMBIA: *66*. **3–5**
RSO: *77* **1–3**
Picture Sleeves
COLUMBIA: *80–81* **1–3**
LPs: 10/12-Inch 33rpm
A&M: *71* **10–15**
ASYLUM: *74*. **8–10**
COLUMBIA (2618; "Gene
Clark"): *67*. **20–30**
(Monaural issue.)
COLUMBIA (9418; "Gene
Clark"): *67*. **20–30**
(Stereo issue.)
COLUMBIA (31123;
"Early L.A. Sessions"):
72 .... **10–12**
RSO: *77* **5–8**
TAKOMA: *84*. **5–8**
Also see BYRDS, The

CLARK, Petula (Pet Clark)
Singles: 7-Inch
CORAL: *53–54* **8–10**
DUNHILL: *74*. **2–3**
ERIC: *83* **1–3**
IMPERIAL: *59–60*. **4–6**
JANUS: *76* **2–3**
KING: *54* **8–10**
LAURIE: *62–63* **3–5**

Price Range

LONDON: *62* **$3–5**
MGM (12000 series): *55*............ **5–8**
MGM (14000 series):
  72–74 .... **2–3**
SCOTTI BROTHERS: *82* **1–3**
WARNER BROS: *64–69*............ **2–4**
WARWICK: *61*.................... **3–5**

EPs: 7-Inch 33/45rpm
WARNER BROS: *65–66*............ **4–8**
  (Jukebox issues only.)

LPs: 10/12-Inch 33rpm
GNP/CRESCENDO: *73* **8–10**
IMPERIAL: *65*.................. **15–20**
LAURIE: *65* **15–20**
MGM: *72*....................... **8–10**
PREMIER: *64*.................. **15–20**
SUNSET: *66* **10–12**
WARNER BROS: *65–71*......... **10–12**

CLARK, Roy
Singles: 7-Inch
ABC: *74–79*...................... **1–3**
ABC/DOT: *75–77*................. **2–3**
CAPITOL: *61–66* **3–5**
CHURCHILL: *82–84*............. **1–3**
DOT: *68–74*...................... **2–4**
MCA: *79–81* **1–3**
SONGBIRD: *81* **1–3**
TOWER: *67*...................... **2–4**

LPs: 10/12-Inch 33rpm
ABC: *77–79*..................... **5–10**
ABC/DOT: *74–77*................ **6–10**
CAPITOL (300 series): *69* **10–12**
CAPITOL (1700 through
  2500 series): *62–66* **12–18**
  (With a "T" or "ST" prefix.)
CAPITOL (2400 series): *81* **5–8**
  (With an "SM" prefix.)
CAPITOL (11000 series):
  74–75 .... **8–12**
CAPITOL (12000 through
  16000 series): *80–81* **5–8**
CHURCHILL: *82*................. **5–8**
DOT: *68–74*..................... **8–12**
MCA: *79–84* **4–8**
PICKWICK/HILLTOP:
  66 .... **10–15**
SONGBIRD: *81* **5–8**
TOWER: *67–68*................. **10–15**
WORD: *75*....................... **5–8**

Price Range

CLARK, Sanford
Singles: 7-Inch
ABC: *74*......................... **$1–3**
DOT (15000 series): *56*........... **10–12**
  (Maroon labels.)
DOT (15000 series, except
  15738): *56–58*.................. **5–8**
  (Black labels.)
DOT (15738; "Modern
  Romance"): *58*................. **35–45**
JAMIE: *58–60*.................... **5–8**
LHI: *67–68* **3–5**
MCI: *55* **35–40**
RAMCO: *66* **4–6**
TREY: *61* **3–5**
WARNER BROS: *64–65*........... **3–5**
  Also see CASEY, Al

CLARK, Sanford, & Duane Eddy
Singles: 7-Inch
JAMIE (1107; "Sing 'Em
  Some Blues"): *58*............... **6–10**
  Also see CLARK, Sanford
  Also see EDDY, Duane

CLARK SISTERS, The
Singles: 12-Inch 33/45rpm
ELEKTRA: *83* **4–6**
Singles: 7-Inch
ELEKTRA: *83* **1–3**

CLARKE, Allan
Singles: 7-Inch
ASYLUM: *76*..................... **2–3**
ATLANTIC: *78* **2–3**
ELEKTRA: *80* **1–3**
EPIC: *72* **2–4**
LPs: 10/12-Inch 33rpm
ASYLUM: *76*.................... **8–10**
ATLANTIC: *78* **5–8**
ELEKTRA: *80* **5–8**
EPIC: *72* **10–12**
  Also see HOLLIES, The

CLARKE, Stanley (Stan Clarke)
Singles: 12-Inch 33/45rpm
EPIC: *83–85* **4–6**
NEMPEROR: *79* **4–6**
Singles: 7-Inch
EPIC: *80–85* **1–3**
NEMPEROR: *75–79* **2–3**

Price Range

LPs: 10/12-Inch 33rpm
EPIC: 80–85 .... **$5–8**
NEMPEROR: 74–78 .... **8–10**
POLYDOR: 73 .... **10–12**
Also see RETURN TO FOREVER

CLARKE, Stanley, & George Duke
Singles: 12-Inch 33/45rpm
EPIC: 83 .... **4–6**
Singles: 7-Inch
EPIC: 81–84 .... **1–3**
LPs: 10/12-Inch 33rpm
EPIC: 81–83 .... **5–8**
Also see CLARKE, Stanley
Also see DUKE, George

CLARKE, Tony
Singles: 7-Inch
CHESS: 64–65.................... **3–5**
CHICKORY: 70.................. **2–4**
ERIC: 78 .... **1–3**
M-S: 68......................... **3–5**

CLASH, The
Singles: 12-Inch 33/45rpm
EPIC: 81–82 .... **5–8**
Singles: 7-Inch
EPIC (1178; "Gates Of
   The West"): 79 .... **4–6**
   (Promotional issue only.)
EPIC (50000 series, except
   50738): 79–85................. **2–3**
EPIC (50738; "White Man
   In Hammersmith
   Palais"): 79.................... **5–8**
LPs: 10/12-Inch 33rpm
EPIC (952; "If Music
   Could Talk"): 81 .... **15–20**
   (Promotional issue only.)
EPIC (30000 series, except
   37037): 78–85................. **5–8**
EPIC (37037; "Sadinista"):
   82 .... **10–12**
EPIC/NU-DISC: 80............... **5–8**
Members: Mick Jones; Joe Strummer; Nick
Sheppard; Pete Howard; Vince White.
Also see BIG AUDIO DYNAMITE

CLASSIC SULLIVANS, The
Singles: 7-Inch
KWANZA: 73.................... **2–3**

Price Range

CLASSICS, The
Singles: 7-Inch
ALCAR: 63.................... **$15–20**
STARR: 60 .... **75–90**
Members: Lou Christie; Kay Chick; Shirley
Herbert; Ken Krease.
Also see CHRISTIE, Lou
Also see LUGEE & THE LIONS

CLASSICS, The
Singles: 7-Inch
COLLECTABLES: 83 .... **1–3**
DART: 60–61 .... **10–15**
ERIC: 82 .... **1–3**
MERCURY: 61.................. **10–12**
MUSIC NOTE: 63 .... **4–6**
MUSICTONE.................... **4–6**
PICCOLO: 65 .... **3–5**
STORK: 64 .... **3–5**
STREAM LINE: 61 .... **3–5**
Members: Emil Stuccio; Tony Victor; John
Gamble; Jamie Troy.

CLASSICS IV, The (Dennis Yost & The Classics IV; The Classics)
Singles: 7-Inch
ARLEN: 64..................... **10–15**
CAPITOL: 66–67 .... **8–10**
IMPERIAL: 67–70............... **3–5**
LIBERTY: 70 .... **2–4**
MGM: 75....................... **2–3**
MGM/SOUTH: 72–73 .... **2–3**
UNITED ARTISTS: 71............ **2–3**

LPs: 10/12-Inch 33rpm
ACCORD: 81 .... **5–8**
IMPERIAL: 68–69............... **12–15**
LIBERTY (10000 series):
   82–83 .... **5–8**
LIBERTY (11000 series):
   70 .... **10–12**
MGM/SOUNDS OF THE
   SOUTH: 73 .... **8–10**
SUNSET: 70 .... **10–12**
UNITED ARTISTS: 75........... **8–10**
Members: Dennis Yost; James Cobb; Dean
Daughtry; Wally Eaton; Auburn Burrell; Kim
Venable; Joe Wilson.
Also see ATLANTA RHYTHM SECTION,
The
Also see CANDYMEN, The
Also see YOST, Dennis

CLAY, Cassius (Cassius Marcellus Clay, Jr; Muhammed Ali)
Singles: 7-Inch
COLUMBIA (43007;
"Stand By Me"): *64* **$8–10**
COLUMBIA (75717; "Will
The Real Sonny Liston
Please Fall Down"): *64* **25-35**
(Promotional issue only.)
Picture Sleeves
COLUMBIA (43007;
"Stand By Me"): *64* **15–20**
LPs: 10/12-Inch 33rpm
COLUMBIA: *63* **30–40**

CLAY, Judy
Singles: 7-Inch
ATLANTIC: *69–70* **2–3**
EMBER: *61–62* **3–5**
SCEPTER: *64–66* **3–5**
STAX: *68–69* **2–4**
Also see BELL, William, & Judy Clay
Also see VERA, Billy, & Judy Clay

CLAY, Otis
Singles: 7-Inch
COTILLION: *68–71* **2–4**
DAKAR: *69* **2–4**
ELKA: *75* **2–3**
HI: *72–73* **2–3**
KAYVETTE: *77* **2–3**
ONE-DERFUL: *65–67* **3–5**
LPs: 10/12-Inch 33rpm
HI: *73–77* **8–10**

CLAY, Tom (Tom Clay & The Blackberries)
Singles: 7-Inch
CHANT **4–8**
MOTOWN: *81* **2–3**
MOWEST: *71* **2–4**
LPs: 10/12-Inch 33rpm
MOWEST: *71* **10–12**

CLAYDERMAN, Richard
LPs: 10/12-Inch 33rpm
COLUMBIA: *84* **4–8**

CLAYTON, Merry
Singles: 7-Inch
CAPITOL: *63–65* **3–5**

MCA: *80* **$1–3**
ODE '70: *70–76* **2–3**
LPs: 10/12-Inch 33rpm
MCA: *80* **5–8**
ODE (34000 series): *77* **5–8**
ODE (77000 series): *71–75* **10–12**
Also see BEACH BOYS, The
Also see SCOTT, Tom
Also see SMITH, Leslie, & Merry Clayton
Also see WYCOFF, Michael

CLAYTON, Willie
Singles: 7-Inch
COMPLEAT: *85* **1–3**

CLAYTON-THOMAS, David
Singles: 7-Inch
COLUMBIA: *72* **2–4**
DECCA: *69* **2–5**
RCA VICTOR: *73* **2–4**
LPs: 10/12-Inch 33rpm
ABC: *78* **5–8**
COLUMBIA: *72* **10–12**
DECCA: *69* **15–18**
RCA VICTOR: *73–74* **8–10**
Also see BLOOD, SWEAT & TEARS

CLEAN LIVING
Singles: 7-Inch
VANGUARD: *72* **2–4**
LPs: 10/12-Inch 33rpm
VANGUARD: *72–73* **8–10**

CLEAR LIGHT
Singles: 7-Inch
ELEKTRA: *67* **3–5**
LPs: 10/12-Inch 33rpm
ELEKTRA: *67* **12–15**
Members: Cliff DeYoung; Douglas Lubahn;
Michael Ney; Ralph Schuckett; Bob Seal; Dallas Taylor.

CLEFS OF LAVENDER HILL, The
Singles: 7-Inch
DATE: *66–67* **3–5**
THAMES: *66* **8–10**

CLEFTONES, The
Singles: 7-Inch
ABC: *73* **1–3**
GEE (Red label): *56–58* **5–8**
GEE (Gray label): *61–63* **3–5**

Price Range

ROULETTE **$1–3**
LPs: 10/12-Inch 33rpm
GEE (705; "Heart &
Soul"): *61* **40–50**
GEE (707; "For
Sentimental Reasons"):
62 .... **30–40**
(Monaural issue.)
GEE (707; "For
Sentimental Reasons"):
62 .... **75–100**
(Stereo issue.)
ROULETTE: *58–60* **4–6**
WARE: *64* **3–5**
　Members: Herbie Cox; Berman Patterson; Bill
　McClain; Charles James; Warren Corbin; Pat
　Span; Eugene Pearson.
　Also see HARPTONES, The / The Cleftones

CLEMMONS, Angela
Singles: 12-Inch 33/45rpm
PORTRAIT: *82*. **4–6**
Singles: 7-Inch
EPIC: *80* **1–3**
PORTRAIT: *82*. **1–3**
LPs: 10/12-Inch 33rpm
PORTRAIT: *82*. **5–8**

CLEMONS, Clarence (Clarence Clemons & The Red Bank Rockers)
Singles: 7-Inch
COLUMBIA: *83–85* **1–3**
LPs: 10/12-Inch 33rpm
COLUMBIA: *83–85* **5–8**
　Also see BROWNE, Jackson
　Also see FRANKLIN, Aretha
　Also see SPRINGSTEEN, Bruce

CLIFF, Jimmy
Singles: 12-Inch 33/45rpm
COLUMBIA: *83–84* **4–6**
Singles: 7-Inch
A&M: *69–70* **2–4**
COLUMBIA: *82–84* **1–3**
MANGO: *73* **2–3**
MCA: *81* **1–3**
REPRISE: *74–77*. **2–3**
VEEP: *67–68* **3–5**
LPs: 10/12-Inch 33rpm
A&M: *70* **12–15**
COLUMBIA: *82* **5–8**
ISLAND: *74* **8–10**

Price Range

MCA: *80–81* **$5–8**
REPRISE: *73–76*. **8–10**
VEEP: *69*. **15–20**
WARNER BROS: *78* **5–8**

CLIFFORD, Buzz (Buzz Clifford With The Teenagers)
Singles: 7-Inch
BOW. **4–6**
CAPITOL: *67* **2–4**
COLUMBIA (41876;
"Baby Sittin' Boogie"):
60 .... **10–15**
(With a "3" prefix. Compact 33 Single.)
COLUMBIA (41979;
"Simply Because"): *61* **25–30**
(With a "3" prefix. Compact 33 Single.)
COLUMBIA (42019; "I'll
Never Forget"): *61* **25–30**
(With a "3" prefix. Compact 33 Single.)
COLUMBIA (42290;
"Forever"): *62*. **25–30**
(With a "3" prefix. Compact 33 Single.)
COLUMBIA (41774;
"Hello Mr. Moonlight"):
60 .... **8–10**
(With a "4" prefix.)
COLUMBIA (41876;
"Baby Sitter Boogie"): *60*. **15–20**
(Note slightly different title. With a "4" prefix.)
COLUMBIA (41876;
"Baby Sittin' Boogie"):
61 .... **3–5**
(With a "4" prefix.)
COLUMBIA (41979;
"Simply Because"): *61* **15–20**
(With a "4" prefix.)
COLUMBIA (42019; "I'll
Never Forget"): *61* **15–20**
(With a "4" prefix.)
COLUMBIA (42177;
"Moving Day"): *61*. **3–5**
(With a "4" prefix.)
COLUMBIA (42290;
"Forever"): *62*. **15–20**
(With a "4" prefix.)
DOT: *69–70*. **2–3**
ERIC: *83* **1–3**
RCA VICTOR: *66* **2–4**
ROULETTE: *62–63* **4–6**
Picture Sleeves
COLUMBIA: *61–62* **15–20**

Price Range

LPs: 10/12-Inch 33rpm
COLUMBIA: *61* $40–50
DOT: *69* 12–15
Also see TEENAGERS, The

CLIFFORD, Linda
Singles: 12-Inch 33/45rpm
CAPITOL: *82* 4–6
RSO: *79* 4–6
RED LABEL: *85* 4–6
Singles: 7-Inch
CAPITOL: *80–82* 1–3
CURTOM: *77–78* 2–3
GEMIGO: *75* 2–3
PARAMOUNT: *74* 2–3
POLYDOR: *73* 2–3
RSO: *79–80* 1–3
RED LABEL: *84–85* 1–3
LPs: 10/12-Inch 33rpm
CAPITOL: *80–82* 5–8
CURTOM: *77–80* 8–10
PARAMOUNT: *74* 2–3
RSO: *79–80* 5–8
Also see MAYFIELD, Curtis, & Linda Clifford

CLIFFORD, Mike
Singles: 7-Inch
AIR: *71* 2–3
AMERICAN INT'L: *70* 2–3
CAMEO: *65–66* 3–5
COLUMBIA: *61–62* 3–5
LIBERTY: *59* 3–5
SIDEWALK: *67–68* 2–4
UNITED ARTISTS: *62–65* 3–5
Picture Sleeves
COLUMBIA: *61* 3–5
LPs: 10/12-Inch 33rpm
UNITED ARTISTS: *65* 15–20

CLIFFORD, Mike, & Patience & Prudence
Singles: 7-Inch
LIBERTY: *59* 3–5
Also see CLIFFORD, Mike
Also see PATIENCE & PRUDENCE

CLIMAX
Singles: 7-Inch
ARISTA: *81* 1–3
BELL: *71* 2–3
CAROUSEL: *70–71* 2–3

Price Range

FLASHBACK: *73* $1–3
PARAMOUNT: *70* 2–4
PATTI PLATTERS: *67* 3–5
ROCKY ROAD: *72* 2–3
LPs: 10/12-Inch 33rpm
ROCKY ROAD: *72* 12–15
Members: Sonny Geraci; John Bahler; Tom
Bahler; Jon Jon Gultman.
Also see LOVE GENERATION
Also see OUTSIDERS, The

CLIMAX BLUES BAND, The
Singles: 7-Inch
SIRE: *71–79* 2–3
WARNER BROS: *79–82* 1–3
LPs: 10/12-Inch 33rpm
SIRE (Except 6000 series):
69–76 10–15
SIRE (6000 series): *77–78* 8–10
VIRGIN: *83* 5–8
WARNER BROS: *79–81* 5–8
Members: The Climax Chicago Blues Band;
Colin Cooper; John Cuffley; Peter Haycock;
Derek Holt; Richard Jones; Arthur Wood.

CLINE, Patsy
Singles: 7-Inch
CORAL: *55–56* 4–6
DECCA (25000 series):
65–69 2–4
DECCA (29963 through
30846): *57–59* 4–6
DECCA (30929; "Gotta
Lot Of Rhythm In My
Soul"): *59* 8–12
DECCA (31000 series):
59–64 3–5
EVEREST (2000 series):
62–64 3–5
EVEREST (20005; "I
Don't Wanta"): *62* 8–12
FOUR STAR (Except 1000
series): *56* 4–6
FOUR STAR (1000 series):
78 1–3
MCA: *73–80* 1–3
STARDAY (7000 series):
65 3–5
STARDAY (8000 series):
71 2–3
Picture Sleeves
DECCA: *57–63* 4–6

Price Range

EPs: 7-Inch 33/45rpm
CORAL: *58* $15–20
DECCA: *57–65* 10–15
FOUR STAR: *57* 20–30
(Promotional issue only.)
LPs: 10/12-Inch 33rpm
ACCORD: *81* 5–8
ALBUM GLOBE 5–8
ALLEGIANCE: *84.* 5–8
COLUMBIA: *69* 12–15
(Columbia Musical Treasury issue.)
COUNTRY FIDELITY:
   82 5–8
DECCA (4200 series):
   61–62 20–25
DECCA (4500 series): *64* 15–20
DECCA (4800 series): *67* 10–15
DECCA (8600 series): *57* 25–35
EVEREST (300 series): *75* 5–8
EVEREST (1200 series):
   62–64 15–20
51 WEST: *82* 5–8
H.S.R.D: *84* 8–10
LONGINES. 8–12
MCA: *80–84* 5–10
METRO: *65.* 12–18
PICKWICK/HILLTOP:
   65–68 10–12
SEARS 10–15
VOCALION: *65–69* 10–15
Also see HAGGARD, Merle / Patsy Cline
Also see REEVES, Jim, & Patsy Cline

CLINE, Patsy / Cowboy Copas / Hawkshaw Hawkins
LPs: 10/12-Inch 33rpm
STARDAY: *65* 12–18
Also see CLINE, Patsy
Also see COPAS, Cowboy
Also see HAWKINS, Hawkshaw

CLINTON, George, Band
Singles: 12-Inch 33/45rpm
CAPITOL: *82–83* 4–6
Singles: 7-Inch
ABC: *74* 2–3
CAPITOL: *83–85* 1–3
LPs: 10/12-Inch 33rpm
ABC: *74* 8–10
CAPITOL: *82–85* 5–8
INVICTUS: *73* 10–12

Price Range

Also see PARLIAMENTS, The

CLIQUE, The
Singles: 7-Inch
ABC: *73* $1–3
FRETONE: *74.* 2–3
MERCURY: *69.* 2–4
SASSY: *67* 4–6
SCEPTER: *67* 3–5
WHITE WHALE: *69–71* 3–5
LPs: 10/12-Inch 33rpm
WHITE WHALE: *69* 20–25

CLIQUES, The (Featuring Jesse Belvin)
Singles: 7-Inch
MODERN: *56.* 8–10
Also see BELVIN, Jesse
Also see CHURCH, Eugene

CLOCKS, The
Singles: 7-Inch
BOULEVARD: *82* 1–3
LPs: 10/12-Inch 33rpm
BOULEVARD: *82* 5–8

CLOCKWORK
Singles: 12-Inch 33/45rpm
PRIVATE 1: *84.* 4–6
Singles: 7-Inch
PRIVATE 1: *84.* 1–3

CLOONEY, Rosemary
Singles: 7-Inch
APCO: *75* 1–3
COLUMBIA (38000
   through 40000 series):
   50–57 3–5
CORAL: *59* 2–4
DOT: *68.* 2–3
MGM: *59–65* 2–4
RCA VICTOR: *60–61* 2–4
REPRISE: *63–64.* 2–4
Picture Sleeves
RCA VICTOR: *60* 2–4
EPs: 7-Inch 33/45rpm
COLUMBIA: *51–56* 5–10
MGM: *58–60.* 5–8
LPs: 10/12-Inch 33rpm
COLUMBIA (500 through
   1200 series): *54–58* 15–25

Price Range

CONCORD JAZZ: *78–83* **$5–8**
CORAL: *59* **10–15**
HARMONY: *59–68* **8–12**
MGM (Except 1000 series):
  59–62 .... **10–15**
MGM (1000 series): *67*. **8–12**
RCA VICTOR: *60–63* **10–12**
REPRISE: *63–64*. **8–12**
  Also see BOYD, Jimmy, & Rosemary Clooney
  Also see HERMAN, Woody

CLOONEY, Rosemary, & Bing Crosby
Singles: 7-Inch
RCA VICTOR: *59* **2–4**

LPs: 10/12-Inch 33rpm
CAMDEN: *69*. **6–10**
CAPITOL (2300 series): *65* **8–12**
CAPITOL (11000 series):
  77 .... **5–8**
  Also see CROSBY, Bing

CLOONEY, Rosemary, & Jose Ferrer
EPs: 7-Inch 33/45rpm
MGM: *58*. **12–18**
  Also see FERRER, Jose

CLOONEY, Rosemary, & Dick Haymes
LPs: 10/12-Inch 33rpm
EXACT: *80* **5–8**
  Also see HAYMES, Dick

CLOONEY, Rosemary, & Guy Mitchell (With Joanne Gilbert)
EPs: 7-Inch 33/45rpm
COLUMBIA (377; "Red
  Garters"): *54* **12–18**
  (Soundtrack.)

LPs: 10/12-Inch 33rpm
COLUMBIA (6282; "Red
  Garters"): *54* **40–50**
  (10-Inch LP. Soundtrack.)
  Also see MITCHELL, Guy

CLOONEY, Rosemary, & Perez Prado
Singles: 7-Inch
RCA VICTOR: *60* **2–4**

Price Range

LPs: 10/12-Inch 33rpm
RCA VICTOR: *60* **$10–12**
  Also see CLOONEY, Rosemary
  Also see PRADO, Perez

CLOUD, Christopher (Tommy Boyce)
Singles: 7-Inch
CHELSEA: *72–73*. **2–4**
LPs: 10/12-Inch 33rpm
CHELSEA: *73*. **10–15**
  Also see BOYCE, Tommy

CLOUT
Singles: 7-Inch
EPIC: *78–79* **2–3**
LPs: 10/12-Inch 33rpm
EPIC: *79–80* **5–8**

CLOVERS, The
Singles: 7-Inch
ATLANTIC (900 series,
  except 934 & 944): *52–53*. **20–25**
ATLANTIC (934; "Don't
  You Know I Love
  You"): *51* **60–75**
ATLANTIC (944; "Fool,
  Fool, Fool"): *51*. **40–50**
ATLANTIC (1000 series,
  except 1000): *53–56*. **8–12**
ATLANTIC (1000; "Good
  Lovin"): *53*. **20–25**
ATLANTIC (1100 series):
  56–58 .... **5–8**
ATLANTIC (2000 series):
  61 .... **3–5**
BRUNSWICK: *63*. **3–5**
JOSIE: *68*. **3–5**
POPLAR: *58*. **5–8**
PORT: *65*. **3–5**
PORWIN: *63*. **3–5**
UNITED ARTISTS: *59–61* **4–6**
WINLEY: *61–62*. **3–5**
EPs: 7-Inch 33/45rpm
ATLANTIC: *56–57* **40–50**
LPs: 10/12-Inch 33rpm
ATCO: *71* **10–12**
ATLANTIC (1200 series):
  56 .... **75–90**
ATLANTIC (8000 series):
  57 .... **50–60**
  (Black labels.)

Price Range   *Price Range*

ATLANTIC (8000 series):
59 .... **$25–30**
(Red labels.)
GRAND PRIX: *64*.............. **10–12**
POPLAR: *58*.................... **50–60**
TRIP: *72* **8–10**
UNITED ARTISTS: *59–60*....... **35–40**
Members: John "Buddy" Bailey; Harold Winley; Harold Lucas; Bill Harris; Matthew McQuater; Charlie White; Billy Mitchell.
Also see JACKSON, Willis
Also see MITCHELL, Billy

CLUB HOUSE
Singles: 12-Inch 33/45rpm
ATLANTIC: *83* **4–6**
Singles: 7-Inch
ATLANTIC: *83* **1–3**

Coasters, 20 charted singles (1956–71), no charted LPs.

COASTERS, The
Singles: 7-Inch
ATCO (6000 series): *56* **10–15**
(Maroon label.)
ATCO (6000 series): *56–57* **5–8**
(Yellow & white label.)
ATCO (6100 series): *57–61* **4–6**
ATCO (6200 through 6400
series): *61–66* **3–5**
DATE: *67–68*..................... **3–5**
KING: *71–73*..................... **2–4**
TURNTABLE: *69*................. **2–4**
EPs: 7-Inch 33/45rpm
ATCO: *58–59*.................... **25–35**

LPs: 10/12-Inch 33rpm
ATCO (100 series, except
101): *59–71*................. **$20–30**
ATCO (101; "The
Coasters"): *58* **35–45**
(Yellow label.)
ATCO (101; "The
Coasters"): *59* **20–30**
(Yellow & white label.)
ATCO (300 series): *71* **10–12**
ATLANTIC: *82* **10–12**
CLARION: *64*................... **12–15**
KING: *71* **10–12**
POWER PAK: *83*................ **5–8**
TRIP: *72–76* **8–10**
Members: Bobby Nunn; Leon Hughes; Carl Gardner; Billy Guy; Adolph Jacobs; Cornel Gunter; Will Jones; Earl Carroll; Ronnie Bright.
Also see HENDRICKS, Bobby
Also see NUNN, Bobby
Also see ROBINS, The

COASTERS, The / The Crew-Cuts / The Chiffons
LPs: 10/12-Inch 33rpm
EXACT: *80* **5–8**
Also see CHIFFONS, The
Also see CREW-CUTS, The

COASTERS, The / The Drifters
LPs: 10/12-Inch 33rpm
TVP **10–12**
(A TV mail-order LP offer.)
Also see COASTERS, The
Also see DRIFTERS, The

COATES, Odia
Singles: 12-Inch 33/45rpm
EPIC: *77* **4–6**
Singles: 7-Inch
BUDDAH: *73*.................... **2–3**
EPIC: *78* **2–3**
UNITED ARTISTS: *74–75*.......... **2–3**
LPs: 10/12-Inch 33rpm
UNITED ARTISTS: *75*............ **8–10**
Also see ANKA, Paul, & Odia Coates

COBB, Joyce
Singles: 7-Inch
CREAM: *79–80*................... **1–3**
TRUTH: *75* **2–3**

Price Range   *Price Range*

COBHAM, Billy (Billy Cobham's Glass Menagerie; Billy Cobham With The George Duke Band)
Singles: 12-Inch 33/45rpm
COLUMBIA: 80 .... $4–6
Singles: 7-Inch
ATLANTIC: 75–77 2–3
COLUMBIA: 78–80 1–3
LPs: 10/12-Inch 33rpm
ATLANTIC: 73–79 5–8
COLUMBIA: 77–80 5–8
ELEKTRA: 82–83 5–8
Also see DUKE, George
Also see SINGLETON, Charlie

COCCIANTE, Richard
Singles: 7-Inch
20TH CENTURY-FOX:
76 1–3

COCHISE (With Mick Grabham)
Singles: 7-Inch
UNITED ARTISTS: 71 2–4
EPs: 7-Inch 33/45rpm
UNITED ARTISTS: 71 10–12
LPs: 10/12-Inch 33rpm
UNITED ARTISTS: 71 10–12

COCHRAN, Eddie
Singles: 7-Inch
CREST: 56 80–100
LIBERTY (54000 series):
62 4–6
LIBERTY (55056; "Sittin' In The Balcony"): 57 8–10
LIBERTY (55070; "Mean When I'm Mad"): 58 8–12
LIBERTY (55087; "Drive In Show"): 57 10–12
LIBERTY (55112; "Twenty Flight Rock"): 58 15–20
LIBERTY (55123; "Jeannie Jeannie Jeannie"): 58 15–20
LIBERTY (55138; "Pretty Girl"): 58 8–10
LIBERTY (55144; "Summertime Blues"): 58 8–10
LIBERTY (55166; "C'mon Everybody"): 58 8–10

LIBERTY (55177; "Teenage Heaven"): 59 .... $8–10
LIBERTY (55203; "Somethin' Else"): 59 10–12
(With horizontal silver lines.)
LIBERTY (55203; "Somethin' Else"): 59 5–8
(Without horizontal silver lines.)
LIBERTY (55217; "Hallelujah, I Love Her So"): 59 5–8
LIBERTY (55242; "Cut Across Shorty"): 60 8–12
(Green label.)
LIBERTY (55242; "Cut Across Shorty"): 61 5–8
(Black label.)
LIBERTY (55278; "Sweetie Pie"): 60 8–10
LIBERTY (55389; "Weekend"): 61 15–20

Picture Sleeves
LIBERTY (55070; "Mean When I'm Mad"): 58 40–50

EPs: 7-Inch 33/45rpm
LIBERTY: 58 50–75

LPs: 10/12-Inch 33rpm
LIBERTY (3000 series, except 3061): 60–62 40–50
LIBERTY (3061; "Singin' To My Baby"): 58 75–100
(Green label.)
LIBERTY (3061; "Singin' To My Baby"): 60 25–30
(Black label.)
LIBERTY (10000 series): 81–83 5–8
SUNSET: 66 12–15
UNITED ARTISTS: 71–75 10–12
Also see COCHRAN BROTHERS, The

COCHRAN, Hank
Singles: 7-Inch
CAPITOL: 78 1–3
DOT: 70 2–3
ELEKTRA: 80 1–3
GAYLORD: 62–63 3–5
LIBERTY: 62–63 3–5
MONUMENT: 67–68 2–3
RCA VICTOR: 64–66 2–4

Price Range

Price Range

LPs: 10/12-Inch 33rpm

CAPITOL: 78 .... $5–8
ELEKTRA: 80 5–8
MONUMENT: 68. 10–12
RCA VICTOR: 65 12–18
Also see COCHRAN BROTHERS, The

COCHRAN, Hank, & Willie Nelson
Singles: 7-Inch

CAPITOL: 78 1–3
Also see COCHRAN, Hank
Also see NELSON, Willie

COCHRAN, Wayne (Wayne Cochran & The C.C. Riders)
Singles: 7-Inch

BETHLEHEM: 70 2–3
CHESS: 67–68 2–4
DECK 2–4
EPIC: 72 2–4
KING (5000 series): 63–65 4–6
KING (6000 series): 65–71 3–5
MERCURY: 65–67 3–5
SCOTTIE: 59. 5–8
SOFT: 65 3–5

Picture Sleeves

CHESS: 67 2–4
MERCURY: 65 3–5

LPs: 10/12-Inch 33rpm

BETHLEHEM: 70 12–15
CHESS: 68 15–18
EPIC: 72 8–10
KING: 70 12–15

COCHRAN BROTHERS, The
Singles: 7-Inch

EKKO (1000 series): 56 60–75
EKKO (3000 series): 56 75–100
Members: Eddie Cochran; Hank Cochran (not really brothers).
Also see COCHRAN, Eddie
Also see COCHRAN, Hank

COCK ROBIN
Singles: 12-Inch 33/45rpm

COLUMBIA: 85 4–6
Singles: 7-Inch
COLUMBIA: 85 1–3
LPs: 10/12-Inch 33rpm
COLUMBIA: 85 5–8

COCKBURN, Bruce
Singles: 7-Inch

GOLD MOUNTAIN: 84 .... $1–3
MILLENNIUM: 80 1–3
LPs: 10/12-Inch 33rpm
EPIC: 71–72 10–12
GOLD MOUNTAIN: 84 5–8
ISLAND: 77–78 8–10
MILLENNIUM: 80–81 5–8
TRUE NORTH: 77–78 8–10

COCKER, Joe
Singles: 7-Inch

A&M: 68–78 2–4
ASYLUM: 78–79. 2–3
CAPITOL: 84–85 1–3
ISLAND: 83 1–3
PHILIPS: 65 6–10

Picture Sleeves

A&M: 69–74 1–3

LPs: 10/12-Inch 33rpm

A&M (Except 3100 series):
   69–77 10–12
A&M (3100 series): 82 5–8
ASYLUM (Except picture
   discs): 78–79. 5–8
ASYLUM (Picture discs):
   79 20–25
   (Promotional issues only.)
CAPITOL: 84–85 5–8
Also see BOWIE, David / Joe Cocker / The Youngbloods
Also see CRUSADERS, The
Also see RUSSELL, Leon

COCKER, Joe, & Jennifer Warnes
Singles: 7-Inch

ISLAND: 82 1–3
Picture Sleeves
ISLAND: 82 .... INC
Also see COCKER, Joe
Also see WARNES, Jennifer

COCO, El: see EL COCO

CODAY, Bill
Singles: 7-Inch

CRAJON: 71 2–4
EPIC: 73–75 2–3
GALAXY: 71 2–4

**CODY, Commander: see
COMMANDER CODY**

COE, David Allan
Singles: 7-Inch
COLUMBIA: *74–85* $1–3
SSS INT'L: *71–72* 2–4
LPs: 10/12-Inch 33rpm
COLUMBIA: *72–84* 5–10
SSS INT'L (9;
"Penitentiary Blues"): *70* 20–30

COE, David Allan, & Bill Anderson
Singles: 7-Inch
COLUMBIA: *80* 1–3
Also see ANDERSON, Bill
Also see COE, David Allan
Also see JONES, George, & David Allan Coe
Also see NELSON, Willie / Jerry Lee Lewis /
Carl Perkins / David Allan Coe

COFFEE
Singles: 7-Inch
DELITE: *80–82* 1–3

**COFFEY, Dennis (Dennis Coffey &
The Detroit Guitar Band; Dennis
Coffey & The Lyman Woodward Trio)**
Singles: 7-Inch
MAVERICK: *69* 2–4
SUSSEX: *70–74* 2–3
WARNER BROS: *74* 2–3
20TH CENTURY/
WESTBOUND: *75–76* 2–3
WESTBOUND: *77–78* 1–3
LPs: 10/12-Inch 33rpm
SUSSEX: *70–75* 10–12
20TH CENTURY/
WESTBOUND: *75–76* 8–10
WESTBOUND: *77* 5–8

COHEN, Leonard
Singles: 7-Inch
COLUMBIA: *68–73* 2–4
LPs: 10/12-Inch 33rpm
COLUMBIA: *68–85* 10–12
WARNER BROS: *77* 8–12

COHEN, Myron
LPs: 10/12-Inch 33rpm
RCA VICTOR: *66* 10–12

COLD BLOOD
Singles: 7-Inch
ABC: *75* $2–3
REPRISE: *72–73* 2–4
SAN FRANCISCO: *70* 3–5
LPs: 10/12-Inch 33rpm
ABC: *76* 8–10
REPRISE: *72–73* 10–12
SAN FRANCISCO: *69–70* 12–15
WARNER BROS: *74* 8–10
Members: Lydia Pense; Michael Andreas; Rod
Ellicott; Frank Davis; Jerry Jonutz; Danny
Hull; Larry Field.

COLD CHISEL
Singles: 7-Inch
ELEKTRA: *81* 1–3
LPs: 10/12-Inch 33rpm
ELEKTRA: *80–82* 5–8
Members: Don Walker; Jimmy Barnes; Steve
Prestwich; Phil Small; Ian Moss.

COLDER, Ben (Sheb Wooley)
Singles: 7-Inch
MGM: *62–73* 2–4
SUNBIRD: *80* 1–3
LPs: 10/12-Inch 33rpm
MGM (Except 4100 series):
66–73 10–15
MGM (4100 series): *61–63* 15–20
Also see WOOLEY, Sheb

**COLE, Ann (Ann Cole & The
Suburbans)**
Singles: 7-Inch
BATON: *56–57* 5–8
MGM: *60* 3–5
ROULETTE: *62* 3–5
SIR: *59–60* 4–6
TIMELY: *54* 5–8

COLE, Bobby
Singles: 7-Inch
DATE: *68–69* 2–4

**COLE, Cozy (Cozy Cole & His All
Stars)**
Singles: 7-Inch
ARTISTIQUE: *61* 2–4
BETHLEHEM: *63* 2–4
CHARLIE PARKER: *62* 2–4

Price Range

CORAL: *62–67*	$2–3
KING: *59–60.*	2–4
LOVE: *58–59.*	3–6
MGM: *54.*	4–6
RANDOM: *60.*	2–4

Picture Sleeves

RANDOM: *60.*	2–4

EPs: 7-Inch 33/45rpm

AFTER HOURS: *55*	15–20
MGM: *54*	15–20

LPs: 10/12-Inch 33rpm

AFTER HOURS: *55*	25–30
CHARLIE PARKER: *62*	15–20
COLUMBIA: *66*	10–15
CORAL: *62–64*	15–20
EVEREST: *74*	8–10
FELSTED: *59*	15–20
KING: *59–60.*	20–25
LOVE: *59.*	20–25
PARIS: *58*	20–25
SAVOY: *72–77*	8–12
TRIP: *74*	8–10

COLE, Cozy, & Illinois Jacquet
LPs: 10/12-Inch 33rpm

AUDITION: *55.*	25–30

Also see COLE, Cozy
Also see JACQUET, Illinois

COLE, Nat "King" (The King Cole Trio)
Singles: 7-Inch

CAPITOL (Except 900
through 4600 series):
61–69 2–3
CAPITOL (900 through
4600 series): *50–61* 3–6
(Purple labels.)

Picture Sleeves

CAPITOL: *59–66*	2–4

EPs: 7-Inch 33/45rpm

CAPITOL: *50–60*	5–10

LPs: 10/12-Inch 33rpm

CAPITOL (Except 100
through 2900 series):
61–82 5–10

Price Range

CAPITOL (100 through
300 series): *50–52* $20–35
(With an "H" prefix. 10-Inch LPs.)
CAPITOL (100 through
300 series): *52–53* 15–30
(With a "T" prefix.)
CAPITOL (400 through
2900 series): *52–68* 10–25

CROWN: *64*	8–12
MCA: *73*	5–8
MARK '56: *76.*	5–8
SCORE: *57*	15–20
VSP: *66*	10–15

Also see KENTON, Stan
Also see MARTIN, Dean, & Nat "King" Cole

COLE, Nat "King," & George Shearing
LPs: 10/12-Inch 33rpm

CAPITOL: *61*	15–25

Also see COLE, Nat "King"
Also see SHEARING, George

COLE, Natalie
Singles: 12-Inch 33/45rpm

EPIC: *83*	4–6
MODERN: *85*	4–6

Singles: 7-Inch

CAPITOL: *75–80*	2–3
EPIC: *83*	1–3
MODERN: *85*	1–3

LPs: 10/12-Inch 33rpm

CAPITOL: *75–82*	8–12
EPIC: *83*	5–8
MODERN: *85*	5–8

Also see BRYSON, Peabo, & Natalie Cole

COLE, Sami Jo
Singles: 7-Inch

ELEKTRA: *81*	1–3

COLE, Tony
Singles: 7-Inch

20TH CENTURY-FOX:
72–74 2–3

LPs: 10/12-Inch 33rpm

20TH CENTURY-FOX:
73 8–10

Price Range

COLEMAN, Albert (Albert Coleman's Atlanta Pops)
Singles: 7-Inch
EPIC: *82* **$1–3**

COLEMAN, Durell
Singles: 7-Inch
ISLAND: *85* **1–3**

LPs: 10/12-Inch 33rpm
ISLAND: *85* **5–8**

COLLAGE
Singles: 12-Inch 33/45rpm
CONSTELLATION: *86*............ **4–6**
MCA: *85* **4–6**
SOLAR: *83* **4–6**

Singles: 7-Inch
CONSTELLATION: *86*............ **1–3**
MCA: *85* **1–3**
SOLAR: *82–83* **1–3**

LPs: 10/12-Inch 33rpm
CONSTELLATION: *86*............ **5–8**
SOLAR: *81–83* **5–8**

COLLAY & THE SATELLITES
Singles: 7-Inch
SHO-BIZ: *60*..................... **5–8**

COLLEY, Keith
Singles: 7-Inch
CHALLENGE: *66–70* **3–5**
COLUMBIA: *68*.................. **2–4**
ERA: *61–62*...................... **3–5**
UNICAL: *63–64* **3–5**
VEE JAY: *65*..................... **3–5**

COLLIER, Mitty
Singles: 7-Inch
CHESS: *61–68*.................... **3–5**
ENTRANCE: *72*................... **2–4**
ERIC: *78* **1–3**
PEACHTREE: *69–70*.............. **2–4**

LPs: 10/12-Inch 33rpm
CHESS: *65–66*................... **15–20**
GOSPEL ROOTS: *79*.............. **5–8**

Albert Collins, one charted single (1972), no charted LPs.

Price Range

COLLINS, Albert (Albert Collins & The Ice Breakers)
Singles: 7-Inch
GREAT SCOTT................. **$8–10**
HALL: *64* **4–6**
HALL WAY: *63*................... **5–8**
IMPERIAL: *69*................... **2–4**
KANGAROO: *58*............... **12–15**
LIBERTY: *70* **2–4**
TCF HALL: *65–66*................. **3–5**
TUMBLEWEED: *72–73* **2–3**
20TH CENTURY-FOX:
   68 .... **2–4**

LPs: 10/12-Inch 33rpm
ALLIGATOR: *79–84*............... **5–8**
BLUE THUMB: *69* **10–12**
BRYLEN: *84*..................... **5–8**
IMPERIAL: *69–70*............... **10–12**
TCF HALL: *65*................. **30–35**
TUMBLEWEED: *71* **10–12**

COLLINS, Dave & Ansell
Singles: 7-Inch
BIG TREE: *71–72* **2–4**

LPs: 10/12-Inch 33rpm
BIG TREE: *71* **10–12**
   Also see COLLINS, Dave

Price Range

COLLINS, Dorothy
Singles: 7-Inch
AUDIOVOX: *54–55* **$3–5**
CORAL: *55–56* **2–4**
DECCA: *52* **3–5**
GOLD EAGLE: *61* **2–3**
MGM: *50–51* **3–5**
ROULETTE: *63* **2–3**
TOP RANK: *59–60* **2–4**
EPs: 7-Inch 33/45rpm
CORAL: *55–56* **5–8**
MGM: *55* **5–8**
LPs: 10/12-Inch 33rpm
CORAL: *55–57* **10–15**
MOTIVATION: *62*. **8–12**
TOP RANK: *60* **10–12**
VOCALION: *65* **5–10**

COLLINS, Judy
Singles: 7-Inch
ELEKTRA: *64–84* **2–3**
Picture Sleeves
ELEKTRA (Except "The
  Hostage"): *69–84*. **1–3**
ELEKTRA ("The
  Hostage"): *73*. **2–5**
  (Promotional issue only.)
LPs: 10/12-Inch 33rpm
ELEKTRA (Except 200 &
  300 series): *67–84* **10–12**
ELEKTRA (200 series):
  61–64 . . . . **20–25**
ELEKTRA (300 series):
  65–72 . . . . **15–20**

COLLINS, Judy, & T.G. Sheppard
Singles: 7-Inch
ELEKTRA: *84* **1–3**
  Also see COLLINS, Judy
  Also see SHEPPARD, T.G.

COLLINS, Keanya
Singles: 7-Inch
BLUE ROCK: *69* **2–4**
ITCO: *69* **2–4**

COLLINS, Lyn (Lyn Collins & The Famous Flames)
Singles: 7-Inch
PEOPLE: *72–76* **2–3**

Price Range

LPs: 10/12-Inch 33rpm
PEOPLE: *72–75* **$10–12**
  Also see BROWN, James & Lyn Collins

COLLINS, Phil
Singles: 12-Inch 33/45rpm
ATLANTIC: *84–86* **4–6**
Singles: 7-Inch
ATLANTIC: *81–86* **1–3**
Picture Sleeves
ATLANTIC: *81–86* . . . . **INC**
LPs: 10/12-Inch 33rpm
ATLANTIC: *81–86* **5–8**
  Also see BAILEY, Philip, & Phil Collins
  Also see BAND AID
  Also see BRAND X
  Also see GENESIS

COLLINS, Rodger (Roger Collins)
Singles: 7-Inch
FANTASY: *73*. **2–3**
GALAXY: *66–73* **3–5**
POMPEII: *69*. **2–4**

COLLINS, William: see BOOTSY'S RUBBER BAND

COLLINS & COLLINS
Singles: 7-Inch
A&M: *80* **1–3**
LPs: 10/12-Inch 33rpm
A&M: *80* **5–8**

COLOMBO, Chris: see COLUMBO, Chris

COLONEL ABRAMS: see ABRAMS, Colonel

COLORS
Singles: 12-Inch 33/45rpm
FIRST TAKE: *83* **4–6**
Singles: 7-Inch
BECKET: *82* **1–3**

COLTER, Jessi
Singles: 7-Inch
CAPITOL: *75–82* **1–3**
RCA VICTOR: *69–72* **2–4**
LPs: 10/12-Inch 33rpm
CAPITOL: *75–81* **6–10**

Price Range

RCA VICTOR: *70* **$8–12**
Also see JENNINGS, Waylon, & Jessi Colter

COLTRANE, Alice
LPs: 10/12-Inch 33rpm
IMPULSE: *71–74* **8–10**
WARNER BROS: *77–78* **5–10**

COLTRANE, Alice, & Carlos Santana
LPs: 10/12-Inch 33rpm
COLUMBIA: *74* **6–10**
Also see COLTRANE, Alice
Also see SANTANA

COLTRANE, Chi
Singles: 7-Inch
CLOUDS: *78* **1–3**
COLUMBIA: *72–73* **2–4**

LPs: 10/12-Inch 33rpm
CLOUDS: *77* **5–8**
COLUMBIA: *72–73* **8–10**

COLTRANE, John (The John Coltrane Trio; The John Coltrane Quartet)
Singles: 7-Inch
ATLANTIC: *60–61* **2–4**
IMPULSE: *62* **2–3**
PRESTIGE: *57–63* **2–4**

LPs: 10/12-Inch 33rpm
ATLANTIC (300 series):
73 . . . . **8–12**
ATLANTIC (1300 & 1400
series): *59–66* **15–20**
ATLANTIC (1500 series):
69–70 . . . . **8–12**
ATLANTIC (1600 series):
75 . . . . **5–10**
ATLANTIC (90000 series):
82 . . . . **5–8**
BETHLEHEM (6000
series): *63* **12–18**
(Maroon label.)
BETHLEHEM (6000
series): *76* **10–12**
(Gray label.)

Price Range

BLUE NOTE (400 series):
75 . . . . **$8–10**
BLUE NOTE (1500 series):
60 . . . . **15–25**
(Label reads "Blue Note Records Inc. - New
York, USA.")
BLUE NOTE (1500 series):
66 . . . . **10–20**
(Label shows Blue Note Records as a division
of either Liberty or United Artists.)
COLTRANE: *66* **50–75**
IMPULSE (6 through 95):
61–65 . . . . **12–20**
IMPULSE (9000 & 9100
series): *66–72* **10–15**
IMPULSE (9200 & 9300
series): *73–79* **8–12**
NEW JAZZ: *63* **10–15**
PABLO: *77–83* **6–10**
PRESTIGE (O20 through
2507): *81–83* **6–10**
PRESTIGE (7000 & 7100
series): *56–60* **20–30**
(Yellow label.)
PRESTIGE (7200 series):
61–64 . . . . **15–20**
(Yellow label.)
PRESTIGE (7000 through
7400 series): *64–66* **10–15**
(Blue label.)
PRESTIGE (7500 through
7800 series): *68–70* **8–12**
PRESTIGE (24000 series):
72–83 . . . . **8–12**
RIVERSIDE: *82* **5–8**
ROULETTE: *63* **10–20**
SAVOY: *76–77* **8–12**
SOLID STATE: *68* **8–12**
TRIP: *73* **5–10**
UNITED ARTISTS (5600
series): *72* **8–12**
UNITED ARTISTS (14000
& 15000 series): *62* **10–15**
Also see ADDERLY, Julian "Cannonball," &
John Coltrane
Also see ELLINGTON, Duke, & John Col-
trane

COLTRANE, John, & Miles Davis
LPs: 10/12-Inch 33rpm
PRESTIGE: *64* **10–15**
Also see DAVIS, Miles

Price Range *Price Range*

COLTRANE, John, & Thelonious Monk
LPs: 10/12-Inch 33rpm
JAZZLAND: *61* **$15–25**
MILESTONE: *73* **8–12**
RIVERSIDE (Except 039):
  65–68 .... **10–15**
RIVERSIDE (039;
  "Thelonious Monk &
  John Coltrane"): *82*............. **5–8**
  Also see COLTRANE, John
  Also see MONK, Thelonious

COLTS, The
Singles: 7-Inch
ANTLER: *59*.................. **10–12**
MAMBO: *55* **40–50**
PLAZA: *62* **3–5**
VITA: *55–56* **15–20**
  Members: Joe Crunby; Rubin Crunby; Leroy
  Smith; Carl Moland.

COLUMBO, Chris (The Chris Colombo Quintet)
Singles: 7-Inch
BATTLE: *62* **2–4**
MAXX: *64*. **2–3**
STRAND: *63*................... **2–4**
LPs: 10/12-Inch 33rpm
MERCURY: *75*.................. **5–8**
STRAND: *63*.................. **10–15**

COMATEENS, The
Singles: 12-Inch 33/45rpm
MERCURY: *83–84*............... **4–6**
Singles: 7-Inch
MERCURY: *83–84*............... **1–3**
LPs: 10/12-Inch 33rpm
CACHALOT: *81*................. **5–8**
MERCURY: *83*................. **5–8**

COMER, Tony & Crosswinds
Singles: 7-Inch
VIDCOM: *84*.................... **1–3**

COMMANDER CODY (Commander Cody & His Lost Planet Airmen)
Singles: 7-Inch
ABC: *75* **2–3**
ARISTA: *77* **2–3**
DOT: *73–74*.................... **2–3**

MCA: *83* **$1–3**
PARAMOUNT: *71–74*............. **2–4**
WARNER BROS: *75*............... **2–3**
LPs: 10/12-Inch 33rpm
ARISTA: *78* **5–8**
PARAMOUNT: *71–74*........... **10–12**
WARNER BROS: *75*............. **8–10**

COMMODORES, The
Singles: 7-Inch
MOTOWN: *74–85*................. **1–3**
MOWEST: *72* **2–4**
LPs: 10/12-Inch 33rpm
MOTOWN (Except 39):
  75–85 .... **8–10**
MOTOWN (39; 1978
  "Platinum Tour"): *78* **15–20**
  (Promotional issue only.)
  Members: Lionel Richie; William King; Ron-
  ald LaPread; Tommy McClary; Walter Orange;
  Milan Williams.
  Also see RICHIE, Lionel

COMMON SENSE
Singles: 7-Inch
BC: *81* **1–3**

COMO, Perry
Singles: 7-Inch
RCA VICTOR (0100
  through 0900 series):
  69–73 .... **1–3**
RCA VICTOR (3800
  through 7100 series):
  50–58 .... **3–5**
RCA VICTOR (7200
  through 9700 series):
  58–69 .... **2–4**
RCA VICTOR (10000
  through 13000 series):
  74–83 .... **1–3**
Picture Sleeves
RCA VICTOR (3800
  through 7100 series):
  53–58 .... **3–5**
RCA VICTOR (7200
  through 9700 series):
  58–69 .... **2–4**
EPs: 7-Inch 33/45rpm
RCA VICTOR: *52–61* **5–10**

COMO, Perry, & Jaye P. Morgan
Singles: 7-Inch
RCA VICTOR: 55 . . . . $3–5
   Also see COMO, Perry
   Also see MORGAN, Jaye P.

COMPAGNONS DE LA CHANSON, Les: see LES COMPAGNONS DE LA CHANSON

COMSTOCK, Bobby (Bobby Comstock & The Counts)
Singles: 7-Inch
ASCOT: *64–66* **3–5**
ATLANTIC: *60* **4–6**
BLAZE: *59* **4–6**
ERIC: *73* **1–3**
FESTIVAL: *61* **3–5**
JUBILEE: *60–63* **4–6**
LAWN: *62–64* **3–5**
MOHAWK: *61* **3–5**
TRIUMPH: *59* **4–6**
LPs: 10/12-Inch 33rpm
ASCOT: *66* **30–35**
BLAZE. **50–75**

CON FUNK SHUN
Singles: 12-Inch 33/45rpm
MERCURY: *83–85* **4–6**
Singles: 7-Inch
FRETONE: *74.* **2–4**
MERCURY: *77–85* **1–3**
LPs: 10/12-Inch 33rpm
51 WEST: *83* **5–8**
MERCURY: *76–85* **5–8**

CONCEPT
Singles: 7-Inch
TUCKWOOD: *85* **1–3**

CONDUCTOR
Singles: 7-Inch
MONTAGE: *82.* **1–3**
LPs: 10/12-Inch 33rpm
MONTAGE: *82.* **5–8**

CONEY HATCH
LPs: 10/12-Inch 33rpm
MERCURY: *83–85* **5–8**

LPs: 10/12-Inch 33rpm
CAMDEN: *60–74* $5–10
RCA VICTOR (0100
   through 4000 series):
   73–83 . . . . **5–10**
   (With an "AFL1," "ANL1," "APL1,"
   "AQL1," "AYL1" or "CPL1" prefix.)
RCA VICTOR (400
   through 1900 series):
   52–58 . . . . **12–20**
   (With an "LPM" prefix.)
RCA VICTOR (2000
   through 2900 series):
   59–63 . . . . **10–15**
   (With an "LPM" or "LSP" prefix.)
RCA VICTOR (LPM-3100
   series): *53–54* **15–25**
   (10-Inch LPs. With an LPM prefix.)
RCA VICTOR (3300
   through 4500 series):
   64–71 . . . . **8–12**
   (With an "LPM" or "LSP" prefix.)

COMO, Perry, & Eddie Fisher
Singles: 7-Inch
RCA VICTOR: *52* **3–5**
   Also see FISHER, Eddie

COMO, Perry, & The Fontane Sisters
Singles: 7-Inch
RCA VICTOR: *50–51* **3–5**
   Also see FONTANE SISTERS, The

Price Range

CONLEE, John
Singles: 7-Inch
ABC: 78 . . . . $1–3
ABC/DOT: 76–77 2–3
MCA: 79–85 1–3
LPs: 10/12-Inch 33rpm
ABC: 78 8–10
MCA: 79–83 5–8

CONLEY, Arthur
Singles: 7-Inch
ATCO: 67–70 3–5
CAPRICORN: 71–74 2–4
FAME: 66 3–5
JOTIS: 66 3–5
LPs: 10/12-Inch 33rpm
ATCO: 67–69 12–20
Also see SOUL CLAN, The

CONNIE
Singles: 12-Inch 33/45rpm
SUNNYVIEW: 85 4–6

CONNIFF, Ray, Orchestra & Chorus
Singles: 7-Inch
COLUMBIA: 56–82 1–3
Picture Sleeves
COLUMBIA: 60–64 1–3
EPs: 7-Inch 33/45rpm
COLUMBIA: 56–59 4–6
LPs: 10/12-Inch 33rpm
COLUMBIA: 57–82 5–15
HARMONY: 69 4–8

CONNOR, Chris
Singles: 7-Inch
ATLANTIC: 56–62 2–4
BETHLEHEM (1200 &
1300 series): 54–55 3–5
BETHLEHEM (3000
series): 64 2–3
FM: 63 2–3
EPs: 7-Inch 33/45rpm
ATLANTIC: 56–57 5–10
BETHLEHEM: 54–56 8–12
LPs: 10/12-Inch 33rpm
ABC-PARAMOUNT:
65–66 8–12
ATLANTIC (1200 & 1300
series): 56–59 15–25

Price Range

ATLANTIC (8000 series):
56–62 . . . . $15–25
BETHLEHEM (Except
1000 series): 55–60 15–25
(Maroon label.)
BETHLEHEM (1000
series): 54 40–60
(10-Inch LPs.)
BETHLEHEM (6000
series): 78 10–12
(Gray label.)
FM: 63 10–15

CONNOR, Chris, & Maynard Ferguson
Singles: 7-Inch
ATLANTIC: 61 2–4
LPs: 10/12-Inch 33rpm
ATLANTIC: 61 12–20
ROULETTE: 58 20–30
Also see CONNOR, Chris
Also see FERGUSON, Maynard
Also see SIMONE, Nina, Chris Connor & Carmen McRae

CONNORS, Norman
Singles: 7-Inch
ARISTA: 78–80 1–3
BUDDAH: 74–77 2–3
LPs: 10/12-Inch 33rpm
ARISTA: 78–80 5–8
BUDDAH: 75–78 10–12
NOVUS: 81 5–8
Members: Michael Henderson; Pharoah Sanders.
Also see AQUARIAN DREAM
Also see HENDERSON, Michael

CONTI, Bill
Singles: 7-Inch
ARISTA: 82 1–3
UNITED ARTISTS: 77–78 1–3
LPs: 10/12-Inch 33rpm
MCA: 79 5–10
UNITED ARTISTS: 78–79 8–12

CONTINENTAL 4, The (The Continental Four)
Singles: 7-Inch
JAY WALKING: 71–72 2–4
LPs: 10/12-Inch 33rpm
JAY WALKING: 71 10–15

Price Range

CONTINO, Dick
Singles: 7-Inch
DOT: 66–67..................... **$2–3**
MERCURY: 54–64................ **2–4**
EPs: 7-Inch 33/45rpm
MERCURY: 55–59................ **5–8**
LPs: 10/12-Inch 33rpm
DOT: 64–66..................... **5–10**
HAMILTON: 64–66.............. **5–10**
MERCURY: 56–63............... **8–12**
WING: 63 .... **6–10**

CONTOURS, The
Singles: 7-Inch
GORDY: 62–67.................. **3–5**
MOTOWN (400 series): 82 .... **1–3**
MOTOWN (1008; "Whole
Lotta Woman"): 61.......... **100–125**
MOTOWN (1012;
"Funny"): 61............... **150–175**
ROCKET: 80..................... **1–3**
LPs: 10/12-Inch 33rpm
GORDY: 62 .... **35–40**
MOTOWN: 82................... **5–8**

CONTROLLERS, The (The Controllers With Valerie DeMece)
Singles: 7-Inch
JUANA: 76–82 .... **2–3**
MCA: 85 .... **1–3**
LPs: 10/12-Inch 33rpm
JUANA: 77–79 .... **8–10**
WINDHAM HILL: 85.............. **5–8**

CONVERTION
Singles: 7-Inch
SAM: 81........................ **1–3**
VANGUARD: 83.................. **1–3**
LPs: 10/12-Inch 33rpm
VANGUARD: 83................. **5–8**

CONWAY BROTHERS, The
Singles: 7-Inch
PAULA: 85...................... **1–3**

COODER, Ry
Singles: 7-Inch
MUSICOR: 66................... **3–5**
REPRISE: 69–72................. **2–4**
WARNER BROS: 77–82........... **1–3**

Price Range

LPs: 10/12-Inch 33rpm
REPRISE: 72–76................. **$8–10**
WARNER BROS: 77–82........... **5–8**
Also see CAPTAIN BEEFHEART

COOK, Tony
Singles: 12-Inch 33/45rpm
HALFMOON: 84.................. **4–6**

COOKE, SAM (Sam Cooke & The Soul Stirrers)
Singles: 7-Inch
CHERIE: 71 .... **2–4**
COLLECTABLES: 81 .... **1–3**
KEEN (2000 series): 58–60 .... **8–10**
(With a "5" prefix. Stereo singles.)
KEEN (2000 & 4000
series): 57–61 .... **4–6**
(With a "3" prefix.)
RCA VICTOR (7000
series): 60–61 .... **8–10**
(With a "61" prefix. Stereo singles.)
RCA VICTOR (7000 &
8000 series): 60–66 .... **3–5**
(With a "47" prefix.)
SPECIALTY (500 & 600
series): 57–59 .... **4–6**
SPECIALTY (900 series):
70–72 .... **2–3**
Picture Sleeves
RCA VICTOR: 60–65 .... **5–8**
EPs: 7-Inch 33/45rpm
KEEN: 57–59 .... **15–20**
RCA VICTOR: 61–63 .... **12–15**
LPs: 10/12-Inch 33rpm
CAMDEN: 68–74................ **8–10**
CANDLELITE................... **15–20**
(A mail-order offer.)
CHERIE: 71 .... **8–10**
FAMOUS: 69................... **12–15**
KEEN: 58–60 .... **20–30**
PHOENIX 10: 81................ **5–8**
RCA VICTOR (2000 &
3000 series): 60–68 .... **15–30**
(With an "LPM" or "LSP" prefix.)
RCA VICTOR (2000
through 5000 series):
78–85 .... **5–8**
(With an "AFL1," "ANL1" or "AYL1" prefix.)
SAR: 61 .... **3–5**
SPECIALTY: 69–85.............. **5–12**

Price Range

TRIP: *72–76* **$8–10**
UPFRONT: *73* **8–10**
    Also see ANKA, Paul / Sam Cooke / Neil
    Sedaka
    Also see RAWLS, Lou

COOKE, Sam / Rod Lauren / Neil Sedaka / The Browns
EPs: 7-Inch 33/45rpm
RCA VICTOR: *60* **8–15**
    Also see BROWNS, The
    Also see LAUREN, Rod
    Also see SEDAKA, Neil

COOKE, Sam / Lloyd Price / Larry Williams
LPs: 10/12-Inch 33rpm
SPECIALTY: *60*................. **20–25**
    Also see COOKE, Sam
    Also see PRICE, Lloyd
    Also see WILLIAMS, Larry

COOKE, Samona
Singles: 7-Inch
EPIC: *76–77* **2–3**

COOKER (Norman Des Rosiers)
Singles: 7-Inch
SCEPTER: *73–74* **2–3**
LPs: 10/12-Inch 33rpm
SCEPTER: *74* **8–10**

COOKIE & HIS CUPCAKES (Terry "Cookie" Clinton)
Singles: 7-Inch
CHESS: *63*........................ **3–5**
JUDD: *59* **8–10**
KHOURY'S: *59* **10–15**
LYRIC: *63–64*.................... **8–10**
MERCURY: *61*.................... **3–5**
PAULA: *65–68* **3–5**

COOKIES, The (Featuring Earl-Jean McCree)
Singles: 7-Inch
ABC: *74*......................... **1–3**
DIMENSION: *62–64* **4–6**
ERIC: *73* **1–3**
MCA: *83* **1–3**
    Also see EARL-JEAN
    Also see KING, Carole / Little Eva / The
    Cookies

Price Range

COOL HEAT
Singles: 7-Inch
FOWARD: *70*.................... **$2–4**
    Also see WIND

COOLEY, Eddie (Eddie Cooley & The Dimples)
Singles: 7-Inch
ABC: *73*......................... **1–3**
ROULETTE: *60* **3–5**
ROYAL ROOST: *56–57* **5–8**
TRIUMPH: *59* **4–6**

COOLIDGE, Rita
Singles: 7-Inch
A&M: *71–80* **1–3**
PEPPER: *68–69*................... **3–5**
Picture Sleeves
A&M: *72–80* **1–3**
LPs: 10/12-Inch 33rpm
A&M: *71–83* **6–10**
Promotional LPs
A&M ("In-Store
    Sampler-Rita Coolidge")......... **8–12**
    Also see CAMPBELL, Glen, & Rita Coolidge

COOLIDGE, Rita, & Kris Kristofferson
Singles: 7-Inch
A&M: *73–74* **2–3**
MONUMENT: *74–75*.............. **2–3**
Picture Sleeves
A&M: *73* **2–3**
LPs: 10/12-Inch 33rpm
A&M: *73–79* **8–10**
MONUMENT: *74*................. **8–10**
    Also see COOLIDGE, Rita
    Also see KRISTOFFERSON, Kris

COOPER, Alice (The Alice Cooper Group)
Singles: 12-Inch 33/45rpm
WARNER BROS: *80* **10–15**
    (Promotional issue only.)
Singles: 7-Inch
ATLANTIC: *75* **2–4**
STRAIGHT: *69–70*.............. **12–15**
WARNER BROS: *70–80*........... **2–4**
Promotional Singles
ATLANTIC: *75* **4–6**
WARNER BROS: *70–80*........... **5–8**

Price Range

Picture Sleeves
WARNER BROS: *72–80* $2–5
EPs: 7-Inch 33/45rpm
WARNER BROS: *73* **15–20**
(Jukebox issues only.)
LPs: 10/12-Inch 33rpm
ATLANTIC: *75–78* **5–8**
MFSL: *80* **10–15**
WARNER BROS (Except
1883, 2567 & 2623):
73–84 . . . . **8–12**
WARNER BROS (1883;
"Love It To Death"): *71* **20–25**
(Black cover has Cooper's right thumb showing
through his wrap. Does NOT have white block
reading "Including Their Hit I'm Eighteen.")
WARNER BROS (1883;
"Love It To Death"): *71* **15–18**
(Black cover has Cooper's right thumb showing
through his wrap. Has white block reading "In-
cluding Their Hit I'm Eighteen." Also includes
issue with huge white stripes at top and bottom
of cover.)
WARNER BROS (1883;
"Love It To Death"): *71* **5–8**
(Black cover does NOT have Cooper's right
thumb showing through his wrap. Has the
white block reading "Including Their Hit I'm
Eighteen.")
WARNER BROS (2567;
"Killer"): *71* **15–18**
(With poster & 1972 calendar.)
WARNER BROS (2567;
"Killer"): *72* **5–8**
(Without poster & calendar.)
WARNER BROS (2623;
"School's Out"): *72* **25–30**
(With panties attached. Back cover does not list
titles.)
WARNER BROS (2623;
"School's Out"): *72* **15–18**
(With panties attached. Back cover lists titles.)
WARNER BROS (2623;
"School's Out"): *72* **5–8**
(With no paper panties. Back cover lists titles.)
WARNER
BROS/STRAIGHT
(1051; "Pretties For
You"): *69* **15–18**
WARNER
BROS/STRAIGHT
(1845; "Easy Action"):
70 . . . . **30–35**

Price Range

(With the name "Alice Cooper" in black letters
on front cover.)
WARNER
BROS/STRAIGHT
(1845; "Easy Action"):
70 . . . . **$5–8**
(With the name "Alice Cooper" in white letters
on front cover.)

Promotional LPs
CHELSEA PROD
("Allison's Tea House"):
74 . . . . **25–30**
STRAIGHT (1845; "Easy
Action"): *70* **25–30**
STRAIGHT (1883; "Love
It To Death"): *71* **20–25**
WARNER BROS (White
label promos): *71–78* **20–25**
WARNER
BROS./STRAIGHT
("Pretties For You"): *69* **25–30**
Also see BILLION DOLLAR BABIES, The
Also see FROST
Also see NAZZ
Also see SPIDERS, The

COOPER, Les, & The Soul Rockers
Singles: 7-Inch
ABC: *73* **2–3**
ARRAWAK: *65* **3–5**
ATCO: *69* **2–4**
EVERLAST: *62* **3–5**
SAMAR: *66* **3–5**

Price Range

LPs: 10/12-Inch 33rpm
EVERLAST: *63*.................. **$40–50**

COOPER, Pat
LPs: 10/12-Inch 33rpm
UNITED ARTISTS: *66–69*......... **8–15**

COOPER BROTHERS, The
Singles: 7-Inch
CAPRICORN: *78–79*.............. **1–3**

LPs: 10/12-Inch 33rpm
CAPRICORN: *78–79*.............. **5–8**
Also see BLACK OAK ARKANSAS / The
Cooper Brothers

COPAS, Cowboy
Singles: 7-Inch
KING (900 through 1500
series): *50–55*.................. **4–6**
KING (4800 through 5200
series): *55–59*.................. **3–5**
KING (5300 through 5700
series): *60–63*.................. **2–4**
STARDAY (400 through
700 series): *60–66*............... **2–4**
STARDAY (7000 series):
64.......................... **2–3**
STARDAY (8000 series):
71.......................... **1–3**

EPs: 7-Inch 33/45rpm
KING: *57*..................... **15–20**
STARDAY: *60*................. **10–12**

LPs: 10/12-Inch 33rpm
GUEST STAR.................. **10–15**
KING (500 series): *57*........... **30–40**
KING (600 through 800
series): *59–64*................. **25–35**
KING (1000 series): *69*........... **8–12**
NASHVILLE: *68–70*............. **8–12**
PICKWICK/HILLTOP:
66......................... **10–12**
STARDAY (100 & 200
series): *60–64*............... **20–25**
STARDAY (300 series):
65–67..................... **12–20**
STARDAY (400 series):
68–70..................... **8–12**

Price Range

COPAS, Cowboy / Hawkshaw Hawkins
LPs: 10/12-Inch 33rpm
KING: *63–66*.................. **$10–15**
Also see CLINE, Patsy / Cowboy Copas /
Hawkshaw Hawkins
Also see COPAS, Cowboy
Also see HAWKINS, Hawkshaw

COPELAND, Ken
Singles: 7-Inch
DOT: *58*......................... **4–6**
IMPERIAL: *57*................... **4–6**
LIN (5007; "Pledge Of
Love"): *57*.................... **8–10**
LIN (5007; "Fanny
Brown"): *58*.................. **12–15**

COPELAND, Stewart
LPs: 10/12-Inch 33rpm
A&M: *83*....................... **5–8**
Also see POLICE, The

COPELAND, Stewart, & Standard Ridgway
Singles: 7-Inch
A&M: *83*....................... **1–3**
Also see COPELAND, Stewart
Also see WALL OF VOODOO

COPELAND, Vivian
Singles: 7-Inch
D'ORO: *69*...................... **2–3**
MALA: *67*...................... **3–5**

COREA, Chick
Singles: 7-Inch
POLYDOR: *79*................... **1–3**
LPs: 10/12-Inch 33rpm
BLUE NOTE: *75–78*............. **8–12**
ECM: *75–80*.................... **6–10**
ELEKTRA: *83*.................. **5–8**
PACIFIC JAZZ: *81*.............. **5–8**
POLYDOR: *76–78*.............. **6–10**
VERVE: *76*..................... **5–8**
WARNER BROS: *80–81*........... **5–8**
Also see RETURN TO FOREVER

COREA, Chick, & Lionel Hampton
LPs: 10/12-Inch 33rpm
WHO'S WHO IN JAZZ:
81.......................... **5–8**
Also see HAMPTON, Lionel

Price Range

COREA, Chick, & Herbie Hancock
LPs: 10/12-Inch 33rpm
POLYDOR: 79 . . . . $8–12
Also see COREA, Chick
Also see HANCOCK, Herbie, & Chick Corea

COREY, Jill
Singles: 7-Inch
COLUMBIA: 54–60 2–5
MERCURY: 62 2–4
EPs: 7-Inch 33/45rpm
COLUMBIA: 55–57 6–10
LPs: 10/12-Inch 33rpm
COLUMBIA: 56–57 10–15

CORLEY, Al
Singles: 7-Inch
MERCURY: 85 1–3

CORLEY, Bob
Singles: 7-Inch
RCA VICTOR: 56 3–5
STARS: 55 4–6

CORNBREAD & BISCUITS
Singles: 7-Inch
MASKE: 60 3–5

CORNELIUS BROTHERS & SISTER ROSE, The
Singles: 7-Inch
UNITED ARTISTS: 70–74 2–4
LPs: 10/12-Inch 33rpm
UNITED ARTISTS: 72–76 10–12

CORNELL, Don
Singles: 7-Inch
ABC-PARAMOUNT: 65 2–3
CORAL: 52–57 3–5
DOT: 59–60 2–4
JAYBEE: 69 1–3
JUBILEE: 62 2–3
SIGNATURE: 59–60 2–4
20TH CENTURY-FOX:
   64 2–3
EPs: 7-Inch 33/45rpm
CORAL: 54–56 5–10
LPs: 10/12-Inch 33rpm
ABC-PARAMOUNT: 66 5–10

Price Range

CORAL: 54–57 . . . . $10–15
DOT: 59 8–12
MOVIETONE: 66 5–10
SIGNATURE: 59 6–10
VOCALION: 59 8–12

CORNELL, Don, Johnny Desmond & Alan Dale
Singles: 7-Inch
CORAL: 53 3–5
EPs: 7-Inch 33/45rpm
CORAL: 54 5–10
Also see CORNELL, Don
Also see DALE, Alan
Also see DESMOND, Johnny

CORNER BOYS, The
Singles: 7-Inch
NEPTUNE: 69 2–4

CORPORATION, The
Singles: 7-Inch
CAPITOL: 69 2–4
MUSICOR: 70 2–4
LPs: 10/12-Inch 33rpm
AGE OF AQUARIUS: 69 15–20
CAPITOL: 69 12–15

CORSAIRS, The (Featuring Jay "Bird" Uzzell)
Singles: 7-Inch
CHESS: 62 3–5
ERIC: 78 1–3
SMASH: 61 3–5
TUFF: 61–64 4–6

CORTEZ, Dave "Baby" (Baby Cortez)
Singles: 7-Inch
ABC: 74 1–3
ALL PLATINUM: 72 2–4
ARGO: 64 3–5
CHESS: 63 3–5
CLOCK: 59–62 4–6
COLLECTABLES: 81 1–3
EMIT: 62 3–5
ERIC: 73 1–3
FIRE: 60 4–6
JULIA: 62 15–20
OKEH (7100 series): 58 8–10
OKEH (7200 series): 64 3–5

Price Range

ROULETTE: *65–68* **$3–5**
SOUND: *71* **2–4**
T-NECK: *69* **2–4**
WINLEY: *62* **3–5**

EPs: 7-Inch 33/45rpm
CLOCK: *59–61* **15–20**
RCA VICTOR (4300
   series): *59* **15–20**
   (With an "EPA" prefix. Monaural issue.)
RCA VICTOR (4300
   series): *59* **20–30**
   (With an "ESP" prefix. Stereo issue.)

LPs: 10/12-Inch 33rpm
CHESS: *62* **25–30**
CLOCK: *60–63* **25–30**
CORONET **10–12**
CROWN: *63* **12–15**
DESIGN **10–12**
METRO: *65* **12–15**
RCA VICTOR: *59* **25–30**
ROULETTE: *65–66* **15–20**
   Also see ISLEY BROTHERS, The, & Dave
   "Baby" Cortez

CORY
Singles: 7-Inch
PHANTOM: *77* **2–3**

CORYELL, Larry
LPs: 10/12-Inch 33rpm
VANGUARD: *69* **8–12**
   Also see ELEVENTH HOUR
   Also see MOUZON, Alphonse, & Larry
   Coryell

COSBY, Bill
Singles: 7-Inch
CAPITOL: *76–78* **1–3**
UNI: *69–70* **2–4**
WARNER BROS: *65–67* **3–5**

LPs: 10/12-Inch 33rpm
CAPITOL: *76–78* **5–8**
MCA **5–8**
MOTOWN: *82* **5–8**
PARTEE **6–10**
TETRAGRAMMATON:
   69 .... **6–10**
UNI: *69–72* **6–10**
WARNER BROS. (Except
   249): *64–70* **10–15**

Price Range

WARNER BROS. (249;
   "Best Of Bill Cosby"):
   69 .... **$15–20**
   (Promotional issue only.)

COSTA, Don, Orchestra
Singles: 7-Inch
ABC-PARAMOUNT:
   56–57 .... **2–4**
COLUMBIA: *62–63* **2–3**
DCP: *64–65* **1–3**
ESSEX: *55* **2–4**
JAMIE: *59* **2–4**
MGM: *66–72* **1–3**
MERCURY: *68* **1–3**
UNITED ARTISTS: *59–62* **2–4**
VERVE: *67* **1–3**
Picture Sleeves
UNITED ARTISTS: *60* **2–4**
LPs: 10/12-Inch 33rpm
ABC-PARAMOUNT:
   56–61 .... **10–15**
COLUMBIA: *62–63* **8–10**
DCP: *64–65* **5–10**
HARMONY: *65* **5–10**
MERCURY: *68–69* **5–10**
UNITED ARTISTS: *59–62* **8–12**
VERVE: *67* **5–10**

COSTANDINOS, Alec R., & The Syncophonic Orchestra
LPs: 10/12-Inch 33rpm
CASABLANCA: *78* **5–8**

COSTELLO, Elvis (Elvis Costello & The Attractions)
Singles: 12-Inch 33/45rpm
COLUMBIA: *83* **5–8**
Singles: 7-Inch
CBS (Black vinyl): *79* **2–3**
CBS (Colored vinyl): *79* **8–10**
COLUMBIA: *77–85* **2–4**
EPs: 7-Inch 33/45rpm
COLUMBIA: *80* **5–8**
LPs: 10/12-Inch 33rpm
COLUMBIA (Black vinyl):
   77–85 .... **6–12**
COLUMBIA (Colored
   vinyl): *79* **20–30**
COLUMBIA/COSTELLO:
   78 .... **20–25**

Price Range

Price Range

Promotional EPs
COLUMBIA: *78–80* **$10–15**
Promotional LPs
COLUMBIA (Picture Disc;
"My Aim Is
True"/"This Year's
Model"): *79* **100-125**
COLUMBIA (529; "Live
At Hollywood High"):
79 .... **20–30**
COLUMBIA (958; "Tom
Snyder Interview"): *81* **20–30**
COLUMBIA (1318;
"Almost Blue"): *81* **25–30**
COLUMBIA/COSTELLO
("Taking Liberties"): *80* **30–35**
 Also see NICK & ELVIS

COTTON, Gene
Singles: 7-Inch
ABC: *75–77* **2–3**
ARIOLA AMERICA:
77–79 .... **1–3**
KNOLL: *81–82* **1–3**
MYRRH: *74* **1–3**
LPs: 10/12-Inch 33rpm
ABC: *76–77* **8–10**
ACCORD: *83* **5–8**
ARIOLA AMERICA:
78–79 .... **5–8**
BUDDAH: *74–75* **8–10**
CAPITOL: *71* **8–10**
IMPACT **15–20**
KNOLL: *81–82* **5–8**
MYRRH: *73* **8–10**

COTTON, Gene, & Kim Carnes
Singles: 7-Inch
ARIOLA AMERICA: *78* **2–3**
 Also see CARNES, Kim
 Also see COTTON, Gene

COTTON, James (The James Cotton Blues Band)
Singles: 12-Inch 33/45rpm
ERECT: *82* **4–6**
Singles: 7-Inch
BUDDAH: *75* **2–3**
LOMA: *66* **5–8**
SUN: *54* **100–125**
VERVE/FOLKWAYS: *67* **2–4**

VERVE/FORECAST:
67–69 .... **$2–4**
LPs: 10/12-Inch 33rpm
ACCORD: *83* **5–8**
ALLIGATOR: *84* **5–8**
BUDDAH: *74–76* **10–12**
CAPITOL: *71* **10–12**
ERECT: *82* **5–8**
INTERMEDIA: *84* **5–8**
VANGUARD: *68* **10–15**
VERVE/FOLKWAYS: *67* **10–15**
VERVE/FORECAST:
68–69 .... **10–15**

COTTON, Josie
Singles: 7-Inch
ELEKTRA (Black vinyl):
82 .... **1–3**
ELEKTRA (Colored
vinyl): *82* **2–4**
LPs: 10/12-Inch 33rpm
ELEKTRA: *82* **5–8**

COTTON, LLOYD & CHRISTIAN
Singles: 7-Inch
20TH CENTURY-FOX:
75–76 .... **2–4**
LPs: 10/12-Inch 33rpm
20TH CENTURY-FOX:
75–76 .... **8–10**
 Members: Darryl Cotton; Michael Lloyd; Chris Christian.

COUCHOIS
Singles: 7-Inch
WARNER BROS: *79–80* **1–3**
LPs: 10/12-Inch 33rpm
WARNER BROS: *79–80* **5–8**

COUGAR, John (John Cougar Mellencamp)
Singles: 7-Inch
RIVA: *79–85* **1–3**
LPs: 10/12-Inch 33rpm
MAIN MAN: *83* **5–8**
RIVA: *79–85* **5–8**

COULTER, Clifford
Singles: 7-Inch
COLUMBIA: *80* **1–3**

Price Range

LPs: 10/12-Inch 33rpm
COLUMBIA: *80* **$5–8**

COUNT BASIE: see BASIE, Count

COUNT FIVE, The
Singles: 7-Inch
DOUBLE SHOT: *66–69.* **5–8**
LPs: 10/12-Inch 33rpm
DOUBLE SHOT: *66.* **30–40**

COUNTRY BOYS & CITY GIRLS (Featuring Lee Maye)
Singles: 7-Inch
HAPPY FOX: *76* **2–4**

COUNTRY COALITION, The
Singles: 7-Inch
ABC: *70–73* **2–4**
ABC/BLUESWAY: *70.* **2–4**

COUNTRY HAMS, The
Singles: 7-Inch
EMI: *74* **8–10**
Promotional Singles
EMI: *74* **15–20**
Picture Sleeves
EMI: *74* **20–30**
Members: Paul McCartney & Wings; Chet Atkins; Floyd Cramer.
Also see ATKINS, Chet
Also see CRAMER, Floyd
Also see McCARTNEY, Paul

COUNTRY JOE & THE FISH
Singles: 7-Inch
VANGUARD: *67–69.* **4–6**
Picture Sleeves
VANGUARD: *60.* **4–6**
EPs: 7-Inch 33/45rpm
RAG BABY **25–30**
LPs: 10/12-Inch 33rpm
FANTASY: *77.* **8–10**
VANGUARD (Except 9266): *67–71.* **10–15**
VANGUARD (9266; "I Feel Like I'm Fixin' To Die"): *67* **20–30**
(With cut-out pictures and poster game.)

Price Range

VANGUARD (9266; "I Feel Like I'm Fixin' To Die"): *67* **$12–15**
(Without pictures and poster.)
Also see McDONALD, Country Joe

COUNTS, The
Singles: 7-Inch
DOT (1199; "Hot Tamales"): *54.* **8–12**
DOT (1188; "Darling Dear"): *53* **20–25**
DOT (1210; "My Dear, My Darling"): *54.* **25–30**
DOT (1226; "Baby, I Want You"): *54* **20–25**
DOT (1235; "Let Me Go Lover"): *54.* **8–12**
DOT (1243; "From This Day On"): *55.* **10–15**
DOT (1265; "Sally Walker"): *55.* **10–15**
DOT (1275; "Heartbreaker"): *56* **10–15**
DOT (16000 series): *60.* **3–5**

COUNTS, The
Singles: 7-Inch
AWARE: *74* **2–3**
WESTBOUND: *72* **2–4**
LPs: 10/12-Inch 33rpm
AWARE: *75* **8–10**
AWARE/GRC: *73* **8–10**
GRC: *73.* **8–10**
WESTBOUND: *72* **8–10**

COURTNEY, David
LPs: 10/12-Inch 33rpm
UNITED ARTISTS: *75* **8–10**

COURTNEY, Lou (Lew Courtney)
Singles: 7-Inch
BUDDAH: *69* **2–5**
EPIC: *73–75* **2–3**
IMPERIAL: *63–64* **3–5**
PHILIPS: *65* **3–5**
POP SIDE: *67.* **3–5**
RAYS: *73.* **2–3**
RIVERSIDE: *66–67* **3–5**
VERVE: *68* **2–5**

Price Range

LPs: 10/12-Inch 33rpm
EPIC: 74 .... $8–10
RCA VICTOR: 76 8–10
RIVERSIDE: 67 15–20

COURTSHIP
Singles: 7-Inch
CAPITOL: 70 2–4
TAMLA: 72 2–3

COUSIN ICE
Singles: 7-Inch
URBAN ROCK: 85 4–6

COVAY, Don (Don Covay & The Goodtimers; Don Covay & The Jefferson Lemon Blues Band)
Singles: 7-Inch
ATLANTIC: 65–70 3–5
BIG TOP: 60 4–6
CAMEO: 62–63 3–5
COLUMBIA: 61 3–5
LANDA: 64 3–5
MERCURY: 72–75 2–3
NEWMAN: 80 1–3
PARKWAY: 63–64 3–5
PHILADELPHIA INT'L:
   76 2–3
ROSEMART: 64 3–5
LPs: 10/12-Inch 33rpm
ATLANTIC: 65–69 15–20
JANUS: 72 8–10
MERCURY: 74 8–10
PHILADELPHIA INT'L:
   76 8–10
   Also see GOODTIMERS, The
   Also see PRETTY BOY
   Also see SOUL CLAN, The

COVEN (Featuring Teresa Kelly)
Singles: 7-Inch
BUDDAH: 74 2–3
MGM: 71–73 2–4
MERCURY: 69 2–4
SGC: 68 3–5
WARNER BROS: 71–73 2–4
LPs: 10/12-Inch 33rpm
BUDDAH: 74 8–10
MGM: 71–72 10–12
MERCURY: 69 12–15

RCA VICTOR
WALLY COX
STAR OF
"MR. PEEPERS"
ON NBC-TV
WHAT A
CRAZY GUY
(DUFO)
TAVERN IN
THE TOWN

Price Range

COWBOY COPAS: see COPAS, Cowboy

COWBOY CHURCH SUNDAY SCHOOL, The
Singles: 7-Inch
DECCA: 54–55 .... $2–4
VOSS: 54 3–5
EPs: 7-Inch 33/45rpm
DECCA: 55 5–8

COWSILLS, The
Singles: 7-Inch
JODA: 65 4–6
LONDON: 71–72 2–3
MGM: 67–71 2–4
PHILIPS: 66–67 3–5
Picture Sleeves
MGM: 67–69 3–5
PHILIPS: 66 5–8
LPs: 10/12-Inch 33rpm
LONDON: 71 8–10
MGM: 67–71 10–12
WING: 68 10–12

COX, Wally
Singles: 7-Inch
ARVEE: 60 2–4
GEORGE: 61 2–4
RCA VICTOR (5278;
"What A Crazy Guy"):
   53 3–5
WAND: 70 1–3

Price Range

Price Range

Picture Sleeves

RCA VICTOR (5278;
"What A Crazy Guy"):
53 .... **$6–10**

COYOTE SISTERS, The
Singles: 7-Inch
MOROCCO: *84*.................... **1–3**
LPs: 10/12-Inch 33rpm
MOROCCO: *84*.................... **5–8**
Members: Leah Kunkel; Marty Gwinn; Renee Armand.

CRABBY APPLETON
Singles: 7-Inch
ELEKTRA: *70–72* **2–4**
LPs: 10/12-Inch 33rpm
ELEKTRA: *70–71* **8–10**

CRACK THE SKY
Singles: 7-Inch
LIFESONG: *76–79*................ **2–3**
LPs: 10/12-Inch 33rpm
LIFESONG (Except 8000
series): *75–78* **10–15**
LIFESONG (8000 series):
81 .... **5–8**

CRADDOCK, Billy "Crash" ("Crash" Craddock)
Singles: 7-Inch
ABC: *72–78*...................... **1–3**
ABC/DOT: *75–77*................. **2–3**
CAPITOL: *78–82* **1–3**
CARTWHEEL: *71–72* **2–3**
CEE CEE: *83*..................... **1–3**
CHART: *67–73*................... **2–3**
COLONIAL: *58* **8–10**
COLUMBIA: *59–60*.............. **4–6**
DATE: *58* **5–8**
KING (Except 5912):
64–65 .... **3–5**
KING (5912; "Betty
Betty"): *64* **10–12**
MERCURY: *61–62*................ **3–5**
Picture Sleeves
COLUMBIA: *59* **6–10**
EPs: 7-Inch 33/45rpm
ABC: *74*......................... **4–6**

(Jukebox issue only.)
LPs: 10/12-Inch 33rpm
ABC: *72–78*.................... **$6–10**
ABC/AT EASE: *78* **10–12**
(Special issue for the Armed Forces.)
ABC/DOT: *76–77*................ **6–10**
CAPITOL: *78–83* **5–8**
CARTWHEEL: *71–72* **10–12**
CHART: *73*...................... **8–12**
HARMONY: *73* **10–12**
KING: *64* **40–50**
STARDAY **8–10**
MCA: *82* **5–10**

CRAMER, Floyd
Singles: 7-Inch
ABBOTT: *53–54*.................. **3–5**
MGM: *55–57*..................... **2–4**
RCA VICTOR: *60–81* **1–3**
Picture Sleeves
RCA VICTOR: *60–68* **1–3**
EPs: 7-Inch 33/45rpm
MGM: *57*....................... **5–10**
RCA VICTOR: *61–63* **5–10**
LPs: 10/12-Inch 33rpm
ALSHIRE: *68* **8–12**
CAMDEN: *65–74*................. **6–12**
MGM (3500 series): *57*........... **18–20**
MGM (4200 series): *64*........... **12–15**
MGM (4600 series): *70*........... **8–12**
RCA VICTOR (0100
through 4000 series):
73–81 .... **5–10**
(With an "AHL1," "ANL1," "APD1,"
"APL1," or "AYL1" prefix.)
RCA VICTOR (2000
through 4000 series):
60–73 .... **10–20**
(With an "LPM" or "LSP" prefix.)
Also see COUNTRY HAMS, The

CRAMPTON SISTERS, The
Singles: 7-Inch
ABC: *66*......................... **3–5**
DCP: *64*......................... **3–5**

CRANE, Les
Singles: 7-Inch
WARNER BROS: *71*............... **2–3**
LPs: 10/12-Inch 33rpm
WARNER BROS: *71*.............. **6–10**

Price Range

CRAWFORD, Caroline
Singles: 7-Inch
MERCURY: *78–79*. $1–3
LPs: 10/12-Inch 33rpm
MERCURY: *78–79*. 5–8

CRAWFORD, Carolyn
Singles: 7-Inch
MOTOWN: *63–64*. 8–10
PHILADELPHIA INT'L:
  74–75 2–3

CRAWFORD, Hank
Singles: 7-Inch
ATLANTIC: *61–70* 2–4
KUDU: *72*. 2–3
LPs: 10/12-Inch 33rpms
ATLANTIC: *61–73* 10–20
KUDU: *72–76*. 10–12

CRAWFORD, Johnny
Singles: 7-Inch
ABC: *73*. 2–3
COLLECTABLES: *81* 1–3
DEL-FI: *61–64* 3–5
SIDEWALK: *67–68* 3–5
WYNNE: *60* 5–8
Picture Sleeves
DEL-FI: *61–63* 6–10
SIDEWALK: *68* 4–6
LPs: 10/12-Inch 33rpm
DEL-FI: *62–63* 20–25
GUEST STAR: *63* 15–20
RHINO: *82* 5–8
SUPREME: *66*. 15–20

CRAWFORD, Randy
Singles: 12-Inch 33/45rpm
WARNER BROS: *83*. 4–6
Singles: 7-Inch
COLUMBIA: *72–73* 2–3
MCA: *81* 1–3
WARNER BROS: *77–83*. 1–3
LPs: 10/12-Inch 33rpm
RCA VICTOR: *84* 5–8
WARNER BROS: *76–81*. 8–10
  Also see CRUSADERS, The
  Also see JARREAU, Al, & Randy Crawford
  Also see SPRINGFIELD, Rick, & Randy
  Crawford

Price Range

CRAWLER: see BACK STREET CRAWLER

CRAYTON, Pee Wee
Singles: 7-Inch
ALADDIN: *51* $20–25
EDCO. 10–12
FLAIR. 10–12
FOX 8–10
GUYDEN: *61* 3–5
IMPERIAL: *54–55*. 10–15
JAMIE: *61*. 3–5
MODERN: *51*. 15–20
POST: *55* 8–10
RECORDED IN
  HOLLYWOOD: *54*. 20–25
SMASH: *62* 3–5
VEE JAY: *56–57*. 5–8
LPs: 10/12-Inch 33rpm
CROWN: *59* 35–40
VANGUARD: *71*. 8–10

CRAZY ELEPHANT
Singles: 7-Inch
BELL: *69–70*. 3–5
SPHERE SOUND: *69* 2–4
LPs: 10/12-Inch 33rpm
BELL: *69*. 12–15

CRAZY HORSE
Singles: 7-Inch
EPIC: *72* 2–4
M.O.C.. 3–5
REPRISE: *71–72*. 2–4
LPs: 10/12-Inch 33rpm
EPIC: *72–76* 8–10
RCA VICTOR: *78* 5–8
REPRISE: *71–72*. 10–12
  Also see YOUNG, Neil

CRAZY OTTO
Singles: 7-Inch
DECCA: *55–61*. 2–4
MGM: *62*. 2–3
EPs: 7-Inch 33/45rpm
DECCA: *55–58* 5–8
LPs: 10/12-Inch 33rpm
DECCA: *55–61* 8–12
MGM: *63*. 6–10
VOCALION: *59* 8–10

Price Range

CREACH, Papa John
Singles: 7-Inch
BUDDAH: 76 . . . . $2–3
DJM: 79 1–3
GRUNT: 71–72 2–4
LPs: 10/12-Inch 33rpm
BUDDAH: 75–77 10–12
DJM: 77–78 8–10
GRUNT: 71–74 12–15
Also see JEFFERSON STARSHIP

CREAM
Singles: 7-Inch
ATCO: 67–70 4–6
EPs: 7-Inch 33/45rpm
ATCO ("Goodbye
  Cream"): 69 8–12
  (Promotional issue only.)
LPs: 10/12-Inch 33rpm
ATCO: 67–72 15–20
POLYDOR: 72–73 10–12
RSO (Except 015): 72–83 5–8
RSO (015; "Classic Cuts"):
  75 35–40
  (Promotional issue only.)
SPRINGBOARD 10–12
  Members: Eric Clapton; Jack Bruce; Ginger
  Baker.
  Also see BAKER, Ginger
  Also see BRUCE, Jack
  Also see CLAPTON, Eric

CREATIVE SOURCE
Singles: 7-Inch
POLYDOR: 75 2–3
SUSSEX: 73–74 2–3
LPs: 10/12-Inch 33rpm
POLYDOR: 75–76 8–10
SUSSEX: 74 10–12

CREEDENCE CLEARWATER REVIVAL
Singles: 7-Inch
FANTASY (Except 2832):
  69–80 2–4
FANTASY (2832; "45
  Revolutions Per
  Minute"): 69 15–20
  (Promotional issue only.)
SCORPIO (412;
  "Porterville"): 67 15–25

Price Range

Picture Sleeves
FANTASY: 69–76 . . . . $3–5
LPs: 10/12-Inch 33rpm
FANTASY (Except 4500
  series): 68–73 10–12
FANTASY (4500 series):
  80–82 8–10
K-TEL: 78 8–10
MFSL: 79 15–18
  Also see FOGERTY, John
  Also see FOGERTY, Tom
  Also see GOLLIWOGS, The
  Also see HARRISON, Don

CREME D'COCOA
Singles: 7-Inch
VENTURE: 78–80 1–3
LPs: 10/12-Inch 33rpm
VENTURE: 79 8–10

CRENSHAW, Marshall
Singles: 12-Inch 33/45rpm
WARNER BROS: 82 5–8
Singles: 7-Inch
WARNER BROS: 82–85 1–3
LPs: 10/12-Inch 33rpm
WARNER BROS: 82–85 5–8

CREOLE, Kid: see KID CREOLE

CRESCENDOS, The (With Dale Ward)
Singles: 7-Inch
ABC: 73 1–3
MCA: 84 1–3
NASCO: 57–58 5–8
SCARLET: 60–61 5–8
TAP 4–6
Picture Sleeves
NASCO: 58 15–20
TAP 10–15
LPs: 10/12-Inch 33rpm
GUEST STAR 20–25
  Also see WARD, Dale

CRESCENTS, The (Chiyo & The Crescents)
Singles: 7-Inch
BREAK OUT: 63 4–6
ERA: 63 3–5

Price Range

CRESTS, The
Singles: 7-Inch

ABC: *73*	$1–3
APT: *65*	4–6
CAMEO: *63–64.*	4–6
COED (Except 501): *58–62*	5–8
COED (501; "Pretty Little Angel"): *58.*	25–30
COLLECTABLES: *81–83*	1–3
CORAL: *64*	15–20
ERIC: *73*	1–3
JOYCE 103; ("Sweetest One"): *57*	40–50

(With the oversize letter "Y" in the Joyce logo.)

JOYCE 103; "Sweetest One")	10–15

(With all of the letters the same size in the Joyce logo.)

JOYCE 105; "No One To Love"): *57*	50–60
KING TUT	3–5
MUSICTONE: *62*	3–5
SELMA: *62–63*	8–10
TIMES SQUARE: *62–64*	4–6
TRANS ATLAS: *62*	4–6
UNITED ARTISTS: *62*	12–15

EPs: 7-Inch 33/45rpm

COED: *59*	60–75

LPs: 10/12-Inch 33rpm

COED: *60–61.*	100–125
COLLECTABLES: *83*	5–8
POST	8–10

Members: Johnny Maestro; Tom Gough; Harold Torres; Jay Carter.
Also see MAESTRO, Johnny

CRETONES, The
Singles: 7-Inch

PLANET: *80*	1–3

LPs: 10/12-Inch 33rpm

PLANET: *81*	5–8

CREW-CUTS, The
Singles: 7-Inch

ABC-PARAMOUNT: *63*	3–5
CHESS: *64*	3–5
FIREBIRD: *70*	2–4
MERCURY: *54–57.*	4–6
RCA VICTOR: *58–60*	3–5
VEE JAY: *63.*	3–5
WARWICK: *60–61.*	3–5

Price Range

WHALE: *62*	$3–5

EPs: 7-Inch 33/45rpm

MERCURY: *54–57.*	10–15

LPs: 10/12-Inch 33rpm

MERCURY: *55–56.*	20–25
RCA VICTOR: *59–60*	15–20
WING: *59–60*	15–20

Members: Roy Perkins; John Perkins; Rudi Maugeri; Pat Barrett.
Also see COASTERS, The / The Crew-Cuts / The Chiffons

CREWE, Bob (The Bob Crewe Generation; Bob Crew & The Rays)
Singles: 7-Inch

ABC-PARAMOUNT: *61*	3–5
DYNO VOICE: *66–68*	1–3
CORAL: *56*	4–6
CREWE: *71*	2–3
ELEKTRA: *76–77*	1–3
ERIC: *73*	1–3
JUBILEE: *54*	5–8
MELBA: *57*	4–6
METROMEDIA: *72.*	2–3
SPOTLIGHT	10–15
20TH CENTURY-FOX: *76*	1–3
U.T.: *59*	4–6
VIK: *57*	4–6
WARWICK: *59–61.*	3–5

Picture Sleeves

DYNO VOICE: *67*	1–3

LPs: 10/12-Inch 33rpm

CGC: *70*	10–12

Price Range

DYNO VOICE: *67–68* **$10–12**
ELEKTRA: *76–77* **8–10**
GAMBLE: *69* **2–3**
PHILIPS: *67* **10–15**
WARWICK: *60–61.* **15–20**
    Also see LA ROSA, Julius, & The Bob Crew
    Generation

CRICKETS, The
Singles: 7-Inch
BARNABY: *72.* **15–20**
BRUNSWICK (55124;
    "Love's Made A Fool Of
    You"): *59* **12–15**
BRUNSWICK (55153;
    "When You Ask About
    Love"): *59* **12–15**
CORAL: *63* **12–15**
    (Records by Buddy Holly & The Crickets, even
    if shown only as by The Crickets, are listed in
    the BUDDY HOLLY section of this guide.)
LIBERTY: *61–65* **8–12**
MGM: *73.* **10–12**
MUSIC FACTORY: *68* **12–15**
Promotional Singles
BRUNSWICK (55124;
    "Love's Made A Fool Of
    You"): *59* **15–20**
BRUNSWICK (55153;
    "When You Ask About
    Love"): *59* **15–20**
CORAL: *60.* **20–25**
EPs: 7-Inch 33/45rpm
B.H.M.S.: *78* **3–5**
CORAL (81192; "The
    Crickets"): *63.* **40–50**
    (With Buddy Holly on one track, "It's Too
    Late.")
LPs: 10/12-Inch 33rpm
BARNABY: *70.* **15–20**
CORAL: *60.* **40–50**
    (Records by Buddy Holly & The Crickets, even
    if shown only as by The Crickets, are listed in
    the BUDDY HOLLY section of this guide.)
KOALA. **8–10**
LIBERTY: *62–64* **25–30**
VERTIGO: *74.* **12–15**
    Members: Sonny Curtis; Jerry Naylor; Glen D.
    Hardin; Jerry Allison; Joe Mauldin; Earl Sinks;
    David Box.
    Also see CURTIS, Sonny
    Also see HOLLY, Buddy

Price Range

    Also see IVAN
    Also see JENNINGS, Waylon
    Also see NAYLOR, Jerry
    Also see PRESLEY, Elvis
    Also see VEE, Bobby, & The Crickets

CRISS, Peter
Singles: 7-Inch
CASABLANCA: *79–80* **$1–3**
LPs: 10/12-Inch 33rpm
CASABLANCA (Except
    picture discs): *78–80* **5–8**
CASABLANCA (Picture
    discs): *79* **10–15**
    Also see KISS

CRITTERS, The
Singles: 7-Inch
KAPP: *65–69.* **3–5**
MCA: *84* **1–3**
PRANCER: *68* **3–5**
PROJECT 3: *67–69.* **3–5**
Picture Sleeves
KAPP: *66* **4–6**
LPs: 10/12-Inch 33rpm
BACK-TRAC: *85* **5–8**
KAPP: *66* **25–30**
PROJECT 3: *68.* **15–20**
    Also see 4 SEASONS, The

CROCE, Jim
Singles: 7-Inch
ABC: *72–74* **2–4**
LIFESONG: *75–76.* **2–3**
Picture Sleeves
ABC: *73* **2–4**
EPs: 7-Inch 33/45rpm
ABC: *73* **10–12**
    (Jukebox issue only.)
LPs: 10/12-Inch 33rpm
ABC: *72–74* **10–12**
CASHWEST: *77* **8–10**
COMMAND: *74–75* **12–15**
LIFESONG: *75–78* **8–10**

CROCE, Jim & Ingrid (Jim & Ingrid)
Singles: 7-Inch
CAPITOL: *69* **10–15**
LPs: 10/12-Inch 33rpm
CAPITOL: *69* **30–35**
    Also see CROCE, Jim

Price Range

Price Range

CROCHET, Cleveland (Cleveland Crochet & The Sugar Bees)
Singles: 7-Inch
GOLDBAND: *60–61* $3–5
LPs: 10/12-Inch 33rpm
GOLDBAND: *61* 30–35

CROCKETT, G.L. (G. Davy Crockett)
Singles: 7-Inch
CHECKER: *65* 15–20
CHIEF: *57* 30–40
4 BROTHERS: *65* 3–5

CROCKETT, Howard
Singles: 7-Inch
DOT: *73* 2–3

CROOK, General
Singles: 7-Inch
CAPITOL: *69* 2–4
WAND: *74* 2–3
LPs: 10/12-Inch 33rpm
CAPITOL: *70* 10–15
WAND: *74* 10–12

CROSBY, Beverly
Singles: 7-Inch
BAREBACK: *77* 1–3

CROSBY, Bing (Bing Crosby & The Andrews Sisters)
Singles: 7-Inch
AMOS: *69* 1–3
CAPITOL: *63* 2–3
COLUMBIA: *59* 2–4
DAYBREAK: *71* 1–3
DECCA (23700 through
  25600 series): *51–65* 2–4
  (Includes 45rpm reissues of 1940's material, originally issued on 78rpm.)
DECCA (27000 through
  30000 series): *50–59* 3–5
KAPP: *57* 2–4
LONDON: *77* 1–3
MGM: *60* 2–4
POLYDOR: *78* 1–3
RCA VICTOR: *60* 2–4
REPRISE: *64–67* 2–3
UNITED ARTISTS: *75* 1–3

Picture Sleeves
DECCA: *53–57* $3–5
KAPP: *57* 2–4
EPs: 7-Inch 33/45rpm
BRUNSWICK: *55* 5–10
COLUMBIA: *50–52* 8–12
DECCA: *50–59* 6–12
RCA VICTOR: *57* 5–8
LPs: 10/12-Inch 33rpm
AMOS: *69* 8–10
ARGO: *76* 10–15
BIOGRAPH: *73* 5–10
BRUNSWICK: *55* 15–20
CAPITOL (2300 series): *65* 8–12
CAPITOL (11000 series):
  77–78 5–8
CITADEL: *78* 5–8
COLUMBIA (43; "Bing In
  Hollywood"): *67* 10–15
COLUMBIA (6000 series):
  50 15–25
COLUMBIA (35000
  series): *78–79* 5–10
DECCA (100 series): *54–65* 10–25
DECCA (4000 series):
  61–64 8–12
DECCA (5000 series):
  50–55 15–25
  (10-Inch LPs.)
DECCA (8000 series):
  54–59 10–20
  (Black label with silver print.)
DECCA (8000 series):
  60–72 8–12
  (Black label with horizontal rainbow stripe.)
DECCA (8700 series): *64* 6–10
DECCA (9000 series):
  61–62 10–15
  (Decca LP numbers in this series preceded by a "7" or a "DL-7" are stereo issues.)
ENCORE: *68* 8–10
GOLDEN: *57* 10–15
HARMONY (7000 series):
  57 10–15
HARMONY (11000
  series): *69* 5–10
LONDON: *77* 5–8
MCA: *77–82* 5–10
MGM: *61–64* 10–12
METRO: *65* 5–10
P.I.P.: *71* 5–10

Price Range

POLYDOR: *77* **$5–8**
RCA VICTOR (500 series):
72 .... **6–10**
RCA VICTOR (1400
through 2000 series):
57–59 .... **10–15**
(With an "LPM" or "LSP" prefix.)
RCA VICTOR (2000
series): *77* **5–8**
(With a "CPL1" prefix.)
REPRISE: *64.* **8–12**
20TH CENTURY-FOX:
79 .... **5–8**
UNITED ARTISTS: *76* **5–8**
VOCALION (3600 series):
57 .... **10–15**
VOCALION (3700 series):
66 .... **5–10**
WARNER BROS: *60–62* **10–15**
Also see LEE, Peggy
Also see YOUNG, Victor

CROSBY, Bing & Gary
Singles: 7-Inch
DECCA: *50–51* **3–5**

CROSBY, Bing, & Louis Armstrong
Singles: 7-Inch
CAPITOL: *56* **3–5**
MGM: *60.* **2–4**
LPs: 10/12-Inch 33rpm
MGM (100 series): *70.* **5–10**
MGM (3800 series): *60.* **10–20**
SOUNDS RARE: *83* **5–8**
Also see ARMSTRONG, Louis

CROSBY, Bing, & Count Basie
LPs: 10/12-Inch 33rpm
DAYBREAK: *72* **8–12**
Also see BASIE, Count

CROSBY, Bing, & Rosemary Clooney
LPs: 10/12-Inch 33rpm
CAMDEN: *69.* **5–10**
CAPITOL: *65* **8–12**
Also see CLOONEY, Rosemary

CROSBY, Bing, & Grace Kelly
Singles: 7-Inch
CAPITOL: *56* **3–5**

Price Range

CROSBY, Bing, & Frank Sinatra
Singles: 7-Inch
CAPITOL: *56* **$3–5**
Also see SINATRA, Frank

CROSBY, Bing, & Orson Welles
LPs: 10/12-Inch 33rpm
DECCA (6000; "The Small
One - The Happy
Prince"): *50* **10–25**
Also see CROSBY, Bing
Also see WELLES, Orson

CROSBY, Chris
Singles: 7-Inch
ATLANTIC: *67* **3–5**
CHALLENGE: *64–65* **3–5**
COLUMBIA: *69.* **2–4**
DORE: *61* **3–5**
MGM: *64.* **3–5**
WARNER BROS: *63.* **3–5**
Picture Sleeves
MGM: *64.* **3–5**
LPs: 10/12-Inch 33rpm
MGM: *64.* **15–18**

CROSBY, David
Singles: 7-Inch
ATLANTIC: *71* **2–4**
LPs: 10/12-Inch 33rpm
ATLANTIC: *71* **10–12**
Also see BYRDS, The
Also see SLICK, Grace

CROSBY, David, & Graham Nash
Singles: 7-Inch
ABC: *75–77* **2–3**
ATLANTIC: *72* **2–4**
LPs: 10/12-Inch 33rpm
ABC: *75–78.* **8–10**
ATLANTIC: *72* **10–12**

CROSBY, STILLS & NASH
Singles: 7-Inch
ATLANTIC: *69–82* **2–4**
Picture Sleeves
ATLANTIC: *70–82* **2–4**
LPs: 10/12-Inch 33rpm
ATLANTIC (Except 8000
series): *77–83* **8–10**

Price Range

Price Range

ATLANTIC (8000 series):
69 .... **$12–15**
Members: David Crosby; Stephen Stills; Graham Nash.

CROSBY, STILLS, NASH & YOUNG
Singles: 7-Inch
ATLANTIC: 70 .... **2–4**
Picture Sleeves
ATLANTIC: 70 .... **2–4**
EPs: 7-Inch 33/45rpm
ATLANTIC: 70 .... **10–12**
(Jukebox issue only.)
LPs: 10/12-Inch 33rpm
ATLANTIC (Except 19000
series): 70–74 .... **8–10**
ATLANTIC (19000 series):
81 .... **5–8**
Promotional LPs
ATLANTIC (165;
"Celebration Copy") **25–30**
Members: David Crosby; Stephen Stills; Graham Nash; Neil Young.
Also see CROSBY, David
Also see CROSBY, STILLS & NASH
Also see NASH, Graham
Also see STILLS, Stephen
Also see YOUNG, Neil

CROSS, Christopher
Singles: 7-Inch
COLUMBIA: 85 .... **1–3**
WARNER BROS: 80–85 .... **1–3**
Picture Sleeves
WARNER BROS: 80–81 .... **1–3**
LPs: 10/12-Inch 33rpm
COLUMBIA: 85 .... **5–8**
WARNER BROS: 80–85 .... **5–8**

CROSS, Jimmy
Singles: 7-Inch
CHICKEN: 65. .... **3–5**
RECORDO: 61 .... **4–6**
RED BIRD: 65 .... **3–5**
TOLLIE: 64. .... **3–5**

CROSS COUNTRY (The Tokens)
Singles: 7-Inch
ATCO: 73–74. .... **2–4**
LPs: 10/12-Inch 33rpm
ATCO: 73 .... **10–12**

Also see TOKENS, The

CROUCH, Andre (Andre Crouch & The Disciples)
Singles: 7-Inch
LIGHT: 76–80. .... **$1–3**
WARNER BROS: 81 .... **1–3**
LPs: 10/12-Inch 33rpm
ACCORD: 82 .... **5–8**
LIGHT: 68–82. .... **5–10**
WARNER BROS: 81 .... **5–8**

CROW (David Wagner)
Singles: 7-Inch
AMARET: 69–72 .... **2–4**
LPs: 10/12-Inch 33rpm
AMARET: 69–73 .... **10–15**

CROWD PLEASERS, The
Singles: 7-Inch
WESTBOUND: 79 .... **1–3**
LPs: 10/12-Inch 33rpm
WESTBOUND: 79 .... **5–8**

CROWELL, Rodney
Singles: 7-Inch
WARNER BROS: 78–82 .... **1–3**
LPs: 10/12-Inch 33rpm
WARNER BROS: 78–81 .... **5–8**

CROWN HEIGHTS AFFAIR, The
Singles: 7-Inch
DELITE: 75–80. .... **1–3**
RCA VICTOR: 73–74 .... **2–3**
LPs: 10/12-Inch 33rpm
DELITE: 75–82. .... **5–8**
RCA VICTOR: 74–78 .... **10–12**

CROWS, The
Singles: 7-Inch
RAMA (3; "Seven Lonely
Days"): 53 .... **100–125**
RAMA (5; "Gee" - black
vinyl): 53 .... **25–30**
RAMA (5; "Gee" - colored
vinyl): 53 .... **75–90**
RAMA (10;
"Heartbreaker" - black
vinyl): 53 .... **125–150**

Price Range

RAMA (10;
"Heartbreaker" - colored
vinyl): *53* **$225–250**
RAMA (29; "Baby"): *54* **60–75**
RAMA (30; "Miss You" -
black vinyl): *54* **100–125**
RAMA (30; "Miss You" -
colored vinyl): *54*............. **225–250**
RAMA (50; "Baby Doll"):
54 .... **60–75**
TICO (Black vinyl): *51*............ **60–75**
TICO (Colored vinyl): *51*....... **100–125**
  Members: Sonny Norton; Harold Major; Jerry
  Hamilton; Mark Jackson; Bill Davis.
  Also see JEWELS, The
  Also see HARPTONES, The / The Crows

CRUDUP, Big Boy (Arthur "Big Boy" Crudup)
Singles: 7-Inch
FIRE: *62* **4–6**
GROOVE: *53–54*................ **10–15**
RCA VICTOR (4000 &
5000 series): *52–53* **15–20**
  (With a "47" prefix.)
RCA VICTOR (50-0000;
"That's All Right"): *50* **30–35**
RCA VICTOR (50-0001
through 50-0141): *50–51*........ **20–25**
EPs: 7-Inch 33/45rpm
CAMDEN **25–30**
LPs: 10/12-Inch 33rpm
DELMARK: *69*................. **10–12**
FIRE: *62* **125–150**
RCA VICTOR: *71* **10–12**
TRIP: *75* **8–10**
  Also see JAMES, Elmore

CRUISE, Pablo: see PABLO CRUISE

CRUM, Simon (Ferlin Husky)
Singles: 7-Inch
CAPITOL: *55–63* **4–6**
LPs: 10/12-Inch 33rpm
CAPITOL: *63* **50–75**
  Also see HUSKY, Ferlin

CRUSADERS, The
Singles: 7-Inch
ABC: *78*........................ **1–3**

Price Range

BLUE THUMB: *72–77* **$2–3**
CHISA: *71*...................... **2–4**
MCA: *79–85* **1–3**
LPs: 10/12-Inch 33rpm
BLUE THUMB: *73–77* **10–12**
MCA: *79–85* **8–10**
MOTOWN: *73*................. **10–12**
MOWEST: *72* **10–12**
  Also see COCKER, Joe
  Also see CRAWFORD, Randy
  Also see HOOPER, Stix
  Also see JAZZ CRUSADERS, The
  Also see SAMPLE, Joe

CRUSADERS, The, & B.B. King
Singles: 7-Inch
MCA: *82* **1–3**
LPs: 10/12-Inch 33rpm
MCA: *82* **8–10**
  Also see CRUSADERS, The
  Also see KING, B.B.

CRYAN' SHAMES, The
Singles: 7-Inch
COLUMBIA: *66–70*................ **3–5**
DESTINATION: *66*................ **3–5**
Picture Sleeves
COLUMBIA
LPs: 10/12-Inch 33rpm
BACK-TRAC: *85*.................. **5–8**
COLUMBIA (Except 2589
& 9389): *67–69* **15–20**
COLUMBIA (2589; "Sugar
& Spice"): *66*.................. **20–25**
  (Monaural issue.)
COLUMBIA (9389; "Sugar
& Spice"): *66*.................. **20–30**
  (Stereo issue.)

CRYSTAL, Billy
Singles: 12-Inch 33/45rpm
A&M: *85* **4–6**
Singles: 7-Inch
A&M: *85* **1–3**

CRYSTAL GAYLE
Singles: 7-Inch
COLUMBIA: *79–82*................ **1–3**
DECCA: *70–72*................... **2–4**
ELEKTRA: *82* **1–3**
MCA: *77* **1–3**
UNITED ARTISTS: *74–80*.......... **2–3**

Price Range

Picture Sleeves
COLUMBIA: *79–82* . . . . **$INC**
UNITED ARTISTS: *77–79* **1–3**
LPs: 10/12-Inch 33rpm
COLUMBIA: *79–83* **5–8**
ELEKTRA: *82* **5–8**
LIBERTY: *80–82* **5–8**
MCA: *78* **5–8**
UNITED ARTISTS: *75–80* **6–10**
WARNER BROS: *83* **5–8**
Also see RABBITT, Eddie, & Crystal Gayle

CRYSTAL GAYLE & TOM WAITS
LPs: 10/12-Inch 33rpm
COLUMBIA: *82* **5–8**
Also see CRYSTAL GAYLE
Also see WAITS, Tom

CRYSTAL GRASS
Singles: 7-Inch
POLYDOR: *75* **2–3**
PRIVATE STOCK: *76*. **2–3**
LPs: 10/12-Inch 33rpm
MERCURY: *78*. **5–8**
POLYDOR: *75* **8–10**

CRYSTAL MANSION, The
Singles: 7-Inch
CAPITOL: *68–70* **2–4**
COLOSSUS: *70–71* **2–4**
RARE EARTH: *72* **2–3**
20TH CENTURY-FOX:
    79 . . . . **1–3**
LPs: 10/12-Inch 33rpm
CAPITOL: *69* **12–15**
RARE EARTH: *72* **10–12**
20TH CENTURY-FOX:
    79 . . . . **5–8**
Also see CASWELL, Johnny

CRYSTALS, The
Singles: 7-Inch
INDIGO: *61* **8–10**
MICHELLE: *67* **3–5**
PAVILLION: *82*. **2–3**
PHILLES (Except 105 &
    111): *61–64*. **5–10**
PHILLES (105; "He Hit
    Me"): *62*. **15–20**
PHILLES (111; "Let's
    Dance The Screw"): *63*. **350–375**

Price Range

(White label promotional issue only. Light blue
labels are counterfeit copies.)
UNITED ARTISTS: *65–66* **$4–6**
LPs: 10/12-Inch 33rpm
PHILLES (4000; "The
    Crystals Twist
    Uptown"): *62*. **75–100**
PHILLES (4001; "He's A
    Rebel"): *63*. **60–75**
PHILLES (4003; "The
    Crystals"): *63*. **60–75**
Also see LOVE, Darlene
Also see RONETTES, The / The Crystals /
Darlene Love / Bob B. Soxx & The
Blue Jeans

CUBA, Joe (The Joe Cuba Sextet)
Singles: 7-Inch
ROULETTE: *71* **2–3**

CUES, The
Singles: 7-Inch
CAPITOL: *55–56* **8–15**
JUBILEE: *55*. **5–8**
LAMP: *54* **8–10**
PREP: *57*. **4–6**
Members: Ollie Jones; Jimmy Breedlove; Abe
DeCosta; Robey Kirk; Eddie Barnes.

CUFF LINKS, The (Ron Dante)
Singles: 7-Inch
ATCO: *72* **2–3**
DECCA: *69–71* **2–4**
MCA: *84* **1–3**
LPs: 10/12-Inch 33rpm
DECCA: *69–70* **12–15**

CUGINI
Singles: 7-Inch
SCOTTI BROTHERS: *79* **1–3**

CULTURE CLUB, The (Featuring Boy George)
Singles: 12-Inch 33/45rpm
EPIC: *82–83* **4–6**
VIRGIN: *83–85*. **4–6**
Singles: 7-Inch
EPIC: *82* **1–3**
LPs: 10/12-Inch 33rpm
EPIC: *83* **5–8**
VIRGIN (Except picture
    discs): *82–84*. **5–8**

BRENDA

KC-115

RECORDS

THE CUPIDS

Price Range

VIRGIN (Picture discs): *83* **$8–10**
    Also see BAND AID

CUMMINGS, Burton
Singles: 7-Inch
ALFA: *81* **1–3**
PORTRAIT: *76–78*................ **2–3**

Picture Sleeves
ALFA: *81* **1–3**

EPs: 7-Inch 33/45rpm
PORTRAIT: *77*.................... **2–5**
    (Issued with paper sleeve.)

LPs: 10/12-Inch 33rpm
ALFA: *81* **5–8**
PORTRAIT: *76–78*................ **8–10**
    Also see GUESS WHO, The

CUNHA, Rick
Singles: 7-Inch
COLUMBIA: *75*.................... **2–3**
GRC: *74*.......................... **2–3**

LPs: 10/12-Inch 33rpm
COLUMBIA: *75*.................... **8–10**
GRC: *74*.......................... **10–12**
    Also see JENNINGS, Waylon

CUPIDS, The
Singles: 7-Inch
AANKO: *63* **20–25**
KC: *63* **5–8**

Price Range

CURB, Mike (Mike Curb & The Rebalairs; The Mike Curb Congregation)
Singles: 7-Inch
MGM: *70*........................ **$2–3**
SMASH: *64* **3–5**
TOWER........................... **3–5**
LPs: 10/12-Inch 33rpm
BUENA VISTA **8–12**
MGM: *71*........................ **5–8**
    Also see DAVIS, Sammy, Jr.; ALLAN, Davies
    Also see LEGRAND, Michel, & The Mike
    Curb Congregation

CURE
Singles: 12-Inch 33/45rpm
SIRE: *83–85* **4–6**
Singles: 7-Inch
SIRE: *83–85* **1–3**
LPs: 10/12-Inch 33rpm
A&M: *81* **8–10**
ELEKTRA: *85* **5–8**
PVC: *80* **8–10**
SIRE: *83–85* **5–8**
    Members: Robert Smith; Laurence Tolhurst.

CURTIS, Sonny
Singles: 7-Inch
A&M: *72* **10–15**
CAPITOL: *75–76* **8–12**
CORAL (61023; "The Best
  Way To Hold A Girl"):
   53 .... **10–20**
CORAL (62207; "Red
  Headed Stranger"): *60* **15–20**
DIMENSION: *63–64* **5–8**
DOT: *58*......................... **10–15**
ELEKTRA: *79–81* **2–3**
LIBERTY: *64* **10–15**
MERCURY: *73*................... **8–10**
OVATION: *70*................... **10–15**
VIVA: *66–69* **8–10**
LPs: 10/12-Inch 33rpm
ELEKTRA: *79–81* **8–10**
IMPERIAL: *64*.................. **20–25**
VIVA: *68–69* **15–20**
    Also see CRICKETS, The

CURTIS, T.C.
Singles: 12-Inch 33/45rpm
SIRE: *85* **4–6**

Price Range

Price Range

CURTIS LEE: see LEE, Curtis

CURTOLA, Bobby
Singles: 7-Inch
DEL-FI: *61–63* $3–5
KING: *67* 3–5
TARTAN AMERICAN:
   66 3–5
Picture Sleeves
DEL-FI: *61–62* 4–6

CYCLONES, The (Featuring Bill Taylor)
Singles: 7-Inch
TROPHY: *58*. 10–12

CYMANDE
Singles: 7-Inch
JANUS: *72–73*. 2–4
LPs: 10/12-Inch 33rpm
JANUS: *72–74*. 10–12

CYMARRON
Singles: 7-Inch
ENTRANCE: *71–72*. 2–4
LPs: 10/12-Inch 33rpm
ENTRANCE: *71*. 10–12

CYMBAL, Johnny
Singles: 7-Inch
AMARET: *69* 2–4
COLUMBIA: *66*. 3–5
DCP: *65*. 3–5
KAPP: *63–64*. 4–6
KEDLEN: *63*. 8–10
MCA: *84* 1–3
MGM: *60–61*. 4–6
MUSICOR: *67*. 3–5
VEE JAY: *63*. 4–6
LPs: 10/12-Inch 33rpm
KAPP: *63* 30–35
   Also see DEREK

CYMONE, Andre
Singles: 12-Inch 33/45rpm
COLUMBIA: *82–85*. 4–6
Singles: 7-Inch
COLUMBIA: *82–85*. 2–3
LPs: 10/12-Inch 33rpm
COLUMBIA: *82–85*. 5–8

CYRKLE, The
Singles: 7-Inch
COLUMBIA: *65–68* $3–5
Picture Sleeves
COLUMBIA: *66–68* 3–5
LPs: 10/12-Inch 33rpm
COLUMBIA: *66–67* 20–25
FLYING DUTCHMAN/
  AMSTERDAM (12007;
  "The Minx"): *70* 20–25
  (Soundtrack.)
  Also see REVERE, Paul, & The Raiders / The
  Cyrkle

D

D., Eddie: see EDDIE D.

"D" TRAIN
Singles: 12-Inch 33/45rpm
PRELUDE: *81–85*. 4–6
Singles: 7-Inch
PRELUDE: *81–85*. 1–3
LPs: 10/12-Inch 33rpm
PRELUDE: *82–85*. 5–8

DFX2
Singles: 7-Inch
MCA: *83* 1–3
LPs: 10/12-Inch 33rpm
MCA: *83* 5–8

DMX, Davy: see DAVY DMX

DADDY DEWDROP
Singles: 7-Inch
CAPITOL: *75* 2–3
INPHASION: *78–79*. 2–3
SUNFLOWER: *70–72* 2–4
SUNFLOWER/MGM: *73* 2–3
LPs: 10/12-Inch 33rpm
SUNFLOWER: *71* 12–15

DADDY O's, The
Singles: 7-Inch
CABOT: *58* 4–6

Price Range

DAHL, Steve, & The Teenage Radiation
Singles: 7-Inch
COHO: *79* $2–3
OVATION: *79*. 2–3
Picture Sleeves
OVATION: *79*. 2–3

DAISY DILLMAN BAND, The: see DILLMAN BAND, The

DALBELLO
Singles: 12-Inch 33/45rpm
CAPITOL: *84* 4–6
Singles: 7-Inch
CAPITOL: *84* 1–3

DALE, Alan
Singles: 7-Inch
ABC-PARAMOUNT: *64*. 1–3
COLUMBIA: *50–51* 3–5
CORAL (60000 & 61000 series): *52–56* 2–4
CORAL (62000 series): *63*. 2–3
DECCA: *52* 3–5
EMKAY: *62* 2–3
FTP: *61* 2–3
MGM: *59* 2–3
SINCLAIR: *61* 2–3
EPs: 7-Inch 33/45rpm
CORAL: *52–56* 6–10
LPs: 10/12-Inch 33rpm
CORAL: *55–56* 12–20
FORD: *63* 6–10
UNITED ARTISTS: *60* 8–12
Also see CORNELL, Don, Johnny Desmond & Alan Dale

DALE, Dick (Dick Dale & His Del-tones)
Singles: 7-Inch
ACCENT: *68*. 4–6
CAPITOL: *63–64* 5–8
CONCERT ROOM: *63* 4–6
COUGAR: *67* 3–5
CUPID: *60*. 10–12
DEL-TONE (5012 through 5014): *59–60*. 25–30
DEL-TONE (5017 through 5028): *61–63*. 8–12

Price Range

GNP/CRESCENDO: *75* $2–4
SATURN: *63*. 8–10
YES. 3–5
Promotional Singles
CAPITOL ("Thunder Wave"/"Spanish Kiss"):
64 5–8
(Bonus single, packaged with an LP by Jerry Cole & His Spacemen.)
CAPITOL (2320; "Peppermint Man"): *63* 25–35
(Compact 33 Single)
UNITED STATES ARMY (1301; "Enlistment Twist"): *62* 5–8
Picture Sleeves
CAPITOL (Except 2320): *63* 8–12
CAPITOL (2320; "Peppermint Man"): *63* 35–45
(Promotional Compact 33 Single sleeve.)
LPs: 10/12-Inch 33rpm
ACCENT: *67*. 15–18
BALBOA: *83*. 5–8
CAPITOL (1886; "Surfer's Choice"): *63*. 15–25
CAPITOL (1930; "King Of The Surf Guitar"): *63*. 30–35
CAPITOL (2002; "Checkered Flag"): *63* 25–35
CAPITOL (2053; "Mr. Eliminator"): *64*. 30–35
CAPITOL (2111; "Summer Surf"): *64* 30–35
(Includes the bonus single by Jerry Cole & His Spacemen.)
CAPITOL (2111; "Summer Surf"): *64* 20–30
(Without the bonus single by Jerry Cole & His Spacemen.)
CAPITOL (2293; "Rock Out With Dick Dale Live At Ciro's"): *65* 30–35
CLOISTER: *63* 15–20
DEL-TONE (1001; "Surfer's Choice"): *61*. 30–40
DEL-TONE (1886; "Surfer's Choice"): *63*. 20–25
DIPLOMAT: *63* 12–15
DUBTONE: *63* 15–20
GNP/CRESCENDO: *75* 8–12

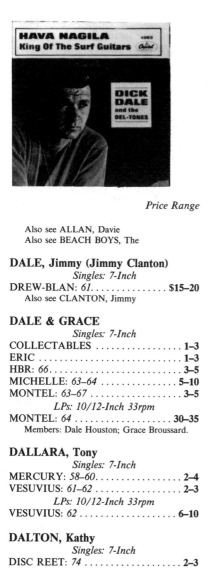

HAVA NAGILA
King Of The Surf Guitars

DICK DALE
and the
DEL-TONES

Price Range

Also see ALLAN, Davie
Also see BEACH BOYS, The

DALE, Jimmy (Jimmy Clanton)
Singles: 7-Inch
DREW-BLAN: *61*............... $15–20
Also see CLANTON, Jimmy

DALE & GRACE
Singles: 7-Inch
COLLECTABLES 1–3
ERIC 1–3
HBR: *66*....................... 3–5
MICHELLE: *63–64* 5–10
MONTEL: *63–67* 3–5
LPs: 10/12-Inch 33rpm
MONTEL: *64* 30–35
Members: Dale Houston; Grace Broussard.

DALLARA, Tony
Singles: 7-Inch
MERCURY: *58–60*................ 2–4
VESUVIUS: *61–62* 2–3
LPs: 10/12-Inch 33rpm
VESUVIUS: *62* 6–10

DALTON, Kathy
Singles: 7-Inch
DISC REET: *74* 2–3
LPs: 10/12-Inch 33rpm
DISC REET: *73–74* 8–10

DALTON & DUBARRI
Singles: 7-Inch
ABC: *76*........................ 2–3
COLUMBIA: *73–74*............... 2–3

Price Range

HILLTAK: *79*................... $1–3
LPs: 10/12-Inch 33rpm
ABC: *76*........................ 8–10
COLUMBIA: *73–74*............. 10–12
HILLTAK: *79*................... 5–8

DALTREY, Roger
Singles: 7-Inch
A&M: *75–76* 2–3
ATLANTIC: *84–85* 1–3
MCA: *73–82* 1–3
MCA/GOLDHAWKE:
75–77 2–3
ODE: *72–73*..................... 2–4
POLYDOR: *80–81* 2–3
TRACK: *73*...................... 2–3
LPs: 10/12-Inch 33rpm
ATLANTIC: *84–85* 5–8
MCA: *71–82* 10–12
TRACK: *73*.................... 10–12
Also see WHO, The

DALTREY, Roger, & Rick Wakeman
Singles: 7-Inch
A&M: *75* 2–3
LPs: 10/12-Inch 33rpm
A&M: *75* 8–10
Also see WAKEMAN, Rick

DALTREY, Roger, & Steve Gibbons
Singles: 12-Inch 33/45rpm
MCA............................. 5–8
(Promotional issue only.)
Also see DALTREY, Roger
Also see GIBBONS, Steve, Band

DAMIAN, Michael
Singles: 7-Inch
LEG: *81*........................ 1–3

DAMARIS
Singles: 7-Inch
COLUMBIA: *84*.................. 1–3

DAMIANO, Joe (Josef Damiano)
Singles: 7-Inch
CHANCELLOR: *59–60*............ 3–5

DAMION & DENITA
LPs: 10/12-Inch 33rpm
ROCKET: *80*..................... 5–8

Price Range

Price Range

DAMITA JO (Damita Joe)
Singles: 7-Inch
EPIC: *65–67* $2–3
MELIC: *64* 2–3
MERCURY: *60–64*. 2–4
RANWOOD: *68–71* 1–3
VEE JAY: *65*. 2–3
Picture Sleeves
EPIC: *65* 2–3
MERCURY: *61–63*. 2–4
EPs: 7-Inch 33/45rpm
MERCURY: *60–61*. 5–8
LPs: 10/12-Inch 33rpm
CAMDEN: *65*. 6–10
EPIC: *65–67* 8–12
MERCURY: *61–63*. 12–18
RANWOOD: *68* 5–8
VEE JAY: *65*. 8–12
Also see BENTON, Brook, & Damita Jo

DAMITA JO & BILLY ECKSTINE
Singles: 7-Inch
MERCURY: *63*. 2–3
Also see ECKSTINE, Billy

DAMITA JO & STEVE GIBSON & THE RED CAPS
Singles: 7-Inch
ABC-PARAMOUNT: *61*. 4–6
LPs: 10/12-Inch 33rpm
ABC-PARAMOUNT: *61*. 25–35
Also see DAMITA JO
Also see GIBSON, Steve

DAMNATION (Featuring Adam Blessing)
Singles: 7-Inch
UNITED ARTISTS: *71–72*. 2–4
LPs: 10/12-Inch 33rpm
UNITED ARTISTS: *69–71*. 10–15

DAMON, Liz (Liz Damon's Orient Express)
Singles: 7-Inch
ABC: *73*. 1–3
ANTHEM: *71–72* 2–4
MAKAHA: *70*. 3–5
WHITE WHALE: *70*. 2–3
LPs: 10/12-Inch 33rpm
WHITE WHALE: *71*. 8–12

DAMONE, Vic
Singles: 7-Inch
CAPITOL: *61–64* $2–3
COLUMBIA: *56–61*. 2–4
DOLTON: *62*. 2–3
MGM: *72–73*. 2–3
MERCURY: *50–55*. 2–4
RCA VICTOR: *66–69* 1–3
REBECCA: *77*. 1–3
UNITED TALENT: *70*. 1–3
WARNER BROS: *65–66*. 2–3
EPs: 7-Inch 33/45rpm
COLUMBIA: *56–58* 5–8
MERCURY: *50–56*. 6–10
LPs: 10/12-Inch 33rpm
CAPITOL: *62–64* 8–12
COLUMBIA (1000
  through 1500 series):
  58–61 10–15
COLUMBIA (1900 series):
  62 8–12
COLUMBIA (8000
  through 8300 series):
  58–61 10–15
COLUMBIA (8700 series):
  62 8–12
DOLTON: *64*. 6–10
HARMONY: *66–67* 5–8
MERCURY (Except 25000
  series): *69* 6–10
MERCURY (25000 series):
  50–56 12–20
RCA VICTOR: *66–68* 5–10
WARNER BROS: *65*. 5–10
WING: *59–63* 6–10

DANA, Bill (Jose Jimenez)
Singles: 7-Inch
A&M: *65–66* 2–4
KAPP: *61–63*. 2–5
SIGNATURE: *60* 3–5
Picture Sleeves
KAPP: *61–62*. 3–5
LPs: 10/12-Inch 33rpm
A&M: *68* 8–12
CAPITOL: *70* 6–10
HBR: *66*. 8–10
KAPP: *60–64*. 10–15
ROULETTE: *61* 12–18
SIGNATURE: *60* 20–25

Price Range

DANA, Vic
Singles: 7-Inch
CASINO: 76 . . . . **$1–3**
COLUMBIA: 71 . . . . **1–3**
DOLTON: 61–65. . . . . **2–4**
LIBERTY: 68–70 . . . . **2–3**
MGM: 75 . . . . **1–3**
Picture Sleeves
DOLTON: 62–66. . . . . **2–4**
LPs: 10/12-Inch 33rpm
DOLTON: 61–65. . . . . **10–15**
LIBERTY: 67–70 . . . . **8–12**
SUNSET: 67 . . . . **6–10**

DANCER, PRANCER & NERVOUS
Singles: 7-Inch
CAPITOL: 59 . . . . **3–5**
Picture Sleeves
CAPITOL: 59 . . . . **3–5**

DANDERLIERS, The
Singles: 7-Inch
B&F: 61 . . . . **4–6**
STATES (Black vinyl):
 55–56 . . . . **30–40**
STATES (Colored vinyl):
 55 . . . . **100–150**
Members: Dallas Taylor; James Campbell;
Richard Thomas; Walter Stephenson; Bernard
Dixon; Louis Johnson.

DANDLEERS, The: see DANLEERS, The

DANGERFIELD, Rodney
Singles: 12-Inch 33/45rpm
RCA VICTOR: 83 . . . . **4–6**
Singles: 7-Inch
RCA VICTOR: 83 . . . . **1–3**
LPs: 10/12-Inch 33rpm
DECCA: 66 . . . . **15–20**
CASABLANCA: 80 . . . . **5–8**
RCA VICTOR: 83 . . . . **5–8**
RHINO: 80 . . . . **5–8**

DANIELS, Charlie, Band (Charley Daniels & The Jaguars)
Singles: 7-Inch
EPIC: 76–85 . . . . **1–3**
KAMA SUTRA: 73–76 . . . . **2–3**
PAULA (200 series): 66 . . . . **3–5**

Price Range

PAULA (400 series): 76 . . . . **$2–3**
LPs: 10/12-Inch 33rpm
CAPITOL (11000 series):
 75 . . . . **8–10**
CAPITOL (16000 series):
 80 . . . . **5–8**
EPIC (Except 273): 76–85 . . . . **5–8**
EPIC (273; "Everything
You Always Wanted To
 Hear"): 77 . . . . **8–12**
(Promotional issue only.)
KAMA SUTRA: 73–76 . . . . **10–12**

DANKO, Rick
Singles: 7-Inch
ARISTA: 78 . . . . **2–3**
LPs: 10/12-Inch 33rpm
ARISTA: 77 . . . . **8–10**
Also see BAND, The

DANKWORTH, Johnny (Johnnie Dankworth)
Singles: 7-Inch
CAPITOL: 55–56 . . . . **2–4**
FONTANA: 63–66 . . . . **2–3**
20TH CENTURY-FOX:
 66 . . . . **2–3**
LPs: 10/12-Inch 33rpm
FONTANA (Except 7559):
 64–69 . . . . **6–10**
FONTANA (7559; "The
 Idol"): 66 . . . . **15–20**
(Soundtrack.)
ROULETTE: 60–61 . . . . **10–15**
TOP RANK: 60 . . . . **10–15**

DANLEERS, The (The Dandleers)
Singles: 7-Inch
ABC: 75 . . . . **1–3**
AMP 3: 58 . . . . **8–10**
EPIC: 60 . . . . **4–6**
EVEREST: 61 . . . . **4–6**
LE MANS: 64 . . . . **3–5**
MERCURY: 58–59. . . . . **5–8**
SMASH: 64 . . . . **3–5**
Members: Bill Carey; Daniel Webb.

DANNY & THE JUNIORS (Featuring Danny Rapp)
Singles: 7-Inch
ABC: 73 . . . . **1–3**

Price Range   *Price Range*

ABC-PARAMOUNT:
57–59 .... $5–8
CRUNCH: *73* 2–4
GUYDEN: *62* 4–6
LUB: *68* 2–4
MCA. 1–3
MERCURY: *64.* 3–5
RONN: *68* 3–5
ROULETTE 1–3
SINGULAR (Blue label):
57 25–35
SINGULAR (Black label) 2–3
SWAN: *60–62* 4–6
    EPs: 7-Inch 33/45rpm
ABC-PARAMOUNT: *57.* 35–45
    Picture Sleeves
SWAN: *60–62* 15–20
    LPs: 10/12-Inch 33rpm
MCA. 5–8
  Also see CANNON, Freddy

DANSE SOCIETY
    Singles: 12-Inch 33/45rpm
ARISTA: *84* 4–6
    Singles: 7-Inch
ARISTA: *84* 1–3

DANTE (Dante & The Evergreens; Dante & His Friends)
    Singles: 7-Inch
A&M: *66* 3–5
DECCA: *60–61* 4–6
IMPERIAL: *61–62* 4–6
MADISON: *60–61* 4–6
TIDE: *60* 4–6
    LPs: 10/12-Inch 33rpm
MADISON: *61* 45–50

DARENSBOURG, Joe, & His Dixie Flyers
    Singles: 7-Inch
LARK: *58–59* 2–4
    LPs: 10/12-Inch 33rpm
DIXIELAND JUBILEE:
75 5–8
GHB: *77.* 5–8

DARIAN, Fred (Freddy Darian)
    Singles: 7-Inch
DEL-FI: *60* 3–5
GARDENA: *61.* 3–5

JAF: *61–63* $3–5
MAHALO: *63* 3–5
OKEH: *59* 4–6
RCA VICTOR: *59* 4–6
UNITED ARTISTS: *63* 3–5

DARIN, Bobby (Bobby Darin & The Jaybirds; Bobby Darin & The Rinky Dinks; Bob Darin)
    Singles: 7-Inch
ATCO (Except stereo
  singles): *57–65* 5–8
ATCO (Stereo singles): *59* 15–20
  (With an "SD" prefix.)
ATLANTIC: *65–67* 3–5
CAPITOL: *62–65* 4–6
DECCA (Except 30737):
56–57 15–20
DECCA (30737; "Dealer
  In Dreams"): *59* 8–10
DIMENSION: *70* 3–5
DIRECTION: *68–70.* 3–5
MOTOWN: *71–72.* 2–4
    Picture Sleeves
ATCO: *59–62.* 6–10
CAPITOL: *62–65* 4–8
    EPs: 7-Inch 33/45rpm
ATCO: *58–60.* 20–30
CAPITOL
  CUSTOM/SCRIPTO: *63* 15–25
DECCA (2676; "Bobby
  Darin"): *60.* 30–50
    LPs: 10/12-Inch 33rpm
ATCO (Except 102 & 131):
59–67 20–30
ATCO (102; "Bobby
  Darin"): *58.* 35–45
ATCO (131; "The Bobby
  Darin Story"): *61* 35–40
  (White cover.)
ATCO (131; "The Bobby
  Darin Story"): *72* 8–12
  (Black cover.)
ATLANTIC: *66–67* 15–25
BAINBRIDGE: *81.* 5–8
CANDLELITE: *76.* 12–15
CAPITOL: *62–66* 15–25
CLARION: *64.* 15–18
DIRECTION: *68–70.* 12–15
IMPERIAL HOUSE: *76* 12–15
MOTOWN (100 series): *82* 5–8

Price Range

MOTOWN (700 & 800
  series): *72–74* **$10–12**
WARNER BROS: *76* **15–20**
  Also see DING DONGS, The
  Also see RINKY DINKS, The

DARLIN, Florraine
Singles: 7-Inch
EPIC: *62–63* **3–5**
RIC: *64* **3–5**

DARNEL, Bill
Singles: 7-Inch
CORAL: *50–51* **3–5**
DECCA: *52–53* **3–5**
LONDON (Except 1665):
  56 . . . . **3–5**
LONDON (1665;
  "Rock-A-Boogie Baby"):
  56 . . . . **6–10**
X: *54–55* **4–8**
EPs: 7-Inch 33/45rpm
X: *55* **10–15**
LPs: 10/12-Inch 33rpm
X: *55* **20–30**

DARNELL, Larry
Singles: 7-Inch
ANNA: *60* **10–12**
ARGO: *60* **3–5**
DELUXE: *57* **5–8**
OKEH: *51–53* **8–10**
REGAL (3300 series): *51* **8–12**
WARWICK: *59* **4–6**
EPs: 7-Inch 33/45rpm
EPIC: *61* **15–20**

DARRELL, Johnny
Singles: 7-Inch
CAPRICORN: *74–75* **1–3**
CARTWHEEL: *71–72* **1–3**
GUSTO: *78* **1–3**
MONUMENT: *73* **1–3**
UNITED ARTISTS: *65–70* **2–3**
Picture Sleeves
UNITED ARTISTS: *67* **2–4**
LPs: 10/12-Inch 33rpm
CAPRICORN: *75* **6–10**
GUSTO **5–8**
SUNSET: *68–70* **6–10**
UNITED ARTISTS: *66–70* **8–12**

Price Range

DARRELL, Johnny / George Jones / Willie Nelson
LPs: 10/12-Inch 33rpm
SUNSET: *69* **$8–10**
  Also see DARRELL, Johnny
  Also see JONES, George
  Also see NELSON, Willie

DARREN, James (Jimmy Darren)
Singles: 7-Inch
ABC: *74* **1–3**
BUDDAH: *70* **2–4**
COLPIX (Except stereo
  singles): *58–64* **4–6**
COLPIX (Stereo singles):
  58–64 . . . . **8–12**
  (With an "SCP" prefix.)
ERIC **1–3**
KIRSHNER: *71–72* **2–4**
MCA **1–3**
MGM: *73* **2–3**
PRIVATE STOCK: *75–77* **2–3**
RCA VICTOR: *78* **2–3**
WARNER BROS: *65–68* **3–5**

Picture Sleeves
COLPIX: *58–61* **4–8**

LPs: 10/12-Inch 33rpm
COLPIX: *60–62* **15–25**
KIRSHNER: *71–72* **10–15**
WARNER BROS: *67* **15–20**

Price Range

Price Range

DARREN, James / Shelley Fabares / Paul Petersen
LPs: 10/12-Inch 33rpm
COLPIX: 63–64................ $20–30
    Also see DARREN, James
    Also see FABARES, Shelley
    Also see PETERSEN, Paul

DARTELLS, The (Featuring Doug Phillips)
Singles: 7-Inch
ARLEN (Black vinyl): 63 8–10
ARLEN (Colored vinyl):
  63 20–25
DOT: 63–64..................... 4–6
HBR: 66....................... 3–5
LPs: 10/12-Inch 33rpm
DOT: 63...................... 25–30

DASH, Sarah
Singles: 7-Inch
KIRSHNER: 79 1–3
LPs: 10/12-Inch 33rpm
KIRSHNER: 78 5–8
    Also see LABELLE, Patti

DAVE & SUGAR (Dave Rowland & Sugar)
Singles: 7-Inch
ELEKTRA: 81 1–3
RCA VICTOR: 75–82 1–3
LPs: 10/12-Inch 33rpm
ELEKTRA: 81 5–8
RCA VICTOR: 76–82 5–10
    Members: Dave Rowland; Vicki Hackeman-Baker; Jackie Frantz; Sue Powell; Melissa Dean; Jamie Kaye.
    Also see PRIDE, Charley

DAVID, F.R.
Singles: 7-Inch
CARRERE AMERICA:
  83 1–3
LPs: 10/12-Inch 33rpm
CARRERE AMERICA:
  83 5–8

DAVID, Geater
Singles: 7-Inch
HOUSE OF ORANGE: 70 2–4

DAVID & JONATHAN
Singles: 7-Inch
AMY: 68 .... $3–5
CAPITOL: 66–67 4–6
20TH CENTURY-FOX:
  66 4–6
Picture Sleeves
CAPITOL: 66 4–6
LPs: 10/12-Inch 33rpm
CAPITOL: 66 20–25
    Members: Roger Greenaway; Roger Cook.
    Also see WHITE PLAINS

DAVID & LEE
Singles: 7-Inch
G.S.P: 62 12–18
    Members: David Gates; Leon Russell.
    Also see GATES, David
    Also see RUSSELL, Leon

DAVIDSON, John
Singles: 7-Inch
COLUMBIA: 66–71 2–3
MERCURY: 73................... 1–3
20TH CENTURY-FOX:
  73–77 1–3
Picture Sleeves
COLUMBIA: 66–69 2–3
LPs: 10/12-Inch 33rpm
COLPIX: 65 10–15
COLUMBIA: 66–80 5–10
HARMONY: 72 4–6
MERCURY: 73................... 5–8
20TH CENTURY-FOX:
  74–76 5–8

DAVIE, Hutch (Hutch Davie & His Honky-Tonkers)
Singles: 7-Inch
ATCO: 58–59.................... 3–5
CLARIDGE: 66 2–4
DYNO VOICE: 68................. 2–3
LPs: 10/12-Inch 33rpm
ATCO: 59 20–25

DAVIES, Dave
Singles: 7-Inch
REPRISE: 67–68................. 15–20
WARNER BROS: 83............... 1–3
LPs: 10/12-Inch 33rpm
RCA VICTOR: 80–81 8–10

Price Range

WARNER BROS: *83* **$5–8**
Also see KINKS, The

DA VINCI, Paul
Singles: 7-Inch
MERCURY: *72–74* **2–3**

DAVIS, Betty
Singles: 7-Inch
ISLAND: *75–76* **2–3**
JUST SUNSHINE: *73–74* **2–4**

LPs: 10/12-Inch 33rpm
ISLAND: *75* **5–8**
JUST SUNSHINE: *73–74* **6–10**

DAVIS, Billy
Singles: 7-Inch
ABC: *75* **2–3**
COBBLESTONE: *69* **2–4**
HI: *68* **3–5**

DAVIS, Carl, & The Chi-Sound Orchestra
Singles: 7-Inch
CHI-SOUND: *77* **2–3**

DAVIS, Danny (Danny Davis & The Nashville Brass; The Danny Davis Orchestra; Danny Davis & The Titans; Danny Davis & The Nashville Strings)
Singles: 7-Inch
BLUE JAY: *54* **2–4**
CABOT: *59* **2–4**
HICKORY: *54* **2–4**
LIBERTY: *59* **2–3**
MGM (11000 series):
51–53 . . . . **2–5**
MGM (13000 series):
62–65 . . . . **2–3**
RCA VICTOR: *69–84* **1–3**
THUNDER: *59* **2–4**
VERVE: *61* **2–3**

LPs: 10/12-Inch 33rpm
MGM: *61–65* **8–15**
RCA VICTOR: *69–84* **5–10**

Price Range

DAVIS, Danny, The Nashville Brass, & Willie Nelson
Singles: 7-Inch
RCA VICTOR: *80* **$1–3**
LPs: 10/12-Inch 33rpm
RCA VICTOR: *80* **5–8**
Also see DAVIS, Danny
Also see LOCKLIN, Hank
Also see NELSON, Willie, Danny Davis & The
Nashville Brass
Also see NEWMAN, Jimmy C., Danny Davis
& The Nashville Brass

DAVIS, John, & The Monster Orchestra
Singles: 12-Inch 33/45rpm
COLUMBIA: *79* **4–6**
Singles: 7-Inch
COLUMBIA: *78–79* **1–3**
SAM: *76–78* **2–3**
LPs: 10/12-Inch 33rpm
COLUMBIA: *79* **5–8**

DAVIS, Krystal
Singles: 12-Inch 33/45rpm
URBAN ROCK: *85* **4–6**

DAVIS, Mac
Singles: 7-Inch
CAPITOL: *65* **3–5**
COLUMBIA: *70–78* **2–3**
CASABLANCA: *80–85* **1–3**
JAMIE: *62* **4–6**
VEE JAY: *63* **4–6**
Picture Sleeves
COLUMBIA: *70–75* **1–3**
LPs: 10/12-Inch 33rpm
ACCORD: *82* **5–8**
CASABLANCA: *81–85* **5–8**
COLUMBIA: *70–83* **8–10**
TRIP: *73* **8–10**

DAVIS, Miles (The Miles Davis Sextet)
Singles: 7-Inch
BLUE NOTE (1600 series):
54–56 . . . . **3–5**
COLUMBIA (02000
through 03000 series):
81–83 . . . . **1–3**

Price Range   *Price Range*

COLUMBIA (10000
  series): *75* **$1–3**
COLUMBIA (41000
  through 46000 series):
  61–74 . . . . **2–3**
PRESTIGE (100 through
  400 series): *57–66* **2–4**
PRESTIGE (700 through
  900 series): *52–55* **3–5**

EPs: 7-Inch 33/45rpm
BLUE NOTE: *52* **15–20**
CAPITOL: *54* **10–20**
COLUMBIA: *59* **6–10**
PRESTIGE: *52–53* **12–20**

LPs: 10/12-Inch 33rpm
BLUE NOTE (100 series):
  73 . . . . **8–12**
BLUE NOTE (1500 series):
  56–58 . . . . **25–50**
  (Label gives New York street address for Blue
  Note Records.)
BLUE NOTE (1500 series):
  58 . . . . **15–25**
  (Label reads "Blue Note Records Inc. - New
  York, USA.")
BLUE NOTE (1500 series):
  66 . . . . **10–20**
  (Label shows Blue Note Records as a division
  of either Liberty or United Artists.)
BLUE NOTE (5000 series):
  52–54 . . . . **60–90**
  (10-Inch LPs.)
CAPITOL (400 series): *54* **50–75**
  (10-Inch LPs.)
CAPITOL (700 series): *56* **20–30**
CAPITOL (1900 series): *63* **8–12**
CAPITOL (11000 series):
  72 . . . . **5–10**
CAPITOL (16000 series):
  81 . . . . **4–6**
COLUMBIA (20; "Friday
  & Saturday Nights In
  Person"): *61* **20–30**
  (Monaural issue.)
COLUMBIA (26; "Bitches
  Brew"): *70* **8–12**
COLUMBIA (820; "Friday
  & Saturday Nights In
  Person"): *61* **25–35**
  (Stereo issue.)

COLUMBIA (900 through
  1600 series): *57–61* **$15–25**
  (With six black Columbia "eye" logos on red
  label.)
COLUMBIA (1800
  through 2300 series):
  61–65 . . . . **10–20**
COLUMBIA (8000
  through 8400 series):
  58–61 . . . . **20–30**
  (With six black Columbia "eye" logos on red
  label.)
COLUMBIA (8600
  through 9800 series):
  61–69 . . . . **10–20**
COLUMBIA (10000
  series): *73* **6–10**
COLUMBIA (30000 series,
  except 36976): *70–85* **6–12**
COLUMBIA (36976; "The
  Miles Davis Collection"):
  80 . . . . **30–40**
  (A 6-LP set.)
COLUMBIA (40000
  series): *81* **8–12**
DEBUT (043; "Blue
  Moods"): *83* **5–8**
DEBUT (120; "Blue
  Moods"): *55* **40–50**
FANTASY: *62* **15–20**
FONTANA: *65* **10–15**
MOODSVILLE: *63* **15–20**
NEW JAZZ: *64* **10–15**
PRESTIGE (004 through
  093): *80–85* **5–8**
PRESTIGE (100 series):
  52–54 . . . . **50–75**
  (10-Inch LPs.)
PRESTIGE (7007 through
  7166): *55–59* **20–30**
  (Yellow label.)
PRESTIGE (7168 through
  7281): *60–64* **12–20**
  (Yellow label.)
PRESTIGE (7000 through
  7600 series): *64–69* **6–12**
  (Blue label.)
PRESTIGE (7700 through
  7800 series): *70–71* **6–12**
PRESTIGE (24000 series):
  72–78 . . . . **8–12**
SAVOY: *61* **12–20**

Price Range

TRIP: 73 .... $5–10
UNITED ARTISTS: 71 8–10
    Also see COLTRANE, John, & Miles Davis
    Also see FORREST, Jimmy

DAVIS, Miles, & Thelonious Monk
LPs: 10/12-Inch 33rpm
COLUMBIA: 64 10–20
    Also see DAVIS, Miles
    Also see MONK, Thelonious

DAVIS, Miz
Singles: 7-Inch
NOW: 76 2–3

DAVIS, Paul
Singles: 7-Inch
ARISTA: 81–82 1–3
BANG: 68–81 2–3
FLASHBACK: 82 1–3
SOLID GOLD: 73 1–3
LPs: 10/12-Inch 33rpm
ARISTA: 81 5–8
BANG: 72–82 10–12

DAVIS, Ruth
Singles: 7-Inch
CLARIDGE: 78 2–3
    Also see KIRKLAND, Bo, & Ruth Davis

DAVIS, Sammy, Jr. (Sammy Davis)
Singles: 7-Inch
DECCA (25500 series): 62 2–3
DECCA (29000 through
    31000 series): 54–60 2–5
DECCA (32000 series): 69 2–3
ECOLOGY: 71 1–3
MGM: 71–79 1–3
VERVE: 60 2–3
REPRISE: 61–71 2–3
20TH CENTURY-FOX:
    75–76 1–3
WARNER BROS: 77 1–3
EPs: 7-Inch 33/45rpm
CAPITOL: 54 4–6
DECCA: 54–55 6–10
LPs: 10/12-Inch 33rpm
DECCA (100 series): 66 8–12
DECCA (4000 series):
    61–65 8–12

Price Range

DECCA (8100 through
    8700 series): 54–58 .... $15–25
DECCA (8900 series): 59 10–15
MCA: 77 5–10
MGM: 72–73 5–10
HARMONY: 69–71 5–10
MOTOWN: 70 6–10
RCA VICTOR (1086;
    "The Three Penny
    Opera"): 64 15–25
REPRISE: 61–69 10–18
20TH CENTURY-FOX
    (Except 5014): 76 5–8
20TH CENTURY-FOX
    (5014; "Of Love &
    Desire"): 64 25–35
    (Soundtrack.)
WARNER BROS: 77 5–8
UNITED ARTISTS (5187;
    "Salt & Pepper"): 68 10–15
    (Soundtrack.)
VOCALION: 68 5–10
    Also see CURB, Mike

DAVIS, Sammy, Jr., & Laurindo Almeida
LPs: 10/12-Inch 33rpm
REPRISE: 67 8–12
    Also see ALMEIDA, Laurindo

DAVIS, Sammy, Jr., & Count Basie
Singles: 7-Inch
VERVE: 65 1–3

Price Range

Price Range

LPs: 10/12-Inch 33rpm
MGM: 73..................... **$6–10**
VERVE: 65 .... **10–15**
Also see BASIE, Count
Also see SINATRA, Frank, & Sammy Davis, Jr.

DAVIS, Sammy, Jr., & Carmen McRae
Singles: 7-Inch
DECCA: 55...................... **2–4**
EPs: 7-Inch 33/45rpm
DECCA: 59...................... **5–8**
LPs: 10/12-Inch 33rpm
DECCA: 59..................... **12–18**
Also see McRAE, Carmen

DAVIS, Skeeter
Singles: 7-Inch
MERCURY: 76–77................. **1–3**
PART TWO: 80 .... **1–3**
RCA VICTOR (Except
7400 through 9600
series): 69–74 .... **1–3**
RCA VICTOR (7400
through 8300 series):
59–64 .... **3–5**
RCA VICTOR (8400
through 9600 series):
64–68 .... **1–3**
Picture Sleeves
RCA VICTOR: 63 .... **3–5**
EPs: 7-Inch 33/45rpm
RCA VICTOR: 63 .... **5–10**
LPs: 10/12-Inch 33rpm
CAMDEN: 65–74................. **5–10**
GUSTO: 78 .... **5–8**
RCA VICTOR (2000 &
3000 series, except 3790):
60–68 .... **10–15**
RCA VICTOR (3790;
"Skeeter Davis Sings
Buddy Holly"): 67.............. **20–30**
TUDOR: 84...................... **5–8**
Also see BARE, Bobby, & Skeeter Davis
Also see HAMILTON, George, IV, & Skeeter Davis
Also see JENNINGS, Waylon
Also see POSEY, Sandy / Skeeter Davis
Also see WAGONER, Porter, & Skeeter Davis

DAVIS, Spencer (The Spencer Davis Group; Spencer Davis & Peter Jameson)
Singles: 7-Inch
ALLEGIANCE: 84................ **$1–3**
ATCO: 66 .... **3–5**
FONTANA: 64................... **4–6**
UNITED ARTISTS: 66–72.......... **3–5**
VERTIGO: 73–74................. **2–3**
Picture Sleeves
UNITED ARTISTS: 66–67.......... **3–5**
LPs: 10/12-Inch 33rpm
ALLEGIANCE: 84................ **5–8**
DATE: 70 .... **10–12**
FONTANA: 66.................. **20–30**
MEDIARTS: 71 .... **10–12**
RHINO: 84 .... **5–8**
UNITED ARTISTS: 67–75........ **20–30**
VERTIGO: 73–74................ **10–12**
WING **10–15**
Also see WINWOOD, Steve

DAVIS, Tim
Singles: 7-Inch
METROMEDIA: 72–73............. **2–3**
LPs: 10/12-Inch 33rpm
METROMEDIA: 72–74............ **8–10**

DAVIS, Tyrone
Singles: 7-Inch
ABC: 68......................... **3–5**
COLUMBIA: 76–81 .... **1–3**
DAKAR: 68–77 .... **2–3**
EPIC: 83 .... **1–3**
HIGHRISE: 82–83 .... **1–3**
OCEAN FRONT: 83–84 .... **1–3**
LPs: 10/12-Inch 33rpm
COLUMBIA: 76–81 .... **8–10**
DAKAR: 69–76 .... **10–15**
EPIC: 83 .... **5–8**
HIGHRISE: 82................... **5–8**

DAVY DMX
Singles: 12-Inch 33/45rpm
CBS ASSOCIATED: 84............. **4–6**
Singles: 7-Inch
CBS ASSOCIATED: 84............. **1–3**

Price Range

DAWN
Singles: 7-Inch
ARISTA: 75 .... $2–3
ELEKTRA: 76–77 2–3
Members: Joyce Wilson; Telma Hopkins.
Also see DAWN (With Tony Orlando)

DAWN (With Tony Orlando)
Singles: 7-Inch
BELL: 70–72 2–4
LPs: 10/12-Inch 33rpm
BELL: 70–71 10–12
Members: Tony Orlando; Joyce Wilson; Telma Hopkins.
Also see DAWN
Also see ORLANDO, Tony, & Dawn

DAWSON, Cliff
Singles: 7-Inch
BOARDWALK: 82 1–3

DAWSON, Cliff, & Renee Diggs
Singles: 7-Inch
BOARDWALK: 83 1–3
Also see DAWSON, Cliff
Also see STARPOINT

DAY, Arlan
Singles: 7-Inch
PASHA: 81 1–3

DAY, Bobby (Bobby Day & The Satellites; Bobby Day & The Blossoms; Bobby Byrd)
Singles: 7-Inch
CLASS: 57–59 5–8
RCA VICTOR: 63–64 3–5
RENDEZVOUS: 60–62 4–6
SURE SHOT: 67 3–5
LPs: 10/12-Inch 33rpm
CLASS: 59 45–55
RHINO: 84 5–8
Also see BYRD, Bobby

DAY, Dennis
Singles: 7-Inch
CAPITOL: 56 2–4
RCA VICTOR: 50–54 2–4
SHAMROCK: 59 2–3
EPs: 7-Inch 33/45rpm
CAPITOL: 56 4–6
RCA VICTOR: 50–59 4–8

Price Range

LPs: 10/12-Inch 33rpm
BLUEBIRD: 60 .... $5–10
CAMDEN: 64–66 5–10
CAPITOL: 56 10–15
REPRISE: 63 5–10
ROULETTE: 63 8–12

DAY, Doris
Singles: 7-Inch
COLUMBIA (38000 & 39000 series): 50–53 3–6
COLUMBIA (40000 through 44000 series): 54–67 2–5
Picture Sleeves
COLUMBIA: 57–61 2–5
EPs: 7-Inch 33/45rpm
COLUMBIA (Except 540): 50–59 5–10
COLUMBIA (540; "Love Me Or Leave Me"): 55 12–15
LPs: 10/12-Inch 33rpm
COLUMBIA (600 through 1200 series): 55–59 15–25
COLUMBIA (1400 through 2100 series): 60–64 10–15
COLUMBIA (8000 through 8900 series): 58–64 12–18
COLUMBIA (2200 through 2300 series): 64–65 8–12
COLUMBIA (9000 through 9100 series): 64–65 8–12
COLUMBIA (6000 series): 50–54 15–25
(10-Inch LPs.)
HARMONY: 66–72 5–10

DAY, Doris, & Don Cherry
EPs: 7-Inch 33/45rpm
COLUMBIA: 56 8–12
Also see CHERRY, Don

DAY, Doris, & Andre Previn
LPs: 10/12-Inch 33rpm
COLUMBIA: 62 10–20
Also see PREVIN, Andre

Price Range

DAY, Doris, & Johnnie Ray
Singles: 7-Inch
COLUMBIA: 52–53 . . . . $3–6
Also see RAY, Johnnie

DAY, Doris / Frank Sinatra
LPs: 10/12-Inch 33rpm
COLUMBIA (6000 series):
   55 20–35
   (10-Inch LPs.)
   Also see DAY, Doris
   Also see SINATRA, Frank

DAY, Morris
Singles: 12-Inch 33/45rpm
WARNER BROS: 85 4–6
   Singles: 7-Inch
WARNER BROS: 85 1–3
   LPs: 10/12-Inch 33rpm
WARNER BROS: 85 5–8
   Also see TIME, The

DAYBREAK
Singles: 7-Inch
PRELUDE: 80. 1–3
UNI: 70 2–4

DAYE, Cory
Singles: 7-Inch
N.Y.I.: 79. 1–3
   LPs: 10/12-Inch 33rpm
N.Y.I.: 79. 5–8
   Also see DR. BUZZARD'S ORIGINAL
   SAVANNAH BAND

DAYE, Johnny
Singles: 7-Inch
JOMADA: 65–66 3–5
PARKWAY: 66 3–5
STAX: 68. 3–5

DAYTON
Singles: 7-Inch
CAPITOL: 82–84 1–3
LIBERTY: 81–82 1–3
UNITED ARTISTS: 80 1–3
   LPs: 10/12-Inch 33rpm
CAPITOL: 83 5–8
LIBERTY: 81–82 5–8
UNITED ARTISTS: 80 5–8

Price Range

DAZZ BAND
Singles: 12-Inch 33/45rpm
MOTOWN: 80–85. . . . . $4–6
   Singles: 7-Inch
MOTOWN: 80–85. 1–3
   LPs: 10/12-Inch 33rpm
MOTOWN: 80–85. 5–8
   Also see KINSMAN DAZZ

**D'COCOA, Creme: see CREME
D'COCOA**

DEACONS, The
Singles: 7-Inch
SHAMA: 68 3–5

DEAD BOYS, The
Singles: 7-Inch
SIRE: 77–78 1–3
   LPs: 10/12-Inch 33rpm
SIRE: 77–78 8–10

**DEAD OR ALIVE (Featuring Pete
Burns)**
Singles: 12-Inch 33/45rpm
EPIC: 84–85 4–6
   Singles: 7-Inch
EPIC: 84–85 1–3
   LPs: 10/12-Inch 33rpm
EPIC: 84–85 5–8

DEADLY NIGHTSHADE
Singles: 7-Inch
PHANTOM: 76. 2–3
   LPs: 10/12-Inch 33rpm
PHANTOM: 76. 8–10

**DEAL, Bill (Bill Deal & The
Rhondels)**
Singles: 7-Inch
BUDDAH: 71–72 2–3
COLLECTABLES 1–3
ERIC 1–3
HERITAGE: 68–70 3–5
POLYDOR: 70–73 2–3
RED LION: 79. 2–3
   Picture Sleeves
HERITAGE: 69 4–6
   LPs: 10/12-Inch 33rpm
HERITAGE: 69 12–15

Price Range

RHINO: *86* **$5–8**

DEAN, Alan
Singles: 7-Inch
LONDON: *51* **3–5**
MGM: *51–56* **2–4**

DEAN, Debbie
Singles: 7-Inch
MOTOWN: *61–62* **10–15**
TREVA: *66* **3–5**
V.I.P.: *66–68* **3–5**
Picture Sleeves
MOTOWN: *62* **20–30**

DEAN, Hazell (Hazel Dean)
Singles: 12-Inch 33/45rpm
QUALITY: *84* **4–6**
Singles: 7-Inch
LONDON: *76* **1–3**

DEAN, Jimmy (Jimmie Dean)
Singles: 7-Inch
CASINO: *76* **1–3**
COLUMBIA (40000
  through 43000 series,
  except 42175): *57–66* **2–4**
COLUMBIA (42175; "Big
  Bad John"): *61* **4–6**
  (With words: "At the bottom of this mine lies
  one hell of a man.")
COLUMBIA (42175; "Big
  Bad John"): *61* **2–4**
  (With words: "At the bottom of this mine lies
  a big, big man.")
COLUMBIA (45000
  through 46000 series): *74* **1–3**
FOUR STAR (1600 series):
  54 . . . . **4–6**
FOUR STAR (1700 series):
  59 . . . . **3–5**
KING: *64* **2–3**
MERCURY: *56* **3–5**
RCA VICTOR: *66–71* **2–3**
Picture Sleeves
COLUMBIA (Except
  41025): *59–66* **3–5**
COLUMBIA (41025;
  "Little Sandy
  Sleighfoot"): *57* **8–12**

Price Range

EPs: 7-Inch 33/45rpm
COLUMBIA: *57* **$6–10**

LPs: 10/12-Inch 33rpm
ACCORD: *82* **5–8**
BRYLEN **5–8**
CASINO: *76* **5–8**
COLUMBIA (1000 series):
  57 . . . . **15–25**
COLUMBIA (1500
  through 2500 series):
  61–66 . . . . **10–20**
  (Monaural issues.)
COLUMBIA (8000 & 9000
  series): *61–68* **10–20**
  (With a "CS" prefix. Stereo issues.)
COLUMBIA (9200 series) **5–8**
  (With a "PC" prefix.)
COLUMBIA (10000
  series): *73* **6–10**
GRT: *77* **5–8**
GUEST STAR **8–10**
HARMONY: *60–69* **8–12**
KING: *61* **12–18**
MERCURY: *57* **15–20**
PICKWICK/HILLTOP:
  65 . . . . **10–12**
RCA VICTOR: *67–71* **8–12**
SPIN-O-RAMA **8–10**
WING: *64* **8–12**
WYNCOTE **8–10**

DEAN, Jimmy / Johnny Horton
LPs: 10/12-Inch 33rpm
STARDAY: *65* **15–20**
  Also see HORTON, Johnny

DEAN, Jimmy, & Dottie West
Singles: 7-Inch
RCA VICTOR: *71* **2–3**

LPs: 10/12-Inch 33rpm
RCA VICTOR: *70* **8–10**
  Also see DEAN, Jimmy
  Also see WEST, Dottie

DEAN & JEAN
Singles: 7-Inch
EMBER: *59–62* **4–6**
RUST: *63–65* **3–5**

Price Range

Price Range

DEAN & MARC
Singles: 7-Inch
BULLSEYE: 59. . . . . $4–6
HICKORY: 63–65 3–5
MAY: 63 3–5
Members: Dean Mathis; Marc Mathis.
Also see NEWBEATS, The

DEANE, Shelbra
Singles: 7-Inch
CASINO: 76–77 1–3

DE BARGE (The DeBarges; El DeBarge With DeBarge)
Singles: 12-Inch 33/45rpm
GORDY: 85–86. 4–6
Singles: 7-Inch
GORDY: 81–86. 1–3
LPs: 10/12-Inch 33rpm
GORDY: 81–86. 5–8
MOTOWN. 4–6

DEBBIE DEB
Singles: 12-Inch 33/45rpm
JAMPACKED: 85 4–6
SUNNYVIEW: 84. 4–6

DE BLANC
Singles: 7-Inch
ARISTA: 75–76. 2–3

DE BURGH, Chris
Singles: 7-Inch
A&M: 75–84 1–3
LPs: 10/12-Inch 33rpm
A&M: 76–84 8–10

DE CARO, Nick, Orchestra
Singles: 7-Inch
A&M: 67–69 2–3
LPs: 10/12-Inch 33rpm
A&M: 69 6–10
BLUE THUMB: 77 5–8

DE CASTRO, Peggy
Singles: 7-Inch
SPOTLITE: 62. 2–3
Also see DE CASTRO SISTERS, The

DE CASTRO SISTERS, The
Singles: 7-Inch
ABC-PARAMOUNT: 58. . . . . $2–4
ABBOTT: 54–56 2–4
CAPITOL: 60–61 2–3
RCA VICTOR: 56 2–4
TICO: 52 3–5
ZODIAC: 77 1–3
LPs: 10/12-Inch 33rpm
ABBOTT: 56. 20–30
CAPITOL: 60–61 12–18
20TH CENTURY-FOX:
65 8–12
Members: Peggy DeCastro; Babette DeCastro;
Cherie DeCastro.
Also see DE CASTRO, Peggy

DECO
Singles: 12-Inch 33/45rpm
QWEST: 84–85 4–6
Singles: 7-Inch
QWEST: 84–85 1–3
LPs: 10/12-Inch 33rpm
QWEST: 84 5–8

DEE, Dave, Dozy, Beaky, Mick & Tich
Singles: 7-Inch
ATLANTIC: 83 1–3
FONTANA: 66–67. 4–6
IMPERIAL: 67–68. 3–5
LPs: 10/12-Inch 33rpm
FONTANA: 67. 20–30
IMPERIAL: 68. 15–25

DEE, Jackie (Jackie DeShannon)
Singles: 7-Inch
GONE: 57 20–25
LIBERTY: 58 15–20
Also see DE SHANNON, Jackie

DEE, Jimmy (Jimmy Dee & The Offbeats)
Singles: 7-Inch
CUTIE: 63 3–5
DOT: 57–58 6–10
INNER-GLO 35–45
SCOPE 8–10
TNT: 57–59 20–30

Price Range

DEE, Joey (Joey Dee & The Starliters; Joey Dee & The New Starliters)
Singles: 7-Inch
ABC: 73 . . . . $1–3
JUBILEE: 66–67 3–5
ROULETTE: 61–63 3–5
SCEPTER: 60 4–6
TONSIL RECORDS: 70 2–4
VASELINE HAIR
    TONIC: 62 8–10
Picture Sleeves
ROULETTE: 62 4–6
EPs: 7-Inch 33/45rpm
DIPLOMAT: 62 10–12
LPs: 10/12-Inch 33rpm
ACCORD: 82 5–8
ROULETTE: 61–63 15–25
SCEPTER: 62 15–25

DEE, Joey, & The Starliters / Dion
Singles: 7-Inch
MONUMENT: 61 4–6
Also see DION

DEE, Johnny (John D. Loudermilk)
Singles: 7-Inch
COLONIAL: 57 5–8
DOT: 58 4–6
Also see LOUDERMILK, John D.

DEE, Kiki
Singles: 7-Inch
LIBERTY: 68 3–5
MCA: 73–77 2–3
POSSE: 81 1–3
RCA VICTOR: 81 1–3
RARE EARTH: 71 2–3
ROCKET: 73–79 1–3
TAMLA: 70 2–4
WORLD PACIFIC: 66 3–5
LPs: 10/12-Inch 33rpm
LIBERTY (7600 series): 69 15–20
LIBERTY (10000 series):
    81 5–8
MCA/ROCKET: 73–74 8–12
RCA VICTOR: 81 5–8
ROCKET: 77–78 8–10
TAMLA: 70 15–20
Also see JOHN, Elton, & Kiki Dee

Price Range

DEE, Lenny
Singles: 7-Inch
DECCA: 59–61 . . . . $2–3
EPs: 7-Inch 33/45rpm
DECCA: 59 3–6
LPs: 10/12-Inch 33rpm
DECCA: 55–70 5–15

DEE, Lola
Singles: 7-Inch
MERCURY: 54–56 2–4
WING: 55–56 2–4

DEE, Neecy
Singles: 12-Inch 33/45rpm
TNT: 85 4–6

DEE, Tommy, (Tommy Dee With Carol Kay & The Teen-Aires)
Singles: 7-Inch
CHALLENGE: 60 6–10
CREST (Except stereo
    singles): 59 4–6
CREST (Stereo singles): 59 15–20
PIKE: 61 3–5
SIMS: 66 3–5

DEE JAY & THE RUNAWAYS
Singles: 7-Inch
COULEE 8–10
SMASH: 66 3–5
SONIC: 68 3–5

Price Range

DEELE
Singles: 7-Inch
SOLAR: *83–85* **$1–3**
LPs: 10/12-Inch 33rpm
SOLAR: *85* **5–8**

DEEP PURPLE
Singles: 7-Inch
GRP: *73* **2–4**
MERCURY: *84–85*................ **1–3**
TETRAGRAMMATON:
68–69 .... **5–10**
WARNER BROS: *70–73*........... **3–5**
WARNER
BROS./PURPLE: *74–75* **2–4**
Picture Sleeves
TETRAGRAMMATON:
68 .... **5–10**
LPs: 10/12-Inch 33rpm
MERCURY: *84*................... **5–8**
PORTRAIT: *82*.................. **5–8**
SCEPTER/CITATION: *72*......... **8–10**
TETRAGRAMMATON:
68–69 .... **20–30**
WARNER BROS (Except
3000 series): *70–74* **15–20**
WARNER BROS (3000
series): *77*..................... **5–8**
WARNER
BROS./PURPLE: *74–80* **10–12**
Members: Ritchie Blackmore; Rod Evans; Ian
Paice; Jon Lord; Nick Simper; Roger Glover;
Ian Gillan; David Coverdale.
Also see BLACKMORE, Ritchie
Also see CAPTAIN BEYOND
Also see GILLAN, Ian
Also see GLOVER, Roger
Also see TRAPEZE
Also see WHITESNAKE

DEEP VELVET
Singles: 7-Inch
AWARE: *73* **2–3**

**DEES, Rick (Rick Dees & His Cast
Of Idiots)**
Singles: 12-Inch 33/45rpm
RSO: *78* **4–6**
STAX: *78*........................ **4–6**
Picture Sleeves
STAX: *78*........................ **1–3**
Singles: 7-Inch
ATLANTIC: *86* **1–3**

Price Range

RSO (Except 860): *76–77*......... **$1–3**
RSO (860; "He Ate Too
Many Jelly Donuts"): *77* **4–6**
RSO/POLYDOR: *76–77* **1–3**
STAX: *78*........................ **1–3**
LPs: 10/12-Inch 33rpm
ATLANTIC: *85* **5–8**
RSO: *77*........................ **8–10**

DEES, Sam
Singles: 7-Inch
ATLANTIC: *73–75* **2–3**
CHESS: *71*....................... **2–3**
LOLO: *69* **2–4**
POLYDOR: *78* **1–3**

DEES, Sam, & Betty Swann
Singles: 7-Inch
BIG TREE: *76* **2–3**
Also see DEES, Sam
Also see SWANN, Betty

DEF LEPPARD
Singles: 7-Inch
MERCURY: *80–84*................ **1–3**
EPs: 7-Inch 33/45rpm
BLUDGEON RIFFOLA:
78 .... **10–15**
LPs: 10/12-Inch 33rpm
MERCURY: *80–83*................ **5–8**

**DE FRANCO FAMILY, The
(Featuring Tony DeFranco)**
Singles: 7-Inch
20TH CENTURY-FOX
(Except 2214): *73–74*............. **2–3**
20TH CENTURY-FOX
(2214; "We Belong
Together"): *75*.................. **3–5**
LPs: 10/12-Inch 33rpm
20TH CENTURY-FOX:
73–74 .... **8–10**

DE JOHN SISTERS, The
Singles: 7-Inch
COLUMBIA: *57*................... **2–4**
EPIC: *54–56* **2–4**
OKEH: *53* **3–5**
SUNBEAM: *59*................... **2–4**
UNITED ARTISTS: *60*............. **2–3**
LPs: 10/12-Inch 33rpm
UNITED ARTISTS: *60*.......... **10–20**

Price Range

Members: Julie DeGiovanni; Dux DeGiovanni.

DEJONAY, Zena
Singles: 12-Inch 33/45rpm
TVI: *84*. **$4–6**

DEKKER, Desmond, & The Aces
Singles: 7-Inch
UNI: *69–70* **2–4**

LPs: 10/12-Inch 33rpm
UNI: *69* **15–18**

DELACARDOS, The
Singles: 7-Inch
ELGEY: *59* **10–12**
IMPERIAL: *63*. **4–6**
SHELL: *61–62*. **3–5**
UNITED ARTISTS: *61*. **6–10**

DELANEY & BONNIE (Delaney & Bonnie & Friends)
Singles: 7-Inch
ATCO: *70–72*. **2–4**
COLUMBIA: *72–73* **2–4**
ELEKTRA: *69* **3–5**
INDEPENDENCE: *67*. **4–6**
STAX: *68–69*. **3–5**

LPs: 10/12-Inch 33rpm
ATCO: *70–72*. **10–12**
COLUMBIA: *72* **10–12**
ELEKTRA: *69* **10–15**
GNP/CRESCENDO: *70* **10–12**
STAX: *69*. **10–15**
Members: Delaney Bramlett; Bonnie Bramlett.
Also see BAD HABITS, The
Also see BRAMLETT, Bonnie
Also see BRAMLETT, Delaney
Also see CLAPTON, Eric
Also see LANI & BONI
Also see SHINDOGS, The
Also see WHITLOCK, Bobby

DELBERT & GLEN
Singles: 7-Inch
CLEAN: *72–73* **2–4**

LPs: 10/12-Inch 33rpm
CLEAN: *72–73* **10–12**
Members: Delbert McClinton; Glen Clark.
Also see McCLINTON, Delbert

Price Range

DELEGATES, The
Singles: 7-Inch
MAINSTREAM: *72*. **$5–8**
LPs: 10/12-Inch 33rpm
MAINSTREAM: *73*. **10–15**

DELEGATION, The
Singles: 12-Inch 33/45rpm
SHADYBROOK: *77*. **4–6**
Singles: 7-Inch
MCA: *76* **2–3**
MERCURY: *80–81*. **1–3**
SHADYBROOK: *77–79*. **1–3**
LPs: 10/12-Inch 33rpm
MERCURY: *80–81*. **5–8**
SHADYBROOK: *79*. **5–8**

DELFONICS, The
Singles: 7-Inch
CAMEO: *67* **3–5**
COLLECTABLES **1–3**
MOON SHOT: *68*. **3–5**
PHILLY GROOVE: *68–73* **2–3**
ROULETTE: *73* **1–3**
LPs: 10/12-Inch 33rpm
KORY: *77*. **8–10**
PHILLY GROOVE: *68–74* **8–10**
POOGIE: *81* **5–8**
Also see HARRIS, Major

DELIVERANCE
Singles: 7-Inch
COLUMBIA: *80*. **1–3**

DELLS, The
Singles: 12-Inch 33/45rpm
ABC: *79*. **4–6**
Singles: 7-Inch
A&M: *76* **2–3**
ABC: *73–78* **1–3**
ARGO: *62* **4–6**
CADET: *67–75* **3–5**
CHESS: *73*. **2–4**
COLLECTABLES **1–3**
MCA: *79* **1–3**
MERCURY: *75–77*. **2–3**
PRIVATE I: *84*. **1–3**
20TH CENTURY-FOX:
80–82 . . . . **1–3**
VEE JAY (134; "Tell The
World"): *55* **175–200**
(Black vinyl.)

Price Range

VEE JAY (134; "Tell The
World"): 55 .... $300–325
   (Colored vinyl.)
VEE JAY (166; "Dreams
Of Contentment"): 55 40–50
VEE JAY (200 series):
   56–58 8–12
VEE JAY (300 series,
except 300): 59–61 5–8
VEE JAY (300; "Wedding
Day"): 58 20–30
VEE JAY (500 through
700 series): 64–65 4–6

LPs: 10/12-Inch 33rpm

ABC: 78 8–10
BUDDAH: 69 10–15
CADET: 68–75 10–15
LOST-NITE: 81 6–10
MERCURY: 75–77 10–12
PRIVATE I: 84 5–8
TRIP: 73 10–12
20TH CENTURY-FOX:
   80–81 5–8
UPFRONT: 68 10–12
VEE JAY (1000 series): 59 60–70
VEE JAY (1100 series): 65 20–25
    Members: Johnny Funches; Mike McGill; Mar-
    vin Junior; Vern Allison; Johnny Carter.
    Also see EL RAYS, The
    Also see EVERETT, Betty, & Jerry Butler
    Also see SOUTH, Joe / The Dells

DELLS, The, & The Dramatics
Singles: 7-Inch
CADET: 75 1–3
    Also see DELLS, The
    Also see DRAMATICS, The

DE LORY, Al
Singles: 7-Inch
CAPITOL: 68–71 1–3
EUREKA: 61 2–4
PHI DAN: 65 2–3

LPs: 10/12-Inch 33rpm
CAPITOL: 69–70 5–10

DELPHS, Jimmy
Singles: 7-Inch
CARLA: 67 3–5
KAREN: 68 3–5

Price Range

DEL-VIKINGS, The (The Dell-Vikings)
Singles: 7-Inch
ABC: 75 .... $1–3
ABC-PARAMOUNT:
   61–63 5–8
ALPINE: 60 8–10
BIM BAM BOOM: 72 2–3
BLUE SKY 2–4
BROADCAST 2–4
COLLECTABLES 1–3
DOT: 57–60 4–6
FEE BEE: 56–57 20–30
GATEWAY: 64 4–6
LUNIVERSE: 57 12–15
MERCURY 57–63
SCEPTER: 72 2–3

EPs: 7-Inch 33/45rpm
DOT: 57 25–30
MERCURY: 57 20–25

LPs: 10/12-Inch 33rpm
CROWN (5368; "The
Del-Vikings & The
Sonnets"): 63 20–25
    (Tracks shown as by The Sonnets on this LP are
    actually by The Meadowlarks and by The
    Sounds.)
DOT: 66 50–60
LUNIVERSE: 57 100–125
MERCURY: 57–58 60–75
    Members: Kripps Johnson; Norman Wright;
    Clarence Quick; Don Jackson; Gus Backus; Bill
    Blakely; David Lerchey.

DE MARCO, Ralph
Singles: 7-Inch
GUARANTEED: 59 .... $2–4
SHELLEY: 60.................... 2–4
20TH CENTURY-FOX:
  62 2–3

DE MATTEO, Nicky (Nicky DeMatteo & The Sorrows)
Singles: 7-Inch
ABC-PARAMOUNT: 61............ 3–5
CAMEO: 65–66................... 5–8
DIAMOND: 63................... 3–5
END: 58........................ 8–10
GUYDEN: 60.................... 3–5
PARIS: 59...................... 4–6
TORE: 59 4–6

DEMENSIONS, The (The Dimensions)
Singles: 7-Inch
COLLECTABLES 1–3
CORAL (Except 65600
  series): 61–63.................. 6–10
CORAL (65600 series): 67........... 3–5
MOHAWK: 60–61 5–8
Picture Sleeves
CORAL: 63..................... 8–12
LPs: 10/12-Inch 33rpm
CORAL: 63..................... 60–75

DENNY, Martin
Singles: 7-Inch
LIBERTY (55000 series):
  59–67 2–4
LIBERTY (56000 series):
  69 1–3
LIBERTY (77000 series):
  59–60 4–6
  (Stereo singles.)
Picture Sleeves
LIBERTY: 59–63 2–4
LPs: 10/12-Inch 33rpm
FIRST AMERICAN: 81 5–8
LIBERTY: 59–69 8–12
SUNSET: 66–68 5–10
UNITED ARTISTS: 74–80.......... 5–8
  Also see BAJA MARIMBA BAND, The
  Also see ZENTER, Si

DENNY, Sandy
Singles: 7-Inch
A&M: 72–73 .... $2–4
LPs: 10/12-Inch 33rpm
A&M: 71–72 8–10
ISLAND: 74–76 8–10
  Also see FAIRPORT CONVENTION

DENVER, John
Singles: 7-Inch
RCA VICTOR (Except
  0067 through 0955):
  74–86 1–3
RCA VICTOR (0067
  through 0955): 70–74 3–5
Picture Sleeves
RCA VICTOR: 74–86 1–3
LPs: 10/12-Inch 33rpm
HJD 40–50
RCA VICTOR: 70–86 6–10
  Also see MITCHELL, Chad, Trio

DENVER, John, & Emmylou Harris
Singles: 7-Inch
RCA VICTOR: 83 1–3
  Also see HARRIS, Emmylou

DENVER, John, & The Muppets
Singles: 7-Inch
RCA VICTOR: 79 1–3
LPs: 10/12-Inch 33rpm
RCA VICTOR: 79–83 5–8
  Also see MUPPETS, The

DENVER, John, & Olivia Newton-John
Singles: 7-Inch
RCA VICTOR: 75 2–3
  Also see NEWTON-JOHN, Olivia

DENVER, John, & Placido Domingo
Singles: 7-Inch
COLUMBIA: 82.................... 1–3
  Also see DOMINGO, Placido

DENVER, BOISE & JOHNSON (With John Denver)
Singles: 7-Inch
REPRISE: 68..................... 3–5
  Also see DENVER, John

Price Range

DEODATO (Eumir Deodato)
Singles: 12-Inch 33/45rpm
WARNER BROS: *84* $4–6
Singles: 7-Inch
CTI: *73–77* 2–3
MCA: *74–76* 2–3
WARNER BROS: *78–84* 1–3
LPs: 10/12-Inch 33rpm
CTI: *73–74* 8–10
MCA: *76* 6–10
MUSE: *73* 8–10
WARNER BROS: *78–82* 5–8

DEPECHE MODE
Singles: 12-Inch 33/45rpm
SIRE: *81–85* 4–6
Singles: 7-Inch
SIRE: *81–85* 1–3
LPs: 10/12-Inch 33rpm
SIRE: *81–85* 5–8

DEREK (Johnny Cymbal)
Singles: 7-Inch
BANG: *68–69* 3–5
SOLID GOLD: *73* 1–3
Also see CYMBAL, Johnny

DEREK & CYNDI
Singles: 7-Inch
THUNDER: *74* 2–3
Picture Sleeves
THUNDER: *74* 2–3

DEREK & THE DOMINOS
Singles: 7-Inch
ATCO: *70–72* 2–4
RSO: *73* 2–3
LPs: 10/12-Inch 33rpm
ATCO: *70–71* 20–30
POLYDOR: *74* 8–10
RSO: *77* 5–8
Members: Eric Clapton; Jim Gordon; Carl
Radle; Bobby Whitlock; Duane Allman
Also see ALLMAN, Duane
Also see CLAPTON, Eric
Also see WHITLOCK, Bobby

**DERRINGER, Rick (Derringer; Rick
Derringer & The McCoys)**
Singles: 7-Inch
BLUE SKY: *74–80* 2–3

Price Range

EPIC: *83* $1–3
LPs: 10/12-Inch 33rpm
BLUE SKY: *73–81* 8–12
MERCURY: *74* 10–12
PASSPORT: *83* 5–8
Also see McCOYS, The

**DERRINGER, Rick, & The Edgar
Winter Group**
LPs: 10/12-Inch 33rpm
BLUE SKY: *75* 8–10
Also see DERRINGER, Rick
Also see WINTER, Edgar

DE SANTO, Sugar Pie
Singles: 7-Inch
BRUNSWICK: *67–68* 3–5
CADET: *66* 3–5
CHECK: *60* 4–6
CHECKER: *63–66* 3–5
GEDINSON: *62* 3–5
SOUL CLOCK: *69* 2–4
VELTONE: *60* 4–6
WAX: *64* 3–5
EPs: 7-Inch 33/45rpm
CHECKER: *61* 12–15
LPs: 10/12-Inch 33rpm
CHECKER: *61* 25–30
Also see JAMES, Etta, & Sugar Pie DeSanto

DE SARIO, Teri
Singles: 7-Inch
CASABLANCA: *78* 1–3
LPs: 10/12-Inch 33rpm
CASABLANCA: *80* 5–8

DE SARIO, Teri, & K.C.
Singles: 7-Inch
CASABLANCA: *79–80* 1–3
Also see DE SARIO, Teri
Also see K.C. & THE SUNSHINE BAND

DE SHANNON, Jackie
Singles: 7-Inch
AMHERST: *78* 2–3
ATLANTIC: *72–74* 2–5
CAPITOL: *71* 3–5
COLUMBIA (Except
10221): *75* 2–3
COLUMBIA (10221; "Boat
To Sail"): *76* 10–12
(With Brian Wilson.)

Price Range

EDISON INT'L: *60*	$10–15
IMPERIAL: *65–70*	3–5
LIBERTY: *60–70*	5–8
MGM: *65*	4–6
RCA VICTOR: *80*	2–3

Picture Sleeves

LIBERTY: *63*	8–10

LPs: 10/12-Inch 33rpm

AMHERST: *77*	8–10
ATLANTIC: *72–74*	10–12
CAPITOL: *71*	12–15
COLUMBIA: *75*	10–12
IMPERIAL: *65–70*	18–25
LIBERTY (3000 & 7000 series): *63–64*	25–35
LIBERTY (10000 series): *82*	5–8
SUNSET: *68–71*	10–15
UNITED ARTISTS: *75*	8–10

Also see DEE, Jackie
Also see SHANNON, Jackie

DESMOND, Johnny
Singles: 7-Inch

COLUMBIA: *59–60*	2–3
CORAL: *52–56*	2–4
DIAMOND: *62*	1–3
EDGEWOOD: *62*	1–3
MGM: *50–51*	2–4
RCA VICTOR: *63*	1–3
20TH CENTURY-FOX: *64*	1–3
VIGOR: *73*	1–3

Picture Sleeves

CORAL: *55*	2–4

EPs: 7-Inch 33/45rpm

CORAL: *54–56*	5–8
MGM: *52*	5–8

LPs: 10/12-Inch 33rpm

CAMDEN: *53–54*	10–20
COLUMBIA: *59–60*	5–10
CORAL: *55–56*	10–20
LION: *56*	10–15
MGM: *55*	10–20
MAYFAIR: *58*	10–15
MOVIETONE: *66*	5–8
VOCALION: *66*	5–10

Also see CORNELL, Don, Johnny Desmond & Alan Dale

Price Range

DESMOND, Paul (The Paul Desmond Quartet)
Singles: 7-Inch

A&M: *69–70*	$1–3
RCA VICTOR: *62–63*	2–3

LPs: 10/12-Inch 33rpm

A&M: *69–76*	6–12
CTI: *75*	6–10
CAMDEN: *73*	5–10
DISCOVERY: *81*	5–8
FANTASY (21; "Paul Desmond"): *54*	40–60
(10-Inch LP.)	
FANTASY (220; "Paul Desmond"): *56*	20–25
RCA VICTOR (2400 & 2500 series): *62–63*	10–20
RCA VICTOR (2800 series): *78*	5–8
RCA VICTOR (3300 & 3400 series): *65–66*	10–15
WARNER BROS: *60*	15–25

Also see BRUBECK, Dave, & Paul Desmond
Also see MULLIGAN, Gerry, & Paul Desmond

DESTINATION
Singles: 7-Inch

A.V.I.: *77*	2–3

LPs: 10/12-Inch 33rpm

A.V.I.: *77*	8–10

DESTINATION
Singles: 12-Inch 33/45rpm

BUTTERFLY: *79*	4–6

Singles: 7-Inch

BUTTERFLY: *79*	1–3

LPs: 10/12-Inch 33rpm

BUTTERFLY: *79*	5–8

DET REIRRUC & THE CLUB RAPPERS
Singles: 12-Inch 33/45rpm

CLUB: *85*	4–6

DETECTIVE
Singles: 7-Inch

SWAN SONG: *77–78*	1–3

LPs: 10/12-Inch 33rpm

SWAN SONG: *77*	10–12

Price Range

DETERGENTS, The
Singles: 7-Inch
KAPP: *66* **$4–6**
ROULETTE: *64–65* **4–6**
Picture Sleeves
ROULETTE: *64–65* **6–10**
LPs: 10/12-Inch 33rpm
ROULETTE: *65* **20–30**

DETROIT (The Detroit Wheels)
Singles: 7-Inch
INFERNO: *68*................... **3–5**
PARAMOUNT: *70–71*.............. **2–3**
LPs: 10/12-Inch 33rpm
PARAMOUNT: *71–72*............ **10–12**
Also see RYDER, Mitch, & The Detroit
Wheels

DETROIT EMERALDS, The
Singles: 7-Inch
RIC-TIC: *68* **3–5**
WESTBOUND: *70–78* **2–4**
LPs: 10/12-Inch 33rpm
WESTBOUND: *71–78* **10–12**

**DETROIT WHEELS, The: see
DETROIT**

DETROYT
Singles: 7-Inch
TABU: *84* **1–3**

DE VAUGHN, William
Singles: 7-Inch
ROXBURY: *74*................... **2–3**
TEC: *80* **1–3**
LPs: 10/12-Inch 33rpm
ROXBURY: *74*.................. **8–10**
TEC: *80* **5–8**

DEVO
Singles: 12-Inch 33/45rpm
WARNER BROS: *80–85*............ **4–6**
Singles: 7-Inch
ASYLUM: *81*.................... **1–3**
BOOJI BOY **2–3**
FULL MOON: *81*................. **1–3**
WARNER BROS: *78–85*........... **1–3**
Picture Sleeves
WARNER BROS: *79–85*.......... **INC**

Price Range

LPs: 10/12-Inch 33rpm
WARNER BROS: *78–84*......... **$6–10**

**DE VOL, Frank, Orchestra (Frank
De Vol & The Rainbow Strings)**
Singles: 7-Inch
ABC-PARAMOUNT:
64–65 .... **2–3**
CAPITOL: *50–56* **2–4**
COLGEMS: *68* **2–3**
COLUMBIA: *59–62*............... **2–3**
KEM: *55* **2–4**
LPs: 10/12-Inch 33rpm
ABC-PARAMOUNT:
65–66 .... **5–10**
COLGEMS (108; "Guess
Who's Coming To
Dinner"): *68*.................. **20–25**
(Soundtrack.)
COLGEMS (5006; "The
Happening"): *67* **15–20**
(Soundtrack.)
COLUMBIA: *59–63*.............. **8–10**
HARMONY: *65* **5–8**

DE VONS, The
Singles: 7-Inch
KING: *69* **2–4**

DE VORZON, Barry
Singles: 7-Inch
COLUMBIA: *59–61*.............. **6–10**
RCA VICTOR: *57–59* **6–10**
WARNER BROS: *81*.............. **1–3**
Also see BARRY & THE TAMERLANES

**DE VORZON, Barry, & Perry
Botkin, Jr.**
Singles: 7-Inch
A&M: *76–77* **1–3**
Picture Sleeves
A&M: *76* **1–3**
Also see DE VORZON, Barry

DEVOTIONS, The
Singles: 7-Inch
DELTA: *61* **40–50**
KAPE............................ **3–5**
ROULETTE (Except 4406
& 4541): *64* **8–10**

Price Range

ROULETTE (4406; "Rip
Van Winkle"): *61* $20–25
(White label.)
ROULETTE (4541; "Rip
Van Winkle"): *64* 3–5
(Orange label.)
Members: Joe Pardo; Frank Pardo; Bob Weisbrod; Ray Sanchez; Bob Havorka; Louis DeCarlo; Larry Frank.

DEXY'S MIDNIGHT RUNNERS
Singles: 7-Inch
EMI AMERICA: *81* 1–3
MERCURY: *82–83* 1–3
LPs: 10/12-Inch 33rpm
EMI AMERICA: *81* 5–8
MERCURY: *82* 5–8

DEY, Tracey
Singles: 7-Inch
AMY: *63–65* 3–5
COLUMBIA: *66* 3–5
LIBERTY: *63* 4–6
VEE JAY: *62* 5–8

DE YOUNG, Cliff
Singles: 7-Inch
MCA: *73–75* 2–3
LPs: 10/12-Inch 33rpm
MCA: *73–75* 10–12

DE YOUNG, Dennis
Singles: 7-Inch
A&M: *83–84* 1–3
LPs: 10/12-Inch 33rpm
A&M: *84* 5–8
Also see STYX

DIAMOND, Gregg (Gregg Diamond's Starcruiser; Gregg Diamond's Bionic Boogie)
Singles: 12-Inch 33/45rpm
POLYDOR: *79* 4–6
Singles: 7-Inch
MARLIN: *78* 1–3
POLYDOR: *79–80* 1–3
LPs: 10/12-Inch 33rpm
MARLIN: *78* 5–8
MERCURY: *79* 5–8
POLYDOR: *77–78* 5–8

Price Range

DIAMOND, Joel (The Joel Diamond Experience)
Singles: 12-Inch 33/45rpm
CASABLANCA: *79* $4–6
Singles: 7-Inch
ATLANTIC: *82* 1–3
CASABLANCA: *79–84* 1–3
MOTOWN: *81* 1–3
LPs: 10/12-Inch 33rpm
CASABLANCA: *79* 8–10

DIAMOND, Leo
Singles: 7-Inch
RCA VICTOR: *55* 2–4

DIAMOND, Neil
Singles: 7-Inch
BANG: *66–73* 3–6
CAPITOL: *80–81* 1–3
COLUMBIA (Except
42809): *73–85* 2–3
COLUMBIA (42809;
"Clown Town"): *63* 75–100
COLUMBIA (42809;
"Clown Town"): *63* 50–75
(Promotional issue. White label.)
MCA: *73* 2–3
UNI: *68–72* 3–5
Picture Sleeves
CAPITOL: *80–81* 1–3
COLUMBIA: *73–85* 2–3
UNI: *68–70* 3–5
LPs: 10/12-Inch 33rpm
BANG: *66–73* 15–30
CAPITOL: *80* 5–8
COLUMBIA (Except
40000 series): *73–85* 5–8
COLUMBIA (40000
series): *78–82* 10–15
(Half-speed mastered LPs.)
FROG KING (1; "Early
Classics"): *78* 15–25
(Includes music & lyrics songbook.)
MCA: *72–81* 6–10
MFSL: *80* 15–20
UNI: *70–72* 15–30
Also see NEIL & JACK
Also see STREISAND, Barbra, & Neil Diamond

Price Range

Price Range

DIAMOND REO
Singles: 7-Inch
BIG TREE: 75 .... $2–3
BUDDAH: 77..................... 2–3

LPs: 10/12-Inch 33rpm
BIG TREE: 75 8–10
KAMA SUTRA: 76............... 8–10
PICCADILLY: 79 5–8

DIAMONDS, The
Singles: 7-Inch
CORAL: 55–56................... 5–8
MERCURY: 56–62................ 3–6

Picture Sleeves
MERCURY: 58.................... 4–6

EPs: 7-Inch 33/45rpm
BRUNSWICK: 57............... 10–15
MERCURY: 56–61.............. 10–15

LPs: 10/12-Inch 33rpm
MERCURY: 56–60.............. 20–30
WING: 59 15–20
Members: David Somerville; Phil Leavitt; Bill Reed; Ted Kowalski.

DIAMONDS, The, & Pete Rugolo
LPs: 10/12-Inch 33rpm
MERCURY: 59.................. 45–55
Also see DIAMONDS, The

DIANE RAY: see RAY, Diane

DIBANGO, Manu
Singles: 7-Inch
ATLANTIC: 73 .... $2–3
LPs: 10/12-Inch 33rpm
ATLANTIC: 73 8–10

DICK & DEE DEE
Singles: 7-Inch
DOT: 68–69...................... 3–5
LAMA: 61...................... 10–15
LIBERTY: 61–62................. 5–8
UNITED ARTISTS 2–3
WARNER BROS: 62–69........... 4–6
Picture Sleeves
WARNER BROS: 63–64........... 5–8
LPs: 10/12-Inch 33rpm
LIBERTY: 62 30–40
WARNER BROS: 63–65......... 20–25
Members: Dick St. John; Dee Dee Sperling.

DICK & DON: see ADDRISI BROTHERS, The

DICK LEE: see LEE, Dick

DICKENS, Jimmy (Little Jimmy Dickens)
Singles: 7-Inch
COLUMBIA (10000
series): 76...................... 1–3
COLUMBIA (20000 &
21000 series): 50–56 5–10

Price Range

COLUMBIA (40000
series): *56* **$4–6**
COLUMBIA (41000 series,
except 41173): *57–60.* **4–6**
COLUMBIA (41173; "I
Got A Hole In My
Pocket"): *57.* **20–30**
COLUMBIA (42000
through 44000 series):
60–67 . . . . **3–5**
DECCA: *67–69* **2–4**
LITTLE GEM: *75* **1–3**
PARTRIDGE: *80* **1–3**
STARDAY: *73* **1–3**
UNITED ARTISTS: *70–72* **2–3**

EPs: 7-Inch 33/45rpm

COLUMBIA (Except 2800
series): *52–57* **15–20**
COLUMBIA (2800 series):
57–58 . . . . **10–15**

LPs: 10/12-Inch 33rpm

COLUMBIA (1047;
"Raisin' The Dickens"):
57 . . . . **40–50**
COLUMBIA (1500
through 2500 series):
60–66 . . . . **10–20**
(Monaural issues.)
COLUMBIA (8300
through 9600 series):
60–68 . . . . **12–20**
(Stereo issues.)
COLUMBIA (10000 &
11000 series): *70–73* **6–10**
COLUMBIA (38000
series): *84* **5–8**
DECCA: *68–69* **10–12**
GUSTO **5–8**
HARMONY (7000 series):
64–65 . . . . **10–15**
HARMONY (9000 series):
54 . . . . **20–30**
(10-Inch LPs.)
HARMONY (11000
series): *67* **8–12**
QCA: *75* **6–10**

DICKEY DOO & THE DONT'S
(Featuring Gerry Granahan)
Singles: 7-Inch
ASCOT: *65* **3–5**

Price Range

DANNA: *67* **$3–5**
SWAN: *58–59* **5–8**
UNITED ARTISTS: *60–61* **5–8**
LPs: 10/12-Inch 33rpm
UNITED ARTISTS: *60* **25–35**
Also see GRANAHAN, Gerry

DICKIE LEE: see LEE, Dickie

DICTATORS, The
Singles: 7-Inch
ASYLUM: *77.* **2–3**
LPs: 10/12-Inch 33rpm
ASYLUM: *77–78.* **8–10**
EPIC: *75* **10–12**

DIDDLEY, Bo
Singles: 7-Inch
ABC: *74* **1–3**
CHECKER (800 series):
55–58 . . . . **8–10**
CHECKER (900 series):
59–62 . . . . **4–6**
CHECKER (1000 through
1200 series): *62–69* **3–5**
CHESS: *71–72* **2–4**
RCA VICTOR: *76* **2–3**
EPs: 7-Inch 33/45rpm
CHESS (5125; "Bo
Diddley"): *58* **25–30**
(This EP was issued with two different covers;
one of the conventional cardboard style, the
other made of paper.)
LPs: 10/12-Inch 33rpm
ACCORD: *82* **5–8**
CHECKER: *57–69* **15–25**
CHESS (Except 1400
series): *71–74* **10–15**
CHESS (1400 series): *58.* **25–30**
RCA VICTOR: *76* **8–10**
Also see BELMONTS, The, Freddy Cannon &
Bo Diddley
Also see BERRY, Chuck, & Bo Diddley
Also see MOONGLOWS, The

DIDDLEY, Bo, Howlin' Wolf &
Muddy Waters
LPs: 10/12-Inch 33rpm
CHECKER: *68* **15–20**
Also see DIDDLEY, Bo
Also see HOWLIN' WOLF
Also see MUDDY WATERS

Price Range

DIESEL
Singles: 7-Inch
REGENCY: *81* $2–3
LPs: 10/12-Inch 33rpm
REGENCY: *81* 8–10

DIFFORD & TILBROOK
Singles: 7-Inch
A&M: *84* 1–3
LPs: 10/12-Inch 33rpm
A&M: *84* 5–8
Members: Chris Difford; Glenn Tillbrook
Also see SQUEEZE

DIFOSCO
Singles: 7-Inch
EARTHQUAKE: *71* 2–4
ROXBURY: *76* 1–3
20TH CENTURY-FOX:
78 1–3

DILLARD, Varetta (Varetta Dillard & The Roamers)
Singles: 7-Inch
CUB: *60–61* 4–6
GROOVE: *55–56* 5–10
RCA VICTOR: *57* 5–10
SAVOY: *53–55* 5–10
TRIUMPH: *59* 4–6

DILLARDS, The
Singles: 7-Inch
ANTHEM: *71–72* 2–3
CAPITOL: *65* 2–4
ELEKTRA: *63–69* 2–4
POPPY: *74* 2–3
UNITED ARTISTS: *75* 2–3
WHITE WHALE: *70* 2–3
LPs: 10/12-Inch 33rpm
ANTHEM: *72* 6–10
ELEKTRA (200 series):
63–65 20–30
(Gold label.)
ELEKTRA (7-200 series):
63–65 20–30
(Gold label.)
ELEKTRA (7-200 series) 10–15
(Brown label.)
ELEKTRA (74000 series):
68 8–12
FLYING FISH: *77–81* 5–8

Price Range

POPPY: *73* $8–12
20TH CENTURY-FOX:
73 8–12
Members: Doug Dillard; Rodney Dillard; Dean Webb; Mitch Jayne.

DILLARDS, The, & John Hartford
LPs: 10/12-Inch 33rpm
FLYING FISH 5–8
Also see DILLARDS, The
Also see HARTFORD, John

DILLMAN BAND, The (The Daisy Dillman Band)
Singles: 7-Inch
RCA: *81* 1–3
UNITED ARTISTS: *77–78* 2–3
LPs: 10/12-Inch 33rpm
RCA: *81* 5–8
UNITED ARTISTS: *78* 5–8

DI MEOLA, Al
Singles: 7-Inch
COLUMBIA: *76–84* 1–3
LPs: 10/12-Inch 33rpm
COLUMBIA: *76–83* 5–8
Also see RETURN TO FOREVER

DING DONGS, The (Featuring Bobby Darin)
Singles: 7-Inch
BRUNSWICK: *58* 50–60
Also see DARIN, Bobby

DINNING, Mark
Singles: 7-Inch
CAMEO: *64* 3–5
HICKORY: *65–66* 3–5
MGM (Except 12980):
57–63 4–6
MGM (12980; "Top 40, News, Weather & Sports"): *61* 5–10
(With mention of "Patrice Lumumba" in lyrics.)
MGM (12980; "Top 40, News, Weather & Sports"): *61* 4–6
(With no mention of "Patrice Lumumba" in lyrics.)
UNITED ARTISTS: *67–68* 3–5

Price Range

Price Range

Picture Sleeves

MGM: *60* **$5–8**

LPs: 10/12-Inch 33rpm

MGM (3828; "Teen
Angel"): *60* **35–40**

MGM (3855; "Wanderin"):
60 . . . . **25–30**

DINO, DESI & BILLY

Singles: 7-Inch

COLUMBIA: *69* **2–4**

UNI: *69* **3–5**

REPRISE (Except 0965):
64–69 . . . . **4–6**

REPRISE (0965; "Lady
Love"): *70* **10–15**

Picture Sleeves

REPRISE: *65–68* **4–6**

LPs: 10/12-Inch 33rpm

REPRISE: *65–66* **15–20**

UNI: *69* **12–15**

Members: Dino Martin; Desi Arnaz, Jr; Billy
Hinsche.

DINO, Kenny

Singles: 12-Inch 33/45rpm

KDK PRODUCTIONS
("Love Songs For
Seka"): *80* **20–30**

(Picture disc with photo of Seka.)

Singles: 7-Inch

COLUMBIA: *64* **3–5**

DOT: *61* **3–5**

MUSICOR: *61–62* **4–6**

SMASH: *63–64* **3–5**

DINO, Paul

Singles: 7-Inch

ENTRE: *63* **3–5**

PROMO: *60–61* **3–5**

DIO

Singles: 7-Inch

WARNER BROS: *85–86* **1–3**

LPs: 10/12-Inch 33rpm

WARNER BROS: *85–86* **5–8**

DION (Dion DiMuci)

Singles: 7-Inch

BIG TREE/SPECTOR: *76* **2–3**

COLUMBIA (40000
series): *62* **$15–20**

(With a "3" prefix. Compact 33 Singles.)

COLUMBIA (40000
series): *62–65* **4–6**

(With a "4" prefix.)

LAURIE: *60–69* **4–6**

LIFESONG: *78–79* **2–3**

SPECTOR: *75* **2–3**

WARNER BROS: *69–79* **2–4**

WARNER
BROS./SPECTOR: *75* **2–3**

Picture Sleeves

COLUMBIA (Except
42662): *64–66* **5–8**

COLUMBIA (42662;
"Ruby Baby"): *62* **20–30**

(Promotional issue sleeve sent with "Ruby
Baby," but does not list title or number. Simply
reads, "Dion Is Now On Columbia Records.")

COLUMBIA (42662;
"Ruby Baby"): *62* **5–8**

(Commercially issued sleeve.)

LAURIE: *60–62* **5–10**

LPs: 10/12-Inch 33rpm

ABEL **8–10**

ARISTA: *77* **8–12**

COLUMBIA: *63–73* **15–20**

DAYSPRING: *80* **5–8**

LAURIE (Except 2047):
61–63 . . . . **20–25**

LAURIE (2047; "Dion"):
68 . . . . **10–15**

LIFESONG: *78* **5–8**

WARNER BROS: *69–76* **10–15**

Also see DEE, Joey, & The Starliters / Dion

DION & THE BELMONTS
(Featuring Dion DiMuci)

Singles: 7-Inch

ABC: *66–67* **3–5**

COLLECTABLES **1–3**

LAURIE (Gray label): *58* **15–20**

LAURIE (Blue label): *58* **12–15**

LAURIE (Red & white
label, except stereo
singles): *58–60* **4–6**

LAURIE (Stereo singles):
59 . . . . **20–25**

(With an "S" prefix.)

MOHAWK: *57* **25–30**

DION AND BELMONTS

LAURIE
3035

"EVERY LITTLE THING I DO"
"A LOVER'S PRAYER"

Price Range

Picture Sleeves
LAURIE: 59–60 .... **$10–12**
EPs: 7-Inch 33/45rpm
LAURIE: 59 .... **20–30**
LPs: 10/12-Inch 33rpm
ABC: 67 .... **15–20**
ARISTA: 84 .... **8–12**
GRT: 75 .... **8–10**
LAURIE (2002;
"Presenting Dion & The
Belmonts"): 59 .... **30–40**
LAURIE (2006; "Wish
Upon A Star"): 60 .... **30–35**
LAURIE (2013; "Dion
With The Belmonts"): 62 .... **20–30**
LAURIE (2016; "By
Special Request"): 62 .... **20–30**
LAURIE (4001;
"Everything You Always
Wanted To Hear"): 76 .... **8–12**
LAURIE (6000; "60
Greatest") **12–15**
PICKWICK: 75 .... **8–10**
WARNER BROS: 73 .... **8–10**
Also see BELMONTS, The

DION & THE TIMBERLANES
(Featuring Dion DiMuci)
Singles: 7-Inch
JUBILEE: 57 .... **12–15**
MOHAWK: 57 .... **30–35**
VIRGO: 73 .... **2–3**
Also see DION

Price Range

DIONNE & FRIENDS
Singles: 7-Inch
ARISTA: 85 .... **$1–3**
Members: Dionne Warwick; Elton John; Stevie
Wonder; Gladys Knight.
Also see JOHN, Elton
Also see KNIGHT, Gladys
Also see WARWICK, Dionne
Also see WONDER, Stevie

DIPLOMATS, The
Singles: 7-Inch
AROCK: 64 .... **3–5**
DYNAMO: 68–69 .... **3–5**
MAY: 61 .... **4–6**
MINIT: 66 .... **3–5**
WAND: 65 .... **3–5**

DIRECT CURRENT
Singles: 7-Inch
TEC: 79 .... **1–3**

DIRE STRAITS
Singles: 12-Inch 33/45rpm
WARNER BROS: 83 .... **4–6**
Singles: 7-Inch
WARNER BROS: 79–85 .... **1–3**
Picture Sleeves
WARNER BROS: 80 .... **INC**
LPs: 10/12-Inch 33rpm
WARNER BROS: 78–85 .... **5–8**

DIRT BAND, The: see NITTY
GRITTY DIRT BAND, The

DIRKSEN, Senator Everett
McKinley
Singles: 7-Inch
CAPITOL: 66 .... **2–4**
Picture Sleeves
CAPITOL: 66 .... **2–4**
LPs: 10/12-Inch 33rpm
BELL: 70 .... **5–10**
CAPITOL: 66–67 .... **10–15**

DISCO FOUR, The
Singles: 12-Inch 33/45rpm
PROFILE: 83 .... **4–6**
Singles: 7-Inch
PROFILE: 82–83 .... **1–3**

LPs: 10/12-Inch 33rpm
DECCA (DL-8938; "Carl
 Dobkins, Jr."): *59* **$30–40**
 (Monaural issue.)
DECCA (DL7-8938; "Carl
 Dobkins, Jr."): *59* **40–50**
 (Stereo issue.)

DOCKETT, Jimmy
Singles: 7-Inch
HULL: *64–65*. **3–5**

DR. BUZZARD'S ORIGINAL SAVANNAH BAND
Singles: 7-Inch
RCA VICTOR: *76–80* **2–3**
LPs: 10/12-Inch 33rpm
ELEKTRA: *79* **5–8**
PASSPORT. **5–8**
RCA VICTOR: *76–80* **8–10**
 Also see DAYE, Cory
 Also see KID CREOLE & THE COCONUTS

DOCTOR FEELGOOD (Doctor Feelgood & The Interns)
Singles: 7-Inch
COLUMBIA: *65–66* **3–5**
EPIC. **2–3**
MASTER SOUND: *67*. **3–5**
OKEH: *62–63* **4–6**
1-2-3: *68*. **3–5**
LPs: 10/12-Inch 33rpm
OKEH: *62* **20–25**
NUMBER ONE **15–20**
 Also see PIANO RED

DR. HOOK (Doctor Hook & The Medicine Show)
Singles: 7-Inch
CAPITOL: *75–80* **2–3**
CASABLANCA: *80–82* **1–3**
COLUMBIA: *71–74* **2–3**
Picture Sleeves
CAPITOL: *75–80* **1–3**
COLUMBIA: *71–72* **2–3**
LPs: 10/12-Inch 33rpm
CAPITOL: *75–81* **8–10**
CASABLANCA: *80–82* **5–8**
COLUMBIA (Except
 34147): *72–74*. **15–20**

COLUMBIA (34147; "Best
 Of Dr. Hook"): *76* **$5–8**
 Also see BEACH BOYS, The
 Also see SAWYER, Ray

DR. J.R. KOOL & THE OTHER ROXANNES
Singles: 12-Inch 33/45rpm
COMPLEAT: *85*. **4–6**
Singles: 7-Inch
COMPLEAT: *85*. **1–3**
LPs: 10/12-Inch 33rpm
COMPLEAT: *85*. **5–8**

DR. JECKYLL & MR. HYDE
Singles: 12-Inch 33/45rpm
PROFILE: *83–84* **4–6**
Singles: 7-Inch
PROFILE: *83–84* **1–3**
LPs: 10/12-Inch 33rpm
PROFILE: *84* **5–8**

DR. JOHN (Mac Rebennack)
Singles: 7-Inch
ATCO: *72–74*. **2–4**
COLUMBIA: *82* **1–3**
HORIZON: *79*. **2–3**
RCA VICTOR: *78* **2–3**
WARNER BROS: *81* **1–3**
LPs: 10/12-Inch 33rpm
A&M: *79* **8–10**
ACCORD: *81* **5–8**
ACE **10–12**
ATCO (Except 200 & 300
 series): *72–74* **8–10**
ATCO (200 & 300 series):
 68–71 . . . . **12–15**
BAROMETER: *74* **10–12**
CLEANCUTS: *82–84* **5–8**
KARATE: *78* **8–10**
SPRINGBOARD: *72* **10–12**
TRIP: *75–76* **8–10**
UNITED ARTISTS: *75*. **8–10**
 Also see BLOOMFIELD, Mike, Dr. John &
 John Paul Hammond
 Also see REBENNACK, Mac
 Also see SAHM, Doug

Price Range

DOLPHINS, The
Singles: 7-Inch
EMPRESS: *61* $4–6
FRATERNITY: *64–65* 3–5
GEMINI: *62* 4–6
LAURIE: *63* 4–6
SHAD: *60* 10–12
YORKSHIRE: *66* 4–6

DOMINATRIX
Singles: 12-Inch 33/45rpm
STREETWISE: *84* 4–6

DOMINGO, Placido
Singles: 7-Inch
COLUMBIA: *81–84* 1–3
LPs: 10/12-Inch 33rpm
COLUMBIA: *81–84* 5–8
RCA VICTOR: *82* 5–8
Also see DENVER, John, & Placido Domingo

DOMINO, Fats
Singles: 7-Inch
ABC: *73* 2–3
ABC-PARAMOUNT:
 63–64 3–5
BROADMOOR: *67* 3–5
IMPERIAL (5099; "Korea
 Blues"): *52* 125–150
IMPERIAL (5167; "You
 Know I Miss You"): *52* 100–125
IMPERIAL (5180; "Goin'
 Home"): *52.* 40–50
IMPERIAL (5197 through
 5251): *52–53* 25–35
 (Black vinyl.)
IMPERIAL (5197 through
 5251): *52–53* 55–65
 (Colored vinyl.)
IMPERIAL (5262 through
 5340): *53–55* 15–20
 (Black vinyl.)
IMPERIAL (5262 through
 5340): *53–55* 30–40
 (Colored vinyl.)
IMPERIAL (5348 through
 5454): *55–57* 5–10
IMPERIAL (5467 through
 5900 series): *57–63* 4–6
IMPERIAL (66000 series):
 64 3–5

Price Range

MERCURY: *65* $3–5
REPRISE: *68–70.* 3–5
UNITED ARTISTS: *74* 2–3
WARNER BROS: *80* 2–3

Picture Sleeves
IMPERIAL: *57–59* 8–12
MERCURY: *65* 6–10

EPs: 7-Inch 33/45rpm
ABC-PARAMOUNT:
 64–65 12–15
IMPERIAL (Red Script
 label): *56–60* 30–40
IMPERIAL (Maroon
 label): *56–57.* 12–18
MERCURY: *65.* 15–20
 (Jukebox issues only.)

LPs: 10/12-Inch 33rpm
ABC-PARAMOUNT:
 63–65 15–20
CANDLELITE: *76* 12–15
EVEREST: *74–77* 8–10
GRAND AWARD 10–15
HARLEM HIT PARADE:
 75 8–10
HARMONY: *69* 10–15
IMPERIAL (Except 9004
 through 9103): *60–63* 20–30
IMPERIAL (9004 through
 9103): *56–60.* 30–40
LIBERTY: *80–81* 5–8
MERCURY: *65.* 15–20
 (Listing above is for "Fats Domino '65." How-
 ever, March, '66 Mercury catalogs show MG-
 21065 & SR-61065, "Fats Domino, Southland
 U.S.A.," as issued. It may not have actually
 been released, but if it does exist its value range
 could be $100-$150.)
REPRISE: *68–71.* 15–20
SUNSET: *66–71* 12–15
UNITED ARTISTS: *71–80* 8–10
Also see PRICE, Lloyd

DOMINOES, The
Singles: 7-Inch
FEDERAL (12001; "Do
 Something For Me"): *50* 150–175
FEDERAL (12022; "Sixty
 Minute Man"): *51* 50–75
FEDERAL (12039; "I Am
 With You"): *51* 100–125

Price Range

FEDERAL (12059; "That's
What You're Doing To
Me"): *52*.................. **$200–225**
FEDERAL (12068; "Have
Mercy Baby"): *52* **50–75**
FEDERAL (12072; "Love,
Love, Love"): *52* **40–50**
(Later Federal numbers are listed under Billy
Ward & The Dominoes.)
GUSTO **1–3**
Members: Billy Ward; Clyde McPhatter;
Charlie White; William Lamont; Bill Brown.
Also see LITTLE ESTHER & THE DOMI-
NOES
Also see McPHATTER, Clyde
Also see WARD, Billy, & The Dominoes

DON & JUAN
Singles: 7-Inch
BIG TOP: *61–63*.................. **4–6**
ERIC **1–3**
MALA: *63–65*..................... **3–5**
TWIRL: *66* **3–5**
Members: Roland Trone: Claude Johnson.
Also see GENIES, The

DON & THE GOODTIMES
(Featuring Don Gallucci)
Singles: 7-Inch
DUNHILL: *65.*.................... **4–6**
EPIC: *67–68* **3–5**
JERDEN: *66*...................... **4–6**
WAND: *64* **4–6**
Picture Sleeves
EPIC: *67* **5–8**
LPs: 10/12-Inch 33rpm
BURDETTE: *66* **30–35**
EPIC: *67* **15–20**
PANORAMA **20–25**
WAND: *67* **20–25**
Also see KINGSMEN, The
Also see TOUCH

DON, DICK & JIMMY
Singles: 7-Inch
CROWN: *54–55* **4–6**
DOT: *54*......................... **4–6**
LPs: 10/12-Inch 33rpm
CROWN: *57* **20–25**
DOT: *59* **15–20**
MODERN **25–30**
VERVE: *59* **15–20**

Price Range

Members: Don Ralke; Dick Crow; Jimmy
Styne.

DONALDSON, Bo, & The Heywoods
Singles: 7-Inch
ABC: *73–75*..................... **$2–3**
CAPITOL: *76* **2–3**
FAMILY: *72–74*.................. **2–4**
PLAYBOY: *77* **2–3**
Picture Sleeves
ABC: *74*........................ **1–3**
LPs: 10/12-Inch 33rpm
ABC: *74*........................ **6–10**
FAMILY: *73*.................... **8–12**

DONALDSON, Lou (The Lou
Donaldson Quintet)
Singles: 7-Inch
ARGO: *63–65* **2–3**
BLUE NOTE (100 through
300 series): *73–74* **1–3**
BLUE NOTE (1500 &
1600 series): *52–58* **3–5**
BLUE NOTE (1700
through 1900 series):
58–72 .... **2–4**
LPs: 10/12-Inch 33rpm
ARGO: *63–65* **10–20**
BLUE NOTE: *64–80* **8–15**
(Label shows Blue Note Records as a division
of either Liberty or United Artists.)
BLUE NOTE (1500 series):
57–58 .... **25–50**
(Label gives New York street address for Blue
Note Records.)
BLUE NOTE (1500 series):
58 .... **15–25**
(Label reads "Blue Note Records Inc. - New
York, USA.")
BLUE NOTE (1500 series):
66 .... **10–20**
(Label shows Blue Note Records as a division
of either Liberty or United Artists.)
BLUE NOTE (4000 &
84000 series): *58–63* **15–25**
(Label reads "Blue Note Records Inc. - New
York, U.S.A.")
BLUE NOTE (5000 series):
52–54 .... **50–75**
(10-Inch LPs.)
CADET: *65–71* **8–12**
COTILLION: *76–77*.............. **5–8**

Price Range

SUNSET: *69–71* **$5–10**
TRIP: *79* **5–8**

DONEGAN, Lonnie (Lonnie Donegan & His Skiffle Group)
Singles: 7-Inch

ABC: *76* **1–3**
APT: *62* **3–5**
ATLANTIC: *60–61* **3–5**
DOT: *61* **3–5**
FELSTED: *61* **3–5**
HICKORY: *64–65* **3–5**
LONDON: *56* **5–8**
MCA **2–3**
MERCURY: *56* **4–6**

LPs: 10/12-Inch 33rpm

ABC-PARAMOUNT: *63* **15–20**
ATLANTIC: *60* **20–25**
DOT (3159; "Lonnie
   Donegan"): *59* **20–30**
DOT (3394; "Lonnie
   Donegan"): *61* **15–25**
UNITED ARTISTS: *77* **10–12**

DONNA LYNN: see LYNN, Donna

DONNER, Ral (Ral Donner & The Starfires; Ral Donner With Scotty Moore, D.J. Fontana & The Jordanaires)
Singles: 7-Inch

ABC: *73* **1–3**
CHICAGO FIRE: *74* **5–8**
END: *63* **10–12**
EVA-TONE/GOLDMINE:
   79 . . . . **2–3**
   (Soundsheet.)
FONTANA: *64–65* **10–15**
GONE (5102; "Girl Of My
   Best Friend"): *60* **20–25**
   (Black label.)
GONE (5100 series, except
   5108 & 5119): *61–62* **4–6**
   (Multi-color labels.)
GONE (5108; "To
   Love"/"And Then"): *61* **15–20**
   (Shortly after this release, "You Don't Know
   What You've Got" was issued using the same
   catalog number.)

Price Range

GONE (5108; "You Don't
   Know What You've
   Got"): *61* **$4–6**
GONE (5119; "School Of
   Heartbreakers"): *61* **15–20**
MJ: *70* **3–5**
MID-EAGLE: *68–76* **3–5**
RED BIRD: *66* **75–100**
REPRISE: *62–63* **12–20**
RISING SONS: *68* **3–5**
ROULETTE: *71* **2–3**
SCOTTIE: *59* **40–50**
SMASH: *65* **15–20**
   (Promotional issue only.)
STARFIRE (Except
   picture discs): *78–79* **2–3**
STARFIRE (Picture discs):
   79 . . . . **4–6**
SUNLIGHT: *72* **5–8**
TAU: *63* **15–20**
THUNDER: *78* **2–3**

Picture Sleeves

MJ: *70* **5–8**
REPRISE: *63* **25–35**
STARFIRE: *78–79* . . . . **INC**

LPs: 10/12-Inch 33rpm

AUDIO RESEARCH: *80* **12–15**
GONE (5012; "Takin' Care
   Of Business"): *61* **50–60**
GONE (5033; "Elvis
   Scrapbook") **10–15**
GYPSY: *79* **8–12**
STARFIRE: *82* **8–10**
   Also see PRESLEY, Elvis

Price Range

DONNER, Ral / Ray Smith / Bobby Dale
LPs: 10/12-Inch 33rpm
CROWN: *63* **$15–20**
Also see DONNER, Ral
Also see SMITH, Ray

DONNIE & THE DREAMERS
Singles: 7-Inch
DECCA: *61* **10–15**
WHALE: *61* **10–15**

DONOVAN (Donovan P. Leitch)
Singles: 7-Inch
ALLEGIANCE: *83* **1–3**
ARISTA: *77* **2–3**
EPIC: *66–76* **3–5**
HICKORY: *65–68* **4–6**

Picture Sleeves
EPIC: *66–70* **4–8**

LPs: 10/12-Inch 33rpm
ALLEGIANCE: *83* **5–8**
ARISTA: *77* **8–10**
BELL: *73* **10–12**
COLUMBIA: *73* **5–10**
EPIC: *67–76* **12–15**
HICKORY: *65–69* **15–20**
JANUS: *70–71* **10–12**
KORY: *77* **5–8**
PYE: *76* **8–10**

DOO, Dickey: see DICKEY DOO & THE DON'TS

DOOBIE BROTHERS, The
Singles: 12-Inch 33/45rpm
WARNER BROS: *79* **4–6**

Singles: 7-Inch
ASYLUM: *80* **1–3**
SESAME STREET: *81* **1–3**
WARNER BROS: *71–83* **1–3**

Picture Sleeves
WARNER BROS: *72–80* **1–3**

LPs: 10/12-Inch 33rpm
NAUTILUS: *80* **5–8**
PICKWICK: *80* **6–10**

Price Range

WARNER BROS: *71–83* **$8–12**
Members: Michael McDonald; Tom Johnson; Patrick Simmons.
Also see JOHNSON, Tom
Also see McDONALD, Michael
Also see SIMMONS, Patrick

DOOBIE BROTHERS, The, James Hall & James Taylor
Singles: 7-Inch
ASYLUM: *80* **1–3**
Also see TAYLOR, James

DOOBIE BROTHERS, The, & Nicolette Larson
Singles: 7-Inch
WARNER BROS: *79* **1–3**
Also see LARSON, Nicolette

DOOBIE BROTHERS, The / Kate Taylor & The Simon-Taylor Family
Singles: 7-Inch
WARNER BROS: *80* **2–3**
Picture Sleeves
WARNER BROS: *80* **2–3**
Also see DOOBIE BROTHERS, The
Also see SIMON SISTERS, The
Also see TAYLOR, James
Also see TAYLOR, Kate
Also see TAYLOR, Livingston

DOOLITTLE BAND, The (Dandy & The Doolittle Band)
Singles: 7-Inch
COLUMBIA: *80* **1–3**

DOORS, The
Singles: 7-Inch
ELEKTRA (Except 45000 series): *79–83* **2–3**
ELEKTRA (45000 series): *67–72* **4–6**
Picture Sleeves
ELEKTRA: *67–78* **5–8**
LPs: 10/12-Inch 33rpm
ELEKTRA (500 series): *78–80* **5–8**
ELEKTRA (4007; "The Doors"): *67* **15–20**
ELEKTRA (4014; "Strange Days"): *67* **15–20**

Price Range

(Elektra 4000 series numbers were mono issues. Stereo numbers were preceeded by a "7.")

ELEKTRA (5035; "Best
Of The Doors"): *73* **$15–20**
ELEKTRA (EKS-6001;
"Weird Scenes Inside
The Gold Mine"): *72* **12–15**
ELEKTRA (8E-6001;
"Weird Scenes Inside
The Gold Mine"): *73* **8–12**
ELEKTRA (9002;
"Absolutely Live"): *70* **15–20**
ELEKTRA (74024;
"Waiting For The Sun"):
68 .... **15–20**
ELEKTRA (75005; "The
Soft Parade"): *69*.............. **12–15**
ELEKTRA (75007;
"Morrison Hotel/Hard
Rock Cafe"): *70*................ **12–15**
ELEKTRA (74079; "Doors
13"): *70* **12–15**
ELEKTRA (75011; "L.A.
Woman"): *71*................. **15–20**
(With die-cut cover.)
ELEKTRA (75011; "L.A.
Woman") **5–8**
(With standard cover.)
ELEKTRA (75017; "Other
Voices"): *71* **8–12**
ELEKTRA (75038; "Full
Circle"): *72*................... **8–12**
ELEKTRA (60000 series):
84–85 .... **5–8**
MFSL: *76*...................... **15–18**
Members: Jim Morrison; Robbie Krieger; Ray
Manzarek; John Densmore.
Also see MANZAREK, Ray

DORADOS, El: see EL DORADOS, The

DORE, Charlie
Singles: 7-Inch
CHRYSALIS: *81*.................. **1–3**
ISLAND: *80–81* **1–3**

LPs: 10/12-Inch 33rpm
ISLAND: *80–81* **5–8**

Price Range

DORMAN, Harold
Singles: 7-Inch
ABC: *73*........................ **$1–3**
COLLECTABLES **1–3**
RITA: *60*....................... **4–6**
SANTO: *62* **3–5**
SUN: *61–62* **3–5**
TINCE: *60*...................... **4–6**

DORSEY, Jimmy, Orchestra & Chorus
Singles: 7-Inch
ABC: *73*........................ **1–3**
BELL: *54*....................... **2–4**
COLUMBIA: *50–52*.............. **2–4**
DECCA: *51–67*................... **2–4**
DOT: *63*........................ **1–3**
EPIC: *59* **2–4**
FRATERNITY: *57–60*............. **2–4**
MGM: *54*....................... **2–4**

EPs: 7-Inch 33/45rpm
COLUMBIA: *52–56*.............. **4–6**

LPs: 10/12-Inch 33rpm
COLUMBIA: *55–56*............. **10–20**
CORAL: *54*.................... **10–20**
DECCA: *57–66*................. **10–20**
EPIC: *59* **8–12**
FRATERNITY: *57*............... **10–20**
HINDSIGHT: *81* **5–8**
LION: *56*...................... **10–20**
MCA: *75* **5–8**

Price Range

DORSEY, Lee
Singles: 7-Inch
ABC: 78 .... $1–3
ABC-PARAMOUNT: 60 4–6
AMY: 65–69 3–5
CONSTELLATION: 64 3–5
FLASHBACK: 65 1–3
FURY: 61–63 4–6
GUSTO 1–3
POLYDOR: 70–72 2–3
REX: 57 15–20
ROULETTE 1–3
SANSU: 67 3–5
SMASH: 63 3–5
SPRING: 71 2–3
VALIANT: 58 10–15
LPs: 10/12-Inch 33rpm
AMY: 66 20–25
FURY: 62 30–35
POLYDOR: 70 10–12
SPHERE SOUND: 67 15–20

DORSEY, Tommy, Orchestra (The Tommy Dorsey Orchestra Starring Warren Covington)
Singles: 7-Inch
DECCA: 52–64 2–4
MCA: 73 1–3
RCA VICTOR: 50–57 2–4
EPs: 7-Inch 33/45rpm
COLUMBIA: 52–56 4–6
DECCA: 52–63 4–6
RCA VICTOR: 51–61 4–6
LPs: 10/12-Inch 33rpm
ACCORD: 82 5–8
BRIGHT ORANGE: 73 5–10
CAMDEN (Except 200
    series): 61–73 5–10
CAMDEN (200 series):
    53–55 10–20
COLPIX: 58–63 10–20
CORAL: 73 5–8
DECCA: 52–60 10–20
GOLDEN MUSIC
    SOCIETY: 56 15–20
HARMONY: 65–72 5–10
MCA: 75–81 5–8
MOVIETOWN: 67 8–10
RCA VICTOR: 51–82 10–20
SPRINGBOARD: 77 6–10

Price Range

20TH CENTURY-FOX:
    59–73 .... $10–15
    Also see SINATRA, Frank

DOSS, Kenny
Singles: 7-Inch
BEARSVILLE: 80 1–3
LPs: 10/12-Inch 33rpm
BEARSVILLE: 80 5–8

DOTTIE & RAY
Singles: 7-Inch
LE SAGE: 65 3–5

DOUBLE ENTENTE
Singles: 12-Inch 33/45rpm
COLUMBIA: 84 4–6
Singles: 7-Inch
COLUMBIA: 84 1–3

DOUBLE EXPOSURE
Singles: 7-Inch
SALSOUL: 76–79 1–3
LPs: 10/12-Inch 33rpm
SALSOUL: 78–79 8–10

DOUBLE IMAGE
Singles: 7-Inch
CBS ASSOCIATED: 83 1–3
CURB: 83 1–3
LPs: 10/12-Inch 33rpm
ECM: 79 5–8

DOUBLE VISION
Singles: 12-Inch 33/45rpm
PROFILE: 84 4–6

DOUCETTE (Jerry Doucette)
Singles: 7-Inch
MUSHROOM: 77–79 1–3
LPs: 10/12-Inch 33rpm
MUSHROOM: 78–79 5–8

DOUGLAS, Carl (Carl Douglas & The Big Stampede)
Singles: 7-Inch
ERIC 1–3
OKEH: 66–67 3–5
20TH CENTURY-FOX:
    74–75 2–3

LPs: 10/12-Inch 33rpm
20TH CENTURY-FOX:
  74 . . . . **$10–15**

DOUGLAS, Carol
Singles: 12-Inch 33/45rpm
MIDSONG INT'L **78**
Singles: 7-Inch
MIDLAND INT'L: *74–79* **2–3**
RCA VICTOR: *76* **2–3**
20TH CENTURY-FOX:
  81 . . . . **1–3**
Picture Sleeves
MIDLAND INT'L: *77–88* **1–3**
LPs: 10/12-Inch 33rpm
MIDLAND INT'L: *76–80* **8–10**

DOUGLAS, Mike
Singles: 7-Inch
BLUE RIVER: *66* **2–4**
DECCA: *69* **1–3**
EPIC: *65–67* **2–4**
IMAGE: *77* **1–3**
MGM: *71–73* **1–3**
PROJECT 3: *68* **2–3**
STAX: *74* **1–3**
Picture Sleeves
EPIC: *65–66* **2–4**
LPs: 10/12-Inch 33rpm
ATLANTIC: *76* **5–8**
EPIC: *65–67* **10–15**
HARMONY: *68* **8–12**
Also see BAILEY, Pearl, & Mike Douglas

DOUGLAS, Ronny (Ronny Douglas & Bobby Lonero)
Singles: 7-Inch
COLUMBIA: *71–72* **2–3**
DECCA: *63* **3–5**
EPIC: *65* **3–5**
EVEREST: *61* **4–6**

DOVALE, Debbie
Singles: 7-Inch
ROULETTE: *63–64* **3–5**

DOVE, Ronnie (Ronnie Dove & The Beltones)
Singles: 7-Inch
ABC: *74* **1–3**
DECCA (31000 series): *61* **6–10**

DECCA (32000 & 33000
  series): *71–73* **$2–3**
DIAMOND: *64–70* **3–5**
ERIC **1–3**
HITSVILLE: *76* **2–3**
JALO: *62* **6–10**
MC: *78* **2–3**
MCA: *73* **1–3**
MELODYLAND: *75–76* **2–3**
MOTION: *81* **2–3**
MOON SHINE: *83* **1–3**
SWAN: *63* **3–5**
WRAYCO: *71* **2–3**

Picture Sleeves
DIAMOND: *65–66* **3–5**

LPs: 10/12-Inch 33rpm
CERTRON: *70* **10–12**
DIAMOND: *65–70* **12–18**
MCA: *73* **8–10**

DOVELLS, The
Singles: 7-Inch
ABKCO: *83* **2–3**
COLLECTABLES **1–3**
DECCA: *70* **3–5**
EVENT: *70–74* **3–5**
MGM: *66–73* **3–5**
PARKWAY (Except 819
  & 827): *62–63* **3–5**
PARKWAY (819; "No No
  No"): *61* **6–10**
PARKWAY (827; "Bristol
  Stomp"/"Out In The
  Cold"): *61* **5–8**
PARKWAY (827; "Bristol
  Stomp"/"Letters Of
  Love"): *61* **3–5**
VERVE: *73* **2–3**
Picture Sleeves
PARKWAY: *62–63* **4–6**

LPs: 10/12-Inch 33rpm
DOVCO: *76* **5–8**
PARKWAY: *61–63* **20–25**
WYNCOTE: *65* **10–15**
Members: Len Barry; Arnie Satin; Jerry Sum-
mers; Danny Brooks; Mike Dennis.
Also see BARRY, Len
Also see MAGISTRATES, The
Also see ORLONS, The / The Dovells

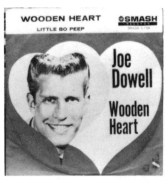

Price Range

DOWELL, Joe
Singles: 7-Inch
JOURNEY: *73.* $2–3
MONUMENT: *66.* 3–5
SMASH: *61–63* 4–6
Picture Sleeves
JOURNEY: *73.* 2–3
SMASH: *61–62* 3–5
LPs: 10/12-Inch 33rpm
SMASH: *61–62* 15–20
WING: *66* 10–12

DOWNING, Al (Big Al Downing)
Singles: 7-Inch
CARLTON: *58–59* 6–10
CHALLENGE: *58* 10–15
CHESS (1000 series): *62.* 3–5
CHESS (2000 series): *75.* 2–3
COLUMBIA: *64* 3–5
HOUSE OF THE FOX: *71* 2–4
JANUS: *74* 2–3
KANSOMA: *62.* 3–5
LENOX: *63* 3–5
POLYDOR: *76* 2–3
TEAM: *82–84* 1–3
V-TONE: *61* 3–5
WARNER BROS: *78–80* 1–3
WHITE ROCK: *58.* 30–35
LPs: 10/12-Inch 33rpm
TEAM: *83–85* 5–8
Also see PHILLIPS, Little Esther, & Big Al
Downing

Price Range

DOWNING, Don
Singles: 7-Inch
ABNER: *62* $3–5
CHAN 3–5
SCEPTER: *74* 2–3
LPs: 10/12-Inch 33rpm
ROADSHOW: *79* 5–8

DOZIER, Gene, & The Brotherhood
Singles: 7-Inch
MINIT: *67–68* 3–5
LPs: 10/12-Inch 33rpm
MINIT: *67.* 10–15

DOZIER, Lamont
Singles: 12-Inch 33/45rpm
WARNER BROS: *79* 4–6
Singles: 7-Inch
ABC: *73–76* 2–3
COLUMBIA: *81* 1–3
INVICTUS: *72* 2–4
LPs: 10/12-Inch 33rpm
ABC: *73–74* 8–10
COLUMBIA: *81* 5–8
INVICTUS: *74* 8–10
M&M: *82* 5–8
WARNER BROS: *76–79* 8–10
Also see HOLLAND, Eddie, & Lamont Dozier

DRAFI
Singles: 7-Inch
LONDON: *66–67* 4–6

Price Range

DRAGON
Singles: 12-Inch 33/45rpm
POLYDOR: 84 . . . . $4–6

Singles: 7-Inch
POLYDOR: 83–84 1–3
PORTRAIT: 78–79. 1–3

LPs: 10/12-Inch 33rpm
POLYDOR: 83 5–8
PORTRAIT: 78. 5–8

DRAKE, Charlie
Singles: 7-Inch
UNITED ARTISTS
  (Except 398): 61–62. 3–5
UNITED ARTISTS (398;
  "My Boomerang Won't
  Come Back"): 61 10–15
  (With "Practiced till I was BLACK in the face"
  lyrics.)
UNITED ARTISTS (398;
  "My Boomerang Won't
  Come Back"): 61 3–5
  (With "Practiced till I was BLUE in the face"
  lyrics.)

DRAKE, Guy
Singles: 7-Inch
MALLARD: 71. 2–3
ROYAL AMERICAN: 70. 2–4

LPs: 10/12-Inch 33rpm
OVATION: 74. 5–8
ROYAL AMERICAN: 70. 15–20

DRAKE, Pete
Singles: 7-Inch
SMASH: 64–65 2–4
STARDAY: 66 2–3
STOP: 68–70 1–3

LPs: 10/12-Inch 33rpm
CANAAN: 68. 8–12
CUMBERLAND: 63 12–18
PICKWICK/HILLTOP:
  67 8–12
MOUNTAIN DEW 8–10
SMASH: 64–65 10–15
STARDAY: 62–65 15–25
STOP: 70. 6–10

Price Range

DRAMATICS, The (Featuring Ron Banks)
Singles: 7-Inch
ABC: 75–77. $2–3
CADET: 74 2–3
MAINSTREAM: 75. 2–3
SPORT: 67. 3–5
VOLT: 71–73. 2–3

LPs: 10/12-Inch 33rpm
ABC: 75–78. 8–10
CADET: 74 8–10
CAPITOL: 82 5–8
MCA: 80 5–8
STAX: 77–78. 8–10
VOLT: 72–74. 10–12
  Also see BANKS, Ron
  Also see DELLS, The / The Dramatics

DRAPER, Rusty
Singles: 7-Inch
MERCURY: 52–62. 2–5
MONUMENT: 63–70. 2–3

EPs: 7-Inch 33/45rpm
MERCURY: 54–56. 5–10

LPs: 10/12-Inch 33rpm
GOLDEN CREST: 73 5–10
HARMONY: 72 5–10
MERCURY: 54–62. 10–20
MONUMENT: 65–75. 8–12
WING: 63–64 8–12

DREAM SYNDICATE, The
LPs: 10/12-Inch 33rpm
A&M: 84 5–8
SLASH. 5–8
  Also see TEXTONES, The

DREAM WEAVERS, The (Featuring Wade Buff)
Singles: 7-Inch
DECCA: 55–56 3–5

EPs: 7-Inch 33/45rpm
DECCA: 56. 10–15

DREAMBOY
Singles: 7-Inch
QWEST: 83–84 1–3

LPs: 10/12-Inch 33rpm
QWEST: 83–84 5–8

Price Range

Price Range

DREAMLOVERS, The
Singles: 7-Inch
CAMEO: *64* **$4–6**
CASINO **6–10**
COLLECTABLES **1–3**
COLUMBIA: *63* **20–25**
END: *62*......................... **3–5**
HERITAGE: *61–62* **4–6**
MERCURY: *66–67*............... **5–8**
SWAN: *63*....................... **3–5**
V-TONE: *60–61*................... **5–8**
WARNER BROS: *65*............. **3–5**

LPs: 10/12-Inch 33rpm
COLUMBIA: *63*................. **25–35**
Also see CHECKER, Chubby

DREAMS
Singles: 7-Inch
COLUMBIA: *71–72*............... **2–4**
D.C: *69*.......................... **3–5**

LPs: 10/12-Inch 33rpm
COLUMBIA: *70–71* **10–15**
Also see BRECKER BROTHERS, The

DREGS, The: see DIXIE DREGS, The

DRENNON, Eddie, & B.B.S. Unlimited
Singles: 7-Inch
FRIENDS & CO: *75* **2–3**

DRESSLER, Len
Singles: 7-Inch
CAPITOL: *63* **3–5**
MERCURY: *56*................... **4–6**

DREW, Patti (Patti Drew & The Drew-Vels)
Singles: 7-Inch
CAPITOL: *67–68* **3–5**
QUILL: *65*........................ **4–6**

LPs: 10/12-Inch 33rpm
CAPITOL: *69–70* **12–15**
Also see DREW-VELS, The

DREW-VELS, The (With Patti Drew)
Singles: 7-Inch
CAPITOL: *63–64* **4–6**

LPs: 10/12-Inch 33rpm
CAPITOL (2804; "Tell
Him"): *67*................... **$20–30**
Also see DREW, Patti

DREWS, J.D.
Singles: 7-Inch
UNICORN: *80* **1–3**

DRIFTER, Dixie: see DIXIE DRIFTER,, The

DRIFTERS, The
Singles: 7-Inch
ATLANTIC (1006 through
1029): *53–54*.................. **15–20**
ATLANTIC (1043 through
1078): *54–55*.................. **8–10**
ATLANTIC (1089 through
2127): *56–62*.................. **5–8**
ATLANTIC (2134 through
2786): *62–71*.................. **3–5**
BELL: *73–74*..................... **2–4**

Picture Sleeves
ATLANTIC: *64* **4–6**

EPs: 7-Inch 33/45rpm
ATLANTIC: *55–58* **25–35**

LPs: 10/12-Inch 33rpm
ATCO: *71* **10–12**
ATLANTIC (Except 8003
& 8022): *59–68* **25–35**
ATLANTIC (8003; "Clyde
McPhatter & The
Drifters"): *56* **75–100**
(Black label.)
ATLANTIC (8003; "Clyde
McPhatter & The
Drifters"): *59*................. **30–40**
(Red label.)
ATLANTIC (8022;
"Rockin' & Driftin"): *58* **35–45**
(Black label.)
ATLANTIC (8022;
"Rockin' & Driftin"): *59* **25–35**
(Red label.)
CLARION: *64*................... **15–20**
GUSTO: *80* **5–8**
TRIP: *76* **5–8**

Price Range

Price Range

Members: Clyde McPhatter; Bill Pinckney; Andrew Thrasher; Gerhart Thrasher; Willie Ferbie; Jimmy Oliver; David Baughan; Bobby Lee Hollis; Bobby Hendricks; Tommy Evans; Johnny Williams; Gene Pearson; Abdul Samad.
Also see COASTERS, The / The Drifters
Also see HENDRICKS, Bobby
Also see KING, Ben E.
Also see McPHATTER, Clyde

DRIFTERS, The / Lesley Gore / Roy Orbison / Los Bravos
EPs: 7-Inch 33/45rpm
SWINGERS FOR COKE:
66 . . . . **$8–15**
(Promotional issue only. Each artist sings a song about Coca Cola.)
Also see DRIFTERS, The
Also see GORE, Lesley
Also see LOS BRAVOS
Also see ORBISON, Roy

DRUPI
Singles: 7-Inch
A&M: 73 . . . . **1–3**

DRUSKY, Roy
Singles: 7-Inch
CAPITOL: 76 . . . . **1–3**
DECCA: 60–62 . . . . **2–5**
MERCURY: 63–72 . . . . **2–4**
PLANTATION: 79–80 . . . . **1–3**
EPs: 7-Inch 33/45rpm
DECCA: 61–63 . . . . **4–8**
LPs: 10/12-Inch 33rpm
CAPITOL: 76 . . . . **5–10**
DECCA: 61–62 . . . . **12–20**
HARMONY: 65 . . . . **10–12**
MCA **4–8**
MERCURY: 64–72 . . . . **8–15**
PICKWICK/HILLTOP **8–12**
PLANTATION: 79–80 . . . . **5–8**
SCORPION: 76 . . . . **5–10**
VOCALION: 70 . . . . **8–12**
WING: 64–66 . . . . **10–15**
Also see WELLS, Kitty, & Roy Drusky

DUALS, The
Singles: 7-Inch
ARC: 59 . . . . **4–6**
COLLECTABLES **1–3**
STAR REVUE: 61 . . . . **15–20**
SUE: 61 . . . . **4–6**

LPs: 10/12-Inch 33rpm
SUE: 61 . . . . **$40–50**

DUBS, The
Singles: 7-Inch
ABC-PARAMOUNT:
59–61 . . . . **5–8**
CLIFTON: 73 . . . . **2–3**
END: 62 . . . . **4–6**
GONE (Except 5002):
58–62 . . . . **6–10**
GONE (5002; "Don't Ask
Me To Be Lonely"): 57 . . . . **10–15**
JOHNSON (Except 102):
73 . . . . **2–4**
JOHNSON (102; "Don't
Ask Me To Be Lonely"):
57 . . . . **150–200**
JOSIE: 63 . . . . **3–5**
MARK-X: 60 . . . . **4–6**
ROULETTE **1–3**
WILSHIRE: 63 . . . . **5–8**

LPs: 10/12-Inch 33rpm
CANDLELITE **10–15**
Members: Richard Blandon; Cordell Brown; Cleveland Still; Jake Miller; Tom Gardner; Tom Grate.

DUBS, The / The Shells
LPs: 10/12-Inch 33rpm
CANDLELITE **8–10**
JOSIE **45–50**
Also see DUBS, The
Also see SHELLS, The

DUBSET
Singles: 12-Inch 33/45rpm
ELEKTRA: 84 . . . . **4–6**

DUCES OF RHYTHM & TEMPO TOPPERS (Featuring Little Richard)
Singles: 7-Inch
PEACOCK: 53–54 . . . . **35–40**
Also see LITTLE RICHARD

DUCHIEN, Armand
Singles: 12-Inch 33/45rpm
A&M: 84 . . . . **4–6**

Price Range

DUDEK, Les
Singles: 7-Inch
COLUMBIA: 77–78 . . . . $1–3
LPs: 10/12-Inch 33rpm
COLUMBIA: 75–81 8–10
Also see ALLMAN BROTHERS BAND, The

DUDLEY, Dave
Singles: 7-Inch
COLUMBIA: 78 1–3
GOLDEN WING: 63 3–5
JUBILEE: 62 3–5
KING (Except 5000
series): 55–56 4–6
KING (5000 series): 63 2–4
MERCURY: 63–73 2–3
NRC: 59 4–6
NEW STAR: 62 4–6
RICE: 73–78 1–3
STARDAY: 60 3–5
SUN: 79–80 1–3
UNITED ARTISTS: 75–76 1–3
VEE: 61 4–6
LPs: 10/12-Inch 33rpm
GOLDEN WING: 63 25–30
MERCURY: 64–73 10–15
MOUNTAIN DEW: 69 8–12
NASHVILLE: 68 8–12
PLANTATION: 81 5–8
RICE: 78 1–3
SUN: 80 5–8
UNITED ARTISTS: 75–76 8–12
WING: 68 8–12

DUDLEY, Dave, & Tom T. Hall
Singles: 7-Inch
MERCURY: 70 2–3
Also see HALL, Tom T.

DUDLEY, Dave / Link Wray
LPs: 10/12-Inch 33rpm
GUEST STAR: 63 10–15
Also see DUDLEY, Dave
Also see WRAY, Link

DU DROPPERS, The
Singles: 7-Inch
GROOVE (Except 0013):
54–55 15–20
GROOVE (0013; "Just
Whisper"): 54 30–35

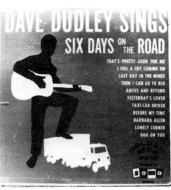

Price Range

RCA VICTOR: 53 . . . . $10–15
RED ROBIN (Black
vinyl): 52–53 25–30
RED ROBIN (Colored
vinyl): 52–53 75–90
EPs: 7-Inch 33/45rpm
GROOVE: 55 50–60
Members: Julius Ginyard; Willie Ray; Eddie
Hashaw; Harvey Ray; Bob Kornegay; Prentice
Moreland; Joe Van Loan; Charlie Hughes.
Also see GALE, Sunny, & The Du Droppers

DUKAYS, The (Featuring Gene Chandler)
Singles: 7-Inch
NAT: 61–62 5–8
VEE JAY: 62 3–5
Also see CHANDLER, Gene

DUKE, Doris
Singles: 7-Inch
CANYON: 70 2–3

DUKE, George
Singles: 12-Inch 33/45rpm
EPIC: 83 4–6
Singles: 7-Inch
EPIC: 77–83 1–3
LPs: 10/12-Inch 33rpm
ELEKTRA: 85 5–8
EPIC: 77–83 5–8
MPS/BASF: 74–76 8–10
Also see CLARKE, Stanley, & George Duke
Also see COBHAM, Billy
Also see MOTHERS OF INVENTION, The

DUKE, Patty
Singles: 7-Inch
UNITED ARTISTS: 65–68 . . . . **$3–5**
Picture Sleeves
UNITED ARTISTS: 65 . . . . **3–5**
LPs: 10/12-Inch 33rpm
UNITED ARTISTS: 65–68 . . . . **15–20**

DUKE & THE DRIVERS
Singles: 7-Inch
ABC: 75 . . . . **2–3**
LPs: 10/12-Inch 33rpm
ABC: 76 . . . . **8–10**

DUKE JUPITER
Singles: 7-Inch
COAST TO COAST: 82 . . . . **1–3**
MOROCCO: 84–85 . . . . **1–3**
LPs: 10/12-Inch 33rpm
COAST TO COAST:
82–83 . . . . **5–8**
MERCURY: 80 . . . . **5–8**
MOROCCO: 84 . . . . **5–8**

DUKE OF EARL, The (Gene Chandler)
Singles: 7-Inch
VEE JAY: 62 . . . . **3–5**
Also see CHANDLER, Gene

DUKES OF DIXIELAND, The
LPs: 10/12-Inch 33rpm
AUDIO FIDELITY: 55–61 . . . . **5–15**
COLUMBIA: 62 . . . . **4–8**
EPIC: 56 . . . . **5–12**
RCA VICTOR: 59 . . . . **5–10**

DUNCAN SISTERS, The
Singles: 12-Inch 33/45rpm
EAR MARC: 79 . . . . **4–6**
Singles: 7-Inch
EAR MARC: 79–80 . . . . **1–3**

DUNDAS, David
Singles: 7-Inch
CHRYSALIS: 76–77 . . . . **2–3**
LPs: 10/12-Inch 33rpm
CHRYSALIS: 77 . . . . **8–10**

DUNLAP, Gene (Gene Dunlap & The Ridgeways)
Singles: 12-Inch 33/45rpm
CAPITOL: 82 . . . . **$4–6**
Singles: 7-Inch
CAPITOL: 81–83 . . . . **1–3**
LPs: 10/12-Inch 33rpm
CAPITOL: 81–83 . . . . **5–8**
Also see AYERS, Roy
Also see WYNNE, Philippe

DUNN & BRUCE STREET
Singles: 7-Inch
DEVAKI: 81–82 . . . . **1–3**
Members: Dunn Pearson; Bruce Gray.

DUNN & McCASHEN
Singles: 7-Inch
CAPITOL: 69–70 . . . . **2–3**
LPs: 10/12-Inch 33rpm
CAPITOL: 69–70 . . . . **10–12**
COLUMBIA: 71 . . . . **12–15**

DUPREE, Champion Jack (Jack Dupree & His Band; Jack Dupree & Mr. Bear)
Singles: 7-Inch
ATLANTIC: 61 . . . . **3–5**
EVERLAST: 64 . . . . **3–5**
FEDERAL: 61 . . . . **3–5**
GROOVE: 56 . . . . **8–10**
GUSTO **1–3**
KING: 53–55 . . . . **8–10**
RED ROBIN: 53–58 . . . . **50–60**
VIK: 57 . . . . **8–10**
LPs: 10/12-Inch 33rpm
ARCHIVE OF FOLK
  MUSIC: 68 . . . . **10–12**
ATLANTIC (Except 8019
  & 8255): 61 . . . . **25–30**
ATLANTIC (8019; "Blues
  From The Gutter"): 59 . . . . **40–45**
  (Green label.)
ATLANTIC (8019; "Blues
  From The Gutter"): 59 . . . . **20–25**
  (Black label.)
ATLANTIC (8019; "Blues
  From The Gutter"): 59 . . . . **15–20**
  (Red label.)
ATLANTIC (8255; "Blues
  From The Gutter"): 70 . . . . **8–10**

Price Range

BLUE HORIZON: *69* **$10–12**
EVEREST **8–12**
FOLKWAYS: *61.* **20–25**
GNP/CRESCENDO: *74* **8–10**
JAZZMAN: *82* **5–8**
KING (700 series): *61* **40–45**
KING (1000 series): *70* **10–12**
LONDON: *69* **10–12**
OKEH: *63* **25–30**
STORYVILLE: *82* **5–8**
　　Also see McGHEE, Brownie

DUPREE, Champion Jack, & Mickey Baker
　　LPs: 10/12-Inch 33rpm
SIRE: *69* **10–12**
　　Also see BAKER, Mickey
　　Also see DUPREE, Champion Jack

DUPREE, Robbie
　　Singles: 7-Inch
ELEKTRA: *80–81* **1–3**
　　Picture Sleeves
ELEKTRA: *80* . . . . **INC**
　　LPs: 10/12-Inch 33rpm
ELEKTRA: *80–81* **5–8**

DUPREES, The
　　Singles: 7-Inch
COED: *62–65.* **4–6**
COLLECTABLES **1–3**
COLUMBIA: *65–67* **5–8**
ERIC **1–3**
HERITAGE: *68–70* **3–5**
RCA VICTOR: *75* **3–5**
　　Picture Sleeves
HERITAGE: *68* **3–5**
　　LPs: 10/12-Inch 33rpm
COED: *62–63.* **35–45**
HERITAGE: *68* **12–15**
POST **10–12**
　　Members: Joey Vann; Mike Kelly.
　　Also see ITALIAN ASPHALT & PAVE-
　　MENT COMPANY, The

DURAN DURAN
　　Singles: 12-Inch 33/45rpm
CAPITOL: *83–85* **4–6**
　　Singles: 7-Inch
CAPITOL: *83–85* **1–3**
HARVEST: *81–82.* **1–3**

Price Range

　　Picture Sleeves
CAPITOL: *83–85* . . . . **$INC**
　　LPs: 10/12-Inch 33rpm
CAPITOL: *83–85* **5–8**
HARVEST: *82.* **5–8**
　　Members: John Taylor, Andy Taylor; Simon
　　LeBon.
　　Also see ARCADIA
　　Also see BAND AID
　　Also see POWER STATION

DURANTE, Jimmy
　　Singles: 7-Inch
DECCA: *51–59* **2–5**
WARNER BROS: *63–70* **2–3**
　　EPs: 7-Inch 33/45rpm
DECCA: *54–56* **5–10**
MGM: *53–55* **5–10**
VARSITY: *55* **5–10**
　　LPs: 10/12-Inch 33rpm
DECCA (9000 series):
　　54–56 . . . . **15–25**
DECCA (78000 series): *70* **8–12**
HARMONY: *68* **8–12**
LIGHT: *71* **5–10**
LION: *56* **15–20**
MGM (3200 series): *55.* **15–25**
MGM (4200 series): *64.* **10–15**
ROULETTE: *61* **15–20**
WARNER BROS: *63–67* **10–15**

DURY, Ian, & The Blockheads
　　Singles: 7-Inch
STIFF: *79–81.* **1–3**
　　LPs: 10/12-Inch 33rpm
POLYDOR: *81* **5–8**
STIFF: *78–82.* **5–8**
　　Also see JANKEL, Chas

DUSK
　　Singles: 7-Inch
BELL: *71–72* **2–3**

DUVALL, Huelyn
　　Singles: 7-Inch
CHALLENGE (Except
　　1012 with blue label):
　　58–60 . . . . **15–20**
CHALLENGE (1012;
　　"Comin' Or Goin"): *58* **25–35**
　　(Blue label.)
STARFIRE: *59* **30–35**

Price Range

DYKE & THE BLAZERS
Singles: 7-Inch
ARTCO: *67* $8–10
ORIGINAL SOUND:
   67–69 3–5

LPs: 10/12-Inch 33rpm
ORIGINAL SOUND:
   67–69 30–35

DYLAN, Bob (Bob Dylan With The Band)
Singles: 7-Inch
ASYLUM: *74.* 3–5
COLUMBIA (10106;
  "Tangled Up In Blue"):
  75 8–10
COLUMBIA (10217;
  "Million Dollar Bash"):
  75 8–10
COLUMBIA (10245;
  "Hurricane"): *75* 2–4
COLUMBIA (10298;
  "Mozambique"): *75.* 2–4
COLUMBIA (10454; "Rita
  Mae"): *77.* 8–10
COLUMBIA (10805;
  "Baby Stop Crying"): *78* 4–6
COLUMBIA (10851;
  "Changing Of The
  Guards"): *78* 5–8
COLUMBIA (11000
  series): *79–80* 2–4
COLUMBIA (18-0000
  series): *81* 2–3
COLUMBIA (38-0000
  series): *84* 1–3
COLUMBIA (42656;
  "Mixed Up Confusion"):
  63 250–300
COLUMBIA (42856;
  "Blowin' In The Wind"):
  63 125–175
COLUMBIA (43242;
  "Subterranean Homesick
  Blues"): *65* 10–15
   (Gray label.)
COLUMBIA (43242;
  "Subterranean Homesick
  Blues"): *65* 4–6
   (Red label.)

Price Range

COLUMBIA (43346; "Like
  A Rolling Stone"): *65* $4–6
COLUMBIA (43389;
  "Positively 4th Street"):
  65 10–15
   (Gray label.)
COLUMBIA (43389;
  "Positively 4th Street"):
  65 4–6
   (Red label.)
COLUMBIA (43477; "Can
  You Please Crawl Out
  Your Window"): *65* 10–15
COLUMBIA (43683; "I
  Want You"): *66.* 4–6
COLUMBIA (43541; "One
  Of Us Must Know"): *66* 8–10
COLUMBIA (43592;
  "Rainy Day Women
  #12 & 35"): *66.* 4–6
COLUMBIA (43792; "Just
  Like A Woman"): *66* 4–6
COLUMBIA (44069;
  "Lepord-Skin Pill-Box
  Hat"): *67* 8–10
COLUMBIA (44826; "I
  Threw It All Away"): *69* 5–8
COLUMBIA (44926; "Lay
  Lady, Lay"): *69.* 4–6
COLUMBIA (45004;
  "Tonight I'll Be Staying
  Here With You"): *69* 5–8
COLUMBIA (45199;
  "Wigwam"): *69* 8–10
COLUMBIA (45516;
  "George Jackson"): *71* 8–10
COLUMBIA (45913;
  "Knockin' On Heaven's
  Door"): *73* 2–4
COLUMBIA (45982; "A
  Fool Such As I"): *73* 3–5

Picture Sleeves
COLUMBIA (11235;
  "Slow Train"): *80* 5–8
COLUMBIA (43242;
  "Subterranean Homesick
  Blues"): *65* 200–250
   (Promotional issue picture sleeve.)
COLUMBIA (43242;
  "Subterranean Homesick
  Blues"): *65* 30–40
   (Columbia "Hit Pack" picture sleeve.)

Price Range

COLUMBIA (43389;
"Positively 4th Street"):
65 .... **$15–20**
COLUMBIA (43683; "I
Want You"): *66*............... **15–20**
COLUMBIA (18-0000
series): *81* **4–6**

Promotional Singles

ASYLUM: *74*..................... **5–8**
COLUMBIA (25; "All The
Tired Horses"): *70*............. **25–35**
COLUMBIA (1039; "If
Not For You"): *71* **25–35**
COLUMBIA (10106;
"Tangled Up In Blue"):
75 .... **10–15**
COLUMBIA (10245;
"Hurricane"): *75*............... **10–15**
COLUMBIA (10245;
"Hurricane"): *75*............... **20–25**
(Compact 33 Single.)
COLUMBIA (10298;
"Mozambique"): *75*............. **5–8**
COLUMBIA (10454; "Rita
Mae"): *77*.................... **10–15**
COLUMBIA (10805;
"Baby Stop Crying"): *78* **10–15**
COLUMBIA (11000
series): *79–80*................... **4–6**
COLUMBIA (42856;
"Blowin' In The Wind"):
63 .... **200–275**
(Price includes a biographical insert, which
represents $75-$100 of the value.)
COLUMBIA (43242;
"Subterranean Homesick
Blues"): *65*.................... **25–30**
COLUMBIA (43346; "Like
A Rolling Stone"): *65*........... **20–25**
COLUMBIA (43389;
"Positively 4th Street"):
65 .... **20–25**
COLUMBIA (43389;
"Positively 4th Street"):
65 .... **75–100**
(Outtake promo. Actually contains an alternate
take of "Can You Please Crawl Out Your Win-
dow.")

Price Range

COLUMBIA (43477; "Can
You Please Crawl Out
Your Window"): *65* **$25-30**
COLUMBIA (43683; "I
Want You"): *66*................ **20–25**
COLUMBIA (43541; "One
Of Us Must Know"): *66* **25–30**
COLUMBIA (43592;
"Rainy Day Women
#12 & 35"): *66*............... **20–25**
COLUMBIA (43792; "Just
Like A Woman"): *66* **20–25**
COLUMBIA (44069;
"Lepord-Skin Pill-Box
Hat"): *67* **20–25**
COLUMBIA (44826; "I
Threw It All Away"): *69*....... **15–20**
COLUMBIA (44926; "Lay
Lady, Lay"): *69*............... **15–18**
COLUMBIA (45004;
"Tonight I'll Be Staying
Here With You"): *69* **15–20**
COLUMBIA (45199;
"Wigwam"): *69*............... **15–20**
COLUMBIA (45409;
"Watching The River
Flow"): *71* **15–20**
COLUMBIA (45516;
"George Jackson"): *71* **15–20**
COLUMBIA (45913;
"Knockin' On Heaven's
Door"): *73* **10–15**

Price Range

COLUMBIA (45982; "A
Fool Such As I"): *73* **$10–15**

EPs: 7-Inch 33/45rpm
COLUMBIA (319; "Step
Lively"): *65* **75–100**
COLUMBIA (9128;
"Bringing It All Back
Home"): *65.* **100–125**
(Jukebox issue only.)

LPs: 10/12-Inch 33rpm
ASYLUM (201; "Before
The Flood"): *74.* **10–15**
ASYLUM (1003; "Planet
Waves"): *74.* **15–20**
(Without cut corner.)
ASYLUM (1003; "Planet
Waves"): *74.* **8–10**
(With cut corner.)
ASYLUM (1003; "Planet
Waves"): *74.* **15–20**
(With an "EQ" prefix. Quad LP.)
COLUMBIA
(C2L-41/C2S-841;
"Blonde On Blonde"): *66.* **25–35**
(With "female photos.")
COLUMBIA
(C2L-41/C2S-841;
"Blonde On Blonde"): *66.* **10–12**
(With Dylan photo replacing female photos.)
COLUMBIA
(CL-1779/CS-8579; "Bob
Dylan"): *62* **80–100**
(Red & black label with six Columbia "eye"
boxes.)
COLUMBIA
(CL-1779/CS-8579; "Bob
Dylan"): *62* **20–30**
(Red label, without six Columbia "eye" boxes.)
COLUMBIA
(CL-1986/CS-8786; "The
Freewheelin' Bob
Dylan"): *63* **750–1000**
(With the tracks: "Let Me Die In My Foot-
steps," "Talkin' John Birch Society Blues,"
"Gamblin' Willie's Dead Man's Hand" and
"Rocks & Gravel," which may also be shown as
"Solid Gravel.")
Note: We suggest verification of the above
tracks by listening to the LP, rather than ac-
cepting the information printed on the label.

Price Range

COLUMBIA
(CL-1986/CS-8786; "The
Freewheelin' Bob
Dylan"): *63* **$25–35**
(Reissued with the above tracks replaced by
four others.)
COLUMBIA
(CL-2105/CS-8905; "The
Times They Are
A-Changin'"): *64* **20–30**
COLUMBIA
(CL-2193/CS-8993;
"Another Side Of Bob
Dylan"): *64* **15–20**
COLUMBIA
(CL-2328/CS-9128;
"Bringin' It All Back
Home"): *65.* **15–25**
COLUMBIA
(CL-2389/CS-9189;
. "Highway 61
Revisited"): *65.* **75–100**
(With an alternate take of "From A Buick 6."
The alternate take begins with a harmonica riff
and that pressing has a "-1" at the end of the
matrix number, stamped in the vinyl trailoff.)
COLUMBIA
(CL-2389/CS-9189;
"Highway 61
Revisited"): *65.* **10–15**
COLUMBIA
(KCL-2663/KCS-9463;
"Bob Dylan's Greatest
Hits"): *67.* **15–25**
COLUMBIA (CL-2804;
"John Wesley Harding" -
mono): *68.* **50–60**
COLUMBIA (CS-9604;
"John Wesley Harding" -
stereo): *68.* **10–15**
COLUMBIA (KCS-9825;
"Nashville Skyline"): *68* **8–12**
COLUMBIA (Q-30000
series - quad issues):
74–75 . . . . **20–30**
COLUMBIA (30050; "Self
Portrait"): *70* **50–60**
(With "360-Degree Stereo" at bottom of label.)
COLUMBIA (30050; "Self
Portrait"): *70* **10–12**
(Without "360-Degree Stereo" at bottom of
label.)

Price Range

COLUMBIA (30290
through 32747): *70–73* **$6–10**
COLUMBIA (33235;
"Blood On The
Tracks"): *75* **25–35**
(With a mural pictured on the back cover.)
COLUMBIA (33235;
"Blood On The
Tracks"): *75* **8–12**
(With liner notes on the back cover.)
COLUMBIA (33893
through 38819): *76–83* **6–10**
COLUMBIA (38830;
"Biography"): *85* **10–15**
(Boxed set, includes 36-page booklet.)
COLUMBIA (39944; "Real
Live"): *84* **5–8**
COLUMBIA (40110;
"Empire Burlesque"): *85* **5–8**
COLUMBIA (HC-40000
series - half-speed
mastered): *81–82* **15–20**
FOLKWAYS (5322; "Bob
Dylan Vs. A.J.
Weberman") **75–100**
ISLAND: *74* **20–30**

Promotional LPs

ASYLUM (201; "Before
The Flood"): *74* **20–30**
(White label.)
ASYLUM (1003; "Planet
Waves"): *74* **20–30**
(White label.)
COLUMBIA (422;
"Renaldo & Clara: *76* **20–25**
COLUMBIA (798;
"Saved"): *80* **25–30**
COLUMBIA (1259;
"Dylan London
Interview"): *80* **20–30**
COLUMBIA (1263; "Shot
Of Love"): *81* **25–30**
COLUMBIA (1471;
"Electric Lunch"): *83* **10–15**
COLUMBIA (1770;
"Infidels"): *83* **10–15**
COLUMBIA
(C2L-41/C2S-841;
"Blonde On Blonde"): *66* **60–75**
(White label.)

Price Range

COLUMBIA
(CL-1779/CS-8579; "Bob
Dylan"): *62* **$100–125**
(White label.)
COLUMBIA
(CL-1986/CS-8786; "The
Freewheelin' Bob
Dylan"): *63* **750–1000**
(White label. With the tracks: "Let Me Die In
My Footsteps," "Talkin' John Birch Society
Blues," "Gamblin' Willie's Dead Man's Hand"
and "Rocks & Gravel," which may also be
shown as "Solid Gravel.")
Note: We suggest verification of the above
tracks by listening to the LP, rather than ac-
cepting the information printed on the label.
COLUMBIA
(CL-1986/CS-8786; "The
Freewheelin' Bob
Dylan"): *63* **75–100**
(White label reissue, with the above tracks re-
placed by four others.)
COLUMBIA
(CL-2105/CS-8905; "The
Times They Are
A-Changin'"): *64* **60–75**
(White label.)
COLUMBIA
(CL-2193/CS-8993;
"Another Side Of Bob
Dylan"): *64* **60–75**
(White label.)
COLUMBIA
(CL-2328/CS-9128;
"Bringin' It All Back
Home"): *65* **60–75**
(White label.)
COLUMBIA
(CL-2389/CS-9189;
"Highway 61
Revisited"): *65* **60–75**
(White label.)
COLUMBIA
(KCL-2663/KCS-9463;
"Bob Dylan's Greatest
Hits"): *67* **60–75**
(White label.)
COLUMBIA (CL-2804;
"John Wesley Harding"):
68 .... **50–60**
(White label.)

Price Range

COLUMBIA (KCS-9825;
"Nashville Skyline"): *68* **$50–60**
(White label.)
COLUMBIA (30050; "Self
Portrait"): *70* **50–60**
(White label.)
COLUMBIA (30290
through 32747): *70–73* **15–20**
(White labels.)
COLUMBIA (33235;
"Blood On The
Tracks"): *75* **20–25**
(White label.)
COLUMBIA (33893
through 38819): *76–83* **10–15**
(White labels.)
COLUMBIA (39944; "Real
Live"): *84* **10–15**
(White label.)
COLUMBIA (FC-40000
series): *85* **5–8**
COLUMBIA (HC-40000
series - half-speed
mastered): *81–82* **15–20**
FOLKWAYS (5322; "Bob
Dylan Vs. A.J.
Weberman") **75–100**
ISLAND: *74* **20–30**
Also see BAND, The
Also see BELAFONTE, Harry
Also see SAHM, Doug
Also see U.S.A. FOR AFRICA

DYLAN, Bob, & The Heartbreakers / Michael Rubini
Singles: 7-Inch
MCA: *86* **1–3**
Also see DYLAN, Bob
Also see PETTY, Tom, & The Heartbreakers

DYNAMIC BREAKERS, The
Singles: 12-Inch 33/45rpm
SUNNYVIEW: *85* **4–6**

Singles: 7-Inch
SUNNYVIEW: *85* **1–3**

DYNAMIC CORVETTES, The
Singles: 7-Inch
ABET: *75* **2–3**

Price Range

DYNAMIC SUPERIORS, The
Singles: 7-Inch
MOTOWN: *74* **$2–3**

LPs: 10/12-Inch 33rpm
MOTOWN: *74–77* **8–10**

DYNAMICS, The
Singles: 7-Inch
ARC: *59* **4–6**
BIG TOP: *63–64* **3–5**
CAPRI: *59* **4–6**
DELTA: *59* **4–6**
DYNAMIC: *59–62* **8–12**
GUARANTEED: *59* **4–6**
IMPALA: *59* **12–15**
LAVERE: *61* **3–5**
LI BAN: *62* **3–5**
LIBERTY: *63* **3–5**
REPRISE: *63* **8–10**
SEECO: *59* **5–8**
U.S.A.: *64* **3–5**

DYNA-SORES, The
Singles: 7-Inch
RENDEZVOUS: *60* **5–8**

DYNASTY
Singles: 7-Inch
SOLAR: *80* **1–3**

LPs: 10/12-Inch 33rpm
SOLAR: *79–82* **5–8**

DYNATONES, The
Singles: 7-Inch
HBR: *66* **3–5**
ST. CLAIR: *66* **5–8**

LPs: 10/12-Inch 33rpm
HBR: *66* **20–25**

DYNELL, Johnny, & The New York 88
Singles: 12-Inch 33/45rpm
ACME: *83–84* **4–6**

DYSON, Clifton
LPs: 10/12-Inch 33rpm
AFTER HOURS: *82* **5–8**
NETWORK: *82* **5–8**

Price Range

DYSON, Ronnie
Singles: 12-Inch 33/45rpm
COTILLION: 83 . . . . $4–6
Singles: 7-Inch
COLUMBIA: 69–76 2–3
COTILLION: 83 1–3
Picture Sleeves
COLUMBIA: 73–75 2–3
LPs: 10/12-Inch 33rpm
COLUMBIA: 70–79 8–10
COTILLION: 82–83 5–8

E

E., Sheila (Shelia Escovedo)
Singles: 12-Inch 33/45rpm
WARNER BROS: 84–85 4–6
Singles: 7-Inch
PAISLEY PARK: 85 1–3
WARNER BROS: 84–85 1–3
LPs: 10/12-Inch 33rpm
PAISLEY PARK: 85 5–8
WARNER BROS: 84 5–8
Also see KRUSH GROOVE ALL-STARS, The
Also see PRINCE

EAGER, Brenda Lee (Brenda Lee Eager & Peaches)
Singles: 12-Inch 33/45rpm
PRIVATE I: 84 4–6
Singles: 7-Inch
MERCURY: 72–74 2–4
PLAYBOY: 75 2–3
PRIVATE I: 84 1–3
Also see BUTLER, Jerry, & Brenda Lee Eager

EAGLES, The
Singles: 7-Inch
ASYLUM: 72–80 2–4
FULL MOON: 81 1–3
Picture Sleeves
ASYLUM: 72–80 2–4
LPs: 10/12-Inch 33rpm
ASYLUM: 72–82 8–12
Members: Don Felder; Glenn Frey; Don Henley; Randy Meisner; Timothy B. Schmit; Joe Walsh.
Also see FELDER, Don
Also see FREY, Glenn

Price Range

Also see HENLEY, Don
Also see LEADON, Bernie
Also see LEE, Johnny / Eagles
Also see MEISNER, Randy
Also see NEWMAN, Randy
Also see POCO
Also see RONSTADT, Linda
Also see SCHMIT, Timothy B.
Also see SIMMONS, Patrick
Also see VITALE, Joe
Also see WALSH, Joe

EARLAND, Charles (Charles Earland's Odyssey; Charlie Earland, Jr.)
Singles: 7-Inch
COLUMBIA: 81–82 . . . . $1–3
MERCURY: 76 1–3
PRESTIGE: 70–74 2–3
QUAKER TOWN: 64 2–4
LPs: 10/12-Inch 33rpm
COLUMBIA: 80 5–8
MERCURY: 76–78 5–8
MUSE: 80 5–8
PRESTIGE: 70–75 5–10
RARE BIRD: 71 5–10
TRIP: 73 5–10

EARLE, Steve (Steve Earle & The Dukes)
Singles: 12-Inch 33/45rpm
MCA: 86 4–6
Singles: 7-Inch
EPIC: 84–85 2–3
MCA: 86 1–3
Picture Sleeves
EPIC: 84 . . . . INC
EPs: 7-Inch 33/45rpm
LSI: 82 4–6
LPs: 10/12-Inch 33rpm
MCA: 86 5–8

EARL-JEAN (Earl Jean McCree)
Singles: 7-Inch
COLPIX: 64 3–5
Also see COOKIES, The

EARLS, The
Singles: 12-Inch 33/45rpm
WOODBURY: 76–77 6–10
Singles: 7-Inch
ABC: 68 5–8

Price Range

ATLANTIC **$1–3**
BARRY: *63* **3–5**
CLIFTON: *74* **2–3**
COLLECTABLES **1–3**
COLUMBIA: *76* **2–4**
MR. "G": *67* **5–8**
OLD TOWN (Light blue
   label): *63* **15–20**
OLD TOWN (Multi-color
   label, except 1130):
   63–65 .... **8–12**
OLD TOWN (1130;
   "Remember Then"): *62* **4–6**
ROME (101; "Life Is But a
   Dream"/"It's You"): *61* **15–20**
ROME (101; "Life Is But a
   Dream"/"Without
   You"): *61* **10–15**
ROME (102; "Lookin' For
   My Baby"): *61* **10–15**
ROME (112; "Little Boy &
   Girl"): *76* **2–4**
ROME (114; "All Through
   Our Teens"): *76* **2–4**
   (Black vinyl.)
ROME (114; "All Through
   Our Teens"): *76* **4–6**
ROME (5117; "My Heart's
   Desire"): *62* **15–20**
   (Colored vinyl.)
ROME/POWER
   MARTIN: *76* **2–4**
WOODBURY: *76* **2–3**

LPs: 10/12-Inch 33rpm
CRYSTAL BALL................ **8–10**
OLD TOWN: *63* **75–100**
   Members: Larry Chance; Robert Del Din; Jack
   Wray; Ed Harder.

EARONS, The
   Singles: 12-Inch 33/45rpm
ISLAND: *84* **4–6**

   Singles: 7-Inch
BOARDWALK: *83* **1–3**
ISLAND: *84* **1–3**

EARTH OPERA
   Singles: 7-Inch
ELEKTRA: *67–69* **3–5**

Price Range

   LPs: 10/12-Inch 33rpm
ELEKTRA: *68–69* **$10–12**

**EARTH QUAKE: see
EARTHQUAKE**

EARTH, WIND & FIRE
   Singles: 12-Inch 33/45rpm
COLUMBIA: *75–83* **4–6**
   Singles: 7-Inch
ARC: *78–82* **1–3**
COLUMBIA: *73–84* **1–3**
WARNER BROS: *71* **2–3**
   Picture Sleeves
COLUMBIA: *74–80* **1–3**
   LPs: 10/12-Inch 33rpm
COLUMBIA (Except
   40000 series): *72–84* **8–12**
COLUMBIA (40000
   series): *81–82* **15–18**
   (Half-speed mastered LPs.)
COLUMBIA/ARC
   (Except picture discs):
   75–81 .... **8–10**
COLUMBIA/ARC
   (Picture discs): *79* **10–15**
WARNER BROS: *71–74* **12–15**
   Also see BAILEY, Philip

**EARTH, WIND & FIRE & THE
EMOTIONS**
   Singles: 12-Inch 33/45rpm
ARC: *79* **4–6**
   Singles: 7-Inch
ARC: *79–80* **1–3**
   LPs: 10/12-Inch 33rpm
ARC: *79* **5–8**
   Also see EMOTIONS, The

**EARTH, WIND & FIRE &
RAMSEY LEWIS**
   Singles: 7-Inch
COLUMBIA **74–75**
   Also see EARTH, WIND & FIRE
   Also see LEWIS, Ramsey

EARTHQUAKE (Earth Quake)
   Singles: 7-Inch
A&M: *72* **2–4**
BESERKLEY: *76–77* **2–3**
   LPs: 10/12-Inch 33rpm
A&M: *71–78* **10–12**

Price Range

BESERKLEY: *76–80* **$8–10**

EAST, Thomas (Thomas East & The Fabulous Playboys)
Singles: 7-Inch
LION: *73* **2–3**
MGM: *73* **2–3**
TODDLIN' TOWN: *68–69* **2–4**

EAST COAST
Singles: 7-Inch
RSO: *79* **1–3**

EAST L.A. CAR POOL
Singles: 7-Inch
GRC: *75* **2–3**

EASTBOUND EXPRESSWAY
Singles: 7-Inch
AVI: *78–79* **2–3**

EASTON, Elliot
Singles: 7-Inch
ELEKTRA: *85* **1–3**
LPs: 10/12-Inch 33rpm
ELEKTRA: *85* **5–8**
Also see CARS, The

EASTON, Sheena
Singles: 12-Inch 33/45rpm
EMI AMERICA: *81–85* **4–6**
Singles: 7-Inch
EMI AMERICA: *81–85* **1–3**
LIBERTY: *81* **1–3**
Picture Sleeves
EMI AMERICA: *81–85* **1–3**
LPs: 10/12-Inch 33rpm
EMI AMERICA: *81–85* **5–8**

EASTON, Sheena, & Kenny Rogers
Singles: 7-Inch
LIBERTY: *83* **1–3**
LPs: 10/12-Inch 33rpm
LIBERTY: *84* **5–8**
Also see EASTON, Sheena
Also see ROGERS, Kenny

EASTWOOD, Clint
Singles: 7-Inch
CAMEO: *63* **4–6**
CERTRON: *70* **2–4**
GOTHIC: *61* **5–8**

Price Range

PARAMOUNT: *69* **$2–4**
WARNER BROS: *81* **1–3**
Picture Sleeves
CAMEO: *63* **15–20**
LPs: 10/12-Inch 33rpm
CAMEO: *63* **25–40**
Also see CHARLES, Ray, & Clint Eastwood
Also see HAGGARD, Merle, & Clint Eastwood

EASTWOOD, Clint, & T.G. Sheppard
Singles: 7-Inch
WARNER BROS: *84* **1–3**
Also see EASTWOOD, Clint
Also see SHEPPARD, T.G.

EASY STREET
Singles: 7-Inch
CAPRICORN: *76* **2–3**
LPs: 10/12-Inch 33rpm
CAPRICORN: *76–77* **8–10**

EASYBEATS, The
Singles: 7-Inch
ASCOT: *66* **8–10**
RARE EARTH: *69* **3–5**
UNITED ARTISTS: *67–69* **4–6**
LPs: 10/12-Inch 33rpm
RARE EARTH: *70* **10–15**
UNITED ARTISTS: *67–68* **30–40**
Also see FLASH & THE PAN

EBB TIDE
Singles: 7-Inch
SOUND GEMS: *75–76* **2–3**

EBN/OZN
Singles: 12-Inch 33/45rpm
ELEKTRA: *84* **4–6**
Singles: 7-Inch
ELEKTRA: *84* **1–3**
LPs: 10/12-Inch 33rpm
ELEKTRA: *84* **5–8**
Members: Ebn; Ozn.

EBONEE WEBB (Ebony Web)
Singles: 7-Inch
CAPITOL: *81–84* **1–3**

Price Range

HI: *70–72* **$2–4**

LPs: 10/12-Inch 33rpm
CAPITOL: *81–84* **5–8**

EBONY
Singles: 12-Inch 33/45rpm
QUALITY/RFC: *84* **4–6**

EBONY, IVORY & JADE
Singles: 7-Inch
COLUMBIA: *75* **2–3**

EBONY RHYTHM FUNK CAMPAIGN, The
Singles: 7-Inch
MCA: *72* **2–3**

LPs: 10/12-Inch 33rpm
UNI: *72* **6–10**

EBONY WEB: see EBONEE WEBB

EBONYS, The
Singles: 7-Inch
BUDDAH: *76* **2–3**
PHILADELPHIA INT'L:
71–74 . . . . **2–3**

LPs: 10/12-Inch 33rpm
PHILADELPHIA INT'L:
73 . . . . **8–10**

ECHO & THE BUNNYMEN
Singles: 12-Inch 33/45rpm
SIRE: *81–84* **5–8**

Singles: 7-Inch
SIRE: *81–84* **1–3**

LPs: 10/12-Inch 33rpm
SIRE: *81–84* **5–8**

ECHOES, The
Singles: 7-Inch
ASCOT: *65* **6–10**
COLUMBIA: *60* **4–6**
DOLTON: *60.* **4–6**
FELSTED: *61* **5–8**
SRG: *61* **10–15**
SEG-WAY: *60–61.* **5–8**
SWAN: *58* **4–6**

Price Range

ECKSTINE, Billy
Singles: 7-Inch
A&M: *76* **$1–3**
ENTERPRISE: *70–74* **1–3**
MGM (10000 through
12000 series): *50–56* **2–4**
MERCURY: *59–64.* **2–3**
MOTOWN: *65–68.* **2–4**
RCA VICTOR: *56* **2–4**
ROULETTE: *59–60* **2–4**

EPs: 7-Inch 33/45rpm
EMARCY: *54–55* **10–15**
KING: *54* **10–15**
MGM: *50–56.* **8–12**
RENDITION: *50* **15–25**

LPs: 10/12-Inch 33rpm
AUDIO LAB: *60* **10–20**
EMARCY (26000 series):
54–55 . . . . **25–50**
(10-Inch LPs.)
EMARCY (36000 series):
54–56 . . . . **15–25**
ENTERPRISE: *71–74* **5–10**
KING (265 series): *54* **40–60**
(10-Inch LP.)
MGM (100 & 200 series):
52–53 . . . . **25–50**
(10-Inch LPs.)
MGM (3100 & 3200
series): *54–55* **15–25**
MERCURY: *57–64.* **10–20**
METRO: *65.* **8–12**
MOTOWN: *65–69.* **10–15**
NATIONAL (2000 series):
50 . . . . **30–60**
(10-Inch LP.)
REGENT: *56–57.* **15–25**
ROULETTE: *60* **10–20**
SAVOY: *76–79* **8–10**
TRIP: *75* **5–8**
WING: *67* **6–10**
Also see BASIE, Count, & Billy Eckstine
Also see DAMITA JO & BILLY ECKSTINE

ECKSTINE, Billy, & Quincy Jones
Singles: 7-Inch
MERCURY: *62.* **2–4**

LPs: 10/12-Inch 33rpm
MERCURY: *62.* **12–20**
Also see JONES, Quincy

Price Range

ECKSTINE, Billy, & Sarah Vaughan
Singles: 7-Inch
MERCURY: 57–59 . . . . $2–4
LPs: 10/12-Inch 33rpm
LION: 59 12–15
MERCURY: 57 15–20
  Also see ECKSTINE, Billy
  Also see VAUGHAN, Sarah

ECSTASY, PASSION & PAIN
(Featuring Barbara Roy)
Singles: 12-Inch
ROULETTE: 84 4–6
Singles: 7-Inch
ROULETTE: 74–76 2–3
LPs: 10/12-Inch 33rpm
ROULETTE: 74 8–10
  Also see ROY, Barbara

EDDIE & BETTY
Singles: 7-Inch
LARK: 59 4–6
SIX THOUSAND: 57 5–8
WARNER BROS: 59 4–6
LPs: 10/12-Inch 33rpm
WARNER BROS: 59 15–20
  Members: Eddie Cole; Betty Cole.

EDDIE & DUTCH
Singles: 7-Inch
IVANHOE: 70 2–3

EDDIE & ERNIE
Singles: 7-Inch
CHESS: 66 3–5
EASTERN: 65–66 3–5
REVUE: 69 2–4

EDDIE & FREDDIE
Singles: 7-Inch
OCTOBER: 77 2–3

EDDIE & THE TIDE (Eddie Rice)
Singles: 7-Inch
ATCO: 85 1–3

EDDIE D.
Singles: 12-Inch 33/45rpm
PHILLY WORLD: 85 4–6
Singles: 7-Inch
PHILLY WORLD: 85 1–3

Duane Eddy, 27 charted singles (1958–64), 10 charted LPs (1959–64).

Price Range

EDDY, Duane (Duane Eddy & The Rebels; Duane Eddy & The Rebelettes; Duane Eddy & His Rock-a-billies)
Singles: 7-Inch
BIG TREE: 72 . . . . $2–4
COLPIX: 65–66 4–6
CONGRESS: 70 2–4
ELEKTRA: 77 2–3
FORD: 57 25–30
GREGMARK (5;
  "Caravan"): 61 5–8
  (Shown as by Duane Eddy, but was actually Al Casey.)
JAMIE (Except stereo
  singles): 58–62 4–6
JAMIE (Stereo singles):
  59–60 15–20
RCA VICTOR: 61–65 4–6
REPRISE: 66–68 3–5
UNI: 70 2–4

Picture Sleeves
COLPIX: 66 15–20
JAMIE: 59–61 10–20
RCA VICTOR: 62–63 5–10

EPs: 7-Inch 33/45rpm
JAMIE: 59–60 15–25

Price Range

Price Range

**RCA
VICTOR/WURLITZER
DISCOTHEQUE
MUSIC:** *64* **$15–20**

LPs: 10/12-Inch 33rpm
COLPIX: *65* **25–30**
JAMIE (Except 3000, 3011
& 3026): *59–63* **30–40**
JAMIE (3000; "Have
Twangy Guitar Will
Travel"): *58* **40–50**
(White cover.)
JAMIE (3000; "Have
Twangy Guitar Will
Travel"): *58* **30–35**
(Red cover.)
JAMIE (3011; "Song Of
Our Heritage" with
gatefold cover): *60*............. **30–40**
JAMIE (3011; "Song Of
Our Heritage" with
standard cover): *61* **15–20**
JAMIE (3026; "16 Greatest
Hits"): *64*.................... **15–20**
RCA VICTOR (LPM/LSP
series): *62–66* **25–30**
RCA VICTOR (ANL
series): *78* **5–8**
REPRISE: *66–67*................ **15–20**
SIRE: *75* **10–12**
Also see BLOSSOMS, The
Also see CASEY, Al
Also see CLARK, Sanford, & Duane Eddy
Also see JIMMY & DUANE
Also see THOMAS, B.J.

EDELMAN, Randy
Singles: 7-Inch
ARISTA: *77–79*................... **1–3**
LION: *73*........................ **2–3**
MGM: *73*....................... **2–3**
SUNFLOWER: *71–72* **2–4**
20TH CENTURY-FOX:
74–76 .... **2–3**

LPs: 10/12-Inch 33rpm
ARISTA: *77–79*................... **5–8**
LION: *73*....................... **8–10**
MGM: *72*...................... **8–10**
SUNFLOWER: *71* **8–10**
20TH CENTURY-FOX:
74–78 .... **8–10**

EDEN'S CHILDREN
Singles: 7-Inch
ABC: *68* **$2–4**

LPs: 10/12-Inch 33rpm
ABC: *68*....................... **10–15**

**EDGE, Graeme (The Graeme Edge
Band)**
Singles: 7-Inch
LONDON: *77*.................... **1–3**
THRESHOLD: *74*................. **2–3**

LPs: 10/12-Inch 33rpm
LONDON: *77*.................... **8–10**
THRESHOLD: *75*................. **8–10**
Also see GURVITZ, Adrian
Also see MOODY BLUES, The

EDISON LIGHTHOUSE
Singles: 7-Inch
BELL: *70–71*..................... **2–4**

EDMUNDS, Dave
Singles: 7-Inch
COLUMBIA: *80–85*............... **1–3**
MAM: *70–71*..................... **3–5**
RCA VICTOR: *73–74* **3–5**
SWAN SONG: *77–81*.............. **2–3**

Promotional Singles
COLUMBIA (1576; "Run
Rudolph Run"): *82* **3–5**
(Compact 33 Single.)
COLUMBIA (03428; "Run
Rudolph Run"): *82* **2–4**

Picture Sleeves
SWAN SONG: *81*................. **2–3**

LPs: 10/12-Inch 33rpm
ATLANTIC (320; "College
Network") **35–40**
(Promotional issue only.)
COLUMBIA: *80–83* **5–8**
MAM: *72*...................... **30–40**
RCA VICTOR (4000
series): *82* **5–8**
RCA VICTOR (5000
series) **10–12**
SWAN SONG: *77–81*.............. **8–10**
Also see LEWIS, Huey, & The News
Also see LOVE SCULPTURE

COLUMBIA

® Columbia, Marcas Reg.

DAVE EDMUNDS BAND

33⅓ RPM
DEMONSTRATION
NOT FOR SALE
STEREO

AE7 1576
ZSM 170736
℗ 1-82 CBS Inc
Time: 3:35

**RUN RUDOLPH RUN From the
soundtrack album of the
film "Party Party"**
J. Marks - M. Brodsky

Publisher St. Nicholas Music
(ASCAP)

Produced by Dave Edmunds

Price Range

EDMUNDS, Dave, & Carlene Carter
Singles: 7-Inch
WARNER BROS: 80 . . . . $1–3
Also see CARTER, Carlene

EDMUNDS, Dave, & Nick Lowe
Singles: 7-Inch
COLUMBIA: 81 1–3
EPs: 7-Inch 33/45rpm
COLUMBIA: 80–83 5–8
Also see EDMUNDS, Dave
Also see LOWE, Nick
Also see ROCKPILE

EDSELS, The
Singles: 7-Inch
ABC: 75 1–3
CAPITOL: 61–62 3–5
DOT: 62 5–8
DUB (2843; "Lama Rama
  Ding Dong"): 58 20–30
DUB (2843; "Rama Lama
  Ding Dong"): 58 8–12
  (Note variation in title.)
EMBER: 61 4–6
ROULETTE (4000 series):
  59 10–12
TAMMY: 60–61 5–8
TWIN: 61 4–6

EDWARD BEAR
Singles: 7-Inch
CAPITOL: 70–74 2–3

Price Range

Picture Sleeves
CAPITOL: 72–73 . . . . $2–3
LPs: 10/12-Inch 33rpm
CAPITOL: 70–73 8–10

EDWARDS, Alton
Singles: 12-Inch 33/45rpm
COLUMBIA: 82 4–6
Singles: 7-Inch
COLUMBIA: 82 1–3

EDWARDS, Bobby
Singles: 7-Inch
BLUEBONNET: 59 3–5
CAPITOL: 61–63 2–4
CHART: 68 1–3
CREST: 61 3–5
MANCO: 62 3–5
MUSICOR: 65 2–3

EDWARDS, Dee
Singles: 12-Inch 33/45rpm
COTILLION: 79 4–6
Singles: 7-Inch
COTILLION: 78–80 1–3
D TOWN: 65 3–5
RCA VICTOR: 72 2–4
LPs: 10/12-Inch 33rpm
COTILLION: 80 5–8

EDWARDS, Dennis
Singles: 12-Inch 33/45rpm
GORDY: 84 4–6
Singles: 7-Inch
GORDY: 84–85 1–3
MOTOWN 1–3
LPs: 10/12-Inch 33rpm
GORDY: 84–85 5–8
Also see TEMPTATIONS, The

EDWARDS, Jayne
Singles: 12-Inch 33/45rpm
PROFILE: 83–84 4–6
Singles: 7-Inch
PROFILE: 83–84 1–3
LPs: 10/12-Inch 33rpm
PROFILE: 84 5–8

Price Range   *Price Range*

EDWARDS, Jimmy (Jimmie Edwards)
Singles: 7-Inch
MERCURY: *57–58* $4–6
RCA VICTOR: *59–60* 3–5

EDWARDS, John
Singles: 7-Inch
AWARE: *73–74* 2–3
BELL: *72* 2–4
COTILLION: *76–77* 2–3
LPs: 10/12-Inch 33rpm
AWARE: *74* 5–10
CREED: *75* 5–10
GENERAL/GRC: *74* 5–10

EDWARDS, Jonathan
Singles: 7-Inch
ATCO: *72–73* 2–3
CAPRICORN: *71* 2–3
WARNER BROS: *77* 2–3
LPs: 10/12-Inch 33rpm
ATCO: *72–74* 8–10
CAPRICORN: *71* 10–12
REPRISE: *74* 8–10
WARNER BROS: *77* 8–10

EDWARDS, Tom
Singles: 7-Inch
CORAL: *57* 3–5

EDWARDS, Tommy
Singles: 7-Inch
MGM (10000 & 11000
   series): *51–55* 3–5
MGM (12000 & 13000
   series): *55–65* 2–4
MGM (50000 series): *59* 5–8
   (Stereo singles.)
Picture Sleeves
MGM: *60* 4–6
EPs: 7-Inch 33/45rpm
MGM (Except 1001): *59* 8–12
MGM (1001; "It's All In
   The Game"): *52* 10–15
LPs: 10/12-Inch 33rpm
LION: *59* 10–15
MGM: *59–63* 10–20
METRO: *65* 8–12
REGENT 10–15

EDWARDS, Vincent
Singles: 7-Inch
CAPITOL: *62* $2–4
COLPIX: *65* 2–4
DECCA (Except stereo
   singles): *62–63* 2–4
DECCA (Stereo 33
   singles): *62* 4–6
RUSS-FI (1; "Oh Babe"):
   59 4–6
RUSS-FI (7001; "Why Did
   You Leave Me"): *62* 3–5
Picture Sleeves
COLPIX: *65* 2–4
DECCA: *62* 2–4
EPs: 7-Inch 33/45rpm
DECCA: *62* 8–10
LPs: 10/12-Inch 33rpm
DECCA: *62–63* 10–15

EGAN, Walter
Singles: 7-Inch
COLUMBIA: *77–79* 1–3
LPs: 10/12-Inch 33rpm
COLUMBIA: *77–80* 5–8
   Also see BUCKINGHAM, Lindsey
   Also see NICKS, Stevie

EGG CREAM (Featuring Andy Adams)
Singles: 7-Inch
PYRAMID: *77* 1–3
LPs: 10/12-Inch 33rpm
PYRAMID: *77* 5–8

EGYPTIAN LOVER
Singles: 7-Inch
EGYPTIAN: *84* 1–3
FREAK BEAT: *84* 2–3
LPs: 10/12-Inch 33rpm
EGYPTIAN: *85* 5–8

8TH DAY, The (The Eighth Day)
Singles: 7-Inch
A&M: *83* 1–3
INVICTUS: *71–72* 2–4
KAPP: *67–68* 3–5
Picture Sleeves
KAPP: *67* 3–5
LPs: 10/12-Inch 33rpm
A&M: *83* 5–8

Price Range

INVICTUS: *71–73* **$8–10**
KAPP: *68* **10–15**

EL CHICANO
Singles: 7-Inch
GORDO: *70* **3–5**
KAPP/GORDO: *70–72* **2–4**
MCA: *73–75* **2–3**
RFR: *82* **1–3**
SHADYBROOK: *77–78* **1–3**
LPs: 10/12-Inch 33rpm
KAPP: *70–72* **10–12**
MCA: *73–74* **8–10**
Also see TIERRA

EL COCO (Coco)
Singles: 12-Inch 33/45rpm
A.V.I.: *78–85* **4–6**
Singles: 7-Inch
A.V.I.: *75–85* **1–3**
LPs: 10/12-Inch 33rpm
A.V.I.: *75–85* **5–8**

EL DEBARGE: see DE BARGE

EL DORADOS, The
Singles: 7-Inch
COLLECTABLES **1–3**
VEE JAY (100 series,
 except 115, 118 & 127):
 55–56 . . . . **10–15**
VEE JAY (115; "Baby I
 Need You"): *54* **15–20**
 (Black vinyl.)
VEE JAY (115; "Baby I
 Need You"): *54* **60–75**
 (Colored vinyl.)
VEE JAY (118; "Annie's
 Answer"): *54* **30–35**
 (Black vinyl. With Hazel McCollum.)
VEE JAY (118; "Annie's
 Answer"): *54* **75–100**
 (Colored vinyl. With Hazel McCollum.)
VEE JAY (127; "One
 More Chance"): *54* **60–75**
VEE JAY (200 series,
 except 263): *56–57* **10–15**
VEE JAY (263; "3
 Reasons Why"): *58* **20–25**
VEE JAY (302; "Lights
 Are Low"): *58* **25–30**

Price Range

LPs: 10/12-Inch 33rpm
LOST-NITE: *81* **$5–8**
VEE JAY (1001; "Crazy
 Little Mama"): *59* **125–150**
 (This LP also contains two tracks by The Mag-
 nificants.)
 Members: Pirkle Lee Moses, Jr.; Arthur Bas-
 sett; Louis Bradley; James Maddox; Jewel
 Jones; Richard Nickens; Johnny Carter; Ted
 Long; John McCall; Douglas Brown.
 Also see MAGNIFICENTS, The

ELAINE & ELLEN
Singles: 7-Inch
OVATION: *80* **1–3**

ELBERT, Donnie
Singles: 7-Inch
ALL PLATINUM: *72* **2–3**
AVCO: *72* **2–3**
BULLET: *70* **2–4**
CUB: *63* **3–5**
DELUXE: *57* **4–6**
GATEWAY: *64–65* **3–5**
GUSTO **1–3**
JALYNNE: *61–62* **3–5**
VEE JAY: *60* **3–5**
LPs: 10/12-Inch 33rpm
ALL PLATINUM: *71* **10–12**
DELUXE: *71* **10–15**
KING: *59* **30–40**
SUGARHILL: *81* **5–8**
TRIP: *72* **8–10**

ELBOW BONES & THE
RACKETEERS
Singles: 12-Inch 33/45rpm
EMI AMERICA: *83* **4–6**

ELECTRIC EXPRESS
Singles: 7-Inch
LINCO: *71* **2–3**

ELECTRIC FLAG, The (The Electric
Flag Music Band)
Singles: 7-Inch
ATLANTIC: *74–75* **2–3**
COLUMBIA: *67* **3–5**
SIDEWALK: *67* **8–10**
Picture Sleeves
COLUMBIA: *67* **3–5**

Price Range

LPs: 10/12-Inch 33rpm
ATLANTIC: *74* **$8–10**
COLUMBIA: *68–71* **10–12**
   Also see BLOOMFIELD, Mike, & Nick Graventes
   Also see MILES, Buddy, Express

ELECTRIC INDIAN, The
Singles: 7-Inch
MARMADUKE: *69* **5–8**
UNITED ARTISTS: *69* **2–4**
LPs: 10/12-Inch 33rpm
UNITED ARTISTS: *69* **10–12**

ELECTRIC LIGHT ORCHESTRA, The (ELO)
Singles: 12-Inch 33/45rpm
JET: *78* **8–12**
Singles: 7-Inch
JET: *77–84* **2–3**
JET/CBS: *79* **2–3**
JET/UNITED ARTISTS:
   77 . . . . **2–3**
MCA: *80* **1–3**
UNITED ARTISTS: *72–77* **2–4**
Picture Sleeves
JET: *78–79* **2–3**
JET/UNITED ARTISTS:
   77 . . . . **2–3**
MCA: *80* **1–3**
UNITED ARTISTS: *72–77* **2–4**
LPs: 10/12-Inch 33rpm
COLUMBIA/JET (Except
   40000 series): *78–81* **5–8**
COLUMBIA/JET (40000
   series): *80–81* **15–18**
   (Half-speed mastered LPs.)
UNITED ARTISTS: *72–75* **10–12**
UNITED ARTISTS/JET:
   76–77 . . . . **8–10**
   (Black vinyl.)
UNITED ARTISTS/JET:
   76–77 . . . . **25–30**
   (Colored vinyl. Promotional issues only.)
   Also see LYNNE, Jeff
   Also see NEWTON-JOHN, Olivia, & The
   Electric Light Orchestra
   Also see WOOD, Roy

ELECTRIC MIND
Singles: 12-Inch 33/45rpm
EMERGENCY: *83* **4–6**

Price Range

ELECTRIC PRUNES, The
Singles: 7-Inch
REPRISE (Except 0300 &
   0400 series): *67–69* **$6–10**
REPRISE (0300 & 0400
   series): *65–66* **15–20**
LPs: 10/12-Inch 33rpm
REPRISE: *67–69* **20–25**

ELECTRONIC CONCEPT ORCHESTRA, The (Featuring Eddie Higgins)
LPs: 10/12-Inch 33rpm
LIMELIGHT: *69* **5–10**
MERCURY: *70* **5–10**

ELEGANTS, The (Vito & The Elegants)
Singles: 7-Inch
ABC: *73* **1–3**
ABC-PARAMOUNT: *61* **10–12**
APT (Except 25005): *59* **10–15**
APT (25005; "Little Star"):
   58 . . . . **20–25**
   (With silver letters on an all-black label.)
APT (25005; "Little Star"):
   58 . . . . **5–8**
   (With a multi-color label.)
BIM BAM BOOM: *74* **5–8**
   (Black vinyl.)
BIM BAM BOOM: *74* **2–4**
   (Colored vinyl.)
HULL: *60* **25–30**
LAURIE: *65* **8–12**
MCA **1–3**
PHOTO: *63* **8–10**
ROULETTE: *71* **1–3**
UNITED ARTISTS: *60–61* **10–12**
Picture Sleeves
PHOTO: *63* **30–40**
   (Price includes special insert, which represents
   $10-$15 of the value.)
   Members: Vito Picone; Frank Tardagno; Carman Romano; Jimmy Moschella; Artie Venosa.
   Also see BARBARIANS, The

ELEKTRIK DRED
Singles: 7-Inch
SOUNDS OF FLORIDA:
   83 . . . . **1–3**

Price Range

ELEKTRO, Eve
Singles: 12-Inch 33/45rpm
BLACK SUIT: *84*................ $4–6

ELEPHANT'S MEMORY
Singles: 7-Inch
APPLE: *72* 3–5
BUDDAH: *69*.................... 3–5
METROMEDIA: *70–71*............ 2–4
RCA VICTOR: *74* 2–3

Picture Sleeves
METROMEDIA: *70*............... 2–4

LPs: 10/12-Inch 33rpm
APPLE: *72* 10–15
BUDDAH: *69–74* 10–15
METROMEDIA: *70*............. 10–12
MUSE.......................... 8–10
RCA VICTOR: *74* 8–10

ELEVENTH HOUR, The (With Larry Coryell)
Singles: 7-Inch
20TH CENTURY-FOX:
74–75 2–3

LPs: 10/12-Inch 33rpm
20TH CENTURY-FOX:
74 8–10
Also see CORYELL, Larry

ELGART, Larry (Larry Elgart & His Manhattan Swing Orchestra)
Singles: 7-Inch
DECCA: *54–55*.................. 2–4
MGM: *61–62*................... 2–3
RCA VICTOR: *59–83* 1–3

EPs: 7-Inch 33/45rpm
BRUNSWICK: *54*................ 5–10
DECCA: *54–55*.................. 5–10

LPs: 10/12-Inch 33rpm
BRUNSWICK: *54*............... 15–25
(10-Inch LPs.)
CAMDEN: *60–73*................ 5–10
DECCA: *54–55* 10–20
MGM: *60–62*................... 8–12
RCA VICTOR: *59–83* 5–10

Price Range

ELGART, Les (Les Elgart & His Orchestra)
Singles: 7-Inch
COLUMBIA (40000 series,
except 40180): *53–62*............ $2–4
COLUMBIA (40180;
"Bandstand Boogie"): *54* 15–20
("Bandstand Boogie" was the familiar American Bandstand TV show theme.)
COLUMBIA (56767;
"Bandstand Twist"): *62* 5–8
(Promotional issue only.)
GOLD-MOR: *73*.................. 1–3
EPs: 7-Inch 33/45rpm
COLUMBIA: *53–59*.............. 5–10
LPs: 10/12-Inch 33rpm
COLUMBIA: *53–62*.............. 10–20
HARMONY: *66* 5–10

ELGART, Les & Larry
Singles: 7-Inch
COLUMBIA: *64–68*.............. 2–3
SWAMPFIRE: *69*............... 1–3
LPs: 10/12-Inch 33rpm
COLUMBIA (Except
38000 series): *57–68* 8–15
COLUMBIA (38000
series): *82*...................... 5–8
HARMONY: *68–73* 5–10
SWAMPFIRE: *70*............... 5–8
Also see ELGART, Larry
Also see ELGART, Les

Price Range

ELGINS, The (With Saundra Mallet)
Singles: 7-Inch
V.I.P.: *66–71* $3–5
LPs: 10/12-Inch 33rpm
V.I.P.: *66* 15–20

ELI'S SECOND COMING
Singles: 7-Inch
SILVER BLUE: *76–78* 2–3

ELLEDGE, Jimmy
Singles: 7-Inch
FOUR STAR: *75* 1–3
HICKORY: *65–67* 2–3
LITTLE DARLIN': *68* 1–3
RCA VICTOR: *61–64* 2–4
SIMS: *64* 2–4
Picture Sleeves
RCA VICTOR: *62–63* 3–5

ELLIMAN, Yvonne
Singles: 7-Inch
DECCA: *71–72* 2–3
MCA. 1–3
RSO: *74–79* 1–3
LPs: 10/12-Inch 33rpm
DECCA: *72* 12–15
MCA: *73* 8–10
RSO: *77–79* 5–8
Also see BISHOP, Stephen, & Yvonne Elliman

ELLINGTON, Duke
Singles: 7-Inch
BELL: *73* 1–3
BETHLEHEM: *58–60* 2–4
CAPITOL (2000 series):
 53–56 3–5
COLUMBIA (33000
 series): *76* 1–3
COLUMBIA (39000
 series): *50–53* 3–5
COLUMBIA (40000
 through 42000 series):
 58–61 2–4
RCA VICTOR (0300
 series): *74* 1–3
RCA VICTOR (4000
 through 6000 series):
 51–55 3–5
REPRISE: *67*. 2–3

Price Range

EPs: 7-Inch 33/45rpm
BRUNSWICK: *54*. $6–12
CAPITOL: *53–56* 6–12
COLUMBIA: *50–56* 8–15
RCA VICTOR: *52–60* 6–15

LPs: 10/12-Inch 33rpm
ALLEGIANCE: *84*. 5–8
ALLEGRO: *54* 25–40
 (10-Inch LPs.)
ATLANTIC: *71–82* 5–10
BASF: *73* 5–10
BETHLEHEM: *56–57* 15–25
BRIGHT ORANGE: *73* 5–10
BRUNSWICK (54000
 series): *56* 15–25
BRUNSWICK (58000
 series): *54* 25–40
 (10-Inch LPs.)
CAMDEN (400 series): *58*. 15–25
CAPITOL (400 series): *53* 25–40
 (With an "H" prefix. 10-Inch LPs.)
CAPITOL (400 through
 600 series): *55–57* 25–40
CAPITOL (1600 series): *61* 10–20
 (With a "T" prefix.)
CAPITOL (11000 series):
 72–77 5–10
CAPITOL (16000 series):
 81 4–6
COLUMBIA (27; "The
 Ellington Era, Volume
 1): *63* 25–40
COLUMBIA (39; "The
 Ellington Era, Volume 2:
 1927-1940): *66* 25–40
COLUMBIA (500 through
 900 series): *54–57* 15–25
COLUMBIA (1085
 through 2029, except
 1360): *57–63*. 10–20
 (Monaural issues.)
COLUMBIA (1360;
 "Anatomy Of A
 Murder"): *59* 35–45
 (Soundtrack. Monaural issue.)
COLUMBIA (4000 series):
 55 25–40
COLUMBIA (6000 series):
 50 25–40
 (10-Inch LPs.)

Price Range

COLUMBIA (8053
through 9600, except
8166): *57–68*.................. **$10–20**
(Stereo issues.)
COLUMBIA (8166;
"Anatomy Of A
Murder"): *59*.................. **45-55**
(Soundtrack. Stereo issue.)
COLUMBIA (14000
series): *79*..................... **5–10**
(Columbia Special Products series.)
COLUMBIA (32000
through 38000 series):
73–82........................ **5–10**
DECCA: *67–70*.................. **8–15**
DOCTOR JAZZ: *84*............... **5–8**
EVEREST: *70–73*................ **5–10**
FANTASY: *71–75*................ **6–12**
FLYING DUTCHMAN:
69........................... **5–10**
HARMONY: *67–71*.............. **5–10**
IMPULSE (Except 9200
series): *62*.................... **12–20**
IMPULSE (9200 series): *73*........ **8–12**
ODYSSEY: *68*................... **8–12**
PABLO: *76–80*.................. **5–8**
PRESTIGE: *73–77*............... **6–12**
RCA VICTOR (500 series):
64–69....................... **10–20**
RCA VICTOR (0700
through 2000 series):
75–78........................ **5–8**
(With an "ANL1" or "APL1" prefix.)
RCA VICTOR (1000
series): *54*.................... **25–40**
(With an "LJM" or "LPT" prefix.)
RCA VICTOR (1300
through 2800 series):
57–66....................... **10–20**
(With an "LPM" or "LSP" prefix.)
RCA VICTOR (3000
series): *52–53*................. **25–40**
(10-Inch LPs.)
RCA VICTOR (3500
through 3900 series):
66–68........................ **8–12**
RCA VICTOR (4000
series): *81*.................... **8–10**
RCA VICTOR (6009;
"The Indispensible Duke
Ellington"): *61*................. **20–30**

Price Range

RCA VICTOR (6042;
"This Is Duke
Ellington"): *71*............... **$10–15**
REPRISE: *63–68*................ **10–20**
RIVERSIDE (Except 100
series): *62–64*................. **10–20**
RIVERSIDE (100 series):
56–59 .... **15–25**
RON-LETTE: *58*................ **15–25**
SOLID STATE: *70*............... **5–10**
SUNSET: *69* **5–10**
TRIP: *75–76* **5–8**
UNITED ARTISTS
(Except 14000 & 15000
series): *72*.................... **5–10**
UNITED ARTISTS (14000
& 15000 series): *62* **15–25**
VERVE: *67* **10–12**
X: *54*......................... **25–40**
(10-Inch LPs.)
Also see ARMSTRONG, Louis, & Duke Ellington
Also see BASIE, Count, & Duke Ellington
Also see BREWER, Teresa, & Duke Ellington
Also see FITZGERALD, Ella, & Duke Ellington
Also see HIBBLER, Al, & Duke Ellington
Also see SINATRA, Frank, & Duke Ellington

ELLINGTON, Duke, & John Coltrane
LPs: 10/12-Inch 33rpm
IMPULSE: *63* **15–25**
Also see COLTRANE, John

ELLINGTON, Duke, & Johnny Hodges
LPs: 10/12-Inch 33rpm
PRESTIGE: *81* **8–10**
VERVE (Except 8800
series): *59–60*................. **15–30**
VERVE (8800 series): *73* **8–12**
Also see ELLINGTON, Duke
Also see HODGES, Johnny

ELLIOT, Cass (Mama Cass)
Singles: 7-Inch
DUNHILL: *68–70*................. **2–4**
RCA VICTOR: *71–73* **2–3**
LPs: 10/12-Inch 33rpm
DUNHILL: *68–72*............... **10–15**
RCA VICTOR: *72–73* **10–12**

Price Range   *Price Range*

Also see BIG THREE, The
Also see MAMAS & THE PAPAS, The
Also see MASON, Dave, & Mama Cass

ELLIS, Ray, Orchestra
Singles: 7-Inch
MGM: *59–60* $2–3
RCA VICTOR: *61* 2–3
LPs: 10/12-Inch 33rpm
HARMONY: *59* 4–8
MGM: *59–60* 5–10
RCA VICTOR: *61* 4–8

ELLIS, Shirley
Singles: 7-Inch
COLUMBIA: *67* 2–4
CONGRESS: *63–65* 3–5
Picture Sleeves
CONGRESS: *64–65* 4–6
LPs: 10/12-Inch 33rpm
COLUMBIA: *67* 15–20
CONGRESS: *64–65* 20–25

ELLISON, Lorraine
Singles: 7-Inch
LOMA: *67–68* 2–4
MERCURY: *65–66* 3–5
SHARP: *63* 3–5
WARNER BROS: *66–69* 2–4
LPs: 10/12-Inch 33rpm
WARNER BROS (1000
  series): *67–69* 15–20
WARNER BROS (2000
  series): *74* 8–10

ELMO & ALMO
Singles: 7-Inch
DADDY BEST: *67* 2–4

ELUSION
Singles: 7-Inch
COTILLION: *81* 1–3
LPs: 10/12-Inch 33rpm
COTILLION: *81* 5–8

ELY, Joe
Singles: 7-Inch
MCA: *77–81* 1–3
SOUTHCOAST: *81* 1–3

LPs: 10/12-Inch 33rpm
MCA: *77–81* $1–3
SOUTHCOAST: *81* 5–8

EMERSON, Keith
LPs: 10/12-Inch 33rpm
BACKSTREET: *81* 5–10

EMERSON, Keith, & The Nice
Singles: 7-Inch
MERCURY: *72* 2–4
LPs: 10/12-Inch 33rpm
MERCURY: *72* 12–15
Also see EMERSON, Keith
Also see NICE, The

EMERSON, LAKE & PALMER
Singles: 7-Inch
ATLANTIC: *77–80* 1–3
COTILLION: *71–72* 2–3
MANTICORE: *74* 2–3
LPs: 10/12-Inch 33rpm
ATLANTIC (Except 281):
  77–80 8–10
ATLANTIC (281;
  "Emerson, Lake &
  Palmer"): *77* 12–15
(With The London Philharmonic Orchestra.
Also contains interviews with the three members. Promotional issue only.)
COTILLION: *71–72* 12–15
MANTICORE: *73–74* 10–12
Members: Keith Emerson; Greg Lake; Carl Palmer.
Also see ASIA
Also see EMERSON, Keith
Also see LAKE, Greg

EMMERSON, Les
Singles: 7-Inch
LION: *73* 2–3

EMOTIONS, The
Singles: 7-Inch
BRAINSTORM: *68* 3–5
CALLA: *65* 4–6
KAPP: *62–63* 4–6
KARATE: *64* 4–6
20TH CENTURY-FOX:
  63–64 5–8
VARDAN: *65* 3–5

Price Range

Price Range

LPs: 10/12-Inch 33rpm
MAGIC CARPET **$8–10**
Members: Joe Favale; Tony Maltese; Don Colluri; Larry Cusamanno; Joe Nigro; Sal Covais.

EMOTIONS, The
Singles: 12-Inch 33/45rpm
RED LABEL: *84* **4–6**
Singles: 7-Inch
ARC: *80–81*..................... **1–3**
COLUMBIA: *76–81* **1–3**
STAX: *77–79*.................... **1–3**
MOTOWN: *85*.................... **1–3**
RED LABEL: *84* **1–3**
TWIN STACKS: *68*............... **3–5**
VOLT: *69–74*.................... **2–3**
LPs: 10/12-Inch 33rpm
COLUMBIA: *76–81* **5–8**
MOTOWN: *85*.................... **5–8**
RED LABEL: *84* **5–8**
STAX: *77–79*.................... **5–8**
VOLT: *69–74*................... **10–12**
Members: Sheila Hutchinson; Wanda Hutchinson; Jeanette Hutchinson.
Also see EARTH, WIND & FIRE & THE EMOTIONS

EMPERORS, The
Singles: 7-Inch
BRUNSWICK: *67*................. **3–5**
MALA: *66–67*.................... **3–5**
TWO PLUS TWO: *66* **3–5**

ENCHANTERS, The
Singles: 7-Inch
BALD EAGLE: *58*................. **4–6**
BAMBOO: *61* **4–6**
EPSOM: *62* **3–5**
J.J. & M.: *62* **8–10**
LOMA: *65–66*................... **3–5**
MUSITRON: *61* **3–5**
ORBIT: *59*.................... **10–12**
SHARP: *60* **5–8**
STARDUST **10–15**
TOM TOM: *63* **5–8**
WARNER BROS: *64*.............. **3–5**

ENDGAMES
Singles: 12-Inch 33/45rpm
FLIP: *83* **4–6**
MCA: *83* **4–6**

Singles: 7-Inch
MCA: *84* **$1–3**
LPs: 10/12-Inch 33rpm
MCA: *84* **5–8**

ENCHANTMENT
Singles: 7-Inch
COLUMBIA: *82–84*............... **1–3**
DESERT MOON: *76*.............. **2–3**
RCA VICTOR: *80* **1–3**
ROADSHOW: *77–78*............. **1–3**
UNITED ARTISTS: *76–77*......... **1–3**
LPs: 10/12-Inch 33rpm
COLUMBIA: *82*.................. **5–8**
RCA VICTOR: *80* **5–8**
ROADSHOW: *77–78*............. **8–10**
UNITED ARTISTS: *77*........... **8–10**

ENERGETICS, The
Singles: 7-Inch
ATLANTIC: *79* **1–3**
LPs: 10/12-Inch 33rpm
ATLANTIC: *79* **5–8**

ENERGY
Singles: 7-Inch
SHOUT: *74* **2–3**

ENGLAND DAN & JOHN FORD COLEY
Singles: 7-Inch
A&M: *71–77* **2–4**
BIG TREE: *76–80* **1–3**
MCA: *80* **1–3**
LPs: 10/12-Inch 33rpm
A&M: *71–73* **10–12**
BIG TREE: *76–79* **8–10**
MCA: *80* **5–8**
Members: Dan Seals; John Ford Coley.
Also see SEALS, Dan
Also see SOUTHWEST F.O.B.

ENGLISH, Barbara Jean
Singles: 7-Inch
ALITHIA: *73–74* **2–3**
LPs: 10/12-Inch 33rpm
ALITHIA: *73* **8–10**

ENGLISH, Jackie
Singles: 7-Inch
VENTURE: *80* **1–3**

ENGLISH, Scott (Scott English & The Accents; Scott English & The Dedications)
Singles: 7-Inch
DOT: *60* $8–10
JANUS (Except 171): *72* 2–3
JANUS (171; "Brandy"):
   71 8–10
JOKER: *62* 4–6
SPOKANE: *64* 4–6
SULTAN: *63* 8–10

ENGLISH BEAT, The
Singles: 12-Inch 33/45rpm
I.R.S.: *83–85* 4–6
Singles: 7-Inch
I.R.S.: *83–85* 1–3
LPs: 10/12-Inch 33rpm
I.R.S.: *82–85* 5–8
SIRE: *80–81* 5–8

ENGLISH CONGREGATION, The
Singles: 7-Inch
ATCO: *72* 2–3
SIGNPOST: *73* 2–3
LPs: 10/12-Inch 33rpm
SIGNPOST: *73* 8–10

ENNIS, Ethel
Singles: 7-Inch
BASF: *73* 1–3
RCA VICTOR: *64–66* 2–3
SPIRAL: *71–72* 1–3
LPs: 10/12-Inch 33rpm
BASF: *73* 5–10
CAMDEN: *73* 5–8
RCA VICTOR: *64–65* 10–15

ENO, Brian (Eno)
Singles: 7-Inch
ISLAND: *72* 2–3
LPs: 10/12-Inch 33rpm
ANTILLES: *73–78* 8–10
EDITIONS E.G.: *81–82* 5–8
ISLAND: *73–78* 8–10
PVC: *79* 5–8
SIRE: *81* 5–8
   Also see FRIPP & ENO
   Also see ROXY MUSIC

ENTERTAINERS IV, The
Singles: 7-Inch
DORE: *66* $3–5

ENTWISTLE, John (John Entwistle's Rigor Mortis; John Entwistle's Ox)
Singles: 7-Inch
DECCA: *72* 2–4
TRACK: *73* 2–3
LPs: 10/12-Inch 33rpm
ATCO: *81* 5–8
DECCA: *71–72* 10–15
MCA/TRACK: *73–75* 8–10
   Also see TOWNSHEND, Pete, & Ronnie Lane
   Also see WHO, The

EON
Singles: 7-Inch
ARIOLA AMERICA: *78* 1–3
LPs: 10/12-Inch 33rpm
ARIOLA AMERICA: *78* 5–8
SCEPTER: *73* 8–10

EPIC SPLENDOR, The
Singles: 7-Inch
HOT BISCUIT: *67–68* 3–5
Picture Sleeves
HOT BISCUIT: *67* 3–5

EPOQUE, Belle: see BELLE EPOQUE

EPPS, Preston
Singles: 7-Inch
ADMIRAL: *65* 3–5
EMBASSY: *62* 3–5
JO JO: *69* 2–4
MAJESTY 3–5
ORIGINAL SOUND
  (Except stereo singles):
   59–61 4–6
ORIGINAL SOUND
  (Stereo singles): *59* 8–10
EPs: 7-Inch 33/45rpm
ORIGINAL SOUND: *60* 10–15
LPs: 10/12-Inch 33rpm
ORIGINAL SOUND:
   60–63 20–25
TOP RANK: *61* 25–30

Price Range

EQUALS, The (With Eddy Grant)
Singles: 7-Inch
PRESIDENT: 67–68. . . . . $3–5
RCA VICTOR: 68 2–4
LPs: 10/12-Inch 33rpm
LAURIE: 67 20–25
PRESIDENT: 68–69. 15–20
RCA VICTOR: 68 10–12
Also see GRANT, Eddy

ERAMUS HALL
Singles: 12-Inch 33/45rpm
CAPITOL: 84 4–6
Singles: 7-Inch
CAPITOL: 84 1–3
LPs: 10/12-Inch 33rpm
CAPITOL: 84 5–8

ERIC
Singles: 12-Inch 33/45rpm
MEMO: 84. 4–6

ERNIE (Jim Henson) / The Sesame Street Kids
Singles: 7-Inch
COLUMBIA: 70 2–3
Also see HENSON, Jim

ERUPTION
Singles: 12-Inch 33/45rpm
ARIOLA AMERICA: 78 4–6
Singles: 7-Inch
ARIOLA AMERICA: 78 1–3
LPs: 10/12-Inch 33rpm
ARIOLA AMERICA: 78 5–8

ERWIN, Dee (Big Dee Erwin)
Singles: 7-Inch
CUB: 68. 3–5
ROULETTE: 65 3–5
Also see IRWIN, Big Dee

ESCORTS, The
Singles: 7-Inch
ALITHIA: 73–74 2–4
LPs: 10/12-Inch 33rpm
ALITHIA: 73–74 8–10

ESCOVEDO, Coke
Singles: 7-Inch
MERCURY: 76–77. 1–3

Price Range

LPs: 10/12-Inch 33rpm
MERCURY: 76–77. . . . . $5–8
Also see AZTECA
Also see SANTANA

ESMERALDA, Santa (Featuring Leroy Gomez)
Singles: 12-Inch 33/45rpm
CASABLANCA: 77–78 4–6
Singles: 7-Inch
CASABLANCA: 77–78 2–3
LPs: 10/12-Inch 33rpm
CASABLANCA: 77–80 5–8

ESPOSITO, Joe "Bean"
Singles: 7-Inch
CASABLANCA: 83 1–3
Also see BROOKLYN DREAMS

ESQUIRES, The
Singles: 7-Inch
BUNKY: 67–68. 3–5
CAPITOL: 69 2–4
COLUMBIA: 66 3–5
DOT: 66. 3–5
JU-PAR: 76. 2–3
LAMARR: 71 2–3
SALEM: 65 3–5
TOWER: 65. 3–5
WAND: 68–69. 3–5
LPs: 10/12-Inch 33rpm
BUNKY: 68 12–15

ESSENCE
Singles: 7-Inch
EPIC: 75–77 2–3
LPs: 10/12-Inch 33rpm
SAVOY: 78 5–8

ESSEX, The (Featuring Anita Humes)
Singles: 7-Inch
BANG: 66 3–5
ROULETTE: 63–64 4–6
LPs: 10/12-Inch 33rpm
ROULETTE: 63–64 15–20

ESSEX, David
Singles: 7-Inch
COLUMBIA: 73–76 2–3
RSO: 79 1–3
UNI: 67 4–6

Price Range

Picture Sleeves
UNI: *67* **$4–6**
LPs: 10/12-Inch 33rpm
COLUMBIA: *73–75* **8–10**
MERCURY: *83*................... **5–8**

ETERNALS, The
Singles: 7-Inch
COLLECTABLES **1–3**
HOLLYWOOD: *59*................ **5–8**
WARWICK: *60*.................. **4–6**
Members: Charles Girona; Alex Miranda; Fred
Hodge; Ernie Sierra; Arnold Torres; George
Villanueva.

ETERNITY'S CHILDREN
Singles: 7-Inch
A&M: *67* **3–5**
TOWER: *68–69*................... **3–5**
Picture Sleeves
TOWER: *68*..................... **3–5**
LPs: 10/12-Inch 33rpm
TOWER: *68*.................... **15–20**

ETHICS, The
Singles: 7-Inch
VENT: *68–69*..................... **2–4**

ETTA & HARVEY
Singles: 7-Inch
CHESS: *60*....................... **3–5**
Members: Etta James; Harvey Fuqua.
Also see HARVEY & THE MOONGLOWS
Also see JAMES, Etta

ETZEL, Roy
Singles: 7-Inch
HICKORY: *63* **2–3**
MGM: *65–67*..................... **2–3**
PRESIDENT: *61*.................. **2–4**
TIME: *61*........................ **2–4**
LPs: 10/12-Inch 33rpm
MGM: *65*....................... **8–12**

EUBANKS, Jack
Singles: 7-Inch
MONUMENT: *61–64*.............. **2–3**
LPs: 10/12-Inch 33rpm
MONUMENT: *66*................. **8–12**

EUCLID BEACH BAND, The
Singles: 7-Inch
EPIC/CLEVELAND
  INT'L: *78–79*.................. **$1–3**
SCENE: *78* **2–3**
LPs: 10/12-Inch 33rpm
EPIC: *79* **5–8**

EUROGLIDERS (Featuring Grace Knight)
Singles: 7-Inch
COLUMBIA: *84*.................. **1–3**
LPs: 10/12-Inch 33rpm
COLUMBIA: *84*.................. **5–8**

EURYTHMICS, The
Singles: 12-Inch 33/45rpm
RCA VICTOR: *83–85* **4–6**
Singles: 7-Inch
RCA VICTOR: *83–85* **1–3**
LPs: 10/12-Inch 33rpm
RCA VICTOR: *83–85* **5–8**
Members: Annie Lennox; Dave Stewart.
Also see FRANKLIN, Aretha
Also see TOURISTS, The

EURYTHMICS, The, & Aretha Franklin
Singles: 12-Inch 33/45rpm
RCA VICTOR: *85* **4–6**
Singles: 7-Inch
RCA VICTOR: *85* **1–3**
Also see EURYTHMICS, The
Also see FRANKLIN, Aretha

EVANS, Linda
Singles: 7-Inch
ARIOLA: *79*..................... **1–3**

EVANS, Margie
Singles: 7-Inch
ICA: *77* **2–3**
UNITED ARTISTS: *73*............. **2–3**

EVANS, Paul (Paul Evans & The Curls)
Singles: 7-Inch
ATCO: *59–60*.................... **3–5**
CARLTON: *61–62* **3–5**
CINNAMON INT'L: *80* **1–3**
COLLECTABLES **1–3**

Price Range

COLUMBIA: *68* **$2–4**
DECCA: *58* **4–6**
DOT: *73* **2–3**
EPIC: *64–65* **3–5**
GUARANTEED: *59–60* **4–6**
KAPP: *62–63* **3–5**
LAURIE: *71* **2–3**
MERCURY: *74–75* **2–3**
MUSICOR: *77* **2–3**
RCA VICTOR: *57* **4–6**
RANWOOD: *72* **2–3**
SPRING: *78–79* **1–3**
LPs: 10/12-Inch 33rpm
CARLTON: *61* **25–30**
GUARANTEED: *60* **30–35**
KAPP: *64–66* **20–25**

EVASIONS, The
Singles: 7-Inch
SAM: *81* **1–3**

EVE ELEKTRO: see ELEKTRO, Eve

EVERETT, Betty (Betty Everett & The Daylighters)
Singles: 7-Inch
ABC: *66–67* **3–5**
C.J.: *61–64* **4–6**
COBRA: *57–58* **10–12**
COLLECTABLES **1–3**
ERIC **1–3**
FANTASY: *70–74* **2–3**
ONE-DERFUL: *62* **3–5**
UNI: *68–69* **2–4**
VEE JAY: *63–65* **3–5**
LPs: 10/12-Inch 33rpm
FANTASY: *75* **8–10**
SUNSET: *68* **10–12**
UNI: *69* **10–12**
VEE JAY: *64* **15–20**
Also see BUTLER, Jerry, & Betty Everett

EVERETT, Betty / Ketty Lester
LPs: 10/12-Inch 33rpm
GRAND PRIX **10–12**
Also see LESTER, Ketty

EVERETT, Betty / The Impressions
LPs: 10/12-Inch 33rpm
CUSTOM **10–12**

Price Range

Also see EVERETT, Betty
Also see IMPRESSIONS, The

EVERLY, Don
Singles: 7-Inch
ABC/HICKORY: *75–77* **$2–3**
ODE: *70–74* **2–4**
LPs: 10/12-Inch 33rpm
ABC/HICKORY: *76–77* **8–10**
ODE: *70–74* **8–10**
Also see HARRIS, Emmylou

EVERLY, Phil
Singles: 7-Inch
CAPITOL: *83* **1–3**
CURB: *80–81* **1–3**
ELEKTRA: *79* **2–3**
PYE: *73–76* **2–3**
RCA VICTOR: *73* **2–4**
LPs: 10/12-Inch 33rpm
ELECTRA: *79* **5–8**
PYE: *75–76* **8–10**
RCA VICTOR: *73* **8–10**

EVERLY BROTHERS, The
Singles: 7-Inch
BARNABY: *70–76* **2–3**
CADENCE (Silver & maroon label): *57–61* **5–8**
CADENCE (Red label): *61–62* **3–5**
COLUMBIA: *56* **30–40**
ERIC **1–3**
MERCURY: *84–86* **1–3**
RCA VICTOR: *72–73* **2–3**
WARNER BROS (Except stereo singles): *60–74* **3–5**
WARNER BROS (Stereo singles): *60* **10–15**
(With an "S" prefix.)
Picture Sleeves
CADENCE: *57–60* **10–20**
WARNER BROS: *60–66* **8–12**
EPs: 7-Inch 33/45rpm
CADENCE: *57–61* **20–30**
WARNER BROS: *60* **15–20**
LPs: 10/12-Inch 33rpm
ARISTA: *84* **8–12**
BARNABY (Except 4000 series): *70–74* **8–12**

Price Range

BARNABY (4000 series):
77 . . . . **$6–10**
CADENCE (3003; "The
Everly Brothers"): *58* **45–55**
CADENCE (3016; "Songs
Our Daddy Taught Us"):
58 . . . . **45–55**
CADENCE (3025; "The
Everly Brothers Best"):
59 . . . . **50–60**
(With blue cover.)
CADENCE (3040; "The
Fabulous Style Of The
Everly Brothers"): *60* **45–55**
CADENCE (3059; "Folk
Songs"): *62* **35–40**
CADENCE (3062; "15
Everly Hits"): *63* **35–40**
CADENCE (25040; "The
Fabulous Style Of The
Everly Brothers"): *60* **55–65**
CANDLELITE: *76* **10–15**
HARMONY: *68–70* **10–12**
MERCURY: *84* **5–8**
PAIR: *84* **8–12**
PASSPORT: *84–86* **5–8**
RCA VICTOR: *72* **8–12**
RHINO (Except picture
discs): *85* **5–8**
RHINO (Picture discs): *85* **8–10**
RONCO **8–10**
WARNER BROS. (135;
"Souvenir Sampler-10
Songs"): *61* **30–40**
(Promotional issue only.)
WARNER BROS (1381;
"It's Everly Time"): *60* **25–30**
WARNER BROS (1395;
"A Date With The
Everly Brothers): *60* **30–40**
(With gatefold cover & wallet photos.)
WARNER BROS (1395;
"A Date With The
Everly Brothers): *61* **15–20**
(With standard cover.)
WARNER BROS (1418;
"Both Sides Of An
Evening"): *61* **25–30**
WARNER BROS (1430;
"Instant Party"): *62* **20–30**

Price Range

WARNER BROS (1471;
"Golden Hits"): *62* **$20–30**
WARNER BROS (1483;
"Christmas With The
Everly Brothers"): *61* **20–25**
WARNER BROS (1513;
"Great Country Hits"):
63 . . . . **20–25**
WARNER BROS (1554;
"Very Best Of The
Everly Brothers"): *64* **15–20**
(Yellow cover.)
WARNER BROS (1554;
"Very Best Of The
Everly Brothers"): *64* **10–15**
(Blue cover.)
WARNER BROS (1578;
"Rock 'N Soul"): *65* **20–25**
WARNER BROS (1585;
"Gone Gone Gone"): *65* **20–25**
WARNER BROS (1605;
"Beat & Soul"): *65* **15–20**
WARNER BROS (1620;
"In Our Image"): *66* **15–20**
WARNER BROS (1646;
"Two Yanks In
London"): *66* **15–20**
WARNER BROS (1676;
"The Hit Sound Of The
Everly Brothers"): *67* **15–20**
WARNER BROS (1708;
"The Everly Brothers
Sing"): *67* **15–20**

Price Range   *Price Range*

WARNER BROS (1752;
  "Roots"): *68*. **$15–20**
WARNER BROS (1858;
  "The Everly Brothers
  Show"): *70*. **12–15**
  Members: Don Everly; Phil Everly.
  Also see EVERLY, Don
  Also see EVERLY, Phil

EVERY FATHER'S TEENAGE SON
Singles: 7-Inch
BUDDAH: *67*. **3–5**

EVERY MOTHER'S SON
Singles: 7-Inch
MGM: *67–68*. **3–5**
POLYDOR **1–3**
Picture Sleeves
MGM: *67*. **3–5**
LPs: 10/12-Inch 33rpm
MGM: *67*. **15–20**

EVERYTHING IS EVERYTHING
Singles: 7-Inch
VANGUARD
  APOSTOLIC: *69*. **3–5**
LPs: 10/12-Inch 33rpm
VANGUARD: *69*. **15–20**

EXCELLENTS, The
Singles: 7-Inch
BLAST (Red label): *62*. **20–25**
BLAST (Red & white
  label): *62–63*. **8–10**
COLLECTABLES **1–3**
MERMAID. **25–30**
OLD TIMER: *64* **3–5**
  Also see EXCELLONS, The

EXCELLONS, The (The Excellents)
Singles: 7-Inch
BOBBY: *64* **10–12**
  Also see EXCELLENTS, The

EXCELS, The
Singles: 7-Inch
GONE: *60* **4–6**
R.S.V.P.: *61* **5–8**

EXCITERS, The
Singles: 7-Inch
BANG: *66* **$3–5**
LIBERTY **1–3**
ROULETTE: *64* **3–5**
RCA VICTOR: *68–69* **3–5**
SHOUT: *66–67* **3–5**
TODAY: *70*. **2–4**
UNITED ARTISTS: *62–63*. **4–6**
Picture Sleeves
ROULETTE: *64* **3–5**
LPs: 10/12-Inch 33rpm
RCA VICTOR: *69* **10–12**
ROULETTE: *66* **15–20**
SUNSET: *70* **10–12**
TODAY: *71*. **8–10**
UNITED ARTISTS: *63* **25–35**
  Members: Brenda Reid; Herb Rooney.
  Also see BRENDA & HERB

EXECUTIVE
Singles: 7-Inch
20TH CENTURY-FOX:
  81 . . . . **1–3**

EXECUTIVE SUITE
Singles: 7-Inch
BABYLON: *73–74* **2–3**
UNITED ARTISTS: *75* **2–3**

EXILE
Singles: 7-Inch
ATCO: *77* **1–3**
COLUMBIA: *69–70*. **2–4**
WARNER BROS/CURB:
  78–81 . . . . **1–3**
WOODEN NICKEL:
  72–73 . . . . **2–3**
LPs: 10/12-Inch 33rpm
RCA VICTOR: *78* **5–8**
WARNER BROS: *78–81* **5–8**
WOODEN NICKEL: *73* **8–10**

EXITS, The
Singles: 7-Inch
GEMINI: *67* **3–5**

EXOTIC GUITARS, The
Singles: 7-Inch
RANWOOD: *68–70* **2–3**

"JOHNNY ANGEL" (P 621)
Shelley Fabares
of THE DONNA REED SHOW
Produced by TONY OWEN

Price Range

FABIAN / Frankie Avalon
LPs: 10/12-Inch 33rpm
CHANCELLOR: *60*. **$30–35**
MCA: *85* **5–8**
Also see AVALON, Frankie
Also see FABIAN

FABRIC, Bent
Singles: 7-Inch
ATCO: *62–65*. **2–3**
Picture Sleeves
ATCO: *62* **2–3**
LPs: 10/12-Inch 33rpm
ATCO: *62–63*. **6–10**
Also see BILK, Mr. Acker, & Bent Fabric

FABRIQUE, Tina
Singles: 12-Inch 33/45rpm
PRISM: *84*. **4–6**

FABULOUS COUNTS, The
Singles: 7-Inch
MOIRA: *68–70* **2–4**
LPs: 10/12-Inch 33rpm
COTILLION: *69*. **10–12**

FABULOUS FARQUAHR
(Farquahr)
Singles: 7-Inch
ELEKTRA: *71* **2–3**
VERVE/FORECAST:
68–69 . . . . **3–5**
WARNER BROS: *70*. **2–4**
LPs: 10/12-Inch 33rpm
ELEKTRA: *70* **8–10**
VERVE/FORECAST: *69* **10–12**

FABULOUS POODLES, The
Singles: 7-Inch
EPIC: *79* **1–3**
LPs: 10/12-Inch 33rpm
EPIC: *76–79* **5–8**

FABULOUS RHINESTONES, The
Singles: 7-Inch
JUST SUNSHINE: *72* **2–4**
LPs: 10/12-Inch 33rpm
JUST SUNSHINE: *72–73* **8–10**

Price Range

FABULOUS THUNDERBIRDS, The
Singles: 7-Inch
CBS ASSOCIATED: *86*. **$1–3**
CHRYSALIS: *79–81*. **1–3**
LPs: 10/12-Inch 33rpm
CBS ASSOCIATED: *86*. **5–8**
CHRYSALIS: *79–81*. **5–8**
TAKOMA: *79*. **5–8**
Members: Jimmie Vaughan; Preston Hubbard;
Fran Christina; Kim Wilson.
Also see SANTANA

FACE TO FACE
Singles: 12-Inch 33/45rpm
EPIC: *84* **4–6**
PORTRAIT: *84*. **4–6**
Singles: 7-Inch
EPIC: *84* **1–3**
PORTRAIT: *84*. **1–3**
LPs: 10/12-Inch 33rpm
EPIC: *84* **5–8**

FACENDA, Tommy
Singles: 7-Inch
ATLANTIC: *59* **8–12**
LEGRANDE: *59*. **4–6**
NASCO: *58* **4–6**

FACES, The
Singles: 7-Inch
IGUANA: *65*. **8–10**
REGINA: *65*. **8–10**
WARNER BROS: *71–75*. **2–4**
LPs: 10/12-Inch 33rpm
MERCURY: *73*. **8–10**
WARNER BROS: *71–76*. **10–15**
Members: Rod Stewart; Ron Wood; Ronnie
Lane.
Also see McLAGAN, Ian
Also see SMALL FACES
Also see STEWART, Rod
Also see WOOD, Ron

FACTS OF LIFE, The
Singles: 7-Inch
KAYVETTE: *76–77*. **2–3**
LPs: 10/12-Inch 33rpm
KAYVETTE: *77*. **8–10**

FAGEN, Donald
Singles: 7-Inch
WARNER BROS: *82–83*. **1–3**

Price Range

LPs: 10/12-Inch 33rpm
WARNER BROS: 82 . . . . $5–8
Also see STEELY DAN

FAGEN, Donald, & Walter Becker
LPs: 10/12-Inch 33rpm
PVC: 85 5–8
Also see FAGEN, Donald

FAGIN, Joe
Singles: 7-Inch
MILLENNIUM: 82 1–3

FAIR, Yvonne
Singles: 7-Inch
DADE: 63 3–5
KING: 62 3–5
MOTOWN: 74–76 2–3
SMASH: 66 3–5
SOUL: 70 2–4
LPs: 10/12-Inch 33rpm
MOTOWN: 76 5–8

FAIRCHILD, Barbara
Singles: 7-Inch
COLUMBIA: 69–78 1–3
DOWN HOME: 80 1–3
KAPP: 68 2–4
LPs: 10/12-Inch 33rpm
AUDIO: 82 5–8
COLUMBIA: 70–78 8–12
PAID: 81 5–8
Also see WALKER, Billy, & Barbara Fairchild

FAIRPORT CONVENTION
Singles: 7-Inch
A&M: 71–72 2–4
LPs: 10/12-Inch 33rpm
A&M: 69–74 10–12
COTILLION: 70 10–15
ISLAND: 74–75 8–10
Also see DENNY, Sandy
Also see MATTHEWS, Ian
Also see THOMPSON, Richard

FAIRWEATHER (Andy
Fairweather-Low)
LPs: 10/12-Inch 33rpm
NEON: 71 8–10
Also see FAIRWEATHER-LOW, Andy

Price Range

FAIRWEATHER-LOW, Andy
Singles: 7-Inch
A&M: 75–77 . . . . $2–3
LPs: 10/12-Inch 33rpm
A&M: 74–76 8–10
WARNER BROS: 80 5–8
Also see WILLIE & THE POOR BOYS

FAITH, Adam
Singles: 7-Inch
AMY: 64–65 3–5
CAPITOL: 65–66 3–5
CUB: 59 4–6
DOT: 62 3–5
LPs: 10/12-Inch 33rpm
AMY: 65 25–30
MGM: 61 25–30
WARNER BROS: 74 8–10

FAITH, Gene
Singles: 7-Inch
VIRTUE: 69–70 2–4

FAITH, Percy, Orchestra
Singles: 7-Inch
COLUMBIA: 50–76 1–3
Picture Sleeves
COLUMBIA: 60 2–4
EPs: 7-Inch 33/45rpm
COLUMBIA: 50–59 4–6
LPs: 10/12-Inch 33rpm
COLUMBIA: 51–82 5–15
HARMONY: 68–72 5–10
Also see SANDERS, Felicia

FAITH BAND, The
Singles: 7-Inch
MERCURY/VILLAGE:
  78–79 1–3
VILLAGE: 78 2–3
LPs: 10/12-Inch 33rpm
BROWN BAG: 73 10–12
MERCURY: 78–79 5–8
VILLAGE: 77 8–10

FAITH, HOPE & CHARITY
Singles: 7-Inch
MAXWELL: 70 2–4
RCA VICTOR: 75–77 2–3
20TH CENTURY-FOX:
  78–80 1–3

LPs: 10/12-Inch 33rpm
RCA VICTOR: 75 .... **$8–10**
SUSSEX: 72 .... **8–10**
20TH CENTURY-FOX:
  80 .... **5–8**

FAITHFULL, Marianne
Singles: 12-Inch 33/45rpm
ISLAND: 83 .... **4–6**
Singles: 7-Inch
ISLAND: 79 .... **1–3**
LONDON (Except 1022):
  64–72 .... **3–6**
LONDON (1022; "Sister
  Morphine"): 69 .... **45–55**
  (With The Rolling Stones.)
Picture Sleeves
LONDON: 65 .... **3–5**
LPs: 10/12-Inch 33rpm
ISLAND: 79–83 .... **5–8**
LONDON: 65–69 .... **15–20**
Also see ROLLING STONES, The

FALANA, Lola
Singles: 7-Inch
RCA VICTOR: 75 .... **1–3**
REPRISE: 67 .... **2–3**

FALCO
Singles: 12-Inch 33/45rpm
A&M: 83–84 .... **4–6**
Singles: 7-Inch
A&M: 83–84 .... **1–3**
LPs: 10/12-Inch 33rpm
A&M: 83–84 .... **5–8**

FALCONS, The
Singles: 7-Inch
ANNA: 60 .... **30–35**
ATLANTIC: 62–63 .... **3–5**
BIG WHEEL: 66 .... **3–5**
CHESS: 59 .... **4–6**
FALCON: 57 .... **15–20**
FLICK (Except 001): 59 .... **8–10**
FLICK (001; "You're So
  Fine"): 59 .... **35–40**
KUDO: 58 .... **8–10**
LIBERTY **1–3**
LU PINE: 62–64 .... **3–5**
MERCURY: 56 .... **15–20**
SILHOUETTE: 57 .... **20–25**

UNART: 59 .... **$4–6**
UNITED ARTISTS: 59–60 .... **4–6**
  Members: Wilson Pickett; Eddie Floyd; Arnet
  Robinson; Joe Stubbs; Ben Rice; Lance Finnie.
  Also see FLOYD, Eddie
  Also see PICKETT, Wilson

FALLING PEBBLES, The (The Buckinghams)
Singles: 7-Inch
ALLEY CAT **12–15**
  Also see BUCKINGHAMS, The

FALTERMEYER, Harold
Singles: 7-Inch
MCA: 85 .... **1–3**
  Also see LABELLE, Patti, & Harold Falter-
  meyer

FALTSKOG, Agnetha
Singles: 7-Inch
POLYDOR: 83 .... **1–3**

LPs: 10/12-Inch 33rpm
POLYDOR: 83 .... **5–8**
  Also see ABBA

FAME: see KIDS FROM "FAME"

FAME, Georgie (Georgie Fame & The Blue Flames)
Singles: 7-Inch
EPIC: 68–70 .... **3–5**
IMPERIAL: 65–67 .... **3–5**
ISLAND: 75 .... **2–3**

EPs: 7-Inch 33/45rpm
EPIC: 68 .... **4–8**
  (Jukebox issues only.)
LPs: 10/12-Inch 33rpm
EPIC: 68–70 .... **10–15**
IMPERIAL: 65–66 .... **15–20**
ISLAND: 75 .... **8–10**

FAMILY
Singles: 7-Inch
LITTLE CITY: 77 .... **2–3**
UNITED ARTISTS: 71–73 .... **2–4**
LPs: 10/12-Inch 33rpm
REPRISE: 68–70 .... **15–20**
UNITED ARTISTS: 71–73 .... **10–12**

Price Range

FAMILY
Singles: 12-Inch 33/45rpm
PAISLEY PARK: 85 .... $4–6
Singles: 7-Inch
PAISLEY PARK: 85 1–3
LPs: 10/12-Inch 33rpm
PAISLEY PARK: 85 5–8

FAMILY PLANN
Singles: 7-Inch
DRIVE: 75 2–3

FANCY
Singles: 7-Inch
BIG TREE: 74 2–3
LPs: 10/12-Inch 33rpm
BIG TREE: 74 8–10
POISON RING: 71 10–15
RCA VICTOR: 79 5–8

FANNY
Singles: 7-Inch
CASABLANCA: 74–75 2–3
REPRISE: 70–73 2–3
LPs: 10/12-Inch 33rpm
CASABLANCA: 74 8–10
REPRISE: 70–73 10–12

FANTASTIC FIVE KEYS, The
Singles: 7-Inch
CAPITOL: 62 3–5
Also see FIVE KEYS, The

FANTASTIC FOUR, The
Singles: 7-Inch
EASTBOUND: 73–74 2–3
RIC-TIC: 66–68 3–5
SOUL: 68–70 2–4
WESTBOUND: 75–79 1–3
LPs: 10/12-Inch 33rpm
SOUL: 69 10–12
20TH CENTURY-FOX/
  WESTBOUND: 76 8–10
WESTBOUND: 75–78 8–10

FANTASTIC JOHNNY C., The
(Johnny Corley)
Singles: 7-Inch
KAMA SUTRA: 70 2–4
PHIL L.A OF SOUL:
  67–73 3–5

Price Range

LPs: 10/12-Inch 33rpm
PHIL L.A OF SOUL: 68 .... $15–20

FANTASTICS, The
Singles: 7-Inch
BELL: 71–72 2–3
DERAM: 69 2–4

FANTASY
Singles: 7-Inch
IMPERIAL: 69 2–4
LIBERTY: 70 2–3
LPs: 10/12-Inch 33rpm
LIBERTY: 70 10–12

FANTASY
Singles: 12-Inch 33/45rpm
QUALITY: 83 4–6
Singles: 7-Inch
PAVILLION: 81 1–3

FANTAYZEE, Haysi: see HAYSI
FANTAYZEE

FARAGHER BROTHERS, The
Singles: 7-Inch
ABC: 76–77 2–3
POLYDOR: 79 1–3
LPs: 10/12-Inch 33rpm
ABC: 79 5–8
POLYDOR: 78–79 5–8

FARDON, Don
Singles: 7-Inch
CHELSEA: 73 2–3
GNP/CRESCENDO: 68 3–5
LPs: 10/12-Inch 33rpm
DECCA: 70 10–12
GNP/CRESCENDO: 68 15–18

FARGO, Donna
Singles: 7-Inch
ABC: 78 1–3
ABC/DOT: 74–77 1–3
CHALLENGE: 68 2–4
DECCA: 72 2–3
DOT: 72–74 2–3
MCA: 81 1–3
RCA VICTOR: 82 1–3
RAMCO: 67 3–5

Price Range

Price Range

FEATHER
Singles: 7-Inch
WHITE WHALE: 70 . . . . $2–3
LPs: 10/12-Inch 33rpm
COLUMBIA: 70 10–12

FEATHERBED (Featuring Barry Manilow)
Singles: 7-Inch
BELL: 71 12–15
Also see MANILOW, Barry

FEE WAYBILL: see WAYBILL, Fee

FEEL
Singles: 12-Inch 33/45rpm
SUTRA: 83 4–6
Singles: 7-Inch
SUTRA: 82–83 1–3

FEELGOOD, DR.: see DR. FEELGOOD

FELDER, Don
Singles: 7-Inch
ASYLUM: 83 1–3
FULL MOON/ASYLUM:
81 1–3
MCA 1–3
Picture Sleeves
FULL MOON/ASYLUM:
81 . . . . INC
LPs: 10/12-Inch 33rpm
ASYLUM: 83 5–8
Also see EAGLES, The

FELDER, Wilton
Singles: 7-Inch
ABC: 78 1–3
MCA: 79–85 1–3
LPs: 10/12-Inch 33rpm
ABC: 78 5–8
MCA: 80–85 5–8
PACIFIC JAZZ: 69 8–12
Also see TASTE OF HONEY & WILTON
FELDER

FELDER, Wilton, & Bobby Womack
Singles: 7-Inch
MCA: 80 1–3
Also see FELDER, Wilton

Also see WOMACK, Bobby

FELDMAN, Victor (The Victor Feldman All Stars; The Victor Feldman Quartet; The Victor Feldman Trio; Vic Feldman)
Singles: 7-Inch
AVA: 63 . . . . $2–3
INFINITY: 62 2–3
PACIFIC JAZZ: 66 2–3
VEE JAY: 64 2–3
LPs: 10/12-Inch 33rpm
AVA: 63 12–20
CONTEMPORARY:
58–60 15–25
INTERLUDE: 59 15–20
MODE: 58 20–30
PACIFIC JAZZ: 67–68 10–15
PALTO ALTO: 83–84 5–8
RIVERSIDE: 61 15–20
VEE JAY: 59–65 15–25
WORLD PACIFIC: 62 15–25

FELICIANO, Jose
Singles: 7-Inch
ALA: 80 1–3
MOTOWN: 81–83 1–3
PRIVATE STOCK: 76–77 1–3
RCA VICTOR: 64–75 2–4
LPs: 10/12-Inch 33rpm
CAMDEN: 72 8–10
MOTOWN: 81 5–8
PRIVATE STOCK: 76–77 6–10
RCA VICTOR: 65–76 8–15

FELICIANO, Jose, & Quincy Jones
LPs: 10/12-Inch 33rpm
RCAVICTOR (4096; "Mac
Kenna's Gold"): 69 20–25
(Soundtrack.)
Also see FELICIANO, Jose
Also see JONES, Quincy

FELIX & JARVIS
Singles: 7-Inch
RFC/QUALITY: 82–83 1–3

FELLER, Dick
Singles: 7-Inch
ASYLUM: 74–75 1–3
UNITED ARTISTS: 72–80 2–3

Price Range

LPs: 10/12-Inch 33rpm
ASYLUM: 75. . . . . **$6–10**
AUDIOGRAPH ALIVE:
    84 . . . . **5–8**
UNITED ARTISTS: 73 . . . . **8–12**

FELLINI, Suzanne
Singles: 7-Inch
CASABLANCA: 80 . . . . **1–3**
    LPs: 10/12-Inch 33rpm
CASABLANCA: 80 . . . . **5–8**

FELONY
Singles: 7-Inch
ROCK 'N' ROLL: 83–84 . . . . **1–3**
    LPs: 10/12-Inch 33rpm
ROCK 'N' ROLL: 83 . . . . **5–8**

FELTS, Narvel
Singles: 7-Inch
ABC: 76 . . . . **2–3**
ABC/DOT: 75–77 . . . . **2–3**
CINNAMON: 73–74 . . . . **2–3**
COLLAGE: 79 . . . . **2–3**
COMPLEAT: 82–83 . . . . **1–3**
EVERGREEN: 82–83 . . . . **1–3**
GMC: 81 . . . . **1–3**
GROOVE: 63 . . . . **3–5**
HI (2100 series): 67 . . . . **3–5**
HI (2300 series): 76 . . . . **2–3**
KARI: 80 . . . . **1–3**
LOBO: 82 . . . . **1–3**
MCA: 79 . . . . **1–3**
MERCURY: 57 . . . . **5–8**
PINK: 59–60 . . . . **4–6**
    LPs: 10/12-Inch 33rpm
ABC: 78 . . . . **5–8**
ABC/DOT: 75–77 . . . . **8–10**
CINNAMON: 73–74 . . . . **8–10**
HI: 76 . . . . **8–10**

FELTS, Narvel / Red Sovine / Mel Tillis
LPs: 10/12-Inch 33rpm
POWER PAK **5–8**
    Also see FELTS, Narvel
    Also see SOVINE, Red

FENDER, Freddy
Singles: 7-Inch
ABC: 76–79 . . . . **2–3**

Price Range

ABC/DOT: 75–77 . . . . **$2–3**
ARV INT'L: 75 . . . . **2–3**
ARGO: 60 . . . . **8–10**
DUNCAN: 59 . . . . **10–15**
GRT: 75–76 . . . . **2–3**
GOLDBAND **4–6**
IMPERIAL: 60 . . . . **8–10**
MCA: 82 . . . . **1–3**
NORCO: 63–65 . . . . **4–6**
STARFLITE: 79–80 . . . . **2–3**
WARNER BROS: 83 . . . . **1–3**
    LPs: 10/12-Inch 33rpm
ABC: 78–79 . . . . **5–8**
ABC/DOT: 75–77 . . . . **8–10**
ACCORD: 81 . . . . **5–8**
GRT: 75 . . . . **8–10**
STARFLITE: 80 . . . . **5–8**

FENDERMEN, The
Singles: 7-Inch
COLLECTABLES **1–3**
CUCA: 60 . . . . **25–35**
DAB **3–5**
ERA: 72 . . . . **1–3**
ERIC **1–3**
SOMA: 60–61 . . . . **4–6**
    LPs: 10/12-Inch 33rpm
SOMA: 60 . . . . **325–350**
    Members: Phil Humphrey; Jim Sundquist.

FERGUSON, Helena
Singles: 7-Inch
COMPASS: 67–68 . . . . **3–5**

Price Range

FERGUSON, Jay
Singles: 7-Inch
ASYLUM: 77–79. . . . . $2–3
LPs: 10/12-Inch 33rpm
ASYLUM: 76–79. 8–10
CAPITOL: 80–82 5–8
Also see JO JO GUNNE
Also see SPIRIT

FERGUSON, Johnny
Singles: 7-Inch
MGM: 59–60. 3–5

FERGUSON, Maynard (The Maynard Ferguson Sextet)
Singles: 12-Inch 33/45rpm
COLUMBIA: 79. 4–6
Singles: 7-Inch
CAMEO: 63 2–3
CAPITOL: 50–51 3–5
COLUMBIA: 71–82. 1–3
EMARCY: 54 3–5
MERCURY: 55. 2–4
ROULETTE: 59–62 2–4
EPs: 7-Inch 33/45rpm
EMARCY: 54–57 5–15
LPs: 10/12-Inch 33rpm
BETHLEHEM: 78 5–8
CAMEO: 63 12–20
COLUMBIA: 71–82. 5–10
EMARCY (400 series): 76. 5–10
EMARCY (1000 series): 81. 5–8
EMARCY (26000 series):
  54 30–50
  (10-Inch LPs.)
EMARCY (36000 series):
  55–57 20–40
ENTERPRISE: 68 8–12
MAINSTREAM (300
  series): 71–72. 6–10
MAINSTREAM (6000
  series): 64. 15–20
  (Stereo issues.)
MAINSTREAM (56000
  series): 64. 12–20
  (Monaural issues.)
MERCURY: 60. 12–20
PALTO ALTO: 83 5–8
PRESTIGE: 69. 8–12
ROULETTE: 59–72 10–20
SKYLARK: 53 20–40

Price Range

TRIP: 74 . . . . $5–8
Also see BASIE, Count, & Maynard Ferguson
Also see CONNOR, Chris, & Maynard Ferguson
Also see KENTON, Stan
Also see MANN, Herbie, & Maynard Ferguson

FERKO STRING BAND, The
Singles: 7-Inch
ARGO: 63. 2–3
MEDIA: 55. 2–4
SAVOY: 55 2–4

LPs: 10/12-Inch 33rpm
ABC-PARAMOUNT: 63. 10–15
ALSHIRE: 76 4–6
REGENT: 56–59. 12–20
SURE: 65–73. 6–12

FERRANTE & TEICHER
Singles: 7-Inch
ABC-PARAMOUNT:
  58–62 2–3
COLUMBIA: 53. 2–4
ENTRE: 53 3–5
UNITED ARTISTS: 59–79. 1–3

Picture Sleeves
UNITED ARTISTS: 60–69. 2–3

EPs: 7-Inch 33/45rpm
MGM: 54. 4–6

LPs: 10/12-Inch 33rpm
ABC: 73–76. 5–10
ABC-PARAMOUNT:
  58–66 8–15
COLUMBIA: 55–73 8–15
HARMONY: 64–70 5–10
LIBERTY: 81–84 5–8
MGM: 54. 12–20
METRO: 66. 5–10
MISTLETOE: 75. 4–6
SUNSET: 70–71 5–10
WESTMINSTER: 55–58 12–20
UNART: 67. 5–10
UNITED ARTISTS: 60–80. 5–15
Members: Arthur Ferrante; Louis Teicher.

FERRARI
Singles: 12-Inch 33/45rpm
SUGAR HILL: 82 4–6

Price Range   *Price Range*

FERRER, Jose (Jose Ferrer & The Ferrers)
Singles: 7-Inch
COLUMBIA: *54–55* $2–4
EPIC: *68* 1–3
RCA VICTOR: *60* 2–3
Picture Sleeves
RCA VICTOR: *60* 2–3
LPs: 10/12-Inch 33rpm
MGM: *62–65* 6–12
Also see CLOONEY, Rosemary, & Jose Ferrer

FERRY, Bryan
Singles: 12-Inch 33/45rpm
WARNER BROS: *85* 4–6
Singles: 7-Inch
ATLANTIC: *74–79* 2–3
WARNER BROS: *85* 1–3
LPs: 10/12-Inch 33rpm
ATLANTIC: *72–78* 10–12
WARNER BROS: *85* 5–8
Also see ROXY MUSIC

FESTIVAL
Singles: 7-Inch
RSO: *80* 1–3
LPs: 10/12-Inch
RSO: *80* 5–8

FEVA, Sandra
Singles: 7-Inch
VENTURE: *79–81* 1–3

FEVER
Singles: 12-Inch 33/45rpm
FANTASY: *79–82* 4–6
Singles: 7-Inch
FANTASY: *79–82* 1–3
LPs: 10/12-Inch 33rpm
FANTASY: *79–80* 5–8

FEVER TREE, The
Singles: 7-Inch
AMPEX: *70* 3–5
MAINSTREAM: *67* 5–8
UNI: *68–69* 5–8
LPs: 10/12-Inch 33rpm
AMPEX: *70* 12–15
MCA: *76* 8–10
UNI: *68–70* 15–20

FIDELITYS, The
Singles: 7-Inch
BATON: *58* $4–6
SIR: *59–60* 4–6

FIEDLER, Arthur: see BOSTON POPS ORCHESTRA, The

FIELD, Sally
Singles: 7-Inch
COLGEMS: *67–68* 2–4
Picture Sleeves
COLGEMS: *67* 2–4
LPs: 10/12-Inch 33rpm
COLGEMS: *67* 12–18

FIELDS, Ernie
Singles: 7-Inch
CAPITOL: *64* 2–4
RENDEZVOUS: *59–62* 3–5
LPs: 10/12-Inch 33rpm
RENDEZVOUS: *60* 30–40

FIELDS, Kim
Singles: 7-Inch
CRITIQUE: *84* 1–3

FIELDS, Richard "Dimples"
Singles: 7-Inch
BOARDWALK: *81–83* 1–3
RCA VICTOR: *84–85* 1–3
LPs: 10/12-Inch 33rpm
BOARDWALK: *81–82* 5–8
RCA VICTOR: *84* 5–8

FIELDS, W.C.
LPs: 10/12-Inch 33rpm
AMERICAN: *75* 5–8
COLUMBIA: *69–77* 6–10
DECCA: *68* 8–12
HARMONY: *70* 6–10
HUDSON: *60* 15–20

FIELDS, W.C., & Mae West
LPs: 10/12-Inch 33rpm
HARMONY: *70* 6–10
PROSCENIUM: *60* 15–20
Also see FIELDS, W.C.
Also see WEST, Mae

Price Range

FIESTA
Singles: 7-Inch
ARISTA: 78 .... $1–3

FIESTAS, The
Singles: 7-Inch
ATLANTIC 1–3
COLLECTABLES 1–3
OLD TOWN (1000 series):
   59–60 4–6
OLD TOWN (1100 series):
   61–65 3–5
RESPECT: 75 2–3
STRAND: 61..................... 3–5
VIGOR: 74 1–3
   Members: Tom Bullock; Eddie Morris; Sam In-
   galls; Preston Love.
   Also see ROBERT & JOHNNY / The Fiestas

FIFTH DIMENSION, The
Singles: 7-Inch
ABC: 75–76....................... 1–3
ARISTA: 75 2–3
BELL: 70–74..................... 2–4
MOTOWN: 78–79................. 1–3
SOUL CITY: 66–70 2–4
SUTRA: 83 1–3

Picture Sleeves
SOUL CITY: 67–69 2–4

LPs: 10/12-Inch 33rpm
ARISTA: 75 8–10
BELL: 70–74..................... 8–10
KORY: 77........................ 8–10
MOTOWN: 78–79................. 5–8
RHINO: 86 5–8
SOUL CITY: 67–70 10–15
   Members: Marilyn McCoo; Billy Davis, Jr.; La-
   monte McLemore; Florence LaRue; Ron
   Townson.
   Also see McCOO, Marilyn, & Billy Davis, Jr.

FIFTH ESTATE, The
Singles: 7-Inch
JUBILEE: 67–69.................. 3–5
RED BIRD: 66.................... 3–5

LPs: 10/12-Inch 33rpm
JUBILEE: 67.................... 20–25

Price Range

50 GUITARS OF TOMMY GARRETT, The
Singles: 7-Inch
LIBERTY: 66–68 .... $1–3
LPs: 10/12-Inch 33rpm
LIBERTY: 61–71 5–10
MUSICOR: 76–78................. 4–6
UNITED ARTISTS: 73............. 5–8
   Also see GARRETT, Tommy

52ND STREET
Singles: 12-Inch 33/45rpm
A&M: 83 4–6
PROFILE: 84 4–6

FIGURES ON THE BEACH
Singles: 12-Inch 33/45rpm
METRO AMERICAN: 84 4–6

FILE 13
Singles: 12-Inch 33/45rpm
PROFILE: 84 4–6

FINISHED TOUCH
Singles: 7-Inch
MOTOWN: 78..................... 1–3
LPs: 10/12-Inch 33rpm
MOTOWN: 78..................... 5–8

FINN, Tim
Singles: 7-Inch
A&M: 83 1–3
LPs: 10/12-Inch 33rpm
A&M: 83 5–8
   Also see SPLIT ENZ

FINNEGAN, Larry
Singles: 7-Inch
CORAL: 62....................... 3–5
OLD TOWN: 62–63................ 3–5
RIC: 64 4–8

FINNEY, Albert
Singles: 7-Inch
MOTOWN: 77..................... 1–3
LPs: 10/12-Inch 33rpm
MOTOWN: 77..................... 5–8

FIONA (Fiona Flanagan)
Singles: 7-Inch
ATLANTIC: 84–85 1–3

Price Range

LPs: 10/12-Inch 33rpm
ATLANTIC: *84–85* **$5–8**

FIRE & RAIN
LPs: 10/12-Inch 33rpm
MERCURY: *73*.................. **8–10**

FIRE INC.
Singles: 7-Inch
MCA: *84* **1–3**

FIREBALLET
Singles: 7-Inch
PASSPORT: *75–76*............... **1–3**

LPs: 10/12-Inch 33rpm
PASSPORT: *75–76*.............. **8–10**

FIREBALLS, The (With Jimmy Gilmer)
Singles: 7-Inch
ATCO: *67–70*.................... **3–5**
DOT: *63–67*..................... **4–6**
KAPP: *59* **35–50**
TOP RANK (Except stereo
singles): *59–61* **5–8**
TOP RANK (Stereo
singles): *59–60* **12–15**
   (With an "ST" following the number.)
WARWICK: *61*................... **4–6**

EPs: 7-Inch 33/45rpm
TOP RANK: *60* **25–35**

LPs: 10/12-Inch 33rpm
ATCO: *68* **10–12**
TOP RANK: *60* **35–45**
WARWICK: *61*................. **45–55**
   Also see GILMER, Jimmy, & The Fireballs

FIREFALL (Featuring Rick Roberts)
Singles: 7-Inch
ATLANTIC: *76–81* **1–3**

Picture Sleeves
ATLANTIC: *78* **1–3**

LPs: 10/12-Inch 33rpm
ATLANTIC: *76–82* **5–8**
   Also see ABBA / The Spinners / Firefall /
   England Dan & John Ford Coley

Fireflies, two charted singles (1959–60), no charted LPs.

Price Range

FIREFLIES, The (Featuring Ritchie Adams)
Singles: 7-Inch
CANADIAN
   AMERICAN: *60*............... **$4–6**
ERIC **1–3**
HAMILTON: *63*.................. **3–5**
RIBBON: *59–60* **5–8**
TAURUS: *62–64*................. **8–12**

LPs: 10/12-Inch 33rpm
TAURUS: *61*................... **75–90**

FIREFLY
Singles: 7-Inch
A&M: *75* **2–3**
EMERGENCY: *81*................. **1–3**

FIRESIGN THEATRE, The
Singles: 7-Inch
COLUMBIA: *69*.................. **2–4**

LPs: 10/12-Inch 33rpm
BUTTERFLY: *77*................. **5–8**
COLUMBIA: *69–74*.............. **8–12**
EPIC: *74* **5–10**
RHINO: *79–82* **5–8**

FIRM, The
Singles: 7-Inch
ATLANTIC: *85–86* **1–3**

Price Range

Price Range

LPs: 10/12-Inch 33rpm
ATLANTIC: 85–86 . . . . **$5–8**
Members: Jimmy Page; Paul Rodgers; Tony Franklin; Chris Slade.
Also see BAD COMPANY
Also see MANN, Manfred
Also see PAGE, Jimmy

FIRST CHOICE
Singles: 12-Inch 33/45rpm
FIRST CHOICE: 83 . . . . **4–6**
SALSOUL: 84 . . . . **4–6**
Singles: 7-Inch
GOLD MINE: 77 . . . . **2–3**
PHILLY GROOVE: 73–74 . . . . **2–4**
LPs: 10/12-Inch 33rpm
GOLD MIND: 77–80 . . . . **5–8**
KORY: 77 . . . . **8–10**
PHILLY GROOVE: 73–74 . . . . **8–10**

FIRST CLASS
Singles: 7-Inch
ALL PLATINUM: 76–77 . . . . **2–3**
PRIVATE STOCK/UK:
76 . . . . **1–3**
TODAY: 74 . . . . **2–4**
UK: 74–75 . . . . **2–3**
LPs: 10/12-Inch 33rpm
ALL PLATINUM: 76 . . . . **5–8**
PARK-WAY: 80 . . . . **5–8**
SUGARHILL: 81 . . . . **5–8**
UK: 74 . . . . **8–10**

FIRST EDITION, The
Singles: 7-Inch
REPRISE: 67–68 . . . . **3–6**
LPs: 10/12-Inch 33rpm
REPRISE: 67–68 . . . . **12–15**
Members: Kenny Rogers; Mike Settle; Thelma Lou Camacho; Terry Williams; Mickey Jones.
Also see NEW CHRISTY MINSTRELS, The
Also see ROGERS, Kenny, & The First Edition

FIRST FAMILY, The
Singles: 7-Inch
POLYDOR: 74 . . . . **2–4**

FIRST FIRE
LPs: 10/12-Inch 33rpm
TORTOISE INT'L: 78 . . . . **5–8**

FIRST FOUR, The
Singles: 7-Inch
STRATA: 65 . . . . **$3–5**

FIRST GEAR
LPs: 10/12-Inch 33rpm
MYRRH: 72 . . . . **8–10**

FIRST LOVE
Singles: 12-Inch 33/45rpm
CHYCAGO INT'L: 82 . . . . **4–6**
Singles: 7-Inch
CHYCAGO INT'L: 82 . . . . **1–3**
CIM: 83 . . . . **1–3**
DAKAR: 80 . . . . **1–3**
LPs: 10/12-Inch 33rpm
CHYCAGO INT'L: 82 . . . . **5–8**

FISCHOFF, George (George Fischoff Keyboard Komplex; George Fischoff & The Peppers; George Fischoff & The Luv Ens)
Singles: 7-Inch
COLUMBIA: 77 . . . . **1–3**
DRIVE: 79 . . . . **1–3**
HERITAGE: 81 . . . . **1–3**
P.I.P.: 75 . . . . **1–3**
RANWOOD: 76 . . . . **1–3**
REWARD: 84 . . . . **1–3**
UNITED ARTISTS: 72–74 . . . . **2–3**

FISHER, Eddie
Singles: 7-Inch
ABC-PARAMOUNT: 61 . . . . **2–3**
DOT: 65–66 . . . . **2–3**
MUSICOR: 69 . . . . **1–3**
RCA VICTOR (3000
through 6000 series):
50–57 . . . . **3–5**
RCA VICTOR (7000
through 9000 series):
57–68 . . . . **2–4**
RAMROD: 60–63 . . . . **2–3**
7 ARTS: 61 . . . . **2–3**
TRANS ATLAS: 62 . . . . **2–3**
Picture Sleeves
RCA VICTOR (5000
series): 53–55 . . . . **5–10**
RCA VICTOR (6000
series): 55–57 . . . . **3–5**

Price Range

EPs: 7-Inch 33/45rpm
RCA VICTOR: *51–58* **$5–10**
LPs: 10/12-Inch 33rpm
CAMDEN: *63* **6–10**
DOT: *65–67* **8–12**
HAMILTON: *66* **6–10**
RCA VICTOR (Except
1100 series): *51–72* **10–20**
RCA VICTOR (1100
series): *75* **5–8**
RAMROD: *60–63* **10–15**
Also see COMO, Perry, & Eddie Fisher

FISHER, Mary Ann
Singles: 7-Inch
FIRE: *59–60* **3–5**
IMPERIAL: *62* **3–5**
SEG-WAY: *61* **3–5**

FISHER, Toni (Miss Toni Fisher)
Singles: 7-Inch
BIG TOP: *62* **3–5**
CAPITOL: *67* **2–4**
COLLECTABLES **1–3**
COLUMBIA: *61* **3–5**
ERA: *72* **1–3**
SIGNET: *59–64* **3–5**
SMASH: *63* **3–5**

FISHER, Willie
Singles: 7-Inch
TIGRESS: *77* **1–3**

FITZGERALD, Ella
Singles: 7-Inch
CAPITOL: *67–68* **1–3**
DECCA: *50–67* **2–5**
PABLO: *75* **1–3**
REPRISE: *69–71* **1–3**
VERNE: *54* **3–5**
VERVE (10000 series):
56–59 .... **2–4**
VERVE (10100 throughh
10300 series): *60–65* **1–3**
Picture Sleeves
VERVE: *59–60* **2–4**
EPs: 7-Inch 33/45rpm
DECCA: *50–58* **15–30**
VERVE: *56–61* **10–25**
LPs: 10/12-Inch 33rpm
ATLANTIC: *72* **5–10**

Price Range

BAINBRIDGE: *81* **$5–8**
CAPITOL (2000 series):
67–68 .... **8–12**
CAPITOL (11000 series):
78 .... **5–8**
CAPITOL (16000 series):
82 .... **4–6**
COLUMBIA: *73* **5–8**
CORAL: *73* **4–6**
DECCA (156; "The Best
Of Ella Fitzgerald"): *58* **25–35**
(Black label with silver print.)
DECCA (156; "The Best
Of Ella Fitzgerald"): *65* **15–20**
(Black label with horizontal rainbow band.)
DECCA (4000 series):
61–67 .... **10–20**
DECCA (5000 series):
50–51 .... **40–60**
(10-Inch LPs.)
DECCA (8000 series):
55–59 .... **20–40**
EVEREST: *73* **5–8**
MCA: *76–82* **5–8**
MGM: *70* **6–12**
MPS: *72* **6–10**
METRO: *65–66* **10–15**
OLYMPIC: *74* **5–8**
PABLO: *75–83* **5–8**
REPRISE: *69–71* **8–12**
VERVE (2500 & 2600
series): *76–82* **5–10**
(Reads "Manufactured By MGM Record
Corp.," or mentions either Polydor or Poly-
gram at bottom of label.)
VERVE (4001 through
4009): *56* **25–50**
(Reads "Verve Records, Inc." at bottom of
label.)
VERVE (4010; "Ella
Fitzgerald Sings The
Duke Ellington Song
Book"): *56* **75-125**
(A 4-LP set.)
VERVE (4019; "Ella
Fitzgerald Sings The
Irving Berlin Song
Book"): *58* **20-40**
VERVE (4029; "Ella
Fitzgerald Sings The
George & Ira Gershwin
Songbook"): *59* **40-60**

Price Range

(Boxed five mono LP set, containing individual LPs 4024 through 4028.)
VERVE (4036 through
4071): *59–66.* **$10–20**
VERVE (6000 series):
57–59 . . . . **20–35**
(Reads "Verve Records, Inc." at bottom of label.)
VERVE (6100 series): *60* **15–20**
(Reads "Verve Records, Inc." at bottom of label.)
VERVE (8200 series): *58* **20–30**
(Reads "Verve Records, Inc." at bottom of label.)
VERVE (64036 through
64071): *59–66.* **10–20**
VERVE (67000 & 68000
series): *67–73* **8–15**
VERVE (2610000 series):
83 . . . . **20–30**
VOCALION: *67* **6–10**
Also see RIDDLE, Nelson

FITZGERALD, Ella, & Louis Armstrong
LPs: 10/12-Inch 33rpm
METRO: *67.* **5–10**
VERVE: *56* **20–40**
Also see ARMSTRONG, Louis

FITZGERALD, Ella, & Count Basie
LPs: 10/12-Inch 33rpm
PABLO: *79* **5–8**
VERVE: *63* **12–20**
Also see BASIE, Count

FITZGERALD, Ella / Bill Doggett
LPs: 10/12-Inch 33rpm
VERVE: *62* **10–20**
Also see DOGGETT, Bill

FITZGERALD, Ella, & Duke Ellington
Singles: 7-Inch
VERVE: *66* **2–3**

LPs: 10/12-Inch 33rpm
VERVE: *65–67* **10–20**
Also see ELLINGTON, Duke

FITZGERALD, Ella / Billie Holiday
LPs: 10/12-Inch 33rpm
MCA: *76* **$5–8**
VERVE: *58* **20–40**

FITZGERALD, Ella / Billie Holiday / Lena Horne
LPs: 10/12-Inch 33rpm
COLUMBIA: *56* **25–50**
Also see HOLIDAY, Billie
Also see HORNE, Lena

FITZGERALD, Ella, & The Ink Spots
EPs: 7-Inch 33/45rpm
DECCA: *53* **5–10**
Also see INK SPOTS, The

FITZGERALD, Ella, & Antonio Carlos Jobim
LPs: 10/12-Inch 33rpm
PABLO: *81* **5–8**
Also see JOBIM, Antonio Carlos

FITZGERALD, Ella, & Peggy Lee
LPs: 10/12-Inch 33rpm
DECCA (8166; "Pete
Kelly's Blues"): *56* **30–50**
Also see LEE, Peggy

FITZGERALD, Ella, & Oscar Peterson
LPs: 10/12-Inch 33rpm
PABLO: *76* **5–8**
Also see FITZGERALD, Ella
Also see PETERSON, Oscar

FIVE AMERICANS, The
Singles: 7-Inch
ABC-PARAMOUNT: *65* **4–6**
ABNAK (Except 109):
67–69 . . . . **3–5**
ABNAK (109; "I See The
Light"): *65* **12–15**
HBR: *65–66.* **3–5**
JETSTAR: *65* **4–6**

Price Range

Picture Sleeves
ABNAK: *68* **$8–10**
HBR: *66* **10–12**

LPs: 10/12-Inch 33rpm
ABNAK: *67–68* **20–30**
HBR: *66* **20–25**

FIVE BLOBS, The (With Bernie Nee)
Singles: 7-Inch
COLUMBIA: *58* **4–6**
JOY: *59* **4–6**

FIVE BY FIVE
Singles: 7-Inch
PAULA: *67–70* **3–5**

LPs: 10/12-Inch 33rpm
PAULA: *69* **15–20**

5 CHANELS, The
Singles: 7-Inch
DEB: *58* **5–8**

FIVE DU-TONES, The
Singles: 7-Inch
ONE-DERFUL: *63–65* **3–5**

FIVE EMPREES, The
Singles: 7-Inch
FREEPORT: *65–66* **3–5**
SMASH: *66* **3–5**

LPs: 10/12-Inch 33rpm
FREEPORT: *65–66* **25–35**
Also see FIVE EMPRESSIONS, The

FIVE EMPRESSIONS, The
Singles: 7-Inch
FREEPORT: *65* **6–10**
Also see FIVE EMPREES, The

FIVE FLIGHTS UP
Singles: 7-Inch
T.A: *70–71* **2–4**

Five Keys, six charted singles (1951–57), no charted LPs.

Price Range

FIVE KEYS, The
Singles: 7-Inch
ALADDIN (3085 through
  3118): *51–52* **$175–200**
ALADDIN (3127 through
  3136): *52* **350–375**
ALADDIN (3158 through
  3175): *52–53* **175–200**
ALADDIN (3190; "These
  Foolish Things"): *53* **375–425**
ALADDIN (3204 through
  3312): *53–56* **150–175**
CAPITOL: *54–57* **8–12**
GROOVE (0031; "I'll
  Follow You"): *51* **1000–1200**
  (Believed to exist only on promotional copy.)
GUSTO **1–3**
IMPERIAL: *62* **2–3**
KING: *59–64* **8–12**
LANDMARK: *73* **2–3**

EPs: 7-Inch 33/45rpm
CAPITOL (572; "The Five
  Keys"): *55* **35–40**
CAPITOL (828; "The Five
  Keys On Stage"): *57* **45–55**
  (Covers picture a group member's thumb in a
  phallic-like position.)

LPs: 10/12-Inch 33rpm
ALADDIN: *56* **150–200**

Price Range

CAPITOL (828; "The Five
Keys On Stage" -
original cover): *57* **$100–125**
(Original cover pictures a group member's
thumb in a phallic position.)
CAPITOL (828; "The Five
Keys On Stage" -
reworked cover): *57*. **75–90**
(Reworked cover removes member's thumb
from picture.)
CAPITOL (1769; "The
Fantastic Five Keys"):
62 . . . . **50–75**
(With a "T" prefix.)
CAPITOL (1769; "The
Fantastic Five Keys"):
77 . . . . **8–10**
(With an "M" prefix.)
HARLEM HIT PARADE:
72 . . . . **10–12**
KING: *60* **100–125**
SCORE: *57* **75–100**
Members: Rudy West; Ripley Ingram; Mary-
land Pierce; Dickie Smith; Bernie West; Ulysses
Hicks; Ray Loper; Thomas Threat.
Also see FANTASTIC FIVE KEYS, The

FIVE MAN ELECTRICAL BAND, The
Singles: 7-Inch
CAPITOL: *68–69* **3–5**
LION: *72–73* **2–3**
LIONEL: *71* **2–3**
MGM: *70* **4–6**
POLYDOR: *74* **2–3**
LPs: 10/12-Inch 33rpm
CAPITOL: *69* **12–15**
LION: *73* **10–12**
LIONEL: *70–71*. **10–12**
MGM: *70* **10–12**

FIVE ROYALES, The (The 5 Royales)
Singles: 7-Inch
ABC-PARAMOUNT: *62*. **3–5**
APOLLO (Black vinyl):
51–55 . . . . **15–20**
APOLLO (Colored vinyl):
52 . . . . **35–45**
GUSTO **1–3**
HOME OF THE BLUES:
60–62 . . . . **3–5**

Price Range

KING (4000 series): *54–56* **$5–8**
KING (5000 series): *57–64* **3–5**
SMASH: *64–65* **3–5**
TODD: *63* **3–5**
VEE JAY: *61–62*. **3–5**
LPs: 10/12-Inch 33rpm
APOLLO: *55*. **150–175**
KING (Except 955): *57–60* **60–75**
KING (955; "24 All Time
Hits"): *66*. **20–30**
Members: Lowman Pauling; John Tanner;
Scoop Carter; Otto Jeffries; Jim Moore.

FIVE SATINS, The
Singles: 7-Inch
ABC: *73* **1–3**
CANDLELITE. **2–4**
CHANCELLOR: *62*. **4–6**
COLLECTABLES **1–3**
CUB: *60–61* **8–10**
EMBER: *56–61* **6–10**
ELEKTRA: *82* **2–3**
FIRST: *59* **5–8**
FLASHBACK: *65*. **2–4**
KIRSHNER: *73–74* **2–3**
RCA VICTOR: *71* **2–3**
ROULETTE: *64* **3–5**
STANDORD (100; "All
Mine"): *56* **60–75**
STANDORD (200; "In
The Still Of The Nite"):
56 . . . . **100–125**
TIME MACHINE **2–4**
TIMES SQUARE: *62–64*. **3–5**
UNITED ARTISTS: *61* **10–12**
WARNER BROS: *63* **3–5**
EPs: 7-Inch 33/45rpm
EMBER (Red label): *60* **25–30**
EMBER (Black or "logs"
label): *60–61*. **12–15**
LPs: 10/12-Inch 33rpm
CELEBRITY
SHOWCASE: *70* **10–12**
EMBER (100; "The Five
Satins Sing"): *57* **100–125**
(Red label. Cover pictures the group on the
front.)
EMBER (100; "The Five
Satins Sing"): *58* **40–50**
("Logs" label.)

EMBER (100; "The Five
   Satins Sing"): *60* $20–25
   (Black label.)
EMBER (401; "The Five
   Satins Encore"): *60* 40–50
   (Black label.)
EMBER (401; "The Five
   Satins Encore"): *61* 20–25
   ("Logs" label.)
LOST-NITE: *81*. 6–10
MT. VERNON 20–25
RELIC 8–10
   Members: Fred Parris; Bill Baker; Ed Martin;
   Louis Peebles; Stan Dortch; Jim Freeman; Tom
   Killebrew; Al Denby; Jess Murphy; Wes
   Forbes; Richard Freeman.
   Also see BLACK SATIN
   Also see GRANAHAN, Gerry
   Also see NEW YORK CITY
   Also see NEW YORKERS, The
   Also see PARRIS, Fred
   Also see SOUTHSIDE JOHNNY & THE AS-
   BURY DUKES

FIVE SPECIAL
Singles: 7-Inch
ELEKTRA: *79–80* 1–3
LPs: 10/12-Inch 33rpm
ELEKTRA: *79* 5–8

FIVE STAIRSTEPS, The (The Stairsteps; The Five Stairsteps & Cubie)
Singles: 7-Inch
BUDDAH: *67–68* 2–4
COLLECTABLES 1–3
CURTOM: *68–69* 2–4
WINDY C: *66–67*. 3–5
Picture Sleeves
BUDDAH: *67–68* 2–4
LPs: 10/12-Inch 33rpm
BUDDAH: *68–70* 10–12
CURTOM: *69* 8–10
WINDY C: *67*. 10–12
   Also see INVISIBLE MAN'S BAND, The
   Also see STAIRSTEPS, The

FIVE STAR
Singles: 12-Inch 33/45rpm
RCA VICTOR: *85* 4–6
Singles: 7-Inch
RCA VICTOR: *85* 1–3

LPs: 10/12-Inch 33rpm
RCA VICTOR: *85* $5–8

5000 VOLTS
Singles: 7-Inch
PHILIPS: *75* 2–3
PRIVATE STOCK: *76*. 1–3

FIXX, The
Singles: 12-Inch 33/45rpm
MCA: *82–84* 4–6
Singles: 7-Inch
MCA: *82–84* 1–3
LPs: 10/12-Inch 33rpm
MCA: *82–84* 5–8

FLACK, Roberta
Singles: 7-Inch
ATLANTIC: *69–82* 1–3
MCA: *81* 1–3
VIVA: *83* 1–3
Picture Sleeves
ATLANTIC: *78–82* 1–3
LPs: 10/12-Inch 33rpm
ATLANTIC: *69–82* 6–10
VIVA: *83* 5–8
   Also see BRYSON, Peabo, & Roberta Flack
   Also see McCANN, Les

FLACK, Roberta, & Donny Hathaway
Singles: 7-Inch
ATLANTIC: *71–80* 1–3
LPs: 10/12-Inch 33rpm
ATLANTIC: *72–80* 6–10
   Also see HATHAWAY, Donny

FLACK, Roberta, & Eric Mercury
Singles: 7-Inch
ATLANTIC: *83* 1–3
   Also see FLACK, Roberta
   Also see MERCURY, Eric

FLAGG, Fannie
LPs: 10/12-Inch 33rpm
RCA VICTOR: *67–77* 6–12
SUNFLOWER: *71* 6–10

FLAME
Singles: 7-Inch
BROTHER: *70–71* 10–12

Price Range

Price Range

LPs: 10/12-Inch 33rpm
BROTHER: 70 .... **$15–18**
Also see BEACH BOYS, The

FLAMIN' GROOVIES, The
Singles: 7-Inch
BOMP: 75 .... **2–3**
EPIC: 69–70 .... **3–5**
KAMA SUTRA: 71 .... **3–5**

LPs: 10/12-Inch 33rpm
BUDDAH: 77 .... **10–12**
EPIC: 69 .... **35–45**
KAMA SUTRA (2021;
  "Flamingo"): 70 .... **20–25**
  (Pink label.)
KAMA SUTRA (2021;
  "Flamingo") **10–12**
  (Blue label.)
KAMA SUTRA (2031;
  "Teenage Head"): 71 .... **15–20**
  (Pink label.)
KAMA SUTRA (2031;
  "Teenage Head") **10–12**
  (Blue label.)
SIRE: 76–79 .... **10–12**

FLAMING EMBER
Singles: 7-Inch
HOT WAX: 69–70 .... **2–3**

LPs: 10/12-Inch 33rpm
HOT WAX: 70–71 .... **10–15**

Flamingos, 13 charted singles (1956–70), no charted LPs.

FLAMINGOS, The
Singles: 7-Inch
ABC: 73 .... **$1–3**
CHANCE (1133;
  "Someday, Someway"):
  53 .... **275–300**
  (Colored vinyl.)
CHANCE (1133;
  "Someday, Someway"):
  53 .... **150–175**
  (Black vinyl.)
CHANCE (1140; "That's
  My Desire"): 53 .... **225–250**
  (Colored vinyl.)
CHANCE (1140; "That's
  My Desire"): 53 .... **125–150**
  (Black vinyl.)
CHANCE (1145; "Golden
  Teardrops"): 53 .... **325–350**
  (Colored vinyl.)
CHANCE (1145; "Golden
  Teardrops"): 53 .... **175–200**
  (Black vinyl.)
CHANCE (1149 through
  1162): 53–54 .... **125–150**
CHECKER (815;
  "When"): 55 .... **15–20**
CHECKER (821; "Please
  Come Back Home"): 55 .... **25–30**
CHECKER (830; "I'll Be
  Home"): 56 .... **20–25**
CHECKER (837 through
  1091): 56–64 .... **8–12**
CHESS: 73 .... **1–3**
COLLECTABLES **1–3**
DECCA: 57–59 .... **5–8**
END (Except stereo
  singles): 58–62 .... **4–6**
END (Stereo singles): 59 .... **10–15**
JULMAR: 69 .... **3–5**
PARROT (808; "Dream Of
  A Lifetime"): 54 .... **200–225**
  (Colored vinyl.)
PARROT (808; "Dream Of
  A Lifetime"): 54 .... **125–150**
  (Black vinyl.)
PARROT (811; "I Really
  Don't Want To Know"):
  55 .... **350–400**
PARROT (812; "I'm
  Yours"): 55 .... **200–225**
  (Colored vinyl.)

Price Range

PARROT (812; "I'm
   Yours"): *55*. **$125–150**
  (Black vinyl.)
PHILIPS: *66* **3–5**
POLYDOR: *70* **2–4**
RONZE: *71–76* **2–4**
ROULETTE (Except 4000
  series): *71* **2–4**
ROULETTE (4000 series):
  63 . . . . **3–5**
TIMES SQUARE: *64*. **3–5**
VEE JAY: *61*. **3–5**
WORLDS: *75* **2–3**

EPs: 7-Inch 33/45rpm
END (Monaural): *59* **15–20**
END (Stereo): *59*. **25–30**

LPs: 10/12-Inch 33rpm
CHECKER (1433; "The
  Flamingos"): *59*. **35–45**
  (Monaural issue.)
CHECKER (3005; "The
  Flamingos"): *59*. **20–25**
  (Stereo issue.)
CHESS: *76*. **8–10**
CONSTELLATION: *64*. **15–20**
END (Except 304): *60–62* **25–30**
END (304; "Flamingo
  Serenade"): *59* **20–25**
  (Monaural issue.)
END (304; "Flamingo
  Serenade"): *59* **45–50**
  (Stereo issue.)
LOST-NITE: *81*. **5–8**
MEKA **10–12**
PHILLIPS: *66*. **15–20**
RONZE: *72* **10–12**
SOLID SMOKE: *82* **5–8**
  Members: Solly McElroy; John Carter; Zeke
  Carey; Jake Carey; Paul Wilson; Nate Nelson;
  Tommy Hunt; Terry Johnson.
  Also see HUNT, Tommy

FLAMINGOS, The / The Moonglows
LPs: 10/12-Inch 33rpm
VEE JAY: *62*. **30–40**
  Also see FLAMINGOS, The
  Also see MOONGLOWS, The

FLANAGAN, Ralph
Singles: 7-Inch
CORAL: *61* **2–3**

Price Range

IMPERIAL: *59*. **$2–3**
RCA VICTOR: *50–57* **2–4**
EPs: 7-Inch 33/45rpm
CAMDEN: *54*. **4–6**
RCA VICTOR: *51–57* **4–6**
LPs: 10/12-Inch 33rpm
CAMDEN: *54*. **5–10**
GOLDEN ERA: *76* **4–6**
IMPERIAL: *58–59*. **5–10**
RCA VICTOR: *51–57* **5–10**

FLARES, The
Singles: 7-Inch
COLLECTABLES **1–3**
FELSTED: *60–61* **3–5**
PRESS: *62–63* **3–5**
Picture Sleeves
FELSTED: *60* **10–15**
LPs: 10/12-Inch 33rpm
PRESS: *61* **20–25**
  Members: Aaron Collins; Willie Davis; Tom
  Miller; Randy Jones.
  Also see CADETS, The

FLASH
Singles: 7-Inch
CAPITOL: *72* **2–3**
LPs: 10/12-Inch 33rpm
CAPITOL (11000 series):
  77 . . . . **5–8**
  (With an "SM" prefix.)
CAPITOL (11000 series):
  72–73 . . . . **8–10**
  (With an "SMAS" & "ST" prefix.)
  Also see BANKS, Peter

FLASH & THE PAN
Singles: 12-Inch 33/45rpm
EPIC: *81–83* **4–6**
Singles: 7-Inch
EPIC: *79–83* **1–3**
LPs: 10/12-Inch 33rpm
EPIC: *79–82* **5–8**
  Members: Harry Vanda; George Young.
  Also see EASYBEATS, The

FLASH CADILLAC & THE
CONTINENTAL KIDS
Singles: 7-Inch
EPIC: *72–74* **2–4**
PRIVATE STOCK: *74–77*. **2–4**

Price Range   *Price Range*

LPs: 10/12-Inch 33rpm
EPIC: *72–74* **$10–12**
PRIVATE STOCK: *75.* **8–10**
   Also see WOLFMAN JACK

FLATT, Lester, & Earl Scruggs
Singles: 7-Inch
COLUMBIA (20000 &
  21000 series): *51–56* **4–6**
COLUMBIA (40000
  through 42000 series):
  56–63 .... **3–5**
COLUMBIA (43000
  through 45000 series):
  64–67 .... **2–4**
Picture Sleeves
COLUMBIA: *62–67* **3–5**
MERCURY: *68.* **2–4**
EPs: 7-Inch 33/45rpm
COLUMBIA: *57–60* **8–12**
LPs: 10/12-Inch 33rpm
COLUMBIA (30; "Flatt &
  Scruggs"): *75* **8–12**
COLUMBIA (400 series):
  69 .... **12–15**
COLUMBIA (1000 & 2000
  series, except 1019):
  60–68 .... **10–20**
COLUMBIA (1019;
  "Foggy Mountain
  Jamboree"): *57.* **25–35**
COLUMBIA (8000 & 9000
  series): *60–70* **10–20**
  (With a "CS" prefix.)
COLUMBIA (8000 & 9000
  series) **5–8**
  (With a "PC" prefix.)
COLUMBIA (10000
  series): *73* **6–12**
COLUMBIA (30000
  through 37000 series):
  70–82 .... **5–12**
COUNTY **5–10**
EVEREST: *71–82* **5–10**
51 WEST **5–8**
HARMONY: *60–71* **8–15**
MERCURY (20000 series):
  58–63 .... **20–30**
  (Monaural issues.)
MERCURY (60000 series):
  63 .... **20–30**

(Stereo issues.)
MERCURY (61000 series):
  68 .... **$10–15**
NASHVILLE: *70* **8–10**
PICKWICK/HILLTOP:
  68 .... **8–12**
POWER PAK **5–8**
ROUNDER
WING: *68* **8–12**
  Also see SCRUGGS, Earl

FLATT, Lester, Earl Scruggs, & Doc Watson
LPs: 10/12-Inch 33rpm
COLUMBIA: *67* **10–15**
  Also see FLATT, Lester, & Earl Scruggs
  Also see WATSON, Doc

FLAVOR
Singles: 7-Inch
COLUMBIA: *68* **2–4**
Picture Sleeves
COLUMBIA: *68* **2–4**
LPs: 10/12-Inch 33rpm
JU-PAR: *77* **8–10**

FLAVOUR, La: see LA FLAVOUR

FLEETWOOD, Mick
LPs: 10/12-Inch 33rpm
RCA VICTOR: *81* **5–8**
  Also see FLEETWOOD MAC

FLEETWOOD MAC
Singles: 7-Inch
BLUE HORIZON: *70* **4–6**
DJM: *73* **4–6**
EPIC (Except 11029):
  68–69 .... **5–8**
EPIC (11029;
  "Albatross"/"Black
  Magic Woman"): *73* **2–3**
REPRISE: *69–76.* **2–4**
WARNER BROS: *77–85* **1–3**
Picture Sleeves
WARNER BROS: *77–83* **1–3**
LPs: 10/12-Inch 33rpm
BLUE HORIZON: *69–71* **20–25**
EPIC (Except 33740):
  68–69 .... **20–25**

Price Range

Price Range

EPIC (33740; "English
Rose"): *73* **$8–12**
(Price range also includes reissue 2-LP set,
"Fleetwood Mac/English Rose," which carries
the same catalog number and was issued in
1974.)
MFSL: *78*...................... **15–18**
NAUTILUS: *79*.................. **15–18**
REPRISE: *69–77*................. **8–12**
SIRE: *75–77* **8–10**
WARNER BROS: *77–85*........... **8–12**
Members: Mick Fleetwood; Stevie Nicks;
Christine McVie; John McVie; Lindsay Buck-
ingham; Peter Green; Danny Kirwin; Jeremy
Spencer.
Also see BUCKINGHAM, Lindsay
Also see BUCKINGHAM NICKS
Also see FLEETWOOD, Mick
Also see GREEN, Peter
Also see McVIE, Christine
Also see NICKS, Stevie
Also see WELCH, Bob

FLEETWOODS, The
Singles: 7-Inch
DOLPHIN: *59*.................... **8–12**
DOLTON (1; "Come
Softly To Me"): *59* **6–10**
DOLTON (3;
"Graduation's Here"): *59*.......... **3–6**
(Monaural issue.)
DOLTON (3;
"Graduation's Here"): *59*....... **10–15**
(Stereo issue. With an "S" prefix.)
DOLTON (5 through 315):
59–66 .... **3–5**
LIBERTY (55000 series):
59 .... **4–6**
LIBERTY (77000 series):
59 .... **10–15**
(Stereo singles.)
UNITED ARTISTS: *74*............ **1–3**
Picture Sleeves
DOLTON: *60–62*................. **5–8**
EPs: 7-Inch 33/45rpm
DOLTON: *60*................... **15–20**
LPs: 10/12-Inch 33rpm
DOLTON: *59–65*................ **15–20**
LIBERTY: *82–83* **5–8**
SUNSET: *66* **10–15**
UNITED ARTISTS: *75*........... **8–10**
Members: Gary Troxel; Barbara Ellis;
Gretchen Christopher.

FLEMONS, Wade (Wade Flemons & The Newcomers)
Singles: 7-Inch
VEE JAY (Maroon label):
58–59 .... **$4–6**
VEE JAY (Black label):
61–63 .... **3–5**
LPs: 10/12-Inch 33rpm
VEE JAY (Maroon label):
59 .... **40–50**
VEE JAY (Black label): *61* **15–20**

FLESHTONES, The (With Jonithan Weiss)
Singles: 7-Inch
I.R.S.: *81–82* **1–3**
LPs: 10/12-Inch 33rpm
I.R.S.: *81–82* **5–8**

FLETCHER, Darrow
Singles: 7-Inch
CROSSOVER: *75–79* **2–3**
GROOVY: *66* **3–5**
REVUE: *68*..................... **2–4**
UNI: *70–71* **2–3**

FLETCHER, Lois
Singles: 7-Inch
PLAYBOY: *74* **2–3**

FLINT, Shelby
Singles: 7-Inch
VALIANT: *60–66*................. **3–5**
LPs: 10/12-Inch 33rpm
VALIANT (400 series):
61–63 .... **20–25**
VALIANT (25000 series):
66 .... **15–20**

FLIP CARTRIDGE: see CARTRIDGE, Flip

FLIRTATIONS, The
Singles: 7-Inch
DERAM: *69* **3–5**
PARROT: *68*.................... **2–4**
LPs: 10/12-Inch 33rpm
DERAM: *69* **15–18**

Price Range

FLOATERS, The
Singles: 7-Inch
ABC: 77–79 . . . . **$1–3**
Picture Sleeves
ABC: 77–78 . . . . **1–3**
LPs: 10/12-Inch 33rpm
ABC: 77–79 . . . . **5–8**

FLOCK, The
Singles: 7-Inch
COLUMBIA: 70 . . . . **3–5**
DESTINATION: 66–67 . . . . **5–8**
U.S.A: 68 . . . . **4–6**
LPs: 10/12-Inch 33rpm
COLUMBIA: 69–71 . . . . **10–15**
MERCURY: 75 . . . . **8–10**

FLOCK OF SEAGULLS, A
Singles: 12-Inch 33/45rpm
JIVE: 82–83 . . . . **4–6**
Singles: 7-Inch
ARISTA: 84 . . . . **1–3**
JIVE: 82–83 . . . . **1–3**
LPs: 10/12-Inch 33rpm
JIVE: 82–83 . . . . **5–8**

FLOOD, Dick (Dick Flood & The Pathfinders)
Singles: 7-Inch
EPIC: 61–62 . . . . **2–4**
KAPP: 65 . . . . **2–4**
MONUMENT: 59–60 . . . . **3–5**
NASCO: 71–72 . . . . **1–3**
NUGGET: 68 . . . . **2–3**
TOTEM: 67 . . . . **2–4**

FLOYD, Eddie
Singles: 7-Inch
ATLANTIC: 65 . . . . **3–5**
MALACO: 77 . . . . **2–3**
MERCURY: 78 . . . . **1–3**
SAFICE: 64 . . . . **4–6**
STAX: 66–75 . . . . **3–5**
LPs: 10/12-Inch 33rpm
ATCO: 74 . . . . **8–10**
MALACO: 77 . . . . **5–8**
STAX: 67–79 . . . . **10–15**
Also see FALCONS, The
Also see MOORE, Dorothy, & Eddie Floyd

Price Range

FLOYD, Eddie, & Mavis Staples
Singles: 7-Inch
STAX: 69 . . . . **$2–3**
Also see FLOYD, Eddie
Also see STAPLES, Mavis

FLOYD, King: see KING FLOYD

FLYING BURRITO BROTHERS, The
Singles: 7-Inch
A&M: 69–70 . . . . **2–4**
COLUMBIA: 76 . . . . **2–3**
LPs: 10/12-Inch 33rpm
A&M: 69–76 . . . . **10–15**
COLUMBIA: 75–76 . . . . **8–10**
REGENCY: 80 . . . . **5–8**
Also see BURRITO BROTHERS, The
Also see HILLMAN, Chris
Also see PARSONS, Gram

FLYING LIZARDS, The
Singles: 7-Inch
VIRGIN: 79 . . . . **1–3**
Picture Sleeves
VIRGIN: 79 . . . . **1–3**
LPs: 10/12-Inch 33rpm
VIRGIN: 80 . . . . **5–8**

FLYING MACHINE, The
Singles: 7-Inch
CONGRESS: 69–70 . . . . **3–5**
RAINY DAY: 67 . . . . **3–5**
LPs: 10/12-Inch 33rpm
JANUS: 69 . . . . **10–15**
Also see TAYLOR, James

FOCUS
Singles: 7-Inch
ATCO: 75 . . . . **2–3**
SIRE: 73 . . . . **2–3**
LPs: 10/12-Inch 33rpm
ATCO: 74–75 . . . . **8–10**
SIRE: 72–77 . . . . **8–10**
Also see AKKERMAN, Jan

FOCUS & P.J. PROBY
LPs: 10/12-Inch 33rpm
HARVEST: 78 . . . . **5–8**
Also see FOCUS
Also see PROBY, P.J.

Price Range

Price Range

FOGELBERG, Dan
Singles: 7-Inch
COLUMBIA: 73 . . . . $4–6
EPIC: 74–75 2–3
FULL MOON/EPIC:
  75–82 1–3
FULL MOON: 82–85 1–3
Picture Sleeves
FULL MOON/EPIC: 80 . . . . INC
LPs: 10/12-Inch 33rpm
COLUMBIA: 72 10–15
EPIC: 74–78 8–10
EPIC/FULL MOON:
  75–82 8–10
FULL MOON: 82–85 5–8

FOGELBERG, Dan, & Tim Weisberg
Singles: 7-Inch
FULL MOON/EPIC:
  78–80 1–3
LPs: 10/12-Inch 33rpm
FULL MOON/EPIC: 78 5–8
  Also see FOGELBERG, Dan
  Also see WEISBERG, Tim

FOGERTY, John
Singles: 7-Inch
ASYLUM: 75–76 2–3
FANTASY: 73 2–4
WARNER BROS: 84–85 1–3
Picture Sleeves
WARNER BROS: 85 . . . . INC
LPs: 10/12-Inch 33rpm
ASYLUM: 75–76 10–15
WARNER BROS: 85 5–8
  Also see BLUE RIDGE RANGERS, The
  Also see CREEDENCE CLEARWATER RE-
  VIVAL

FOGERTY, Tom (Tom Fogerty & The Blue Velvets)
Singles: 7-Inch
FANTASY: 71–73 2–4
ORCHESTRA 12–15
Picture Sleeves
FANTASY: 71 2–4
LPs: 10/12-Inch 33rpm
FANTASY: 72–81 8–10
  Also see CREEDENCE CLEARWATER RE-
  VIVAL
  Also see SAUNDERS, Merl

FOGHAT
Singles: 7-Inch
BEARSVILLE: 72–80 . . . . $1–3
Picture Sleeves
BEARSVILLE: 79 1–3
LPs: 10/12-Inch 33rpm
BEARSVILLE: 72–82 6–10
  Also see SAVOY BROWN
  Also see WISHBONE ASH

FOLEY, Ellen
Singles: 7-Inch
CLEVELAND INT'L:
  79–81 1–3
LPs: 10/12-Inch 33rpm
CLEVELAND INT'L:
  79–81 5–8
  Also see MEAT LOAF

FOLEY, Red
Singles: 7-Inch
DECCA (25000 series):
  61–67 2–3
DECCA (27000 through
  30000 series): 50–59 3–5
DECCA (31000 through
  32000 series): 60–67 2–4
DECCA (46000 series): 68 1–3
MCA: 73 1–3
EPs: 7-Inch 33/45rpm
DECCA: 53–59 5–10
LPs: 10/12-Inch 33rpm
CORAL: 73 4–6
COUNTRY MUSIC: 76 6–10
DECCA (100 series): 64 15–20
DECCA (4000 series,
  except 4140): 61–67 12–20
DECCA (4140;
  "Company's Comin' "):
  61 20–30
DECCA (5300 series):
  51–54 35–45
  (10-Inch LPs.)
DECCA (8294; "Souvenir
  Album"): 58 20–30
DECCA (8296; "Beyond
  The Sunset"): 58–65 10–15
DECCA (8700 series): 58 12–20
DECCA (8806; "My
  Keepsake Album"): 58 20–30

RED FOLEY EXCLUSIVE MANAGEMENT ABC-TV'S "JUBILEE U.S.A."
DECCA RECORDS TOP TALENT also RADIO'S "RED FOLEY SHOW"

Price Range

DECCA (8847; "Let's All
  Sing With Red Foley"):
  59 . . . . $10–18
DECCA (8900 series): 59 10–18
DECCA (75000 series):
  68–69 8–12
DECCA/DICKIES ("Red
  Foley's Dickies Souvenir
  Album"): 58 40–50
  (Decca Special Products issue for the Dickies
  Company.)
MCA 4–6
PICKWICK/HILLTOP:
  66 8–12
VOCALION: 65–71 6–12
  Also see KERR, Anita
  Also see WELLS, Kitty, & Red Foley

FOLKSWINGERS, The
Singles: 7-Inch
WORLD PACIFIC: 66 2–4
LPs: 10/12-Inch 33rpm
WORLD PACIFIC: 63–66 10–18
  Members: Glen Campbell; Tut Taylor; Harihar
  Rao.
  Also see CAMPBELL, Glen
  Also see SHANK, Bud

FONTAINE, Eddie
Singles: 7-Inch
ARGO: 58–59 10–15
CHANCELLOR: 58 15–20

Price Range

DECCA: 56–57 . . . . $5–8
LIBERTY: 65 3–5
SUNBEAM: 59 12–15
VIK 4–6
WARNER BROS: 62–63 3–5
X 4–6

FONTAINE, Frankie
Singles: 7-Inch
ABC-PARAMOUNT:
  62–65 2–4
CAPITOL: 63 2–4
Picture Sleeves
ABC-PARAMOUNT: 62 2–4
CAPITOL: 63 2–4
LPs: 10/12-Inch 33rpm
ABC-PARAMOUNT:
  62–66 10–20
MGM: 67 6–10

FONTANA, Wayne
Singles: 7-Inch
BRUT: 73 2–4
MGM: 66–67 3–5
METROMEDIA: 69 3–5
LPs: 10/12-Inch 33rpm
MGM: 67 12–15

**FONTANA, Wayne, & The
Mindbenders**
Singles: 7-Inch
FONTANA: 65 4–6
LPs: 10/12-Inch 33rpm
FONTANA: 65 30–35
  Also see FONTANA, Wayne
  Also see MINDBENDERS, The

FONTANE SISTERS, The
Singles: 7-Inch
DOT: 54–60 3–6
RCA VICTOR: 51–54 5–8
Picture Sleeves
RCA VICTOR: 54 5–8
EPs: 7-Inch 33/45rpm
DOT: 56–57 8–12
LPs: 10/12-Inch 33rpm
DOT: 56–63 15–20
  Members: Bea Fontane; Marge Fontane; Geri
  Fontane.
  Also see COMO, Perry, & The Fontane Sisters

Price Range

FOOLS, The
Singles: 12-Inch 33/45rpm
PVC **$4–6**
Singles: 7-Inch
EMI AMERICA: *80–81*............ **1–3**
Picture Sleeves
EMI AMERICA: *80*.............. **INC**
LPs: 10/12-Inch 33rpm
EMI AMERICA (Except
9393/4): *80–81*................. **5–8**
EMI AMERICA (9393/4
"April Fools Day"): *80* **10–15**
(Promotional issue only.)

FOOLS GOLD
Singles: 7-Inch
COLUMBIA: *77*.................. **2–3**
MORNING SKY: *76*.............. **2–3**
LPs: 10/12-Inch 33rpm
COLUMBIA: *77*.................. **8–10**
MORNING SKY: *76*.............. **8–10**

FORBERT, Steve
Singles: 7-Inch
NEMPEROR: *79–82* **1–3**
LPs: 10/12-Inch 33rpm
NEMPEROR: *79–82* **5–8**

FORCE MDs, The
Singles: 12-Inch 33/45rpm
TOMMY BOY: *84–86* **4–6**
Singles: 7-Inch
TOMMY BOY: *84–86* **2–3**
LPs: 10/12-Inch 33rpm
TOMMY BOY: *84–86* **5–8**

FORD, Dee Dee: see GARDNER, Don, & Dee Dee Ford

FORD, Frankie
Singles: 7-Inch
ABC: *73–74*..................... **1–3**
ACE: *58–60*..................... **5–8**
COLLECTABLES: *81* **1–3**
CONSTELLATION: *63*............ **3–5**
DOUBLOON: *67* **3–5**
IMPERIAL: *60–62*................ **4–6**
PAULA: *71*..................... **2–4**
SYC: *82* **2–3**

Price Range

Picture Sleeves
ACE: *60*....................... **$8–12**
EPs: 7-Inch 33/45rpm
ACE: *59*....................... **15–20**
LPs: 10/12-Inch 33rpm
ACE: *59*....................... **40–45**
BRIARMEADE: *76*............... **8–10**
Also see SMITH, Huey

FORD, Lita
Singles: 7-Inch
MERCURY: *84*................... **1–3**
LPs: 10/12-Inch 33rpm
MERCURY: *84*................... **5–8**
Also see RUNAWAYS, The

FORD, Mary: see PAUL, Les, & Mary Ford

FORD, Pennye
Singles: 12-Inch 33/45rpm
TOTAL EXPERIENCE:
84–85 .... **4–6**
Singles: 7-Inch
TOTAL EXPERIENCE:
84–85 .... **1–3**
LPs: 10/12-Inch 33rpm
TOTAL EXPERIENCE:
85 .... **5–8**

FORD, Tennessee Ernie
Singles: 7-Inch
CAPITOL (1275 through
2900 series): *50–54* **4–8**
(Purple labels. Ford's many "Boogie" titles represent the higher end of this price range.)
CAPITOL (2000 through
4100 series): *70–75* **1–3**
(Orange labels.)
CAPITOL (3000 through
4400 series): *54–60* **2–4**
CAPITOL (4500 through
5700 series): *61–67* **1–3**
Picture Sleeves
CAPITOL: *55–60*................. **3–5**
EPs: 7-Inch 33/45rpm
CAPITOL (Except 413):
55–61 .... **5–10**
CAPITOL (413;
"Backwoods Boogie &
Blues"): *53* **15–25**

Price Range

LPs: 10/12-Inch 33rpm
CAPITOL (Except 888):
56–80 . . . . **$5–15**
CAPITOL (888; "Ol'
Rockin' Ern"): 57 . . . . **25–35**
Also see LEE, Brenda / Tennessee Ernie Ford
Also see STARR, Kay, & Tennessee Ernie Ford

FORD, Tennessee Ernie, & Glen Campbell
LPs: 10/12-Inch 33rpm
CAPITOL: 75 . . . . **10–12**
Also see CAMPBELL, Glen

FORECAST
Singles: 12-Inch 33/45rpm
RCA VICTOR: 83 . . . . **4–6**
Singles: 7-Inch
ARIOLA: 80 . . . . **1–3**
RCA VICTOR: 83 . . . . **1–3**
LPs: 10/12-Inch 33rpm
RCA VICTOR: 83 . . . . **5–8**

FOREIGNER
Singles: 7-Inch
ATLANTIC: 77–85 . . . . **1–3**
ATLANTIC/WARNER:
79 . . . . **1–3**
Picture Sleeves
ATLANTIC: 78–85 . . . . **1–3**
LPs: 10/12-Inch 33rpm
ATLANTIC (Except
picture discs): 77–84 . . . . **5–8**
ATLANTIC (Picture
discs): 79 . . . . **20–25**
GEFFEN: 85 . . . . **5–8**
Members: Lou Gramm; Rick Wills; Mick
Jones; Dennis Elliott; Ian McDonald; Al
Greenwood.
Also see BAD COMPANY
Also see NEW JERSEY MASS CHOIR, The
Also see SPYS, The

FOREVER MORE
Singles: 7-Inch
RCA VICTOR: 69–70 . . . . **2–4**
LPs: 10/12-Inch 33rpm
RCA VICTOR: 69–70 . . . . **10–15**

FORMATIONS, The
Singles: 7-Inch
BANK: 68 . . . . **5–8**

Price Range

MGM: 68–69 . . . . **$3–5**

FORREST
Singles: 12-Inch 33/45rpm
PROFILE: 83 . . . . **4–6**

FORREST, Jimmy
Singles: 7-Inch
PRESTIGE: 61–62 . . . . **2–4**
TRIUMPH: 59 . . . . **3–5**
UNITED (Black vinyl):
52–55 . . . . **5–8**
UNITED (Colored vinyl):
52 . . . . **10–12**
LPs: 10/12-Inch 33rpm
NEW JAZZ: 60–64 . . . . **15–25**
PRESTIGE: 61–62 . . . . **15–25**
(Yellow label.)
PRESTIGE: 64 . . . . **10–15**
(Blue label.)
UNITED: 57 . . . . **60–75**
Also see DAVIS, Miles

FORTUNES, The
Singles: 7-Inch
CAPITOL: 71–74 . . . . **2–3**
LONDON **1–3**
PRESS: 65–66 . . . . **4–6**
UNITED ARTISTS: 67–68 . . . . **3–5**
WORLD PACIFIC: 70 . . . . **2–3**
LPs: 10/12-Inch 33rpm
CAPITOL: 71–73 . . . . **8–10**
COCA-COLA **25–35**
PRESS: 65 . . . . **25–30**
WORLD PACIFIC: 70 . . . . **8–10**

FORUM, The
Singles: 7-Inch
MIRA: 67 . . . . **3–5**
PENTHOUSE: 66 . . . . **5–8**
LPs: 10/12-Inch 33rpm
MIRA: 67 . . . . **15–20**
Members: Phil Campos; Rene Nole; Riselle
Vaine.

FOSTER, Bruce
Singles: 7-Inch
MILLENNIUM: 77 . . . . **1–3**
Picture Sleeves
MILLENNIUM: 77 . . . . **INC**

Price Range

FOSTER, David
Singles: 7-Inch
ATLANTIC: *85* $1–3
LPs: 10/12-Inch 33rpm
ATLANTIC: *86* 5–8

FOSTER, David, & Olivia Newton-John
Singles: 7-Inch
ATLANTIC: *86* 1–3
Also see FOSTER, David
Also see NEWTON-JOHN, Olivia

FOTOMAKER
Singles: 7-Inch
ATLANTIC: *78–79* 2–3
LPs: 10/12-Inch 33rpm
ATLANTIC: *78–79* 5–8
Members: Gene Cornish; Dino Dannelli; Wally Bryson.
Also see BULLDOG
Also see RASCALS, The

FOUNDATIONS, The
Singles: 7-Inch
UNI: *67–71* 3–5
LPs: 10/12-Inch 33rpm
UNI: *68–69* 15–20

FOUNTAIN, Pete
Singles: 7-Inch
CORAL: *58–62* 2–3
LPs: 10/12-Inch 33rpm
CORAL: *59–69* 5–15
FIRST AMERICAN: *78* 4–6
Also see HIRT, Al, & Pete Fountain
Also see LEE, Brenda, & Pete Fountain

FOUNTAIN, Roosevelt, & The Pens of Rhythm
Singles: 7-Inch
PRINCE-ADAMS: *62–63* 3–5

FOUR ACES, The
Singles: 7-Inch
ABC PARAMOUNT: *60*............ 2–4
DECCA (25000 series):
61–64 2–3
DECCA (27000 & 28000 series): *51–53* 5–8

Price Range

DECCA (29000 through 31000 series): *54–60* $4–6
FLASH: *50* 10–15
MERION: *52*. 10–15
RADNOR: *69*. 1–3
VICTORIA (Black vinyl):
51 10–15
VICTORIA (Colored vinyl): *51* 20–30
Picture Sleeves
ABC-PARAMOUNT: *60*............ 2–4
EPs: 7-Inch 33/45rpm
DECCA: *52–59* 10–20
LPs: 10/12-Inch 33rpm
ACCORD: *81–82* 5–8
DECCA (8100 through 8500 series): *55–56* 15–25
DECCA (8600 through 8900 series): *57–59* 10–20
MCA: *74* 5–10
UNITED ARTISTS: *61*........... 10–15
VOCALION: *69* 5–10
Members: Al Alberts; Louis Silvestri; Dave Mahoney; Sol Vocarro.

FOUR ACES, The / The Four Lads / The Four Preps
LPs: 10/12-Inch 33rpm
EXACT: *80* 5–8
Also see FOUR ACES, The
Also see FOUR LADS, The
Also see FOUR PREPS, The

FOUR BLAZES, The (Featuring Tommy Braden)
Singles: 7-Inch
UNITED (100 series):
52–54 25–30
(Colored vinyl.)
UNITED (100 series, except 114): *52–54*............. 10–15
(Black vinyl.)
UNITED (114; "Mary Jo"): *52*. 25–30

FOUR BUDDIES, The (The Four Buds)
Singles: 7-Inch
SAVOY (700 series): *50–51* 50–60
SAVOY (817; "Heart & Soul"): *51*. 50–60

Price Range

SAVOY (845; "You're Part
Of Me"): *52* **$35–40**
SAVOY (866; "What's The
Matter With Me"): *52* **35–40**
SAVOY (888; "My
Mother's Eyes"): *53* **20–25**
 Members: Leon Harrison; Greg Carroll; Bert
 Palmer; Tommy Smith.

FOUR COINS, The
Singles: 7-Inch
COLUMBIA: *67* **2–3**
EPIC: *54–59* **2–4**
JOY: *64* **1–3**
JUBILEE: *61–62* **2–3**
MGM: *60–61* **2–3**
VEE JAY: *62–63* **2–3**
   Picture Sleeves
EPIC: *57* **2–4**
  EPs: 7-Inch 33/45rpm
EPIC: *55–58* **5–10**
  LPs: 10/12-Inch 33rpm
EPIC: *55–58* **10–15**
MGM: *61* **8–12**
ROULETTE: *65* **6–10**

FOUR DATES, The
Singles: 7-Inch
CHANCELLOR: *58* **5–8**
 Also see FABIAN

FOUR ESQUIRES, The
Singles: 7-Inch
ROULETTE **1–3**
TERRACE: *63* **3–5**

450 SL
Singles: 7-Inch
GOLDEN BOY: *85* **1–3**

FOUR FELLOWS, The
Singles: 7-Inch
DERBY: *54* **20–25**
GLORY (Except 231):
55–57 .... **8–12**
GLORY (231; "I Wish I
Didn't Know You"): *55* **15–18**
 Members: David Jones; Ted Williams; Larry
 Banks; Jim McGowan.
 Also see McLAURIN, Bette

Price Range

FOUR FRESHMEN, The
Singles: 7-Inch
CAPITOL: *50–65* **$2–4**
DECCA: *67* **2–3**
LIBERTY: *68* **1–3**
   Picture Sleeves
CAPITOL: *63* **2–4**
  EPs: 7-Inch 33/45rpm
CAPITOL: *54–59* **4–8**
  LPs: 10/12-Inch 33rpm
CAPITOL ("SM" prefix):
75–79 .... **5–8**
CAPITOL ("T" or "ST"
prefix): *54–64* **10–15**
LIBERTY: *68–82* **5–10**
SUNSET: *70* **5–8**
 Members: Don Barbour; Ross Barbour; Ken
 Errair; Bob Flanagan.

FOUR JACKS & A JILL
Singles: 7-Inch
RCA: *68* **3–5**
  LPs: 10/12-Inch 33rpm
RCA VICTOR: *68* **10–15**

FOUR KNIGHTS, The
Singles: 7-Inch
CAPITOL (346; "Spotlight
Songs"): *52* **20–30**
 (Boxed set of three 45rpm singles.)
CAPITOL (1000 & 2000
series): *51–54* **6–10**
CAPITOL (3000 series):
55–57 .... **4–6**

Price Range

CORAL (61000 & 62000
series): *58–59* **$5–8**
DECCA (48018; "He'll
Understand And Say
Well Done"): *52* **20–25**
(45rpm reissue of a 1947 78rpm.)
SOUVENIR: *62* **3–5**

EPs: 7-Inch 33/45rpm
CAPITOL: *52–54* **35–45**

LPs: 10/12-Inch 33rpm
CAPITOL: *52* **50–75**

FOUR LADS, The
Singles: 7-Inch
COLUMBIA: *52–60* **2–4**
DOT: *62* **2–3**
FONA: *77–78* **1–3**
KAPP: *60–61* **2–4**
OKEH: *52* **3–5**
UNITED ARTISTS: *63–69* **1–3**

Picture Sleeves
COLUMBIA: *57–59* **2–4**
KAPP: *60* **2–4**

EPs: 7-Inch 33/45rpm
COLUMBIA: *55–59* **4–8**

LPs: 10/12-Inch 33rpm
COLUMBIA: *54–60* **10–15**
DOT: *62–63* **8–12**
KAPP: *61* **8–12**
HARMONY: *69* **5–10**
UNITED ARTISTS: *64* **6–10**

Price Range

Members: Frankie Busseri; Jimmy Arnold;
Connie Coderini; Bernie Toorish.
Also see FOUR ACES, The / The Four Lads
/ The Four Preps
Also see LAINE, Frankie, & The Four Lads
Also see RAY, Johnnie

FOUR LOVERS, The
Singles: 7-Inch
EPIC: *57* **$150–175**
RCA VICTOR: *56–57* **15–20**
EPs: 7-Inch 33/45rpm
RCA VICTOR (47; "The
Four Lovers/Homer &
Jethro"): *56* **20–25**
(Promotional issue only. Not issued with
cover.)
RCA VICTOR (64; "The
Four Lovers/Teddi
King"): *56* **20–25**
(Promotional issue only. Not issued with
cover.)
RCA VICTOR (869; "The
Four Lovers"): *56* **100–125**
RCA VICTOR (871;
"Joyride"): *56* **75–100**
LPs: 10/12-Inch 33rpm
RCA VICTOR: *56* **250–300**
Members: Frankie Valli; Tom Devito; Nick
Devito; Hank Majewski.
Also see HOMER & JETHRO
Also see 4 SEASONS, The
Also see VALLI, Frankie

FOUR PENNIES, The (The Chiffons)
Singles: 7-Inch
LAURIE **2–3**
RUST: *63* **10–15**
Also see CHIFFONS, The

FOUR PREPS, The
Singles: 7-Inch
CAPITOL (Purple labels):
56–61 .... **4–6**
CAPITOL (Orange &
yellow labels): *62–67* **3–5**
Picture Sleeves
CAPITOL: *61* **3–5**
EPs: 7-Inch 33/45rpm
CAPITOL: *56–58* **8–10**
LPs: 10/12-Inch 33rpm
CAPITOL: *58–67* **10–20**

Price Range

Members: Bruce Belland; Glen Larson; Marv Ingraham; Ed Cobb.
Also see FOUR ACES, The / The Four Lads / The Four Preps

4 SEASONS, The (The Four Seasons; Frankie Valli & The 4 Seasons)

Singles: 7-Inch
BOB CREWE PRESENTS:
  70 .... **$10–12**
  (Promotional issue only.)
COLLECTABLES: *81* **1–3**
COLUMBIA (6675; "Big
  Man's World"): *64* **20–30**
  (Promotional soundsheet.)
CREWE: *69*. **3–5**
GONE: *61* **20–25**
GORDA: *65* **4–6**
MOTOWN: *73*. **5–8**
MOWEST: *72* **5–8**
OLDIES 45: *62–63* **3–5**
PHILIPS (40166 through
  40662): *64–69*. **3–5**
PHILIPS (40688; "Lay Me
  Down"): *70*. **15–20**
PHILIPS (40694; "Where
  Are My Dreams"): *70*. **20–25**
RAINBOW: *62* **3–5**
SEASONS 4-EVER (Black
  vinyl): *71* **4–6**
SEASONS 4-EVER
  (Colored vinyl): *71* **10–12**
VEE JAY (456 through
  562): *62–63*. **4–6**
VEE JAY (576;
  "Stay"/"Peanuts"): *63* **40–50**
VEE JAY (582;
  "Stay"/"Goodnight My
  Love"): *64* **3–5**
VEE JAY (597; "Alone" -
  yellow label): *64*. **10–12**
VEE JAY (597; "Alone" -
  black label): *64*. **4–6**
VEE JAY (608 through
  719): *64–66*. **5–8**
WABC RADIO: *64* **50–60**
  (Special products custom pressing.)
WXYZ-DETROIT: *65* **25–30**
  (Special products custom pressing.)
WARNER BROS: *75–80*. **2–3**
WIBBAGE: *65* **25–30**

Price Range

(Special products custom pressing.)

Picture Sleeves
PHILIPS (Except 40524):
  64–68 .... **$6–10**
PHILIPS (40524;
  "Saturday's Father"): *68* **15–20**
  (Fold-out sleeve.)
PHILIPS (40524;
  "Saturday's Father"): *68* **5–8**
  (Standard sleeve.)
VEE JAY: *64*. **8–12**

EPs: 7-Inch 33/45rpm
PHILIPS: *68* **15–20**
VEE JAY: *64*. **15–20**

LPs: 10/12-Inch 33rpm
ARISTA: *84* **8–12**
K-TEL: *77*. **15–20**
LONGINES. **20–25**
  (TV mail-order offer.)
MCA: *85* **5–8**
MOTOWN: *80*. **5–8**
MOWEST **10–12**
PHILLIPS (124; "Dawn &
  11 Other Great Hits"):
  64 .... **15–20**
PHILLIPS (129; "Born To
  Wander"): *64*. **15–20**
PHILLIPS (146; "Rag
  Doll"): *64*. **15–20**
PHILLIPS (150; "All The
  Song Hits"): *64* **15–20**
PHILLIPS (164; "The 4
  Seasons Entertain You"):
  65 .... **15–20**
PHILLIPS (193; "The 4
  Seasons Sing Big Hits By
  Burt Bacharach, Hal
  David & Bob Dylan"):
  65 .... **45-55**
  (With photos of the group on the front and back
  cover.)
PHILLIPS (193; "The 4
  Seasons Sing Big Hits By
  Burt Bacharach, Hal
  David & Bob Dylan"):
  65 .... **12-15**
  (Does not have group photos on front and back
  cover.)
PHILLIPS (196; "Gold
  Vault Of Hits"): *65*. **15–20**

Price Range

VEE JAY (1100 series):
64–65 .... **$15–20**
WARNER BROS: *75–81* **8–10**
Members: Frankie Valli; Tom Devito; Nick
Devito; Hank Majewski; Bob Gaudio; Charlie
Calello; Nick Massi; Joe Long; Don Ciccione;
Bill Deloach; Paul Wilson.
Also see BEATLES, The / The 4 Seasons
Also see CRITTERS, The
Also see FOUR LOVERS, The
Also see ROYAL TEENS, The
Also see SANTOS, Larry
Also see VALLI, Frankie
Also see WONDER WHO, The

4 SEASONS, The / The Shirelles
Singles: 7-Inch
COKE: *65* **20–30**
(Coca-Cola radio spots. Issued to radio stations
only.)
Also see SHIRELLES, The

4 SEASONS, The / Ray Stevens
Singles: 7-Inch
OLDIES 45: *63* **5–8**
Also see 4 SEASONS, The
Also see STEVENS, Ray

FOUR SONICS, The
Singles: 7-Inch
SPORT: *68.* **3–5**

FOUR SPORTSMEN
Singles: 7-Inch
SUNNYBROOK: *60–62.* **4–6**

FOUR TOPS, The
Singles: 12-Inch 33/45rpm
ABC: *77–78* **4–6**
Singles: 7-Inch
ABC: *75–79* **2–3**
CASABLANCA: *81–82* **2–3**
CHESS: *56* **35–40**
COLUMBIA (41755;
"Ain't That Love"): *60* **20–25**
COLUMBIA (43356;
"Ain't That Love"): *65* **4–6**
DUNHILL: *72–74.* **2–3**
MOTOWN (400 series) **1–3**
MOTOWN (1000 through
1200 series): *64–72* **3–5**
MOTOWN (1700 series):
83–85 .... **1–3**

Price Range

PHILLIPS (201; "Working
My Way Back To
You"): *66* **$15–20**
PHILLIPS (221; "2nd
Gold Vault Of Hits"): *66* **15–20**
PHILLIPS (222; "Lookin'
Back"): *66* **15–20**
PHILLIPS (223;
"Christmas Album"): *66* **12–15**
PHILLIPS (243; "New
Gold Hits"): *67* **15–20**
PHILLIPS (290; "Genuine
Imitation Life Gazette"):
69 .... **35–45**
(With yellow cover.)
PHILLIPS (290; "Genuine
Imitation Life Gazette"):
69 .... **10–12**
(With white cover.)
PHILLIPS (341; "Half &
Half"): *70.* **10–12**
PHILLIPS (2-6501;
"Edizone D'Oro"): *68.* **20–25**
PICKWICK: *70* **8–10**
PRIVATE STOCK: *75.* **10–12**
SEARS: *70.* **20–25**
VEE JAY (1000 series
except 1082 & 1088):
62–63 .... **30–35**
VEE JAY (1082;
"Folk-Nanny"): *64* **30–40**
VEE JAY (1082; "Stay &
Other Great Hits"): *64* **15–20**
(Repackage of "Folk-Nanny.")
VEE JAY (1088; "More
Golden Hits"): *64* **15–20**

Price Range

RSO: *82* **$2–3**
RIVERSIDE: *62* **20–25**
Picture Sleeves
MOTOWN: *66–70.* **3–5**
LPs: 10/12-Inch 33rpm
ABC: *75–78* **8–10**
CASABLANCA: *81–82* **5–8**
COMMAND: *74* **10–12**
DUNHILL: *72–74.* **8–10**
MOTOWN (Except 100 &
200 series): *64–72* **10–20**
MOTOWN (100 & 200
series): *82–84* **5–8**
NATURAL RESOURCES:
78 . . . . **8–10**
WORKSHOP: *62* **100–125**
Members: Levi Stubbs; Lawrence Payton;
Abdul "Duke" Fakir; Obie Benson.
Also see SUPREMES, The, & The Four Tops

FOUR TOPS, The / The Temptations
LPs: 10/12-Inch 33rpm
SILVER EAGLE: *87* **6–10**
Also see FOUR TOPS, The
Also see TEMPTATIONS, The

FOUR TUNES, The
Singles: 7-Inch
JUBILEE: *53–57* **4–6**
KAY-RON **5–8**
RCA VICTOR (3881
through 4102): *50–51* **15–20**
RCA VICTOR (4241
through 4305): *51* **10–15**
RCA VICTOR (4427; "I'll
See You In My
Dreams"): *51* **15–20**
RCA VICTOR (4489
through 5532): *52–53* **5–8**
RCA VICTOR (50-0000
series): *49–51* **25–35**
VIRGO: *72* **1–3**
EPs: 7-Inch 33/45rpm
RCA VICTOR: *54* **25–30**
LPs: 10/12-Inch 33rpm
JUBILEE **30–35**
Members: Jim Nabbie; Danny Owens; Pat Best;
Jimmy Gordon; Deek Watson.

FOUR VOICES, The
Singles: 7-Inch
COLUMBIA: *55–60* **3–5**

Price Range

PEACOCK: *62* **$2–3**

FOUR-EVERS, The
Singles: 7-Inch
CHATTAHOOCHEE: *64* **3–5**
COLUMBIA (Except
42303): *66* **3–5**
COLUMBIA (42303; "You
Belong To Me"): *62* **20–25**
CONSTELLATION: *65* **10–12**
JAMIE: *63* **5–8**
RED BIRD: *66* **10–12**
SMASH (1887; "Please Be
Mine"): *63* **5–8**
SMASH (1887; "Be My
Girl"): *64* **3–5**

FOWLEY, Kim
Singles: 7-Inch
CAPITOL: *72–73* **2–4**
CORBY: *65* **8–10**
IMPERIAL: *68–69* **3–5**
LIVING LEGEND: *65–66* **8–10**
LOMA: *66* **4–6**
REPRISE: *67.* **3–5**
TOWER: *67.* **3–5**
LPs: 10/12-Inch 33rpm
CAPITOL: *72–74* **10–12**
IMPERIAL: *68–69* **15–20**
PVC: *79* **5–8**
TOWER: *67.* **15–20**
Also see KING LIZARD

FOX
Singles: 7-Inch
ARIOLA/GTO: *75.* **2–3**
GTO: *74.* **2–4**
LPs: 10/12-Inch 33rpm
ARIOLA AMERICA: *75* **8–10**

FOX, Charles
Singles: 7-Inch
HANDSHAKE: *81.* **1–3**

FOX, Virgil
LPs: 10/12-Inch 33rpm
DECCA: *71* **5–10**

FOXX, Inez (Inez & Charlie Foxx)
Singles: 7-Inch
DYNAMO: *67–70.* **3–5**

Price Range

MUSICOR: *66–68*................ **$3–5**
SUE: *65* **3–5**
SYMBOL: *63–64*................. **4–6**
VOLT: *72–73*................... **2–4**
UNITED ARTISTS: *74*............ **2–3**
LPs: 10/12-Inch 33rpm
DYNAMO: *67*................... **10–15**
SUE: *65* **20–25**
SYMBOL: *63*................... **25–30**
VOLT: *73*...................... **8–10**
Also see PLATTERS, The / Inez & Charlie
Foxx / The Jive Five / Tommy Hunt

FOXX, Redd (Redd Foxx & Hattie Noel)
Singles: 7-Inch
DOOTO: *57–61*.................. **2–4**
DOOTONE: *56–57*............... **3–5**
EPs: 7-Inch 33/45rpm
DOOTO: *57–61*.................. **5–8**
DOOTONE: *56–57*............... **5–10**
LPs: 10/12-Inch 33rpm
ATLANTIC: *75* **5–8**
AUTHENTIC: *55–56*............ **15–25**
DOOTO: *60–74*................. **5–15**
DOOTONE: *57*................. **10–20**
KING: *69–71*................... **5–10**
LAFF: *79*...................... **5–8**
LOMA: *66–68*.................. **8–12**
RCA VICTOR: *72* **5–10**
WARNER BROS: *69*............. **8–10**

FOXY
Singles: 7-Inch
DASH: *76–80*................... **1–3**
LPs: 10/12-Inch 33rpm
DASH: *78–80*................... **5–8**
Also see OXO

FOZZIE BEAR: see KERMIT / Fozzie Bear

FRAMPTON, Peter
Singles: 7-Inch
A&M: *74–81* **2–5**
Picture Sleeves
A&M: *76–81* **2–4**
LPs: 10/12-Inch 33rpm
A&M (Except picture
discs): *73–82*................ **6–12**
A&M ("I'm In You"): *77* **50–60**

Price Range

(Picture disc.)
A&M ("Frampton Comes
Alive"): *79*.................. **$15–20**
(Picture disc. Promotional issue only.)
Also see FRAMPTON'S CAMEL
Also see STARR, Ringo

FRAMPTON'S CAMEL (Peter Frampton)
Singles: 7-Inch
A&M: *72–73* **5–8**
Also see FRAMPTON, Peter
Also see HUMBLE PIE

FRANCE JOLI: see JOLI, France

FRANCHI, Sergio
Singles: 7-Inch
LAX: *79*...................... **1–3**
METROMEDIA: *71–72*........... **1–3**
RCA VICTOR: *62–67* **2–3**
UNITED ARTISTS: *69–70*........ **1–3**
LPs: 10/12-Inch 33rpm
FOUR CORNERS: *66*............ **6–10**
RCA VICTOR: *62–77* **5–15**
UNITED ARTISTS: *70*........... **5–10**

FRANCIS, Connie
Singles: 7-Inch
GSF: *73* **2–3**
MGM (3000 series): *71*.......... **2–3**
MGM (12122 through
12555): *55–57*............... **10–15**
MGM (12588 through
13116): *58–63*............... **4–6**
MGM (13127 through
14034): *64–69*............... **3–5**
MGM (14500 series): *81*......... **1–3**
MGM (50000 series):
59–60...................... **10–15**
(Stereo singles.)
POLYDOR: *83* **1–3**
Picture Sleeves
MGM (12700 through
12900 series): *58–61* **5–10**
MGM (13000 & 14000
series): *61–69*............... **3–5**
EPs: 7-Inch 33/45
MGM: *58–62*.................. **10–15**
LPs: 10/12-Inch 33rpm
LEO **12–15**

Price Range

LION **$12–15**
MGM (100 series): *70.* **10–15**
MGM (3700 series): *58–60.* **20–30**
MGM (3800 & 3900
  series): *60–61* **15–25**
MGM (4000 series): *62–69.* **12–18**
MGM (5400 series) **5–8**
MGM (10000 series): *71.* **8–12**
METRO: *65–66.* **10–15**
POLYDOR: *83* **5–8**
SESSIONS: *75.* **8–10**
  Also see RAINWATER, Marvin, & Connie
  Francis

FRANCIS, Connie, & Hank Williams, Jr.
LPs: 10/12-Inch 33rpm
MGM: *64.* **15–25**
  Also see FRANCIS, Connie
  Also see WILLIAMS, Hank, Jr.

FRANKE & THE KNOCKOUTS
Singles: 7-Inch
MCA: *84* **2–3**
MILLENNIUM: *81–82* **2–3**
LPs: 10/12-Inch 33rpm
MCA: *84* **5–8**
MILLENNIUM: *81–82* **5–8**

FRANKIE & THE SPINDELS
Singles: 7-Inch
ROC-KER: *68.* **3–5**

FRANKIE GOES TO HOLLYWOOD
Singles: 12-Inch 33/45rpm
ISLAND: *84–85* **4–6**
Singles: 7-Inch
ISLAND: *84–85* **1–3**
LPs: 10/12-Inch 33rpm
ISLAND: *84* **5–8**
  Members: Holly Johnson; Paul Rutherford.

FRANKLIN, Aretha
Singles: 12-Inch 33/45rpm
ARISTA: *84–85.* **4–6**
Singles: 7-Inch
ARISTA: *80–83.* **1–3**
ATLANTIC (2000 series):
  67–74 . . . . **3–5**

Price Range

ATLANTIC (3000 series):
  74–77 . . . . **$2–3**
CHECKER: *60* **5–8**
COLUMBIA (Except
  44000 series): *60–67* **3–5**
COLUMBIA (44000
  series): *67–68* **2–4**
CHESS: *73* **1–3**
Picture Sleeves
COLUMBIA: *62–63* **3–5**
LPs: 10/12-Inch 33rpm
ARISTA: *80–83.* **5–8**
ATLANTIC: *67–79* **8–12**
CANDLELITE: *77.* **8–10**
CHECKER: *65* **12–15**
COLUMBIA (12; "Aretha
  Franklin"): *68* **10–15**
COLUMBIA (1612
  through 2281): *61–64* **12–20**
COLUMBIA (2300
  through 2700 series):
  65–67 . . . . **10–15**
. COLUMBIA (8402
  through 9081): *61–64* **12–25**
  (With a "CS" prefix.)
COLUMBIA (9100
  through 9700 series):
  65–69 . . . . **10–15**
  (With a "CS" prefix.)
COLUMBIA (10000
  series): *73* **5–10**
COLUMBIA (30000
  series): *72–82* **5–10**
HARMONY: *68–71* **10–12**
UPFRONT: *79* **5–8**
  Also see CLEMONS, Clarence
  Also see EURYTHMICS, The, & Aretha
  Franklin
  Also see SANTANA
  Also see SWEET INSPIRATIONS, The
  Also see WOLF, Peter

FRANKLIN, Aretha, & George Benson
Singles: 7-Inch
ARISTA: *81* **1–3**
  Also see BENSON, George

Price Range

EPs: 7-Inch 33/45rpm
CAPITOL: *54* **$5–10**
Also see CARR, Joe "Fingers"
Also see FRAZIER, Dallas

FREBERG, Stan (The Stan Freberg Show)

Singles: 7-Inch

BELFAST SPARKLING
WATER (1515;
"Invisible Bubbles") **50–75**
(Contains product commercials for radio station use.)

BIG SOUND (2; "Jockey's
Little Helper") **35–50**
(Contains product commercials for radio station use.)

BUBBLE UP (2227;
"Music To Bubble Up
By") **20–30**
(Contains product commercials for radio station use.)

BUTTERNUT COFFEE
(2000; "Instant Sales For
Instant Butternut By
Instant Freberg") **40–50**
(Contains product commercials for radio station use.)

BUTTERNUT COFFEE
(2237; "Amazing
Butternut Coffee") **25–35**
(Contains product commercials for radio station use.)

CAPITOL (415;
"Wun'erful Wun'erful"):
57 .... **10–15**
(One-sided disc. Promotional issue only.)

CAPITOL (1200 through
3100 series, except 2125):
50–54 .... **10–20**

CAPITOL (2125; "Abe
Snake For President"):
52 .... **30–40**

CAPITOL (3200 through
5700 series): *54–66* **5–10**

COCA COLA BOTTLING
CO. (2227; "Music To
Bubble-Up By") **30–50**
(Contains product commercials for radio station use.)

CONTADINA (4476; "The
Whole Peeled Bounce") **35–50**

Price Range

(Contains product commercials for radio station use. With The Hi Lo's.)

MILKY WAY (23300;
"Tom Sweet & His
Milky Way Machine") **$35–50**

PITTSBURGH PAINT (1/
2; "Four Pittsburgh
Paint commercials") **20–30**
(Contains product commercials for radio station use.)

RADIO (2225; "Who
Listens To Radio") **25–40**
(Contains promotional spots for using radio advertising.)

SOUTHERN BAPTIST
CHURCH (101578;
"Southern Baptist Radio
& TV Commission") **15-20**
(Contains product commercials for radio station use.)

STAINLESS STEEL
(1369; "Stainless Steel") **35–50**
(Contains product commercials for radio station use.)

STAN FREBERG ON
COMMERCIALS
("Rubblemeyer Farms") **40–60**
(Promotional issue only. Contains radio commercial parodies, comparing the right and wrong approach to producing radio spots.)

TERMINIX (3540; "Floor
Show, Now Going On
At Your House") **30–40**
(Contains product commercials for radio station use.)

UNITED
PRESBYTERIAN
CHURCH (101578;
"The Presbyterian
Church") **15–20**
(Contains product commercials for radio station use.)

ZEE (2020; "Zee With
Freberg – Hey You Up
There") **35–50**
(Contains product commercials for radio station use.)

ZEE (24005; "Zee Spot
Commercials") **35–50**
(Contains product commercials for radio station use.)

Price Range

Picture Sleeves

BUBBLE UP (2227;
"Music To Bubble Up
By") **$85–100**
(Fold-open sleeve for product commercial disc.)

CAPITOL (415;
"Wun'erful Wun'erful"):
57 .... **15–20**
(Promotional issue only.)

CAPITOL (4097; "Green
Christmas"): *58* **6–12**

CAPITOL (4329; "The Old
Payola Roll Blues"): *60* **15–20**

CAPITOL (5726;
"Flackman & Reagan"):
66 .... **10–15**

PITTSBURGH PAINT (1/
2; "Four Pittsburgh
Paint commercials") **20–30**
(Sleeve for product commercial disc. Reads:
"The Stations Representatives Assn. presents:
Some Exciting new commercials for Radio!")

RADIO (2225; "Who
Listens To Radio") **25–40**
(Sleeve for product commercial disc.)

SOUTHERN BAPTIST
CHURCH (101578;
"Southern Baptist Radio
& TV Commission") **15-20**
(Sleeve for product commercial disc.)

TERMINIX (3540; "Floor
Show") **10–20**
(Sleeve for product commercial disc.)

ZEE (2020; "Zee Here, Mr.
Freberg") **35–50**
(Sleeve for product commercial disc.)

EPs: 7-Inch 33/45rpm

CAPITOL (496; "Any
Requests"): *54* **20–30**

CAPITOL (628; "Real St.
George"): *55*. **15–25**

CAPITOL (731; "Elderly
Man River"): *58* **35–50**

CAPITOL (732; "The Best
Of The Stan Freberg
Show"): *58* **40–50**
(Promotional issue only.)

CAPITOL (1101;
"Omaha"): *59*. **15–25**

Price Range

CAPITOL (1589; "Stan
Freberg"): *61* **$25–40**
(Compact 33 issue.)

SWIMSUITSMANSHIP
(2080;
"Swimsuitsmanship") **100–125**
(Promotional issue only. Cover reads: "Fit
Facts & Figures...You & Rose Marie Reid.")

UNITED
PRESBYTERIAN
CHURCH (1400 "Is
God Dead?") **30–45**
(Contains product commercials for radio sta-
tion use.)

LPs: 10/12-Inch 33rpm

BEKINS (27713; "Bekins
Presents The Sound Of
Moving") **35–50**
(Contains product commercials for radio sta-
tion use.)

BUTTERNUT COFFEE
(2000; "Instant Butternut
Coffee") **40–60**
(Contains product commercials for radio station use.)

CAPITOL (777; "A
Child's Garden Of
Freberg"): *57*. **20–40**

CAPITOL (1035; "The
Best Of The Stan
Freberg Shows"): *58* **40–60**

CAPITOL (1242; "Stan
Freberg With The
Original Cast"): *59* **20–35**
(With a "T" prefix.)

CAPITOL (1242; "Stan
Freberg With The
Original Cast"): *69* **12–20**
(With a "DT" prefix.)

CAPITOL (1242; "Stan
Freberg With The
Original Cast"): *75* **5–8**
(With an "SM" prefix.)

CAPITOL (1573; "Stan
Freberg Presents The
United States Of
America, Volume 1 -
The Early Years"): *61*. **25-25**
(With a "W" or "SW" prefix.)

CAPITOL (1694; "Face
The Funnies"): *62* **25–35**

Price Range

CAPITOL (1816;
"Madison Avenue
Werewolf"): *62.* **$25–35**
CAPITOL (2020; "Best Of
Stan Freberg"): *64.* **15–25**
CAPITOL (2551; "Freberg
Underground): *66* **15–25**
  (With a "T" or "ST" prefix.)
CAPITOL (2551; "Freberg
Underground): *75* **5–8**
  (With an "SM" prefix.)
CAPITOL (3264; "Mickey
Mouse's Birthday
Party"): *63* **15–25**
CAPITOL (11000 series):
78 . . . . **5–8**
CAPITOL (80700; "Uncle
Stan Wants You"): *61.* **60–80**
  (Promotional issue for the LP series, "Stan Fre-
  berg Presents The United States Of America.")
COCA COLA (2468; "The
Freedle Family Singers") **175–200**
COLUMBIA (105948;
"Hey, Look Us Over") **60–75**
  (Promotional issue only. With booklet.)
KAISER FOIL (22077; "A
Kaiser Foil Salesman
Faces Life") **125–175**
  (A 10-Inch LP. Contains product commercials
  for radio station use.)
MEADOWGOLD (2152;
"Meadowgold Dairies") **85–100**
  (Contains product commercials for radio sta-
  tion use.)
OREGON (2039; "Oregon
Soundtrack") **125–150**
  (Contains product commercials for radio sta-
  tion use. Includes press kit.)
RADIO (3; "Radio
Briefings") **35–50**
  (Contains promotional spots for using radio ad-
  vertising.)
RADIO (1499; "More
Here Than Meets The
Ear") **30–45**
  (Contains promotional spots for using radio ad-
  vertising.)
RADIO (2226; "Who
Listens To Radio") **35–50**
  (Contains promotional spots for using radio ad-
  vertising.)

Price Range

TV GUIDE (2889; "TV
Guide Spots") **$60–75**
  (Contains product commercials for radio sta-
  tion use.)
Note: Advertising agency discs, containing
commercials for radio station use, are listed by
product name since there are no label names
used.
Members: Stan Freberg; Daws Butler; June
Foray; George Burns; Jesse White; Peter Leeds;
Paul Frees; Billy May.

FRED, John (John Fred & His Playboy Band)
Singles: 7-Inch
JEWEL: *64–65.* **5–8**
MONTEL: *59–62* **10–12**
N-JOY **8–10**
PAULA: *65–69* **3–5**
UNI: *69–70* **2–4**
LPs: 10/12-Inch 33rpm
PAULA: *66–68* **20–25**
UNI: *70* **15–20**

FRED & THE NEW J.B.s
Singles: 7-Inch
PEOPLE: *75* **2–3**

FREDDIE & THE DREAMERS
Singles: 7-Inch
CAPITOL: *63–64* **15–20**
ERIC **1–3**
MERCURY: *64–65.* **3–5**
SUPER K: *70* **2–4**
TOWER: *65.* **3–5**

Price Range

Picture Sleeves
MERCURY: 65................... $4–6

EPs: 7-Inch 33/45rpm
MERCURY (74;
"Interview With The
Dreamers"): 65 20–25
(Promotional issue only.)

LPs: 10/12-Inch 33rpm
CAPITOL: 76–79 8–10
MERCURY: 65–66.............. 20–25
TOWER: 65.................... 20–25
Also see JONES, Tom / Freddie & The Dream-
ers / Johnny Rivers

FREDERICK
Singles: 12-Inch 33/45rpm
HEAT: 85 4–6

FREDERICK II
Singles: 7-Inch
VULTURE: 71 2–4

FREE
Singles: 7-Inch
A&M: 70–71 2–4
ISLAND: 72 2–3

LPs: 10/12-Inch 33rpm
A&M: 69–75 10–15
ISLAND: 73 8–10
Members: Andy Fraser; Paul Rodgers: Simon
Kirke; Paul Kosoff.
Also see BACK STREET CRAWLER
Also see BAD COMPANY
Also see FRASER, Andy
Also see KOSSOFF, Paul
Also see KOSSOFF/KIRKE/TETSU/RAB-
BIT
Also see RODGERS, Paul

FREE EXPRESSION
Singles: 7-Inch
VANGUARD: 81................. 1–3

FREE MOVEMENT, The
Singles: 7-Inch
COLUMBIA: 71.................. 2–3
DECCA: 71..................... 2–3

LPs: 10/12-Inch 33rpm
COLUMBIA: 72................. 8–10

Price Range

FREEMAN, Bobby
Singles: 7-Inch
ABC: 73...................... $1–3
AUTUMN: 63–64................. 3–5
DOUBLE SHOT: 69–70............ 2–4
GUSTO 1–3
JOSIE: 58–62.................. 5–8
KING: 60–65................... 4–6
LOMA: 67..................... 3–5
VIRGO: 72.................... 1–3

LPs: 10/12-Inch 33rpm
AUTUMN: 64................... 20–25
JOSIE: 65.................... 15–20
JUBILEE (1000 series): 59........ 35–45
JUBILEE (5000 series): 62........ 20–25
KING: 65 30–35

FREEMAN, Ernie
Singles: 7-Inch
AVA: 64...................... 3–5
IMPERIAL: 57–62............... 4–6
LIBERTY: 62 3–5
LPs: 10/12-Inch 33rpm
DUNHILL: 67.................. 10–12
IMPERIAL: 57–62.............. 15–20
LIBERTY: 62–63.............. 12–15
Also see OTIS, Johnny
Also see SIR CHAUNCEY
Also see WITHERSPOON, Jimmy

FREEMAN, John
Singles: 7-Inch
DAKAR: 77 1–3

Price Range

Price Range

FREESTYLE EXPRESS
Singles: 7-Inch
MUSIC: *84–85*.................... **$1–3**

FREEZ
Singles: 12-Inch 33/45rpm
STREETWISE: *83* **4–6**
Singles: 7-Inch
STREETWISE: *83* **1–3**
LPs: 10/12-Inch 33rpm
STREETWISE: *83* **5–8**
Also see ROCCA, John

FREHLEY, Ace
Singles: 7-Inch
CASABLANCA: *78* **1–3**
LPs: 10/12-Inch 33rpm
CASABLANCA (Except
picture discs): *78* **5–8**
CASABLANCA (Picture
discs): *78* **10–15**
Also see KISS

FRENCH, Don
Singles: 7-Inch
LANCER: *59*.................... **8–12**

FRESH BAND, The
Singles: 12-Inch 33/45rpm
ARE 'N BE: *84*.................... **4–6**

FRESH 3 MCs
Singles: 7-Inch
PROFILE: *84* **1–3**

FREY, Glenn
Singles: 12-Inch 33/45rpm
MCA: *84–85* **4–6**
Singles: 7-Inch
ASYLUM: *82*.................... **1–3**
MCA: *84–85* **1–3**
Picture Sleeves
MCA: *85* .... **INC**
LPs: 10/12-Inch 33rpm
ASYLUM: *82*.................... **5–8**
MCA: *84–85* **5–8**
Also see EAGLES, The

FRIDA
Singles: 7-Inch
ATLANTIC: *82* **1–3**

LPs: 10/12-Inch 33rpm
ATLANTIC: *82* **$5–8**
Also see ABBA

FRIEDMAN, Dean
Singles: 7-Inch
LIFESONG: *77–78*................ **1–3**
LPs: 10/12-Inch 33rpm
LIFESONG: *77–78*................ **5–8**
RECORD CO-OP: *82*.............. **5–8**

FRIEDMAN, Kinky
Singles: 7-Inch
ABC: *75*......................... **1–3**
EPIC: *76* **1–3**
SUNRISE: *83*..................... **1–3**
LPs: 10/12-Inch 33rpm
ABC: *74*........................ **5–10**
EPIC: *76* **5–8**
VANGUARD: *73*................. **6–10**

FRIEND & LOVER
Singles: 7-Inch
ABC: *67*......................... **3–5**
CADET CONCEPT................ **2–4**
VERVE/FORECAST: *68* **3–5**
LPs: 10/12-Inch 33rpm
VERVE/FORECAST: *68* **12–15**
Members: James Post; Cathy Post.

FRIENDS OF DISTINCTION, The
Singles: 7-Inch
RCA VICTOR: *69–73* **2–3**
LPs: 10/12-Inch 33rpm
RCA VICTOR: *69–73* **10–12**

FRIJID PINK
Singles: 7-Inch
LION: *72*........................ **2–4**
LONDON **1–3**
PARROT: *69–71*.................. **3–5**
LPs: 10/12-Inch 33rpm
FANTASY: *74*.................... **8–10**
LION: *72*........................ **8–10**
PARROT: *70*................... **12–15**

FRIPP, Robert
LPs: 10/12-Inch 33rpm
EDITIONS E.G: *79–81* **5–8**
POLYDOR: *79–81* **5–8**
Also see KING CRIMSON

Price Range

FRIPP, Robert, & Andy Summers
LPs: 10/12-Inch 33rpm
A&M: *83–84* **$5–8**
Also see FRIPP, Robert
Also see POLICE, The

FRIPP & ENO
LPs: 10/12-Inch 33rpm
ANTILLES: *73* **8–10**
Members: Robert Fripp; Brian Eno.
Also see ENO, Brian
Also see FRIPP, Robert

FRIZZELL, Lefty
Singles: 7-Inch
ABC: *73–75* **1–3**
COLUMBIA (20000 &
  21000 series): *50–56* **4–6**
COLUMBIA (40000 &
  41000 series): *56–61* **3–5**
COLUMBIA (42000
  through 45000 series):
  61–72 . . . . **2–4**
EPs: 7-Inch 33/45rpm
COLUMBIA: *51–59* **10–20**
LPs: 10/12-Inch 33rpm
ABC: *73–77* **8–12**
COLUMBIA (CG series):
  75 . . . . **10–12**
COLUMBIA (1000 & 2000
  series, except 1342):
  64–67 . . . . **10–20**
COLUMBIA (1342; "The
  One & Only Lefty
  Frizzell"): *59* **20–30**
COLUMBIA (8000 & 9000
  series): *64–67* **10–20**
  (With a "CS" prefix.)
COLUMBIA (8000 & 9000
  series) **5–8**
  (With a "PC" prefix.)
COLUMBIA (9000 series):
  51–52 . . . . **35–50**
  (10-Inch LPs. With an "HL" prefix.)
COLUMBIA (10000
  series): *73–83* **5–12**
COLUMBIA (30000
  series): *75–82* **5–12**
HARMONY (7200 series):
  60 . . . . **15–20**
HARMONY (11000
  series): *66–68* **8–15**

LEFTY FRIZZELL
America's Greatest Song Stylist

AMERICANA

Price Range

MCA: *82* **$5–8**
ROUNDER: *80–83* **5–8**
Also see PRICE, Ray / Lefty Frizzell / Carl
Smith
Also see ROBBINS, Marty / Lefty Frizzell /
Carl Smith

FROGMEN, The
Singles: 7-Inch
ASTRA: *61* **10–15**
CANDIX: *61* **5–8**
SCOTT: *64* **4–6**
TEE JAY: *64* **4–6**

FROMAN, Jane
Singles: 7-Inch
CAPITOL: *52–56* **2–4**

EPs: 7-Inch 33/45rpm
CAPITOL: *52–56* **5–10**

LPs: 10/12-Inch 33rpm
CAPITOL: *52–56* **15–25**

FROST (Dick Wagner & Frost)
Singles: 7-Inch
DATE: *68* **4–6**
VANGUARD: *69–70* **3–5**

LPs: 10/12-Inch 33rpm
VANGUARD: *69–70* **12–15**
Also see COOPER, Alice

Price Range

Price Range

FROST, Frank, With The Night Hawks
Singles: 7-Inch
JEWEL: 66–67................... **$3–5**
PHILLIPS INT'L: 61.............. **4–6**
LPs: 10/12-Inch 33rpm
CHARLY **5–8**
JEWEL: 74 .... **8–10**
PHILLIPS INT'L: 61.......... **200–225**

FROST, Max, & The Troopers
Singles: 7-Inch
SIDEWALK: 68................... **3–5**
TOWER: 68–69.................. **3–5**
LPs: 10/12-Inch 33rpm
TOWER: 68.................... **12–15**

FROST, Thomas & Richard
Singles: 7-Inch
IMPERIAL: 69................... **2–3**
LPs: 10/12-Inch 33rpm
UNI: 72 .... **8–10**

FUGS, The
Singles: 7-Inch
ESP: 66.......................... **4–6**
LPs: 10/12-Inch 33rpm
BROADSIDE: 66 .... **30–35**
ESP: 66–67.................... **20–25**
PVC **5–8**
REPRISE: 67–70............... **10–15**

FULL FORCE
Singles: 12-Inch 33/45rpm
COLUMBIA: 85................... **4–6**
Singles: 7-Inch
COLUMBIA: 85................... **1–3**
LPs: 10/12-Inch 33rpm
COLUMBIA: 85................... **5–8**
Also see LISA LISA & CULT JAM WITH
FULL FORCE

FULLER, Bobby (The Bobby Fuller Four; Bobby Fuller & The Embers)
Singles: 7-Inch
ABC: 73........................ **1–3**
HI-TONE........................ **3–5**
DONNA: 65 .... **25–35**
EASTWOOD: 62................ **15–20**
ERIC **1–3**
EXETER (Except 124): 64 .... **15–20**

EXETER (124; "I Fought
   The Law"): 64 .... **$30–40**
LIBERTY: 65 .... **8–10**
MUSTANG: 65–66................ **4–6**
TODD **15–18**
YUCCA: 62..................... **20–30**
LPs: 10/12-Inch 33rpm
MUSTANG (900; "KRLA
   King Of The Wheels"):
   66 .... **50–60**
MUSTANG (901; "I
   Fought The Law"): 66 .... **30–35**
RHINO: 82 .... **5–8**
VOXX: 84 .... **5–8**

FULLER, Jerry
Singles: 7-Inch
CHALLENGE (Except
   59052): 60–66.................. **4–6**
CHALLENGE (59052;
   "Betty My Angel"): 59.......... **10–12**
COLUMBIA: 70.................. **2–4**
LIN: 58–59 .... **10–12**
LPs: 10/12-Inch 33rpm
LIN: 60 .... **25–35**
MCA: 79 .... **5–8**

FULLER, Jerry, & Diane Maxwell
Singles: 7-Inch
CHALLENGE: 60 .... **3–5**
Also see FULLER, Jerry
Also see MAXWELL, Diane

FULSON, Lowell (Lowell Folsom; Lowel Fulsom)
Singles: 7-Inch
ALADDIN (3088 through
   3104): 51 .... **30–35**
(Black vinyl.)
ALADDIN (3104;
   "Stormin' & Rainin"): 53........ **50–75**
(Colored vinyl.)
ALADDIN (3200 series):
   53–54 .... **15–20**
CASH: 57....................... **8–12**
CHECKER (Except 800
   series): 59–62.................. **4–6**
CHECKER (800 series):
   54–58 .... **5–8**
HOLLYWOOD: 55................ **5–8**
JEWEL: 69 .... **2–4**

Price Range

Also see FURIOUS FIVE, The
Also see SUGARHILL GANG, The

FURYS, The
Singles: 7-Inch
MACK IV: 63 . . . . $4–6

FUSE ONE
LPs: 10/12-Inch 33rpm
CTI: 82 5–8

FUTURES, The
Singles: 7-Inch
PHILADELPHIA INT'L:
    81 1–3

FUZZ, The
Singles: 7-Inch
CALLA: 71 2–3
ROULETTE 1–3
LPs: 10/12-Inch 33rpm
CALLA: 71 10–12

G

G., Kenny (Kenny Gorelick)
Singles: 7-Inch
ARISTA: 83–85 1–3
LPs: 10/12-Inch 33rpm
ARISTA: 83–85 5–8

G.L.O.B.E. & WHIZ KID
Singles: 12-Inch 33/45rpm
TOMMY BOY: 83 4–6
Singles: 7-Inch
TOMMY BOY: 83 1–3

GQ
Singles: 7-Inch
ARISTA: 79–82 1–3
LPs: 10/12-Inch 33rpm
ARISTA: 79–81 5–8

G.T.
Singles: 7-Inch
A&M: 83 1–3

GABOR SZABO: see SZABO, Gabor

Price Range

GABRIEL
Singles: 7-Inch
ABC: 76–77 . . . . $2–3
EPIC: 78–79 1–3
LPs: 10/12-Inch 33rpm
ABC: 75–76 8–10
EPIC: 78 2–3

GABRIEL, Peter
Singles: 7-Inch
ATCO: 77 2–3
ATLANTIC: 78 1–3
GEFFEN: 82–85 1–3
MERCURY: 80 1–3
LPs: 10/12-Inch 33rpm
ATCO: 77 10–12
ATLANTIC: 78 8–10
GEFFEN: 82–85 5–8
MERCURY: 80 5–8
Also see GENESIS

GABRIEL & THE ANGELS
Singles: 7-Inch
AMY: 61 20–25
NORMAN: 61–62 5–8
SWAN: 62–63 4–6

GADABOUTS, The
Singles: 7-Inch
JARO: 60 3–5
MERCURY: 54–56 5–8
WING: 55 4–6

GADSON, James
Singles: 7-Inch
CREAM: 72 2–4

GADSON, Mel
Singles: 7-Inch
BIG TOP: 60 4–6

GAGE, Yvonne
Singles: 7-Inch
CIM: 84 1–3

GAGNON, Andre
Singles: 7-Inch
LONDON: 76 2–3

GAIL, Sunny: see GALE, Sunny

Price Range

GAINES, Earl
Singles: 7-Inch
DELUXE: 68–69. . . . . $2–4
HBR: 66. 3–5
HOLLYWOOD: 67. 3–5
SEVENTY SEVEN: 73 2–3
LPs: 10/12-Inch 33rpm
DELUXE: 69. 10–15
EXCELLO: 62. 3–5

GAINES, Rosie
Singles: 7-Inch
EPIC: 85 1–3

GALE, Eric
Singles: 7-Inch
COLUMBIA: 78–80. 1–3
LPs: 10/12-Inch 33rpm
COLUMBIA: 77–80. 5–8
ELEKTRA: 83 5–8
KUDU: 73. 8–10
Also see GRUSIN, Dave

GALE, Sunny (Sunny Gale & The Saints & Sinners Dixieland Band; Sunny Gail)
Singles: 7-Inch
BLAINE: 65 2–4
CANADIAN
  AMERICAN: 63–64. 2–4
DECCA: 56–59. 2–4
RCA VICTOR (4000
  through 6000 series):
  52–56 3–5
RCA VICTOR (9000
  series): 68 2–3
RIVERSIDE: 63 2–4
TERRACE: 62 2–4
THIMBLE: 74. 1–3
WARWICK: 60–61. 2–4
LPs: 10/12-Inch 33rpm
CANADIAN
  AMERICAN: 64. 10–15
Also see WILCOX, Eddie

GALE, Sunny, & The Du Droppers
Singles: 7-Inch
RCA VICTOR: 53 10–12
Also see DU DROPPERS, The
Also see GALE, Sunny

Price Range

GALENS, The
Singles: 7-Inch
CHALLENGE: 63–65 . . . . $3–5

GALLAGHER, Rory
LPs: 10/12-Inch 33rpm
ATCO: 71–72. 10–12
CHRYSALIS: 75–80. 5–8
MERCURY: 82. 5–8
POLYDOR: 72–75 8–10
Also see TASTE

GALLAGHER & LYLE
Singles: 7-Inch
A&M: 73–78 2–3
LPs: 10/12-Inch 33rpm
A&M: 73–78 8–10
CAPITOL (10000 series):
  77 5–8
  (With an "SM" prefix.)
CAPITOL (11000 series):
  72 8–12
  (With an "ST" prefix.)
  Members: Ben Gallagher; Graham Lyle.
  Also see McGUINNESS-FLINT

GALLAHADS, The
Singles: 7-Inch
CAPITOL: 55 5–8
JUBILEE: 56. 5–8
VIK: 57 4–6

GALLERY
Singles: 7-Inch
SUSSEX: 72. 2–3
Picture Sleeves
SUSSEX: 72. 2–3
LPs: 10/12-Inch 33rpm
SUSSEX: 72–73. 10–12

GALLOP, Frank
Singles: 7-Inch
ABC-PARAMOUNT: 58. 3–5
KAPP: 66 2–4
MUSICOR: 66. 2–3
Picture Sleeves
MUSICOR: 66. 2–4
LPs: 10/12-Inch 33rpm
MUSICOR: 66. 8–12

Price Range

GAMBLE, Dee Dee Sharp: see SHARP, Dee Dee

GAMMA
Singles: 7-Inch
ELEKTRA: 79–82 .... $1–3
LPs: 10/12-Inch 33rpm
ELEKTRA: 79–82 5–8
Also see MONTROSE

GANG OF FOUR, The
Singles: 12-Inch 33/45rpm
WARNER BROS: 80–84 4–6
Singles: 7-Inch
WARNER BROS: 80–84 1–3
LPs: 10/12-Inch 33rpm
WARNER BROS: 80–83 5–8
Also see SHRIEKBACK

GANG'S BACK, The
Singles: 7-Inch
HANDSHAKE: 82 1–3

GANGSTERS, The
Singles: 7-Inch
HEAT: 79–81 1–3

GANTS, The
Singles: 7-Inch
LIBERTY: 65–67 4–6
LPs: 10/12-Inch 33rpm
LIBERTY: 65–66 15–20

GAP, Billy & Baby: see BILLY & BABY GAP

GAP BAND, The
Singles: 12-Inch 33/45rpm
PASSPORT: 83 4–6
TOTAL EXPERIENCE:
  82–85 4–6
Singles: 7-Inch
A&M: 75 2–3
MERCURY: 79–84 1–3
PASSPORT: 83 1–3
SHELTER: 74 2–3
TATTOO: 77 1–3
TOTAL EXPERIENCE:
  82–85 1–3

Price Range

LPs: 10/12-Inch 33rpm
MERCURY: 79–80 .... $5–8
PASSPORT: 83 5–8
SHELTER: 74 8–10
TATTOO: 77 8–10
TOTAL EXPERIENCE:
  82–85 5–8

GARCIA, Jerry (Jerry Garcia & Robert Hunter)
Singles: 7-Inch
DOUGLAS: 73 3–5
ROUND: 74–75 3–5
WARNER BROS: 72 3–5

LPs: 10/12-Inch 33rpm
ARISTA: 78–82 5–8
ROUND: 74–75 8–10
UNITED ARTISTS: 76 8–10
WARNER BROS: 72 8–10
Also see GRATEFUL DEAD, The
Also see HART, Mickey
Also see IT'S A BEAUTIFUL DAY
Also see SAUNDERS, Merl

GARDNER, Dave (Brother Dave Gardner)
Singles: 7-Inch
OJ: 57 3–5
RCA VICTOR: 59–61 2–4

LPs: 10/12-Inch 33rpm
CAMDEN: 73 5–10
CAPITOL: 63 12–20
RCA VICTOR: 60–64 10–20
TOWER: 67 8–15

GARDNER, Don, & Dee Dee Ford
Singles: 7-Inch
FIRE: 62 4–6
FLASHBACK: 65 1–3
KC: 62 3–5
LUDIX: 63 3–5
RED TOP: 63 3–5
TRU-GLO-TOWN: 66 3–5

LPs: 10/12-Inch 33rpm
FIRE: 62 35–45
SUE: 66 15–20
Also see WASHINGTON, Baby, & Don Gardner

Price Range

GARDNER, Joanna
Singles: 7-Inch
PHILLY WORLD: *84* **$1–3**

GARDNER, Reggie
Singles: 7-Inch
CAPITOL: *71* **2–3**

GARDNER, Taana
Singles: 7-Inch
WEST END: *81* **1–3**

GARFUNKEL, Art
Singles: 7-Inch
COLUMBIA: *73–81* **1–3**
Picture Sleeves
COLUMBIA: *81* **1–3**
LPs: 10/12-Inch 33rpm
COLUMBIA (30000
series): *73–81* **8–12**
(With an "FC," "JC," "KC" or "PC" prefix.)
COLUMBIA (30000
series): *73–75* **10–15**
(With a "CQ" or "PCQ" prefix. Quad issues.)
COLUMBIA (47000
series): *78* **12–15**
(Half-speed mastered LPs.)
Also see GARR, Artie
Also see SIMON & GARFUNKEL
Also see TAYLOR, James

GARI, Frank
Singles: 7-Inch
ATLANTIC: *62* **3–5**
CAPITOL: *68* **2–4**
CRUSADE: *60–62* **3–5**
RIBBON: *59* **4–6**
Picture Sleeves
CRUSADE: *61–62* **5–8**

GARLAND, Judy
Singles: 7-Inch
ABC: *67* **2–4**
CAPITOL: *56–63* **3–5**
COLUMBIA (40000
series): *53–54* **5–10**
DECCA (29000 series): *55* **4–8**
WARNER BROS: *63* **3–5**
EPs: 7-Inch 33/45rpm
CAPITOL (676; "Miss
Show Business"): *55* **10–20**

CAPITOL (734; "Judy"):
56 . . . . **$10–20**
CAPITOL (835; "Alone"):
57 . . . . **10–20**
CAPITOL (1569; "Judy At
Carnegie Hall"): *62* **10–15**
COLUMBIA (1201; "A
Star Is Born"): *54* **15–20**
(Soundtrack.)
COLUMBIA (2598; "Judy
Garland"): *57*. **20–30**
COLUMBIA (7621; "Born
In A Trunk"): *56* **10–15**
DECCA (620; "Judy
Garland At The Palace/
Greatest Performances"):
55 . . . . **10–20**
DECCA (661; "The
Wizard Of Oz"): *51* **15–25**
DECCA (2050; "Judy
Garland, Volume 2"): *53* **12–20**
MGM (268; "If You Feel
Like Singing, Sing"): *54* **10–20**
MGM (1038; "Get
Happy"): *55*. **10–20**
MGM (1116; "Look For
The Silver Lining"): *55*. **10–20**
MGM (1122; "Judy
Garland"): *55*. **10–20**

LPs: 10/12-Inch 33rpm
ABC (620; Judy Garland
At Home At The
Palace"): *67* **10–15**
ABC (30007; "Judy
Garland - The ABC
Collection"): *76* **5–10**
CAPITOL (676; "Miss
Show Business"): *55* **25–40**
(With a "W" prefix.)
CAPITOL (676; "Miss
Show Business"): *63* **10–20**
(With an "SW" prefix.)
CAPITOL (734; "Judy"):
56 . . . . **25–35**
(With a "T" prefix.)
CAPITOL (734; "Judy"):
63 . . . . **10–20**
(With a "DT" prefix.)
CAPITOL (835; "Alone"):
57 . . . . **25–35**
(With a "T" prefix.)

Price Range

CAPITOL (835; "Alone"):
63 .... **$10–20**
(With a "DT" prefix.)
CAPITOL (1036; "Judy In
Love"): 58 .... **20–35**
CAPITOL (1118; "Garland
At The Grove"): 59 .... **20–35**
CAPITOL (1467; "Judy
Garland - That's
Entertainment"): 60. .... **20–35**
CAPITOL (1569; "Judy At
Carnegie Hall"): 61 .... **20–35**
CAPITOL (1710; "The
Garland Touch"): 62. .... **20–30**
CAPITOL (1861; "I Could
Go On Singing"): 63 .... **25–35**
(Soundtrack.)
CAPITOL (1941; "Our
Love Letter"): 63. .... **15–20**
(With John Ireland.)
CAPITOL (1999; "The
Hits Of Judy Garland"):
64 .... **20–30**
(With a "T" or "ST" prefix.)
CAPITOL (1999; "The
Hits Of Judy Garland"):
75 .... **5–8**
(With an "SM" prefix.)
CAPITOL (2062; "Just For
Openers"): 64. .... **15–25**
CAPITOL (2988; "Judy
Garland - Deluxe Set"):
68 .... **20–35**
CAPITOL (11763;
"Alone"): 78. .... **5–8**
CAPITOL (11876; "Judy -
That's Entertainment"):
79 .... **5–8**
CAPITOL (12034; "Just
For Openers"): 80 .... **5–8**
CAPITOL (16175; "The
Hits Of Judy Garland"):
81 .... **4–6**
COLUMBIA (762; "Born
In A Trunk"): 56 .... **30–45**
COLUMBIA (1101; "A
Star Is Born"): 58 .... **20–30**
(Soundtrack.)
COLUMBIA (1201; "A
Star Is Born"): 54 .... **40–55**
(Soundtrack. Deluxe boxed edition.)

Price Range

COLUMBIA (8740; "A
Star Is Born"): 63 .... **$20–30**
(Soundtrack. Reprocessed stereo.)
COLUMBIA (10011; "A
Star Is Born"): 73 .... **5–10**
(Soundtrack.)
COLUMBIA/CSP (8740;
"A Star Is Born") **5–10**
(Soundtrack. Reprocessed stereo.)
DECCA (75; "Collector's
Items: 1936-1945"): 70 .... **15–25**
DECCA (172; "The Best
Of Judy Garland"): 63 .... **15–20**
DECCA (4199; "The
Magic Of Judy
Garland"): 61. .... **15–20**
DECCA (5152; "The
Wizard Of Oz"): 51 .... **40–60**
(10-Inch LP.)
DECCA (6020; "Judy
Garland At The
Palace"): 55 .... **35–45**
DECCA (8190; "Judy
Garland - Greatest
Performances"): 55 .... **35–45**
DECCA (8387; "The
Wizard Of Oz"): 56 .... **30–40**
(One side of this LP is "The Song Hits From
Pinocchio," which does not feature Judy Gar-
land.)
DECCA (75150; "Judy
Garland's Greatest
Hits"): 69. .... **8–12**
DECCA (78387; "The
Wizard Of Oz"): 67 .... **10–15**

Price Range

HARMONY (11366; "A
Star Is Born"): *69* **$10–15**
JUNO (1000; "Judy -
London 1969"): *69* **8–12**
(Reissued in 1979 using the same catalog number. If there is a difference in label or cover design on the reissue, we are not yet aware of it.)
MCA (4003; "The Best Of
Judy Garland"): *73* **10–15**
MGM (1; "Golden Years
At MGM"): *69* **15–25**
MGM (21; "The Pirate"):
51 . . . . **40–60**
(Soundtrack, with Gene Kelly. 10-Inch LP.)
MGM (82; "Judy Garland
Sings"): *51* **60–90**
MGM (113; "Judy
Garland"): *70*. **8–12**
MGM (3149; "Judy
Garland"): *54*. **35–45**
MGM (3234; "The
Pirate"): *55*. **20–35**
(Soundtrack, with Gene Kelly.)
MGM (3771; "Words &
Music"): *60* **15–25**
MGM (3989; "The Judy
Garland Story, Volume
1"): *61* **15–20**
MGM (4005; "The Judy
Garland Story, Volume
2"): *61* **15–20**
MGM (4204; "The Very
Best Of Judy Garland"):
64 . . . . **12–20**
METRO (505; "Judy
Garland"): *65*. **10–15**
METRO (581; "Judy
Garland In Song"): *66* **10–15**
TRIP (9; "16 Greatest Hits
- Judy Garland"): *76*. **5–8**

GARLAND, Judy, & Liza Minnelli
Singles: 7-Inch
CAPITOL: *65* **2–4**

LPs: 10/12-Inch 33rpm
CAPITOL (2295; "Live At
The London
Palladium"): *65* **15–20**
CAPITOL (11191; "Live
At The London
Palladium"): *73* **5–8**

Price Range

Also see GARLAND, Judy
Also see MINNELLI, Liza

GARLOW, Clarence
Singles: 7-Inch
ALADDIN: *52* **$20–25**
FEATURE: *54*. **15–20**
FLAIR: *54*. **25–30**
FOLK STAR: *54* **12–16**
GOLDBAND: *56–57* **5–8**

GARNER, Erroll (The Erroll Garner Trio)
Singles: 7-Inch
ABC-PARAMOUNT:
61–62 . . . . **2–3**
COLUMBIA: *50–70* **2–4**
MGM: *66–69*. **2–3**
MERCURY (70000 series):
54 . . . . **2–4**
MERCURY (72000 &
73000 series): *63–71* **2–3**
REPRISE: *63*. **2–3**

EPs: 7-Inch 33/45rpm
ATLANTIC: *52–56* **5–10**
BRUNSWICK: *53*. **5–10**
COLUMBIA: *50–75* **5–15**
EMARCY: *56* **5–10**
KING: *54* **5–10**
MERCURY: *54–56*. **5–10**
SAVOY: *51–55* **5–10**

LPs: 10/12-Inch 33rpm
ABC-PARAMOUNT: *61*. **10–20**
ATLANTIC (100 series):
50–52 . . . . **20–40**
(10-Inch LPs.)
ATLANTIC (1200 series):
56 . . . . **10–20**
BARONET: *61* **10–20**
BLUE NOTE (5000 series):
52–53 . . . . **20–40**
(10-Inch LPs.)
COLUMBIA (500 through
1500 series): *54–61* **10–20**
COLUMBIA (2500 series):
56 . . . . **15–25**
(10-Inch LPs.)
COLUMBIA (6000 series):
50–51 . . . . **20–40**
(10-Inch LPs.)

Price Range

COLUMBIA (8000 series):
60 .... $10–20
COLUMBIA (9000 series):
70 5–10
COLUMBIA SPECIAL
  PRODUCTS: 79 5–8
DIAL: 50 25–50
  (10-Inch LPs.)
EMARCY (26000 series):
54 20–35
  (10-Inch LPs.)
EMARCY (36000 series):
55–56 15–25
ENRICA: 59 15–20
EVEREST: 70 5–10
GRAND AWARD: 56 15–25
HARMONY: 68 5–10
JAZZTONE: 57 15–20
KING (200 series): 54 20–35
  (10-Inch LPs.)
KING (500 series): 58 12–20
LONDON: 72–73 5–10
MGM: 65–68 8–15
MERCURY (20000 series):
54–63 10–25
  (Monaural issues.)
MERCURY (25000 series):
51 20–40
  (10-Inch LPs.)
MERCURY (60000 series):
62–63 10–20
  (Stereo issues.)
MERCURY (61000 series):
70 5–10
REPRISE: 63 10–20
RONDO-LETTE: 58 15–20
ROOST: 52 20–40
  (10-Inch LPs.)
ROOST (2000 series): 56 15–25
SAVOY (1100 series): 78 5–8
SAVOY (2000 series): 76 5–10
SAVOY (12000 series): 55 15–25
SAVOY (15000 series):
50–51 20–40
  (10-Inch LPs.)
TRIP: 74 5–8
WING: 62 10–15
  Also see STARR, Kay / Erroll Garner

Price Range

**GARNETT, Gale (Gale Garnett &
The Gentle Reign)**
Singles: 7-Inch
COLUMBIA: 68 .... $2–3
RCA VICTOR: 64–67 2–4
Picture Sleeves
RCA VICTOR: 64 2–4
LPs: 10/12-Inch 33rpm
COLUMBIA: 68–69 8–12
RCA VICTOR: 64–66 8–12

GARR, Artie (Art Garfunkel)
Singles: 7-Inch
OCTAVIA: 61 15–20
WARWICK: 59 20–25
  Also see GARFUNKEL, Art

GARRAFFA, Donna
Singles: 12-Inch 33/45rpm
ARTIST INT'L: 85 4–6

GARRETT, Lee
Singles: 7-Inch
CHRYSALIS: 76 2–3

GARRETT, Leif
Singles: 7-Inch
ATLANTIC: 77–78 1–3
SCOTTI BROS: 78–81 1–3
Picture Sleeves
ATLANTIC: 77–78 1–3
SCOTTI BROS: 78–81 1–3
LPs: 10/12-Inch 33rpm
ATLANTIC: 77 5–8
SCOTTI BROS: 78–80 5–8
  Also see CHIC / Roberta Flack / Leif Garrett
  / Genesis

GARRETT, Scott (Scott Garret)
Singles: 7-Inch
LAURIE (Except 3029): 59 4–6
LAURIE (3029; "Love
  Story"): 59 12–15
  (With The Mystics.)
OKEH: 60 3–5
  Also see MYSTICS, The

GARRETT, Siedah
Singles: 12-Inch 33/45rpm
QWEST: 85 4–6

Price Range

TAMLA (54041; "Let
Your Conscience Be
Your Guide"): *61* **$20–25**
TAMLA (54055;
"Sandman"): *62* **45–55**
TAMLA (54063; "Taking
My Time"): *62* **10–12**
TAMLA (54068 through
54170): *62–68* **4–6**
TAMLA (54176 through
54280): *62–68* **3–5**
Picture Sleeves
MOTOWN: *64–77* **2–5**
LPs: 10/12-Inch 33rpm
COLUMBIA: *82–85* **5–8**
KORY: *76–77* **8–10**
MOTOWN: *64–83* **8–12**
NATURAL RESOURCES:
78 .... **5–8**
TAMLA (221 through
251): *61–64* **25–35**
TAMLA (252 through
299): *64–69* **15–20**
TAMLA (300 series):
70–81 .... **8–12**
Also see MARTHA & THE VANDELLAS
Also see MOONGLOWS, The
Also see SPINNERS, The

**GAYE, Marvin / Gladys Knight &
The Pips**
Singles: 7-Inch
MOTOWN: *68* **3–5**
Also see KNIGHT, Gladys

GAYE, Marvin, & Diana Ross
Singles: 7-Inch
MOTOWN: *73–74* **2–3**
Also see ROSS, Diana

GAYE, Marvin, & Tammi Terrell
Singles: 7-Inch
TAMLA: *67–70* **3–5**
LPs: 10/12-Inch 33rpm
MOTOWN: *80–82* **5–8**
TAMLA: *67–70* **10–15**
Also see TERRELL, Tammi

GAYE, Marvin, & Mary Wells
Singles: 7-Inch
MOTOWN: *64* **3–5**

Price Range

Picture Sleeves
MOTOWN: *64* **$4–6**
LPs: 10/12-Inch 33rpm
MOTOWN: *64* **20–25**
Also see WELLS, Mary

GAYE, Marvin, & Kim Weston
Singles: 7-Inch
TAMLA: *64–67* **3–5**
LPs: 10/12-Inch 33rpm
TAMLA: *66* **20–25**
Also see GAYE, Marvin
Also see WESTON, Kim

**GAYLE, Crystal: see CRYSTAL
GAYLE**

GAYLORD, Ronnie
Singles: 7-Inch
MERCURY: *54–55* **3–5**
WING: *55–56* **3–5**
EPs: 7-Inch 33/45rpm
MERCURY: *55* **5–10**
Also see GAYLORDS, The

GAYLORD & HOLIDAY
Singles: 7-Inch
NATURAL RESOURCES:
77 .... **1–3**
PALMER: *67* **2–3**
PRODIGAL: *76* **1–3**
VERVE: *66* **2–3**
LPs: 10/12-Inch 33rpm
NATURAL RESOURCES:
76 .... **5–8**
PRODIGAL: *75* **5–8**
VMI: *72* **5–10**
Members: Ronnie Gaylord; Burt Holiday.
Also see GAYLORD, Ronnie
Also see GAYLORDS, The

GAYLORDS, The
Singles: 7-Inch
MERCURY: *52–62* **3–5**
TIME: *64* **2–3**
EPs: 7-Inch 33/45rpm
MERCURY: *54–56* **5–10**
LPs: 10/12-Inch 33rpm
MERCURY: *54–63* **10–20**
TIME: *64* **8–15**
WING: *59–64* **8–15**
Members: Ronnie Gaylord; Burt Holiday.

Price Range

Also see GAYLORD, Ronnie
Also see GAYLORD & HOLIDAY

GAYNOR, Gloria
Singles: 12-Inch 33/45rpm
POLYDOR: 78 . . . . $4–6
SILVER BLUE: 83 4–6

Singles: 7-Inch
COLUMBIA: 73 2–3
JOCIDA: 65 3–5
MGM: 74–75 2–3
POLYDOR: 78–79 1–3

LPs: 10/12-Inch 33rpm
ATLANTIC: 82 5–8
MGM: 75 8–10
POLYDOR: 77–80 5–8

GAYTEN, Paul
Singles: 7-Inch
ANNA: 59–60 4–6
ARGO: 57–58 5–8
CHECKER (801 through
836): 55–56 10–15
CHECKER (872 through
880): 57–58 4–6
OKEH: 52–55 8–10

G-CLEFS, The
Singles: 7-Inch
LOMA: 66 3–5
PARIS: 57 5–8
PILGRIM: 56 5–8
REGINA: 64 3–5
ROULETTE 1–3
TERRACE: 61–63 4–6
VEEP: 65–66 3–5
Also see CANNON, Freddy

GEDDES, David
Singles: 7-Inch
ATCO: 75 2–3
BIG TREE: 75 2–3
H&L: 77 2–3
ZODIAC: 77 2–3

LPs: 10/12-Inch 33rpm
BIG TREE: 75 8–10

GEE, Spoonie: see SPOONIE GEE

GEILS, J., Band, (Geils)
Singles: 12-Inch 33/45rpm
EMI AMERICA: 82–84 . . . . $4–6
Singles: 7-Inch
ATLANTIC: 71–78 2–3
EMI AMERICA: 78–84 1–3
Picture Sleeves
ATLANTIC: 73–78 2–3
EMI AMERICA: 78–84 . . . . INC
LPs: 10/12-Inch 33rpm
ATLANTIC (Black vinyl):
70–80 8–12
ATLANTIC (Colored
vinyl): 73 15–20
EMI AMERICA: 78–84 5–8
Also see WOLF, Peter

GEM
Singles: 7-Inch
STREETKING: 84 1–3

GENE & DEBBE
Singles: 7-Inch
HICKORY: 70 2–4
TRX: 67–69 3–5
LPs: 10/12-Inch 33rpm
TRX: 68 15–20
Members: Gene Thomas; Debbe Nevills.
Also see THOMAS, Gene

GENE & EUNICE
Singles: 7-Inch
ALADDIN: 55 8–10
CASE: 59 4–6
COLLECTABLES 1–3
COMBO: 55 8–10
ERA: 72 1–3
LILLY: 62 3–5
EPs: 7-Inch 33/45rpm
CASE: 59 15–25
(Issued with a paper sleeve.)
Members: Gene Forrest; Eunice Levy.

GENE & JERRY: see CHANDLER, Gene, & Jerry Butler

GENE & TOMMY
Singles: 7-Inch
ABC: 67 3–5
Members: Terry Cashman; Tommy West.
Also see CASHMAN & WEST

Price Range

GENE & WENDELL
Singles: 7-Inch
PHILIPS: 62–63 .... $3–5
RAY STAR: 61–62. 3–5

GENE THE HAT
Singles: 7-Inch
CHECKER: 61 3–5
DEAUVILLE: 62 3–5
GEE: 62 3–5

GENELLS, The
Singles: 7-Inch
DEWEY: 63 5–8

GENERAL CAINE: see CAINE, General

GENERAL PUBLIC, The
Singles: 12-Inch 33/45rpm
I.R.S.: 84–85 4–6
Singles: 7-Inch
I.R.S.: 84–85 1–3
LPs: 10/12-Inch 33rpm
I.R.S.: 84 5–8

GENESIS
Singles: 7-Inch
ATCO: 76–77. 2–3
ATLANTIC: 78–83 1–3
BUDDAH: 69 5–8
CHARISMA: 73 4–6
MERCURY: 68. 10–15
PARROT: 68. 10–15
SCEPTER: 71 2–4
Picture Sleeves
ATLANTIC: 78–83 1–3
LPs: 10/12-Inch 33rpm
ABC: 74 10–12
ATCO: 74–79. 8–12
ATLANTIC: 73–83 5–8
BUDDAH: 76 10–12
CHARISMA: 72–79 10–12
IMPULSE: 70 15–20
LONDON: 74 10–15
LONDON COLLECTOR:
77 8–10
MCA: 78 5–8
Also see BANKS, Tony
Also see CHIC / Roberta Flack / Leif Garrett / Genesis

Price Range

Also see COLLINS, Phil
Also see GABRIEL, Peter
Also see HACKETT, Steve
Also see PHILLIPS, Anthony
Also see RUTHERFORD, Mike

GENIES, The
Singles: 7-Inch
ERIC $1–3
HOLLYWOOD: 59. 4–6
SHAD: 59 4–6
WARWICK: 60–61. 8–10
Members: Eugene Pitt; Jay Washington; Claude Johnson; Roland Trone.
Also see DON & JUAN
Also see JIVE FIVE, The

GENTLE GIANT
Singles: 7-Inch
CAPITOL: 74–78 2–3
COLUMBIA: 72–73 2–4

LPs: 10/12-Inch 33rpm
CAPITOL: 74–80 5–8
COLUMBIA: 72–73 8–10
VERTIGO: 71 10–12

GENTLE PERSUASION
Singles: 7-Inch
CAPITOL: 83 1–3

GENTRY, Bobbie
Singles: 7-Inch
BRUNSWICK: 75. 2–3
CAPITOL: 67–76 2–4
WARNER BROS: 76–78 1–3

Picture Sleeves
CAPITOL: 67–72 2–4
LPs: 10/12-Inch 33rpm
CAPITOL (Except "SM"
series): 67–71 8–15
CAPITOL ("SM" series):
81 5–8
WARNER BROS. ("Ode
To Billie Joe: Special
Radio Salute To Bobbie
Gentry"): 76. 15-20
(Promotional issue only.)
Also see CAMPBELL, Glen, & Bobbie Gentry
Also see REYNOLDS, Jody, & Bobbie Gentry

Price Range

GENTRYS, The (With Larry Raspberry)
Singles: 7-Inch
BELL: *68* **$3–5**
CAPITOL: *72* **2–3**
MGM: *65–67* **3–5**
STAX: *74* **2–3**
SUN: *70–71* **2–4**
(Black vinyl.)
SUN: *71* **8–15**
(Colored vinyl. Promotional issues only.)
YOUNGSTOWN: *65* **12–15**
Picture Sleeves
MGM: *66* **3–5**
LPs: 10/12-Inch 33rpm
MGM: *65–70* **15–20**
SUN: *70* **10–15**

GENTY
Singles: 7-Inch
VENTURE: *80* **1–3**

GEORGE, Barbara
Singles: 7-Inch
AFO: *61–62* **3–5**
SUE: *62–63* **3–5**
UNITED ARTISTS: *74* **1–3**
LPs: 10/12-Inch 33rpm
AFO: *62* **30–40**

GEORGE, Lowell
Singles: 7-Inch
WARNER BROS: *78–79* **1–3**
LPs: 10/12-Inch 33rpm
WARNER BROS: *78–79* **5–8**
Also see LITTLE FEAT

GEORGE & GENE: see JONES, George, & Gene Pitney

GERARD, Danyel
Singles: 7-Inch
COLUMBIA: *72* **3–5**
MGM/VERVE: *72* **2–4**
LPs: 10/12-Inch 33rpm
VERVE: *71* **8–10**

GERRARD, Donny
Singles: 7-Inch
GREEDY: *76–77* **2–3**
ROCKET: *76* **2–3**

Price Range

LPs: 10/12-Inch 33rpm
GREEDY **$8–10**
Also see SKYLARK

GERRY & THE PACEMAKERS (Featuring Gerry Marsden)
Singles: 7-Inch
ERIC **1–3**
LAURIE (Except 3100
series): *64–67* **4–6**
LAURIE (3100 series): *63* **8–10**
LPs: 10/12-Inch 33rpm
ACCORD: *81* **5–8**
CAPITOL: *79* **5–8**
LAURIE: *64–66* **15–20**
Also see MARTIN, George, & His Orchestra

GESTURES, The
Singles: 7-Inch
SOMA: *64–65* **3–5**

GET WET
Singles: 7-Inch
BOARDWALK: *81* **1–3**
LPs: 10/12-Inch 33rpm
BOARDWALK: *81* **5–8**

GETZ, Stan (The Stan Getz Quintet)
Singles: 7-Inch
CLEF: *53–54* **3–5**
COLUMBIA: *75–80* **1–3**
DAWN: *54* **3–5**
MGM: *65* **2–3**
MERCURY: *53* **3–5**
NORGRAN: *54–55* **3–5**
PRESTIGE: *50–53* **3–5**
ROOST: *50–53* **3–5**
VERVE: *60–72* **1–3**

EPs: 7-Inch 33/45rpm
CLEF: *53* **10–20**
DALE: *51* **15–25**
NORGRAN (100 series):
55 .... **10–15**
NORGRAN (2000 series):
54 .... **20–40**
(Boxed set series.)
PRESTIGE: *50* **15–25**
ROOST: *51–52* **15–25**

Price Range

Price Range

LPs: 10/12-Inch 33rpm

AMERICAN
  RECORDING
  SOCIETY: *57*................ **$20–30**
BARONET: *62*.................. **10–20**
BLUE RIBBON: *61*.............. **10–20**
CLEF (100 series): *53*............ **60–80**
  (10-Inch LPs.)
COLUMBIA: *74–82*.............. **5–10**
CONCORD JAZZ: *81*............. **5–8**
DALE: *51* **75–100**
  (10-Inch LPs.)
INNER CITY: *78*................ **5–8**
JAZZ MAN: *82*.................. **5–8**
JAZZTONE: *57*................. **15–25**
MGM (Except 4312): *70* **5–10**
MGM (4312; "Mickey
  One"): *65* ...:............ **15–20**
  (Soundtrack.)
METRO: *65*................... **10–15**
MODERN: *56*.................. **20–30**
NEW JAZZ: *59*................. **15–25**
NORGRAN (4; "Stan
  Getz"): *53* **75–100**
  (10-Inch LP.)
NORGRAN (1000 series):
  54–56 .... **30–50**
NORGRAN (2000 series):
  54 .... **100–125**
  (Boxed set series.)
PRESTIGE (100 series): *52*....... **75–100**
  (10-Inch LPs.)
PRESTIGE (7002 through
  7022): *56* **25–50**
  (Yellow label.)
PRESTIGE (7252 through
  7256): *56* **25–50**
  (Yellow label.)
PRESTIGE (7000 series):
  64–68 .... **8–18**
  (Blue label.)
PRESTIGE (24000 series):
  72–79 .... **8–12**
ROOST (400 series): *51–52* **60–90**
  (10-Inch LPs.)
ROOST (2000 series):
  58–64 .... **12–25**
ROULETTE: *71–72* **8–12**
SAVOY (1100 series): *77*........... **5–8**
SAVOY (9000 series): *53*.......... **60–80**
  (10-Inch LPs.)
SEECO: *54*.................... **50–75**

(10-Inch LPs.)
VSP: *66–67* **$8–12**
VERVE: *58–60* **15–30**
  (Reads "Verve Records, Inc." at bottom of
  label.)
VERVE: *61–72* **10–20**
  (Reads "MGM Records - A Division Of Metro-
  Goldwyn-Mayer, Inc." at bottom of label.)
VERVE: *73–84* **5–10**
  (Reads "Manufactured By MGM Record
  Corp.," or mentions either Polydor or Poly-
  gram at bottom of label.)
  Also see BENNETT, Tony
  Also see HOLIDAY, Billie, & Stan Getz
  Also see TJADER, Cal, & Stan Getz

GETZ, Stan, & Laurindo Almeida
Singles: 7-Inch
VERVE: *66* **2–3**
LPs: 10/12-Inch 33rpm
VERVE: *66* **8–15**
  Also see ALMEIDA, Laurindo

GETZ, Stan, & Charlie Byrd
Singles: 7-Inch
MGM: *78*....................... **1–3**
VERVE: *62* **2–3**
LPs: 10/12-Inch 33rpm
VERVE: *62* **10–20**
  Also see BYRD, Charlie

GETZ, Stan, & Astrud Gilberto
Singles: 7-Inch
MGM: *78*....................... **1–3**
VERVE: *64–65* **2–3**
LPs: 10/12-Inch 33rpm
VERVE: *64* **10–20**
  Also see GILBERTO, Astrud

GETZ, Stan, & Gerry Mulligan
LPs: 10/12-Inch 33rpm
VERVE: *58–60* **20–30**
  (Reads "Verve Records, Inc." at bottom of
  label.)
VERVE: *61–63* **10–20**
  (Reads "MGM Records - A Division Of Metro-
  Goldwyn-Mayer, Inc." at bottom of label.)
  Also see MULLIGAN, Gerry

GETZ, Stan, & Oscar Peterson
LPs: 10/12-Inch 33rpm
VERVE: *60* **15–25**

Price Range

(Reads "Verve Records, Inc." at bottom of label.)
VERVE: *61–81* **$8–18**
(Reads "MGM Records - A Division Of Metro-Goldwyn-Mayer, Inc." at bottom of label.)
Also see GETZ, Stan
Also see PETERSON, Oscar

GIBB, Andy
Singles: 7-Inch
RSO: *77–81* **1–3**
Picture Sleeves
RSO: *77–78* **1–3**
LPs: 10/12-Inch 33rpm
RSO: *77–80* **5–8**
Also see BEE GEES, The
Also see NEWTON-JOHN, Olivia, & Andy Gibb

GIBB, Andy, & Victoria Principal
Singles: 7-Inch
RSO: *81* **1–3**
Picture Sleeves
RSO: *81* **1–3**
Also see GIBB, Andy

GIBB, Barry
Singles: 7-Inch
ATCO: *77* **2–3**
MCA: *84* **1–3**
LPs: 10/12-Inch 33rpm
MCA: *84* **5–8**
Also see BEE GEES, The
Also see STREISAND, Barbra, & Barry Gibb
Also see WARWICK, Dionne

GIBB, Maurice
Singles: 7-Inch
ATCO: *70* **2–3**
Also see BEE GEES, The

GIBB, Robin
Singles: 7-Inch
ATCO: *69–71*. **2–3**
MIRAGE: *84*. **1–3**
POLYDOR: *83* **1–3**
RSO: *78* **1–3**
SESAME STREET: *78*. **1–3**
LPs: 10/12-Inch 33rpm
ATCO: *70* **8–10**
MIRAGE: *84*. **5–8**
POLYDOR: *83* **5–8**
Also see BEE GEES, The

Price Range

Also see LEVY, Marcy, & Robin Gibb

GIBBONS, Steve, Band
Singles: 7-Inch
MCA/GOLD HAWKE:
76–78 .... **$1–3**
POLYDOR: *78* **1–3**
LPs: 10/12-Inch 33rpm
MCA: *76–77* **8–10**
POLYDOR: *78–80* **5–8**
Also see DALTREY, Roger, & Steve Gibbons

GIBBS, Doug
Singles: 7-Inch
OAK: *72* **2–3**

GIBBS, Georgia
Singles: 7-Inch
BELL: *64–66* **2–3**
CORAL: *50–51* **3–5**
EPIC: *63–64* **2–4**
IMPERIAL: *60*. **2–4**
KAPP: *59* **2–4**
MERCURY: *51–57*. **3–5**
RCA VICTOR: *57–67* **2–4**
ROULETTE: *58–59* **2–4**
EPs: 7-Inch 33/45rpm
MERCURY: *54–56*. **5–10**
LPs: 10/12-Inch 33rpm
BELL: *66*. **8–12**
CORAL: *54* **15–20**
EPIC: *63* **8–15**
IMPERIAL: *60*. **10–15**
MERCURY: *54–56*. **12–20**
SUNSET: *66* **8–12**

GIBBS, Terri
Singles: 7-Inch
MCA: *81–83* **1–3**
TEM: *82*. **1–3**
LPs: 10/12-Inch 33rpm
MCA: *81–83* **5–8**
PHONORAMA: *84* **5–8**

GIBSON, Beverly Ann
Singles: 7-Inch
JUBILEE: *63*. **3–5**

GIBSON, Don
Singles: 7-Inch
ABC/HICKORY: *75–78* **1–3**

Price Range

COLUMBIA (20000
  series): *52–54* **$4–8**
HICKORY: *70–72* **2–3**
MCA: *79* **1–3**
MGM (12000 series):
  55–56 . . . . **4–6**
RCA VICTOR (0400
  series): *51* **5–10**
RCA VICTOR (4300 &
  4400 series): *51–52* **5–10**
RCA VICTOR (7100
  through 7900 series):
  58–61 . . . . **3–5**
RCA VICTOR (8000
  through 9000 series):
  62–70 . . . . **2–4**
WARNER BROS: *80* **1–3**
  Picture Sleeves
RCA VICTOR: *63* **2–4**
  EPs: 7-Inch 33/45rpm
COLUMBIA: *57* **12–18**
RCA VICTOR: *58–59* **8–15**
  LPs: 10/12-Inch 33rpm
ABC/HICKORY: *75–78* **6–10**
CAMDEN: *65–74* **10–15**
HARMONY (7300 series):
  65 . . . . **12–18**
HARMONY (31000
  series): *72* **5–10**
HICKORY: *70–72* **8–12**
HICKORY/MGM: *73–75* **6–10**
LION: *58* **25–35**
MGM: *70* **8–12**
METRO: *65* **12–18**
RCA VICTOR (Except
  1700 through 2000
  series): *60–70* **10–20**
RCA VICTOR (1700
  through 2000 series):
  58–59 . . . . **20–30**

GIBSON, Don, & Dottie West
  Singles: 7-Inch
RCA VICTOR: *69–70* **2–4**
  LPs: 10/12-Inch 33rpm
RCA VICTOR: *69* **8–12**
  Also see WEST, Dottie

GIBSON, Don, & Sue Thompson
  Singles: 7-Inch
HICKORY: *71–75* **2–3**

Price Range

  LPs: 10/12-Inch 33rpm
HICKORY: *73* **$8–12**
HICKORY/MGM: *75* **5–10**
  Also see GIBSON, Don
  Also see THOMPSON, Sue

GIBSON, Ginny
  Singles: 7-Inch
ABC-PARAMOUNT: *56* **3–5**
DERBY: *52* **3–5**
MGM: *51–55* **3–5**
  EPs: 7-Inch 33/45rpm
JD **5–8**

GIBSON, Johnny (The Johnny Gibson Trio)
  Singles: 7-Inch
BIG TOP: *61–63* **3–5**
TWIRL **3–5**
  Also see JOHNNY & THE HURRICANES

GIBSON, Steve (Steve Gibson & The Red Caps; Steve Gibson & The Original Red Caps)
  Singles: 7-Inch
ABC-PARAMOUNT:
  56–60 . . . . **5–8**
BANDBOX: *62* **3–5**
HI LO: *58* **5–8**
HUNT: *59* **4–6**
JAY DEE: *54* **6–10**
MERCURY (8069 through
  8093): *48* **25–30**
MERCURY (8100 series):
  48–50 . . . . **15–20**
MERCURY (70000 series):
  54 . . . . **15–20**
RCA VICTOR (3986;
  "The Thing"): *50* **30–35**
RCA VICTOR (4294;
  "Shame"): *51* **30–35**
RCA VICTOR (4670
  through 5130): *52–53* **12–15**
RCA VICTOR (5900 &
  6000 series): *55* **5–8**
RCA VICTOR (50-0000
  series): *51* **15–20**
ROSE: *59* **4–6**
STAGE **8–10**
  EPs: 7-Inch 33/45rpm
MERCURY **20–25**

Price Range

LPs: 10/12-Inch 33rpm
MERCURY $75–100
Also see DAMITA JO & STEVE GIBSON &
THE RED CAPS
Also see GREGG, Bobby

GIBSON BROTHERS, The
Singles: 12-Inch 33/45rpm
ISLAND: *79* 4–6
Singles: 7-Inch
ISLAND: *79* 1–3

**GIDEA PARK (Featuring Adrian
Baker)**
Singles: 7-Inch
PROFILE: *82* 1–3

GILBERTO, Astrud
Singles: 7-Inch
CTI 71
VERVE: *67–70* 2–3
LPs: 10/12-Inch 33rpm
IMAGE: *78* 5–8
PERCEPTION: *72* 5–10
VERVE: *65–70* 8–15
Also see GETZ, Stan, & Astrud Gilberto
Also see JOBIM, Antonio Carlos
Also see JONES, Quincy
Also see WANDERLEY, Walter

**GILBERTO, Astrud, & Stanley
Turrentine**
LPs: 10/12-Inch 33rpm
CTI: *71* 8–12
Also see GILBERTO, Astrud
Also see TURRENTINE, Stanley

GILDER, Nick
Singles: 7-Inch
CHRYSALIS: *76–79* 1–3
Picture Sleeves
CHRYSALIS: *78* 1–3
LPs: 10/12-Inch 33rpm
CASABLANCA: *80* 5–8
CHRYSALIS: *77–79* 5–8
Also see SWEENY TODD

**GILKYSON, Terry (Terry Gilkyson
& The Easy Riders; Terry Gilkyson
& The South Coasters)**
Singles: 7-Inch
COLUMBIA: *54–57* 3–5

Price Range

DECCA: *51–52* $4–6
Picture Sleeves
COLUMBIA: *57* 4–6
EPs: 7-Inch 33/45rpm
COLUMBIA: *57* 5–8
DECCA: *51–53* 5–10
LPs: 10/12-Inch 33rpm
DECCA (5000 series):
51–53 15–25
(10-Inch LPs.)
KAPP: *60–63* 10–20
Also see MARTIN, Dean

GILL, Johnny
Singles: 7-Inch
COTILLION: *83–85* 1–3
LPs: 10/12-Inch 33rpm
COTILLION: *83–85* 5–8
Also see LATTISAW, Stacy, & Johnny Gill

GILLAN, Ian (Gillan)
Singles: 7-Inch
OYSTER: *76* 1–3
LPs: 10/12-Inch 33rpm
ISLAND: *77–78* 5–8
OYSTER: *76* 8–10
VIRGIN: *80* 5–8
Also see DEEP PURPLE

GILLEY, Mickey
Singles: 7-Inch
ACT 1: *66* 4–6
ASTRO (Except 100
series): *71–73* 2–4
ASTRO (100 series): *63–65* 10–12

Price Range

DARYL: *63* $4–6
DOT: *58* 40–50
EPIC: *78–85* 1–3
ERIC: *64* 4–6
GOLDBAND: *64* 3–5
GRT: *70* 2–4
KHOURY'S: *59* 15–20
LYNN: *60–61* 10–15
MINOR: *57* 50–60
PAULA (Except 400
    series): *66–68* 3–5
PAULA (400 series): *74–84* 1–3
PLAYBOY: *74–77* 2–3
POTOMAC: *60* 10–15
PRINCESS: *62* 5–8
RESCO: *74* 2–4
REX: *58* 15–20
SABRA: *61* 8–10
SAN: *63* 8–12
SUPREME: *62* 5–8
TCF HALL: *65* 3–5

LPs: 10/12-Inch 33rpm

ASTRO (Except 101):
    73–78 8–10
ASTRO (101; "Lonely
    Wine"): *64* 40–50
EPIC: *79–85* 5–8
PAULA (Except 2000
    series): *81* 5–8
PAULA (2195; "Down
    The Line"): *67* 20–25
PAULA (2224; "Mickey
    Gilley At His Best"): *74* 10–12
PAULA (2234; "Mickey
    Gilley"): *78* 8–10
PLAYBOY: *74–78* 8–12
    Also see CHARLES, Ray, & Mickey Gilley
    Also see HAGGARD, Merle / Mickey Gilley
    / Willie Knight

GILLEY, Mickey, & Johnny Lee
Singles: 7-Inch

EPIC: *81* 1–3
    Also see LEE, Johnny
    Also see NELSON, Willie / Johnny Lee /
    Mickey Gilley

GILLEY, Mickey, & Charly McClain
Singles: 7-Inch

EPIC: *83–84* 1–3
    Also see GILLEY, Mickey

GILMER, Jimmy (Jimmy Gilmer & The Fireballs)
Singles: 7-Inch

ABC: *74* $1–3
ATCO: *68* 3–5
DECCA: *59* 8–10
DOT: *63–66* 3–5
HAMILTON: *63* 4–6
WARWICK: *60* 8–10

LPs: 10/12-Inch 33rpm

ATCO: *68–69* 10–12
CROWN: *63* 15–18
DOT (Except 3577 &
    25577): *63–68* 20–25
DOT (3577; "Buddy's
    Buddy"): *64* 40–50
    (Monaural issue.)
DOT (25577; "Buddy's
    Buddy"): *64* 75–90
    (Stereo issue.)
    Also see FIREBALLS, The
    Also see JIM & MONICA

GILMOUR, David
Singles: 7-Inch

COLUMBIA: *78–84* 1–3
LPs: 10/12-Inch 33rpm
COLUMBIA: *78* 5–8
    Also see PINK FLOYD

GILREATH, James
Singles: 7-Inch

JOY: *63–64* 3–5

GILSTRAP, Jim
Singles: 7-Inch

BELL: *74* 2–3
ROXBURY: *75–76* 2–3
LPs: 10/12-Inch 33rpm
ROXBURY: *75–76* 5–8

GINIE LYNN: see LYNN, Ginie

GIOVANNI, Nikki, & The New York Community Choir
LPs: 10/12-Inch 33rpm
RIGHT-ON: *71* 4–8

GINO & GINA
Singles: 7-Inch
BRUNSWICK: *61* 3–5

Price Range

MERCURY: *58*. **$4–6**

GIRLFRIENDS, The
Singles: 7-Inch
COLPIX: *63–64*. **5–8**
MELIC: *63* **5–8**
PIONEER: *60*. **5–8**

GIRLS CAN'T HELP IT
LPs: 10/12-Inch 33rpm
SIRE: *84* **5–8**

GIRLSCHOOL
Singles: 7-Inch
MERCURY: *82*. **1–3**
LPs: 10/12-Inch 33rpm
MERCURY: *82*. **5–8**
STIFF AMERICA: *82* **5–8**

GIRLTALK
Singles: 7-Inch
GEFFEN: *84*. **1–3**

GIUFFRIA (Gregg Giuffria)
Singles: 7-Inch
MCA: *84–85* **1–3**
LPs: 10/12-Inch 33rpm
MCA: *84* **5–8**
Also see ANGEL

GIVENS FAMILY, The
Singles: 7-Inch
SUGAR HILL: *85* **1–3**

GLADIOLAS, The
Singles: 7-Inch
EXCELLO: *57–58*. **8–10**
Members: Maurice Williams; Norman Wade;
Bill Massey; Willie Jones; Earl Gainey; Bobby
Robinson.
Also see WILLIAMS, Maurice, & The Zodiacs

GLADSTONE
Singles: 7-Inch
ABC: *72*. **2–3**
LPs: 10/12-Inch 33rpm
ABC: *72–73* **8–10**

GLAHE, Will, & His Orchestra
Singles: 7-Inch
LONDON: *55–60* **2–4**

Price Range

LPs: 10/12-Inch 33rpm
LONDON: *55–60* **$5–15**

**GLASS BOTTLE, The (Featuring
Gary Criss)**
Singles: 7-Inch
AVCO: *71* **2–3**
AVCO EMBASSY: *71* **2–3**

GLASS FAMILY
Singles: 7-Inch
JDC: *78* **2–3**

GLASS HARP (With Phil Keaggy)
LPs: 10/12-Inch 33rpm
DECCA: *71–72*. **8–10**
MCA. **5–8**

GLASS HOUSE
Singles: 7-Inch
INVICTUS: *69–72* **2–4**
LPs: 10/12-Inch 33rpm
INVICTUS: *71–72* **8–10**
KIRSHNER: *71* **8–10**

GLASS MOON
Singles: 7-Inch
RADIO: *82* **1–3**
LPs: 10/12-Inch 33rpm
RADIO: *80–82* **5–8**

**GLAZER, Tom (Tom Glazer & The
Children's Do-Re-Mi Chorus)**
Singles: 7-Inch
COLUMBIA: *53–55* **2–4**
CORAL: *56*. **2–4**
KAPP: *63–64*. **2–4**
UNITED ARTISTS: *66–67* **2–3**
Picture Sleeves
KAPP: *63* **2–4**
LPs: 10/12-Inch 33rpm
CAMDEN: *64–65*. **5–10**
KAPP: *63–64*. **8–12**
COLUMBIA: *55* **8–15**
HARMONY: *59* **8–15**
MERCURY: *55*. **10–20**
MOTIVATION: *62*. **5–10**
RIVERSIDE: *61* **8–12**
UNITED ARTISTS: *66* **8–12**
WASHINGTON: *59*. **8–15**

WONDERLAND: *63* $6–12

GLEASON, Jackie (Jackie Gleason's Orchestra)
Singles: 7-Inch
CAPITOL: *52–62* 2–3
DECCA (27000 series): *51* 2–5
EPs: 7-Inch 33/45rpm
CAPITOL: *53–60* 3–6
LPs: 10/12-Inch 33rpm
CAPITOL: *53–69* 5–15

GLENCOVES, The
Singles: 7-Inch
SELECT: *63–64* 3–5

GLENN, Darrell
Singles: 7-Inch
COLUMBIA: *66–67* 2–3
DOT: *56* 3–5
FASHION: *60* 2–4
LONGHORN: *65* 2–4
POMPEII: *68–69* 2–3
RCA VICTOR: *54* 3–5
ROBBIE: *64* 2–4
VALLEY: *53* 3–5
LPs: 10/12-Inch 33rpm
NRC: *59* 12–20

GLENN, Lloyd
Singles: 7-Inch
ALADDIN: *56–59* 5–8
HOLLYWOOD: *54* 5–8
IMPERIAL: *62* 3–5
SWING TIME: *52–54* 15–20
LPs: 10/12-Inch 33rpm
ALADDIN (Black vinyl):
56 30–40
ALADDIN (Colored
vinyl): *56* 70–80
BLACK & BLUE: *77* 8–10
IMPERIAL: *62* 15–20
SCORE: *57* 30–40
SWING TIME 100–125
Also see FULSON, Lowell

GLITTER, Gary (Gary Glitter & The Glitter Band)
Singles: 7-Inch
ARISTA: *75* 2–3
BELL: *72–74* 2–3

LPs: 10/12-Inch 33rpm
BELL: *72* $8–10
EPIC: *81* 5–8
Also see GLITTER BAND, The

GLITTER BAND, The
Singles: 7-Inch
ARISTA: *75–76* 2–3
LPs: 10/12-Inch 33rpm
ARISTA: *76* 8–10
Member: Pete Gill.
Also see GLITTER, Gary
Also see MOTORHEAD

GLORIES, The
Singles: 7-Inch
DATE: *67–68* 3–5

GLOVER, Roger
Singles: 7-Inch
21: *84* 1–3
U.K.: *75* 8–10
LPs: 10/12-Inch 33rpm
POLYDOR: *78* 5–8
21: *84* 5–8
U.K.: *75* 8–10
Also see DEEP PURPLE
Also see RAINBOW

GO WEST
Singles: 7-Inch
CHRYSALIS: *85* 1–3
LPs: 10/12-Inch 33rpm
CHRYSALIS: *85* 5–8

GOANNA
Singles: 7-Inch
ATCO: *83* 1–3
LPs: 10/12-Inch 33rpm
ATCO: *83* 5–8

GODFREY, Arthur
Singles: 7-Inch
COLUMBIA: *50–56* 3–5
CONTEMPO: *63–64* 2–3
DECCA (29000 series): *55* 3–5
MGM: *66* 2–3
MTA: *69* 1–3
SIGNATURE: *60* 2–4
VEE JAY: *65* 2–3
EPs: 7-Inch 33/45rpm
COLUMBIA: *52–56* 5–8

Price Range

LPs: 10/12-Inch 33rpm
ADMIRAL: 67 . . . . **$8–12**
CAMDEN: 66–67 . . . . **8–12**
CAPITOL: 62 . . . . **8–15**
COLUMBIA: 53–61 . . . . **10–20**
CONTEMPO **8–15**
HARMONY: 59 . . . . **10–15**
RCA VICTOR: 73 . . . . **5–8**
SIGNATURE: 60 . . . . **8–15**
Also see MARINERS, The

GODFREY, Ray
Singles: 7-Inch
ABC: 67 . . . . **3–5**
COLUMBIA: 67 . . . . **3–5**
J&J: 60 . . . . **4–6**
PEACH: 62 . . . . **8–10**
SIMS: 63 . . . . **3–5**
SPRING: 70 . . . . **2–4**
TOLLIE: 65 . . . . **3–5**
YONAH: 61 . . . . **4–6**

GODLEY, Kevin, & Lol Creme
(Godley & Creme)
Singles: 12-Inch 33/45rpm
POLYDOR: 85 . . . . **4–6**

Singles: 7-Inch
MERCURY: 77 . . . . **2–3**
POLYDOR: 85 . . . . **1–3**

LPs: 10/12-Inch 33rpm
MERCURY: 77 . . . . **10–15**
MIRAGE: 82 . . . . **5–8**
POLYDOR: 85 . . . . **5–10**
Also see 10CC

GODSPELL (Robin Lamont & Original "Godspell" Cast)
Singles: 7-Inch
BELL: 72 . . . . **2–3**

GODWIN, Peter
Singles: 12-Inch 33/45rpm
POLYDOR: 83 . . . . **4–6**

GODZ, The
Singles: 7-Inch
MILLENNIUM: 78 . . . . **2–3**

Price Range

LPs: 10/12-Inch 33rpm
CASABLANCA: 78 . . . . **$5–8**
MILLENNIUM/
  CASABLANCA: 78 . . . . **5–8**

GOFFIN, Louise
Singles: 7-Inch
ASYLUM: 79 . . . . **1–3**
ELEKTRA: 79 . . . . **1–3**

LPs: 10/12-Inch 33rpm
ASYLUM: 79–81 . . . . **5–8**

GO-GOs, The
Singles: 12-Inch 33/45
I.R.S.: 82 . . . . **4–6**

Singles: 7-Inch
I.R.S. (Except 8001): 81–85 . . . . **1–3**
I.R.S. (8001; "We Got The
  Beat"): 82 . . . . **6–10**
(Picture disc.)

Picture Sleeves
I.R.S.: 81–85 . . . . **1–3**

LPs: 10/12-Inch 33rpm
I.R.S.: 81–85 . . . . **5–8**
Members: Belinda Carlisle; Charlotte Caffey;
Jane Wiedlin; Margot Olaverria; Elissa Bello;
Gina Schook; Kathy Valentine.
Also see TEXTONES, The
Also see WIEDLIN, Jane

GOLD, Andrew
Singles: 7-Inch
ASYLUM: 76–78 . . . . **1–3**

Picture Sleeves
ASYLUM: 77–78 . . . . **1–3**

LPs: 10/12-Inch 33rpm
ASYLUM: 75–80 . . . . **5–8**
Also see WAX

GOLD, Marty, & His Orchestra
Singles: 7-Inch
KAPP: 58–59 . . . . **2–3**
RCA VICTOR: 60–61 . . . . **2–3**

EPs: 7-Inch 33/45rpm
KAPP: 59 . . . . **3–6**
VIK: 56–57 . . . . **4–8**

Price Range

LPs: 10/12-Inch 33rpm
KAPP: *59* $4–8
RCA VICTOR: *59–63* 4–8
VIK: *56–57* 5–10

GOLDDIGGERS, The
Singles: 7-Inch
METROMEDIA: *69*............... 1–3
RCA VICTOR: *72* 1–3

LPs: 10/12-Inch 33rpm
METROMEDIA: *69*.............. 6–10
RCA VICTOR: *71* 5–10
Also see MARTIN, Dean

GOLDE, Frannie
Singles: 7-Inch
ATLANTIC: *77* 1–3
BIG TREE: *76* 2–3
PORTRAIT: *79*................... 1–3

GOLDEN EARRING
Singles: 7-Inch
ATLANTIC: *70* 2–4
MCA: *76–78* 2–3
POLYDOR (2000 series):
 79 1–3
POLYDOR (14000 series):
 69 3–5
TRACK: *74–75*................... 2–3
21: *82–85* 1–3

LPs: 10/12-Inch 33rpm
ATLANTIC: *69* 15–20
CAPITOL (Except 11315):
 67–74 30–35
CAPITOL (11315;
 "Golden Earring"): *74* 10–12
MCA: *75–81* 6–10
POLYDOR: *79–80* 5–8
TRACK (396;
 "Moontan"): *73*............... 18–20
 (With nude showgirl on cover.)
TRACK (396;
 "Moontan"): *73*............... 10–12
 (Showgirl not nude on cover.)
21: *82–85* 5–8

GOLDEN GATE STRINGS, The
LPs: 10/12-Inch 33rpm
EPIC: *67* 5–10

Bobby Goldsboro, 26 charted singles (1962–73), 10 charted LPs (1967–74).

Price Range

GOLDSBORO, Bobby
Singles: 7-Inch
CURB: *80–82*.................... $2–3
EPIC: *77* 1–3
LAURIE: *62–63* 3–5
UNITED ARTISTS
 (Except 600 through 900
 series): *63–66* 2–4
UNITED ARTISTS (600
 through 900 series):
 63–64 3–5
VISTA: *74* 2–3

Picture Sleeves
UNITED ARTISTS
 (Except 700 series):
 66–74 2–4
UNITED ARTISTS (700
 series): *64* 5–8

LPs: 10/12-Inch 33rpm
CURB: *80–82*.................... 5–8
EPIC: *77* 8–10
K-TEL 5–8
LIBERTY: *81* 5–8
UNITED ARTISTS: *64–76* 10–15
Also see REEVES, Del, & Bobby Goldsboro

GOLLIWOGS, The
Singles: 7-Inch
FANTASY: *65*.................. 15–20
SCORPIO: *65–67* 15–20

Price Range   *Price Range*

LPs: 10/12-Inch 33rpm
FANTASY: 75. . . . . **$8–10**
Also see CREEDENCE CLEARWATER RE-
VIVAL

GOMM, Ian
Singles: 7-Inch
STIFF: 79 . . . . **1–3**
LPs: 10/12-Inch 33rpm
STIFF: 79–80. . . . . **5–8**

GONE ALL STARS, The
Singles: 7-Inch
GONE: 58 . . . . **8–10**
ROULETTE: 71 . . . . **1–3**
EPs: 7-Inch 33/45rpm
GONE: 58 . . . . **15–20**

GONZALES, Terri
Singles: 7-Inch
BECKET: 82. **1–3**

GONZALEZ
Singles: 12-Inch 33/45rpm
CAPITOL: 79 . . . . **4–6**
Singles: 7-Inch
CAPITOL: 78–79 . . . . **1–3**
LPs: 10/12-Inch 33rpm
CAPITOL: 78–80 . . . . **5–8**

GOODEES, The
Singles: 7-Inch
HIP: 68–69 . . . . **4–6**
LPs: 10/12-Inch 33rpm
HIP: 69 . . . . **10–12**

GOODIE
Singles: 12-Inch 33/45rpm
TOTAL EXPERIENCE:
82–84 . . . . **4–6**
Singles: 7-Inch
TOTAL EXPERIENCE:
82–84 . . . . **1–3**
LPs: 10/12-Inch 33rpm
TOTAL EXPERIENCE:
83 . . . . **5–8**

GOODIES, The
Singles: 7-Inch
20TH CENTURY-FOX:
75 . . . . **2–3**

GOODING, Cuba
Singles: 12-Inch 33/45rpm
STREETWISE: 83 . . . . **$4–6**
Singles: 7-Inch
MOTOWN: 78–79. . . . . **1–3**
STREETWISE: 83 . . . . **1–3**
LPs: 10/12-Inch 33rpm
MOTOWN: 78–79. . . . . **5–8**
Also see MAIN INGREDIENT, The

GOODMAN, Benny, Orchestra
Singles: 7-Inch
CHESS: 59. . . . . **2–3**
COLUMBIA: 50–56 . . . . **2–3**
COMMAND: 67. . . . . **1–3**
DECCA: 62 . . . . **1–3**
EPs: 7-Inch 33/45rpm
BRUNSWICK: 54. . . . . **4–8**
CAPITOL: 55–56 . . . . **4–8**
COLUMBIA: 50–58 . . . . **4–8**
DECCA (798; "The Benny
Goodman Story"): 56 . . . . **10–15**
MGM: 59. . . . . **4–6**
RCA VICTOR: 50–59 . . . . **4–8**
LPs: 10/12-Inch 33rpm
ABC: 76. . . . . **5–8**
BRIGHT ORANGE: 73 . . . . **5–8**
BRUNSWICK: 54. . . . . **10–20**
CAMDEN: 63–65. . . . . **5–10**
CAPITOL: 55–78 . . . . **5–15**
CENTURY: 79 . . . . **5–8**
CHESS: 59. **5–15**
COLPIX: 62 . . . . **8–12**
COLUMBIA: 50–82. . . . . **5–15**
COMMAND: 67. . . . . **5–10**
DECCA (188; "The Benny
Goodman Story,
Volumes 1 & 2") **25–35**
DECCA (8252; "The
Benny Goodman Story,
Volume 1"): 56 . . . . **20–30**
DECCA (8253; "The
Benny Goodman Story,
Volume 2"): 56 . . . . **20–30**
DECCA (7-8252; "The
Benny Goodman Story,
Volume 1"): 59 . . . . **15–20**
(Reprocessed stereo reissue.)
DECCA (7-8253; "The
Benny Goodman Story,
Volume 2"): 59 . . . . **15–20**
(Reprocessed stereo reissue.)

Price Range

EVEREST: *73* **$5–8**
HARMONY: *59–60* **5–10**
LONDON: *72–78* **5–10**
LONDON/PHASE 4:
  71–72 .... **5–10**
MCA: *80* **5–8**
MGM: *59* **5–15**
MARK '56: *77.* **5–8**
MEGA: *72–74.* **5–8**
PAUSA: *83* **5–8**
PRESTIGE: *69* **5–10**
QUINTESSENCE: *79.* **4–8**
RCA VICTOR: *50–78* **5–15**
SUNBEAM: *73* **5–8**
X: *54.* **10–15**
  Also see BASIE, Count, & Benny Goodman
  Also see LEE, Peggy

GOODMAN, Dickie
Singles: 7-Inch
AUDIO SPECTRUM: *64* **8–10**
CASH: *75.* **3–5**
COTIQUE: *69.* **3–5**
DIAMOND: *62.* **4–6**
EXTRAN: *82.* **2–3**
HOTLINE: *79.* **2–4**
J.M.D.: *62* **12–15**
JANUS: *77* **2–4**
M.D.: *65.* **8–10**
MARK-X: *61.* **10–12**
MONTAGE: *82.* **2–3**
PRELUDE: *80.* **2–3**
RAINY WEDNESDAY:
  73–75 .... **2–4**
RAMGO **8–10**
RED BIRD: *66.* **8–10**
RHINO: *84* **1–3**
RORI: *61.* **8–10**
SHARK: *79.* **2–4**
SHOCK: *77.* **2–4**
20TH CENTURY-FOX:
  63 .... **4–6**
TWIRL: *66* **10–12**
WACKO: *81* **2–3**

LPs: 10/12-Inch 33rpm
CASH: *75.* **18–20**
COMET: *64.* **12–15**
IX CHAINS: *73* **8–10**
RHINO: *83* **5–8**
RORI: *62.* **35–40**

Price Range

Also see BUCHANAN & GOODMAN

GOODMAN, Jerry, & Jan Hammer
LPs: 10/12-Inch 33rpm
NEMPEROR: *74* **$8–10**
  Also see HAMMER, Jan

GOODMAN, Steve
Singles: 7-Inch
ASYLUM: *75–81.* **1–3**
BUDDAH: *72–73* **2–3**
LPs: 10/12-Inch 33rpm
ASYLUM: *80.* **5–8**
BUDDAH: *71–76* **8–12**
RED PAJAMAS: *83.* **5–8**

GOODMAN, Steve, & Phoebe Snow
Singles: 7-Inch
ASYLUM: *80.* **1–3**
  Also see GOODMAN, Steve
  Also see SNOW, Phoebe

GOODTIMERS, The (Featuring Don Covay)
Singles: 7-Inch
ARNOLD: *61* **4–6**
EPIC: *61* **3–5**
  Also see COVAY, Don

GOODWIN, Don
Singles: 7-Inch
SILVER BLUE: *73.* **2–3**

GOODWIN, Ron, Orchestra
Singles: 7-Inch
CAPITOL: *56–59* **2–4**
KING: *61* **2–3**
LPs: 10/12-Inch 33rpm
CAPITOL: *57–60* **5–15**

GOODY GOODY
Singles: 7-Inch
ATLANTIC: *78* **1–3**
LPs: 10/12-Inch 33rpm
ATLANTIC: *78* **5–8**

GOON SQUAD, The
Singles: 12-Inch 33/45rpm
EPIC: *85* **4–6**
Singles: 7-Inch
EPIC: *85* **1–3**

Price Range

GOOSE CREEK SYMPHONY
(Goose Creek)
Singles: 7-Inch
CAPITOL: *70–72* **$2–4**

LPs: 10/12-Inch 33rpm
CAPITOL: *70–72* **10–12**
COLUMBIA: *74* **8–10**
RLO **8–10**

GORDON, Barry
Singles: 7-Inch
ABC: *68* **2–3**
CAPITOL: *71* **1–3**
CADENCE: *62* **2–4**
DUNHILL: *68.* **2–3**
ERA: *59* **2–4**
MGM: *55–56* **3–5**
MERCURY: *61.* **2–4**
UNITED ARTISTS: *64–66* **2–4**

Picture Sleeves
MGM: *56* **3–5**

LPs: 10/12-Inch 33rpm
UNITED ARTISTS: *66* **8–15**

GORDON, Robert (Robert Gordon & Link Wray)
Singles: 7-Inch
PRIVATE STOCK: *77–78* **2–3**
RCA VICTOR: *79–81* **1–3**

Picture Sleeves
PRIVATE STOCK: *79* **2–3**

LPs: 10/12-Inch 33rpm
PRIVATE STOCK: *77–78* **8–10**
RCA VICTOR (Except
  colored vinyl): *79–82.* **5–8**
RCA VICTOR (Colored
  vinyl): *79* **10–15**
  Also see WRAY, Link

GORDON, Roscoe
Singles: 7-Inch
ABC-PARAMOUNT:
  62–63 .... **3–5**
CHESS: *52* **35–45**
COLLECTABLES: *81* **1–3**
DUKE (106 through 129):
  53–54 .... **20–25**

Price Range

DUKE (300 series): *60* **$4–6**
FLIP (227; "Just Love Me
  Baby"): *55* **50–75**
FLIP (237; "The
  Chicken"): *56.* **35–40**
RPM (322 through 336):
  50 .... **30–35**
RPM (344 through 384):
  51–53 .... **20–25**
SUN (Except 227 & 237):
  56–58 .... **5–8**
SUN (227; "Just Love Me
  Baby"): *55* **50–75**
SUN (237; "The
  Chicken"): *56.* **35–40**
VEE JAY: *59–61.* **4–6**

GORE, Lesley
Singles: 7-Inch
A&M: *75–76* **2–4**
CREWE: *70–71* **2–4**
MERCURY: *63–69.* **3–5**
MOWEST: *72* **2–4**

Picture Sleeves
MERCURY: *63–67.* **5–10**

LPs: 10/12-Inch 33rpm
A&M: *75* **8–10**
MERCURY: *63–80.* **20–25**
MOWEST: *72* **8–10**
POLYDOR: *85* **5–8**
WING: *67–69* **10–15**
  Also see BILLY & SUE
  Also see CHRISTIE, Lou, & Leslie Gore
  Also see DRIFTERS, The / Leslie Gore / Roy
  Orbison / Los Bravos

GORE, Michael
Singles: 7-Inch
CAPITOL: *84* **1–3**

GORL, Robert
Singles: 7-Inch
ELEKTRA: *84* **1–3**

Eydie Gorme, 17 charted singles (1956–72), 16 charted LPs (1957–70). (Includes issues shown as by Steve Lawrence & Eydie Gorme.)

Price Range

GORME, Eydie
Singles: 7-Inch
ABC-PARAMOUNT:
  55–62 .... $2–4
CALENDAR: 67 1–3
COLUMBIA: 62–68 2–4
CORAL: 53–55 3–5
MGM: 71–73 1–3
RCA VICTOR: 69–70 1–3
UNITED ARTISTS: 60–76 1–3

Picture Sleeves
COLUMBIA: 62–63 2–4

Price Range

LPs: 10/12-Inch 33rpm
ABC-PARAMOUNT:
  57–65 .... $8–15
APPLAUSE: 81. 4–6
COLUMBIA: 63–73 8–15
HARMONY: 68–71 5–10
MGM: 71 5–10
RCA VICTOR: 68–70 5–10
UNITED ARTISTS: 61–62 8–15
VOCALION: 63 6–10
  Also see LAWRENCE, Steve, & Eydie Gorme

GOUDREAU, Barry
Singles: 7-Inch
PORTRAIT: 79. 1–3
LPs: 10/12-Inch 33rpm
PORTRAIT: 79. 5–8
  Also see BOSTON

GOULET, Robert
Singles: 7-Inch
ABC: 74 1–3
ARTISTS OF AMERICA:
  75 1–3
COLUMBIA: 61–70 2–4
MGM: 73 1–3
MERLIN: 71 1–3
PARAMOUNT: 74. 1–3
Picture Sleeves
COLUMBIA: 62–65 2–4
LPs: 10/12-Inch 33rpm
ARTISTS OF AMERICA:
  76 5–8
COLUMBIA: 61–73 5–15
HARMONY: 71–72 5–10
MERLIN: 71 5–10
ORINDA: 78. 5–8

GRACE, Fredi, & Rhinestone
Singles: 7-Inch
RCA VICTOR: 82 1–3

GRACE, Leda
Singles: 7-Inch
POLYDOR: 81 1–3

GRACIE, Charlie
Singles: 7-Inch
ABKCO: 75. 1–3
CADILLAC: 54 40–50
CAMEO: 57–59. 4–6

Price Range

CORAL: *59* **$4–6**
DIAMOND: *65*. **3–5**
FELSTED: *61* **3–5**
PRESIDENT: *62*. **3–5**
ROULETTE: *59–61* **3–5**
20TH CENTURY: *56*. **20–25**

GRADUATES, The
Singles: 7-Inch
CORSICAN: *59*. **5–8**
SHAN-TODD: *59*. **5–8**

GRAHAM, Larry (Larry Graham & Graham Central Station; Graham Central Station)
Singles: 7-Inch
WARNER BROS: *74–83* **1–3**
Picture Sleeves
WARNER BROS: *80* .... **INC**
LPs: 10/12-Inch 33rpm
WARNER BROS: *73–83* **5–10**
Also see SLY & THE FAMILY STONE

GRAINGERS, The
Singles: 7-Inch
BC: *81* **1–3**

GRAMMER, Billy
Singles: 7-Inch
DECCA: *61–66*. **2–4**
EPIC: *66–67* **2–3**
EVEREST: *60* **2–4**
MERCURY: *68–69*. **2–3**
MONUMENT (Except 400
    series): *75–76* **1–3**
MONUMENT (400 series):
    59–63 .... **2–4**
RICE: *67* **2–3**
STOP: *69* **2–3**
EPs: 7-Inch 33/45rpm
DECCA: *64* **4–6**
LPs: 10/12-Inch 33rpm
CLASSIC CHRISTMAS:
    77 .... **5–8**
DECCA: *62–64*. **10–15**
EPIC: *67* **8–12**
MONUMENT (14000;
    "Travelin' On"): *59* **12–18**
MONUMENT (18039;
    "Travelin' On"): *66*. **8–12**
STONEWAY: *75*. **5–10**

Price Range

VOCALION: *68* **$6–12**
    Also see CASH, Johnny / Billy Grammer / The
    Wilburn Brothers

GRANAHAN, Gerry
Singles: 7-Inch
CANADIAN
    AMERICAN: *60*. **3–5**
CAPRICE (Except 108):
    61 .... **3–5**
CAPRICE (108; "Dance
    Girl, Dance"): *61*. **25–30**
    (With The Wildwoods, who were actually The
    Five Satins.)
GONE: *59–60* **4–6**
SUNBEAM: *58–59* **4–6**
Picture Sleeves
GONE: *60* **4–6**
    Also see DICKY DOO & THE DON'TS
    Also see FIVE SATINS, The

GRANATA, Rocca, & The International Quintet
Singles: 7-Inch
LAURIE: *59* **2–4**

GRAND CANYON
Singles: 7-Inch
BANG: *74* **2–3**
FAITHFUL VIRTUE: *70* **2–3**

GRAND FUNK RAILROAD (Grand Funk)
Singles: 7-Inch
CAPITOL: *69–76* **2–4**
FULL MOON: *81*. **1–3**
MCA: *76–77* **1–3**
Picture Sleeves
CAPITOL: *72–76* **2–4**
FULL MOON: *81*. .... **INC**
MCA: *76* **1–3**
LPs: 10/12-Inch 33rpm
CAPITOL (Except 12000
    & 16000 series): *69–76* **8–10**
CAPITOL (12000 & 16000
    series): *80–81* **5–8**
FULL MOON: *81–83*. **5–8**
MCA: *76* **8–10**
    Members: Mark Farner; Don Brewer; Mel
    Schacher; Craig Frost.
    Also see KNIGHT, Terry

Price Range   *Price Range*

GRANDMASTER FLASH & THE FURIOUS FIVE (Grandmaster Melle Mel & The Furious Five; Grandmaster & Melle Mel; Grandmaster Flash)
Singles: 12-Inch 33/45
ATLANTIC: 84 .... $4–6
ELEKTRA: 85 4–6
SUGAR HILL: 80–85 4–6
Singles: 7-Inch
SUGAR HILL: 80–85 1–3
LPs: 10/12-Inch 33rpm
SUGAR HILL: 82–85 5–8
Also see MELLE MEL & DUKE BOOTEE

GRANDMIXER D. ST.
Singles: 12-Inch 33/45rpm
ISLAND: 83 4–6
Singles: 7-Inch
ISLAND: 83 1–3

GRANT, Amy
Singles: 7-Inch
A&M: 85–86 1–3
Picture Sleeves
A&M: 85–86 .... INC
LPs: 10/12-Inch 33rpm
A&M: 85–86 5–8
MYRRH: 80–85 5–8

GRANT, David
Singles: 12-Inch 33/45rpm
CHRYSALIS: 83................... 4–6
Singles: 7-Inch
CHRYSALIS: 83................... 1–3
Also see LINX

GRANT, Earl
Singles: 7-Inch
DECCA: 58–70................... 2–4
PRINCE: 56 3–5
EPs: 7-Inch 33/45rpm
DECCA: 59–62................... 4–8
LPs: 10/12-Inch 33rpm
DECCA: 59–70................... 5–15
MCA: 76 5–8
VOCALION: 69–70 5–10

GRANT, Eddy
Singles: 12-Inch 33/45rpm
EPIC: 80–82 .... $4–6
PORTRAIT: 83–85................ 4–6
Singles: 7-Inch
EPIC: 79–80 1–3
PORTRAIT: 83–85................ 1–3
LPs: 10/12-Inch 33rpm
EPIC: 79–80 5–8
PORTRAIT: 83–85................ 5–8
Also see EQUALS, The

GRANT, Eleanor
Singles: 7-Inch
CBS ASSOCIATED: 84–85.......... 1–3
CATAWBA: 83.................... 1–3
COLUMBIA: 76................... 2–3

GRANT, Gogi
Singles: 7-Inch
CHARTER: 63 2–4
ERA: 55–56..................... 3–5
LIBERTY: 60–61 2–4
MONUMENT: 66–67............... 2–3
PETE: 68–69.................... 2–3
RCA VICTOR: 52–58 3–5
20TH CENTURY-FOX:
   61–62 2–3
EPs: 7-Inch 33/45rpm
RCA VICTOR (Except
   1030): 57–58.................. 5–8
RCA VICTOR (1030;
   "The Helen Morgan
   Story"): 57................... 20–30
   (Soundtrack.)
LPs: 10/12-Inch 33rpm
CHARTER: 64 8–12
ERA: 56–61..................... 10–20
LIBERTY: 60 8–15
PETE: 68–70.................... 6–10
RCA VICTOR (Except
   1030): 57–59.................. 10–20
RCA VICTOR (1030;
   "The Helen Morgan
   Story"): 57................... 50–75
   (Soundtrack.)

GRANT, Janie
Singles: 7-Inch
CAPRICE: 61–62................. 4–6
PARKWAY: 66 3–5

Price Range

UNITED ARTISTS: *63–65* **$3–5**
Also see RAY, James

GRANT, Tom
Singles: 7-Inch
WMOT: *81* **1–3**

GRAPEFRUIT
Singles: 7-Inch
EQUINOX: *68.* **3–5**
LPs: 10/12-Inch 33rpm
DUNHILL: *68.* **10–12**
RCA VICTOR: *69* **10–12**

GRAPPELLI, Stephane, & David Grisman
LPs: 10/12-Inch 33rpm
WARNER BROS: *81.* **5–8**
Also see GRISMAN, David

GRASS ROOTS, The (Featuring Rob Grill)
Singles: 7-Inch
ABC: *70.* **1–3**
DUNHILL: *65–74.* **3–5**
HAVEN: *75–76.* **2–3**
MCA: *82* **1–3**
Picture Sleeves
DUNHILL: *67–70.* **3–5**
LPs: 10/12-Inch 33rpm
ABC: *76.* **8–10**
COMMAND: *74.* **8–10**
DUNHILL: *66–73.* **10–15**
HAVEN: *75.* **8–10**
MCA: *82* **5–8**

GRATEFUL DEAD, The (Featuring Jerry Garcia)
Singles: 7-Inch
ARISTA: *77–80.* **1–3**
GRATEFUL DEAD:
73–76 .... **2–3**
SCORPIO: *66* **35–45**
WARNER BROS: *67–73* **4–6**
WARNER BROS./
FILLMORE: *72* **2–3**
Picture Sleeves
ARISTA: *80* **1–3**
LPs: 10/12-Inch 33rpm
ARISTA: *77–81.* **5–8**

Price Range

GRATEFUL DEAD:
73–76 .... **$10–12**
MFSL: *78.* **10–15**
PRIDE: *73.* **12–15**
SUNFLOWER: *70–71* **20–25**
WARNER BROS. (1600 &
1700 series): *67–69* **20–25**
(With Warner Bros./Seven "W7" label.)
WARNER BROS. (1800
series, except 1830): *70* **15–20**
(With Warner Bros./Seven "W7" label.)
WARNER BROS. (1830;
"Live Dead"): *69* **20–25**
(With Warner Bros./Seven "W7" label.)
WARNER BROS. (1900
series): *71* **10–12**
WARNER BROS. (2600
series): *72* **15–18**
WARNER BROS. (2700 &
3000 series): *74–77* **8–12**
Also see GARCIA, Jerry
Also see HART, Mickey
Also see WEIR, Bob

GRAVES, Billy
Singles: 7-Inch
MONUMENT (Except
401): *59–66.* **3–5**
MONUMENT (401; "The
Shag"): *59* **5–8**

GRAVES, Carl
Singles: 7-Inch
A&M: *74* **2–3**
ARIOLA AMERICA:
75–77 .... **2–3**

GRAY, Claude
Singles: 7-Inch
COLUMBIA: *64–66* **2–3**
COUNTRY INT'L: *81.* **1–3**
D: *59–60.* **3–5**
DECCA: *66–71* **2–3**
GRANNY WHITE: *76–82* **1–3**
MERCURY: *60–64.* **2–4**
MILLION: *72–73* **1–3**
LPs: 10/12-Inch 33rpm
DECCA: *67–68.* **8–12**
MERCURY: *62.* **12–18**
MILLION: *72* **5–10**

Price Range

Price Range

PICKWICK/HILLTOP:
67 .... **$8–12**

GRAY, Dolores
Singles: 7-Inch
DECCA: 51–55 3–5

GRAY, Diva, & Oyster
Singles: 7-Inch
COLUMBIA: 79–80 1–3
LPs: 10/12-Inch 33rpm
COLUMBIA: 79 5–8

GRAY, Dobie
Singles: 12-Inch 33/45rpm
INFINITY: 79 4–6
Singles: 7-Inch
ARISTA: 83 1–3
CAPITOL: 67 3–5
CAPRICORN: 76–77 2–3
CHARGER: 64–66 3–5
COLLECTABLES: 81 1–3
CORDAK: 62–64 3–5
DECCA: 73 2–3
ERIC 1–3
INFINITY: 78–79 2–3
JAF: 63 4–6
MCA: 73–75 2–3
REAL FINE: 62 4–6
ROBOX: 81 1–3
STRIPE: 60–61 8–10
WHITE WHALE: 69 3–5
LPs: 10/12-Inch 33rpm
CAPRICORN: 76 8–10
CHARGER: 65 15–20
DECCA: 73 8–10
INFINITY: 79 6–10
MCA: 73–74 8–10
ROBOX: 81 5–8
STRIPE 10–12

GRAY, Glen, & The Casa Loma Orchestra
Singles: 7-Inch
CAPITOL: 56–58 2–4
DECCA: 55 2–4
EPs: 7-Inch 33/45rpm
CAPITOL: 56–58 3–6
LPs: 10/12-Inch 33rpm
CAPITOL: 56–61 5–15

GRAY, Maureen
Singles: 7-Inch
CHANCELLOR: 61–62 .... $3–5
LANDA: 62 3–5
MERCURY: 63–64 3–5

GREAN, Charles (The Charles Randolph Grean Sounde)
Singles: 7-Inch
DOT: 67 2–3
RANWOOD: 69–79 1–3
LPs: 10/12-Inch 33rpm
RANWOOD: 69–70 6–12

GREASE BAND, The (With Henry McCullough)
Singles: 7-Inch
SHELTER: 71 2–4
LPs: 10/12-Inch 33rpm
SHELTER: 71 8–10
Also see McCARTNEY, Paul

GREAT BELIEVERS, The
Singles: 7-Inch
CASCADE: 64 30–35
Member: Johnny Winter.
Also see WINTER, Johnny

GREAT!! SOCIETY!!, The (Featuring Grace Slick)
Singles: 7-Inch
COLUMBIA: 68 8–10
NORTHBEACH: 66 40–50
Also see JEFFERSON AIRPLANE, The
Also see SLICK, Grace

GREAT WHITE
Singles: 7-Inch
EMI AMERICA: 84 1–3
LPs: 10/12-Inch 33rpm
EMI AMERICA: 84 5–8

GREAVES, R.B.
Singles: 7-Inch
ATCO: 69–70 2–4
BAREBACK: 77 2–3
MGM: 73 2–3
MIDSONG: 80 1–3
SUNFLOWER: 72 2–3
20TH CENTURY-FOX:
74 2–3

Price Range

LPs: 10/12-Inch 33rpm
ATCO: 69 . . . . **$12–15**

GRECCO, Cyndi
Singles: 7-Inch
PRIVATE STOCK: 76–77. . . . . **1–3**

Buddy Greco, one charted single (1962), no charted LPs.

GRECO, Buddy (The Buddy Greco Trio)
Singles: 7-Inch
CORAL: 51–55. . . . . **3–5**
EPIC: 58–67 . . . . **2–4**
HERALD: 59 . . . . **2–4**
KAPP: 56 . . . . **2–4**
MGM: 71–72. . . . . **1–3**
REPRISE: 66–68. . . . . **2–3**
SCEPTER: 69 . . . . **1–3**
Picture Sleeves
EPIC: 64–65 . . . . **2–4**
EPs: 7-Inch 33/45rpm
CORAL: 55. . . . . **5–8**
LPs: 10/12-Inch 33rpm
CORAL: 55. **10–20**
EPIC: 60–66 . . . . **8–15**
HARMONY: 68 . . . . **8–12**
KAPP: 61 . . . . **8–15**
REPRISE: 67. . . . . **8–12**

Price Range

SCEPTER: 69–73 . . . . **$5–10**
VOCALION: 64 . . . . **8–12**

GRECH, Rick
LPs: 10/12-Inch 33rpm
RSO: 73 . . . . **5–8**

GREELEY, George
Singles: 7-Inch
WARNER BROS: 59–62 . . . . **2–3**
EPs: 7-Inch 33/45rpm
CAPITOL: 56 . . . . **4–8**
LPs: 10/12-Inch 33rpm
CAPITOL: 56 . . . . **5–15**
RAVE: 56 . . . . **8–18**
WARNER BROS: 59–61 . . . . **5–10**

GREEN, Al (Al Greene & The Soul Mates)
Singles: 7-Inch
BELL: 72–73. **2–3**
FLASHBACK. **1–3**
HI: 70–78. . . . . **2–3**
HOT LINE: 67 . . . . **4–6**
MOTOWN: 82–85. . . . . **1–3**
LPs: 10/12-Inch 33rpm
BELL: 71. . . . . **8–10**
HI: 69–78. . . . . **10–12**
HOT LINE: 67 . . . . **20–25**
KORY: 77 . . . . **8–10**
MOTOWN: 82–85. . . . . **5–8**
MYRRH: 80–83 . . . . **5–8**

GREEN, Darren
Singles: 7-Inch
RCA VICTOR: 73–74 . . . . **2–3**

GREEN, Garland
Singles: 7-Inch
OCEAN FRONT: 83 . . . . **1–3**
RCA VICTOR: 77 . . . . **1–3**
SPRING: 74–75. . . . . **2–3**
UNI: 69 . . . . **3–5**
LPs: 10/12-Inch 33rpm
RCA VICTOR: 74–78 . . . . **8–10**
UNI: 70 . . . . **10–12**

GREEN, Grant
LPs: 10/12-Inch 33rpm
BLUE NOTE: 61–65 . . . . **10–20**

Price Range

Price Range

(Label reads "Blue Note Records Inc. - New York, U.S.A.")
BLUE NOTE: *66* **$8–12**
(Label reads "Blue Note Records - A Division Of Liberty Records Inc.")
BLUE THUMB: *71* **5–10**
VERVE: *65* **10–18**

GREEN, Jack
Singles: 7-Inch
RCA VICTOR: *80* **1–3**
LPs: 10/12-Inch 33rpm
RCA VICTOR: *80* **5–8**
Also see PRETTY THINGS, The
Also see T-REX

GREEN, Peter
LPs: 10/12-Inch 33rpm
REPRISE: *71*. **8–10**
SAIL: *79–80* **5–8**
Also see BOYD, Eddie
Also see FLEETWOOD MAC

GREEN, Sonny
Singles: 7-Inch
HILL: *73* **2–3**

GREEN BERETS, The
Singles: 7-Inch
UNI: *70* **2–3**

GREEN RIVER BOYS, The: see CAMPBELL, Glen

GREENBAUM, Norman
Singles: 7-Inch
GREGAR: *69–70* **4–6**
REPRISE: *70–71*. **3–5**
LPs: 10/12-Inch 33rpm
GREGAR: *70* **15–20**
REPRISE: *69–72*. **12–15**
Also see DR. WEST'S MEDICINE SHOW & JUNK BAND

GREENBERG, Steve
Singles: 7-Inch
TRIP: *69* **3–5**

GREENE, Al: see GREEN, Al

GREENE, Barbara
Singles: 7-Inch
ATCO: *63* **$4–6**
RENEE: *68* **2–4**
VIVID: *64* **3–5**

GREENE, Jack (Jack Greene & The Jolly Green Giants)
Singles: 7-Inch
DECCA: *65–72* **2–3**
EMH: *83–84* **1–3**
FRONTLINE: *80* **1–3**
MCA: *73–74* **1–3**
LPs: 10/12-Inch 33rpm
CORAL: *73* **4–6**
DECCA: *66–71* **8–12**
51 WEST: *84* **5–8**
FRONTLINE: *80* **5–8**
MCA: *73* **5–10**

GREENE, Jack, & Jeannie Seely
Singles: 7-Inch
DECCA: *69–72* **2–3**
LPs: 10/12-Inch 33rpm
DECCA: *70–72* **8–10**
MCA: *73* **4–6**
PINNACLE: *78*. **5–8**
RDS: *79* **5–8**
Also see GREENE, Jack
Also see SEELY, Jeannie

GREENE, Laura
Singles: 7-Inch
SOUND TREK: *80*. **1–3**

GREENE, Lorne
Singles: 7-Inch
COLUMBIA: *69* **2–3**
GRT: *70–71*. **1–3**
RCA VICTOR: *62–66* **2–4**
Picture Sleeves
RCA VICTOR: *63–65* **2–4**
LPs: 10/12-Inch 33rpm
CAMDEN: *70*. **5–10**
MGM: *71*. **5–10**
RCA VICTOR: *63–66* **8–15**

GREENWICH, Ellie (Ellie Gaye)
Singles: 7-Inch
BELL: *69*. **3–5**
RED BIRD: *65*. **4–6**

Price Range

RCA VICTOR................... $8–12
UNITED ARTISTS: 67............. 3–5
VERVE: 70–73 2–4
LPs: 10/12-Inch 33rpm
UNITED ARTISTS: 68........... 15–20
VERVE: 73 10–12
Also see ARCHIES, The
Also see BONDS, Gary "U.S."
Also see RAINDROPS, The

GREENWOOD, Lee (The Lee Greenwood Affair)
Singles: 7-Inch
DOT: 69......................... 2–4
MCA: 81–84 1–3
PARAMOUNT: 71................. 2–3
LPs: 10/12-Inch 33rpm
MCA: 82–84 5–8
Also see MANDRELL, Barbara, & Lee Greenwood

GREENWOOD COUNTY SINGERS, The (The Greenwoods)
Singles: 7-Inch
DECCA: 64–66.................... 2–4
KAPP: 64–66..................... 2–4
LPs: 10/12-Inch 33rpm
DECCA: 64...................... 10–15
KAPP: 64–66.................... 10–15
RCA VICTOR: 70 8–12

GREER, John (Big John Greer)
Singles: 7-Inch
RCA VICTOR (Black
  vinyl): 50–53................... 8–12
RCA VICTOR (Colored
  vinyl): 49–50.................. 15–20

GREGG, Bobby (Bobby Gregg & His Friends)
Singles: 7-Inch
COTTON: 62...................... 5–8
EPIC: 62–66 4–6
LPs: 10/12-Inch 33rpm
EPIC: 63 25–30
Also see GIBSON, Steve

GREGORY, Dick
Singles: 7-Inch
VEE JAY: 62...................... 2–4

Price Range

LPs: 10/12-Inch 33rpm
COLPIX: 61–64................ $10–20
POPPY: 69–73.................... 8–15
VEE JAY: 62–64................. 10–20

GREY & HANKS
Singles: 7-Inch
RCA VICTOR: 78–80 1–3
LPs: 10/12-Inch 33rpm
RCA VICTOR: 79–80 5–8
Members: Zane Grey; Len Hanks.

GRIFFIN
Singles: 7-Inch
QWEST: 84 1–3

GRIFFIN, Billy
Singles: 7-Inch
COLUMBIA: 83–84 1–3
LPs: 10/12-Inch 33rpm
COLUMBIA: 84 5–8

GRIFFIN, Merv (Merv Griffin & The Griffin Family Singers)
Singles: 7-Inch
CAMEO: 63–64.................... 2–4
CARLTON: 61 2–4
COLUMBIA: 53 3–5
CORAL: 66....................... 2–3
DOT: 68......................... 2–3
GRIFFIN: 73 1–3
MGM: 65–67...................... 2–3
MERCURY: 62..................... 2–4
METROMEDIA: 70................. 1–3
RCA VICTOR: 51–52 3–5
EPs: 7-Inch 33/45rpm
RCA VICTOR (3000
  series): 52.................... 5–10
LPs: 10/12-Inch 33rpm
CAMEO: 64 8–15
CARLTON: 61 10–20
MGM: 65–66.................... 8–15
METROMEDIA: 69............... 5–10
RCA VICTOR (3000
  series): 52................... 15–25
(10-Inch LPs.)
Also see MARTIN, Freddy, & His Orchestra

GRIFFIN, Reggie, & Technofunk
Singles: 7-Inch
SWEET MOUNTAIN: 82........... 1–3

Price Range

GRIFFIN BROTHERS, The (The Griffin Brothers Featuring Tommy Brown; The Griffin Brothers Featuring Margie Day)
Singles: 7-Inch
DOT (1100 series, except
1108): *51–53*................ **$10–15**
DOT (1108; "Ace In The
Hole"): *52* **15–20**
DOT (16000 series): *60*............. **4–6**
Members: Jimmy Griffin; Edward "Buddy" Griffin.

GRIFFITH, Andy (Deacon Andy Griffith)
Singles: 7-Inch
CAPITOL (2500 series): *69*.......... **1–3**
CAPITOL (2600 through
3600 series): *53–57* **5–15**
CAPITOL (4000 & 5000
series): *59–63* **4–6**
(Purple or orange/yellow swirl labels.)
CAPITOL (4000 series): *76*.......... **2–3**
(Orange labels.)
COLONIAL: *53* **15–20**
COLUMBIA: *72*................. **5–10**
EPs: 7-Inch 33/45rpm
CAPITOL: *54–61* **10–20**
LPs: 10/12-Inch 33rpm
CAPITOL (1100 through
1600 series): *59–61* **15–25**
CAPITOL (2000 series):
64–67 .... **10–20**
COLUMBIA: *72*................. **5–10**

GRIFFITH, Johnny, Inc.
Singles: 7-Inch
RCA VICTOR: *73* **2–3**

GRIM REAPER
Singles: 7-Inch
RCA VICTOR: *85* **1–3**
LPs: 10/12-Inch 33rpm
RCA VICTOR: *85* **5–8**

GRIN (With Nils Lofgren)
Singles: 7-Inch
A&M: *74* **2–3**
SPINDIZZY: *71–72* **2–3**
LPs: 10/12-Inch 33rpm
A&M: *73* **8–10**

Price Range

COLUMBIA **$5–8**
SPINDIZZY: *71–72* **8–10**
Also see LOFGREN, Nils

GRINDERSWITCH
Singles: 7-Inch
ATCO: *77–78*.................... **2–3**
LPs: 10/12-Inch 33rpm
ATCO: *77* **8–10**
CAPRICORN: *74–76*............. **8–10**

GRISMAN, David
LPs: 10/12-Inch 33rpm
WARNER BROS: *81*.............. **5–8**
Also see GRAPPELLI, Stephane, & David Grisman

GROCE, Larry
Singles: 7-Inch
PEACEABLE: *75*................. **2–3**
WARNER BROS: *75*.............. **2–3**
LPs: 10/12-Inch 33rpm
DAYBREAK: *71–72* **8–10**
WARNER BROS: *76*............. **8–10**

GROSS, Henry
Singles: 7-Inch
A&M: *74–75* **2–3**
LIFESONG: *76–78*................ **1–3**
LPs: 10/12-Inch 33rpm
ABC-PARAMOUNT: *71*........... **8–10**
A&M: *73–75* **8–10**
CAPITOL: *81* **5–8**
LIFESONG: *76–78* **8–10**
Also see SHA NA NA

GROVE, Harry, Trio
Singles: 7-Inch
LONDON: *52* **2–4**
LPs: 10/12-Inch 33rpm
LONDON: *52* **10–15**

GROUND HOG
Singles: 7-Inch
GEMIGO: *74*.................... **2–3**

GRUSIN, Dave (The Dave Grusin Quintet; Dave Grusin & The NY/LA Dream Band)
Singles: 7-Inch
DECCA: *68–69*.................... **2–3**

Price Range

EPIC: *63* **$2–4**
WARNER BROS: *83* **1–3**
LPs: 10/12-Inch 33rpm
COLUMBIA: *65* **10–20**
EPIC: *62* **15–25**
GRP: *80–83* **5–8**
POLYDOR: *77* **5–8**
SHEFFIELD LAB: *77–82* **8–15**
Also see BISHOP, Stephen
Also see GALE, Eric
Also see RITENOUR, Lee

GUARALDI, Vince (The Vince Guaraldi Trio)
Singles: 7-Inch
FANTASY: *62–66* **2–4**
LPs: 10/12-Inch 33rpm
FANTASY (3200 series):
56–58 .... **15–25**
FANTASY (3300 series):
62–66 .... **10–20**
FANTASY (8000 series):
62 .... **15–25**
FANTASY (8300 series):
63–66 .... **10–20**
WARNER BROS: *68–69* **8–12**

GUARD, Dave, & The Whiskeyhill Singers
Singles: 7-Inch
CAPITOL: *62* **3–5**
LPs: 10/12-Inch 33rpm
CAPITOL: *62* **15–20**
Also see KINGSTON TRIO, The

GUESS WHO, The
Singles: 7-Inch
AMY: *67* **8–10**
FONTANA: *69* **5–8**
HILLTAK: *78–79* **2–3**
RCA VICTOR: *69–76* **3–5**
SCEPTER: *65–73* **5–8**
Picture Sleeves
RCA VICTOR: *70* **3–5**
LPs: 10/12-Inch 33rpm
HILLTAK: *79* **5–8**
MGM: *69* **12–15**
PICKWICK: *72* **8–10**
PIP: *71* **8–10**
PRIDE: *73* **8–10**

Price Range

RCA VICTOR (Except
AYL1 & LSP series):
73–80 .... **$10–12**
RCA VICTOR (AYL1
series): *80* **5–8**
RCA VICTOR (LSP
series): *69–72* **12–15**
SCEPTER: *73* **8–10**
SPRINGBOARD: *72* **8–10**
WAND: *69* **12–15**
Also see BACHMAN, Randy
Also see CUMMINGS, Burton
Also see WOLFMAN JACK

GUIDRY, Greg
Singles: 7-Inch
COLUMBIA: *82* **1–3**
LPs: 10/12-Inch 33rpm
COLUMBIA: *82* **5–8**

GUITAR, Bonnie
Singles: 7-Inch
ABC: *74* **1–3**
COLUMBIA: *72* **1–3**
DOLTON: *59* **3–5**
DOT (15000 series): *57–59* **3–5**
DOT (16000 series): *66–67* **2–4**
FABOR: *64* **2–3**
FOUR STAR: *75* **1–3**
JERDEN: *63* **2–4**
MCA: *74* **1–3**
PARAMOUNT: *70* **1–3**
RCA VICTOR: *61–62* **2–4**
RADIO **5–8**
LPs: 10/12-Inch 33rpm
CAMDEN: *69* **6–12**
DOT (Except 3069): *59–68* **10–15**
DOT (3069; "Moonlight &
Shadows"): *57* **15–20**
HAMILTON: *65* **8–12**
PARAMOUNT: *70* **8–12**
PICKWICK: *70* **6–12**

GUITAR SLIM (Johnny Winter)
Singles: 7-Inch
DIAMOND: *62* **50–75**
Also see WINTER, Johnny

GUNHILL ROAD
Singles: 7-Inch
KAMA SUTRA: *73* **2–3**

Price Range

MERCURY: 72.................... **$2–3**
    LPs: 10/12-Inch 33rpm
KAMA SUTRA: 72............... **8–10**
MERCURY: 71.................. **8–10**

GUNTER, Shirley (Shirley Gunter & The Flairs; Shirley Gunter & The Queens)
    Singles: 7-Inch
FLAIR: 55....................... **5–8**
MODERN: 56..................... **5–8**
TANGERINE: 65.................. **3–5**

GURVITZ, Adrian
    Singles: 7-Inch
JET: 79.......................... **1–3**
    Also see BAKER-GURVITZ ARMY, The
    Also see EDGE, Graeme

GUTHRIE, Arlo
    Singles: 7-Inch
REPRISE: 69–77.................. **2–3**
    LPs: 10/12-Inch 33rpm
REPRISE: 70–76.................. **8–10**
WARNER BROS **77–78**
    Also see SEEGER, Pete, & Arlo Guthrie

GUTHRIE, Gwen
    Singles: 12-Inch 33/45rpm
GARAGE: 85 .... **4–6**
    Singles: 7-Inch
GARAGE: 85 .... **1–3**
ISLAND: 82–85 .... **1–3**
    LPs: 10/12-Inch 33rpm
GARAGE: 85 .... **5–8**
ISLAND: 85 .... **5–8**
    Also see HOWARD, George
    Also see LIMIT

GUY, Bob (Frank Zappa)
    Singles: 7-Inch
DONNA: 61 .... **12–15**
    Also see ZAPPA, Frank

GUY, Buddy (Buddy Guy & His Band)
    Singles: 7-Inch
ARTISTIC: 58–59.................. **5–8**
CHESS: 60–65.................... **3–5**
    LPs: 10/12-Inch 33rpm
BLUE THUMB: 70 .... **8–10**

Price Range

CHESS: 69..................... **$10–12**
VANGUARD: 68............... **12–15**
    Also see WELLS, Junior, & Buddy Guy

GYPSIES, The
    Singles: 7-Inch
CAPRICE: 66 .... **3–5**
OLD TOWN: 64–66................ **3–5**

GYPSY
    Singles: 7-Inch
METROMEDIA: 70................ **2–4**
RCA VICTOR: 72 .... **2–3**
    LPs: 10/12-Inch 33rpm
METROMEDIA: 70–71........... **8–10**
RCA VICTOR: 72–73 .... **8–10**
    Also see WALSH, James, Gypsy Band

H

HACKETT, Buddy
    Singles: 7-Inch
CORAL: 53–56 .... **3–5**
LAUREL: 60...................... **2–4**
    LPs: 10/12-Inch 33rpm
CORAL: 65 .... **8–15**
DOT: 59........................ **10–15**

HACKETT, Steve
    Singles: 7-Inch
CHARISMA: 80................... **1–3**
CHRYSALIS: 76–79............... **2–3**
EPIC: 81 .... **1–3**
    LPs: 10/12-Inch 33rpm
CHARISMA: 80................... **5–8**
CHRYSALIS: 76–79............... **5–8**
EPIC: 81 .... **5–8**
    Also see GENESIS

HAGAR, Sammy
    Singles: 7-Inch
CAPITOL: 76–79 .... **2–3**
GEFFEN: 82–85 .... **1–3**
    LPs: 10/12-Inch 33rpm
CAPITOL: 77–82 .... **5–8**
GEFFEN: 82–85.................. **5–8**
    Also see MONTROSE

Price Range

HAGAR, SCHON, AARONSON, SHRIEVE
Singles: 7-Inch
GEFFEN: *85* **$1–3**
LPs: 10/12-Inch 33rpm
GEFFEN: *85* **5–8**
Members: Sammy Hagar; Neal Schon; Ken Aaronson; Michael Shrieve.
Also see HAGAR, Sammy
Also see SCHON, Neal, & Jan Hammer
Also see SANTANA

HAGEN, Nina (The Nina Hagen Band)
Singles: 12-Inch 33/45rpm
COLUMBIA: *84–85* **4–6**
Singles: 7-Inch
COLUMBIA: *80–85* **1–3**
LPs: 10/12-Inch 33rpm
COLUMBIA: *80–83* **5–8**

HAGGARD, Merle (Merle Haggard & The Strangers)
Singles: 7-Inch
CAPITOL: *65–77* **2–4**
COLUMBIA: *83* **1–3**
EPIC: *81–85* **1–3**
MCA: *77–85* **1–3**
MERCURY: *83* **1–3**
TALLY: *63–65* **5–10**
Picture Sleeves
CAPITOL: *67–71* **2–4**
MCA: *77–80* .... **INC**
EPs: 7-Inch 33/45rpm
CAPITOL: *71* **5–8**
(Jukebox issues only.)
LPs: 10/12-Inch 33rpm
ALBUM GLOBE **5–8**
CAPITOL (168 through
735): *69–71* **8–15**
(With a "T," "ST," "STBB" or "SWBB" prefix.)
CAPITOL (168 through
735): *69–71* **4–8**
(With an "SM" prefix.)
CAPITOL (796; "Merle Haggard's Strangers & Friends Honky Tonkin' "): *71* **20–30**
CAPITOL (803; "Land Of Many Churches"): *71* **50–65**

CAPITOL (823; "Truly The Best Of Merle Haggard"): *71* **$40–60**
CAPITOL (882 through The Best Of Merle Haggard"): *71* **40–60**
CAPITOL (2300 through 2900 series): *65–68* **15–25**
(With a "T," "ST" or "SKAO" prefix.)
CAPITOL (2700 through 2900 series). **4–8**
(With an "SM" prefix.)
CAPITOL (11000 through 16000 series): *72–82* **4–8**
EPIC: *81–85* **5–8**
MCA: *77–84* **4–8**
MERCURY: *83* **5–8**
PICKWICK/HILLTOP. **8–12**
SONGBIRD: *81* **5–8**

HAGGARD, Merle / Patsy Cline
LPs: 10/12-Inch 33rpm
OUT OF TOWN DIST: *82* **5–8**
Also see CLINE, Patsy

HAGGARD, Merle, & Clint Eastwood
Singles: 7-Inch
ELEKTRA: *80* **1–3**
Picture Sleeves
ELEKTRA: *80* .... **INC**
Also see EASTWOOD, Clint

HAGGARD, Merle / Mickey Gilley / Willie Knight
LPs: 10/12-Inch 33rpm
OUT OF TOWN DIST: *82* **5–8**
Also see GILLEY, Mickey

HAGGARD, Merle / Sonny James
LPs: 10/12-Inch 33rpm
CAPITOL **12–15**
Also see JAMES, Sonny

HAGGARD, Merle, & George Jones
Singles: 7-Inch
EPIC: *82* **1–3**
LPs: 10/12-Inch 33rpm
EPIC: *82* **5–8**
Also see JONES, George

Price Range　　　　　　　　*Price Range*

HAGGARD, Merle, & Willie Nelson
Singles: 7-Inch
EPIC: *83* **$1–3**
LPs: 10/12-Inch 33rpm
EPIC: *83* **5–8**
　　Also see NELSON, Willie

HAGGARD, Merle, & Johnny Paycheck
Singles: 7-Inch
EPIC: *81* **1–3**
　　Also see HAGGARD, Merle
　　Also see PAYCHECK, Johnny

HAHN, Carol
Singles: 12-Inch 33/45rpm
NICKLE: *83* **4–6**

HAHN, Joyce
Singles: 7-Inch
CADENCE: *57* **2–4**

HAIRCUT ONE HUNDRED
(Featuring Nick Heyward)
Singles: 7-Inch
ARISTA: *82* **1–3**
LPs: 10/12-Inch 33rpm
ARISTA: *82* **5–8**
　　Also see HEYWARD, Nick

HAIRSTON, Curtis
Singles: 12-Inch 33/45rpm
PRETTY PEARL: *83* **4–6**

HALEY, Bill (Bill Haley & The Comets; Bill Haley & The Saddlemen)
Singles: 7-Inch
APT: *65* **10–15**
ARZEE: *77* **2–3**
DECCA (29000 series):
　54–56 .... **10–15**
　　(With silver lines on both sides of the name Decca.)
DECCA (29000 series):
　54–56 .... **6–10**
　　(With a star and silver lines under the name Decca.)
DECCA (30000 & 31000
　series): *56–64* **4–6**
DECCA (72000 series): *69* **3–5**

ESSEX (303; "Rock The
　Joint"): *52* **$150–175**
　　(Colored vinyl.)
ESSEX (303; "Rock The
　Joint"): *52* **50–60**
　　(Black vinyl.)
ESSEX (305; "Rocking
　Chair On The Moon"):
　52 .... **50–60**
ESSEX (310; "Real Rock
　Drive"): *52* **30–35**
ESSEX (321; "Crazy Man
　Crazy"): *53* **30–35**
ESSEX (327; "Fractured"):
　53 .... **30–35**
ESSEX (332; "Live It
　Up"): *53* **25–30**
ESSEX (340; "Ten Little
　Indians"): *53* **25–30**
ESSEX (348; "Chattanooga
　Choo-Choo"): *54* **25–30**
ESSEX (374; "Jukebox
　Cannonball"): *54* **25–30**
ESSEX (381; "Rocket 88"):
　54 .... **100–125**
ESSEX (399; "Rock The
　Joint"): *55* **20–25**
GONE: *61* **10–12**
HOLIDAY: *51–52* **150–175**
JANUS: *71* **2–3**
KASEY: *61* **5–8**
LOGO: *61* **5–8**
MCA: *74* **1–3**
NEWTOWN: *63–64* **5–8**
TRANSWORLD (200 &
　300 series): *54* **60–75**
TRANSWORLD (700
　series): *53* **35–45**
UNITED ARTISTS: *69* **3–5**
WARNER BROS: *60* **10–12**
Picture Sleeves
DECCA: *57–58* **10–15**
EPs: 7-Inch 33/45rpm
DECCA: *55–59* **20–25**
ESSEX: *54* **35–45**
TRANSWORLD: *55* **25–30**
LPs: 10/12-Inch 33rpm
ACCORD: *81–82* **5–8**
ALSHIRE: *70–79* **8–10**
AMBASSADOR **10–12**
CORAL: *73* **8–10**

Price Range

HALL, Daryl (Daryl Hall With Gulliver)

Singles: 7-Inch

HALL, Daryl, & John Oates (Hall & Oates)

Singles: 12-Inch 33/45rpm

HALL, Daryl, & Ruth Copeland

Singles: 7-Inch

Price Range

HALL, Ellis, Jr.
Singles: 7-Inch
H.C.R.C.: 83 .... $1–3

HALL, Jimmy
Singles: 7-Inch
EPIC: 80–82 1–3
LPs: 10/12-Inch 33rpm
EPIC: 80 5–8
Also see WET WILLIE

HALL, John, Band
Singles: 7-Inch
ASYLUM: 78. 2–3
COLUMBIA: 79 1–3
EMI AMERICA: 81–83. 1–3
LPs: 10/12-Inch 33rpm
ASYLUM: 78. 5–8
COLUMBIA: 70. 8–10
EMI AMERICA: 81–82. 5–8
Also see ORLEANS

HALL, Lani
Singles: 7-Inch
A&M: 71–85 1–3
Picture Sleeves
A&M: 80 .... INC
LPs: 10/12-Inch 33rpm
A&M: 72–85 5–8
Also see MENDES, Sergio

HALL, Lani, & Herb Alpert
Singles: 7-Inch
A&M: 81 1–3
Also see ALPERT, Herb
Also see HALL, Lani

HALL, Larry
Singles: 7-Inch
GOLD LEAF: 62 3–5
HOT: 59. 8–10
STRAND: 59–62. 4–6
LPs: 10/12-Inch 33rpm
STRAND: 60. 35–45

HALL, Randy
Singles: 7-Inch
MCA: 84 1–3
LPs: 10/12-Inch 33rpm
MCA: 84 5–8

Price Range

HALL, Tom T. (Tom T. Hall & The Storytellers)
Singles: 7-Inch
MERCURY: 67–84. .... $1–3
RCA VICTOR: 77–81 1–3
LPs: 10/12-Inch 33rpm
MERCURY (500 through
1100 series): 73–77 5–10
MERCURY (5000 through
8000 series): 78–84 5–8
MERCURY (61000 series):
69–71 8–15
MERCURY (81000 series):
83–84 5–8
OUT OF TOWN DIST: 82 5–8
RCA VICTOR: 78–81 4–8
Also see DUDLEY, Dave, & Tom T. Hall
Also see PAGE, Patti, & Tom T. Hall

HALL, Tom T., & Earl Scruggs
Singles: 7-Inch
COLUMBIA: 82 1–3
LPs: 10/12-Inch 33rpm
COLUMBIA: 82 5–8
Also see HALL, Tom T.
Also see FLATT, Lester, & Earl Scruggs

HALL & OATES: see HALL, Daryl, & John Oates

HALLORAN, Jack, Singers
Singles: 7-Inch
DOT: 63 2–3

HALOS, The
Singles: 7-Inch
7 ARTS: 61 4–6
TRANS ATLAS: 62. 3–5
LPs: 10/12-Inch 33rpm
WARWICK: 62. 35–40

HAMBLIN, Stuart
Singles: 7-Inch
BLUEBIRD: 59. 2–4
COLUMBIA: 50–62 2–5
CORAL: 59 2–4
KAPP: 66 2–3
LAMB & LION: 74 1–3
RCA VICTOR (0500
series): 71 1–3

Price Range

Price Range

RCA VICTOR (5000 &
  6000 series): *54–56* $2–4
    EPs: 7-Inch 33/45rpm
COLUMBIA: *58–59* 5–8
RCA VICTOR: *54–60* 5–12
    LPs: 10/12-Inch 33rpm
CAMDEN: *59–66* 6–12
COLUMBIA: *61–62* 8–15
CORAL: *60* 12–15
KAPP: *66* 8–12
LAMB & LION: *74* 4–6
RCA VICTOR: *54–57* 10–20
SACRED 4–8
WORD 4–8

HAMILTON, Bobby
Singles: 7-Inch
APT: *58–59* 5–8
DECCA: *59* 4–6
DIANA: *59* 4–6

HAMILTON, Chico (The Chico Hamilton Trio; The Chico Hamilton Quartet; The Chico Hamilton Quintet; Chico Hamilton & The Players)
Singles: 7-Inch
COLUMBIA: *61* 2–3
CORAL: *62* 2–3
ENTERPRISE: *74* 1–3
IMPULSE: *64–67* 1–3
PACIFIC JAZZ (600
  series): *54–55* 3–5
PACIFIC JAZZ (88000
  series): *66* 1–3
    EPs: 7-Inch 33/45rpm
DECCA: *57* 5–15
PACIFIC JAZZ: *55–56* 10–20
    LPs: 10/12-Inch 33rpm
BLUE NOTE: *75* 5–8
COLUMBIA: *60–62* 15–25
CROWN: *63* 10–15
DECCA: *57* 25–35
DISCOVERY: *81* 5–8
ELEKTRA: *80* 5–8
EVEREST: *79* 5–8
FLYING DUTCHMAN:
  71 5–10
IMPULSE: *63–71* 10–20
INSTANT: *64* 10–15
MERCURY: *77* 5–8

ODYSSEY: *68* $8–12
PACIFIC JAZZ (17; "The
  Chico Hamilton Trio"):
  55 40–60
  (10-Inch LP.)
PACIFIC JAZZ (39;
  "Spectacular Chico
  Hamilton"): *62*................ 10–15
PACIFIC JAZZ (1200
  series): *55–57* 20–40
PACIFIC JAZZ (20000
  series): *68* 8–12
REPRISE: *63*.................... 10–20
SESAC: *59* 30–40
  (Promotional issue only.)
SOLID STATE: *68–69* 8–12
SUNSET: *68* 5–10
WARNER BROS. (1200 &
  1300 series): *58–59* 20–30
WORLD PACIFIC (1000
  & 1200 series): *58–60* 20–30
  Also see ALMEIDA, Laurindo / Chico Hamilton

HAMILTON, Chico, & Charles Lloyd
LPs: 10/12-Inch 33rpm
COLUMBIA: *68* 8–10
  Also see HAMILTON, Chico
  Also see LLOYD, Charles, Quartet

HAMILTON, George, IV
Singles: 7-Inch
ABC: *78* 1–3
ABC/DOT: *77*.................... 1–3
ABC-PARAMOUNT:
  56–60 4–6
COLONIAL: *56* 20–25
GRT: *76*........................ 2–3
MCA: *79–80* 1–3
RCA VICTOR: *61–74* 2–4
    EPs: 7-Inch 33/45rpm
ABC-PARAMOUNT: *58*........... 8–10
    LPs: 10/12-Inch 33rpm
ABC: *72–77*..................... 8–10
ABC-PARAMOUNT:
  58–63 25–35
CAMDEN: *68–73*................. 8–10
HARMONY: *70* 8–10
LAMB & LION: *74* 8–10
MCA: *80* 5–8

Price Range

RCA VICTOR (APLI
  series): *74–76* **$8–10**
RCA VICTOR (LPM &
  LSP series): *61–73* **10–15**
  Also see ANKA, Paul, George Hamilton IV &
  Johnny Nash

HAMILTON, George, IV, & Skeeter Davis
  LPs: 10/12-Inch 33rpm
RCA VICTOR: *70* **10–12**
  Also see DAVIS, Skeeter
  Also see HAMILTON, George, IV

HAMILTON, Roy
  Singles: 7-Inch
AGP: *69* **1–3**
CAPITOL: *67* **2–3**
EPIC: *54–62* **3–6**
MGM: *63–65* **3–5**
RCA VICTOR: *65–67* **2–4**

  Picture Sleeves
EPIC: *60–62* **3–5**

  EPs: 7-Inch 33/45rpm
EPIC: *55–59* **10–12**

  LPs: 10/12-Inch 33rpm
EPIC: *55–67* **10–20**
MGM: *63–64* **10–15**
RCA VICTOR: *66* **8–12**

HAMILTON, Russ
  Singles: 7-Inch
KAPP: *57–64* **4–6**
MGM: *60* **3–5**

  LPs: 10/12-Inch 33rpm
KAPP: *57* **30–35**

HAMILTON, JOE FRANK & DENNISON
  Singles: 7-Inch
PLAYBOY: *76–77* **2–3**
  Picture Sleeves
PLAYBOY: *76* **2–3**
  LPs: 10/12-Inch 33rpm
PLAYBOY: *76–77* **8–10**
  Members: Dan Hamilton; Joe Frank Carollo;
  Alan Dennison.

Hamilton, Joe Frank & Dennison, eight charted singles (1971–76), three charted LPs (1971–75). (Includes issues shown as by Hamilton, Joe Frank & Reynolds.)

Price Range

HAMILTON, JOE FRANK & REYNOLDS
  Singles: 7-Inch
ABC: *72* **$2–3**
DUNHILL: *71* **2–3**
PLAYBOY: *75–76* **2–3**
  Picture Sleeves
PLAYBOY: *76* **2–3**
  LPs: 10/12-Inch 33rpm
DUNHILL: *71–72* **8–10**
PLAYBOY: *75–77* **8–10**
  Members: Dan Hamilton; Joe Frank Carollo;
  Tom Reynolds.
  Also see HAMILTON, JOE FRANK & DEN-
  NISON
  Also see T-BONES, The

HAMLISCH, Marvin
  Singles: 12-Inch 33/45rpm
UNITED ARTISTS: *77* **4–6**
  Singles: 7-Inch
A&M: *74–76* **1–3**
ARISTA: *79* **1–3**
MCA: *74–83* **1–3**
PLANET: *80* **1–3**
UNITED ARTISTS: *71–77* **1–3**
  LPs: 10/12-Inch 33rpm
MCA: *74* **5–10**
SOUTHERN CROSS: *83* **5–8**

Price Range

HAMMEL, Karl, Jr.
Singles: 7-Inch
ARLISS (1007; "Summer
Souvenirs"): *61*................... **$3–5**
ARLISS (1011; "Sittin'
Alphabetically"): *61* **12–15**
LAURIE: *63* **3–5**
20TH CENTURY-FOX:
66 .... **3–5**

HAMMER, Jan (The Jan Hammer Group)
Singles: 12-Inch 33/45rpm
MCA: *85* **4–6**
Singles: 7-Inch
ASYLUM: *79*...................... **1–3**
MCA: *85* **1–3**
NEMPEROR: *76–78* **1–3**
LPs: 10/12-Inch 33rpm
ECM............................. **5–8**
MPS: *76*......................... **5–8**
NEMPEROR: *74–76* **5–10**
VANGAURD: *77*.................. **5–8**
Also see BECK, Jeff
Also see GOODMAN, Jerry, & Jan Hammer
Also see SCHON, Neal, & Jan Hammer

HAMMOND, Albert
Singles: 7-Inch
EPIC: *76* **2–3**
MUMS: *72–75*..................... **2–3**
LPs: 10/12-Inch 33rpm
COLUMBIA: *81–82*................ **5–8**
EPIC: *77* **8–10**
MUMS: *72–74*..................... **8–10**
Also see MAGIC LANTERNS, The
Also see SPRINGSTEEN, Bruce / Albert
Hammond / Loudon Wainwright, III / Taj
Mahal

HAMPSHIRE, Keith
Singles: 7-Inch
A&M: *72–74* **2–3**
RCA VICTOR: *71* **2–3**

HAMPTON, Lionel (Lionel Hampton & His Orchestra; The Lionel Hampton Quartet; The Lionel Hampton All Star Alumni Big Band)
Singles: 7-Inch
CLEF: *55*......................... **2–4**

Price Range

BRUNSWICK: *74*................. **$1–3**
COLUMBIA: *76*................... **1–3**
DECCA: *50–53*.................... **2–4**
GLAD HAMP: *60–67* **2–3**
IMPULSE: *65* **2–3**
MGM: *51–61*...................... **2–4**
NORGREN: *56*.................... **2–4**
EPs: 7-Inch 33/45rpm
CLEF: *53–56*..................... **10–20**
COLUMBIA: *56*.................. **5–15**
DECCA: *53–53*................... **5–15**
EMARCY: *56*..................... **5–15**
EPIC: *56* **5–10**
GLAD HAMP: *62* **5–8**
MGM: *56*......................... **5–15**
MERCURY: *55*.................... **5–15**
NORGREN: *55*.................... **10–20**
RCA VICTOR: *54–57* **5–15**
LPs: 10/12-Inch 33rpm
AMERICAN
RECORDING
SOCIETY: *56*.................. **40–60**
AUDIO FIDELITY: *57–59*........ **15–20**
BLUE NOTE (5000 series):
53 .... **40–60**
(10-Inch LPs.)
BRUNSWICK: *74*................. **5–8**
CAMDEN (400 & 500
series): *58–59*................. **10–20**
CLEF (100 series): *53*............. **30–50**
(10-Inch LPs.)
CLEF (600 & 700 series):
53–56 .... **20–35**
COLUMBIA (1300
through 1600 series):
59–61 .... **10–20**
(Monaural issues.)
COLUMBIA (8100
through 8400 series):
59–61 .... **15–25**
(Stereo issues.)
CONTEMPORARY: *55*.......... **20–35**
CORAL: *63*...................... **15–20**
DECCA (4000 series):
61–63 .... **15–20**
DECCA (5000 & 7000
series): *51–53*.................. **20–30**
(10-Inch LPs.)
DECCA (8200 series): *56*.......... **20–30**
DECCA (9000 series): *58*.......... **15–25**
DECCA (79000 series): *69*......... **8–12**

EMARCY (26000 series):
53 .... **$30–40**
(10-Inch LPs.)
EMARCY (36000 series):
56 .... **15–25**
EPIC (3000 series): 56 .... **15–25**
EPIC (16000 & 17000
series): 62 .... **15–20**
GENE NORMAN
PRESENTS: 57................ **20–30**
GLAD HAMP (1001
through 1009): 61–65 .... **10–15**
GLAD HAMP (1020 &
1021): 80 .... **5–8**
GLAD HAMP (3000
series): 62 .... **10–15**
HARMONY (7000 series):
58–61 .... **10–20**
HARMONY (32000
series): 73..................... **5–8**
IMPULSE: 65 .... **10–20**
LAURIE: 78 .... **5–8**
MCA: 75–82 .... **5–8**
MGM (200 series): 51............. **20–30**
(10-Inch LPs.)
MGM (3300 series): 56........... **15–25**
MUSE: 79 .... **5–8**
NORGREN (1000 series):
55 .... **30–50**
PERFECT: 59................... **20–30**
RCA VICTOR (1000
series): 54..................... **20–30**
RCA VICTOR (1400
through 2300 series):
57–61 .... **15–25**
RCA VICTOR (3900
series): 68..................... **8–15**
RCA VICTOR (5536;
"The Complete Lionel
Hampton: 1937-1941"):
76 .... **45–60**
(A 6-LP boxed set.)
SUTRA: 81 .... **5–8**
VERVE (2500 series): 82 .... **5–10**
VERVE (8100 & 8200
series): 56–58 .... **20–30**
(Reads "Verve Records, Inc." at bottom of
label.)
WHO'S WHO IN JAZZ:
78–81 .... **5–8**
Also see COREA, Chick, & Lionel Hampton

HAMPTON, Lionel, & Dinah Washington
LPs: 10/12-Inch 33rpm
DECCA (8000 series): 54........ **$20–30**
Also see HAMPTON, Lionel
Also see WASHINGTON, Dinah

HANCOCK, Herbie
Singles: 12-Inch 33/45rpm
COLUMBIA: 79–85 .... **4–6**
Singles: 7-Inch
BLUE NOTE: 62–65 .... **2–3**
COLUMBIA: 74–85 .... **1–3**
WARNER BROS: 69–72............ **2–3**
LPs: 10/12-Inch 33rpm
BLUE NOTE: 62–65 .... **15–25**
(Label reads "Blue Note Records Inc. - New
York, U.S.A.")
BLUE NOTE: 66–71 .... **8–15**
(Label shows Blue Note Records as a division
of either Liberty or United Artists.)
COLUMBIA: 73–85 .... **5–10**
WARNER BROS: 70–74.......... **8–15**
Also see SANTANA
Also see SUMMERS, Bill

HANCOCK, Herbie, & Chick Corea
LPs: 10/12-Inch 33rpm
COLUMBIA: 79.................. **5–8**
Also see COREA, Chick, & Herbie Hancock

HANCOCK, Herbie, & Willie Bobo
LPs: 10/12-Inch 33rpm
BLUE NOTE: 73................. **5–10**
Also see HANCOCK, Herbie
Also see BOBO, Willie

HANDY, John (The John Handy Quartet; The John Handy Quintet)
Singles: 7-Inch
IMPULSE: 76–77 .... **1–3**
COLUMBIA: 66–69................ **2–3**
LPs: 10/12-Inch 33rpm
IMPULSE: 76–77 .... **5–10**
COLUMBIA **66–68**
RCA VICTOR: 67 .... **8–15**
ROULETTE (52000
series): 60.................... **15–25**
ROULETTE (52100
series): 66–67................. **10–15**
WARNER BROS: 78.............. **5–8**

HANDY, John, III
LPs: 10/12-Inch 33rpm
ROULETTE (100 series):
76 . . . . $5–8
ROULETTE (52000
series): *60* 15–25
ROULETTE (52100
series): *66–67* 10–15

HANNIBAL, King: see KING HANNIBAL

HANSON & DAVIS
Singles: 12-Inch 33/45rpm
FRESH: *85* 4–6

HANSSON, Bo
Singles: 7-Inch
CHARISMA: *73* 2–3
SIRE: *76–77* 2–3
LPs: 10/12-Inch 33rpm
FAMOUS CHARISMA:
72–73 8–10
PVC: *79* 5–8
SIRE: *76–77* 8–10

HAPPENINGS, The (Featuring Bob Miranda)
Singles: 7-Inch
ABC: *73* 1–3
B.T. PUPPY: *66–69* 3–5
BIG TREE: *72* 2–3
JUBILEE: *69–71* 3–5
MIDLAND INT'L: *77* 2–3
MUSICORE: *72* 2–3
VIRGO: *72* 1–3
Picture Sleeves
B.T. PUPPY: *67* 4–6
LPs: 10/12-Inch 33rpm
B.T. PUPPY: *66–68* 12–15
JUBILEE: *69* 10–12
Also see TOKENS, The / The Happenings

HARBOR, Pearl: see PEARL HARBOR

HARD TIMES, The
Singles: 7-Inch
WORLD PACIFIC: *66–68* 3–5

Price Range

LPs: 10/12-Inch 33rpm
WORLD PACIFIC: *66–68* $12–15

HARDCASTLE, Paul
Singles: 12-Inch 33/45rpm
CHRYSALIS: *85* 4–6
PROFILE: *84* 4–6
Singles: 7-Inch
CHRYSALIS: *85* 1–3
PROFILE: *84–85* 1–3
LPs: 10/12-Inch 33rpm
PROFILE: *85* 5–8

HARDEN TRIO, The
Singles: 7-Inch
COLUMBIA: *65–68* 2–4
PAPA JOE: *72* 2–3
LPs: 10/12-Inch 33rpm
COLUMBIA: *66–68* 10–15
HARMONY: *70* 8–12
Members: Arlene Harden; Bobby Harden; Robbie Harden.

HARDIN, Tim
Singles: 7-Inch
COLUMBIA: *69–72* 2–4
VERVE/FOLKWAYS:
66–70 2–4
VERVE/FORECAST:
67–71 2–4
LPs: 10/12-Inch 33rpm
ATCO: *67* 8–15
COLUMBIA: *69–81* 6–12
MGM: *70–74* 6–10
POLYDOR: *81* 5–8
VERVE/FOLKWAYS:
66–69 10–15

HARDLY-WORTHIT PLAYERS, The (Featuring Senator Bobby & Senator McKinley)
Singles: 7-Inch
PARKWAY: *67* 3–5
LPs: 10/12-Inch 33rpm
PARKWAY: *66–67* 10–20
Also see SENATOR BOBBY

HARDY, Hagood
Singles: 7-Inch
CAPITOL: *75–78* 1–3
HERITAGE: *71* 2–3

Price Range

Price Range

LPs: 10/12-Inch 33rpm
CAPITOL: *75–76* **$4–8**

HARDY BOYS, The
Singles: 7-Inch
RCA VICTOR: *69–70* **2–3**
LPs: 10/12-Inch 33rpm
RCA VICTOR: *69–70* **8–10**

HARLEM RIVER DRIVE
Singles: 7-Inch
ARISTA: *75* **2–3**
ROULETTE: *72* **2–4**

HARLEY, Steve (Steve Harley & Cockney Rebel)
Singles: 7-Inch
CAPITOL: *78* **1–3**
EMI: *75–77* **2–3**
LPs: 10/12-Inch 33rpm
CAPITOL: *78* **5–8**
EMI: *75–77* **5–8**

HARMONICATS, The (Jerry Murad's Harmonicats)
Singles: 7-Inch
COLUMBIA: *61–67* **2–3**
MERCURY: *50–60* **2–4**
EPs: 7-Inch 33/45rpm
MERCURY: *50–61* **3–6**
LPs: 10/12-Inch 33rpm
COLUMBIA: *61–67* **5–10**
HARMONY: *50* **5–10**
MERCURY: *50–69* **8–15**
WING: *59–64* **8–12**
Members: Jerry Murad; Al Fiore; Don Les.

HARNELL, Joe (Joe Harnell & His Orchestra; Joe Harnell & His Trio)
Singles: 7-Inch
COLUMBIA: *66–68* **2–3**
EPIC: *59–60* **2–3**
KAPP: *61–65* **2–3**
MCA: *78* **1–3**
MEDALLION: *61–62* **2–3**
MOTOWN: *69–70* **1–3**
LPs: 10/12-Inch 33rpm
CAPITOL: *77* **4–8**
COLUMBIA: *66* **5–10**
EPIC: *59–63* **8–12**

KAPP: *63–66* **$8–12**
MEDALLION: *61* **6–10**
MOTOWN: *70* **5–10**

HARNEY, Ben, & Sheryl Lee Ralph
Singles: 7-Inch
GEFFEN: *83* **1–3**

HAROLD, Prince: see PRINCE HAROLD

HARPER, Janice
Singles: 7-Inch
CAPITOL: *58–60* **2–4**
PREP: *57* **3–5**

HARPERS BIZARRE
Singles: 7-Inch
FOREST BAY CO.: *76* **2–3**
WARNER BROS: *67–72* **2–4**
EPs: 7-Inch 33/45rpm
WARNER BROS: *68* **4–8**
(Jukebox issues only.)
LPs: 10/12-Inch 33rpm
FOREST BAY CO.: *76* **8–10**
WARNER BROS: *67–68* **10–12**

HARPO, Slim
Singles: 7-Inch
ABC: *73* **1–3**
EXCELLO (2100 series,
   except 2113): *59–61* **4–6**
EXCELLO (2113; "I'm A
   King Bee"): *57* **8–10**
EXCELLO (2200 series):
   62–68 .... **3–5**
EXCELLO (2300 series):
   69–71 .... **2–4**
LPs: 10/12-Inch 33rpm
EXCELLO (Except 8003 &
   8005): *68–70* **10–12**
EXCELLO (8003;
   "Raining In My Heart"):
   61 .... **25–30**
EXCELLO (8005; "Baby,
   Scratch My Back"): *66* **15–20**

HARPTONES, The
Singles: 7-Inch
AMBIENT SOUND: *82* **2–3**

Price Range

ANDREA: *56* $12–15
BRUCE (Except 101):
  54–55 25–35
BRUCE (101; "A Sunday
  Kind Of Love"): *53*. 125–150
  ("Bruce" in script lettering.)
BRUCE (101; "A Sunday
  Kind Of Love"): *53*. 20–25
  ("Bruce" in block lettering.)
COED: *60* 3–5
COMPANION: *61–62* 10–15
CUB: *61*. 3–5
GEE: *57*. 8–10
KT: *63* 10–12
PARADISE: *56*. 35–45
RAMA: *56–57*. 10–15
RAVEN: *62*. 10–12
ROULETTE: *71* 1–3
TIP TOP: *56* 5–8
WARWICK: *59–60*. 5–8
      EPs: 7-Inch 33/45rpm
BRUCE: *54* 350–400
      LPs: 10/12-Inch 33rpm
AMBIENT SOUND: *82* 5–8
HARLEM HIT PARADE 8–10
RARE BIRD. 6–10
RELIC 5–8
  Members: Willie Winfield; Nicky Clark; Bill
  Brown; Bill Dempsey; Bill Galloway; Raoul
  Cita; Jimmy Beckum; Lynn Daniels; Vicki Bur-
  gess; Margaret Moore; Fred Taylor.

HARPTONES, The / The Cleftones
Singles: 7-Inch
ROULETTE 1–3
  Also see CLEFTONES, The

HARPTONES, The / The Crows
LPs: 10/12-Inch 33rpm
ROULETTE: *72* 12–15
  Also see CROWS, The

HARPTONES, THE / The Paragons
LPs: 10/12-Inch 33rpm
MUSICNOTE: *64*. 18–20
  Also see HARPTONES, The
  Also see PARAGONS, The

HARRELL, Grady
Singles: 7-Inch
MCA: *85* 1–3

Price Range

HARRIS, Betty
Singles: 7-Inch
JUBILEE: *63–64*. $3–5
SSS INT'L: *69*. 2–3
SANSU: *66–68*. 2–4

HARRIS, Bobby
Singles: 7-Inch
ATLANTIC: *65* 3–5
  Also see LUNDY, Pat, & Bobby Harris

HARRIS, Brenda Jo
Singles: 7-Inch
ROULETTE: *68* 2–4

HARRIS, Damon
Singles: 12-Inch 33/45rpm
WMOT: *78–79*. 4–6
Singles: 7-Inch
WMOT: *78–79*. 1–3
LPs: 10/12-Inch 33rpm
WMOT: *78* 5–8

HARRIS, David
Singles: 7-Inch
PLEASURE: *74*. 2–3

HARRIS, Eddie
Singles: 7-Inch
ABC: *73*. 1–3
ATLANTIC: *65–77* 1–3
COLUMBIA: *64*. 2–3
VEE JAY: *61–63*. 2–4

Price Range

WARNER BROS: *81* **$1–3**

LPs: 10/12-Inch 33rpm
ANGELACO: *81* **5–8**
ATLANTIC: *65–81* **6–12**
BUDDAH: *69* **8–12**
COLUMBIA: *64–68* **10–20**
GNP/CRESCENDO: *73* **5–8**
HARMONY: *72* **5–10**
RCA VICTOR: *78* **5–8**
SUNSET: *69* **5–10**
TRIP: *73* **5–8**
VEE JAY (3016 through
  3028): *61–62* **20–35**
VEE JAY (3031 through
  3034): *63* **15–25**
  Also see McCANN, Les, & Eddie Harris

HARRIS, Eddie, & John Klemmer
LPs: 10/12-Inch 33rpm
CRUSADERS: *82* **5–8**
  Also see KLEMMER, John

HARRIS, Emmylou (Emmylou Harris & The Hot Band)
Singles: 7-Inch
JUBILEE: *69–70* **5–8**
REPRISE (Except 1341):
  75–77 .... **2–3**
REPRISE (1341; "Light Of
  The Stable"): *75* **4–6**
WARNER BROS: *77–85* **1–3**

Picture Sleeves
REPRISE: *75–77* **2–3**
WARNER BROS: *80–85* .... **INC**

LPs: 10/12-Inch 33rpm
EMUS: *79* **10–15**
JUBILEE: *69* **25–30**
REPRISE: *75* **8–10**
WARNER BROS: *77–85* **5–8**
  Emmylou's Hot Band included James Burton,
  Glen D. Hardin, Emory Gordy & Ronnie Tutt,
  all previously with Elvis Presley's band.
  Also see DENVER, John
  Also see EVERLY, Don
  Also see ORBISON, Roy, & Emmylou Harris
  / Craig Hundley
  Also see OWENS, Buck, & Emmylou Harris
  Also see PARSONS, Gram
  Also see PARTON, Dolly
  Also see PRESLEY, Elvis

Price Range

Also see RONSTADT, Linda, & Emmylou
Harris
Also see TUCKER, Tanya
Also see WINCHESTER, Jesse
Also see YOUNG, Neil

HARRIS, Gene (Gene Harris & The Three Sounds)
Singles: 7-Inch
BLUE NOTE: *71–77* **$1–3**
LPs: 10/12-Inch 33rpm
BLUE NOTE: *71–77* **5–10**

HARRIS, Huey "Baby"
Singles: 7-Inch
PROFILE: *85* **1–3**

HARRIS, Major
Singles: 7-Inch
ATLANTIC: *75–76* **2–3**
OKEH: *69* **2–4**
POP ART: *83* **1–3**
WMOT: *76–81* **2–3**

LPs: 10/12-Inch 33rpm
ATLANTIC: *75* **8–10**
RCA VICTOR: *78* **5–8**
WMOT: *76* **8–10**
  Also see DELFONICS, The

HARRIS, Peppermint: see PEPPERMINT HARRIS

HARRIS, Phil
Singles: 7-Inch
COLISEUM: *68* **2–3**
MEGA: *73* **1–3**
MONTCLARE: *76* **1–3**
RCA VICTOR: *50–54* **3–5**
REPRISE: *62* **2–3**
VISTA: *67–70* **2–3**

EPs: 7-Inch 33/45rpm
RCA VICTOR: *53–60* **5–10**

LPs: 10/12-Inch 33rpm
CAMDEN: *63* **8–12**
MEGA: *72–74* **5–10**
RCA VICTOR (1900
  series): *59* **10–20**
RCA VICTOR (3000
  series): *53–54* **20–30**
ZODIAC: *77* **5–8**

Price Range

HARRIS, Richard
Singles: 7-Inch
ATLANTIC: *74–75* $2–3
DUNHILL: *68–75*. 2–4

Picture Sleeves
DUNHILL (4134; "Mac
Arthur Park"): *68* 3–5
(Promotional issue only.)

EPs: 7-Inch 33/45rpm
DUNHILL: *68*. 4–6
(Jukebox issues only.)

LPs: 10/12-Inch 33rpm
ATLANTIC: *74–75* 6–10
DUNHILL: *70–73*. 8–12

HARRIS, Rolf
Singles: 7-Inch
EPIC (Except 9721): *63–66* 3–5
EPIC (9721; "Ringo For
President"): *64*. 5–8
MGM: *70*. 2–4
20TH CENTURY-FOX:
60–61 5–8

Picture Sleeves
EPIC: *63–64* 4–6

LPs: 10/12-Inch 33rpm
EPIC: *63–64* 15–20

HARRIS, Sam
Singles: 12-Inch 33/45rpm
MOTOWN: *84*. 4–6

Singles: 7-Inch
MOTOWN: *84*. 1–3

LPs: 10/12-Inch 33rpm
MOTOWN: *84*. 5–8

**HARRIS, Thurston (Thurston Harris
& The Sharps)**
Singles: 7-Inch
ALADDIN: *57–61* 4–6
CUB: *62*. 3–5
DOT: *62–63* 3–5
IMPERIAL: *63* 3–5
REPRISE: *64*. 3–5

HARRIS, Tony
Singles: 7-Inch
EBB: *56–57* 4–6

Price Range

**HARRIS, Wynonie (Wynonie Harris
& Lucky Millinder)**
Singles: 7-Inch
KING (Colored vinyl): *51* $75–100
KING (4210 through
4724): *51–54*. 25–35
(Black vinyl.)
KING (4763 through
4839): *54–55*. 12–15
KING (4900 & 5000
series): *56–57*. 5–8
KING (5100 through 5400
series): *58–60*. 3–5
ROULETTE: *60* 3–5
EPs: 7-Inch 33/45rpm
KING. 40–50
LPs: 10/12-Inch 33rpm
KING (1000 series): *72* 12–15
Also see MILLINDER, Lucky, & His Orchestra

HARRIS, Wynonie / Roy Brown
LPs: 10/12-Inch 33rpm
KING (600 series): *58–59* 60–75

**HARRIS, Wynonie / Roy Brown /
Eddie Vinson**
LPs: 10/12-Inch 33rpm
KING: *60* 35–45
Also see BROWN, Roy
Also see HARRIS, Wynonie

HARRISON, Don, Band
Singles: 7-Inch
ATLANTIC: *76* 2–3
LPs: 10/12-Inch 33rpm
ATLANTIC: *76* 8–10
MERCURY: *77*. 8–10
Members: Don Harrison; Doug Clifford; Stu Cook.
Also see CREEDENCE CLEARWATER REVIVAL

HARRISON, George
Singles: 12-Inch 33/45rpm
COLUMBIA (2085; "I
Don't Want To Do It"):
85 15–18
DARK HORSE
(PRO-A-949; "All Those
Years Ago"): *81*. 25–30
(Promotional issue only.)

Price Range

Price Range

Singles: 7-Inch
APPLE: *70–75* **$3–5**
CAPITOL STARLINE: *77* **2–3**
DARK HORSE: *76–82* **2–3**

Picture sleeves
APPLE (Except 1877):
  70–75 . . . . **6–10**
APPLE (1877; "Dark
  Horse"): *74* **12–15**
DARK HORSE (Except
  8844): *76–82* **5–8**
DARK HORSE (8844;
  "Love Comes To
  Everyone"): *79* **100–125**

LPs: 10/12-Inch 33rpm
APPLE: *68–78* **10–15**
CAPITOL (Except 3385):
  75–81 . . . . **5–8**
CAPITOL (3385; "Concert
  For Bangla Desh"): *81* **10–12**
DARK HORSE: *74–82* **8–10**
ZAPPLE: *69* **12–15**

Promotional LPs
DARK HORSE ("Dark
  Horse Radio Special"):
  74 . . . . **70–80**
DARK HORSE (649;
  "Presents A Personal
  Music Dialogue With
  George Harrison At
  33-1/3"): *76* **40–50**
  Also see BEATLES, The
  Also see BROMBERG, David
  Also see SCOTT, Tom

HARRISON, Noel
Singles: 7-Inch
LONDON: *65–67* **3–5**
REPRISE: *67–70* **2–4**

LPs: 10/12-Inch 33rpm
LONDON: *66–67* **15–1**
REPRISE: *67–69* **10–1**
RIVERSIDE **10–12**
  Also see LEGRAND, Michel, & Noel Harrison

HARRISON, Reggie: see HIPPIES, The / Reggie Harrison

HARRISON, Wes
LPs: 10/12-Inch 33rpm
PHILIPS: *63* **$10–1**

HARRISON, Wilbert (Wilbert Harrison & The Roamers; Wilburt Harrison)
Singles: 7-Inch
ABC: *73* **1–3**
BRUNSWICK: *74* **2–3**
CONSTELLATION: *64* **3–5**
DELUXE: *52–53* **25–30**
DOC: *62* **3–5**
FURY: *59–62* **4–6**
GLADES: *59* **5–8**
NEPTUNE: *61* **3–5**
PORT: *65* **3–5**
ROCKIN': *52* **35–45**
ROULETTE: *67* **3–5**
SSS INT'L: *71* **2–3**
SAVOY (1100 series): *54* **8–10**
SAVOY (1500 series): *59* **4–6**
SEA HORN: *63* **3–5**
SUE: *69* **2–4**

LPs: 10/12-Inch 33rpm
BUDDAH: *71* **8–10**
CHELSEA: *77* **8–10**
JUGGERNAUT: *71* **8–10**
SPHERE SOUND: *65* **25–30**
SUE: *70* **12–15**
WET SOUL: *70* **10–12**

HARRY, Debbie
Singles: 12-Inch 33/45rpm
CHRYSALIS: *81–83* **4–6**
GEFFEN: *85* **4–6**
Singles: 7-Inch
CHRYSALIS: *81–83* **1–3**
GEFFEN: *85* **1–3**
Picture Sleeves
CHRYSALIS: *81* . . . . **INC**
LPs: 10/12-Inch 33rpm
CHRYSALIS: *81* **5–8**
  Also see BLONDIE
  Also see WIND IN THE WILLOWS

HART, Corey
Singles: 7-Inch
EMI AMERICA: *84–85* **1–3**
LPs: 10/12-Inch 33rpm
EMI AMERICA: *84–85* **5–8**

HART, Freddie (Freddie Hart & The Heartbeats)

Singles: 7-Inch

CAPITOL (2500 through
   3000 series): *53–55* **$4–8**
   (Purple labels.)
CAPITOL (2600 through
   4600 series): *70–79* **2–3**
   (Orange labels.)
COLUMBIA: *56–63* **3–5**
KAPP: *65–72*..................... **2–4**
MCA: *73* **1–3**
MONUMENT: *63–64*............... **2–3**
SUNBIRD: *80–81*................. **1–3**

Picture Sleeves

KAPP: *68* **2–4**
SUNBIRD: *80*.................... **INC**

LPs: 10/12-Inch 33rpm

BRYLEN: *84*..................... **5–8**
CAPITOL: *70–79* **5–10**
COLUMBIA (1700 series):
   62 .... **20–25**
COLUMBIA (13000
   series): *72* **10–12**
CORAL: *73*...................... **4–8**
HARMONY: *67–73* **8–12**
KAPP: *65–69*.................... **8–15**
MCA: *75* **8–12**
PICKWICK/HILLTOP............ **8–12**
SUNBIRD: *80*.................... **5–8**
VOCALION: *72* **8–10**

HART, Freddie / Sammi Smith / Jerry Reed

LPs: 10/12-Inch 33rpm

HARMONY: *72* **6–10**
   Also see HART, Freddie
   Also see REED, Jerry
   Also see SMITH, Sammi

HART, Mickey (With Jerry Garcia)

Singles: 7-Inch

WARNER BROS: *71–72*............ **2–4**

LPs: 10/12-Inch 33rpm

WARNER BROS: *72*............. **10–12**
   Also see GARCIA, Jerry
   Also see GRATEFUL DEAD, The

HART, Rita

Singles: 12-Inch 33/45rpm

ENVELOPE: *84* **4–6**

HART, Rod

Singles: 7-Inch

IBC: *80*......................... **$1–3**
PHOENIX SUN: *68*............... **2–3**
PLANTATION: *76–77*.............. **2–3**

LPs: 10/12-Inch 33rpm

PLANTATION: *76*................. **5–8**

HARTFORD, John

Singles: 7-Inch

AMPEX: *71*...................... **2–3**
RCA VICTOR: *66–70* **2–4**

LPs: 10/12-Inch 33rpm

FLYING FISH: *76–84*.............. **5–8**
RCA VICTOR: *67–70* **8–12**
WARNER BROS: *71–72*........... **8–10**
   Also see DILLARDS, The, & John Hartford

HARTLEY, Keef, Band

LPs: 10/12-Inch 33rpm

DERAM: *69–73* **10–12**
   Also see MAYALL, John

HARTMAN, Dan

Singles: 12-Inch 33/45rpm

BLUE SKY: *78–81*................. **4–6**
MCA: *84–85* **4–6**

Singles: 7-Inch

BLUE SKY: *76–81*................. **2–3**
MCA: *84–85* **1–3**
PORTRAIT: *81*.................... **1–3**

LPs: 10/12-Inch 33rpm

BLUE SKY (Except 246):
   76–81 .... **5–8**
BLUE SKY (246; "Who Is
   Dan Hartman"): *75* **8–12**
   (Promotional issue only.)
MCA: *84–85* **5–8**
   Also see WINTER, Edgar

HARVEST, Barclay James: see BARCLAY JAMES HARVEST

HARVEST, King: see KING HARVEST

HARVEY (Harvey Fuqua)

Singles: 7-Inch

CHESS: *59*....................... **3–5**
TRI-PHI: *62–63* **3–5**
   Also see HARVEY & THE MOONGLOWS
   Also see NEW BIRTH

Price Range

HARVEY, Alex (The Sensational Alex Harvey Band)
Singles: 7-Inch
ATLANTIC: 75 . . . . $2–3
CAPITOL: 72 2–4
VERTIGO: 73–75 2–3

LPs: 10/12-Inch 33rpm
CAPITOL: 72 8–12
ATLANTIC: 75 8–10
VERTIGO: 73–75 8–10

HARVEY, Steve
Singles: 12-Inch 33/45rpm
LONDON: 84 4–6

Singles: 7-Inch
LONDON: 84 1–3

HARVEY & THE MOONGLOWS (Featuring Harvey Fuqua)
Singles: 7-Inch
CHESS: 58–59 4–6
   Also see ETTA & HARVEY
   Also see HARVEY
   Also see MOONGLOWS, The

HARVEY BOYS, The
Singles: 7-Inch
CADENCE: 57 3–5

HASHIM
Singles: 12-Inch 33/45rpm
CUTTING EDGE: 84 4–6

HASLAM, Annie
Singles: 7-Inch
SIRE: 77 2–3

LPs: 10/12-Inch 33rpm
SIRE: 77 8–10
   Also see RENAISSANCE

HASSAN & 7-11
Singles: 7-Inch
EASY STREET: 84 1–3

HATCHER, Roger
Singles: 7-Inch
BROWN DOG: 76 2–3

Bobby Hatfield, 22 charted singles (1963–74), 15 charted LPs (1965–74). (Includes issues shown as by The Righteous Brothers.)

Price Range

HATFIELD, Bobby
Singles: 7-Inch
MOONGLOW: 63 . . . . $3–5
VERVE: 68–69 2–4
WARNER BROS: 72 2–3
LPs: 10/12-Inch 33rpm
MGM: 71 10–12
   Also see RIGHTEOUS BROTHERS, The

HATHAWAY, Donny
Singles: 7-Inch
ATCO: 69–78 2–4
CURTOM: 72 2–3
LPs: 10/12-Inch 33rpm
ATCO: 70–78 8–10
ATLANTIC: 80 5–8
   Also see FLACK, Roberta, & Donny Hathaway

HATHAWAY, Donny, & Margie Joseph
Singles: 7-Inch
ATCO: 72 2–3
   Also see HATHAWAY, Donny
   Also see JOSEPH, Margie

HAVENS, Richie
Singles: 7-Inch
A&M: 77 2–3

Price Range

DOUGLAS: *68* **$3–5**
ELEKTRA: *80* **1–3**
MGM: *70* **2–4**
ODE '70: *72* **2–3**
STORMY FOREST: *70–74* **2–3**
VERVE/FOLKWAYS:
   66–67 . . . . **3–5**
VERVE/FORECAST: *68* **3–5**
   LPs: 10/12-Inch 33rpm
A&M: *77* **8–10**
DOUGLAS: *68* **12–15**
ELEKTRA: *80* **5–8**
MGM: *70* **8–10**
ODE '70: *73* **8–10**
STORMY FOREST: *69–74* **10–12**
VERVE/FOLKWAYS: *67* **12–15**
VERVE/FORECAST:
   67–68 . . . . **12–15**

HAWK, The (Jerry Lee Lewis)
Singles: 7-Inch
PHILLIPS INT'L: *60* **8–10**
  Also see LEWIS, Jerry Lee

HAWKINS, Dale (Dale Hawkins With The Escapades)
Singles: 7-Inch
ABC-PARAMOUNT: *65* **3–5**
ATLANTIC: *61–62* **3–5**
BELL: *69* **3–5**
CHECKER (800 series):
   56–57 . . . . **12–15**
   (Maroon label with "checkerboard" logo at top.)
CHECKER (800 series):
   58–61 . . . . **5–8**
   (Maroon label with Checker name on side.)
LINCOLN **3–5**
TILT: *61* **3–5**
ZONK: *62* **4–6**
  Picture Sleeves
CHECKER: *60* **15–20**
   LPs: 10/12-Inch 33rpm
BELL: *69* **10–12**
CHESS: *58* **100–125**
ROULETTE: *62* **30–35**

HAWKINS, Edwin, Singers
Singles: 7-Inch
BUDDAH: *71–72* **2–3**
PAVILION: *69* **2–3**

Price Range

   LPs: 10/12-Inch 33rpm
BUDDAH: *71–72* **$8–12**
PAVILION: *69* **10–12**
  Also see MELANIE
  Also see MORRISON, Dorothy

HAWKINS, Erskine
Singles: 7-Inch
BRUNSWICK: *53* **4–6**
DECCA: *56* **3–5**
CORAL: *52–54* **3–5**
KING (Black vinyl): *51–52* **8–10**
KING (Colored vinyl):
   51–52 . . . . **15–20**
RCA VICTOR: *50–52* **4–6**
   EPs: 7-Inch 33/45rpm
RCA VICTOR: *59* **8–10**
   LPs: 10/12-Inch 33rpm
CORAL: *54* **15–25**
DECCA: *61* **10–15**
IMPERIAL: *62* **15–25**
RCA VICTOR: *60* **15–20**

HAWKINS, Erskine, & The Four Hawks
Singles: 7-Inch
KING: *53* **25–30**
  Also see HAWKINS, Erskine

HAWKINS, Hawkshaw
Singles: 7-Inch
COLUMBIA: *59–62* **3–5**
KING (900 through 1100
   series): *50–53* **4–6**
KING (5000 series): *60–64* **2–4**
RCA VICTOR: *55–59* **3–5**
STARDAY: *71* **1–3**
   EPs: 7-Inch 33/45rpm
KING: *53* **5–10**
   LPs: 10/12-Inch 33rpm
CAMDEN: *64–66* **10–15**
GLADWYNNE **40–60**
HARMONY: *63* **10–15**
KING (500 series): *58–59* **20–30**
KING (800 series): *63–64* **15–25**
KING (1000 series): *69* **8–12**
LA BREA **40–50**
NASHVILLE: *69* **8–12**
STARDAY **5–8**
  Also see CLINE, Patsy / Cowboy Copas / Hawkshaw Hawkins

Price Range

Also see COPAS, Cowboy / Hawkshaw Hawkins

HAWKINS, Jennell
Singles: 7-Inch
AMAZON: *61–63* $3–5
DYNAMIC: *61* 3–5
DYNAMITE: *61* 3–5
LPs: 10/12-Inch 33rpm
AMAZON: *61–62* 20–25

HAWKINS, Ronnie (Ronnie Hawkins & The Hawks)
Singles: 7-Inch
COTILLION: *70–71* 2–4
HAWK 5–8
MONUMENT: *72–73* 2–4
ROULETTE (Except
stereo singles): *59–63* 5–8
ROULETTE (Stereo
singles): *59* 20–25
(With an "SSR" prefix.)
LPs: 10/12-Inch 33rpm
ACCORD: *83* 5–8
COTILLION: *70–71* 8–10
MONUMENT: *72–75* 8–10
ROULETTE (25000
series): *59–60* 40–50
ROULETTE (42000
series): *70* 20–25
UNITED ARTISTS: *79* 5–8
Also see BAND, The
Also see LENNON, John / Ronnie Hawkins
Also see LEVON & THE HAWKS

HAWKINS, Roy
Singles: 7-Inch
KENT: *62* 3–5
MODERN (Except 826):
51–54 12–15
MODERN (826; "The
Thrill Is Gone"): *51* 20–25
RPM: *54* 8–10
RHYTHM 15–20

HAWKINS, Sam (Sam Hawkins & The Crystals)
Singles: 7-Inch
ARNOLD: *63* 3–5
BLUE CAT: *65* 3–5
DECCA: *59–61* 4–6

Price Range

GONE: *59* $4–6

HAWKS, The
Singles: 7-Inch
COLUMBIA: *81* 1–3
LPs: 10/12-Inch 33rpm
COLUMBIA: *81* 5–8

HAWKWIND
Singles: 7-Inch
ATCO: *75* 2–3
UNITED ARTISTS: *71–73* 2–3
LPs: 10/12-Inch 33rpm
ATCO: *75* 8–10
SIRE: *78* 5–8
UNITED ARTISTS: *71–74* 10–15
Also see MOTORHEAD

HAWLEY, Deane
Singles: 7-Inch
DORE: *59–61* 3–5
LIBERTY: *61–62* 3–5
SUNDOWN 3–5
VALOR 5–8
WARNER BROS: *64* 3–5

HAYES, Bill
Singles: 7-Inch
ABC-PARAMOUNT: *57* 3–5
BARNABY: *76* 1–3
CADENCE: *55–56* 4–6
DAYBREAK: *74* 1–3
KAPP: *59* 2–4
MGM: *55* 4–6
SHAW: *65* 2–3
Picture Sleeves
CADENCE: *55* 8–12
EPs: 7-Inch 33/45rpm
MGM: *55* 10–15
LPs: 10/12-Inch 33rpm
ABC-PARAMOUNT: *57* 20–25
DAYBREAK: *74* 5–10
KAPP: *60* 8–15

HAYES, Isaac
Singles: 7-Inch
ABC: *77* 1–3
BRUNSWICK: *64* 3–5
ENTERPRISE: *69–74* 2–3
HBS/ABC: *75–76* 2–3
POLYDOR: *78–80* 1–3

Price Range

SAN AMERICAN: *70* **$2–4**
STAX: *78* **1–3**

LPs: 10/12-Inch 33rpm
ABC-PARAMOUNT:
  75–77 . . . . **8–10**
ATLANTIC: *72* **8–10**
ENTERPRISE: *68–75* **10–12**
POLYDOR: *77–81* **5–8**
STAX: *77–82* **5–8**

HAYES, Isaac, & Millie Jackson
Singles: 7-Inch
POLYDOR: *79–80* **1–3**
LPs: 10/12-Inch 33rpm
POLYDOR: *79* **5–8**
  Also see JACKSON, Millie

HAYES, Isaac, & David Porter
Singles: 7-Inch
ENTERPRISE: *72* **2–3**
  Also see PORTER, David

HAYES, Isaac, & Dionne Warwick
Singles: 7-Inch
ABC: *77* **1–3**
  Also see HAYES, Isaac
  Also see WARWICK, Dionne

HAYES, Linda (Linda Hayes & The Platters; Linda Hayes With The Flairs)
Singles: 7-Inch
ANTLER: *56* **10–15**
DECCA: *55* **10–12**
KING: *55* **12–15**
  Also see PLATTERS, The

HAYES, Peter Lind, & Mary Healy
Singles: 7-Inch
COLUMBIA: *55* **2–4**
ESSEX: *53* **2–4**
KAPP: *56* **2–4**

HAYES, Richard
Singles: 7-Inch
ABC-PARAMOUNT: *56* **2–4**
COLUMBIA: *60–61* **2–3**
CONTEMPO: *64* **1–3**
DECCA: *61* **2–3**
MERCURY: *50–55* **2–4**

Price Range

EPs: 7-Inch 33/45rpm
MERCURY: *54* **$3–6**
LPs: 10/12-Inch 33rpm
MERCURY: *55* **5–15**

HAYES, Richard, & Kitty Kallen
Singles: 7-Inch
MERCURY: *50–51* **2–4**
  Also see HAYES, Richard
  Also see KALLEN, Kitty

HAYMAN, Richard, Orchestra (Richard Hayman & Jan August)
Singles: 7-Inch
COMMAND: *69* **1–3**
MGM: *65* **1–3**
MERCURY: *50–62* **2–4**
MUSICOR: *73* **1–3**
EPs: 7-Inch 33/45rpm
MERCURY: *51–59* **3–6**
LPs: 10/12-Inch 33rpm
ASCOT: *64* **5–10**
COMMAND: *69* **5–10**
MAINSTREAM: *67* **5–10**
MERCURY: *51–64* **8–15**
TIME: *63–64* **5–10**
WING: *62–64* **5–10**
  Also see AUGUST, Jan

HAYMES, Dick
Singles: 7-Inch
CAPITOL: *56* **2–4**
GNP/CRESCENDO: *75* **1–3**
DECCA: *50–54* **2–4**
WARWICK: *60* **2–3**
EPs: 7-Inch 33/45rpm
CAPITOL: *56* **4–6**
DECCA: *50–54* **4–8**
LPs: 10/12-Inch 33rpm
AUDIOPHILE: *78* **5–8**
CAPITOL: *56* **8–15**
CORAL: *73* **4–6**
DAYBREAK: *74* **5–10**
DECCA: *50–54* **10–20**
GLENDALE: *84* **5–8**
MCA: *76–83* **5–8**
WARWICK: *60* **8–15**
  Also see CLOONEY, Rosemary, & Dick Haymes
  Also see JAMES, Harry, & Dick Haymes
  Also see MERMAN, Ethel, & Dick Haymes

Price Range

HAYSI FANTAYZEE
Singles: 7-Inch
RCA VICTOR: 83 .... $1–3
LPs: 10/12-Inch 33rpm
RCA VICTOR: 83 5–8
Members: Kate Garner; Jeremiah Healy

HAYWARD, Justin
Singles: 7-Inch
COLUMBIA: 78 1–3
DERAM: 77 2–3
LPs: 10/12-Inch 33rpm
DERAM: 77–80 5–8

HAYWARD, Justin, & John Lodge
Singles: 7-Inch
THRESHOLD: 75. 2–3
LPs: 10/12-Inch 33rpm
MAPCITY..................... 10–12
THRESHOLD: 75. 12–15
Also see HAYWARD, Justin
Also see LODGE, John
Also see MOODY BLUES, The

HAYWARD, Leon: see HAYWOOD, Leon

HAYWOOD, Leon (Leon Hayward)
Singles: 12-Inch 33/45rpm
CASABLANCA: 83 4–6
MCA: 79 4–6
20TH CENTURY-FOX:
   80 4–6
Singles: 7-Inch
ATLANTIC: 71–72 2–3
CAPITOL: 69–70 2–3
CASABLANCA: 83 1–3
COLUMBIA: 76–77 2–3
DECCA: 67–68 2–4
EPIC: 80–81 1–3
FAT FISH: 66. 3–5
GALAXY: 67 2–4
IMPERIAL: 65–66 3–5
MCA: 77–79 1–3
MODERN: 84 1–3
20TH CENTURY-FOX:
   74–80 2–3
LPs: 10/12-Inch 33rpm
CASABLANCA: 83 5–8
DECCA: 67 8–12
GALAXY: 67 8–12

Price Range

MCA: 78–79 .... $5–8
20TH CENTURY-FOX:
   73 5–10

HAZARD, Robert
Singles: 7-Inch
RCA VICTOR: 83 1–3
LPs: 10/12-Inch 33rpm
RCA VICTOR: 83 5–8

HAZE
Singles: 7-Inch
ASI: 75....................... 2–3

HAZELWOOD, Lee
Singles: 7-Inch
CAPITOL: 72 2–3
JAMIE: 60. 3–5
LHI: 68 2–3
MCA: 79–80 1–3
MGM: 66–67. 2–4
REPRISE: 65–68. 2–4
SMASH: 61 3–5
LPs: 10/12-Inch 33rpm
CAPITOL: 72 8–10
MGM: 66–67. 10–15
MERCURY: 63. 10–15
REPRISE: 64–65. 10–15
Also see ANN-MARGRET & LEE HAZEL-WOOD
Also see SHACKLEFORDS, The
Also see SINATRA, Nancy, & Lee Hazelwood

HEAD, Murray (Murray Head With The Trinidad Singers)
Singles: 12-Inch 33/45rpm
CHESS: 85. 4–6
Singles: 7-Inch
A&M: 76 1–3
CAPITOL: 67 2–4
CHESS: 85. 1–3
DECCA: 69–71 2–3
Picture Sleeves
DECCA: 70–71 2–3
LPs: 10/12-Inch 33/45
A&M: 76 8–10
COLUMBIA: 72 5–10

Price Range

HEAD, Roy (Roy Head & The Traits)

Singles: 7-Inch

ABC: *73–79* $1–3
ABC/DOT: *76–77.* 2–3
AVION: *83* 1–3
BACK BEAT: *65–67* 3–5
CHURCHILL: *81* 1–3
DUNHILL: *70.* 2–3
ELEKTRA: *79–80* 1–3
MEGA: *74.* 2–3
MERCURY: *68.* 2–4
NSD: *82* 1–3
SCEPTER: *65–66* 3–5
SHANNON: *75.* 2–3
TMI: *71–73* 2–3

LPs: 10/12-Inch 33/45

ABC: *73–78* 8–10
DUNHILL: *70.* 10–12
ELEKTRA: *79–80* 5–8
SCEPTER: *65* 15–20
TMI: *72* 8–10
TNT: *65* 100–150
Also see TRAITS, The

HEAD EAST

Singles: 7-Inch

A&M: *75–79* 1–3

LPs: 10/12-Inch 33/45

A&M: *76–80* 5–8
ALLEGIANCE: *83.* 5–8

HEADBOYS, The

Singles: 7-Inch

RSO: *79* 1–3

LPs: 10/12-Inch 33/45

RSO: *79* 5–8

HEADHUNTERS, The

Singles: 7-Inch

FENTON 3–5

LPs: 10/12-Inch 33/45

ARISTA: *78* 5–8

HEADPINS, The

Singles: 7-Inch

ATCO: *82* 1–3
SGR: *83* 1–3

LPs: 10/12-Inch 33/45

ATCO: *82* 5–8

Price Range

HEAP, Jimmy (Jimmy Heap & The Melody Masters)

Singles: 7-Inch

CAPITOL: *53–55* $6–10
D: *59.* 5–10
DART: *60* 4–6
FAME (502; "Little
    Jewell"): *58.* 100–150
IMPERIAL: *60.* 4–6

HEART

Singles: 12-Inch 33/45rpm

MUSHROOM: *76.* 4–6
PORTRAIT: *77–79.* 4–6

Promotional 12-Inch singles

MUSHROOM (7023,
    "Dreamboat Annie"): *76* 8–10
PORTRAIT (16445,
    "Straight On"): *78.* 8–10

Singles: 7-Inch

CAPITOL: *85–86* 1–3
EPIC: *81–83* 1–3
MUSHROOM: *76–79.* 2–3
PORTRAIT: *77–79.* 2–3

Picture Sleeves

CAPITOL: *85–86* .... INC

LPs: 10/12-Inch 33/45

CAPITOL: *85–86* 5–8
EPIC: *80–82* 5–8
MUSHROOM (Except
    picture discs): *76–79* 8–10
MUSHROOM (MRS-1-SP;
    "Magazine"): *78* 8–12
    (Picture Disc.)
MUSHROOM (MRS-2-SP;
    "Dreamboat Annie"): *79* 10–15
    (Picture Disc.)
PORTRAIT (30000 series):
    77–81 5–8
PORTRAIT (40000 series):
    81 12–15
    (Half-speed mastered LPs.)
    Members: Nancy Wilson; Ann Wilson; Mark
    Andes; Howard Leese; Denny Carmassi.
    Also see BORDERSONG
    Also see WILSON, Ann & The Daybreaks

Price Range

Price Range

HEART BEATS QUINTET, The (With Russell Jacquet & His Orchestra)
Singles: 7-Inch

NETWORK **$30–40**
Members: James Sheppard; Albert Crump; Vernon Walker; Wally Roker; Rob Adams.
Also see HEARTBEATS, The
Also see JACQUET, Illinois

HEARTBEATS, The
Singles: 7-Inch

GEE: *57–60* **4–6**
GUYDEN: *59* **4–6**
HULL (711; "Crazy For
 You"): *55* **35–40**
 (Pink label.)
HULL (713; "Darling How
 Long"): *56* **25–30**
HULL (716; "People Are
 Talking"): *56* **35–40**
HULL (720; "A Thousand
 Miles Away"): *56* **50–60**
 (Black label.)
HULL (720; "A Thousand
 Miles Away"): *56* **10–12**
 (Red label.)
RAMA: *56–60* **5–8**
ROULETTE (4000 series):
 58–59 .... **4–6**
 (Roulette reissues have a "1981" copyright date at the bottom of back cover, and are currently available for $5-$8.)
LPs: 10/12-Inch 33/45

EMUS. **8–10**
ROULETTE: *60* **40–50**
Members: James Sheppard; Albert Crump; Vernon Walker; Wally Roker; Rob Adams.
Also see HEART BEATS QUINTET, The

HEARTBEATS, The / Shep & The Limelights
LPs: 10/12-Inch 33/45

ROULETTE (115; "Echoes
 Of A Rock Era"). **25–35**
Also see HEARTBEATS, The
Also see SHEP & THE LIMELIGHTS

HEARTS, The
Singles: 7-Inch

BATON: *55–56* **5–8**
J&S: *56–57* **5–8**

HEARTS, The
Singles: 7-Inch

TUFF: *63* **$3–5**
Members: Baby Washington; Rex Garvin; Pat Ford.
Also see GARVIN, Rex, & The Mighty Cravers
Also see WASHINGTON, Baby

HEARTSFIELD
Singles: 7-Inch

MERCURY: *74* **2–3**
LPs: 10/12-Inch 33/45

COLUMBIA: *77* **5–8**
MERCURY: *73–75*. **8–10**

HEARTSMAN, Johnny
Singles: 7-Inch

MUSIC CITY: *57* **5–8**

HEAT
Singles: 7-Inch

MCA: *79–81* **1–3**
LPs: 10/12-Inch 33/45

MCA: *79–81* **5–8**

HEATH, Ted
Singles: 7-Inch

LONDON: *50–61* **2–3**
EPs: 7-Inch 33/45rpm

LONDON: *51–56* **3–6**
LPs: 10/12-Inch 33rpm

LONDON: *50–62* **5–15**
RICHMOND: *62* **4–8**

HEATH, Walter
Singles: 7-Inch

BUDDAH: *74* **2–3**

HEATH BROTHERS, The
Singles: 7-Inch

COLUMBIA: *79–81* **1–3**
LPs: 10/12-Inch 33/45

COLUMBIA: *79–81* **5–8**

HEATHERTON, Joey
Singles: 7-Inch

CORAL: *64–65* **2–4**
DECCA: *66* **2–4**
MGM: *72–73* **2–3**

Picture Sleeves
CORAL: *64* $2–4
MGM: *72* 2–3
LPs: 10/12-Inch 33rpm
MGM: *72* 8–12

HEATWAVE
Singles: 12-Inch 33/45rpm
EPIC: *77–82* 4–6
Singles: 7-Inch
EPIC: *77–82* 1–3
LPs: 10/12-Inch 33/45
EPIC: *77–82* 5–8

HEAVEN & EARTH
Singles: 7-Inch
GEC: *76* 2–3
MERCURY: *78–80* 1–3
TEC: *80* 1–3
WMOT: *81* 1–3
LPs: 10/12-Inch 33/45
MERCURY: *78–79* 5–8
WMOT: *81* 5–8
Members: Dwight Dukes; Dean Williams;
James Dukes; Keith Steward.

HEAVEN BOUND (With Tony Scotti)
Singles: 7-Inch
MGM: *71* 2–3
LPs: 10/12-Inch 33rpm
MGM: *72* 8–12

HEAVEN 17
Singles: 12-Inch 33/45rpm
ARISTA: *83–84* 4–6
Singles: 7-Inch
ARISTA: *83–84* 1–3
LPs: 10/12-Inch 33/45
ARISTA: *83* 8–10
Also see BAND AID

HEBB, Bobby
Singles: 7-Inch
BOOM: *66* 3–5
CADET: *72* 2–3
FM: *61* 3–5
LAURIE: *75* 2–3
PHILIPS: *66* 3–5
RICH: *60* 3–5
SCEPTER: *66* 3–5

Picture Sleeves
PHILIPS: *66* $3–5
LPs: 10/12-Inch 33/45
EPIC: *70* 10–12
PHILLIPS: *66* 15–20

HEDGEHOPPERS ANONYMOUS
Singles: 7-Inch
PARROT: *65–66* 4–6
Also see KING, Jonathan

HEFTI, Neal (Neal Hefti & His Orchestra; The Neal Hefti Quintet)
Singles: 7-Inch
COLUMBIA: *65* 1–3
CORAL: *51–59* 2–4
DOT: *67–68* 1–3
EPIC: *55–56* 2–4
RCA VICTOR: *66* 2–4
REPRISE: *62* 2–3
UNITED ARTISTS: *65–66* 1–3
Picture Sleeves
RCA VICTOR: *66–67* 2–4
EPs: 7-Inch 33/45rpm
CORAL: *52–56* 3–6
X: *55* 4–6
LPs: 10/12-Inch 33rpm
COLUMBIA: *60* 8–15
CORAL: *52–60* 10–20
DOT (803; "Barefoot In
The Park"): *67* 20–25
(Soundtrack.)
EPIC: *56* 10–15
LIBERTY (413;
"Synanon"): *65* 15–25
(Soundtrack.)
RCA VICTOR (1121;
"Boeing Boeing"): *66* 20–25
(Soundtrack.)
RCA VICTOR (3573;
"Batman"): *66* 15–20
(Soundtrack.)
RCA VICTOR (3621;
"Hefti In Gotham
City"): *66* 10–20
RCA VICTOR (3750; "Oh
Dad, Poor Dad, Mama's
Hung You In The Closet
& I'm Feeling So Sad"):
67 15-20
(Soundtrack.)

Price Range

REPRISE: *62*. **$8–15**
20TH CENTURY-FOX:
   64 . . . . **8–12**
UNITED ARTISTS (119;
   "How To Murder Your
   Wife"): *65* **10–15**
   (Soundtrack.)
UNITED ARTISTS (139;
   "Duel At Diablo"): *66* **15–20**
   (Soundtrack.)
UNITED ARTISTS (573;
   "Definitely Hefti"): *67* **8–15**
WARNER BROS. (1572;
   "Sex & The Single
   Girl"): *64* **20–25**
   (Soundtrack.)
X: *55*. **10–15**

HEIGHT, Donald
Singles: 7-Inch

JUBILEE: *63*. **3–5**
KING: *60* **3–5**
OLD TOWN: *64*. **3–5**
RCA VICTOR: *65* **3–5**
ROULETTE: *65* **3–5**
SHOUT: *66–68* **2–4**
SOOZEE: *62* **3–5**

HEIGHT, Ronnie
Singles: 7-Inch

BAMBOO: *61* **3–5**
DORE: *59* **4–6**
ERA: *59–61*. **3–5**

HEINTJE
Singles: 7-Inch
MGM: *70*. **2–3**
LPs: 10/12-Inch 33rpm
MGM: *70*. **8–10**

HELIX
LPs: 10/12-Inch 33rpm
CAPITOL: *83–84* **5–8**

HELLO PEOPLE, The
Singles: 7-Inch
ABC/DUNHILL: *75–76* **2–3**
PHILIPS: *68* **3–5**
Picture Sleeves
PHILIPS: *68* **3–5**

Price Range

LPs: 10/12-Inch 33/45
ABC/DUNHILL: *74* **$8–10**
ABC-PARAMOUNT: *75*. **8–10**
MEDIARTS: *70* **12–15**
PHILLIPS: *68*. **12–15**

HELM, Levon (Levon Helm & The RCO All-Stars)
Singles: 7-Inch

A&M: *80* **1–3**
ABC: *78*. **1–3**
CAPITOL: *82* **1–3**
MCA: *80* **1–3**
LPs: 10/12-Inch 33/45
ABC-PARAMOUNT:
   77–78 . . . . **5–8**
CAPITOL: *82* **5–8**
MCA: *80* **5–8**
   Also see BAND, The
   Also see CASH, Johnny, & Levon Helm
   Also see LEVON & THE HAWKS

HELMS, Bobby
Singles: 7-Inch

BLACK ROSE: *83–84* **1–3**
CAPITOL: *70* **2–3**
CERTRON: *70* **2–3**
COLUMBIA: *64*. **2–4**
DECCA (Except 29947):
   57–62 . . . . **3–5**
DECCA (29947;
   "Tennessee Rock &
   Roll"): *56*. **8–10**
GUSTO: *74* **1–3**
KAPP: *65–67*. **2–3**
LARRICK: *75*. **2–3**
LITTLE DARLIN': *67–79* **1–3**
MILLION: *72*. **2–3**
MISTLETOE: *74*. **1–3**
Picture Sleeves
DECCA: *57*. **4–6**
EPs: 7-Inch 33/45rpm
DECCA: *57–59* **12–15**
LPs: 10/12-Inch 33/45
CERTRON: *70* **8–10**
COLUMBIA: *63* **12–15**
DECCA: *57*. **25–30**
HARMONY: *67* **10–12**
KAPP: *66* **10–12**
LITTLE DARLIN': *68* **10–12**
MCA: *83* **5–8**

Price Range

MISTLETOE: *74.* **$5–8**
VOCALION: *65* **10–12**
   Also see KERR, Anita

HELMS, Jimmie
Singles: 7-Inch
EAST WEST **10–15**
FOREST: *63* **3–5**
SCOTTIE: *59.* **4–6**
SYMBOL: *63.* **3–5**

HENDERSON, Finis
Singles: 7-Inch
MOTOWN: *83.* **1–3**
LPs: 10/12-Inch 33rpm
MOTOWN: *83.* **5–8**

HENDERSON, Joe
Singles: 7-Inch
ABC: *73* **1–3**
KAPP: *64* **3–5**
RIC: *64* **3–5**
TODD: *62–63* **3–5**
VIRGO: *72* **1–3**
LPs: 10/12-Inch 33/45
TODD: *62* **20–25**

HENDERSON, Michael
Singles: 7-Inch
BUDDAH: *76–83* **1–3**
LPs: 10/12-Inch 33rpm
BUDDAH: *76–83* **8–12**
   Also see CONNORS, Norman
   Also see HYMAN, Phyllis, & Michael Henderson

HENDERSON, Ron, & Choice Of Colour
Singles: 7-Inch
CHELSEA: *77.* **2–3**

HENDERSON, Skitch, Orchestra
Singles: 7-Inch
CAPITOL: *50–51* **2–4**
COLUMBIA: *65–69* **1–3**
EPs: 7-Inch 33/45rpm
CAPITOL: *54* **5–10**
DECCA: *56* **5–10**
LPs: 10/12-Inch 33rpm
CAPITOL: *50–54* **10–25**
COLUMBIA: *62–69* **8–12**

Price Range

DECCA: *56* **$10–20**
HARMONY: *72* **5–8**
SEECO: *55.* **10–20**
VOCALION: *66* **5–10**

HENDERSON, Willie (Willie Henderson & The Soul Explosions)
Singles: 7-Inch
BRUNSWICK: *70.* **2–3**
PLAYBOY: *74* **2–3**
LPs: 10/12-Inch 33/45
BRUNSWICK: *69–74.* **10–12**

HENDERSON, Wayne (Wayne Henderson & The Freedom Sounds)
Singles: 7-Inch
POLYDOR: *78–79* **1–3**
LPs: 10/12-Inch 33/45
ABC: *77.* **5–8**
ATLANTIC: *67–68* **8–12**
POLYDOR: *78–79* **5–8**
   Also see AYERS, Roy, & Wayne Henderson
   Also see CONNORS, Norman

HENDRICKS, Bobby
Singles: 7-Inch
MGM: *63.* **3–5**
MERCURY: *61.* **3–5**
SUE: *58–60* **4–6**
   Also see COASTERS, The
   Also see DRIFTERS, The

HENDRIX, Jimi
Singles: 7-Inch
AUDIO FIDELITY **10–12**
REPRISE (Except 0572 &
  0665): *67–72.* **5–8**
REPRISE (0572; "Hey
  Joe"): *67.* **15–20**
REPRISE (0665; "Up
  From The Skies"): *68* **10–15**
TRIP: *72* **2–4**
LPs: 10/12-Inch 33/45
ACCORD: *81* **5–8**
CAPITOL: *70* **8–12**
CRAWDADDY: *75* **200–250**
PICKWICK: *75* **5–8**
REPRISE (840; "Jimi
  Hendrix - Christmas
  Medley"): *79* **40–50**
   (Promotional issue only.)

Price Range

REPRISE (2025; "Smash
  Hits"): *69* **$25–35**
(Orange & brown label. Price includes bonus
poster, which represents about $15-$20 of the
value.)
REPRISE (2025; "Smash
  Hits"): *71* **8–10**
(Brown label.)
REPRISE (2029; "Historic
  Performances"): *71* **8–10**
REPRISE (2034; "The Cry
  Of Love"): *71* **8–10**
REPRISE (2040; "Rainbow
  Bridge"): *71* **10–15**
REPRISE (2049; "In The
  West"): *72* **10–15**
REPRISE (2103; "War
  Heroes"): *72* **10–15**
REPRISE (2204; "Crash
  Landing"): *75* **10–15**
REPRISE (2229;
  "Midnight Lightning"):
  75 . . . . **10–15**
REPRISE (2245; "Essential
  Jimi Hendrix"): *78* **8–12**
REPRISE (2276; "Smash
  Hits"): *77* **5–8**
REPRISE (2293; "Essential
  Jimi Hendrix, Vol. 2"):
  79 . . . . **5–8**
REPRISE (2299; "Nine To
  The Universe"): *80* **5–8**
REPRISE (6261; "Are You
  Experienced"): *67* **15–20**
(Orange & brown label.)
REPRISE (6261; "Are You
  Experienced"): *71* **5–8**
(Brown label.)
REPRISE (R-6281; "Axis:
  Bold As Love"): *68* **150–200**
(Monaural issue.)
REPRISE (RS-6281; "Axis:
  Bold As Love"): *68* **15–20**
(Orange & brown label. Stereo issue.)
REPRISE (RS-6281; "Axis:
  Bold As Love"): *71* **5–8**
(Brown label.)
REPRISE (6307; "Electric
  Ladyland"): *68* **12–15**
(Orange & brown label.)
REPRISE (6307; "Electric
  Ladyland"): *71* **8–10**

Price Range

(Brown label.)
REPRISE (22306; "Jimi
  Hendrix Concerts"): *82* **$8–10**
RHINO: *82* **5–8**
SHOUT: *72* **8–10**
SPRINGBOARD: *72* **8–10**
TRIP: *72–74* **8–10**
UNITED ARTISTS: *75* **8–10**
Also see MILES, Buddy
Also see REDDING, Otis / Jimi Hendrix

HENDRIX, Jimi, & The Isley Bros.
  LPs: 10/12-Inch 33/45
T-NECK: *71* **10–15**
Also see ISELY BROTHERS, The

HENDRIX, Jimi, & Curtis Knight
  LPs: 10/12-Inch 33/45
CAPITOL (659;
  "Flashing"): *70* **8–10**
CAPITOL (2856; "Get
  That Feeling"): *67* **10–15**
CAPITOL (2894;
  "Flashing"): *68* **10–15**
51 WEST: *82* **5–8**

HENDRIX, Jimi, & Little Richard
  Singles: 7-Inch
ALANNA: *72* **3–5**
  LPs: 10/12-Inch 33/45
ALANNA: *72* **10–12**
EVEREST: *74* **6–10**
PICKWICK: *73* **6–10**
Also see LITTLE RICHARD

**HENDRIX, Jimi, & Lonnie
Youngblood**
  LPs: 10/12-Inch 33/45
MAPLE: *71* **20–25**
Also see HENDRIX, Jimi
Also see YOUNGBLOOD, Lonnie

HENDRIX, Patti
  Singles: 7-Inch
HILLTAK: *78* **1–3**
20TH CENTURY-FOX:
  74 . . . . **2–3**

HENDRYX, Nona
  Singles: 12-Inch 33/45rpm
RCA VICTOR: *83–85* **4–6**

Price Range

Price Range

Singles: 7-Inch
EPIC: 77 .... $2–3
RCA VICTOR: 83–85 1–3

LPs: 10/12-Inch 33rpm
EPIC: 77 5–8
RCA VICTOR: 83–84 5–8
Also see LABELLE, Patti

HENHOUSE FIVE PLUS TWO, The (With Ray Stevens)
Singles: 7-Inch
WARNER BROS./AHAB:
  76–77 2–3
Also see STEVENS, Ray

HENLEY, Don
Singles: 12-Inch 33/45rpm
GEFFEN: 85 4–6

Singles: 7-Inch
ASYLUM: 82–83. 1–3
GEFFEN: 84–85 1–3

LPs: 10/12-Inch 33/45
ASYLUM: 82–83. 5–8
GEFFEN: 84–85 5–8
Also see EAGLES, The
Also see NICKS, Stevie, & Don Henley

HENRY, Clarence (Clarence "Frogman" Henry)
Singles: 7-Inch
ARGO (5200 series): 56–58 5–8
ARGO (5300 & 5400
  series): 59–63 4–6
DIAL: 67. 3–5
PARROT: 64–66. 3–5
CHESS: 73. 2–3
ERIC: 73 1–3

LPs: 10/12-Inch 33/45
ARGO: 61 35–50
ROULETTE: 69 15–20

HENSLEY, Ken
Singles: 7-Inch
MERCURY: 73. 2–3

LPs: 10/12-Inch 33/45
MERCURY: 73. 8–10
WARNER BROS: 75 8–10
Also see URIAH HEEP

HENSON, Jim (Jim Henson's Muppets)
Singles: 7-Inch
COLUMBIA: 72 .... $1–3
SIGNATURE: 60 3–5
Singles: 12-Inch 33/45rpm
COLUMBIA: 71 5–8
Also see ERNIE
Also see KERMIT / Fozzie Bear
Also see MUPPETS, The

HERB THE "K"
Singles: 7-Inch
PRIVATE I: 85. 1–3

HERMAN, Keith
Singles: 7-Inch
RADIO: 79 1–3

HERMAN, Woody, & His Orchestra
Singles: 7-Inch
CADET: 69 1–3
CAPITOL: 54–56 2–4
CENTURY: 79 1–3
CHURCHILL: 79. 1–3
COLUMBIA: 65–76 1–3
FANTASY: 73–74. 1–3
MCA: 73 1–3
MARS: 52–53 2–4
PHILIPS: 62 1–3
EPs: 7-Inch 33/45rpm
CAPITOL: 55–56 5–10
COLUMBIA: 52–54 8–12
DECCA: 56 5–10
MGM: 55 5–10
LPs: 10/12-Inch 33rpm
ACCORD: 82 5–8
ATLANTIC (1300 series):
  60 10–20
ATLANTIC (90000 series):
  82 5–8
BRIGHT ORANGE: 73 5–8
CADET: 69–71 8–12
CAPITOL: 72–75 5–8
  (With an "M" or "SM" prefix.)
CAPITOL: 55–62 10–25
  (With a "T" or "ST" prefix.)
CENTURY: 78 5–8
CHESS: 76. 5–8
COLUMBIA (2300 & 2400
  series): 65–66 5–15

Price Range

COLUMBIA (2500 series):
52–54 .... **$15–25**
(10-Inch LPs.)
COLUMBIA (6000 series):
52–55 .... **15–25**
COLUMBIA (9000 series):
65–67 .... **5–15**
COLUMBIA (32000
series): 74...................... **5–8**
CONCORD JAZZ: 81–83 .... **5–8**
CROWN: 59 .... **10–15**
DECCA (4000 series): 64.......... **8–15**
DECCA (8000 series): 56......... **10–25**
EVEREST (Except 200 &
300 series): 59–63 .... **10–20**
EVEREST (200 & 300
series): 74–78 .... **5–8**
FPM: 75.......................... **5–8**
FANTASY: 71–81................ **5–10**
HARMONY: 72 .... **5–8**
JAZZLAND: 60 .... **10–20**
MGM: 55....................... **10–25**
METRO: 65..................... **5–12**
PHILIPS: 62–65 .... **10–15**
ROULETTE: 59 .... **10–20**
SURREY: 66.................... **8–12**
TREND: 81..................... **5–8**
TRIP: 75 .... **5–8**
VSP: 66–67 .... **8–12**
VERVE: 63–68 .... **8–15**
WHO'S WHO IN JAZZ:
78 .... **5–8**
Also see BYRD, Charlie, & Woody Herman
Also see CLOONEY, Rosemary

HERMAN'S HERMITS (Featuring Peter Noone)
Singles: 7-Inch
BUDDAH: 74–76.................. **2–3**
MGM: 64–69..................... **3–5**
PRIVATE STOCK: 75.............. **2–3**
Picture Sleeves
MGM: 65–67..................... **4–6**
LPs: 10/12-Inch 33/45
ABKCO: 73–76.................. **5–8**
MGM: 65–68................... **12–15**
Also see PAGE, Jimmy

HERNANDEZ, Patrick
Singles: 12-Inch 33/45rpm
COLUMBIA: 79.................. **4–6**

Price Range

Singles: 7-Inch
COLUMBIA: 79................. **$1–3**
LPs: 10/12-Inch 33/45
COLUMBIA: 79.................. **5–8**

HESITATIONS, The
Singles: 7-Inch
B.T. PUPPY: 68 .... **2–3**
GWP: 69 .... **2–3**
KAPP: 66–68.................... **2–4**
LPs: 10/12-Inch 33/45
KAPP: 67–68.................... **8–10**

HEWETT, Howard
Singles: 7-Inch
ELEKTRA: 85 .... **1–3**

HEYETTES, The
Singles: 7-Inch
LONDON: 76.................... **2–3**
Picture Sleeves
LONDON: 76.................... **2–3**
LPs: 10/12-Inch 33rpm
LONDON: 76................... **5–10**

HEYWARD, Nick
Singles: 7-Inch
ARISTA: 83–84................... **1–3**
LPs: 10/12-Inch 33rpm
ARISTA: 83 .... **5–8**
Also see HAIRCUT ONE HUNDRED

HEYWOOD, Eddie
Singles: 7-Inch
DECCA: 53...................... **2–4**
LIBERTY: 61–63 .... **1–3**
MERCURY: 55–61................. **2–4**
20TH CENTURY-FOX:
63 .... **1–3**
EPs: 7-Inch 33/45rpm
COLUMBIA: 52................... **4–8**
DECCA: 56...................... **4–8**
MERCURY: 55–56................. **4–8**
LPs: 10/12-Inch 33rpm
BRUNSWICK: 55................ **10–15**
CAPITOL: 67–69 .... **5–10**
COLUMBIA: 52................. **10–20**
CORAL: 55.................... **10–15**
DECCA: 56.................... **10–15**
EPIC: 56 .... **10–15**
LIBERTY: 62–63 .... **8–12**

Price Range

Price Range

MERCURY: *55–60*. **$10–15**
RCA VICTOR: *59* **10–12**
SUNSET: *66* **5–10**
VOCALION: *66* **5–10**
WING: *59–64* **8–12**
 Also see WINTERHALTER, Hugo, & His Orchestra

HIBBLER, Al
Singles: 7-Inch
ALADDIN: *56* **3–5**
ATLANTIC (900 series):
 51 . . . . **15–25**
ATLANTIC (1000 series):
 55 . . . . **8–15**
CLEF: *54* **3–5**
COLUMBIA: *50* **3–5**
DECCA: *55–59* **2–5**
MCA: *74* **1–3**
MERCURY: *52–56*. **3–5**
NORGRAN: *54–55* **3–5**
ORIGINAL: *55*. **5–8**
REPRISE: *61–62*. **2–4**
SATIN: *66*. **2–3**
TOP RANK: *60* **2–4**
VEGAS: *67* **2–3**
EPs: 7-Inch 33/45rpm
CLEF: *51*. **10–15**
DECCA: *55–57* **5–10**
NORGRAN: *53* **10–15**
RCA VICTOR: *55* **5–10**
LPs: 10/12-Inch 33rpm
ATLANTIC: *56* **10–20**
CLEF
DECCA (8000 series):
 56–59 . . . . **10–20**
DECCA (75000 series): *69*. **5–10**
LMI: *65* **8–12**
MCA: *76* **5–10**
NORGRAN: *53* **20–40**
REPRISE: *61*. **8–15**
TRIP: *77* **4–8**
VERVE: *55* **10–20**
 Also see HOLIDAY, Billie, & Al Hibbler

HIBBLER, Al, & Duke Ellington
Singles: 7-Inch
COLUMBIA (33000
 series): *76* **1–3**
LPs: 10/12-Inch 33rpm
COLUMBIA: *56* **10–20**

Also see ELLINGTON, Duke
Also see HIBBLER, Al

HICKEY, Ersel
Singles: 7-Inch
APOLLO: *62* **$3–5**
BLACK CIRCLE: *72*. **2–3**
EPIC (Except 9278, 9298
 & 9309): *58–60* **5–8**
EPIC (9278; "Goin' Down
 That Road"): *58* **8–10**
EPIC (9298; "You Never
 Can Tell"): *58* **8–10**
EPIC (9309; "You Threw
 A Dart"): *59* **8–10**
JANUS: *71* **2–3**
KAPP: *61* **4–6**
LAURIE: *63* **3–5**
MAGNUM: *84* **1–3**
RAMESES: *76*. **2–3**
TOOT. **8–10**
UNIFAX: *74* **2–3**
EPs: 7-Inch 33/45rpm
EPIC: *58* **20–25**

HICKS, Clair
Singles: 12-Inch 33/45rpm
KN: *84*. **4–6**

HICKS, Dan, & His Hot Licks
Singles: 7-Inch
BLUE THUMB: *73–74* **2–3**
LPs: 10/12-Inch 33rpm
BLUE THUMB: *71–72* **8–10**
EPIC: *69* **10–12**
WARNER BROS: *78*. **5–8**

HIDDEN STRENGTH
Singles: 7-Inch
UNITED ARTISTS: *76*. **2–3**

HI-FI FOUR, The
Singles: 7-Inch
KING: *56* **4–6**

HIGGINS, Bertie
Singles: 7-Inch
KAT FAMILY: *81–82*. **1–3**
LPs: 10/12-Inch 33rpm
KAT FAMILY: *82*. **5–8**

Price Range

HIGGINS, Monk (Monk Higgins & The Specialties)
Singles: 7-Inch
CHESS: 67....................... $2–4
SOLID STATE: 68................. 2–3
ST. LAWRENCE: 66............... 3–5
UNITED ARTISTS: 72–73.......... 2–4
LPs: 10/12-Inch 33rpm
BUDDAH: 74..................... 5–8
SOLID STATE: 69................ 8–12
UNITED ARTISTS: 72............ 8–10
Also see MASON, Barbara

HIGH INERGY
Singles: 12-Inch 33/45rpm
GORDY: 83 4–6
Singles: 7-Inch
GORDY: 77–83................... 1–3
LPs: 10/12-Inch 33rpm
GORDY: 77–83................... 5–8
Also see ROBINSON, Smokey, & Barbara Mitchell

HIGH KEYS, The
Singles: 7-Inch
ATCO: 63–64..................... 3–5
VERVE: 66 3–5

HIGHLIGHTS, The (With Frank Pizani)
Singles: 7-Inch
BALLY: 56–58 5–8
Also see PIZANI, Frank

HIGHTOWER, Willie
Singles: 7-Inch
CAPITOL: 69 3–5
FAME: 70 2–4

HIGHWAYMEN, The
Singles: 7-Inch
ABC-PARAMOUNT:
  65–66 2–3
LIBERTY: 81 1–3
UNITED ARTISTS: 61–64.......... 3–5
LPs: 10/12-Inch 33rpm
ABC-PARAMOUNT: 66........... 8–15
LIBERTY: 82 4–8
UNITED ARTISTS: 61–65........ 10–20

Price Range

HILL, Bunker
Singles: 7-Inch
MALA (Except 464): 62 .... $3–5
MALA (464; "The Girl
  Can't Dance"): 63............... 8–10

HILL, Dan
Singles: 7-Inch
EPIC: 80–81 1–3
20TH CENTURY-FOX:
  75–79 1–3
LPs: 10/12-Inch 33rpm
EPIC: 80–81 5–8
20TH CENTURY-FOX:
  75–80 6–9

HILL, David
Singles: 7-Inch
KAPP: 59 4–6
RCA VICTOR: 57–58 4–6

HILL, Jessie
Singles: 7-Inch
DOWNEY: 64..................... 3–5
MINIT: 60–62................... 3–5
LPs: 10/12-Inch 33rpm
BLUE THUMB: 72 8–10

HILL, Lonnie
Singles: 7-Inch
URBAN SOUND: 84–85............ 1–3
LPs: 10/12-Inch 33rpm
URBAN SOUND: 85.............. 5–8

HILL, Z.Z.
Singles: 7-Inch
COLUMBIA: 77–78................ 1–3
HILL: 71–73 2–3
KENT: 64–71 3–5
M.H.: 63....................... 3–5
M.H.R.: 75..................... 2–3
MALACO: 82–84 1–3
MESA: 64 3–5
MANKIND: 71–72................. 2–3
UNITED ARTISTS: 73–75.......... 2–3
LPs: 10/12-Inch 33rpm
COLUMBIA: 78–79................ 5–8
KENT: 69–71 10–12
MALACO: 82–84 5–8
MANKIND: 71.................... 8–10

Price Range

UNITED ARTISTS: *72–75* **$8–10**

HILLAGE, Steve
LPs: 10/12-Inch 33rpm
ATLANTIC: *76–77* **8–10**
VIRGIN: *75* **8–10**

HILLMAN, Chris
Singles: 7-Inch
ASYLUM: *76–77*. **2–3**
LPs: 10/12-Inch 33rpm
ASYLUM: *76–77*. **5–8**
SUGAR HILL: *82–84* **5–8**
Also see BYRDS, The
Also see FLYING BURRITO BROTHERS, The
Also see McGUINN, CLARK & HILLMAN
Also see SOUTHER-HILLMAN-FURAY BAND, The

HILLSIDE SINGERS, The
Singles: 7-Inch
METROMEDIA: *71–72*. **2–3**
LPs: 10/12-Inch 33rpm
METROMEDIA: *71*. **8–12**

HILLTOPPERS, The (The Hill Toppers)
Singles: 7-Inch
ABC: *74*. **1–3**
DOT (15000 series): *52–60*. **3–5**
DOT (16000 series): *63*. **2–4**
3-J: *66*. **2–3**
EPs: 7-Inch 33/45rpm
DOT: *54–56*. **5–10**
LPs: 10/12-Inch 33rpm
DOT: *54–56*. **10–20**
SOUVENIR: *73*. **8–15**
Members: Jimmy Sacca; Billy Vaughn; Don McGuire; Sy Spiegleman.
Also see VAUGHN, Billy

HINE, Eric
Singles: 7-Inch
MONTAGE: *81*. **1–3**

HINES, J., & The Fellows
Singles: 7-Inch
DELUXE: *73*. **2–4**

Price Range

HINTON, Joe (Little Joe Hinton)
Singles: 7-Inch
ARVEE: *61* **$4–6**
BACKBEAT: *59–65* **3–5**
HOTLANTA: *74*. **8–10**
Picture Sleeves
BACKBEAT: *59–65* **4–8**
LPs: 10/12-Inch 33rpm
BACKBEAT: *65*. **15–20**
DUKE: *73* **8–10**

HIPPIES, The / Reggie Harrison
Singles: 7-Inch
PARKWAY (863;
"Memory Lane"): *63*. **3–5**
Also see STEREOS, The
Also see TAMS, The

HIROSHIMA
Singles: 12-Inch 33/45rpm
EPIC: *85* **4–6**
Singles: 7-Inch
ARISTA: *80–84*. **1–3**
EPIC: *85* **1–3**
LPs: 10/12-Inch 33rpm
ARISTA: *84* **5–8**
EPIC: *85* **5–8**

HIRT, Al
Singles: 7-Inch
CORAL: *65*. **2–3**
GWP: *69–70* **1–3**
MONUMENT: *74*. **1–3**
RCA VICTOR: *61–68* **2–3**
Picture Sleeves
RCA VICTOR: *61–66* **2–3**
EPs: 7-Inch 33/45rpm
RCA VICTOR: *62* **4–6**
LPs: 10/12-Inch 33rpm
ACCORD: *82* **4–8**
AUDIO FIDELITY: *59–61*. **10–15**
CAMDEN: *67–71*. **5–10**
GWP: *70–71* **5–8**
METRO: *65*. **5–10**
MONUMENT: *74*. **4–8**
RCA VICTOR: *61–78* **5–15**
VOCALION: *70* **5–8**
Also see ANN-MARGRET & AL HIRT

Price Range

HIRT, Al, & Pete Fountain
Singles: 7-Inch
CORAL: *61* $2–3
EPs: 7-Inch 33/45rpm
CORAL: *62* 4–6
LPs: 10/12-Inch 33rpm
CORAL: *61–62* 8–15
MGM: *64* 8–15
MONUMENT: *75* 5–10
Also see FOUNTAIN, Pete

HIRT, Al / Henry Mancini / Perez Prado
LPs: 10/12-Inch 33rpm
RCA VICTOR: *63* 8–15
Also see MANCINI, Henry
Also see PRADO, Perez

HIRT, Al, & Hugo Montenegro
LPs: 10/12-Inch 33rpm
RCA VICTOR (4275;
"Viva Max"): *70* 12–15
(Soundtrack.)
Also see MONTENEGRO, Hugo

HIRT, Al, & Boots Randolph
Singles: 7-Inch
MONUMENT: *75* 1–3
Also see HIRT, Al
Also see RANDOLPH, Boots

HO, Don (Don Ho & The Aliis)
Singles: 7-Inch
MEGA: *74–75* 1–3
REPRISE: *65–71* 2–3
LPs: 10/12-Inch 33rpm
MEGA: *74* 4–8
REPRISE: *65–70* 5–10

HODGE, Chris
Singles: 7-Inch
APPLE: *72–73* 3–5
RCA VICTOR: *73–75* 2–3
Picture Sleeves
APPLE: *72* 3–5

HODGES, Charles
Singles: 7-Inch
ALTO: *65* 3–5
CALLA: *70* 2–4
Also see HUNT, Geraldine, & Charlie Hodges

Price Range

HODGES, Eddie
Singles: 7-Inch
AURORA: *65–66* $3–5
BARNABY: *76* 1–3
CADENCE: *61–62* 5–8
COLUMBIA: *62–63* 3–5
DECCA: *59* 4–6
MGM: *64* 3–5
Picture Sleeves
CADENCE: *61* 5–8
Also see MILLS, Hayley, & Eddie Hodges

HODGES, Johnny
Singles: 7-Inch
CLEF: *53–56* 3–5
COLUMBIA: *51* 3–5
GROOVE: *56* 3–5
MERCURY: *51–53* 3–5
NORGRAN: *54–56* 3–5
VMC: *68* 2–3
VERVE: *57–67* 2–4
EPs: 7-Inch 33/45rpm
ATLANTIC: *54* 10–20
EPIC: *55* 10–20
NORGRAN: *54* 20–30
RCA VICTOR (3000
series): *52* 25–50
LPs: 10/12-Inch 33rpm
AMERICAN
RECORDING
SOCIETY: *57.* 20–30
CLEF (100 series): *52.* 75–100
(10-Inch LP.)
ENCORE: *68.* 8–15
EPIC (3100 series): *55* 25–35
EPIC (22000 series): *74* 5–8
IMPULSE: *65* 10–15
INSTANT: *64* 10–18
MCA: *82* 5–8
NORGRAN (1; "Swing
With Johnny Hodges"):
53 75–100
(10-Inch LP.)
NORGRAN (1000 through
1048): *54–55.* 50–75
NORGRAN (1055 through
1061): *55–56.* 25–50
PABLO: *78* 5–8
RCA VICTOR (500 series):
66 8–15

Price Range

RCA VICTOR (3000
series): *52* **$75–100**
(10-Inch LP.)
RCA VICTOR (3800
series): *67* **8–15**
VSP: *66–67* **8–15**
VERVE: *57–60* **20–40**
(Reads "Verve Records, Inc." at bottom of
label.)
VERVE: *61–69* **10–20**
(Reads "MGM Records - A Division Of Metro-
Goldwyn-Mayer, Inc." at bottom of label.)
VERVE: *74–79* **5–10**
(Reads "Manufactured By MGM Record
Corp.," or mentions either Polydor or Poly-
gram at bottom of label.)
Also see ELLINGTON, Duke, & Johnny
Hodges
Also see MULLIGAN, Gerry, & Johnny
Hodges

HODGES, Johnny, & Lawrence Welk
LPs: 10/12-Inch 33rpm
DOT: *66*. **10–15**
Also see WELK, Lawrence

HODGES, Johnny, & Wild Bill Davis
LPs: 10/12-Inch 33rpm
RCA VICTOR: *65–67* **10–15**
VERVE: *61–66* **10–20**
Also see HODGES, Johnny

HODGES, JAMES & SMITH
Singles: 12-Inch 33/45rpm
LONDON: *79* **4–6**

Singles: 7-Inch
LONDON: *76–79* **2–3**

LPs: 10/12-Inch 33rpm
LONDON: *78* **5–8**
Members: Pat Hodges; Denita James; Jessica
Smith.

HODGSON, Roger
Singles: 7-Inch
A&M: *84* **1–3**

LPs: 10/12-Inch 33rpm
A&M: *84* **5–8**
Also see SUPERTRAMP

Price Range

HOG HEAVEN
Singles: 7-Inch
ROULETTE: *71* **$2–3**
LPs: 10/12-Inch 33rpm
ROULETTE: *71* **10–12**
Also see JAMES, Tommy, & The Shondells

HOGG, Smokey (Andrew Hogg)
Singles: 7-Inch
CROWN: *54* **20–25**
EBB: *58* **8–10**
FEDERAL: *53* **20–25**
IMPERIAL (5200 series):
53 . . . . **12–15**
MERCURY: *51*. **20–25**
METEOR: *54*. **20–25**
MODERN (884 through
924): *51–52*. **15–18**
RAY'S RECORD: *52*. **20–25**
SHOW TIME: *54* **25–30**
LPs: 10/12-Inch 33rpm
CROWN: *62* **15–20**
KENT **10–12**
TIME: *62*. **30–35**
UNITED **5–8**

HOLDEN, Ron (Ron Holden & The Thunderbirds)
Singles: 7-Inch
ABC: *73*. **1–3**
CHALLENGE: *67* **3–5**
DONNA: *60–61* **5–8**
ELDO: *61* **4–6**
NITE OWL: *60*. **20–25**
NOW: *74* **2–3**
RAMPART: *65*. **3–5**
LPs: 10/12-Inch 33rpm
DONNA: *60* **45–55**
Also see ROSIE & RON

HOLIDAY, Billie
Singles: 7-Inch
CLEF: *53–55*. **4–6**
COLUMBIA (30000
series): *51–52* **4–6**
DECCA (27000 series):
50–52 . . . . **4–6**
DECCA (48000 series):
51–52 . . . . **4–6**
KENT: *73* **1–3**
MGM: *59*. **3–5**

Price Range

MERCURY (89000 series):
52–53 .... **$4–6**
UNITED ARTISTS: *72* **1–3**
VERVE: *59–62* **3–5**

EPs: 7-Inch 33/45rpm
CLEF: *53–54* **10–25**
COLUMBIA: *54–58* **10–25**
DECCA: *56* **5–15**

LPs: 10/12-Inch 33rpm
ALADDIN: *56* **40–60**
AMERICAN
RECORDING
SOCIETY: *56.* **30–50**
ATLANTIC: *72* **5–10**
CLEF (100 series): *53–54* **75–125**
(10-Inch LPs.)
CLEF (600 & 700 series):
55–56 .... **30–50**
COLUMBIA (21; "The
Golden Years"): *62* **20–40**
(3-LP boxed set.)
COLUMBIA (40; "The
Golden Years, Volume
2"): *66* **20–35**
(3-LP boxed set.)
COLUMBIA (600 series):
54 .... **40–60**
(Red label with gold colored printing.)
COLUMBIA (600 series):
56 .... **20–40**
(Red label with black and white printing.)
COLUMBIA (2600 series):
67 .... **8–15**
COLUMBIA (6000 series):
50 .... **75–125**
(10-Inch LPs.)
COLUMBIA (1100 series):
58 .... **25–40**
COLUMBIA (30000
series): *72–73* **8–15**
COMMODORE (20000
series): *50* **75–100**
(10-Inch LPs.)
COMMODORE (30000
series): *59* **20–40**
DECCA (100 series): *65* **10–15**
DECCA (5000 series): *52* **75–100**
(10-Inch LPs.)
DECCA (8000 series):
56–58 .... **25–50**
DECCA (75000 series): *68* **8–15**

Price Range

ESP: *71–73* **$8–12**
EVEREST: *73–75* **5–8**
HARMONY: *73* **5–8**
JAZZTONE: *56.* **20–35**
JOLLY ROGER: *54* **40–60**
KENT: *73* **5–8**
MCA: *73* **5–10**
MGM (100 series): *70.* **6–10**
MGM (3700 series): *59* **20–35**
MGM (4900 series): *74* **5–8**
MAINSTREAM: *65* **10–20**
METRO: *65* **10–20**
MONMOUTH-
EVERGREEN: *72* **5–10**
PARAMOUNT: *73.* **5–8**
RIC: *64* **10–20**
SCORE: *57* **25–50**
SOLID STATE: *69* **8–12**
TRIP: *73* **5–8**
UNITED ARTISTS (5600
series): *72* **5–10**
UNITED ARTISTS (14000
& 15000 series): *62* **20–30**
VSP: *66* **8–15**
VERVE: *57–60* **20–40**
(Reads "Verve Records, Inc." at bottom of label.)
VERVE: *61–72* **10–25**
(Reads "MGM Records - A Division Of Metro-Goldwyn-Mayer, Inc." at bottom of label.)
VERVE: *73–84* **5–10**
(Reads "Manufactured By MGM Record Corp.," or mentions either Polydor or Polygram at bottom of label.)
Also see FITZGERALD, Ella / Billie Holiday / Lena Horne

HOLIDAY, Billie, & Stan Getz
LPs: 10/12-Inch 33rpm
DALE: *51* **75–100**
Also see GETZ, Stan

HOLIDAY, Billie, & Al Hibbler
LPs: 10/12-Inch 33rpm
IMPERIAL: *62* **15–25**
SUNSET: *67* **8–15**
Also see HIBBLER, Al
Also see HOLIDAY, Billie

HOLIDAY, Chico
Singles: 7-Inch
CORAL: *61–63* **2–4**

Price Range

Price Range

EPIC (Except 32061):
67–78 .... **$10–15**
EPIC (32061; "Greatest
Hits"): 73 .... **6–10**
IMPERIAL: 64–67 .... **20–25**
LIBERTY: 84 .... **5–8**
    Also see CLARKE, Allan
    Also see NASH, Graham
    Also see SPRINGSTEEN, Bruce / Johnny
    Winter / The Hollies

HOLLIES, The / Peter Sellers
Singles: 7-Inch
UNITED ARTISTS
(50079; "After The
Fox"): 66 .... **12–15**
LPs: 10/12-Inch 33rpm
UNITED ARTISTS (286;
"After The Fox"): 74 .... **8–10**
(Soundtrack.)
UNITED ARTISTS (4148;
"After The Fox"): 66 .... **15–20**
(Soundtrack.)
UNITED ARTISTS (5148;
"After The Fox"): 66 .... **20–25**
(Soundtrack.)
    Also see HOLLIES, The

HOLLOWAY, Brenda
Singles: 7-Inch
BREVIT: 63 .... **3–5**
CATCH: 64 .... **3–5**
DONNA: 62 .... **4–6**
TAMLA: 64–67 .... **3–5**
LPs: 10/12-Inch 33rpm
TAMLA: 65 .... **20–25**

HOLLOWAY, Loleatta (Loleatta Holloway & The Salsoul Orchestra)
Singles: 12-Inch 33/45rpm
SALSOUL: 83 .... **4–6**
STREETWISE: 84 .... **4–6**
Singles: 7-Inch
AWARE: 73–75 .... **2–3**
GRC: 73 .... **2–3**
GALAXY: 71 .... **2–4**
GOLD MIND: 76–77 .... **1–3**
SALSOUL: 77–83 .... **1–3**
LPs: 10/12-Inch 33rpm
GOLD MINE: 77 .... **5–8**
    Also see SALSOUL ORCHESTRA, The

HOLLOWAY, Loleatta, & Bunny Sigler
Singles: 7-Inch
GOLD MIND: 78 .... **$1–3**
    Also see HOLLOWAY, Loleatta
    Also see SIGLER, Bunny

HOLLY, Buddy (Buddy Holly & The Crickets; Buddy Holly & The Three Tunes)
Singles: 12-Inch 33/45rpm
SOLID SMOKE: 79 .... **1–3**

Singles: 78rpm
BRUNSWICK: 57–58 .... **40–50**
CORAL (Except 61852):
57–58 .... **40–50**
CORAL (61852; "Words
Of Love"): 57 .... **60–75**
DECCA: 56–58 .... **50–75**
    All Buddy Holly 78rpms were simultaneously
    issued on 45rpm.

Singles: 7-Inch
BRUNSWICK: 57–58 .... **8–10**
CORAL (61852; "Words
Of Love"): 57 .... **100–125**
CORAL (61885; "Peggy
Sue"): 57 .... **8–10**
CORAL (61947; "Listen
To Me"): 58 .... **8–10**
CORAL (61985; "Rave
On"): 58 .... **12–15**
CORAL (62006; "Early In
The Morning"): 58 .... **10–12**
CORAL (62051;
"Heartbeat"): 58 .... **10–12**
CORAL (62074; "It
Doesn't Matter
Anymore"): 59 .... **8–10**
CORAL (62143; "Peggy
Sue Got Married"): 59 .... **15–20**
CORAL (62210; "True
Love Ways"): 60 .... **20–25**
CORAL (62329;
"Reminiscing"): 62 .... **15–20**
CORAL (62352; "Bo
Diddley"): 63 .... **25–30**
CORAL (62369; "Brown
Eyed Handsome Man"):
63 .... **20–25**

Price Range

CORAL (62390; "Rock
Around With Ollie
Vee"): *64* $25–30
CORAL (62407; "Maybe
Baby"): *64* 20–25
CORAL (62448; "Slippin'
& Sliddin'"): *65* 40–50
CORAL (62554; "Rave
On"): *68* 15–18
CORAL (62558; "Love Is
Strange"): *69* 8–10
CORAL (65618; "That'll
Be The Day"): *69* 5–8
DECCA (29854; "Blue
Days - Black Nights"):
56 60–70
DECCA (30166; "Modern
Don Juan"): *56* 40–50
DECCA (30434; "That'll
Be The Day"): *57* 75–100
DECCA (30543; "Love
Me"): *58* 35–45
DECCA (30650;
"Ting-A-Ling"): *58* 40–50
MCA: *73–78* 2–3

Promotional singles

BRUNSWICK: *57–58* 35–45
CORAL (Except 61852):
57–69 15–20
CORAL (61852; "Words
Of Love"): *57* 80–100
DECCA (Except 29854 &
30434): *56–58* 35–45
DECCA (29854; "Blue
Days - Black Nights"):
56 50–60
DECCA (30434; "That'll
Be The Day"): *57* 50–60

Picture sleeves

CORAL (62558; "Love Is
Strange"): *69* 10–15
MCA: *78* 3–5

EPs: 7-Inch 33/45rpm

BRUNSWICK: *57–58* 80–100
CORAL (Except 81169):
59–63 80–100
CORAL (81169; "Listen
To Me"): *58* 125–150
DECCA (2575; "That'll Be
The Day'): *58* 225–275
(With liner notes on the back cover.)

Price Range

DECCA (2575; "That'll Be
The Day'): *58* $175–225
(With EP ads on the back cover.)

LPs: 10/12-Inch 33rpm

BRUNSWICK: *57* 125–150
CORAL (8; "The Best Of
Buddy Holly"): *66* 50–60
CORAL (CRL-57210;
"Buddy Holly"): *58* 75–100
(Maroon label.)
CORAL (CRL-572179;
"The Buddy Holly
Story" - maroon label):
59 40–50
(Maroon label. With red & black print on the
back cover.)
CORAL (CRL-572179;
"The Buddy Holly
Story"): *59* 30–40
(Maroon label. With black print on the back
cover.)
CORAL (CRL-572179;
"The Buddy Holly
Story"): *63* 25–30
(With pictures of other LPs on the back cover.)
CORAL (CRL-57326;
"The Buddy Holly Story
Vol. II"): *60* 50–60
(Maroon label.)
CORAL (CRL-57405;
"Buddy Holly And The
Crickets"): *62* 40–50
(Maroon label.)
CORAL (CRL-57426;
"Reminiscing"): *63* 40–50
(Maroon label.)

Price Range

CORAL (CRL-57450;
"Showcase"): *64*. **$40–50**
CORAL (CRL-57463;
"Holly In The Hills"):
65 . . . . **40–50**
CORAL (CRL-57492;
"Buddy Holly's Greatest
Hits"): *67* **25–35**
CORAL (CRL-757504;
"Giant"): *69*. **25–35**
DECCA (207; "A Rock &
Roll Collection"): *72*. **15–20**
DECCA (8707; "That'll Be
The Day"): *58* **150–175**
(Black label.)
MCA (Except 6-80000):
75–83 . . . . **8–12**
MCA (6-80000; "The
Complete Buddy Holly"
6-LP set): *81*. **30–40**
VOCALION (3811; "The
Great Buddy Holly"): *67* **90–110**
(Monaural.)
VOCALION (73811; "The
Great Buddy Holly"): *67* **80–100**
(Reprocessed stereo.)
VOCALION (73923;
"Good Rockin' Buddy
Holly"): *71*. **30–40**

Promotional LPs

BRUNSWICK: *57*. **200–250**
CORAL (Except 757504):
58–65 . . . . **50–75**
CORAL (757504;
"Giant"): *69*. **35–45**
DECCA: *58* **150–175**
(Pink label.)
Also see CRICKETS, The
Also see JENNINGS, Waylon
Also see PETTY, Norman, Trio

HOLLY & THE ITALIANS
(Featuring Holly Beth Vincent)
Singles: 7-Inch
VIRGIN: *82* **1–3**

LPs: 10/12-Inch 33rpm
VIRGIN: *82* **5–8**

HOLLYRIDGE STRINGS, The (Stu Phillips & The Hollyridge Strings)
Singles: 7-Inch
CAPITOL: *61–68* **$2–4**
LPs: 10/12-Inch 33rpm
CAPITOL: *64–78* **5–15**

HOLLYWOOD ARGYLES, The
(With Gary Paxton)
Singles: 7-Inch
ABC: *74*. **1–3**
CHATTAHOOCHEE: *65* **3–5**
ERA: *72*. **1–3**
FELSTED: *63* **3–5**
FINER ARTS: *61*. **3–5**
LUTE: *60*. **4–6**
PAXLEY: *61*. **4–6**
LPs: 10/12-Inch 33rpm
LUTE: *60*. **150–175**
Also see NEW HOLLYWOOD ARGYLES,
The
Also see SKIP & FLIP

HOLLYWOOD FLAMES, The
Singles: 7-Inch
ATCO: *59–60*. **4–6**
CHESS: *61*. **3–5**
DECCA: *54–55* **30–35**
EBB: *57–59* **5–8**
GOLDIE: *62* **3–5**
LUCKY: *54*. **75–100**
SWING TIME: *53* **125–150**
SYMBOL: *65–66*. **3–5**
VEE JAY: *63*. **3–5**
Members: David Ford; Bobby Byrd; Gaynel
Hodge; Clyde Tillis; Earl Nelson; Curtis Wil-
liams; Don Height; Ray Brewster; John Berry;
George Home.
Also see DAY, Bobby
Also see NELSON, Earl

HOLLYWOOD STARS, The
Singles: 7-Inch
ARISTA: *77* **1–3**
LPs: 10/12-Inch 33rpm
ARISTA: *77* **8–10**
Also see KINKS, The / The Hollywood Stars

HOLLYWOOD STUDIO ORCHESTRA, The
Singles: 7-Inch
UNITED ARTISTS: *59*. **1–3**

Price Range

LPs: 10/12-Inch 33rpm
UNITED ARTISTS: *61* **$5–12**

HOLM, Michael
Singles: 7-Inch
MERCURY: *74*. **2–3**

HOLMAN, Eddie
Singles: 7-Inch
ABC: *69–71* **2–4**
ASCOT: *63* **3–5**
BELL: *68*. **3–5**
PARKWAY: *65–67* **3–5**
SALSOUL: *77*. **1–3**
SILVER BLUE: *74*. **2–3**
LPs: 10/12-Inch 33rpm
ABC-PARAMOUNT: *70*. **10–12**
SALSOUL: *77*. **5–8**

HOLMES, Cecil (Cecil Holmes' Soulful Sounds)
Singles: 7-Inch
BUDDAH: *73* **2–3**
LPs: 10/12-Inch 33rpm
BUDDAH: *73* **6–12**

HOLMES, Clint
Singles: 7-Inch
EPIC: *73* **2–3**
LPs: 10/12-Inch 33rpm
EPIC: *73* **10–12**

HOLMES, Jake
Singles: 7-Inch
COLUMBIA: *71–72* **2–3**
POLYDOR: *70*. **2–3**
TOWER: *67*. **2–4**
Picture Sleeves
TOWER: *67*. **2–4**
LPs: 10/12-Inch 33rpm
POLYDOR: *70* **8–12**

HOLMES, Jan
Singles: 7-Inch
JAY JAY: *85*. **1–3**

HOLMES, Leroy, Orchestra
Singles: 7-Inch
MGM: *51–61*. **2–3**
METRO: *59*. **1–3**

Price Range

EPs: 7-Inch 33/45rpm
MGM: *52–56*. **$3–6**
LPs: 10/12-Inch 33rpm
LION: *59–60*. **5–10**
MGM: *52–62*. **5–15**
UNITED ARTISTS: *67–68* **4–8**

HOLMES, Richard "Groove"
Singles: 7-Inch
BLUE NOTE: *71* **2–3**
FLYING DUTCHMAN:
76 . . . . **1–3**
PACIFIC JAZZ: *61–69* **2–4**
PRESTIGE: *66–69* **2–4**
LPs: 10/12-Inch 33rpm
BLUE NOTE: *71* **5–10**
FLYING DUTCHMAN:
75–76 . . . . **5–8**
GROOVE MERCHANT:
72–75 . . . . **5–10**
LOMA: *66* **10–15**
MUSE: *78–80*. **5–8**
PACIFIC JAZZ (Except
20000 series): *61–62* **15–25**
PACIFIC JAZZ (20000
series): *68–69* **8–15**
PRESTIGE: *66–70* **8–15**
VERSATILE: *78*. **5–8**
WARNER BROS: *64*. **10–20**
WORLD PACIFIC JAZZ:
70 . . . . **8–12**
Also see AMMONS, Gene, & Richard "Groove" Holmes
Also see JONES, Brenda, & "Groove" Holmes
Also see McGRIFF, Jimmy
Also see WITHERSPOON, Jimmy

HOLMES, Richard "Groove," & Les McCann
LPs: 10/12-Inch 33rpm
PACIFIC JAZZ: *62* **15–25**
Also see HOLMES, Richard "Groove"
Also see McCANN, Les

HOLMES, Rupert
Singles: 7-Inch
EPIC: *74–76* **2–3**
INFINITY: *79*. **1–3**
MCA: *80–81* **1–3**
PRIVATE STOCK: *78*. **1–3**

Price Range   *Price Range*

Picture Sleeves
EPIC: 75 . . . . **$2–3**

LPs: 10/12-Inch 33rpm
ELEKTRA: *81* **5–8**
EPIC: *74–75* **8–10**
INFINITY: *79.* **5–8**
MCA: *80* **5–8**
PRIVATE STOCK: *78.* **5–8**
   Also see STREET PEOPLE, The

HOMBRES, The
Singles: 7-Inch
VERVE/FORECAST:
   67–68 . . . . **3–5**

LPs: 10/12-Inch 33rpm
VERVE/FORECAST: *67* **15–20**

HOMER & JETHRO
Singles: 7-Inch
BLUEBIRD: *59.* **3–5**
KING: *63* **2–4**
RCA VICTOR (0300 &
   0400 series): *50* **4–8**
RCA VICTOR (0500
   series): *71* **2–3**
RCA VICTOR (4200
   through 7500 series):
   51–59 . . . . **3–5**
RCA VICTOR (7600
   through 9900 series):
   59–70 . . . . **2–4**

EPs: 7-Inch 33/45rpm
AUDIO LAB: *59* **10–15**
KING: *58* **10–15**
RCA VICTOR: *53–57* **10–20**

Picture Sleeves
RCA VICTOR (5000
   series): *53* **5–8**
RCA VICTOR (8000
   series): *64* **3–5**

LPs: 10/12-Inch 33rpm
AUDIO LAB: *58* **20–30**
CAMDEN: *62–71* **10–18**
DIPLOMAT **8–12**
GUEST STAR: *63* **10–15**
KING (600 series): *59* **20–25**
KING (800 series): *63* **12–18**
KING (1000 series): *67* **8–12**
NASHVILLE: *69* **8–12**
RCA VICTOR (1400 &
   1500 series): *57* **25–40**

RCA VICTOR (1400
   through 1800 series):
   57–58 . . . . **$25–40**
RCA VICTOR (2100
   through 2900 series):
   60–64 . . . . **12–20**
RCA VICTOR (3100
   series): *53* **40–50**
   (10-Inch LP.)
RCA VICTOR (3300
   through 4600 series):
   65–72 . . . . **8–15**
   Members: Henry "Homer" Haynes; Kenneth
   "Jethro" Burns.
   Also see FOUR LOVERS, The

HONDELLS, The
Singles: 7-Inch
AMOS: *69–70* **4–6**
COLUMBIA: *67–68* **4–6**
MERCURY (Except 72563
   & 72605): *64–66* **8–12**
MERCURY (72563;
   "Younger Girl"): *67* **5–8**
MERCURY (72605;
   "Kissin' My Life
   Away"): *67.* **5–8**

Promotional Singles
MERCURY (72324; "Hot
   Rod High"): *67* **5–8**
   (White label. Shows "Hot Rod High" as the
   "A" side instead of "Little Honda.")

Picture Sleeves
MERCURY: *64–65* **10–15**

LPs: 10/12-Inch 33rpm
MERCURY: *64–65* **20–30**
   Members: Gary Usher; Chuck Girard; Brian
   Wilson.
   Also see ALLAN, Davie
   Also see BEACH BOYS, The
   Also see WILSON, Brian

HONEY CONE, The
Singles: 7-Inch
HOT WAX: *69–76* **2–4**

LPs: 10/12-Inch 33rpm
HOT WAX: *70–72* **8–10**

HONEYCOMBS, The
Singles: 7-Inch
INTERPHON: *64–65* **5–8**
WARNER BROS: *65–66* **3–5**

Price Range

Price Range

Picture Sleeves
INTERPHON: *64*. $5–10
LPs: 10/12-Inch 33rpm
INTERPHON: *64*. 20–25
VEE JAY: *64*. 35–45
Members: Honey; John; Martin; Denis; Alan.

HONEYCONES, The
Singles: 7-Inch
EMBER: *58–59*. 4–6

HONEYCUTT, Miki
Singles: 7-Inch
PAULA: *77*. 2–3

HONEYDRIPPERS, The
Singles: 7-Inch
ESPARANZA: *84–85*. 1–3
Picture Sleeves
ESPARANZA: *84–85*. . . . . INC
LPs: 10/12-Inch 33rpm
ESPARANZA: *84*. 5–8
Members: Jeff Beck; Jimmy Page; Robert Plant; Nile Rodgers.
Also see BECK, Jeff
Also see CHIC
Also see PAGE, Jimmy
Also see PLANT, Robert
Also see RODGERS, Nile

HONEYMOON SUITE
Singles: 7-Inch
WARNER BROS: *84*. 1–3
LPs: 10/12-Inch 33rpm
WARNER BROS: *84*. 5–8

HOOK, Dr.: see DR. HOOK

HOOKER, Frank, & The Positive People
Singles: 7-Inch
PANORAMA: *79–80*. 1–3

HOOKER, John Lee
Singles: 7-Inch
ABC: *71–73*. 2–3
BATTLE: *62*. 3–5
BLUESWAY: *67–69*. 3–5
CHART: *53*. 5–8
CHESS (1513; "Walkin'
The Boogie"): *52*. 30–35

CHESS (1562; "It's My
Own Fault"): *54* $15–20
CHESS (1900 series): *66*. 3–5
FEDERAL: *60* 3–5
FORTUNE: *60* 3–5
GALAXY: *63* 3–5
HI-Q: *61*. 3–5
JVB: *53*. 20–25
JEWEL: *70–77*. 2–3
LAUREN: *61*. 3–5
MODERN (800 series):
51–52 25–30
MODERN (900 series):
53–56 20–25
SPECIALTY: *54*. 10–12
STARDAY: *70* 2–4
STAX: *69*. 2–4
VEE JAY (Maroon label):
55–60 4–6
VEE JAY (Black label):
60–65 3–5

EPs: 7-Inch 33/45rpm
IMPULSE: *66* 8–10
(Jukebox issue only.)

LPs: 10/12-Inch 33rpm
ABC: *71–74*. 8–12
ARCHIVE OF FOLK
MUSIC: *68*. 10–12
ATCO: *63* 25–30
ATLANTIC: *72* 8–10
BATTLE 10–12
BLUESWAY: *66–73*. 10–15
BRYLEN: *84*. 5–8
BUDDAH: *69*. 12–15
CHESS (1400 series):
61–63 20–30
CHESS (1500 series): *66*. 15–18
CROWN: *62–63* 10–15
CUSTOM. 12–15
EVEREST: *79–83* 5–8
EXODUS. 8–10
FANTASY: *72–77*. 8–10
FORTUNE: *69* 8–12
GNP/CRESCENDO: *74* 8–10
GALAXY: *63* 20–25
GREEN BOTTLE: *72* 10–12
IMPULSE: *66* 12–15
JEWEL: *71* 10–12
KENT: *71* 10–12
KING (700 series): *61* 20–25
KING (1000 series): *70* 10–12

Vee-Jay RECORDS

60-1384
Vocal

Disc Jockey
Advanced Sample

Time 2:27
Conrad BMI

NO SHOES
(J. Hooker)
JOHN LEE HOOKER
VJ 349

Price Range

MCA: *83*	**$5–8**
MUSE: *80*	**5–8**
SPECIALTY: *70*	**10–12**
STAX (2000 series): *69*	**10–12**
STAX (4000 series): *77*	**8–10**
TOMATO: *78*	**5–8**
TRADITION: *69*	**10–12**
TRIP: *73–78*	**8–10**
UNITED	**10–12**
UNITED ARTISTS: *71–73*	**12–15**
VEE JAY (1007; "I'm John Lee Hooker"): *59* (Maroon label.)	**30–35**
VEE JAY (1007; "I'm John Lee Hooker"): *61* (Black label.)	**15–20**
VEE JAY (1023 through 1043): *60–62*	**25–30**
VEE JAY (1049 through 1078): *62–64*	**15–20**
VERVE/FOLKWAYS: *66*	**10–15**
WAND	**70**

Also see McGHEE, Sticks / John Lee Hooker
Also see WILLIAMS, Johnny

HOOKER, John Lee, & Canned Heat
Singles: 7-Inch

UNITED ARTISTS: *71*	**2–3**

LPs: 10/12-Inch 33rpm

LIBERTY: *71*	**10–12**
RHINO: *82*	**5–8**

Also see CANNED HEAT
Also see HOOKER, John Lee

Price Range

HOOPER, Stix
Singles: 7-Inch

MCA: *79–82*	**$1–3**

LPs: 10/12-Inch 33rpm

MCA: *79–82*	**5–8**

Also see BUTLER, Jerry, & Stix Hooper
Also see CRUSADERS, The

HOOTERS, The
Singles: 7-Inch

COLUMBIA: *85*	**1–3**
MONTAGE: *83*	**1–3**

LPs: 10/12-Inch 33rpm

COLUMBIA: *85*	**5–8**

Also see LAUPER, Cyndi

HOPE, Ellie
Singles: 12-Inch 33/45rpm

QUALITY: *83*	**4–6**

HOPE, Lynn (The Lynn Hope Quintet)
Singles: 7-Inch

ALADDIN: *54–56*	**4–6**
KING: *60*	**3–5**

LPs: 10/12-Inch 33rpm

ALADDIN (707; "Lynn Hope & His Tenor Sax"): *55*	**35–45**
ALADDIN (850; "Lynn Hope"): *56*	**25–35**
IMPERIAL: *62*	**12–15**
KING: *61*	**15–18**
SCORE: *57*	**20–25**

HOPKIN, Mary (Mark Hopkins)
Singles: 7-Inch

APPLE: *68–72*	**3–5**
ESKEE: *66*	**3–5**
RCA VICTOR: *76*	**2–3**

Picture Sleeves

APPLE: *68–70*	**3–5**

LPs: 10/12-Inch 33rpm

AIR: *72*	**8–10**
APPLE: *69–72*	**10–12**

HOPKINS, Lightnin'
Singles: 7-Inch

ACE: *56*	**5–8**
ALADDIN (3063; "Shotgun"): *50*	**20–25**

Price Range

ALADDIN (3077 through
  3262): *51–54* **$12–18**
ARHOOLIE: *65* **3–5**
BLUESVILLE: *60–63* **3–5**
CANDID: *60–62* **3–5**
CHART: *55* **5–8**
DART: *60* **3–5**
DECCA: *53* **10–12**
FIRE: *61* **3–5**
FLASHBACK: *65.* **1–3**
HARLEM: *49–50* **25–30**
HERALD (400 series):
  54–58 . . . . **5–8**
HERALD (500 series):
  59–60 . . . . **4–6**
IMPERIAL: *62* **3–5**
IVORY: *61* **3–5**
JAX (Colored vinyl): *49–50* **35–40**
JEWEL: *68–72.* **2–4**
KENT **2–4**
KIMBERLEY: *60.* **3–5**
LIGHTNING: *49* **15–18**
MERCURY: *52.* **15–20**
PRESTIGE: *60–67* **3–5**
RPM (337 through 351):
  51–52 . . . . **20–25**
RPM (359 through 398):
  52–53 . . . . **15–20**
SHAD: *59* **4–6**
SITTIN' IN WITH
  (Colored vinyl): *49–51* **35–40**
TNT: *53* **25–30**
VAULT: *70* **2–3**

LPs: 10/12-Inch 33rpm

ARHOOLIE: *68* **10–15**
BARNABY: *71* **8–10**
BULLDOG: *65* **12–15**
CANDID: *61.* **20–25**
CHARLEY: *84* **5–8**
CROWN: *61* **20–25**
DART **10–15**
EVEREST (241; "Lightnin'
  Hopkins"): *69.* **10–12**
EVEREST (342;
  "Autobiography In
  Blues"): *79* **5–8**
FANTASY: *72–81.* **8–10**
FIRE: *62* **50–60**
GUEST STAR: *64* **15–20**
HARLEM HITPARADE **5–8**
HERALD: *60* **75–90**

Price Range

IMPERIAL: *62* **$20–25**
INTERNATIONAL
  ARTISTS: *68.* **20–25**
JAZZ MAN: *82.* **5–8**
JEWEL: *67–70.* **10–12**
MAINSTREAM: *71–74* **8–10**
MOUNT VERNON **15–20**
OLYMPIC: *73.* **8–10**
POPPY: *69* **12–15**
PRESTIGE: *65–70* **10–15**
PRESTIGE/
  BLUESVILLE: *61–64* **20–25**
RHINO: *82* **5–8**
SCORE **40–50**
TIME: *60–62* **25–30**
TOMATO: *77* **5–8**
TRADITION (1035
  through 1040): *60* **20–25**
TRADITION (1056
  through 2000): *67–72* **10–12**
TRIP: *71–78* **5–8**
UNITED **8–10**
VAULT: *69* **10–12**
VEE JAY: *62.* **20–25**
VERVE: *62* **15–20**
VERVE/FOLKWAYS:
  65–67 . . . . **12–15**

HOPKINS, Lightnin,' & Sonny Terry
LPs: 10/12-Inch 33rpm
PRESTIGE
  BLUESVILLE: *61–63* **15–20**
  Also see HOPKINS, Lightnin'
  Also see TERRY, Sonny

HOPKINS, Nicky
Singles: 7-Inch
COLUMBIA: *72* **2–3**

LPs: 10/12-Inch 33rpm
COLUMBIA: *73* **8–10**
ROLLING STONE: *72* **10–12**
  Also see LORD SUTCH
  Also see QUICKSILVER
  Also see ROLLING STONES, The

HORAN, Eddie
Singles: 7-Inch
HDM: *78* **1–3**

Price Range

Price Range

HORN, Paul
Singles: 7-Inch
MUSHROOM: 78 . . . . $1–3

HORNE, Jimmy "Bo"
Singles: 12-Inch 33/45rpm
SUNSHINE SOUND: 79 4–6
Singles: 7-Inch
ALSTON: 75–77 2–4
SUNSHINE SOUND:
    77–80 1–3
LPs: 10/12-Inch 33rpm
SUNSHINE SOUND:
    78–80 5–8

HORNE, Lena
Singles: 7-Inch
BUDDAH: 71 1–3
CHARTER: 63 2–4
GRYPHON: 76 1–3
MCA: 78 1–3
RCA VICTOR (4000
    through 7000 series):
    52–61 3–5
20TH CENTURY-FOX:
    63–64 2–4
UNITED ARTISTS: 65–66 2–3
Picture Sleeves
RCA VICTOR: 62 2–4
EPs: 7-Inch 33/45rpm
MGM: 54–55 5–10
RCA VICTOR: 56–59 5–10
LPs: 10/12-Inch 33rpm
BUDDAH: 71 5–10
CAMDEN: 56 10–20
CHARTER: 63 10–15
GRYPHON: 75–76 5–8
MGM: 54–55 10–20
QWEST: 81 5–10
RCA VICTOR: 52–63 10–20
SPRINGBOARD: 77 4–8
20TH CENTURY-FOX:
    64 8–15
UNITED ARTISTS: 65–66 8–15
    Also see FITZGERALD, Ella / Billie Holiday
    / Lena Horne

HORNE, Lena, & Michel Legrand
LPs: 10/12-Inch 33rpm
GRYPHON: 75 5–8
    Also see LEGRAND, Michel

HORNE, Lena, & Gabor Szabo
Singles: 7-Inch
SKYE: 70 . . . . $1–3
LPs: 10/12-Inch 33rpm
BUDDAH: 70–76 6–12
SKYE: 70 6–12
    Also see HORNE, Lena
    Also see SZABO, Gabor

HORSLIPS
Singles: 7-Inch
DJM (Black vinyl): 77–79 2–3
DJM (Colored vinyl): 77 3–5
    (Promotional issues only.)
MERCURY: 79 2–3
RCA VICTOR: 75 2–3
LPs: 10/12-Inch 33rpm
ATCO: 73–74 10–12
DJM: 77–79 5–8
MERCURY: 79–80 5–8
RCA VICTOR: 74 8–10

HORTON, Jamie
Singles: 7-Inch
ERIC: 68 1–3
JOY: 59–61 3–5

HORTON, Johnny
Singles: 7-Inch
ABBOTT: 53 15–20
COLUMBIA (20000
    series): 56 5–8
COLUMBIA (40000 series,
    except 40813): 57 4–6
COLUMBIA (40813; "I'm
    Coming Home"): 57 8–10
COLUMBIA (41000 series,
    except 41043 & 41110):
    57–61 4–6
COLUMBIA (41043;
    "Lover's Rock"): 57 10–15
COLUMBIA (41110;
    "Honky Tonk Hardwood
    Floor"): 58 20–25
COLUMBIA (42000
    through 44000 series):
    61–67 2–5
DOT: 59 4–6
MERCURY: 54–55 8–10
Picture Sleeves
COLUMBIA: 59–64 6–10

Price Range

Price Range

DOT: *59*. **$5–8**

EPs: 7-Inch 33/45rpm
COLUMBIA: *57–60*. **10–15**
MERCURY: *55*. **15–20**
SESAC: *59*. **25–30**
(Promotional issues only.)

LPs: 10/12-Inch 33rpm
BRIAR INT'L. **60–75**
COLUMBIA (1300
   through 1700 series):
   60–62 . . . . **20–30**
   (With a "CL" prefix.)
COLUMBIA (8000 series):
   60–63 . . . . **25–30**
   (With a "CS" prefix.)
COLUMBIA (8000 series) **5–8**
   (With a "PC" prefix.)
COLUMBIA (9000 series):
   65–69 . . . . **15–20**
   (With a "CS" prefix.)
COLUMBIA (30000
   series): *71*. **10–15**
CROWN: *63* **12–15**
CUSTOM. **8–12**
DOT: *59*. **15–20**
HARMONY: *70–71* **10–12**
MERCURY: *59*. **25–30**
PICKWICK/HILLTOP:
   65–68 . . . . **10–15**
SEARS. **10–15**
   (Promotional issue only.)
SESAC: *59*. **100–125**
   (Promotional issue only.)
   Also see DEAN, Jimmy / Johnny Horton

HORTON, Johnny / Sonny James
LPs: 10/12-Inch 33rpm
CUSTOM. **8–12**
   Also see JAMES, Sonny
   Also see HORTON, Johnny

HOSANNA
Singles: 7-Inch
CALLA: *76* **2–3**

HOT
Singles: 7-Inch
BIG TREE: *77–79* **1–3**

LPs: 10/12-Inch 33rpm
BIG TREE: *77–79* **5–8**

HOT BUTTER
Singles: 7-Inch
MUSICOR: *72*. **$2–3**
LPs: 10/12-Inch 33rpm
MUSICOR: *72–74*. **8–10**

HOT CHOCOLATE
Singles: 7-Inch
APPLE: *69* **3–5**
BIG TREE: *75–77* **1–3**
EMI AMERICA: *82*. **1–3**
INFINITY: *78–79*. **1–3**
RAK: *72–73* **2–3**
LPs: 10/12-Inch 33rpm
BIG TREE: *74–77* **8–10**
EMI AMERICA: *82*. **5–8**
INFINITY: *78–79*. **5–8**

HOT CUISINE
Singles: 7-Inch
PRELUDE: *81*. **1–3**

HOT LINE
Singles: 12-Inch 33/45rpm
MEMO: *84*. **4–6**
Singles: 7-Inch
RED COACH: *74*. **2–4**

HOT SAUCE
Singles: 7-Inch
VOLT: *72–74*. **2–3**

HOT STREAK
Singles: 12-Inch 33/45rpm
EASY STREET: *83* **4–6**

HOT TUNA
Singles: 7-Inch
GRUNT: *71–76*. **2–3**
LPs: 10/12-Inch 33rpm
GRUNT: *72–78*. **8–12**
RCA VICTOR (3000
   series): *81* **5–8**
RCA VICTOR (4000
   series): *70–71* **10–15**
   Members: Paul Cassady; Jorma Kaukonen.
   Also see KAUKONEN, Jorma

HOTBOX
Singles: 12-Inch 33/45rpm
POLYDOR: *84* **4–6**

Price Range

Singles: 7-Inch
POLYDOR: *84* **$1–3**

HOTEL
Singles: 7-Inch
MCA: *79–80* **1–3**
MERCURY: *78*.................... **1–3**
LPs: 10/12-Inch 33rpm
MCA: *79–80* **5–8**

HOTLEGS
Singles: 7-Inch
CAPITOL (Except 3043):
70–71 .... **2–5**
CAPITOL (3043; "Run
Baby, Run"): *71* **10–15**
LPs: 10/12-Inch 33rpm
CAPITOL: *71* **15–20**
Members: Eric Stewart; Kevin Godley; Lol Cream.
Also see 10CC

HOT-TODDYS, The
Singles: 7-Inch
CORSICAN: *59*................... **4–6**
SHAN-TODD: *59*................ **10–12**
STRAND: *60*..................... **4–6**
Also see ROCKIN' REBELS, The

HOUR GLASS
Singles: 7-Inch
LIBERTY: *68* **8–10**
Picture Sleeves
LIBERTY: *68* **10–15**
LPs: 10/12-Inch 33rpm
LIBERTY: *67–68* **15–20**
UNITED ARTISTS: *73* **10–12**
Members: Duane Allman; Gregg Allman.
Also see ALLMAN BROTHERS, The

HOUSTON, Cissy (Sissie Houston)
Singles: 7-Inch
COLUMBIA: *79–80*............... **1–3**
COMMONWEALTH
UNITED: *70*.................... **2–3**
JANUS: *71* **2–3**
KAPP: *67* **3–5**
PRIVATE STOCK: *77–78*.......... **1–3**
LPs: 10/12-Inch 33rpm
COLUMBIA: *79–80*............... **5–8**
JANUS: *70* **8–10**
PRIVATE STOCK: *77–78*.......... **5–8**

Price Range

Also see BOWIE, David
Also see MANN, Herbie, & Cissy Houston
Also see SWEET INSPIRATIONS, The

HOUSTON, David
Singles: 7-Inch
BLACK ROSE: *82*............... **$1–3**
COLONIAL: *78* **2–3**
COUNTRY INT'L: *80*............. **1–3**
DERRICK: *79*.................... **1–3**
ELEKTRA: *78–79* **1–3**
EXCELSIOR: *81*.................. **1–3**
EPIC: *63–76* **2–4**
NRC: *59*........................ **3–5**
PHILLIPS
INTERNATIONAL: *61*.......... **4–6**
RCA VICTOR (6611;
"Sugar Sweet"): *56* **10–15**
RCA VICTOR (6696;
"Blue Prelude"): *56*............. **5–8**
RCA VICTOR (6927;
"One & Only"): *57* **15–20**
RCA VICTOR (7001;
"Teenage Frankie &
Johnny"): *57*................... **8–10**
SOUNDWAVES: *83*............... **1–3**
STARDAY: *77*................... **1–3**
SUN (400 series): *66*.............. **2–4**
SUN (1100 series): *72*.............. **1–3**
Picture Sleeves
EPIC: *66–69* **2–4**
LPs: 10/12-Inch 33rpm
CAMDEN: *66*.................... **8–12**
COLUMBIA: *73*.................. **6–10**
DELTA: *82*...................... **5–8**
EPIC: *64–76* **5–15**
EXACT: *80* **5–8**
EXCELSIOR: *81*.................. **5–8**
51 WEST: *84*.................... **5–8**
GUSTO: *78* **5–8**
HARMONY: *70–72* **8–12**
STARDAY: *77* **6–10**
Also see JAMES, Sonny / David Houston

HOUSTON, David, & Barbara Mandrell
Singles: 7-Inch
EPIC: *70–74* **2–4**
LPs: 10/12-Inch 33rpm
EPIC: *72–75* **8–15**
Also see MANDRELL, Barbara

Price Range

HOUSTON, David, & Tammy Wynette
Singles: 7-Inch
EPIC: 67 . . . . $2–4
LPs: 10/12-Inch 33rpm
EPIC: 67 . . . . **8–12**
51 WEST: 82 . . . . **5–8**
Also see HOUSTON, David
Also see WYNETTE, Tammy

HOUSTON, Don
Singles: 7-Inch
THUNDER: 59 . . . . **4–6**

HOUSTON, Thelma (Thelma Houston & Pressure Cooker)
Singles: 12-Inch 33/45rpm
MCA: 83 . . . . **4–6**
Singles: 7-Inch
CAPITOL: 66 . . . . **3–5**
DUNHILL (Except 11): 70 . . . . **2–4**
DUNHILL (11;
"Everybody Gets To Go
To The Moon") **69**
(Special Apollo 11 Mission promotional issue. Price includes paper sleeve.)
MCA: 83 . . . . **1–3**
MOTOWN: 74–78 . . . . **1–3**
MOWEST: 71–73 . . . . **2–4**
RCA VICTOR: 80–81 . . . . **1–3**
TAMLA: 76–79 . . . . **2–3**
LPs: 10/12-Inch 33rpm
DUNHILL: 69 . . . . **10–12**
MCA: 83 . . . . **5–8**
MOTOWN: 81–82 . . . . **5–8**
MOWEST: 72 . . . . **8–10**
RCA VICTOR: 80–81 . . . . **5–8**
SHEFFIELD (2; "I've Got
The Music In Me"): 74 . . . . **25–30**
SHEFFIELD (200; "I've
Got The Music In Me"):
82 . . . . **5–8**
TAMLA: 76–79 . . . . **5–8**
MYRRH: 74 . . . . **8–10**
Also see BUTLER, Jerry, & Thelma Houston

HOUSTON, Whitney
Singles: 7-Inch
ARISTA: 85–86 . . . . **1–3**
LPs: 10/12-Inch 33rpm
ARISTA: 85–86 . . . . **5–8**

Price Range

Also see PENDERGRASS, Teddy

HOWARD, Camille (The Camille Howard Trio)
Singles: 7-Inch
FEDERAL: 53 . . . . $10–12
IMPERIAL: 53 . . . . **6–10**
SPECIALTY: 51–53 . . . . **8–10**
VEE JAY: 56 . . . . **5–8**

HOWARD, Don
Singles: 7-Inch
ESSEX: 52 . . . . **3–5**
MERCURY: 56 . . . . **2–4**

HOWARD, Eddy
Singles: 7-Inch
MERCURY: 50–61 . . . . **2–4**
MISHAWAKA: 72 . . . . **1–3**
EPs: 7-Inch 33/45rpm
MERCURY: 50–59 . . . . **4–8**
LPs: 10/12-Inch 33rpm
IMPERIAL: 61 . . . . **8–15**
MERCURY: 50–65 . . . . **8–18**
WING: 60–63 . . . . **5–10**

HOWARD, George (George Howard With Gwen Guthrie)
Singles: 7-Inch
PALO ALTO: 83 . . . . **1–3**
TBA: 84 . . . . **1–3**
LPs: 10/12-Inch 33rpm
PALO ALTO: 83 . . . . **5–8**
TBA: 84–85 . . . . **5–8**
Also see GUTHRIE, Gwen

HOWE, Steve, Band
Singles: 7-Inch
ATLANTIC: 75–79 . . . . **1–3**
LPs: 10/12-Inch 33rpm
ATLANTIC: 75–79 . . . . **5–8**
Also see ASIA

HOWLIN' WOLF (Chester Burnett)
Singles: 7-Inch
CHESS (1528; "My Last
Affair"): 53 . . . . **20–25**
CHESS (1557 through
1593): 53–55 . . . . **8–12**
CHESS (1600 series):
55–57 . . . . **5–8**

Price Range

CHESS (1700 through 1900
  series): *58–66* $3–5
CHESS (2000 series):
  67–71 2–3
  LPs: 10/12-Inch 33rpm
CADET: *69* 10–12
CHESS (Except 1400 &
  1500 series): *71–77* 8–10
CHESS (1400 series):
  58–62 35–45
CHESS (1500 series, except
  1502): *67–69* 15–20
CHESS (1502; "Real Folk
  Blues"): *66* 25–30
CROWN: *62* 15–20
CUSTOM 10–12
KENT: *67* 10–15
UNITED 8–10
  Also see BERRY, Chuck, & Howlin' Wolf
  Also see DIDDLEY, Bo, Howlin' Wolf &
  Muddy Waters
  Also see ROBINSON, Freddy
  Also see WATERS, Muddy, & Howlin' Wolf

HUANG CHUNG: see WANG CHUNG

HUBBARD, Freddie
  Singles: 12-Inch 33/45rpm
FANTASY: *81* 4–6
  Singles: 7-Inch
ATLANTIC: *69* 2–3
BLUE NOTE: *61–64* 2–4
COLUMBIA: *74–76* 1–3
  LPs: 10/12-Inch 33rpm
ATLANTIC: *67–76* 8–15
BLUE NOTE: *60–65* 15–25
  (Label reads "Blue Note Records Inc. - New
  York, U.S.A.")
BLUE NOTE: *66–76* 8–15
  (Label shows Blue Note Records as a division
  of either Liberty or United Artists.)
CTI: *70–75* 5–10
COLUMBIA: *74–83* 5–8
ELEKTRA: *82* 5–8
ENJA: *81* 5–8
FANTASY: *81–83* 5–8
IMPULSE: *63–73* 10–20
LIBERTY: *81* 5–8
PABLO: *82–83* 5–8
PAUSA: *82* 5–8

Price Range

HUBBARD, Freddie, & Oscar Peterson
  LPs: 10/12-Inch 33rpm
PABLO: *80* $5–8
  Also see PETERSON, Oscar

HUBBARD, Freddie, & Stanley Turrentine
  LPs: 10/12-Inch 33rpm
CTI: *74* 5–8
  Also see HUBBARD, Freddie
  Also see TURRENTINE, Stanley

HUDMON, R.B., Jr.
  Singles: 7-Inch
ATLANTIC: *76–77* 2–3
CAPITOL: *71* 2–4
COTILLION: *78* 1–3
1-2-3: *68–70* 2–4
  LPs: 10/12-Inch 33rpm
COTILLION: *78* 5–8

HUDSON, Al (Al Hudson & The Soul Partners)
  Singles: 12-Inch 33/45rpm
ABC: *77* 4–6
  Singles: 7-Inch
ABC: *76–77* 1–3
ATCO: *75–76* 2–3
  LPs: 10/12-Inch 33rpm
ABC: *77* 8–10
  Also see ONE WAY

HUDSON, David
  Singles: 7-Inch
ALSTON: *80* 1–3
  LPs: 10/12-Inch 33rpm
ALSTON: *80* 5–8

HUDSON, "Emperor" Bob, & Lawrence Welk
  Singles: 7-Inch
RANWOOD: *72* 2–3
  Also see HUDSON & LANDRY
  Also see WELK, Lawrence

HUDSON, Pookie (Pookie Hudson & The Spaniels)
  Singles: 7-Inch
CHESS: *66* 3–5
DOUBLE-L: *63* 3–5

NEPTUNE: *61* $3–5
PARKWAY: *62* 3–5
Also see SPANIELS, The

HUDSON & LANDRY
Singles: 7-Inch
DORE: *71–74* 2–3
LPs: 10/12-Inch 33rpm
DORE: *71–75* 5–10
Members: Bob Hudson; Ron Landry.
Also see HUDSON, "Emperor" Bob, & Lawrence Welk

HUDSON BROTHERS, The
Singles: 7-Inch
ARISTA: *76–78*................... 1–3
CASABLANCA: *74* 2–3
ROCKET: *74–76*.................. 2–3
Picture Sleeves
ROCKET: *75*.................... INC
LPs: 10/12-Inch 33rpm
CASABLANCA: *74* 8–10
PLAYBOY: *72* 8–10
ROCKET: *74–75*................. 8–10
Members: Bill Hudson; Brett Hudson; Mark Hudson.

HUES CORPORATION, The
Singles: 7-Inch
RCA VICTOR: *73–75* 2–3
WARNER BROS: *77* 2–3
LPs: 10/12-Inch 33rpm
RCA VICTOR: *73–77* 8–10
WARNER BROS: *77–78*........... 5–8

HUFF, Terry (Terry Huff & Special Delivery)
Singles: 7-Inch
MAINSTREAM: *76*................ 2–3
PHILADELPHIA INT'L:
80 1–3
LPs: 10/12-Inch 33rpm
MAINSTREAM: *76*............... 5–8

HUGHES, Freddie (Fred Hughes)
Singles: 7-Inch
BRUNSWICK: *69–71*.............. 2–4
COLLECTABLES: *81* 1–3
EXODUS: *66*.................... 3–5
MINASA: *65*.................... 3–5
VEE JAY: *65*.................... 3–5

WAND: *68–69*................... $3–5
LPs: 10/12-Inch 33rpm
BRUNSWICK: *70*................ 8–12
WAND: *68* 10–15

HUGHES, Jimmy
Singles: 7-Inch
COLLECTABLES: *81* 1–3
FAME: *64–67*................... 3–5
GUYDEN: *62*................... 3–5
VOLT: *69*...................... 2–3
LPs: 10/12-Inch 33rpm
ATCO: *67* 10–15
STAX: *85*...................... 5–8
VEE JAY: *64*.................. 15–20
VOLT: *69*..................... 10–12

HUGO & LUIGI
Singles: 7-Inch
MERCURY: *55–56*................ 2–4
RCA VICTOR: *59–60* 2–3
LPs: 10/12-Inch 33rpm
FORUM: *60* 5–10
MERCURY: *56*.................. 5–15
RCA VICTOR: *60–63* 5–10
WING: *60* 5–10

HUGHES, Rhetta (Rhetta Hughes & Tennyson Stephens)
Singles: 12-Inch 33/45rpm
ARIA: *83*...................... 4–6
Singles: 7-Inch
ARIA: *83*...................... 1–3
COLUMBIA: *67–68* 3–5
SUTRA: *80* 1–3
TETRAGRAMMATON:
68–69 2–3
LPs: 10/12-Inch 33rpm
COLUMBIA: *65*................ 12–18
SUTRA: *80* 5–8
TETRAGRAMMATON:
69 10–12

HUGHES-THRALL
Singles: 7-Inch
BOULEVARD: *82* 1–3
Members: Glenn Hughes; Pat Thrall.

HULIN, T.K.
Singles: 7-Inch
SMASH: *63* 3–5

Price Range

L.K.: *63* **$15–20**
LPs: 10/12-Inch 33rpm
STARLITE **10–12**

HULLABALOOS, The
Singles: 7-Inch
ROULETTE: *64–65* **4–6**
Picture Sleeves
ROULETTE: *64–65* **5–10**
LPs: 10/12-Inch 33rpm
ROULETTE: *65* **25–30**

HUMAN BEINZ (Human Beinz With The Mammals)
Singles: 7-Inch
CAPITOL: *67–69* **4–6**
GATEWAY: *66–67.* **5–8**
Picture Sleeves
CAPITOL: *68* **4–6**
LPs: 10/12-Inch 33rpm
CAPITOL: *68* **20–25**
GATEWAY: *68.* **25–30**

HUMAN BODY
Singles: 7-Inch
BEARSVILLE: *84* **1–3**

HUMAN LEAGUE, The
Singles: 12-Inch 33/45rpm
A&M: *82–85* **4–6**
Singles: 7-Inch
A&M: *82–85* **1–3**
Picture Sleeves
A&M: *82–85* .... **INC**
LPs: 10/12-Inch 33rpm
A&M: *82–85* **5–8**
Also see LEAGUE UNLIMITED ORCHESTRA, The
Also see MORODER, Giorgio, & Phil Oakey

HUMBLE PIE
Singles: 7-Inch
A&M: *71–75* **2–4**
ATCO: *80* **1–3**
IMMEDIATE: *69.* **4–6**
LPs: 10/12-Inch 33rpm
A&M: *70–82* **8–12**
ACCORD: *82* **5–8**
ATCO: *80–81.* **5–8**
IMMEDIATE: *68–72* **12–15**
Also see FRAMPTON, Peter

Price Range

Also see SMALL FACES

HUMPERDINCK, Engelbert
Singles: 7-Inch
EPIC: *76–83* **$1–3**
PARROT: *67–73.* **2–3**
Picture Sleeves
PARROT: *67–71.* **2–3**
LPs: 10/12-Inch 33rpm
EPIC: *76–83* **5–10**
PARROT: *67–74.* **8–15**

HUMPHREY, Bobbi
Singles: 12-Inch 33/45rpm
EPIC: *78–79* **4–6**
Singles: 7-Inch
BLUE NOTE: *72–76* **2–3**
EPIC: *77–79* **1–3**
LPs: 10/12-Inch 33rpm
BLUE NOTE: *71–76* **5–10**
EPIC: *78–79* **5–8**

HUMPHREY, Della
Singles: 7-Inch
ARCTIC: *68* **3–5**

HUMPHREY, Paul, & His Cool Aid Chemists
Singles: 7-Inch
LIZARD: *70–71* **2–4**
LPs: 10/12-Inch 33rpm
LIZARD: *71* **8–12**

HUMPHRIES, Teddy
Singles: 7-Inch
KING: *59* **3–5**

HUNT, Geraldine
Singles: 7-Inch
ABC: *67* **2–4**
BOMBAY: *64* **3–5**
CHECKER: *62* **3–5**
PRISM: *80.* **1–3**
ROULETTE: *70–73* **2–4**

HUNT, Geraldine, & Charlie Hodges
Singles: 7-Inch
CALLA: *70* **2–4**
Also see HODGES, Charles
Also see HUNT, Geraldine

Price Range

HUNT, Pee Wee
Singles: 7-Inch
CAPITOL: *50–62* **$2–4**
SAVOY: *51* **3–5**
EPs: 7-Inch 33/45rpm
CAPITOL: *50–56* **4–8**
SAVOY: *51* **5–10**
LPs: 10/12-Inch 33rpm
CAPITOL: *78* **4–8**
(With an "SM" prefix.)
CAPITOL: *50–63* **10–20**
(With a "T" or "ST" prefix.)
GLENDALE: *78*. **4–8**
SAVOY: *51* **20–30**

HUNT, Tommy
Singles: 7-Inch
ATLANTIC: *65* **3–5**
CAPITOL: *66* **3–5**
DYNAMO: *67*. **3–5**
SCEPTER: *61–63* **4–6**
LPs: 10/12-Inch 33rpm
DYNAMO: *67*. **10–15**
SCEPTER: *62* **20–25**
Also see FLAMINGOS, The
Also see PLATTERS, The / Inez & Charlie
Foxx / The Jive Five / Tommy Hunt

HUNTER, Ian
Singles: 7-Inch
CHRYSALIS: *79*. **1–3**
COLUMBIA: *75* **2–3**
LPs: 10/12-Inch 33rpm
CHRYSALIS: *79–81*. **5–8**
COLUMBIA: *75–79* **8–10**
Also see MOTT THE HOOPLE

HUNTER, Ivory Joe (Ivory Joe Hunter & The Ivorytones)
Singles: 7-Inch
ATLANTIC: *55–58* **5–8**
CAPITOL: *61–62* **3–5**
DOT: *58–59*. **4–6**
GOLDISC: *60*. **3–5**
KING (4424 through
  4455): *51* **20–25**
KING (5200 series): *59* **5–8**
MGM (500 series): *78*. **1–3**
MGM (8000 series): *49*. **10–12**
MGM (10000 & 11000
  series): *49–54* **8–10**

Price Range

PARAMOUNT: *73*. **$2–3**
SMASH: *63* **3–5**
SOUND STAGE 7: *68*. **3–5**
VEE JAY: *62*. **3–5**
VEEP: *67* **3–5**
EPs: 7-Inch 33/45rpm
ATLANTIC: *58* **15–20**
KING. **25–30**
MGM: *57*. **20–25**
LPs: 10/12-Inch 33rpm
ATLANTIC (Black label):
  58 .... **25–30**
ATLANTIC (Red label):
  59 .... **15–20**
DOT: *64*. **15–20**
EPIC: *71* **8–10**
EVEREST: *74* **8–10**
GOLDISC: *61*. **20–25**
GRAND PRIX. **10–15**
KING: *58* **25–30**
LION **15–20**
MGM: *57*. **50–60**
PARAMOUNT: *74*. **8–10**
SAGE: *59*. **20–25**
SMASH: *63* **15–18**
SOUND: *57*. **30–35**
Also see CHARLES, Ray / Ivory Joe Hunter
/ Jimmy Rushing

HUNTER, Ivory Joe / Memphis Slim
LPs: 10/12-Inch 33rpm
STRAND. **10–12**

HUNTER, John
Singles: 7-Inch
PRIVATE I: *84–85*. **1–3**
LPs: 10/12-Inch 33rpm
PRIVATE I: *85*. **5–8**

HUNTER, Tab
Singles: 7-Inch
DOT: *56–62*. **3–5**
WARNER BROS. (Except
  stereo singles): *58–59*. **3–5**
WARNER BROS. (Stereo
  singles): *59* **5–8**
(With an "S" prefix.)
Picture Sleeves
WARNER BROS: *58–60*. **4–6**

Price Range

LPs: 10/12-Inch 33rpm
DOT: 59.............................$25–30
WARNER BROS: 58–60..........25–35

HUNTER, Ty (Ty Hunter & The Voice Masters)
Singles: 7-Inch
ANNA: 60.........................5–8
CHECK MATE: 61...............4–6
CHESS: 62–64....................3–5
Also see VOICE MASTERS, The

HUNTLEY, Chet, & David Brinkley
LPs: 10/12-Inch 33rpm
RCA VICTOR: 64–66.............8–15

HURD, Debra
Singles: 7-Inch
GEFFEN: 83.......................1–3

HURT, Jim
Singles: 7-Inch
SCOTTI BROTHERS: 80...........1–3

HURT 'EM BAD & THE S.C. BAND
Singles: 7-Inch
PROFILE: 82.....................1–3

HUSKY, Ferlin (Ferlin Husky & The Hush Puppies; Ferlin Husky & The Coon Creek Girls; Ferlin & Bettie Husky; Ferlin Huskey)
Singles: 7-Inch
ABC: 73–75........................1–3
CAPITOL (2000 through
  3400): 67–72....................2–3
  (Orange labels.)
CAPITOL (2300 through
  4300): 52–60....................3–5
  (Purple labels.)
CAPITOL (4400 through
  5900): 60–67....................2–4
CACHET: 80.......................1–3
FIRST GENERATION:
  78..............................1–3
KING: 60–61.......................2–4
EPs: 7-Inch 33/45rpm
CAPITOL: 57–60...................8–15

STEREO   KING

FERLIN HUSKEY

COUNTRY TUNES SUNG FROM THE HEART

Price Range

Picture Sleeves
CAPITOL: 62–68.................$2–4
LPs: 10/12-Inch 33rpm
ABC: 73–75.......................5–10
AUDIOGRAPH ALIVE:
  82..............................5–8
CAPITOL (700 & 800
  series): 56–57..................25–40
CAPITOL (1200 through
  2800 series): 60–68............10–20
  (With a "T" or "ST" prefix.)
CAPITOL (1200 through
  2800 series): 68–75............5–10
  (With a "DT" or "SM" prefix.)
KING (600 & 700 series):
  59–60...........................25–35
PICKWICK........................6–12
PICKWICK/HILLTOP:
  65..............................8–12
  Also see CRUM, Simon
  Also see OWENS, Buck / Faron Young / Ferlin Husky
  Also see PRESTON, Terry
  Also see SHEPARD, Jean, & Ferlin Husky

HUTCH, Willie
Singles: 7-Inch
DUNHILL: 65......................3–5
MAVERICK: 68.....................3–5
MOTOWN: 73–82....................2–3
RCA VICTOR: 69...................2–4
WHITFIELD: 78–79................1–3
LPs: 10/12-Inch 33rpm
MOTOWN: 73–82....................5–10

Price Range

RCA VICTOR: *69* **$10–12**
WHITFIELD: *78–79* **5–8**

HUTSON, Leroy (Leroy Hutson & The Free Spirit Symphony)
Singles: 7-Inch
CURTOM: *73–78* **2–3**
LPs: 10/12-Inch 33rpm
CURTOM: *73–78* **8–10**
Also see IMPRESSIONS, The

HUTTON, Danny
Singles: 7-Inch
HBR: *65* **3–5**
MGM: *66* **3–5**
Picture Sleeves
HBR: *65* **5–8**
MGM: *66* **3–5**
LPs: 10/12-Inch 33rpm
MGM: *70* **8–10**
Also see THREE DOG NIGHT

HYDE, Paul, & The Payolas
Singles: 7-Inch
A&M: *85* **1–3**
LPs: 10/12-Inch 33rpm
A&M: *85* **5–8**

HYLAND, Brian
Singles: 7-Inch
ABC: *73* **1–3**
ABC-PARAMOUNT:
   61–64 . . . . **3–5**
DOT: *67–69* **3–5**
KAPP: *60–61* **4–6**
LEADER: *60* **5–8**
MCA: *73* **1–3**
PHILIPS: *64–67* **3–5**
ROULETTE **1–3**
UNI: *70–72* **2–4**
Picture Sleeves
ABC-PARAMOUNT:
   61–63 . . . . **5–8**
KAPP (Except 352): *60–61* **6–10**
KAPP (352; "Four Little
   Heels"): *60* **10–12**
   (Black & white sleeve. Promotional issue only.)
KAPP (352; "Four Little
   Heels"): *60* **5–8**
   (Color sleeve.)
PHILIPS: *64–67* **3–5**

Price Range

LPs: 10/12-Inch 33rpm
ABC-PARAMOUNT:
   61–64 . . . . **$20–25**
DOT: *69* **10–12**
KAPP: *60* **25–30**
PHILIPS: *64–66* **15–20**
PRIVATE STOCK: *77* **5–8**
UNI: *71* **8–10**
WING: *67* **10–12**

HYMAN, Dick (The Dick Hyman Trio; Dick Hyman & His Electric Eclectics)
Singles: 7-Inch
COLUMBIA: *74–75* **1–3**
COMMAND: *61–70* **2–3**
EVEREST: *60* **2–3**
MGM: *54–62* **2–4**
RCA VICTOR: *62* **2–3**

LPs: 10/12-Inch 33rpm
ATLANTIC: *75* **5–8**
COLUMBIA: *74* **5–8**
COMMAND: *60–73* **5–15**
EVEREST: *60* **5–10**
FAMOUS DOOR: *73* **5–8**
MCA: *77* **5–10**
MGM: *54–63* **10–20**
PROJECT 3: *71* **5–8**
RCA VICTOR: *80–83* **4–8**
SUNSET: *66* **5–10**

HYMAN, Phyllis
Singles: 12-Inch 33/45rpm
ARISTA: *83* **4–6**

Singles: 7-Inch
ARISTA: *78–83* **1–3**
BUDDAH: *77* **1–3**
DESERT MOON: *76* **2–3**

LPs: 10/12-Inch 33rpm
ARISTA: *79–83* **5–8**
BUDDAH: *77* **5–8**

HYMAN, Phyllis, & Michael Henderson
Singles: 7-Inch
ARISTA: *81* **1–3**
Also see HENDERSON, Michael
Also see HYMAN, Phyllis

I

I LEVEL
Singles: 12-Inch 33/45rpm
VIRGIN: *82–84*.................. **$4–6**
Singles: 7-Inch
VIRGIN: *82–84*.................. **1–3**
LPs: 10/12-Inch 33rpm
VIRGIN: *83* **5–8**

I.R.T. (Interboro Rhythm Team)
Singles: 12-Inch 33/45rpm
RCA VICTOR: *84* **4–6**
Singles: 7-Inch
RCA VICTOR: *84* **1–3**

IAN, Janis
Singles: 7-Inch
CAPITOL: *71* **2–3**
CASABLANCA: *80* **1–3**
COLUMBIA: *74–81* **1–3**
POLYDOR: *78* **1–3**
VERVE/FOLKWAYS:
66–67 .... **3–5**
VERVE/FORECAST:
68–69 .... **2–4**
LPs: 10/12-Inch 33rpm
CAPITOL: *71–75* **8–12**
COLUMBIA: *74–81* **8–10**
MGM: *70*........................ **8–10**
POLYDOR: *75* **8–10**
VERVE/FOLKWAYS: *67*........ **10–15**
VERVE/FORECAST:
68–69 .... **10–15**

ICICLE WORKS
Singles: 7-Inch
ARISTA: *84* **1–3**
LPs: 10/12-Inch 33rpm
ARISTA: *84* **5–8**

ICEHOUSE
Singles: 12-Inch 33/45rpm
CHRYSALIS: *81–84*............. **4–6**
Singles: 7-Inch
CHRYSALIS: *81–84*............. **1–3**
LPs: 10/12-Inch 33rpm
CHRYSALIS: *81–84*............. **5–8**

ICON
LPs: 10/12-Inch 33rpm
CAPITOL: *85* **$5–8**
Members: Steve Clifford; Dan Wexler; Pat
Dixon; John Aquilino; Tracy Wallach; Jerry
Harrison.

IDEALS, The
Singles: 7-Inch
SATELLITE: *66*.................. **3–5**

IDES OF MARCH, The (With Jim Peterik)
Singles: 7-Inch
KAPP: *69* **3–5**
PARROT: *66–67*................. **5–8**
RCA VICTOR: *72–73* **2–4**
WARNER BROS: *69–71*......... **3–5**
LPs: 10/12-Inch 33rpm
RCA VICTOR: *72–73* **8–12**
WARNER BROS: *70–71*........ **10–15**
Also see SURVIVOR

IDLE RACE
Singles: 7-Inch
LIBERTY: *67* **10–15**
LPs: 10/12-Inch 33rpm
LIBERTY: *69* **25–30**
SUNSET: *72* **8–12**
Members: Jeff Lynne; Greg Masters; Roger
Spencer; Dave Pritchard.
Also see LYNNE, Jeff

IDOL, Billy
Singles: 12-Inch 33/45rpm
CHRYSALIS: *81–85*.............. **4–6**
Singles: 7-Inch
CHRYSALIS: *81–85*.............. **1–3**
LPs: 10/12-Inch 33rpm
CHRYSALIS: *82–85*.............. **5–8**

IF
Singles: 7-Inch
CAPITOL: *70–74* **2–4**
METROMEDIA: *72*............... **2–3**
LPs: 10/12-Inch 33rpm
CAPITOL: *69–74* **10–12**
METROMEDIA: *72–73*.......... **8–10**

Price Range

Price Range

IFIELD, Frank
Singles: 7-Inch
CAPITOL: 63–65 .... **$2–4**
HICKORY: 66–71 .... **2–3**
MAM: 71 .... **2–3**
VEE JAY: 62–63. .... **3–5**
WARNER BROS: 79 .... **1–3**
LPs: 10/12-Inch 33rpm
CAPITOL: 63 .... **10–12**
HICKORY: 66–68 .... **8–10**
VEE JAY: 62. .... **10–15**
Also see BEATLES, The / Frank Ifield

IGLESIAS, Julio
Singles: 7-Inch
COLUMBIA: 83–84 .... **1–3**
LPs: 10/12-Inch 33rpm
COLUMBIA: 83–84 .... **5–8**

IGLESIAS, Julio, & Willie Nelson
Singles: 7-Inch
COLUMBIA: 84 .... **1–3**
Also see NELSON, Willie

IGLESIAS, Julio, & Diana Ross
Singles: 7-Inch
COLUMBIA: 84 .... **1–3**
Also see IGLESIAS, Julio
Also see ROSS, Diana

IGGY & THE STOOGES: see POP, Iggy

IKETTES, The
Singles: 7-Inch
ATCO: 61–62. .... **3–5**
INNIS: 64 .... **3–5**
MODERN: 64–66 .... **3–5**
PHI-DAN **3–5**
POMPEII: 68. .... **3–5**
TEENA: 63 .... **3–5**
UNITED ARTISTS: 71–72 .... **2–4**
LPs: 10/12-Inch 33rpm
MODERN: 65. .... **15–20**
UNITED ARTISTS: 73–75 .... **8–10**
Also see TURNER, Ike & Tina

ILLINOIS SPEED PRESS, The (With Paul Cotton)
Singles: 7-Inch
COLUMBIA: 68–70 .... **3–5**

LPs: 10/12-Inch 33rpm
COLUMBIA: 69–70 .... **$10–15**
Also see POCO

ILLUSION
Singles: 7-Inch
ISLAND: 77–78 .... **1–3**
LPs: 10/12-Inch 33rpm
ISLAND: 77–78 .... **5–8**

ILLUSION
Singles: 7-Inch
SUGAR HILL: 82 .... **1–3**

ILLUSION, The
Singles: 7-Inch
DYNO VOICE: 68 .... **3–5**
STEED: 69–71. .... **2–4**
LPs: 10/12-Inch 33rpm
STEED: 69–70. .... **12–15**

ILLUSTRATED MAN
Singles: 7-Inch
CAPITOL: 84 .... **1–3**

IMAGINATION
Singles: 12-Inch 33/45rpm
ELEKTRA: 84 .... **4–6**
Singles: 7-Inch
ELEKTRA: 83 .... **1–3**
MCA: 82–83 .... **1–3**
LPs: 10/12-Inch 33rpm
MCA: 82 .... **5–8**

IMPACT
Singles: 7-Inch
ATCO: 76 .... **2–3**
FANTASY: 77–78. .... **2–3**
LPs: 10/12-Inch 33rpm
ATCO: 75 .... **8–10**
FANTASY: 77. .... **5–8**

IMPALAS, The (Featuring Joe "Speedo" Frazier)
Singles: 7-Inch
CUB (Except 9022): 59–60. .... **5–8**
CUB (9022; "I Ran All
The Way Home"): 59 .... **12–15**
CUB (9022; "Sorry I Ran
All The Way Home"):
59 .... **5–8**

Price Range

(The difference between the two previous listings is the use of the word "Sorry" in the title.)
HAMILTON: *59* **$4–6**
MGM: *64–78* **1–3**

EPs: 7-Inch 33/45rpm
CUB: *59* **40–50**

LPs: 10/12-Inch 33rpm
CUB (CUB-8003; "Sorry I
Ran All The Way
Home"): *59* **75–90**
(Monaural issue.)
CUB (CUBS-8003; "Sorry
I Ran All The Way
Home"): *59* **100–125**
(Stereo issue.)

IMPALAS, The / Horst Jankowski & His Orchestra
Singles: 7-Inch
COLLECTABLES: *85* **1–3**
(Contains the true stereo version of "I Ran All The Way Home.")
Also see IMPALAS, The
Also see JANKOWSKI, Horst, & His Orchestra

IMPERIALS, The
Singles: 7-Inch
CAPITOL: *63* **3–5**
CARLTON: *61* **3–5**
END (1027; "Tears On My
Pillow"): *58* **10–12**
(Reissues were shown as by "Little Anthony & The Imperials.")
LIBERTY: *58* **4–6**
Also see LITTLE ANTHONY & THE IMPERIALS

IMPERIALS, The
Singles: 7-Inch
OMNI: *78* **2–3**

IMPRESSIONS, The
Singles: 12-Inch 33/45rpm
20TH CENTURY-FOX:
  79 . . . . **4–6**
Singles: 7-Inch
ABC: *66–68* **3–5**
ABC-PARAMOUNT:
  61–66 . . . . **4–6**
ABNER: *59–60* **5–8**
COTILLION: *76–77* **2–3**

Price Range

CURTOM: *68–76* **$2–4**
SWIRL: *62* **3–5**
20TH CENTURY-FOX:
  81 . . . . **1–3**
VEE JAY (400 series): *62* **4–6**
Picture Sleeves
CURTOM: *68* **2–4**
LPs: 10/12-Inch 33rpm
ABC: *66–76* **10–15**
ABC-PARAMOUNT:
  63–66 . . . . **15–20**
COTILLION: *76* **8–10**
CURTOM: *68–76* **8–10**
MCA: *82* **5–8**
PICKWICK: *75* **8–10**
SCEPTER/CITATION **8–10**
SIRE: *76* **8–10**
20TH CENTURY-FOX:
  79–81 . . . . **5–8**
UPFRONT **8–10**
Members: Curtis Mayfield; Sam Gooden; Fred Cash.
Also see EVERETT, Betty / The Impressions
Also see HUTSON, Leroy
Also see MAYFIELD, Curtis

IMPRESSIONS, The / Jerry Butler
LPs: 10/12-Inch 33rpm
SIRE: *77* **5–8**
Also see BUTLER, Jerry
Also see IMPRESSIONS, The

IN CROWD, The
Singles: 7-Inch
BRENT: *65* **3–5**
MUSICOR: *65* **4–6**
SWAN: *65* **3–5**
TOWER: *65–66* **3–5**
VIVA: *66–67* **3–5**

INCREDIBLE BONGO BAND, The
Singles: 7-Inch
MGM: *73* **2–3**
PRIDE: *72–74* **2–3**
LPs: 10/12-Inch 33rpm
PRIDE: *73–74* **8–10**

INCREDIBLE STRING BAND, The
LPs: 10/12-Inch 33rpm
ELEKTRA: *67–72* **8–12**
REPRISE: *72–74* **8–12**

Price Range

INCREDIBLES, The
Singles: 7-Inch
AUDIO ARTS: *66–68* **$3–5**
CLASS: *66* **3–5**
TETRAGRAMMATON:
  69 .... **2–4**
LPs: 10/12-Inch 33rpm
AUDIO ARTS: *70* **10–12**

INDEEP
Singles: 12-Inch 33/45rpm
SOUND OF NEW YORK:
  83–84 .... **4–6**
Singles: 7-Inch
SOUND OF NEW YORK:
  83 .... **1–3**
LPs: 10/12-Inch 33rpm
SOUND OF NEW YORK:
  83 .... **5–8**

INDEPENDENTS, The
Singles: 7-Inch
WAND: *72–74* **2–3**
LPs: 10/12-Inch 33rpm
WAND: *72–74* **8–10**

INDIA
Singles: 12-Inch 33/45rpm
WEST END: *83* **4–6**

INDIOS TABAJARAS, Los: see LOS INDIOS TABAJARAS

INDIVIDUALS, The
Singles: 7-Inch
P.I.P.: *75* **2–3**

INDUSTRY
Singles: 7-Inch
CAPITOL: *83* **1–3**

INFINITY
Singles: 7-Inch
FOUNTAIN: *69* **2–4**
MERCURY: *70* **2–3**
UNI: *72* **2–3**
  Also see BUTLER, Billy

INGMANN, Jorgen
Singles: 7-Inch
ATCO: *60–66* **$2–4**
MERCURY: *56* **2–4**
PARROT: *64* **2–3**
UNITED ARTISTS
  INT'L: *68* **2–3**
LPs: 10/12-Inch 33rpm
ATCO: *62* **20–30**
MERCURY: *56* **15–25**
UNITED ARTISTS
  INT'L: *68* **8–12**

INGRAM
Singles: 7-Inch
H&L: *77* **1–3**
LPs: 10/12-Inch 33rpm
H&L: *77* **8–10**

INGRAM, James
Singles: 12-Inch 33/45rpm
QWEST: *83* **4–6**
Singles: 7-Inch
QWEST: *83* **1–3**
LPs: 10/12-Inch 33rpm
QWEST: *83* **5–8**
  Also see AUSTIN, Patti, & James Ingram
  Also see JONES, Quincy, & James Ingram
  Also see ROGERS, Kenny, Kim Carnes & James Ingram
  Also see U.S.A. FOR AFRICA

INGRAM, James, & Michael McDonald
Singles: 7-Inch
QWEST: *83* **1–3**
  Also see INGRAM, James
  Also see McDONALD, Michael

INGRAM, Luther (Luther Ingram & The G-Men)
Singles: 7-Inch
DECCA: *65* **3–5**
HIB: *67* **3–5**
KO KO: *67–78* **2–4**
SMASH: *66* **3–5**
LPs: 10/12-Inch 33rpm
KO KO: *71–76* **8–10**
  Note: The Ko Ko label name may be shown as one word on some issues.

Price Range

INK SPOTS, The
Singles: 7-Inch
DECCA (25000 through
31000 series): *50–61* **$2–4**
GRAND AWARD: *56*. **3–5**
VERVE: *60* **2–3**
X-TRA: *60*. **2–4**
EPs: 7-Inch 33/45rpm
DECCA: *54–56* **5–15**
GRAND AWARD: *56*. **5–15**
LPs: 10/12-Inch 33rpm
CORAL: *73* **4–6**
CROWN: *59* **5–15**
DECCA (100 series): *65*. **10–20**
DECCA (4000 series): *63* **10–20**
(Decca LP numbers in this series preceded by
a "7" or a "DL-7" are stereo issues.)
DECCA (5000 series):
51–53 .... **20–30**
(10-Inch LPs.)
DECCA (7000 & 8000
series): *54–59* **15–25**
EVEREST: *82* **5–8**
EXACT: *80* **5–8**
GRAND AWARD: *56–59*. **10–20**
MCA: *73* **5–8**
PAULA: *72*. **5–8**
VERVE: *56–60* **15–25**
VOCALION: *59–65* **8–15**
WALDORF MUSIC
HALL: *55* **20–30**
Members: Bill Kenny; Orville Jones; Herb
Kenny; Charlie Fuqua; Deek Watson; Billy
Bowen.
Also see FITZGERALD, Ella, & The Ink
Spots
Also see KENNY, Bill

INK SPOTS, The
Singles: 7-Inch
KING (1200 & 1300 series,
except 1336): *53–54* **12–15**
KING (1336; "Melody Of
Love"): *54* **25–30**
KING (1400 series): *54–55* **20–25**
KING (1500 series): *55* **12–15**
KING (4000 series, except
4670): *55* **12–15**
KING (4670; "Here In My
Lonely Room"): *54*. **40–50**
EPs: 7-Inch 33/45rpm
KING: *57* **30–40**

Price Range

LPs: 10/12-Inch 33rpm
KING (500 series): *57* **$75–100**
KING (600 series): *59* **40–60**
Members: James Holmes; Charlie Fuqua;
Harry Jackson; Isaac Royal; Leon Antoine.

INK SPOTS, The (Featuring Joe Van Loan)
Singles: 7-Inch
FORD: *62* **3–5**

INMAN, Autry
Singles: 7-Inch
DECCA (28000 & 29000
series): *56* **3–5**
EPIC: *67–69* **2–3**
GLAD: *60* **3–5**
JUBILEE: *65–69*. **2–4**
MERCURY: *62*. **2–4**
MILLION: *72* **1–3**
SIMS: *63–64* **2–4**
UNITED ARTISTS: *60* **2–4**
LPs: 10/12-Inch 33rpm
ALSHIRE: *69* **8–12**
EPIC: *68* **8–12**
GUEST STAR. **8–12**
JUBILEE: *64–69*. **10–20**
MOUNTAIN DEW: *63*. **15–25**
SIMS: *64* **15–20**

INMATES, The
Singles: 7-Inch
POLYDOR/RADAR: *79* **1–3**
LPs: 10/12-Inch 33rpm
POLYDOR: *79–80* **5–8**

INNER CITY JAM BAND, The
Singles: 7-Inch
BAREBACK: *77*. **2–3**

INNER LIFE
Singles: 12-Inch 33/45rpm
SALSOUL: *83* **4–6**
Singles: 7-Inch
PERSONAL: *84* **1–3**
PRELUDE: *79–80*. **1–3**
SALSOUL: *83* **1–3**

INNERVISION
Singles: 7-Inch
ARIOLA AMERICA: *77* **2–3**

Price Range

INVITATIONS, The
Singles: 7-Inch
DIAMOND: 68 . . . . $3–5
DYNO VOICE: 65–66 3–5
MGM: 66 3–5

INVITATIONS, The
Singles: 7-Inch
SILVER BLUE: 74 2–3

INXS
Singles: 12-Inch 33/45rpm
ATCO: 84 4–6
Singles: 7-Inch
ATCO: 83–85 1–3
ATLANTIC: 85–86 1–3
LPs: 10/12-Inch 33rpm
ATCO: 83–85 5–8
ATLANTIC: 85–86 5–8
Members: Michael Hutchence; Tim Farriss; Andrew Farriss; Jon Farriss; Garry Gary Beers; Kirk Pengilly.

IRIS, Donnie
Singles: 7-Inch
HME: 85 1–3
MCA: 80–83 1–3
LPs: 10/12-Inch 33rpm
HME: 85 5–8
MCA: 80–83 5–8
MIDWEST: 80 5–8
Also see JAGGERZ, The

IRISH ROVERS, The
Singles: 7-Inch
DECCA: 68–70 2–3
LPs: 10/12-Inch 33rpm
DECCA: 68–72 8–15
MCA: 73–77 5–8
SANDCASTLE: 76 5–8
Also see ROVERS, The

IRON BUTTERFLY
Singles: 7-Inch
ATCO: 68–71 3–5
MCA: 75 2–3
LPs: 10/12-Inch 33rpm
ATCO (Except 227): 68–71 10–15
ATCO (227; "Heavy"): 68 15–20
MCA: 75 8–10
Members: Doug Ingle; Mike Pinera; Larry Reinhardt.

Price Range

Also see PINERA, Mike

IRON MAIDEN
LPs: 10/12-Inch 33rpm
CAPITOL (Except picture discs): 82–85 . . . . $5–8
CAPITOL (Picture discs): 82 8–10
HARVEST: 80–82 5–8

IRONHORSE (With Randy Bachman)
Singles: 7-Inch
SCOTTI BROS: 79–80 1–3
LPs: 10/12-Inch 33rpm
SCOTTI BROS: 79–80 5–8
Also see BACHMAN, Randy

IRWIN, Big Dee (Dee Irwin; Big Dee Irwin With Little Eva)
Singles: 7-Inch
DIMENSION: 63–64 3–5
FAIRMOUNT: 66 3–5
IMPERIAL: 68 2–4
ROTATE: 65 3–5
Also see ERWIN, Dee
Also see LITTLE EVA
Also see PASTELLS, The

ISLANDERS, The (Featuring Randy Starr)
Singles: 7-Inch
MAYFLOWER: 59 4–6
Also see STARR, Randy

ISLEY BROTHERS, The
Singles: 12-Inch 33/45rpm
T-NECK: 79–83 4–6
Singles: 7-Inch
ATLANTIC: 61–65 3–5
CINDY: 58 12–15
GONE: 58 8–10
MARK-X: 60 4–6
RCA VICTOR (0500 series): 61 2–3
(With a "447" prefix. Black label with dog on top.)
RCA VICTOR (7000 series): 59–60 4–6
(With a "47" prefix.)
RCA VICTOR (7000 series): 59–60 8–10
(With a "61" prefix. Stereo singles.)

Price Range

T-NECK (Except 501):
  69–84 .... **$1–3**
T-NECK (501; "Testify"):
  64 .... **4–6**
TAMLA: *66–69*................... **3–5**
TEENAGE: *57* **45–55**
UNITED ARTISTS: *63–64* **3–5**
VEEP: *66* **3–5**
WAND: *62–63*.................... **3–5**

EPs: 7-Inch 33/45rpm
RCA VICTOR/
  WURLITZER: *64*............... **5–8**
  (Promotional issue only.)

LPs: 10/12-Inch 33rpm
BUDDAH: *76*................... **10–12**
CAMDEN: *73–75*................ **8–10**
MOTOWN: *80–82*................ **5–8**
PHILADELPHIA INT'L:
  78 .... **5–8**
PICKWICK **8–10**
RCA VICTOR: *59* **30–35**
SCEPTER: *66* **10–15**
SUNSET: *69* **8–10**
T-NECK: *69–84* **8–10**
TAMLA: *66–69*................. **12–15**
TRIP: *76* **8–10**
UNITED ARTISTS (500
  series): *75*..................... **8–10**
UNITED ARTISTS (6000
  series): *63* **20–25**
WAND: *62* **15–20**
WARNER BROS: *85*.............. **5–8**
  Members: Ron Isley; Rudy Isley; O'Kelly Isley;
  Ernie Isley; Marvin Isley.
  Also see HENDRIX, Jimi, & The Isley Brothers
  Also see ISLEY-JASPER-ISLEY

ISLEY BROTHERS, The / The Chiffons
LPs: 10/12-Inch 33rpm
SPINORAMA: *63*............... **10–15**
  Also see CHIFFONS, The

ISLEY BROTHERS, The, & Dave "Baby" Cortez
LPs: 10/12-Inch 33rpm
T-NECK: *69* **8–10**
  Also see CORTEZ, Dave "Baby"

Price Range

ISLEY BROTHERS, The / Marvin & Johnny
LPs: 10/12-Inch 33rpm
CROWN: *63* **$8–10**
  Also see MARVIN & JOHNNY

ISLEY-JASPER-ISLEY
Singles: 12-Inch 33/45rpm
CBS ASSOCIATED: *85*............. **4–6**
Singles: 7-Inch
CBS ASSOCIATED: *85*............. **1–3**
LPs: 10/12-Inch 33rpm
CBS ASSOCIATED: *85*............. **5–8**
  Members: Marvin Isley; Chris Isley; Ernie
  Isley.
  Also see ISLEY BROTHERS, The

ITALIAN ASPHALT & PAVEMENT COMPANY, The (The Duprees)
Singles: 7-Inch
COLOSSUS: *70*................... **2–4**
Picture Sleeves
COLOSSUS: *70*................... **2–4**
LPs: 10/12-Inch 33rpm
COLOSSUS: *70*.................. **8–10**
  Also see DUPREES, The

IT'S A BEAUTIFUL DAY (Featuring David LaFlamme)
Singles: 7-Inch
COLUMBIA: *69–73* **3–5**
SAN FRANCISCO
  SOUND **8–10**
LPs: 10/12-Inch 33rpm
COLUMBIA (1000 series):
  70 .... **12–18**
COLUMBIA (9000 series):
  69 .... **25–30**
COLUMBIA (30000
  series): *71–73* **10–12**
SAN FRANCISCO
  SOUND: *70*................... **10–15**
Promotional LPs
COLUMBIA (32660; "A
  1001 nights"): *73*.............. **30–40**
  Also see GARCIA, Jerry
  Also see LA FLAMME, David
  Also see PABLO CRUISE

Price Range

IVAN (Jerry Ivan Allison)
Singles: 7-Inch
CORAL (62017; "Real
Wild Child"): *59* **$35–40**
CORAL (62081; "Frankie
Frankenstein"): *59*.............. **40–50**
CORAL (65607; "Real
Wild Child"): *67* **15–20**
Also see CRICKETS, The

IVAN / Johnny Tillotson
Singles: 7-Inch
OLDIES 45: *64* **3–5**
Also see IVAN
Also see TILLOTSON, Johnny

IVES, Burl (Burl Ives & The Trinidaddies)
Singles: 7-Inch
BELL: *70* **1–3**
BIG TREE: *71* **1–3**
BUENA VISTA: *63* **2–4**
COLUMBIA (39000
series): *50–51* **3–5**
COLUMBIA (44000
series): *68–69* **2–3**
COLUMBIA (70000
series): *69* **1–3**
CYCLONE: *70* **1–3**
DECCA (25000 series):
66–69 .... **2–3**
DECCA (28000 through
31000 series): *52–66* **3–5**
DECCA (32000 & 33000
series): *67–73* **2–3**
DISNEYLAND: *64* **2–3**
MCA: *73–74* **1–3**
MONKEY JOE: *78* **1–3**
Picture Sleeves
BUENA VISTA: *63* **2–4**
DECCA: *62* **3–5**
UNITED ARTISTS: *62* **2–4**
EPs: 7-Inch 33/45rpm
COLUMBIA: *51–55* **5–15**
DECCA: *51–65* **5–15**
LPs: 10/12-Inch 33rpm
BELL: *71* **5–8**
CAEDMON: *72* **4–6**
COLUMBIA (600 series):
55 .... **15–20**

Price Range

COLUMBIA (1400 series):
60 .... **$10–20**
COLUMBIA (2500 series):
55 .... **15–25**
(10-Inch LPs.)
COLUMBIA (6000 series):
50–51 .... **15–25**
COLUMBIA (9000 series):
68–69 .... **8–12**
CORAL: *73* **4–6**
DECCA (100 series): *61* **10–20**
DECCA (4000 series):
62–68 .... **8–15**
(Decca LP numbers in this series preceded by
a "7" or a "DL-7" are stereo issues.)
DECCA (5000 series):
51–53 .... **15–25**
(10-Inch LPs.)
DECCA (5000 series): *68* **8–12**
(12-Inch LPs.)
DECCA (8000 series):
55–59 .... **10–20**
DISNEYLAND: *63–64* **8–12**
EVEREST: *78* **5–8**
HARMONY: *59–70* **8–15**
MCA: *73–75* **5–8**
SUNSET: *70* **5–10**
UNART: *67*........................ **6–12**
UNITED ARTISTS: *59–62* **10–20**
WORD: *63–66* **5–10**
Also see MILLS, Hayley, & Burl Ives

Price Range

IVEYS, The
Singles: 7-Inch
APPLE: *69* $5–8
Also see BADFINGER

IVY LEAGUE, The (Featuring John Carter)
Singles: 7-Inch
CAMEO: *65–66*.................. 3–5
LPs: 10/12-Inch 33rpm
CAMEO: *65* 15–18
Also see OHIO EXPRESS, The

IVY THREE, The
Singles: 7-Inch
SHELL (Except 723):
60–61 4–6
SHELL (723; "Hush Little
Baby"): *60* 8–10

J

J. BIRD: see BIRD, J.

J.B.s, The (J.B.'s Internationals)
Singles: 7-Inch
PEOPLE: *72–76* 2–3
POLYDOR: *77–78* 1–3
LPs: 10/12-Inch 33rpm
PEOPLE: *72–75* 5–8
Also see BROWN, James

J.D. DREWS: see DREWS, J.D.

JACK, Ballin': see BALLIN' JACK

JACKIE & THE STARLITES
Singles: 7-Inch
FIRE/FURY (1000; "They
Laughed At Me"): *57*.......... 40–50
FURY: *62* 8–10
HULL: *64* 10–15
MASCOT: *62–63*................ 15–20
LPs: 10/12-Inch 33rpm
LOST-NITE: *81*.................. 5–8

JACKIE LEE: see LEE, Jackie

Price Range

JACKS, The
Singles: 7-Inch
KENT: *60* $3–5
RPM (Except 428 & 433):
55–56 10–15
RPM (428; "Why Don't
You Write Me"/"Smack
Dab In The Middle"): *55*........ 25–30
RPM (428; "Why Don't
You Write Me"/"My
Darling"): *55* 20–25
(Note different flip side.)
RPM (433; "I'm
Confessin"): *55*................ 20–25
LPs: 10/12-Inch 33rpm
BEST 12–25
CROWN (5372; "The
Jacks"): *62* 35–40
RPM: *56* 75–90
RELIC 10–12
Members: Willie Davis; Ted Taylor; Aaron
Collins; Will Jones; Lloyd McCraw; Prentice
Moreland.
Also see ANKA, Paul
Also see CADETS, The

JACKS, Susan
Singles: 7-Inch
EPIC: *80* 1–3
MERCURY: *75–76*................ 2–3
LPs: 10/12-Inch 33rpm
EPIC: *80* 5–8
Also see POPPY FAMILY, The

JACKS, Terry
Singles: 7-Inch
BELL: *74*....................... 2–3
FLASHBACK: *75*................. 1–3
LONDON: *73* 2–3
PRIVATE STOCK: *75–76*.......... 2–3
LPs: 10/12-Inch 33rpm
BELL: *74*...................... 8–10
Also see POPPY FAMILY, The

JACKSON, Bull Moose (Bull Moose Jackson & His Buffalo Bearcats)
Singles: 7-Inch
KING (4100 series): *51* 8–10
KING (4400 & 4500 series,
except 4524 & 4580):
51–52 5–8

Price Range

KING (4524; "Nosey
Joe"): *52*. **$20–25**
KING (4580; "Big Ten
Inch Record"): *52*. **25–35**
KING (4600 through 4800
series): *53–55*. **5–8**
SEVEN ARTS: *61*. **3–5**
WARWICK: *60*. **3–5**
EPs: 7-Inch 33/45rpm
KING. **20–25**
LPs: 10/12-Inch 33rpm
AUDIO LAB. **50–60**

JACKSON, Chuck
Singles: 7-Inch
ABC: *73–74*. **1–3**
ALL PLATINUM: *75–77*. **1–3**
BELTONE: *61*. **3–5**
DAKAR: *72*. **2–3**
EMI AMERICA: *80*. **1–3**
MOTOWN: *68*. **2–4**
SCEPTER: *73*. **2–3**
SUGAR HILL: *81*. **1–3**
VIBRATION: *77*. **1–3**
V.I.P.: *69–71*. **2–3**
WAND: *61–67*. **3–5**
Picture Sleeves
WAND: *63*. **3–5**
LPs: 10/12-Inch 33rpm
ABC: *73*. **8–10**
ALL PLATINUM: *76*. **8–10**
EMI-AMERICA: *80*. **5–8**
GUEST STAR. **8–10**
MOTOWN: *68–69*. **10–15**
SCEPTER: *72*. **8–10**
SPINORAMA. **10–12**
UNITED ARTISTS: *75*. **8–10**
V.I.P.: *70*. **8–10**
WAND (Except 680):
61–67. . . . . **15–20**
WAND (680; "Dedicated
To The King"): *66*. **20–25**
Also see BONDS, Gary "U.S."

JACKSON, Chuck, & Maxine Brown
Singles: 7-Inch
WAND: *65–67*. **3–5**
LPs: 10/12-Inch 33rpm
WAND: *65–66*. **15–20**
Also see BROWN, Maxine

Price Range

JACKSON, Chuck, & Tammi Terrell
LPs: 10/12-Inch 33rpm
WAND: *67*. **$15–20**
Also see JACKSON, Chuck
Also see TERRELL, Tammi

JACKSON, Clarence
Singles: 7-Inch
R&R: *85*. **1–3**

JACKSON, Deon
Singles: 7-Inch
ABC: *75*. **1–3**
ATLANTIC: *63–64*. **3–5**
CARLA: *66–69*. **3–5**
LPs: 10/12-Inch 33rpm
ATCO: *66*. **15–20**

JACKSON, Ernest
Singles: 7-Inch
STONE: *73*. **2–3**

JACKSON, Freddie
Singles: 12-Inch 33/45rpm
CAPITOL: *85*. **4–6**
Singles: 7-Inch
CAPITOL: *85*. **1–3**
LPs: 10/12-Inch 33rpm
CAPITOL: *85*. **5–8**

JACKSON, George
Singles: 7-Inch
ATLANTIC: *53*. **8–10**
CAMEO: *66*. **3–5**
DOT: *65*. **3–5**
FAME: *69*. **2–4**
HI: *72–73*. **2–3**
MERCURY: *67–68*. **3–5**
PUBLIC: *68*. **3–5**
RPM: *55*. **5–8**

JACKSON, J.J. (J.J. Jackson & The Jackels; J.J. Jackson & The Jackals)
Singles: 7-Inch
ABC: *73*. **1–3**
CALLA: *66–67*. **3–5**
EVEREST: *62*. **3–5**
LOMA: *67–68*. **3–5**
MAGNA-GLIDE: *75*. **2–3**
PRELUDE: *59*. **4–6**
STORM: *59*. **5–8**

Price Range

WARNER BROS: *69* **$2–3**
    LPs: 10/12-Inch 33rpm
CALLA: *67* **15–25**
CONGRESS: *68* **15–25**
PERCEPTION: *69–70* **10–15**
WARNER BROS: *69* **10–12**

JACKSON, Janet
    Singles: 12-Inch 33/45rpm
A&M: *82–85* **4–6**
    Singles: 7-Inch
A&M: *82–85* **1–3**
    LPs: 10/12-Inch 33rpm
A&M: *82–85* **5–8**

JACKSON, Jenny
    Singles: 7-Inch
FARR: *76* **2–3**

JACKSON, Jermaine
    Singles: 12-Inch 33/45rpm
ARISTA: *84–85*. **4–6**
MOTOWN: *80–83*. **4–6**
    Singles: 7-Inch
ARISTA: *84* **2–3**
MOTOWN: *72–83*. **2–3**
    Picture Sleeves
MOTOWN: *81*. .... **INC**
    LPs: 10/12-Inch 33rpm
ARISTA: *84* **5–8**
MOTOWN: *72–82*. **5–8**
    Also see JACKSONS, The

JACKSON, Jermaine, & Michael Jackson
    Singles: 12-Inch 33/45rpm
ARISTA: *84* **4–6**
    Also see JACKSON, Michael

JACKSON, Jermaine, & Pia Zadora
    Singles: 7-Inch
CURB: *85* **1–3**
    Also see JACKSON, Jermaine
    Also see ZADORA, Pia

JACKSON, Joe
    Singles: 12-Inch 33/45rpm
A&M: *82–85* **4–6**
    Singles: 7-Inch
A&M: *79–85* **1–3**

Price Range

    Picture Sleeves
A&M: *80–85* .... **$INC**
    LPs: 10/12-Inch 33rpm
A&M: *79–85* **5–8**

JACKSON, La Toya
    Singles: 12-Inch 33/45rpm
LARC: *83* **4–6**
PRIVATE I: *84*. **4–6**
    Singles: 7-Inch
LARC: *83* **1–3**
POLYDOR: *80–81* **1–3**
PRIVATE I: *84–85*. **1–3**
    LPs: 10/12-Inch 33rpm
POLYDOR: *80–81* **5–8**
PRIVATE I: *84*. **5–8**

JACKSON, Mahalia
    Singles: 7-Inch
APOLLO (200 through 500
  series): *50–59* **2–4**
APOLLO (600 through 700
  series): *59–62* **2–3**
COLUMBIA: *55–70*. **2–4**
GRAND AWARD: *58–59*. **2–4**
KENWOOD: *64–69* **1–3**
    EPs: 7-Inch 33/45rpm
APOLLO: *54–59*. **5–10**
COLUMBIA: *55–60* **5–10**
    LPs: 10/12-Inch 33rpm
APOLLO: *54–61*. **10–20**
CAEDMON: *73* **4–6**
COLUMBIA (600 through
  2100 series): *55–64* **10–20**
COLUMBIA (2400
  through 2600 series):
  66–67 .... **5–15**
COLUMBIA (8100
  through 8900 series):
  59–64 .... **10–20**
COLUMBIA (9200
  through 9900 series):
  66–69 .... **5–15**
COLUMBIA (10000
  series): *73* **4–8**
COLUMBIA (30000
  series): *71–72* **5–10**
GRAND AWARD: *56*. **15–20**
HARMONY: *68–72* **5–8**
KENWOOD: *64–73* **5–10**
PRIORITY: *82* **4–6**

Price Range　　　　　　　　　　　　　*Price Range*

JACKSON, Michael
Singles: 12-Inch 33/45rpm
EPIC: *79–84* **$4–6**
Singles: 7-Inch
EPIC: *79–85* **1–3**
MOTOWN: *71–84*. **1–3**
Picture Sleeves
EPIC: *82* **1–3**
LPs: 10/12-Inch 33rpm
EPIC (30000 series): *79–85* **5–8**
EPIC (40000 series): *80* **10–15**
(Half-speed mastered LPs.)
MOTOWN: *72–85*. **6–10**
　　Also see JACKSON, Jermaine, & Michael
　　Jackson
　　Also see JACKSONS, The
　　Also see JONES, Quincy
　　Also see McCARTNEY, Paul, & Michael Jack-
　　son
　　Also see ROCKWELL
　　Also see ROSS, Diana, & Michael Jackson
　　Also see U.S.A. FOR AFRICA

JACKSON, Mick
Singles: 7-Inch
ATCO: *78* **1–3**

JACKSON, Millie
Singles: 7-Inch
MGM: *69*. **2–4**
SPRING: *71–83*. **1–3**
LPs: 10/12-Inch 33rpm
SPRING: *73–83*. **5–8**
POLYDOR: *79* **5–8**
　　Also see HAYES, Isaac, & Millie Jackson

JACKSON, Python Lee: see
PYTHON LEE JACKSON

JACKSON, Rebbie
Singles: 12-Inch 33/45rpm
COLUMBIA: *84* **4–6**
Singles: 7-Inch
COLUMBIA: *84* **1–3**
LPs: 10/12-Inch 33rpm
COLUMBIA: *84* **5–8**

JACKSON, Randy
Singles: 7-Inch
EPIC. **78**

JACKSON, Roddy (Sonny Bono)
Singles: 7-Inch
SPECIALTY **$58–59**
　　Also see SONNY

JACKSON, Shawn
Singles: 7-Inch
PLAYBOY **74**

JACKSON, Stonewall
Singles: 7-Inch
COLUMBIA (Except
　41000 series): *61–73* **2–3**
COLUMBIA (41000
　series): *58–61* **3–5**
FIRST GENERATION:
　81 .... **1–3**
GRT: *74*. **1–3**
LITTLE DARLIN': *78–79* **1–3**
MGM: *73* **1–3**
PHONORAMA: *83* **1–3**
EPs: 7-Inch 33/45rpm
COLUMBIA: *59*. **5–10**
LPs: 10/12-Inch 33rpm
AUDIOGRAPH ALIVE:
　82 .... **5–8**
COLUMBIA (1300 series):
　59 .... **15–20**
COLUMBIA (1700
　through 2700 series):
　62–67 .... **8–15**
COLUMBIA (8100 series):
　59 .... **15–25**
COLUMBIA (8500
　through 9900 series):
　62–70 .... **8–15**
COLUMBIA (10000
　series): *73* **5–8**
COLUMBIA (30000
　series): *70–72* **5–10**
GRT: *75–76*. **5–10**
HARMONY: *66–74* **6–12**
LITTLE DARLIN': *79* **5–8**
MYRRH: *76* **5–8**
PHONORAMA. **5–8**
RURAL RHYTHM **5–10**
SUNBIRD: *80*. **5–8**

JACKSON, Walter
Singles: 7-Inch
BRUNSWICK: *73*. **2–3**

Price Range

	Price Range
CHI-SOUND: *76–78*	$2–3
COLUMBIA (02000 series): *81*	1–3
COLUMBIA (42000 series): *62–63*	3–5
COTILLION: *69*	2–3
EPIC: *66–68*	3–5
KELLI-ARTS: *83*	1–3
OKEH: *64–67*	3–5
20TH CENTURY-FOX: *79*	1–3

Picture Sleeves

OKEH: *66–67*	3–5

LPs: 10/12-Inch 33rpm

CHI-SOUND: *76–78*	8–10
COLUMBIA: *81*	5–8
EPIC: *77*	8–10
OKEH: *65–69*	12–15
20TH CENTURY-FOX: *79*	5–8

Wanda Jackson, five charted singles (1964–76), no charted LPs.

JACKSON, Wanda (Wanda Jackson & The Party Timers)

Singles: 7-Inch

ABC: *75*	1–3
CAPITOL (2000 through 3000 series): *67–72*	2–3
(Orange or orange/yellow labels.)	
CAPITOL (3400 through 4500 series): *56–61*	6–10
(Purple labels.)	

Price Range

	Price Range
CAPITOL (4600 through 5900 series): *61–67*	$2–4
MYRRH: *73–75*	1–3

Picture Sleeves

CAPITOL: *62–66*	2–5

EPs: 7-Inch 33/45rpm

CAPITOL: *58*	15–25

LPs: 10/12-Inch 33rpm

CAPITOL (100 through 600 series): *69–71*	8–12
CAPITOL (1041; "Wanda Jackson"): *58*	40–50
CAPITOL (1384; "Rockin' With Wanda"): *60*	50–60
CAPITOL (1511; "There's A Party Goin' On"): *61*	60–75
CAPITOL (1596; "Right Or Wrong"): *61*	25–35
CAPITOL (1700 through 1900 series): *62–63*	10–20
CAPITOL (2030; "Two Sides Of Wanda Jackson"): *64*	35–45
CAPITOL (2300 through 2900 series): *65–68*	8–15
CAPITOL (11000 series): *72–73*	5–8
DECCA: *62*	40–50
GUSTO: *80*	5–8
MYRRH: *73–76*	5–8
PICKWICK/HILLTOP: *65–68*	8–12
VOCALION: *69*	8–12
WORD: *77*	4–6

JACKSON, Willis (Willis "Gator Tail" Jackson)

Singles: 7-Inch

ATLANTIC (900 series): *51–53*	15–20
CADET: *66*	2–3
DELUXE: *53*	5–8
FIRE: *59*	4–6
PRESTIGE: *59–69*	2–4
VERVE: *64*	2–4

LPs: 10/12-Inch 33rpm

ATLANTIC: *75*	5–8
AUDIO-LAB: *59*	15–25
CADET: *66*	10–20
COTILLION: *76*	5–8

Price Range

MGM: *64* **$10–20**
MOODSVILLE: *62* **15–20**
MUSE: *76–81* **5–8**
PRESTIGE (2500 series):
  82 . . . . **5–8**
PRESTIGE (7100 & 7200
  series): *59–64* **15–25**
  (Yellow label.)
PRESTIGE (7100 & 7200
  series): *65* **10–20**
  (Blue label.)
PRESTIGE (7300 through
  7800 series): *65–71* **8–15**
TRIP: *73* **5–10**
VERVE: *64–69* **10–20**
  Also see CLOVERS, The
  Also see McDUFF, Brother Jack, & Willis
  Jackson

JACKSON SISTERS, The
Singles: 7-Inch
PROPHESY: *73* **1–3**

JACKSONS, The (The Jackson 5)
Singles: 12-Inch 33/45rpm
EPIC: *79–84* **4–6**
Singles: 7-Inch
DYNAMO: *71* **3–5**
EPIC: *76–81* **1–3**
MOTOWN: *69–75* **2–3**
STEEL-TOWN: *68* **25–35**
Picture Sleeves
EPIC: *76–81* . . . . **INC**
MOTOWN: *69–75* **2–3**
LPs: 10/12-Inch 33rpm
EPIC (30000 series, except
  picture discs): *76–84* **5–8**
EPIC (Picture discs): *79* **10–15**
EPIC (40000 series): *81* **10–15**
  (Half-speed mastered LPs.)
MOTOWN (Except 700
  series): *75–84* **5–8**
MOTOWN (700 series,
  except 713): *69–74* **8–12**
MOTOWN (713;
  "Christmas Won't Be
  The Same This Year"):
  70 . . . . **12–15**
    Members: Michael Jackson; Jermaine Jackson;
    Jackie Jackson; Marlon Jackson; Tito Jackson;
    Randy Jackson.
    Also see JACKSON, Jermaine

Price Range

  Also see JACKSON, Michael
  Also see RIPPLES & WAVES PLUS MI-
  CHAEL, The
  Also see WONDER, Stevie

JACOBI, Lou
LPs: 10/12-Inch 33rpm
CAPITOL: *66* **$8–12**
VERVE: *67* **8–12**

JACOBS, Debbie
Singles: 12-Inch 33/45rpm
PERSONAL: *84* **4–6**
Singles: 7-Inch
MCA: *79–80* **1–3**

JACOBS, Dick, & His Orchestra
Singles: 7-Inch
CORAL: *54–62* **2–4**
EPs: 7-Inch 33/45rpm
CORAL: *56* **3–6**
LPs: 10/12-Inch 33rpm
CORAL: *56–60* **5–15**
VOCALION: *60* **4–8**

JACOBS, Hank
Singles: 7-Inch
IMPERIAL: *62* **3–5**
SUE: *63–64* **3–5**
LPs: 10/12-Inch 33rpm
SUE: *64* **15–20**

JACQUET, Illinois (Illinois Jacquet & His All Stars; The Jacque Rabbit; With Russell Jacquet)
Singles: 7-Inch
ALADDIN (3100 & 3200
  series): *53–54* **10–15**
ARGO: *63–65* **2–4**
PRESTIGE: *68–69* **2–3**
RCA VICTOR (50-0000
  series): *51* **15–20**
VERVE: *62* **2–4**
EPs: 7-Inch 33/45rpm
APOLLO: *50* **45–55**
CLEF: *51–54* **20–30**
RCA VICTOR: *53* **20–30**
SAVOY: *50–53* **20–30**
LPs: 10/12-Inch 33rpm
ACCORD: *82* **5–8**
ALADDIN (700 series): *54* **50–75**

Price Range

ALADDIN (800 series): *56* **$50–60**
APOLLO (104; "Jam
  Session"): *50.* **125–150**
ARGO: *63–65* **10–20**
CLEF (100 series): *51–52.* **40–60**
  (10-Inch LPs.)
CLEF (600 & 700 series):
  54–56 . . . . **30–50**
EPIC: *63* **15–20**
GRAND AWARD: *56.* **20–30**
IMPERIAL: *62* **15–20**
JRC: *79* **5–8**
PRESTIGE: *69–75* **8–12**
RCA VICTOR (3200
  series): *53* **35–50**
  (10-Inch LPs.)
ROULETTE: *60* **15–25**
SAVOY (500 series): *52* **30–50**
SAVOY (15000 series): *50* **40–60**
TRIP: *79* **5–8**
VERVE (2500 series): *82* **5–10**
VERVE (8000 series):
  57–58 . . . . **25–50**
  (Reads "Verve Records, Inc." at bottom of label.)
VERVE (8000 series):
  61–65 . . . . **10–20**
  (Reads "MGM Records - A Division Of Metro-Goldwyn-Mayer, Inc." at bottom of label.)
  Also see COLE, Cozy, & Illinois Jacquet
  Also see DOGGETT, Bill
  Also see HEART BEATS QUINTET, The

JACQUET, Illinois / Lester Young
EPs: 7-Inch 33/45rpm
ALADDIN: *54* **30–40**
LPs: 10/12-Inch 33rpm
ALADDIN (701; "Battle
  Of The Saxes"): *54* **50–75**
  (10-Inch LP. Black vinyl.)
ALADDIN (701; "Battle
  Of The Saxes"): *54* **125–150**
  (10-Inch LP. Colored vinyl.)
ALADDIN (800 series): *56* **50–60**
  Also see JACQUET, Illinois

JADE WARRIOR
Singles: 7-Inch
VERTIGO: *71–72* **2–4**
LPs: 10/12-Inch 33rpm
ANTILLES: *78* **5–8**
ISLAND: *74–76* **8–10**

Price Range

VERTIGO: *71–72* **$10–12**

JAGGER, Chris
LPs: 10/12-Inch 33rpm
ASYLUM: *73–74.* **8–10**

Mick Jagger, two charted singles (1985), one charted LP (1985).

JAGGER, Mick
Singles: 12-Inch 33/45rpm
COLUMBIA (2060;
  "Lucky In Love"): *85* **4–6**
  (With special cover.)
COLUMBIA (2060;
  "Lucky In Love"): *85* **12–15**
  (Promotional issue with special cover.)
COLUMBIA (5181; "Just
  Another Night"): *85* **4–6**
  (With special cover.)
COLUMBIA (5181; "Just
  Another Night"): *85* **10–15**
  (Promotional issue with special cover.)
Singles: 7-Inch
COLUMBIA: *85* **1–3**
LPs: 10/12-Inch 33rpm
COLUMBIA: *85* **5–8**
LONDON
  WAVELENGTH (006;
  "The Mick Jagger
  Special"): *81* **50–75**
  (Promotional issue only.)
ROLLING STONES (164;
  "Interview With Mick
  Jagger"): *71* **50–75**
  (Promotional issue only.)

Price Range

Also see BOWIE, David, & Mick Jagger
Also see ROLLING STONES, The
Also see TOSH, Peter, & Mick Jagger
Also see WEST, Leslie

JAGGERZ, The
Singles: 7-Inch
KAMA SUTRA: *70* $2–3
WOODEN NICKEL: *75* 2–3
LPs: 10/12-Inch 33rpm
KAMA SUTRA: *70* 10–15
WOODEN NICKEL: *75* 8–10
Also see IRIS, Donnie
Also see Q

JAGS, The
Singles: 7-Inch
ISLAND: *80* 1–3
LPs: 10/12-Inch 33rpm
ISLAND: *80–81* 5–8

JAISUN
Singles: 7-Inch
JETT SETT: *78* 2–3

JAK
Singles: 7-Inch
EPIC: *84* 1–3

JAKKI
Singles: 7-Inch
PYRAMID: *76* 1–3

JAM, The
Singles: 7-Inch
POLYDOR: *78–83* 1–3
LPs: 10/12-Inch 33rpm
POLYDOR: *77–83* 5–8
Also see STYLE COUNCIL

JAMAL, Ahmad (The Ahmad Jamal Trio; The Ahmad Jamal Quintet)
Singles: 7-Inch
ARGO: *57–65* 2–4
CADET: *66–68* 2–3
CHESS: *73* 1–3
PARROTT: *55* 3–5
20TH CENTURY-FOX:
73–80 1–3
EPs: 7-Inch 33/45rpm
ARGO: *59–61* 8–15

Price Range

LPs: 10/12-Inch 33rpm
ABC: *68* $8–12
ARGO (610 through 662):
56–60 20–40
ARGO (667 through 758):
61–65 10–20
CADET: *65–73* 8–15
CATALYST: *76* 5–8
CHESS: *76* 5–10
EPIC (600 series): *63–65* 10–20
EPIC (3200 series): *56* 20–30
EPIC (3600 series): *59* 15–25
IMPULSE: *69–73* 8–15
MOTOWN: *80* 5–8
PERSONAL CHOICE: *82* 5–8
SHUBRA: *83* 5–8
20TH CENTURY-FOX:
73–80 5–8
WHO'S WHO IN JAZZ:
81 5–8

JAMES, Bob (The Bob James Trio)
Singles: 7-Inch
CTI: *74–77* 1–3
COLUMBIA: *79–83* 1–3
TAPPAN ZEE/
COLUMBIA: *77–85* 1–3
Picture Sleeves
COLUMBIA: *79–80* . . . . INC
LPs: 10/12-Inch 33rpm
CTI: *74–77* 5–10
COLUMBIA: *83* 5–8
ESP: *65* 10–15
MERCURY: *63* 15–20
TAPPAN ZEE/
COLUMBIA: *77–85* 5–10

JAMES, Bob, & Earl Klugh
Singles: 7-Inch
CAPITOL: *82* 1–3
TAPPAN ZEE/
COLUMBIA: *79* 1–3
LPs: 10/12-Inch 33rpm
CAPITOL: *82* 5–8
Also see JAMES, Bob
Also see KLUGH, Earl

JAMES, Elmore (Elmore James & His Broomdusters; Elmo James)
Singles: 7-Inch
ACE: *53* 60–75

Price Range

	Price Range
CHECKER: 53	$50–60
CHESS: 60	4–6
CHIEF: 57–60	8–10
ENJOY: 65	3–5
FIRE: 60–62	4–6
FLAIR (1011 through 1031): 54–55	20–30
FLAIR (1039 through 1079): 55–56	15–20
FLASHBACK: 65	1–3
JEWEL: 66–67	3–5
KENT: 60–67	3–5
METEOR: 53	40–50
M-PAC	3–5
S&M	4–6
SOUND	3–5
SPHERE SOUND: 65	3–5
VEE JAY: 57	5–8

LPs: 10/12-Inch 33rpm

BELL: 68–69	10–12
BLUE HORIZON	10–12
CHESS: 69	10–12
CROWN: 61	40–50
INTERMEDIA: 84	5–8
KENT: 64–69	10–15
KENT "TREASURE SERIES": 86	5–8
SPHERE SOUND	20–25
TRIP: 71–78	8–10
UNITED	10–12
UPFRONT	8–10

Also see CRUDUP, Big Boy

JAMES, Etta (Etta "Miss Peaches" James)

Singles: 7-Inch

ABC: 74	1–3
ARGO: 60–64	3–5
CADET: 67–72	2–4
CHESS: 73–76	2–3
KENT: 58–60	3–5
MODERN (900 series): 55–56	5–8
MODERN (1000 series): 57–58	4–6
T-ELECTRIC: 80	1–3
WARNER BROS: 78	2–3

LPs: 10/12-Inch 33rpm

ARGO: 61–65	20–25
CADET: 67–71	10–15
CHESS: 71–76	10–12

Price Range

	Price Range
CROWN: 61–63	$15–18
INTERMEDIA: 84	5–8
T-ELECTRIC: 80	5–8
UNITED	10–12
WARNER BROS: 78	5–8
WESTBOUND	8–10

Also see ETTA & HARVEY

JAMES, Etta, & Sugar Pie DeSanto

Singles: 7-Inch

CADET: 65–66	3–5

Also see DE SANTO, Sugar Pie
Also see JAMES, Etta

JAMES, Harry, & His Orchestra

Singles: 7-Inch

COLUMBIA (33000 series): 76	1–3
COLUMBIA (38000 through 40000 series): 50–56	2–4
DOT: 65–66	1–3
GOLD-MOR: 73	1–3
MGM: 59–63	2–3

EPs: 7-Inch 33/45rpm

COLUMBIA: 50–56	4–8

LPs: 10/12-Inch 33rpm

BAINBRIDGE: 83	4–8
BRIGHT ORANGE: 73	4–8
CAPITOL (600 through 1500 series): 55–61	8–15
(With a "T" or "ST" prefix.)	
CAPITOL (1500 series): 62	8–10
(With a "DT" prefix.)	
CAPITOL (1500 series): 77	4–8
(With an "M" prefix.)	
COLUMBIA: 50–67	8–15
COLUMBIA SPECIAL PRODUCTS: 79	4–8
DOT: 66–67	5–10
HARMONY: 59–72	8–12
LONDON: 68	5–10
MGM: 59–65	8–15
METRO: 65–67	5–10
SHEFFIELD LAB: 77–79	5–10
Also see KALLEN, Kitty	
Also see SINATRA, Frank	

JAMES, Harry, & Dick Haymes

LPs: 10/12-Inch 33rpm

CIRCLE: 81	5–8

Also see HAYMES, Dick
Also see JAMES, Harry, & His Orchestra

Price Range

JAMES, Jesse
Singles: 7-Inch
20TH CENTURY-FOX:
  67–75 .... **$2–4**
UNI: *69* **2–4**
ZEA (ZAY): *70–71* **2–4**
  LPs: 10/12-Inch 33rpm
20TH CENTURY-FOX:
  67 .... **8–10**

JAMES, Jimmy, & The Vagabonds
Singles: 7-Inch
ATCO: *67–68* **3–5**
PYE: *75–76* **2–3**
  LPs: 10/12-Inch 33rpm
ATCO: *67* **10–15**
PYE: *76* **5–8**

JAMES, Joni
Singles: 7-Inch
MGM: *52–64* **2–4**
  Picture Sleeves
MGM: *57–62* **2–4**
  EPs: 7-Inch 33/45rpm
MGM: *53–59* **5–10**
  LPs: 10/12-Inch 33rpm
MGM (200 series): *54* **10–20**
MGM (3200 through 4100
  series): *55–63* **10–20**
MGM (4200 series): *64–65* **8–15**

JAMES, Rick (Rick James & The Stone City Band)
Singles: 12-Inch 33/45rpm
GORDY: *79–85* **4–6**
MOTOWN: *80–85* **4–6**
  Singles: 7-Inch
GORDY: *78–85* **1–3**
  Picture Sleeves
GORDY: *79–85* .... **INC**
  LPs: 10/12-Inch 33rpm
GORDY: *78–83* **5–8**
  Also see STONE CITY BAND, The
  Also see TEMPTATIONS, The, & Rick James

JAMES, Rick, & Smokey Robinson
Singles: 7-Inch
GORDY: *83* **1–3**
  Also see JAMES, Rick

Price Range

Also see ROBINSON, Smokey

JAMES, Sonny (Sonny James & The Southern Gentlemen)
Singles: 7-Inch
CAPITOL (2000 through
  3900): *67–74* **$2–3**
  (Orange labels.)
CAPITOL (2600 through
  3800): *52–57* **3–5**
  (Purple labels.)
CAPITOL (3900 through
  5900): *57–67* **2–4**
COLUMBIA: *72–78* **1–3**
DIMENSION: *82* **1–3**
DOT: *62* **2–4**
GROOVE: *61* **3–5**
MONUMENT: *79* **1–3**
NRC: *60* **3–5**
RCA VICTOR: *61–62* **3–5**
  Picture Sleeves
CAPITOL: *59–72* **2–4**
COLUMBIA: *72–75* **1–3**
DIMENSION: *76* **1–3**
NRC: *60* **3–5**
  EPs: 7-Inch 33/45rpm
CAPITOL: *57–58* **8–15**
  LPs: 10/12-Inch 33rpm
ABC: *77* **5–8**
BROOKVILLE: *75* **8–12**
CAMDEN **8–12**
CAPITOL (100 through
  800): *68–71* **8–12**
CAPITOL (700 through
  900): *57–58* **20–30**
CAPITOL (1100 series): *59* **15–25**
CAPITOL (2000 through
  2800): *64–68* **8–15**
CAPITOL (11000 series):
  72–73 .... **5–8**
COLUMBIA: *72–78* **5–10**
CROWN **8–12**
DIMENSION: *82* **5–8**
DOT: *62* **15–20**
GUEST STAR **10–15**
HAMILTON: *65* **8–12**
MONUMENT: *79* **5–8**
PICKWICK: *76* **5–8**
PICKWICK/HILLTOP:
  69 .... **8–12**
TVP: *75* **8–12**

Price Range

Also see HAGGARD, Merle / Sonny James
Also see HORTON, Johnny / Sonny James

JAMES, Sonny / David Houston
LPs: 10/12-Inch 33rpm
PICKWICK/HILLTOP:
   67 . . . . **$8–12**
   Also see HOUSTON, David
   Also see JAMES, Sonny

JAMES, Tommy (Tommy James & The Shondells)
Singles: 7-Inch
ABC: *73* **1–3**
FANTASY: *75–80.* **1–3**
MCA: *74* **2–3**
MILLENNIUM: *79–81* **1–3**
ROULETTE: *66–73* **3–5**

Picture Sleeves
ROULETTE: *66–67* **4–6**

LPs: 10/12-Inch 33rpm
FANTASY: *76–80.* **8–10**
MILLENNIUM: *80–81* **5–8**
ROULETTE: *66–72* **10–15**
SCEPTER: *73* **8–10**
SCEPTER/CITATION: *82* **5–8**
TWENTY-ONE: *83* **5–8**
   Also see HOG HEAVEN
   Also see SHONDELLS, The

JAMES BOYS, The
Singles: 7-Inch
PHIL L.A. OF SOUL: *68* **2–4**

JAMES GANG, The
Singles: 7-Inch
ABC: *70–72* **2–4**
ATCO: *74–75.* **2–3**
BLUESWAY: *69.* **3–5**

LPs: 10/12-Inch 33rpm
ABC: *70–73* **10–12**
ATCO: *74–76.* **8–10**
BLUESWAY: *69.* **10–15**
COMMAND: *74.* **8–10**
MCA. **5–8**
   Members: Joe Walsh; Tommy Bolin; Dominic Troiano.
   Also see BOLIN, Tommy
   Also see WALSH, Joe

Price Range

JAMESON, Cody
Singles: 7-Inch
ATCO: *77* **$2–3**

JAMESTOWN MASSACRE, The
Singles: 7-Inch
WARNER BROS: *72.* **2–3**

JAMIE & JANE
Singles: 7-Inch
DECCA: *59* **10–15**
   Members: Gene Pitney; Ginny Arnell.
   Also see ARNELL, Ginny
   Also see PITNEY, Gene

JAMIES, The
Singles: 7-Inch
EPIC (9000 series): *58–63* **4–6**
EPIC (11000 series): *74* **1–3**
UNITED ARTISTS: *59* **4–6**

Picture Sleeves
EPIC: *62* **6–10**

JAMMERS, The
Singles: 7-Inch
SALSOUL: *82–83* **1–3**

JAMUL
LPs: 10/12-Inch 33rpm
LIZARD: *70* **10–12**

JAN & ARNIE
Singles: 7-Inch
ARWIN: *58.* **10–12**
DOT: *60.* **8–10**
DORE (522; "Baby Talk"):
   59 . . . . **80–100**
   (Actually by Jan & Dean but shown on first pressings as by Jan & Arnie.)
EPs: 7-Inch 33/45rpm
DOT: *60.* **80–100**
   Members: Jan Berry; Arnie Ginsburg.
   Also see BERRY, Jan
   Also see JAN & DEAN
   Also see RITUALS, The

JAN & DEAN
Singles: 7-Inch
CHALLENGE (Except
   9111): *61* **5–8**

Price Range

CHALLENGE (9111;
"Heart & Soul"/"Those
Words"): *61* **$25–30**
CHALLENGE (9111;
"Heart &
Soul"/"Midsummer
Night's Dream"): *61* **5–8**
(Note different flip side.)
COLUMBIA: *67* **12–15**
DORE: *59–61* **8–18**
J&D: *66* **20–25**
JAN & DEAN: *66* **45–50**
LIBERTY (Except 55522):
61–66 .... **5–8**
LIBERTY (55522; "She's
Still Talkin' Baby Talk"):
62 .... **20–25**
MAGIC LAMP: *66* **15–20**
ODE: *75* **20–25**
UNITED ARTISTS: *72–76* **8–10**
WARNER BROS: *67–68* **25–30**

Picture Sleeves

DORE (555; "We Go
Together"): *60* **20–25**
DORE (576; "Gee"): *60* **35–45**
LIBERTY (Except 55766
& 55849): *63–65* **10–15**
LIBERTY (55766; "From
All Over The World"):
65 .... **40–60**
LIBERTY (55849; "Folk
City"): *65* **20–25**
UNITED ARTISTS: *71* **5–8**

LPs: 10/12-Inch 33rpm

COLUMBIA (9461; "Save
For A Rainy Day"): *67* **350–400**
(Promotional issue only.)
DEADMAN'S CURVE: *81* **15–20**
DESIGN/STEREO
SPECTRUM: *64* **10–15**
DORE: *60* **100–125**
(Price includes a 12x12 Jan & Dean color
photo, which represents about $25-$35 of the
value.)
EXACT: *80* **5–8**
IMPERIAL HOUSE: *80* **5–8**
INTERNATIONAL
AWARD SERIES **8–10**
J&D: *67* **175–200**
L-J: *63* **35–45**

Price Range

LIBERTY (LN series):
81–82 .... **$5–8**
LIBERTY (LRP & LST
series, except 414): *62–66* **20–30**
LIBERTY (414; "Pop
Symphony Number 1"):
65 .... **40–50**
(With an "LRP-3" prefix, for mono, or an
"LST-7" prefix for stereo issues.)
MAGIC CARPET **10–12**
RHINO: *82* **5–8**
SUNSET: *67* **10–15**
UNITED ARTISTS: *71–79* **10–12**
Members: Jan Berry; Dean Torrence.
Also see BERRY, Jan
Also see JAN & ARNIE

JAN & DEAN / The Beach Boys
LPs: 10/12-Inch 33rpm
EXACT: *81* **5–8**
Also see BEACH BOYS, The

JAN & DEAN / Roy Orbison
LPs: 10/12-Inch 33rpm
COKE: *65* **20–30**
(Coca-Cola radio spots. Issued to radio stations
only.)
Also see JAN & DEAN
Also see ORBISON, Roy

JAN & KJELD
Singles: 7-Inch
ALONCA: *66* **2–4**
IMPERIAL: *59* **3–5**
JARO INT'L: *60* **3–5**
KAPP: *60–61* **3–5**
Picture Sleeves
JARO INT'L: *60* **4–6**
KAPP: *60* **4–6**
LPs: 10/12-Inch 33rpm
KAPP: *60* **15–20**

JANE, Baby: see BABY JANE

JANIS, Johnny
Singles: 7-Inch
ABC-PARAMOUNT: *57* **5–8**
BOMARC: *59–60* **4–6**
COLUMBIA: *60* **3–5**
CORAL: *55* **5–8**
MONUMENT: *66–68* **3–5**

Price Range

Price Range

LPs: 10/12-Inch 33rpm
ABC-PARAMOUNT: 57......... **$20–25**
COLUMBIA: *61*............... **15–18**
MONUMENT: *65*.............. **10–15**

JANKEL, Chas
Singles: 12-Inch 33/45rpm
A&M: *83*...................... **4–6**
Singles: 7-Inch
A&M: *82*...................... **1–3**
LPs: 10/12-Inch 33rpm
A&M: *82*...................... **5–8**
Also see DURY, Ian, & The Blockheads

JANKOWSKI, Horst, & His Orchestra
Singles: 7-Inch
MERCURY: *65–68*.............. **2–3**
LPs: 10/12-Inch 33rpm
MERCURY: *65–69*.............. **5–15**
Also see IMPALAS, The / Horst Jankowski & His Orchestra

JARMELS, The
Singles: 7-Inch
LAURIE: *61–63* **4–6**

JARRE, Jean-Michael
Singles: 7-Inch
POLYDOR: *78*.................. **1–3**
LPs: 10/12-Inch 33rpm
DREYFUS: *85*.................. **5–8**
POLYDOR: *78–81* **5–8**
Also see U.S.A. FOR AFRICA

JARREAU, Al
Singles: 7-Inch
REPRISE: *76*................... **2–3**
WARNER BROS: *77–86*.......... **1–3**
LPs: 10/12-Inch 33rpm
REPRISE: *76*................... **5–8**
WARNER BROS: *77–86*.......... **5–8**
Also see U.S.A. FOR AFRICA

JARREAU, Al, & Randy Crawford
Singles: 7-Inch
WARNER BROS: *82*.............. **1–3**
Also see CRAWFORD, Randy
Also see JARREAU, Al

JARRETT, Keith
LPs: 10/12-Inch 33rpm
ATLANTIC: *75* **$6–10**
ECM: *76–80*.................... **6–10**
IMPULSE: *75–77* **6–10**

JARVIS, Carol
Singles: 7-Inch
DOT: *57–59*.................... **4–6**
ERA: *60–61*.................... **3–5**

JARVIS, Marion
Singles: 7-Inch
ROXBURY: *74*.................. **2–4**

JASMIN
Singles: 12-Inch 33/45rpm
TVI: *84*....................... **4–6**

JASON & THE SCORCHERS
LPs: 10/12-Inch 33rpm
EMI AMERICA: *84–85*........... **5–8**

JAY, Morty (Morty Jay & The Surfin' Cats)
Singles: 7-Inch
LEGEND: *63*................... **5–8**
20TH CENTURY-FOX:
63 .... **2–4**

JAY, Dee: see DEE JAY

JAY, Jazzy: see JAZZY JAY

JAY & THE AMERICANS
(Featuring Jay Black)
Singles: 7-Inch
FUTURA: *72*.................... **2–3**
UNITED ARTISTS
(Except 300 through 600
series): *64–71* **3–5**
UNITED ARTISTS (300
through 600 series):
61–63 .... **4–6**
Picture Sleeves
UNITED ARTISTS: *65–66*......... **3–5**
LPs: 10/12-Inch 33rpm
SUNSET: *69–70* **10–12**
UNART: *68*.................... **8–12**

Price Range

UNITED ARTISTS (222;
  "She Cried"): *62* **$20–25**
  (With a "UAL" prefix, for mono, or "UAS" for stereo.)
UNITED ARTISTS (300;
  "At The Cafe Wha"): *63* **20–25**
  (With a "UAL" prefix, for mono, or "UAS" for stereo.)
UNITED ARTISTS (300
  series): *75* **5–8**
  (With a "UA-LA" prefix.)
UNITED ARTISTS (400
  through 700 series):
  65–70 . . . . **10–15**
  (With a "UAL" prefix, for mono, or "UAS" for stereo.)
UNITED ARTISTS (1000
  series): *80* **5–8**
  (With an "LM" prefix.)
  Also see BLACK, Jay

JAY & THE TECHNIQUES
(Featuring Jay Proctor)
Singles: 7-Inch
EVENT: *76* **2–4**
GORDY: *72* **2–3**
SMASH: *67–69* **3–5**
Picture Sleeves
SMASH: *67–68* **3–5**
LPs: 10/12-Inch 33rpm
EVENT: *75* **8–10**
SMASH: *67–68* **15–20**

JAYE, Jerry
Singles: 7-Inch
COLUMBIA: *75* **2–3**
HI (2100 series): *67–68* **3–5**
HI (2300 series): *76–77* **2–3**
LABEL: *59* **4–6**
MEGA: *71–74* **2–3**
RAINTREE: *72* **2–3**
STEPHANY **5–8**
LPs: 10/12-Inch 33rpm
HI (32000 series): *67* **15–20**
HI (32100 series): *76* **5–8**

JAYHAWKS, The
Singles: 7-Inch
ALADDIN: *57* **8–10**
EASTMAN: *59* **5–8**
FLASH (Except 105): *56* **5–8**

Price Range

FLASH (105; "Counting
  My Teardrops"): *56* **$50–60**
  Members: James Johnson; Carl Fisher; Dave
  Govan; Carver Bunkern; Richard Owens.
  Also see MARATHONS, The
  Also see VIBRATIONS, The

JAYNETTES, The
Singles: 7-Inch
J&S: *65* **3–5**
TUFF: *63–64* **3–5**
LPs: 10/12-Inch 33rpm
TUFF: *63* **30–35**

JAZZ CRUSADERS, The
Singles: 7-Inch
CHISA: *70–71* **1–3**
PACIFIC JAZZ: *62–68* **2–4**
WORLD PACIFIC: *64–65* **2–3**
LPs: 10/12-Inch 33rpm
BLUE NOTE: *75–80* **5–10**
CHISA: *70* **8–12**
LIBERTY: *70* **8–12**
PACIFIC JAZZ (27
  through 87): *61–64* **20–35**
PACIFIC JAZZ (10000 &
  20000 series): *65–69* **10–20**
PAUSA: *82* **5–8**
WORLD PACIFIC: *65* **8–15**
  Members: Wilton Felder; Nesbert Hooper;
  Wayne Henderson; Joe Sample.
  Also see CRUSADERS, The
  Also see McCANN, Les

JAZZY JAY
Singles: 7-Inch
ATLANTIC: *84* **1–3**

JEAN, Cathy: see CATHY JEAN

JEAN, Earl: see EARL-JEAN

JEAN & THE DARLINGS
Singles: 7-Inch
VOLT: *67–69* **3–5**

JECKYLL, Dr.: see DR. JECKYLL

JEFF & ALETA
Singles: 7-Inch
SRI: *80* **1–3**

Price Range

JEFFERSON
Singles: 7-Inch
DECCA: *69* **$2–4**
JANUS: *69* **2–4**
LPs: 10/12-Inch 33rpm
JANUS: *69* **10–12**

JEFFERSON, Morris
Singles: 7-Inch
PARACHUTE: *78* **1–3**
LPs: 10/12-Inch 33rpm
PARACHUTE: *78* **5–8**

JEFFERSON AIRPLANE
Singles: 7-Inch
GRUNT: *71–73* **2–4**
RCA VICTOR (Except
8700 & 8800 series):
67–70 .... **4–6**
RCA VICTOR (8700 &
8800 series): *66* **8–10**
Picture Sleeves
GRUNT: *71* **2–4**
RCA VICTOR: *68–69* **4–6**
LPs: 10/12-Inch 33rpm
GRUNT (Except 1000
series): *73–82* **6–10**
GRUNT (1000 series):
71–72 .... **10–15**
PAIR: *84* **8–10**
RCA VICTOR (0320;
"Volunteers"): *73* **12–15**
(With an "APD1" prefix. Quad issue.)
RCA VICTOR (1511;
"After Bathing At
Baxters"): *67* **15–20**
(Black label. With an "LOP" or "LSO" prefix.)
RCA VICTOR (1511;
"After Bathing At
Baxters"): *71* **8–12**
(Orange label. With an "AFL1" prefix.)
RCA VICTOR (3584;
"Jefferson Airplane
Takes Off"): *66* **25–30**
(Black label. Has 12 tracks. With an "LPM" or
"LSP" prefix.)
RCA VICTOR (3584;
"Jefferson Airplane
Takes Off"): *66* **15–20**
(Black label. Has 11 tracks. With an "LPM" or
"LSP" prefix.)

Price Range

RCA VICTOR (3584;
"Jefferson Airplane
Takes Off"): *66* **$10–12**
(Orange Label. With an "AYL1" prefix.)
RCA VICTOR (3661;
"Worst Of Jefferson
Airplane"): *80* **5–8**
(With an "AYL1" prefix.)
RCA VICTOR (3766;
"Surrealistic Pillow"): *67* **15–20**
(Black label. With an "LPM" or "LSP" prefix.)
RCA VICTOR (3766;
"Surrealistic Pillow"): *69* **10–12**
(Orange label. With an "AYL1" prefix.)
RCA VICTOR (3797;
"Crown Of Creation"):
80 .... **5–8**
(With an "AYL1" prefix.)
RCA VICTOR (3798;
"Bless Its Pointed Little
Head"): *80* **5–8**
(With an "AYL1" prefix.)
RCA VICTOR (3867;
"Volunteers"): *81* **5–8**
(With an "AYL1" prefix.)
RCA VICTOR (4058;
"Crown Of Creation"):
68 .... **10–15**
(With an "LSP" prefix.)
RCA VICTOR (4238;
"Volunteers"): *69* **10–15**
(With an "LSP" prefix.)
RCA VICTOR (4448;
"Blows Against The
Empire"): *70* **10–15**
(Price includes booklet insert, which represents
about $3-$5 of the value. With an "LSP" pre-
fix.)
RCA VICTOR (4448;
"Blows Against The
Empire"): *70* **50–60**
(Clear vinyl. Promotional issue only.)
RCA VICTOR (4459;
"Worst Of Jefferson
Airplane"): *70* **8–10**
(With an "LSP" prefix.)
Members: Grace Slick, Marty Balin & Paul
Kantner.
Also see BALIN, Marty
Also see GREAT!! SOCIETY!!, The
Also see JEFFERSON STARSHIP
Also see KAUKONEN, Jorma
Also see KANTNER, Paul, & Grace Slick

Price Range

Also see QUICKSILVER
Also see SLICK, Grace

JEFFERSON STARSHIP
Singles: 7-Inch
GRUNT: *74–83*................... **$1–3**
Picture Sleeves
GRUNT: *77–83*.................... **2–3**
LPs: 10/12-Inch 33rpm
GRUNT (Except picture
discs): *74–85*.................... **6–12**
GRUNT (Picture discs): *79*........ **15–20**
(With a "CYL1" prefix.)
RCA VICTOR: *81* **5–8**
Also see CREACH, Papa John
Also see JEFFERSON AIRPLANE, The
Also see KANTNER, Paul, & Jefferson Starship
Also see STARSHIP

JEFFREE
Singles: 7-Inch
MCA: *78–79* **1–3**
LPs: 10/12-Inch 33rpm
MCA: *79* **5–8**

JEFFREY, Joe (The Joe Jeffrey Group)
Singles: 7-Inch
WAND: *69* **2–4**
LPs: 10/12-Inch 33rpm
WAND: *69* **10–15**

JEFFREYS, Garland
Singles: 7-Inch
A&M: *77–79* **1–3**
ARISTA: *75* **2–3**
ATLANTIC: *73* **2–4**
EPIC: *81–83* **1–3**
LPs: 10/12-Inch 33rpm
A&M: *77–79* **5–8**
ATLANTIC: *73* **8–10**
EPIC: *81–83* **5–8**

JELLY BEANS, The
Singles: 7-Inch
ESKEE: *65* **3–5**
RED BIRD: *64*.................... **4–6**

JELLYBEAN
Singles: 12-Inch 33/45rpm
EMI AMERICA: *84–85*............. **4–6**

Price Range

Singles: 7-Inch
EMI AMERICA: *84–85*............ **$1–3**
LPs: 10/12-Inch 33rpm
EMI AMERICA: *84*............... **5–8**

JENKINS, Donald (Donald Jenkins & The Delighters)
Singles: 7-Inch
CORTLAND: *63*.................. **4–6**
DUCHESS: *65*.................... **3–5**

JENKINS, Gordon, & His Orchestra
Singles: 7-Inch
COLUMBIA: *64*................... **1–3**
DECCA: *50–56*................... **2–4**
KAPP: *60–64*.................... **2–3**
TIME: *62*....................... **2–3**
X: *55*.......................... **2–4**
EPs: 7-Inch 33/45rpm
DECCA: *51–56*.................. **5–10**
LPs: 10/12-Inch 33rpm
CAPITOL (700 series): *56*........ **12–20**
(With a "T" prefix.)
CAPITOL (700 series): *61*......... **8–15**
(With a "DT" prefix.)
CAPITOL (700 series): *75*.......... **4–8**
(With an "SM" prefix.)
COLUMBIA: *62–63*.............. **8–15**
CORAL: *73*..................... **4–6**
DECCA: *51–63*.................. **8–18**
(Decca LP numbers in this series preceded by a "7" or a "DL-7" are stereo issues.)
DOT: *66*....................... **5–10**
GWP: *71* **5–10**
MCA: *73–75* **4–8**
SUNSET: *67* **5–10**
TIME: *62–64*.................... **8–15**
Also see ARMSTRONG, Louis
Also see BOONE, Pat
Also see LEE, Peggy
Also see WEAVERS, The

JENKINS, Gus (Gus Jinkins)
Singles: 7-Inch
CATALINA: *63* **3–5**
COMBO: *54*...................... **20–25**
FLASH: *56–57*................... **4–6**
GENERAL ARTIST:
64–69 .... **3–5**
PIONEER INT'L: *59–62*........... **3–5**
SAR: *64* **3–5**
TOWER: *64–65*.................. **3–5**

Price Range

JENKINS, Norma
Singles: 7-Inch
DESERT MOON: *76* $2–3

JENNIFER (Jennifer Warnes)
Singles: 7-Inch
PARROT: *67–70* 3–5
LPs: 10/12-Inch 33rpm
PARROT: *68–70* 12–18
Also see WARNES, Jennifer

JENNINGS, Waylon (Waylon Jennings & The Waylors; Waylon Jennings & The Kimberlys; Waylon Jennings & The Crickets)
Singles: 7-Inch
A&M (Except 722): *64* 8–10
A&M (722; "Rave On"):
63 10–15
BAT: *62* 10–15
BRUNSWICK (55130;
"Jole Blon"): *59* 80–100
(Maroon label. With Buddy Holly & King Curtis.)
BRUNSWICK (55130;
"Jole Blon"): *59* 60–80
(Yellow label. Promotional issue only.)
RCA VICTOR (Except
8500 through 9600
series): *69–80* 1–3
RCA VICTOR (8500
through 9600 series):
65–68 3–5
RAMCO: *67* 5–10
TREND '61: *61* 15–20
TREND '63: *63* 30–35
Picture Sleeves
RCA VICTOR: *80* 1–3
LPs: 10/12-Inch 33rpm
A&M: *69* 25–30
BAT: *64* 150–200
CAMDEN: *67–76* 8–15
MCA 4–6
PICKWICK: *75* 5–10
RCA VICTOR (0500
through 3300 series):
74–79 5–10
RCA VICTOR (3400
series, except 3406): *79* 5–8
RCA VICTOR (3406;
"Greatest Hits"): *79* 12–18

Price Range

(Picture disc.)
RCA VICTOR (3500
through 3900 series):
66–68 . . . . $15–25
(With an "LPM" or "LSP" prefix.)
RCA VICTOR (3600
through 3900 series):
80–81 4–8
(With an "AYL1" or "AHL1" prefix.)
RCA VICTOR (4000
through 4100 series):
68–69 10–20
(With an "LPM" or "LSP" prefix.)
RCA VICTOR (4000
through 4300 series):
81–82 4–8
(With an "AYL1" prefix.)
RCA VICTOR (4400
through 4800 series):
70–73 8–15
(With an "LSP" prefix.)
RCA VICTOR (4400
through 4800 series): *83* 4–8
(With an "AHL1" prefix.)
SOUNDS: *64* 125–150
TIME-LIFE: *81* 5–8
VOCALION: *69* 15–20
Also see CASH, Johnny, & Waylon Jennings
Also see CUNHA, Rick
Also see DAVIS, Skeeter
Also see HOLLY, Buddy
Also see KIMBERLYS, The
Also see KING CURTIS
Also see U.S.A. FOR AFRICA

Price Range   *Price Range*

JENNINGS, Waylon, & Jesse Colter
Singles: 7-Inch
RCA VICTOR: 69–71 . . . . $2–4
LPs: 10/12-Inch 33rpm
RCA VICTOR: 81 5–8
Also see COLTER, Jesse

JENNINGS, Waylon / Johnny Paycheck
LPs: 10/12-Inch 33rpm
OUT OF TOWN DIST: 82 5–8
Also see PAYCHECK, Johnny

JENNINGS, Waylon, & Jerry Reed
Singles: 7-Inch
RCA VICTOR: 83 1–3
Also see REED, Jerry

JENNINGS, Waylon, & Willie Nelson (Waylon & Willie)
Singles: 7-Inch
COLUMBIA: 83 1–3
RCA VICTOR: 76–82 1–3
LPs: 10/12-Inch 33rpm
AURA: 83 5–8
RCA VICTOR (Except
  colored vinyl): 78–83 5–8
RCA VICTOR (Colored
  vinyl): 78 20–25
  (Promotional issues only.)
  Also see JENNINGS, Waylon
  Also see NELSON, Willie

JENSEN, Kris
Singles: 7-Inch
A&M: 70 2–4
COLPIX: 59 4–6
HICKORY: 62–65 3–5
KAPP: 61 3–5
LEADER: 60–61 3–5
Picture Sleeves
HICKORY: 62–64 4–6
LPs: 10/12-Inch 33rpm
HICKORY: 62 35–40

JEROME, Henry, & His Orchestra
Singles: 7-Inch
DECCA: 60–64 1–3
LPs: 10/12-Inch 33rpm
DECCA: 60–64 5–12
ROULETTE: 59 5–15

JERRY, Mungo: see MUNGO JERRY

JERRY O
Singles: 7-Inch
SHOUT: 67 . . . . $3–5
WHITE WHALE: 69 2–4

JESSE & MARVIN
Singles: 7-Inch
SPECIALTY (Black vinyl):
  52 5–8
SPECIALTY (Colored
  vinyl): 52 25–30
  Members: Jesse Belvin; Marvin Phillips.
  Also see BELVIN, Jesse
  Also see MARVIN & JOHNNY

JESSE'S GANG
Singles: 7-Inch
JES SAY: 85 4–6

JESTERS, The
Singles: 7-Inch
ABC: 73 1–3
AMY: 62 3–5
CYCLONE: 58 12–15
LOST-NITE: 63 3–5
WINLEY (Except 218):
  57–61 5–8
WINLEY (218; "So
  Strange"): 57 15–20
LPs: 10/12-Inch 33rpm
LOST-NITE: 81 5–8
  Members: Len McKay; Adam Jackson; Jimmy
  Smith; Noel Grant; Leo Vincent; Melvin Lewis;
  Don Lewis.
  Also see PARAGONS, The / The Jesters

JETE, Le: see LE JETE

JETHRO TULL (Featuring Ian Anderson)
Singles: 7-Inch
CHRYSALIS: 72–84 1–3
CHRYSALIS/REPRISE:
  69–72 2–4
LPs: 10/12-Inch 33rpm
CHRYSALIS (Except CH4
  series): 73–84 6–10

Price Range

CHRYSALIS (CH4 series):
73–74 .... **$10–12**
MFSL: *80–82*.................. **12–15**
REPRISE: *69–72*............... **10–15**
REPRISE/CHRYSALIS
(2106; "Living In The
Past"): *72*................... **15–20**
(Price range includes bonus color booklet.)
Also see WILD TURKEY

JETS, The
Singles: 12-Inch 33/45rpm
MCA: *85* **4–6**
Singles: 7-Inch
MCA: *85* **1–3**
LPs: 10/12-Inch 33rpm
MCA: *85* **5–8**

JETT, Joan, & The Blackhearts
Singles: 12-Inch 33/45rpm
MCA: *83* **4–6**
Singles: 7-Inch
BLACKHEART: *83*............... **1–3**
BOARDWALK: *81–82* **2–3**
MCA: *83* **1–3**
Picture Sleeves
BOARDWALK: *81–82* **2–3**
LPs: 10/12-Inch 33rpm
BLACKHEART: *80–83*............ **5–8**
BOARDWALK: *81–82* **5–8**
MCA: *83–84* **5–8**
Also see RUNAWAYS, The

JEWELS, The (The Crows)
Singles: 7-Inch
RAMA: *53*..................... **250–300**
(Colored vinyl.)
Also see CROWS, The

JEWELS, The
Singles: 7-Inch
DIMENSION: *64–65* **3–5**

JIGSAW
Singles: 7-Inch
CHELSEA: *75–76*................. **2–3**
20TH CENTURY-FOX:
77–78 .... **1–3**
LPs: 10/12-Inch 33rpm
CHELSEA: *75*................... **8–10**
ELEKTRA: *82* **5–8**

Price Range

20TH CENTURY-FOX:
77 .... **$5–8**

JILL & RAY
Singles: 7-Inch
LE CAM: *62*................... **10–15**
Members: Jill Jackson; Ray Hildebrand.
Also see PAUL & PAULA

JIM & JEAN
Singles: 7-Inch
VERVE/FORECAST: *68* **2–4**
Members: Jim Glover; Jean Glover.

JIM & MONICA (With Jimmy Gilmer)
Singles: 7-Inch
BETTY: *64* **3–5**
Also see GILMER, Jimmy

JIMENEZ, Jose: see DANA, Bill

JIMMY & DUANE
Singles: 7-Inch
EB X. PRESTON.............. **75–100**
Members: Jimmy Delbridge; Duane Eddy.
Also see EDDY, Duane

JIMMY LEE: see LEE, Jimmy

JINKINS, Gus: see JENKINS, Gus

JIVE BOMBERS, The (Featuring Clarence "Bad Boy" Palmer)
Singles: 7-Inch
CITATION: *52*................. **20–25**
MIDDLE TONE: *64* **3–5**
SAVOY: *56–59* **5–8**

JIVE FIVE, The
Singles: 7-Inch
AMBIENT SOUND: *82* **2–3**
BELTONE: *61–63*................ **4–6**
DECCA: *70*..................... **3–5**
MUSICOR: *67–68*................ **3–5**
SKETCH: *64*................... **8–10**
UNITED ARTISTS: *64–66*........ **3–5**
LPs: 10/12-Inch 33rpm
AMBIENT SOUND: *82* **5–8**
RELIC........................ **8–10**
UNITED ARTISTS: *65*.......... **25–35**

Price Range

Members: Eugene Pitt; Norm Johnson; Richard Harris; Jerry Hannah; Billy Prophet; Johnny Watson; Casey Spencer; Webster Harris.
Also see GENIES, The
Also see PLATTERS, The / Inez & Charlie Foxx / The Jive Five / Tommy Hunt

JIVIN' GENE (Jivin' Gene & The Jokers)
Singles: 7-Inch
ABC: *73* $1–3
CHESS: *64* 3–5
HALL WAY: *64* 3–5
JIN: *59* 8–10
MERCURY: *59–62* 4–6
TFC/HALL: *65* 3–5

JO, Damita: see DAMITA JO

JO, Marcy: see MARCY JOE

JO, Sami: see SAMI JO

JO ANN & TROY
Singles: 7-Inch
ATLANTIC: *64* 8–10
Members: Jo Ann Campbell; Troy Seals.
Also see CAMPBELL, Jo Ann

JO JO GUNNE (Featuring Jay Ferguson)
Singles: 7-Inch
ASYLUM: *72* 2–3
LPs: 10/12-Inch 33rpm
ASYLUM (Except 5071):
72–74 8–10
ASYLUM (5071; "Jumpin'
The Gunne"): *73* 10–12
(With gatefold cover.)
ASYLUM (5071; "Jumpin'
The Gunne"): *73* 6–10
(With standard cover.)
Also see FERGUSON, Jay

JOBIM, Antonio Carlos
Singles: 7-Inch
A&M: *67* 2–3
CTI: *70* 1–3
MCA: *74* 1–3
VERVE: *63–64* 2–4

Price Range

LPs: 10/12-Inch 33rpm
A&M: *67–70* $8–12
CTI: *70–71* 8–12
CAPITOL: *64* 10–20
DISCOVERY: *82* 5–8
MCA: *73* 5–8
VERVE (Except 3000
series): *63* 10–20
VERVE (3000 series): *82* 5–8
WARNER BROS: *65–80* 8–15
Also see FITZGERALD, Ella, & Antonio Carlos Jobim
Also see GILBERTO, Astrud
Also see SINATRA, Frank, & Antonio Carlos Jobim

JOBOXERS, The
Singles: 7-Inch
RCA VICTOR: *83* 1–3
LPs: 10/12-Inch 33rpm
RCA VICTOR: *83* 5–8

JOE, Billy: see BILLY JOE

JOE, Marcy: see MARCY JOE

JOE & ANN
Singles: 7-Inch
ACE: *60–62* 4–6

JOE & EDDIE
Singles: 7-Inch
CAPITOL: *59* 3–5
GNP/CRESCENDO:
62–65 2–4
LPs: 10/12-Inch 33rpm
GNP/CRESCENDO:
63–66 8–15
Members: Joe Gilbert; Eddie Brown.

JOEL, Billy
Singles: 12-Inch 33/45rpm
COLUMBIA: *83* 4–6
Singles: 7-Inch
COLUMBIA: *73–86* 1–3
FAMILY: *71–73* 3–5
Picture Sleeves
COLUMBIA: *79–85* 1–3
LPs: 10/12-Inch 33rpm
COLUMBIA (30000
series): *73–86* 5–8
(With an "FC," "KC" or "TC" prefix.)

Price Range

COLUMBIA (30000
series): *74–76* **$10–15**
(With a "CQ" or "PCQ" prefix. Quad issues.)
COLUMBIA (40000
series): *80–85* **10–12**
(Half-speed mastered LPs.)
FAMILY
PRODUCTIONS: *71* **20–25**

Promotional LPs

COLUMBIA (326;
"Souvenir"): *75* **20–25**
Also see ATTILA
Also see KHAN, Steve
Also see U.S.A. FOR AFRICA

JOHANSEN, David
Singles: 7-Inch
BLUE SKY: *78–82* **1–3**

LPs: 10/12-Inch 33rpm
BLUE SKY: *78–82* **5–8**
Also see NEW YORK DOLLS, The

JOHN, Dr.: see DR. JOHN

JOHN, Elton
Singles: 7-Inch
CONGRESS: *69–70* **12–15**
DJM: *69* **15–18**
GEFFEN: *81–86* **1–3**
MCA: *72–80* **1–3**
MCA/ROCKET: *76–77* **2–3**
ROCKET: *76* **2–3**
UNI: *70–72* **2–3**
VIKING: *69* **20–25**

Picture Sleeves
GEFFEN: *81–86* **1–3**
MCA (Except 40364):
74–80 .... **1–3**
MCA (40364; WFIL radio
"Philadelphia
Freedom"): *75* **25–30**
(Promotional issue only.)

EPs: 7-Inch 33/45rpm
MCA: *73* **8–10**
(Jukebox issue only.)
UNI: *70* **10–12**
(Jukebox issue only.)

LPs: 10/12-Inch 33rpm
GEFFEN: *81–86* **5–8**
MCA ("A Single Man"):
79 .... **10–15**

Price Range

(Picture disc.)
MCA (2100 through 2130):
73–75 .... **$6–10**
MCA (2142; "Captain
Fantastic & The Brown
Dirt Cowboy"): *75* **10–12**
(Includes poster, lyrics booklet, bio scrapbook
and comic insert. Deduct $3-$5 if these items
are missing.)
MCA ("Captain
Fantastic"): *79* **35–45**
(Picture disc. Promotional issue only.)
MCA ("Captain
Fantastic"): *79* **25–40**
(Colored vinyl. Promotional issue only.)
MCA (2163 through 5121):
75–80 .... **5–8**
MCA (10003; "Goodbye
Yellow Brick Road"): *73* **10–12**
MCA (37000 series): *79* **4–6**
MCA/ROCKET (Except
1953): *76–77.* **10–12**
MCA/ROCKET (1953;
"Get Up And Dance"):
77 .... **20–25**
(Promotional issue only.)
NAUTILUS: *82.* **12–18**
(Half-speed mastered LPs.)
UNI: *70–72* **12–15**
Also see DIONNE & FRIENDS
Also see OLSSON, Nigel
Also see SEDAKA, Neil
Also see STARR, Ringo

JOHN, Elton, & Kiki Dee
Singles: 7-Inch
ROCKET: *76.* **2–3**

Picture Sleeves
ROCKET: *76.* **2–3**
Also see DEE, Kiki

JOHN, Elton, & Lesley Duncan
Singles: 7-Inch
MCA (1938; "Love Song"):
76 .... **10–15**
(Promotional issue only.)

JOHN, Elton / Tina Turner
Singles: 7-Inch
POLYDOR: *75* **20–25**
(Promotional issue only.)
Also see JOHN, Elton
Also see TURNER, Tina

Price Range   *Price Range*

JOHN, Little Willie
Singles: 7-Inch
GUSTO **$1–3**
KING (4818 through
5394): *56–60.* **4–6**
KING (5428 through
5949): *61–64.* **3–5**
EPs: 7-Inch 33/45rpm
KING: *58* **20–25**
LPs: 10/12-Inch 33rpm
BLUESWAY: *73* **8–10**
KING (500 through 700
series, except 564): *58–61* **20–25**
KING (564; "Fever"): *56.* **30–35**
(With brown cover.)
KING (564; "Fever"): *59.* **15–20**
(With blue cover.)
KING (800 through 1000
series): *62–70.* **15–20**
Also see WILLIAMS, Paul

JOHN, Mable
Singles: 7-Inch
STAX: *66–68.* **3–5**
TAMLA (54031; "Who
Wouldn't Love A Man
Like That"): *60* **25–30**
TAMLA (54040; "No
Love"): *61* **15–20**
TAMLA (54050; "Take
Me"): *61.* **15–20**
TAMLA (54081; "Who
Wouldn't Love A Man
Like That"): *63* **8–10**

JOHN, Pope: see POPE JOHN

JOHN, Robert (Bobby Pedrick, Jr.)
Singles: 12-Inch 33/45
CBS ASSOCIATED: *84.* **4–6**
Singles: 7-Inch
A&M: *70–71* **2–4**
ARIOLA: *78* **2–3**
ATLANTIC: *72* **2–3**
COLUMBIA: *68–69.* **3–5**
EMI AMERICA: *79–80.* **1–3**
MOTOWN: *83.* **1–3**
LPs: 10/12-Inch 33rpm
COLUMBIA: *68* **10–15**
EMI AMERICA: *79–82.* **5–8**
HARMONY: *72* **8–10**

Also see PEDRICK, Bobby

JOHN & ERNEST
Singles: 7-Inch
RAINY WEDNESDAY:
73 . . . . **$2–4**
Members: John Free; Ernest Smith.

JOHNNIE & JOE
Singles: 7-Inch
ABC-PARAMOUNT: *60.* **3–5**
AMBIENT SOUND: *82* **2–3**
CHESS: *60.* **4–6**
(Blue or multi-color labels.)
CHESS: *57.* **8–10**
(Silver & blue label.)
J&S (Except 1664): *57–59* **5–8**
J&S (1664; "Over The
Mountain"): *57* **25–30**
(First pressings had thick & thin horizontal
lines across the label.)
J&S (1664; "Over The
Mountain"): *62* **4–6**
(Without the horizontal lines across the label.)
LPs: 10/12-Inch 33rpm
AMBIENT SOUND: *82* **5–8**
Members: Johnnie Richardson; Joe Rivers.

JOHNNY & THE DISTRACTIONS
Singles: 7-Inch
A&M: *82* **1–3**
LPs: 10/12-Inch 33rpm
A&M: *82* **5–8**

JOHNNY & THE EXPRESSIONS
Singles: 7-Inch
JOSIE: *65–66.* **3–5**

JOHNNY & THE HURRICANES
(Johnny Paris)
Singles: 7-Inch
ABC: *73.* **1–3**
ATILA: *64.* **3–5**
BIG TOP: *60–63.* **4–6**
JA-DA **3–5**
JEFF: *64* **4–6**
MALA: *63.* **3–5**
TWIRL: *59* **10–15**
WARWICK (Except stereo
singles): *59–60* **5–8**
WARWICK (Stereo
singles): *59* **15–20**
(With an "S" prefix.)

Price Range

Picture Sleeves
BIG TOP: *60–61*................ **$6–12**
WARWICK: *60*................... **8–12**
EPs: 7-Inch 33/45rpm
WARWICK: *59*................. **25–35**
LPs: 10/12-Inch 33rpm
ATILA........................ **30–35**
BIG TOP: *60*.................. **45–55**
TWIRL....................... **40–45**
WARWICK: *59–60*.............. **50–60**
Also see GIBSON, Johnny

JOHNNY & THE JAMMERS
(Featuring Johnny Winter)
Singles: 7-Inch
DART: *59* **75–100**
Also see WINTER, Johnny

JOHNNY AVERAGE BAND, The
(Featuring Nikki Wills)
Singles: 7-Inch
BEARSVILLE: *81* **1–3**
LPs: 10/12-Inch 33rpm
BEARSVILLE: *81* **5–8**

JOHNNY LEE: see LEE, Johnny

JOHNNY T. ANGEL
Singles: 7-Inch
BELL: *74*....................... **2–3**

JOHNS, Sammy
Singles: 7-Inch
GRC: *73–75*...................... **2–3**
REAL WORLD: *80*............... **1–3**
WARNER/CURB: *76* **2–3**
LPs: 10/12-Inch 33rpm
GRC: *75*........................ **8–10**

JOHNSON, Al
Singles: 7-Inch
COLUMBIA: *80*.................. **1–3**
LPs: 10/12-Inch 33rpm
COLUMBIA: *80*.................. **5–8**

JOHNSON, Al, & Jean Carn
Singles: 7-Inch
COLUMBIA: *80*.................. **1–3**
Also see CARN, Jean
Also see JOHNSON, Al

Price Range

JOHNSON, Benny
Singles: 7-Inch
TODAY: *73*..................... **$2–3**

JOHNSON, Betty
Singles: 7-Inch
ATLANTIC: *58–60* **3–5**
BALLY: *56–57* **4–6**
BELL: *71*........................ **2–4**
COED: *60* **3–5**
DOT: *60*........................ **3–5**
RCA VICTOR (6000
series): *55*...................... **4–6**
RCA VICTOR (8000
series): *63*...................... **2–4**
REPUBLIC: *60–61*............... **3–5**
WORLD ARTISTS: *63* **2–4**
EPs: 7-Inch 33/45rpm
RCA VICTOR: *57* **4–6**
LPs: 10/12-Inch 33rpm
ATLANTIC: *58–59* **15–20**
BALLY: *57* **20–25**

JOHNSON, Bubber (Bubber Johnson
& The Dreamers)
Singles: 7-Inch
KING (4000 series): *55–56* **5–8**
KING (5000 series): *57–60* **4–6**
MERCURY: *52*.................. **20–25**
LPs: 10/12-Inch 33rpm
KING (500 series): *57* **30–35**
KING (600 series): *59* **20–25**

JOHNSON, Buddy (Buddy Johnson
& His Orchestra)
Singles: 7-Inch
ATLANTIC: *53* **4–6**
DECCA (24996 through
29058): *50–54*................. **5–8**
MERCURY: *53–56*................ **4–6**
RCA VICTOR: *56* **4–6**
ROULETTE: *59* **3–5**
WING: *56* **4–6**
LPs: 10/12-Inch 33rpm
FORUM...................... **10–15**
MERCURY: *55–60*.............. **25–30**
WING (Except 12005): *63*........ **10–15**
WING (12005; "Rock 'N
Roll Stage Show"): *56*.......... **25–30**
Also see PRYSOCK, Arthur

Price Range   *Price Range*

JOHNSON, Buddy & Ella
Singles: 7-Inch
MERCURY: *56–61*............... $3–5
ROULETTE: *59*.................. 3–5

LPs: 10/12-Inch 33rpm
MERCURY: *58*.................. 20–25
ROULETTE: *59*................. 20–25
Also see JOHNSON, Buddy

JOHNSON, Danny
Singles: 7-Inch
FIRST AMERICAN: *79*............ 1–3

LPs: 10/12-Inch 33rpm
FIRST AMERICAN: *79*............ 5–8

JOHNSON, General
Singles: 7-Inch
ARISTA: *76–78*.................. 2–3
Also see CHAIRMEN OF THE BOARD, The
Also see SHOWMEN, The

JOHNSON, Howard
Singles: 12-Inch 33/45rpm
A&M: *82–85*..................... 4–6

Singles: 7-Inch
A&M: *82–85*..................... 1–3

LPs: 10/12-Inch 33rpm
A&M: *82–85*..................... 5–8
Also see NITEFLYTE

JOHNSON, Janice Marie
Singles: 7-Inch
CAPITOL: *84*.................... 1–3

JOHNSON, Jesse (Jesse Johnson's Revue)
Singles: 12-Inch 33/45rpm
A&M: *85*........................ 4–6

Singles: 7-Inch
A&M: *85*........................ 1–3
OLD TOWN: *66*.................. 3–5

LPs: 10/12-Inch 33rpm
A&M: *85*........................ 5–8
Also see TIME, The

JOHNSON, Jimmy
Singles: 7-Inch
MAGNUM: *65*.................... 3–5

JOHNSON, Kevin
Singles: 7-Inch
MAINSTREAM: *73*.............. $2–3

JOHNSON, L.V.
Singles: 7-Inch
ICA: *80–81*...................... 1–3

JOHNSON, Lonnie (Lonnie Johnson & Victoria Spivey)
Singles: 7-Inch
FEDERAL: *60*................... 3–5
GROOVE: *55*.................... 5–8
KING (4201; "Tomorrow
  Night"): *51*................. 12–15
KING (4500 through 4600
  series): *51–53*.............. 10–12
KING (4700 through 4900
  series): *54–56*................ 5–8
KING (5000 series): *57–65* 3–5
KING (6000 series): *70* 2–4
PRESTIGE: *60–64* 3–5
RAMA (Black vinyl): *56*...... 10–12
RAMA (Colored vinyl): *56* 20–25

EPs: 7-Inch 33/45rpm
KING: *54* 20–25

LPs: 10/12-Inch 33rpm
COLLECTOR'S
  CLASSICS.................... 10–15
KING (Except 520): *66–70* 10–15
KING (520; "Lonesome
  Road"): *54*.................... 60–75
PRESTIGE: *69* 10–12
PRESTIGE
  BLUESVILLE: *60–63*.......... 15–20

JOHNSON, Lou
Singles: 7-Inch
BIG HILL: *64–66*................. 3–5
BIG TOP: *62–67*.................. 3–5
COTILLION: *68–69*................ 2–4
HILLTOP: *64* 3–5

LPs: 10/12-Inch 33rpm
COTILLION: *69*................. 10–12
VOLT: *71*........................ 8–10

JOHNSON, Marv
Singles: 7-Inch
GORDY: *65–68*................... 3–5

Price Range

TAMLA (101; "Come To
  Me"): *59*................... **$125–150**
UNITED ARTISTS: *59–64*.......... **3–5**
  EPs: 7-Inch 33/45rpm
UNITED ARTISTS: *60*........... **20–25**
  LPs: 10/12-Inch 33rpm
UNITED ARTISTS: *60–62*........ **25–30**

JOHNSON, Michael
  Singles: 7-Inch
ATCO: *73* **2–4**
EMI AMERICA: *78–80*............ **1–3**
  Picture Sleeves
EMI AMERICA: *78*................ **1–3**
  LPs: 10/12-Inch 33rpm
ATCO: *73* **8–10**
EMI AMERICA: *78–82*............ **5–8**

JOHNSON, Orlando, & Trance
  Singles: 12-Inch 33/45rpm
EASYSTREET: *83* **4–6**

JOHNSON, Robert
  Singles: 7-Inch
INFINITY: *78*.................... **2–3**
  LPs: 10/12-Inch 33rpm
INFINITY: *78*.................... **5–8**

JOHNSON, Rozetta
  Singles: 7-Inch
CLINTONE: *70* **2–3**

JOHNSON, Ruby
  Singles: 7-Inch
NEBS: *65*........................ **3–5**
VOLT: *66*........................ **3–5**

JOHNSON, Syl
  Singles: 12-Inch 33/45rpm
BOARDWALK: *82* **4–6**
  Singles: 7-Inch
FEDERAL: *59–62* **3–5**
HI: *73–76*........................ **2–3**
SHAMA: *77* **2–3**
TMP-TING: *65*................... **3–5**
TWILIGHT: *67–68*................ **3–5**
TWINIGHT: *69* **2–4**
  LPs: 10/12-Inch 33rpm
HI: *73–75*........................ **8–10**
TWINIGHT: *68* **10–12**

Price Range

JOHNSTON, Tom
  Singles: 7-Inch
WARNER BROS: *79–81*........... **$1–3**
  LPs: 10/12-Inch 33rpm
WARNER BROS: *81*............... **5–8**
  Also see DOOBIE BROTHERS, The

JOINER, ARKANSAS JUNIOR
HIGH SCHOOL BAND, The
  Singles: 7-Inch
LIBERTY: *60–61* **3–5**

JOLI, France
  Singles: 12-Inch 33/45rpm
EPIC: *83–85* **4–6**
  Singles: 7-Inch
EPIC: *83–85* **1–3**
PRELUDE: *79–82*.................. **2–3**
  LPs: 10/12-Inch 33rpm
EPIC: *83–85* **5–8**
PRELUDE: *79–80*.................. **5–8**

JOLO
  Singles: 12-Inch 33/45rpm
MEGATONE: *84* **4–6**

JOLLY, Pete (The Pete Jolly Trio)
  Singles: 7-Inch
A&M: *68–69* **1–3**
AVA: *63–64*...................... **2–4**
COLUMBIA: *66*................... **1–3**
MAINSTREAM: *69*................ **1–3**
  LPs: 10/12-Inch 33rpm
A&M: *68–71* **8–12**
AVA: *63–64*..................... **10–20**
CHARLIE PARKER: *62* **15–20**
COLUMBIA: *65*................. **10–20**
MGM: *63*........................ **8–15**
METROJAZZ: *60*............... **15–25**
RCA VICTOR (1100
  through 1300 series):
  55–57 .... **20–30**
TRIP: *75* **5–8**

JON & ROBIN (Jon & Robin & The
In Crowd)
  Singles: 7-Inch
ABNAK: *67–68*................... **3–5**
  LPs: 10/12-Inch 33rpm
ABNAK: *67–68*................. **15–18**
  Members: Jon Abnor; Robin Abnor.

Price Range

JON & VANGELIS
Singles: 7-Inch
POLYDOR: *80–83* **$1–3**

LPs: 10/12-Inch 33rpm
POLYDOR: *80–83* **5–8**
Members: Jon Anderson; Vangelis.
Also see ANDERSON, Jon

JONAE, Gwen
Singles: 12-Inch 33/45rpm
ARIAL: *83* **4–6**
C&M: *83* **4–6**

JONES, Brenda
Singles: 7-Inch
FLYING DUTCHMAN:
76 . . . . **2–3**
MERCURY: *74*. **2–3**
WAVE: *82* **1–3**

JONES, Brenda, & "Groove" Holmes
Singles: 7-Inch
FLYING DUTCHMAN:
76 . . . . **2–3**
Also see HOLMES, Richard "Groove"
Also see JONES, Brenda

JONES, Brian
LPs: 10/12-Inch 33rpm
ROLLING STONES
(49100; "Pipes Of Pan"):
71 . . . . **10–15**
Promotional LPs
ROLLING STONES
(49100; "Pipes Of Pan"):
71 . . . . **30–35**
(Price range includes poster and cue sheets.)
Also see ROLLING STONES, The

JONES, Corky (Buck Owens)
Singles: 7-Inch
DIXIE: *56* **25–35**
PEP: *56* **50–75**
Also see OWENS, Buck

JONES, Davy (David Jones)
Singles: 7-Inch
BELL: *71–72*. **2–4**
COLPIX: *65* **5–8**
MGM: *72–73* **2–4**

Price Range

Picture Sleeves
COLPIX: *64–65*. **$8–12**
LPs: 10/12-Inch 33rpm
BELL: *71* **15–20**
COLPIX: *65* **20–25**
Also see MONKEES, The

JONES, Davey, & Mickey Dolenz
Singles: 7-Inch
BELL: *71* **2–4**
Also see JONES, Davey
Also see DOLENZ, Mickey

JONES, Etta
Singles: 7-Inch
KING: *61–62*. **2–4**
PRESTIGE: *60–65* **2–4**
20TH CENTURY-FOX/
WESTBOUND: *75* **1–3**

LPs: 10/12-Inch 33rpm
GRAND PRIX. **8–12**
KING (500 series): *58* **20–40**
KING (700 series): *61* **15–25**
MUSE: *77–81*. **5–8**
PRESTIGE (7100 & 7200
series): *60–63* **20–30**
(Yellow labels.)
PRESTIGE (7100 & 7200
series): *65* **10–20**
(Blue labels.)
PRESTIGE (7400 through
7700 series): *67–70* **8–15**
ROULETTE: *66* **8–15**
20TH CENTURY-FOX/
WESTBOUND: *75* **5–8**

JONES, George (George Jones & The Jones Boys)
Singles: 7-Inch
D: *65–66*. **2–4**
EPIC: *72–82* **1–3**
MERCURY (71000 &
72000 series): *57–64* **3–6**
MUSICOR: *65–71*. **2–4**
RCA VICTOR: *72–74* **1–3**
STARDAY (Except 100 &
200 series): *64–71* **1–3**
STARDAY (100 & 200
series): *54–57* **4–6**
UNITED ARTISTS: *62–67*. **3–5**

Price Range

Price Range

WHITE LIGHTNING.......... **$12–18**
WING: *64–68* **8–12**
WING/PICKWICK............... **4–6**
Also see CHARLES, Ray, George Jones & Chet Atkins
Also see DARRELL, Johnny / George Jones / Willie Nelson
Also see HAGGARD, Merle, & George Jones
Also see PARTON, Dolly / George Jones
Also see JONES, Thumper

JONES, George, & David Allan Coe
Singles: 7-Inch
COLUMBIA: *81* **1–3**
Also see COE, David Allan

JONES, George, & Melba Montgomery
Singles: 7-Inch
MUSICOR: *66–67*................. **2–4**
UNITED ARTISTS: *63–66* **2–4**

LPs: 10/12-Inch 33rpm
BUCKBOARD: *76*................ **5–8**
GUEST STAR.................. **20–30**
LIBERTY: *82* **4–6**
MUSIC DISC: *69* **6–10**
MUSICOR: *66–74*................ **8–12**
MUSICOR/RCA
VICTOR: *74* **8–10**
UNITED ARTISTS (200 series): *73*...................... **5–8**
UNITED ARTISTS (3000 & 6000 series): *63–66* **10–15**
Also see MONTGOMERY, Melba

JONES, George, & Johnny Paycheck
Singles: 7-Inch
EPIC: *78–80* **1–3**

LPs: 10/12-Inch 33rpm
EPIC: *80* **5–8**
Also see PAYCHECK, Johnny

JONES, George, & Gene Pitney (George & Gene)
Singles: 7-Inch
MUSICOR: *65–66*................. **3–5**

Picture Sleeves
MUSICOR: *65*.................... **3–5**

LPs: 10/12-Inch 33rpm
DESIGN **6–10**

INTERNATIONAL
AWARD **$8–10**
MUSIC DISC: *69* **10–12**
MUSICOR (3044; "George Jones & Gene Pitney"):
65 .... **15–20**
(Front cover shows title as "For The First Time! Two Great Stars, George Jones & Gene Pitney.")
MUSICOR (3044; "George Jones & Gene Pitney"):
65 .... **12–15**
(Front cover shows title as "Recorded In Nashville, Tennessee, George Jones & Gene Pitney.")
MUSICOR (3065; "It's Country Time Again"):
65 .... **12–15**
Also see PITNEY, Gene

JONES, George, Gene Pitney & Melba Montgomery
LPs: 10/12-Inch 33rpm
MUSICOR: *66*................... **12–15**
(Contains duets by these artists, but there are no tracks where all three perform together.)
Also see MONTGOMERY, Melba

JONES, George, & Ernest Tubb
Singles: 7-Inch
FIRST GENERATION:
81 .... **1–3**

JONES, George, & Tammy Wynette (George, Tammy & Tina)
Singles: 7-Inch
EPIC: *71–80* **2–3**

LPs: 10/12-Inch 33rpm
COLUMBIA: *81*.................. **5–8**
EPIC: *71–81* **8–12**
TVP **5–8**
Also see JONES, George
Also see WYNETTE, Tammy

JONES, Glenn
Singles: 12-Inch 33/45rpm
RCA VICTOR: *83–85* **4–6**
Singles: 7-Inch
RCA VICTOR: *83–85* **1–3**
LPs: 10/12-Inch 33rpm
RCA VICTOR: *83–84* **5–8**
Also see WARWICK, Dionne, & Glenn Jones

Price Range

JONES, Grace
Singles: 12-Inch 33/45rpm
ISLAND: *83* $4–6
MANHATTAN: *85* 4–6
Singles: 7-Inch
BEAM JUNCTION: *76–77* 2–3
ISLAND: *78–83* 1–3
MANHATTAN: *85* 1–3
LPs: 10/12-Inch 33rpm
ISLAND: *77–82* 5–8
MANHATTAN: *85* 5–8

JONES, Howard
Singles: 12-Inch 33/45rpm
ELEKTRA: *83–85* 4–6
Singles: 7-Inch
ELEKTRA: *83–85* 1–3
LPs: 10/12-Inch 33rpm
ELEKTRA: *83–85* 5–8

JONES, Ignatius
Singles: 12-Inch 33/45rpm
WARNER BROS: *83* 4–6
Singles: 7-Inch
WARNER BROS: *83* 1–3

JONES, Jack
Singles: 7-Inch
CAPITOL: *59–60* 2–4
KAPP: *60–67* 2–3
POLYDOR: *83* 1–3
RCA VICTOR: *67–77* 1–3
Picture Sleeves
CAPITOL: *59* 2–4
KAPP: *63–69* 2–3
LPs: 10/12-Inch 33rpm
CAMDEN: *73* 4–8
CAPITOL: *59–64* 10–15
KAPP: *61–69* 8–15
MCA: *77* 5–8
MGM: *79* 4–8
RCA VICTOR: *67–77* 5–10

JONES, Jimmy (Jimmy Jones & The Jones Boys; Jimmy Jones & The Pretenders)
Singles: 7-Inch
ABC-PARAMOUNT: *60* 5–8
ARROW: *57* 20–25

Price Range

BELL: *67* $3–5
CONCHILLO: *76* 2–3
CUB: *59–62* 3–5
EPIC: *59* 3–5
MGM: *78* 1–3
PARKWAY: *66* 3–5
RAMA: *56* 40–50
ROULETTE: *65* 3–5
SAVOY: *60* 4–6
VEE JAY: *63* 3–5
Picture Sleeves
CUB: *60* 5–8
LPs: 10/12-Inch 33rpm
JEN JILLUS: *77* 5–8
MGM: *60* 35–40

JONES, Joe
Singles: 7-Inch
ABC: *73* 1–3
RIC: *60* 4–6
ROULETTE: *60–61* 3–5
LPs: 10/12-Inch 33rpm
PRESTIGE: *69* 10–12
ROULETTE: *61* 25–30

JONES, Johnny
Singles: 7-Inch
FURY: *68* 3–5

JONES, Jonah (The Jonah Jones Quartet)
Singles: 7-Inch
BETHLEHEM: *59* 2–4
CAPITOL: *58–63* 2–4
DECCA: *65* 1–3
GROOVE: *56* 2–4
EPs: 7-Inch 33/45rpm
BETHLEHEM: *55* 8–12
CAMDEN: *69* 5–10
CAPITOL: *58–59* 5–10
GROOVE: *56* 5–10
RCA VICTOR: *59* 5–10
LPs: 10/12-Inch 33rpm
ANGEL: *56* 15–25
BETHLEHEM: *55–60* 15–30
CAPITOL (1000 through
2800 series): *58–67* 10–20
(With a "T" or "ST" prefix.)
CAPITOL (1600 series): *77* 4–8
(With an "SM" prefix.)

Price Range

CAPITOL (11000 series):
75 .... **$5–8**
DECCA: *65–67* **8–15**
GROOVE: *56.* **15–25**
INNER CITY: *81* **5–8**
MOTOWN: *69.* **8–12**
RCA VICTOR: *59–63* **12–20**
Also see CHRISTY, June

JONES, Kay Cee
Singles: 7-Inch
AMERICAN: *56.* **5–8**
CHANCELLOR: *59* **4–6**

JONES, Klinte
Singles: 7-Inch
OH MY: *84* **4–6**

JONES, Linda
Singles: 7-Inch
COTIQUE: *69.* **2–4**
LOMA: *67–68* **3–5**
NEPTUNE: *69* **2–4**
TURBO: *72* **2–3**
WARNER BROS: *69.* **2–4**
LPs: 10/12-Inch 33rpm
LOMA: *67* **12–15**
TURBO: *72* **8–10**

JONES, Quincy
Singles: 7-Inch
A&M: *69–81* **1–3**
ABC: *68* **2–3**
BELL: *69.* **2–3**
COLGEMS: *68* **2–3**
IMPULSE: *62* **2–4**
RCA VICTOR: *69* **2–3**
REPRISE: *72.* **1–3**
UNI: *69* **2–3**
UNITED ARTISTS: *70.* **1–3**
Picture Sleeves
A&M: *77–81* **1–3**
COLGEMS: *68* **2–3**
LPs: 10/12-Inch 33rpm
A&M: *69* **5–10**
ABC (7; "For Love Of
Ivy"): *68.* **12–15**
(Soundtrack.)
ABC (700 series): *73* **8–12**

Price Range

ABC-PARAMOUNT:
56–57 .... **$30–50**
ALLEGIANCE: *84.* **5–8**
COLGEMS: *68* **20–25**
EMARCY: *56* **25–50**
IMPULSE (11; "The
Quintessence"): *62* **15–25**
IMPULSE (9300 series): *78* **8–12**
LIBERTY: *67* **12–15**
MERCURY (Black label):
59–63 .... **20–35**
MERCURY (Red label):
64–72 .... **10–20**
PRESTIGE (100 series): *53* **100–150**
(10-Inch LPs.)
TRIP: *74–76* **5–8**
UNITED ARTISTS: *70* **10–15**
VERVE: *67* **15–20**
WING: *69* **6–12**
Also see ASHFORD & SIMPSON
Also see AUSTIN, Patti
Also see BROTHERS JOHNSON, The
Also see ECKSTINE, Billy, & Quincy Jones
Also see FELICIANO, Jose, & Quincy Jones
Also see GILBERTO, Astrud
Also see JACKSON, Michael
Also see KHAN, Chaka
Also see RIPERTON, Minnie
Also see U.S.A. FOR AFRICA
Also see WASHINGTON, Dinah

JONES, Quincy, & James Ingram
Singles: 7-Inch
A&M: *81* **1–3**
Also see INGRAM, James
Also see JONES, Quincy

JONES, Rickie Lee
Singles: 7-Inch
WARNER BROS: *79–84* **1–3**
LPs: 10/12-Inch 33rpm
WARNER BROS: *79–84* **5–8**

JONES, Spencer
Singles: 12-Inch 33/45rpm
NEXT PLATINUM: *83.* **4–6**

**JONES, Spike (Spike Jones & The
City Slickers)**
Singles: 7-Inch
LIBERTY: *59–65* **3–5**

Price Range

Price Range

RCA VICTOR (0500
series): *71* **$2–4**
RCA VICTOR (3600
through 6000 series):
50–55 .... **5–10**
WARNER BROS: *59* **4–6**
Picture Sleeves
RCA VICTOR: *53–54* **8–15**
EPs: 7-Inch 33/45rpm
RCA VICTOR: *51–59* **15–25**
VERVE: *56–57* **10–20**
LPs: 10/12-Inch 33rpm
GLENDALE: *78*.................. **5–8**
LIBERTY: *60–65* **12–20**
MGM: *70*....................... **8–12**
RCA VICTOR (18; "Spike
Jones Plays The
Charleston"): *51*............... **50–75**
RCA VICTOR (1000
series): *75*..................... **5–8**
RCA VICTOR (2200
series): *60*.................... **15–25**
RCA VICTOR (2300
series): *77*..................... **5–8**
RCA VICTOR (3000 &
3100 series): *52–53* **30–50**
RCA VICTOR (3200
series): *71*..................... **8–12**
RCA VICTOR (3700
series): *80* **4–8**
RCA VICTOR (3800
series): *67*.................... **10–15**
(With an "LPM" or "LSP" prefix.)
RCA VICTOR (3800
series): *81*..................... **5–8**
(With an "AYL1" prefix.)
UNITED ARTISTS: *75*............. **5–8**
VERVE (Except 8500
series): *56–59* **20–30**
VERVE (8500 series): *63* **12–20**
WARNER BROS: *59–60*.......... **15–25**
Also see KATZ, Mickey, & His Orchestra

JONES, Tamiko
Singles: 7-Inch
A&M: *68–69* **2–4**
ARISTA: *75* **2–3**
ATLANTIC: *66* **3–5**
ATLANTIS: *77*.................... **2–3**
CONTEMPO: *76*.................. **2–3**
DECEMBER: *67*................... **3–5**

GOLDEN WORLD: *66*........... **$3–5**
POLYDOR: *79*................... **1–3**
20TH CENTURY-FOX:
74 .... **2–3**
LPs: 10/12-Inch 33rpm
A&M: *68* **10–12**
DECEMBER: *68*................. **10–12**

JONES, Tamiko, & Herbie Mann
Singles: 7-Inch
ATLANTIC: *66* **3–5**
LPs: 10/12-Inch 33rpm
ATLANTIC: *67* **8–15**
Also see JONES, Tamiko
Also see MANN, Herbie

JONES, Thelma
Singles: 7-Inch
BARRY: *66–68*.................... **3–5**
COLUMBIA: *78*................... **2–3**

JONES, Thumper (George Jones)
Singles: 7-Inch
STARDAY (240;
"Rock-It"): *56* **45–55**
EPs: 7-Inch 33/45rpm
DIXIE (502; "Thumper
Jones"): *58*.................... **15–25**
(Contains three Jones tracks. Not issued with
cover.)
LPs: 10/12-Inch 33rpm
TEENAGE HEAVEN **8–12**
Also see JONES, George

JONES, Tom
Singles: 7-Inch
EPIC: *76–80* **1–3**
LONDON: *77*..................... **2–3**
MCA: *79* **1–3**
MERCURY: *81–85*................. **1–3**
PARROT: *65–75*................... **2–4**
SYMBOL: *65*...................... **3–5**
TOWER: *65*....................... **3–5**
Picture Sleeves
PARROT: *65–71*................... **2–4**
LPs: 10/12-Inch 33rpm
EPIC: *70–75* **8–12**
LONDON: *78* **5–8**
MERCURY: *81–85*................. **5–8**
PARROT: *65–74*................. **10–20**

Price Range

JONES, Tom / Freddie & The Dreamers / Johnny Rivers
LPs: 10/12-Inch 33rpm
TOWER: 65 .... **$15–20**
   Also see FREDDIE & THE DREAMERS
   Also see JONES, Tom
   Also see RIVERS, Johnny

JONES GIRLS, The
Singles: 7-Inch
CURTOM: 75 .... **2–3**
EPIC: 81 .... **1–3**
PARAMOUNT: 74 .... **2–3**
PHILADELPHIA INT'L:
   79–82 .... **1–3**
RCA VICTOR: 83 .... **1–3**
LPs: 10/12-Inch 33rpm
PHILADELPHIA INT'L:
   79–81 .... **5–8**
RCA VICTOR: 83 .... **5–8**

JONESES, The
Singles: 7-Inch
MERCURY: 74–83 .... **1–3**
VMP: 72 .... **2–3**
Picture Sleeves
MERCURY: 75 .... **1–3**
LPs: 10/12-Inch 33rpm
EPIC: 77 .... **5–8**
MERCURY: 74–83 .... **5–8**

JONZUN CREW, The (Featuring Michael Jonzun)
Singles: 12-Inch 33/45rpm
TOMMY BOY: 82–85 .... **4–6**
Singles: 7-Inch
TOMMY BOY: 82–85 .... **1–3**
LPs: 10/12-Inch 33rpm
TOMMY BOY: 83–85 .... **5–8**

JOPLIN, Janis
Singles: 7-Inch
COLUMBIA: 69–72 .... **5–8**
SIMON & SHUSTER
   ("Janis") **3–5**
   (Soundsheet. Included with the book "Janis.")
LPs: 10/12-Inch 33rpm
COLUMBIA (9000 series):
   69 .... **12–18**
   (With a "CS" prefix.)
COLUMBIA (9000 series) **5–8**

(With a "PC" prefix.)
COLUMBIA (30000
   series): 71–75 .... **$10–15**
   (With a "KC" or "PG" prefix.)
COLUMBIA (30000
   series): 74 .... **12–18**
   (With a "CQ" prefix. Quad issue.)
COLUMBIA (30000
   series): 82–84 .... **5–8**
   (With a "PC" prefix.)
   Also see BIG BROTHER & THE HOLDING
   COMPANY

JORDAN, Jerry (The Jordans)
Singles: 7-Inch
MCA: 75–76 .... **1–3**
LPs: 10/12-Inch 33rpm
MCA: 75–76 .... **5–8**

JORDAN, Lonnie
Singles: 7-Inch
BOARDWALK: 82 .... **1–3**
MCA: 78 .... **1–3**
UNITED ARTISTS: 76–77 .... **2–3**
LPs: 10/12-Inch 33rpm
MCA: 78 .... **5–8**
   Also see WAR

JORDAN, Louis (Louis Jordan & His Tympani 5)
Singles: 7-Inch
ALADDIN: 54–55 .... **8–10**
DECCA (23000 through
   30000 series): 50–54 .... **8–12**
LOU-WA: 60 .... **3–5**
MERCURY: 56–58 .... **5–8**
PZAZZ: 68 .... **2–4**
TANGERINE: 62–66 .... **2–4**
WARWICK: 60–61 .... **3–5**
X: 55 .... **5–8**
EPs: 7-Inch 33/45rpm
DECCA **15–20**
MERCURY: 57 .... **15–20**
LPs: 10/12-Inch 33rpm
CLASSICAL JAZZ: 82 .... **5–8**
DECCA (5035; "Greatest
   Hits"): 68 .... **10–15**
DECCA (8500 series): 56 .... **30–35**
MCA: 75–80 .... **5–8**
MERCURY: 57–58 .... **25–30**
SCORE **55–65**

Price Range

TANGERINE: *64*............... **$12–15**
TRIP: *75* **8–10**
WING: *63* **12–15**

JORDAN, Tenita
Singles: 7-Inch
CBS ASSOCIATED: *85*............. **1–3**

JORDANS, The: see JORDAN, Jerry

JOSEPH, David
Singles: 12-Inch 33/45rpm
MANGO: *83*..................... **4–6**
Singles: 7-Inch
MANGO: *83* **1–3**

JOSEPH, Margie (Margie Joseph & Blue Magic)
Singles: 12-Inch 33/45rpm
H.C.R.C.: *83* **4–6**
Singles: 7-Inch
ATCO: *75* **2–3**
ATLANTIC: *72–78* **2–3**
COTILLION: *76–84*............... **1–3**
H.C.R.C.: *82–83* **1–3**
OKEH: *68* **3–5**
VOLT: *68–71*..................... **2–4**
LPs: 10/12-Inch 33rpm
ATLANTIC: *73–74* **8–10**
H.C.R.C.: *83* **5–8**
VOLT: *71*....................... **10–12**
Also see BLUE MAGIC
Also see HATHAWAY, Donny, & Margie Joseph

JOSIAS, Cory
Singles: 12-Inch 33/45rpm
SIRE: *83* **4–6**

JOURNEY (Featuring Steve Perry & Neal Schon)
Singles: 7-Inch
COLUMBIA: *74–83* **2–4**
GEFFEN: *85*..................... **1–3**
Picture Sleeves
COLUMBIA: *80–81* .... **INC**
LPs: 10/12-Inch 33rpm
COLUMBIA (662; "Live
  Sampler"): *75* **12–15**
  (Promotional issue only.)

Price Range

COLUMBIA (914;
  "Journey"): *75*............... **$12–15**
  (Promotional issue only.)
COLUMBIA (30000
  series): *75–82* **5–10**
COLUMBIA (40000
  series): *81–82* **12–15**
  (Half-speed mastered LPs.)
  Also see CAIN, Jonathan
  Also see PERRY, Steve
  Also see SCHON, Neal, & Jan Hammer

JOVI, Bon: see BON JOVI

JOY, Roddie
Singles: 7-Inch
PARKWAY: *66–67* **3–5**
RED BIRD: *65*................... **3–5**

JOY OF COOKING, The (With Terry Garthwaite)
Singles: 7-Inch
BROWNSVILLE: *71* **2–4**
CAPITOL: *71–73* **2–3**
FANTASY: *77–78*................. **1–3**
LPs: 10/12-Inch 33rpm
CAPITOL: *71–72* **8–10**

JUDAS PRIEST
Singles: 7-Inch
COLUMBIA: *79–84*............... **1–3**
Picture Sleeves
COLUMBIA: *81* .... **INC**
LPs: 10/12-Inch 33rpm
COLUMBIA (Except
  picture discs): *77–84* **5–8**
COLUMBIA (Picture
  discs): *84* **8–10**
JANUS: *76* **6–10**
OVATION: *80*.................... **5–8**
RCA VICTOR: *83–84* **5–8**
VISA: *78–81* **5–8**
  Members: Rob Halford; K.K. Downing; Glenn
  Tipton; Ian Hill; Dave Holland.

JUDDS, The
Singles: 7-Inch
RCA VICTOR: *84–85* **1–3**
LPs: 10/12-Inch 33rpm
RCA VICTOR: *83–85* **5–8**
  Members: Naomi Judd; Wynonna Judd.

Price Range

JUICY
Singles: 12-Inch 33/45rpm
ATLANTIC: *83–84* **$4–6**
PRIVATE I: *85*. **4–6**
Singles: 7-Inch
ARISTA: *83* **1–3**
ATLANTIC: *83–84* **1–3**
PRIVATE I: *85*. **1–3**
LPs: 10/12-Inch 33rpm
ARISTA: *83* **5–8**
ATLANTIC: *84* **5–8**
Members: Jerry Barnes; Katreese Barnes.

JUKES, The: see SOUTHSIDE JOHNNY & THE ASBURY JUKES

JULIA LEE: see LEE, Julia

JULIAN, Don (Don Julian & The Larks)
Singles: 7-Inch
DYNAMITE: *62*. **3–5**
JERK: *65*. **3–5**
ORIGINAL SOUND:
58–60 . . . . **5–8**
LPs: 10/12-Inch 33rpm
AMAZON: *63*. **25–30**
Also see LARKS, The

JULIAN, Don & The Meadowlarks
Singles: 7-Inch
DOOTO: *57*. **15–20**
DOOTONE: *55–56*. **25–30**
ORIGINAL SOUND:
58–59 . . . . **5–8**
RPM: *54* **75–100**
EPs: 7-Inch 33/45rpm
DOOTO. **12–15**
DOOTONE: *56*. **25–30**
Also see JULIAN, Don
Also see PENGUINS, The / The Meadowlarks
/ The Medallions / The Dootones

JULIE (Julie Budd)
Singles: 7-Inch
TOM CAT: *76*. **2–3**

JULUKA
Singles: 7-Inch
WARNER BROS: *83–84*. **1–3**

Price Range

LPs: 10/12-Inch 33rpm
WARNER BROS: *83–84*. **$5–8**

JUMBO
Singles: 7-Inch
PRELUDE: *77*. **2–3**

JUMP 'N THE SADDLE
Singles: 7-Inch
ATLANTIC: *83* **1–3**

JUNE & DONNIE
Singles: 7-Inch
CURTOM: *68* **2–4**

JUNIE (Walter Morrison)
Singles: 7-Inch
COLUMBIA: *81*. **1–3**
EASTBOUND: *74*. **2–4**
20TH CENTURY-FOX/
WESTBOUND: *75–76* **2–3**
LPs: 10/12-Inch 33rpm
20TH CENTURY-FOX/
WESTBOUND: *76* **5–8**
Also see FUNKADELIC
Also see OHIO PLAYERS

JUNIOR (Junior Giscombe)
Singles: 12-Inch 33/45rpm
LONDON: *84* **4–6**
MERCURY: *83*. **4–6**
Singles: 7-Inch
LONDON: *84* **1–3**
MERCURY: *82–83*. **1–3**
LPs: 10/12-Inch 33rpm
MERCURY: *82–83*. **5–8**

JU-PAR UNIVERSAL ORCHESTRA, The
Singles: 7-Inch
JU-PAR: *77*. **2–3**

JUPITER, Duke: see DUKE JUPITER

JUST US
Singles: 7-Inch
ATLANTIC: *71* **2–3**
COLPIX: *66* **2–4**
KAPP: *66–67*. **2–4**
MINUTEMAN: *66*. **3–5**

Price Range

EPIC (304; "Side Trips"):
67 .... **$30–40**
(With an "LN-24" for mono or "BN-26" for stereo issues.)
EPIC (333; "A Beacon
From Mars"): 67 .... **30–40**
(With an "LN-24" for mono or "BN-26" for stereo issues.)
EPIC (26467; "Incredible
Kaleidoscope"): 69 .... **15–20**
EPIC (26508; "Bernice"):
70 .... **15–20**
PACIFIC ARTS: 78 .... **5–8**

KALIN TWINS, The
Singles: 7-Inch
DECCA: 58–62 .... **4–6**
Picture Sleeves
DECCA: 59 .... **5–8**
LPs: 10/12-Inch 33rpm
DECCA: 58 .... **20–25**
VOCALION: 66 .... **10–15**
Members: Hal Kalin; Herb Kalin.

KALLEN, Kitty
Singles: 7-Inch
BELL: 67 .... **2–3**
DECCA: 54–59 .... **2–4**
COLUMBIA (40000
series): 54 .... **3–5**
COLUMBIA (41000
series): 59–61 .... **2–4**
MGM: 65 .... **2–3**
MERCURY: 51–54 .... **3–5**
PHILIPS: 66 .... **2–3**
RCA VICTOR: 63 .... **2–4**
20TH-CENTURY-FOX: 64 .... **2–3**
UNITED ARTISTS: 65 .... **2–3**
EPs: 7-Inch 33/45rpm
DECCA: 54–56 .... **5–10**
COLUMBIA: 54 .... **5–10**
MERCURY: 55 .... **5–10**
LPs: 10/12-Inch 33rpm
COLUMBIA: 60–61 .... **10–20**
DECCA: 56 .... **15–25**
MCA: 83 .... **4–8**
MOVIETONE: 67 .... **8–12**
RCA VICTOR: 63 .... **10–15**
20TH-CENTURY-FOX: 64 .... **8–15**
VOCALION: 59 .... **10–15**
WING: 63 .... **8–15**

Price Range

Also see ANN-MARGRET / Kitty Kallen / Della Reese
Also see HAYES, Richard, & Kitty Kallen
Also see JAMES, Harry, & His Orchestra

KALLMANN, Gunter, Chorus
Singles: 7-Inch
4 CORNERS: 65–68 .... **$2–4**
LPs: 10/12-Inch 33rpm
4 CORNERS: 65–68 .... **6–12**
POLYDOR: 70 .... **5–10**

KALYAN
Singles: 7-Inch
MCA: 77 .... **2–3**
LPs: 10/12-Inch 33rpm
MCA: 77 .... **8–10**

KAMON, Karen
Singles: 7-Inch
COLUMBIA: 84 .... **1–3**

KAMIKAZE
Singles: 12-Inch 33/45rpm
A&M: 84 .... **4–6**
Singles: 7-Inch
A&M: 84 .... **1–3**

KANE, Madleen
Singles: 12-Inch 33/45rpm
CHALET: 82 .... **4–6**
TSR: 85 .... **4–6**
Singles: 7-Inch
CHALET: 82 .... **1–3**
WARNER BROS: 78–79 .... **1–3**
Picture Sleeves
WARNER BROS: 78–79 .... **1–3**
LPs: 10/12-Inch 33rpm
CHALET: 82 .... **5–8**
WARNER BROS: 78–79 .... **5–8**

KANE, Paul (Paul Simon)
Singles: 7-Inch
TRIBUTE: 63 .... **25–30**
(Copies on Tribute showing "Paul Simon" as the artist are bootleg issues.)
Also see SIMON, Paul

KANO
Singles: 7-Inch
EMERGENCY: 80 .... **1–3**
MIRAGE: 81 .... **1–3**

LPs: 10/12-Inch 33rpm
EMERGENCY: *81* **$5–8**
MIRAGE: *81* **5–8**

KANSAS
Singles: 7-Inch
CBS ASSOCIATED: *83* **1–3**
KIRSHNER: *74–82* **1–3**

LPs: 10/12-Inch 33rpm
BURNS MEDIA: *78* **15–20**
  (Promotional issue only.)
KIRSHNER ("Point Of
  Know Return" - picture
  disc): *79* **50–75**
  (Promotional issue only.)
KIRSHNER (555; "Two
  For The Show"): *78* **10–15**
  (Promotional issue only.)
KIRSHNER (30000 series):
  74–82 .... **8–10**
KIRSHNER (40000 series):
  81–82 .... **10–15**
  (Half-speed mastered LPs.)
  Also see STREETS, The

KANTNER, Paul, & Grace Slick
Singles: 7-Inch
GRUNT: *72* **3–5**

LPs: 10/12-Inch 33rpm
GRUNT (Except 4000
  series): *71–73* **8–10**
GRUNT (4000 series): *82* **5–8**
  Also see JEFFERSON AIRPLANE, The
  Also see SLICK, Grace

KANTNER, Paul, & The Jefferson Starship
Singles: 7-Inch
RCA VICTOR: *71* **2–4**
  Also see KANTNER, Paul
  Also see JEFFERSON STARSHIP, The

KAPLAN, Gabriel
Singles: 7-Inch
ABC: *74* **2–3**
ELEKTRA: *76–77* **1–3**

Picture Sleeves
ELEKTRA: *77* **1–3**

LPs: 10/12-Inch 33rpm
ABC: *74* **6–10**

KAREN, Kenny
Singles: 7-Inch
BIG TREE: *73* **$2–3**

KARI, Sax (Sax Kari & The Quailtones)
Singles: 7-Inch
CHECKER: *54* **8–10**
CONTOUR: *59* **4–6**
GREAT LAKES: *54* **10–12**
JOSIE: *55* **35–40**
STATES: *53* **10–12**

KARL, Frankie, & The Dreams
Singles: 7-Inch
D.C.: *68* **3–5**

KARMA
LPs: 10/12-Inch 33rpm
A&M: *77* **8–10**

KASANDRA (Kasandrea & The Midnight Riders)
Singles: 7-Inch
CAPITOL: *68* **3–5**
IMPERIAL: *60* **4–6**

LPs: 10/12-Inch 33rpm
CAPITOL: *68* **10–12**

KASENETZ-KATZ SINGING ORCHESTRAL CIRCUS, The (The Kasenetz-Katz Super Cirkus; The Kasenetz-Katz Fighter Squadron)
Singles: 7-Inch
BELL (966; "When He
  Comes"): *71* **5–8**
  (With 10CC.)
BUDDAH: *68* **3–5**
EPIC: *77* **2–3**
MAGNA-GLIDE: *75* **2–3**
SUPER K: *69–71* **2–4**

LPs: 10/12-Inch 33rpm
BUDDAH: *68* **10–12**
  Also see MUSIC EXPLOSION, The
  Also see 1910 FRUITGUM COMPANY, The
  Also see OHIO EXPRESS, The
  Also see 10CC

KASHIF
Singles: 12-Inch 33/45rpm
ARISTA: *83–85*. **$4–6**
Singles: 7-Inch
ARISTA: *83–85*. **1–3**
LPs: 10/12-Inch 33rpm
ARISTA: *83–85*. **5–8**

KATFISH
Singles: 7-Inch
BIG TREE: *75* **2–3**

KATRINA & THE WAVES
Singles: 7-Inch
CAPITOL: *85* **1–3**
LPs: 10/12-Inch 33rpm
CAPITOL: *85* **5–8**

KATZ, Mickey, & His Orchestra
Singles: 7-Inch
CAPITOL: *51–62* **3–5**
EPs: 7-Inch 33/45rpm
CAPITOL: *53–56* **5–10**
LPs: 10/12-Inch 33rpm
CAPITOL (Except
SM-298): *53–65* **10–20**
CAPITOL (SM-298): *78*. **5–8**
Also see JONES, Spike

KAUKONEN, Jorma (Jorna Kaukonen & Vital Parts)
Singles: 7-Inch
GRUNT: *73*. **2–3**
LPs: 10/12-Inch 33rpm
GRUNT: *73*. **8–10**
RCA VICTOR: *81* **5–8**
Also see HOT TUNA
Also see JEFFERSON AIRPLANE, The

KAY, John
Singles: 7-Inch
DUNHILL: *72–73*. **2–3**
MERCURY: *78*. **2–3**
LPs: 10/12-Inch 33rpm
COLUMBIA: *69* **10–12**
DUNHILL: *72–73*. **8–10**
MERCURY: *78*. **5–8**
Also see STEPPENWOLF

KAY GEES, The: see KAY-GEES, The

KAYAK
Singles: 7-Inch
JANUS: *78* **$2–3**
MERCURY: *80*. **1–3**
LPs: 10/12-Inch 33rpm
HARVEST: *74*. **8–10**
JANUS (Except picture
discs): *75–79*. **8–10**
JANUS ("Phantom Of The
Night"): *79*. **25–30**
(Picture disc. Promotional issue only.)
MERCURY: *80*. **5–8**
Also see WERNER, Max

KAYE, Danny
Singles: 7-Inch
DECCA: *50–56*. **3–5**
REPRISE: *62*. **2–4**
Picture Sleeves
REPRISE: *62*. **4–6**
EPs: 7-Inch 33/45rpm
DECCA: *50–56*. **8–15**
LPs: 10/12-Inch 33rpm
DECCA: *50–67*. **10–20**
(Decca LP numbers in this series preceded by
a "7" or a "DL-7" are stereo issues.)
GOLDEN: *62* **5–10**
HARMONY: *64* **5–10**

KAYE, Danny, & Louis Armstrong
Singles: 7-Inch
DOT: *59–64*. **2–4**
Picture Sleeves
DOT: *59*. **2–4**
Also see ARMSTRONG, Louis
Also see KAYE, Danny

KAYE, Mary (The Mary Kaye Trio)
Singles: 7-Inch
CAMELOT: *67*. **2–3**
CAPITOL: *52* **3–5**
DECCA: *55–56* **2–4**
LECTRON: *65* **2–3**
RCA VICTOR: *54* **2–4**
VERVE: *60* **2–4**
WARNER BROS: *59*. **2–4**
EPs: 7-Inch 33/45rpm
DECCA: *56*. **5–10**
LPs: 10/12-Inch 33rpm
COLUMBIA: *62* **5–15**
DECCA: *56*. **10–20**

Price Range

MOVIETONE: *67* **$8–12**
20TH CENTURY-FOX:
  64 . . . . **8–15**
VERVE: *60–62* **10–15**
WARNER BROS: *59* **10–20**
  Also see BYRNES, Edd "Kookie," With Joanie
  Sommers & The Mary Kaye Trio

KAYE, Sammy, & His Orchestra
Singles: 7-Inch
COLUMBIA: *50–60* **2–4**
DECCA: *60–70* **1–3**
PROJECT 3: *72* **1–3**
EPs: 7-Inch 33/45rpm
COLUMBIA: *50–60* **5–10**
DECCA: *64* **4–6**
RCA VICTOR: *52–53* **5–10**
LPs: 10/12-Inch 33rpm
CAMDEN: *53–56* **8–15**
COLUMBIA: *50–62* **10–15**
DECCA: *60–70* **8–15**
  (Decca LP numbers in this series preceded by
  a "7" or a "DL-7" are stereo issues.)
HARMONY: *59–68* **5–10**
MCA: *74* **5–10**
PROJECT 3: *72* **5–8**
RCA VICTOR: *68–72* **5–10**
VOCALION: *71* **5–10**

KAY-GEES, The
Singles: 7-Inch
DE-LITE: *78* **2–3**
GANG: *74–76* **2–3**
LPs: 10/12-Inch 33rpm
GANG: *75* **5–8**

KAYLI, Bob
Singles: 7-Inch
ANNA: *59* **15–20**
CARLTON: *58* **5–8**
GORDY: *62* **20–25**
TAMLA: *61* **15–20**

K-DOE, Ernie (Ernest Kador; Ernie Kado)
Singles: 7-Inch
DUKE: *64–69* **3–5**
EMBER: *59–61* **4–6**
INSTANT: *63–64* **3–5**
MINIT: *59–63* **4–6**
SPECIALTY: *55* **8–10**

Price Range

LPs: 10/12-Inch 33rpm
JANUS: *71* **$8–10**
MINIT: *61* **35–45**
  Also see BLUE DIAMONDS, The
  Also see SPELLMAN, Benny

KEANE BROTHERS, The
Singles: 12-Inch 33/45rpm
ABC: *79* **4–6**
Singles: 7-Inch
ABC: *79* **1–3**
20TH CENTURY-FOX:
  76 . . . . **2–3**
LPs: 10/12-Inch 33rpm
ABC: *79* **5–8**

KEEL
Singles: 7-Inch
GOLD MOUNTAIN:
  84–85 . . . . **1–3**
LPs: 10/12-Inch 33rpm
GOLD MOUNTAIN: *85* **5–8**

KEITH
Singles: 7-Inch
DISCREET: *71–74* **2–3**
MERCURY: *66–68* **3–5**
RCA VICTOR: *69* **2–4**
Picture Sleeves
MERCURY: *66–68* **3–5**
LPs: 10/12-Inch 33rpm
MERCURY: *67* **12–15**
RCA VICTOR: *69* **10–12**

KELLEM, Manny, & His Orchestra
Singles: 7-Inch
EPIC: *68* **1–3**
LPs: 10/12-Inch 33rpm
EPIC: *68* **5–10**

KELLER, Jerry
Singles: 7-Inch
CAPITOL: *61* **3–5**
CORAL: *63–64* **3–5**
KAPP (Except stereo
  singles): *59–60* **4–6**
KAPP (Stereo singles): *59* **8–10**
  (With a "KS" prefix.)
RCA VICTOR: *67* **3–5**
REPRISE: *65* **3–5**

Price Range

Picture Sleeves
KAPP: *59* $5–10
LPs: 10/12-Inch 33rpm
KAPP: *60* 20–25

KELLUM, Murry
Singles: 7-Inch
CINNAMON: *74* 2–3
EPIC: *71–72* 2–4
MUSIC MILL: *76*................. 2–3
PLANTATION: *78*................ 1–3
RANWOOD: *76*.................. 2–3
LPs: 10/12-Inch 33rpm
PLANTATION: *78*................ 5–8

KELLUM, Murry / Glenn Sutton
Singles: 7-Inch
ABC: *73*........................ 1–3
M.O.C. (Except 658):
63–64 3–5
M.O.C. (658; "I Dreamed I
Was A Beatle"): *64*.............. 8–10
Also see KELLUM, Murry
Also see SUTTON, Glenn

KELLY, Casey
Singles: 7-Inch
ELEKTRA: *72–73* 2–3
PRIVATE STOCK: *77*............. 2–3
LPs: 10/12-Inch 33rpm
ELEKTRA: *72* 8–10

**KELLY, Grace: see CROSBY, Bing,
& Grace Kelly**

KELLY, Herman, & Life
Singles: 7-Inch
ALSTON: *78*..................... 2–3

KELLY, J., & The Premiers
Singles: 7-Inch
ROADSHOW: *74*................. 2–3

KELLY, Monty, & His Orchestra
Singles: 7-Inch
CARLTON: *59–60* 2–4
LPs: 10/12-Inch 33rpm
ALSHIRE: *72*.................... 4–8
CARLTON: *59*.................. 10–20

Price Range

KELLY, Paul
Singles: 7-Inch
DIAL: *65–68*.................... $3–5
HAPPY TIGER: *70*............... 2–4
PHILIPS: *66–68* 3–5
WARNER BROS: *73–76*........... 2–3
LPs: 10/12-Inch 33rpm
HAPPY TIGER: *70*.............. 8–10
WARNER BROS: *72–76*.......... 8–10
Also see TEX, Joe

KELLY BROTHERS, The
Singles: 7-Inch
EXCELLO: *67–69*................. 3–5
SIMS: *65–67* 3–5
LPs: 10/12-Inch 33rpm
EXCELLO: *68*.................. 12–15

KENDALL, Jeannie (Jeanie Kendall)
Singles: 7-Inch
DOT: *72–73*..................... 2–4
Also see KENDALLS, The

KENDALL SISTERS, The
Singles: 7-Inch
ARGO: *57–58* 3–5

KENDALLS, The
Singles: 7-Inch
DOT: *72–73*..................... 2–4
MERCURY: *81–82*................ 1–3
OVATION: *77–80*................ 1–3
STOP: *70* 2–4
UNITED ARTISTS: *75–76*.......... 2–3
LPs: 10/12-Inch 33rpm
DOT: *72*....................... 8–12
GUSTO: *78* 5–8
MERCURY: *81–82*................ 5–8
OVATION: *77–80*............... 5–10
STOP: *70*..................... 10–15
POWER PAK: *74*................. 5–8
Members: Jeannie Kendall; Royce Kendall.
Also see KENDALL, Jeannie

KENDRICK, Nat, & The Swans
Singles: 7-Inch
DADE (1000 series): *59–60*.......... 4–6
DADE (5000 series): *63*............. 3–5

Price Range

KENDRICKS, Eddie
Singles: 7-Inch
ARISTA: *78–80*. **$1–3**
ATLANTIC: *80–81* **1–3**
CORNER STREET: *84* **1–3**
TAMLA: *71–77*. **2–3**
LPs: 10/12-Inch 33rpm
ARISTA: *78* **5–8**
ATLANTIC: *81* **5–8**
MOTOWN: *75–82*. **5–8**
MS. DIXIE: *83* **5–8**
TAMLA: *71–78*. **8–10**
Also see HALL, Daryl, & John Oates
Also see TEMPTATIONS, The

KENDRICKS, Linda
Singles: 12-Inch 33/45rpm
AIRWAVE: *84* **4–6**
Singles: 7-Inch
AIRWAVE: *84* **1–3**

KENNEDY, Edward M.
LPs: 10/12-Inch 33rpm
RCA VICTOR: *65* **8–15**

KENNEDY, Jacqueline
LPs: 10/12-Inch 33rpm
AUDIO FIDELITY (703;
"Jacqueline Kennedy"):
66 . . . . **8–15**
(LP contains Jackie's story as well as excerpts
of some of her speeches given as First Lady.)

KENNEDY, John Fitzgerald
LPs: 10/12-Inch 33rpm
CAEDMON: *64* **5–10**
CHALLENGE: *64* **8–15**
COLPIX: *64* **10–20**
COLUMBIA: *65*. **10–20**
DECCA: *63*. **10–20**
DIPLOMAT: *63* **5–15**
DOCUMENTARIES
UNLIMITED: *63* **10–20**
GATEWAY: *64*. **8–15**
HARMONIA: *64* **8–15**
LEGACY: *65*. **10–20**
PALACE: *64*. **8–15**
PHILIPS: *64* **8–15**
PICKWICK: *63* **8–12**
PREMIER: *63*. **10–20**
RCA VICTOR: *64* **8–15**

JOHN FITZGERALD KENNEDY
A Memorial Album

Price Range

REGINA: *64*. **$5–15**
SOMERSET: *63* **5–15**
20TH CENTURY-FOX:
63 . . . . **10–20**
Note: Most of the albums listed above were
released as a tribute of some type to President
Kennedy after his assassination on November
22, 1963. Most contain excerpts of his speeches.

KENNEDY, John Fitzgerald /
Richard M. Nixon
LPs: 10/12-Inch 33rpm
COLUMBIA: *68*. **10–15**
Also see KENNEDY, John Fitzgerald

KENNEDY, Joyce
Singles: 7-Inch
A&M: *84* **1–3**
LPs: 10/12-Inch 33rpm
A&M: *84* **5–8**
Also see MOTHER'S FINEST

KENNEDY, Joyce, & Jeffrey
Osborne
Singles: 7-Inch
A&M: *84* **1–3**
Also see KENNEDY, Joyce
Also see OSBORNE, Jeffrey

KENNEDY, Mike
Singles: 7-Inch
ABC: *72* **2–3**
LPs: 10/12-Inch 33rpm
ABC: *72* **8–10**
Also see LOS BRAVOS

Price Range

KENNEDY, Ray
Singles: 7-Inch
ARC: *80*........................ **$1–3**
LPs: 10/12-Inch 33rpm
CREAM: *72* **10–12**
Also see KGB

KENNEDY, Robert Francis
LPs: 10/12-Inch 33rpm
COLUMBIA: *68*................. **8–15**

KENNER, Chris
Singles: 7-Inch
BATON: *55*..................... **10–12**
IMPERIAL: *57–58*................ **5–8**
INSTANT: *61–64*.................. **3–5**
PRIGAN: *61*..................... **4–6**
UPTOWN: *65*..................... **3–5**
LPs: 10/12-Inch 33rpm
ATLANTIC: *66* **15–20**

KENNY, Bill (Bill Kenny & The Song Spinners)
Singles: 7-Inch
DECCA: *50–53*.................... **3–5**
MERCURY: *62*.................... **2–4**
TEL: *59* **2–4**
VIK: *56* **2–4**
WARWICK: *60*.................... **2–4**
X: *55*........................... **2–4**
LPs: 10/12-Inch 33rpm
DECCA (5000 series): *51*.......... **10–20**
(10-Inch LPs.)
MERCURY: *62*................. **10–15**
Also see INK SPOTS, The

KENNY & THE CADETS (The Beach Boys)
Singles: 7-Inch
RANDY (Black vinyl): *61*....... **225–250**
RANDY (Colored vinyl):
61 .... **325–350**
Also see BEACH BOYS, The

KENNY G. see G., Kenny

KENT, Al
Singles: 7-Inch
BARITONE: *60* **3–5**
RIC-TIC: *67* **3–5**
WIZARD: *59*..................... **4–6**

Price Range

KENTON, Stan, & His Orchestra
Singles: 7-Inch
CAPITOL: *50–68* **$2–4**
EPs: 7-Inch 33/45rpm
CAPITOL: *50–59* **5–15**
LPs: 10/12-Inch 33rpm
BRIGHT ORANGE: *73* **5–8**
CAPITOL (100 series): *75*........... **4–8**
(With an "SM" prefix.)
CAPITOL (100 through
500 series): *50–54* **25–50**
(10-Inch LPs.)
CAPITOL (300 series): *69*.......... **5–10**
CAPITOL (600 through
1200 series): *56–59* **15–25**
CAPITOL (1300 through
2900 series): *60–68* **10–20**
CAPITOL (11000 & 12000
series): *72–80*................... **5–8**
CAPITOL (16000 series):
81 .... **4–6**
CREATIVE WORLD:
71–80 .... **5–8**
HINDSIGHT: *84* **4–8**
LONDON: *72–77* **5–8**
MARK '56: *77*.................... **5–8**
Also see CHRISTY, June
Also see COLE, Nat "King"
Also see FERGUSON, Maynard
Also see RITTER, Tex

KERMIT (Jim Henson)
Singles: 7-Inch
ATLANTIC: *79* **1–3**
Also see HENSON, Jim

KERMIT / Fozzie Bear (Jim Henson)
Singles: 7-Inch
ATLANTIC: *80* **1–3**
Also see KERMIT
Also see HENSON, Jim

KERR, Anita (The Anita Kerr Singers; The Anita Kerr Quartette)
Singles: 7-Inch
AMPEX: *71*...................... **1–3**
DECCA: *51–72*................... **2–4**
DOT: *69–70*..................... **1–3**
RCA VICTOR: *63–75* **2–3**
WARNER BROS: *66–68*............ **2–3**

Price Range

KIDS NEXT DOOR, The
Singles: 7-Inch
4 CORNERS OF THE
  WORLD: *65* **$3–5**

KIHN, Greg, Band
Singles: 12-Inch 33/45rpm
BESERKLEY: *78–83* **4–6**
Singles: 7-Inch
BESERKLEY: *78–83* **1–3**
EMI AMERICA: *85*. **1–3**
Picture Sleeves
BESERKLEY: *81* .... **INC**
LPs: 10/12-Inch 33rpm
BESERKLEY: *76–83* **8–10**
EMI AMERICA: *85*. **5–8**

KILGORE, Theola
Singles: 7-Inch
KT: *64* **3–5**
SEROCK: *63* **3–5**

KIM, Andy
Singles: 7-Inch
ABC: *74* **1–3**
CAPITOL: *74–76* **2–3**
RED BIRD: *65* **4–6**
STEED: *68–71* **2–3**
TCF: *64* **3–5**
20TH CENTURY-FOX:
  68 .... **2–3**
UNI: *72–73* **2–3**
UNITED ARTISTS: *63* **3–5**
Picture Sleeves
CAPITOL: *74* **2–3**
STEED: *69*. **2–3**
LPs: 10/12-Inch 33rpm
CAPITOL: *74–75* **8–10**
DUNHILL: *74*. **8–10**
STEED: *68–71*. **10–12**
UNI: *72–73* **8–10**
Also see ARCHIES, The

KIMBERLY, Adrian
Singles: 7-Inch
CALLIOPE: *61* **2–4**

KIMBERLYS, The
Singles: 7-Inch
COLUMBIA: *65–66* **2–4**
HAPPY TIGER: *70–71* **2–3**

Price Range

RCA VICTOR: *69* **$2–3**
LPs: 10/12-Inch 33rpm
HAPPY TIGER: *70* **8–12**
Also see JENNINGS, Waylon

KIMBLE, Neal
Singles: 7-Inch
VENTURE: *68* **3–5**

KIME, Warren, & His Brass Impact Orchestra
LPs: 10/12-Inch 33rpm
COMMAND: *67*. **5–10**

KING (Paul King)
Singles: 12-Inch 33/45rpm
EPIC: *85* **4–6**
Singles: 7-Inch
EPIC: *85* **1–3**
LPs: 10/12-Inch 33rpm
ELEKTRA: *80–81* **5–8**
EPIC: *85* **5–8**

KING, Albert
Singles: 7-Inch
BOBBIN: *59–62*. **4–6**
COUN-TREE: *65* **3–5**
KING: *61–63*. **3–5**
PARROT: *53*. **40–50**
STAX: *66–74*. **3–5**
TOMATO: *78–79* **2–3**
UTOPIA: *76–77* **2–3**
LPs: 10/12-Inch 33rpm
ATLANTIC: *69–82* **8–10**
KING (800 series): *63* **35–45**
KING (1000 series): *69* **10–12**
STAX (Except 700 & 2000
  series): *72–81* **8–10**
STAX (700 series): *67*. **12–15**
STAX (2000 series): *68–71*. **10–12**
TOMATO: *77–79* **5–8**
UTOPIA: *76–77* **8–10**
  Also see LITTLE MILTON & ALBERT
  KING

KING, Albert, & Otis Rush
LPs: 10/12-Inch 33rpm
CHESS: *69*. **10–12**
  Also see KING, Albert
  Also see RUSH, Otis

Price Range

KING, Bobby (Featuring Alfie Silas)
Singles: 7-Inch
MOTOWN: *84*.................. **$1–3**
   Also see SILAS, Alfie

KING, Carole
Singles: 7-Inch
ABC: *74*.......................... **1–3**
ABC-PARAMOUNT:
   58–59 .... **25–30**
ALPINE: *60* **35–40**
ATLANTIC: *82–83* **1–3**
AVATAR: *77–78* **2–3**
CAPITOL: *77–80* **1–3**
COMPANION: *62* **20–25**
DIMENSION (Except
   2000): *62–63*................ **8–10**
DIMENSION (2000; "It
   Might As Well Rain
   Until September"): *62*............ **4–6**
ODE: *71–76*...................... **2–3**
RCA VICTOR: *59* **20–25**
TOMORROW: *66*................. **8–10**

Picture Sleeves
AVATAR: *77* **2–3**
CAPITOL: *80* **1–3**
ODE: *71–75*...................... **2–3**

LPs: 10/12-Inch 33rpm
ATLANTIC: *82–83* **5–8**
CAPITOL (Except 11000
   series): *80*...................... **5–8**
CAPITOL (11000 series):
   77–79 .... **8–10**
EMUS: *79* **5–8**
EPIC/ODE (30000 series):
   78–80 .... **5–8**
EPIC/ODE (40000 series):
   80 .... **12–15**
   (Half-speed mastered LPs.)
ODE: *70–77*.................... **10–12**

KING, Carole / Little Eva / The Cookies
LPs: 10/12-Inch 33rpm
DIMENSION: *63* **40–50**
   Also see COOKIES, The
   Also see KING, Carole
   Also see LITTLE EVA

Price Range

KING, Claude
Singles: 7-Inch
CINNAMON: *74* **$2–3**
COLUMBIA: *61–71* **2–4**
TRUE: *77–80*..................... **1–3**
Picture Sleeves
COLUMBIA: *61–69* **2–4**
LPs: 10/12-Inch 33rpm
COLUMBIA: *62–70* **10–15**
GUSTO: *80* **5–8**
HARMONY: *68* **8–12**
TRUE: *77* **8–10**
   Also see YOUNG, Faron / Carl Perkins /
   Claude King

KING, Earl
Singles: 7-Inch
ACE: *56–57*.................... **10–12**
IMPERIAL: *60–62*................ **3–5**
KING: *55* **5–8**
REX: *61*........................ **3–5**
SPECIALTY: *54–55*............. **12–15**
   Also see SMITH, Huey

KING, Evelyn "Champagne"
Singles: 12-Inch 33/45rpm
PRIVATE I: *85*................... **4–6**
RCA VICTOR: *78–85* **4–6**
Singles: 7-Inch
RCA VICTOR: *78–85* **1–3**
Picture Sleeves
RCA VICTOR: *78–85* **1–3**
LPs: 10/12-Inch 33rpm
RCA VICTOR: *77–85* **5–8**

KING, Freddie (Freddy King; Freddie King & Lulu Reed)
Singles: 7-Inch
COTILLION: *68–70*................ **2–3**
EL-BEE: *56*.................... **50–60**
FEDERAL: *60–65* **3–5**
GUSTO: *78* **1–3**
KING: *69* **2–3**
LPs: 10/12-Inch 33rpm
COTILLION: *69–70*............. **10–15**
FEDERAL: *62* **20–25**
KING (700 series): *61* **35–40**
KING (800 series): *62–63* **20–25**
KING (900 series): *65–66* **15–20**
KING (1000 series): *69* **12–15**
MCA............................ **5–8**

Price Range

RSO: *74–77* **$8–10**
SHELTER: *71–75* **8–10**
   Also see ROGERS, Jimmy, & Freddie King

KING, Freddie / Lulu (Reed) / Sonny Thompson
LPs: 10/12-Inch 33rpm
KING: *62* **25–30**
   Also see KING, Freddie
   Also see THOMPSON, Sonny

KING, Johnny
Singles: 7-Inch
DOT: *58* **4–6**
GUY: *61* **3–5**
MONTICELLO: *59* **4–6**
TIARA: *59* **4–6**

KING, Jonathan
Singles: 7-Inch
PARROT: *65–72* **3–5**
UK: *73–74* **2–3**
UK/BIG TREE: *75* **2–3**
LPs: 10/12-Inch 33rpm
PARROT: *67* **25–30**
UK: *72–73* **10–12**
   Also see HEDGEHOPPERS ANONYMOUS

KING, Marcel
Singles: 12-Inch 33/45rpm
A&M: *84* **4–6**
Singles: 7-Inch
A&M: *84* **1–3**

KING, Morgana
Singles: 7-Inch
MAINSTREAM: *64* **2–4**
MERCURY: *56* **2–4**
PARAMOUNT: *73–74* **2–3**
REPRISE: *66–67* **2–3**
20TH CENTURY-FOX:
  59 .... **2–4**
VERVE: *68* **2–3**
WING: *56* **2–4**
Picture Sleeves
PARAMOUNT: *73* **2–3**
LPs: 10/12-Inch 33rpm
ASCOT: *65–66* **10–20**
CAMDEN: *60* **10–20**
EMARCY: *56* **20–30**

Price Range

MAINSTREAM (300
  series): *72* **$5–10**
MAINSTREAM (6000
  series): *64–65* **10–20**
MUSE: *79–82* **5–8**
PARAMOUNT: *73* **5–10**
REPRISE: *65–67* **10–20**
TRIP: *74* **5–8**
UNITED ARTISTS: *59* **15–25**
VERVE: *68* **8–15**
WING: *65* **10–15**

KING, Pee Wee (Pee Wee King With Redd Stewart; Pee Wee King & The New Golden West Cowboys)
Singles: 7-Inch
BRIAR: *61* **2–4**
JARO: *60* **2–4**
CUCA: *64–66* **2–4**
LANDA: *61* **2–4**
RCA VICTOR: *50–55* **3–5**
STARDAY: *64–71* **2–4**
TODD: *59* **2–4**
LPs: 10/12-Inch 33rpm
BRIAR: *62* **40–50**
CAMDEN: *65–71* **8–15**
CAPITOL: *66* **12–18**
NASHVILLE **8–12**
RCA VICTOR: *77* **5–8**
STARDAY (200 series): *64* **12–15**
STARDAY (900 series): *75* **8–10**

KING, Peggy
Singles: 7-Inch
BUENA VISTA: *62* **2–3**
BULLET: *71* **1–3**
COLUMBIA: *54–56* **2–4**
MGM: *52* **2–4**
ROULETTE: *61* **2–4**
EPs: 7-Inch 33/45rpm
COLUMBIA: *55* **5–10**
LPs: 10/12-Inch 33rpm
COLUMBIA: *55* **10–20**
IMPERIAL: *59* **10–15**
   Also see VALE, Jerry, Peggy King & Felicia Sanders

KING, Rev. Martin Luther, Jr.
Singles: 7-Inch
DOOTO: *68* **2–3**
GORDY: *68* **2–3**

Price Range

MERCURY: 68. . . . . $2–3
LPs: 10/12-Inch 33rpm
BUDDAH: 69. 8–15
CREED: 69–71 8–12
DOTTO: 62–68 8–15
EXCELLO: 68. 8–15
GORDY: 63–68. 8–15
MERCURY: 68. 8–15
MR. MAESTRO: 63. 10–15
NASHBORO: 72. 5–8
20TH CENTURY-FOX:
  63–68 8–15
UNART: 68. 8–12
  Note: The above recordings contain speeches or
  excerpts of speeches by King.
  Also see LANDS, Liz / Martin Luther King

KING, Sleepy: see SLEEPY KING

KING, Willard (Will King)
Singles: 7-Inch
CAPITOL: 73 2–3
TOTAL EXPERIENCE:
  85 1–3

KING BISCUIT BOY (King Biscuit Boy With Crowbar)
Singles: 7-Inch
EPIC: 75 2–3
PARAMOUNT: 70–73. 2–4
LPs: 10/12-Inch 33rpm
EPIC: 74 8–10
PARAMOUNT: 70–73. 10–15

KING COLE TRIO, The: see COLE, Nat "King"

KING CRIMSON
Singles: 12-Inch 33/45rpm
WARNER BROS: 84. 4–6
Singles: 7-Inch
ATLANTIC: 70–74 2–3
WARNER BROS: 81–84. 1–3
LPs: 10/12-Inch 33rpm
ATLANTIC (Except 18000
  & 19000 series): 69–74 10–15
ATLANTIC (18000 &
  19000 series): 74–75 8–10
WARNER BROS: 81–82. 5–8
WIZARDO 10–12
WORLD RECORD CLUB. 12–15

Price Range

Members: Greg Lake; Robert Fripp; Boz Burrell.
Also see BAD COMPANY
Also see FRIPP, Robert
Also see LAKE, Greg

KING CURTIS (King Curtis & The Kingpins; King Curtis & The Nobel Knights)
Singles: 7-Inch
ABC-PARAMOUNT: 60. . . . . $3–5
ALCOR: 62. 3–5
ATCO: 59–71. 3–5
CAPITOL: 62–65 3–5
ENJOY: 62 3–5
EVEREST: 61 3–5
GEM: 54 20–25
KING: 62 3–5
MONARCH: 53 25–30
NEW JAZZ: 61. 3–5
TRU-SOUND: 61–63 3–5

EPs: 7-Inch 33/45rpm
ATCO: 68 3–5
  (Jukebox issues only.)
CAPITOL: 63 10–12

LPs: 10/12-Inch 33rpm
ATCO (113; "Have Tenor
  Sax, Will Blow"): 59. 25–30
ATCO (189 through 385):
  66–72 10–15
CAMDEN: 68. 10–12
CAPITOL (2000 series):
  64–68 12–15
CAPITOL (11000 series):
  78–79 5–8
CLARION. 8–10
ENJOY: 62 25–30
EVEREST: 61 20–25
MOUNT VERNON 10–12
NEW JAZZ: 60. 20–25
PRESTIGE (7200 series):
  62 15–20
PRESTIGE (7700 series):
  69–70 8–12
TRU-SOUND: 62. 15–20
  Also see COASTERS, The
  Also see JENNINGS, Waylon
  Also see KING PINS, The
  Also see SHARPE, Ray
  Also see SHIRELLES, The, & King Curtis

KING FAMILY, The
Singles: 7-Inch
WARNER BROS: *65* $2–3
LPs: 10/12-Inch 33rpm
CAPITOL: *65* 5–15
WARNER BROS: *65* 5–15

KING FLOYD
Singles: 7-Inch
CHIMNEYVILLE: *70–75* 2–4
ORIGINAL SOUND: *64* 3–5
UPTOWN: *66* 3–5
LPs: 10/12-Inch 33rpm
ATCO: *73* 8–10
CHIMNEYVILLE 8–10
PULSAR: *69* 10–12

KING HANNIBAL
Singles: 7-Inch
AWARE: *73* 2–3
LPs: 10/12-Inch 33rpm
AWARE: *73* 8–10

KING HARVEST
Singles: 7-Inch
A&M: *75–76* 2–3
PERCEPTION: *72–73* 2–3
LPs: 10/12-Inch 33rpm
A&M: *75* 10–12
PERCEPTION: *73* 8–10

KING LIZARD (Kim Fowley)
Singles: 7-Inch
ORIGINAL SOUND: *75* 2–3
Also see FOWLEY, Kim

KING PINS, The
Singles: 7-Inch
ATCO: *67* 3–5
FEDERAL: *63–64* 3–5
MGM: *66* 3–5
VEE JAY: *63* 3–5
LPs: 10/12-Inch 33rpm
KING: *63* 20–25
Also see KING CURTIS
Also see LEE, T.C., & The King Pins

KING PLEASURE: see PLEASURE, King

KING RICHARD'S FLUEGEL KNIGHTS
Singles: 7-Inch
MTA: *66–68* $2–3
LPs: 10/12-Inch 33rpm
MTA: *67–70* 5–10

KINGBEES, The
Singles: 7-Inch
RSO: *80–81* 1–3
Picture Sleeves
RSO: *80–81* .... INC
LPs: 10/12-Inch 33rpm
RSO: *80–81* 5–8
Members: Jamie; Michael; Rex.

KINGFISH (With Bob Weir)
Singles: 7-Inch
JET: *78* 2–3
ROUND: *76* 2–3
LPs: 10/12-Inch 33rpm
JET: *78* 5–8
ROUND: *76* 8–10
TOWNHOUSE: *81* 5–8
UNITED ARTISTS: *77* 8–10
Also see WEIR, Bob

KINGS, The
Singles: 7-Inch
ELEKTRA: *80* 1–3
LPs: 10/12-Inch 33rpm
ELEKTRA: *80* 5–8

KINGSMEN, The
Singles: 7-Inch
EAST WEST: *58* 5–8
Also see HALEY, Bill

KINGSMEN, The (With Jack Ely & Lynn Easton)
Singles: 7-Inch
CAPITOL: *72* 2–4
EARTH: *69* 3–5
ERIC 1–3
JALYNNE: *61* 10–12
JERDEN: *63* 15–25
WAND (Except 1107 & 1115): *63–68* 5–8
WAND (1107; "It's Only The Dog"): *65* 8–10

WAND (1115; "Killer
Joe"): 65 .... **$8–10**
LPs: 10/12-Inch 33rpm
ARISTA: *81* **8–10**
HEAVY WEIGHT: *67*............ **20–25**
RHINO **5–8**
SCEPTER/CITATION: *72*......... **8–12**
WAND (657; "The
Kingsmen In Person"):
64 .... **30–35**
WAND (659; "The
Kingsmen, Vol. 2"): *64*.......... **35–45**
(Without "Death Of An Angel.")
WAND (659; "The
Kingsmen, Vol. 2"): *64*.......... **25–35**
(With "Death Of An Angel.")
WAND (662; "The
Kingsmen, Vol. 3"): *65*.......... **25–30**
WAND (670 through 681):
65–67 .... **20–25**
Also see DON & THE GOODTIMES

KINGSTON TRIO, The
Singles: 7-Inch
CAPITOL: *58–64* **4–6**
DECCA: *64–66*................... **3–5**
Picture Sleeves
CAPITOL: *60–62* **4–6**
DECCA: *66–66*................... **3–5**
EPs: 7-Inch 33/45rpm
CAPITOL: *58–61* **8–15**
LPs: 10/12-Inch 33rpm
CAPITOL (500 series): *70*.......... **8–15**
CAPITOL (900 through
1500 series): *58–61* **20–25**
CAPITOL (1600 through
2200 series, except 2180):
61–65 .... **15–20**
CAPITOL (2180; "The
Folk Era"): *64*................ **15–35**
(3-LP set with bound-in booklet.)
CAPITOL (11000 series):
79 .... **5–8**
CAPITOL (16000 series):
81 .... **4–6**
DECCA: *64–65*................. **15–20**
INTERMEDIA: *85*................ **5–8**
NAUTILUS: *79*.................. **5–8**
TETRAGRAMMATON:
69 .... **10–15**
XERES: *82* **5–8**

Members: John Stewart; Dave Guard; Nick
Reynolds; Bob Shane.
Also see BEATLES, The / The Beach Boys /
The Kingston Trio
Also see GUARD, Dave, & The Whiskeyhill
Singers
Also see NEW KINGSTON TRIO, The
Also see STEWART, John
Also see STEWART, John, & Nick Reynolds

KINKS, The (Featuring Ray Davies)
Singles: 7-Inch
ARISTA: *77–85*.................. **$1–3**
CAMEO (308; "Long Tall
Sally"): *64* **50–60**
CAMEO (345; "Long Tall
Sally"): *65* **35–40**
CAMEO (348; "You Still
Want Me"): *65*................. **75–90**
ERIC **1–3**
RCA VICTOR: *72–76* **3–5**
REPRISE (0306 through
0647): *65–67*................. **5–8**
REPRISE (0691 through
0847): *68–69*.................. **10–12**
REPRISE (0930 through
1017): *70–71*................... **3–5**

Promotional Singles
REPRISE (0306 through
0647): *65–67*................. **10–12**
REPRISE (0691 through
0847): *68–69*................. **10–15**
REPRISE (0930 through
1017): *70–71*................... **4–8**

Price Range

Price Range

EPs: 7-Inch 33/45rpm

ARISTA (22; "The Kinks
Misfit Record"): *78* **$20–25**
(Promotional issue only.)
CAMEO: *78* **4–6**

Picture Sleeves

ARISTA: *80* **1–3**

LPs: 10/12-Inch 33rpm

ARISTA: *77–84* **5–8**
COMPLEAT **5–8**
MFSL: *81* **12–15**
PICKWICK: *72* **6–10**
PYE: *75–76* **8–10**
RCA VICTOR (Except
AYL1 series): *71–76* **10–15**
RCA VICTOR (AYL1
series): *80–82* **5–8**
REPRISE (2127; "The
Great Lost Kinks
Album"): *73* **20–30**
REPRISE (R-6143; "You
Really Got Me"): *64* **40–50**
REPRISE (RS-6143; "You
Really Got Me"): *64* **20–30**
REPRISE (R-6158; "Kinks
Size"): *65* **40–50**
REPRISE (RS-6158;
"Kinks Size"): *65* **20–30**
REPRISE (R-6173; "Kinda
Kinks"): *65* **40–50**
REPRISE (RS-6173;
"Kinda Kinks"): *65* **20–30**
REPRISE (R-6184; "Kinks
Kingdom"): *65* **40–50**
REPRISE (RS-6184;
"Kinks Kingdom"): *65* **20–30**
REPRISE (R-6197; "The
Kink Kontroversy"): *66* **40–50**
REPRISE (RS-6197; "The
Kink Kontroversy"): *66* **20–30**
REPRISE (R-6217; "The
Kink's Greatest Hits"):
66 . . . . **40–50**
REPRISE (RS-6217; "The
Kink's Greatest Hits"):
66 . . . . **20–30**
(Reprise 6143 through 6217 require separate
pricing for mono, indicated with an "R" prefix,
and for stereo, shown by an "RS".)
REPRISE (6228; "Face To
Face"): *66* **20–30**

REPRISE (6260; "The
Live Kinks"): *67* **$20–30**
REPRISE (6279;
"Something Else"): *67* **20–30**
REPRISE (6327; "Village
Green Preservation
Society"): *69* **25–35**
REPRISE (6366;
"Arthur"): *69* **15–20**
(Price includes lyrics insert.)
REPRISE (6423; "Lola Vs.
The Powerman"): *69* **12–15**
(Blue & white cover.)
REPRISE (6423; "Lola Vs.
The Powerman"): *69* **6–10**
(Black, blue & white cover.)
REPRISE (6454; "The
Kink Kronikles"): *69* **8–12**
(Original Reprise Kinks LPs from the sixties
were on a multi-colored label. All 11 of these
LPs have been repressed on the brown Reprise
label.)

Promotional LPs

ARISTA (Except 69):
77–84 . . . . **10–15**
ARISTA (69; "Low Budget
Radio Interview"): *79* **40–50**
REPRISE (2127; "The
Great Lost Kinks
Album"): *73* **50–75**
REPRISE (6000 series -
mono issues): *64–68* **50–60**
REPRISE (6000 series -
stereo issues): *64–72* **30–40**
WARNER BROS. (328;
"Then Now &
In-Between"): *69* **60–75**
(For the LP only.)
WARNER BROS. (328;
Complete "Kinks Kit"):
69 . . . . **275–300**
(Boxed set, includes "Then Now & In-
Between" LP as well as other promotional
materials.)
Also see DAVIES, Dave

KINKS, The / The Hollywood Stars
Singles: 7-Inch

ARISTA (5;
"Sleepwalker"): *77* **8–10**
Also see HOLLYWOOD STARS, The
Also see KINKS, The

Price Range   *Price Range*

KINNEY, Fern
Singles: 7-Inch
ATLANTIC: 68 .... **$3–5**
MALACO: 79–80 .... **1–3**

KINSMAN DAZZ
Singles: 7-Inch
20TH CENTURY-FOX:
78–79 .... **2–3**
LPs: 10/12-Inch 33rpm
20TH CENTURY-FOX:
79 .... **5–8**
Also see DAZZ BAND

KIRBY, Kathy
Singles: 7-Inch
ASCOT: 67 .... **2–4**
LONDON: 62–65 .... **3–5**
PARROT: 65–66.................. **3–5**

KIRK, Jim, & The TM Singers
Singles: 7-Inch
CAPITOL: 80 .... **2–3**

KIRKLAND, Bo
Singles: 7-Inch
CLARIDGE: 75 .... **2–3**

KIRKLAND, Bo, & Ruth Davis
Singles: 7-Inch
CLARIDGE: 75–78 .... **2–3**
Also see DAVIS, Ruth
Also see KIRKLAND, Bo

KIRTON, Lew
Singles: 7-Inch
MARLIN: 77..................... **2–3**

KISS
Singles: 12-Inch 33/45rpm
MERCURY: 85.................... **4–6**
Singles: 7-Inch
CASABLANCA: 74–82 .... **1–3**
MERCURY: 83–85................. **1–3**
Picture Sleeves
CASABLANCA: 75–78 .... **1–3**
LPs: 10/12-Inch 33rpm
CASABLANCA (Except
7032): 74–82 .... **6–10**
CASABLANCA (7032;
"The Originals"): 76 .... **15–20**

MERCURY: 83–85................ **$5–8**
Promotional LPs
CASABLANCA (76; "Kiss
Tour Album"): 76 .... **15–20**
CASABLANCA (20137;
"Criss-Frehley-Simmons-
Stanley"): 78.................. **12–15**
Members: Gene Simmons; Ace Frehley; Paul
Stanley; Peter Criss; Bruce Kulick; Eric Carr.
Also see CRISS, Peter
Also see FREHLEY, Ace
Also see SIMMONS, Gene
Also see STANLEY, Paul

KISSING THE PINK
Singles: 7-Inch
ATLANTIC: 83 .... **1–3**
LPs: 10/12-Inch 33rpm
ATLANTIC: 83 .... **5–8**

KISSOON, Katie
Singles: 12-Inch 33/45rpm
JIVE: 84........................ **4–6**

KISSOON, Mac & Katie
Singles: 7-Inch
ABC: 71........................ **2–4**
BELL: 72....................... **2–3**
MCA/STATE: 75–76.............. **2–3**
Also see KISSOON, Katie
Also see WATERS, Roger

KITT, Eartha
Singles: 12-Inch 33/45rpm
STREETWISE: 83 .... **4–6**
Singles: 7-Inch
DECCA: 65...................... **2–4**
KAPP: 59–66.................... **2–4**
RCA VICTOR: 53–57 .... **2–4**
STREETWISE: 83 .... **1–3**
Picture Sleeves
RCA VICTOR: 54–55 .... **3–5**
EPs: 7-Inch 33/45rpm
RCA VICTOR: 53–57 .... **5–10**
LPs: 10/12-Inch 33rpm
CAEDMON: 69 .... **5–10**
DECCA: 65...................... **10–15**
GNP/CRESCENDO: 65 .... **10–15**
KAPP: 59–60.................... **10–20**
MGM: 62 .... **10–20**
PHILIPS: 68 .... **8–15**
RCA VICTOR: 53–57 .... **15–25**

Price Range

LPs: 10/12-Inch 33rpm
BRUT: 73 .... $8–12

KLEIN & MBO
Singles: 12-Inch 33/45rpm
ATLANTIC: 83 4–6
Singles: 7-Inch
ATLANTIC: 83 1–3

KLEMMER, John
Singles: 7-Inch
ABC: 76 1–3
LPs: 10/12-Inch 33rpm
ABC: 75–79 5–10
CADET CONCEPT: 69 8–12
CHESS: 76 8–12
ELEKTRA: 80–83 5–8
MCA: 79–82 5–10
NAUTILUS: 80–81 5–8
NOVUS: 79 5–8
Also see HARRIS, Eddie, & John Klemmer

KLINT, Pete, Quintet
Singles: 7-Inch
MERCURY: 67 2–3

KLIQUE
Singles: 12-Inch 33/45rpm
MCA: 81–85 4–6
Singles: 7-Inch
MCA: 81–85 1–3
LPs: 10/12-Inch 33rpm
MCA: 81–85 5–8

KLOCKWISE
Singles: 7-Inch
SINBAN: 84–85 1–3

KLOWNS, The
Singles: 7-Inch
RCA VICTOR: 70 2–3
LPs: 10/12-Inch 33rpm
RCA VICTOR: 70 8–10

KLUGH, Earl
Singles: 7-Inch
BLUE NOTE: 76–77 1–3
CAPITOL: 83–84 1–3
LIBERTY: 81 1–3
UNITED ARTISTS: 78–80 1–3

Price Range
STANYAN: 72 .... $5–10

KITTY & THE HAYWOODS
Singles: 7-Inch
MERCURY: 77 2–3
LPs: 10/12-Inch 33rpm
MERCURY: 77 8–10

KIX
Singles: 7-Inch
ATLANTIC: 81–83 1–3
LPs: 10/12-Inch 33rpm
ATLANTIC: 81–83 5–8

KLAATU
Singles: 7-Inch
CAPITOL: 77–80 1–3
ISLAND: 75 2–3
Picture Sleeves
CAPITOL: 77 .... INC
LPs: 10/12-Inch 33rpm
CAPITOL: 76–80 5–8

KLEEER
Singles: 7-Inch
ATLANTIC: 79–85 1–3
LPs: 10/12-Inch 33rpm
ATLANTIC: 79–85 5–8

KLEIN, Robert
Singles: 7-Inch
BRUT: 73 3–5
CASABLANCA: 79 2–3

Price Range

LPs: 10/12-Inch 33rpm
BLUE NOTE: 76–77 .... $5–10
CAPITOL: 83–84 5–8
LIBERTY: 80–81 5–8
UNITED ARTISTS: 78–80 5–10
WARNER BROS: 85 5–8
Also see JAMES, Bob, & Earl Klugh
Also see LAWS, Hubert, & Earl Klugh

KLYMAXX
Singles: 12-Inch 33/45rpm
CONSTELLATION: 84–85 4–6
MCA: 84 4–6
Singles: 7-Inch
CONSTELLATION: 84–85 1–3
SOLAR: 81–83 1–3
LPs: 10/12-Inch 33rpm
CONSTELLATION: 85 5–8
SOLAR: 81–83 5–8

KNACK, The
Singles: 7-Inch
CAPITOL (4000 series):
79–81 2–4
Picture Sleeves
CAPITOL: 79–81 2–4
LPs: 10/12-Inch 33rpm
CAPITOL: 79–81 8–10
Also see SKY

**KNICKERBOCKERS, The
(Featuring Buddy Randall)**
Singles: 7-Inch
CHALLENGE: 65–67 4–6
ERIC 1–3
LPs: 10/12-Inch 33rpm
CHALLENGE (Except
622): 65 25–30
CHALLENGE (622;
"Lies"): 66 30–40

KNIGHT, Frederick
Singles: 7-Inch
JUANA: 81 1–3
MAXINE: 69 2–4
STAX: 72 2–3
TRUTH: 75 2–3
LPs: 10/12-Inch 33rpm
STAX: 73 8–10

Price Range

**KNIGHT, Gladys (Gladys Knight &
The Pips)**
Singles: 12-Inch 33/45rpm
COLUMBIA: 79–85 .... $4–6

Singles: 7-Inch
ABC: 73 1–3
BUDDAH: 73–79 2–3
COLUMBIA: 79–85 1–3
ENJOY: 64 3–5
ERIC: 78 1–3
FLASHBACK: 67 1–3
FURY: 61–63 4–6
MAXX: 64–65 3–5
SOUL (Except 35023 &
35033): 67–74 2–3
SOUL (35023 & 35033): 66 3–5
VEE JAY: 61–63 4–6

Picture Sleeves
BUDDAH: 73–75 2–3
COLUMBIA: 81 1–3

LPs: 10/12-Inch 33rpm
ACCORD: 81–82 5–8
ALLEGIANCE: 84 5–8
BELL: 68–75 10–12
BUDDAH: 73–78 8–10
COLUMBIA: 79–85 5–8
51 WEST 5–8
FURY: 62 40–50
LOST-NITE: 81 5–8
MAXX 10–15
MCP: 76 8–10
MOTOWN (Except 792):
80–82 5–8
MOTOWN (792;
"Anthology"): 74 8–10
NATURAL RESOURCES:
78 5–8
PICKWICK: 73 8–10
SOUL: 67–75 10–15
SPHERE SOUND: 65 15–18
SPRINGBOARD: 75 8–10
TRIP: 73 8–10
UNITED ARTISTS: 75 10–12
UPFRONT 10–12
VEE JAY: 75 10–12
Also see DIONNE & FRIENDS
Also see GAYE, Marvin / Gladys Knight &
The Pips
Also see PIPS, The

Price Range *Price Range*

KNIGHT, Gladys, & Johnny Mathis
Singles: 7-Inch
COLUMBIA: *80* **$1–3**
Also see KNIGHT, Gladys
Also see MATHIS, Johnny

KNIGHT, Jean (Jean Knight & Premium)
Singles: 7-Inch
CHELSEA: *75* **2–3**
COTILLION: *81* **1–3**
DIAL: *74* **2–4**
MIRAGE: *85* **5–8**
STAX: *71–73* **2–4**
TRIBE: *65* **3–5**
LPs: 10/12-Inch 33rpm
STAX: *71* **10–12**

KNIGHT, Jerry
Singles: 7-Inch
A&M: *80–83* **1–3**
Picture Sleeves
A&M: *80* . . . . **INC**
LPs: 10/12-Inch 33rpm
A&M: *80–81* **5–8**
Also see OLLIE & JERRY
Also see RAYDIO

KNIGHT, Marie
Singles: 7-Inch
DIAMOND: *63* **3–5**
MERCURY: *56* **8–10**
MUSICOR: *65–66* **3–5**
OKEH: *61–65* **3–5**
WING: *56* **6–10**
Picture Sleeves
OKEH: *61* **3–5**
LPs: 10/12-Inch 33rpm
CARLTON: *60* **20–25**
Also see MARIE & REX

KNIGHT, Robert
Singles: 7-Inch
DOT: *61* **4–6**
ELF: *68–69* **3–5**
MONUMENT: *74* **2–4**
RISING SONS: *67–68* **3–5**
LPs: 10/12-Inch 33rpm
MONUMENT: *67* **12–15**

KNIGHT, Sonny
Singles: 7-Inch
A&M: *63–64* **$3–5**
ALADDIN: *53* **10–15**
AURA: *64–65* **3–5**
DOT (Maroon label): *56* **5–8**
EASTMAN: *59* **4–6**
FIFO: *61* **3–5**
MERCURY: *62* **3–5**
SPECIALTY: *57* **5–8**
STARLA (Except 1):
58–59 . . . . **8–10**
STARLA (1; "Dedicated
To You"): *57* **10–12**
VITA: *56* **12–15**
WORLD PACIFIC
(Except 403): *66* **3–5**
WORLD PACIFIC (403;
"If You Want This
Love"): *64* **4–6**
(Reissued several months later on Aura 403.)
Picture Sleeves
AURA: *65* **3–5**
LPs: 10/12-Inch 33rpm
AURA: *64* **15–20**

KNIGHT, Terry (Terry Knight & The Pack)
Singles: 7-Inch
ABKCO: *75* **2–3**
CAMEO: *67* **3–5**
CAPITOL: *69* **3–5**
FRATERNITY: *67* **3–5**
LUCKY ELEVEN: *66–67* **4–6**
LPs: 10/12-Inch 33rpm
ABKCO: *72* **10–15**
CAMEO: *67* **25–30**
LUCKY ELEVEN: *66* **20–25**
Also see GRAND FUNK RAILROAD

KNIGHT BROTHERS, The
Singles: 7-Inch
CHECKER: *63–66* **3–5**
MERCURY: *67–68* **2–4**

KNIGHTSBRIDGE STRINGS, The
Singles: 7-Inch
MONUMENT: *66* **1–3**
TOP RANK: *59–60* **2–3**
LPs: 10/12-Inch 33rpm
MONUMENT: *66–69* **5–10**

Price Range

PURIST: *64*.................... $5–10
RIVERSIDE: *62–64* 5–12
TOP RANK: *59–60* 5–15
　Also see RANDOLPH, Boots

KNOBLOCK, Fred
Singles: 7-Inch
SCOTTI BROS: *80–82*............. 1–3
LPs: 10/12-Inch 33rpm
SCOTTI BROS: *80–82*............. 5–8

KNOBLOCK, Fred, & Susan Anton
Singles: 7-Inch
SCOTTI BROS: *80*................ 1–3
　Also see ANTON, Susan
　Also see KNOBLOCK, Fred

KNOCKOUTS, The
Singles: 7-Inch
MGM: *61*........................ 3–5
SHAD: *59–60*.................... 8–10
TRIBUTE: *64–65* 3–5
LPs: 10/12-Inch 33rpm
TRIBUTE: *64* 45–50

KNOX, Buddy (Buddy Knox & The Rhythm Orchids)
Singles: 7-Inch
ABC: *73*........................ 1–3
BLUE MOON: *57*.............. 125–150
LIBERTY: *60–64* 4–6
REPRISE: *65–66*................. 3–5
ROULETTE (4000 series):
　57 10–12
　(With the "roulette wheel" label.)
ROULETTE (4000 series):
　57–58 5–8
　(Orange label. No "roulette wheel.")
ROULETTE (4082 through
　4262): *58–60*.................. 4–6
RUFF: *65*....................... 3–5
UNITED ARTISTS: *68–71*.......... 2–4
Picture Sleeves
LIBERTY: *61* 6–10
EPs: 7-Inch 33/45rpm
ROULETTE: *57* 20–25
LPs: 10/12-Inch 33rpm
ACCORD: *82–83* 5–8
LIBERTY: *62* 20–25
ROULETTE: *57* 50–60
UNITED ARTISTS: *69*.......... 10–12

Price Range

KNOX, Buddy / Jimmy Bowen
Singles: 7-Inch
TRIPLE-D: *57*................. $75–100
LPs: 10/12-Inch 33rpm
MURRAY HILL 5–8
ROULETTE: *58* 50–60
　Also see BOWEN, Jimmy
　Also see KNOX, Buddy

KOFFMAN, Moe, (The Moe Koffman Quartette; The Moe Koffman Quintet; The Moe Koffman Septette)
Singles: 7-Inch
ABC: *73*........................ 1–3
ASCOT: *62* 2–3
ATCO: *65* 2–3
GOLD EAGLE: *61* 2–3
JUBILEE: *58–68*................. 2–4
PALETTE: *60–63*................. 2–4
VIRGO: *72* 1–3
LPs: 10/12-Inch 33rpm
ASCOT: *62* 10–15
JANUS: *78* 5–8
JUBILEE: *68*................... 8–12
UNITED ARTISTS: *62–63*....... 10–20

KOFFIE
Singles: 12-Inch 33/45rpm
PAN DISC: *83* 4–6

KOMIKO
Singles: 7-Inch
SAM: *82*........................ 1–3

KOKOMO (James Wisner)
Singles: 7-Inch
FELSTED: *61–62* 2–4
Picture Sleeves
FELSTED: *61* 3–5
LPs: 10/12-Inch 33rpm
FELSTED: *61* 15–20

KOKOMO
Singles: 7-Inch
COLUMBIA: *75–76*............... 2–3
LPs: 10/12-Inch 33rpm
COLUMBIA: *75–76* 8–10

Price Range   *Price Range*

KOTTKE, Leo
Singles: 7-Inch
CAPITOL: 75 . . . . $2–3
LPs: 10/12-Inch 33rpm
CAPITOL (Except 16000
series): 71–76 8–10
CAPITOL (16000 series):
71–76 5–8
CHRYSALIS: 76–81 5–8
OBLIVION 15–20
SYMPOSIUM: 70 10–12
TAKOMA: 71–74 8–12

KRAFTWERK
Singles: 12-Inch 33/45rpm
WARNER BROS: 83 4–6
Singles: 7-Inch
CAPITOL: 76–78 2–3
VERTIGO: 75 2–3
WARNER BROS: 81–83 1–3
Picture Sleeves
WARNER BROS: 81–83 1–3
LPs: 10/12-Inch 33rpm
CAPITOL: 75–78 8–10
MERCURY: 77 5–8
VERTIGO: 73–74 8–10
WARNER BROS: 80–81 5–8

KRAMER, Billy J., & The Dakotas
Singles: 7-Inch
ERIC 1–3
IMPERIAL: 64–66 4–6
LIBERTY (55586; "Do
You Want To Know A
Secret"/"I'll Be On My
Way"): 63 8-12
LIBERTY (55626; "Bad
To Me"): 64 8–10
LIBERTY (55643; "I'll
Keep You Satisfied"): 64 8–10
LIBERTY (55667; "Do
You Want To Know A
Secret"/"Bad To Me"):
64 5–8
(The original 1963 issue coupled "Do You
Want To Know A Secret" with "I'll Be On My
Way.")
Picture Sleeves
IMPERIAL: 64 5–8
LPs: 10/12-Inch 33rpm
CAPITOL: 78–79 8–10

IMPERIAL: 64–65 . . . . $20–30

KRANZ, George
Singles: 12-Inch 33/45rpm
PERSONAL: 83 4–6
Singles: 7-Inch
PERSONAL: 83 1–3

KRISTOFFERSON, Kris
Singles: 7-Inch
COLUMBIA: 77–81 1–3
EPIC: 67 3–5
MONUMENT: 70–81 1–3
LPs: 10/12-Inch 33rpm
COLUMBIA: 77–81 5–8
MONUMENT: 70–76 6–10
Also see COOLIDGE, Rita, & Kris Kristoffer-
son

KROKUS
Singles: 7-Inch
ARIOLA AMERICA: 81 1–3
ARISTA: 82–84 1–3
LPs: 10/12-Inch 33rpm
ARIOLA AMERICA: 81 5–8
ARISTA: 82–84 5–8

KRUSH GROOVE ALL STARS
Singles: 12-Inch 33/45rpm
WARNER BROS: 85 4–6
Also see BLOW, Kurtis
Also see E., Sheila
Also see FAT BOYS, The
Also see RUN D.M.C.

KRYSTAL
Singles: 7-Inch
EPIC: 84 1–3
SPRING: 79 2–3

KRYSTAL GENERATION, The
Singles: 7-Inch
BUDDAH: 69 2–4
MR. CHAND: 71 2–3

KRYSTOL
Singles: 12-Inch 33/45rpm
EPIC: 84 4–6
Singles: 7-Inch
EPIC: 84–85 1–3

Price Range

KUBAN, Bob (Bob Kuban & The In-Men; The Bob Kuban Band)
Singles: 7-Inch
ERIC $1–3
MUSICLAND U.S.A.
(Except 20,001): *66–67* 3–5
MUSICLAND U.S.A.
(20,001; "The Cheater"):
66 8–10
(With "Vocal by Walter Scott" shown on both sides of disc.)
MUSICLAND U.S.A.
(20,001; "The Cheater"):
66 3–5
(With "Vocal by Walter Scott" shown only on flip side, "Try Me Baby.")
MUSICLAND U.S.A.
(20,001; "The Cheater"):
66 3–5
(With "Vocal by Walter Scott" not shown on either side.)
NORMAN: *65–66*. 4–6
(Walter Scott vocal may be shown as by "Little Walter.")
REPRISE: *70*. 2–4

LPs: 10/12-Inch 33rpm
MUSICLAND U.S.A.: *66* 20–25
Members: Bob Kuban; Walter Scott.

KUF-LINX, The (Featuring Johnny Jennings)
Singles: 7-Inch
CHALLENGE (White label): *58*. 8–10
CHALLENGE (Maroon label): *58*. 4–6

KULIS, Charlie
Singles: 7-Inch
PLAYBOY: *75* 2–3

KWICK
Singles: 12-Inch 33/45rpm
CAPITOL: *83* 4–6

Singles: 7-Inch
CAPITOL: *83* 1–3
EMI AMERICA: *80–82*. 1–3

LPs: 10/12-Inch 33rpm
CAPITOL: *83* 5–8
EMI AMERICA: *80–81*. 5–8

Price Range

KYM
Singles: 12-Inch 33/45rpm
AWARD: *84* $4–6

Singles: 7-Inch
AWARD: *84* 1–3

L

L.A. BOPPERS, The
Singles: 7-Inch
MCA: *82* 1–3
MERCURY: *80–81*. 1–3

LPs: 10/12-Inch 33rpm
MCA: *82* 5–8
MERCURY: *80–81*. 5–8

L.A. JETS, The
Singles: 7-Inch
RCA VICTOR: *76* 2–3

LPs: 10/12-Inch 33rpm
RCA VICTOR: *76* 8–10

L.L. COOL J
Singles: 7-Inch
COLUMBIA: *85* 1–3

LPs: 10/12-Inch 33rpm
COLUMBIA: *85* 5–8

Price Range

L.T.D. (Love, Togetherness & Devotion)
Singles: 7-Inch
A&M: *76–80* $1–3
MONTAGE: *83.* 1–3
Picture Sleeves
A&M: *76–78* 1–3
LPs: 10/12-Inch 33rpm
A&M: *74–81* 8–10
MONTAGE: *83.* 5–8
SPRINGBOARD: *77* 8–10
Also see OSBORNE, Jeffrey

LTG EXCHANGE
Singles: 7-Inch
FANIA: *74* 2–3
WAND: *74* 2–3

LABELLE, Patti (Patti Labelle & The Blue Belles; Labelle)
Singles: 12-Inch 33/45rpm
EPIC: *78–79* 4–6
MCA: *85* 4–6
PHILADELPHIA INT'L:
    83–85 4–6
Singles: 7-Inch
ATLANTIC: *65–70* 2–4
EPIC: *74–80* 1–3
KING: *63* 4–6
MISTLETOE: *73.* 2–3
PHILADELPHIA INT'L:
    81–85 1–3
MCA: *85–86* 1–3
NEWTOWN: *62–63* 4–6
NICETOWN: *64.* 4–6
PARKWAY: *64* 3–5
RCA VICTOR: *73* 2–3
TRIP: *71* 1–3
WARNER BROS: *71–72* 2–3
LPs: 10/12-Inch 33rpm
ATLANTIC: *65–67* 15–20
EPIC: *74–82* 8–10
MCA: *85–86* 5–8
MISTLETOE. 10–15
NEWTOWN: *63.* 30–35
PARKWAY: *64* 20–25
PHILADELPHIA INT'L:
    81–85 5–8
RCA VICTOR (0200
    series): *73* 8–10

Price Range

RCA VICTOR (4100
    series): *82* $5–8
TRIP: *71–75* 8–10
UNITED ARTISTS: *74–75* 8–10
UPFRONT 10–12
WARNER BROS: *71–72* 8–10
Also see BLUE-BELLES, The
Also see DASH, Sarah
Also see HENDRIX, Nona
Also see NYRO, Laura
Also see WOMACK, Bobby, & Patti Labelle

LABELLE, Patti, & Grover Washington, Jr.
Singles: 7-Inch
ELEKTRA: *82* 1–3
Also see WASHINGTON, Grover, Jr.

LABELLE, Patti / Harold Faltermeyer
Singles: 7-Inch
MCA: *85* 1–3
Also see FALTERMEYER, Harold

LABELLE, Patti, & Michael McDonald
Singles: 7-Inch
MCA: *86* 1–3
Also see LABELLE, Patti
Also see McDONALD, Michael

LA BOUNTY, Bill
Singles: 7-Inch
20TH CENTURY-FOX:
    75–76 2–3
WARNER BROS: *78.* 2–3

LABYRINTH (Featuring Julie Loco)
Singles: 7-Inch
21: *85* 1–3

LADD, Cheryl
Singles: 7-Inch
CAPITOL: *76–79* 1–3
Picture Sleeves
CAPITOL: *78–79* 1–3
WARNER BROS: *74.* 2–3
LPs: 10/12-Inch 33rpm
CAPITOL: *78–79* 5–10
Also see VALLI, Frankie, & Cheryl Ladd

Price Range

LADIES CHOICE
Singles: 7-Inch
STREETWISE: *83* $1–3

LADY
Singles: 7-Inch
MEGA: *82* 1–3

LADY FLASH
Singles: 7-Inch
RSO: *76* 2–3
LPs: 10/12-Inch 33rpm
RSO: *76* 8–10
Also see MANILOW, Barry

LAFAYETTES, The
Singles: 7-Inch
RCA VICTOR: *62* 3–5

LA FLAMME, David
Singles: 7-Inch
AMHERST: *76–77* 2–3
Picture Sleeves
AMHERST: *76* 2–3
LPs: 10/12-Inch 33rpm
AMHERST: *76–78* 8–10
Also see IT'S A BEAUTIFUL DAY

LA FLAVOUR
Singles: 12-Inch 33/45rpm
SWEET CITY: *80* 5–8
Singles: 7-Inch
MERCURY: *79* 1–3
SWEET CITY: *80* 1–3
LPs: 10/12-Inch 33rpm
SWEET CITY: *80* 5–8

LA FORGE, Jack (Jack LaForge & His Orchestra)
Singles: 7-Inch
LYRIC: *65–66* 2–3
REGINA: *63–66* 2–3
RIO: *62* 2–4
LPs: 10/12-Inch 33rpm
AUDIO FIDELITY: *66* 6–12
PURPLETONE: *62* 8–15
REGINA: *63–65* 8–15

LA LA, Prince: see PRINCE LA LA

Price Range

LAID BACK
Singles: 12-Inch 33/45rpm
SIRE: *84–85* $4–6
WARNER BROS: *83* 4–6
Singles: 7-Inch
SIRE: *84–85* 1–3
WARNER BROS: *83–84* 1–3
LPs: 10/12-Inch 33rpm
SIRE: *84* 5–8
Members: Timothy Stahl; John Guldberg.

LAINE, Cleo
Singles: 7-Inch
RCA VICTOR: *74–80* 1–3
LPs: 10/12-Inch 33rpm
BUDDAH: *74* 8–10
FONTANA: *66* 10–15
GNP/CRESCENDO: *74* 5–10
QUINTESSENCE: *80* 5–8
RCA VICTOR: *73–80* 5–10
Also see CHARLES, Ray, & Cleo Laine

LAINE, Frankie
Singles: 7-Inch
ABC: *67–69* 2–3
AMOS: *70–71* 2–3
CAPITOL: *64–66* 2–3
COLUMBIA (39000
  through 40000): *51–57* 3–5
COLUMBIA (41000
  through 42000): *57–64* 2–4
MAINSTREAM: *75* 1–3
MERCURY (5000 series):
  50–51 3–5
SUNFLOWER: *72* 1–3
WARNER BROS: *74* 1–3
Picture Sleeves
COLUMBIA: *56* 3–5
EPs: 7-Inch 33/45rpm
COLUMBIA: *52–59* 6–12
MERCURY: *51–54* 8–15
LPs: 10/12-Inch 33rpm
ABC (600 series): *67–69* 8–15
ABC (30000 series): *76* 5–8
AMOS: *70–71* 8–12
CAPITOL: *65* 10–15
COLUMBIA (600 through
  1200 series): *54–58* 12–20
COLUMBIA (1300
  through 1900 series):
  59–63 10–20

Price Range

COLUMBIA (6000 series):
53–54 .... $15–30
(10-Inch LPs.)
COLUMBIA (8100
through 8700 series):
59–63 10–20
HARMONY: 65–71 8–15
HINDSIGHT: 84 4–8
MERCURY (20000 series):
54–61 10–20
MERCURY (25000 series):
51–52 20–30
(10-Inch LPs.)
MERCURY (60000 series):
61 10–20
TOWER: 67..................... 8–15
TRIP: 75 5–8
WING: 60–67 8–15

LAINE, Frankie, & Jimmy Boyd
Singles: 7-Inch
COLUMBIA: 53 3–5
Also see BOYD, Jimmy

LAINE, Frankie, & The Four Lads
Singles: 7-Inch
COLUMBIA: 54 3–5

EPs: 7-Inch 33/45rpm
COLUMBIA: 56 5–15

LPs: 10/12-Inch 33rpm
COLUMBIA: 56 15–20
Also see FOUR LADS, The

Price Range

LAINE, Frankie, & Jo Stafford
Singles: 7-Inch
COLUMBIA: 51–53 .... $3–5
EPs: 7-Inch 33/45rpm
COLUMBIA: 54 5–15
LPs: 10/12-Inch 33rpm
COLUMBIA: 54 15–20
Also see LAINE, Frankie
Also see STAFFORD, Jo

LAKE
Singles: 7-Inch
COLUMBIA: 77–79 1–3
LPs: 10/12-Inch 33rpm
CARIBOU: 81.................... 5–8
COLUMBIA: 77–79 5–8

LAKE, Greg
Singles: 7-Inch
ATLANTIC: 75–77 2–3
CHRYSALIS: 81................. 1–3
LPs: 10/12-Inch 33rpm
CHRYSALIS: 81................. 5–8
Also see EMERSON, LAKE & PALMER
Also see KING CRIMSON

LAKESIDE
Singles: 7-Inch
SOLAR: 77–85 1–3
LPs: 10/12-Inch 33rpm
ABC-PARAMOUNT: 77........... 8–10
SOLAR: 77–82 5–8

LAMAS, Lorenzo
Singles: 7-Inch
SCOTTI BROTHERS:
84–85 1–3

LAMB, Kevin
Singles: 7-Inch
ARISTA: 78 1–3

LAMONT, Lee
Singles: 7-Inch
BACK BEAT: 64–66 3–5

L'AMOUR
Singles: 12-Inch 33/45rpm
BROCCOLLI: 84 4–6

Price Range

Price Range

LAMP SISTERS, The
Singles: 7-Inch
DUKE: *68–69* **$3–5**

LANCE, Herb (Herb Lance & The Classics)
Singles: 7-Inch
DELUXE: *57*..................... **8–10**
MALA: *59–60*.................... **4–6**
PROMO: *61* **4–6**
LPs: 10/12-Inch 33rpm
CHESS: *66*...................... **12–15**

LANCE, Major
Singles: 12-Inch 33/45rpm
KAT FAMILY: *82*................. **4–6**
Singles: 7-Inch
COLUMBIA: *77*................... **2–3**
CURTOM: *70*..................... **2–4**
DAKAR: *69* **2–3**
EPIC: *66* **1–3**
KAT FAMILY: *82*................. **1–3**
MERCURY: *60.*................... **5–8**
OKEH: *63–67*.................... **3–5**
OSIRIS: *75* **2–3**
PLAYBOY: *74–75* **2–3**
SOUL: *78*....................... **2–3**
VOLT: *72*....................... **2–4**
Picture Sleeves
OKEH: *63–64* **4–6**
EPs: 7-Inch 33/45rpm
OKEH: *64* **10–15**
(Jukebox issue only.)
LPs: 10/12-Inch 33rpm
BACK-TRAC: *85* **5–8**
CONTEMPO..................... **10–12**
KAT FAMILY: *83*................. **5–8**
OKEH: *63–64* **15–20**
SOUL: *78*....................... **5–8**

LANDIS, Jerry (Paul Simon)
Singles: 7-Inch
AMY: *62* **10–15**
CANADIAN
  AMERICAN: *61*.............. **10–15**
MGM: *59*........................ **15–20**
WARWICK: *60–61*................ **10–15**
Also see SIMON, Paul

LANDS, Liz
Singles: 7-Inch
GORDY (26; "What He
  Lived For"): *63* **$5–8**
ONE-DERFUL: *67.*................ **3–5**

LANDS, Liz / Martin Luther King
Singles: 7-Inch
GORDY (23; "We Shall
  Overcome"): *63* **8–12**
Also see KING, Rev. Martin Luther, Jr.

LANDS, Liz, & The Temptations
Singles: 7-Inch
GORDY (30; "Keep Me"):
  64 .... **8–12**
Also see LANDS, Liz
Also see TEMPTATIONS, The

LANE, Mickey Lee
Singles: 7-Inch
MALA: *68*....................... **3–5**
SWAN: *64–66*.................... **3–5**

LANE, Robin, & The Chartbusters
Singles: 7-Inch
WARNER BROS: *80–81*............ **1–3**
Picture Sleeves
WARNER BROS: *80*.............. **INC**
LPs: 10/12-Inch 33rpm
WARNER BROS: *80–81*............ **5–8**
Members: Robin Lane; Leroy Radcliffe; Asa
Brebner; Scott Baerenwald; Tim Jackson.

LANE BROTHERS, The
Singles: 7-Inch
LEADER: *60.*.................... **3–5**
RCA VICTOR: *57–58* **4–6**

LANI & BONI
Singles: 7-Inch
GARPAX: *64* **4–6**
Members: Delaney Bramlett; Bonnie Bramlett.
Also see DELANEY & BONNIE

LANIER & CO.
Singles: 7-Inch
LARC: *82–83.*................... **1–3**
LPs: 10/12-Inch 33rpm
LARC: *83* **5–8**

Price Range

LANIN, Lester, & His Orchestra
Singles: 7-Inch
EPIC: *56–62* $2–3
EPs: 7-Inch 33/45rpm
EPIC: *56–58* 3–6
LPs: 10/12-Inch 33rpm
EPIC: *56–62* 5–15

LANSON, Snooky
Singles: 7-Inch
DECCA: *52* 2–4
DOT: *55–56* 2–4
LONDON: *50–51* 3–5
REPUBLIC: *53* 2–4
STARDAY: *68* 1–3
LPs: 10/12-Inch 33rpm
CAMDEN (200 series): *55* 10–20
DOT: *60* 10–15
STARDAY: *68* 5–10

LANZA, Mario
Singles: 7-Inch
RCA VICTOR (0400
  series): *71* 1–3
RCA VICTOR (3200
  through 8500 series):
  51–59 3–5
RCA VICTOR (1300
  series): *50* 4–6
Picture Sleeves
RCA VICTOR (4209;
  "Song Of India"): *51*............. 5–15
  Note: Thus far, this is the earliest 45rpm picture
  sleeve known to exist.
  As an August 1951 issue, it predates "Birds,"
  by Yma Sumac (Capitol 1819), an October 1951
  release, previously thought to be the earliest.
  Yma Sumac is not a charted artist, and is not
  found in this guide. If a sleeve issued earlier
  than "Song Of India" surfaces, we will report
  on it in a future edition of this book.
EPs: 7-Inch 33/45rpm
RCA VICTOR (Except
  1837): *53–61*................... 8–15
RCA VICTOR (1837;
  "The Student Prince"):
  54 15–25
  (Soundtrack.)
LPs: 10/12-Inch 33rpm
CAMDEN (Except 400
  series): *63* 5–15
CAMDEN (400 series): *57* 10–20

Mario Lanza Sings

Price Range

(With a "CAL" prefix.)
CAMDEN (400 series): *63* $8–15
(With a "CAS" prefix.)
RCA VICTOR (75; "The
  Toast Of New Orleans"):
  51 45–60
  (Soundtrack. A 10-Inch LP.)
RCA VICTOR (86 through
  1181): *51–53*.................. 20–30
RCA VICTOR (1750; "A
  Legendary Performer"):
  76 5–8
RCA VICTOR (1837;
  "The Student Prince"):
  54 35–45
  (Soundtrack.)
RCA VICTOR (1860
  through 2090): *54–57* 15–25
  (Black labels.)
RCA VICTOR (1860
  through 2090): *68* 6–12
  (Orange labels.)
RCA VICTOR (2211;
  "Seven Hills Of Rome"):
  58 20–30
  (Soundtrack songs on one side. Other Mario
  Lanza songs on the second side.)
RCA VICTOR (2331
  through 2333): *59* 12–20
  (Black labels.)
RCA VICTOR (2331
  through 2333): *68* 6–12
  (Orange labels.)
RCA VICTOR (2338; "For
  The First Time"): *59*........... 20–30
  (Soundtrack.)

1.

2.

3.

4.

5.

6.

1. All of the Everly Brothers' records on Cadence are valuable, including this 1962 issue. *2.* Sam Cooke's first LP on RCA, released in 1960. *3.* On a 1967 LP, Mr. Spock shared some of his favorite outer space music with first-generation trekers. *4.* Ed Rudy's interviews with the big British groups in 1964 were snapped up by anxious U.S. collectors. *5.* This 1964 LP was the first of a long string of successful releases by Cosby on Warner Brothers. *6.* Pictured is the 1966 Pickwick LP made by the folk duo in the late '50s when they called themselves Tom and Jerry. Legally restrained when it appeared, it was instantly collectible.

1. One of the most successful bands of its kind, this 1969 Paul Revere and the Raiders LP was on the charts for five months. *2.* The pairing of these pop and country stars was so successful that many other labels followed suit. The 1965 LP shown here was the second for Gene and George. *3.* Paul Anka's first 24 hits were on ABC-Paramount. Volume 2 in their "Anka's Big 15" series was issued in 1961. *4.* A 1969 collection of Joe South self-penned classics. "Introspect" was one of the definitive albums of its time. *5.* The "Champagne Music Maker" has 40 chart-making LPs to his credit, including this 1957 Coral release. *6.* The 1959 release shown here, along with its follow-up, "Double Impact," has provided the background music for hundreds of commercials. Great stereo!

1.

2.

3.

4.

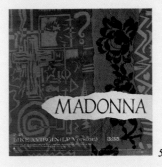

5.

6.

1. "I'll Wait" was the 1984 follow-up to Van Halen's big hit, "Jump." The 12-inch single depicted here was a promotional issue. *2.* Most of Bruce Springsteen's singles were simultaneously issued on 7-inch and 12-inch discs. Pictured is the 1984 "Born in the U.S.A." *3.* The Bangles were one of the best of the girl groups of the '80s. Shown is an advance 12-inch promo pressing. *4.* When a group becomes as collectible as the Rolling Stones, so does work by its individual members. This Jagger single was released in early 1985. *5.* "Like A Virgin" not only put Madonna on the charts and in the news, but eventually into *Penthouse* magazine. *6.* Dolly saddled up many a disco turntable with "Baby I'm Burnin'," a 1978 pink vinyl disc which contrasts nicely with her pink dress.

1.

2.

3.

4.

5.

6.

1. Contains the musical score of "The Wizard of Oz," featuring Judy Garland. Also included are song hits from "Pinocchio." *2.* One of the few mono LPs released in 1968, this Elvis recording is valued at *10 times* the price of the simultaneous stereo release. *3.* Shown here is a special, limited-edition, clear vinyl pressing of Bowie's 1983 release. *4.* Thousands of jazz releases are contained in this guide, including this early Brubeck LP on Columbia from 1955. *5.* This 1981 LP on Plantation was legally recalled almost immediately after release, making it highly collectible. *6.* Dino's recordings for Capitol are among the finest non-rock recordings ever made. Many were reissued on their Tower label subsidiary, like the 1966 offering shown here.

1. EPs

2. 10-inch LPs

1. Extended Play singles, or EPs, enabled the Victrola owner to play many of the same selections issued on Long Play, or LP. Many of the early phonographs had a non-removable 45rpm spindle, designed for records with the large (1½ inch) hole. The EP often would be a mini-LP, containing four to six tracks. Most EPs played at 45rpm, but some were 33s, such as the 1961 Capitol Compact Double of Andy Griffith's comedy hits. On "Pecos Bill," Roy Rogers stars in a wild west adventure for children. The 1957 Jerry Lee Lewis EP is collectible, as is anything on Sun. It was packaged in a paper (not cardboard) sleeve. The Flamingos were one of the first rhythm and blues groups to record in stereo. "Goodnight Sweetheart" was a 1959 issue. The Stan Freberg EP contains radio commercials for the United Presbyterian Church. "Strictly Instrumental," by Bill Haley and His Comets, was another of the early stereo EPs. *2.* The 10-inch LPs were extremely popular from 1948 through 1954. They were easily playable on phonographs that were manufactured to play the 10-inch 78rpm singles. By 1956, the 10-inch LP had pretty much given way to the now-standard 12-inch disc. Some, like the 1951 "Al Jolson," contained recordings from the '40s. The *very first* Long Play 33 appeared in 1948, an innovation from Columbia records. They chose a Frank Sinatra collection, "The Voice," for this landmark release. Note the plain graphics and design on a paper (not cardboard) sleeve. "Lover's Rhapsody" (1953) was one in a series of romantic mood music albums from "The Great One." Gleason placed 22 different LPs on the charts, four of which reached number one. First issued in 1953, "Unforgettable," by Nat "King" Cole, was reissued in the 12-inch format in 1956. Surprisingly, it didn't hit the charts until 1965.

1.

2.

3.

4.

5.

This is a special JOAN BAEZ album. It's for radio airplay and it's not-for-sale. It contains the following previously unreleased "live" songs: "Please Come To Boston" written by Dave Loggins, "Boulder To Birmingham" by Emmylou Harris, "Lily, Rosemary And The Jack Of Hearts," "Love Is Just A Four-Letter Word," and "Forever Young" by Bob Dylan. It also includes Joan's classic rendition of Bob Dylan's "I Shall Be Released" and the stunning "live" performance of her own classic, "Diamonds & Rust." (Continued on back)

6.

1. Annette, from Mouseketeer to beach party queen, is one of the most collectible of the '50s teen female stars. This was issued in 1959. *2.* The promo issue shown here, for radio use only, contains a one-hour interview with Barbra. *3.* Here is a barely recognizable Billy Joel on his first LP, released by Family Productions in 1971. *4.* Fats Domino is still on tour, playing all year round. Pictured is one of his 1961 releases. *5.* Probably the rarest of the original Monkees albums, this was a Special Products Release not sold in record stores. *6.* The Joan Baez promo LP shown here featured some previously unreleased tunes. Created for radio station use, this 1976 release was issued only to dee jays.

1.

2.

3.

4.

5.

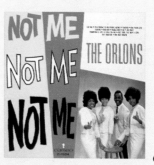

6.

1. An audiophile pressing, this half-speed mastered Nautilus SuperDisc was a reissue of the 1974 release. *2.* Bobby Bland's "Call On Me" and "That's the Way Love Is" were just two of the blues classics heard on the 1963 LP shown here. *3.* Carly Simon started out with her sister Lucy, recording as the Simon Sisters. This LP was issued in 1964. *4.* Though "I'm Telling You Now" was a number-one hit in 1965, Freddie and the Dreamers didn't have enough material for a full LP, so Tower Records included tracks by "Other Great English Stars." *5.* Much of Ray Price's earlier Columbia material was reissued in 1970 on their subsidiary label, Harmony records. *6.* In just two years (1962–1963) Cameo/Parkway released seven Orlons albums. That's more than some artists have in an entire career.

1.

2.

3.

4.

5.

6.

1. For the 1976 LP "Together—Johnny and Edgar Winter," the brothers prepared this promo discussing how they worked together. *2.* Along with the Beach Boys, the Four Seasons were one of the few American groups to hold their own against the British Invasion. *3.* "The Genius" has successfully recorded blues, soul, pop, rock, jazz, and country-western music. His first Top 10 album was this 1960 collection. *4.* The 1957 release shown here remained on the charts for 20 weeks for the native New Yorker with the Jamaican style. Few singers rank above Belafonte in total record sales. *5.* A Columbia release coming four years after Sinatra had left them for Capitol. *6.* The material from all seven of the annual Beatles Fan Club Christmas Message records (1963–69) was packaged together on one special LP.

Price Range

RCA VICTOR (2393
through 2790): *60–64* **$10–20**
(Black labels.)
RCA VICTOR (2393
through 2790): *68* **6–12**
(Orange labels.)
RCA VICTOR (2800
series): *78* **4–8**
RCA VICTOR (2900
through 3200): *68–71* **8–15**
RCA VICTOR (4158;
"The Mario Lanza
Collection"): *81* **35–45**
(5-LP boxed set.)

LARKIN, Billy (Billy Larkin & The Delegates)
Singles: 7-Inch
BRYAN: *75* **2–3**
CASINO: *76* **2–3**
MERCURY: *78–79* **1–3**
SUNBIRD: *81* **1–3**
WORLD PACIFIC: *66* **3–5**

LPs: 10/12-Inch 33rpm
AURA: *65–66* **12–18**
BRYAN: *75* **5–10**
WORLD PACIFIC: *65–69* **10–15**

LARKS, The
Singles: 7-Inch
APOLLO (427 through
435): *51* **175–225**
APOLLO (437; "Darlin"):
52 . . . . **225–250**
APOLLO (475; "Honey
From The Bee"): *55* **40–50**
APOLLO (1180;
"Hopefully Yours"): *51* **175–200**
APOLLO (1184; "My
Reverie" - black vinyl):
51 . . . . **225–250**
APOLLO (1184; "My
Reverie" - colored vinyl):
51 . . . . **400–425**
APOLLO (1189;
"Shadrack"): *52* **200–225**
APOLLO (1190; "Stolen
Love"): *52* **325–350**
APOLLO (1194; "Hold
Me"): *52* **325–350**

Price Range

LLOYDS (108; "Margie"):
54 . . . . **$50–75**
LLOYDS (110; "If It's A
Crime"): *54* **150–175**
LLOYDS (112; "No Other
Girl"): *54* **225–250**
LLOYDS (114; "Forget
It"): *54* **75–100**
LLOYDS (115; "Johnny
Darling"): *54* **75–100**
Members: Gene Mumford; Allen Bunn; Ray
Barnes; Thermon Ruth; Dave McNeil; Hadie
Rowe; Orville Brooks.

LARKS, The (With Don Julian)
Singles: 7-Inch
JERK: *65* **3–5**
MONEY: *64–71* **3–5**

LPs: 10/12-Inch 33rpm
MONEY: *65–67* **15–20**
Also see JULIAN, Don

LARKS, The
Singles: 7-Inch
CROSS FIRE. **5–8**
GUYDEN: *63* **3–5**
SHERYL: *61* **3–5**
STACY: *63* **3–5**
VIOLET: *63* **4–6**

LA ROSA, Julius
Singles: 7-Inch
ABC: *67* **2–3**
BARNABY: *70* **1–3**
CADENCE (1200 series):
53–55 . . . . **3–5**
CADENCE (1400 series):
63–64 . . . . **2–4**
KAPP: *60–62* **2–4**
MGM: *66* **2–3**
METROMEDIA: *70* **1–3**
RCA VICTOR (0900
series): *73* **1–3**
RCA VICTOR (6000 &
7000 series): *56–58* **2–4**
ROULETTE: *59* **2–4**

EPs: 7-Inch 33/45rpm
CADENCE: *54–57* **5–10**
RCA VICTOR: *56* **4–8**

LPs: 10/12-Inch 33rpm
CADENCE: *56* **15–20**

LA ROSA, Julius, & The Bob Crewe Generation

LARRICE

LARRY LEE: see LEE, Larry

LARSEN, Neil

LARSEN-FEITEN BAND, The

LARSON, Nicolette

LA RUE, D.C.

LA SALLE, Denise

LASLEY, David

LASSIES, The

LAST, James

LAST POETS, The

LAST WORD, The

Price Range

LATEEF, Yusef (The Yusef Lateef Quintet)
Singles: 7-Inch
ATLANTIC: *68–70* **$2–3**
IMPULSE: *64* **2–4**
NEW JAZZ: *60*. **2–4**
PRESTIGE: *63–69* **2–4**

LPs: 10/12-Inch 33rpm
ATLANTIC: *68–76* **8–15**
CTI: *77–79*...................... **5–8**
CADET: *69* **8–15**
CHARLIE PARKER: *62* **15–25**
EVEREST: *74* **5–8**
IMPULSE (56 through
  9125): *63–66*. **10–20**
IMPULSE (9200 & 9300
  series): *73–78* **8–12**
MILESTONE: *73* **8–12**
MOODSVILLE: *61*............... **20–30**
NEW JAZZ: *59–61*............... **20–35**
PRESTIGE (7100 series):
  57 .... **25–50**
PRESTIGE (7400 through
  7800 series): *66–71* **8–15**
PRESTIGE (24000 series):
  72–74 .... **8–15**
RIVERSIDE (300 series):
  60 .... **20–30**
    (Riverside 300 series numbers may be preceded
    by a "9" or a "12.")
RIVERSIDE (3000 series):
  68 .... **10–15**
SAVOY (2200 series):
  76–79 .... **8–12**
SAVOY (12000 & 13000
  series): *56–59* **20–40**
TRIP: *73* **5–8**
VERVE: *57* **20–40**

LATIMORE, Benny (Latimore)
Singles: 7-Inch
ATLANTIC: *69* **2–4**
DADE: *67–68* **3–5**
GLADES: *73–79*.................. **1–3**
MALACO: *83* **1–3**

LPs: 10/12-Inch 33rpm
GLADES: *73–78*................. **6–10**
MALACO: *83* **5–8**

Price Range

LATTISAW, Stacy
Singles: 7-Inch
COTILLION: *79–85*.............. **$1–3**

LPs: 10/12-Inch 33rpm
COTILLION: *79–84*.............. **5–8**

LATTISAW, Stacy, & Johnny Gill
Singles: 7-Inch
COTILLION: *84–85*.............. **1–3**

LPs: 10/12-Inch 33rpm
COTILLION: *84*.................. **5–8**
  Also see GILL, Johnny
  Also see LATTISAW, Stacy

LAUPER, Cyndi
Singles: 12-Inch 33/45rpm
PORTRAIT: *83–85*............... **4–6**

Singles: 7-Inch
PORTRAIT: *83–85*............... **1–3**

LPs: 10/12-Inch 33rpm
PORTRAIT: *83–85*............... **5–8**
  Also see HOOTERS, The
  Also see U.S.A. FOR AFRICA

LAURA & JOHNNY
Singles: 7-Inch
SILVER FOX: *69*................. **2–4**

LAURA LEE: See LEE, Laura

LAURAN, Niki
Singles: 12-Inch 33/45rpm
WAVE: *83* **4–6**

LAUREN, Rod
Singles: 7-Inch
CHANCELLOR: *62*............... **3–5**
RCA VICTOR: *59–62* **4–6**

Picture Sleeves
RCA VICTOR: *59–60* **4–8**

LPs: 10/12-Inch 33rpm
RCA VICTOR: *61* **20–25**
  Also see COOKE, Sam / Rod Lauren / Neil
  Sedaka / The Browns

LAURENCE, Paul
Singles: 7-Inch
CAPITOL: *85* **1–3**

Price Range

LAURIE, Annie
Singles: 7-Inch
DELUXE: 57–60. . . . . $5–8
DOVE: 68 2–4
GUSTO: 78 1–3
OKEH: 55 5–8
RITZ: 62 3–5
SAVOY: 56 5–8

LAURIE, Linda
Singles: 7-Inch
ANDIE: 60 3–5
GLORY: 59. 5–8
KEETCH: 64. 3–5
RECONA: 63 3–5
RUST: 60–63. 4–6

LAURIE SISTERS, The
Singles: 7-Inch
MGM: 59–60. 3–5
MERCURY: 54–55. 4–6
PORT: 63. 3–5
VIK: 56 4–6
LPs: 10/12-Inch 33rpm
CAMDEN: 60. 15–20

LAVERNE & SHIRLEY
Singles: 7-Inch
ATLANTIC: 76–77 2–3
LPs: 10/12-Inch 33rpm
ATLANTIC: 76 8–10
Members: Penny Marshall; Cindy Williams.

LAVETTE, Betty (Bettye LaVette)
Singles: 7-Inch
ATCO: 72 2–3
ATLANTIC: 62–63 3–5
BIG WHEEL: 66 3–5
CALLA: 65 3–5
EPIC: 75 2–3
KAREN: 68–69. 2–4
MOTOWN: 81–82. 1–3
SSS INT'L: 71 1–3
SILVER FOX: 69. 2–3
WEST END 2–3
LPs: 10/12-Inch 33rpm
MOTOWN: 81. 5–8

LAWRENCE, Eddie
Singles: 7-Inch
CORAL: 56–63 2–4

Price Range

EPIC: 65 . . . . $2–3
SHASTA: 60 2–4
SIGNATURE: 60. 2–4
Picture Sleeves
CORAL: 56. 3–5
EPIC: 65 2–3
LPs: 10/12-Inch 33rpm
CORAL: 55–62. 10–25
EPIC: 65 8–15
SIGNATURE: 59. 10–20

LAWRENCE, Steve
Singles: 7-Inch
ABC: 73. 1–3
ABC-PARAMOUNT:
  58–60 3–5
CALENDAR: 67–68 2–3
COLUMBIA: 62–68. 2–4
CORAL: 55–59. 3–5
KING (1200 series): 53 4–6
KING (5000 series): 60–64 2–4
KING (15000 series):
  52–53 4–6
MGM: 71–73. 1–3
RCA VICTOR: 69–70 1–3
20TH CENTURY-FOX:
  75–77 1–3
UNITED ARTISTS (200
  & 300 series): 60–61 3–5
UNITED ARTISTS (900
  through 1100 series):
  76–78 1–3
WARNER BROS: 78. 1–3
Picture Sleeves
COLUMBIA: 62–63. 3–5
UNITED ARTISTS: 60–61 4–6
EPs: 7-Inch 33/45rpm
KING: 53 10–15
LPs: 10/12-Inch 33rpm
ABC-PARAMOUNT:
  59–60 15–20
APPLAUSE: 81. 4–8
COLUMBIA: 63–68 10–15
CORAL: 57–63. 15–25
HARMONY: 68–71 6–12
KING: 57 20–25
MGM: 71 5–10
RCA VICTOR: 70 6–12
UNITED ARTISTS: 61–63. 12–15
VOCALION: 66–69 6–12

Price Range

LAWRENCE, Steve, & Eydie Gorme (Steve & Eydie)
Singles: 7-Inch
CALENDAR: 68 .... $2–3
COLUMBIA: 62–67 3–5
CORAL: 55 3–5
MGM: 72–73 1–3
RCA VICTOR: 68–69 1–3
LPs: 10/12-Inch 33rpm
ABC: 73–76 5–10
ABC-PARAMOUNT:
   59–64 10–15
CALENDAR: 68 8–15
COLUMBIA: 63–67 10–15
CORAL: 60 10–15
HARMONY: 71 5–10
MGM: 72–73 5–8
RCA VICTOR: 69–72 6–12
UNITED ARTISTS: 61–62 12–15
   Also see GORME, Eydie
   Also see LAWRENCE, Steve
   Also see OSMONDS, The, Steve Lawrence &
   Eydie Gorme

LAWRENCE, Vicki
Singles: 7-Inch
BELL: 73–74 2–3
FLASHBACK: 74 1–3
PRIVATE STOCK: 75–76 2–3
UNITED ARTISTS: 71 2–4
LPs: 10/12-Inch 33rpm
WINDMILL: 79 5–8

LAWS, Debra
Singles: 7-Inch
ELEKTRA: 80–81 1–3
LPs: 10/12-Inch 33rpm
ELEKTRA: 81 5–8

LAWS, Eloise
Singles: 7-Inch
ABC: 77–78 1–3
CAPITOL: 82 1–3
COLUMBIA: 68–70 2–3
INVICTUS: 75–77 2–3
LIBERTY: 80–81 1–3
MUSIC MERCHANT:
   72–73 2–3
Picture Sleeves
LIBERTY: 80 .... INC

Price Range

LPs: 10/12-Inch 33rpm
ABC: 77–78 .... $8–10
CAPITOL: 82 5–8
INVICTUS: 76 5–8
LIBERTY: 80 5–8

LAWS, Hubert
Singles: 7-Inch
ATLANTIC: 65 2–4
CTI: 70–75 2–3
COLUMBIA: 78 1–3
LPs: 10/12-Inch 33rpm
ATLANTIC: 66–81 8–15
CTI: 70–77 8–15
COLUMBIA: 76–80 5–10
   Also see KLUGH, Earl, & Hubert Laws

LAWS, Ronnie (Ronnie Laws & Pressure)
Singles: 7-Inch
BLUE NOTE: 75–77 2–3
CAPITOL: 83–84 1–3
LIBERTY: 80–81 1–3
UNITED ARTISTS: 75–80 1–3
LPs: 10/12-Inch 33rpm
BLUE NOTE: 75–77 6–12
CAPITOL: 83 5–8
LIBERTY: 81 5–8
UNITED ARTISTS: 75–80 5–10

LAYNA, Magda
Singles: 12-Inch 33/45rpm
MEGATONE: 83 4–6

LAYNE, Joy
Singles: 7-Inch
LUCKY FOUR: 61 3–5
MERCURY: 57 4–6

LAZY RACER
Singles: 7-Inch
A&M: 79–80 1–3
LPs: 10/12-Inch 33rpm
A&M: 79–80 5–8

LEACH, Billy
Singles: 7-Inch
BALLY: 57 4–6

Price Range

LEADON, Bernie (Bernie Leadon & The Michael Georgiades Band)
Singles: 7-Inch
ASYLUM: 77................... **$2–3**
LPs: 10/12-Inch 33rpm
ASYLUM: 77................... **8–10**
Also see EAGLES, The

LEAGUE UNLIMITED ORCHESTRA, The
Singles: 7-Inch
A&M: 82 .... **1–3**
LPs: 10/12-Inch 33rpm
A&M: 82 .... **5–8**
Also see HUMAN LEAGUE

LEAPY LEE
Singles: 7-Inch
CADET: 69..................... **2–4**
DECCA: 68–71 .... **3–5**
MAM: 72....................... **2–3**
MCA: 75 .... **1–3**
Picture Sleeves
MCA: 75 .... **1–3**
LPs: 10/12-Inch 33rpm
DECCA: 68.................... **12–15**

LEAVES, The (With John Beck & Bob Arlin)
Singles: 7-Inch
CAPITOL: 66 .... **4–6**
MIRA (Except 202 & 207):
  66 .... **4–6**
MIRA (202; "Too Many People"/"Love Minus Zero"): 65 .... **8–10**
  (Reissued on Mira 227 with the different flip side, "Girl From The East.")
MIRA (207; "Hey Joe, Where You Gonna Go"):
  65 .... **10–12**
  (Reissued on Mira 222 with the shorter title, "Hey Joe.")
LPs: 10/12-Inch 33rpm
CAPITOL: 67 .... **15–20**
MIRA: 66 .... **25–30**

LEAVILLE, Otis (Otis Leavill)
Singles: 7-Inch
BLUE ROCK: 65 .... **3–5**
BRUNSWICK: 67................ **3–5**

Price Range

COLUMBIA: 66................. **$3–5**
DAKAR: 69–70 .... **2–4**
LIMELIGHT: 64 .... **3–5**
SMASH: 68 .... **3–5**

LEAVY, Calvin
Singles: 7-Inch
BLUE FOX: 70.................. **2–4**

LE BLANC, Lenny
Singles: 7-Inch
BIG TREE: 76–77 .... **2–3**
CAPITOL: 81 .... **1–3**
LPs: 10/12-Inch 33rpm
BIG TREE: 76–77 .... **8–10**
CAPITOL: 81 .... **5–8**

LE BLANC & CARR
Singles: 7-Inch
BIG TREE: 77–78 .... **2–3**
LPs: 10/12-Inch 33rpm
ATLANTIC (003; "Live From The Atlantic Studios"): 78 .... **8–12**
  (Promotional issue only.)
BIG TREE: 77 .... **8–10**
  Members: Lenny LeBlanc; Pete Carr.
  Also see CARR, Pete
  Also see LE BLANC, Lenny

LED ZEPPELIN
Singles: 7-Inch
ATLANTIC (Except 2777): 69–73................. **3–5**
ATLANTIC (2777; "The Immigrant Song"): 70........... **6–10**
  (With "Do What Thou Wilt Shall Be The Whole Of The Law" etched in the vinyl trail-off, which indicates a first pressing. Valued higher than other Atlantic Led Zeppelin singles because the flip, "Hey Hey, What Can I Do," is not available otherwise.)
SWAN SONG: 74–79.............. **2–3**
Promotional Singles
ATLANTIC (175; "Stairway To Heaven"):
  72 .... **30–35**
  (If accompanied by its special promotional sleeve, the price range of this issue would be approximately double.)

Price Range

ATLANTIC (269;
"Stairway To Heaven"):
72 .... **$30–35**
ATLANTIC (1019; "Dazed
& Confused")................. **10–15**
ATLANTIC (Mono/Stereo
and Long/Short version
issues): 69–73................... **5–8**
EPs: 7-Inch 33/45rpm
ATLANTIC (7-7208; "Led
Zeppelin"): 71 .... **35–40**
(May have been a promotional issue only.
"Rock And Roll" & "Black Dog" backed with
"Stairway To Heaven.")
LPs: 10/12-Inch 33rpm
ATLANTIC (7000 series):
70–73 .... **6–10**
ATLANTIC (8000 series):
69 .... **8–12**
ATLANTIC (19000 series):
77 .... **5–8**
MFSL: 80...................... **12–15**
SWAN SONG: 75–79............. **8–12**
Members: Robert Plant; Jimmy Page; John
Paul Jones; John Bonham.
Also see PAGE, Jimmy
Also see PLANT, Robert

LEDERNACKEN
Singles: 12-Inch 33/45rpm
4TH & BROADWAY: 84 .... **4–6**

LEE, Alvin (Alvin Lee & Company; Alvin Lee & Ten Years Later; Alvin Lee & Mylon LeFevre)
Singles: 7-Inch
COLUMBIA: 74.................. **2–3**
RSO: 79 .... **2–3**
LPs: 10/12-Inch 33rpm
ATLANTIC: 80–81 .... **5–8**
COLUMBIA: 73–75 .... **10–12**
LONDON: 78 .... **8–10**
RSO: 77–79 .... **10–12**
Also see TEN YEARS AFTER

LEE, Bobby
Singles: 7-Inch
CUCA: 62 .... **3–5**
DECCA: 60–61................... **3–5**
FALEW: 64...................... **3–5**
PORT: 67....................... **3–5**

Price Range

RAMCO: 67 .... **$3–5**
SUE: 66 .... **3–5**

LEE, Brenda
Singles: 7-Inch
DECCA (30050;
"Jambalaya"): 56............... **15–20**
DECCA (30107 through
30885): 56–59.................. **10–15**
(Price range of 30050 through 30333 is for black
label originals. Decca multi-color labels in that
series are $2-$4 1960s reissues.)
DECCA (30967 through
31570): 59–63................... **4–6**
DECCA (31599 through
32975): 64–72.................. **3–5**
DECCA (88215; "I'm
Gonna Lasso Santa
Claus"): 56.................... **15–20**
(Decca Children's Series issue.)
ELEKTRA: 78 .... **2–3**
MCA: 73–84 .... **1–3**

Picture Sleeves
DECCA (30776; "Rockin'
Around The Christmas
Tree"): 59 .... **10–15**
DECCA (30967; "Sweet
Nothin's"): 59 .... **20–25**
DECCA (31093 through
32428): 60–69................... **5–10**
DECCA (88215; "I'm
Gonna Lasso Santa
Claus"): 56 .... **20–30**
EPs: 7-Inch 33/45rpm
DECCA: 60–65 .... **8–15**
LPs: 10/12-Inch 33rpm
CORAL: 73 .... **5–8**
DECCA (4039 through
4104): 60–61................... **20–25**
DECCA (4176 through
4755): 61–66................... **15–20**
DECCA (4757; "10 Golden
Years"): 66.................... **15–20**
("Deluxe Limited Edition," with gatefold
cover.)
DECCA (4757; "10 Golden
Years")........................ **10–12**
(With standard cover.)
DECCA (4825 through
75232): 66–70.................. **10–15**

Price Range

(Brenda's Decca LPs, 4039 through 4955, with a "DL" prefix were mono. Decca stereo LPs were indicated by a "DL7" prefix.)

MCA (Except 700 series):
73–82 .... **$8–10**
MCA (700 series) **5–8**
VOCALION: *67–70* **10–12**

LEE, Brenda / Tennessee Ernie Ford
LPs: 10/12-Inch 33rpm
DECCA (9226; "The
Brenda Lee/Tennessee
Ernie Ford Show For
Christmas Seals") **20-30**
(Promotional issue only.)
Also see FORD, Tennessee Ernie

LEE, Brenda, & Pete Fountain
LPs: 10/12-Inch 33rpm
DECCA: *68* **8–15**
Also see FOUNTAIN, Pete

LEE, Brenda, & The Oak Ridge Boys
Singles: 7-Inch
MCA: *82* **1–3**
Also see OAK RIDGE BOYS, The

LEE, Brenda, & Willie Nelson
Singles: 7-Inch
MONUMENT: *83*................. **1–3**
Also see LEE, Brenda
Also see NELSON, Willie

LEE, Curtis
Singles: 7-Inch
ABC: *74*.......................... **1–3**
DUNES: *60–63* **5–8**
HOT: *60*........................ **15–20**
MCA............................. **1–3**
MIRA: *67* **3–5**
ROJAC: *67* **3–5**
SABRA: *61* **10–15**
WARRIOR: *59*................. **10–15**
Picture Sleeves
DUNES: *61* **10–15**

LEE, Dick
Singles: 7-Inch
ABC: *67*.......................... **2–4**
BLUE BELL: *61*.................. **3–5**
CAPITOL: *68* **2–3**
CENTAUR: *59*................... **3–5**

Price Range

DOT: *66*........................ **$2–4**
ESSEX: *54* **3–5**
FELSTED: *60* **3–5**
KAPP: *69* **2–3**
MGM: *59*........................ **3–5**
METRO: *65*...................... **2–4**
ROULETTE: *62–63* **2–4**
20TH CENTURY-FOX:
65 .... **2–4**
VIK: *56* **3–5**
X: *55*............................ **3–5**

LEE, Dickey (Dickey Lee With The Collegiates)
Singles: 7-Inch
ABC: *73*.......................... **1–3**
ATCO: *68* **3–5**
DIAMOND: *69*.................... **3–5**
DICKIE LEE STORY: *77*........ **10–15**
(Identified as "The Dickie Lee Story," since no label name appears on this disc. Promotional issue only.)
DOT: *60*......................... **8–10**
ERIC **1–3**
MERCURY: *79–82*................. **1–3**
RCA VICTOR: *70–78* **1–3**
SMASH: *62–64* **3–5**
SUN (280; "Good
Lovin' "): *57* **8–12**
SUN (297; "Dreamy
Nights"): *57*.................... **15–20**
TCF: *65* **3–5**
TCF HALL: *64–65*................ **3–5**
TAMPA: *57*.................... **12–15**
TRACIE: *67* **3–5**
LPs: 10/12-Inch 33rpm
RCA VICTOR: *71–76* **6–12**
MERCURY: *79–80*................ **5–8**
SMASH: *62*..................... **20–25**
TCF HALL: *65*................. **15–20**

LEE, Jackie (Earl Nelson)
Singles: 7-Inch
FAYETTE: *64*..................... **3–5**
KEYMAN: *67–68*................. **3–5**
MIRWOOD: *65–66*................ **3–5**
SWAN: *59*........................ **4–6**
UNI: *70* **2–4**
LPs: 10/12-Inch 33rpm
MIRWOOD: *66*................. **15–20**
Also see BOB & EARL

Price Range

Price Range

LEE, Jackie, & His Orchestra
Singles: 7-Inch
CORAL: 53 . . . . **$2–4**

LEE, Jimmy, & Artis
Singles: 7-Inch
MODERN: 52 . . . . **25–30**

LEE, Johnny
Singles: 7-Inch
ABC/DOT: 75. . . . . **2–3**
ASTRO: 80 . . . . **1–3**
ASYLUM: 80–82. . . . . **1–3**
EPIC: 81 . . . . **1–3**
FULL MOON: 80–83. . . . . **1–3**
GRT: 76–78. . . . . **2–3**
WARNER BROS: 83 . . . . **1–3**

Picture Sleeves
ASYLUM: 80. **INC**

LPs: 10/12-Inch 33rpm
ACCORD: 83 . . . . **5–8**
ASYLUM: 80–81. . . . . **5–8**
FULL MOON: 80–84. . . . . **5–8**
GRT: 77. . . . . **6–10**
JMS. **8–12**
PLANTATION: 81. . . . . **4–8**
Also see GILLEY, Mickey, & Johnny Lee

LEE, Johnny / Eagles
Singles: 7-Inch
ASYLUM: 80–81. . . . . **1–3**

Picture Sleeves
ASYLUM: 80. **1–3**
Also see EAGLES, The
Also see LEE, Johnny

LEE, Julia
Singles: 7-Inch
CAPITOL: 52 . . . . **10–15**

LEE, Larry (Larry Lee & Frankie Valli)
Singles: 7-Inch
COLUMBIA: 82 . . . . **1–3**
GENIUS **4–6**
Also see OZARK MOUNTAIN DARE-
DEVILS, The
Also see VALLI, Frankie

LEE, Laura
Singles: 7-Inch
ARIOLA AMERICA: 76 . . . . **$2–3**
CHESS: 67–69. . . . . **3–5**
COTILLION: 69. . . . . **2–4**
HOT WAX: 71–72 . . . . **2–3**
INVICTUS: 74 . . . . **2–3**
RIC TIC: 66 . . . . **3–5**

LPs: 10/12-Inch 33rpm
CHESS: 72. . . . . **8–10**
HOT WAX: 72–73 . . . . **8–10**
INVICTUS: 74 . . . . **8–10**

LEE, Leapy: see LEAPY LEE

LEE, Leon
Singles: 7-Inch
CROSSOVER: 74 . . . . **2–4**

LEE, Michele
Singles: 7-Inch
ABC-PARAMOUNT:
62–63 . . . . **3–5**
COLUMBIA: 65–69 . . . . **3–5**
LPs: 10/12-Inch 33rpm
COLUMBIA: 66–68 . . . . **10–15**

LEE, Nickie
Singles: 7-Inch
DADE: 67 . . . . **3–5**
MALA: 68–69 . . . . **3–5**

LEE, Peggy
Singles: 7-Inch
A&M: 75 . . . . **1–3**
ATLANTIC: 74 . . . . **1–3**
CAPITOL (1400 through
1600 series): 51 . . . . **4–6**
CAPITOL (2100 through
3400 series): 68–72 . . . . **2–3**
CAPITOL (3900 through
5900 series): 58–67 . . . . **2–4**
COLUMBIA: 76. . . . . **1–3**
DECCA (25000 series): 64. . . . . **2–4**
DECCA (28000 series):
52–54 . . . . **3–5**
EPs: 7-Inch 33/45rpm
CAPITOL (Except 100
series): 57–59 . . . . **5–15**
CAPITOL (100 series): 50 . . . . **15–25**

Price Range

DECCA (2000 series): *52* **$15–30**
   LPs: 10/12-Inch 33rpm
ATLANTIC: *74* **5–8**
CAPITOL (100 & 200
   series): *50* **30–50**
   (10-Inch LPs.)
CAPITOL (100 through
   810): *69–71* **5–10**
CAPITOL (864 through
   1100 series): *57–59* **15–30**
CAPITOL (1300 through
   2800 series): *60–68* **10–20**
   (With a "T" or "ST" prefix.)
CAPITOL (1500 through
   1800 series): *75–77* **5–8**
   (With an "SM" prefix.)
CAPITOL (11000 series):
   72–79 .... **5–8**
CAPITOL (16000 series):
   80 .... **4–8**
DRG: *79* **5–8**
DECCA (100 series): *60–66* **10–20**
DECCA (4000 series): *64* **10–20**
DECCA (5000 series):
   54–55 .... **30–50**
   (10-Inch LPs.)
DECCA (8000 series):
   55–59 .... **15–30**
GLENDALE: *82* **4–8**
HARMONY (7000 series):
   58 .... **10–15**
HARMONY (30000
   series): *70* **5–10**
MERCURY: *77* **5–8**
VOCALION: *66–70* **6–12**
   Also see CROSBY, Bing
   Also see FITZGERALD, Ella, & Peggy Lee
   Also see GOODMAN, Benny, Orchestra
   Also see JENKINS, Gordon, & His Orchestra

LEE, Peggy, & George Shearing
Singles: 7-Inch
CAPITOL: *59* **2–4**
   LPs: 10/12-Inch 33rpm
CAPITOL (1219; "Beauty
   & The Beat"): *59* **20–30**
   (With Capitol logo on left side of label.)
CAPITOL (1219; "Beauty
   & The Beat"): *62* **10–20**
   (With Capitol logo at the top of label.)
   Also see LEE, Peggy
   Also see SHEARING, George

Price Range

LEE, Roberta
Singles: 7-Inch
DECCA: *51–54* **$3–5**
TEMPO: *50–51* **4–6**
TOWER: *68* **1–3**
X: *54* **3–5**

LEE, Toney
Singles: 12-Inch 33/45rpm
RADAR: *83* **4–6**
Singles: 7-Inch
CRITIQUE: *85* **1–3**

LEE & PAUL
Singles: 7-Inch
COLUMBIA: *59–65* **3–5**
   Members: Lee Pockriss; Paul Vance.
   Also see VANCE, Paul

LEFEVRE, Raymond, & His Orchestra
Singles: 7-Inch
ATLANTIC: *61* **2–3**
4 CORNERS: *67–68* **2–3**
JAMIE: *60* **2–3**
KAPP: *58–66* **2–4**
MERCURY: *60* **2–3**
VERVE: *62* **2–3**
   LPs: 10/12-Inch 33rpm
ATLANTIC: *61* **8–15**
BUDDAH: *71–72* **5–10**
4 CORNERS: *67–68* **5–10**

Price Range

KAPP: *59–66*..................... **$8–15**
MONUMENT: *67*................ **6–12**

LEFT BANKE, The (Featuring Michael Brown)
Singles: 7-Inch
CON AMERICA: *78*.............. **2–3**
SMASH (Except 2243):
66–69......................... **3–5**
SMASH (2243; "Myrah"):
69........................... **20–30**
Picture Sleeves
SMASH: *67*...................... **3–5**
LPs: 10/12-Inch 33rpm
RHINO: *85*...................... **5–8**
SMASH: *67–69*................. **15–20**
MERCURY: *81*................... **5–8**
Also see STORIES, The

LEGACY
Singles: 7-Inch
BRUNSWICK: *82*................. **1–3**
PRIVATE I: *85*................... **1–3**

LEGRAND, Michel, & His Orchestra
Singles: 7-Inch
A&M: *83*........................ **1–3**
BELL: *71–72*..................... **1–3**
COLUMBIA: *55–59*.............. **2–4**
DECCA: *68*...................... **1–3**
FLASHBACK: *73*................. **1–3**
MCA: *73–76*..................... **1–3**
MGM: *67–68*..................... **1–3**
PHILIPS: *63–66*................. **2–3**
20TH CENTURY-FOX:
77........................... **1–3**
UNITED ARTISTS: *70*............ **1–3**
WARNER BROS: *68–76*.......... **1–3**
Picture Sleeves
MGM: *67*........................ **1–3**
EPs: 7-Inch 33/45rpm
COLUMBIA: *56–59*.............. **5–10**
LPs: 10/12-Inch 33rpm
BELL: *72–74*.................... **5–10**
COLUMBIA (Except
3140): *55–71*................. **10–20**
COLUMBIA (3140; "How
To Save A Marriage &
Ruin Your Life"): *68* **35–40**
(Soundtrack.)
GRYPHON: *75–79*................ **5–8**

Price Range

HARMONY: *66–74*............. **$5–10**
KORY: *77*....................... **4–8**
MCA: *73–76*.................... **8–15**
MGM (14; "Ice Station
Zebra"): *68*.................. **40–50**
(Soundtrack.)
MERCURY: *65*.................. **8–15**
PABLO: *83*..................... **4–8**
PHILIPS: *62–64*................. **8–15**
SPRINGBOARD: *77*.............. **4–8**
20TH CENTURY-FOX:
77.......................... **5–10**
UNITED ARTISTS: *69*........... **6–12**
VERVE: *68–72*.................. **8–15**
WARNER BROS: *71–76*.......... **6–12**
Also see HORNE, Lena, & Michel Legrand
Also see VAUGHAN, Sarah

LEGRAND, Michel, & The Mike Curb Congregation
LPs: 10/12-Inch 33rpm
AMERICAN INT'L (1039;
"Wuthering Heights"):
71.......................... **15–20**
(Soundtrack.)
Also see CURB, Mike

LEGRAND, Michel, & Noel Harrison
LPs: 10/12-Inch 33rpm
UNITED ARTISTS (295;
"The Thomas Crown
Affair"): *74*.................... **5–10**
(Soundtrack.)
UNITED ARTISTS (5182;
"The Thomas Crown
Affair"): *68*.................. **12–18**
(Soundtrack.)
Also see HARRISON, Noel

LEGRAND, Michel, & Matt Monro
LPs: 10/12-Inch 33rpm
DECCA (9160; "A Matter
Of Innocence"): *68* **15–25**
(Soundtrack.)
Also see LEGRAND, Michel
Also see MONRO, Matt

LEHRER, Tom
Singles: 7-Inch
REPRISE: *69*..................... **2–4**

Price Range

LPs: 10/12-Inch 33rpm
REPRISE: 65–66 . . . . $10–20

LE JETE
Singles: 12-Inch 33/45rpm
MEGATONE: 83 4–6

LEMMONS, Billy
Singles: 7-Inch
ARIOLA AMERICA: 77 2–3

LEMON PIPERS, The (Featuring Ivan Browne)
Singles: 7-Inch
BUDDAH: 67–69 3–5
ERIC: 78 1–3

Picture Sleeves
BUDDAH: 68 4–6

LPs: 10/12-Inch 33rpm
BUDDAH: 68 12–15
Also see 1910 FRUITGUM COMPANY, The
/ The Lemon Pipers
Also see RAM JAM

LENNON, John (John & Yoko; The Plastic Ono Band)
Singles: 12-Inch 33/45rpm
GEFFEN (919; "Starting
Over"): 80 30–40
(Promotional issue only.)
GEFFEN (1079; "Happy
Xmas"): 82 25–30
(Price range includes special sleeve. Promotional issue only.)

Singles: 7-Inch
APPLE (1809; "Give Peace
A Chance"): 69 3–4
APPLE (1813; "Cold
Turkey"): 69 5–8
APPLE (1818; "Instant
Karma"): 70 2–4
APPLE (1827; "Mother"):
70 3–5
APPLE (1830; "Power To
The People"): 71 2–4
APPLE (1840; "Imagine"):
71 2–4
APPLE (1842; "Happy
Xmas"): 71 8–12

Price Range

APPLE (1848; "Woman Is
The Nigger Of The
World"): 72 . . . . $2–4
(With Elephant's Memory.)
APPLE (1868; "Mind
Games"): 73 2–4
APPLE (1874; "Whatever
Gets You Through The
Night"): 74 2–4
APPLE (1878; "#9
Dream"): 74 2–4
APPLE (1881; "Stand By
Me"): 75 2–4
CAPITOL: 78–84 2–3
GEFFEN (0408; "Starting
Over"): 83 2–3
GEFFEN (0415;
"Watching The
Wheels"): 83 2–3
GEFFEN (29855; "Happy
Xmas"): 82 2–3
GEFFEN (49604; "Starting
Over"): 80 2–3
GEFFEN (49644;
"Woman"): 80 2–3
GEFFEN (49695;
"Watching The
Wheels"): 81 2–3
POLYDOR: 84 2–3

Promotional Singles
APPLE (1809; "Give Peace
A Chance"): 69 8–10
APPLE (1813; "Cold
Turkey"): 69 20–25
APPLE (1818; "Instant
Karma"): 70 20–25
(With "Instant Karma" on both sides of disc.)
APPLE (1818; "Instant
Karma"): 70 125–175
(With "Instant Karma" only on one side of
disc. Flip side is a blank pressing.)
APPLE (1827; "Mother"):
70 20–25
APPLE (1830; "Power To
The People"): 71 15–20
APPLE (1833; "Ain't That
A Shame"): 75 80–100
APPLE (1840; "Imagine"):
71 10–15
APPLE (1842; "Happy
Xmas"): 71 150–200
(White label with black print.)

Price Range

APPLE (1848; "Woman Is
The Nigger Of The
World"): *72* **$12–15**
APPLE (1868; "Mind
Games"): *73* **10–12**
APPLE (1874; "Whatever
Gets You Through The
Night"): *74* **10–15**
APPLE (1878; "#9
Dream"): *74* **10–15**
APPLE (1878; "What You
Got"): *74* **40–50**
(There were two separate promo singles using
the same 1878 catalog number. On commercial
issues these tracks were back to back.)
APPLE (1881; "Stand By
Me"): *75* **10–15**
APPLE (1883; "Slippin' &
Slidin'): *75* **75–90**
GEFFEN (29855; "Happy
Xmas"): *82* **5–8**
GEFFEN (49604; "Starting
Over"): *80* **10–12**
GEFFEN (49644;
"Woman"): *80* **8–10**
GEFFEN (49695;
"Watching The
Wheels"): *81* **10–12**
KYA ("KYA 1969 Peace
Talk"): *69* **50–60**
(Radio KYA's Tom Campbell & Bill Holley's
telephone interview with John Lennon.)
POLYDOR: *84* **2–3**
WHAT'S IT ALL ABOUT **15–20**

Picture Sleeves

APPLE (1809; "Give Peace
A Chance"): *69* **15–20**
APPLE (1813; "Cold
Turkey"): *69* **40–60**
APPLE (1818; "Instant
Karma"): *70* **15–20**
APPLE (1827; "Mother"):
70 .... **40–60**
APPLE (1830; "Power To
The People"): *71* **15–20**
APPLE (1842; "Happy
Xmas"): *71* **10–12**
APPLE (1848; "Woman Is
The Nigger Of The
World"): *72* **10–15**

Price Range

APPLE (1868; "Mind
Games"): *73* **$5–8**
GEFFEN (29855; "Happy
Xmas"): *82* **2–3**
GEFFEN (49604; "Starting
Over"): *80* **2–4**
GEFFEN (49644;
"Woman"): *80* **2–4**
GEFFEN (49695;
"Watching The
Wheels"): *81* **2–4**
LPs: 10/12-Inch 33rpm
ADAM VIII LTD: *75* **80–90**
APPLE (Except 3361 &
3362): *71–75* **10–15**
APPLE (3361; "Wedding
Album"): *69* **75–90**
(Price range is for complete boxed set with all
inserts.)
APPLE (3362; "Live Peace
In Toronto"): *70* **30–40**
(With 16-page calendar.)
APPLE (3362; "Live Peace
In Toronto"): *70* **15–20**
(Without 16-page calendar.)
APPLE/
TETRAGRAMMATON
(5001; "Two Virgins"):
68 .... **80–100**
(With brown paper outer sleeve.)
APPLE/
TETRAGRAMMATON
(5001; "Two Virgins") **5–8**
(Reissue, with brown paper outer sleeve that
does NOT cover entire jacket.)
APPLE/
TETRAGRAMMATON
(5001; "Two Virgins"):
68 .... **50–60**
(Without brown paper outer sleeve.)
CAPITOL: *75–80* **8–10**
GEFFEN: *80–82* **8–10**
NAUTILUS SUPER
DISC: *82* **12–15**
POLYDOR: *84* **5–8**
ZAPPLE: *69* **30–35**
Promotional LPs
APPLE (3392; "Sometime
In New York City"): *72* **125–150**
(Issued on a white label.)
GEFFEN (2023; "John
Lennon Collection"): *82* **12–15**
(Quiex II "Limited Edition Pressing.")

Price Range

Also see BEATLES, The
Also see ELEPHANT'S MEMORY
Also see ONO, Yoko

LENNON, John / Ronnie Hawkins
Promotional Singles:
COTILLION: 70................ $30–35
(John Lennon promotes a 1970 Ronnie Hawkins LP on Cotillion.)
Also see HAWKINS, Ronnie
Also see LENNON, John

LENNON, Julian
Singles: 12-Inch 33/45rpm
ATLANTIC: 85................... 5–8
Singles: 7-Inch
ATLANTIC: 84–85 1–3
Picture Sleeves
ATLANTIC: 84–85 .... INC
LPs: 10/12-Inch 33rpm
ATLANTIC: 84–85 5–8

LENNON SISTERS, The
Singles: 7-Inch
BRUNSWICK: 59................. 2–4
CORAL: 56...................... 2–4
DOT: 58–67..................... 2–4
MERCURY: 68................... 2–3
LPs: 10/12-Inch 33rpm
DOT: 59–67..................... 5–15
HAMILTON: 64................. 5–12
MERCURY: 68–69............... 8–12
RANWOOD: 68–81 4–8
VOCALION: 69–70 5–10
WING: 69 5–10
Members: Kathy Lennon; Peggy Lennon; Janet Lennon; Dianne Lennon.
Also see WELK, Lawrence

LEON LEE: see LEE, Leon

LEONETTI, Tommy
Singles: 7-Inch
ATLANTIC: 60 2–4
CAPITOL: 54–56 3–5
COLUMBIA: 67–73 2–3
DECCA: 68–69................... 2–4
EPIC: 74 1–3
RCA VICTOR: 59–77 2–4
20TH CENTURY-FOX:
  77 1–3

Price Range

Picture Sleeves
COLUMBIA: 68................. $2–3
LPs: 10/12-Inch 33rpm
CAMDEN: 59.................... 8–15
RCA VICTOR: 64–67 8–15

LE PAMPLEMOUSSE
Singles: 12-Inch 33/45rpm
A.V.I.: 78–85..................... 4–6
Singles: 7-Inch
A.V.I.: 77–85..................... 1–3
LPs: 10/12-Inch 33rpm
A.V.I.: 78–85..................... 5–8

LEPPARD, Def: see DEF LEPPARD

LE ROUX (Louisiana's LeRoux)
Singles: 7-Inch
CAPITOL: 78..................... 2–3
RCA VICTOR: 82–83 1–3
LPs: 10/12-Inch 33rpm
CAPITOL: 78–81 5–8
RCA VICTOR: 82 5–8

LES COMPAGNONS DE LA CHANSON
Singles: 7-Inch
CAPITOL: 59–60 2–4

LESEAR, Anne
Singles: 7-Inch
H.C.R.C.: 84 1–3

LESTER, Bobby
Singles: 7-Inch
CHECKER: 59.................... 4–6
COLUMBIA: 70.................. 2–4
LPs: 10/12-Inch 33rpm
COLUMBIA: 70................. 10–15

LESTER, Bobby, & The Moonglows
Singles: 7-Inch
CHESS: 62....................... 3–5
LPs: 10/12-Inch 33rpm
CHESS: 62...................... 25–30
Also see MOONGLOWS, The

**LESTER, Bobby, & The
Moonlighters**
Singles: 7-Inch
CHECKER: *54* $10–12
Also see LESTER, Bobby

LESTER, Jerry
Singles: 7-Inch
CORAL: *50* 4–6

LESTER, Ketty
Singles: 7-Inch
COLLECTABLES 1–3
ERA: *62–63* 3–5
EVEREST: *62* 3–5
PETE: *68–69* 2–4
RCA VICTOR: *64* 3–5
TOWER: *65–66* 3–5
LPs: 10/12-Inch 33rpm
ERA: *62* 20–25
PETE: *69* 10–12
RCA VICTOR: *64–65* 10–15
SHEFFIELD: *77* 8–10
TOWER: *66* 10–15
Also see EVERETT, Betty, & Ketty Lester

LET'S ACTIVE
LPs: 10/12-Inch 33rpm
I.R.S.: *84* 5–8

LETTERMEN, The
Singles: 7-Inch
CAPITOL: *61–76* 2–4
WARNER BROS: *60* 3–5
Picture Sleeves
CAPITOL: *61–68* 2–4
LPs: 10/12-Inch 33rpm
CAPITOL: *62–80* 5–15
Members: Tony Butala; James Pike; Robert Engemann; Gary Pike; Red Saber; Don Campo.
Also see PETER & GORDON / The Lettermen
Also see TONY, BOB & JIMMY

LEVEL 42
Singles: 7-Inch
A&M: *84* 1–3
LPs: 10/12-Inch 33rpm
A&M: *84* 5–8
POLYDOR: *82* 5–8

LEVERT
Singles: 7-Inch
TEMPRE: *85* $1–3

**LEVINE, Hank (Hank Levine & The
Minature Men)**
Singles: 7-Inch
ABC-PARAMOUNT: *61* 2–4
DOLTON: *62–63* 2–4
TOPS: *60* 3–5

**LEVON & THE HAWKS (Featuring
Levon Helm)**
Singles: 7-Inch
ATCO: *65–68* 5–8
Also see BAND, The
Also see HELM, Levon
Also see HAWKINS, Ronnie

LEVY, Marcy, & Robin Gibb
Singles: 7-Inch
RSO: *80* 1–3
Picture Sleeves
RSO: *80* 1–3
Also see GIBB, Robin

LEWIS, Barbara
Singles: 7-Inch
ATLANTIC: *62–67* 3–5
ENTERPRISE: *70–71* 2–3
REPRISE: *73* 2–3
LPs: 10/12-Inch 33rpm
ATLANTIC (Except
8286): *63–68* 15–20
ATLANTIC (8286; "Best
Of Barbara Lewis"): *71* 10–12
ENTERPRISE: *70* 10–12
SOLID SMOKE 8–10

LEWIS, Bobby
Singles: 7-Inch
ABC-PARAMOUNT: *64* 3–5
BELTONE: *61–62* 4–6
ERIC 1–3
LANA 1–3
ROULETTE: *59* 4–6
LPs: 10/12-Inch 33rpm
BELTONE: *61* 35–40

Price Range   *Price Range*

LEWIS, Gary, & The Playboys
Singles: 7-Inch
LIBERTY (Except 56144):
64–69 .... **$3–5**
LIBERTY (56144; "I Saw
Elvis Presley Last
Night"): 69. .... **10–12**

Picture Sleeves
LIBERTY: 65–67 .... **3–6**

EPs: 7-Inch 33/45rpm
LIBERTY (227; "Doin'
The Flake"): 65 .... **5–10**
(Liberty/Kellogg's Premium Record. Issued
with paper sleeve.)

LPs: 10/12-Inch 33rpm
GUSTO: 72 .... **5–8**
LIBERTY (Except 10000
series): 65–69 .... **15–20**
LIBERTY (10000 series):
81 .... **5–8**
SUNSET: 69 .... **12–15**
UNITED ARTISTS
(Except 1000 series): 75 .... **8–10**
UNITED ARTISTS (1000
series): 81 .... **5–8**

LEWIS, Huey, & The News
Singles: 12-Inch 33/45rpm
CHRYSALIS: 84–85. .... **4–6**

Singles: 7-Inch
CHRYSALIS: 80–85. .... **1–3**

Promotional Singles
CHRYSALIS (43065; "Hip
To Be Square"): 85 .... **10–15**
(Four disc set, each of a different color vinyl.)

LPs: 10/12-Inch 33rpm
CHRYSALIS: 80–85. .... **5–8**
Members: Huey Lewis; Bill Gibson; Mario
Cipollina; Sean Hopper; Chris Hayes; Johnny
Colla.
Also see CLOVER
Also see EDMUNDS, Dave
Also see SAN FRANCISCO ALL STARS,
The
Also see U.S.A. FOR AFRICA

LEWIS, J.G.
Singles: 7-Inch
IX CHAINS: 76 .... **2–3**

LEWIS, Jerry
Singles: 7-Inch
CAPITOL: 50–53 .... **$3–5**
DECCA: 56–62 .... **2–4**
DOT: 60. .... **2–4**
LIBERTY: 63 .... **2–4**
EPs: 7-Inch 33/45rpm
CAPITOL: 56 .... **5–12**
DECCA: 56 .... **5–10**
LPs: 10/12-Inch 33rpm
CAPITOL: 64 .... **10–15**
DECCA: 56 .... **15–25**
DOT: 60. .... **10–15**
VOCALION: 66 .... **8–12**
Also see MARTIN, Dean, & Jerry Lewis

LEWIS, Jerry Lee (Jerry Lee Lewis & His Pumping Piano)
Singles: 7-Inch
BUDDAH: 71 .... **2–3**
ELEKTRA: 79–82 .... **2–3**
MCA: 82–83 .... **1–3**
MERCURY: 70–82. .... **2–3**
SSS/SUN: 69–84 .... **1–3**
(Includes numbers below 100 and over 1000.)
SMASH (1857 through
2122): 63–67. .... **4–6**
SMASH (2146 through
2257): 68–70. .... **2–4**
SUN (259; "Crazy Arms"):
56 .... **10–12**
SUN (267 through 296):
56–58 .... **5–8**
SUN (300 series): 58–65 .... **3–5**
Picture Sleeves
SUN: 57–58 .... **10–20**
EPs: 7-Inch 33/45rpm
MERCURY: 71–72. .... **15–20**
(Promotional issues only.)
SSS/SUN: 69. .... **15–20**
(Jukebox issues only.)
SMASH: 64–65 .... **20–25**
SUN: 57–58 .... **20–25**
(Sun EP 107, "The Great Ball Of Fire," was
issued with a paper sleeve.)
LPs: 10/12-Inch 33rpm
ACCORD: 81–82 .... **5–8**
AURA: 82 .... **5–8**
BUCKBOARD: 75 .... **8–10**
CHARLY **5–8**
ELEKTRA: 79–82 .... **5–8**

Price Range

EVEREST: *75* **$8–10**
HILLTOP: *72* **10–12**
KOALA: *79* **5–8**
MCA: *82–84* **5–8**
MERCURY (SR series,
  except 61318 & 61343):
  70–72 . . . . **12–15**
MERCURY (SR-61318;
  "In Loving Memories"):
  71 . . . . **15–20**
MERCURY (SR-61343;
  "Touching Home"): *71* **15–20**
  (Cover is mostly an artist's drawing with a
  small photo of Lewis on the right side.)
MERCURY (SR-61343;
  "Touching Home"): *71* **12–15**
  (Cover pictures Lewis standing in front of a
  brick wall.)
MERCURY (SRM1 series):
  72–78 . . . . **8–10**
MERCURY (SRM2 series):
  73 . . . . **15–20**
OUT OF TOWN DIST: *82* **5–8**
PICKWICK: *70–74* **10–12**
POLYSTAR **8–10**
POWER PAK: *74*. **8–10**
RHINO: *83* **8–10**
SSS/SUN: *69–84* **5–8**
SEARS **10–12**
SMASH (040; "The
  Golden Hits Of Jerry
  Lee Lewis"): *64* **20–25**
SMASH (040; "The
  Golden Rock Hits Of
  Jerry Lee Lewis") **10–12**
  (Reissue, using a slightly different title.)
SMASH (056 through 086):
  64–66 . . . . **20–25**
SMASH (097; "Soul My
  Way"): *67*. **25–30**
  (Smash numbers 040 through 097 were pre-
  ceeded by a "27" for mono issues or a "67" for
  stereo releases.)
SMASH (7000 series): *82* **5–8**
SMASH (67104 through
  67131): *68–70*. **10–15**
SUN (1230; "Jerry Lee
  Lewis"): *58*. **45–55**
SUN (1265; "Jerry Lee's
  Greatest"): *62*. **35–45**
SUNNYVALE: *77* **8–10**

Price Range

TRIP: *74* **$8–10**
WING (Except PKW2
  series): *66–67* **12–15**
WING (PKW2 series): *69* **20–25**

Promotional LPs
MERCURY (690; "Jerry
  Lee Lewis Radio
  Special"): *73*. **35–40**
  Also see HAWK, The
  Also see NELSON, Willie / Jerry Lee Lewis /
  Carl Perkins / David Allan Coe

LEWIS, Jerry Lee, & Friends
Singles: 7-Inch
SSS/SUN: *80* **2–3**
  (Shown on one side as by Jerry Lee Lewis &
  Orion, and on the other as Charlie Rich &
  Orion.)

LPs: 10/12-Inch 33rpm
SSS/SUN: *78* **8–10**
  Members: Jerry Lee Lewis; Jimmy Ellis;
  Charlie Rich.
  Also see RICH, Charlie

LEWIS, Jerry Lee / Curly Bridges / Frank Motley
LPs: 10/12-Inch 33rpm
DESIGN: *63* **10–15**

LEWIS, Jerry Lee / Johnny Cash
LPs: 10/12-Inch 33rpm
SSS/SUN: *71* **8–10**
  Also see CASH, Johnny
  Also see PERKINS, Carl, Jerry Lee Lewis, Roy
  Orbison & Johnny Cash

LEWIS, Jerry Lee & Linda Gail
Singles: 7-Inch
SMASH: *69–70* **2–4**
SUN: *63* **3–5**

LPs: 10/12-Inch 33rpm
SMASH: *69* **15–20**

LEWIS, Jerry Lee / Roger Miller / Roy Orbison
LPs: 10/12-Inch 33rpm
PICKWICK **8–10**
  Also see MILLER, Roger
  Also see ORBISON, Roy

Price Range

LEWIS, Jerry Lee, Carl Perkins & Charlie Rich
LPs: 10/12-Inch 33rpm
SSS/SUN (1018; "Trio
+"): *78* **$8–10**
  Also see LEWIS, Jerry Lee, & Friends
  Also see PERKINS, Carl

LEWIS, Jerry Lee / Charlie Rich / Johnny Cash
LPs: 10/12-Inch 33rpm
POWER PAK **8–10**
  Also see CASH, Johnny, Carl Perkins & Jerry
  Lee Lewis
  Also see LEWIS, Jerry Lee

LEWIS, Jimmy (Jimmy Lewis & The L.A. Street Band)
Singles: 7-Inch
HOTLANTA: *75.* **2–3**
MCA: *84* **1–3**
LPs: 10/12-Inch 33rpm
HOTLANTA: *74.* **5–10**

LEWIS, Ramsey (The Ramsey Lewis Trio; Ramsey Lewis & Co.)
Singles: 12-Inch 33/45rpm
COLUMBIA: *79–85* **4–6**
Singles: 7-Inch
ABC: *74* **1–3**
ARGO: *58–65* **2–4**
CADET: *65–72* **2–3**
CHESS: *73* **1–3**
COLUMBIA: *72–85* **1–3**
EMARCY: *59* **2–4**
EPs: 7-Inch 33/45rpm
ARGO: *61* **10–15**
LPs: 10/12-Inch 33rpm
ARGO (600 series): *58–62* **20–40**
ARGO (700 series): *62–65* **15–25**
CADET: *65–72* **8–15**
COLUMBIA: *72–85* **5–10**
EMARCY: *59* **20–40**
TRIP: *75* **5–8**
  Members: Ramsey Lewis; Eldee Young; Red
  Holt.
  Also see EARTH, WIND & FIRE & RAM-
  SEY LEWIS
  Also see WILSON, Nancy
  Also see YOUNG-HOLT UNLIMITED

Price Range

LEWIS, Smiley
Singles: 7-Inch
DOT: *64* **$4–6**
IMPERIAL (5194; "The
  Bells Are Ringing"): *52* **35–40**
IMPERIAL (5208 through
  5279): *52–54.* **20–25**
  (Black vinyl.)
IMPERIAL (5200 series):
  53 .... **45–55**
  (Colored vinyl.)
IMPERIAL (5296 through
  5325): *54* **15–20**
IMPERIAL (5349 through
  5418): *55–56.* **8–10**
IMPERIAL (5431 through
  5820): *57–62.* **4–6**
KNIGHT: *59.* **4–6**
LOMA: *65* **3–5**
OKEH: *62* **3–5**
LPs: 10/12-Inch 33rpm
IMPERIAL: *61* **100–125**

LEWIS, Webster (Webster Lewis & The Post-Pop Space Rock Be-Bop Gospel Tabernacle Orchestra & Chorus; Webster Lewis & Love Unlimited Orchestra)
Singles: 12-Inch 33/45rpm
EPIC: *77* **4–6**
UNLIMITED GOLD: *81* **4–6**
Singles: 7-Inch
EPIC: *77–81* **1–3**
UNLIMITED GOLD: *81* **1–3**
LPs: 10/12-Inch 33rpm
EPIC: *78–80* **5–8**
UNLIMITED GOLD: *81* **5–8**

Price Range

Price Range

LEWIS & CLARKE (The Lewis & Clarke Expedition)
Singles: 7-Inch
CHARTMAKER: 66 . . . . **$4–6**
COLGEMS: 67–68 . . . . **3–5**
Picture Sleeves
COLGEMS: 67 . . . . **5–8**
LPs: 10/12-Inch 33rpm
COLGEMS: 67 . . . . **12–15**
Members: Travis Lewis; Boomer Clarke.
Also see MURPHEY, Michael

LIA, Orsa
Singles: 7-Inch
INFINITY: 79. **1–3**
RCA VICTOR: 68 . . . . **2–4**

LIBERACE
Singles: 7-Inch
A.V.I.: 76–77. **1–3**
COLUMBIA (39000
through 41000 series):
52–58 . . . . **2–4**
CORAL: 59–61 . . . . **2–4**
DECCA (28000 series): 52 . . . . **3–5**
DOT: 64–67. . . . . **2–3**
MGM: 73. . . . . **1–3**
WARNER BROS: 71 . . . . **1–3**
EPs: 7-Inch 33/45rpm
COLUMBIA: 52–56 . . . . **5–12**
DECCA (28000 series): 52 . . . . **8–12**
LPs: 10/12-Inch 33rpm
ABC: 74. . . . . **4–8**
A.V.I.: 73–79 . . . . **4–8**
COLUMBIA (500 through
1200 series): 53–58 . . . . **10–20**
COLUMBIA (6000 series):
52 . . . . **15–25**
COLUMBIA (9800 series):
69 . . . . **5–10**
CORAL: 59–64 . . . . **8–15**
DECCA: 72. . . . . **5–10**
DOT: 63–68. **5–15**
FORWARD: 69 . . . . **5–10**
HARMONY: 59–70 . . . . **5–10**
HAMILTON: 65. . . . . **5–10**
MISTLETOE: 74. . . . . **4–8**
PARAMOUNT: 73–74. . . . . **5–10**
TRIP: 76 . . . . **4–8**
VOCALION: 68 . . . . **5–10**
WARNER BROS: 71 . . . . **5–10**

LIEBERMAN, Lori
Singles: 7-Inch
CAPITOL: 72–75 . . . . **$2–3**
MILLENNIUM: 78 . . . . **2–3**
LPs: 10/12-Inch 33rpm
CAPITOL: 72–74 . . . . **8–10**

LIFESTYLE
Singles: 7-Inch
MCA: 77 . . . . **2–3**
LPs: 10/12-Inch 33rpm
MCA: 77 . . . . **8–10**

LIGGETT, Otis
Singles: 12-Inch 33/45rpm
EMERGENCY: 83 . . . . **4–6**
Singles: 7-Inch
EMERGENCY: 83 . . . . **1–3**

LIGGINS, Jimmy
Singles: 7-Inch
ALADDIN: 54 . . . . **12–15**
SPECIALTY (300 & 400
series): 49–54 . . . . **12–15**
(Black vinyl.)
SPECIALTY (Colored
vinyl): 53 . . . . **25–30**

LIGGINS, Joe (Joe Liggins & His Honeydrippers)
Singles: 7-Inch
ALADDIN: 56 . . . . **5–8**
MERCURY: 54. . . . . **5–8**
SPECIALTY: 51–54 . . . . **10–12**
Also see MILTON, Roy / Joe Liggins

LIGHT, Enoch, & His Orchestra
Singles: 7-Inch
COMMAND: 61. . . . . **1–3**
LPs: 10/12-Inch 33rpm
COMMAND: 60–66. . . . . **5–15**
GRAND AWARD: 59. . . . . **5–10**
PROJECT 3: 67–71. . . . . **5–10**

LIGHTFOOT, Gordon (Gord Lightfoot)
Singles: 7-Inch
ABC-PARAMOUNT: 62. . . . . **6–10**
REPRISE: 70–77. . . . . **2–4**
UNITED ARTISTS: 65–69 . . . . **3–6**

Price Range

WARNER BROS (Except
5600 series): *78–83* **$5–8**
WARNER BROS (5600
series): *65* **3–5**
Picture Sleeves
UNITED ARTISTS
(50152; "The Way I
Feel"): *67* **4–8**
LPs: 10/12-Inch 33rpm
REPRISE: *70–76*................. **6–12**
UNITED ARTISTS
(Except 400 series):
70–74 .... **6–12**
UNITED ARTISTS (400
series): *66–69* **10–20**
(U.A. 400 series numbers may be preceded by
a "3," for monaural, or a "6," for stereo issues.)
WARNER BROS: *78–83* **1–3**

LIGHTHOUSE
Singles: 7-Inch
EVOLUTION: *71–72* **2–3**
POLYDOR: *73–74* **2–3**
RCA VICTOR: *69–70* **2–4**
LPs: 10/12-Inch 33rpm
EVOLUTION: *71–72* **10–12**
JANUS: *76* **8–10**
POLYDOR: *73–74* **8–10**
RCA VICTOR: *69–70* **10–15**

LIMAHL (Chris Hamill)
Singles: 12-Inch 33/45rpm
EMI AMERICA: *85*............... **4–6**
Singles: 7-Inch
EMI AMERICA: *85*............... **1–3**
LPs: 10/12-Inch 33rpm
EMI AMERICA: *85*............... **5–8**
Also see KAJAGOOGOO

LIME
Singles: 12-Inch 33/45rpm
PRISM: *83*...................... **4–6**
TSR: *85* **4–6**
Singles: 7-Inch
PRISM: *83*...................... **1–3**
LPs: 10/12-Inch 33rpm
PRISM: *83*...................... **5–8**

LIMELITERS, The
Singles: 7-Inch
ELEKTRA: *60–61* **3–5**

Price Range

RCA VICTOR: *61–64* **$3–5**
WARNER BROS: *68*............... **2–4**
Picture Sleeves
RCA VICTOR: *61–63* **3–5**
LPs: 10/12-Inch 33rpm
CAMDEN: *74*.................... **5–10**
ELEKTRA: *60–61* **15–20**
LEGACY: *70*.................... **8–10**
PICKWICK: *72* **5–8**
RCA VICTOR (Except
ANL1 series): *61–68*............ **8–15**
RCA VICTOR (ANL1
series): *77*..................... **5–8**
STAX: *74*...................... **6–10**
WARNER BROS: *68*............. **8–15**
Members: Glen Yarbrough; Lou Gottlieb; Alex
Hassilev; Ernie Sheldon.
Also see YARBROUGH, Glen

LIMMIE & FAMILY COOKIN'
Singles: 7-Inch
AVCO: *72* **2–3**

LIMIT
Singles: 12-Inch 33/45rpm
PORTRAIT: *84*................... **4–6**
Singles: 7-Inch
ARISTA: *82* **1–3**
PORTRAIT: *84*................... **1–3**
Also see GUTHRIE, Gwen

LIND, Bob
Singles: 7-Inch
CAPITOL: *71* **2–4**
VERVE/FOLKWAYS: *66*........... **3–5**
WORLD PACIFIC: *65–66* **3–5**
LPs: 10/12-Inch 33rpm
CAPITOL: *71* **10–12**
VERVE/FOLKWAYS: *66*........ **10–15**
WORLD PACIFIC: *66* **10–15**
Also see CASCADES, The

LINDEN, Kathy
Singles: 7-Inch
CAPITOL: *62–63* **3–5**
FELSTED: *58–59* **4–6**
MONUMENT: *60–61*.............. **3–5**
NATIONAL **3–5**
RECORD PROD. CORP:
61 .... **3–5**

Price Range

Price Range

Picture Sleeves
MONUMENT: 60–61.............. **$3–5**

LINDISFARNE
Singles: 7-Inch
ATCO: 78 .... **1–3**
ELEKTRA: 72–73 .... **2–3**
LPs: 10/12-Inch 33rpm
ATCO: 78 .... **8–10**
ELEKTRA: 71–74 .... **10–12**

LINDLEY, David
Singles: 7-Inch
ASYLUM: 81..................... **1–3**
LPs: 10/12-Inch 33rpm
ASYLUM: 81..................... **5–8**
Also see BROWNE, Jackson

LINDSAY, Mark
Singles: 7-Inch
COLUMBIA: 69–75............... **2–4**
GREEDY: 76..................... **2–3**
WARNER BROS: 77............... **2–3**
LPs: 10/12-Inch 33rpm
COLUMBIA: 70–71 .... **10–12**
Also see: REVERE, Paul, & The Raiders

LINER
Singles: 7-Inch
ATCO: 79 .... **1–3**
LPs: 10/12-Inch 33rpm
ATCO: 79 .... **5–8**

LINK-EDDY COMBO, The
Singles: 7-Inch
REPRISE: 61.................... **3–5**

LINKLETTER, Art
Singles: 7-Inch
CAPITOL: 69 .... **2–3**
EPs: 7-Inch 33/45rpm
COLUMBIA: 56.................. **5–10**
WORD: 69...................... **3–5**
LPs: 10/12-Inch 33rpm
CAPITOL: 61 .... **8–15**
COLUMBIA: 56................. **10–20**
HARMONY: 59 .... **8–15**
20TH CENTURY-FOX:
    63–66 .... **8–15**
WORD: 68...................... **5–10**

LINX
Singles: 7-Inch
CHRYSALIS: 81................. **$1–3**
Picture Sleeves
CHRYSALIS: 81................. **INC**
LPs: 10/12-Inch 33rpm
CHRYSALIS: 81................. **5–8**
Members: David Grant; Peter Martin.
Also see GRANT, David

LIPPS, INC.
Singles: 7-Inch
CASABLANCA: 79–83 .... **1–3**
LPs: 10/12-Inch 33rpm
CASABLANCA: 79–81 .... **5–8**

LIQUID GOLD
Singles: 12-Inch 33/45rpm
CRITIQUE: 83 .... **4–6**
PARACHUTE: 79 .... **4–6**
Singles: 7-Inch
CRITIQUE: 83 .... **1–3**
PARACHUTE: 79 .... **1–3**
LPs: 10/12-Inch 33rpm
PARACHUTE: 79 .... **5–8**

LIQUID LIQUID
Singles: 12-Inch 33/45rpm
99 RECORDS: 83................. **4–6**

LIQUID SMOKE
Singles: 7-Inch
AVCO EMBASSY: 70 .... **2–3**
LPs: 10/12-Inch 33rpm
AVCO EMBASSY: 70 .... **10–12**

LISA
Singles: 12-Inch 33/45rpm
MOBY DICK: 83–84.............. **4–6**

LISA LISA & CULT JAM WITH FULL FORCE
Singles: 12-Inch 33/45rpm
COLUMBIA: 85.................. **4–6**
Singles: 7-Inch
COLUMBIA: 84–85 .... **1–3**
LPs: 10/12-Inch 33rpm
COLUMBIA: 84–85............... **5–8**
Also see FULL FORCE

Price Range

LITES, Shirley
Singles: 12-Inch 33/45rpm
WEST END: 83 .... $4–6

LITTER, The
Singles: 7-Inch
PROBE: 69 20–40
LPs: 10/12-Inch 33rpm
HEXAGON: 69................ 75–100
PROBE: 69 100–125
WARICK: 68................ 125–150

LITTLE, Rich
Singles: 7-Inch
BOARDWALK: 82 1–3
MERCURY: 71..................... 2–3
LPs: 10/12-Inch 33rpm
BOARDWALK: 82 5–8
CAEDMON: 72 5–10
KARR: 68...................... 8–15
MERCURY: 71.................. 8–10

LITTLE ANTHONY & THE IMPERIALS (Anthony & The Imperials; The Imperials)
Singles: 7-Inch
APOLLO: 61..................... 4–6
AVCO: 74–75..................... 2–4
DCP: 64–66...................... 3–5
END (Except 1027): 58–62 5–8
END (1027; "Tears On My
  Pillow"): 58 10–12
  (Shown as by "The Imperials.")
END (1027; "Tears On My
  Pillow"): 58 5–8
  (Shown as by "Little Anthony & The Imperials.")
JANUS: 71–72.................... 2–4
MCA: 80 1–3
PCM: 83........................ 1–3
PURE GOLD: 76.................. 2–3
ROULETTE: 61–63 4–6
UNITED ARTISTS: 69–70 3–5
VEEP: 66–68 3–5
Picture Sleeves
DCP: 65........................ 5–8
VEEP: 66....................... 4–6
EPs: 7-Inch 33/45rpm
END: 58–59..................... 20–30
LPs: 10/12-Inch 33rpm
ACCORD: 83 5–8

Price Range

AVCO: 74 .... $8–10
DCP: 64–66.................... 15–20
END: 59–60..................... 30–40
FORUM CIRCLE 10–15
LIBERTY: 81 5–8
ROULETTE: 65 20–25
SUNSET: 70 10–12
UNITED ARTISTS
  (Except 1000 series):
  69–74 10–15
UNITED ARTISTS (1000
  series): 80.................... 5–8
VEEP: 66–68 12–15
  Also see IMPERIALS, The

LITTLE ANTHONY & THE IMPERIALS / The Platters
LPs: 10/12-Inch 33rpm
EXACT: 80...................... 5–8
  Also see LITTLE ANTHONY & THE IMPERIALS
  Also see PLATTERS, The

LITTLE BEAVER
Singles: 7-Inch
CAT: 72–76...................... 2–4

LITTLE BILL & THE BLUENOTES
Singles: 7-Inch
DOLTON: 59..................... 4–6

LITTLE BO (Eddie Bo)
Singles: 7-Inch
ACE: 55........................ 20–25
  Also see BO, Eddie

LITTLE BOOKER (James Booker)
Singles: 7-Inch
IMPERIAL: 54.................. 25–30
  Also see BOOKER, James

LITTLE CAESAR
Singles: 7-Inch
BIG TOWN..................... 10–15
RPM........................... 10–12
RECORDED IN
  HOLLYWOOD: 53............. 10–15

Price Range

LITTLE CAESAR & THE CONSULS
Singles: 7-Inch
MALA: 65 . . . . $3–5

LITTLE CAESAR & THE ROMANS
Singles: 7-Inch
DEL-FI: 61 5–8
LPs: 10/12-Inch 33rpm
DEL-FI: 61 35–45
Also see BLUE JAYS, The / Little Caesar & The Romans

LITTLE DIPPERS, The (The Anita Kerr Singers)
Singles: 7-Inch
DOT: 64 2–4
UNIVERSITY: 59–60 3–5
Also see KERR, Anita

LITTLE ESTHER (Little Esther Phillips)
Singles: 7-Inch
ATLANTIC: 64–67 3–5
DECCA: 54 12–15
FEDERAL (12023; "I'm A Bad Girl"): 51 35–40
FEDERAL (12042: "Crying & Sighing"): 51 35–40
FEDERAL (12055 through 12142): 51–53 20–25
Note: Federal 12100 is included in the LITTLE ESTHER & THE ROBINS section.
KUDU: 72–76 2–3
LENOX: 62–63 3–5
SAVOY (1100 series): 56 5–8
SAVOY (1500 series): 58–59 4–6
WARWICK: 60–61 3–5
LPs: 10/12-Inch 33rpm
ATLANTIC (Except 8000 series): 70–76 8–10
ATLANTIC (8000 series): 65–66 12–15
KING: 59 150–175
KUDU: 72–76 8–10
LENOX: 62 20–25
MERCURY: 78–81 5–8
YORKSHIRE 8–10
Also see PHILLIPS, Esther

Price Range

LITTLE ESTHER & BIG AL DOWNING
Singles: 7-Inch
LENOX: 63 . . . . $3–5
Also see DOWNING, Al

LITTLE ESTHER & LITTLE WILLIE LITTLEFIELD
Singles: 7-Inch
FEDERAL: 52 20–25
Also see LITTLEFIELD, Little Willie

LITTLE ESTHER & MEL WALKER
Singles: 7-Inch
FEDERAL: 52 20–25
SAVOY: 50 25–35

LITTLE ESTHER & THE DOMINOES
Singles: 7-Inch
FEDERAL: 51 225–250
Also see DOMINOES, The

LITTLE ESTHER & THE ROBINS
Singles: 7-Inch
FEDERAL (12100; "Saturday Night Daddy"): 52 75–100
SAVOY: 50 30–40
Also see LITTLE ESTHER
Also see OTIS, Johnny
Also see ROBINS, The

LITTLE EVA
Singles: 7-Inch
ABC: 74 1–3
AMY: 65–66 3–5
BELL: 72 2–3
DIMENSION: 62–65 4–6
SPRING: 70 2–4
VERVE: 66 3–5
Picture Sleeves
DIMENSION: 64 8–12
LPs: 10/12-Inch 33rpm
DIMENSION: 62 35–45
Also see IRWIN, Big Dee
Also see KING, Carole / Little Eva / The Cookies

Price Range   *Price Range*

LITTLE FEAT (Featuring Lowell George)
Singles: 7-Inch
WARNER BROS: 70–78 . . . . $2–3
LPs: 10/12-Inch 33rpm
MFSL: 78 20–25
WARNER BROS: 70–81 6–10
Promotional LPs
WARNER BROS (984;
"Hoy Hoy"): 81 10–15
Also see GEORGE, Lowell

LITTLE JO ANN
Singles: 7-Inch
KAPP: 62 3–5

LITTLE JOE & THE THRILLERS (Little Joe; Little Joe The Thriller)
Singles: 7-Inch
ENJOY: 64 3–5
EPIC (9000 series): 58 4–6
MGM: 70–73 2–3
OKEH: 56–61 5–8
REPRISE: 63 3–5
ROSE: 63 3–5
20TH CENTURY-FOX:
61 3–5
EPs: 7-Inch 33/45rpm
EPIC: 58 30–40

LITTLE JOE BLUE
Singles: 7-Inch
CHECKER: 66 3–5
MOVIN': 66 3–5

LITTLE JOEY & THE FLIPS (Joey Hall)
Singles: 7-Inch
JOY: 62 3–5

LITTLE JUNIOR'S BLUE FLAMES (Junior Parker)
Singles: 7-Inch
SUN: 53 30–35
Also see PARKER, Little Junior

LITTLE MAC & THE BOSS SOUNDS (With Ann Mason)
Singles: 7-Inch
ATLANTIC: 65 3–5

LITTLE MILTON
Singles: 7-Inch
BOBBIN: 59–61 . . . . $4–6
CHECKER (1000 & 1100
series): 62–68 3–5
CHECKER (1200 series):
68–71 2–4
CHESS: 73–76 2–3
GLADES: 76–78 2–3
MCA: 83 1–3
MALACO: 84 1–3
METEOR: 57 25–35
STAX: 72–82 1–3
SUN: 53–55 45–55

LPs: 10/12-Inch 33rpm
CHECKER: 65–70 10–15
CHESS: 72–76 10–12
GLADES: 76–77 8–10
MCA: 83 5–8
MALACO: 84 5–8
STAX: 73–81 8–10

LITTLE MILTON & ALBERT KING
LPs: 10/12-Inch 33rpm
STAX: 79 5–8
Also see KING, Albert
Also see LITTLE MILTON

Little Richard, 22 charted singles (1956–70), three charted LPs (1957–71).

Price Range *Price Range*

LITTLE RICHARD (Little Richard & His Band)
Singles: 7-Inch
ABC: *73* $1–3
ATLANTIC: *63* 3–5
BELL: *73* 2–4
BRUNSWICK: *68.* 3–5
CORAL: *63* 3–5
END: *59* 4–6
GREEN MOUNTAIN: *73* 2–4
KENT: *73* 2–4
MANTICORE: *75* 2–3
MERCURY: *61.* 3–5
MODERN: *66–67.* 3–5
OKEH: *66–69* 3–5
PEACOCK: *53–54* 15–20
RCA VICTOR: *51–52* 60–75
REPRISE: *70–72.* 2–4
SPECIALTY (561 through
   664): *56–59.* 5–8
SPECIALTY (670 through
   699): *59–64.* 4–6
SPECIALTY (Boxed sets
   of 6 colored vinyl 45s):
   85 12–15
TRIP: *71* 2–3
VEE JAY: *64.* 3–5

Picture Sleeves
MODERN: *66.* 3–5
OKEH: *66* 3–5
SPECIALTY: *57–58* 8–12

EPs: 7-Inch 33/45rpm
CAMDEN: *56* 25–35
KAMA SUTRA: *70* 12–15
SPECIALTY: *56–57* 20–25

LPs: 10/12-Inch 33rpm
ACCORD: *81* 5–8
BUDDAH: *69* 10–12
CAMDEN (420; "Little
   Richard"): *56* 60–75
CAMDEN (2430; "Every
   Hour"): *70* 10–12
CHARLY 5–8
CORAL: *63* 15–20
CROWN: *63* 15–20
CUSTOM....................... 10–12
EPIC: *71* 10–12
EVEREST: *82* 5–8
EXACT: *80–81* 5–8
51 WEST 5–8

GRT: *77.* $5–8
GOLD DISC................... 10–12
GUEST STAR.................. 10–12
KAMA SUTRA: *70* 10–12
MERCURY: *61.* 20–25
MODERN: *66.* 10–15
OKEH: *67* 10–15
PICKWICK: *72* 10–12
REPRISE: *70–72.* 10–12
ROULETTE: *68* 10–15
SCEPTER 10–12
SPECIALTY (100; "Here's
   Little Richard"): *57.* 50–60
   (First pressings were numbered 100, later issues
   were cataloged as 2100. Prior to this LP, Spe-
   cialty issued a 10-inch LP by Buddy Baker &
   His Orchestra which was also numbered 100.)
SPECIALTY (2100
   through 2104): *57–58* 25–30
SPECIALTY (2111
   through 2136): *63–70* 10–15
   (Specialty LP reissues, using original catalog
   numbers, are currently available.)
SPIN-O-RAMA.................. 10–12
SUMMIT....................... 10–12
TRIP: *71–78* 10–12
20TH CENTURY-FOX:
   63 12–15
UNITED 8–10
UNITED ARTISTS: *75*........... 8–10
UPFRONT: *77* 8–10
VEE JAY: *64–65.* 12–15
VEE JAY/DYNASTY............ 10–12
WING: *64* 12–15
   Also see CANNED HEAT
   Also see DEUCES OF RHYTHM & TEMPO
   TOPPERS, The
   Also see HENDRIX, Jimi, & Little Richard

LITTLE RIVER BAND, The (LRB)
Singles: 12-Inch 33/45rpm
CAPITOL: *83* 4–6

Singles: 7-Inch
CAPITOL: *79–85* 1–3
HARVEST: *76–78.* 2–3

Picture Sleeves
CAPITOL: *81–83* .... INC

LPs: 10/12-Inch 33rpm
CAPITOL: *79–85* 5–8
HARVEST: *75–80.* 5–8
   Also see SHORROCK, Glen

LITTLE ROYAL & THE SWINGMASTERS
Singles: 7-Inch
TRI-US: *72–73*.................. **$2–4**

LITTLE SISTER
Singles: 7-Inch
STONE FLOWER: *70–72* **3–5**
LPs: 10/12-Inch 33rpm
STONE FLOWER: *70* **10–12**

LITTLE STEVEN & THE DISCIPLES OF SOUL
Singles: 7-Inch
EMI AMERICA: *82–84*............. **1–3**
LPs: 10/12-Inch 33rpm
EMI AMERICA: *82–84*............. **5–8**
Also see SPRINGSTEEN, Bruce

LITTLE SYLVIA (Sylvia Vanderpool)
Singles: 7-Inch
CAT: *53*.......................... **5–8**
JUBILEE: *52*.................... **12–15**
Also see SYLVIA

LITTLE WALTER (Little Walter & His Jukes; Little Walter & His Night Caps; Little Walter & His Night Cats; The Little Walter Trio)
Singles: 7-Inch
CHANCE: *52* **100–125**
CHECKER (700 series):
  52–54 .... **8–10**
  (Black vinyl.)
CHECKER (700 series): *54*........ **40–50**
  (Colored vinyl.)
CHECKER (800 series):
  54–58 .... **5–8**
CHECKER (900 through
  1100 series): *58–65* **3–5**
LPs: 10/12-Inch 33rpm
CHESS (Except 1400
  series): *69–74*................. **10–15**
CHESS (1400 series): *63*........... **15–20**
Also see ROBINSON, Freddy

LITTLE WILLIE JOHN: see JOHN, Little Willie

LITTLEFIELD, Little Willie
Singles: 7-Inch
BULLS-EYE: *58*................. **$4–6**
FEDERAL (12100 &
  12200 series): *52–54* **20–25**
FEDERAL (12300 series):
  57–59 .... **5–8**
RHYTHM: *56*................... **15–20**
Also see LITTLE ESTHER & LITTLE WIL-
LIE LITTLEFIELD

LIVE
Singles: 7-Inch
T.S.O.B.: *81*...................... **1–3**

LIVERPOOL FIVE, The
Singles: 7-Inch
RCA VICTOR: *65–67* **3–5**
LPs: 10/12-Inch 33rpm
RCA VICTOR: *66–67* **20–25**

LIVIGNI, John
Singles: 7-Inch
RAINTREE: *75* **2–3**

LIVIN' PROOF
Singles: 7-Inch
JU-PAR: *77*...................... **2–3**

LIVING STRINGS, The
Singles: 7-Inch
COMMAND: *59*.................. **1–3**
GRAND AWARD: *59*............. **1–3**
LPs: 10/12-Inch 33rpm
CAMDEN: *60–62*................. **4–8**
COMMAND: *59*.................. **4–8**
GRAND AWARD: *59*............. **4–8**

LIZARD, King: see KING LIZARD

LLOYD, Charles, Quartet
LPs: 10/12-Inch 33rpm
ATLANTIC: *67* **8–12**
COLUMBIA: *64–65*.............. **8–15**
Also see HAMILTON, Chico, & Charles Lloyd

LLOYD, Ian
Singles: 7-Inch
POLYDOR: *76*.................... **2–3**
SCOTTI BROTHERS: *79* **1–3**

Price Range

LPs: 10/12-Inch 33rpm
SCOTTI BROTHERS: *79* **$5–8**
Also see STORIES, The

LOAF, Meat: see MEAT LOAF

LOBO
Singles: 7-Inch
BIG TREE: *71–75* **2–4**
ELEKTRA: *80* **1–3**
EVERGREEN. **2–3**
FLASHBACK: *73*. **1–3**
MCA: *79* **2–3**
MARIANNE: *77*. **2–3**
WARNER BROS: *76–78* **2–3**
LPs: 10/12-Inch 33rpm
BIG TREE: *71–75* **10–12**
CALUMET: *73* **10–12**
MCA: *79* **5–8**

LOCKLIN, Hank
Singles: 7-Inch
COUNTRY ARTISTS: *83* **1–3**
DECCA (29000 series): *52* **4–6**
FOUR STAR (1500 &
1600 series): *52–54* **4–6**
KING (5000 series): *59* **3–5**
MGM: *74* **1–3**
PLANTATION: *76–77*. **1–3**
RCA VICTOR (0030
through 0900 series):
72–74 . . . . **1–3**
RCA VICTOR (6100
through 7600 series):
55–59 . . . . **3–5**
RCA VICTOR (7700
through 9900 series):
60–71 . . . . **2–3**
EPs: 7-Inch 33/45rpm
RCA VICTOR: *58–61* **8–12**
LPs: 10/12-Inch 33rpm
CAMDEN: *62–74* **8–15**
DESIGN: *62* **10–15**
INTERNATIONAL
AWARD **8–12**
KING (600 & 700 series):
61 . . . . **12–18**
MGM: *75* **5–10**
METRO: *65* **10–15**
PICKWICK/HILLTOP:
65–68 . . . . **8–15**

Price Range

PLANTATION: *77–81* **$5–8**
RCA VICTOR (Except
1600 series): *62–71* **8–15**
RCA VICTOR (1600
series): *58* **20–25**
SEARS **8–12**
WRANGLER: *62* **15–25**
Also see SNOW, Hank / Hank Locklin / Por-
ter Wagoner

LOCKLIN, Hank, With Danny Davis & The Nashville Brass
Singles: 7-Inch
RCA VICTOR: *69–70* **2–3**
LPs: 10/12-Inch 33rpm
RCA VICTOR: *70* **6–10**
Also see DAVIS, Danny
Also see LOCKLIN, Hank

LOCKSMITH
Singles: 7-Inch
ARISTA: *80* **1–3**
LPs: 10/12-Inch 33rpm
ARISTA: *80* **5–8**

LODGE, John
Singles: 7-Inch
LONDON: *77* **2–3**
LPs: 10/12-Inch 33rpm
LONDON: *76* **8–10**
Also see HAYWARD, Justin, & John Lodge
Also see MOODY BLUES, The

LOFGREN, Nils
Singles: 7-Inch
A&M: *75–77* **2–3**
LPs: 10/12-Inch 33rpm
A&M: *75–82* **8–10**
BACKSTREET: *81*. **5–8**
EPIC: *76* **8–10**
Promotional LPs
A&M (8362; "Authorized
Bootleg"): *76* **25–30**
Also see GRIN

LOGG
Singles: 7-Inch
SALSOUL: *81* **1–3**
LPs: 10/12-Inch 33rpm
SALSOUL: *81* **5–8**

Price Range

LOGGINS, Dave
Singles: 7-Inch
EPIC: 74–81 .... **$1–3**
VANGUARD: 72–74 .... **2–3**
LPs: 10/12-Inch 33rpm
CAPITOL: 84 .... **5–8**
EPIC: 74–81 .... **8–10**
VANGUARD: 72 .... **8–10**
Also see MURRAY, Anne, & Dave Loggins

LOGGINS, Kenny
Singles: 7-Inch
COLUMBIA: 77–85 .... **1–3**
LPs: 10/12-Inch 33rpm
COLUMBIA (30000
series): 72–84 .... **8–10**
COLUMBIA (40000
series): 81 .... **10–15**
(Half-speed mastered LPs.)
Also see U.S.A. FOR AFRICA

LOGGINS, Kenny, & Stevie Nicks
Singles: 7-Inch
COLUMBIA: 78 .... **1–3**
Also see NICKS, Stevie

LOGGINS, Kenny, & Steve Perry
Singles: 7-Inch
COLUMBIA: 82 .... **1–3**
Also see LOGGINS, Kenny
Also see PERRY, Steve

LOGGINS & MESSINA
Singles: 7-Inch
COLUMBIA: 72–76 .... **2–3**
LPs: 10/12-Inch 33rpm
COLUMBIA (30000
series): 72–82 .... **8–10**
COLUMBIA (40000
series): 82 .... **10–15**
(Half-speed mastered LPs.)
Members: Kenny Loggins; Jim Messina.
Also see LOGGINS, Kenny
Also see MESSINA, Jim

LOGGINS & MESSINA / David Bromberg
LPs: 10/12-Inch 33rpm
COLUMBIA: 72 .... **8–15**
(Promotional issue only.)
Also see BROMBERG, David
Also see LOGGINS & MESSINA

Price Range

LOLITA
Singles: 7-Inch
4 CORNERS: 65 .... **$2–4**
KAPP: 60–61 .... **3–5**
Picture Sleeves
KAPP: 61 .... **3–5**
LPs: 10/12-Inch 33rpm
KAPP: 61 .... **15–20**

LOMAX, Jackie
Singles: 7-Inch
APPLE: 68–71 .... **3–5**
CAPITOL: 77 .... **2–3**
EPIC: 68 .... **3–5**
WARNER BROS: 71–73 .... **2–4**
LPs: 10/12-Inch 33rpm
APPLE: 69 .... **15–20**
CAPITOL: 76–77 .... **5–10**
WARNER BROS: 71–72 .... **8–12**
Also see BADGER
Also see CLAPTON, Eric
Also see McCARTNEY, Paul
Also see STARR, Ringo

LOMBARDO, Guy (Guy Lombardo & His Royal Canadians)
Singles: 7-Inch
CAPITOL: 59–67 .... **2–4**
DECCA: 50–73 .... **2–4**
EPs: 7-Inch 33/45rpm
CAPITOL: 56–59 .... **4–6**
DECCA: 50–59 .... **4–8**
RCA VICTOR: 60 .... **4–6**
LPs: 10/12-Inch 33rpm
CAMDEN: 54–65 .... **5–15**
CAPITOL: 56–81 .... **5–15**
DECCA: 50–67 .... **5–15**
LONDON: 73 .... **4–8**
MCA: 75 .... **4–8**
RCA VICTOR: 72–77 .... **4–8**
VOCALION: 66–68 .... **5–10**
Also see ANDREWS SISTERS, The & Guy Lombardo
Also see ARMSTRONG, Louis, & Guy Lombardo

LONDON, Julie
Singles: 7-Inch
BETHLEHEM: 59 .... **2–4**
LIBERTY: 55–68 .... **2–4**

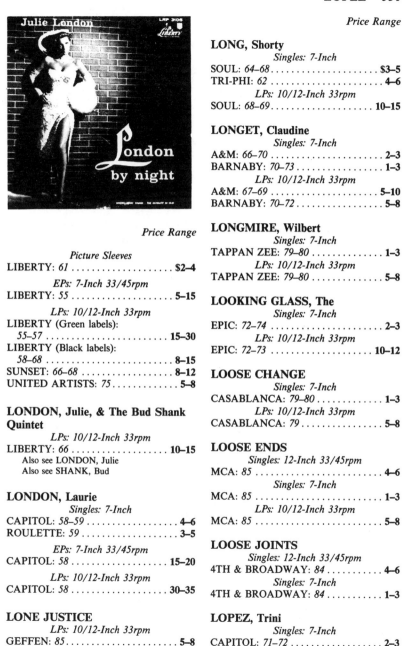

Price Range

D.R.A.: *61*	**$4–6**
GRIFFIN: *73*	**2–3**
KING (5100 series): *58–59*	**8–10**
KING (5200 through 5400 series): *59–61*	**4–6**
KING (5800 series): *63*	**3–5**
MARIANNE: *77.*	**1–3**
PRIVATE STOCK: *75.*	**2–3**
REPRISE: *63–71.*	**3–5**
ROULETTE: *78*	**1–3**
UNITED MODERN: *64*	**3–5**
VOLK	**8–10**

Picture Sleeves

REPRISE: *62–66.*	**3–5**

EPs: 7-Inch 33/45rpm

COLUMBIA/WARNER
BROS. (124178; "Trini
Lopez Sings His Greatest
Hits"): *67* **4–8**
(A Coca-Cola/Fresca premium issue.)
KING: *63* **8–15**
(Includes juke box EPs.)

LPs: 10/12-Inch 33rpm

CAPITOL: *72*	**5–10**
EXACT: *81*	**5–8**
GRIFFIN: *72*	**8–10**
HARMONY: *70*	**8–10**
KING: *63*	**10–15**
REPRISE: *63–69.*	**8–15**
ROULETTE: *78*	**5–8**

LOR, Denise

Singles: 7-Inch

LIBERTY: *56*	**2–4**
MAJAR: *54.*	**3–5**
MERCURY: *55.*	**2–4**

EPs: 7-Inch 33/45rpm

MERCURY: *55.*	**5–8**

LORBER, Jeff (The Jeff Lorber Fusion)

Singles: 12-Inch 33/45rpm

ARISTA: *85*	**4–6**

Singles: 7-Inch

ARISTA: *79–85.*	**1–3**

LPs: 10/12-Inch 33rpm

ARISTA: *79–85.*	**5–8**
INNER CITY: *78.*	**5–10**

Also see UNLIMITED TOUCH

LORD, C.M.

Singles: 12-Inch

MONTAGE: *82–84.*	**$4–6**
WAVE: *83*	**4–6**

Singles: 7-Inch

CAPITOL: *76*	**2–3**
MONTAGE: *82–84.*	**1–3**

LPs: 10/12-Inch 33rpm

CAPITOL: *76*	**8–10**
MONTAGE: *84.*	**5–8**

LORD ROCKINGHAM'S XI

Singles: 7-Inch

LONDON: *58*	**4–6**

LORD SUTCH (Lord Sutch & His Heavy Friends)

LPs: 10/12-Inch 33rpm

COTILLION: *70–72* **15–20**
Also see BECK, Jeff
Also see BLACKMORE, Ritchie
Also see HOPKINS, Nicky
Also see MOON, Keith
Also see PAGE, Jimmy

LORELEIS, The

Singles: 7-Inch

BRUNSWICK: *64.*	**3–5**
SPOTLIGHT: *55.*	**5–8**

LOREN, Bryan

Singles: 12-Inch 33/45rpm

PHILLY WORLD: *83–84*	**4–6**

Singles: 7-Inch

PHILLY WORLD: *83*	**1–3**

LORETTA LYNN: see LYNN, Loretta

LOS ADMIRADORES

LPs: 10/12-Inch 33rpm

COMMAND: *60.*	**8–1**

LOS BRAVOS (Featuring Mike Kennedy)

Singles: 7-Inch

LONDON	**1–3**
PARROT: *68.*	**3–5**
PRESS: *66–68*	**3–5**

LPs: 10/12-Inch 33rpm

PARROT: *68.*	**15–20**

Price Range

PRESS: 66 . . . . $20–25
  Also see DRIFTERS, The / Lesley Gore / Roy
  Orbison / Los Bravos
  Also see KENNEDY, Mike

LOS INDIOS TABAJARAS
Singles: 7-Inch
RCA VICTOR: 63–64 2–4
LPs: 10/12-Inch 33rpm
RCA VICTOR: 63–64 8–15

LOS LOBOS
Singles: 7-Inch
SLASH/WARNER BROS:
  85 1–3
LPs: 10/12-Inch 33rpm
SLASH: 83. 5–8
SLASH/WARNER BROS:
  84 5–8

LOS POP-TOPS: see POP-TOPS, The

LOST GENERATION, The
Singles: 7-Inch
BRUNSWICK: 70–71. 2–4
INNOVATION: 74. 2–4
LPs: 10/12-Inch 33rpm
BRUNSWICK: 70. 10–12

LOU, Bonnie
Singles: 7-Inch
KING: 55 4–6

LOUDERMILK, John D.
Singles: 7-Inch
COLUMBIA: 58–60 5–8
MUSIC IS MEDICINE:
  78–79 2–3
RCA VICTOR: 61–69 3–5
WARNER BROS: 71 2–3
Picture Sleeves
COLUMBIA: 58 5–8
RCA VICTOR: 62 4–6
LPs: 10/12-Inch 33rpm
MUSIC IS MEDICINE: 78 5–8
RCA VICTOR: 61–69 15–20
WARNER BROS: 71 8–12
  Also see DEE, Johnny

Price Range

LOUDNESS
LPs: 10/12-Inch 33rpm
ATCO: 85 . . . . $5–8

LOUISIANA'S LE ROUX: see LE ROUX

LOVE (Featuring Arthur Lee)
Singles: 7-Inch
BLUE THUMB: 69–70 3–5
ELEKTRA: 66–70 5–8
RSO: 74–75 3–5
LPs: 10/12-Inch 33rpm
BLUE THUMB: 69–70 12–15
ELEKTRA: 66–70 20–30
MCA: 82 5–8
RSO: 74 8–10
RHINO (Except picture
  discs): 80 5–8
RHINO (Picture discs): 82 8–10

LOVE, Candace
Singles: 7-Inch
AQUARIUS: 68 3–5

LOVE, Darlene
Singles: 7-Inch
PHILLES (Except 111 &
  123): 63–64. 8–10
PHILLES (111; "The Boy
  I'm Gonna Marry"/"My
  Heart Beat A Little
  Bit"): 63 10-15
PHILLES (111; "The Boy
  I'm Gonna
  Marry"/"Playing For
  Keeps"): 63 8-10
PHILLES (123; "He's A
  Quiet Guy"): 64. 25–30
REPRISE: 66. 4–6
WARNER/SPECTOR:
  74–77 2–4
  Also see BLOSSOMS, The
  Also see BOB B. SOXX & THE BLUE JEANS
  Also see CRYSTALS, The
  Also see RONETTES, The / The Crystals /
  Darlene Love / Bob B. Soxx
  & The Blue Jeans

Price Range

LOVE, Mary
Singles: 7-Inch
JOSIE: 68....................... $3–5
MODERN: 65–66................. 3–5

LOVE, Ronnie
Singles: 7-Inch
DOT: 60–61...................... 4–6
STARTIME: 61.................. 10–15

LOVE, Rudy, & The Love Family
Singles: 7-Inch
CALLA: 76....................... 2–3
LPs: 10/12-Inch 33rpm
CALLA: 76....................... 5–8

LOVE, Vikki, With Nuance
Singles: 12-Inch 33/45rpm
4TH & BROADWAY: 85........... 4–6
Singles: 7-Inch
4TH & BROADWAY: 85........... 1–3
Also see NUANCE

LOVE & KISSES
Singles: 7-Inch
CASABLANCA: 77–79............. 1–3
LPs: 10/12-Inch 33rpm
CASABLANCA: 77–79............ 8–10

LOVE BUG STARSKI
Singles: 12-Inch 33/45rpm
FEVER: 83 4–6

**LOVE CHILD'S AFRO CUBAN
BLUES BAND (Love Child's Latin
Soul Afro Blues Band)**
Singles: 7-Inch
A&M: 69......................... 2–4
ROULETTE: 75 2–3

LOVE CLUB
Singles: 12-Inch 33/45rpm
WEST END: 83 4–6

LOVE COMMITTEE
Singles: 7-Inch
ARIOLA AMERICA:
  75–76 2–3
GOLD MIND: 77–78.............. 2–3

Price Range

LOVE GENERATION
Singles: 7-Inch
IMPERIAL: 67–68................ $3–5
LPs: 10/12-Inch 33rpm
IMPERIAL: 68................... 10–15
UNITED ARTISTS: 77............ 8–10
Also see CLIMAX

LOVE, PEACE & HAPPINESS
Singles: 7-Inch
RCA VICTOR: 71–72 2–3
LPs: 10/12-Inch 33rpm
RCA VICTOR: 71 8–10

**LOVE UNLIMITED (The Love
Unlimited Orchestra)**
Singles: 7-Inch
CASABLANCA 2–3
MCA............................ 2–3
20TH CENTURY-FOX:
  73–77 2–3
UNI: 72 2–4
UNLIMITED GOLD:
  77–84 1–3
LPs: 10/12-Inch 33rpm
20TH CENTURY-FOX:
  74–76 8–10
UNLIMITED GOLD:
  77–84 5–8
Also see WHITE, Barry

LOVELITES, The
Singles: 7-Inch
BANDERA: 67.................... 8–10
LOCK: 69 3–5
LOVELITE: 70–71 2–4
PHI-DAN: 66 8–10
20TH CENTURY-FOX:
  73 2–4
UNI: 69–70 2–4
LPs: 10/12-Inch 33rpm
UNI: 70 10–15

LOVELY, Ike
Singles: 7-Inch
WAND: 73 2–4

LOVERBOY
Singles: 7-Inch
COLUMBIA: 81–85............... 1–3

Price Range

Picture Sleeves
COLUMBIA: *81–85* . . . . **$INC**
LPs: 10/12-Inch 33rpm
COLUMBIA (Except
picture discs): *80–85* **5–8**
COLUMBIA (Picture
discs): *82* **8–12**
Members: Mike Reno; Matthew Frenette; Paul
Dean; Doug Johnson; Scott Smith.
Also see RENO, Mike, & Ann Wilson

LOVERDE
Singles: 12-Inch 33/45rpm
MOBY DICK: *83* **4–6**

LOVERS, The (With Tarheel Slim)
Singles: 7-Inch
ALADDIN: *58* **5–8**
DECCA: *56* **5–8**
IMPERIAL: *62–63* **4–6**
KELLER: *61* **4–6**
LAMP: *57–58* **10–12**
POST: *63* **4–6**
Also see TARHEEL SLIM

LOVERS, The
Singles: 7-Inch
MARLIN: *77* **2–3**

LOVESMITH (Michael Lovesmith)
Singles: 7-Inch
MOTOWN: *81–85* **1–3**
LPs: 10/12-Inch 33rpm
MOTOWN: *81* **5–8**

LOVETTE, Eddie
Singles: 7-Inch
STEADY: *69* **3–5**
LPs: 10/12-Inch 33rpm
STEADY: *70* **8–10**

LOVICH, Lene
Singles: 7-Inch
STIFF: *79–83* **1–3**
LPs: 10/12-Inch 33rpm
STIFF: *79–83* **5–8**

LOVIN' SPOONFUL, The
Singles: 7-Inch
ERIC: *78* **1–3**
KAMA SUTRA: *65–72* **3–5**

Price Range

Picture Sleeves
KAMA SUTRA: *65–67* **$4–6**
LPs: 10/12-Inch 33rpm
BACK-TRAC: *85* **5–8**
BUDDAH: *73* **8–10**
51 WEST **5–8**
GRT: *76* **8–15**
GUSTO **5–8**
KAMA SUTRA (Except
8000 series): *70–76* **10–15**
KAMA SUTRA (8000
series): *65–69* **15–20**
Members: John Sebastian; Zalman Yanovsky;
Joe Butler; Steve Boone.
Also see SEBASTIAN, John

LOW, Gary
Singles: 12-Inch 33/45rpm
QUALITY: *83* **4–6**

LOWE, Bernie (The Bernie Lowe Orchestra)
Singles: 7-Inch
CAMEO: *58–63* **3–5**
LPs: 10/12-Inch 33rpm
CAMEO: *62–63* **12–15**

LOWE, Jim
Singles: 7-Inch
BUDDAH: *68* **2–4**
DECCA: *60–61* **3–5**
DOT (15300 through 16200
series): *55–60* **4–6**
DOT (16600 series): *64* **3–5**
MERCURY: *53–54* **4–6**
20TH CENTURY-FOX:
63 . . . . **3–5**
UNITED ARTISTS: *67* **2–4**
EPs: 7-Inch 33/45rpm
DOT: *57* **10–15**
MERCURY: *56* **10–15**
LPs: 10/12-Inch 33rpm
DOT (3051; "The Green
Door"): *57* **25–30**
DOT (3681; "The Green
Door"): *66* **10–15**
DOT (25681; "The Green
Door"): *66* **10–15**
MERCURY: *56* **20–25**

Price Range

LOWE, Nick (Nick Lowe & Rockpile)
Singles: 7-Inch
COLUMBIA: 78–83 .... $1–3
LPs: 10/12-Inch 33rpm
COLUMBIA: 78–83 8–10
Also see NICK & ELVIS
Also see EDMUNDS, Dave, & Nick Lowe
Also see ROCKPILE

LOWRELL
Singles: 7-Inch
AVI: 78–80 2–3

LOZ NETTO: see NETTO, Loz

LUBOFF, Norman, Choir
Singles: 7-Inch
COLUMBIA: 54–59 2–3
EPs: 7-Inch 33/45rpm
COLUMBIA: 54–59 3–6
LPs: 10/12-Inch 33rpm
COLUMBIA: 54–60 5–15
HARMONY: 61 4–8
RCA VICTOR: 61–62 4–8

LUCAS, Carrie
Singles: 12-Inch 33/45rpm
CONSTELLATION: 84–85 4–6
Singles: 7-Inch
CONSTELLATION: 84–85 1–3
SOLAR: 79–82 1–3
SOUL TRAIN: 77 2–3
LPs: 10/12-Inch 33rpm
CONSTELLATION: 85 5–8
SOLAR: 79–82 5–8
SOUL TRAIN: 77 8–10

LUCAS, Carrie, & The Whispers
Singles: 7-Inch
CONSTELLATION: 85 1–3
Also see LUCAS, Carrie
Also see WHISPERS, The

LUCAS, Frank
Singles: 7-Inch
ICA: 77–78 2–3

LUCAS, Matt
Singles: 7-Inch
DOT: 63–64 3–5

Price Range

SMASH: 63 .... $3–5

LUGEE & THE LIONS
Singles: 7-Inch
ROBBEE: 61 35–40
Members: Lou Christie; Kay Chick; Amy
Sacco; Bill Faveck.
Also see CHRISTIE, Lou
Also see CLASSICS, The

LUGO, Danny, & The Destinations
Singles: 12-Inch 33/45rpm
C&M: 84 4–6

LUKE, Robin
Singles: 7-Inch
BERTRAM
INTERNATIONAL
(Except 206): 58–59 8–10
BERTRAM
INTERNATIONAL
(206; "Susie Darlin"): 58 15–20
DOT: 58–61 4–6
Picture Sleeves
BERTRAM
INTERNATIONAL
(206; "Susie Darlin"): 58 25–30
DOT: 60 8–10
EPs: 7-Inch 33/45rpm
DOT: 60 20–25

LULU (Lulu & The Luvers)
Singles: 7-Inch
ALFA: 81–82 1–3
ATCO: 69–72 2–4
CHELSEA: 73–75 2–4
EPIC: 67–68 3–5
PARROT (9000 series):
64–65 5–8
PARROT (40000 series):
67 3–5
ROCKET: 78 2–4
Picture Sleeves
ALFA: 81 1–3
EPIC: 67–68 3–5
LPs: 10/12-Inch 33rpm
ALFA: 81 5–8
ATCO: 70–72 10–12
CAPRICORN: 74 8–10
CHELSEA: 73–77 10–12
EPIC: 67–70 10–15

Price Range   *Price Range*

HARMONY: 70 .... $10–12
PARROT: 67. 20–25
PICKWICK: 73 8–10
ROCKET: 78. 5–8
Also see CLARK, Dave, Five / Lulu

LUMAN, Bob
Singles: 7-Inch
CAPITOL: 58 8–10
EPIC: 68–77 2–3
HICKORY: 63–70 2–4
IMPERIAL (8311; "Red
  Cadillac & A Black
  Mustache"): 55 15–20
  (Maroon label.)
IMPERIAL (5705; "Red
  Cadillac & A Black
  Mustache"): 60 5–8
  (Black label.)
IMPERIAL (8313; "Red
  Hot"): 55 35–45
  (Maroon label.)
IMPERIAL (8313; "Red
  Hot"): 59 20–25
  (Black label.)
IMPERIAL (8315; "Make
  Up Your Mind Baby"):
  55 15–20
  (Maroon label.)
IMPERIAL (8315; "Make
  Up Your Mind Baby"):
  59 5–8
  (Black label.)
POLYDOR: 77 2–3
WARNER BROS: 59–63 4–6

Picture Sleeves
WARNER BROS: 60–62 6–10

EPs: 7-Inch 33/45rpm
ROLLIN' ROCK 4–6
WARNER BROS: 60 15–20

LPs: 10/12-Inch 33rpm
EPIC: 68–77 10–12
HARMONY: 72 10–12
HICKORY (100 series): 65 12–15
HICKORY (4000 series):
  74 8–10
POLYDOR: 78 8–10
WARNER BROS: 60 25–35

LUMAN, Bob, & Sue Thompson
Singles: 7-Inch
HICKORY: 63 .... $3–5
Also see LUMAN, Bob
Also see THOMPSON, Sue

LUNAR FUNK
Singles: 7-Inch
BELL: 72 2–3

LUND, Art, & His Orchestra
Singles: 7-Inch
CORAL: 52–58 2–4
UNITED ARTISTS: 65 2–3
EPs: 7-Inch 33/45rpm
MGM: 54–55 4–8
LPs: 10/12-Inch 33rpm
MGM: 55 5–15

LUNDBERG, Victor
Singles: 7-Inch
LIBERTY: 67 2–4
LPs: 10/12-Inch 33rpm
LIBERTY: 68 8–15

LUNDY, Pat
Singles: 7-Inch
COLUMBIA: 67–68 2–4
DELUXE: 69. 2–4
HEIDI: 65 3–5
LEOPARD 2–5
PYRAMID: 76 2–3
RCA VICTOR: 73 2–3
TOTO: 62 3–5
VIGOR: 75 1–3
LPs: 10/12-Inch 33rpm
COLUMBIA: 68 10–12
PYRAMID: 76 5–8

LUNDY, Pat, & Bobby Harris
Singles: 7-Inch
HEIDI: 65 3–5
Also see HARRIS, Bobby
Also see LUNDY, Pat

**LUSHUS DAIM & THE PRETTY
VAIN**
Singles: 7-Inch
MOTOWN: 85. 1–3
LPs: 10/12-Inch 33rpm
MOTOWN: 85. 5–8

Price Range

LUTHER
Singles: 7-Inch
COTILLION: 76–77 . . . . $2–3
LPs: 10/12-Inch 33rpm
COTILLION: 77 8–10

LY-DELLS, The
Singles: 7-Inch
MASTER (111; "Genie Of
The Lamp"): 61 20–25
MASTER (251; "Wizard
Of Love"): 61 12–15
ROULETTE: 63 4–6
SCA: 62 4–6
SOUTHERN SOUND: 65 4–6
LPs: 10/12-Inch 33rpm
CLIFTON 8–10

LYLE, Bobby
Singles: 7-Inch
CAPITOL: 78 2–3

LYMAN, Arthur (The Arthur Lyman Group)
Singles: 7-Inch
GNP/CRESCENDO:
64–75 1–3
HI FI: 59–69 2–4
LPs: 10/12-Inch 33rpm
GNP/CRESCENDO:
63–75 8–15
HI FI: 59–69 8–18
OLYMPIC: 79 5–8

LYME & CYBELLE
Singles: 7-Inch
WHITE WHALE: 66–67 3–5

LYMON, Frankie (Frankie Lymon & The Teenagers)
Singles: 7-Inch
ABC: 73 1–3
COLUMBIA: 64 3–5
GEE: 55–59 6–10
ROULETTE: 58–61 4–8
TCF: 64 3–5
EPs: 7-Inch 33/45rpm
GEE: 56 30–40
ROULETTE: 58 25–30

Price Range

LPs: 10/12-Inch 33rpm
GEE (Red label): 57 . . . . $90–100
GEE (Gray label): 61 30–35
ROULETTE (Except
25250): 58 45–50
ROULETTE (25250;
"Frankie Lymon's
Greatest"): 64 25–30
Also see TEENAGERS, The

LYNDELL, Linda
Singles: 7-Inch
VOLT: 68 3–5

LYNN, Barbara
Singles: 7-Inch
ATLANTIC: 67–72 2–4
COLLECTABLES 1–3
JAMIE: 62–65 3–5
TRIBE: 66–67 3–5
LPs: 10/12-Inch 33rpm
ATLANTIC: 68 10–15
JAMIE: 62–64 20–25

LYNN, Cheryl
Singles: 12-Inch 33/45rpm
COLUMBIA: 78–85 4–6
Singles: 7-Inch
COLUMBIA: 78–85 1–3
PRIVATE I: 85 1–3
LPs: 10/12-Inch 33rpm
COLUMBIA: 78–84 5–8

LYNN, Cheryl, & Luther Vandross
Singles: 7-Inch
COLUMBIA: 82 1–3
Also see LYNN, Cheryl
Also see VANDROSS, Luther

LYNN, Donna
Singles: 7-Inch
CAPITOL (Except 5127):
63–65 3–5
CAPITOL (5127; "My
Boyfriend Got A Beatle
Haircut"): 64 5–8
EPIC: 63 3–5
PALMER: 67 3–5
LPs: 10/12-Inch 33rpm
CAPITOL: 64 15–20

Price Range   *Price Range*

LYNN, Ginie
Singles: 7-Inch
ABC: 78 . . . . $2–3

*Loretta Lynn, three charted singles
(1970–75), 13 charted LPs (1967–75).
(Includes issues shown as by Conway Twitty
& Loretta Lynn.)*

LYNN, Loretta (Loretta Lynn & The Coal Miners)
Singles: 7-Inch
DECCA (31000 series):
   62–66 3–5
DECCA (32000 series):
   66–71 2–4
MCA: 73–85 1–3
ZERO: 60–61 10–20
Picture Sleeves
DECCA (31000 series): 66 4–6
DECCA (32000 series): 70 2–4
MCA: 78 1–3
EPs: 7-Inch 33/45rpm
DECCA: 64–65 10–15
LPs: 10/12-Inch 33rpm
CORAL: 73 4–8
COUNTRY MUSIC
   MAGAZINE: 76 12–18
   (Special issue, available through "Country
   Music" magazine's record catalog.)
DECCA (4457; "Loretta
   Lynn Sings"): 63 50–75

DECCA (4541 through
   5000): 64–68 . . . . $15–25
   (Decca numbers in the 4000 & 5000 series
   preceded by a "DL7" are stereo issues.)
DECCA (75084; "Your
   Squaw Is On The
   Warpath"): 69 25–35
   (Includes the song "Barney," which was omit-
   ted from later pressings.)
DECCA (75084; "Your
   Squaw Is On The
   Warpath"): 69 15–20
   (Does not include the song "Barney.")
DECCA (75115 through
   75381): 69–72 10–20
L.L.: 76 20–25
MCA: 73–85 5–10
TEE VEE: 78 8–12
TROLLEY CAR: 81 8–10
VOCALION: 68–72 8–15
Promotional LPs
MCA (1934; "Loretta
   Lynn's Greatest Hits"):
   74 25–35
   (Cover shows title as simply "Loretta Lynn.")
MCA (35013;
   "Allis-Chalmers Presents
   Loretta Lynn"): 78 20–25
MCA (35018; "Crisco
   Presents Loretta Lynn's
   Country Classics"): 79 20-30
   Also see PIERCE, Webb / Loretta Lynn
   Also see TWITTY, Conway

LYNN, Loretta / Tammy Wynette
LPs: 10/12-Inch 33rpm
RADIANT: 81 5–8
   Also see LYNN, Loretta
   Also see WYNETTE, Tammy

LYNN, Vera
Singles: 7-Inch
ARCO: 67 1–3
DJM: 69 1–3
LONDON: 51–64 2–4
UNITED ARTISTS: 67 1–3
EPs: 7-Inch 33/45rpm
LONDON: 52–56 5–10
LPs: 10/12-Inch 33rpm
LONDON: 52–64 8–15
MGM: 61 6–12
UNITED ARTISTS: 67 5–10

Price Range

LYNNE, Gloria
Singles: 7-Inch
CANYON: 70 . . . . **$1–3**
EVEREST: 59–66 . . . . **2–4**
FONTANA: 64–69 . . . . **2–4**
HI FI: 66 . . . . **2–3**
IMPULSE: 76 . . . . **1–3**
MERCURY: 72 . . . . **1–3**
SEECO: 61 . . . . **2–4**

LPs: 10/12-Inch 33rpm
CANYON: 70 . . . . **5–10**
DESIGN: 62 . . . . **10–15**
EVEREST (300 series): 75 . . . . **5–8**
EVEREST (5000 series):
59–60 . . . . **15–25**
EVEREST (5100 & 5200
series): 60–65 . . . . **10–20**
FONTANA: 64–69 . . . . **8–18**
HI FI: 66 . . . . **8–15**
IMPULSE: 76 . . . . **5–8**
MERCURY: 69–72 . . . . **8–12**
SUNSET: 66–67 . . . . **8–12**
UPFRONT: 72 . . . . **5–10**

LYNNE, Jeff (Jeff Lynn)
Singles: 12-Inch 33/45rpm
JET: 77 . . . . **5–8**

Singles: 7-Inch
JET: 77 . . . . **2–4**
TWIN-SPIN: 65 . . . . **8–10**
VIRGIN: 84 . . . . **1–3**
Also see ELECTRIC LIGHT ORCHESTRA,
The
Also see IDLE RACE
Also see MOVE, The

LYNYRD SKYNYRD
Singles: 7-Inch
ATNIA: 78 . . . . **2–3**
MCA: 74–78 . . . . **2–3**

Promotional Singles
MCA (1966; "Gimmie
Back My Bullets"): 77 . . . . **8–10**
(Concert souvenir copy.)

EPs: 7-Inch 33/45rpm
MCA: 76 . . . . **10–15**
(Promotional issue only.)

LPs: 10/12-Inch 33rpm
MCA (2000 & 3000 series,
except 3029): 75–78 . . . . **$8–10**
MCA (3029; "Street
Survivors"): 77 . . . . **30–35**
(Front cover pictures the group in flames.)
MCA (3029; "Street
Survivors"): 77 . . . . **8–10**
(Front cover pictures the group without
flames.)
MCA (5000 series): 79–82 . . . . **5–8**
MCA (6000 series): 76–81 . . . . **10–15**
MCA (10000 series): 79–81 . . . . **10–15**
MCA (37000 series): 79–82 . . . . **5–8**
MCA/SOUNDS OF THE
SOUTH (300 & 400
series): 73–74 . . . . **10–15**

Promotional LPs
MCA (2170; "Gimmie
Back My Bullets"): 76 . . . . **25–30**
(White label. Concert souvenir copy.)
Members: Ronnie Van Zant; Gary Rossington;
Allen Collins; Steve Gaines; Cassie Gaines.
Also see ROSSINGTON-COLLINS BAND,
The

LYTLE, Johnny (The Johnny Lytle Quintet; The Johnny Lytle Trio)
Singles: 7-Inch
PACIFIC JAZZ: 68 . . . . **2–3**
RIVERSIDE: 63 . . . . **2–4**
SOLID STATE: 68 . . . . **2–3**
TUBA: 65–66 . . . . **2–4**

LPs: 10/12-Inch 33rpm
JAZZLAND: 60–62 . . . . **15–25**
MILESTONE: 72 . . . . **5–10**
MUSE: 78–81 . . . . **5–8**
PACIFIC JAZZ: 67 . . . . **8–15**
RIVERSIDE: 63–68 . . . . **10–20**
SOLID STATE: 67–69 . . . . **8–15**
TUBA: 66 . . . . **10–15**

LYTLE, Johnny, & Ray Barretto
LPs: 10/12-Inch 33rpm
JAZZLAND: 62 . . . . **15–25**
Also see BARRETTO, Ray
Also see LYTLE, Johnny

M

M (Robin Scott)
Singles: 12-Inch 33/45rpm
SIRE: 79 .... **$8–10**
Singles: 7-Inch
SIRE: 79–81 .... **1–3**
LPs: 10/12-Inch 33rpm
SIRE: 79–82 .... **6–10**

M., Boney: see BONEY M

MC-5 (Motor City 5)
Singles: 7-Inch
A SQUARE: 67.................. **10–15**
AMG: 66 .... **10–12**
ATLANTIC: 69 .... **4–6**
ELEKTRA: 69 .... **5–8**
Picture Sleeves
A SQUARE: 67.................. **30–40**
LPs: 10/12-Inch 33rpm
ATLANTIC: 70–71 .... **10–15**
ELEKTRA (74042; "Kick
  Out The Jams"): 69............. **30–35**
  (Title track has X-rated intro. Back cover has
  liner notes.)
ELEKTRA (74042; "Kick
  Out The Jams"): 69............. **12–15**
  (Title track has censored intro. Back cover has
  no liner notes.)

MFSB (Mothers, Fathers, Sisters, Brothers)
Singles: 7-Inch
PHILADELPHIA INT'L:
  74–78 .... **2–3**
TSOP: 81 .... **1–3**
LPs: 10/12-Inch 33rpm
PHILADELPHIA INT'L:
  73–78 .... **8–10**
TSOP: 80 .... **5–8**
  Also see THREE DEGREES, The

MGs, The (The Memphis Group)
Singles: 7-Inch
STAX: 73......................... **2–3**
LPs: 10/12-Inch 33rpm
STAX: 73......................... **8–10**
  Also see BOOKER T. & THE MGs

M+M: see MARTHA & THE MUFFINS

MABLEY, Moms
Singles: 7-Inch
MERCURY: 69–71............... **$2–3**
EPs: 7-Inch 33/45rpm
CHESS: 63....................... **5–8**
LPs: 10/12-Inch 33rpm
CHESS: 61–64................... **10–20**
MERCURY: 64–70............... **8–15**

MABLEY, Moms, & Pigmeat Markham
LPs: 10/12-Inch 33rpm
CHESS: 64–71................... **8–15**
  Also see MABLEY, Moms
  Also see MARKHAM, Pigmeat

MABON, Willie (Willie Mabon & His Combo)
Singles: 7-Inch
CHESS (Black vinyl):
  52–56 .... **8–10**
CHESS (Colored vinyl): 53 .... **50–60**
DELTA **3–5**
FEDERAL: 57 .... **5–8**
FORMAL: 62 .... **3–5**
MAD: 60 .... **3–5**
PARROT: 53.................... **60–75**
U.S.A.: 63–65.................. **3–5**

MAC, Fleetwood: see FLEETWOOD MAC

MacARTHUR, James
Singles: 7-Inch
SCEPTER: 62–63 .... **3–5**
TRIODEX: 61.................... **3–5**

MacDONALD, Jeanette, & Nelson Eddy
EPs: 7-Inch 33/45rpm
RCA VICTOR (Except
  220): 61 .... **4–8**
RCA VICTOR (220; "Rose
  Marie"): 52.................... **10–20**
LPs: 10/12-Inch 33rpm
RCA VICTOR (16; "Rose
  Marie"): 52.................... **35–50**
  (10-Inch LP.)

Price Range   *Price Range*

RCA VICTOR (526; "Rose
  Marie"): *66*. **$12–18**
  (Soundtrack.)
RCA VICTOR (1000
  series): *75*. **4–8**
RCA VICTOR (1700
  series): *59*. **10–20**
RCA VICTOR (2400
  series): *77*. **5–8**
RCA VICTOR (3900
  series): *81*. **4–6**

MacDONALD, Ralph
Singles: 12-Inch 33-45rpm
POLYDOR: *84–85*. **4–6**
Singles: 7-Inch
MARLIN: *76–79*. **2–3**
POLYDOR: *84–85*. **1–3**
LPs: 10/12-Inch 33rpm
MARLIN: *76–79*. **6–10**
POLYDOR: *85*. **5–8**

MACEO & ALL THE KINGS MEN
Singles: 7-Inch
EXCELLO: *72*. **2–3**
HOUSE OF FOX: *70*. **2–4**
LPs: 10/12-Inch 33rpm
EXCELLO: *72*. **8–10**

MACEO & THE MACKS
Singles: 7-Inch
PEOPLE: *73–74*. **2–3**
LPs: 10/12-Inch 33rpm
PEOPLE: *74*. **8–10**

MACHINE
Singles: 7-Inch
RCA VICTOR: *79–80*. **1–3**
LPs: 10/12-Inch 33rpm
RCA VICTOR: *80*. **5–8**

MACHINATIONS
Singles: 12-Inch 33/45rpm
A&M: *83*. **4–6**
Singles: 7-Inch
A&M: *83*. **1–3**
LPs: 10/12-Inch 33rpm
A&M: *83*. **5–8**

MacGREGOR, Byron
Singles: 7-Inch
CAPITOL: *75*. **$1–3**
WESTBOUND: *74*. **2–3**
LPs: 10/12-Inch 33rpm
WESTBOUND: *74*. **5–10**

MacGREGOR, Mary
Singles: 7-Inch
ARIOLA: *78*. **1–3**
ARIOLA AMERICA:
  76–77. . . . . **2–3**
RSO: *79–80*. **1–3**
LPs: 10/12-Inch 33rpm
ARIOLA AMERICA: *77*. **8–10**

MACHO
Singles: 7-Inch
PRELUDE: *78*. **1–3**
LPs: 10/12-Inch 33rpm
PRELUDE: *78*. **5–8**

MACK, Lonnie (Lonnie Mack & Pismo)
Singles: 7-Inch
ABC: *73*. **1–3**
CAPITOL: *77*. **2–3**
COLLECTABLES **1–3**
ELEKTRA: *71*. **2–3**
FRATERNITY: *63–68*. **3–5**
ROULETTE: *75*. **1–3**
LPs: 10/12-Inch 33rpm
ALLIGATOR **5–8**
CAPITOL: *77*. **8–10**
ELEKTRA: *69–71*. **10–12**
FRATERNITY: *63*. **20–25**
TRIP: *75*. **8–10**

MACK, Lonnie, & Rusty York
LPs: 10/12-Inch 33rpm
QCA: *73*. **10–12**
  Also see MACK, Lonnie
  Also see YORK, Rusty

MACK, Warner
Singles: 7-Inch
DECCA (Except 30000
  series): *59–73*. **2–4**
DECCA (30000 series):
  57–59. . . . . **3–5**
KAPP: *61–62*. **2–4**

Price Range

Price Range

EPs: 7-Inch 33/45rpm
JAY DEE: 54 .... $5–10
MGM: 57........................ 4–8

LPs: 10/12-Inch 33rpm
CORAL: 62...................... 8–15
MGM: 57–69.................... 5–15

MADNESS
Singles: 12-Inch 33/45rpm
GEFFEN: 83..................... 4–6

Singles: 7-Inch
GEFFEN: 83–84.................. 1–3
SIRE: 80–81 1–3

LPs: 10/12-Inch 33rpm
GEFFEN: 83–84.................. 5–8
SIRE: 80–81 5–8

MADONNA
Singles: 12-Inch 33/45rpm
SIRE: 83–85 4–6

Singles: 7-Inch
GEFFEN: 85..................... 1–3
SIRE: 83–85 2–3

Picture Sleeves
SIRE: 83–85 .... INC

LPs: 10/12-Inch 33rpm
SIRE: 83–85 5–8

MADURA
LPs: 10/12-Inch 33rpm
COLUMBIA: 71–73.............. 10–12

MAESTRO, Johnny
Singles: 7-Inch
APT: 65........................ 8–10
BUDDAH: 71–72................. 5–8
CAMEO: 63–64.................. 8–10
COED (Except 562): 61 10–12
COED (562; "Besame
  Baby"): 61 30–40
COLLECTABLES 1–3
PARKWAY: 66–67 8–10
UNITED ARTISTS: 62.......... 10–12

LPs: 10/12-Inch 33rpm
BUDDAH: 71.................... 15–20
Also see BROOKLYN BRIDGE, The
Also see CRESTS, The
Also see MASTERS, Johnny

MAGGARD, Cledus, & The Citizen's Band
Singles: 7-Inch
MERCURY: 75–79............... $2–3

LPs: 10/12-Inch 33rpm
MERCURY: 76................... 5–10

MAGIC LADY
Singles: 12-Inch 33/45rpm
A&M: 82 4–6

Singles: 7-Inch
A&M: 82 1–3

LPs: 10/12-Inch 33rpm
A&M: 82 5–8
ARISTA: 80 5–8
Also see OSBOURNE, Ozzy

MAGIC LANTERNS, The (With Albert Hammond)
Singles: 7-Inch
ATLANTIC: 68–70 2–4
BIG TREE: 71 2–3
CHARISMA: 72.................. 2–3
EPIC: 66 3–5

LPs: 10/12-Inch 33rpm
ATLANTIC: 69 12–15
CHAPARRAL: 68 45–55
Also see HAMMOND, Albert

MAGIC MUSHROOM, The
Singles: 7-Inch
A&M: 66 3–5
EAST COAST.................... 4–6
PHILIPS: 67 3–5
WARNER BROS: 66.............. 3–5

MAGIC ORGAN (Jerry Smith)
Singles: 7-Inch
RANWOOD: 72–77............... 1–3

LPs: 10/12-Inch 33rpm
RANWOOD: 72–83 4–8
SUNNYVALE: 79 4–6
Also see SMITH, Jerry

MAGIC TOUCH, The
Singles: 7-Inch
BLACK FALCON: 71.............. 2–4

Price Range

Price Range

MAGIC TOUCH, The (Vito & The Salutations)
Singles: 7-Inch
ROULETTE: 73 . . . . **$4–6**
Also see VITO & THE SALUTATIONS

MAGISTRATES, The (Featuring Jean Hillary)
Singles: 7-Inch
MGM: 68–69 . . . . **3–5**
Also see DOVELLS, The

MAGNIFICENT MEN, The
Singles: 7-Inch
CAPITOL: 66–68 . . . . **3–5**
MERCURY: 69 . . . . **2–4**
LPs: 10/12-Inch 33rpm
CAPITOL: 67–68 . . . . **10–15**
MERCURY: 70 . . . . **8–10**

MAGNIFICENTS, The
Singles: 7-Inch
CHECKER: 62 . . . . **3–5**
COLLECTABLES **1–3**
KANSOMA: 62 . . . . **5–8**
VEE JAY (183 through
235): 56–58 . . . . **15–20**
VEE JAY (281; "Don't
Leave Me"): 58 . . . . **20–25**
VEE JAY (367; "Up On
The Mountain"): 60 . . . . **4–6**
(Reissue. This track was first issued in 1956 on
Vee Jay 183.)
Also see EL DORADOS, The

MAGNUM FORCE
Singles: 7-Inch
PAULA: 85 . . . . **1–3**
LPs: 10/12-Inch 33rpm
WIZARD: 78 . . . . **5–8**

MAHAL, TAJ: see TAJ MAHAL

MAHARIS, George
Singles: 7-Inch
EPIC: 62–66 . . . . **2–4**
Picture Sleeves
EPIC: 62–64 . . . . **2–4**
LPs: 10/12-Inch 33rpm
EPIC: 62–66 . . . . **8–15**

MAHOGANY
Singles: 12-Inch 33/45rpm
WEST END: 83 . . . . **$4–6**
Singles: 7-Inch
WEST END: 83 . . . . **1–3**

MAHOGANY RUSH (Featuring Frank Marino)
Singles: 7-Inch
COLUMBIA: 76 . . . . **2–3**
20TH CENTURY-FOX:
74–75 . . . . **2–4**
LPs: 10/12-Inch 33rpm
COLUMBIA: 76 . . . . **8–10**
20TH CENTURY-FOX:
73–75 . . . . **10–12**
Also see MARINO, Frank, & Mahogany Rush

MAHONEY, Skip, & The Casuals
Singles: 7-Inch
ABET: 76–77 . . . . **2–3**
D.C. INT'L: 74 . . . . **2–4**

MAIN INGREDIENT, The (Featuring Cuba Gooding)
Singles: 7-Inch
RCA VICTOR: 69–81 . . . . **2–4**
Picture Sleeves
RCA VICTOR: 70–81 . . . . **2–4**
LPs: 10/12-Inch 33rpm
RCA VICTOR: 70–81 . . . . **8–10**
Also see GOODING, Cuba

MAINSTREETERS, The
Singles: 7-Inch
EVENT: 73 . . . . **2–3**

MAI TAI
Singles: 7-Inch
CRITIQUE: 85 . . . . **1–3**

MAJESTY
Singles: 7-Inch
GOLDEN BOY: 85 . . . . **1–3**

MAJOR LANCE: see LANCE, Major

Price Range   *Price Range*

MAJORS, The
Singles: 7-Inch
IMPERIAL: *62–64* **$4–6**
LPs: 10/12-Inch 33rpm
IMPERIAL: *63* **25–30**
Members: Ricky Cordo; Eugene Glass; Idella
Morris; Frank Troutt; Ronald Gathers.

MAKEBA, Miriam
Singles: 7-Inch
KAPP: *62* **2–4**
MERCURY: *66*. **2–3**
RCA VICTOR: *64* **2–3**
REPRISE: *67–68*. **2–3**
LPs: 10/12-Inch 33rpm
KAPP: *62* **10–20**
MERCURY: *66*. **8–15**
PETERS INT'L: *81* **5–8**
RCA VICTOR: *60–68* **8–18**
REPRISE: *67*. **8–15**
Also see BELEFONTE, Harry, & Miriam
Makeba
Also see MANHATTAN BROTHERS &
MIRIAM MAKEBA, The

**MAKEM, Tommy: see CLANCY
BROTHERS, The**

MALCOLM X.
Singles: 7-Inch
TOMMY BOY: *83–84* **1–3**
LPs: 10/12-Inch 33rpm
DOUGLAS: *68–71* **8–15**

**MALMKVIST, Siw (Siw Malmkvist
& Umberto Marcato)**
Singles: 7-Inch
JUBILEE: *64*. **1–3**
KAPP: *61* **1–3**

MALO
Singles: 7-Inch
TRAQ: *81* **2–3**
WARNER BROS: *72–73* **2–4**
LPs: 10/12-Inch 33rpm
WARNER BROS: *72–74* **8–10**
Also see AZTECA
Also see SANTANA, Jorge

MALTBY, Richard, & His Orchestra
Singles: 7-Inch
COLUMBIA: *59* **$2–3**
ROULETTE: *60–61* **2–3**
VIK: *56* **2–4**
X: *54–55*. **2–4**
Picture Sleeves
VIK: *56* **2–4**
EPs: 7-Inch 33/45rpm
COLUMBIA: *59* **4–8**
VIK: *56* **5–8**
X: *54–55*. **5–8**
LPs: 10/12-Inch 33rpm
CAMDEN: *60–62*. **8–12**
COLUMBIA: *59* **8–15**
HARMONY: *61* **8–12**
ROULETTE: *60–62* **8–15**
VIK: *56* **10–15**
X: *54–55*. **10–20**

MAMA CASS: see ELLIOT, Cass

MAMAS & THE PAPAS, The
Singles: 7-Inch
ABC: *70*. **1–3**
DUNHILL: *65–72*. **3–5**
MCA: *80–82* **1–3**
Picture Sleeves
DUNHILL: *67*. **3–5**
EPs: 7-Inch 33/45rpm
ABC: *71*. **8–15**
(Promotional issues only.)
DUNHILL: *65*. **10–15**
LPs: 10/12-Inch 33rpm
ABC: *76*. **6–10**
DUNHILL: *66–73*. **8–15**
MCA: *80–82* **5–8**
PICKWICK: *72* **6–10**
Members: John Phillips; "Mama" Cass Elliot;
Denny Doherty; Michelle Gilliam.
Also see BIG THREE, The
Also see ELLIOT, Cass
Also see PHILLIPS, John

MAMA'S BOYS
LPs: 10/12-Inch 33rpm
JIVE: *84*. **5–8**

**MAN PARRISH: see PARRISH,
Man**

Price Range

MANCHA, Steve
Singles: 7-Inch
GROOVESVILLE: 65–67 .... $3–5
WHEELSVILLE: 65 4–6
Also see BARNES, J.J., & Steve Mancha

Melissa Manchester, 15 charted singles (1975–85), 13 charted LPs (1973–85). (Includes issue shown as by Melissa Manchester & Peabo Bryson.)

MANCHESTER, Melissa
Singles: 12-Inch 33/45rpm
ARISTA: 82 4–6
CASABLANCA: 84 4–6
MCA: 85 4–6
Singles: 7-Inch
ARISTA: 75–84 1–3
BELL: 74 2–3
CASABLANCA: 84 1–3
MB: 67 3–5
MCA: 85 1–3
LPs: 10/12-Inch 33rpm
ARISTA: 75–83 8–10
BELL: 73–74 10–12
CASABLANCA: 84 5–8
MCA: 79 5–8
Also see NATIONAL LAMPOON

MANCHESTER, Melissa, & Peabo Bryson
Singles: 7-Inch
ARISTA: 81 1–3
Also see BRYSON, Peabo
Also see MANCHESTER, Melissa

Price Range

MANCHILD
Singles: 7-Inch
CHI-SOUND: 77 .... $2–3
LPs: 10/12-Inch 33rpm
CHI-SOUND: 77 8–10
Also see REDD HOTT

MANCINI, Henry (Henry Mancini's Orchestra & Chorus)
Singles: 7-Inch
LIBERTY (1400 series): 82 1–3
LIBERTY (55000 series):
58–59 2–4
RCA VICTOR: 59–85 1–3
UNITED ARTISTS: 78 1–3
WARNER BROS: 79–83 1–3
Picture Sleeves
RCA VICTOR: 59–77 1–3
WARNER BROS: 79 1–3
EPs: 7-Inch 33/45rpm
RCA VICTOR: 60–62 5–15
LPs: 10/12-Inch 33rpm
AVCO EMBASSY: 70 12–18
CAMDEN: 66–74 5–10
LIBERTY (3000 series):
57–59 10–20
LIBERTY (51000 series):
82 4–8
MCA: 75–76 6–12
PARAMOUNT: 70 10–15
RCA VICTOR (0013
through 0098): 72–73 5–10
RCA VICTOR (0231;
"Visions Of Eight"): 73 20–25
(Soundtrack.)
RCA VICTOR (0270;
"Country Gentleman"):
74 5–8
RCA VICTOR (0271;
"Oklahoma Crude"): 73 10–15
(Soundtrack.)
RCA VICTOR (0672
through 1928): 74–76 5–10
RCA VICTOR (1956;
"The Music From Peter
Gunn"): 59 15–20
(TV Soundtrack.)
RCA VICTOR (2040;
"More Music From
Peter Gunn"): 59 15–25
(TV Soundtrack.)

Price Range   *Price Range*

RCA VICTOR (2143;
"The Music From Peter
Gunn"): 77 . . . . $4–8
(TV Soundtrack.)

RCA VICTOR (2147;
"The Blues & The
Beat"): 60 10–20

RCA VICTOR (2198;
"Music From Mr.
Lucky"): 60 10–20
(TV Soundtrack.)

RCA VICTOR (2314;
"High Time"): 60 20–30
(Soundtrack.)

RCA VICTOR (2360; "Mr.
Lucky Goes Latin"): 61 10–20

RCA VICTOR (2362;
"Just You & Me
Together Love"): 77 4–8

RCA VICTOR (2362;
"Breakfast At
Tiffany's"): 61 25–35
(Soundtrack.)

RCA VICTOR (2258;
"Combo"): 62 10–20

RCA VICTOR (2442;
"Experiment In Terror"):
62 35–50
(Cover pictures Lee Remick and her attacker.
Soundtrack.)

RCA VICTOR (2442;
"Experiment In Terror"):
62 25–35
(Cover pictures mannequins. Soundtrack.)

RCA VICTOR (2484;
"Love Story"): 77 4–8
(Soundtrack.)

RCA VICTOR (2559;
"Hatari"): 62 25–35
(Soundtrack.)

RCA VICTOR (2600
series): 63–64 8–15

RCA VICTOR (2755;
"Charade"): 63 20–30
(Soundtrack.)

RCA VICTOR (2795;
"The Pink Panther"): 64 10–20
(Soundtrack.)

RCA VICTOR (2800 &
2900 series): 64–65 8–15

RCA VICTOR (3000
series): 78 4–8

RCA VICTOR (3356;
"The Latin Sound Of
Henry Mancini"): 65 . . . . $8–15

RCA VICTOR (3347;
"Best Of Henry Mancini,
Volume 3"): 79 5–8

RCA VICTOR (3402;
"The Great Race"): 65 25–35
(Soundtrack.)

RCA VICTOR (3500
series): 66 6–12

RCA VICTOR (3612;
"Merry Mancini
Christmas"): 66 6–12

RCA VICTOR (3623;
"Arabesque"): 66 30–40
(Soundtrack.)

RCA VICTOR (3648;
"What Did You Do In
The War Daddy"): 66 20–30
(Soundtrack.)

RCA VICTOR (3667;
"Pure Gold"): 80 4–8

RCA VICTOR (3668;
"Mancini Country"): 80 4–8

RCA VICTOR (3694
through 3713): 66–67 6–12

RCA VICTOR (3756;
"Warm Shade Of
Ivory"): 80 4–8

RCA VICTOR (3802;
"Two For The Road"):
67 15–25
(Soundtrack.)

RCA VICTOR (3822;
"Best Of Henry
Mancini"): 80 4–8

RCA VICTOR (3877;
"Music Of Hawaii"): 81 4–8

RCA VICTOR (3887;
"Encore"): 67 8–15

RCA VICTOR (3954;
"Country Gentleman"):
67 4–8

RCA VICTOR (3997
through 4689): 68–72 5–10

RCA VICTOR (5000
series): 85 4–8

RCA VICTOR (6000
series): 66–72 8–15

SUNSET: 66 5–10

Price Range

UNITED ARTISTS: *70* **$10–12**
WARNER BROS (Except
3339): *59–73* **10–20**
WARNER BROS (3339;
"10"): *79* **5–10**
(Soundtrack.)
Also see HIRT, Al / Henry Mancini / Perez
Prado

MANCINI, Henry, & Charley Pride
LPs: 10/12-Inch 33rpm
DECCA (79185;
"Sometimes A Great
Notion"): *71* **12–18**
(Soundtrack.)
Also see PRIDE, Charley

MANCINI, Henry, & Doc Severinsen
LPs: 10/12-Inch 33rpm
RCA VICTOR (3700
series): *80* **4–8**
Also see MANCINI, Henry
Also see SEVERINSEN, Doc

MANDEL, Harvey
Singles: 7-Inch
PHILIPS: *68* **3–5**
LPs: 10/12-Inch 33rpm
JANUS: *70–74* **8–10**
OVATION: *71* **8–10**
PHILIPS: *68–69* **10–12**
Also see CANNED HEAT

MANDELL, Mike
Singles: 7-Inch
VANGUARD: *81* **1–3**

MANDRE
Singles: 7-Inch
MOTOWN: *77–79* **1–3**
LPs: 10/12-Inch 33rpm
MOTOWN: *77–79* **5–8**

MANDRELL, Barbara
Singles: 7-Inch
ABC: *78–79* **1–3**
ABC/DOT: *75–78* **2–3**
COLUMBIA: *69–75* **2–4**
MCA: *79–85* **1–3**
MOSRITE: *66* **5–8**
Picture Sleeves
MCA: *79–85* **1–3**

Price Range

LPs: 10/12-Inch 33rpm
ABC: *78* **$8–10**
ABC/DOT: *76–77* **8–12**
COLUMBIA: *71–81* **8–15**
MCA: *79–85* **5–10**
SONGBIRD: *82* **5–8**
TIME-LIFE: *81* **5–8**
Also see HOUSTON, David, & Barbara Mandrell

MANDRELL, Barbara, & Lee Greenwood
Singles: 7-Inch
MCA: *84* **1–3**
LPs: 10/12-Inch 33rpm
MCA: *84* **5–8**
Also see GREENWOOD, Lee
Also see MANDRELL, Barbara

MANDRILL
Singles: 7-Inch
ARISTA: *77–80* **1–3**
LIBERTY: *83* **1–3**
MONTAGE: *82* **1–3**
POLYDOR: *71–74* **2–3**
LPs: 10/12-Inch 33rpm
ARISTA: *77–80* **8–10**
LIBERTY: *83* **5–8**
POLYDOR: *71–75* **10–12**
UNITEDARTISTS **75**
Also see MASSER, Michael, & Mandrill

MANFRED MANN: see MANN, Manfred

MANGANO, Silvana
Singles: 7-Inch
MGM: *53* **3–5**

MANGIONE, Chuck (The Chuck Mangione Quintet; Gap & Chuck Mangione)
Singles: 7-Inch
A&M: *75–80* **1–3**
COLUMBIA: *82–84* **1–3**
MERCURY: *71–77* **1–3**
Picture Sleeves
A&M: *78–80* **1–3**
LPs: 10/12-Inch 33rpm
A&M: *75–81* **5–10**
COLUMBIA: *82–84* **5–8**

Price Range

JAZZLAND: *63* $15–25
MERCURY: *71–78*. 6–12
MILESTONE: *77* 5–8
RIVERSIDE: *61* 20–30

MANHATTAN BROTHERS & MIRIAM MAKEBA, The
Singles: 7-Inch
LONDON: *56* 3–5
Also see MAKEBA, Miriam

MANHATTAN TRANSFER, The
Singles: 7-Inch
ATLANTIC: *75–85* 1–3
LPs: 10/12-Inch 33rpm
ATLANTIC: *75–83* 8–10
MFSL: *78*. 12–15
Also see PISTILLI, Gene

MANHATTANS, The
Singles: 12-Inch 33/45rpm
COLUMBIA: *84–85* 4–6
Singles: 7-Inch
AVANTI: *63* 4–6
CAPITOL: *61–62* 5–8
CARNIVAL: *64–69* 3–5
COLUMBIA: *73–85* 1–3
DELUXE: *69–73*. 2–3
LPs: 10/12-Inch 33rpm
CARNIVAL: *66* 15–20
COLUMBIA: *73–83* 8–10
DELUXE: *70–72*. 10–15
SOLID SMOKE: *81* 5–8
Members: George Smith; Ken Kelly; Sonny Bivens; Winfred Scott; Richard Taylor.

MANILOW, Barry
Singles: 12-Inch 33/45rpm
ARISTA: *78–84*. 4–6
Singles: 7-Inch
ARISTA: *74–85*. 1–3
BELL: *73–74* 2–4
FLASHBACK: *76*. 1–3
RCA VICTOR: *86* 1–3
Picture Sleeves
ARISTA: *78–85*. 1–3
LPs: 10/12-Inch 33rpm
ARISTA: *74–84*. 8–10
BELL: *74* 10–15
RCA VICTOR: *86* 5–8
Also see FEATHERBED

Price Range

Also see LADY FLASH

MANN, Barry
Singles: 7-Inch
ABC: *73* $1–3
ABC-PARAMOUNT:
 60–62 5–8
ARISTA: *76* 2–4
CAPITOL: *66–68* 3–5
CASABLANCA: *80* 1–3
COLPIX: *63* 4–6
JDS: *59*. 5–8
MCA. 1–3
NEW DESIGN: *71–72*. 2–4
RCA VICTOR: *74–76* 2–4
RED BIRD: *64* 4–6
ROULETTE 1–3
SCEPTER: *70* 2–4
UNITED ARTISTS: *77–78* 1–3
WARNER BROS: *79*. 1–3
LPs: 10/12-Inch 33rpm
ABC-PARAMOUNT: *62*. 50–60
CASABLANCA: *80* 5–8
NEW DESIGN: *71*. 10–12
RCA VICTOR: *75* 8–10
UNITED ARTISTS: *77*. 8–10

MANN, Bobby (Bobby Bloom)
Singles: 7-Inch
KAMA SUTRA: *66* 3–5
Also see BLOOM, Bobby

MANN, Carl
Singles: 7-Inch
JAXON: *57* 50–60
PHILLIPS INT'L: *59–61*. 5–8
SUN 1–3
LPs: 10/12-Inch 33rpm
CHARLEY 5–8
GRT/SUNNYVALE: *77* 6–10
PHILLIPS INT'L: *60*. 40–50

MANN, Charles
Singles: 7-Inch
ABC: *73* 2–3

MANN, Gloria (Gloria Mann & The Carter Rays)
Singles: 7-Inch
DECCA: *56*. 4–6
DERBY: *56* 5–8

Price Range

JUBILEE: *54*.................... **$8–10**
SLS: *54*...................... **25–30**
SOUND: *54–55*................. **8–10**

MANN, Herbie
Singles: 12-Inch 33/45rpm
ATLANTIC: *83* **4–6**

Singles: 7-Inch
A&M: *68* **2–3**
ATLANTIC: *60–83* **1–3**
BETHLEHEM: *59–62* **2–4**
COLUMBIA: *70*................. **1–3**
EMBRYO: *71* **1–3**
PRESTIGE: *66* **2–3**

LPs: 10/12-Inch 33rpm
A&M: *68* **8–12**
ATLANTIC (300 series):
 72.......................... **8–12**
ATLANTIC (1300 & 1400
 series): *60–65* **10–20**
ATLANTIC (1500 & 1600
 series): *69–76*................ **8–12**
ATLANTIC (8000 series):
 67.......................... **8–15**
ATLANTIC (18000 &
 19000 series): *77–83* **5–10**
BETHLEHEM (24 through
 63): *55–56* **20–40**
BETHLEHEM (1000
 series): *54*.................. **40–60**
 (10-Inch LPs.)
BETHLEHEM (6001;
 "The Bethlehem Years"):
 76 .... **5–8**
BETHLEHEM (6067;
 "The Epitome Of Jazz"):
 63 .... **12–20**
COLUMBIA: *65–81*.............. **8–15**
EMBRYO: *70–71* **8–12**
EPIC: *57–58* **20–35**
FINNADAR: *76*................. **5–10**
INTERLUDE: *59*................ **15–25**
JAZZLAND: *60* **15–25**
MILESTONE: *73* **8–12**
MODE: *57*..................... **25–40**
NEW JAZZ: *58*................. **20–30**
PREMIER: *63*.................. **10–20**
PRESTIGE (7000 series):
 57 .... **30–50**
 (Yellow label.)

Price Range

PRESTIGE (7000 series):
 65–69....................... **$10–20**
 (Blue label.)
RIVERSIDE (03; "Blues
 For Tomorrow"): *82*............ **5–8**
RIVERSIDE (200 & 300
 series): *57*.................... **20–35**
RIVERSIDE (3000 series):
 69.......................... **8–12**
ROULETTE: *67*................. **8–15**
SAVOY (1100 series): *76*.......... **5–8**
SAVOY (12000 series): *57*......... **20–35**
SOLID STATE: *68*............... **8–12**
SURREY: *65*................... **10–15**
UNITED ARTISTS (4000
 & 5000 series): *59* **20–40**
UNITED ARTISTS (5300
 series): *72*.................... **8–10**
UNITED ARTISTS (14000
 & 15000 series): *62–63* **20–35**
VSP: *66*....................... **8–15**
VERVE: *57–61* **15–30**
 (Reads "Verve Records, Inc." at bottom of
 label.)
VERVE: *63* **10–20**
 (Reads "MGM Records - A Division Of Metro-
 Goldwyn-Mayer, Inc." at bottom of label.)
VERVE: *69–73* **5–10**
 (Reads "Manufactured By MGM Record
 Corp.," or mentions either Polydor or Poly-
 gram at bottom of label.)
 Also see JONES, Tamiko, & Herbie Mann

MANN, Herbie, & Cissy Houston
Singles: 7-Inch
ATLANTIC: *76* **2–3**
 Also see HOUSTON, Cissy

MANN, Herbie / Maynard Ferguson
LPs: 10/12-Inch 33rpm
ROULETTE: *71* **8–12**
 Also see FERGUSON, Herbie
 Also see MANN, Herbie

MANN, Johnny, Singers
Singles: 7-Inch
DECCA: *66*..................... **1–3**
EPIC: *72* **1–3**
EUREKA: *60* **2–4**
LIBERTY: *62–68* **2–3**
LPs: 10/12-Inch 33rpm
EPIC: *72* **4–8**

Price Range

LIBERTY: *59–69* **$5–15**
LIGHT: *76* **4–8**
SUNSET: *66–70* **5–10**
UNITED ARTISTS: *71* **5–10**
Also see Zentner, Si

MANN, Manfred (Manfred Mann's Earth Band)
Singles: 7-Inch
ARISTA: *84–85*................... **1–3**
ASCOT: *64–68*.................... **4–6**
MERCURY: *66–69*................ **3–5**
POLYDOR: *71–74* **2–3**
PRESTIGE: *64* **8–10**
UNITED ARTISTS: *66*........... **4–6**
WARNER BROS: *76–81* **1–3**

EPs: 7-Inch 33/45rpm
UNITED ARTISTS
(10030; "Manfred
Mann"): *64*................... **10–20**
(Promotional issue only. Not issued with
cover.)

Picture Sleeves
ASCOT: *64* **8–10**
MERCURY: *68*................... **4–6**

LPs: 10/12-Inch 33rpm
ARISTA: *83* **5–8**
ASCOT: *64–66*.................. **20–30**
CAPITOL: *80* **5–8**
EMI AMERICA: *77*............. **10–12**
JANUS: *74* **12–15**
MERCURY: *68*................. **15–20**
POLYDOR: *70–74* **10–15**
UNITED ARTISTS: *66–68*....... **20–25**
WARNER BROS: *74–81*........... **5–8**
Also see FIRM, The
Also see McGUINNESS-FLINT
Also see NIGHT

MANNA, Charlie
Singles: 7-Inch
DECCA: *61*...................... **2–4**
JUBILEE: *65*.................... **2–4**

Picture Sleeves
DECCA: *61*...................... **3–5**

LPs: 10/12-Inch 33rpm
DECCA: *61–62*.................. **10–20**
VERVE: *66* **8–15**

MANNHEIM STEAMROLLER
LPs: 10/12-Inch 33rpm
AMERICAN
GRAMAPHONE: *83–85*........ **$5–8**

MANONE, Wingy, & His Orchestra
Singles: 7-Inch
COLUMBIA: *54*.................. **2–4**
DECCA: *57*...................... **2–4**
IMPERIAL: *62*................... **1–3**
KEM: *61* **1–3**

EPs: 7-Inch 33/45rpm
COLUMBIA: *54*.................. **4–8**
VIK: *56* **4–6**

LPs: 10/12-Inch 33rpm
IMPERIAL: *62*................... **8–15**
MCA: *83* **4–8**
PRESTIGE: *70* **5–10**
RCA VICTOR: *69* **5–10**
SAVOY: *73* **5–10**
STORYVILLE: *83* **4–8**
VIK: *56* **10–20**

MANTOVANI (Mantovani & His Orchestra)
Singles: 7-Inch
LONDON (Except 1761):
51–65 .... **1–3**
LONDON (1761; "Let Me
Be Loved"): *57*................... **3–5**
Picture Sleeves
LONDON (Except 1761):
57–65 .... **1–3**
LONDON (1761; "Let Me
Be Loved"): *57*................. **10–15**
("Let Me Be Loved" was the main theme from
the film, "The James Dean Story." Sleeve pic-
tures Dean.)
EPs: 7-Inch 33/45rpm
LONDON: *51–59* **3–6**
LPs: 10/12-Inch 33rpm
BAINBRIDGE: *82*................. **4–8**
LONDON: *51–72* **5–15**

MANTRA
Singles: 7-Inch
CASABLANCA: *81* **1–3**
LPs: 10/12-Inch 33rpm
CASABLANCA: *81* **5–8**

Price Range

MANTRONIX
Singles: 12-Inch 33/45rpm
SLEEPING BAG: 85 . . . . **$4–6**

MANU DIBANGO: see DIBANGO, Manu

MANZANERA, Phil (Phil Manzanera Quiet Sun; Phil Manzanera & 801; Manzanera)
Singles: 12-Inch 33/45rpm
EDITIONS E.G.: 82 . . . . **5–8**

LPs: 10/12-Inch 33rpm
ANTILLES **8–10**
ATCO **8–10**
EDITIONS E.G.: 82 . . . . **5–8**
POLYDOR: 78 . . . . **8–10**
Also see ROXY MUSIC

MANZAREK, Ray
Singles: 7-Inch
MERCURY: 73–74 . . . . **2–4**

LPs: 10/12-Inch 33rpm
A&M: 84 . . . . **5–8**
MERCURY: 74–75 . . . . **8–10**
Also see DOORS, The
Also see RICK & THE RAVENS

MARA, Tommy
Singles: 7-Inch
B&F: 60 . . . . **4–6**
FELSTED: 58–59 . . . . **4–6**

MARATHONS, The
Singles: 7-Inch
ARGO: 61 . . . . **4–6**
ARVEE (5027; "Peanut
Butter"): 61 . . . . **5–8**
(Other Arvee releases by the Marathons are actually a different group, and are listed in a separate section that follows.)
CHESS: 61 . . . . **4–6**
PLAZA: 62 . . . . **4–6**

EPs: 7-Inch 33/45rpm
MARK '56 ("Laura
Scudder's Magic
Record"): 69 . . . . **2–3**

(Contains three tunes, one of which was "Peanut Butter," imbedded into a single band on each side of the disc. When the needle began tracking, you never knew which song would play. The other artists heard on this record would be of no interest to collectors. Price includes paper picture sleeve. A Laura Scudder's potato chip mail order coupon giveaway item.)
LPs: 10/12-Inch 33rpm
ARVEE: 61 . . . . **$30–40**
Members: James Johnson; Carl Fisher; Dick Owens; Dave Govan; Don Bradley.
Also see JAYHAWKS, The
Also see VIBRATIONS, The

MARATHONS, The
Singles: 7-Inch
ARVEE (Except 5027):
61–62 . . . . **4–6**
(Arvee 5027 is by a different group of Marathons and is listed in the preceeding section.)

MARCELS, The
Singles: 7-Inch
COLPIX: 61–63 . . . . **6–10**
ERIC **1–3**
QUEEN BEE: 73 . . . . **2–4**
Picture Sleeves
COLPIX: 61–62 . . . . **10–15**
LPs: 10/12-Inch 33rpm
COLPIX (Gold label): 61 . . . . **35–45**
COLPIX (Blue label): 63 . . . . **20–25**
MURRAY HILL **8–10**
Members: Cornelius Harp; Fred Johnson; Ron Mundy; Gene Bricker; Richard Knauss; Walt Maddox; Al Johnson.
Also see FABULOUS MARCELS, The
Also see REGAN, Tommy

MARCH, Little Peggy (Peggy March)
Singles: 7-Inch
RCA VICTOR: 62–71 . . . . **3–5**
Picture Sleeves
RCA VICTOR: 63 . . . . **4–6**
EPs: 7-Inch 33/45rpm
RCA VICTOR: 63 . . . . **15–20**
LPs: 10/12-Inch 33rpm
RCA VICTOR (Except
2732): 65–68 . . . . **15–20**
RCA VICTOR (2732; "I
Will Follow Him"): 63 . . . . **20–25**

Price Range

Price Range

MARCHAN, Bobby (Bobby Marchon; Bobby Marchan & The Tick Tocks)
Singles: 7-Inch

ABC: *73*	$1–3
ACE: *56*	8–10
ALADDIN: *53*	15–20
CAMEO: *66–67*	3–5
DIAL: *64–74*	3–5
DOT: *54*	10–15
FIRE: *59–62*	5–8
FLASHBACK: *65.*	1–3
GALE.	3–5
GAMBLE: *68*	3–5
MERCURY: *77.*	2–3
SPHERE SOUND: *65*	3–5
VOLT: *63.*	3–5

LPs: 10/12-Inch 33rpm

SPHERE SOUND: *64*	20–25

MARCHAN, Bobby, & The Clowns
Singles: 7-Inch

ACE: *59*	5–8

Also see MARCHAN, Bobby
Also see SMITH, Huey

MARCY JO & EDDIE RAMBEAU
Singles: 7-Inch

ROBBEE: *62*	4–6
SWAN: *63*	5–8

Also see MARCY JOE
Also see RAMBEAU, Eddie

MARCY JOE (Marcy Jo)
Singles: 7-Inch

ROBBEE: *61*	4–6
SWAN: *62*	3–5

Also see CHRISTIE, Lou

MARDONES, Benny
Singles: 7-Inch

POLYDOR: *80*	1–3
PRIVATE STOCK: *78.*	1–3

LPs: 10/12-Inch 33rpm

POLYDOR: *80*	5–8

MARESCA, Ernie
Singles: 7-Inch

LAURIE: *66*	4–6
RUST: *64*	5–8
SEVILLE: *60–65*	5–8

Picture Sleeves

SEVILLE: *62*	$5–10

LPs: 10/12-Inch 33rpm

SEVILLE: *62*	30–40

MARGRET, Ann: see
ANN-MARGRET

MARIACHI BRASS (Featuring Chet Baker)
LPs: 10/12-Inch 33rpm

WORLD PACIFIC: *66*	6–12

MARIE, Diane
Singles: 12-Inch 33/45rpm

PRELUDE: *83.*	4–6

MARIE, Teena
Singles: 12-Inch 33/45rpm

EPIC: *83–85*	4–6

Singles: 7-Inch

EPIC: *83–85*	1–3
GORDY: *79–81.*	1–3
MOTOWN.	1–3

LPs: 10/12-Inch 33rpm

EPIC: *83–85*	5–8
GORDY: *79–81.*	5–8

MARIE & REX
Singles: 7-Inch

CARLTON: *59*	5–8

Members: Marie Knight; Rex Garvin.
Also see KNIGHT, Marie

MARIGOLDS, The
Singles: 7-Inch

EXCELLO: *55.*	15–20

Members: Johnny Bragg; Henry Jones; Hal Hebb; Willie Wilson.

MARILLION
Singles: 7-Inch

CAPITOL: *83–85*	1–3

LPs: 10/12-Inch 33rpm

CAPITOL: *83–85*	5–8

MARIMBA CHIAPAS
Singles: 7-Inch

CAPITOL: *56*	2–4

Price Range

MARINERS, The
Singles: 7-Inch
CADENCE: 55–56 .... $2–4
COLUMBIA: 50–55 2–4
EPs: 7-Inch 33/45rpm
COLUMBIA: 51–55 4–8
LPs: 10/12-Inch 33rpm
CADENCE: 56 10–20
COLUMBIA: 51–55 10–20
EPIC: 59 8–15
HARMONY: 59 8–15
Also see GODFREY, Arthur

MARINO, Frank (Frank Marino & Mahogany Rush)
Singles: 7-Inch
COLUMBIA: 77–81 1–3
LPs: 10/12-Inch 33rpm
COLUMBIA: 77–81 5–8
Also see MAHAGONY RUSH

MARK II, The
Singles: 7-Inch
WYE: 60–61 3–5

MARK IV, The
Singles: 7-Inch
COSMIC: 58 4–6
MERCURY (71000 series):
59 4–6
MERCURY (73000 series):
73 2–3
LPs: 10/12-Inch 33rpm
MERCURY: 73 10–12

MARK-ALMOND BAND, The
Singles: 7-Inch
ABC: 75 2–3
BLUE THUMB: 72 2–4
COLUMBIA: 72–73 2–3
LPs: 10/12-Inch 33rpm
A&M: 78 8–10
BLUE THUMB: 70–71 10–12
COLUMBIA: 72–73 8–10
MCA 5–8
PACIFIC ARTS: 81 8–10
Members: Jon Mark; Johnny Almond.

MARKETTS, The (The Mar-Kets)
Singles: 7-Inch
LIBERTY: 62 4–6

Price Range

MERCURY: 73 .... $2–4
UNI: 69 2–4
UNION: 61–62 8–10
WARNER BROS. (Except
5391): 63–66 3–5
WARNER BROS (5391;
"Outer Limits"): 63 5–8
WARNER BROS (5391;
"Out Of Limits"): 63 3–5
WORLD PACIFIC: 67 3–5
LPs: 10/12-Inch 33rpm
DORE: 82 5–8
LIBERTY: 62–63 30–35
MERCURY: 73 10–15
PHONORAMA: 84 5–8
WARNER BROS: 63–66 20–25
WORLD PACIFIC: 67 15–20
Also see NEW MARKETTS

MAR-KEYS, The
Singles: 7-Inch
SATELITE: 61 8–10
STAX: 61–66 3–5
LPs: 10/12-Inch 33rpm
ATLANTIC: 61–62 20–25
STAX: 66–71 10–15

MAR-KEYS, The / Booker T. & The MGs
LPs: 10/12-Inch 33rpm
STAX: 67 12–15
Also see BOOKER T. & THE MGs
Also see MAR-KEYS, The

MARKHAM, Pigmeat
Singles: 7-Inch
ABC: 74 1–3
CHESS: 64–70 2–3
LPs: 10/12-Inch 33rpm
CHESS: 61–69 8–18
JEWEL: 72–73 5–10
Also see MABLEY, Moms, & Pigmeat Markham

MARKS, Guy
Singles: 7-Inch
ABC: 68 2–3
ARIOLA AMERICA: 76 1–3
RADNOR: 70 2–3
LPs: 10/12-Inch 33rpm
ABC: 66–68 8–15

Price Range

Price Range

MARLEY, Bob, & The Wailers (The Wailers)
Singles: 7-Inch
COTILLION: *81*.................. **$1–3**
ISLAND: *76–84* **1–3**
SHELTER: *71*..................... **2–4**
LPs: 10/12-Inch 33rpm
CALLA (1200 series): *76*.......... **10–15**
CALLA (34000 series): *77*.......... **8–10**
COTILLION: *81*................... **5–8**
ISLAND (Except 90000
  series): *75–80* **8–10**
ISLAND (90000 series):
  83–84 .... **5–8**
  Also see TOSH, Peter

MARLO, Micki
Singles: 7-Inch
ABC-PARAMOUNT
  (Except 9841): *57*............... **4–6**
ABC-PARAMOUNT
  (9841; "What You've
  Done To Me"): *57*.............. **8–10**
  (With "vocal assist by Paul Anka.")
ABC-PARAMOUNT
  (9841; "What You've
  Done To Me"): *57*.............. **4–6**
  (With singer humming the lines done by Paul
  Anka on the above pressing.)
CAPITOL: *54–56* **5–8**
LPs: 10/12-Inch 33rpm
ABC-PARAMOUNT: *60*.......... **12–20**
  Also see ANKA, Paul

MARLOWE, Marion
Singles: 7-Inch
CADENCE: *55–56* **2–4**
COLUMBIA: *53–54* **2–4**
EPs: 7-Inch 33/45rpm
COLUMBIA: *53–55* **4–8**
LPs: 10/12-Inch 33rpm
BARNABY: *76*.................... **5–8**
COLUMBIA: *53–55* **10–20**
HARMONY: *60* **8–12**

MARMALADE (Featuring Junior Campbell)
Singles: 7-Inch
ARIOLA AMERICA: *76* **2–3**
EMI: *74* **2–3**
EPIC: *67–69* **4–6**

LONDON: *70–71* **$3–5**
LPs: 10/12-Inch 33rpm
EPIC: *70* **10–12**
G&P: *81*......................... **8–10**
LONDON: *70* **10–15**
  Also see BLUE

MARSALIS, Branford
LPs: 10/12-Inch 33rpm
COLUMBIA: *84*................... **5–8**

MARSALIS, Wynton
LPs: 10/12-Inch 33rpm
COLUMBIA: *82–85* **5–8**
WHO'S WHO IN JAZZ:
  83 .... **5–8**

MARSH, Little Toni
Singles: 12-Inch 33/45rpm
PRISM: *83*....................... **4–6**

MARSHALL-HAIN
Singles: 7-Inch
HARVEST: *78*.................... **1–3**
LPs: 10/12-Inch 33rpm
HARVEST: *78*.................... **5–8**
  Members: Julian Marshall; Kit Hain.
  Also see EYE TO EYE

MARSHALL TUCKER BAND, The
Singles: 7-Inch
CAPRICORN: *73–78*............... **2–3**
WARNER BROS: *79–80*............ **1–3**
Picture Sleeves
WARNER BROS: *79*............... **1–3**
LPs: 10/12-Inch 33rpm
CAPRICORN: *73–78*............. **10–12**
WARNER BROS: *79–83*.......... **8–10**

MARTERIE, Ralph, & His Orchestra
Singles: 7-Inch
MERCURY: *50–60*................ **2–4**
UNITED ARTISTS: *61–62*.......... **2–3**
EPs: 7-Inch 33/45rpm
MERCURY: *50–59*................. **3–6**
LPs: 10/12-Inch 33rpm
MERCURY: *50–60*................ **5–15**
UNITED ARTISTS: *61–62*......... **5–10**
WING: *50–60* **4–8**

Price Range

MARTHA & THE MUFFINS (M + M)
Singles: 12-Inch 33/45rpm
RCA VICTOR: *83–84* **$4–6**
Singles: 7-Inch
DINDISC/VIRGIN: *80*............. **1–3**
RCA VICTOR: *83–84* **1–3**
LPs: 10/12-Inch 33rpm
RCA VICTOR: *83* **5–8**
VIRGIN: *80* **5–8**

MARTHA & THE VANDELLAS (Martha Reeves & The Vandellas)
Singles: 7-Inch
GORDY (7011; "I'll Have
   To Let Him Go"): *62* **8–10**
GORDY (7014 through
   7025): *62–63*.................... **4–6**
GORDY (7027 through
   7110): *64–72*.................... **3–5**
MOTOWN........................ **1–3**
Picture Sleeves
GORDY: *64* **6–10**
LPs: 10/12-Inch 33rpm
GORDY (902 & 907): *63*.......... **35–45**
GORDY (915 through
   925): *65–67*.................... **20–25**
GORDY (926 through
   958): *68–72*.................... **15–20**
MOTOWN (Except 100 &
   200 series): *74* **12–15**
MOTOWN (100 & 200
   series): *81–82*.................. **5–8**
   Also see GAYE, Marvin
   Also see REEVES, Martha

MARTIN, Bobbi
Singles: 7-Inch
BUDDAH: *71–72* **1–3**
CORAL: *61–67*.................... **2–4**
GREEN MENU: *75*................ **1–3**
MGM: *73*........................ **1–3**
MAYPOLE: *60*................... **3–5**
UNITED ARTISTS: *68–70*.......... **2–3**
Picture Sleeves
CORAL: *65* **2–4**
EPs: 7-Inch 33/45rpm
CORAL: *65* **4–6**
LPs: 10/12-Inch 33rpm
BUDDAH: *71*.................... **5–10**
CORAL: *65*...................... **8–15**

Price Range

SUNSET: *71* **$5–10**
UNITED ARTISTS: *68–70*........ **5–10**
VOCALION: *70* **5–10**

MARTIN, Dean
Singles: 7-Inch
CAPITOL (401; "Dean
   Martin Sings"): *53*.............. **15–25**
   (Boxed set of four singles. As a general note,
   Capitol issued a boxed set of four singles and a
   double EP, with an "EBF" prefix, for nearly
   every 10-inch LP, by their most popular artists,
   issued circa 1949-1953. The LP, EP set and four
   singles all contained the same eight tracks.)
CAPITOL (900 through
   2000 series): *50–54* **4–10**
CAPITOL (3000 through
   4500 series): *55–61* **3–6**
REPRISE (Except 40,000
   series): *62–73* **2–5**
REPRISE (40,000 series):
   62 .... **4–8**
   (Stereo 33 singles.)
TEXAS DESERT
   CIRCUS (2160; "Palm
   Springs Salutes Texas
   Desert Circus Week"):
   58 .... **15-25**
   (A one-sided disc, with no actual label name,
   containing a song recorded especially for air
   play in Palm Springs in conjunction with the
   appearance of the circus there.)
WARNER BROS: *83*.............. **1–3**

Picture Sleeves
CAPITOL: *58* **2–4**
REPRISE: *62*.................... **2–3**

EPs: 7-Inch 33/45rpm
CAPITOL (401; "Dean
   Martin Sings"): *53*.............. **15–30**
   (With an "EBF" prefix. Double EP set.)
CAPITOL (400 through
   700 series): *53–56* **10–20**
   (With an "EAP" prefix.)
CAPITOL (800 through
   1200 series): *57–59* **8–15**
CAPITOL (9000 series): *56*........ **10–15**
CAPITOL (Jukebox 33
   Compacts): *64* **5–10**
REPRISE (Jukebox 33
   Compacts): *64–65* **5–10**

Price Range

Price Range

LPs: 10/12-Inch 33rpm

CAPITOL (100 & 300
series): *69* **$8–15**
CAPITOL (401; "Dean
Martin Sings"): *53* **25–35**
(With an "H" prefix. 10-Inch LPs.)
CAPITOL (401; "Dean
Martin Sings"): *55* **20–30**
(With a "T" prefix.)
CAPITOL (523; "Return
To Me"/"You're
Nobody Til Somebody
Loves You"): *70* **8-12**
CAPITOL (576; "Swingin'
Down Yonder"): *55* **15–25**
CAPITOL (800 through
2600 series): *57–66* **10–20**
(With a "T" or "ST" prefix.)
CAPITOL (800 through
2600 series): *63–65* **8–15**
(With a "DT" prefix.)
CAPITOL (2815; "Dean
Martin Deluxe Set"): *67* **15–25**
(3-LP boxed set.)
CAPITOL (2900 series): *68* **8–12**
LONGINES (5234;
"Memories Are Made Of
This"): *73* **40–60**
(5-LP boxed set. Includes booklet.)
LONGINES (5235; "That's
Amore"): *73* **10–15**
PAIR: *83* **6–10**
PICKWICK **5–10**
REPRISE: *63–78* **8–18**
TOWER: *65–66* **20–35**
WARNER BROS: *83* **5–8**
Also see GILKYSON, Terry
Also see GOLDDIGGERS, The
Also see SINATRA, Frank, & Sammy Davis,
Jr. / Dean Martin & Sammy Davis, Jr.
Also see SINATRA, Nancy

MARTIN, Dean, & Nat "King" Cole
Singles: 7-Inch
CAPITOL: *55* **3–5**
Also see COLE, Nat "King"

MARTIN, Dean, & Jerry Lewis
EPs: 7-Inch 33/45rpm
CAPITOL: *56* **8–15**
Also see LEWIS, Jerry
Also see MARTIN, Dean

MARTIN, Derek
Singles: 7-Inch
CRACKERJACK: *63* **$4–6**
ROULETTE: *65* **3–5**
SUE: *66* **3–5**
VOLT: *68* **3–5**

MARTIN, Eric (The Eric Martin Band)
Singles: 7-Inch
CAPITOL: *85* **1–3**
ELEKTRA: *83* **1–3**
LPs: 10/12-Inch 33rpm
ELEKTRA: *83* **5–8**

MARTIN, Freddy, & His Orchestra
Singles: 7-Inch
CAPITOL: *63* **2–3**
DECCA: *67–68* **1–3**
KAPP: *61* **2–3**
RCA VICTOR: *50–56* **2–4**
EPs: 7-Inch 33/45rpm
CAMDEN: *54–56* **4–8**
RCA VICTOR: *50–54* **5–10**
LPs: 10/12-Inch 33rpm
CAMDEN: *54–56* **5–15**
CAPITOL: *59–79* **5–15**
DECCA: *67* **5–10**
KAPP: *61–66* **5–15**
MCA: *73–75* **4–8**
RCA VICTOR: *51–72* **5–15**
Also see GRIFFIN, Merv

MARTIN, George, & His Orchestra
Singles: 7-Inch
UNITED ARTISTS (745;
"Ringo's Theme"): *64* **5–10**
UNITED ARTISTS (750;
"A Hard Day's Night"):
64 . . . . **5–10**
UNITED ARTISTS (800
series): *65* **2–3**
UNITED ARTISTS (50000
series): *67* **2–3**
Picture Sleeves
UNITED ARTISTS (745;
"Ringo's Theme"): *64* **35–40**
UNITED ARTISTS (750;
"A Hard Day's Night"):
64 . . . . **175–200**

Promotional Singles
UNITED ARTISTS (745;
"Ringo's Theme"): *64* **$10–15**
(White label.)

LPs: 10/12-Inch 33rpm
UNITED ARTISTS (377;
"Off The Beatle Track"):
64 .... **30–40**
UNITED ARTISTS (383;
"A Hard Day's Night"):
64 .... **20–30**
UNITED ARTISTS (420;
"George Martin"): *65* **15–25**
UNITED ARTISTS (448;
"Help"): *65.* **20–30**
UNITED ARTISTS (539;
"The Beatle Girls"): *66* **25–35**
UNITED ARTISTS (647;
"London By George"):
68 .... **10–15**
Also see BEATLES, The
Also see GERRY & THE PACEMAKERS

MARTIN, Janis
Singles: 7-Inch
BIG DUTCH: *77* **2–4**
PALETTE: *61* **5–8**
RCA VICTOR (6400 &
6500 series): *56* **10–12**
RCA VICTOR (6652; "My
Boy Elvis"): *56* **12–15**
RCA VICTOR (6700
through 7300 series):
56–58 .... **5–8**

EPs: 7-Inch 33/45rpm
RCA VICTOR: *58* **25–30**

MARTIN, Kenny
Singles: 7-Inch
BIG TOP: *60.* **3–5**
FEDERAL: *59–60* **4–6**
PJ: *66* **3–5**

MARTIN, Moon (John Martin)
Singles: 7-Inch
CAPITOL: *78–79* **1–3**

LPs: 10/12-Inch 33rpm
CAPITOL: *78–82* **5–8**

MARTIN, Nancy
Singles: 7-Inch
ATLANTIC: *82* **$1–3**

MARTIN, Paul
Singles: 7-Inch
ASCOT: *65* **3–5**
IMPEX: *66* **3–5**

MARTIN, Ray, Orchestra
Singles: 7-Inch
RCA VICTOR: *61–62* **2–3**
UNITED ARTISTS: *58* **2–3**
Picture Sleeves
RCA VICTOR: *61* **2–3**
UNITED ARTISTS: *58* **2–3**
LPs: 10/12-Inch 33rpm
CAMDEN: *67–70* **4–8**
LONDON: *63* **5–12**
MONUMENT: *67.* **5–10**
RCA VICTOR: *61* **5–15**

MARTIN, Steve
Singles: 7-Inch
WARNER BROS: *77–79* **2–3**
Picture Sleeves
WARNER BROS: *78* **2–3**
LPs: 10/12-Inch 33rpm
WARNER BROS: *77–81* **5–8**

MARTIN, Tony
Singles: 7-Inch
CHART: *70.* **1–3**
DOT: *61–66.* **2–3**
DUNHILL: *67.* **2–3**
MOTOWN: *64–66.* **2–3**
NAN: *64* **2–3**
PARK AVENUE: *63* **2–3**
RCA VICTOR: *50–60* **2–4**
EPs: 7-Inch 33/45rpm
DECCA: *51–56.* **5–10**
MERCURY: *54–56.* **5–10**
RCA VICTOR: *51–57* **5–10**
LPs: 10/12-Inch 33rpm
CAMDEN: *59–60.* **8–12**
CHART: *70.* **5–8**
CHARTER: *63* **8–12**
CORAL: *73* **4–8**
DECCA: *51–56.* **10–20**
DOT: *61–62.* **8–15**

Price Range

MERCURY: *54–61* **$8–18**
RCA VICTOR: *51–60* **10–20**
20TH CENTURY-FOX:
   64 .... **8–15**
WING: *59–60* **8–12**

MARTIN, Trade
Singles: 7-Inch
COED: *62–64*. **4–6**
GEE: *59*. **4–6**
RCA VICTOR: *66–67* **3–5**
ROULETTE: *60* **4–6**
STALLION. **3–5**
TOOT: *68* **3–5**

LPs: 10/12-Inch 33rpm
BUDDAH: *72*. **10–12**

**MARTIN, Vince (Vince Martin &
The Tarriers; Vince Martin & Fred
Neil)**
Singles: 7-Inch
ABC-PARAMOUNT: *59*. **3–5**
GLORY: *56*. **3–5**
ELEKTRA: *64* **2–3**

LPs: 10/12-Inch 33rpm
CAPITOL: *73* **5–8**
ELEKTRA: *64* **8–15**
Also see TARRIERS, The

MARTINDALE, Wink
Singles: 7-Inch
ABC/DOT: *76*. **1–3**
DOT: *59–66*. **3–5**
RANWOOD: *73* **1–3**

Picture Sleeves
DOT: *59–60*. **3–5**

LPs: 10/12-Inch 33rpm
DOT: *59–66*. **15–20**
HAMILTON: *64*. **10–15**

**MARTINDALE, Wink, & Robin
Ward**
Singles: 7-Inch
DOT: *63–64*. **3–5**

LPs: 10/12-Inch 33rpm
DOT: *64*. **15–20**
Also see MARTINDALE, Wink
Also see WARD, Robin

Price Range

MARTINE, Layng, Jr.
Singles: 7-Inch
BARNABY: *71*. **$2–4**
DATE: *66* **4–6**
GENERAL INT'L: *66*. **3–5**
PLAYBOY: *76* **2–3**
Also see MORRISON, Professor

MARTINO, Al
Singles: 7-Inch
B.B.S.: *52*. **3–6**
CAPITOL: *52–81* **2–4**
20TH CENTURY-FOX:
   59–64 .... **2–4**
Picture Sleeves
CAPITOL: *63–66* **2–4**
LPs: 10/12-Inch 33rpm
CAPITOL: *62–80* **5–15**
MOVIETONE: *67*. **5–10**
SPRINGBOARD: *78* **4–8**
20TH CENTURY-FOX:
   59–65 .... **8–18**

MARVELETTES, The
Singles: 7-Inch
MOTOWN. **1–3**
TAMLA: *61–71*. **3–5**
Picture Sleeves
TAMLA: *61–64*. **5–8**
LPs: 10/12-Inch 33rpm
MOTOWN (Except 100
   series): *75* **12–15**
MOTOWN (100 series): *82* **5–8**

Price Range

TAMLA (228 through
243): *61–63*. **$30–35**
TAMLA (253 through
288): *66–68*. **20–25**
TAMLA (300 series): *70* **12–15**
Members: Gladys Horton; Kathy Anderson;
Georgeanna Tillman; Wanda Young; Juanita
Cowart.

MARVELOWS, The (The Mighty Marvellows)
Singles: 7-Inch
ABC: *66* **3–5**
ABC-PARAMOUNT:
64–66 . . . . **3–5**
LPs: 10/12-Inch 33rpm
ABC: *68* **12–15**

MARVIN & JOHNNY
Singles: 7-Inch
ALADDIN: *56* **8–10**
ERIC **1–3**
FELSTED: *63* **3–5**
FIREFLY: *60* **5–8**
JAMIE: *61* **4–6**
MODERN: *54–56* **15–20**
RAYS: *54* **8–10**
SPECIALTY (Black vinyl):
53–55 . . . . **10–12**
SPECIALTY (Colored
vinyl): *53* **20–25**
LPs: 10/12-Inch 33rpm
CROWN: *63* **20–25**
Members: Marvin Phillips; Johnny Dean.
Also see ISLEY BROTHERS, The / Marvin &
Johnny
Also see JESSE & MARVIN
Also see PHILLIPS, Marvin

MARX, Groucho
Singles: 7-Inch
A&M: *73* **1–3**
LPs: 10/12-Inch 33rpm
A&M: *72* **5–10**
DECCA: *69* **6–12**

MARY JANE GIRLS, The (Featuring Jo Jo McDuffie)
Singles: 12-Inch 33/45rpm
GORDY: *83–85*. **4–6**
MOTOWN: *85*. **4–6**

Price Range

Singles: 7-Inch
GORDY: *83–85*. **$1–3**
LPs: 10/12-Inch 33rpm
GORDY: *83–85*. **5–8**

MAS, Carolyn
Singles: 7-Inch
MERCURY: *79*. **1–3**
LPs: 10/12-Inch 33rpm
MERCURY: *79*. **5–8**

MASCARA
Singles: 12-Inch 33/45rpm
OH MY: *84* **4–6**

MASEKELA, Hugh (Hugh Masekela & The Union Of South Africa)
Singles: 12-Inch 33/45rpm
JIVE AFRIKA: *84* **4–6**
Singles: 7-Inch
BLUE THUMB: *74* **1–3**
CASABLANCA: *75–77* **1–3**
CHISA: *67–71* **2–3**
JIVE AFRIKA: *84* **1–3**
MGM: *66–68* **2–3**
MERCURY: *63–68*. **2–3**
UNI: *67–69* **2–3**
LPs: 10/12-Inch 33rpm
BLUE THUMB: *72–74* **5–10**
CASABLANCA: *75–77* **5–10**
CHISA: *67–71* **8–15**
IMPULSE: *78* **5–10**
MGM: *66–68* **8–15**
MERCURY: *63–67*. **8–18**
UNI: *67–69* **8–12**
UPFRONT: *77* **5–8**
VERVE: *68* **8–15**
WING: *68* **6–12**
Also see ALPERT, Herb, & Hugh Masekela

MASHMAKHAN
Singles: 7-Inch
EPIC: *70* **2–4**
JAMIE: *69*. **3–5**
LPs: 10/12-Inch 33rpm
EPIC: *70–71* **10–12**

MASKED MARAUDERS, The
Singles: 7-Inch
DEITY: *69*. **4–6**

Price Range

LPs: 10/12-Inch 33rpm
DEITY: *69*. **$15–20**

MASKMAN & THE AGENTS
Singles: 7-Inch
DYNAMO: *68–69*. **3–5**
GAMA: *68* **3–5**

LPs: 10/12-Inch 33rpm
DYNAMO: *69*. **10–15**

MASON, Barbara (Barbara Mason & The Futures)
Singles: 12-Inch 33/45rpm
WEST END: *83–84* **4–6**

Singles: 7-Inch
ARCTIC: *64–68* **3–5**
BUDDAH: *71–75* **2–4**
CHARGER: *65* **3–5**
CRUSADER: *64* **4–6**
NATIONAL GENERAL:
  70 . . . . **2–3**
PHONORAMA: *84* **1–3**
PRELUDE: *78*. **1–3**
WMOT: *80–81*. **1–3**
WEST END: *83–84* **1–3**

LPs: 10/12-Inch 33rpm
ARCTIC: *65–68* **15–20**
BUDDAH: *72–75* **8–10**
GNC: *70* **10–12**
NATIONAL GENERAL:
  70 . . . . **10–12**
PHONORAMA: *84* **5–8**
PRELUDE: *78*. **8–10**
WMOT: *81* **8–10**
WARNER BROS: *77*. **8–10**
WIND: *81* **8–10**
  Also see HIGGINS, Monk

MASON, Barbara, & Bunny Sigler
Singles: 7-Inch
WARNER BROS: *77*. **2–3**
  Also see MASON, Barbara
  Also see SIGLER, Bunny

MASON, Bonnie Jo (Cher)
Singles: 7-Inch
ANNETTE: *64* **20–25**
  Also see CHER

Price Range

MASON, Dave
Singles: 7-Inch
ABC: *74*. **$2–3**
BLUE THUMB: *70–78* **2–4**
COLUMBIA: *73–81*. **1–3**
MARBLE: *83* **1–3**
LPs: 10/12-Inch 33rpm
ABC: *75*. **8–10**
BLUE THUMB (19;
  "Alone Together"): *70* **10–12**
  (Black vinyl.)
BLUE THUMB (19;
  "Alone Together"): *70* **20–25**
  (Colored vinyl.)
BLUE THUMB (34
  through 54): *72–73* **10–12**
BLUE THUMB (800
  series): *75*. **8–10**
BLUE THUMB (6000
  series): *74–78*. **8–10**
COLUMBIA: *73–81*. **8–10**
ISLAND: *83* **5–8**
  Also see MERRYWEATHER, Neil
  Also see TRAFFIC

MASON, Dave, & Cass Elliot
Singles: 7-Inch
DUNHILL: *70–71*. **2–4**
LPs: 10/12-Inch 33rpm
BLUE THUMB: *71* **12–15**
  Also see ELLIOT, Cass
  Also see MASON, Dave

MASON, Harvey
Singles: 7-Inch
ARISTA: *76–81*. **1–3**
LPs: 10/12-Inch 33rpm
ARISTA: *78–81*. **5–8**

MASON, Jackie
Singles: 7-Inch
VERVE: *62* **2–4**
LPs: 10/12-Inch 33rpm
VERVE: *62–64* **8–18**

MASON, Nick (Nick Mason's Fictitious Sports; Nick Mason & Rick Fenn)
Singles: 12-Inch 33/45rpm
COLUMBIA: *85*. **4–6**

Singles: 7-Inch
COLUMBIA: *81–85* **$1–3**
LPs: 10/12-Inch 33rpm
COLUMBIA: *81–85* **5–8**
Also see PINK FLOYD

MASON, Vaughan (Vaughan Mason & Crew)
Singles: 12-Inch 33/45rpm
BRUNSWICK: *80*. **4–6**
Singles: 7-Inch
BRUNSWICK: *80–81*. **1–3**
LPs: 10/12-Inch 33rpm
BRUNSWICK: *80*. **5–8**

MASON, Vaughan, & Butch Dayo
Singles: 12-Inch 33/45rpm
SALSOUL: *83* **4–6**
Singles: 7-Inch
SALSOUL: *82–83* **1–3**
LPs: 10/12-Inch 33rpm
SALSOUL: *83* **5–8**
Also see MASON, Vaughan, & Crew

MASON DIXON DANCE BAND, The
Singles: 7-Inch
ALEXANDER STREET:
   79 .... **1–3**

MASON PROFFIT
Singles: 7-Inch
AMPEX: *71* **2–3**
HAPPY TIGER: *70* **2–4**
LPs: 10/12-Inch 33rpm
AMPEX: *71*. **6–10**
HAPPY TIGER: *70–71* **8–12**
WARNER BROS: *72–73* **6–10**
Members: John Talbot; Terry Talbot.

MASQUERADERS, The
Singles: 7-Inch
AGP: *69*. **2–4**
BELL: *68* **3–5**
TOWER: *66*. **3–5**

MASQUERADERS, The
Singles: 7-Inch
BANG: *80* **1–3**
HOT BUTTERED SOUL:
   75–76 .... **2–3**

MASS PRODUCTION
Singles: 7-Inch
COTILLION: *76–83* **$1–3**
LPs: 10/12-Inch 33rpm
COTILLION: *76–83* **5–8**

MASSER, Michael, & Mandrill
Singles: 7-Inch
ARISTA: *77* **2–3**
Also see MANDRILL

MASSEY, Wayne
Singles: 7-Inch
POLYDOR: *80* **1–3**

MASSIAH, Maurice
Singles: 12-Inch 33/45rpm
RFC/QUALITY: *83*. **4–6**

MASTERPIECE
Singles: 7-Inch
WHITFIELD: *80* **1–3**
LPs: 10/12-Inch 33rpm
WHITFIELD: *80* **5–8**

MASTERS, Johnny (Johnny Maestro)
Singles: 7-Inch
COED: *60* **10–12**
Also see MAESTRO, Johnny

MASTERS, Sammy
Singles: 7-Inch
DOT: *60–66*. **3–5**
4 STAR: *57* **20–30**
GALAHAD: *62–72*. **3–5**
KAPP: *64* **3–5**
LODE: *60–61*. **4–6**
WARNER BROS: *60*. **3–5**

MATHEWS, Tobin (Tobin Mathews & Co.; Tobin Matthews)
Singles: 7-Inch
CHIEF: *60–61*. **3–5**
COLUMBIA: *63* **3–5**
U.S.A.: *61* **3–5**

MATHIS, Johnny
Singles: 7-Inch
COLUMBIA (40000
   series): *57* **3–5**

Price Range

COLUMBIA (41000 &
  42000 series): *58–63* $2–4
MERCURY: *63–66* 2–3
Picture Sleeves
COLUMBIA (40000
  series): *57* 3–5
COLUMBIA (41000 &
  42000 series): *58–63* 2–4
MERCURY: *63–66* 2–3
EPs: 7-Inch 33/45rpm
COLUMBIA (Except 8800
  series): *57–59* 5–10
COLUMBIA (8871
  through 8873): *56* 10–20
LPs: 10/12-Inch 33rpm
COLUMBIA (Except 887):
  57–85 5–15
COLUMBIA (887;
  "Johnny Mathis"): *56* 25–50
MERCURY: *64–67* 5–15
    Also see KNIGHT, Gladys, & Johnny Mathis

MATHIS, Johnny, & Dionne Warwick
Singles: 7-Inch
ARISTA: *82* 1–3
    Also see WARWICK, Dionne

MATHIS, Johnny, & Deniece Williams
Singles: 7-Inch
COLUMBIA: *78–84* 1–3
LPs: 10/12-Inch 33rpm
COLUMBIA: *78* 5–8

Price Range

Also see MATHIS, Johnny
Also see WILLIAMS, Deniece

MATLOCK, Ronn
Singles: 7-Inch
COTILLION: *79* $2–3

MATTHEWS, David
LPs: 10/12-Inch 33rpm
CTI: *77* 5–8
    Also see WASHINGTON, Grover, Jr.

MATTHEWS, Ian
Singles: 7-Inch
DECCA: *70* 2–4
COLUMBIA: *76–77* 2–3
ELEKTRA: *73* 2–4
MUSHROOM: *78–79* 1–3
VERTIGO: *71–72* 2–3
LPs: 10/12-Inch 33rpm
COLUMBIA: *77* 8–10
ELEKTRA: *73–74* 8–10
MUSHROOM (Except
  picture discs): *78* 8–10
MUSHROOM ("Stealin'
  Home" picture disc): *78* 35–40
VERTIGO: *71–72* 10–12
    Also see FAIRPORT CONVENTION
    Also see MATTHEWS' SOUTHERN COMFORT

MATTHEWS, Milt
Singles: 7-Inch
H&L: *78* 2–3

MATTHEWS' SOUTHERN COMFORT (Featuring Ian Matthews)
Singles: 7-Inch
DECCA: *71* 2–4
LPs: 10/12-Inch 33rpm
DECCA: *70–71* 10–12
MCA: *78* 5–8
    Also see MATTHEWS, Ian
    Also see SOUTHERN COMFORT

MATYS BROS., The
Singles: 7-Inch
SELECT: *62* 2–4

Price Range

MAUDS, The
Singles: 7-Inch
DUNWICH: 67................... $4–6
MERCURY: 67–69................. 3–5
RCA VICTOR: 70 2–4
LPs: 10/12-Inch 33rpm
MERCURY: 67................. 15–20

MAURIAT, Paul, & His Orchestra
Singles: 7-Inch
PHILIPS: 67–71 1–3
Picture Sleeves
PHILIPS: 68..................... 1–3
LPs: 10/12-Inch 33rpm
PHILIPS: 67–69 5–10

MAXAYN
Singles: 7-Inch
CAPRICORN: 73................. 2–4

MAXWELL, Robert (Bobby Maxwell)
Singles: 7-Inch
DECCA: 64..................... 2–3
MGM: 57....................... 2–4
MERCURY: 52................... 2–4
TEMPO: 51–52 2–4
EPs: 7-Inch 33/45rpm
MGM: 57....................... 3–6
MERCURY: 52................... 4–8
TEMPO: 51–52 5–10
LPs: 10/12-Inch 33rpm
DECCA: 64..................... 5–12
MGM: 57...................... 10–15
TEMPO: 52.................... 10–20

MAXWELL, Diane
Singles: 7-Inch
CAPITOL: 61 3–5
CHALLENGE: 59 4–6
LPs: 10/12-Inch 33rpm
CHALLENGE: 59 30–35
Also see FULLER, Jerry, & Diane Maxwell

MAY, Billy, & His Orchestra
Singles: 7-Inch
CAPITOL: 50–56 2–4
EPs: 7-Inch 33/45rpm
CAPITOL: 50–56 4–8
LPs: 10/12-Inch 33rpm
CAPITOL: 50–56 5–15

Price Range

MAY, Brian (Brian May & Friends)
Singles: 7-Inch
CAPITOL: 83 .... $1–3
LPs: 10/12-Inch 33rpm
CAPITOL: 83 5–8
Also see QUEEN
Also see REO SPEEDWAGON
Also see VAN HALEN

MAYALL, John (John Mayall & The Blues Breakers Featuring Eric Clapton)
Singles: 7-Inch
IMMEDIATE: 67................. 4–6
LONDON: 66–68 4–6
POLYDOR: 69–74 2–4
LPs: 10/12-Inch 33rpm
ABC: 76–78..................... 8–10
BLUE THUMB: 74 8–10
DJM: 79........................ 8–10
LONDON: 67–78 10–15
MCA........................... 5–8
POLYDOR: 69–74 10–12
Also see BRUCE, Jack
Also see CLAPTON, Eric
Also see HARTLEY, Keef, Band
Also see TAYLOR, Mick

MAYANA
Singles: 12-Inch 33/45rpm
ATLANTIC: 83 4–6
Singles: 7-Inch
ATLANTIC: 83 1–3

MAYER, Nathaniel (Nathaniel Mayer & The Fabulous Twilights; Nathaniel Mayer & The Fortune Braves)
Singles: 7-Inch
FORTUNE (400 series): 62 5–8
FORTUNE (500 series):
62–69 3–5
UNITED ARTISTS: 62............. 4–6
LPs: 10/12-Inch 33rpm
FORTUNE: 64 30–40

MAYFIELD, Curtis
Singles: 7-Inch
BOARDWALK: 81–82 1–3
CURTOM: 70–80 1–3
RSO: 80 1–3

Price Range

Picture Sleeves
CURTOM: 71–78 .... $1–3

LPs: 10/12-Inch 33rpm
ABC: 73 12–15
BOARDWALK: 81–82 5–8
CURTOM: 70–78 10–12
RSO: 79–80 5–8
 Also see IMPRESSIONS, The
 Also see REED, Jimmy

MAYFIELD, Curtis, & Linda Clifford
Singles: 7-Inch
CURTOM: 79–80 1–3

LPs: 10/12-Inch 33rpm
RSO: 80 5–8
 Also see CLIFFORD, Linda
 Also see MAYFIELD, Curtis

MAYFIELD, Percy
Singles: 7-Inch
ATLANTIC: 74 2–3
BRUNSWICK: 68 2–4
IMPERIAL: 59 4–6
RCA VICTOR: 70 2–3
SPECIALTY (300 series):
 50–51 15–20
SPECIALTY (400 series):
 51–54 10–15
 (Black vinyl.)
SPECIALTY (400 series):
 54 20–25
 (Colored vinyl.)
SPECIALTY (500 series):
 55 8–10
SPECIALTY (600 series):
 60 4–6
TANGERINE: 62–67 3–5

LPs: 10/12-Inch 33rpm
BRUNSWICK: 69 12–15
RCA VICTOR: 70–71 10–12
SPECIALTY: 70 8–10
 (Specialty LP reissues, using original catalog numbers, are currently available.)
TANGERINE: 66–67 15–20

MAZE (Featuring Frankie Beverly)
Singles: 12-Inch 33/45rpm
CAPITOL: 84 4–6
Singles: 7-Inch
CAPITOL: 77–85 1–3

Price Range

Picture Sleeves
CAPITOL: 81 .... $1–3

LPs: 10/12-Inch 33rpm
CAPITOL: 78–85 6–10
MTA 10–12

MBULU, Letta
Singles: 7-Inch
A&M: 77 2–3

LPs: 10/12-Inch 33rpm
A&M: 77 5–8

McANALLY, Mac
Singles: 7-Inch
ARIOLA: 78 1–3
ARIOLA AMERICA: 77 2–3

LPs: 10/12-Inch 33rpm
ARIOLA AMERICA: 78 5–8

McCALL, Al
Singles: 7-Inch
PROFILE: 83 1–3

McCALL, C.W.
Singles: 7-Inch
MGM: 74–75 2–3
POLYDOR: 76 1–3

LPs: 10/12-Inch 33rpm
MGM: 75 5–10
POLYDOR: 76–79 5–8

McCALL, Cash
Singles: 7-Inch
THOMAS: 66 3–5

McCALL, Toussaint
Singles: 7-Inch
COLLECTABLES 1–3
RONN: 67–68 3–5

LPs: 10/12-Inch 33rpm
RONN: 67 10–12

McCALLUM, David
Singles: 7-Inch
CAPITOL: 66 2–4
Picture Sleeves
CAPITOL: 66 2–4
LPs: 10/12-Inch 33rpm
CAPITOL: 66 5–15

Price Range

McCANN, Les
LPs: 10/12-Inch 33rpm
ATLANTIC: *69–75* **$5–10**
LIMELIGHT: *65* **10–20**
PACIFIC JAZZ: *60–65* **15–25**
  Also see FLACK, Roberta
  Also see HOLMES, Richard "Groove," & Les
  McCann
  Also see JAZZ CRUSADERS, The
  Also see RAWLS, Lou, & Les McCann Ltd.

McCANN, Les, & Eddie Harris
Singles: 7-Inch
ATLANTIC: *69–70* **2–3**
LPs: 10/12-Inch 33rpm
ATLANTIC: *69–71* **5–10**
  Also see HARRIS, Eddie
  Also see McCANN, Les

McCANN, Peter
Singles: 7-Inch
COLUMBIA: *79* **1–3**
20TH CENTURY-FOX:
77 . . . . **2–3**
LPs: 10/12-Inch 33rpm
20TH CENTURY-FOX:
77 . . . . **8–10**

McCARTNEY, Paul (Paul McCartney & Wings; Paul & Linda McCartney; Wings)
Singles: 12-Inch 33/45rpm
COLUMBIA (775
"Coming Up"): *80.* **45–55**
COLUMBIA (05077; "No
More Lonely Nights"):
84 . . . . **4–6**
COLUMBIA (10940;
"Goodnight Tonight"):
79 . . . . **8–10**
COLUMBIA (39927; "No
More Lonely Nights"):
84 . . . . **8–10**
Promotional 12-Inch Singles
CAPITOL (8574; "Maybe
I'm Amazed"): *77* **35–40**
COLUMBIA (03019;
"Take It Away"): *82.* **5–8**
COLUMBIA (10940;
"Goodnight Tonight"):
79 . . . . **12–15**

Price Range

Singles: 7-Inch
APPLE (1829; "Another
Day"): *71* **$2–4**
APPLE (1837; "Uncle
Albert-Admiral Halsey"):
71 . . . . **2–4**
APPLE (1847; "Give
Ireland Back To The
Irish"): *72* **2–4**
APPLE (1851; "Mary Had
A Little Lamb"): *72* **2–4**
APPLE (1857; "Hi Hi
Hi"): *72* **2–4**
APPLE (1861; "My
Love"): *73* **2–4**
APPLE (1863; "Live & Let
Die"): *73* **2–4**
APPLE (1869; "Helen
Wheels"): *73.* **2–4**
APPLE (1871;
"Jet"/"Mamunia"): *74* **5–8**
APPLE (1871; "Jet"/"Let
Me Roll It"): *74* **2–4**
APPLE (1873; "Band On
The Run"): *74* **2–4**
APPLE (1875; "Junior's
Farm"): *74* **2–4**
CAPITOL (1829; "Another
Day") **2–3**
CAPITOL (1839; "Uncle
Albert-Admiral Halsey") **2–3**
CAPITOL (1847; "Give
Ireland Back To The
Irish") **2–3**
CAPITOL (1851; "Mary
Had A Little Lamb") **2–3**
CAPITOL (1857; "Hi Hi
Hi") **2–3**
CAPITOL (1861; "My
Love") **2–3**
CAPITOL (1863; "Live &
Let Die") **2–3**
CAPITOL (1869; "Helen
Wheels") **2–3**
CAPITOL (1871; "Jet") **2–3**
CAPITOL (1873; "Band
On The Run") **2–3**
CAPITOL (1875; "Junior's
Farm") **2–3**

Price Range

Price Range

CAPITOL (4091; "Listen
To What The Man
Said"): 75 . . . . $2–3
CAPITOL (4145; "Letting
Go"): 75 2–3
CAPITOL (4175; "Venus
& Mars Rock Show"):
75 2–3
CAPITOL (4256; "Silly
Love Songs."): 76 3–5
(Capitol custom label.)
CAPITOL (4256; "Silly
Love Songs."). 2–3
(Black label.)
CAPITOL (4293; "Let 'Em
In"): 76. 3–5
(Capitol custom label.)
CAPITOL (4293; "Let 'Em
In"). 2–3
(Black label.)
CAPITOL (4385; Maybe
I'm Amazed"): 77. 2–3
CAPITOL (4504; "Mull Of
Kintyre"): 77. 2–3
CAPITOL (4559; "With A
Little Luck"): 78 2–3
CAPITOL (4594; "I've
Had Enough"): 78. 2–3
CAPITOL (4625; "London
Town"): 78. 2–3
COLUMBIA (02171; "Silly
Love Songs"): 81 2–3
COLUMBIA (03018;
"Take It Away"): 82. 2–3
COLUMBIA (03235; "Tug
Of War"): 82 2–3
COLUMBIA (04296; "So
Bad"): 83 2–3
COLUMBIA (04581; "No
More Lonely Nights"):
84 2–3
COLUMBIA (10939;
"Goodnight Tonight"):
79 2–3
COLUMBIA (11020;
"Getting Closer"): 79 2–3
COLUMBIA (11070;
"Arrow Through Me"):
79 2–3

COLUMBIA (11162;
"Wonderful
Christmastime"): 79 . . . . $2–3
COLUMBIA (11263;
"Coming Up"): 80. 2–3
COLUMBIA (11335;
"Waterfalls"): 80. 2–3
COLUMBIA (33405;
"Goodnight Tonight"):
80 2–3
COLUMBIA (33409; "My
Love"): 80 2–3
COLUMBIA (33408;
"Uncle Albert-Admiral
Halsey"): 80. 2–3
COLUMBIA (33409;
"Band On The Run"):
80 2–3

Promotional Singles

APPLE (1829; "Another
Day"): 71 15–20
APPLE (1839; "Uncle
Albert-Admiral Halsey"):
71 15–20
APPLE (1847; "Give
Ireland Back To The
Irish"): 72 15–20
APPLE (1851; "Mary Had
A Little Lamb"): 72 15–20
APPLE (1857; "Hi Hi
Hi"): 72 10–15
APPLE (1861; "My
Love"): 73 10–15
APPLE (1863; "Live & Let
Die"): 73 10–15
APPLE (1869; "Helen
Wheels"): 73. 10–15
APPLE (1871; "Jet"): 74 10–15
APPLE (1873; "Band On
The Run"): 74 10–15
APPLE (1875; "Junior's
Farm"): 74 10–15
APPLE (6787; "Country
Dreamer"): 73 20–25
CAPITOL (4091; "Listen
To What The Man
Said"): 75 8–10
CAPITOL (4145; "Letting
Go"): 75 8–10

Price Range

CAPITOL (4175; "Venus
& Mars Rock Show"):
75 .... **$8–10**
CAPITOL (4256; "Silly
Love Songs."): 76 .... **8–10**
CAPITOL (4293; "Let 'Em
In"): 76....................... **8–10**
CAPITOL (4594; "I've
Had Enough"): 78............... **8–10**
(Add $3-$5 if accompanied by special promo-
tional flyer.)
CAPITOL (4625; "London
Town"): 78.................... **8–10**
CAPITOL (8570/1;
"Maybe I'm Amazed"):
77 .... **5–8**
CAPITOL (8746/7; "Mull
Of Kintyre"): 77 .... **8–10**
CAPITOL (8812; "With A
Little Luck"): 78 .... **8–10**
COLUMBIA (1204
"Coming Up"): 80............... **4–6**
COLUMBIA (03018;
"Take It Away"): 82............. **4–6**
COLUMBIA (03235; "Tug
Of War"): 82 .... **4–6**
COLUMBIA (04296; "So
Bad"): 83 .... **4–6**
COLUMBIA (04581; "No
More Lonely Nights"):
84 .... **4–6**
COLUMBIA (10939;
"Goodnight Tonight"):
79 .... **5–8**
COLUMBIA (11020;
"Getting Closer"): 79 .... **5–8**
COLUMBIA (11070;
"Arrow Through Me"):
79 .... **5–8**
COLUMBIA (11162;
"Wonderful
Christmastime"): 79 .... **8–10**
COLUMBIA (11263;
"Coming Up"): 80.............. **8–10**
COLUMBIA (11335;
"Waterfalls"): 80............... **5–8**

Picture Sleeves
APPLE (1847; "Give
Ireland Back To The
Irish"): 72 .... **10–12**

Price Range

APPLE (1851; "Mary Had
A Little Lamb"): 72 .... **$15–20**
("Little Woman Love" printed on reverse side
of sleeve.)
APPLE (1851; "Mary Had
A Little Lamb"): 72 .... **10–12**
("Little Woman Love" not printed on reverse
side of sleeve.)
CAPITOL (4091; "Listen
To What The Man
Said"): 75.................... **3–5**
CAPITOL (4504; "Mull Of
Kintyre"): 77.................. **8–10**
COLUMBIA (03018;
"Take It Away"): 82............. **5–8**
(Reads "Not For Sale" on back side. Promo-
tional issue only.)
COLUMBIA (03018;
"Take It Away"): 82............. **2–4**
COLUMBIA (11020;
"Getting Closer"): 79 .... **20–25**
COLUMBIA (11162;
"Wonderful
Christmastime"): 79 .... **3–5**
COLUMBIA (11263
"Coming Up"): 80.............. **3–5**
COLUMBIA (11335;
"Waterfalls"): 80.............. **12–15**

LPs: 10/12-Inch 33rpm
APPLE (3363;
"McCartney"): 70 .... **12–15**
(Label shows Paul's full name beneath LP title.)
APPLE (3363;
"McCartney"): 70 .... **10–12**
(Label doesn't show Paul's name beneath LP
title.)
APPLE (3375; "Ram"): 71 .... **10–15**
APPLE (3386; "Wild
Life"): 71 .... **10–15**
APPLE (3409; "Red Rose
Speedway"): 73 .... **10–15**
APPLE (3415; "Band On
The Run"): 73................. **10–15**
(Price includes bonus poster.)
CAPITOL (3363;
"McCartney") **8–10**
CAPITOL (3375; "Ram") **8–10**
CAPITOL (3386;
"Wildlife") **8–10**
CAPITOL (3409; "Red
Rose Speedway")................ **8–10**

Price Range

CAPITOL (3415; "Band
On The Run")................ **$8–10**
(Price includes bonus poster.)
CAPITOL (11525; "Wings
At The Speed Of
Sound"): 76 .... **8–10**
CAPITOL (11593; "Wings
Over America"): 76............ **12–15**
CAPITOL (11905;
"Greatest Hits"): 78 .... **5–8**
(Price includes bonus poster.)
CAPITOL (11419; "Venus
And Mars"): 75............... **10–12**
(Price includes bonus posters & stickers.)
CAPITOL (11777;
"London Town"): 78 .... **10–12**
(Price includes bonus poster.)
CAPITOL (11901; "Band
On The Run" - picture
disc): 78 .... **18–20**
COLUMBIA (36057;
"Back To The Egg"): 79 .... **5–8**
COLUMBIA (36478;
"McCartney"): 80 .... **5–8**
COLUMBIA (36479;
"Ram"): 80.................... **5–8**
COLUMBIA (36480;
"Wild Life"): 80 .... **5–8**
COLUMBIA (36481; "Red
Rose Speedway"): 80............ **5–8**
COLUMBIA (36482;
"Band On The Run"):
80 .... **5–8**
COLUMBIA (36511;
"McCartney II"): 80........... **12–15**
(Issued with bonus single, 1204, "Coming Up,"
which represents $4-$6 of the above price
range.)
COLUMBIA (36801;
"Venus And Mars"): 80.......... **5–8**
(Price includes bonus posters.)
COLUMBIA (36987; "The
McCartney Interview"):
80 .... **8–10**
COLUMBIA (37409;
"Wings At The Speed Of
Sound"): 81 .... **5–8**
COLUMBIA (37462; "Tug
Of War"): 82 .... **5–8**
(With Stevie Wonder on "Ebony And Ivory.")
COLUMBIA (39149;
"Pipes Of Peace"): 83........... **5–8**

Price Range

(With Michael Jackson on "Say Say Say",)
COLUMBIA (39613;
"Give My Regards To
Broad Street"): 84.............. **$5–8**
COLUMBIA (46482;
"Band On The Run"):
80 .... **10–15**
(Half-speed mastered.)
LIBERTY (50100; "Live
And Let Die"): 84............... **5–8**
(With McCartney on title track only.)
LONDON (76007; "The
Family Way" - mono):
67 .... **50–60**
LONDON (82007; "The
Family Way" - stereo):
67 .... **60–70**
UNITED ARTISTS (100;
"Live And Let Die"): 73 .... **15–20**
(Copies of this LP with cut corners are valued
at about one-half of the above price range. With
McCartney on title track only.)

Promotional LPs

APPLE (3375; "Ram"): 71 ...... **80–100**
(Monaural issue.)
APPLE (6210; "Brung To
Ewe By"): 71................ **175–200**
COLUMBIA (821; "The
McCartney Interview"):
80 .... **40–50**
COLUMBIA (36057;
"Back To The Egg"): 79 .... **15–20**
COLUMBIA (36511;
"McCartney II"): 80........... **15–20**
Also see BEATLES, The
Also see COUNTRY HAMS, The
Also see GREASE BAND, The
Also see LOMAX, Jackie
Also see NEWMAN, Thunderclap
Also see PERKINS, Carl
Also see SUZY & THE RED STRIPES

McCARTNEY, Paul, & Michael Jackson

Singles: 12-Inch 33/45rpm
COLUMBIA (04169; "Say
Say Say"): 83................... **5–8**
Singles: 7-Inch
COLUMBIA (04168; "Say
Say Say"): 83................... **2–3**
EPIC (03288; "The Girl Is
Mine"): 82 .... **2–3**

Promotional Singles
COLUMBIA (04168; "Say
Say Say"): *83* **$4–6**
EPIC (03288; "The Girl Is
Mine"): *82* **4–6**
Also see JACKSON, Michael

McCARTNEY, Paul, & Stevie Wonder
Singles: 12-Inch 33/45rpm
COLUMBIA (02878;
"Ebony And Ivory"): *82* **5–8**
Promotional 12-Inch Singles
COLUMBIA (1444;
"McCartney"): *82* **30–40**
Singles: 7-Inch
COLUMBIA (02860;
"Ebony And Ivory"): *82* **2–3**
Promotional Singles:
COLUMBIA (02860;
"Ebony And Ivory"): *82* **4–6**
Picture Sleeves
COLUMBIA (02860;
"Ebony And Ivory"): *82* **2–4**
Promotional Picture Sleeves
COLUMBIA (02860;
"Ebony And Ivory"): *82* **5–8**
Note: On all of the above, Stevie Wonder appears only on the track "Ebony And Ivory."
Also see McCARTNEY, Paul
Also see WONDER, Stevie

McCLAIN, Alton, & Destiny
Singles: 7-Inch
POLYDOR: *79–81* **1–3**
LPs: 10/12-Inch 33rpm
POLYDOR: *79–81* **5–8**
Also see BRISTOL, Johnny, & Alton McClain

McCLAIN, Janice
Singles: 7-Inch
RFC: *80* **1–3**

McCLARY, Thomas
Singles: 7-Inch
MOTOWN: *84–85* **1–3**

McCLINTON, Delbert
Singles: 7-Inch
BOBILL: *67* **3–5**
BROWNFIELD: *65* **3–5**

CAPITOL: *80–81* **$1–3**
CAPRICORN: *78* **1–3**
LPs: 10/12-Inch 33rpm
ACCORD: *81* **5–8**
CAPITOL: *81* **5–8**
INTERMEDIA: *84* **5–8**
MCA: *81* **5–8**
Also see DELBERT & GLEN
Also see RONDELLS, The

McCLINTON, O.B.
Singles: 7-Inch
MERCURY: *76* **2–3**
LPs: 10/12-Inch 33rpm
ENTERPRISE: *72–74* **8–10**

McCLURE, Bobby
Singles: 7-Inch
CHECKER: *66–67* **3–5**
Also see BASS, Fontella, & Bobby McClure

McCONNELL, C. Lynda
Singles: 12-Inch 33/45rpm
ATLANTIC: *84* **4–6**
Singles: 7-Inch
ATLANTIC: *84* **1–3**

McCOO, Marilyn
Singles: 7-Inch
RCA VICTOR: *83* **1–3**
LPs: 10/12-Inch 33rpm
RCA VICTOR: *83* **5–8**

McCOO, Marilyn, & Billy Davis, Jr.
Singles: 12-Inch 33/45rpm
COLUMBIA: *79* **4–6**
Singles: 7-Inch
ABC: *76–78* **1–3**
COLUMBIA: *78* **1–3**
LPs: 10/12-Inch 33rpm
ABC: *76* **8–10**
COLUMBIA: *78* **5–8**
Also see FIFTH DIMENSION, The
Also see McCOO, Marilyn

McCORMICK, Gayle
Singles: 7-Inch
DECCA: *72* **2–4**
DUNHILL: *71–72* **2–4**
MCA: *73* **2–3**

Price Range

LPs: 10/12-Inch 33rpm
DECCA: 72 . . . . $10–12
DUNHILL: 71. 10–12
FANTASY: 74. 8–10
Also see SMITH

McCOY, Charlie
Singles: 7-Inch
CADENCE: 61 2–4

LPs: 10/12-Inch 33rpm
EPIC: 82 5–8
MONUMENT: 69–78. 5–10

McCOY, Freddie
Singles: 7-Inch
PRESTIGE: 67 2–4

McCOY, Van (Van McCoy & The Soul City Symphony)
Singles: 12-Inch 33/45rpm
MCA: 79 4–6

Singles: 7-Inch
AMHERST 1–3
AVCO: 74–75. 2–3
CGC: 70. 2–4
COLUMBIA: 65–66 3–5
EPIC: 69 2–4
H&L: 76. 2–3
LIBERTY: 62 3–5
MCA: 78–79 1–3
ROCK 'N: 61 5–8
SILVER BLUE: 73. 2–4

LPs: 10/12-Inch 33rpm
AVCO: 74–75. 8–10
BUDDAH: 72–75 8–10
COLUMBIA: 66 12–15
H&L: 76. 8–10
MCA: 77–79 8–10

McCOYS, The
Singles: 7-Inch
BANG: 65–67 4–6
MERCURY: 68. 3–5
SOLID GOLD: 73 1–3

LPs: 10/12-Inch 33rpm
BANG: 65–66 20–25
MERCURY: 68–69. 15–20
Also see DERRINGER, Rick

Price Range

McCRACKLIN, Jimmy (Jimmy McCracklin & His Blues Blasters; Jimmie McCracklin)
Singles: 7-Inch
ART-TONE: 61–62. . . . . $4–6
CHECKER: 58 5–8
CHESS: 62. 3–5
GEDINSON'S: 61. 3–5
HI: 60. 4–6
HOLLYWOOD: 55. 8–10
IMPERIAL: 62–67. 3–5
IRMA. 8–10
KENT: 62 3–5
LIBERTY: 70 2–4
MERCURY: 59–61. 5–8
MINIT: 67–70. 3–5
MODERN (900 series): 54. 10–12
PEACOCK: 52–54 5–8

LPs: 10/12-Inch 33rpm
CHESS: 62. 25–30
CROWN: 61 15–20
IMPERIAL: 63–66. 15–20
MINIT: 67–69. 12–15
STAX: 72–81. 8–10
Also see BROWN, Charles, & Jimmy McCracklin

McCRAE, George
Singles: 7-Inch
GOLD MOUNTAIN: 84. 1–3
T.K.: 74–79 2–3

LPs: 10/12-Inch 33rpm
CAT: 76. 8–10
GOLD MOUNTAIN: 84. 5–8
T.K.: 74–77 8–10

McCRAE, George & Gwen
Singles: 7-Inch
CAT: 76. 2–3
Also see McCRAE, George
Also see McCRAE, Gwen

McCRAE, Gwen
Singles: 7-Inch
ATLANTIC: 81–83 1–3
BLACK JACK: 84. 1–3
CAT: 74–75. 2–3

LPs: 10/12-Inch 33rpm
ATLANTIC: 81–83 5–8
CAT: 74–76. 8–10
Also see McCRAE, George & Gwen

Price Range

McCRARYS, The
Singles: 7-Inch
CAPITOL: 80–82 . . . . $1–3
PORTRAIT: 78–79 1–3
LPs: 10/12-Inch 33rpm
CAPITOL: 80 5–8
PORTRAIT: 78 5–8
Members: Sam McCrary; Linda McCrary; Al
McCrary; Charity McCrary.

McCULLOUGH, Ullanda
Singles: 7-Inch
ATLANTIC: 81 1–3

McCURN, George
Singles: 7-Inch
A&M: 63–64 3–5
LIBERTY: 62 3–5
REPRISE: 66 2–4
LPs: 10/12-Inch 33rpm
A&M: 63 15–20

McDANIEL, Donna
Singles: 7-Inch
MIDLAND INT'L: 77 2–3

McDANIELS, Gene
Singles: 7-Inch
COLUMBIA: 66–67 2–4
LIBERTY: 60–65 3–5
MGM: 73 2–4
ODE '70: 75 2–4
LPs: 10/12-Inch 33rpm
LIBERTY: 60–67 15–20
ODE '70: 75 8–10
SUNSET: 66 10–15
UNITED ARTISTS: 75 8–10

McDEVITT, Charles, Skiffle Group
Singles: 7-Inch
CHIC: 57 3–5

McDONALD, Country Joe
Singles: 7-Inch
FANTASY: 75–79 2–4
VANGUARD: 71–74 3–5
LPs: 10/12-Inch 33rpm
FANTASY: 75–79 6–10
MFSL: 80 12–15
VANGUARD: 69–76 8–12
Also see COUNTRY JOE & THE FISH

Price Range

McDONALD, Kathi
Singles: 7-Inch
CAPITOL: 74 . . . . $2–4
LPs: 10/12-Inch 33rpm
CAPITOL: 74 12–15
Also see BALDRY, Long John, & Kathi Mc-
Donald

McDONALD, Michael
Singles: 7-Inch
WARNER BROS: 82–85 1–3
Picture Sleeves
WARNER BROS: 82–85 1–3
LPs: 10/12-Inch 33rpm
WARNER BROS: 82 5–8
Also see DOOBIE BROTHERS, The
Also see LABELLE, Patti, & Michael McDon-
ald
Also see MEMPHIS HORNS, The
Also see STEELY DAN
Also see WOOD, Lauren

McDONALD, Michael, & James Ingram
Singles: 7-Inch
QWEST: 83 1–3
Also see INGRAM, James
Also see McDONALD, Michael

McDOWELL, Ronnie
Singles: 7-Inch
EPIC: 79–85 1–3
GRT: 77 2–4
SCORPION: 77–79 2–4
LPs: 10/12-Inch 33rpm
DICK CLARK: 79 8–10
EPIC: 79–85 5–8
SCORPION: 77–79 10–12

McDUFF, Brother Jack
Singles: 7-Inch
CADET: 68 2–3
BLUE NOTE: 69 2–3
LPs: 10/12-Inch 33rpm
BLUE NOTE: 69 8–12
PRESTIGE (7000 series):
60–64 25–50
(Yellow labels.)
PRESTIGE (7000 series):
64–65 10–20
(Blue labels.)
Also see BENSON, George
Also see BURRELL, Kenny, & Jack McDuff

Price Range   *Price Range*

McDUFF, Brother Jack, & Gene Ammons
LPs: 10/12-Inch 33rpm
PRESTIGE: *61* $20–40
(Yellow label.)
Also see AMMONS, Gene

McDUFF, Brother Jack, & Willis Jackson
LPs: 10/12-Inch 33rpm
PRESTIGE: *66* 10–15
Also see JACKSON, Willis
Also see McDUFF, Brother Jack

McFADDEN, Bob (Bob McFadden & Dor)
Singles: 7-Inch
BRUNSWICK: *59*. 5–8
CORAL: *60* 4–6
Picture Sleeves
BRUNSWICK: *59*. 5–8
Also see McKUEN, Rod

McFADDEN & WHITEHEAD
Singles: 12-Inch 33/45rpm
PHILADELPHIA INT'L:
79 4–6
SUTRA 4–6
Singles: 7-Inch
CAPITOL: *82–83* 1–3
PHILADELPHIA INT'L:
79 1–3
SUTRA 1–3
TSOP: *80* 1–3
LPs: 10/12-Inch 33rpm
CAPITOL: *83* 5–8
PHILADELPHIA INT'L:
79 5–8
TSOP: *80*. 5–8
Members: Gene McFadden; John Whitehead.

McFARLAND, Gary
LPs: 10/12-Inch 33rpm
SKYE: *69*. 8–12

McGEE, Parker
Singles: 7-Inch
BIG TREE: *77* 2–3
LPs: 10/12-Inch 33rpm
BIG TREE: *76* 5–8

McGHEE, Brownie (Brownie McGhee & His Jook Block Busters; Brownie McGhee & His Sugar Men)
Singles: 7-Inch
DOT: *53*. $10–12
HARLEM: *52* 25–30
JACKSON (Colored vinyl):
52 40–50
JAX (Colored vinyl): *52*. 35–40
RED ROBIN: *53* 60–75
SAVOY (800 series): *51–52* 8–10
SAVOY (1100 through
1500 series): *55–59* 5–8
LPs: 10/12-Inch 33rpm
FOLKWAYS (Except 20,
30 & 2000 series). 8–10
FOLKWAYS (20, 30 &
2000 series): *54–55* 20–35
STORYVILLE. 5–8
VANGUARD 8–10
Note: Though perhaps not credited, many of
the above feature Sonny Terry on harmonica.
Also see DUPREE, Champion Jack

McGHEE, Brownie, & Sonny Terry
Singles: 7-Inch
PRESTIGE: *60–62* 3–5
LPs: 10/12-Inch 33rpm
A&M: *73* 8–10
BLUESWAY: *69–73*. 10–12
EVEREST: *69* 10–12
FANTASY (3000 series):
61–62 15–20
(Black vinyl.)
FANTASY (3000 series):
61–62 25–30
(Colored vinyl.)
FANTASY (8000 series):
62 15–20
FANTASY (24000 series):
72–81 8–10
FOLKWAYS (2000 &
3000 series): *55–61* 20–25
FOLKWAYS (31000
series) 8–10
FONTANA: *69*. 10–15
MAINSTREAM (6000
series): *65* 15–20
MAINSTREAM (300
series): *71* 8–10

MUSE: *81* **$5–8**
OLYMPIC: *73*................... **8–10**
PRESTIGE (1000 series):
  60 .... **25–30**
PRESTIGE (7000 series):
  69–70 .... **8–10**
PRESTIGE
  BLUESVILLE: *60–62*........... **20–25**
PRESTIGE FOLKLORE **12–15**
ROULETTE: *59*................. **25–30**
SAVOY (1100 series): *84*........... **5–8**
SAVOY (12000 series): *73*.......... **8–10**
SAVOY (14000 series): *58*........ **25–30**
SMASH: *65*.................... **15–20**
VERVE: *61*..................... **20–25**
VERVE/FOLKWAYS: *65*........ **15–20**
WORLD PACIFIC: *60*.......... **25–30**
   Also see McGHEE, Brownie
   Also see TERRY, Sonny

McGHEE, Sticks (Sticks McGhee & His Buddies; Sticks McGhee & The Ramblers)
Singles: 7-Inch
ATLANTIC (955 & 991):
  52–53 .... **25–30**
GUSTO **1–3**
HERALD: *60* **5–8**
KING: *53–55*................... **15–20**
LONDON: *51* **30–35**
SAVOY: *55* **8–10**

McGHEE, Sticks / John Lee Hooker
LPs: 10/12-Inch 33rpm
AUDIO LAB: *59* **25–35**
   Also see HOOKER, John Lee
   Also see McGHEE, Sticks

McGILPIN, Bob
Singles: 7-Inch
BUTTERFLY: *78*................. **1–3**

LPs: 10/12-Inch 33rpm
BUTTERFLY (Black
  vinyl): *78–79*................. **5–8**
BUTTERFLY (Colored
  vinyl): *78* **12–15**
CASABLANCA: *80*............... **5–8**

McGOVERN, Maureen
Singles: 7-Inch
CASABLANCA **$1–3**
EPIC: *78* **1–3**
MAIDEN VOYAGE **2–3**
20TH CENTURY-FOX:
  73–75 .... **2–3**
WARNER BROS: *79–80*........... **1–3**
WOODEN NICKEL: *73*............ **2–4**
LPs: 10/12-Inch 33rpm
20TH CENTURY-FOX:
  73–75 .... **8–10**
WARNER BROS: *79*............... **5–8**

McGRIFF, Edna
Singles: 7-Inch
CAPITOL: *4–65*.................. **3–5**
JUBILEE (Black vinyl):
  51–53 .... **10–15**
JUBILEE (Colored vinyl):
  53 .... **25–30**
WILLOW: *61*.................... **4–6**

McGRIFF, Edna, & Sonny Til
Singles: 7-Inch
JUBILEE: *52*................... **15–20**
   Also see McGRIFF, Edna
   Also see TIL, Sonny

McGRIFF, Jimmy (The Jimmy McGriff Trio)
Singles: 7-Inch
BLUE NOTE: *71* **2–3**
CAPITOL: *70–71* **2–3**
COLLECTABLES **1–3**
GROOVE MERCHANT:
  75 .... **2–3**
JELL (100 series): *62* **5–8**
JELL (500 series): *65* **3–5**
MILESTONE: *83* **1–3**
SOLID STATE: *66–70*............. **2–4**
SUE: *62–64* **3–5**
UNITED ARTISTS: *71–78*......... **1–3**
LPs: 10/12-Inch 33rpm
BLUE NOTE: *70–71* **8–12**
51 WEST **5–8**
GROOVE MERCHANT:
  71–76 .... **8–10**
LRC: *77–78*..................... **8–10**
MILESTONE: *81–83* **5–8**
SOLID STATE: *66–70*........... **10–15**

Price Range

SOUL SUGAR: *70* **$10–12**
SUE: *62–65* **15–30**
UNITED ARTISTS: *71* **8–12**
VEEP: *68* **10–12**
    Also see HOLMES, Richard "Groove"
    Also see PARKER, Little Junior, & Jimmy McGriff

McGUFFEY LANE
Singles: 7-Inch
ATCO: *81–82* **1–3**

McGUINN, Roger
Singles: 7-Inch
COLUMBIA: *73–77* **2–3**
    LPs: 10/12-Inch 33rpm
COLUMBIA: *77* **8–10**

McGUINN, CLARK & HILLMAN
Singles: 7-Inch
CAPITOL: *79* **1–3**
    LPs: 10/12-Inch 33rpm
CAPITOL: *79–82* **5–8**
    Members: Roger McGuinn; Gene Clark; Chris Hillman.
    Also see BEEFEATERS, The
    Also see BYRDS, The

McGUINN & HILLMAN
LPs: 10/12-Inch 33rpm
CAPITOL: *80* **5–8**
    Members: Roger McGuinn; Chris Hillman.
    Also see HILLMAN, Chris
    Also see McGUINN, Roger

McGUINNESS-FLINT
Singles: 7-Inch
CAPITOL: *70–71* **2–4**
    LPs: 10/12-Inch 33rpm
CAPITOL: *70–71* **10–12**
    Members: Tom McGuinness; Hughie Flint.
    Also see GALLAGHER & LYLE
    Also see MANN, Manfred

McGUIRE, Barry (Barry McGuire & The Horizon Singers)
Singles: 7-Inch
ABC: *70* **1–3**
DUNHILL: *65–66* **3–5**
HORIZON: *63* **3–5**
ODE '70: *70* **2–3**
MCA **1–3**

Price Range

MOSAIC: *61–62* **$4–6**
MYRRH: *73* **1–3**
ROULETTE **1–3**
    Picture Sleeves
DUNHILL: *65* **4–6**
    LPs: 10/12-Inch 33rpm
BIRDWING: *80* **5–8**
DUNHILL: *65* **15–20**
HORIZON: *63* **15–20**
MYRRH: *73–75* **5–8**
ODE '70: *70* **8–10**
SPARROW: *79* **5–8**
SURREY: *65* **12–15**
    Also see NEW CHRISTY MINSTRELS, The

McGUIRE, Barry, & Barry Kane
Singles: 7-Inch
HORIZON: *62* **3–5**
    LPs: 10/12-Inch 33rpm
HORIZON: *62* **15–20**
SURREY: *66* **12–15**

McGUIRE, Phyllis
Singles: 7-Inch
REPRISE: *64–65* **2–4**
ORPHEUM: *68* **2–3**
    LPs: 10/12-Inch 33rpm
ABC-PARAMOUNT: *66* **10–15**
    Also see McGUIRE SISTERS, The

McGUIRE SISTERS, The
Singles: 7-Inch
ABC-PARAMOUNT: *66* **2–4**
CORAL (Except 61000 series): *58–65* **3–5**
CORAL (61000 series): *54–58* **4–6**
MCA **1–3**
REPRISE: *63–65* **3–5**
    Picture Sleeves
CORAL: *56–61* **4–6**
    EPs: 7-Inch 33/45rpm
CORAL: *55–60* **8–12**
    LPs: 10/12-Inch 33rpm
ABC-PARAMOUNT: *66* **10–15**
CORAL (6; "Best Of The McGuire Sisters"): *65* **12–20**
CORAL (56000 series): *55* **25–30**
CORAL (57000 series): *56–65* **15–20**
MCA: *78* **5–8**

Price Range

VOCALION: *60–67* **$10–15**
　　Members: Phyllis McGuire; Dorothy McGuire;
　　Christine McGuire.
　　Also see McGUIRE, Phyllis

McIAN, Peter
Singles: 7-Inch
COLUMBIA/ARC: *80*.............. **1–3**
LPs: 10/12-Inch 33rpm
COLUMBIA/ARC: *80*.............. **5–8**

McKEE, Lonett
Singles: 7-Inch
SUSSEX: *74*...................... **2–3**

McKENDREE SPRING
Singles: 7-Inch
DECCA: *69–72*................... **2–4**
MCA: *73* **2–3**
PYE: *76* **2–3**
LPs: 10/12-Inch 33rpm
DECCA: *69–72*................. **10–15**
MCA: *73* **8–10**
PYE: *75* **8–10**

McKENZIE, Bob & Doug
Singles: 7-Inch
MERCURY: *82*................... **1–3**
LPs: 10/12-Inch 33rpm
MERCURY: *81*................... **5–8**

McKENZIE, Scott (McKenzie's Musicians)
Singles: 7-Inch
CAPITOL: *65–67* **3–5**
EPIC: *67–72* **3–5**
ODE: *67–71*...................... **3–5**
LPs: 10/12-Inch 33rpm
ODE (44000 series): *67*........... **15–20**
ODE (34000 series): *77*............ **8–10**
ODE (77000 series): *70*........... **10–15**

McKUEN, Rod (Rod McKuen & The Keytones; Rod McKuen & The Horizon Singers)
Singles: 7-Inch
A&M: *63* **3–5**
BUDDAH: *73–74* **2–3**
DECCA: *59*...................... **4–6**
HORIZON: *63*.................... **3–5**
JUBILEE: *62*..................... **4–6**

Price Range

KAPP: *61* **$3–5**
LIBERTY: *56*.................... **5–8**
RCA VICTOR: *66–67* **3–5**
SPIRAL: *61–62*.................. **4–6**
VISTA: *71* **2–4**
WARNER BROS: *68–72*........... **2–4**

Picture Sleeves
VISTA: *71*...................... **2–4**
WARNER BROS: *71*.............. **2–4**

LPs: 10/12-Inch 33rpm
DECCA (4900 series): *68*......... **10–12**
DECCA (8800 series): *59*.......... **20–25**
DECCA (75000 series): *69*........ **10–12**
CAPITOL: *64* **15–20**
HARMONY: *71* **8–10**
HI FI: *58–59* **20–25**
EPIC (600 & 3800 series):
　62 .... **15–20**
EPIC (26000 series): *68* **10–12**
EVEREST: *68*.................. **10–12**
HORIZON: *63*.................. **15–20**
IN: *64*......................... **15–20**
JUBILEE: *62*................... **20–25**
KAPP (1200 & 3200
　series): *61*................. **15–20**
KAPP (1500 & 3500
　series): *67*.................. **10–15**
LIBERTY (Except 3011):
　67 .... **10–15**
LIBERTY (3011; "Songs
　For A Lazy Afternoon"):
　56 .... **25–35**
RCA VICTOR: *65–68* **10–15**
STANYAN: *66–72* **10–15**
SUNSET: *70* **8–10**
TRADITION: *68* **10–12**
VISTA: *71* **8–10**
WARNER BROS: *67–76*......... **8–12**
　Also see McFADDEN, Bob
　Also see SAN SEBASTIAN STRINGS, The

McLAGAN, Ian
Singles: 7-Inch
MERCURY: *79*................... **1–3**

LPs: 10/12-Inch 33rpm
MERCURY: *79*................... **5–8**
　Also see FACES
　Also see SMALL FACES

Price Range   *Price Range*

McLAREN, Malcom (Malcom McClaren & The World's Famous Supreme Team)
Singles: 12-Inch 33/45rpm
ISLAND: *83–84* $4–6
Singles: 7-Inch
ISLAND: *83–84* 1–3
LPs: 10/12-Inch 33rpm
ISLAND: *84* 5–8
Also see WORLD'S FAMOUS SUPREME TEAM, The

McLAUGHLIN, John
LPs: 10/12-Inch 33rpm
COLUMBIA: *72–83* 5–10
DOUGLAS: *72* 8–12
POLYDOR: *69–72* 8–15

McLAIN, Tommy
Singles: 7-Inch
COLLECTABLES 1–3
JIN: *66* 5–8
MSL: *66* 3–5

McLANE, Jimmy
Singles: 7-Inch
SWAY: *61* 3–5

McLAREN, Malcom (Malcom McLaren & The World's Famous Supreme Band)
Singles: 12-Inch 33/45rpm
ISLAND: *83–85* 4–6
Singles: 7-Inch
ISLAND: *83–85* 1–3
LPs: 10/12-Inch 33rpm
ISLAND: *83–85* 5–8

McLAURIN, Bette
Singles: 7-Inch
CENTER: *54* 4–6
CORAL: *54* 4–6
DERBY: *52* 10–25
GLORY: *56* 8–10
JUBILEE: *54–55* 4–6
Also see FOUR FELLOWS, The

McLEAN, Don
Singles: 7-Inch
ARISTA: *78* 1–3
LIBERTY 1–3

MILLENNIUM: *81–83* $1–3
RCA VICTOR: *83* 1–3
UNITED ARTISTS: *71–75* 2–3
Picture Sleeves
UNITED ARTISTS: *71–73* 2–3
LPs: 10/12-Inch 33rpm
CASABLANCA: *79* 8–10
LIBERTY: *82–83* 5–8
MILLENNIUM: *81* 5–8
UNITED ARTISTS: *71–74* 10–12

McLEAN, Penny
Singles: 7-Inch
ATCO: *75–76*..................... 2–3

McLEAN, Phil
Singles: 7-Inch
VERSATILE: *61–62*............... 4–6

McLOLLIE, Oscar (Oscar McLollie & The Honey Jumpers; Oscar Lollie; Oscar McLollie & Nancy Lamarr)
Singles: 7-Inch
CLASS: *57–59*.................... 4–6
MERCURY (70000 series):
 56 5–8
MODERN (Except 902):
 53–55 8–10
MODERN (902; "The
 Honey Jump"): *52*............. 10–15
SAHARA: *63*..................... 3–5
WING: *56* 5–8

McLOLLIE, Oscar, & Jeanette Baker
Singles: 7-Inch
CLASS: *58*....................... 4–6
Also see McLOLLIE, Oscar

McMAHON, Gerard
Singles: 7-Inch
FULL MOON: *83*.................. 1–3
LPs: 10/12-Inch 33rpm
FULL MOON: *83*.................. 5–8

McNALLY, Larry John
Singles: 7-Inch
ARC: *81*......................... 1–3

Price Range

McNAMARA, Robin
Singles: 7-Inch
STEED: *69–71* $2–4
LPs: 10/12-Inch 33rpm
STEED: *70* 10–15

McNEELY, Big Jay (Big Jay McNeely & His Blue Jays; Big Jay McNeely With Little Sonny Warner)
Singles: 7-Inch
BAYOU: *53* 20–25
FEDERAL: *52–54* 8–12
IMPERIAL (5200 series):
53 10–15
SWINGIN': *59–61* 4–6
VEE JAY: *55* 8–10
WARNER BROS: *63* 3–5
LPs: 10/12-Inch 33rpm
FEDERAL (96; "Big Jay
McNeely"): *54* 90–100
FEDERAL (530; "Big Jay
In 3-D"): *56* 60–75
KING: *59* 25–30
SAVOY (15000 series): *58* 75–90
WARNER BROS: *63* 20–25
Also see OTIS, Johnny

McNEELY, Big Jay / Paul Williams
Singles: 7-Inch
SAVOY (1100 series): *55* 5–8
(Reissue of tracks originally on 78rpm only.)
Also see McNEELY, Big Jay
Also see WILLIAMS, Paul

McNEIR, Ronnie
Singles: 7-Inch
CAPITOL: *84* 1–3
PRODIGAL: *75* 2–3
LPs: 10/12-Inch 33rpm
CAPITOL: *84* 5–8

McNICHOL, Kristy & Jimmy
Singles: 7-Inch
RCA VICTOR: *78* 1–3
Picture Sleeves
RCA VICTOR: *78* 1–3

M'COOL, Shamus
Singles: 7-Inch
PERSPECTIVE: *81* 2–3

Price Range

McPHATTER, Clyde
Singles: 7-Inch
AMY: *65–67* $3–5
ATLANTIC (1000 series):
56–58 8–10
ATLANTIC (2000 series):
58–60 5–8
DECCA: *70* 3–5
DERAM: *68–69* 3–5
MGM: *59–60* 4–6
MERCURY: *60–65* 4–6
Picture Sleeves
MGM: *60* 5–8
MERCURY: *60–65* 4–6
EPs: 7-Inch 33/45rpm
ATLANTIC: *58–59* 25–30
LPs: 10/12-Inch 33rpm
ALLEGIANCE 5–8
ATLANTIC (8024; "Love
Ballads"): *58* 35–45
(Black label.)
ATLANTIC (8024; "Love
Ballads"): *59* 20–25
(Red label.)
ATLANTIC (8031;
"Clyde"): *59* 30–35
ATLANTIC (8077; "Best
Of Clyde McPhatter"):
63 25–30
DECCA: *70* 15–20
MGM: *59–60* 25–30
MERCURY: *60–64* 20–25
WING: *62* 20–25
Also see DOMINOES, The
Also see DRIFTERS, The

McPHERSON, Wyatt "Earp"
Singles: 7-Inch
SAVOY: *61* 3–5

McPHERSON, Wyatt "Earp," & Paul Williams
Singles: 7-Inch
BATTLE: *63* 3–5
Also see McPHERSON, Wyatt "Earp"
Also see WILLIAMS, Paul

McRAE, Carmen
Singles: 7-Inch
COLUMBIA: *62* 2–4
DECCA: *55–57* 2–4

Price Range

VENUS: *54* $3–5

Picture Sleeves
COLUMBIA: *62* 2–4

LPs: 10/12-Inch 33rpm
BETHLEHEM (1000
  series): *54* 40–60
  (10-Inch LPs.)
COLUMBIA: *61–65* 15–25
DECCA (8100 through
  8800 series): *55–58* 25–50
  (Black & silver label.)
DECCA (8100 through
  8800 series): *64* 10–20
  (Black label with horizonal rainbow stripe.)
FOCUS: *65* 10–20
KAPP: *58–59* 20–35
MAINSTREAM: *65–67* 10–20
TIME: *63* 15–25
  Also see DAVIS, Sammy, Jr., & Carmen
  McRae
  Also see SIMONE, Nina, Chris Connor & Car-
  men McRae

McSHANN, Jay (Jay McShann & His Orchestra; Jay McShann & His Combo; Jay McShann & his Trio; The Jay McShann Quartet; Jay McShann's Kansas City Stompers; Jay McShann & His Jazz Men or Jay McShann's Sextet; Jay McShann & Priscilla Bowman)
Singles: 7-Inch
VEE JAY: *55–56* 5–8

EPs: 7-Inch 33/45rpm
DECCA: *54* 30–35

LPs: 10/12-Inch 33rpm
CAPITOL: *67* 12–15
DECCA (5000 series): *54* 125–150
DECCA (9000 series): *68* 10–12
  Also see WITHERSPOON, Jimmy

McVIE, Christine
Singles: 7-Inch
WARNER BROS: *84* 1–3

LPs: 10/12-Inch 33rpm
WARNER BROS: *84* 5–8
  Also see FLEETWOOD MAC
  Also see PERFECT, Christine
  Also see NEWMAN, Randy

Price Range

McWILLIAMS, Paulette
Singles: 7-Inch
FANTASY: *77* $2–3

MEAD, Sister Janet
Singles: 7-Inch
A&M: *74* 1–3

MEADER, Vaughn
LPs: 10/12-Inch 33rpm
CADENCE: *62–63* 10–20

MEAGAN
Singles: 7-Inch
NEXT PLATINUM: *84* 4–6

MEAN MACHINE
Singles: 7-Inch
SUGAR HILL: *81* 1–3

MEAT LOAF (Marvin Lee Aday)
Singles: 7-Inch
EPIC: *77–83* 1–3
RSO: *74* 2–4

LPs: 10/12-Inch 33rpm
CLEVELAND INT'L:
  81–83 5–8
EPIC (30000 series, except
  picture discs): *77–80* 5–8
EPIC (34974; "Bat Out Of
  Hell"): *77* 15–20
  (With bats on front cover.)

Price Range

EPIC (34974; "Bat Out Of
   Hell"): *77*. **$25–30**
   (Promotional issue. Without bats on front
   cover.)
EPIC (40000 series): *80* **12–15**
   (Half-speed mastered LPs.)
   Also see FOLEY, Ellen
   Also see STONEY & MEATLOAF

MECO (Meco Monardo)
   Singles: 12-Inch 33/45rpm
ARISTA: *83* **4–6**
   Singles: 7-Inch
ARISTA: *82–83*. **1–3**
MILLENNIUM: *77–78* **1–3**
RSO: *80* **1–3**
   LPs: 10/12-Inch 33rpm
ARISTA: *82–84*. **5–8**
MILLENNIUM: *77–78* **5–8**
RSO: *80* **5–8**
   Also see STAR WARS INTERGALACTIC
   DROID CHOIR & CHORALE, The

MEDLEY, Bill
   Singles: 7-Inch
A&M: *71–73* **2–4**
LIBERTY: *81* **1–3**
MGM: *68*. **3–5**
PARAMOUNT: *71*. **2–4**
PLANET: *82–83* **1–3**
RCA VICTOR: *83–84* **1–3**
REPRISE: *65*. **4–6**
UNITED ARTISTS: *78–80*. **1–3**
VERVE: *67* **3–5**
   LPs: 10/12-Inch 33rpm
A&M: *71–73* **8–10**
LIBERTY: *81* **5–8**
MGM: *68–70*. **12–15**
PLANET: *82* **8–10**
RCA VICTOR: *83–84* **5–8**
UNITED ARTISTS: *78–80*. **8–10**
   Also see RIGHTEOUS BROTHERS, The

MEDLIN, Joe
   Singles: 7-Inch
BRUNSWICK: *61*. **3–5**
MERCURY: *59–60*. **4–6**

MEGATONS, The
   Singles: 7-Inch
CHECKER: *62* **3–5**
DODGE: *62* **8–10**
FOREST: *63* **3–5**

Price Range

JELL: *62* **$3–5**

MEGATRONS, The
   Singles: 7-Inch
ACOUSTICON: *59*. **4–6**
AUDICON: *59–61* **4–6**

MEISNER, Randy
   Singles: 7-Inch
ASYLUM: *78*. **2–3**
EPIC: *80–82* **1–3**
   LPs: 10/12-Inch 33rpm
ASYLUM: *78*. **8–10**
EPIC: *80–82* **5–8**
   Also see EAGLES, The
   Also see POCO

MEL & TIM
   Singles: 7-Inch
BAMBOO: *69–70* **2–4**
COLLECTABLES **1–3**
ERIC **1–3**
STAX: *72–74*. **2–3**
   LPs: 10/12-Inch 33rpm
BAMBOO: *70* **10–15**
STAX: *72–74*. **8–10**
   Members: Mel Harden; Tim McPherson.

MELACHRINO, George, & His Orchestra
   Singles: 7-Inch
RCA VICTOR: *50–59* **2–3**
   EPs: 7-Inch 33/45rpm
RCA VICTOR: *50–59* **3–6**
   LPs: 10/12-Inch 33rpm
RCA VICTOR: *50–61* **5–15**

MELANIE (Melanie & The Edwin Hawkins Singers)
   Singles: 7-Inch
ABC: *75*. **1–3**
ATLANTIC: *77* **2–3**
BUDDAH: *69–73* **2–4**
CASABLANCA: *74* **2–3**
COLUMBIA: *67–68* **3–5**
ERIC: *78* **1–3**
MCA. **1–3**
MIDSONG INT'L: *78* **1–3**
NEIGHBORHOOD: *71–75*. **2–3**
PORTRAIT: *81*. **1–3**
TOMATO: *78–79* **1–3**

Price Range

Picture Sleeves

BUDDAH: *70–73* $2–4
NEIGHBORHOOD: *72–73* 2–3

LPs: 10/12-Inch 33rpm

ABC: *75* 8–10
ACCORD: *81–82* 5–8
ATLANTIC: *76* 8–10
BLANCHE: *82* 5–8
BUDDAH: *69–77* 10–15
51 WEST: *79* 5–8
MCA/MIDSONG: *77–78* 5–9
NEIGHBORHOOD: *71–75* 8–10
PICKWICK: *71* 8–10
TOMATO: *79* 5–8
Also see HAWKINS, Edwin, Singers

MELLAA
Singles: 7-Inch
LARC: *83* 1–3

MELLE MEL & DUKE BOOTEE
Singles: 12-Inch 33/45rpm
SUGAR HILL: *82* 4–6
Also see GRANDMASTER FLASH & THE
FURIOUS FIVE

**MELLENCAMP, John Cougar: see
COUGAR, John**

**MELLO-KINGS, The (The
Mellokings; The Mellotones)**
Singles: 7-Inch
COLLECTABLES 1–3
FLASHBACK: *65* 1–3
HERALD (Except 502):
 57–61 6–10
HERALD (502; "Tonite
 Tonite"): *57* 25–30
 (With the group shown as "The Mellotones.")
HERALD (502; "Tonite
 Tonite"): *57* 12–15
 (With the group shown as "The Mello-Kings."
 With logo in script print inside the flag.)
HERALD (502; "Tonite
 Tonite") 5–8
 (With the group shown as "The Mello-Kings."
 With logo in block print inside the flag.)
LESCAY: *62* 4–6
EPs: 7-Inch 33/45rpm
HERALD: *60* 30–40

Price Range

LPs: 10/12-Inch 33rpm

HERALD: *60* $60–75
 Members: Larry Esposita; Bob Scholl; Jerry
 Scholl; Eddie Quinn; Neil Areana.

MELLO-MOODS, The
Singles: 7-Inch
HAMILTON: *53* 175–200
PRESTIGE: *52–53* 200–225
RED ROBIN (105;
 "Where Are You"): *52* 275–300
 Members: Ray Wooten; Bobby Williams;
 Monte Owens; Bobby Baylor; Jimmy Bethea.

MELLO-TONES, The
Singles: 7-Inch
FASCINATION: *57* 20–25
GEE: *57* 5–8

MELODIANS, The
Singles: 12-Inch 33/45rpm
REAL AUTHENTIC
 SOUND: *84* 4–6
LPs: 10/12-Inch 33rpm
REAL AUTHENTIC
 SOUND: *84* 5–8

**MELVIN, Harold (Harold Melvin &
The Bluenotes)**
Singles: 12-Inch 33/45rpm
PHILADELPHIA INT'L:
 80 4–6
SOURCE: *79–80* 4–6
Singles: 7-Inch
ABC: *77–78* 1–3
ARCTIC: *67* 3–5
LANDA: *64–65* 4–6
MCA: *81* 1–3
PHILADELPHIA INT'L:
 72–79 2–3
PHILLY WORLD: *84–85* 1–3
SOURCE: *79–80* 1–3
Picture Sleeves
PHILADELPHIA INT'L:
 72–75 2–3
LPs: 10/12-Inch 33rpm
ABC: *77* 8–10
MCA: *81* 5–8
PHILADELPHIA INT'L:
 72–76 8–10
PHILLY WORLD: *84–85* 5–8

Price Range

SOURCE: *80* **$5–8**
  Also see BLUENOTES, The
  Also see PAIGE, Sharon
  Also see PENDERGRASS, Teddy

MEMPHIS HORNS, The
Singles: 7-Inch
RCA VICTOR: *76–78* **1–3**

LPs: 10/12-Inch 33rpm
RCA VICTOR: *77–78* **5–8**
  Also see McDONALD, Michael
  Also see POINTER SISTERS, The

MEN AT WORK
Singles: 12-Inch 33/45rpm
COLUMBIA: *82–83* **4–6**

Singles: 7-Inch
COLUMBIA: *82–83* **1–3**

LPs: 10/12-Inch 33rpm
COLUMBIA (1650;
  "Cargo - World Premier
  Weekend"): *83* **10–15**
  (Promotional issue only.)
COLUMBIA (30000
  series): *82–83* **5–8**
COLUMBIA (40000
  series): *83* **12–15**
  (Half-speed mastered LPs.)

MEN WITHOUT HATS
Singles: 12-Inch 33/45rpm
BACKSTREET: *83* **4–6**
MCA: *83–84* **4–6**

Singles: 7-Inch
BACKSTREET: *83* **1–3**
MCA: *83–84* **1–3**

LPs: 10/12-Inch 33rpm
BACKSTREET: *83* **5–8**
MCA: *84* **5–8**

MENAGE
Singles: 12-Inch 33/45rpm
PROFILE: *83–85* **4–6**

Singles: 7-Inch
PROFILE: *83–85* **1–3**

LPs: 10/12-Inch 33rpm
PROFILE: *83* **5–8**

Price Range

MENDES, Sergio (Sergio Mendes & Brasil '66; Sergio Mendes & Brasil '77)
Singles: 12-Inch 33/45rpm
A&M: *82* **$4–6**

Singles: 7-Inch
A&M (807 through 1257):
  66–71 . . . . **2–3**
A&M (1279 through 2700
  series): *71–85* **1–3**
ATLANTIC: *67–68* **2–3**
BELL: *73* **2–3**
ELEKTRA: *75–80* **1–3**

Picture Sleeves
A&M (807 through 1257):
  66–71 . . . . **2–3**

LPs: 10/12-Inch 33rpm
A&M (Except 4100 series):
  69–84 . . . . **6–10**
A&M (4100 series): *66–69* **10–15**
ATLANTIC: *66–67* **10–15**
BELL: *73–74* **8–10**
ELEKTRA: *75–79* **8–10**
EVEREST: *74* **8–10**
PHILIPS: *68* **10–12**
  Also see ADDERLEY, Julian "Cannonball,"
  & Sergio Mendes
  Also see HALL, Lani

MENUDO
Singles: 7-Inch
RCA VICTOR: *84–85* **1–3**

LPs: 10/12-Inch 33rpm
RCA VICTOR: *84* **5–8**

MERC & MONK
Singles: 7-Inch
MANHATTAN: *85* **1–3**
  Members: Eric Mecury; Thelonious Monk.
  Also see MERCURY, Eric
  Also see MONK, Thelonious

MERCURY, Eric
LPs: 10/12-Inch 33rpm
AVCO EMBASSY: *69* **10–12**
CAPITOL: *81* **5–8**
ENTERPRISE: *72–73* **8–10**
  Also see FLACK, Roberta, & Eric Mercury
  Also see MERC & MONK

Price Range

MERCURY, Freddie
Singles: 12-Inch 33/45rpm
COLUMBIA: 84 . . . . $4–6
Singles: 7-Inch
COLUMBIA: 84–85 1–3
LPs: 10/12-Inch 33rpm
COLUMBIA: 85 5–8
Also see QUEEN

MERCURY, Freddie / Giorgio Moroder
Singles: 12-Inch 33/45rpm
COLUMBIA: 84 4–6
Also see MERCURY, Freddie
Also see MORODER, Giorgio

MERCY
Singles: 7-Inch
SUNDI: 69 3–5
WARNER BROS: 69 3–5
LPs: 10/12-Inch 33rpm
SUNDI: 69 15–20
WARNER BROS: 69 10–15

MERMAIDS, The: see MURMAIDS, The

MERMAN, Ethel, & Dick Haymes
Singles: 7-Inch
DECCA: 51 3–5
Also see HAYMES, Dick

MERRY-GO-ROUND, The (Featuring Emitt Rhodes)
Singles: 7-Inch
A&M: 67–69 3–5
LPs: 10/12-Inch 33rpm
A&M: 67 12–15
RHINO: 85 5–8
Also see RHODES, Emitt

MERRYWEATHER, Neil (Merryweather)
Singles: 7-Inch
CAPITOL: 69 2–4
LPs: 10/12-Inch 33rpm
CAPITOL: 69 10–15
MERCURY: 74–75 10–12
Also see MASON, Dave
Also see MILLER, Steve

Price Range

MERRYWEATHER, Neil, & John Richardson
LPs: 10/12-Inch 33rpm
KENT: 72 . . . . $10–12

MERRYWEATHER & CAREY
LPs: 10/12-Inch 33rpm
RCA VICTOR: 71 8–10
Members: Neil Merryweather; Lynn Carey.
Also see MERRYWEATHER, Neil

MESA
Singles: 7-Inch
ARIOLA AMERICA: 77 2–3

MESSENGERS, The
Singles: 7-Inch
BEAM: 64 4–6
ERA: 65 3–5
MGM: 64–65 3–5
RARE EARTH: 71 2–4
SOUL: 67 3–5
LPs: 10/12-Inch 33rpm
RARE EARTH (S-509;
"The Messengers"): 69 8–12
(Standard cover.)
RARE EARTH (RS-509;
"The Messengers"): 69 12–15
(Round-top cover.)

MESSINA, Jim (Jim Messina & The Jesters)
Singles: 7-Inch
AUDIO FIDELITY: 64 8–10
COLUMBIA: 79–80 1–3
FEATURE: 64 8–10
ULTIMA: 64 8–10
WARNER BROS: 81–83 1–3
LPs: 10/12-Inch 33rpm
AUDIO FIDELITY: 64 25–30
COLUMBIA: 79 5–8
THIMBLE: 73 10–12
WARNER BROS: 81–83 5–8
Also see BUFFALO SPRINGFIELD
Also see LOGGINS & MESSINA
Also see POCO
Also see YOUNG, Neil, & Jim Messina

MESSINA, Jim, & Pauline Wilson
Singles: 7-Inch
WARNER BROS: 81 1–3
Also see MESSINA, Jim

Price Range

METALLICA
LPs: 10/12-Inch 33rpm
ELEKTRA: *84* **$5–8**
ENIGMA: *84.* **5–8**
MEGAFORCE: *84* **8–10**

METERS, The
Singles: 7-Inch
JOSIE: *69–71.* **2–4**
REPRISE: *74–76.* **2–3**
WARNER BROS: *77* **2–3**

LPs: 10/12-Inch 33rpm
ISLAND: *75* **8–10**
JOSIE: *69–70.* **10–12**
REPRISE: *72–74.* **8–10**
VIRGO: *75* **8–10**
WARNER BROS: *77* **8–10**
Also see NEVILLE BROTHERS, The

METHENY, Pat
Singles: 7-Inch
ECM: *79–84.* **1–3**

LPs: 10/12-Inch 33rpm
ECM: *76–84.* **5–10**
EMI AMERICA: *85.* **5–8**
WARNER BROS: *83* **5–8**
Also see BOWIE, David, & The Pat Metheny Group

METROS, The
Singles: 7-Inch
JUST. **12–15**
1-2-3: *69.* **2–4**
RCA VICTOR: *66–67* **3–5**

LPs: 10/12-Inch 33rpm
RCA VICTOR: *67* **10–15**

MIAMI (Featuring Robert Moore)
Singles: 7-Inch
DRIVE: *74–76.* **2–4**

LPs: 10/12-Inch 33rpm
DRIVE: *76* **5–10**

MIAMI DISCO BAND, The
(Featuring Beverly Barkley)
Singles: 7-Inch
SALSOUL: *79.* **1–3**

Price Range

MIAMI SOUND MACHINE, The
Singles: 12-Inch 33/45rpm
EPIC: *84–85* **$4–6**
Singles: 7-Inch
EPIC: *84–85* **1–3**
LPs: 10/12-Inch 33rpm
EPIC: *84* **5–8**
Members: Marcos Avila; Kiki Garcia; Gloria Estefan; Emilio Estefan, Jr.

MICHAELS, Lee
Singles: 7-Inch
A&M: *67–71* **3–5**
COLUMBIA: *73* **2–4**
Picture Sleeves
A&M: *70–71* **3–5**
LPs: 10/12-Inch 33rpm
A&M (Except 3158): *67–73* **10–15**
A&M (3158; "Lee
  Michaels"): *82* **5–8**
COLUMBIA: *73–75* **10–12**
Promotional LPs
COLUMBIA ("Lee
  Michaels In Hawaii"): *75* **35–45**

MICHELE LEE: see LEE, Michele

MICKEY & SYLVIA
Singles: 7-Inch
ALL PLATINUM: *69* **2–4**
GROOVE: *56.* **5–8**
RCA VICTOR (7800
  series): *61* **5–10**
  (With a "37" prefix. Compact 33 Singles.)
RCA VICTOR (7700
  through 8500 series):
  60–65 .... **3–5**
  (With a "47" prefix.)
RCA VICTOR (7800
  series): *60* **5–10**
  (With a "61" prefix. Stereo singles.)
RAINBOW: *55* **8–10**
VIK: *57–58* **5–8**
WILLOW: *61–62.* **4–6**
EPs: 7-Inch 33/45rpm
GROOVE: *57.* **25–30**
VIK: *58* **20–25**
LPs: 10/12-Inch 33rpm
CAMDEN: *65.* **20–25**
RCA VICTOR: *73* **10–12**
VIK: *58* **50–60**

Price Range

Members: Mickey Baker; Sylvia Vanderpool.
Also see DUPREE, Champion Jack, & Mickey Baker
Also see LITTLE SYLVIA
Also see SYLVIA

MIDLER, Bette
Singles: 7-Inch
ATLANTIC: 72–85 .... $1–3
Picture Sleeves
ATLANTIC: 72–85 1–3
LPs: 10/12-Inch 33rpm
ATLANTIC: 72–85 5–8
Also see REDD, Sharon
Also see U.S.A. FOR AFRICA

MIDNIGHT OIL
Singles: 12-Inch 33/45rpm
COLUMBIA: 84 4–6
Singles: 7-Inch
COLUMBIA: 84 1–3
LPs: 10/12-Inch 33rpm
COLUMBIA: 84 5–8

MIDNIGHT STAR
Singles: 12-Inch 33/45rpm
SOLAR: 84 4–6
Singles: 7-Inch
SOLAR: 80–85 1–3
LPs: 10/12-Inch 33rpm
SOLAR: 82–85 5–8

MIDNIGHT STRING QUARTET, The
LPs: 10/12-Inch 33rpm
VIVA: 66–68 4–8

MIDNIGHTERS, The
Singles: 7-Inch
FEDERAL (12169 through
 12243): 54–55 8–18
FEDERAL (12251 through
 12339): 56–58 5–8
Members: Henry Booth; Hank Ballard; Sonny Woods; Charles Sutton; Lawson Smith; Alonzo Tucker.
Note: May be shown on some releases as "The Midnighters, Formerly The Royals."
Also see BALLARD, Hank, & The Midnighters
Also see ROYALS, The

Price Range

MIDNITERS, Thee: see THEE MIDNITERS

MIDWAY
Singles: 12-Inch 33/45rpm
PERSONAL: 84 .... $4–6
Singles: 7-Inch
PERSONAL: 84 1–3

MIGHTY CLOUDS OF JOY, The
Singles: 12-Inch 33/45rpm
EPIC: 79 4–6
Singles: 7-Inch
ABC: 76–77 1–3
DUNHILL: 74–75 1–3
EPIC: 79–80 1–3
MYRRH: 82 1–3
PEACOCK: 61–73 1–3
LPs: 10/12-Inch 33rpm
ABC: 75–76 4–6
DUNHILL: 74 4–8
EPIC: 79 5–8
MYRRH: 81–83 4–6
PEACOCK: 65–73 5–10
PRIORITY: 82 4–8

MIGHTY FLEA, The
Singles: 7-Inch
ELDO: 67 3–5

MIGHTY FIRE
Singles: 7-Inch
ELEKTRA: 81–82 1–3
ZEPHYR: 80 2–3
LPs: 10/12-Inch 33rpm
ELEKTRA: 81–82 5–8

MIGHTY HANNIBAL
Singles: 7-Inch
DECCA: 65 3–5
JOSIE: 66–67 3–5
LOMA: 68 3–5
SHURFINE: 66 3–5

MIGHTY POPE
Singles: 7-Inch
PRIVATE STOCK: 77 2–3

Price Range

MIKE & BILL
Singles: 7-Inch
ARISTA: 75 .... $2–4

MIKKI
Singles: 7-Inch
EMERALD INT'L: 82–83 1–3
POP ART: 84 1–3

MILBURN, Amos
Singles: 7-Inch
ALADDIN (3014;
"Chicken Shack
Boogie"): 50 35–45
ALADDIN (3018;
"Bewildered"): 50 15–20
ALADDIN (3068 through
3197): 50–53 15–20
ALADDIN (3200 & 3300
series): 53–57 10–15
IMPERIAL: 62 3–5
KING (5000 series): 60–61 4–6
KING (6000 series): 67 3–5
LE CAM: 62 3–5
MOTOWN: 63 12–15

LPs: 10/12-Inch 33rpm
ALADDIN (700 series): 55 125–150
(Black vinyl.)
ALADDIN (700 series): 55 150–175
(Colored vinyl.)
ALADDIN (800 series): 56 70–175
IMPERIAL: 62 25–30
MOTOWN: 63 75–100
SCORE: 57 40–50
Also see BROWN, Charles, & Amos Milburn

MILES, Buddy (The Buddy Miles Express; The Buddy Miles Band)
Singles: 7-Inch
CASABLANCA: 75–76 2–3
COLUMBIA: 73–74 2–4
MERCURY: 68–71 2–4

LPs: 10/12-Inch 33rpm
CASABLANCA: 75 8–10
COLUMBIA: 73–74 8–10
MERCURY: 68–72 12–15
Also see ELECTRIC FLAG, The
Also see HENDRIX, Jimi
Also see SANTANA, Carlos, & Buddy Miles

Price Range

MILES, Garry (Garry Miles & The Statues; Gary Miles)
Singles: 7-Inch
LIBERTY: 60–68 .... $3–5
Picture Sleeves
LIBERTY: 60 8–12
EPs: 7-Inch 33/45rpm
LIBERTY: 60 20–25
Also see STATUES, The

MILES, John
Singles: 12-Inch 33/45rpm
LONDON: 77–80 5–8
Singles: 7-Inch
ARISTA: 78 2–3
LONDON: 76–77 2–3
LPs: 10/12-Inch 33rpm
ARISTA: 78 5–8
LONDON: 78–80 5–8

MILES, Lenny
Singles: 7-Inch
GROOVE: 62 3–5
SCEPTER: 61 3–5

MILITELLO, Bobby (Featuring Jean Carn)
Singles: 7-Inch
GORDY: 82–83 1–3
LPs: 10/12-Inch 33rpm
GORDY: 82–83 5–8
Also see CARN, Jean

MILLER, Chuck
Singles: 7-Inch
MERCURY: 55–58 5–8
LPs: 10/12-Inch 33rpm
MERCURY: 56 25–30

MILLER, Clint
Singles: 7-Inch
ABC-PARAMOUNT: 58 5–8
BIG TOP: 59 4–6
HEADLINE: 60–61 4–6
LENOX: 62 3–5

MILLER, Frankie
Singles: 7-Inch
COLUMBIA: 54–56 3–5
STARDAY: 59–67 2–5
UNITED ARTISTS: 62 2–4

Price Range

EPs: 7-Inch 33/45rpm
STARDAY: *60* **$5–8**

LPs: 10/12-Inch 33rpm
AUDIO LAB: *63* **12–18**
STARDAY: *61–65* **10–20**
UNITED ARTISTS: *62* **12–18**

MILLER, Frankie (The Frankie Miller Band)
Singles: 7-Inch
CAPITOL: *82* **1–3**
CHRYSALIS: *75–79*.............. **2–3**

LPs: 10/12-Inch 33rpm
CAPITOL: *82* **5–8**
CHRYSALIS: *73–80*.............. **8–10**

MILLER, Glenn, & His Orchestra (The New Glenn Miller Orchestra With Ray McKinley; Buddy DeFranco & The Glenn Miller Orchestra)
Singles: 7-Inch
EPIC: *65–69* **1–3**
RCA VICTOR: *50–67* **2–4**

EPs: 7-Inch 33/45rpm
EPIC: *54–56* **5–15**
RCA VICTOR (Except
  6700 series): *50–61* **5–10**
RCA VICTOR (6700
  series): *53* **20–40**

LPs: 10/12-Inch 33rpm
BRIGHT ORANGE: *73* **4–8**
CAMDEN: *63–74*................. **5–10**
COLUMBIA: *82*................... **5–8**
EPIC (1000 & 3000 series):
  54–56 .... **15–25**
EPIC (16000 series): *60* **10–20**
EPIC (24000 & 26000
  series): *65–66* **5–10**
EVEREST (Except 4004):
  82 .... **4–8**
EVEREST (4004; "Glenn
  Miller"): *82* **15–25**
  (A 5-LP set.)
GREAT AMERICAN
  GRAMOPHONE: *77*............ **5–10**
HARMONY: *70* **4–8**
KORY: *77*........................ **4–8**
MOVIETONE: *67*................. **8–12**

Price Range

RCA VICTOR (16 through
  30): *51–52* **$25–50**
  (10-Inch LPs.)
RCA VICTOR (0600
  through 3800 series):
  74–81 .... **5–10**
  (With an "ANL," "AYL" or "CPL" prefix.)
RCA VICTOR (3000
  series): *52–54*.................. **20–40**
  (10-Inch LPs.)
RCA VICTOR (1000
  through 1500 series):
  54–57 .... **10–20**
  (Black labels.)
RCA VICTOR (1100
  through 1500 series): *68* **4–8**
  (Orange labels.)
RCA VICTOR (1600
  through 3900 series):
  58–68 .... **5–15**
  (Black labels. With an "LPM" or "LSP" prefix.)
RCA VICTOR (1900
  through 4100 series):
  68–69 .... **4–8**
  (Orange labels.)
RCA VICTOR (5000
  series): *75–80*.................. **6–12**
RCA VICTOR (6000
  series): *69–73*.................. **8–15**
RCA VICTOR (6100
  series): *59–63*................. **15–30**
RCA VICTOR (6700
  series): *53–62*................. **60–80**
  (5-LP set, with booklet and special gold or silver case.)
SPRINGBOARD: *77*.............. **4–6**
20TH CENTURY-FOX
  (100 series): *59*................ **20–30**
20TH CENTURY-FOX
  (900 series): *73*................. **5–10**
20TH CENTURY-FOX
  (3000 series): *59*............... **15–20**
20TH CENTURY-FOX
  (3100 series): *65*............... **10–15**
20TH CENTURY-FOX
  (4100 series): *65*............... **10–15**
20TH CENTURY-FOX
  (72000 series): *73*............... **6–10**

Price Range

MILLER, Jody
Singles: 7-Inch
CAPITOL: 63–70 . . . . $2–5
EPIC: 70–79 1–3

Picture Sleeves
CAPITOL: 65 3–5

LPs: 10/12-Inch 33rpm
CAPITOL (1900 series): 63 15–20
CAPITOL (2300 through
   2900 series): 65–69 12–15
CAPITOL (11000 series):
   73 5–10
EPIC: 70–77 5–10
PICKWICK/HILLTOP:
   66 10–15
      Also see PAYCHECK, Johnny, & Jody Miller

MILLER, Marcus
Singles: 12-Inch 33/45rpm
WARNER BROS: 83–84 4–6

Singles: 7-Inch
WARNER BROS: 83–84 1–3

MILLER, Mitch (Mitch Miller's Orchestra & Chorus; Mitch Miller & The Sing-Along Gang)
Singles: 7-Inch
COLUMBIA: 50–65 2–4
DECCA: 65–66 1–3
DIAMOND: 68 1–3
GOLD-MOR: 73 1–3
UNITED ARTISTS: 68 1–3

Picture Sleeves
COLUMBIA: 59–63 2–4

EPs: 7-Inch 33/45rpm
COLUMBIA: 55–61 4–8

LPs: 10/12-Inch 33rpm
ATLANTIC: 70 4–8
COLUMBIA (Except 2780
   /6380): 56–82 5–15
COLUMBIA (2780;
   "Major Dundee"): 65 35–45
   (Soundtrack. Monaural.)
COLUMBIA (6380;
   "Major Dundee"): 65 45–55
   (Soundtrack. Stereo.)
DECCA: 66 5–10
HARMONY: 65–71 5–10

Price Range

MILLER, Mrs. Elva (Mrs. Miller)
Singles: 7-Inch
AMARET: 69–70 . . . . $3–5
CAPITOL: 66 4–6

LPs: 10/12-Inch 33rpm
AMARET: 69 12–15
CAPITOL: 66–67 20–25

MILLER, Ned
Singles: 7-Inch
CAPITOL (2000 series): 68 2–3
CAPITOL (4600 series): 61 3–5
CAPITOL (5400 & 5800
   series): 65–67 2–4
DOT (15000 series, except
   15601): 57 3–5
DOT (15601; "From A
   Jack To A King"): 57 4–6
FABOR: 62–65 2–4
JACKPOT: 59 3–5
REPUBLIC: 69–70 1–3

LPs: 10/12-Inch 33rpm
CAPITOL: 65–67 10–15
FABOR (Black vinyl): 63 15–20
FABOR (Colored vinyl):
   63 25–30
PLANTATION: 81 5–8
REPUBLIC: 70 8–10

MILLER, Roger
Singles: 7-Inch
COLUMBIA: 73–74 1–3
DECCA: 59 4–6
ELEKTRA: 81 1–3
MERCURY: 70–72 2–3
MUSICOR: 65 2–4
RCA VICTOR (7000
   series): 60–63 3–5
RCA VICTOR (8000
   series): 65 2–4
SMASH: 64–76 2–4
STARDAY: 65 2–4
WINDSONG: 77 1–3

Picture Sleeves
SMASH: 64–68 3–5

LPs: 10/12-Inch 33rpm
CAMDEN: 64–65 10–12
COLUMBIA: 73 6–10
EVEREST: 75 5–8
MERCURY: 72 6–10

Price Range

PICKWICK **$8–10**
SMASH (Except 7000
  series): *64–70* **10–12**
SMASH (7000 series): *82* **5–8**
STARDAY: *65* **10–15**
20TH CENTURY-FOX:
  79 .... **5–8**
WINDSONG: *77*. **5–8**
WING: *69* **8–12**
  Also see LEWIS, Jerry Lee / Roger Miller /
  Roy Orbison
  Also see NELSON, Willie, & Roger Miller

MILLER, Steve, Band
Singles: 12-Inch 33/45rpm
CAPITOL: *81–85* **4–6**
Singles: 7-Inch
CAPITOL (2100 series): *68* **8–10**
CAPITOL (2200 series): *68* **5–8**
CAPITOL (2400 through
  2600 series): *69* **4–6**
CAPITOL (2800 through
  3300 series): *70–72* **3–5**
CAPITOL (3700 through
  4400 series): *73–77* **2–4**
CAPITOL (5000 series):
  81–85 .... **1–3**
LPs: 10/12-Inch 33rpm
CAPITOL (184 through
  748): *69–71*. **10–12**
CAPITOL (2900 series): *68* **12–15**
CAPITOL (11000 through
  16000 series, except
  picture discs): *72–84* **6–10**
CAPITOL (Picture discs):
  78 .... **15–20**
MFSL: *78*. **12–15**
Picture Sleeves
CAPITOL: *80–85* **1–3**
Promotional LPs
CAPITOL (11872;
  "Greatest Hits"): *78* **20–30**
  (Colored vinyl.)
  Also see MERRYWEATHER, Neil
  Also see SCAGGS, Boz

MILLER, Steve, Band / The Band / Quicksilver Messenger Service
LPs: 10/12-Inch 33rpm
CAPITOL: *69* **35–45**
  (A 3-LP set, with one LP by each group.)
  Also see BAND, The
  Also see MILLER, Steve, Band

Price Range

Also see QUICKSILVER

MILLINDER, Lucky, & His Orchestra
Singles: 7-Inch
KING (4400 series): *51* **$15–20**
  (Black vinyl.)
KING (4400 series): *51* **25–30**
  (Colored vinyl.)
KING (4500 series): *52* **10–12**
KING (4700 & 4800
  series): *55* **5–8**
KING (5200 series): *59* **3–5**
RCA VICTOR (50-0000
  series): *51* **15–20**
TODD: *59* **3–5**
WARWICK: *60*. **3–5**
EPs: 7-Inch 33/45rpm
KING. **15–20**
  Also see HARRIS, Wynonie

MILLS, Frank
Singles: 7-Inch
POLYDOR: *78–79* **1–3**
SUNFLOWER: *72* **2–3**
LPs: 10/12-Inch 33rpm
CAPITOL: *85* **5–8**
POLYDOR: *79* **5–8**
  Also see BELLS, The

MILLS, Gary
Singles: 7-Inch
IMPERIAL: *60*. **4–6**
LONDON: *62* **3–5**
TOP RANK: *60* **3–5**

MILLS, Hayley (Hayley Mills & Maurice Chevalier; Hayley Mills & Jimmie Bean)
Singles: 7-Inch
BUENA VISTA: *61–62* **4–6**
MAINSTREAM: *66* **3–5**
Picture Sleeves
BUENA VISTA: *61–62* **6–10**
EPs: 7-Inch 33/45rpm
DISNEYLAND: *60* **15–20**
LPs: 10/12-Inch 33rpm
BUENA VISTA: *62* **20–25**
MAINSTREAM (6090;
  "Gypsy Girl"): *66*. **15–25**
  (Soundtrack.)
  Also see ANNETTE & HAYLEY MILLS

Price Range

MILLS, Hayley, & Eddie Hodges
Singles: 7-Inch
BUENA VISTA: *63* $4–6

Picture Sleeves
BUENA VISTA: *64* 4–6
Also see HODGES, Eddie

MILLS, Hayley, & Burl Ives (With Eddie Hodges & Deborah Walley)
Singles: 7-Inch
BUENA VISTA (4023;
  "Summer Magic"): *64* 3–5
  (Alcoa Wrap promotional issue.)

Picture Sleeves
BUENA VISTA (4023;
  "Summer Magic"): *64* 5–8
  (Alcoa Wrap promotional issue.)
  Also see IVES, Burl
  Also see MILLS, Hayley

MILLS, Stephanie
Singles: 12-Inch 33/45rpm
CASABLANCA: *82–85* 4–6
MCA: *85* 4–6
20TH CENTURY-FOX:
  79–81 4–6

Singles: 7-Inch
ABC: *74* 2–3
CASABLANCA: *82–86* 1–3
MCA: *85* 1–3
MOTOWN: *75* 2–3
PARAMOUNT: *74* 2–3
20TH CENTURY-FOX:
  79–81 1–3

LPs: 10/12-Inch 33rpm
ABC: *75* 8–10
CASABLANCA: *82–85* 5–8
MOTOWN (800 series): *75* 8–10
MOTOWN (6000 series):
  82 5–8
20TH CENTURY-FOX:
  80–81 5–8

MILLS, Stephanie, & Teddy Pendergrass
Singles: 7-Inch
20TH CENTURY-FOX:
  81 1–3

Price Range

Also see MILLS, Stephanie
Also see PENDERGRASS, Teddy

MILLS, Yvonne, & The Sensations
Singles: 7-Inch
ATCO: *56–58* $8–10
Also see SENSATIONS, The

MILLS BROTHERS, The
Singles: 7-Inch
ABC: *64* 1–3
DECCA: *50–61* 2–4
DOT (15000 series): *58–59* 2–4
DOT (17000 series): *68–69* 1–3
MCA: *73–74* 1–3
PARAMOUNT: *71–72* 1–3
RANWOOD: *73–76* 1–3

EPs: 7-Inch 33/45rpm
DECCA: *50–63* 4–8
DOT: *58–59* 3–5

LPs: 10/12-Inch 33rpm
ABC: *74* 4–8
DECCA (100 series): *66* 8–15
DECCA (4000 series):
  61–67 8–15
DECCA (5000 series):
  51–55 15–25
DECCA (7000 series): *55* 15–20
DECCA (8000 series):
  55–59 10–20
DECCA (75000 series): *70* 5–10
DOT: *58–70* 5–15
EVEREST: *75–77* 4–8
GNP/CRESCENDO: *73* 5–8
PARAMOUNT: *72–74* 5–10
RANWOOD: *74–81* 4–8
SONGBIRD: *74* 4–6
VOCALION: *66–69* 5–10
  Members: Herb Mills; Harry Mills; Donald
  Mills; John Mills.

MILLS BROTHERS, The, & Louis Armstrong
Singles: 7-Inch
DECCA: *61* 2–4
Also see ARMSTRONG, Louis

MILLS BROTHERS, The, & Count Basie
LPs: 10/12-Inch 33rpm
ABC: *74* 4–8
DOT: *68* 5–10

Price Range

Also see BASIE, Count
Also see MILLS BROTHERS, The

MILSAP, Ronnie
Singles: 7-Inch
BOBLO: 77 .... $2–4
CHIPS: 70 3–5
FESTIVAL: 77 2–4
RCA VICTOR: 74–85 1–3
SCEPTER: 65–69 3–5
WARNER BROS (5000
  series): 63 5–8
WARNER BROS (8000
  series): 76 2–3
Picture Sleeves
RCA VICTOR: 79–85 1–3
LPs: 10/12-Inch 33rpm
BUCKBOARD: 76 8–10
CRAZY CAJUN: 75 8–10
51 WEST 5–8
HSRD: 82 8–10
RCA VICTOR: 74–83 6–10
TRIP: 76 8–10
WARNER BROS: 71–75 8–10

MILTON, Roy (Roy Milton & His Band; Roy Milton & His Solid Senders; The Roy Milton Sextet)
Singles: 7-Inch
CENCO: 61 3–5
DOOTONE: 55–56 5–8
KING (4900 & 5000
  series): 56–58 4–6
KING (5600 series): 62 3–5
SPECIALTY (414 through
  438): 50–52 8–10
SPECIALTY (446;
  "Believe Me, Baby"): 52 25–30
SPECIALTY (458; "Some
  Day"): 53 8–10
  (Black vinyl.)
SPECIALTY (458; "Some
  Day"): 53 15–20
  (Colored vinyl.)
SPECIALTY (464; "Let
  Me Give You All My
  Love"): 54 8–10
  (Black vinyl.)
SPECIALTY (464; "Let
  Me Give You All My
  Love"): 54 15–20

(Colored vinyl.)
SPECIALTY (480 through
  545): 54–55 .... $5–8
WARWICK: 60 3–5
LPs: 10/12-Inch 33rpm
KENT: 63 15–20

MILTON, Roy / Joe Liggins
Singles: 7-Inch
SPECIALTY: 53 10–12
  Also see LIGGINS, Joe
  Also see MILTON, Roy

MIMMS, Garnet (Garnet Mimms & The Enchanters)
Singles: 7-Inch
ARISTA: 77 2–3
GSF: 72 2–4
LIBERTY: 81 1–3
UNITED ARTISTS: 63–66 3–5
VEEP: 66 3–5
VERVE: 68–70 2–4
Picture Sleeves
UNITED ARTISTS: 63 3–5
LPs: 10/12-Inch 33rpm
ARISTA: 78 8–10
GRAND PRIX: 63 10–15
GUEST STAR: 63 12–15
UNITED ARTISTS: 63–66 20–25

MINA
Singles: 7-Inch
TIME: 61 2–4

MINDBENDERS, The (With Eric Stewart)
Singles: 7-Inch
FONTANA: 65–67 4–6
LPs: 10/12-Inch 33rpm
FONTANA: 66 20–25
  Also see FONTANA, Wayne, & The Mindbenders

MINEO, Sal
Singles: 7-Inch
DECCA: 64 3–5
EPIC: 57–59 4–6
FONTANA: 65 3–5
Picture Sleeves
EPIC: 57–59 5–10

Price Range

EPs: 7-Inch 33/45rpm
EPIC: *57–58* **$15–20**
LPs: 10/12-Inch 33rpm
EPIC: *58* **25–30**

MINIATURE MEN, The
Singles: 7-Inch
DOLTON: *62.* **3–5**
Also see LEVINE, Hank

MINISTRY
Singles: 12-Inch 33/45rpm
ARISTA: *83* **4–6**
Singles: 7-Inch
ARISTA: *83* **1–3**
LPs: 10/12-Inch 33rpm
ARISTA: *83* **5–8**

MINK DE VILLE
Singles: 7-Inch
ATLANTIC: *81–84* **1–3**
CAPITOL: *77–78* **2–3**
LPs: 10/12-Inch 33rpm
ATLANTIC: *81–83* **5–8**
CAPITOL: *77–82* **5–8**

MINNELLI, Liza
Singles: 7-Inch
A&M: *68–71* **2–4**
ABC: *73* **2–3**
CADENCE: *63* **4–6**
CAPITOL (4900 through
5700 series): *63–65* **2–5**
COLUMBIA: *72–75* **2–3**
UNITED ARTISTS: *77* **1–3**
LPs: 10/12-Inch 33rpm
A&M: *68–73* **10–15**
ABC (752; "Cabaret"): *72* **10–15**
(Soundtrack. With Joel Grey.)
ARISTA (4069; "Lucky
Lady"): *76* **8–10**
(Soundtrack.)
CADENCE (4012; "Best
Foot Forward"): *63.* **40–60**
(Original cast.)
CAPITOL (2100 & 2400
series): *64–66* **10–20**
(With a "T" or "ST" prefix.)
CAPITOL (2200 series): *78* **5–8**
CAPITOL (11000 series):
72–78 .... **5–10**

Price Range

COLUMBIA: *72–77* **$6–12**
DRG (6101; "The Act"):
78 .... **8–10**
MCA (752; "Cabaret") **5–8**
(Soundtrack. With Joel Grey.)
STET **8–10**
Also see GARLAND, Judy, & Liza Minnelli

MINOR DETAIL
Singles: 7-Inch
POLYDOR: *83–84* **1–3**
LPs: 10/12-Inch 33rpm
POLYDOR: *83* **5–8**
Members: John Hughes; Willie Hughes.

MIRABAI
LPs: 10/12-Inch 33rpm
ATLANTIC: *75* **5–10**

MIRACLES, The (Smokey Robinson & The Miracles; The Miracles Featuring Bill Smokey Robinson)
Singles: 12-Inch 33/45rpm
COLUMBIA: *77* **4–6**
Singles: 7-Inch
CHESS (119; "Bad Girl"):
84 .... **1–3**
CHESS (1734; "Bad Girl"):
59 .... **10–15**
CHESS (1768; "All I
Want"): *60* **8–10**
COLUMBIA: *77–78* **2–3**
END: *58.* **10–15**
MOTOWN (G1; "Bad
Girl"): *59* **275–300**
MOTOWN (400 & 500
series) **1–3**
MOTOWN (2207; "Bad
Girl"): *59* **300–325**
ROULETTE **1–3**
STANDARD GROOVE
(13090; "I Care About
Detroit"): *68.* **60–75**
(Promotional issue only.)
TAMLA (009; "The
Christmas Song"): *63* **125–150**
(Promotional issue only.)
TAMLA (54028; "Way
Over There"/"Depend
On Me"): *60.* **60–70**

Price Range

(With an alternate take of "Way Over There,"
not available elsewhere.)
TAMLA (54028; "Way
Over There"/"Depend
On Me"): *60*. $20–25
(With the hit version of "Way Over There," the
same as is heard on their Tamla LPs.)
TAMLA (54028; "The
Feeling Is So
Fine"/"You Can Depend
On Me"): *60*. **325-350**
(Issued twice, first with the standard version of
"You Can Depend On Me," and then with an
alternate take of the tune. The alternate take
can be identified by the letter "A" following the
matrix number in the trail-off. There is no re-
portable difference in value.)
TAMLA (54034; "Shop
Around"): *60*. **80–100**
(With horizontal lines across top half of label.
Contains an alternate version of "Shop
Around." Matrix number is 45-H55518 A-2.
Shows writer as "Gordt" instead of Gordy.)
TAMLA (54034; "Shop
Around"): *60*. **25–30**
(Same as above, but with Tamla globe logo and
no lines on label.)
TAMLA (54034; "Shop
Around"): *60*. **4–6**
(Contains the hit version of "Shop Around."
Matrix number is 45-L1 3. Properly shows
writer as Gordy. Copies exist of the record, as
described here, but with the H-55518-A2 ma-
trix. We don't yet know which version of "Shop
Around" is on this variation.)
TAMLA (54036; "Ain't It
Baby"): *61* **8–10**
TAMLA (54044; "Mighty
Good Lovin'"): *61* **5–8**
TAMLA (54048;
"Everybody's Gotta Pay
Some Dues"): *61* **5–8**
TAMLA (54053 through
54069): *62* **4–6**
TAMLA (54073 through
54194): *62–70*. **3–5**
TAMLA (54199 through
54268): *70–76*. **2–4**

Picture Sleeves

TAMLA (54044; "Mighty
Good Lovin'"): *61* **15–20**
TAMLA (54059; "I'll Try
Something New"): *62* **15–20**

I'LL TRY SOMETHING NEW
YOU NEVER MISS A GOOD THING
The Miracles

Price Range

TAMLA (54073 through
54194): *62–70*. $4–6
LPs: 10/12-Inch 33rpm
COLUMBIA: *77–78* **8–10**
MOTOWN (Except 793):
82–84 . . . . **5–8**
MOTOWN (793;
"Anthology"): *74*. **12–15**
NATURAL RESOURCES:
78 . . . . **5–8**
TAMLA (220; "Hi! We're
The Miracles"): *61* **45–50**
TAMLA (223; "Cookin'
With The Miracles"): *62* **40–45**
TAMLA (224; "Shop
Around"): *62* **40–45**
TAMLA (230; "I'll Try
Something New"): *62* **35–40**
TAMLA (236; "Christmas
With The Miracles"): *63* **35–40**
TAMLA (238 through
254): *63–65*. **25–35**
TAMLA (267 through
297): *65–69*. **15–20**
TAMLA (301 through
344): *70–76*. **10–15**
Members: William "Smokey" Robinson; Pete
Moore; Bobby Rogers; Ron White; Claudette
Rogers.
Also see ROBINSON, Smokey
Also see RON & BILL

MIRAN, Wayne, & Rush Release
Singles: 7-Inch
ROULETTE: *75* **2–4**

Price Range

MIRETTES, The
Singles: 7-Inch
REVUE: 67–69 . . . . $3–5
UNI: 69 2–4

LPs: 10/12-Inch 33rpm
REVUE: 68 12–15
UNI: 69 10–12

MISS ABRAMS: see ABRAMS, Miss

MISS TONI FISHER, see FISHER, Miss Toni

MISSING PERSONS
Singles: 12-Inch 33/45rpm
CAPITOL: 82–84 4–6

Singles: 7-Inch
CAPITOL: 82–84 1–3

Picture Sleeves
CAPITOL: 82–84 1–3

EPs: 7-Inch 33/45rpm
KOMOS: 80. 5–8

LPs: 10/12-Inch 33rpm
CAPITOL: 82–84 5–8
Members: Dale Bozzio; Terry Bozzio; Warren Cuccurullo.
Also see MOTHERS OF INVENTION, The

MISSION
Singles: 7-Inch
PARAMOUNT: 74. 2–4

MISSOURI
Singles: 7-Inch
PANAMA: 78. 2–3
POLYDOR: 79 1–3

LPs: 10/12-Inch 33rpm
PANAMA: 77. 8–10
POLYDOR: 79 5–8

MR. BIG
Singles: 7-Inch
ARISTA: 77 2–3

Price Range

LPs: 10/12-Inch 33rpm
ARISTA: 76 . . . . $8–10

MR. MISTER
Singles: 7-Inch
RCA VICTOR: 84–85 1–3
LPs: 10/12-Inch 33rpm
RCA VICTOR: 84–85 5–8
Members: Richard Page; Pat Mastelotto; Steve Farris; Steve George.
Also see PAGES, The

MR. T. (Lawrence Tero)
Singles: 12-Inch 33/45rpm
COLUMBIA (Except picture discs): 84 4–6
COLUMBIA (Picture discs): 84 5–8
Singles: 7-Inch
COLUMBIA: 84 1–3
MCA: 84 1–3
LPs: 10/12-Inch 33rpm
COLUMBIA: 84 5–8
MCA: 84 5–8

MISTRESS
Singles: 7-Inch
RSO: 79 1–3
LPs: 10/12-Inch 33rpm
RSO: 79 5–8

MITCHELL, Billy (The Billy Mitchell Group)
Singles: 7-Inch
CALLA: 69 2–4
JUBILEE: 61. 3–5
UNITED ARTISTS: 60 3–5
WARWICK: 59. 4–6
Also see CLOVERS, The
Also see MORRIS, Joe, & His Orchestra

MITCHELL, Bobby (Bobby Mitchell & The Toppers)
Singles: 7-Inch
IMPERIAL (5236; "I'm Cryin"): 53 60–75
IMPERIAL (5250; "One Friday Morning"): 53 55–65
IMPERIAL (5270; "Baby's Gone"): 54 35–40

Price Range

IMPERIAL (5282; "Angel
Child"): *54* $35–40
IMPERIAL (5295; "The
Wedding Bells Are
Ringing"): *54* 20–25
IMPERIAL (5309; "I'm A
Young Man"): *54* 35–40
IMPERIAL (5326; "I Wish
I Knew"): *55* 15–20
IMPERIAL (5346; "I
Cried"): *55* 15–20
IMPERIAL (5378 through
5558): *56–58.* 8–12
IMPERIAL (5900 series):
63 3–5
RON: *61.* 3–5
SHOW-BIZ: *59* 5–8

MITCHELL, Chad
Singles: 7-Inch
AMY: *68–69* 2–4
WARNER BROS: *66–67.* 3–5
LPs: 10/12-Inch 33rpm
BELL: *69.* 10–12
WARNER BROS: *66–67.* 12–15
Also see MITCHELL, Chad, Trio

MITCHELL, Chad, Trio (The Mitchell Trio)
Singles: 7-Inch
COLPIX: *59–61.* 4–6
KAPP: *61–63.* 3–5
MAY: *62* 3–5
MERCURY: *63–66.* 3–5
REPRISE: *67.* 2–4
Picture Sleeves
KAPP: *61* 4–6
MERCURY: *63–66.* 3–5
LPs: 10/12-Inch 33rpm
COLPIX: *60* 20–25
KAPP: *61–64.* 15–20
MERCURY: *63–66.* 15–20
REPRISE: *67.* 15–20
Members: Chad Mitchell; Joe Frazier; Mike
Kobluk; John Denver.
Also see DENVER, John
Also see MITCHELL, Chad

MITCHELL, Chad, Trio, & The Gatemen
LPs: 10/12-Inch 33rpm
COLPIX: *64* 15–20

Price Range

Also see MITCHELL, Chad, Trio

MITCHELL, Freddie, & Orchestra
Singles: 7-Inch
ABC-PARAMOUNT:
57–61 .... $3–5
BRUNSWICK: *53.* 4–6
CORAL: *53* 4–6
DERBY: *49–52* 4–6
MERCURY: *52.* 5–8
ROCK 'N ROLL 5–8
LPs: 10/12-Inch 33rpm
VIK 20–25

MITCHELL, Guy
Singles: 7-Inch
COLUMBIA: *50–62* 2–5
ERIC: *83* 1–3
JOY: *62–63* 2–4
REPRISE: *66.* 2–3
STARDAY: *67–69* 2–3
Picture Sleeves
COLUMBIA: *56–62* 3–6
EPs: 7-Inch 33/45rpm
COLUMBIA: *54–57* 5–12
LPs: 10/12-Inch 33rpm
COLUMBIA (6000 series):
53 15–25
(10-Inch LPs.)
NASHVILLE: *70* 6–10
STARDAY: *68–69* 8–12
Also see CLOONEY, Rosemary, & Guy Mitchell

MITCHELL, Guy, & Mindy Carson
Singles: 7-Inch
COLUMBIA: *52–53* 2–4
Also see CARSON, Mindy

MITCHELL, Guy / Eileen Rodgers
EPs: 7-Inch 33/45rpm
COLUMBIA: *56* 5–8
Also see RODGERS, Eileen
Also see MITCHELL, Guy

MITCHELL, Joni (Joni Mitchell & The L.A. Express)
Singles: 7-Inch
ASYLUM: *72–80.* 1–3
ELEKTRA: *75* 2–3
GEFFEN: *82–83.* 1–3
REPRISE: *68–72.* 2–4

Price Range

LPs: 10/12-Inch 33rpm
ASYLUM: *72–80*. **$8–10**
GEFFEN: *82*. **5–8**
REPRISE: *68–71*. **10–12**

MITCHELL, Kim
Singles: 7-Inch
BRONZE: *85*. **1–3**

MITCHELL, McKinley
Singles: 7-Inch
BOXER: *59*. **8–10**
CHIMNEYVILLE: *77–78*. **2–3**
ONE-DERFUL: *62–65*. **4–6**

MITCHELL, Philip (Prince Philip Mitchell)
Singles: 7-Inch
ATLANTIC: *78–79*. **1–3**
EVENT: *75*. **2–4**

MITCHELL, Rubin
Singles: 7-Inch
CAPITOL: *67–68*. **2–4**
LPs: 10/12-Inch 33rpm
CAPITOL: *67*. **8–15**

MITCHELL, Willie (Willie Mitchell & The Four Kings)
Singles: 7-Inch
HI: *62–69*. **3–5**
HOME OF THE BLUES:
60–61. . . . . **4–6**
MOTOWN. **1–3**
STOMPER TIME. **15–20**
Picture Sleeves
HI: *68*. **3–5**
LPs: 10/12-Inch 33rpm
BEARSVILLE: *81* **5–8**
HI (010 through 039):
63–67 . . . . **15–20**
HI (042 through 056):
68–71 . . . . **10–15**
(Hi 010 through 042 used a "12" prefix to indicate mono or a "32" prefix to indicate stereo releases.)
HI (8000 series): *77*. **5–8**
MOTOWN: *82*. **8–10**

MITCHELL TRIO, The: see MITCHELL, Chad, Trio

Price Range

MITCHUM, Robert
Singles: 7-Inch
CAPITOL (Purple label):
58 . . . . **$4–8**
CAPITOL (Orange/yellow
label): *62*. **3–5**
MONUMENT: *67*. **2–3**
LPs: 10/12-Inch 33rpm
MONUMENT: *67*. **10–15**

MIXTURES, The
Singles: 7-Inch
SIRE: *71* **2–4**

MOB, The
Singles: 7-Inch
COLOSSUS: *71–72*. **2–4**
MERCURY: *68*. **3–5**
PRIVATE STOCK: *76–77*. **2–3**
Picture Sleeves
COLOSSUS: *71–72*. **2–4**
LPs: 10/12-Inch 33rpm
COLOSSUS: *71*. **10–12**
PRIVATE STOCK: *75*. **8–10**

MOBY GRAPE
Singles: 7-Inch
COLUMBIA: *67–69*. **4–6**
Picture Sleeves
COLUMBIA: *67*. **20–25**
LPs: 10/12-Inch 33rpm
COLUMBIA (Except 2698
& 9498): *68–72* **10–15**
COLUMBIA (2698 &
9498; "Moby Grape"):
67 . . . . **25–30**
(Cover pictures Don Stevenson's middle finger over washboard. Price includes bonus poster, which represents about $8-$10 of the value.)
COLUMBIA (2698/9498;
"Moby Grape"): *67*. **10–15**
(Cover pictures Don Stevenson's hand closed. Price includes bonus poster, which represents about $4-$6 of the value.The "26" prefix indicates mono, the "94" stereo.)
ESCAPE: *78* **8–10**
HARMONY: *70–71* **10–12**
REPRISE: *71*. **10–12**
SAN FRANCISCO
SOUND: *83*. **10–15**

Price Range

Price Range

Promotional LPs
COLUMBIA (MGS-1;
  "Grape Jam"): *68* **$10–15**
  (With Mike Bloomfield & Al Kooper.)
ESCAPE (95018; "Live
  Grape"): *78* **15–20**
  (Colored vinyl.)
  Also see BLOOMFIELD, Mike, & Al Kooper

MOCEDADES
Singles: 7-Inch
TARA: *74* **2–3**
LPs: 10/12-Inch 33rpm
TARA: *74* **5–10**

MODEL 500
Singles: 12-Inch 33/45rpm
METROPLEX: *85* **4–6**

MODERN ENGLISH
Singles: 12-Inch 33/45rpm
SIRE: *82–84* **4–6**
Singles: 7-Inch
SIRE: *82–84* **1–3**
LPs: 10/12-Inch 33rpm
SIRE: *83* **5–8**

MODERN ROCKETRY
Singles: 12-Inch 33/45rpm
MEGATONE: *83* **4–6**

MODERNAIRES, The (The Modernaires With Paula Kelly)
Singles: 7-Inch
CAPITOL: *69* **1–3**
COLUMBIA (38000
  series): *50* **3–5**
CORAL: *51–56* **2–4**
MERCURY: *59* **2–3**
UNITED ARTISTS: *62* **2–3**
EPs: 7-Inch 33/45rpm
CORAL: *51–55* **3–5**
LPs: 10/12-Inch 33rpm
COLUMBIA: *50–66* **5–15**
CORAL: *51–55* **8–15**
LIBERTY: *84* **4–8**
MERCURY: *60* **5–12**
ROSS: *79* **4–8**
UNITED ARTISTS: *61–62* **5–10**
WING: *62* **5–10**

MODUGNO, Domenico
Singles: 7-Inch
DECCA: *58–64* **$2–4**
MCA: *78* **1–3**
MGM: *66* **1–3**
RCA VICTOR: *68–72* **1–3**
UNITED ARTISTS
  INT'L: *67* **1–3**
EPs: 7-Inch 33/45rpm
DECCA: *58* **4–8**
LPs: 10/12-Inch 33rpm
DECCA: *58–61* **10–20**
RCA VICTOR: *66* **5–10**
UNITED ARTISTS
  INT'L: *67* **4–8**

MODULATIONS, The
Singles: 7-Inch
BUDDAH: *74–75* **2–4**

MOJO MEN, The (The Mojo; Mojo)
Singles: 7-Inch
AUTUMN: *65–66* **8–10**
GRT: *69* **3–5**
REPRISE: *66–68* **4–6**

MOLLY HATCHET (Featuring Danny Joe Brown & Jimmy Farrar)
Singles: 7-Inch
EPIC: *79–85* **1–3**
LPs: 10/12-Inch 33rpm
EPIC: *78–85* **5–8**
Promotional LPs
EPIC (Picture discs, except
  1320): *78–81* **15–20**
EPIC (1320; "Molly
  Hatchet" picture disc):
  78 .... **25–30**
EPIC (1339; "Molly
  Hatchet"): *81* **10–12**
  Also see BROWN, Danny Joe

MOM & DADS, The
Singles: 7-Inch
GNP/CRESCENDO:
  71–75 .... **1–3**
LPs: 10/12-Inch 33rpm
GNP/CRESCENDO:
  71–81 .... **4–8**

Price Range

MOMENT OF TRUTH
Singles: 7-Inch
ROULETTE: 75 . . . . $2–4

MOMENTS, The
Singles: 7-Inch
ERA: 63–64 3–5
HIT: 63 3–5
WORLD ARTISTS: 64 3–5
Also see SHACKLEFORDS, The

MOMENTS, The (The Moments & Whatnauts)
Singles: 7-Inch
STANG: 68–78 2–4
SUGAR HILL: 80–81 1–3
LPs: 10/12-Inch 33rpm
STANG: 70–78 8–10
VICTORY: 82 5–8
Also see O'JAYS, The / The Moments
Also see RAY, GOODMAN & BROWN
Also see SYLVIA & THE MOMENTS

MONAE, Tia
Singles: 12-Inch 33/45rpm
FIRST TAKE: 84 4–6

MONARCHS, The
Singles: 7-Inch
ERWIN: 64 3–5
MONUMENT 1–3
SOUND STAGE 7: 64 3–5

MONDAY, Julie
Singles: 7-Inch
RAINBOW: 66 3–5
SSS INT'L: 68 2–4

MONDAY AFTER
Singles: 7-Inch
BUDDAH: 76 2–4

MONEY, Eddie (Eddie Money & Zane Buzby)
Singles: 12-Inch 33/45rpm
COLUMBIA: 84 4–6
Singles: 7-Inch
COLUMBIA: 78–84 1–3
POLYDOR: 85 1–3
Picture Sleeves
COLUMBIA: 82–84 1–3

Price Range

LPs: 10/12-Inch 33rpm
COLUMBIA: 77–84 . . . . $6–9
POLYDOR: 85 5–8

MONEY, Eddie, & Valerie Carter
Singles: 7-Inch
COLUMBIA: 80 1–3
Also see CARTER, Valerie
Also see MONEY, Eddie

MONGO SANTAMARIA: see SANTAMARIA, Mongo

MONITORS, The
Singles: 7-Inch
BUDDAH: 72 2–4
MOTOWN 1–3
SOUL: 68 2–4
V.I.P.: 65–68 3–5
LPs: 10/12-Inch 33rpm
SOUL: 69 12–15

MONK, T.S. (Thelonious Monk, Jr.)
Singles: 7-Inch
MIRAGE: 80–82 1–3
LPs: 10/12-Inch 33rpm
MIRAGE: 81–82 5–8

MONK, Thelonious
Singles: 7-Inch
COLUMBIA: 63–69 2–4
PRESTIGE: 60–00 2–4
EPs: 7-Inch 33/45rpm
PRESTIGE: 52 10–25
LPs: 10/12-Inch 33rpm
BLACK LION: 74 6–10
BLUE NOTE (100 through
500 series): 73–76 8–12
BLUE NOTE (1500 series):
56 25–50
(Label reads "Blue Note Records Inc. - New
York, U.S.A.")
BLUE NOTE (1500 series):
58 15–25
(Label reads "Blue Note Records Inc. - N.Y.,
U.S.A.")
BLUE NOTE: 63 10–20
(Label reads "Blue Note Records - A Division
Of Liberty Records Inc.")
BLUE NOTE (5000 series):
52 150–200
(10-Inch LPs.)

Price Range

Price Range

COLUMBIA (1900
through 2600 series):
63–67 . . . . **$10–20**
(Monaural issues.)
COLUMBIA (8700
through 9800 series):
63–69 . . . . **10–20**
(Stereo issues.)
COLUMBIA (32000
through 38000 series):
74–83 . . . . **6–12**
EVEREST: 78 . . . . **5–8**
MILESTONE: 75–84 . . . . **6–12**
PAUSA: 83 . . . . **5–8**
PRESTIGE (100 series):
52–54 . . . . **50–80**
(10-Inch LPs.)
PRESTIGE (7000 series):
56–62 . . . . **20–40**
(Yellow labels.)
PRESTIGE (7000 through
7600 series): 65–69 . . . . **10–20**
(Blue labels.)
PRESTIGE (7700 & 7800
series): 70–71 . . . . **8–15**
PRESTIGE (24000 series):
72 . . . . **8–15**
RIVERSIDE (010 through
103): 82–84. . . . . **5–8**
RIVERSIDE (200 & 300
series): 55–60 . . . . **25–50**
(Riverside 200 & 300 series numbers may be
preceded by a "12.")
RIVERSIDE (400 series):
62–67 . . . . **15–25**
RIVERSIDE (1100 series):
58–60 . . . . **20–40**
RIVERSIDE (3000 series):
68–69 . . . . **10–20**
RIVERSIDE (9400 series):
62–63 . . . . **15–25**
TOMATO: 78 . . . . **5–10**
TRIP: 73 . . . . **5–10**
Also see COLTRANE, John, & Thelonious
Monk
Also see DAVIS, Miles, & Thelonious Monk
Also see MERC & MONK
Also see MULLIGAN, Gerry, & Thelonious
Monk

MONK, Thelonious, & Sonny Rollins
EPs: 7-Inch 33/45rpm
PRESTIGE: 52 . . . . **$25–50**
LPs: 10/12-Inch 33rpm
PRESTIGE (100 series): 52 . . . . . . **100–150**
(10-Inch LPs.)
PRESTIGE (7000 series):
57–59 . . . . **25–50**
RIVERSIDE (200 series):
57–58 . . . . **25–50**
RIVERSIDE (1100 series):
58 . . . . **20–40**

MONKEES, The
Singles: 7-Inch
ARISTA (0200 series): 76 . . . . **3–5**
ARISTA (9000 series): 76 . . . . **2–3**
COLGEMS: 66–70 . . . . **5–8**
FLASHBACK: 73. . . . . **2–4**
Picture Sleeves
COLGEMS (1000 series):
66–68 . . . . **5–15**
COLGEMS (5000 series):
69–70 . . . . **5–10**
LPs: 10/12-Inch 33rpm
ARISTA (4000 series): 76 . . . . **8–10**
ARISTA (8000 series): 86 . . . . **5–8**
BELL: 73 . . . . **12–15**
COLGEMS (101; "The
Monkees"): 66 . . . . **30–35**
(With the track "Papa Jean's Blues.")
COLGEMS (101; "The
Monkees"): 66 . . . . **20–25**
(Does not contain the track "Papa Jean's
Blues.")
COLGEMS (102 through
109): 67–68. . . . . **15–20**
COLGEMS (113; "Instant
Replay"): 69. . . . . **30–35**
COLGEMS (115 & 117):
69 . . . . **20–25**
COLGEMS (329; "Golden
Hits") **45–55**
(RCA Special Products issue.)
COLGEMS (1001; "A
Barrel Full Of
Monkees"): 71 . . . . **25–30**
COLGEMS (5008;
"Head"): 68 . . . . **35–40**
LAURIE HOUSE: 73. . . . . **20–25**
(Mail-order LP offer.)

Price Range

Price Range

RCA VICTOR (7000
   series) **$8–10**
RHINO: *82–84* **5–8**
   Members: Michael Nesmith; Davy Jones;
   Mickey Dolenz; Peter Tork.
   Also see DOLENZ, Mickey
   Also see DOLENZ, JONES & TORK
   Also see JONES, Davy
   Also see NESMITH, Michael

MONOTONES, The
Singles: 7-Inch
ARGO (Except 5339):
   58–59 .... **5–8**
ARGO (5339; "Tell It To
   The Judge"): *59* **12–15**
CHESS: *73* **1–3**
COLLECTABLES **1–3**
ERIC **1–3**
HICKORY: *64–65* **3–5**
HULL (735; "Reading The
   Book Of Love"): *60.* **25–30**
HULL (743; "Daddy's
   Home But Momma's
   Gone"): *61* **8–10**
MASCOT: *57.* **60–75**
ROULETTE: *73* **1–3**
   Members: Warren Davis; Frank Smith; John
   Raynes; George Malone; Charles Patrick;
   James Patrick.

MONRO, Matt
Singles: 7-Inch
CAPITOL: *66–72* **2–3**
LIBERTY: *62–66* **2–4**
UNITED ARTISTS: *74* **1–3**
WARWICK: *61.* **2–4**
LPs: 10/12-Inch 33rpm
CAPITOL: *67–70* **8–12**
LIBERTY: *62–66* **8–18**
WARWICK: *61.* **10–20**
   Also see BARRY, John
   Also see LEGRAND, Michel, & Matt Monro

MONROE, Marilyn
Singles: 7-Inch
RCA VICTOR: *54–55* **4–6**
20TH CENTURY-FOX:
   62 .... **3–5**
UNITED ARTISTS: *59* **4–6**
Picture Sleeves
RCA VICTOR: *54–55* **5–15**

EPs: 7-Inch 33/45rpm
MGM (208; "Gentlemen
   Prefer Blondes"): *53* **$15–25**
   (Soundtrack. With Jane Russell.)
RCA VICTOR (593;
   "There's No Business
   Like Show Business"): *55* **10–20**
UNITED ARTISTS: *59* **15–25**
LPs: 10/12-Inch 33rpm
ASCOT (13500; "Some
   Like It Hot"): *64.* **15–20**
   (Monaural issue. Soundtrack.)
ASCOT (16500; "Some
   Like It Hot"): *64.* **25–30**
   (Stereo issue. Soundtrack.)
COLUMBIA (1527; "Let's
   Make Love"): *60* **20–30**
   (Monaural issue. Soundtrack.)
COLUMBIA (8327; "Let's
   Make Love"): *60* **30–40**
   (Stereo issue. Soundtrack.)
COLUMBIA/CSP (8327;
   "Let's Make Love") **8–10**
   (Soundtrack. With Yves Montand & Frankie
   Vaughan.)
MGM (208; "Gentlemen
   Prefer Blondes"): *53* **50–75**
MGM (3231; "Gentlemen
   Prefer Blondes"): *55* **25–40**
   (Soundtrack. With Jane Russell.)
MOVIETONE: *67.* **10–20**
STET **5–10**
20TH CENTURY-FOX:
   62 .... **15–30**
UNITED ARTISTS (272;
   "Some Like It Hot"): *74* **8–10**
   (Soundtrack.)
UNITED ARTISTS (4030;
   "Some Like It Hot"): *59* **30–50**
   (Monaural issue. Soundtrack.)
UNITED ARTISTS (5030;
   "Some Like It Hot"): *59* **40–60**
   (Stereo issue. Soundtrack.)

MONROE, Vaughn
Singles: 7-Inch
DOT: *62–63* **2–4**
JUBILEE: *61* **2–3**
MGM: *60* **2–3**
RCA VICTOR: *50–59* **2–4**
ROD: *68.* **1–3**
UNITED ARTISTS: *60* **2–3**

Picture Sleeves
RCA VICTOR: 57 . . . . $2–4

EPs: 7-Inch 33/45rpm
CAMDEN: 56 4–8
RCA VICTOR: 50–56 5–10

LPs: 10/12-Inch 33rpm
CAMDEN: 56 5–15
DOT: 62–64 8–15
HAMILTON: 65 5–10
KAPP: 65 5–10
RCA VICTOR (11 through
3066): 50–53 15–25
(10-Inch LPs.)
RCA VICTOR (1400
through 1700 series):
56–58 10–20
(12-Inch LPs.)
RCA VICTOR (1100
series): 75 4–8
RCA VICTOR (3800
series): 67 5–10
RCA VICTOR (6000
series): 72 5–10

MONROES, The
Singles: 7-Inch
ALFA: 82 1–3

LPs: 10/12-Inch 33rpm
ALFA: 82 5–8

MONTANA ORCHESTRA, The
LPs: 10/12-Inch 33rpm
MJS: 81 5–8

MONTANA SEXTET
Singles: 12-Inch 33/45rpm
PHILLY SOUND: 83 4–6

MONTANAS, The
Singles: 7-Inch
INDEPENDENCE: 67–69 4–6
WARNER BROS: 66–68 3–5

MONTCLAIRS, The
Singles: 7-Inch
PAULA: 71–74 2–4

LPs: 10/12-Inch 33rpm
PAULA: 72 8–12

MONTE, Lou
Singles: 7-Inch
GWP: 72 . . . . $1–3
RCA VICTOR (5382
through 6600 series):
53–56 4–6
RCA VICTOR (6700
through 7600 series,
except 6704): 56–60 3–5
RCA VICTOR (6704;
"Elvis Presley For
President"): 56 12–15
RCA VICTOR (8700
through 9000 series):
65–67 2–4
RAGALIA: 69 2–3
REPRISE: 62–65 3–5
ROULETTE: 60–61 3–5
Picture Sleeves
REPRISE: 62–63 3–5
EPs: 7-Inch 33/45rpm
RCA VICTOR: 57–59 8–10
LPs: 10/12-Inch 33rpm
CAMDEN: 58 15–20
HARMONY: 68 10–12
RCA VICTOR (1600
through 1900 series):
57–59 20–25
RCA VICTOR (3000
series): 66–67 12–15
ROULETTE: 60 15–20
REPRISE: 61–65 15–20

MONTENEGRO, Hugo (Orchestra & Chorus)
Singles: 7-Inch
RCA VICTOR: 64–75 1–3
TIME: 61–63 2–3
20TH CENTURY-FOX:
59 2–3
LPs: 10/12-Inch 33rpm
CAMDEN: 62 5–10
GWP: 70 5–10
MAINSTREAM: 67–68 5–10
MOVIETONE: 67 5–10
RCA VICTOR (0025
through 2300 series):
72–77 4–8
RCA VICTOR (1113;
"Hurry Sundown"): 67 35–50
(Soundtrack.)

Price Range

RCA VICTOR (2900
  series): *64* **$5–15**
RCA VICTOR (3475;
  "The Man From
  Uncle"): *65*. **25–40**
  (Soundtrack.)
RCA VICTOR (3574;
  "The Man From Uncle,
  Volume 2"): *66* **35–45**
  (Soundtrack.)
RCA VICTOR (3500
  through 4600 series):
  66–71 . . . . **5–15**
RCA VICTOR (6000
  series): *71* **5–10**
TIME: *60–64* **8–15**
20TH CENTURY-FOX:
  59–68 . . . . **5–15**
  Also see HIRT, Al, & Hugo Montenegro

MONTEZ, Chris
Singles: 7-Inch
A&M: *65–68* **3–5**
COLLECTABLES **1–3**
ERA: *72* **2–3**
ERIC **1–3**
JAMIE: *73* **2–3**
MONOGRAM: *62–64* **4–6**
PARAMOUNT: *71–73* **2–3**

LPs: 10/12-Inch 33rpm
A&M: *66–67* **12–15**
MONOGRAM: *63* **35–45**
  Also see CHRIS & KATHY

MONTGOMERY, Melba
Singles: 7-Inch
CAPITOL: *69–76* **1–3**
ELEKTRA: *73–75* **1–3**
MUSICOR: *66–69* **2–4**
UNITED ARTISTS (500
  through 900 series):
  63–66 . . . . **2–4**
UNITED ARTISTS (1000
  through 1100 series): *77* **1–3**

Picture Sleeves
MUSICOR: *66* **2–4**

LPs: 10/12-Inch 33rpm
CAPITOL: *69–75* **6–10**
ELEKTRA: *73–75* **5–10**
MUSICOR: *66–68* **10–15**

Price Range

UNART: *67* **$6–12**
UNITED ARTISTS
  (Except 600 series): *64* **10–20**
UNITED ARTISTS (600
  series): *78* **5–8**
  Also see JONES, George, Gene Pitney & Melba
  Montgomery
  Also see JONES, George, & Melba Montgom-
  ery
  Also see PITNEY, Gene, & Melba Montgom-
  ery
  Also see WEST, Dottie / Melba Montgomery

MONTGOMERY, Tammy
Singles: 7-Inch
CHECKER: *64* **3–5**
SCEPTER: *61* **3–5**
TRY ME: *63* **3–5**
WAND: *62* **3–5**

MONTGOMERY, Wes (The Wes Montgomery Quartet)
Singles: 7-Inch
A&M: *67–70* **2–3**
PACIFIC JAZZ: *60* **2–4**
RIVERSIDE: *61–64* **2–4**
VERVE: *65–68* **2–3**

LPs: 10/12-Inch 33rpm
A&M: *67–70* **8–15**
ACCORD: *82* **5–8**
BLUE NOTE: *75* **6–12**
MGM: *70* **8–12**
MILESTONE: *73–83* **8–15**
PACIFIC JAZZ (5;
  "Montgomeryland"): *60* **15–25**
PACIFIC JAZZ (10000 &
  20000 series): *66–68* **10–15**
RIVERSIDE (034 through
  089): *82–83* **5–8**
RIVERSIDE (300 & 400
  series): *59–67* **15–25**
RIVERSIDE (3000 series):
  68–69 . . . . **10–15**
VERVE: *65–72* **8–18**
  (Reads "MGM Records - A Division Of Metro-
  Goldwyn-Mayer, Inc." at bottom of label.)
VERVE: *73–84* **5–10**
  (Reads "Manufactured By MGM Record
  Corp.," or mentions either Polydor or Poly-
  gram at bottom of label.)
  Also see MONTGOMERY BROTHERS, The

Price Range

Price Range

MONTGOMERY, Wes, & Jimmy Smith
LPs: 10/12-Inch 33rpm
VERVE: 66–69 .... **$8–15**
Also see MONTGOMERY, Wes
Also see SMITH, Jimmy

MONTGOMERY BROTHERS, The
Singles: 7-Inch
RIVERSIDE: 61 .... **2–4**
LPs: 10/12-Inch 33rpm
FANTASY: 60–62. .... **15–25**
PACIFIC JAZZ: 61 .... **15–25**
RIVERSIDE: 61 .... **15–25**
WORLD PACIFIC: 58 .... **20–40**
Members: Wes Montgomery; Buddy Montgomery; Monk Montgomery.
Also see MONTGOMERY, Wes
Also see SHEARING, George, & The Montgomery Brothers

MONTRE-EL, Jackie
Singles: 7-Inch
ABC: 68 .... **3–5**

MONTROSE (With Ronnie Montrose & Sammy Hagar)
Singles: 7-Inch
WARNER BROS: 74–77 .... **2–3**
LPs: 10/12-Inch 33rpm
WARNER BROS: 73–78 .... **6–10**
Also see HAGAR, Sammy

MONTROSE, Ronnie
Singles: 7-Inch
WARNER BROS: 78 .... **2–3**
LPs: 10/12-Inch 33rpm
WARNER BROS: 78 .... **5–8**
Also see GAMMA
Also see MONTROSE
Also see WINTER, Edgar

MONTY PYTHON
LPs: 10/12-Inch 33rpm
ARISTA: 75–82. .... **5–8**
MCA: 83 .... **5–8**
PYE: 75 .... **5–10**

MONYAKA
Singles: 12-Inch 33/45rpm
EASY STREET: 83 .... **4–6**

MOODY BLUES, The
Singles: 7-Inch
DERAM: 68–72 .... **$3–5**
LONDON (Except 200 & 9000 series). **1–3**
LONDON (200 series): 78 .... **2–3**
LONDON (9000 series, except 9726): 65–66. .... **8–10**
LONDON (9726; "Go Now"): 65 .... **4–6**
THRESHOLD (600 series): 81–85 .... **1–3**
THRESHOLD (67000 series): 70–72 .... **2–4**
Picture Sleeves
THRESHOLD (600 series): 81–85 .... **1–3**
THRESHOLD (67000 series): 70–72 .... **2–4**
LPs: 10/12-Inch 33rpm
DERAM (18012; "Days Of Future Passed"): 68. .... **10–15**
(Reissues, using the same catalog number, are currently available.)
DERAM (18017; "In Search Of The Lost Chord"): 68 .... **10–15**
(With gatefold cover. Reissues, using standard cover, are currently available.)
DERAM (18025; "On The Threshold Of A Dream"): 69. .... **10–15**
(With gatefold cover. Reissues, using standard cover, are currently available.)
DERAM (18051; "In The Beginning"): 69 .... **12–15**
LONDON (Except 428): 77–78 .... **8–10**
LONDON (428; "Go Now"): 65 .... **20–25**
(Reissues, using the same catalog number, are currently available.)
THRESHOLD: 69–83. .... **8–12**
Members: John Lodge; Justin Hayward; Graeme Edge; Ray Thomas; Michael Pinder; Patrick Moraz.
Also see EDGE, Graeme
Also see HAYWARD, Justin, & John Lodge
Also see LODGE, John
Also see MORAZ, Patrick
Also see PINDER, Michael
Also see THOMAS, Ray

Price Range

MOON, Keith
Singles: 7-Inch
TRACK: *75* $2–4
LPs: 10/12-Inch 33rpm
MCA: *75* 8–10
Also see LORD SUTCH
Also see WHO, The

MOONEY, Art, & His Orchestra
Singles: 7-Inch
DECCA: *61–62* 1–3
KAPP: *64–65* 1–3
MGM (Except 12312):
50–64 2–4
MGM (12312; "Rebel
Without A Cause"/"East
Of Eden"): *56* 4–6
RIVERSIDE: *62* 2–3
Picture Sleeves
MGM (12312; "Rebel
Without A Cause"/"East
Of Eden"): *56* 10–15
(Billed as a "Tribute To James Dean.")
EPs: 7-Inch 33/45rpm
MGM: *55–56* 4–8
LPs: 10/12-Inch 33rpm
DECCA: *62* 5–10
KAPP: *64* 5–10
MGM: *55–61* 5–15
RCA VICTOR: *67* 5–8

MOONGLOWS, The
Singles: 7-Inch
BIG P: *71* 3–5
CHAMPAGNE: *52* 175–200
CHANCE (1147; "Whistle
My Love"): *53* 375–400
(Colored vinyl.)
CHANCE (1150; "Just A
Lonely Christmas"): *53* 200–225
CHANCE (1152; "Secret
Love"): *54* 200–225
(Blue & silver label.)
CHANCE (1152; "Secret
Love"): *54* 150–175
(Yellow & black label.)
CHANCE (1152; "I Was
Wrong"): *54* 150–175
(Yellow & black label.)
CHANCE (1152; "I Was
Wrong"): *55* 120–125

Price Range

(White & black label.)
CHANCE (1161; "219
Train"): *54* $250–275
CHESS (1581; "Sincerely"):
54 25–30
CHESS (1589; "Most Of
All"): *54* 30–35
CHESS (1598; "Foolish
Me"): *55* 10–12
CHESS (1605; "Starlite"):
55 15–20
CHESS (1611; In My
Diary"): *55* 20–25
CHESS (1619 through
1689): *56–58* 6–10
CHESS (1700 series): *58* 4–6
CRIMSON 3–5
LANA: *64* 3–5
RCA VICTOR: *72* 2–4
TIMES SQUARE: *64* 3–5
VEE JAY: *61* 3–5

EPs: 7-Inch 33/45rpm
CHESS: *59* 25–35

LPs: 10/12-Inch 33rpm
CHESS (701; "The
Moonglows") 10–15
CHESS (1430; "Look, It's
The Moonglows"): *59* 40–50
CONSTELLATION: *64* 15–20
LOST-NITE: *81* 5–8
RCA VICTOR: *72* 10–15

Price Range   *Price Range*

Members: Harvey Fuqua; Bobby Lester; Alex
Graves; Prentiss Barnes; Marvin Gaye; Reese
Palmer; James Knowland; Chester Simmons;
George Thorpe; Dock Greene; Berle Ashton.
Also see DIDDLEY, Bo
Also see FLAMINGOS, The / The Moonglows
Also see GAYE, Marvin
Also see HARVEY & THE MOONGLOWS
Also see LESTER, Bobby

MOONLION
Singles: 7-Inch
P.I.P.: *76* $1–3

MOORE, Bob (Bob Moore & His Orchestra)
Singles: 7-Inch
HICKORY: *65–68* 2–3
MONUMENT: *59–64* 2–4
Picture Sleeves
MONUMENT: *62–63* 2–4
LPs: 10/12-Inch 33rpm
HICKORY: *66* 8–12
MONUMENT: *61–67* 10–20
Also see PRESLEY, Elvis

MOORE, Bobby (Bobby Moore & The Rhythm Aces)
Singles: 12-Inch 33/45rpm
SCEPTER: *75* 5–8
Singles: 7-Inch
CHECKER: *66–68* 3–5
SCEPTER: *75–76* 2–4
LPs: 10/12-Inch 33rpm
CHECKER: *66* 15–20

MOORE, Dorothy (Dorthy Moore)
Singles: 12-Inch 33/45rpm
STREETKING: *84* 4–6
Singles: 7-Inch
GSF: *73* 2–4
HANDSHAKE: *82* 1–3
MALACO: *76–80* 2–3
STREETKING: *84* 1–3
LPs: 10/12-Inch 33rpm
MALACO: *76–78* 5–8
Also see POPPIES, The

MOORE, Dorothy, & Eddie Floyd
Singles: 7-Inch
MALACO: *77* 2–3
Also see FLOYD, Eddie
Also see MOORE, Dorothy

MOORE, Gary
Singles: 7-Inch
JET: *79* $1–3
MIRAGE: *83–84* 1–3
LPs: 10/12-Inch 33rpm
JET: *79* 5–8
MIRAGE: *83–84* 5–8
Also see THIN LIZZY

MOORE, Jackie
Singles: 12-Inch 33/45rpm
COLUMBIA: *79–84* 4–6
Singles: 7-Inch
ATLANTIC: *70–73* 2–4
CATAWBA: *83* 1–3
COLUMBIA: *79–84* 1–3
KAYVETTE: *75–81* 1–3
SHOUT: *68* 3–5
LPs: 10/12-Inch 33rpm
COLUMBIA: *79* 5–8

MOORE, Johnny (Johnny Moore's Three Blazers; Johnny Moore's Blazers; Johnny Moore's New Blazers)
Singles: 7-Inch
BLAZE 8–10
HOLLYWOOD: *55–56* 8–10
MODERN (800 & 900
  series): *53* 8–10
RCA VICTOR (50-0000
  series): *50–51* 12–15
RENDEZVOUS: *60* 4–6
Also see BROWN, Charles
Also see DIXON, Floyd, & Johnny Moore's
Three Blazers

MOORE, Lee
Singles: 7-Inch
SOURCE: *79* 1–3

MOORE, Melba
Singles: 12-Inch 33/45rpm
CAPITOL: *83–84* 4–6
EPIC: *79–80* 4–6
Singles: 7-Inch
BUDDAH: *75–78* 2–3
CAPITOL: *82–85* 1–3
EMI AMERICA: *81–82* 1–3
EPIC: *78–80* 1–3
MERCURY: *69–72* 2–4

Price Range

MUSICOR: 66. . . . . $3–5
    LPs: 10/12-Inch 33rpm
ACCORD: 81 5–8
BUDDAH: 75–79 8–10
CAPITOL: 83–85 5–8
EMI AMERICA: 81. 5–8
EPIC: 79–80. 5–8
MERCURY: 70–72. 10–12
    Also see THOMAS, Lillo, & Melba Moore

MOORE, Tim
    Singles: 7-Inch
ASYLUM: 74–79. 1–3
DUNHILL: 73. 2–4

MORAZ, Patrick
    LPs: 10/12-Inch 33rpm
ATLANTIC: 76 8–10
CHARISMA: 78. 5–8
IMPORT: 77. 8–10
PASSPORT 5–8
    Also see MOODY BLUES, The
    Also see YES

MORGAN, Denroy
    Singles: 12-Inch 33/45rpm
BECKET: 81–82 4–6
    Singles: 7-Inch
BECKET: 81 1–3

MORGAN, Jane
    Singles: 7-Inch
ABC: 67–68 1–3
EPIC: 65–68 2–3
COLPIX: 63–65. 2–4
KAPP: 54–62. 2–4
RCA VICTOR: 69–70 1–3
    EPs: 7-Inch 33/45rpm
KAPP: 55–59. 4–8
    Picture Sleeves
COLPIX: 63 2–4
ELEKTRA: 82 1–3
EPIC: 65 2–4
KAPP: 57–59. 2–4
    LPs: 10/12-Inch 33rpm
ABC: 68 5–8
COLPIX: 63–66. 5–15
EPIC: 65–67 5–10
KAPP: 56–63. 8–18
MCA: 73 4–8

Price Range

RCA VICTOR (Except
  1160): 69–70. . . . . $5–8
RCA VICTOR (1160;
  "Marry Me, Marry
  Me"): 69. 10–15
    (Soundtrack.)
HARMONY: 70 5–8
    Also see WILLIAMS, Roger, & Jane Morgan

MORGAN, Jaye P.
    Singles: 7-Inch
ABC-PARAMOUNT: 65. 2–4
BEVERLY HILLS: 69–72 1–3
MGM: 59–63. 2–4
RCA VICTOR: 54–56 2–4
    EPs: 7-Inch 33/45rpm
DECCA: 55. 5–10
    LPs: 10/12-Inch 33rpm
BAINBRIDGE: 82. 4–8
BEVERLY HILLS: 70. 5–8
MGM: 59–61. 10–15
RCA VICTOR: 55 10–20
    Also see COMO, Perry, & Jaye P. Morgan
    Also see PRESLEY, Elvis

MORGAN, Lee
    Singles: 7-Inch
BLUE NOTE: 64–69 2–4
BUZZ: 79–80. 1–3
VEE JAY: 60. 2–4
    LPs: 10/12-Inch 33rpm
BLUE NOTE (200 series):
  74 6–12
BLUE NOTE (900 & 1000
  series): 79–81 5–8
BLUE NOTE (1500 series):
  56–58 25–50
    (Label gives New York street address for Blue
    Note Records.)
BLUE NOTE (1500 series):
  58 15–25
    (Label reads "Blue Note Records Inc. - New
    York, USA.")
BLUE NOTE (1500 series):
  66 10–20
    (Label shows Blue Note Records as a division
    of either Liberty or United Artists.)
BLUE NOTE (4000 series):
  61 20–40
    (Label gives New York street address for Blue
    Note Records.)

Price Range

BLUE NOTE (4000 series):
62 . . . . $15–25
(Label reads "Blue Note Records Inc. - New York, USA.")

BLUE NOTE (4000 series):
66 10–20
(Label shows Blue Note Records as a division of either Liberty or United Artists.)

BLUE NOTE (4100
through 4200 series): 63 15–25
(Label reads "Blue Note Records Inc. - New York, USA.")

BLUE NOTE (4100
through 4200 series):
66–67 10–20
(Label shows Blue Note Records as a division of either Liberty or United Artists.)

·BLUE NOTE (84000
series): 61 20–40
(Label gives New York street address for Blue Note Records.)

BLUE NOTE (84000
series): 62 15–25
(Label reads "Blue Note Records Inc. - New York, USA.")

BLUE NOTE (84000
series): 66 10–20
(Label shows Blue Note Records as a division of either Liberty or United Artists.)

BLUE NOTE (84100
through 84200 series):
63–69 15–25
(Label reads "Blue Note Records Inc. - New York, USA.")

BLUE NOTE (84100
through 84300 series):
66–70 10–20
(Label shows Blue Note Records as a division of either Liberty or United Artists.)

BLUE NOTE (89000
series): 71 10–15
GNP/CRESCENDO: 73 6–12
JAZZLAND: 62 15–25
MCA: 74 5–8
PACIFIC JAZZ: 81 5–8
PRESTIGE: 81 5–8
SAVOY (12000 series): 56 20–40
SUNSET: 69 5–10
TRADITION: 68 8–15
TRIP: 73 6–10
VEE JAY: 60–65. 15–25

Price Range

MORGAN, Russ, & His Orchestra
Singles: 7-Inch
DECCA: 50–56 . . . . $2–4
EVEREST: 61 2–3
VEE JAY: 64–65. 1–3

EPs: 7-Inch 33/45rpm
DECCA: 51–56 4–8

LPs: 10/12-Inch 33rpm
CAPITOL: 62 5–10
CIRCLE: 81 4–6
DECCA: 51–67 5–15
EVEREST: 60–63 5–12
GNP/CRESCENDO: 73 4–8
MCA: 73 4–8
PICKWICK: 65 4–8
SUNSET: 66 4–8
VEE JAY: 65. 5–10

MORGAN BROTHERS, The
Singles: 7-Inch
MGM: 58–60. 2–4
RCA VICTOR: 55 2–4

MORISETTE, Johnnie
Singles: 7-Inch
SAR: 60–63 4–6

MORLEY, Cozy
Singles: 7-Inch
ABC-PARAMOUNT: 57. 4–6

MORMON TABERNACLE CHOIR, The
Singles: 7-Inch
COLUMBIA: 59 2–3

LPs: 10/12-Inch 33rpm
COLUMBIA: 59–63 5–10
RCA VICTOR: 60 5–10

MORNING MIST
Singles: 7-Inch
EVENT: 71 2–4
Members: Terry Cashman; Tommy West.
Also see CASHMAN & WEST

MORNING, NOON & NIGHT
Singles: 7-Inch
ROADSHOW: 77 2–3

Price Range

MORODER, Giorgio (Giorgio)
Singles: 12-Inch 33/45rpm
COLUMBIA: *84* **$4–6**
MCA: *84* **4–6**
Singles: 7-Inch
BACKSTREET **1–3**
CASABLANCA: *79–80* **1–3**
COLUMBIA: *84* **1–3**
DUNHILL: *72*. **2–4**
EMI AMERICA: *84*. **1–3**
MCA: *84* **1–3**
POLYDOR: *80* **1–3**
VIRGIN. **1–3**
LPs: 10/12-Inch 33rpm
CASABLANCA: *77–79* **8–10**
DUNHILL: *72*. **10–12**
POLYDOR: *80* **5–8**
Also see MERCURY, Freddie / Giorgio Moroder
Also see SUMMER, Donna

MORODER, Giorgio, & Phil Oakey
Singles: 12-Inch 33/45rpm
VIRGIN: *84* **4–6**
Also see HUMAN LEAGUE, The
Also see MORODER, Giorgio

MORRIS, David, Jr.
Singles: 7-Inch
BUDDAH: *76* **2–4**

MORRIS, Gary
Singles: 7-Inch
WARNER BROS: *80–83* **1–3**
LPs: 10/12-Inch 33rpm
WARNER BROS: *82–83* **5–8**
Also see ANDERSON, Lynn, & Gary Morris

MORRIS, Joe, & His Orchestra
Singles: 7-Inch
ATLANTIC (950; "If I
Had Known"): *51* **40–50**
(With vocals by Billy Mitchell & Teddy Smith.)
ATLANTIC (954;
"Someday You'll Be
Sorry"): *52* **20–25**
(With vocal by Billy Mitchell, though not shown as "Featuring" him, as those in the following section.)
ATLANTIC (974; "Bald
Headed Woman"): *52* **20–25**

Price Range

(With vocal by Billy Mitchell, though not shown as "Featuring" him, as those in the following section.)
ATLANTIC (1100 series):
57 .... **$4–6**
HERALD (Black vinyl):
53–54 .... **5–8**
HERALD (Colored vinyl):
54 .... **10–15**
Also see ADAMS, Faye
Also see MITCHELL, Billy

MORRIS, Joe, & His Orchestra
(Featuring Billy Mitchell)
Singles: 7-Inch
ATLANTIC: *51–52* **15–20**
Also see MITCHELL, Billy

MORRIS, Joe, & His Orchestra
(Featuring Laurie Tate)
Singles: 7-Inch
ATLANTIC (965; "Rock
Me Daddy"): *52* **15–20**
Also see MORRIS, Joe, & His Orchestra

MORRIS, Marlowe, Quintet
Singles: 7-Inch
COLUMBIA: *62* **2–4**

MORRISON, Dorthy
Singles: 7-Inch
BUDDAH: *70* **2–4**
ELEKTRA: *69* **2–4**
LPs: 10/12-Inch 33rpm
BUDDAH: *70* **10–12**
Also see HAWKINS, Edwin, Singers

MORRISON, Junie
Singles: 7-Inch
ISLAND: *84* **1–3**

MORRISON, Van
Singles: 7-Inch
BANG: *67–68* **3–5**
MERCURY: *85*. **1–3**
SOLID GOLD: *73* **1–3**
WARNER BROS: *70–83* **1–3**
LPs: 10/12-Inch 33rpm
BANG (200 series): *67–70* **15–20**
BANG (400 series): *74* **10–12**
LONDON: *74* **10–12**
MERCURY: *85*. **5–8**

Price Range   *Price Range*

WARNER BROS: *68–83* **$8–12**
Also see THEM

MORROW, Buddy, & His Orchestra
Singles: 7-Inch
EPIC: *64* **2–4**
MERCURY: *54–62* **2–4**
RCA VICTOR: *50–59* **2–4**
UNITED ARTISTS: *68* **1–3**
WING: *55–56* **2–4**
EPs: 7-Inch 33/45rpm
MERCURY: *54–61* **5–10**
RCA VICTOR: *52–61* **5–10**
LPs: 10/12-Inch 33rpm
EPIC (Except 24095 &
26095): *64–65* **5–15**
EPIC (24095 & 26095;
"Big Band
Beatlemania"): *64* **10–20**
(The "24" indicates monaural, the "26" stereo.)
MERCURY: *54–62* **8–15**
RCA VICTOR (2000 &
2100 series): *59–60* **10–20**
RCA VICTOR (2200 &
0000 series): *60* **5–15**
RCA VICTOR (3100 &
3200 series): *52–54* **15–25**
(10-Inch LPs.)
UNITED ARTISTS: *68* **5–8**
WING: *56* **10–20**

MORSE, Ella Mae (Ella Mae Morse & Freddie Slack)
Singles: 7-Inch
CAPITOL (1600 through
3400 series): *50–56* **3–6**
EPs: 7-Inch 33/45rpm
CAPITOL: *54–55* **5–15**
LPs: 10/12-Inch 33rpm
CAPITOL (H-500 series):
54 . . . . **25–40**
(10-Inch LP.)
CAPITOL (T-500 series):
54 . . . . **20–30**
CAPITOL (1800 series): *62* **8–15**

MORSE, Steve, Band
LPs: 10/12-Inch 33rpm
MUSICIAN/ELEKTRA:
84 . . . . **5–8**
Also see DIXIE DREGS, The

MOSBY, Johnny & Jonie
Singles: 7-Inch
CAPITOL: *67–73* **$2–3**
CHALLENGE: *60* **3–5**
COLUMBIA: *62–66* **2–4**
STARDAY: *65* **2–4**
TOPPA: *61* **3–5**
Picture Sleeves
CAPITOL: *70* **2–3**
LPs: 10/12-Inch 33rpm
CAPITOL: *68–71* **8–12**
COLUMBIA: *65* **10–15**
HARMONY: *70* **6–12**

MOSS, Bill
Singles: 7-Inch
BELL: *69* **2–4**

MOST, Donny
Singles: 7-Inch
UNITED ARTISTS: *76–77* **2–3**
VENTURE: *78* **1–3**
LPs: 10/12-Inch 33rpm
UNITED ARTISTS: *76* **8–10**

MOST, Mickie
Singles: 7-Inch
LAWN: *64* **4–6**

MOTELS, The (Featuring Martha Davis)
Singles: 7-Inch
CAPITOL: *79–84* **1–3**
LPs: 10/12-Inch 33rpm
CAPITOL: *79–84* **5–8**

MOTHER EARTH (Featuring Tracy Nelson)
Singles: 7-Inch
MERCURY: *68–69* **3–5**
REPRISE: *70* **2–4**
UNITED ARTISTS: *68* **4–6**
LPs: 10/12-Inch 33rpm
MERCURY: *68–70* **10–15**
REPRISE: *71* **10–12**
UNITED ARTISTS: *68* **15–20**
Also see NELSON, Tracy

Price Range   *Price Range*

MOTHER'S FINEST
Singles: 12-Inch 33/45rpm
EPIC: 77–79 .... **$4–6**
Singles: 7-Inch
EPIC: 76–79 .... **2–3**
LPs: 10/12-Inch 33rpm
ATLANTIC: 81 .... **5–8**
EPIC: 77–79 .... **5–8**
RCA VICTOR: 72 .... **8–10**
Also see KENNEDY, Joyce

MOTHERLODE
Singles: 7-Inch
BUDDAH: 69..................... **3–5**
LPs: 10/12-Inch 33rpm
BUDDAH: 69–72 .... **10–15**

MOTHERS OF INVENTION, The
(The Mothers)
Singles: 7-Inch
BIZARRE/REPRISE: 70 .... **10–15**
DISCREET: 73 .... **6–10**
VERVE: 66–68 .... **10–20**
Promotional Singles
BIZARRE/REPRISE: 70 .... **12–15**
DISCREET: 73 .... **8–10**
VERVE: 66–68 .... **15–20**
EPs: 7-Inch 33/45rpm
REPRISE (332; "Uncle
Meat"): 69 .... **35–40**
(Promotional issue only.)
LPs: 10/12-Inch 33rpm
BIZARRE (2024; "Uncle
Meat"): 69 .... **20–25**
(Blue label. With 12-page booklet.)
BIZARRE (2024; "Uncle
Meat"): 69 .... **10–15**
(Blue label. Without booklet.)
BIZARRE (2028; "Weasles
Ripped My Flesh"): 70.......... **10–15**
(Blue label.)
BIZARRE (2042; "The
Mothers Live/Fillmore
East"): 71 .... **15–20**
(Blue label.)
BIZARRE (2075; "Just
Another Band From
L.A."): 72 .... **10–12**
(Blue label.)
BIZARRE (2093; "Grand
Wazoo"): 72.................... **10–12**
(Blue label.)

BIZARRE (6370; "Burnt
Weeny Sandwich"): 69 .... **$25–30**
(Blue label. With folder of bonus photos.)
BIZARRE (6370; "Burnt
Weeny Sandwich"): 69 .... **10–15**
(Blue label. Without folder of photos.)
DISCREET: 73 .... **10–12**
MGM: 70–71.................... **25–30**
REPRISE: 73–74................. **8–10**
(Reprise reissues of the Bizarre LPs.)
VERVE (5005; "Freak
Out!"): 66.................... **40–45**
(With mail-order bonus Freak map/poster.)
VERVE (5005; "Freak
Out!"): 66.................... **35–40**
(Without mail-order bonus Freak map/poster.)
VERVE (5013; "Absolutely
Free"): 67.................... **30–35**
VERVE (5045; "We're
Only In It For The
Money"): 67.................... **30–40**
VERVE (5055; "Cruisin'
With Ruben & The
Jets"): 68 .... **30–40**
(With inserts.)
VERVE (5055; "Cruisin'
With Ruben & The
Jets"): 68 .... **25–35**
(Without inserts.)
VERVE (5068;
"Mothermania"): 69 .... **15–20**
VERVE (5074; "XXXX Of
The Mothers"): 69.............. **20–25**
Note: The price range of the Mothers' Verve
LPs is applicable for copies on the blue and the
black Verve labels as well as the white MGM/
Verve labels.
WARNER BROS: 77.............. **8–10**
Promotional LPs
BIZARRE: 69–72 .... **20–30**
(White labels.)
VERVE: 67–69 .... **50–75**
(White or yellow labels.)
Members: Frank Zappa; Jim Black; Roy Estrada; Ray Collins; Elliot Ingber.
Also see CAPTAIN BEEFHEART
Also see DUKE, George
Also see MISSING PERSONS
Also see PRESTON, Billy
Also see RUBEN & THE JETS
Also see ZAPPA, Frank

Price Range

MOTLEY CRUE
Singles: 7-Inch
ELEKTRA: *83–85* $1–3
LPs: 10/12-Inch 33rpm
ELEKTRA: *83–85* 5–8

MOTIVATION
Singles: 7-Inch
DE-LITE: *83* 1–3

MOTORHEAD
Singles: 7-Inch
MERCURY: *80–83* 1–3
LPs: 10/12-Inch 33rpm
MERCURY: *80–83* 5–8
Members: Ian "Lemmy" Kilmister; Phil Campbell; Pete Gill; Mick "Wurzel" Burston.
Also see GLITTER BAND, The
Also see HAWKWIND
Also see SAXON

MOTORS, The
Singles: 7-Inch
VIRGIN: *77–80* 1–3
LPs: 10/12-Inch 33rpm
VIRGIN: *77–80* 8–10

MOTT
Singles: 7-Inch
COLUMBIA: *75–76* 2–3
LPs: 10/12-Inch 33rpm
COLUMBIA: *75–76* 5–8
Also see MOTT THE HOOPLE

MOTT THE HOOPLE (Featuring Ian Hunter)
Singles: 7-Inch
ATLANTIC: *70* 3–5
COLUMBIA: *72–74* 2–4
LPs: 10/12-Inch 33rpm
ATLANTIC: *70–74* 12–15
COLUMBIA: *72–74* 8–10
Also see BRITISH LIONS, The
Also see HUNTER, Ian
Also see MOTT

MOTTOLA, Tony
LPs: 10/12-Inch 33rpm
COMMAND: *62–65* 8–15
PROJECT 3: *67–70* 5–10

Price Range

MOUNTAIN (Featuring Leslie West)
Singles: 7-Inch
WINDFALL: *69–71* $2–4
LPs: 10/12-Inch 33rpm
COLUMBIA: *73–74* 8–10
WINDFALL: *69–72* 10–15
Also see WEST, Leslie
Also see WEST, BRUCE & LAING

MOUTH & MacNEAL
Singles: 7-Inch
PHILIPS: *72* 2–4
Picture Sleeves
PHILIPS: *72* 2–4
LPs: 10/12-Inch 33rpm
PHILIPS: *72–73* 10–12
Members: Will Duyn; Maggie MacNeal.

MOUZON, Alphonse (Alphonse Mouzon Featuring Carol Dennis; Alphonze Mouzon)
Singles: 12-Inch 33/45rpm
PRIVATE I: *84* 4–6
Singles: 7-Inch
BLUE NOTE: *73–74* 2–3
HIGHRISE: *82* 1–3
PRIVATE I: *84* 1–3
LPs: 10/12-Inch 33rpm
BLUE NOTE: *73–76* 5–10
HIGHRISE: *82* 5–8
PAUSA: *81* 5–8
PRIVATE I: *84* 5–8

MOUZON, Alphonse, & Larry Coryell
LPs: 10/12-Inch 33rpm
ATLANTIC: *77* 5–10
Also see CORYELL, Larry
Also see MOUZON, Alphonse

MOVE, The (With Jeff Lynne & Roy Wood)
Singles: 7-Inch
A&M: *67–69* 4–6
CAPITOL: *70* 8–10
DERAM: *67* 4–6
MGM: *71* 8–10
UNITED ARTISTS: *72–73* 3–5
LPs: 10/12-Inch 33rpm
A&M (3181; "Shazam"):
82 5–8

Price Range

A&M (3625; "Best Of The
  Move"): *74* **$15–20**
A&M (4259; "Shazam"):
  69 .... **20–25**
CAPITOL: *71* **20–25**
PICKWICK **10–15**
UNITED ARTISTS: *73* **10–15**
  Also see LYNNE, Jeff
  Also see WOOD, Roy

MOVING PICTURES
  Singles: 7-Inch
NETWORK: *82*. **1–3**
  LPs: 10/12-Inch 33rpm
NETWORK: *82*. **5–8**

MOYET, Alison
  Singles: 12-Inch 33/45rpm
COLUMBIA: *85* **4–6**
  Singles: 7-Inch
COLUMBIA: *85* **1–3**
  LPs: 10/12-Inch 33rpm
COLUMBIA: *85* **5–8**
  Also see YAZ

MOZART, Mickey, Quintet
  Singles: 7-Inch
ROULETTE: *59–61* **2–4**

MR.: see MISTER

MRS. MILLER: see MILLER, Mrs.

MTUME (James Mtume)
  Singles: 12-Inch 33/45rpm
EPIC: *79–84* **4–6**
  Singles: 7-Inch
EPIC: *78–84* **1–3**
  LPs: 10/12-Inch 33rpm
EPIC: *78–84* **5–8**

MUHAMMAD, Idris
  Singles: 12-Inch 33/45rpm
FANTASY: *83*. **4–6**
  Singles: 7-Inch
FANTASY: *80–83*. **1–3**
KUDU: *77–78*. **2–3**
PRESTIGE: *72* **2–3**
  LPs: 10/12-Inch 33rpm
FANTASY: *83*. **5–8**
KUDU: *76*. **8–10**

Price Range

PRESTIGE: *72* **$8–10**

MULDAUR, Maria
  Singles: 7-Inch
REPRISE: *73–76*. **2–3**
WARNER BROS: *78–79* **1–3**
  LPs: 10/12-Inch 33rpm
MYRRH: *82* **5–8**
REPRISE: *73–76*. **8–10**
TAKOMA: *80*. **5–8**
WARNER BROS: *78–79* **5–8**

MULL, Martin (The Martin Mull Orchestra)
  Singles: 7-Inch
ABC: *77*. **2–3**
CAPRICORN: *72–77*. **2–4**
ELEKTRA: *79* **1–3**
  LPs: 10/12-Inch 33rpm
ABC: *77–78*. **8–10**
CAPRICORN: *73*. **8–10**
ELEKTRA: *79* **5–8**
MCA. **5–8**

MULLIGAN, Gerry (Gerry Mulligan Quartet)
  Singles: 7-Inch
PACIFIC JAZZ: *61* **2–4**
PHILIPS: *64* **2–4**
VERVE: *60* **2–4**
  EPs: 7-Inch 33/45rpm
CAPITOL: *53* **20–40**
COLUMBIA: *59*. **10–15**
EMARCY (36000 series):
  56 .... **10–20**
FANTASY: *53*. **20–40**
PACIFIC JAZZ: *53–57* **20–45**
PRESTIGE: *52–53* **25–50**
UNITED ARTISTS: *58*. **10–20**
  LPs: 10/12-Inch 33rpm
A&M: *72* **8–12**
ABC-PARAMOUNT: *58*. **40–60**
BLUE NOTE: *81* **5–8**
CTI: *75*. **6–12**
CAPITOL (400 series): *53* **50–75**
  (10-Inch LP.)
CAPITOL (600 series): *56* **30–50**
CAPITOL (2000 series): *63* **15–25**
CAPITOL (11000 series):
  72 .... **5–10**

Price Range

CHIAROSCURO: *77* **$5–10**
COLUMBIA (1300
  through 8700 series):
  59–63 .... **20–35**
COLUMBIA (34000
  series): *77* **5–8**
CROWN: *63–64* **10–20**
DRG: *80* **5–8**
EMARCY (1000 series): *81* **5–8**
EMARCY (36000 series):
  56–57 .... **25–50**
FANTASY (6; "Gerry
  Mulligan Quartet"): *53* **75–100**
  (10-Inch LP.)
FANTASY (200 series): *56* **25–50**
GRP: *83* **5–8**
GENE NORMAN
  PRESENTS: *52* **50–75**
  (10-Inch LP.)
GENE NORMAN
  PRESENTS: *57–61* **20–40**
  (12-Inch LPs.)
INNER CITY: *80*.................. **5–8**
KIMBERLY: *63* **15–25**
LIMELIGHT (82000 &
  86000 series): *65–66* **10–20**
  (The 82000 series is mono, the 86000 series
  stereo.)
MERCURY (20000 series):
  59 .... **20–40**
ODYSSEY: *68*.................... **8–15**
PACIFIC JAZZ (1
  through 10): *53–54* **60–80**
  (10-Inch LPs.)
PACIFIC JAZZ (7
  through 50): *60–62* **20–40**
  (12-Inch LPs.)
PACIFIC JAZZ (1200
  series): *55–57*................. **25–50**
PACIFIC JAZZ (10000 &
  20000 series): *66* **10–15**
PAUSA: *76* **5–10**
PHILIPS: *63–64* **10–20**
PRESTIGE (003;
  "Mulligan Plays
  Mulligan"): *82*.................. **5–8**
PRESTIGE (100 series):
  52–53 .... **150–200**
  (10-Inch LPs.)
PRESTIGE (7000 series):
  55 .... **25–50**

Price Range

(Yellow label.)
PRESTIGE (7200 series):
  63 .... **$15–25**
  (Yellow label.)
RCA VICTOR (2600
  series): *62* **20–30**
SUNSET: *66* **8–15**
TRIP: *75–76* **5–12**
UNITED ARTISTS (4000
  & 5000 series): *58–61* **20–50**
V.S.P.: *66*...................... **10–20**
VERVE: *58–60* **20–40**
  (Reads "Verve Records, Inc." at bottom of
  label.)
VERVE: *61–72* **10–20**
  (Reads "MGM Records - A Division Of Metro-
  Goldwyn-Mayer, Inc." at bottom of label.)
VERVE: *73–84* **5–10**
  (Reads "Manufactured By MGM Record
  Corp.," or mentions either Polydor or Poly-
  gram at bottom of label.)
WHO'S WHO IN JAZZ:
  78 .... **5–8**
WING: *67* **8–15**
WORLD PACIFIC: *58–59* **25–50**
  Also see BRUBECK, Dave, & Gerry Mulligan
  Also see GETZ, Stan, & Gerry Mulligan

MULLIGAN, Gerry, & Paul Desmond (Gerry Mulligan / Paul Desmond)

LPs: 10/12-Inch 33rpm
FANTASY: *56*.................. **25–50**
  (Colored vinyl.)
RCA VICTOR: *62* **20–30**
VERVE: *58* **20–40**
  (Reads "Verve Records, Inc." at bottom of
  label.)
VERVE: *62* **15–20**
  (Reads "MGM Records - A Division Of Metro-
  Goldwyn-Mayer, Inc." at bottom of label.)
  Also see DESMOND, Paul, & Gerry Mulligan

MULLIGAN, Gerry, & Johnny Hodges

LPs: 10/12-Inch 33rpm
VERVE: *60* **20–40**
  (Reads "Verve Records, Inc." at bottom of
  label.)
VERVE: *64* **15–20**
  (Reads "MGM Records - A Division Of Metro-
  Goldwyn-Mayer, Inc." at bottom of label.)
  Also see HODGES, Johnny

Price Range

MULLIGAN, Gerry, & Thelonious Monk
LPs: 10/12-Inch 33rpm
MILESTONE: 82 . . . . $8–12
RIVERSIDE: 57–58 20–40
Also see MONK, Thelonious

MULLIGAN, Gerry, & Oscar Peterson
LPs: 10/12-Inch 33rpm
VERVE: 57 20–40
(Reads "Verve Records, Inc." at bottom of label.)
VERVE: 63 10–20
(Reads "MGM Records - A Division Of Metro-Goldwyn-Mayer, Inc." at bottom of label.)
Also see PETERSON, Oscar
Also see MULLIGAN, Gerry

MUNDY, Nick
Singles: 7-Inch
COLUMBIA: 84 1–3

MUNGO JERRY
Singles: 7-Inch
BELL: 71–73 2–4
FLASHBACK: 73 1–3
JANUS: 70–71 2–4
PYE: 72–75 2–3
LPs: 10/12-Inch 33rpm
JANUS: 70 10–15

MUNICH MACHINE, The
Singles: 7-Inch
CASABLANCA: 78 1–3
LPs: 10/12-Inch 33rpm
CASABLANCA: 78 5–8

MUPPETS, The (The Sesame Street Muppets)
Singles: 7-Inch
ATLANTIC: 79–81 1–3
SESAME STREET: 78 1–3
Picture Sleeves
ATLANTIC: 79–81 1–3
SESAME STREET: 78 1–3
LPs: 10/12-Inch 33rpm
ARISTA: 77 5–8
ATLANTIC: 79–81 5–8
COLUMBIA: 70–72 5–10
SESAME STREET: 78 5–8

Price Range

WARNER BROS: 71 . . . . $5–10
Also see DENVER, John, & The Muppets
Also see ERNIE
Also see KERMIT
Also see HENSON, Jim

MURAD, Jerry: see HARMONICATS, The

MURDOCK, Lydia
Singles: 7-Inch
TEEN: 83 1–3

MURE, Billy (Billy Mure & The Wild Cats; Billy Mure & The Trumpeteers; Billy Mure & The 7 Karats)
Singles: 7-Inch
DANCO: 65 2–4
EVEREST: 60 2–4
MGM: 60–66 2–4
PARIS: 60 2–5
RCA VICTOR: 57–58 3–6
RIVERSIDE: 63 2–4
SRG: 61 2–4
SPLASH: 58 2–5
STRAND: 61 2–5

EPs: 7-Inch 33/45rpm
RCA VICTOR: 58 8–15

LPs: 10/12-Inch 33rpm
EVEREST: 60–61 15–20
KAPP: 61 15–20
MGM: 59–66 15–20
RCA VICTOR: 57–58 25–30
STRAND: 61 15–20
SUNSET: 67 10–12
UNITED ARTISTS: 59 20–25
Also see TRUMPETEERS, The
Also see WILD-CATS, The

MURMAIDS, The (The Mermaids)
Singles: 7-Inch
CHATTAHOOCHEE:
63–69 4–6
LIBERTY: 68 3–5

LPs: 10/12-Inch 33rpm
CHATTAHOOCHEE: 81 8–10

Price Range

Price Range

MURPHEY, Michael (Michael Martin Murphey)
Singles: 7-Inch
A&M: 72 . . . . **$2–4**
CAPITOL: 74 . . . . **2–3**
EMI AMERICA: 84–85. . . . . **1–3**
EPIC: 74–79 . . . . **1–3**
LIBERTY: 82–84 . . . . **1–3**
Picture Sleeves
EPIC: 74 . . . . **1–3**
LPs: 10/12-Inch 33rpm
A&M: 72–73 . . . . **8–10**
EMI AMERICA: 84–85. . . . . **5–8**
EPIC: 74–78 . . . . **8–10**
LIBERTY: 82 . . . . **5–8**
Also see LEWIS & CLARKE
Also see TRINITY RIVER BOYS, The

MURPHY, Eddie
Singles: 12-Inch 33/45rpm
COLUMBIA: 83–85 . . . . **4–6**
Singles: 7-Inch
COLUMBIA: 83–85 . . . . **1–3**
Picture Sleeves
COLUMBIA: 83–85 . . . . **1–3**
LPs: 10/12-Inch 33rpm
COLUMBIA (Except
picture discs): 82–83 . . . . **5–8**
COLUMBIA (Picture
discs): 83 . . . . **8–10**

MURPHY, Walter (Walter Murphy & The Big Apple Band)
Singles: 12-Inch 33/45rpm
PRIVATE STOCK: 77. . . . . **4–6**
Singles: 7-Inch
MCA: 82 . . . . **1–3**
PRIVATE STOCK: 76–77. . . . . **2–3**
LPs: 10/12-Inch 33rpm
MCA: 82 . . . . **5–8**
PRIVATE STOCK: 76–77. . . . . **5–8**

MURPHYS, The
Singles: 7-Inch
VENTURE: 82 . . . . **1–3**

MURRAY, Anne
Singles: 7-Inch
CAPITOL: 70–86 . . . . **1–3**
Picture Sleeves
CAPITOL: 80–86 . . . . **1–3**

LPs: 10/12-Inch 33rpm
CAPITOL: 70–85 . . . . **$6–10**
Also see CAMPBELL, Glen, & Anne Murray
Also see WINCHESTER, Jesse

MURRAY, Anne, & Dave Loggins
Singles: 7-Inch
CAPITOL: 85 . . . . **1–3**
Also see LOGGINS, Dave
Also see MURRAY, Anne

MURRAY, Mickey
Singles: 7-Inch
SSS INT'L: 67–68 . . . . **3–5**
LPs: 10/12-Inch 33rpm
FEDERAL: 71 . . . . **8–10**
SSS INT'L: 67 . . . . **10–15**

MURRAY, Mickey & Clarence
Singles: 7-Inch
SSS INT'L: 68 . . . . **3–5**
Also see MURRAY, Mickey

MUSCLE SHOALS HORNS, The
Singles: 7-Inch
ARIOLA AMERICA: 77 . . . . **2–3**
BANG: 76 . . . . **2–3**
MONUMENT: 83 . . . . **1–3**
LPs: 10/12-Inch 33rpm
ARIOLA AMERICA: 77 . . . . **5–8**
BANG: 76 . . . . **8–10**
MONUMENT: 83. . . . . **5–8**

MUSIC EXPLOSION, The (Featuring Jamie Lyons)
Singles: 7-Inch
ATTACK: 66. . . . . **8–10**
LAURIE: 67–69 . . . . **3–5**
LPs: 10/12-Inch 33rpm
LAURIE: 67 . . . . **25–30**
Also see KASENETZ-KATZ SINGING OR-
CHESTRAL CIRCUS, The
Also see BLOOM, Bobby

MUSIC MACHINE, The (Featuring Sean Bonniwell)
Singles: 7-Inch
BELL: 69 . . . . **5–8**
ORIGINAL SOUND:
66–67 . . . . **5–8**
WARNER BROS: 68 . . . . **5–8**

Price Range

Price Range

LPs: 10/12-Inch 33rpm
ORIGINAL SOUND: 66 . . . . $25–30
Also see BONNIWELL'S MUSIC MACHINE

MUSIC MAKERS, The
Singles: 7-Inch
GAMBLE: 67–68 3–5
LPs: 10/12-Inch 33rpm
GAMBLE: 68 12–15

MUSICAL YOUTH
Singles: 12-Inch 33/45rpm
MCA: 82–84 4–6
Singles: 7-Inch
MCA: 82–84 1–3
LPs: 10/12-Inch 33rpm
MCA: 82–84 5–8

MUSIQUE
Singles: 12-Inch 33/45rpm
PRELUDE: 78 5–8
Singles: 7-Inch
PRELUDE: 78–79 1–3
LPs: 10/12-Inch 33rpm
PRELUDE: 78 5–8

MUSTANGS, The
Singles: 7-Inch
KEETCH: 64 4–6
PROVIDENCE: 63–64 5–8
SURE SHOT: 64 4–6
VEST 4–6
LPs: 10/12-Inch 33rpm
PROVIDENCE: 64 25–30

MYERS, Alicia
Singles: 12-Inch 33/45rpm
MCA: 81–85 4–6
Singles: 7-Inch
MCA: 81–85 1–3
LPs: 10/12-Inch 33rpm
MCA: 84 5–8

MYLES, Billy
Singles: 7-Inch
COLLECTABLES 1–3
EMBER: 57 8–10
KING: 60 4–6

MYRICK, Gary, & The Figures
Singles: 7-Inch
EPIC: 83–84 . . . . $1–3
LPs: 10/12-Inch 33rpm
EPIC: 83–84 5–8

MYSTIC MERLIN
Singles: 7-Inch
CAPITOL: 80–82 1–3
LPs: 10/12-Inch 33rpm
CAPITOL: 80–82 5–8

MYSTIC MOODS ORCHESTRA, The
LPs: 10/12-Inch 33rpm
PHILIPS: 66–70 4–8
SOUNDBIRD: 78 3–6
WARNER BROS: 72–73 3–6

MYSTICS, The
Singles: 7-Inch
AMBIENT SOUND: 82 2–3
COLLECTABLES 1–3
LAURIE (Except 3104):
   59–61 8–10
LAURIE (3104; "Sunday
   Kind Of Love"): 61 12–15
LPs: 10/12-Inch 33rpm
AMBIENT SOUND: 82 5–8
Also see GARRETT, Scott

MYSTICS, The / The Passions
LPs: 10/12-Inch 33rpm
LAURIE: 79 5–8
Also see MYSTICS, The
Also see PASSIONS, The

MYSTIQUE
Singles: 7-Inch
CURTOM: 77 2–3
LPs: 10/12-Inch 33rpm
CURTOM: 77 5–8

N

N.C.C.U.
Singles: 12-Inch 33/45rpm
UNITED ARTISTS: 77 4–6
Singles: 7-Inch
UNITED ARTISTS: 77 2–3

Price Range

LPs: 10/12-Inch 33rpm
UNITED ARTISTS: 77 . . . . $5–8

NRBQ (New Rhythm & Blues Quintet)
Singles: 7-Inch
BEARSVILLE: 83 1–3
BUDDAH: 74 2–4
COLUMBIA: 69 3–5
KAMA SUTRA: 73 2–4
MERCURY: 78 2–3
RED ROOSTER: 77 2–3
ROUNDER: 80 1–3
Picture Sleeves
RED ROOSTER: 77 2–3
LPs: 10/12-Inch 33rpm
ANNUIT COEPTIS: 76 10–15
BEARSVILLE: 83 5–8
KAMA SUTRA: 72–73 10–12
MERCURY: 78 8–10
COLUMBIA: 69 10–15
RED ROOSTER: 77 8–10
ROUNDER: 79–80 5–8
Also see ANDERSON, Al
Also see PERKINS, Carl, & NRBQ

NV
Singles: 12-Inch 33/45rpm
SIRE: 83–84 4–6
Singles: 7-Inch
SIRE: 83–84 1–3

NABORS, Jim
Singles: 7-Inch
COLUMBIA: 65–74 2–4
RANWOOD: 77 1–3
LPs: 10/12-Inch 33rpm
COLUMBIA: 65–75 5–15
HARMONY: 71 5–10
RANWOOD: 76–82 4–8

NAIROBI & THE AWESOME FOURSOME
Singles: 7-Inch
STREETWISE: 82 1–3

NAKED EYES
Singles: 12-Inch 33/45rpm
EMI AMERICA: 83–84 4–6
Singles: 7-Inch
EMI AMERICA: 83–84 1–3

Price Range

LPs: 10/12-Inch 33rpm
EMI AMERICA: 83 . . . . $5–8
Members: Pete Byrne; Rob Fisher.

NAPOLEON XIV (Jerry Samuels)
Singles: 7-Inch
ERIC: 76 1–3
WARNER BROS (5800
series): 66 5–8
WARNER BROS (7700
series): 73 4–6
LPs: 10/12-Inch 33rpm
WARNER BROS (1661;
"They're Coming To
Take Me Away"): 66 50–60
(With a "W" prefix. Monaural issue.)
WARNER BROS (1661;
"They're Coming To
Take Me Away"): 66 75–100
(With a "WS" prefix. Stereo issue.)
WARNER BROS (1661;
"They're Coming To
Take Me Away"): 66 75–100
(White label. Promotional issue only.)

NASH, Graham
Singles: 7-Inch
ATLANTIC: 71–73 2–4
CAPITOL: 79–80 1–3
LPs: 10/12-Inch 33rpm
ATLANTIC: 71–73 8–10
CAPITOL: 80 8–10
Also see CROSBY, David, & Graham Nash
Also see CROSBY, STILLS & NASH
Also see HOLLIES, The
Also see YOUNG, Neil, & Graham Nash

NASH, Johnny
Singles: 12-Inch 33/45rpm
EPIC: 79 4–6
Singles: 7-Inch
ABC-PARAMOUNT:
57–61 4–6
ARGO: 64–65 3–5
ATLANTIC: 66 3–5
BABYLON: 69 2–4
EPIC: 72–80 1–3
GROOVE: 63–64 3–5
JAD: 68–70 2–4
JANUS: 70 2–4
JODA: 65–66 3–5
MGM: 66–67 3–5

Price Range

WARNER BROS: *62–63* **$3–5**
    Picture Sleeves
ABC-PARAMOUNT:
  59–60 . . . . **4–6**
GROOVE: *63–64.* **4–6**
    LPs: 10/12-Inch 33rpm
ABC-PARAMOUNT:
  58–61 . . . . **15–25**
ARGO: *64* **12–20**
CADET: *73* **10–12**
EPIC: *72–74* **10–12**
JAD: *68–69* **12–15**

NASH, Johnny, & Kim Weston
Singles: 7-Inch
BABYLON: *69* **2–4**
  Also see NASH, Johnny
  Also see WESTON, Kim

NASHVILLE BRASS, The: see DAVIS, Danny

NASHVILLE TEENS, The
Singles: 7-Inch
LONDON: *64–65* **4–6**
MGM: *65–67* **4–6**
UNITED ARTISTS: *72* **3–5**
    LPs: 10/12-Inch 33rpm
LONDON: *64* **20–25**

NATASHA
Singles: 12-Inch 33/45rpm
EMERGENCY: *83* **4–6**

NATIONAL LAMPOON, The
Singles: 7-Inch
BLUE THUMB: *72–73* **3–5**
EPIC (193; "Have A
  Kung-Fu Christmas"):
  75 . . . . **2–4**
  (Promotional issue only.)
    Picture Sleeves
EPIC (193; "Have A
  Kung-Fu Christmas"):
  75 . . . . **4–6**
    LPs: 10/12-Inch 33rpm
BLUE THUMB: *72–74* **10–15**
EPIC: *75–76* **8–10**
IMPORT: *77* **8–10**
LABEL 21 (Except picture
  discs): *80* **5–8**

Price Range

LABEL 21 (Picture discs):
  80 . . . . **$12–15**
NATIONAL LAMPOON:
  74 . . . . **15–20**
PASSPORT **82**
VISA: *78* **5–8**
  Also see BELUSHI, John
  Also see MANCHESTER, Melissa

NATIVE
Singles: 7-Inch
RCA VICTOR: *80* **1–3**
    LPs: 10/12-Inch 33rpm
RCA VICTOR: *80* **5–8**

NATURAL FOUR, The
Singles: 7-Inch
ABC: *69* **2–4**
CURTOM: *74–76* **2–3**
    LPs: 10/12-Inch 33rpm
CURTOM: *74–75* **8–10**

NATURALS, The
Singles: 7-Inch
CALLA: *71* **2–4**
MOTOWN: *72.* **2–3**

NATURE ZONE
Singles: 7-Inch
LONDON: *76* **2–3**

NATURE'S DIVINE
Singles: 7-Inch
INFINITY: *79.* **1–3**
    LPs: 10/12-Inch 33rpm
INFINITY: *79.* **5–8**

NATURE'S GIFT
Singles: 7-Inch
ABC: *74* **2–4**

NAUGHTON, David
Singles: 7-Inch
RSO: *78–79* **1–3**

NAYLOR, Jerry
Singles: 7-Inch
COLUMBIA: *68–71* **2–4**
HITSVILLE: *76* **2–3**
JEREMIAH: *79.* **1–3**
MC: *78* **1–3**

Price Range

MGM: *71–72* $2–3
MELODYLAND: *74–75* 2–3
OAK: *80* 1–3
PACIFIC
    CHALLENGER: *82* 1–3
SKLYA: *61–62* 5–8
SMASH: *65* 3–5
TOWER: *65–68* 2–4
WARNER BROS: *79* 1–3
    Also see ALLAN, Davie
    Also see CRICKETS, The

NAYOBE
Singles: 12-Inch 33/45rpm
THE FEVER: *85* 4–6

NAZARETH
Singles: 7-Inch
A&M: *73–80* 1–3
MCA: *83–84* 1–3
WARNER BROS: *71* 2–4
Picture Sleeves
A&M: *75–80* 1–3
LPs: 10/12-Inch 33rpm
A&M: *73–82* 5–8
MCA: *83–84* 5–8
WARNER BROS: *72* 10–12
    Members: Dan McCafferty; Pete Agnew; Darrell Sweet; Manny Charlton.

NAZTY
Singles: 7-Inch
MANKIND: *76* 2–3
LPs: 10/12-Inch 33rpm
MANKIND: *76* 5–10

NAZZ (Featuring Alice Cooper)
Singles: 7-Inch
VERY RECORD: *67* 175–200
    Also see COOPER, Alice

NAZZ (Featuring Todd Rundgren)
Singles: 7-Inch
SGC: *68–69* 4–6
Picture Sleeves
SGC: *68* 6–12
LPs: 10/12-Inch 33rpm
SGC (5001; "Nazz"): *68* 40–50
SGC (5002; "Nazz-Nazz"):
    69 40–50
    (Black vinyl.)

Price Range

SGC (5002; "Nazz-Nazz"):
    69 .... $50–60
    (Colored vinyl. Pink & orange label. SGC logo is blue. Matrix number is 671531.)
SGC (5002; "Nazz-Nazz"):
    69 75–90
    (Colored vinyl. Mail-order edition. Red & orange label. SGC logo is purple. Matrix number is 671531-MO.)
SGC (5004; "Nazz III"):
    71 40–50
    Also see RUNDGREN, Todd

N'COLE
Singles: 7-Inch
MILLENNIUM: *78* 2–3

NDUGU & THE CHOCOLATE JAM COMPANY
Singles: 7-Inch
EPIC: *80* 1–3

NEELY, Sam
Singles: 7-Inch
A&M: *74–75* 2–3
CAPITOL: *72–73* 2–4
ELEKTRA: *77* 2–3
MCA: *83* 1–3
LPs: 10/12-Inch 33rpm
A&M: *74* 8–10
CAPITOL: *72–73* 8–10

NEIGHBORHOOD, The
Singles: 7-Inch
BIG TREE: *70* 2–4
LPs: 10/12-Inch 33rpm
BIG TREE: *70* 10–12

NEIL & JACK
Singles: 7-Inch
DUEL (508; "You Are My
    Love At Last"): *62* 50–75
DUEL (517; "I'm Afraid"):
    62 50–75
    Members: Neil Diamond; Jack Parker.
    Also see DIAMOND, Neil

NEIL & THE SHOCKING PINKS:
see YOUNG, Neil

Rick Nelson, 53 charted singles (1957–73), 16 charted LPs (1957–81).

Price Range

NEKTAR
Singles: 7-Inch
PASSPORT: 74–75 . . . . $2–4

LPs: 10/12-Inch 33rpm
PASSPORT: 74–76 8–10
POLYDOR: 77 8–10
VISA: 78 8–10

NELSON, Jimmy
Singles: 7-Inch
ALL BOY: 62 4–6
CHESS (1500 series): 53 12–15
CHESS (1800 series): 63 4–6
RPM: 53 12–15
Also see TURNER, Joe / Jimmy Nelson

NELSON, Karen, & Billy T.
Singles: 7-Inch
AMHERST: 77 8–10

NELSON, Phyllis
Singles: 7-Inch
CARRERE: 85 1–3

NELSON, Rick / Joannie Sommers / Dona Jean Young
LPs: 10/12-Inch 33rpm
DECCA: 66 20–25
Also see NELSON, Ricky
Also see SOMMERS, Joannie

Price Range

NELSON, Ricky (Rick Nelson & The Stone Canyon Band)
Singles: 12-Inch 33/45rpm
CAPITOL: 82 . . . . $5–8
Singles: 7-Inch
DECCA: 63–72 3–5
CAPITOL: 82 2–3
EPIC: 77–79 2–4
IMPERIAL (5400 series):
  57 15–20
  (Maroon labels.)
IMPERIAL (5463 through
  5614): 57–59 8–10
  (Black labels.)
IMPERIAL (5663 through
  5985): 60–63 4–6
IMPERIAL (66000 series):
  63–64 3–5
LIBERTY 1–3
MCA: 72–75 2–4
VERVE (10047; "A
  Teenager's Romance"):
  57 10–12
VERVE (10070; "You're
  My One & Only Love"):
  57 10–12
  (One side of this single is by Barney Kessell.)
Picture Sleeves
DECCA: 63 4–6
IMPERIAL: 57–63 5–10

Price Range

Price Range

EPs: 7-Inch 33/45rpm
DECCA: 63–65 .... **$15–20**
IMPERIAL: 57–60 .... **20–30**
VERVE (5048; "Ricky"):
   57 .... **25–30**
LPs: 10/12-Inch 33rpm
CAPITOL: *81* **5–8**
DECCA (4419 through
   4944): *63–67*. **20–25**
   (Decca numbers in this series preceeded by a
   "DL" are mono. Stereo issues are indicated by
   a "DL7" prefix.)
DECCA (75014 through
   75391): *68–72*. **15–20**
EPIC: *77–86* **8–12**
EPIC/NU-DISK: *81*. **8–10**
IMPERIAL (9048 through
   9082): *57–59*. **30–40**
IMPERIAL (9122 through
   9244): *60–63*. **25–30**
   (Imperial 9000 series issues were monaural
   LPs.)
IMPERIAL (12030; "Songs
   By Ricky"): *59*. **30–35**
IMPERIAL (12059; "More
   Songs By Ricky"): *60* **30–35**
   (Black vinyl.)
IMPERIAL (12059; "More
   Songs By Ricky"): *60* **100–125**
   (Colored vinyl. Thus far, colored vinyl copies of
   this LP have always been stereo. If there were
   colored vinyl monos done, we've yet to learn of
   it.)
IMPERIAL (12082
   through 12244): *62–63* **25–30**
   (Imperial 12000 series issues were either stereo
   or reprocessed stereo LPs.)
LIBERTY: *81–83* **5–8**
MCA (Except 1517): *73* **10–12**
MCA (1517; "The Decca
   Years"): *82*. **5–8**
SESSIONS (1003; "Ricky
   Nelson Story"): *76*. **15–20**
   (A 3-LP mail-order offer.)
SUNSET: *66–68* **12–15**
UNITED ARTISTS (330;
   "Very Best Of Rick
   Nelson"): *74*. **10–12**
UNITED ARTISTS (1004;
   "Ricky"): *80*. **8–10**

UNITED ARTISTS (9960;
   "Legendary Masters"):
   71 .... **$12–15**
VERVE (2083; "Teen
   Time"): *57* **35–45**
   (Also contains tracks by Randy Sparks, Jeff
   Allen, Rock Murphy, Gary Williams & Barney
   Kessell.)
   Also see NELSON, Rick / Joannie Sommers
   / Dona Jean Young
   Also see RIVERS, Johnny / Ricky Nelson /
   Randy Sparks
   Also see SOUL SURVIVORS, The

NELSON, Sandy
Singles: 7-Inch
COLLECTABLES **1–3**
ERA: *72*. **1–3**
IMPERIAL: *61–69*. **4–6**
LIBERTY **1–3**
ORIGINAL SOUND: *59*. **5–8**
UNITED ARTISTS: *74*. **1–3**
EPs: 7-Inch 33/45rpm
IMPERIAL: *65*. **8–15**
   (Stereo jukebox "Little LPs.")
LPs: 10/12-Inch 33rpm
IMPERIAL (Except 9105/
   12044): *61–69*. **10–20**
IMPERIAL (9105 &
   12044; "Teen Beat"): *60*. **20–25**
   (Imperial's 9000 series was for mono & 12000
   series for stereo LPs.)
LIBERTY: *82–83* **5–8**
SUNSET: *66–70* **12–15**
UNITED ARTISTS: *75*. **8–10**
   Also see TEDDY BEARS, The

NELSON, Tracy
Singles: 7-Inch
ATLANTIC: *75* **2–4**
CAPITOL: *77* **2–3**
MCA: *75* **2–4**
LPs: 10/12-Inch 33rpm
ADELPHI: *83*. **5–8**
ATLANTIC: *74* **8–10**
COLUMBIA: *73*. **10–12**
FLYING FISH: *78–80*. **5–8**
MCA: *75* **8–10**
PRESTIGE (7303; "Deep
   Are The Roots"): *65*. **15–20**
PRESTIGE (7726; "Deep
   Are The Roots"): *69*. **5–8**

Price Range

REPRISE: *72*..................$10–12
Also see MOTHER EARTH
Also see NELSON, Willie & Tracy

NELSON, Willie
Singles: 7-Inch
AMERICAN GOLD: *76*............2–3
ATLANTIC: *73–75* 1–3
BETTY: *64* 6–10
BELLAIRE (100 series):
  63 15–25
  (Black vinyl.)
BELLAIRE (100 series):
  63 20–40
  (Colored vinyl.)
BELLAIRE (5000 series):
  76 2–3
CAPITOL: *78*.....................1–3
COLUMBIA: *75–84*................1–3
D: *59*...........................8–15
LIBERTY (55000 series):
  61–64 4–6
LIBERTY (56000 series):
  69 2–4
LONE STAR: *78* 2–3
MONUMENT (800 series):
  64 3–5
RCA VICTOR (0100
  through 0800 series)
  69–72 2–4
RCA VICTOR (8500
  through 9900 series):
  65–71 3–5
RCA VICTOR (10000
  through 12000 series):
  75–81 1–3
SONGBIRD: *80* 1–3
UNITED ARTISTS (600
  series): *63*....................4–6
UNITED ARTISTS (700
  through 1200 series):
  76–78 1–3
Picture Sleeves
RCA VICTOR (12000
  series): *81*....................1–3
LPs: 10/12-Inch 33rpm
ACCORD: *83* 5–8
ALLEGIANCE: *83*.................5–8
ATLANTIC: *73–74* 8–12
AURA: *83* 5–8
CAMDEN: *70–74*.................8–12

Price Range

CASINO: *84* $6–10
COLUMBIA (Except
  38250): *75–84*.................5–15
COLUMBIA (38250;
  "Willie Nelson"): *83*...........90–100
  (A 10-LP set.)
DELTA: *82* 5–8
EXACT: *83* 5–8
H.S.R.D.: *84* 8–10
HOT SCHATZ: *84*.................5–8
LIBERTY (3200 series): *62*........25–35
LIBERTY (7200 series): *62*........30–40
LIBERTY (10000 series) 4–8
LONE STAR: *78* 8–12
MCA: *80* 4–8
PICKWICK 8–10
PLANTATION: *82*.................5–8
POTOMAC: *82*...................8–15
RCA VICTOR (1100
  through 3200 series):
  75–79 5–10
RCA VICTOR (3400
  through 4700 series):
  65–72 10–20
  (With an "LPM" or "LSP" prefix.)
RCA VICTOR (3600
  through 4800 series):
  80–83 4–8
  (With an "AYL1" prefix.)
RCA VICTOR/
  CANDELITE: *80* 8–10
SHOTGUN: *77*...................12–18
SONGBIRD: *80* 4–8
SUNSET: *66* 10–18

Price Range

TAKOMA: *83* **$5–8**
TIME-LIFE (16000 series):
  83 .... **12–18**
  (A 3-LP set.)
UNITED ARTISTS: *73–78* **6–12**
  Also see CHARLES, Ray, & Willie Nelson
  Also see COCHRAN, Hank, & Willie Nelson
  Also see DARRELL, Johnny / George Jones
  / Willie Nelson
  Also see DAVIS, Danny, & The Nashville
  Brass, & Willie Nelson
  Also see HAGGARD, Merle, & Willie Nelson
  Also see IGLESIAS, Julio, & Willie Nelson
  Also see JENNINGS, Waylon, & Willie Nelson
  Also see LEE, Brenda, & Willie Nelson
  Also see PRICE, Ray, & Willie Nelson

NELSON, Willie, & Johnny Lee
  LPs: 10/12-Inch 33rpm
QUICKSILVER: *84* **5–8**

**NELSON, Willie / Johnny Lee /
Mickey Gilley**
  LPs: 10/12-Inch 33rpm
PLANTATION: *82*. **5–8**
  Also see GILLEY, Mickey
  Also see LEE, Johnny

**NELSON, Willie / Jerry Lee Lewis
/ Carl Perkins / David Allan Coe**
  LPs: 10/12-Inch 33rpm
PLANTATION: *75*. **5–8**
  Also see LEWIS, Jerry Lee
  Also see PERKINS, Carl

NELSON, Willie, & Dolly Parton
  Singles: 7-Inch
MONUMENT: *82*. **1–3**
  Also see PARTON, Dolly

NELSON, Willie, & Webb Pierce
  Singles: 7-Inch
COLUMBIA: *82* **1–3**
  LPs: 10/12-Inch 33rpm
COLUMBIA: *82* **5–8**
  Also see PIERCE, Webb

NELSON, Willie, & Leon Russell
  Singles: 7-Inch
COLUMBIA: *79* **1–3**
  LPs: 10/12-Inch 33rpm
COLUMBIA: *79*. **5–8**
  Also see RUSSELL, Leon

Price Range

NELSON, Willie, & Roger Miller
  LPs: 10/12-Inch 33rpm
COLUMBIA: *82* **$5–8**
  Also see MILLER, Roger

NELSON, Willie / Faron Young
  LPs: 10/12-Inch 33rpm
ROMULUS **5–8**
  Also see YOUNG, Faron

NELSON, Willie & Tracy
  Singles: 7-Inch
ATLANTIC: *74* **2–4**
  Also see NELSON, Tracy
  Also see NELSON, Willie

NENA
  Singles: 12-Inch 33/45rpm
EPIC: *83–84* **4–6**

  Singles: 7-Inch
EPIC: *83–84* **1–3**

  LPs: 10/12-Inch 33rpm
EPIC: *84* **5–8**

NEON PHILHARMONIC, The
  Singles: 7-Inch
MCA: *76* **2–3**
TRX: *72* **2–4**
WARNER BROS: *69–71* **3–5**

  LPs: 10/12-Inch 33rpm
WARNER BROS: *69* **10–15**

NERO, Peter
  Singles: 7-Inch
ARIOLA AMERICA: *76* **1–3**
ARISTA: *75* **1–3**
COLUMBIA: *69–73* **1–3**
RCA VICTOR: *61–68* **2–4**

  Picture Sleeves
RCA VICTOR: *62–63* **2–3**

  LPs: 10/12-Inch 33rpm
ARISTA: *75* **4–8**
CAMDEN: *67–73* **5–10**
COLUMBIA: *69–75* **5–10**
CONCORD JAZZ: *78* **5–8**
HARMONY: *71* **4–8**
PREMIER: *63*. **10–15**
RCA VICTOR: *61–76* **5–15**

Nervous Norvus, two charted singles (1956), no charted LPs.

Price Range

NERVOUS NORVUS (Jimmy Drake; Nervous Norvus With Red Blanchard)
Singles: 7-Inch
BIG BEN **$10–12**
DOT (15000 series): *56* **10–12**
  (Maroon labels.)
DOT (15000 series): *57* **5–8**
  (Black labels.)
DOT (16000 series): *65* **2–4**
EMBEE: *59* **10–12**

NESMITH, Michael (Michael Nesmith & The First National Band; Michael Nesmith & The Second National Band)
Singles: 7-Inch
EDAN **5–8**
ISLAND: *77* **2–3**
PACIFIC ARTS: *75–79* **2–4**
RCA VICTOR: *70–72* **3–5**
LPs: 10/12-Inch 33rpm
PACIFIC ARTS (Except
  boxed 101): *77–79* **6–10**
PACIFIC ARTS (101;
  "The Prison" - boxed
  edition): *78* **10–15**
  (This LP was also issued in standard LP format. Both issues were packaged with a special book-let.)

Price Range

RCA VICTOR: *70–72* **$10–15**
Promotional LPs
PACIFIC ARTS
("Conversation With
Music-Radio Special"):
79 .... **12–15**
  Also see BLESSING, Michael
  Also see MONKEES, The

NETTO, Loz
Singles: 7-Inch
21: *83* **1–3**
LPs: 10/12-Inch 33rpm
21: *82* **5–8**
  Also see SNIFF 'N THE TEARS

NEVILLE, Aaron
Singles: 7-Inch
AIRECORDS: *63* **3–5**
BELL: *68–69* **2–4**
MERCURY: *72–73* **2–4**
MINIT: *60–63* **4–6**
PAR-LO: *66–67* **3–5**
POLYDOR: *77* **2–3**
SAFARI: *67* **3–5**
LPs: 10/12-Inch 33rpm
MINIT: *67* **15–20**
PAR-LO: *67* **15–20**

NEVILLE BROTHERS, The
Singles: 7-Inch
A&M: *81* **1–3**
LPs: 10/12-Inch 33rpm
A&M: *81* **5–8**
  Members: Aaron Neville; Art Neville; Charles Neville; Cyril Neville.
  Also see METERS, The
  Also see NEVILLE, Aaron

NEW BIRTH (With Harvey Fuqua)
Singles: 7-Inch
ARIOLA AMERICA: *79* **2–3**
BUDDAH: *75* **2–4**
RCA VICTOR: *71–75* **2–4**
WARNER BROS: *76–78* **2–3**
LPs: 10/12-Inch 33rpm
ARIOLA AMERICA: *79* **5–8**
BUDDAH: *75* **8–10**
RCA VICTOR (Except
  LSP series): *73–82* **8–10**
RCA VICTOR (LSP
  series): *70–72* **10–12**

Price Range

WARNER BROS: 77 . . . . **$8–10**
  Also see HARVEY

NEW CACTUS BAND, The
Singles: 7-Inch
ATCO: 73 . . . . **2–4**
LPs: 10/12-Inch 33rpm
ATCO: 73 . . . . **8–10**
  Also see CACTUS

NEW CENSATION, The
Singles: 7-Inch
PRIDE: 74–75 . . . . **2–3**
LPs: 10/12-Inch 33rpm
PRIDE: 74 . . . . **8–10**

NEW CHRISTY MINSTRELS, The
Singles: 7-Inch
COLUMBIA (42000
  series): 62–63 . . . . **3–5**
COLUMBIA (43000 &
  44000 series): 64–69 . . . . **2–4**
GREGAR: 70–72 . . . . **2–3**
WARNER BROS: 79 . . . . **1–3**
Promotional Singles
COLUMBIA (Colored
  vinyl): 63–65 . . . . **4–6**
LPs: 10/12-Inch 33rpm
COLUMBIA (1800
  through 2500 series):
  62–66 . . . . **10–20**
  (Monaural issues.)
COLUMBIA (8600
  through 9300 series):
  62–66 . . . . **10–20**
  (Stereo issues.)
COLUMBIA (9600 & 9700
  series): 68 . . . . **8–15**
GREGAR: 70 . . . . **8–10**
HARMONY: 68–72 . . . . **8–10**
  Members: Randy Sparks; Barry McGuire;
  Kenny Rogers; Mike Settle; Thelma Lou Cama-
  cho; Terry Williams; Mickey Jones.
  Also see FIRST EDITION, The
  Also see McGUIRE, Barry

NEW COLONY SIX, The
Singles: 7-Inch
CENTAUR: 66 . . . . **4–6**
MCA: 74 . . . . **1–3**
MERCURY: 67–70 . . . . **3–5**
SENTAR: 66–67 . . . . **4–6**

Price Range

SUNLIGHT: 71–72 . . . . **$2–4**
TWILIGHT: 73 . . . . **2–4**
Picture Sleeves
MERCURY: 67–68 . . . . **3–5**
LPs: 10/12-Inch 33rpm
MERCURY: 68–69 . . . . **20–25**
SENTAR (101;
  "Breakthrough"): 66 . . . . **70–90**
SENTAR (3001;
  "Colonization"): 67 . . . . **20–30**

NEW EDITION, The
Singles: 12-Inch 33/45rpm
MCA: 84–85 . . . . **4–6**
STREETWISE: 83 . . . . **4–6**
Singles: 7-Inch
MCA: 84–85 . . . . **1–3**
STREETWISE: 83 . . . . **5–8**
LPs: 10/12-Inch 33rpm
MCA: 84–85 . . . . **5–8**
STREETWISE: 83 . . . . **5–8**

NEW ENGLAND
Singles: 7-Inch
ELEKTRA: 80–81 . . . . **1–3**
INFINITY: 79 . . . . **2–3**
LPs: 10/12-Inch 33rpm
ELEKTRA: 80–81 . . . . **5–8**
INFINITY: 79 . . . . **8–10**

NEW ENGLAND CONSERVATORY RAGTIME ENSEMBLE
Singles: 7-Inch
ANGEL: 80 . . . . **1–3**
LPs: 10/12-Inch 33rpm
ANGEL: 73 . . . . **5–8**
GOLDEN CREST: 75 . . . . **4–8**

NEW ESTABLISHMENT, The
Singles: 7-Inch
COLGEMS: 69 . . . . **3–5**
MERCURY: 67 . . . . **3–5**

NEW GUYS ON THE BLOCK, The
Singles: 7-Inch
SUGAR HILL: 83 . . . . **1–3**

Price Range

NEW HOLLYWOOD ARGYLES, The
Singles: 7-Inch
KAMMY: 66 . . . . $3–5
Also see HOLLYWOOD ARGYLES, The

NEW HOPE, The
Singles: 7-Inch
JAMIE: 69–70 3–5
LPs: 10/12-Inch 33rpm
JAMIE: 70 20–25
LIGHT: 72 8–10
Also see KIT KATS, The

NEW HORIZONS
Singles: 7-Inch
COLUMBIA: 83 1–3
LPs: 10/12-Inch 33rpm
COLUMBIA: 83 5–8

NEW JERSEY MASS CHOIR, The
Singles: 12-Inch 33/45rpm
SAVOY: 85 4–6
Also see FOREIGNER

NEW KINGSTON TRIO, The
Singles: 7-Inch
CAPITOL: 71 2–4
Also see KINGSTON TRIO, The

NEW MARKETTS, The
Singles: 7-Inch
SEMINOLE: 76 2–4
LPs: 10/12-Inch 33rpm
CALLIOPE: 77 8–12
Also see MARKETTS, The

NEW ORDER
Singles: 12-Inch 33/45rpm
FACTUS: 83 4–6
QWEST: 85 4–6
STREETWISE: 83 4–6
Singles: 7-Inch
QWEST: 85 1–3
STREETWISE: 83 1–3

NEW RIDERS OF THE PURPLE SAGE, The
Singles: 7-Inch
COLUMBIA: 71–74 2–4
MCA: 76–77 2–3

Price Range

LPs: 10/12-Inch 33rpm
A&M: 81 . . . . $5–8
BUDDAH: 75 8–10
COLUMBIA: 71–74 10–12
MCA: 77 8–10

NEW ROTARY CONNECTION, The
LPs: 10/12-Inch 33rpm
CHESS: 71 8–10
Also see ROTARY CONNECTION, The

NEW SEEKERS, The
Singles: 7-Inch
ELEKTRA: 70–72 2–4
MGM/VERVE: 73 2–3
Picture Sleeves
MGM/VERVE: 73 2–3
EPs: 7-Inch 33/45rpm
COCA-COLA: 69 3–6
(Promotional issue only.)
LPs: 10/12-Inch 33rpm
ELEKTRA: 71–72 10–12
MGM/VERVE: 73 8–10
Also see SEEKERS, The

NEW VAUDEVILLE BAND, The
Singles: 7-Inch
FONTANA: 66–68 2–4
LPs: 10/12-Inch 33rpm
FONTANA: 67 10–15

NEW VENTURES, The: see VENTURES, The

NEW YORK CITI PEECH BOYS, The
Singles: 12-Inch 33/45rpm
GARAGE: 83–84 4–6
ISLAND: 83–84 4–6
Singles: 7-Inch
ISLAND: 83–84 1–3
LPs: 10/12-Inch 33rpm
ISLAND: 84 5–8

NEW YORK CITY
Singles: 7-Inch
CHELSEA: 73–75 2–4
LPs: 10/12-Inch 33rpm
CHELSEA: 73–77 10–12
Also see CADILLACS, The
Also see FIVE SATINS, The

Price Range

NEW YORK COMMUNITY CHOIR, The
Singles: 7-Inch
RCA VICTOR: 77 .... $2–3

NEW YORK DOLLS, The
Singles: 7-Inch
MERCURY: 73–76 3–5
Picture Sleeves
MERCURY: 73 4–6
LPs: 10/12-Inch 33rpm
MERCURY (675; "New
   York Dolls"): 73 15–20
MERCURY (1001; "Too
   Much Too Soon"): 74 10–15
REACH OUT INT'L: 81 5–8
   Also see JOHANSEN, David
   Also see SYLVAIN SYLVAIN
   Also see W.A.S.P.

NEW YORKERS, The
Singles: 7-Inch
WALL: 61 8–10
   Members: Fred Parris; Richard Freeman; Wesley Forbes; Louis Peebles; Silvester Hopkins.
   Also see FIVE SATINS, The

NEW YOUNG HEARTS, The
Singles: 7-Inch
ZEA: 70 2–4

NEWBEATS, The
Singles: 7-Inch
ABC: 74 1–3
HICKORY: 64–72 3–5
PLAYBOY: 74 2–3
LPs: 10/12-Inch 33rpm
HICKORY (Except 128):
   64–65 15–20
HICKORY (128; "Run
   Baby Run"): 65 20–25
   Members: Larry Henley; Dean Mathis; Mark Mathis.
   Also see DEAN & MARC

NEWBERRY, Booker, III
Singles: 12-Inch 33/45rpm
BOARDWALK: 83 4–6
Singles: 7-Inch
BOARDWALK: 83 1–3

Price Range

NEWBURY, Mickey
Singles: 7-Inch
ELEKTRA: 71–73 .... $2–3
HICKORY: 65–68 2–4
MERCURY: 69–70 2–4
RCA VICTOR: 68–70 2–4
Picture Sleeves
RCA VICTOR: 68 2–4
LPs: 10/12-Inch 33rpm
ABC/HICKORY: 77–79 8–10
MCA 5–8
ELEKTRA: 71–73 8–10
MERCURY: 69 10–12
RCA VICTOR: 68–72 10–12

NEWCLEUS
Singles: 12-Inch 33/45rpm
SUNNYVIEW: 83–85 4–6
Singles: 7-Inch
SUNNYVIEW: 83–85 1–3
LPs: 10/12-Inch 33rpm
SUNNYVIEW: 84 5–8

NEWCOMERS, The
Singles: 7-Inch
GIGOLO: 65 3–5
STAX: 71 2–4
TRUTH: 74–75 2–3
VOLT: 69 2–4

NEWHART, Bob
LPs: 10/12-Inch 33rpm
HARMONY: 69 8–15

Price Range

WARNER BROS (1300
through 1500 series):
60–65 . . . . **$15–30**
WARNER BROS (1600
through 1700 series):
66–67 . . . . **10–20**

NEWLEY, Anthony
Singles: 7-Inch
KAPP: 69 . . . . **2–3**
LONDON: 58–63 . . . . **2–5**
MGM: 71–74. . . . . **1–3**
RCA VICTOR: 66–67 . . . . **2–3**
UNITED ARTISTS: 76–77. . . . . **1–3**
WARNER BROS: 68. . . . . **2–3**
LPs: 10/12-Inch 33rpm
BELL: 71. . . . . **8–10**
LONDON: 62–66 . . . . **10–20**
MGM: 71–73. **8–12**
RCA VICTOR: 64–69 . . . . **8–15**
UNITED ARTISTS: 77. . . . . **5–8**

NEWMAN, Jimmy C. (Jimmy Newman; Jimmy C. Newman & Cajun Country)
Singles: 7-Inch
DECCA: 60–71 . . . . **2–4**
DOT: 54–57. . . . . **3–5**
MGM: 58–60. . . . . **3–5**
MONUMENT: 72. . . . . **2–3**
PLANTATION: 76–80. . . . . **1–3**
SHANNON: 73. **2–3**
EPs: 7-Inch 33/45rpm
DECCA: 64 . . . . **5–8**
LPs: 10/12-Inch 33rpm
CROWN **8–12**
DECCA: 62–70. . . . . **10–20**
DELTA: 82 . . . . **5–8**
DOT: 66. . . . . **10–18**
LA LOUISANNE. **5–8**
MGM: 59–62. . . . . **15–25**
PICKWICK/HILLTOP. **8–12**
PLANTATION: 77–81. . . . . **5–8**
SWALLOW. **5–8**

NEWMAN, Jimmy C., Danny Davis & The Nashville Brass
Singles: 7-Inch
RCA VICTOR: 80 . . . . **1–3**
Also see DAVIS, Danny
Also see NEWMAN, Jimmy C.

Price Range

NEWMAN, Randy
Singles: 78rpm
REPRISE: 78. **$4–6**
(Promotional issue only.)

Singles: 7-Inch
CHELSEA: 74. **2–3**
DOT: 62. . . . . **3–5**
REPRISE: 68–78. . . . . **2–4**
WARNER BROS: 77–85 . . . . **1–3**

LPs: 10/12-Inch 33rpm
EPIC (147; "Peyton
Place"): 65 . . . . **20–25**
(TV Soundtrack.)
REPRISE (Except 6286):
70–74 . . . . **6–10**
REPRISE (6286; "Randy
Newman"): 68 . . . . **10–12**
(Cover pictures Randy in sweater & coat.)
REPRISE (6286; "Randy
Newman"): 68 . . . . **12–15**
(Cover picture is a close-up of Randy.)
WARNER BROS: 77–85 . . . . **5–8**
Also see BISHOP, Stephen
Also see EAGLES, The
Also see McVIE, Christine
Also see RONSTADT, Linda
Also see SEGER, Bob

NEWMAN, Randy, & Paul Simon
Singles: 7-Inch
WARNER BROS: 83 . . . . **1–3**
Also see NEWMAN, Randy
Also see SIMON, Paul

NEWMAN, Ted
Singles: 7-Inch
REV: 57. . . . . **4–6**

NEWMAN, Thunderclap
Singles: 7-Inch
MCA. **1–3**
TRACK (2000 series):
69–70 . . . . **4–6**
TRACK (60000 series): 75. . . . . **2–4**

LPs: 10/12-Inch 33rpm
ATLANTIC/TRACK: 70 . . . . **12–15**
MCA/TRACK: 73 . . . . **6–10**
Members: Andy Newman; Jimmy McCulloch;
Speedy Keen.
Also see McCARTNEY, Paul

Price Range

NEWSOME, Bobby
Singles: 7-Inch
SPRING: 72 . . . . $2–4

NEWSOME, Frankie
Singles: 7-Inch
GWP: 69 2–4

NEWTON, Juice
Singles: 7-Inch
CAPITOL: 78–84 1–3
RCA VICTOR: 84–85 1–3
Picture Sleeves
CAPITOL: 78–84 1–3
RCA VICTOR: 84–85 . . . . INC
LPs: 10/12-Inch 33rpm
CAPITOL: 78–84 5–8
RCA VICTOR: 84–85 5–8

NEWTON, Juice, & Silver Spur
Singles: 7-Inch
CAPITOL: 77 2–3
RCA VICTOR: 75–76 2–4
LPs: 10/12-Inch 33rpm
CAPITOL (11000 series):
77 8–10
CAPITOL (16000 series):
81 4–8
RCA VICTOR (1000
series): 75 8–12
RCA VICTOR (4000
series): 81 4–8
Also see NEWTON, Juice

NEWTON, Wayne
Singles: 7-Inch
ARIES II: 79–80 1–3
CAPITOL (Except 5338):
63–71 2–5
CAPITOL (5338; "Comin'
On Too Strong"): 64 10–15
(With Bruce Johnston & Terry Melcher.)
CHALLENGE: 64 3–5
CHELSEA: 72–76 1–3
GEORGE: 62 4–6
MGM: 68 2–3
20TH CENTURY-FOX:
78 1–3
WARNER BROS: 70–77 1–3
Picture Sleeves
CAPITOL: 65–66 2–5

WAYNE NEWTON

Price Range

LPs: 10/12-Inch 33rpm
AIRES II: 79–80 . . . . $5–8
CAMDEN: 74 5–10
CAPITOL (573; "Wayne
Newton"): 70 10–20
(A 3-LP set.)
CAPITOL (1973 through
2797): 63–67 10–20
(With a "T" or "ST" prefix.)
CAPITOL (2300 series): 75 5–8
(With an "SM" prefix.)
CAPITOL (11000 series):
79 5–8
CAPITOL (16000 series):
80 5–8
MGM: 68 8–12
MUSICOR: 79 5–8
20TH CENTURY-FOX:
78 5–8
Also see BRUCE & TERRY

NEWTON BROTHERS, The
Singles: 7-Inch
CAPITOL: 59 4–6
GEORGE (Except 7778):
61 5–8
GEORGE (7778; "Little
Jukebox"): 61 8–10
(Shown as by The Newton Brothers Featuring
Wayne.)
Members: Wayne Newton; Jerry Newton.
Also see NEWTON RASCALS

Price Range

NEWTON RASCALS, The
Singles: 7-Inch
RANGER RECORDS
(401; "If The Easter
Bunny Knew The Fun
He'd Have On Xmas"):
58 . . . . **$10-15**
(Issued with a paper insert, picturing 12-year-old Wayne & 14-year-old Jerry as "The Rascals In Rhythm." The value of the insert is about the same as shown for the disc.)
Members: Wayne Newton; Jerry Newton.
Also see NEWTON, Wayne
Also see NEWTON BROTHERS, The

NEWTON-JOHN, Olivia
Singles: 12-Inch 33/45rpm
MCA (Except 1150): *81–84* **4–6**
MCA (1150; "Twist Of
Fate"): *83* **5–8**
(Promotional issue only.)
Singles: 7-Inch
KIRSHNER: *70* **5–8**
MCA: *73–84* **1–3**
RSO: *78* **1–3**
UNI (55281; "If Not For
You"): *71* **3–5**
UNI (55304; "Banks Of
The Ohio"): *71* **4–6**
UNI (55317; "What Is
Life"): *72* **4–6**
UNI (55348; "Just A Little
Too Much"): *72* **8–10**
Promotional Singles
MCA ("Deeper Than The
Night"): *79* **25–30**
(Picture disc.)
WHAT'S IT ALL
ABOUT: *74* **25–30**
Picture Sleeves
MCA (Except 40418):
73–84 . . . . **2–5**
MCA (40418; "Please Mr.
Please"): *75* **6–10**
EPs: 7-Inch 33/45rpm
MCA: *73* **12–15**
(Promotional issue only.)
LPs: 10/12-Inch 33rpm
MCA (389; "Let Me Be
There"): *73* **10–12**
MCA (411; "If You Love
Me, Let Me Know"): *74* **12–15**

Price Range

(With "I Love You, I Honestly Love You." Note longer title.)
MCA (411; "If You Love
Me, Let Me Know"): *74* **$8–10**
(With "I Honestly Love You." Note shorter title.)
MCA (2000 & 3000 series):
75–78 . . . . **8–10**
MCA (5000 & 6000 series):
80–83 . . . . **5–8**
MCA (37000 series): *80–83* **5–8**
MFSL: *81* **12–15**
UNI: *71* **20–25**
Also see DENVER, John, & Olivia Newton-John
Also see FOSTER, David, & Olivia Newton-John
Also see WILSON, Carl

NEWTON-JOHN, Olivia, & The Electric Light Orchestra
Singles: 7-Inch
MCA: *80* **1–3**
Picture Sleeves
MCA: *80* **1–3**
Also see ELECTRIC LIGHT ORCHESTRA, The

NEWTON-JOHN, Olivia, & Andy Gibb
Singles: 12-Inch 33/45rpm
POLYDOR (104; "Rest
Your Love On Me"): *79* **10–15**
Singles: 7-Inch
RSO: *80* **1–3**
Also see GIBB, Andy

NEWTON-JOHN, Olivia, & Cliff Richard
Singles: 7-Inch
MCA: *80* **1–3**
Picture Sleeves
MCA: *80* **1–3**
Also see RICHARD, Cliff

NEWTON-JOHN, Olivia, & John Travolta
Singles: 7-Inch
RSO: *78* **1–3**
Picture Sleeves
RSO: *78* **1–3**
Also see NEWTON-JOHN, Olivia
Also see TRAVOLTA, John

Price Range

NEXT MOVEMENT
Singles: 7-Inch
NUANCE: *84* **$1–3**

NICE, The (Featuring Keith Emerson)
Singles: 7-Inch
IMMEDIATE: *68*................. **3–5**
MERCURY: *70*................... **2–4**
LPs: 10/12-Inch 33rpm
CHARISMA **8–10**
COLUMBIA **8–10**
IMMEDIATE: *68–71*............ **10–15**
MERCURY: *71–72*.............. **10–12**
SIRE: *75* **10–12**
Also see EMERSON, Keith, & The Nice

NICHOLAS, Paul
Singles: 7-Inch
COLUMBIA: *74*.................. **2–4**
RSO: *76–78* **2–3**
LPs: 10/12-Inch 33rpm
RSO: *77*........................ **5–10**

NICHOLS, Mike, & Elaine May
LPs: 10/12-Inch 33rpm
MERCURY: *59–72*.............. **10–20**

NICK & ELVIS
Singles: 12-Inch 33/45rpm
COLUMBIA: *84*.................. **4–6**
Members: Nick Lowe; Elvis Costello.
Also see COSTELLO, Elvis
Also see LOWE, Nick

NICKIE LEE: see LEE, Nickie

NICKS, Stevie
Singles: 12-Inch 33/45rpm
MODERN: *81–82*................. **5–8**
Singles: 7-Inch
MODERN: *81–84*................. **1–3**
Picture Sleeves
MODERN: *81–84*................. **1–3**
LPs: 10/12-Inch 33rpm
MODERN: *81–83*................. **5–8**
Also see BUCKINGHAM NICKS
Also see EGAN, Walter
Also see FLEETWOOD MAC
Also see LOGGINS, Kenny, & Steve Perry
Also see STEWART, John

Price Range

NICKS, Stevie, & Don Henley
Singles: 7-Inch
MODERN: *81*.................... **$1–3**
Also see HENLEY, Don

NICKS, Stevie, Tom Petty & The Heartbreakers
Singles: 7-Inch
MODERN: *81*.................... **1–3**
Also see NICKS, Stevie
Also see PETTY, Tom, & The Heartbreakers

NICOLE
Singles: 7-Inch
PORTRAIT: *85*................... **1–3**

NIELSEN-PEARSON BAND, The
Singles: 7-Inch
CAPITOL: *80–83* **1–3**
EPIC: *78* **2–3**
LPs: 10/12-Inch 33rpm
CAPITOL: *80–81* **5–8**
EPIC: *78* **5–8**
Members: Reid Nielsen; Mark Pearson.

NIGHT (With Chris Thompson)
Singles: 7-Inch
PLANET: *79–81*.................. **1–3**
Picture Sleeves
PLANET: *80–81*.................. **1–3**
LPs: 10/12-Inch 33rpm
PLANET: *79–80*................. **8–10**
Also see MANN, Manfred
Also see THOMPSON, Chris, & Night

NIGHT RANGER
Singles: 7-Inch
BOARDWALK: *83* **1–3**
MCA: *83–85* **1–3**
LPs: 10/12-Inch 33rpm
BOARDWALK: *82* **8–10**
MCA: *83–84* **5–8**

NIGHTCRAWLERS, The
Singles: 7-Inch
KAPP: *66–67*..................... **4–6**
LEE: *66* **10–12**
LPs: 10/12-Inch 33rpm
KAPP: *67* **25–30**

NIGHTHAWK
Singles: 7-Inch
QUALITY: *82*.................... **1–3**

Price Range

NIGHTHAWKS, The
LPs: 10/12-Inch 33rpm
ADELPHI: *76–82* **$6–10**
ALADDIN: *75* **35–40**
CHESAPEAKE: *83* **5–8**
VARRICK: *83.* **5–8**
MERCURY: *80.* **5–8**

NIGHTINGALE, Maxine
Singles: 7-Inch
A&M: *81* **1–3**
HIGHRISE: *82* **1–3**
RCA VICTOR: *80* **1–3**
UNITED ARTISTS: *76* **2–3**
WINDSONG: *79.* **1–3**
LPs: 10/12-Inch 33rpm
UNITED ARTISTS: *77* **8–10**
WINDSONG: *80.* **5–8**

NIGHTINGALE, Maxine, & Jimmy Ruffin
Singles: 7-Inch
HIGHRISE: *82* **1–3**
Also see NIGHTINGALE, Maxine
Also see RUFFIN, Jimmy

NIGHTINGALE, Ollie
Singles: 7-Inch
MEMPHIS: *71.* **2–4**
PATHFINDER: *78.* **1–3**
PRIDE: *72–73* **2–4**
LPs: 10/12-Inch 33rpm
PRIDE: *73* **8–12**

Price Range

NILE, Willie
Singles: 7-Inch
ARISTA: *80–81* **$1–3**
LPs: 10/12-Inch 33rpm
ARISTA: *80–81* **5–8**

NILSSON (Harry Nilsson & The New Salvation Singers)
Singles: 7-Inch
POLYDOR: *85* **1–3**
RCA VICTOR: *67–77* **2–4**
TOWER (100 series):
64–65 .... **3–5**
TOWER (500 series): *69* **2–4**
Picture Sleeves
RCA VICTOR: *74–77* **2–4**
LPs: 10/12-Inch 33rpm
51 WEST **5–8**
MUSICOR: *77.* **8–10**
POLYDOR: *85* **5–8**
RCA VICTOR (0097
through 0817): *73–75* **8–10**
RCA VICTOR (1003;
"The Point"): *71* **10–12**
RCA VICTOR (1031
through 3811): *76–80* **5–8**
RCA VICTOR (3874;
"Pandemonium Shadow
Show"): *67.* **12–18**
RCA VICTOR (3956;
"Aerial Ballet"): *68.* **12–15**
RCA VICTOR (4197
through 4717): *69–72* **8–12**
SPRINGBOARD: *78* **5–8**
TOWER: *69.* **10–15**
Promotional LPs
RCA VICTOR (567;
"Scatalogue") **25–30**
Also see CHER & NILSSON
Also see STARR, Ringo

NIMOY, Leonard
Singles: 7-Inch
DOT: *67–69* **2–5**
LPs: 10/12-Inch 33rpm
DOT: *67–69.* **10–20**
PARAMOUNT: *74.* **8–12**

9TH CREATION, The
Singles: 7-Inch
HILLTAK: *79–80.* **1–3**

Price Range   *Price Range*

PRELUDE: *77.* **$2–3**

LPs: 10/12-Inch 33rpm
PRELUDE: *77.* **8–10**
RITE TRACK. **10–12**

9.9
Singles: 12-Inch 33/45rpm
RCA VICTOR: *85* **4–6**

Singles: 7-Inch
RCA VICTOR: *85* **1–3**

LPs: 10/12-Inch 33rpm
RCA VICTOR: *85* **5–8**

999
Singles: 7-Inch
POLYDOR: *81* **1–3**

LPs: 10/12-Inch 33rpm
PVC: *79* **5–8**
POLYDOR: *80–81* **5–8**

1910 FRUITGUM COMPANY, The
Singles: 7-Inch
ATTACK: *70.* **3–5**
BUDDAH: *67–69* **3–5**
SUPER K: *70* **3–5**

LPs: 10/12-Inch 33rpm
BUDDAH: *68–70* **12–15**
Also see KASENETZ-KATZ SINGING OR-
CHESTRAL CIRCUS, The

1910 FRUITGUM COMPANY, The
/ The Lemon Pipers
LPs: 10/12-Inch 33rpm
BUDDAH: *68–70* **12–15**
Also see LEMON PIPERS, The
Also see 1910 FRUITGUM COMPANY, The

NINO & THE EBB TIDES
(Featuring Nino Aiello)
Singles: 7-Inch
MADISON: *61* **8–10**
MALA: *64.* **8–10**
MARCO: *61* **5–8**
MR. PEACOCK: *61–62.* **10–12**
MR. PEEKE: *63.* **8–10**
RECORTE (Except 408):
58–59 . . . . **20–25**

RECORTE (408; "The
Real Meaning Of
Christmas"): *58* **$30–35**

NITEFLYTE
Singles: 7-Inch
ARIOLA AMERICA:
79–81 . . . . **1–3**

LPs: 10/12-Inch 33rpm
ARIOLA AMERICA:
79–81 . . . . **5–8**
Also see JOHNSON, Howard

NITE-LITERS, The
Singles: 7-Inch
RCA VICTOR: *71–72* **2–4**

LPs: 10/12-Inch 33rpm
RCA VICTOR: *71–72* **8–10**

NITTY GRITTY DIRT BAND, The
(The Dirt Band)
Singles: 7-Inch
LIBERTY (1000 series):
81–84 . . . . **1–3**
LIBERTY (50000 series):
67–70 . . . . **3–5**
UNITED ARTISTS: *71–80* **2–4**
WARNER BROS: *84–85* **1–3**

Picture Sleeves
LIBERTY (1000 series):
81–84 . . . . **1–3**
LIBERTY (50000 series):
67 . . . . **3–5**
UNITED ARTISTS: *71–80* **2–4**

EPs: 7-Inch 33/45rpm
UNITED ARTISTS (69;
"All The Good Times"):
71 . . . . **20–25**
(Promotional issue only.)

LPs: 10/12-Inch 33rpm
LIBERTY (Except 7000
series): *81* **5–8**
LIBERTY (7501 through
7611): *67–69.* **12–15**
LIBERTY (7642; "Uncle
Charlie"): *70* **12–15**
(With an "LST" prefix.)
LIBERTY (7642; "Uncle
Charlie") **5–8**
(With an "LTAO" prefix.)

Price Range

UNITED ARTISTS (184;
"Stars & Stripes
Forever"): *74* $12–15
(With a "UA-LA" prefix.)
UNITED ARTISTS (184;
"Stars & Stripes
Forever") 8–10
(With an "LWB" prefix.)
UNITED ARTISTS (469;
"Dream"): *75* 8–10
UNITED ARTISTS (670;
"Dirt, Silver & Gold"):
76 15–18
(With a "UA-LA" prefix.)
UNITED ARTISTS (670;
"Dirt, Silver & Gold") 10–12
(With an "LKCL" prefix.)
UNITED ARTISTS (854
through 1042): *78–80* 5–8
UNITED ARTISTS (5500
series): *71* 8–10
UNITED ARTISTS (9800
series): *72* 8–10
WARNER BROS: *84–85* 5–8

Promotional LPs
UNITED ARTISTS (117;
"Interview"): *75* 15–20

NITTY GRITTY DIRT BAND, The, & Linda Ronstadt
Singles: 7-Inch
UNITED ARTISTS: *79* 2–3
Also see NITTY GRITTY DIRT BAND, The
Also see RONSTADT, Linda

NITZINGER (John Nitzinger)
LPs: 10/12-Inch 33rpm
CAPITOL: *72–73* 8–10
20TH CENTURY-FOX:
76 8–10

NITZSCHE, Jack
Singles: 7-Inch
FANTASY: *76.* 1–3
MCA: *78* 1–3
REPRISE: *63–65.* 3–5

Picture Sleeves
REPRISE: *63.* 3–5

LPs: 10/12-Inch 33rpm
MCA: *78* 8–10

Price Range

REPRISE (2000 series): *73* $8–10
REPRISE (6100 series):
63–64 15–20
REPRISE (6200 series): *66* 10–15

NIVENS, Pamela
Singles: 7-Inch
SUN VALLEY: *83* 1–3

NIX, Don
Singles: 7-Inch
CREAM: *76* 2–3
ELEKTRA: *71* 2–4

LPs: 10/12-Inch 33rpm
CREAM: *79* 5–8
ELEKTRA: *71* 8–10
ENTERPRISE: *73* 8–10
Also see ALABAMA STATE TROUPERS,
The

NOBLE, Nick
Singles: 7-Inch
CAPITOL: *73* 1–3
CHESS: *63–64.* 2–4
CHURCHILL: *77.* 1–3
CORAL: *59–66* 2–4
DATE: *67–68.* 2–3
EPIC: *77* 1–3
LIBERTY: *62–63* 2–4
MERCURY: *56–57.* 2–4
TMS: *79* 1–3
20TH CENTURY-FOX:
65 2–3
WING: *55–56* 3–5

LPs: 10/12-Inch 33rpm
COLUMBIA: *69* 8–12
LIBERTY: *63* 10–15
WING: *60* 10–20

NOBLES, Cliff (Cliff Nobels & Co.)
Singles: 7-Inch
ATLANTIC: *66–67* 3–5
PHIL L.A. OF SOUL:
68–69 3–5
ROULETTE: *73* 1–3

LPs: 10/12-Inch 33rpm
MOON SHOT..................... 8–10
PHIL L.A. OF SOUL: *68* 10–15

Price Range

NOGUEZ, Jacky, & His Orchestra
Singles: 7-Inch
JAMIE: *59–60* $2–4
Picture Sleeves
JAMIE: *60* 2–4
LPs: 10/12-Inch 33rpm
JAMIE: *60* 10–20

NOLAN: see PORTER, Nolan

NOLAN, Kenny
Singles: 7-Inch
CASABLANCA: *79–80* 1–3
DOT: *68* 3–5
FORWARD: *69* 3–5
HIGHLAND: *68* 3–5
LION: *72* 2–4
MGM: *71* 2–4
POLYDOR: *78* 2–3
20TH CENTURY-FOX:
   76–77 2–3
LPs: 10/12-Inch 33rpm
CASABLANCA: *79* 5–8
POLYDOR: *78* 8–10
20TH CENTURY-FOX:
   77 8–10

NORMA
Singles: 12-Inch 33/45rpm
ERC: *83* 4–6

NORMA JEAN (Norma Jean Wright)
Singles: 12-Inch 33/45rpm
BEARSVILLE: *79–80* 4–6
Singles: 7-Inch
BEARSVILLE: *78–80* 1–3
LPs: 10/12-Inch 33rpm
BEARSVILLE: *78* 5–8
Note: This singer should not be confused with the country star Norma Jean Taylor, who also recorded as Norma Jean.
Also see CHIC

NORMAN, Jimmy (Jimmy Norman & The Hollywood Teeners; Jimmy Norman & The Viceroys)
Singles: 7-Inch
DOT: *59* 4–6
FUN: *60* 4–6
GOOD SOUND: *61* 4–6

Price Range

JOSIE: *68* $3–5
LITTLE STAR: *62–63* 4–6
MERCURY: *67* 3–5
MUN RAB: *59* 4–6
RAY STAR: *61–62* 3–5
SAMAR: *66* 3–5

NORMAN, Jimmy, & The O'Jays
Singles: 7-Inch
LITTLE STAR: *63* 5–8
Also see NORMAN, Jimmy
Also see O'JAYS, The

NORTH, Freddie
Singles: 7-Inch
A-BET: *67–69* 3–5
CAPITOL: *62* 4–6
RIC: *64* 3–5
MANKIND: *71–76* 2–4
PHILLIPS INT'L: *61* 3–5
LPs: 10/12-Inch 33rpm
A-BET 8–10
MANKIND: *71–75* 8–12
PHONORAMA 5–8

NORTHCOTT, Tom
Singles: 7-Inch
UNI: *71* 2–4
WARNER BROS: *67–69* 3–5
LPs: 10/12-Inch 33rpm
UNI: *71* 8–10

NORTHERN LIGHT
Singles: 7-Inch
COLUMBIA: *75* 2–3
GLACIER: *75–77* 2–4

NORVUS, Nervous: see NERVOUS NORVUS

NORWOOD, Dorothy (Dorothy Norwood & The Norwood Singers)
Singles: 7-Inch
GRC: *72–75* 2–3
JEWEL: *78* 1–3
SAVOY: *63–69* 1–3
LPs: 10/12-Inch 33rpm
JEWEL: *78* 4–8
SAVOY: *63–83* 5–15

Price Range

NOTATIONS, The
Singles: 7-Inch
GEMIGO: 75–76................... $2–3
MERCURY: 77.................... 2–3
SUE: 69 3–5
TWINIGHT: 70 2–4
LPs: 10/12-Inch 33rpm
GEMIGO: 76.................... 8–10

NOVA, Aldo
Singles: 12-Inch 33/45rpm
PORTRAIT: 82................... 5–8
Singles: 7-Inch
PORTRAIT: 82................... 1–3
LPs: 10/12-Inch 33rpm
PORTRAIT: 82–83................ 5–8

NOVAS, The
Singles: 7-Inch
PARROT: 64.................... 5–10

NOVELLE, Jay
Singles: 12-Inch 33/45rpm
EMERGENCY: 84................ 4–6

NOVO COMBO, The (With Mike Shrieve)
LPs: 10/12-Inch 33rpm
POLYDOR: 81 5–8
Also see SANTANA

NU TORNADOS, The
Singles: 7-Inch
CARLTON: 58–59 3–5
FELSTED: 59 3–5

NUANCE (Featuring Vikki Love)
Singles: 12-Inch 33/45rpm
4TH & BROADWAY:
84–85 4–6
Singles: 7-Inch
4TH & BROADWAY:
84–85 1–3
Also see LOVE, Vikki, With Nuance

NUGENT, Ted (Ted Nugent & The Amboy Dukes; Ted Nugent & Brian Howe)
Singles: 7-Inch
ATLANTIC: 84 1–3
DISCREET: 74................... 2–3

Price Range

EPIC: 76–80 .... $1–3
LPs: 10/12-Inch 33rpm
ATLANTIC: 82–84 5–8
DISCREET: 74................... 8–10
EPIC (Except 607): 75–81 6–10
EPIC (607; "State Of
Shock"): 79................... 15–25
(Picture disc.)
MAINSTREAM (10-01;
"Ted Nugent & The
Amboy Dukes"): 82 5–8
MAINSTREAM (421;
"Ted Nugent & The
Amboy Dukes")................. 8–10
POLYDOR: 71 10–12
Also see BAD COMPANY

NUGENT, Ted, & The Amboy Dukes
LPs: 10/12-Inch 33rpm
MAINSTREAM: 76............... 8–10
Also see NUGENT, Ted
Also see AMBOY DUKES, The

NUGGETS, The
Singles: 7-Inch
MERCURY: 79................... 1–3
LPs: 10/12-Inch 33rpm
MERCURY: 79................... 5–8

NUMAN, Gary (Gary Numan & The Tubeway Army)
Singles: 7-Inch
ATCO: 79–81.................... 1–3
LPs: 10/12-Inch 33rpm
ATCO: 79–81.................... 5–8

NUMONICS, The
Singles: 7-Inch
HODISK: 84 1–3

NUNN, Bobby (Bobby Nunn & The Robbins)
Singles: 7-Inch
MOTOWN: 82–84................. 1–3
LPs: 10/12-Inch 33rpm
MOTOWN: 82–84................. 5–8
Also see BYRD, Bobby
Also see COASTERS, The
Also see NUNN, Bobby
Also see ROBINS, The

NURSERY SCHOOL
Singles: 12-Inch 33/45rpm
EPIC: *83* **$4–6**

NUTMEGS, The
Singles: 7-Inch
COLLECTABLES **1–3**
FLASHBACK: *65.* **1–3**
HERALD (Except 574):
55–59 .... **10–15**
HERALD (574; "Rip Van
Winkle"): *62.* **5–8**
TEL: *60* **15–20**
TIMES SQUARE: *63.* **4–6**
EPs: 7-Inch 33/45rpm
HERALD: *60* **30–40**
LPs: 10/12-Inch 33rpm
COLLECTABLES **5–8**
RELIC......................... **8–10**
Members: Leroy Griffin; James Griffin; Bill
Emery; Leroy McNeil; Jim Tyson; Ed Martin;
Sonny Washburn; Harold Jones.

NUTMEGS, The / The Volumes
Singles: 7-Inch
TIMES SQUARE: *63.* **4–6**
Also see NUTMEGS, The
Also see VOLUMES, The

NUTTY SQUIRRELS, The
Singles: 7-Inch
COLUMBIA: *60.* **3–5**
HANOVER: *59–60.* **4–6**
RCA VICTOR: *64* **3–5**
Picture Sleeves
COLUMBIA: *60.* **3–5**
HANOVER: *59.* **4–6**
EPs: 7-Inch 33/45rpm
HANOVER: *60.* **15–20**
LPs: 10/12-Inch 33rpm
COLUMBIA: *61* **20–25**
HANOVER: *60.* **20–25**
MGM: *64.* **15–20**

NYRO, Laura
Singles: 7-Inch
COLUMBIA: *68–71* **2–4**
VERVE/FOLKWAYS:
66–67 .... **3–5**
VERVE/FORECAST:
68–69 .... **2–4**

Picture Sleeves
COLUMBIA: *68* **$2–4**
LPs: 10/12-Inch 33rpm
COLUMBIA: *68–84* **6–10**
VERVE/FOLKWAYS: *67.* **10–15**
VERVE/FORECAST: *69* **8–10**
Also see LABELLE, Patti

NYTRO
Singles: 12-Inch 33/45rpm
WHITFIELD: *79* **4–6**
Singles: 7-Inch
WHITFIELD: *76–79* **1–3**
LPs: 10/12-Inch 33rpm
WHITFIELD: *77–79* **5–8**

O

O., Jerry: see JERRY O

O ROMEO
Singles: 12-Inch 33/45rpm
BOB CAT: *83* **4–6**
OH MY: *84.* **4–6**
Members: Lorilee Svedberg; Dora Suppes;
Terry Weinberg.

O.M.D.
Singles: 12-Inch 33/45rpm
A&M: *84* **4–6**
Singles: 7-Inch
A&M: *84* **1–3**

OAK
Singles: 7-Inch
MERCURY: *79–80.* **1–3**
Also see PINETTE, Rick, & Oak

**OAK RIDGE BOYS, The (The Oak
Ridge Quartet; The Oaks)**
Singles: 7-Inch
ABC: *78–79* **2–3**
ABC/DOT: *77.* **2–3**
CADENCE: *59* **2–4**
COLUMBIA: *73–76* **1–3**
HEARTWARMING: *71* **1–3**
IMPACT: *71* **1–3**
MCA: *79–85* **1–3**
WARNER BROS: *63* **2–3**

Price Range

LPs: 10/12-Inch 33rpm

ABC: 78–79	$5–10
ABC/DOT: 77.	8–10
ACCORD: 81–82	4–8
CADENCE: 58	15–25
CANAAN: 66	8–15
COLUMBIA: 74–83	5–10
EXACT: 83	4–8
51 WEST	5–8
HEARTWARMING: 71–74	5–8
INTERMEDIA	5–8
MCA: 80–85	5–8
NASHVILLE: 70	8–10
OUT OF TOWN DIST: 82	4–8
PHONORAMA.	5–8
POWER PAK	5–8
PRIORITY: 82	4–8
SKYLITE: 64–66	8–15
STARDAY: 65	8–15
UNITED ARTISTS: 66	8–15
WARNER BROS: 63	10–15

Members: William Golden; Duane Allen; Rich Sterban; Joe Bonsall. Members of the group prior to 1977 are not given.
Also see LEE, Brenda, & The Oak Ridge Boys

OAKEY, Philip: see MORODER, Giorgio, & Philip Oakey

OAS, Holly
Singles: 12-Inch 33/45rpm
DND: 84	4–6

O'BANION, John
Singles: 7-Inch
ELEKTRA: 81	1–3

LPs: 10/12-Inch 33/45rpm
ELEKTRA: 81	5–8

O'BRYAN (O'Bryan Burnette)
Singles: 12-Inch 33/45rpm
CAPITOL: 83	4–6

Singles: 7-Inch
CAPITOL: 82–83	1–3

LPs: 10/12-Inch 33/45rpm
CAPITOL: 82–83	5–8

OCASEK, Ric
Singles: 12-Inch 33/45rpm
GEFFEN: 83	4–6

Price Range

Singles: 7-Inch
GEFFEN: 83	$1–3

LPs: 10/12-Inch 33/45rpm
GEFFEN: 83	5–8

Also see CARS, The

OCEAN
Singles: 7-Inch
KAMA SUTRA: 71–72	2–4

LPs: 10/12-Inch 33/45rpm
KAMA SUTRA: 71–72	8–10

OCEAN, Billy
Singles: 12-Inch 33/45rpm
EPIC: 80–82	4–6
JIVE: 84–85	4–6

Singles: 7-Inch
ARIOLA AMERICA: 76	2–3
EPIC: 77–82	1–3
JIVE: 84–85	1–3

LPs: 10/12-Inch 33/45rpm
EPIC: 82	5–8
JIVE: 84	5–8

OCHS, Phil
Singles: 7-Inch
A&M: 67–73	3–5

LPs: 10/12-Inch 33/45rpm
A&M: 67–76	10–15
ELEKTRA: 64–66	15–20

O'CONNELL, Helen
Singles: 7-Inch
CAMEO: 63	2–4
CAPITOL: 51–54	2–4
KAPP: 55	2–4
VIK: 57	2–4

EPs: 7-Inch 33/45rpm
CAPITOL: 54	5–8
VIK: 57	5–8

LPs: 10/12-Inch 33rpm
CAMDEN: 59–62	5–10
CAMEO: 63	8–15
MARK '56: 77.	5–8
VIK: 57	10–20
WARNER BROS: 61	8–15

O'CONNER, Carroll
LPs: 10/12-Inch 33rpm
A&M: 72	5–10
AUDIO FIDELITY: 76	5–10

Price Range

O'CONNER, Carroll, & Jean Stapleton
Singles: 7-Inch
ATLANTIC: 71 .... $2–4
Also see O'CONNER, Carroll

O'DAY, Alan
Singles: 7-Inch
PACIFIC: 77–79.................. 2–3
LPs: 10/12-Inch 33/45rpm
PACIFIC: 77...................... 5–8

O'DAY, Anita
Singles: 7-Inch
CLEF: 53.......................... 3–5
CLOVER: 66....................... 2–4
COLUMBIA: 76.................... 1–3
CORAL: 52........................ 3–5
EMILY: 79 1–3
LONDON: 51 3–5
MERCURY: 52–53................. 3–5
VERVE: 56–62 2–4

EPs: 7-Inch 33/45rpm
CLEF: 53........................ 25–50
COLUMBIA: 74................. 8–10
NORGRAN: 54 20–40

LPs: 10/12-Inch 33rpm
ADVANCE: 51................ 100–175
(10-Inch LP.)
AMERICAN
  RECORDING
  SOCIETY: 57.................. 30–60
ANITA O'DAY
  RECORDS: 72................. 5–10
CLEF: 53....................... 75–100
CORAL: 53 75–125
DOBRE: 78....................... 5–8
EMILY: 79–82..................... 5–8
FLYING DUTCHMAN:
  74 5–8
GNP/CRESCENDO: 79 5–8
MPS: 73.......................... 5–8
NORGRAN (30; "Anita
  O'Day"): 54.................. 50–80
(10-Inch LP.)
NORGRAN (1000 series):
  55–56 30–60
PAUSA: 81 5–8
SIGNATURE: 75.................. 5–8
VERVE (2000 series): 56 25–50

Price Range

(Reads "Verve Records, Inc." at bottom of label.)
VERVE (2100 series):
  58–61 .... $20–40
(Reads "Verve Records, Inc." at bottom of label.)
VERVE (6000 series):
  59–60 20–40
(Reads "Verve Records, Inc." at bottom of label.)
VERVE (8200 through
  8500 series): 59–64 15–30
(Reads "Verve Records, Inc." at bottom of label.)
VERVE: 61–72 10–20
(Reads "MGM Records - A Division Of Metro-Goldwyn-Mayer, Inc." at bottom of label.)
VERVE: 79–82 6–12
(Reads "Manufactured By MGM Record Corp.," or mentions either Polydor or Polygram at bottom of label.)

O'DAY, Anita, & Cal Tjader
LPs: 10/12-Inch 33rpm
VERVE: 62 15–25
(Reads "MGM Records - A Division Of Metro-Goldwyn-Mayer, Inc." at bottom of label.)
Also see O'DAY, Anita
Also see TJADER, Cal

O'DAY, Pat
Singles: 7-Inch
ARGO: 59........................ 2–4
MGM: 53–56...................... 2–4
SEVILLE: 59–60.................. 2–4
LPs: 10/12-Inch 33rpm
GOLDEN CREST: 56 10–20

ODDS & ENDS, The
Singles: 7-Inch
RED BIRD: 66.................... 4–6
SOUTHBAY 2–4
TODAY: 71–72.................... 2–4

O'DELL, Brooks
Singles: 7-Inch
GOLD: 63 3–5

O'DELL, Kenny
Singles: 7-Inch
ABC: 73.......................... 2–3
CAPRICORN: 73–79.............. 1–3
KAPP: 72 2–3

Price Range

MAR-KAY **$4–6**
VEGAS: *67–68* **3–5**
WHITE WHALE: *69* **2–4**

LPs: 10/12-Inch 33/45rpm
CAPRICORN: *74–78* **5–10**
VEGAS: *68* **15–20**

ODETTA (Odetta Holmes)
Singles: 7-Inch
DUNHILL: *69* **2–3**
RCA VICTOR: *63* **2–4**
RIVERSIDE: *62* **2–4**
VANGUARD: *59* **2–4**
VERVE/FOLKWAYS: *66* **2–4**
VERVE/FORECAST: *68* **2–3**

LPs: 10/12-Inch 33rpm
EVEREST: *73* **5–8**
POLYDOR: *70* **5–10**
RCA VICTOR: *62–66* **8–15**
RIVERSIDE (400 series):
     62 . . . . **15–25**
RIVERSIDE (3000 series):
     68 . . . . **8–12**
RIVERSIDE (9400 series):
     62 . . . . **15–25**
TRADITION: *67* **8–12**
UNITED ARTISTS: *76* **5–8**
VANGUARD: *59–67* **8–18**
VERVE/FOLKWAYS: *67* **8–12**

ODYSSEY
Singles: 12-Inch 33/45rpm
RCA VICTOR: *77–82* **4–8**

Singles: 7-Inch
MOWEST: *72* **2–4**
RCA VICTOR: *77–82* **1–3**

LPs: 10/12-Inch 33/45rpm
MOWEST: *72* **10–12**
RCA VICTOR: *77–82* **8–10**
Members: Lillian Lopez; Louise Lopez.

OFARIM, Esther & Abraham (Esther Ofarim; Esther & Abi Ofarim)
Singles: 7-Inch
PHILIPS: *64–68* **2–3**

LPs: 10/12-Inch 33rpm
CAPITOL: *68* **5–10**
PHILIPS: *63–70* **5–10**

Price Range

OFF BROADWAY USA
Singles: 7-Inch
ATLANTIC: *80* **$1–3**
LPs: 10/12-Inch 33/45rpm
ATLANTIC: *80* **5–8**

OFFITT, Lillian
Singles: 7-Inch
CHIEF: *60* **5–8**
EXCELLO: *57* **4–6**

OH ROMEO: see O ROMEO

O'HENRY, Lenny (Lenny O'Henry & The Short Stories)
Singles: 7-Inch
ABC-PARAMOUNT: *61* **8–10**
ATCO: *64–67* **5–8**

OHIO EXPRESS, The (Ohio Ltd.)
Singles: 7-Inch
ATTACK: *70* **2–3**
BUDDAH: *68–73* **2–4**
CAMEO: *67* **3–5**
ERIC: *78* **1–3**
SUPER K: *69–70* **2–4**
LPs: 10/12-Inch 33/45rpm
BUDDAH: *68–70* **10–15**
CAMEO: *68* **15–20**
     Also see IVY LEAGUE, The
     Also see KASENETZ-KATZ SINGING OR-
     CHESTRAL CIRCUS, The
     Also see REUNION
     Also see 10CC

OHIO LTD: see OHIO EXPRESS, The

OHIO PLAYERS, The
Singles: 7-Inch
AIR CITY: *84* **1–3**
ARISTA: *79* **1–3**
BOARDWALK: *81* **1–3**
CAPITOL: *69* **2–4**
COMPASS: *68* **3–5**
MERCURY: *74–78* **1–3**
TANGERINE: *67* **3–5**
WESTBOUND: *71–76* **2–3**
LPs: 10/12-Inch 33/45rpm
ACCORD: *81* **5–8**
ARISTA: *79* **5–8**

Price Range

BOARDWALK: *81* **$5–8**
CAPITOL (192;
"Observations In Time"):
69 .... **10–15**
CAPITOL (11291; "The
Ohio Players"): *74*............. **8–10**
MERCURY: *74–78*.............. **8–10**
TRIP: *72* **8–10**
20TH CENTURY-FOX/
WESTBOUND: *75* **8–10**
UNITED ARTISTS: *75*........... **8–10**
WESTBOUND: *72–75*............ **8–10**
Also see JUNIE

OINGO BOINGO
Singles: 12-Inch 33/45rpm
A&M: *81* **4–6**
MCA: *85* **4–6**
Singles: 7-Inch
A&M: *81–82* **1–3**
MCA: *85* **1–3**
LPs: 10/12-Inch 33/45rpm
A&M: *81–82* **5–8**
I.R.S.: *80* **5–8**
MCA: *85* **5–8**

O'JAYS, The
Singles: 12-Inch 33/45rpm
PHILADELPHIA INT'L:
83 .... **4–6**
Singles: 7-Inch
ALL PLATINUM: *74* **2–3**
APOLLO: *63*................... **5–8**
ASTROSCOPE: *74*.............. **2–3**
BELL: *67–73*.................. **2–4**
IMPERIAL: *63–66*.............. **4–6**
LIBERTY: *81* **1–3**
LITTLE STAR: *63*.............. **5–8**
MINIT: *67*.................... **3–5**
NEPTUNE: *69–70* **2–4**
PHILADELPHIA INT'L:
72–83 .... **1–3**
SARU: *71* **2–3**
TSOP: *80–81* **1–3**
LPs: 10/12-Inch 33/45rpm
BELL (6014; "Back On
Top"): *68* **10–15**
BELL (6082; "The
O'Jays"): *73*................. **8–10**
IMPERIAL: *65*................. **15–20**
KORY: *77*.................... **8–10**

MINIT: *67*................... **$12–15**
PHILADELPHIA INT'L:
72–85 .... **6–10**
SUNSET: *68* **10–12**
TSOP: *80*.................... **5–8**
TRIP: *73* **8–10**
UNITED ARTISTS: *72*........... **8–10**
Members: Bob Massey; Eddie LeVert; Walt
Williams; Bill Powell; Bill Isles.
Also see NORMAN, Jimmy, & The O'Jays
Also see PHILADELPHIA INTERNA-
TIONAL ALL STARS, The

O'JAYS, The / The Moments
LPs: 10/12-Inch 33/45rpm
STANG: *74* **8–10**
Also see O'JAYS, The
Also see MOMENTS, The

O'KAYSIONS, The
Singles: 7-Inch
ABC: *68*..................... **3–5**
COTILLION: *70*............... **2–4**
ROULETTE **1–3**
LPs: 10/12-Inch 33/45rpm
ABC: *68*..................... **15–18**

O'KEEFE, Danny
Singles: 7-Inch
ATLANTIC: *75* **2–3**
JERDEN: *66*................... **3–5**
SIGNPOST: *72* **2–4**
WARNER BROS: *77–78*........... **1–3**
Picture Sleeves
WARNER BROS: *77–78*........... **1–3**
LPs: 10/12-Inch 33/45rpm
ATLANTIC: *73–75* **8–10**
COTILLION: *70*............... **10–12**
FIRST AMERICAN **8–10**
SIGNPOST: *72* **10–12**
WARNER BROS: *77–79*........... **5–8**

OLA & THE JANGLERS
Singles: 7-Inch
GNP/CRESCENDO:
68–69 .... **3–5**
LONDON: *67*.................. **3–5**
LPs: 10/12-Inch 33/45rpm
GNP/CRESCENDO: *69* **12–15**

Price Range

OLD & IN THE WAY
LPs: 10/12-Inch 33rpm
ROUND: 75 . . . . **$5–8**

OLDFIELD, Mike (Mike & Sally Oldfield)
Singles: 7-Inch
EPIC: 81–82 . . . . **1–3**
VIRGIN: 73–82. . . . . **1–3**
LPs: 10/12-Inch 33/45rpm
EPIC: 81–82 . . . . **5–8**
VIRGIN: 73–82. . . . . **6–12**

OLIVER (Bill Oliver Swofford)
Singles: 7-Inch
CREWE: 69–70. . . . . **2–4**
JUBILEE: 69. . . . . **2–4**
LIBERTY **1–3**
PARAMOUNT: 73. . . . . **2–3**
PEOPLE SONG: 82 . . . . **1–3**
UNITED ARTISTS: 70–71 . . . . **2–3**
Picture Sleeves
CREWE: 69. . . . . **2–4**
LPs: 10/12-Inch 33/45rpm
CREWE: 69–70. . . . . **10–12**
UNITED ARTISTS: 71 . . . . **8–10**
Also see BILLY & SUE

OLIVER, David
Singles: 7-Inch
MERCURY: 78–80. . . . . **1–3**
LPs: 10/12-Inch 33rpm
MERCURY: 78–79. . . . . **5–8**

OLIVOR, Jane
Singles: 7-Inch
COLUMBIA: 77–85 . . . . **1–3**
LPs: 10/12-Inch 33/45rpm
COLUMBIA: 77–85 . . . . **5–8**

OLLIE & JERRY
Singles: 12-Inch 33/45rpm
POLYDOR: 84–85 . . . . **4–6**
Singles: 7-Inch
POLYDOR: 84–85 . . . . **1–3**
Members: Ollie Brown; Jerry Knight.
Also see KNIGHT, Jerry

OLLIE & THE NIGHTINGALES
Singles: 7-Inch
STAX: 68. . . . . **3–5**

Price Range

LPs: 10/12-Inch 33/45rpm
STAX: 69. . . . . **$10–12**

OLSON, Rocky
Singles: 7-Inch
CHESS: 59. . . . . **8–10**

OLSSON, Nigel
Singles: 7-Inch
BANG: 78–79 . . . . **1–3**
COLUMBIA: 78 . . . . **1–3**
ROCKET: 75. . . . . **2–3**
UNI: 71–72 . . . . **2–4**
LPs: 10/12-Inch 33/45rpm
BANG: 79–80 . . . . **5–8**
COLUMBIA: 78. . . . . **5–8**
ROCKET: 73–75. . . . . **8–10**
UNI: 71 . . . . **8–10**
Also see JOHN, Elton

OLYMPIC RUNNERS, The
Singles: 7-Inch
LONDON: 74–77 . . . . **2–3**
POLYDOR: 79 . . . . **1–3**
LPs: 10/12-Inch 33/45rpm
LONDON: 74–77 . . . . **8–10**
POLYDOR: 79 . . . . **5–8**

OLYMPICS, The
Singles: 7-Inch
ABC: 73 . . . . **1–3**
ARVEE: 59–65 . . . . **4–6**
COLLECTABLES **1–3**
DEMON: 58–60 . . . . **5–8**
DUO DISC: 64 . . . . **4–6**
ERIC **1–3**
JUBILEE: 69. . . . . **3–5**
LIBERTY: 63 . . . . **2–4**
LOMA: 65 . . . . **3–5**
MGM: 73 . . . . **2–4**
MIRWOOD: 66–67. . . . . **3–5**
PARKWAY: 68 . . . . **3–5**
TITAN: 61. . . . . **4–6**
TRI DISC: 63 . . . . **4–6**
WARNER BROS: 70 . . . . **2–4**
EPs: 7-Inch 33/45rpm
ARVEE: 60 . . . . **20–25**
LPs: 10/12-Inch 33/45rpm
ARVEE: 60–61 . . . . **25–30**
EVEREST: 81 . . . . **5–8**
MIRWOOD: 66. . . . . **12–15**

Price Range

POST **$8–10**
RHINO **5–8**
TRI-DISC: *63* **20–25**
    Members: Walter Ward; Eddie Lewis; Melvin
    King; Charles Figer; Julius McMichaels.
    Also see PARAGONS, The
    Also see REYNOLDS, Jody / The Olympics

O'NEAL, Alexander
Singles: 12-Inch 33/45rpm
TABU: *85* **4–6**
Singles: 7-Inch
TABU: *85* **1–3**
LPs: 10/12-Inch 33rpm
TABU: *85* **5–8**

100 PROOF Aged In Soul
Singles: 7-Inch
HOT WAX: *69–72* **2–4**
LPs: 10/12-Inch 33/45rpm
HOT WAX: *70–73* **10–12**

101 STRINGS
Singles: 7-Inch
SOMERSET: *59* **1–3**
LPs: 10/12-Inch 33rpm
SOMERSET: *59–61* **4–8**
STEREO FIDELITY:
   59–61 . . . . **4–8**

ONE ON ONE
Singles: 7-Inch
KEE WEE: *84* **1–3**

ONE WAY (Featuring Al Hudson)
Singles: 12-Inch 33/45rpm
MCA: *82–85* **4–6**
Singles: 7-Inch
MCA: *79–85* **1–3**
LPs: 10/12-Inch 33/45rpm
MCA: *79–85* **5–8**
    Also see HUDSON, Al

ONO, Yoko (Yoko Ono & The Plastic Ono Band)
Singles: 12-Inch 33/45rpm
POLYDOR: *85* **4–6**
Singles: 7-Inch
APPLE: *71–73* **3–5**
GEFFEN: *81* **2–3**
POLYDOR: *82–85* **1–3**

Price Range

Promotional Singles
GEFFEN: *81* **$5–8**
POLYDOR: *82–84* **4–6**

Picture Sleeves
GEFFEN: *81* **2–4**

LPs: 10/12-Inch 33/45rpm
APPLE: *71–73* **15–20**
GEFFEN: *81* **5–8**
POLYDOR: *82* **5–8**

Promotional LPs
GEFFEN (934; "Walking
  On Thin Ice"): *81* **20–25**
GEFFEN (975; "No No
  No"): *81* **25–30**
    Also see LENNON, John

OPUS SEVEN
Singles: 7-Inch
SOURCE: *79* **1–3**
LPs: 10/12-Inch 33/45rpm
SOURCE: *79* **5–8**

OPUS 10
Singles: 7-Inch
PANDISC: *85* **1–3**

Roy Orbison, 30 charted singles (1956–80), nine charted LPs (1962–66). (Includes issue shown as by Roy Orbison & Emmylou Harris.)

Price Range

Price Range

ORBISON, Roy (Roy Orbison & The Teen Kings; Roy Orbison & The Candymen; Roy Orbison & The Roses)

Singles: 7-Inch

ASYLUM: 78. $2–3
MGM: 65–73. 3–5
MGM CELEBRITY
   SCENE (CSN9-5; "Roy
   Orbison"): 66. 30–40
   (Boxed set of five singles, bio insert & title
   strips. Jukebox issue only.)
MERCURY: 74. 2–3
MONUMENT (409;
   "Paper Boy"): 59. 10–15
MONUMENT (412;
   "Uptown"): 59. 8–10
MONUMENT (421
   through 467): 60–62 4–6
MONUMENT (800 & 900
   series): 63–66 3–5
MONUMENT (500 series):
   63 2–3
MONUMENT (8600
   series): 76 1–3
MONUMENT (8900
   series): 72 1–3
MONUMENT (45000
   series): 76–77 2–3
RCA VICTOR: 58–59 10–15
SSS/SUN 1–3
SUN (200 series): 56–58 10–15
SUN (300 series): 61 5–8

Picture Sleeves

MGM: 65–67. 4–8
MONUMENT (400 series):
   60–62 5–10
MONUMENT (800 series):
   63–64 4–8

EPs: 7-Inch 33/45rpm

MONUMENT (2;
   "Crying"): 62. 10–20
   (Compact 33, "Special Promotional Six-Pac.")

LPs: 10/12-Inch 33rpm

ACCORD: 81 5–8
ASYLUM: 78–79. 5–8
BUCKBOARD 8–10
CANDLELITE MUSIC. 10–15
CHARLY 5–8
DESIGN 10–15

HALLMARK $10–12
MGM (4308 through
   4514): 65–67. 15–20
MGM (4636 through
   4934): 69–73. 10–15
MERCURY: 75. 8–10
MONUMENT (4002;
   "Lonely & Blue" -
   mono): 61. 30–40
MONUMENT (14002;
   "Lonely & Blue" -
   stereo): 61. 45–55
MONUMENT (4007;
   "Crying" - mono): 62 30–35
MONUMENT (14007;
   "Crying" - stereo): 62. 45–50
MONUMENT (4009;
   "Greatest Hits" - mono):
   62 25–30
MONUMENT (14009;
   "Greatest Hits" - stereo):
   62 35–40
MONUMENT (6600
   series) 8–10
MONUMENT (8000;
   "Greatest Hits" - mono):
   63 20–25
MONUMENT (18000;
   "Greatest Hits" - stereo):
   63 30–35
   (Apparently the number of this LP was
   changed when Monument switched from the
   4000/14000 series to the 8000/18000 series.
   We're not positive that both a mono and a
   stereo exist for each series, but both are listed
   until we learn otherwise.)
MONUMENT (8003; "In
   Dreams" - mono): 63 20–25
MONUMENT (18003; "In
   Dreams" - stereo): 63 30–35
MONUMENT (8024;
   "More Greatest Hits" -
   mono): 64. 20–25
MONUMENT (18024;
   "More Greatest Hits" -
   stereo): 64. 25–30
MONUMENT (8035;
   "Orbisongs" - mono): 64 15–20
MONUMENT (18035;
   "Orbisongs" - stereo): 64 20–25

Note: For the sake of continuity, the preceding 14000 & 18000 series stereo issues, requiring separate pricing, are listed directly below their 4000 & 8000 series mono counterpart.

MONUMENT (8023/
  18023; "Early Orbison"):
  64 .... **$20–25**
MONUMENT (8045/
  18045; "Very Best"): *66* **15–20**
  (Blue cover.)
MONUMENT (8045/
  18045; "Very Best"): *66* **12–15**
  (Purple cover.)
MONUMENT (38384;
  "All-Time Greatest
  Hits"): *82* **8–10**
SPECTRUM **15–20**
SSS/SUN: *69*.................... **5–8**
SUN (1260; "Rock
  House"): *61* **60–75**
TRIP: *74* **8–10**
  Also see CANDYMEN, The
  Also see DRIFTERS, The / Lesley Gore / Roy
  Orbison / Los Bravos
  Also see JAN & DEAN / Roy Orbison
  Also see LEWIS, Jerry Lee / Roger Miller /
  Roy Orbison
  Also see PERKINS, Carl, Jerry Lee Lewis, Roy
  Orbison & Johnny Cash
  Also see TEEN KINGS, The

**ORBISON, Roy / Bobby Bare /
Joey Powers**
  LPs: 10/12-Inch 33rpm
CAMDEN: *64*................... **15–20**
  Also see BARE, Bobby
  Also see POWERS, Joey

**ORBISON, Roy, & Emmylou Harris
/ Craig Hundley**
  Singles: 7-Inch
WARNER BROS: *80*.............. **2–3**
  Also see HARRIS, Emmylou
  Also see ORBISON, Roy

ORBIT (Featuring Carol Hall)
  Singles: 12-Inch 33/45rpm
QUALITY/RFC: *82–84*........... **4–6**

  Singles: 7-Inch
QUALITY/RFC: *82–84*........... **1–3**

**ORCHESTRAL MANOEUVERS IN
THE DARK**
  Singles: 7-Inch
A&M: *84–85* **$1–3**
EPIC: *82–83* **1–3**
  LPs: 10/12-Inch 33rpm
A&M: *84* **5–8**
EPIC: *82–83* **5–8**

**ORIGINAL ANIMALS: see
ANIMALS, The**

ORIGINAL CADILLACS, The
  Singles: 7-Inch
JOSIE: *57–58*................... **8–10**
  Members: Earl Carroll; Earl Wade; Charles
  Brooks; Bobby Phillips; Junior Glanton; Ro-
  land Martinez.
  Also see CADILLACS, The

**ORIGINAL CAST, The (Featuring
Kacey Cisyk)**
  Singles: 7-Inch
ARISTA: *77* **2–3**

**ORIGINAL CASTE, The (Featuring
Dixie Lee Innes)**
  Singles: 7-Inch
DOT: *68*........................ **3–5**
T-A: *69–70*..................... **2–4**
  LPs: 10/12-Inch 33rpm
T-A: *70*........................ **10–12**

**ORIGINAL CASUALS, The
(Featuring Gary Mears)**
  Singles: 7-Inch
BACK BEAT: *58* **4–6**
  EPs: 7-Inch 33/45rpm
BACK BEAT: *58* **25–30**

ORIGINALS, The
  Singles: 7-Inch
MOTOWN: *75*.................... **2–3**
PHASE II: *81* **1–3**
SOUL (35029 through
  35061): *67–69*................. **3–5**
SOUL (35066 through
  35119): *69–76*................. **2–3**
  LPs: 10/12-Inch 33rpm
FANTASY: *78–79*................. **5–8**

Price Range

MOTOWN: *74–80.* **$5–8**
SOUL: *69–76*. **8–12**

ORIOLES, The
Singles: 7-Inch
ABNER: *58*. **10–12**
CHARLIE PARKER:
62–63 . . . . **3–5**
JUBILEE (5000; "It's Too
Soon To Know"): *51*. **325–350**
JUBILEE (5005; "Tell Me
So"): *51* **325–350**
JUBILEE (5016; "So
Much"): *51*. **300–325**
JUBILEE (5017; "What
Are You Doing New
Year's Eve"): *51* **175–225**
JUBILEE (5025; "At
Night"): *51*. **200–225**
JUBILEE (5040; "I Cross
My Fingers"): *51*. **200–250**
JUBILEE (5045; "Oh Holy
Night"): *51*. **150–175**
JUBILEE (5051; "I Miss
You So" - black vinyl):
51 . . . . **175–200**
JUBILEE (5051; "I Miss
You So" - colored vinyl):
51 . . . . **325–350**
JUBILEE (5055; "Pal Of
Mine"): *51* **200–225**
JUBILEE (5061; "I'm Just
A Fool In Love"): *51* **200–225**
JUBILEE (5065; "Baby,
Please Don't Go" - black
vinyl): *51* **175–200**
JUBILEE (5065; "Baby,
Please Don't Go" -
colored vinyl): *51*. **275–300**
JUBILEE (5071; "When
You're Not Around"):
51 . . . . **150–175**
JUBILEE (5074; "Trust In
Me"): *52*. **150–175**
JUBILEE (5082; "It's Over
Because We're
Through"): *52* **150–175**
JUBILEE (5084; "Barfly"):
52 . . . . **125–150**

Price Range

JUBILEE (5092; "Don't
Cry Baby" - black vinyl):
52 . . . . **$125–150**
JUBILEE (5092; "Don't
Cry Baby" - colored
vinyl): *52* **275–300**
JUBILEE (5102; "You
Belong To Me"): *52* **125–150**
JUBILEE (5107; "I Miss
You So" - black vinyl):
53 . . . . **150–175**
(Reissued in 1963, using the same catalog num-
ber, and shown as by "Sonny Til & The Ori-
oles".)
JUBILEE (5107; "I Miss
You So" - colored vinyl):
53 . . . . **300–325**
JUBILEE (5108;
"Teardrops On My
Pillow" - black vinyl): *53* **75–100**
JUBILEE (5108;
"Teardrops On My
Pillow" - colored vinyl):
53 . . . . **200–225**
JUBILEE (5115; "Bad
Little Girl"): *53*. **60–75**
JUBILEE (5120; "I Cover
The Waterfront" - black
vinyl): *53* **75–100**
JUBILEE (5120; "I Cover
The Waterfront" -
colored vinyl): *53*. **175–200**
JUBILEE (5122; "Crying
In The Chapel"): *53* **20–25**
JUBILEE (5127; "In The
Mission Of St.
Augustine"): *53* **15–20**
JUBILEE (5134; "There's
No One But You"): *54*. **30–35**
JUBILEE (5137; "Secret
Love"): *54* **15–20**
JUBILEE (5143; "Maybe
You'll Be There"): *54*. **20–25**
JUBILEE (5154; "In The
Chapel In The
Moonlight"): *54*. **20–25**
JUBILEE (5161; "If You
Believe"): *54*. **20–25**
JUBILEE (5172;
"Runaround"): *54* **20–25**

Price Range

JUBILEE (5177; "I Love
You Mostly"): *55* $20–25
JUBILEE (5189; "I Need
You Baby"): *55* 20–25
JUBILEE (5221; "Please
Sing My Blues
Tonight"): *55* 20–25
JUBILEE (5231; "Angel"):
56 15–20
JUBILEE (5300 series): *59* 4–6
  Note: There are probably other Jubilee colored
  vinyl issues, but those noted here are the only
  ones we've verified. Also, some Jubilee tracks
  were reissued, shown as by "Sonny Til & The
  Orioles," and are found in the "Til" section of
  this guide.
VEE JAY (Except 244): *56* 15–20
VEE JAY (244; "Sugar
Girl"): *57* 30–35

Picture Sleeves

JUBILEE (5017; "What
Are You Doing New
Year's Eve"): *54* 150–200
JUBILEE (5045; "Oh Holy
Night"): *54*. 150–200
  (Both Jubilee sleeves were issued in late 1954
  and were sold with 1954 pressings of the discs,
  which would actually be second pressings of the
  two singles. These were blue script Jubilee la-
  bels with the line under the logo.)

EPs: 7-Inch 33/45rpm

JUBILEE 225–275

LPs: 10/12-Inch 33rpm

BIG A RECORDS 20–25
CHARLIE PARKER: *62* 25–35
MURRAY HILL 30–35
  (A 5-LP set.)
ROULETTE 5–8
  Members: Sonny Til & The Orioles; Sonny Til;
  Alex Sharp; George Nelson; John Reed; Tom
  Gaither; Charles Harris; Greg Carroll; Billy
  Adams; Jerry Holman; Al Russell; Jerry Rod-
  riguez; Bill Taylor.
  Also see CADILLACS, The / The Orioles
  Also see TIL, Sonny

ORION THE HUNTER (With Barry Goudreau)

Singles: 7-Inch

PORTRAIT: *84–85*. 1–3

LPs: 10/12-Inch 33rpm

PORTRAIT: *84*. 5–8
  Also see BOSTON

*Tony Orlando, 24 charted singles
(1961–77), 11 charted LPs (1970–76).*

Price Range

ORLANDO, Tony

Singles: 12-Inch 33/45rpm

CASABLANCA: *79* $4–6

Singles: 7-Inch

ATCO: *65* 3–6
CAMEO: *67* 3–6
CASABLANCA: *79–80* 2–3
EPIC (9000 series): *61–64* 3–6
MILE: *59*. 25–30

Promotional Singles

EPIC (55299; "Happy
Times Are Here To
Stay"): *61* 8–10

LPs: 10/12-Inch 33rpm

EPIC (611; "Bless You"):
61 35–40
EPIC (33785; "Before
Dawn"): *75*. 10–12
CASABLANCA: *79–80* 5–8

Picture Sleeves

EPIC: *61–62* 3–6
  Also see SHIELDS, Billy
  Also see WIND

ORLANDO, Tony, & Dawn

Singles: 7-Inch

ARISTA: *75* 2–3
BELL: *71–74*. 2–4
ELEKTRA: *75–78* 2–3

LPs: 10/12-Inch 33rpm

ARISTA: *75–76*. 6–10

Price Range

ASYLUM: 75. . . . . **$6–10**
BELL (6000 series): 70–71 . . . . **10–12**
BELL (1000 series): 73–75 . . . . **8–10**
ELEKTRA: 75–78 . . . . **6–10**
KORY: 74–77 . . . . **8–10**
   Also see DAWN
   Also see ORLANDO, Tony

ORLEANS (With John Hall)
Singles: 7-Inch
ASYLUM: 75–77. . . . . **2–3**
INFINITY: 79. **1–3**

LPs: 10/12-Inch 33rpm
ABC: 73–78 . . . . **10–12**
ASYLUM: 75–76. . . . . **6–10**
INFINITY: 79. **5–8**
RADIO: 82 . . . . **5–8**
   Also see HALL, John

ORLONS, The
Singles: 7-Inch
ABC: 67. . . . . **3–5**
CALLA: 66 . . . . **3–5**
CAMEO (198; "I'll Be
   True"): 61 . . . . **5–8**
CAMEO (211; "Mr. 21"):
   62 . . . . **5–8**
CAMEO (218 through
   384): 62–65. . . . . **3–5**

Picture Sleeves
CAMEO: 62–64. . . . . **4–8**

LPs: 10/12-Inch 33rpm
CAMEO: 62–63. . . . . **20–25**
   Members: Shirley Brickley; Rosetta Hightower;
   Steve Caldwell; Marlena Davis.

ORLONS, The / The Dovells
LPs: 10/12-Inch 33rpm
CAMEO: 63 . . . . **20–25**
   Also see DOVELLS, The
   Also see ORLONS, The

ORPHEUS
Singles: 7-Inch
MGM: 68–69. **2–4**

LPs: 10/12-Inch 33rpm
BELL: 71. . . . . **10–12**
MGM: 68–69. . . . . **10–12**

Price Range

ORRALL, Robert Ellis (Robert Ellis Orrall & Carlene Carter)
Singles: 7-Inch
RCA VICTOR: 81–83 . . . . **$1–3**

LPs: 10/12-Inch 33rpm
RCA VICTOR: 81–83 . . . . **5–8**
   Also see CARTER, Carlene

OSBORNE, Jeffrey
Singles: 12-Inch 33/45rpm
A&M: 82–84 . . . . **4–6**

Singles: 7-Inch
A&M: 82–84 . . . . **1–3**

LPs: 10/12-Inch 33rpm
A&M: 82–83 . . . . **5–8**
   Also see KENNEDY, Joyce, & Jeffrey Osborne
   Also see L.T.D.

OSBORNE & GILES
LPs: 10/12-Inch 33rpm
RED LABEL: 85 . . . . **5–8**
   Members: Billy Osborne; A.Z. Giles.

OSBORNE BROTHERS, The (The Osborne Brothers & Red Allen)
Singles: 7-Inch
CMH: 80 . . . . **1–3**
DECCA: 63–72. . . . . **2–4**
MCA: 73–75 . . . . **1–3**
MGM (100 series): 64. . . . . **2–3**
MGM (12000 & 13000
   series): 59–63 . . . . **3–5**

EPs: 7-Inch 33/45rpm
MGM: 59. . . . . **8–12**

LPs: 10/12-Inch 33rpm
CMH: 76–82 . . . . **5–10**
CORAL: 73 . . . . **4–8**
DECCA: 65–72 . . . . **8–18**
MCA: 73–75 . . . . **5–8**
MGM (100 series): 70. . . . . **5–10**
MGM (3700 series): 59. . . . . **20–30**
MGM (4000 series): 62–63. . . . . **10–20**
ROUNDER **5–8**
SUGAR HILL: 84 . . . . **5–8**
   Members: Bobby Osborne; Sonny Osborne.

OSBOURNE, Ozzy
Singles: 7-Inch
CBS ASSOCIATED: 83–84. . . . . **1–3**
JET: 82. . . . . **1–3**

Price Range

LPs: 10/12-Inch 33rpm
CBS ASSOCIATED: *83–84* **$5–8**
JET: *81–82* **5–8**
    Also see BLACK SABBATH
    Also see MAGIC LANTERNS, The

OSIBISA
Singles: 7-Inch
DECCA: *72* **2–4**
ISLAND: *76–77* **2–3**
MCA **1–3**
WARNER BROS: *73–74* **2–4**
LPs: 10/12-Inch 33rpm
BUDDAH: *73* **8–10**
DECCA: *71–72* **10–12**
ISLAND: *77* **8–10**
MCA **5–8**
WARNER BROS: *73–74* **8–10**

OSIRIS
Singles: 7-Inch
INFINITY: *79* **1–3**
WARNER BROS: *79* **1–3**
LPs: 10/12-Inch 33rpm
INFINITY: *79* **5–8**
WARNER BROS: *79* **5–8**

OSKAR, Lee
Singles: 7-Inch
ELEKTRA: *78–81* **1–3**
UNITED ARTISTS: *76* **2–3**
LPs: 10/12-Inch 33rpm
ELEKTRA: *78–79* **5–8**
UNITED ARTISTS: *76* **8–10**
    Also see WAR

OSMOND, Donny
Singles: 7-Inch
MGM: *71–75* **2–3**
POLYDOR: *76–78* **1–3**
Picture Sleeves
MGM: *71–75* **2–3**
LPs: 10/12-Inch 33rpm
MGM: *71–74* **8–10**
POLYDOR: *77* **5–8**
    Also see OSMONDS, The

OSMOND, Donny & Marie
Singles: 7-Inch
MGM: *74–75* **2–3**
POLYDOR: *76–78* **1–3**

Price Range

LPs: 10/12-Inch 33rpm
MGM: *74–75* **$8–10**
POLYDOR: *76–78* **5–8**
    Also see OSMOND, Donny
    Also see OSMOND, Marie

OSMOND, Jimmy (Little Jimmy Osmond)
Singles: 7-Inch
MGM: *70–75* **2–3**
MERCURY: *78* **1–3**
LPs: 10/12-Inch 33rpm
MGM: *72* **8–10**
    Also see OSMONDS, The

OSMOND, Marie
Singles: 7-Inch
ELEKTRA: *82–84* **1–3**
MGM: *73–75* **2–3**
POLYDOR: *76–78* **1–3**
RCA VICTOR: *84* **1–3**
Picture Sleeves
MGM: *73–75* **2–3**
POLYDOR: *77* **1–3**
RCA VICTOR: *84* .... **INC**
LPs: 10/12-Inch 33rpm
MGM: *74–75* **8–10**
POLYDOR: *77* **5–8**
    Also see OSMOND, Donny & Marie
    Also see OSMONDS, The
    Also see SEALS, Dan, & Marie Osmond

OSMONDS, The (The Osmond Brothers)
Singles: 7-Inch
BARNABY: *68–69* **3–5**
ELEKTRA: *82–83* **1–3**
MGM (13126 through
    14159): *63–70* **3–5**
MGM (14193 through
    14831): *70–75* **2–3**
MERCURY: *79* **1–3**
POLYDOR: *76–77* **1–3**
UNI (55015; "I Can't
    Stop"): *67* **4–6**
UNI (55276; "I Can't
    Stop"): *71* **2–4**
WARNER BROS./CURB:
    83–85 .... **1–3**
Picture Sleeves
MGM: *73–74* **2–3**

Price Range

LPs: 10/12-Inch 33rpm
ELEKTRA: 82 .... **$5–8**
MGM (7; "Preview: The
  Osmond Brothers") **12–15**
  (Promotional issue only.)
MGM (4100 & 4200
  series): 63–65 .... **10–20**
MGM (4724 through
  5012): 70–75. .... **8–10**
MERCURY: 79. .... **5–8**
METRO: 65. .... **10–15**
POLYDOR: 76–77 .... **5–8**
WARNER BROS./CURB:
  83–85 .... **5–8**
  Members: Donny Osmond; Alan Osmond;
  Merrill Osmond; Wayne Osmond; Jimmy Os-
  mond; Marie Osmond.
  Also see OSMOND, Donny
  Also see OSMOND, Jimmy
  Also see OSMOND, Marie

OSMONDS, The, Steve Lawrence & Eydie Gorme
Singles: 7-Inch
MGM: 72. .... **2–3**
  Also see LAWRENCE, Steve, & Eydie Gorme
  Also see OSMONDS, The

O'SULLIVAN, Gilbert
Singles: 7-Inch
EPIC: 77–81 .... **1–3**
MAM: 71–76. .... **2–3**
Picture Sleeves
MAM: 72. .... **2–3**
LPs: 10/12-Inch 33rpm
EPIC: 81 .... **5–8**
MAM: 72. .... **10–12**

OTIS, Johnny (The Johnny Otis Show; Johnny Otis & The Peacocks; The Johnny Otis Quintette)
Singles: 7-Inch
CAPITOL (3799 through
  3802): 57 .... **150–200**
  (Records with special four-pocket cover, titled
  "The Johnny Otis Show.")
CAPITOL (3799 through
  3802): 57 .... **5–8**
  (Individual records only. No cover.)
CAPITOL (3852 through
  4326): 58–60. .... **4–6**
  (Monaural singles.)

Price Range

CAPITOL (4000 series): 59 ...... **$10–15**
  (Stereo singles.)
DIG: 55–59 .... **5–8**
ELDO (105; "The New Bo
  Diddley"): 60. .... **4–6**
ELDO (153; "Long
  Distance"): 67 .... **3–5**
EPIC: 70 .... **2–4**
HAWK SOUND: 75. .... **2–3**
KENT: 69 .... **2–4**
KING: 61–63. .... **3–5**
MERCURY: 51–53. .... **10–12**
OKEH: 69 .... **2–4**
PEACOCK (Except 1625):
  52 .... **10–12**
PEACOCK (1625; "Young
  Girl"): 52. .... **25–30**
SAVOY: 50–54 .... **8–12**

EPs: 7-Inch 33/45rpm
CAPITOL: 58–59 .... **20–25**

LPs: 10/12-Inch 33rpm
ALLIGATOR: 82. .... **5–8**
BLUES SPECTRUM **10–12**
CAPITOL: 58 .... **50–60**
CHARLY **5–8**
DIG: 57. .... **125–150**
EPIC: 70–71 .... **10–12**
JAZZ WORLD: 78. .... **5–10**
KENT: 70 .... **10–12**
SAVOY: 78–80 .... **5–8**

Price Range   *Price Range*

Note: Cross-referenced below are some of the artists who performed with the Johnny Otis Show, or with whom he or his orchestra appears.
Also see ADAMS, Marie
Also see FREEMAN, Ernie
Also see LITTLE ESTHER & THE ROBINS
Also see McNEELY, Big Jay
Also see WATSON, Johnny

OTIS, Johnny, & Preston Love
Singles: 7-Inch
KENT: 70 . . . . $2–4
Also see OTIS, Johnny
Also see OTIS, Shuggie, & Preston Love

OTIS, Shuggie
Singles: 7-Inch
EPIC: 70–74 2–4
LPs: 10/12-Inch 33rpm
EPIC: 70–74 10–12
Also see KOOPER, Al, & Shuggie Otis

OTIS, Shuggie, & Preston Love
Singles: 7-Inch
KENT: 70 2–4
Also see OTIS, Johnny, & Preston Love
Also see OTIS, Shuggie

OTIS & CARLA
Singles: 7-Inch
ATCO: 69 2–4
STAX: 67–68 3–5
LPs: 10/12-Inch 33rpm
STAX: 67 10–15
Members: Otis Redding; Carla Thomas.
Also see REDDING, Otis
Also see THOMAS, Carla

OUTLAWS, The
Singles: 7-Inch
ARISTA: 75–80 1–3
LPs: 10/12-Inch 33rpm
ARISTA: 75–80 5–8
Also see PAUL, Henry, Band

OUTPUT
Singles: 12-Inch 33/45rpm
CBS ASSOCIATED: 83 4–6
Singles: 7-Inch
CBS ASSOCIATED: 83 1–3
TUFF CITY: 84 1–3

OUTSIDERS, The (Featuring Sonny Geraci)
Singles: 7-Inch
BELL: 70 . . . . $2–4
CAPITOL: 66–68 3–5
ELLEN 8–10
KAPP: 70 3–5
KARATE: 64 5–8
Picture Sleeves
CAPITOL: 66–67 4–6
LPs: 10/12-Inch 33rpm
CAPITOL: 66–67 15–20
Also see CLIMAX

OVATIONS, The (Featuring Louis Williams)
Singles: 7-Inch
GOLDWAX: 64–69 3–5

OVATIONS, The
Singles: 7-Inch
CHESS: 75 2–3
MGM: 73 2–4
SOUNDS OF MEMPHIS:
72–73 2–4
LPs: 10/12-Inch 33rpm
MGM: 73 8–10
SOUNDS OF MEMPHIS:
72 10–12

OVERLANDERS, The
Singles: 7-Inch
HICKORY: 64–66 4–6

OVERTON, C.B.
Singles: 7-Inch
SHOCK: 78 2–3

OWEN, B.
Singles: 7-Inch
JANUS: 70 2–4

OWEN, Reg, & His Orchestra
Singles: 7-Inch
PALETTE: 58–62 2–5
LPs: 10/12-Inch 33rpm
PALETTE: 59–60 15–20

Price Range

Price Range

OWENS, Buck (Buck Owens & The Buckaroos)
Singles: 7-Inch
CAPITOL (2000 through
  4000 series): *67–75* $2–3
CAPITOL (4000 series):
  59–63 3–5
CAPITOL (5000 series):
  63–67 2–4
NEW STAR 50–60
PEP: *56–57* 10–15
STARDAY (500 series): *61* 3–5
STARDAY (5000 series):
  64 2–4
WARNER BROS: *76–80*........... 1–3
EPs: 7-Inch 33/45rpm
CAPITOL: *61–65* 10–20
LPs: 10/12-Inch 33rpm
CAPITOL (100 through
  400 series): *68–70* 8–12
CAPITOL (500 series,
  except 574): *70*.................. 8–10
CAPITOL (600 through
  800 series): *70–72* 5–10
CAPITOL (574; "Buck
  Owens"): *70*.................. 12–20
  (A 3-LP set.)
CAPITOL (1400 through
  1900 series): *61–63* 20–30
  (With a "T" or "ST" prefix.)
CAPITOL (1400 series): *69*........ 6–12
  (With a "DT" prefix.)
CAPITOL (2100 through
  2700 series): *64–67* 10–20
CAPITOL (2800 through
  2900 series): *68* 8–12
CAPITOL (2980; "Buck
  Owens Minute
  Masters"): *66*.................. 30–35
  (Promotional issue only.)
CAPITOL (11000 series):
  72–78 5–8
HALL OF MUSIC............... 8–12
LA BREA (8017; "Buck
  Owens"): *61*.................. 50–75
OUT OF TOWN DIST: *82* 5–8
PICKWICK/HILLTOP:
  78 6–10
STARDAY (100 series): *62* 15–25
STARDAY (300 series):
  64–65 10–15

STARDAY (400 series): *75* $6–10
TIME-LIFE: *82*.................. 6–10
TRIP: *76* 5–8
WARNER BROS: *76–77*........... 5–8
  Also see JONES, Corky

OWENS, Buck, & Emmylou Harris
Singles: 7-Inch
WARNER BROS: *79*.............. 1–3
  Also see HARRIS, Emmylou

OWENS, Buck, & Susan Raye
Singles: 7-Inch
CAPITOL: *70–73* 2–3
LPs: 10/12-Inch 33rpm
CAPITOL: *70–73* 5–10
  Also see RAYE, Susan

OWENS, Buck / Faron Young / Ferlin Husky
LPs: 10/12-Inch 33rpm
PICKWICK/HILLTOP:
  65 10–12
  Also see HUSKY, Ferlin
  Also see OWENS, Buck
  Also see YOUNG, Faron

OWENS, Donnie (Donny Owens)
Singles: 7-Inch
ARA............................. 3–5
GUYDEN: *58–59* 4–6
TREY: *60* 4–6

OWENS, Gwen
Singles: 7-Inch
BIG TREE: *79* 1–3
JOSIE: *69*....................... 2–4

OWENS, Tony
Singles: 7-Inch
SOUL SOUND: *67*................ 3–5
SOULIN': *67*..................... 3–5

OXO
Singles: 7-Inch
GEFFEN: *83*..................... 1–3
LPs: 10/12-Inch 33rpm
GEFFEN: *83*..................... 5–8
  Also see FOXY

Price Range

OZARK MOUNTAIN DAREDEVILS, The
Singles: 7-Inch
A&M: *74–78* $2–3
COLUMBIA: *80* 1–3
Picture Sleeves
A&M: *75–76* 2–3
LPs: 10/12-Inch 33rpm
A&M: *73–78* 8–12
COLUMBIA: *80* 5–8
Also see LEE, Larry

OZO
Singles: 7-Inch
DJM: *76* 2–3
LPs: 10/12-Inch 33rpm
DJM: *76* 5–10

OZONE
Singles: 7-Inch
MOTOWN: *80–83* 1–3
LPs: 10/12-Inch 33rpm
MOTOWN: *80–83* 5–8

P

P.F.M. (Premiata Forneria Marconi)
Singles: 7-Inch
ASYLUM: *76–77* 2–3
MANTICORE: *73–75* 2–4
LPs: 10/12-Inch 33rpm
ASYLUM: *76–77* 5–8
MANTICORE: *73–74* 8–10
PETERS INT'L: *76* 5–8

P CREW
Singles: 7-Inch
PRELUDE: *83* 1–3

P. FUNK ALL-STARS, The
Singles: 12-Inch 33/45rpm
UNCLE JAM: *84* 4–6
Singles: 7-Inch
CBS ASSOCIATED: *83* 1–3
HUMP: *82* 1–3
UNCLE JAM: *84* 1–3
LPs: 10/12-Inch 33rpm
CBS ASSOCIATED: *84* 5–8
UNCLE JAM: *84* 5–8

Price Range

PG&E: see PACIFIC GAS & ELECTRIC

PABLO CRUISE
Singles: 7-Inch
A&M: *75–84* $1–3
Picture Sleeves
A&M: *77–84* 1–3
LPs: 10/12-Inch 33rpm
A&M: *75–84* 6–10
MFSL: *78* 10–15
Members: Dave Jenkins; Steve Price; Cory Lerios; Bud Cockrell.
Also see IT'S A BEAUTIFUL DAY

PACIFIC GAS & ELECTRIC (PG&E; The Pacific Gas & Electric Blues Band)
Singles: 7-Inch
BRIGHT ORANGE: *68* 4–6
COLUMBIA: *69–72* 2–4
POWER: *69* 4–6
LPs: 10/12-Inch 33rpm
ABC 8–10
BRIGHT ORANGE: *68* 15–20
COLUMBIA: *69–73* 8–12
POWER: *69* 10–15
Also see SEEGER, Pete, & Pacific Gas & Electric

PACKERS, The
Singles: 7-Inch
HBR: *66* 3–5
IMPERIAL: *69* 2–4
PURE SOUL MUSIC: *65* 3–5
TANGERINE: *68* 2–4
LPs: 10/12-Inch 33rpm
IMPERIAL: *68* 10–12
PURE SOUL MUSIC: *66* 12–15

PAGAN, Bruni
Singles: 7-Inch
ELEKTRA: *79* 1–3

PAGAN, Ralfi
Singles: 7-Inch
FANIA: *71* 2–4

PAGE, Gene
Singles: 7-Inch
ARISTA: *78–80* 1–3
ATLANTIC: *74–75* 2–3

Price Range

LPs: 10/12-Inch 33rpm
ARISTA: 78–80. . . . . $5–8
ATLANTIC: 74–75 8–10

PAGE, Jimmy
    LPs: 10/12-Inch 33rpm
SWAN SONG: 82. 5–8
    Also see FIRM, The
    Also see HERMAN'S HERMITS
    Also see HONEYDRIPPERS, The
    Also see LED ZEPPELIN
    Also see LORD SUTCH
    Also see STEWART, Al
    Also see WILLIE & THE POOR BOYS
    Also see YARDBIRDS, The

PAGE, Jimmy, & Sonny Boy Williamson
    LPs: 10/12-Inch 33rpm
SPRINGBOARD: 72 8–10

PAGE, Jimmy, Sonny Boy Williamson & Brian Auger
    LPs: 10/12-Inch 33rpm
CHARLY 5–8
    Also see AUGER, Brian
    Also see PAGE, Jimmy
    Also see WILLIAMSON, Sonny Boy

PAGE, Patti
    Singles: 7-Inch
AVCO: 74–75. 1–3
COLUMBIA: 63–70 2–4
EPIC: 73 1–3
MERCURY (5000 series):
    50–52 3–5
MERCURY (70000 through 72000 series):
    52–63 2–4
MERCURY (73000 series):
    71 2–3
PLANTATION: 81–82. 1–3
    Picture Sleeves
MERCURY: 54–63. 2–5
    EPs: 7-Inch 33/45rpm
MERCURY: 51–61. 5–10
    LPs: 10/12-Inch 33rpm
ACCORD: 82 4–8
COLUMBIA: 63–70 5–15
EXACT: 80 5–8
HARMONY: 69–70 5–10
MERCURY (100 series):
    69 6–12

Price Range

MERCURY (20000 series):
    55–64 . . . . $10–25
MERCURY (25000 series):
    50–54 15–30
    (10-Inch LPs.)
MERCURY (60000 series):
    58–64 10–25
MERCURY (61000 series):
    71 5–10
PLANTATION: 81. 5–8
WING: 63–65 5–10

PAGE, Patti, & Tom T. Hall
    Singles: 7-Inch
MERCURY: 72. 2–3
    Also see HALL, Tom T.
    Also see PAGE, Patti

PAGES, The
    Singles: 7-Inch
CAPITOL: 81 1–3
EPIC: 79–80 1–3
    LPs: 10/12-Inch 33rpm
CAPITOL: 81 5–8
EPIC: 78–79 5–8
    Members: Richard Page; Steve George; Russell
    Battelene; Jerry Manfredi; Peter Leinheiser.
    Also see MR. MISTER

PAIGE, Sharon (Sharon Paige & Harold Melvin & The Bluenotes)
    Singles: 7-Inch
PHILADELPHIA INT'L:
    75 2–3
SOURCE: 80 1–3

Price Range   *Price Range*

Also see MELVIN, Harold

PAINTER
Singles: 7-Inch
ELEKTRA: *73* $2–4
LPs: 10/12-Inch 33rpm
ELEKTRA: *73* 8–10

PALLAS, Laura
Singles: 12-Inch 33/45rpm
TVI: *84*. 4–6

PALM BEACH BAND BOYS, The
Singles: 7-Inch
RCA VICTOR: *66–67* 2–4
LPs: 10/12-Inch 33rpm
RCA VICTOR: *66–67* 5–10

PALMER, Robert
Singles: 12-Inch 33/45rpm
ISLAND: *83–85* 4–6
Singles: 7-Inch
ISLAND: *75–85* 1–3
LPs: 10/12-Inch 33rpm
ISLAND (Except 819):
75–85 5–8
ISLAND (819; "Secrets"):
79 35–40
(Picture disc. Promotional issue only.)

PAMPLEMOUSSE, Le: see LE PAMPLEMOUSSE

PANIC BUTTON, The
Singles: 7-Inch
CHALOM: *68*. 3–5
GAMBLE: *69* 2–4

PAONE, Nicola
Singles: 7-Inch
ABC-PARAMOUNT: *59*. 2–4
CADENCE: *59* 2–4
EPs: 7-Inch 33/45rpm
CADENCE: *59* 4–8
LPs: 10/12-Inch 33rpm
ABC-PARAMOUNT:
59–60 8–15
ROULETTE: *65* 6–12

PAPER LACE
Singles: 7-Inch
BANG: *72* $2–4
MERCURY: *74–75*. 2–3
LPs: 10/12-Inch 33rpm
MERCURY: *74*. 8–10

PARACHUTE CLUB, The
Singles: 12-Inch 33/45rpm
RCA VICTOR: *83* 4–6
Singles: 7-Inch
RCA VICTOR: *83* 1–3
LPs: 10/12-Inch 33rpm
RCA VICTOR: *83* 5–8

PARADE, The
Singles: 7-Inch
A&M: *67–69* 3–5

PARADISE EXPRESS
Singles: 12-Inch 33/45rpm
FANTASY: *78–81*. 4–6
Singles: 7-Inch
FANTASY: *78–81*. 1–3
LPs: 10/12-Inch 33rpm
FANTASY: *78*. 5–8

PARADONS, The
Singles: 7-Inch
COLLECTABLES 1–3
ERA: *72*. 1–3
MILESTONE: *60–61* 6–10
TUFFEST 15–20
WARNER BROS: *60*. 5–8

PARAGONS, The
Singles: 7-Inch
ABC: *73*. 1–3
BUDDAH: *75*. 2–4
COLLECTABLES 1–3
MUSIC CLEF: *63*. 4–6
MUSICRAFT: *60* 5–8
TAP: *62* 4–6
TIMES SQUARE: *63*. 3–5
VIRGO: *72–73*. 1–3
WINLEY (215;
"Florence"): *57* 12–15
WINLEY (220; "Let's
Start All Over Again"):
57 12–15

WINLEY (223 through
240): *57–60*................... **$8–12**
LPs: 10/12-Inch 33rpm
LOST-NITE: *81*................... **5–8**
RARE BIRD.................... **20–25**
Members: Julius McMichaels; Mack Starr; Al
Brown; Don Travis; Ben Frazier; Bill Witt;
Rick Jackson.
Also see HARPTONES, The / The Paragons
Also see OLYMPICS, The

PARAGONS, The / The Jesters
LPs: 10/12-Inch 33rpm
JUBILEE: *59*................... **25–35**
PAUL WINLEY
PRODUCTIONS: *65* **20–25**
WINLEY: *60*.................. **45–55**
Also see JESTERS, The
Also see PARAGONS, The

PARAMOR, Norrie, & His Orchestra
Singles: 7-Inch
ESSEX: *53*...................... **2–4**
EPs: 7-Inch 33/45rpm
CAPITOL: *56*................... **4–8**
LPs: 10/12-Inch 33rpm
CAPITOL: *55–66*............... **5–15**
ESSEX: *54*...................... **8–15**
HAYNES & SBARRA: *79* **4–8**

PARAMOURS, The
Singles: 7-Inch
MOONGLOW (Black
vinyl): *62* **8–10**
MOONGLOW (Colored
vinyl): *62* **15–20**
SMASH: *61* **10–12**
Members: Bill Medley; Bobby Hatfield.
Also see RIGHTEOUS BROTHERS, The

PARIS (Featuring Bob Welch)
Singles: 7-Inch
CAPITOL: *76* **2–3**
LPs: 10/12-Inch 33rpm
CAPITOL: *76* **8–10**
Also see WELCH, Bob

PARIS SISTERS
Singles: 7-Inch
ABC: *73*......................... **1–3**
CAPITOL: *68* **3–5**

COLLECTABLES **$1–3**
DECCA: *54–58*.................. **5–8**
ERIC **1–3**
GNP/CRESCENDO: *68* **3–5**
GREGMARK: *61–62*.............. **4–6**
IMPERIAL: *57–58*.............. **5–8**
MGM: *64*....................... **3–5**
MERCURY: *64–65*.............. **3–5**
REPRISE: *66–67*................. **3–5**
Picture Sleeves
MGM: *64*....................... **4–6**
MERCURY: *64*.................. **4–6**
LPs: 10/12-Inch 33rpm
REPRISE: *67*................... **15–20**
SIDEWALK **12–15**
UNIFILMS **10–12**
Members: Priscilla; Sherrell; Albeth.
Also see ALLAN, Davie

PARKAYS, The
Singles: 7-Inch
ABC-PARAMOUNT: *61*........... **3–5**
FONTANA: *65*.................. **3–5**

PARKER, Bobby
Singles: 7-Inch
AMANDA: *60*................... **4–6**
V-TONE: *61* **3–5**

PARKER, Fess (Fess Parker & Buddy Ebsen)
Singles: 7-Inch
BUENA VISTA: *63* **2–4**
CASCADE: *59* **3–5**
COLUMBIA: *55*................. **4–6**
DISNEYLAND: *57* **3–5**
GUSTO: *63* **3–5**
RCA VICTOR: *64–69* **2–4**
Picture Sleeves
BUENA VISTA: *63* **3–5**
DISNEYLAND: *57* **4–6**
RCA VICTOR: *64* **2–4**
EPs: 7-Inch 33/45rpm
COLUMBIA: *55*................ **5–15**
LPs: 10/12-Inch 33rpm
COLUMBIA (666; "Davy
Crockett"): *55* **15–30**
DISNEYLAND (1200
series): *64–65* **5–12**
DISNEYLAND (1300
series): *70* **5–10**

DISNEYLAND (1900
series): *63* **$5–15**
DISNEYLAND (3000
series): *55* **10–20**
DISNEYLAND (3900
series): *64* **5–12**
HARMONY: *60* **5–15**
RCA VICTOR: *64* **8–15**

PARKER, Graham (Graham Parker & Rumor; Graham Parker & The Shot)

Singles: 7-Inch
ARISTA: *79–83*. **1–3**
MERCURY (Black vinyl):
76–77 . . . . **2–3**
MERCURY (Colored
vinyl): *77* **2–4**
Picture Sleeves
ARISTA: *80–83*. **1–3**
LPs: 10/12-Inch 33rpm
ARISTA: *78–83*. **5–8**
ELEKTRA: *85* **5–8**
MERCURY: *77–78*. **6–10**
Promotional LPs
ARISTA (41; "Mercury
Poisoning"): *78* **25–35**
ARISTA (63; "Live
Sparks"): *79* **25–35**
Also see RUMOR
Also see SPRINGSTEEN, Bruce

PARKER, Little Junior (Junior Parker; Little Junior & His Blue Flames; Little Junior Parker & The Blue Blowers)

Singles: 7-Inch
ABC: *73* **2–3**
BLUE ROCK: *68–69* **2–4**
CAPITOL: *71* **2–4**
DUKE (100 series): *54–58* **6–10**
DUKE (300 series): *59–66* **3–5**
DUKE (400 series): *67* **2–4**
MCA. **1–3**
MERCURY: *66–68*. **3–5**
MINIT: *69* **2–4**
LPs: 10/12-Inch 33rpm
ABC: *76* **8–10**
BLUE ROCK: *69* **10–12**
BLUESWAY: *73* **8–10**

CAPITOL: *70* **$10–12**
DUKE (76; "Driving
Wheel"): *62* **35–40**
DUKE (83; "Best Of
Junior Parker"): *74* **8–10**
MCA. **5–8**
MERCURY: *67*. **12–15**
MINIT: *69*. **10–12**
Also see BLAND, Bobby / Little Junior Parker
Also see LITTLE JUNIOR'S BLUE FLAMES

PARKER, Little Junior, With Bill Johnson's Blue Flames

Singles: 7-Inch
DUKE: *54* **12–15**

PARKER, Little Junior, & Jimmy McGriff

LPs: 10/12-Inch 33rpm
CAPITOL: *71* **10–12**
UNITED ARTISTS: *71* **10–12**
Also see McGRIFF, Jimmy
Also see PARKER, Little Junior

PARKER, Little Willie, & Lorenzo Smith

Singles: 7-Inch
MAR-VEL: *64*. **3–5**

PARKER, Paul

Singles: 12-Inch 33/45rpm
MEGATONE: *83* **4–6**

PARKER, Ray, Jr. (Ray Parker, Jr. & Raydio)

Singles: 12-Inch 33/45rpm
ARISTA: *84–85*. **4–6**
Singles: 7-Inch
ARISTA: *80–85*. **1–3**
FLASHBACK: *82*. **1–3**
Picture Sleeves
ARISTA: *80–85*. **1–3**
LPs: 10/12-Inch 33rpm
ARISTA: *80–85*. **5–8**
Also see RAYDIO

PARKER, Robert

Singles: 7-Inch
HEAD: *72* **1–3**
IMPERIAL: *62*. **4–6**
ISLAND: *75–76* **2–3**

Price Range

NOLA: *66–67* $3–5
RON: *59–60* 5–8
SILVER FOX: *69* 2–4
LPs: 10/12-Inch 33rpm
NOLA: *66* 15–20
Also see BO, Eddie

PARKER, Winfield
Singles: 7-Inch
ARCTIC: *69* 2–4
GSP: *72* 2–3
RU-JAC: *68* 3–5
SPRING: *71* 2–4

PARKING METER
Singles: 12-Inch 33/45rpm
ATLANTIC: *84* 4–6
Singles: 7-Inch
ATLANTIC: *84* 1–3

PARKS, Michael
Singles: 7-Inch
MGM: *70* 2–4
LPs: 10/12-Inch 33rpm
MGM: *69–70* 10–12
VERVE: *71* 8–10

PARLET
Singles: 7-Inch
CASABLANCA: *78–80* 1–3
LPs: 10/12-Inch 33rpm
CASABLANCA: *79* 5–8

PARLIAMENT (Parliament Thang)
Singles: 12-Inch 33/45rpm
CASABLANCA: *78* 4–6
Singles: 7-Inch
CASABLANCA: *74–81* 1–3
INVICTUS: *70–71* 2–3
LPs: 10/12-Inch 33rpm
CASABLANCA (Except
picture discs): *74–80* 5–8
CASABLANCA (Picture
discs): *79* 10–15
INVICTUS: *70* 8–10
Also see BOOTSY'S RUBBER BAND
Also see BRIDES OF FUNKENSTEIN, The
Also see PARLIAMENTS, The

Price Range

PARLIAMENTS, The
Singles: 7-Inch
ATCO: *69* $2–4
REVILOT: *67–68* 3–5
Also see CLINTON, George, Band
Also see FUNKADELIC
Also see PARLIAMENT

PARR, John
Singles: 12-Inch 33/45rpm
ATLANTIC: *86* 4–6
Singles: 7-Inch
ATLANTIC: *84–86* 1–3
LPs: 10/12-Inch 33rpm
ATLANTIC: *86* 5–8

PARRIS, Fred (Fred Parris & The Satins; Fred Parris & The Scarlets; Fred Parris & Black Satin; Fred Parris & The Restless Hearts; Fred Paris)
Singles: 7-Inch
ATCO: *66* 4–6
BIRTH 3–5
BUDDAH: *75* 2–4
CANDLELITE: *63* 5–8
CHECKER: *65* 4–6
ELEKTRA: *82* 2–3
GREEN SEA: *66* 4–6
KLIK: *58* 30–35
MAMA SADIE: *67* 4–6
RCA VICTOR (9200
series): *67* 3–5
(In 1968, a completely different singer, named
Freddie Paris, recorded for RCA. He had a
9300 series single and an LP on Victor. Note
slightly different spelling.)
LPs: 10/12-Inch 33rpm
ELEKTRA: *82* 5–8
Also see FIVE SATINS, The

PARRISH, Dean
Singles: 7-Inch
BOOM: *66* 3–5
LAURIE: *67* 3–5

PARRISH, Man
Singles: 7-Inch
SUGAR SCOOP: *85* 1–3
LPs: 10/12-Inch 33rpm
IMPORTE: *83* 5–8

Price Range

Price Range

PARSONS, Alan, Project
Singles: 7-Inch
ARISTA: *77–84*.................... **$1–3**
20TH CENTURY-FOX:
76 .... **2–4**

LPs: 10/12-Inch 33rpm
ARISTA: *77–84*.................... **5–8**
20TH CENTURY-FOX:
76–77 .... **8–10**
Also see PILOT

PARSONS, Bill (Bobby Bare)
Singles: 7-Inch
ABC: *73*........................ **1–3**
COLLECTABLES **1–3**
FRATERNITY: *58*............... **8–10**
Also see BARE, Bobby

PARSONS, Bill
Singles: 7-Inch
FRATERNITY: *59*................. **4–6**
STARDAY (Except 526):
61 .... **3–5**
STARDAY (526; "Hot
Rod Volkswagen"): *60* **8–10**

PARSONS, Gram (Gram Parsons & The Fallen Angels)
Singles: 7-Inch
REPRISE: *73*..................... **2–4**
SIERRA: *79* **2–3**

EPs: 7-Inch 33/45rpm
SIERRA: *82* **8–10**
(Promotional issue only.)

LPs: 10/12-Inch 33rpm
REPRISE: *73*..................... **8–10**
SHILOH: *73* **8–12**
SIERRA: *79–82*................... **5–8**
Also see BYRDS, The
Also see FLYING BURRITO BROTHERS,
The
Also see HARRIS, Emmylou

PARTON, Dolly
Singles: 12-Inch 33/45rpm
RCA VICTOR (Black
vinyl): *78–83*................... **4–6**
RCA VICTOR (Colored
vinyl): *78* **8–10**

Singles: 7-Inch
GOLDBAND (1000
series): *59*.................... **$10–20**
MERCURY (71000 series):
62 .... **5–10**
MONUMENT (800
through 1000 series):
65–68 .... **3–5**
RCA VICTOR (0100 &
0200 series): *69–76* **2–4**
RCA VICTOR (9500
through 9900 series):
68–71 .... **2–4**
RCA VICTOR (10000
through 14000 series):
74–85 .... **1–3**

Promotional Singles
RCA VICTOR (Colored
vinyl): *77–85*.................... **3–5**

Picture Sleeves
RCA VICTOR: *69–85* **1–3**

LPs: 10/12-Inch 33rpm
ALSHIRE: *69–71* **8–10**
CAMDEN: *72–78*................ **5–10**
MONUMENT (7600
series): *78* **5–8**
MONUMENT (8085;
"Hello,, I'm Dolly"): *67* **12–20**
(Monaural.)
MONUMENT (18085;
"Hello,, I'm Dolly"): *67* **12–20**
(Stereo.)
MONUMENT (18100
series): *70* **8–12**
MONUMENT (31000
series): *72* **8–15**
MONUMENT (33000
series): *75* **6–10**
RCA VICTOR (0033
through 5000 series):
73–85 .... **5–12**
(With an "AFL1," "AHL1," "APD1,"
"APL1," or "AYL1" prefix.)
RCA VICTOR (3413;
"Great Balls Of Fire"):
79 .... **12–18**
(Picture disc. With a "CPL1" prefix.)
RCA VICTOR (3900
through 4700 series):
68–72 .... **8–15**
(With an "LPM" or "LSP" prefix.)

Price Range

RCA VICTOR (5000
  series): *84* **$5–8**
SOMERSET: *63–68* **10–20**
STEREO-FIDELITY:
  63–68 .... **10–20**
TIME-LIFE: *81*.................... **5–8**
  Also see HARRIS, Emmylou
  Also see NELSON, Willie, & Dolly Parton
  Also see PHILLIPS, Bill, & Dolly Parton
  Also see ROGERS, Kenny, & Dolly Parton
  Also see WAGONER, Porter, & Dolly Parton

PARTON, Dolly / George Jones
LPs: 10/12-Inch 33rpm
STARDAY: *68* **25–35**
  Also see JONES, George

PARTON, Dolly / Kitty Wells
LPs: 10/12-Inch 33rpm
EXACT: *80* **5–8**
  Also see PARTON, Dolly
  Also see WELLS, Kitty

PARTRIDGE FAMILY, The
(Featuring David Cassidy)
Singles: 7-Inch
BELL: *70–73* **2–4**
Picture Sleeves
BELL: *70–73* **2–4**
LPs: 10/12-Inch 33rpm
BELL: *70–74* **8–10**
  Also see CASSIDY, David

PASSIONS, The
Singles: 7-Inch
ABC-PARAMOUNT: *63*.......... **8–10**
AUDICON: *59–61* **10–12**
COLLECTABLES **1–3**
DIAMOND: *63*................... **5–8**
DORE: *58* **8–10**
JUBILEE: *61*..................... **8–10**
LAURIE **1–3**
OCTAVIA: *62*.................. **20–25**
  Members: Jim Gallagher; Tony Armato; Al
  Galione; Vince Acerno; Louis Rotondo.
  Also see MYSTICS, The / The Passions

PASSPORT
Singles: 7-Inch
ATCO: *76* **2–3**
ATLANTIC: *78* **2–3**

Price Range

LPs: 10/12-Inch 33rpm
ATCO: *74–77*................... **$8–10**
ATLANTIC: *78–82* **5–8**
REPRISE: *72*.................... **8–10**

PASTEL SIX, The
Singles: 7-Inch
CHATTAHOOCHEE: *65* **3–5**
DOWNEY: *62–63*................. **4–6**
ERA: *72*........................ **1–3**
ZEN: *62*........................ **4–6**
ZENITH: *63* **4–6**

PASTELS, The (With Big Dee Irwin)
Singles: 7-Inch
ARGO: *58*...................... **8–10**
CHESS: *73*...................... **1–3**
MASCOT: *57*................... **45–50**
  Also see IRWIN, Big Dee

PASTORIUS, Jaco
LPs: 10/12-Inch 33rpm
WARNER BROS: *81*.............. **5–8**
  Also see WEATHER REPORT

PAT & THE SATELLITES
Singles: 7-Inch
ATCO: *59* **4–6**

PAT & THE WILDCATS
Singles: 7-Inch
CRUSADER: *64*.................. **3–5**

PATE, Johnny (The Johnny Pate
Trio)
Singles: 7-Inch
ARGO: *64*....................... **2–4**
FEDERAL: *57–59* **3–5**
GIG: *56* **3–5**
LPs: 10/12-Inch 33rpm
GIG: *56* **20–40**
KING (500 & 600 series):
  58–59 .... **15–30**
SALEM: *58* **15–30**
STEPHENY: *57* **20–40**

PATIENCE & PRUDENCE
Singles: 7-Inch
CHATTAHOOCHEE:
  64–65 .... **3–5**
LIBERTY: *56* **5–8**

UNITED ARTISTS **$1–3**
Also see CLIFFORD, Mike, & Patience & Prudence

PATRIS
Singles: 12-Inch 33/45rpm
EMERGENCY: *85* **4–6**

PATTERSON, Kellee
Singles: 7-Inch
SHADYBROOK: *75–77*. **2–3**

LPs: 10/12-Inch 33rpm
SHADYBROOK: *76–79*. **5–8**
Note: Shadybrook may also be shown as Shady Brook, two words.

PATTON, Robbie
Singles: 7-Inch
ATLANTIC: *83–85* **1–3**
BACKSTREET: *79*. **2–3**
LIBERTY: *81* **1–3**

LPs: 10/12-Inch 33rpm
ATLANTIC: *85* **5–8**
LIBERTY: *81* **5–8**

PATTY & THE EMBLEMS (Patti & The Emblems)
Singles: 7-Inch
COLLECTABLES **1–3**
CONGRESS: *66* **3–5**
HERALD: *64* **4–6**
KAPP: *66–68*. **3–5**

PAUL, Billy
Singles: 12-Inch 33/45rpm
PHILADELPHIA INT'L:
79 . . . . **4–6**

Singles: 7-Inch
FINCH: *60* **8–10**
PHILADELPHIA INT'L:
71–81 . . . . **1–3**

LPs: 10/12-Inch 33rpm
GAMBLE: *67* **12–15**
NEPTUNE: *70* **10–12**
PHILADELPHIA INT'L:
71–80 . . . . **6–10**
Also see PHILADELPHIA INTERNATIONAL ALL STARS, The

PAUL, Henry, Band
Singles: 7-Inch
ATLANTIC: *79–81* **$1–3**

LPs: 10/12-Inch 33rpm
ATLANTIC: *79* **5–8**
Also see OUTLAWS, The

PAUL, Les (The Les Paul Trio)
Singles: 7-Inch
CAPITOL: *50–53* **3–5**
DECCA: *54* **3–5**

EPs: 7-Inch 33/45rpm
DECCA: *50–53* **5–15**

LPs: 10/12-Inch 33rpm
CAPITOL (200 series): *77* **5–8**
CAPITOL (16000 series):
82 . . . . **4–6**
DECCA (5000 series):
50–53 . . . . **20–40**
(10-Inch LPs.)
GLENDALE: *78*. **5–8**
LONDON: *68–79* **6–12**
VOCALION: *68* **6–12**
Also see ATKINS, Chet, & Les Paul

PAUL, Les, & Mary Ford
Singles: 7-Inch
CAPITOL: *50–57* **3–5**
COLUMBIA: *58–64* **2–4**

Picture Sleeves
COLUMBIA: *58–64* **2–4**

EPs: 7-Inch 33/45rpm
CAPITOL: *50–57* **5–15**

LPs: 10/12-Inch 33rpm
CAPITOL (200 series): *78* **5–8**
(With an "SM" prefix.")
CAPITOL (200 through
800 series): *50–56* **15–30**
(With an "H," "T" or "ST" prefix.)
CAPITOL (1400 & 1500
series): *60–61* **10–20**
CAPITOL (11000 series):
74 . . . . **5–8**
COLUMBIA: *61–63* **8–15**
HARMONY: *65* **5–12**
Also see PAUL, Les

PAUL, Pope: see POPE PAUL

Price Range

PAUL & PAULA
Singles: 7-Inch
LE CAM (300 series):
74–82 . . . . **$2–3**
LE CAM (900 series): *63* **8–10**
PHILIPS (40000 series):
62–66 . . . . **3–5**
PHILIPS (44000 series) **2–3**
UNI: *68* **3–5**
UNITED ARTISTS: *70* **2–4**

Picture Sleeves
PHILIPS: *63* **5–8**

LPs: 10/12-Inch 33rpm
PHILIPS: *63* **15–20**
Members: Ray Hildebrand & Jill Jackson.
Also see JILL & RAY
Also see CHANNEL, Bruce / Paul & Paula

PAULETTE SISTERS, The
Singles: 7-Inch
CAPITOL: *55* **4–6**
CONTEMPO: *63* **3–5**
RIBBON: *60* **3–5**
20TH CENTURY-FOX:
61 . . . . **3–5**

PAULSEN, Pat
LPs: 10/12-Inch 33rpm
MERCURY: *68–70* **8–15**

PAUPERS, The
Singles: 7-Inch
VERVE/FOLKWAYS:
66–67 . . . . **3–5**
VERVE/FORECAST:
67–68 . . . . **3–5**

Picture Sleeves
VERVE: *67* **3–5**

LPs: 10/12-Inch 33rpm
VERVE/FORECAST:
67–68 . . . . **10–12**

PAVLOV'S DOG
Singles: 7-Inch
COLUMBIA: *76* **2–3**

LPs: 10/12-Inch 33rpm
ABC: *75* **10–12**
COLUMBIA: *75–76* **8–10**

Price Range

PAVONE, Rita
Singles: 7-Inch
RCA VICTOR: *63–66* **$3–5**

Picture Sleeves
RCA VICTOR: *64–65* **3–5**

LPs: 10/12-Inch 33rpm
RCA VICTOR: *64–67* **10–15**

PAVAROTTI, Luciano
Singles: 7-Inch
LONDON: *79–84* **1–3**

LPs: 10/12-Inch 33rpm
LONDON: *76–84* **5–8**

PAXTON, Tom
Singles: 7-Inch
ASYLUM: *70* **2–4**
ELEKTRA: *67* **3–5**
REPRISE: *71* **2–4**

LPs: 10/12-Inch 33rpm
ANCHOR **8–10**
ELEKTRA: *64–71* **10–15**
FLYING FISH **5–8**
PRIVATE STOCK: *75* **8–10**
REPRISE: *71–73* **10–15**

PAYCHECK, Johnny
Singles: 7-Inch
ABC: *74* **1–3**
CUTLASS: *72* **2–4**
EPIC: *71–82* **1–3**
HILLTOP: *64–66* **3–5**
LITTLE DARLIN' (008
through 0072): *66–69* **2–4**
LITTLE DARLIN' (7000
series): *78–79* **1–3**

LPs: 10/12-Inch 33rpm
ACCORD: *82* **4–8**
ALLEGIANCE: *83* **4–8**
CENTRON: *70* **8–15**
EPIC: *71–83* **5–10**
EXCELSIOR: *80* **5–8**
GUSTO: *83* **4–8**
IMPERIAL: *80* **5–8**
LITTLE DARLIN' (0500
through 0700 series):
79–80 . . . . **5–8**
LITTLE DARLIN' (8000
series): *66–69* **10–18**

Price Range

Price Range

LITTLE DARLIN' (10000
series): *79* **$8–12**
PICKWICK/HILLTOP:
72 .... **6–10**
Also see HAGGARD, Merle, & Johnny Paycheck
Also see JENNINGS, Waylon / Johnny Paycheck
Also see JONES, George, & Johnny Paycheck

PAYCHECK, Johnny, & Jody Miller
Singles: 7-Inch
EPIC: *72* **2–3**
Also see MILLER, Jody
Also see PAYCHECK, Johnny

PAYNE, Freda
Singles: 12-Inch 33/45rpm
CAPITOL: *79* **4–6**
Singles: 7-Inch
ABC: *75* **1–3**
ABC-PARAMOUNT:
62–63 .... **3–5**
CAPITOL: *77–78* **2–3**
DUNHILL: *74.* **2–4**
IMPULSE: *63* **3–5**
INVICTUS: *69–73* **2–4**
MGM: *66.* **3–5**
SUTRA: *82* **1–3**
Picture Sleeves
CAPITOL: *77–78* **2–3**
INVICTUS: *71–73* **2–4**
LPs: 10/12-Inch 33rpm
ABC: *75* **8–10**
CAPITOL: *78–79* **5–8**
DUNHILL: *74.* **8–10**
IMPULSE: *64* **12–18**
INVICTUS: *70–72* **10–12**
MGM: *66–70.* **10–15**
U.S.A.: *71* **10–12**

PAYNE, Scherrie
Singles: 12-Inch 33/45rpm
MEGATONE: *84* **4–6**
Singles: 7-Inch
INVICTUS: *72* **2–4**
MOTOWN: *80.* **1–3**
Also see SUPREMES, The

PAYTON, Lawrence
Singles: 7-Inch
DUNHILL: *73–74.* **2–4**

PEACHES & HERB
Singles: 7-Inch
COLUMBIA: *71–74* **$2–4**
DATE: *66–70.* **3–5**
MCA: *77* **1–3**
MERCURY: *73.* **2–3**
Picture Sleeves
DATE: *67–68.* **3–5**
LPs: 10/12-Inch 33rpm
COLUMBIA: *83* **5–8**
DATE: *67–68.* **10–15**
EPIC: *79* **8–10**
MCA: *77* **8–10**
Members: Francine Barker & Herb Fame.

PEACHES & HERB
Singles: 12-Inch 33/45rpm
POLYDOR: *78–79* **4–6**
Singles: 7-Inch
POLYDOR: *78–83* **1–3**
LPs: 10/12-Inch 33rpm
POLYDOR: *78–81* **5–8**
Members: Linda Green & Herb Fame.

**PEANUT BUTTER CONSPIRACY,
The (Featuring Sandi Robison)**
Singles: 7-Inch
CHALLENGE: *69* **4–6**
COLUMBIA: *67* **4–6**
VAULT: *66* **5–8**
LPs: 10/12-Inch 33rpm
CHALLENGE: *69* **20–25**
COLUMBIA (9000 series):
67–68 .... **20–25**
COLUMBIA (38000
series): *82* **8–10**

PEARL, Leslie
Singles: 7-Inch
RCA VICTOR: *82* **1–3**

**PEARL HARBOR (Pearl Harbor &
The Explosions)**
Singles: 7-Inch
WARNER BROS: *80–81* **1–3**
LPs: 10/12-Inch 33rpm
WARNER BROS: *80–81* **5–8**

PEARLETTES, The
Singles: 7-Inch
CRAIG: *61* **4–6**

Price Range

VEE JAY: *61–62*. **$4–6**

PEARLS BEFORE SWINE
(Featuring Tom Rapp)
Singles: 7-Inch
REPRISE: *69–70*. **3–5**
LPs: 10/12-Inch 33rpm
ADELPHI: *80*. **5–8**
ESP: *67–68*. **15–20**
("One Nation Underground," using the origi-
nal ESP 1054 catalog number, is still shown as
being available. We don't yet know how the
current pressings differ from 1967 originals.)
REPRISE: *69–71*. **10–15**

PEARSON, Duke
Singles: 7-Inch
BLUE NOTE: *60–66* **2–4**
LPs: 10/12-Inch 33rpm
ATLANTIC: *66* **8–15**
BLUE NOTE: *59–61* **20–35**
(Label gives New York street address for Blue
Note Records.)
BLUE NOTE: *63–64* **15–25**
(Label reads "Blue Note Records Inc. - New
York, USA.")
BLUE NOTE: *66–74* **8–18**
(Label shows Blue Note Records as a division
of either Liberty or United Artists.)
PRESTIGE: *70* **8–12**

PEARSON, Mr. Danny
Singles: 7-Inch
UNLIMITED GOLD: *78* **2–3**
LPs: 10/12-Inch 33rpm
UNLIMITED GOLD: *79* **5–8**

PEDICIN, Mike (Michael Pedicin, Jr.; The Mike Pedicin Quintet)
Singles: 12-Inch 33/45rpm
PHILADELPHIA INT'L:
79–82 . . . . **5–8**
Singles: 7-Inch
ABC-PARAMOUNT: *62*. **3–5**
APOLLO: *59*. **8–10**
CAMEO: *57* **4–6**
FEDERAL: *61* **3–5**
PHILADELPHIA INT'L:
79–82 . . . . **1–3**
RCA VICTOR: *56* **4–6**

Price Range

LPs: 10/12-Inch 33rpm
APOLLO: *59*. **$25–30**
PHILADELPHIA INT'L:
79 . . . . **5–8**

PEDRICK, Bobby (Bobby Pedrick, Jr.)
Singles: 7-Inch
BIG TOP: *58–60*. **6–10**
DUEL: *62–63*. **5–8**
MGM: *65*. **4–6**
SHELL: *60*. **10–12**
VERVE: *66* **10–15**
Also see JOHN, Robert

PEEBLES, Ann
Singles: 7-Inch
HI: *69–78*. **2–4**
MOTOWN: *82*. **1–3**
LPs: 10/12-Inch 33rpm
HI: *69–75*. **8–10**
MOTOWN: *82*. **5–8**

PEEK, Dan
Singles: 7-Inch
LAMB & LION: *79* **1–3**
SONGBIRD: *79* **1–3**
Also see AMERICA

PEEK, Paul
Singles: 7-Inch
COLUMBIA: *66*. **3–5**
FAIRLANE: *61* **5–8**
MERCURY: *62–63*. **3–5**
NRC: *58–60*. **6–10**
1-2-3: *69*. **2–4**

PEEL, David, & The Lower East Side
LPs: 10/12-Inch 33rpm
APPLE: *72* **12–15**
ELEKTRA: *68–70* **12–15**

PEELS, The
Singles: 7-Inch
KARATE: *66* **4–6**
LPs: 10/12-Inch 33rpm
KARATE: *66* **55–65**

Price Range

PEERCE, Jan
Singles: 7-Inch
BLUEBIRD: *60.*..................$2–3
RCA VICTOR: *51* 2–4
UNITED ARTISTS: *63*.............2–3

EPs: 7-Inch 33/45rpm
RCA VICTOR: *51* 4–8

LPs: 10/12-Inch 33rpm
RCA VICTOR (Except
2900 series): *51* 10–20
RCA VICTOR (2900
series): *78*.......................4–8
UNITED ARTISTS: *63–65*.........5–15
VANGUARD: *63–67*..............5–15

PEGGY LEE: see LEE, Peggy

PENDERGRASS, Teddy
Singles: 12-Inch 33/45rpm
PHILADELPHIA INT'L:
78–82 4–6

Singles: 7-Inch
ASYLUM: *84–85*...................1–3
PHILADELPHIA INT'L:
77–84 1–3

LPs: 10/12-Inch 33rpm
ASYLUM: *84–85*...................5–8
EPIC: *83* 5–8
PHILADELPHIA INT'L
(30000 series): *77–84*.............6–10
PHILADELPHIA INT'L
(40000 series): *82*..............10–15
(Half-speed mastered series.)

Promotional LPs
PHILADELPHIA INT'L
("Life Is A Song"): *78* 20–30
(Picture disc. Promotional issue only.)
Also see HOUSTON, Whitney
Also see MELVIN, Harold
Also see MILLS, Stephanie, & Teddy Pendergrass
Also see PHILADELPHIA INTERNATIONAL ALL STARS, The

PENDULUM
Singles: 7-Inch
VENTURE: *80* 1–3

LPs: 10/12-Inch 33rpm
VENTURE: *81* 5–8

Price Range

PENGUINS, The
Singles: 7-Inch
ATLANTIC: *57* $5–8
DOOTO (348; "Earth
Angel"): *62*.....................3–5
(Reissue of DooTONE 348.)
DOOTO (400 series):
57–58 12–15
DOOTONE (300 series):
54–55 15–20
(Dootone 345 is found in the following section,
PENGUINS, The / The Dootsie Williams Orchestra.)
MERCURY: *55–57*..............10–15
ORIGINAL SOUND:
63–65 8–12
POWER.........................3–5
SUN STATE: *62*..................3–5
WING: *56* 8–10

Picture Sleeves
POWER.........................3–5

EPs: 7-Inch 33/45rpm
DOOTO: *60*....................10–15
DOOTONE: *55*.................30–40

LPs: 10/12-Inch 33rpm
DOOTO: *59*....................35–45
(Yellow label with red lettering.)
DOOTO.........................8–10
(Multi-color label.)
Members: Cleve Duncan; Curtis Williams;
Dexter Tisby; Bruce Tate; Randy Jones; Ted
Harper; Walter Saulsberry.

PENGUINS, The / The Dootsie
Williams Orchestra
Singles: 7-Inch
DOOTONE (345; "No,
There Ain't No News
Today"): *54* 60–75

PENGUINS, The / The Meadowlarks
/ The Medallions / The Dootones
LPs: 10/12-Inch 33rpm
DOOTONE (Black vinyl):
57 50–75
DOOTONE (Colored
vinyl): *57* 125–150
(Flat maroon label. Later pressings have appeared on a glossy label stock and may, in fact,
be the currently available pressing. Current issues may also be on the multi-color label.)
Also see JULIAN, Don, & The Meadowlarks
Also see PENGUINS, The

Price Range

PENTAGONS, The
Singles: 7-Inch
DONNA: *61* $5–8
ERIC 1–3
FLEET INT'L: *61.* 12–15
JAMIE: *61–62.* 5–8
OLDIES 45: *64* 2–3
SPECIALTY: *58.* 5–8

PENTANGLE
Singles: 7-Inch
REPRISE: *68–69.* 3–5

LPs: 10/12-Inch 33rpm
REPRISE: *68–72.* 10–15
Members: Jacqui McShee; Bert Jansch.

PEOPLE (With Larry Norman)
Singles: 7-Inch
CAPITOL: *67–69* 5–8
PARAMOUNT: *69–70.* 3–5
POLYDOR: *71* 2–4
ZEBRA (102; "Come Back
    Beatles"): *78.* 3–5
    (With note suggesting the Beatles reunite.)

LPs: 10/12-Inch 33rpm
CAPITOL: *68–69* 20–30
PARAMOUNT: *69–70.* 10–15

PEOPLE'S CHOICE, The
Singles: 7-Inch
CASABLANCA: *80* 1–3
PALMER: *67.* 3–5
PHIL L.A. OF SOUL:
    71–73 2–4
PHILADELPHIA INT'L:
    71 2–4
PHILIPS: *69* 2–4
TSOP: *74–77* 2–3

LPs: 10/12-Inch 33rpm
CASABLANCA: *80* 5–8
DECCA: *69.* 10–12
PHILADELPHIA INT'L:
    78 5–8
TSOP: *75* 8–10

PEPPERMINT, Danny, & The Jumping Jacks (Danny Lamego)
Singles: 7-Inch
CARLTON: *61* 5–8

Price Range

LPs: 10/12-Inch 33rpm
CARLTON: *62* $20–25

PEPPERMINT HARRIS (Harrison Nelson)
Singles: 7-Inch
ALADDIN: *51–53* 15–20
CASH: *54.* 10–12
DART: *60* 4–6
DUKE: *60* 4–6
JEWEL: *65–68.* 3–5
MODERN: *51* 12–15
MONEY: *54* 12–15
SITTIN' IN WITH (543;
    "Rainin' In My Heart"):
    51 40–50
X: *55.* 35–40
LPs: 10/12-Inch 33rpm
TIME: *62.* 25–35
Also see NELSON, Peppermint

PEPPERMINT RAINBOW, The
Singles: 7-Inch
DECCA: *68–69* 3–5
Picture Sleeves
DECCA: *69.* 3–5
LPs: 10/12-Inch 33rpm
DECCA: *69.* 10–15

PEPPERMINT TROLLEY COMPANY, The
Singles: 7-Inch
ACTA: *67–68.* 3–5
VALIANT: *66.* 4–6
LPs: 10/12-Inch 33rpm
ACTA: *68* 15–20

PEPPERS, The
Singles: 7-Inch
EVENT: *74–75* 2–3
LPs: 10/12-Inch 33rpm
EVENT: *74* 8–10

PERCELLS, The
Singles: 7-Inch
ABC-PARAMOUNT:
    63–64 4–6

PERCY & THEM
Singles: 7-Inch
PLAYBOY: *73* 2–4

Price Range

PERFECT, Christine (Christine McVie)
Singles: 7-Inch
EPIC: 69 .... $3–5
LPs: 10/12-Inch 33rpm
SIRE (6000 series): 77 5–8
SIRE (7000 series): 76 8–10
Also see McVIE, Christine

PERICOLI, Emilio
Singles: 7-Inch
VESUVIUS: 62 2–4
WARNER BROS: 62–63 2–4
Picture Sleeves
WARNER BROS: 62 2–4
LPs: 10/12-Inch 33rpm
WARNER BROS: 63–66 5–15
VESUVIUS: 62 5–15

PERKINS, Al
Singles: 7-Inch
ATCO: 69–70 2–4
HI: 72 2–3
U.S.A.: 64–65 3–5

PERKINS, Carl (Carl Perkins & The C.P. Express)
Singles: 7-Inch
COLUMBIA (3-41000 &
    3-42000 series): 60–62 10–15
(Compact 33 Singles.)
COLUMBIA (4-41000
    through 4-43000 series):
    58–64 4–6
COLUMBIA (44000 &
    45000 series): 64–72 3–5
DECCA: 63–64 4–6
DOLLIE: 67 3–5
FLIP (501; "Movie
    Magg"): 55 275–325
JET: 79 2–3
MERCURY: 73–77 2–4
SSS/SUN 1–3
SUN (224; "Gone Gone
    Gone"): 56 35–45
SUN (234 through 287):
    56–58 8–15
Picture Sleeves
COLUMBIA: 58–62 10–20

CARL PERKINS
SMASH DEBUT ON
COLUMBIA
JIVE AFTER FIVE
PINK PEDAL PUSHERS

Price Range

EPs: 7-Inch 33/45rpm
COLUMBIA: 58 .... $30–40
SUN: 58 30–40
LPs: 10/12-Inch 33rpm
ACCORD: 82 5–8
ALBUM GLOBE 8–10
ALLEGIANCE: 84 5–8
CHARLY 5–8
COLUMBIA (1234;
    "Whole Lotta Shakin"):
    58 60–75
COLUMBIA (9800 series):
    69 8–12
DESIGN 10–15
DOLLIE: 67 10–15
GRT/SUNNYVALE: 77 8–10
HARMONY: 72 8–10
JET: 78 8–10
KOALA: 80 5–8
MERCURY: 73 8–10
SSS/SUN: 69–84 5–8
SUEDE: 81 8–10
SUN (1225; "Dance
    Album"): 57 140–160
SUN (1225; "Teen Beat"):
    61 45–55
    (Repackage of "Dance Album," using the same
    catalog number.)
TRIP: 74 8–10
Also see McCARTNEY, Paul
Also see NELSON, Willie / Jerry Lee Lewis /
    Carl Perkins / David Allan Coe
Also see YOUNG, Faron / Carl Perkins /
    Claude King

Price Range

Price Range

PERKINS, Carl, Jerry Lee Lewis, Roy Orbison & Johnny Cash
LPs: 10/12-Inch 33rpm
AMERICA: *86* **$20–22**
(Mail-order only edition, includes souvenir booklet and audio cassette with interviews of the singers.)
AMERICA/SMASH: *86* **5–8**
Also see CASH, Johnny, Carl Perkins & Jerry Lee Lewis
Also see LEWIS, Jerry Lee, Carl Perkins & Charlie Rich
Also see ORBISON, Roy

PERKINS, Carl, & NRBQ
Singles: 7-Inch
COLUMBIA: *70* **2–4**

LPs: 10/12-Inch 33rpm
COLUMBIA: *70* **10–15**
Also see NRBQ

George Perkins, one charted single (1970), no charted LPs.

PERKINS, George (George Perkins & The Silver Stars)
Singles: 7-Inch
SILVER FOX: *69* **2–4**
SOUL POWER: *72* **2–4**

LPs: 10/12-Inch 33rpm
CHARLY **5–8**
CRYIN' IN THE
  STREETS: *77* **8–10**

PERKINS, Joe
Singles: 7-Inch
MUSICOR: *65* **$3–5**
SOUND STAGE 7: *63* **3–5**

PERKINS, Tony
Singles: 7-Inch
RCA VICTOR: *57* **3–5**
Picture Sleeves
RCA VICTOR: *57* **4–6**

PERRY, Greg
Singles: 7-Inch
ALFA: *82* **1–3**
CASABLANCA: *74–75* **2–3**
CHESS: *68* **3–5**
RCA VICTOR: *77* **2–3**
LPs: 10/12-Inch 33rpm
CASABLANCA: *75* **8–10**

PERRY, Jeff
Singles: 7-Inch
ARISTA: *75–76* **2–3**
EPIC: *77* **2–3**

PERRY, Joe, Project
Singles: 7-Inch
COLUMBIA: *80–81* **1–3**
LPs: 10/12-Inch 33rpm
COLUMBIA: *80–81* **5–8**
MCA: *83* **5–8**
Also see AEROSMITH

PERRY, Linda
Singles: 7-Inch
MAINSTREAM: *73* **2–3**

PERRY, Roxy
Singles: 12-Inch 33/45rpm
PERSONAL: *83* **4–6**

PERRY, Steve
Singles: 7-Inch
COLUMBIA: *84–85* **1–3**
LPs: 10/12-Inch 33rpm
COLUMBIA: *84–85* **5–8**
Also see JOURNEY
Also see LOGGINS, Kenny, & Steve Perry
Also see U.S.A. FOR AFRICA

Price Range

PERRY & SANLIN
Singles: 7-Inch
CAPITOL: 80 . . . . **$1–3**
LPs: 10/12-Inch 33rpm
CAPITOL: 80 . . . . **5–8**

PERSIANS, The
Singles: 7-Inch
ABC: 68 . . . . **3–5**
CAPITOL: 71–72 . . . . **2–4**
GWP: 69–70 . . . . **2–4**

PERSON, Houston
Singles: 7-Inch
WESTBOUND: 75–76 . . . . **2–3**

PERSUADERS, The
Singles: 7-Inch
ATCO: 71–75 . . . . **2–4**
CALLA: 77 . . . . **2–3**
WIN OR LOSE: 71–72 . . . . **2–4**
LPs: 10/12-Inch 33rpm
ATCO: 73–74 . . . . **8–10**
CALLA: 77 . . . . **8–10**
WIN OR LOSE: 72 . . . . **10–12**

PERSUASIONS, The
Singles: 7-Inch
A&M: 74–75 . . . . **2–4**
CAPITOL: 71–72 . . . . **2–4**
CATAMOUNT **2–4**
MCA: 73 . . . . **2–4**
REPRISE: 70 . . . . **2–4**
TOWER: 65–66 . . . . **3–5**
LPs: 10/12-Inch 33rpm
A&M: 74 . . . . **8–10**
CAPITOL: 71–72 . . . . **6–10**
ELEKTRA: 77 . . . . **8–10**
FLYING FISH: 79 . . . . **5–8**
MCA: 73 . . . . **8–10**
ROUNDER **5–8**
STRAIGHT: 70 . . . . **15–20**

PETER & GORDON
Singles: 7-Inch
CAPITOL: 64–69 . . . . **3–5**
Picture Sleeves
CAPITOL: 64–67 . . . . **4–8**
LPs: 10/12-Inch 33rpm
CAPITOL (2500 series): 77 . . . . **5–10**

Price Range

(With an "SM" prefix.)
CAPITOL (2100 through
2800 series): 64–68 . . . . **$10–20**
(With a "T" or "ST" prefix.)
CAPITOL (16000 series):
80 . . . . **5–8**
Members: Peter Asher; Gordon Waller.

PETER & GORDON / The Lettermen
Singles: 7-Inch
CAPITOL CREATIVE
PRODUCTS: 66 . . . . **4–6**
(A Fritos Company promotional issue.)
Also see LETTERMEN, The
Also see PETER & GORDON

PETER, PAUL & MARY
Singles: 7-Inch
EUGENE McCARTHY
FOR PRESIDENT: 68 . . . . **4–8**
(Promotional release only, issued during
McCarthy's unsuccessful Democratic presiden-
tial nomination campaign. No actual label
name was shown.)
WARNER BROS (5000
series): 62–66 . . . . **3–5**
WARNER BROS (7000
series): 67–70 . . . . **2–4**
Picture Sleeves
WARNER BROS: 62–64 . . . . **4–6**
EPs: 7-Inch 33/45rpm
WARNER BROS: 63–64 . . . . **4–8**
(Jukebox issues only.)
LPs: 10/12-Inch 33rpm
WARNER BROS (1449
through 1648): 62–66 . . . . **12–15**
WARNER BROS (1700
through 2552): 67–70 . . . . **8–12**
(At least four LPs from the 1400-1700 series are
still in print, however originals from that period
are easily identified by their gray or gold labels.)
WARNER BROS (3000
series): 77–78 . . . . **5–8**
Members: Peter Yarrow; Paul Stookey; Mary
Travers.
Also see STOOKEY, Paul
Also see TRAVERS, Mary
Also see YARROW, Peter

PETERS, Bernadette
Singles: 7-Inch
ABC-PARAMOUNT: 65 . . . . **4–6**

Price Range

Also see HUBBARD, Freddie, & Oscar Peterson
Also see MULLIGAN, Gerry, & Oscar Peterson
Also see RIDDLE, Nelson

PETERSON, Oscar, & Buddy DeFranco
Singles: 7-Inch
NORGRAN: 55 .... $3–5
LPs: 10/12-Inch 33rpm
NORGRAN: 54 25–50
VERVE: 57 20–30
(Reads "Verve Records, Inc." at bottom of label.)

PETERSON, Oscar, & Sonny Stitt
LPs: 10/12-Inch 33rpm
VERVE: 60 15–25
(Reads "Verve Records, Inc." at bottom of label.)
Also see PETERSON, Oscar
Also see STITT, Sonny

PETERSON, Ray
Singles: 7-Inch
CLOUD 9: 75 2–3
DECCA: 71 2–4
DUNES: 60–63 4–6
MGM: 64–66 3–5
POLYDOR 1–3
RCA VICTOR (7500
through 7700 series):
59–60 10–15
(With a "61" prefix, indicating stereo singles.)
RCA VICTOR (7500
through 0000 series):
58–63 4–6
(With a "47" prefix.)
RCA VICTOR (8300
series): 64 3–5
REPRISE: 69 2–4
UNI: 70 2–4
Picture Sleeves
DUNES: 60 4–8
MGM: 64 3–5
RCA VICTOR: 59 6–10
EPs: 7-Inch 33/45rpm
RCA VICTOR: 60 15–20
LPs: 10/12-Inch 33rpm
CAMDEN: 66 10–15
DECCA: 71 8–10

MGM: 64–65 .... $20–25
RCA VICTOR: 60 35–40

PETS, The
Singles: 7-Inch
ARWIN: 58 3–5

PETTY, Frank, Trio
Singles: 7-Inch
MGM: 50–57 2–4
EPs: 7-Inch 33/45rpm
MGM: 50–57 4–8
LPs: 10/12-Inch 33rpm
MGM: 50–57 8–15

PETTY, Norman, Trio
Singles: 7-Inch
ABC-PARAMOUNT: 57 4–6
COLUMBIA (Except
41039): 57 4–6
COLUMBIA (41039;
"Moondreams"): 57 20–25
(With Buddy Holly on guitar.)
FELSTED: 62 3–5
JARO: 60 4–6
NOR VA JAK (Except
1325): 57–59 15–20
NOR VA JAK (1325;
"True Love Ways"): 60 25–30
NORMAN: 60 4–6
X: 54–55 5–8
EPs: 7-Inch 33/45rpm
COLUMBIA: 58 20–25
X: 55 15–20
LPs: 10/12-Inch 33rpm
COLUMBIA: 58 30–40
TOP RANK: 60 25–30
VIK 20–25
Members: Norman Petty; Vi Petty; Jack Petty.
Also see HOLLY, Buddy

PETTY, Tom, & The Heartbreakers
Singles: 7-Inch
BACKSTREET: 79–83 1–3
MCA: 85 1–3
SHELTER: 77–78 2–3
Picture Sleeves
BACKSTREET: 79–83 1–3
MCA: 85 .... INC
SHELTER: 77–78 2–3

Price Range

LPs: 10/12-Inch 33rpm
BACKSTREET: 79–82. . . . . **$5–8**
MCA: 85 . . . . **5–8**
SHELTER (Except 12677):
76–78 . . . . **5–8**
SHELTER (12677;
"Official Live 'Leg"): 76 . . . . **10–15**
(Promotional issue only.)
Also see DYLAN, Bob, & The Heartbreakers
/ Michael Rubini
Also see NICKS, Stevie, Tom Petty & The
Heartbreakers

PHELPS, James (Jimmy Phelps & The Du-Ettes)
Singles: 7-Inch
ARGO: 65 . . . . **3–5**
CADET: 66 . . . . **3–5**
FONTANA: 66–67. . . . . **3–5**
MECCA: 60. . . . . **5–8**
PARAMOUNT: 71–72. . . . . **2–4**

PHILADELPHIA INTERNATIONAL ALL STARS, The
Singles: 7-Inch
PHILADELPHIA INT'L:
77 . . . . **2–3**
Members: Archie Bell; The O'Jays; Billy Paul;
Teddy Pendergrass; Lou Rawls; Dee Dee
Sharpe.
Also see BELL, Archie
Also see O'JAYS, The
Also see PAUL, Billy
Also see PENDERGRASS, Teddy
Also see RAWLS, Lou
Also see SHARPE, Dee Dee

PHILADELPHIA STORY
Singles: 7-Inch
H&L: 77. . . . . **2–3**

PHILARMONICS, The
Singles: 7-Inch
CAPRICORN: 77. . . . . **2–3**
LPs: 10/12-Inch 33rpm
CAPRICORN: 77. . . . . **5–8**

PHILLINGANES, Greg
Singles: 12-Inch 33/45rpm
PLANET: 85. . . . . **1–3**

Price Range

Singles: 7-Inch
PLANET: 81–85 . . . . **$1–3**
LPs: 10/12-Inch 33rpm
PLANET: 81–85 . . . . **5–8**

PHILLIPS, Anthony
Singles: 7-Inch
PASSPORT: 77–78 . . . . **1–3**
LPs: 10/12-Inch 33rpm
PASSPORT: 77–78 . . . . **5–10**
Also see GENESIS

PHILLIPS, Bill, & Dolly Parton
Singles: 7-Inch
DECCA (31901; "Don't
Put It Off Until
Tomorrow"): 66. . . . . **3–5**
LPs: 10/12-Inch 33rpm
DECCA (4792; "Don't Put
It Off Until
Tomorrow"): 66. . . . . **15–20**
(Monaural issue.)
DECCA (74792; "Don't
Put It Off Until
Tomorrow"): 66. . . . . **15–25**
(Stereo issue.)
Also see PARTON, Dolly

PHILLIPS, Esther (Little Esther Phillips)
Singles: 7-Inch
ATLANTIC: 64–70 . . . . **3–5**
KUDU: 72–77. . . . . **2–4**
LENOX: 62–63 . . . . **3–5**
MERCURY: 77–79. . . . . **2–3**
ROULETTE: 69 . . . . **2–4**
WINNING: 83 . . . . **1–3**
LPs: 10/12-Inch 33rpm
ATLANTIC: 65–76 . . . . **10–15**
KUDO: 72–76. . . . . **8–10**
LENOX: 62. **18–20**
MERCURY: 77–81. . . . . **5–8**
YORKSHIRE **8–10**
Also see LITTLE ESTHER

PHILLIPS, Esther, & Joe Beck
LPs: 10/12-Inch 33rpm
KUDU: 76. . . . . **8–10**
Also see BECK, Joe

Price Range

PHILLIPS, Esther, & Big Al Downing
Singles: 7-Inch
LENOX: 63 . . . . $3–5
　Also see DOWNING, Al
　Also see PHILLIPS, Esther

PHILLIPS, John
Singles: 7-Inch
ATCO: 74 2–4
COLUMBIA: 73 2–4
DUNHILL: 70 2–4
LPs: 10/12-Inch 33rpm
DUNHILL: 70 10–12
　Also see MAMAS & THE PAPAS, The

PHILLIPS, Little Esther: see PHILLIPS, Esther

PHILLIPS, Phil (Phil Phillips With The Twilights)
Singles: 7-Inch
CLIQUE: 66 3–5
KHOURY'S: 59 45–55
MERCURY (10000 series):
　59 8–10
　(Stereo singles.)
MERCURY (71000 series):
　59–61 4–6

PHILLIPS, Shawn
Singles: 7-Inch
A&M: 70–75 2–4
ASCOT: 64 3–5
LPs: 10/12-Inch 33rpm
A&M: 70–77 8–10
RCA VICTOR: 78–81 5–8

PHILLIPS, Stu: see HOLLYRIDGE STRINGS, The

PHILLIPS, Wes
Singles: 12-Inch 33/45rpm
QUALITY: 84 4–6
Singles: 7-Inch
QUALITY: 84 1–3

PHILLY CREAM
Singles: 12-Inch 33/45rpm
WMOT: 79 4–6

Price Range

Singles: 7-Inch
FANTASY: 79 . . . . $1–3
WMOT: 79 1–3
LPs: 10/12-Inch 33rpm
WMOT: 79 5–8

PHILLY DEVOTIONS, The
Singles: 7-Inch
COLUMBIA: 75–76 2–3

PHOTOGLO, Jim (Photoglo)
Singles: 7-Inch
20TH CENTURY-FOX:
　80–81 1–3
LPs: 10/12-Inch 33rpm
CASABLANCA: 83 5–8
20TH CENTURY-FOX:
　80–81 5–8

PIAF, Edith
Singles: 7-Inch
CAPITOL: 56–61 2–4
COLUMBIA: 50–52 3–5
EPs: 7-Inch 33/45rpm
ANGEL 5–15
COLUMBIA: 50–52 5–15
DECCA (6000 series) 5–15
LPs: 10/12-Inch 33rpm
ANGEL: 55–56 15–25
CAPITOL: 59–82 5–15
COLUMBIA (Except
　37000 series): 50–56 15–30
COLUMBIA (37000
　series): 81 5–8
DECCA (6000 series): 54 20–30
DISCOS: 56 10–20
PHILIPS: 64–67 8–15
RCA VICTOR: 64 8–15
VOX: 53 20–30

PIANO RED (Willie Perryman)
Singles: 7-Inch
CHECKER: 58 5–8
GROOVE: 54–57 6–10
JAX: 59 4–6
RCA VICTOR (4000
　series): 50–52 10–12
RCA VICTOR (5000
　series): 52–53 8–10
RCA VICTOR (6000 &
　7000 series): 57–58 5–8

Price Range

RCA VICTOR (50-0000
  series): *50–51* **$10–15**
  (Black vinyl.)
RCA VICTOR (50-0000
  series): *50–51* **20–25**
  (Colored vinyl.)

EPs: 7-Inch 33/45rpm
GROOVE: *56.* **25–30**
RCA VICTOR (587;
  "Rockin' With Red"): *54* **30–35**
RCA VICTOR (5091;
  "Rockin' With Red"): *59* **20–25**
  (Black label.)
RCA VICTOR (5091;
  "Rockin' With Red"): *59* **30–35**
  (Maroon label.)

LPs: 10/12-Inch 33rpm
ARHOOLIE **8–10**
BLACK LION: *76* **8–10**
GROOVE: *56.* **150–175**
KING: *70* **10–12**
RCA VICTOR: *74* **8–10**
  Also see DR. FEELGOOD

PICKETT, Bobby (Bobby "Boris" Pickett & The Crypt-Kickers)
Singles: 12-Inch 33/45rpm
EASY STREET: *84* **4–6**

Singles: 7-Inch
ANTHEM **3–5**
ATMOSPHERE: *65* **4–6**
CAPITOL: *63–64* **5–8**
EASY STREET: *84* **1–3**
GARPAX (1; "Monster
  Mash"): *62* **8–10**
GARPAX (700 series) **4–6**
GARPAX (44000 series):
  62–64 . . . . **4–6**
LONDON **2–3**
METROMEDIA (0089;
  "Me & My Mummy"):
  68 . . . . **3–5**
METROMEDIA (9989;
  "Me & My Mummy"):
  73 . . . . **2–3**
PARROT: *70–73.* **2–3**
RCA VICTOR: *64* **3–5**
WHITE WHALE: *70.* **2–4**

Picture Sleeves
GARPAX: *62–63* **8–15**

LPs: 10/12-Inch 33rpm
GARPAX: *62* **$25–35**
PARROT: *73.* **8–10**

PICKETT, Wilson
Singles: 7-Inch
ATLANTIC (2200 through
  2400 series): *64–67* **3–5**
ATLANTIC (2500 through
  2900 series): *68–72* **2–4**
BIG TREE: *78* **2–3**
CORRECTONE: *62* **12–15**
CUB: *62* **10–12**
DOUBLE-L: *63.* **4–6**
EMI AMERICA: *79–81.* **1–3**
RCA VICTOR: *73–74* **2–4**
VERVE: *65* **3–5**
WICKED: *75–76.* **2–3**

LPs: 10/12-Inch 33rpm
ATLANTIC (Except 8100
  series): *69–73* **8–12**
ATLANTIC (8100 series):
  65–68 . . . . **15–20**
BIG TREE: *78* **5–8**
BROOKVILLE: *77.* **8–12**
DOUBLE-L: *63.* **25–35**
EMI AMERICA: *79–81.* **5–8**
RCA VICTOR: *73–77* **8–10**
WAND: *68* **10–15**
WICKED: *76.* **8–10**
  Also see FALCONS, The

PICKETTYWITCH (Featuring Polly Brown)
Singles: 7-Inch
JANUS: *70* **2–4**
LPs: 10/12-Inch 33rpm
JANUS: *70* **8–10**
  Also see BROWN, Polly

PIECES OF A DREAM
Singles: 12-Inch 33/45rpm
ELEKTRA: *84* **4–6**
Singles: 7-Inch
ELEKTRA: *81–84* **1–3**
LPs: 10/12-Inch 33rpm
ELEKTRA: *81–84* **5–8**

PIECES OF EIGHT, The
Singles: 7-Inch
A&M: *67–68* **3–5**

Price Range

MALA: *68* $3–5
Also see SWINGIN' MEDALLIONS, The

PIERCE, Webb
Singles: 7-Inch
DECCA (28000 through
30000 series): *52–59* 3–5
DECCA (31000 through
33000 series): *59–73* 2–4
DECCA (46000 series):
51–52 4–8
FOUR STAR: *51–52* 5–10
KING: *60* 3–5
MCA: *73–74* 1–3
PLANTATION: *75–77*. 1–3
SOUNDWAVES: *83* 1–3
EPs: 7-Inch 33/45rpm
DECCA: *53–65* 5–15

LPs: 10/12-Inch 33rpm
CORAL: *73* 4–6
DECCA (100 series): *64*. 15–20
DECCA (4000 through
4800 series): *60–67* 10–20
(Decca LP numbers in this series preceded by
a "7" or a "DL-7" are stereo issues.)
DECCA (5000 series): *53*. 30–50
(10-Inch LPs.)
DECCA (8000 series):
55–59 20–40
DECCA (74000 series): *68*. 8–12
ERA: *77*. 8–10
KING (600 series): *59* 25–35
MCA: *73–78* 5–12
PICKWICK/HILLTOP:
65 10–15
PLANTATION: *76–77*. 5–8
SEARS. 8–12
SKYLITE: *77* 5–8
VOCALION: *66–70* 5–15
Also see NELSON, Willie, & Webb Pierce

PIERCE, Webb / Loretta Lynn
LPs: 10/12-Inch 33rpm
PHILCO/MCA: *59*. 12–18
Also see LYNN, Loretta

PIERCE, Webb / Wynn Stewart
LPs: 10/12-Inch 33rpm
DESIGN: *62* 10–15
Also see STEWART, Wynn

WEBB PIERCE
Exclusive DECCA Recording Artist
OZARK JUBILEE
Springfield Mo

America's
No. 1 Folk Singer

Price Range

PIERCE, Webb, & Kitty Wells
Singles: 7-Inch
DECCA: *64* $2–4
EPs: 7-Inch 33/45rpm
DECCA: *59* 5–10
Also see PIERCE, Webb
Also see WELLS, Kitty

PILOT
Singles: 7-Inch
ARISTA: *77* 2–3
EMI: *75–76* 2–3
LPs: 10/12-Inch 33rpm
EMI: *75–76* 8–10
Also see PARSONS, Alan, Project

PILTDOWN MEN, The
Singles: 7-Inch
CAPITOL: *60–62* 4–8

PINDER, Michael
LPs: 10/12-Inch 33rpm
THRESHOLD: *76*. 8–10
Also see MOODY BLUES, The

PINERA, Mike
Singles: 7-Inch
CAPRICORN: *78*. 2–3
SPECTOR: *80* 1–3
SRI: *79*. 1–3

Price Range

LPs: 10/12-Inch 33rpm
SRI: *79* **$5–8**
Also see BLUES IMAGE, The
Also see CACTUS
Also see IRON BUTTERFLY
Also see RAMATAM

PINETOPPERS, The
Singles: 7-Inch
CORAL: *50–54* **2–4**
DECCA: *54–56* **2–4**
PEER SOUTHERN: *67* **1–3**
EPs: 7-Inch 33/45rpm
CORAL: *50–56* **3–6**
LPs: 10/12-Inch 33rpm
CORAL: *50–56* **5–15**

PINETTE, Rick, & Oak
Singles: 7-Inch
MERCURY: *80*. **1–3**
LPs: 10/12-Inch 33rpm
MERCURY: *80*. **5–8**
Also see OAK

PINK FLOYD
Singles: 7-Inch
CAPITOL: *71–78* **3–5**
COLUMBIA: *75–83* **1–3**
HARVEST: *73–74*. **2–4**
TOWER: *67–68* **6–10**
Picture Sleeves
COLUMBIA: *75–83* **1–3**
LPs: 10/12-Inch 33rpm
CAPITOL (Except picture
   discs): *78–83*. **5–8**
CAPITOL (Picture discs):
   78 .... **20–30**
COLUMBIA (Except
   1636): *75–83*. **6–10**
COLUMBIA (1636; "Final
   Cut"): *83* **12–15**
   (Promotional issue only.)
HARVEST (300 series):
   69–70 .... **18–20**
HARVEST (700 & 800
   series): *71* **10–15**
HARVEST (11000 series):
   72–73 .... **10–15**
HARVEST (16000 series):
   82 .... **5–8**
MFSL: *77*. **15–20**

Price Range

TOWER (Except 5169):
   67–68 .... **$25–30**
TOWER (5169; "More"):
   69 .... **20–25**
   Members: David Gilmour; Roger Waters; Rick
   Wright; Nick Mason; Syd Barrett.
   Also see BARRETT, Syd
   Also see GILMOUR, David
   Also see MASON, Nick
   Also see WATERS, Roger

PINK LADY
Singles: 7-Inch
ELEKTRA: *79* **1–3**
LPs: 10/12-Inch 33rpm
ELEKTRA: *79* **5–8**
   Members: Mie; Kei.

PIPEDREAM
Singles: 12-Inch 33/45rpm
ZOO YORK: *84* **4–6**

PIPER, Wardell
Singles: 7-Inch
MIDSONG INT'L: *79–80* **1–3**

PIPKINS, The
Singles: 7-Inch
CAPITOL: *70* **2–4**
LPs: 10/12-Inch 33rpm
CAPITOL: *70* **10–15**

PIPS, The
Singles: 7-Inch
BRUNSWICK: *58*. **30–35**
CASABLANCA: *78* **2–3**
EVERLAST: *63*. **4–6**
FURY: *62* **4–6**
HUNTOM: *61*. **60–75**
VEE JAY: *61*. **4–6**
   Members: Gladys Knight; Merald Knight; Wil-
   liam Guest; Edward Guest.
   Also see KNIGHT, Gladys

PIRATES, The (The Temptations)
Singles: 7-Inch
MEL-O-DY: *62*. **15–20**
   Also see TEMPTATIONS, The

PITNEY, Gene
Singles: 7-Inch
COLLECTABLES **1–3**

Price Range

EPIC: *77* $2–3
ERIC 1–3
FESTIVAL: *61* 8–10
MUSICOR (1000 series):
　60–65 4–6
MUSICOR (1100 through
　1400 series): *65–72* 3–5
Picture Sleeves
MUSICOR (1000 series):
　60–65 5–10
MUSICOR (1100 through
　1400 series): *66–69* 3–6
EPs: 7-Inch 33/45rpm
MUSICOR (500; "Looking
　Through The Eyes Of
　Love"): *65* 15–20
　(Issued without cover. Promotional issue only.)
LPs: 10/12-Inch 33rpm
COLUMBIA HOUSE............. 10–15
　(Columbia Record Club release.)
DESIGN 8–10
EVEREST: *81* 5–8
MUSIC DISC: *69* 10–12
MUISCOR (1 through 6):
　62–63 15–20
MUISCOR (8 through
　134): *64–67*. 12–15
　(Gene's Musicor LPs 1 through 134 were num-
　bered in the "2000" series for mono and the
　"3000" series for stereo issues.)
MUISCOR (3148 through
　3183): *67–70*. 10–12
MUISCOR (5026; "This Is
　Gene Pitney"): *68* 12–15
　(Columbia Record Club release.)
MUSICOR (5600 series):
　78 6–10
RHINO: *85* 5–8
SPRINGBOARD: *76* 6–10
TRIP: *76* 6–10
51 WEST: *79* 5–8
　Also see BRYAN, Billy
　Also see JAMIE & JANE
　Also see JONES, George, & Gene Pitney

PITNEY, Gene, & Melba Montgomery
Singles: 7-Inch
MUSICOR: *65*. 3–5
LPs: 10/12-Inch 33rpm
BUCKBOARD: *76*. 8–10
MUSICOR: *66*. 12–15

Also see MONTGOMERY, Melba
Also see PITNEY, Gene

PIXIES THREE, The
Singles: 7-Inch
MERCURY: *63–64*. $4–6
Picture Sleeves
MERCURY: *63–64*. 4–8
LPs: 10/12-Inch 33rpm
MERCURY: *64*. 20–25

PIZANI, Frank
Singles: 7-Inch
AFTON: *59*. 3–5
BALLY: *57* 4–6
WARWICK: *59*. 3–5
　Also see HIGHLIGHTS, The

PLACE, Mary Kay
Singles: 7-Inch
COLUMBIA: *76–78* 1–3
LPs: 10/12-Inch 33rpm
COLUMBIA: *76–77*. 5–10

PLANET P PROJECT (Featuring Tony Carey)
Singles: 7-Inch
GEFFEN: *83*. 1–3
MCA. 1–3
LPs: 10/12-Inch 33rpm
GEFFEN: *83*. 5–8
　Also see CAREY, Tony

PLANET PATROL
Singles: 12-Inch 33/45rpm
TOMMY BOY: *84* 4–6
Singles: 7-Inch
TOMMY BOY: *82–84* 1–3
LPs: 10/12-Inch 33rpm
TOMMY BOY: *84* 5–8

PLANT, Robert
Singles: 7-Inch
ATLANTIC: *83* 1–3
ESPARANZA: *83*. 1–3
SWAN SONG: *82*. 1–3
LPs: 10/12-Inch 33rpm
ATLANTIC/
　ESPARANZA: *83*. 5–8
SWAN SONG: *82*. 5–8
　Also see HONEYDRIPPERS, The
　Also see LED ZEPPELIN

Price Range

PLASMATICS, The (Featuring Wendy O. Williams)
LPs: 10/12-Inch 33rpm
CAPITOL: *82* **$5–8**
PVC: *84* **5–8**
STIFF AMERICA: *80–81* **8–10**

PLASTIC BERTRAND
Singles: 7-Inch
SIRE: *78* **2–3**

PLASTIC COW, The
Singles: 7-Inch
DOT: *69* **2–4**

LPs: 10/12-Inch 33rpm
DOT: *69* **10–12**

PLASTIC ONO BAND, The: see LENNON, John

PLATT, Eddie, & His Orchestra
Singles: 7-Inch
ABC-PARAMOUNT: *58* **3–5**
GONE: *58* **3–5**

PLATTERS, The
Singles: 7-Inch
ANTLER: *82* **1–3**
COLLECTABLES **1–3**
FEDERAL (12153; "Give Thanks"): *53* **60–75**
FEDERAL (12164; "I Need You All The Time"): *54* **90–100**
FEDERAL (12181; "Roses Of Picardy"): *54* **60–75**
FEDERAL (12188; "Tell The World"): *54* **25–30**
FEDERAL (12204; "Take Me Back"): *54* **20–25**
FEDERAL (12244; "Only You"): *55* **40–50**
FEDERAL (12250; "Tell The World"): *55* **20–25**
FEDERAL (12271; "I Need You All The Time"): *56* **15–20**
GUSTO **1–3**

MERCURY (10000 series): *58–60* **$8–12**
(Stereo singles.)
MERCURY (70633; "Only You"): *55* **15–20**
(Pink label.)
MERCURY (70633; "Only You"): *55* **4–6**
(Black label.)
MERCURY (70753 through 71904): *55–61* **4–6**
MERCURY (71921 through 72359): *62–64* **3–5**
MUSICOR: *66–71* **3–5**
POWER **3–5**

Picture Sleeves
MERCURY: *60–64* **4–8**

EPs: 7-Inch 33/45rpm
KING: *56* **25–30**
MERCURY: *56–61* **10–15**

LPs: 10/12-Inch 33rpm
EVEREST: *81* **5–8**
FEDERAL: *56* **125–150**
51 WEST **5–8**
KING (600 series): *59* **50–65**
MERCURY (4000 series): *82* **5–8**
MERCURY (8000 series) **5–8**
MERCURY (20146 through 20366): *56–58* **20–25**
MERCURY (20410 through 20983): *59–65* **15–20**
(Monaural issues.)
MERCURY (60043 through 60983): *59–65* **15–20**
(Stereo issues.)
MUSIC DISC: *69* **10–12**
MUSICO: *70* **8–10**
MUSICOR (2000 & 3000 series): *66–69* **10–15**
MUSICOR (4600 series): *77* **10–12**
PICKWICK **8–10**
SPRINGBOARD: *76* **8–10**
TRIP: *76* **8–10**
WING: *62–67* **10–15**
Members: Tony Williams; David Lynch; Herb Reed; Linda Hayes: Gaynel Hodge; Zola Taylor; Paul Robi; Alex Hodge.
Also see HAYES, Linda, & The Platters
Also see LITTLE ANTHONY & THE IMPERIALS / The Platters

Price Range

Note: This section is one of several in this edition wherein there are listings by more than one group, using the same name, that are lumped together because we haven't been able yet to accurately separate them.

PLAYER
Singles: 7-Inch
CASABLANCA: *80* $1–3
RCA VICTOR: *82* 1–3
RSO: *77–78* 2–3
LPs: 10/12-Inch 33rpm
CASABLANCA: *80* 5–8
RSO: *77–78* 5–8
RCA VICTOR: *81* 5–8

PLAYERS ASSOCIATION, The
Singles: 12-Inch 33/45rpm
VANGUARD: *79–80* 4–6
Singles: 7-Inch
VANGUARD: *77–80* 1–3
LPs: 10/12-Inch 33rpm
VANGUARD: *77–80* 5–8

PLAYMATES, The
Singles: 7-Inch
ABC-PARAMOUNT:
   63–64 3–5
BELL: *71* 2–4
COLPIX: *64–65*. 3–5
CONGRESS: *65* 3–5
ROULETTE: *57–63* 4–6
LPs: 10/12-Inch 33rpm
FORUM: *60* 15–20
ROULETTE: *57–61* 20–25
   Members: Donny Conn; Morey Carr; Chic Hetti.

PLEASURE
Singles: 12-Inch 33/45rpm
FANTASY: *76–80*. 4–6
Singles: 7-Inch
FANTASY: *76–80*. 1–3
RCA VICTOR: *82–83* 1–3
LPs: 10/12-Inch 33rpm
FANTASY: *76–80*. 5–8
RCA VICTOR: *82* 5–8

PLEASURE, King
Singles: 7-Inch
PRESTIGE (800 & 900
   series): *52–55* 5–8

Price Range

PLATTERS, The / Inez & Charlie Foxx / The Jive Five / Tommy Hunt
LPs: 10/12-Inch 33rpm
MUSICOR: *67*. $12–15
   Also see FOXX, Inez
   Also see HUNT, Tommy
   Also see JIVE FIVE, The

PLATTERS '65, The
Singles: 7-Inch
ENTREE: *65* 3–5
   Also see PLATTERS, The

PLAYBOYS, The
Singles: 7-Inch
ABC-PARAMOUNT: *59* 5–8
ACE: *64* 3–5
CAMEO: *58* 5–8
CATALINA 4–6
CHANCELLOR: *61–62* 4–6
COTTON: *62*. 5–8
DOLTON: *59*. 4–6
IMPERIAL: *59* 5–8
JEWEL: *64* 3–5
LEGATO: *63*. 4–6
MARTINIQUE (101;
  "Over The Weekend"):
   58 10–15
MARTINIQUE (400;
  "Please Forgive Me"): *59* 8–10
MERCURY: *57*. 4–6
RIK: *59* 4–6
SOUVENIR: *59*. 4–6
TITAN: *65*. 4–6

Price Range

LPs: 10/12-Inch 33rpm
HI-FI: 60 . . . . **$20–40**
PRESTIGE (200 series): 55 . . . . **50–100**
(10-Inch LPs.)
PRESTIGE (7000 series):
57 . . . . **30–60**
UNITED ARTISTS: 62 . . . . **15–25**

PLEASURE & THE BEAST
Singles: 12-Inch 33/45rpm
AIRWAVE: 84 . . . . **4–6**

PLEIS, Jack, & His Orchestra
Singles: 7-Inch
ATCO: 65 . . . . **2–3**
COLUMBIA: 61 . . . . **2–4**
DECCA: 53–60 . . . . **2–4**
LONDON: 50–51 . . . . **2–4**
RANWOOD: 76 . . . . **1–3**
EPs: 7-Inch 33/45rpm
DECCA: 55–57 . . . . **4–8**
LPs: 10/12-Inch 33rpm
CAMEO: 63 . . . . **6–12**
COLUMBIA: 61 . . . . **6–12**
DECCA: 55–57 . . . . **6–15**
RANWOOD: 76 . . . . **5–8**

PLIMSOULS, The
Singles: 7-Inch
GEFFEN: 83 . . . . **1–3**
LPs: 10/12-Inch 33rpm
GEFFEN: 83 . . . . **5–8**
PLANET: 81 . . . . **5–8**

PLUSH
Singles: 7-Inch
RCA VICTOR: 82 . . . . **1–3**
LPs: 10/12-Inch 33rpm
RCA VICTOR: 82 . . . . **5–8**

P-NUT GALLERY, The
Singles: 7-Inch
BUDDAH: 71 . . . . **2–4**

POCKETS, The
Singles: 7-Inch
ARC: 79 . . . . **1–3**
COLUMBIA: 77–78 . . . . **2–3**
LPs: 10/12-Inch 33rpm
ARC: 79 . . . . **5–8**
COLUMBIA: 77–78 . . . . **5–8**

Price Range

POCO
Singles: 7-Inch
ABC: 75–79 . . . . **$2–4**
ATLANTIC: 82–84 . . . . **1–3**
EPIC: 69–75 . . . . **3–5**
MCA: 79–82 . . . . **1–3**
Picture Sleeves
EPIC: 70–72 . . . . **3–5**
MCA: 80 . . . . **2–3**
LPs: 10/12-Inch 33rpm
ABC: 75–78 . . . . **8–10**
ATLANTIC: 82 . . . . **5–8**
EPIC (26460 through
30753): 69–71 . . . . **10–15**
EPIC (31601 through
36210): 71–81 . . . . **6–10**
MCA: 80–82 . . . . **5–8**
MFSL: 78 . . . . **12–15**
Members: Richie Furay; Jim Messina; Rusty
Young; Timothy Schmit; Paul Cotton.
Also see BUFFALO SPRINGFIELD
Also see EAGLES, The
Also see FURRAY, Richie
Also see ILLINOIS SPEED PRESS
Also see MEISNER, Randy
Also see MESSINA, Jim
Also see SCHMIT, Timothy B.

POETS, The
Singles: 7-Inch
CHAIRMAN: 63 . . . . **3–5**
RED BIRD: 65 . . . . **4–6**
SYMBOL: 66 . . . . **3–5**
TRY ME: 63 . . . . **3–5**
VEEP: 68 . . . . **3–5**

POETS, The
Singles: 7-Inch
DYNO VOX: 64 . . . . **3–6**

POINT BLANK
Singles: 7-Inch
ARISTA: 76–77 . . . . **2–3**
MCA: 79–81 . . . . **1–3**
LPs: 10/12-Inch 33rpm
ARISTA: 77 . . . . **5–8**
MCA: 79–82 . . . . **5–8**

POINTER, Bonnie
Singles: 12-Inch 33/45rpm
MOTOWN: 78–81 . . . . **4–6**
PRIVATE I: 84–85 . . . . **4–6**

Price Range

Price Range

Singles: 7-Inch
MOTOWN: *78–81*................. $1–3
PRIVATE I: *84–85*................. 1–3
Promotional Singles
MOTOWN (Colored vinyl):
  78 3–5
LPs: 10/12-Inch 33rpm
MOTOWN: *78–79*................. 5–8
PRIVATE I: *84*.................... 5–8
Also see POINTER SISTERS, The

POINTER, June
Singles: 12-Inch 33/45rpm
PLANET: *83–84*................. 4–6
Singles: 7-Inch
PLANET: *83–84*.................. 1–3
LPs: 10/12-Inch 33rpm
PLANET: *83*..................... 5–8

POINTER, Noel
Singles: 12-Inch 33/45rpm
UNITED ARTISTS: *77*............. 4–6
Singles: 7-Inch
BLUE NOTE: *77* 1–3
LIBERTY: *81* 1–3
UNITED ARTISTS: *78–80*.......... 1–3
LPs: 10/12-Inch 33rpm
BLUE NOTE: *77* 5–10
LIBERTY: *81* 5–8
UNITED ARTISTS: *78–80*.......... 5–8

POINTER SISTERS, The
Singles: 12-Inch 33/45rpm
PLANET: *78–85*................. 4–6
Singles: 7-Inch
ABC: *75–78*...................... 2–3
ATLANTIC: *72* 2–4
BLUE THUMB: *73–78* 2–4
PLANET: *78–85*.................. 1–3
RCA VICTOR: *85* 1–3
Picture Sleeves
PLANET: *78–85*.................. 1–3
LPs: 10/12-Inch 33rpm
BLUE THUMB: *73–77* 8–12
MCA: *81* 5–8
PLANET: *78–84*.................. 5–8
RCA VICTOR: *85* 5–8
Members: Bonnie Pointer; Anita Pointer; Ruth Pointer; June Pointer.
Also see MEMPHIS HORNS, The
Also see POINTER, Bonnie

Also see POINTER, June

POISON
Singles: 7-Inch
ROULETTE $75

POLICE, The
Singles: 7-Inch
A&M: *79–84* 1–3
Picture Sleeves
A&M: *80–84* 1–3
LPs: 10/12-Inch 33rpm
A&M: *79–83* 6–10
Members: Gordon "Sting" Sumner; Andy Summers; Stewart Copeland.
Also see COPELAND, Stewart
Also see STING
Also see FRIPP, Robert, & Andy Summers

POLITICIANS, The (Featuring McKinley Jackson)
Singles: 7-Inch
HOT WAX: *72*.................... 2–4
LPs: 10/12-Inch 33rpm
HOT WAX: *72* 8–10

POLNAREFF, Michel
Singles: 12-Inch 33/45rpm
ATLANTIC: *76* 4–6
Singles: 7-Inch
ATLANTIC: *76* 2–3
4 CORNERS: *67*.................. 2–4
KAPP: *65–66*.................... 3–5
LPs: 10/12-Inch 33rpm
ATLANTIC: *75* 8–10
4 CORNERS: *67*................. 10–15

PONDEROSA TWINS + ONE, The
Singles: 7-Inch
ASTROSCOPE: *72*................. 2–4
HOROSCOPE: *71*................. 2–4
LPs: 10/12-Inch 33rpm
HOROSCOPE: *71*................. 8–10

PONI-TAILS, The
Singles: 7-Inch
ABC: *73*......................... 1–3
ABC-PARAMOUNT:
  57–60 4–8
MCA............................. 1–3
MARC: *57*....................... 6–10

Price Range

POINT: *57* **$6–10**

PONSAR, Serge
Singles: 12-Inch 33/45rpm
WARNER BROS: *83* **4–6**
Singles: 7-Inch
WARNER BROS: *83* **1–3**

PONTY, Jean-Luc
Singles: 7-Inch
ATLANTIC: *76–85* **1–3**
LPs: 10/12-Inch 33rpm
ATLANTIC: *75–85* **5–10**
BLUE NOTE: *76–81* **5–10**
MPS: *72–73* **5–10**
PACIFIC JAZZ: *68–78* **8–18**
PAUSA: *80* **5–8**
PRESTIGE: *70* **8–15**
WORLD PACIFIC: *69* **8–15**

POOLE, Brian (Brian Poole & The Tremeloes)
Singles: 7-Inch
DATE: *66* **4–6**
LONDON: *63* **5–8**
MONUMENT: *64–65* **4–6**
LPs: 10/12-Inch 33rpm
AUDIO FIDELITY: *66–67* **15–20**
Also see TREMELOES, The

POP, Iggy (Iggy & The Stooges)
Singles: 7-Inch
RCA VICTOR: *77* **2–3**
SIAMESE: *77* **2–3**
LPs: 10/12-Inch 33rpm
ANIMAL: *82* **5–8**
ARISTA: *79–81* **5–8**
BOMP (Black vinyl): *78* **8–10**
BOMP (Colored vinyl): *78* **12–15**
COLUMBIA: *73* **12–15**
ENIGMA: *84* **5–8**
IMPORT: *77* **8–10**
RCA VICTOR: *77–78* **5–8**
Also see BOWIE, David / Iggy Pop
Also see STOOGES, The

POP TOPS, The
Singles: 7-Inch
ABC: *71* **2–4**
CALLA: *68* **3–5**

Price Range

POPE JOHN XXIII
LPs: 10/12-Inch 33rpm
MERCURY: *63* **$5–10**

POPE JOHN PAUL II
LPs: 10/12-Inch 33rpm
BETHLEHEM: *79* **4–8**
INFINITY: *79* **4–8**
VOX CHRISTIANA: *79* **4–8**

POPE PAUL VI
LPs: 10/12-Inch 33rpm
AMY: *65* **5–10**
AUDIO FIDELITY: *65* **5–10**
MGM: *65* **5–10**
20TH CENTURY-FOX:
 64 . . . . **5–10**

POPPIES, The (Featuring Dorothy Moore)
Singles: 7-Inch
EPIC: *66* **3–5**
Picture Sleeves
EPIC: *66* **4–6**
LPs: 10/12-Inch 33rpm
EPIC: *66* **20–25**
Also see MOORE, Dorothy

POPPY FAMILY, The
Singles: 7-Inch
LONDON: *70–72* **2–4**
LPs: 10/12-Inch 33rpm
LONDON: *70–71* **10–12**
Members: Susan Jacks; Terry Jacks.
Also see JACKS, Susan
Also see JACKS, Terry

PORTER, David
Singles: 7-Inch
ENTERPRISE: *70–72* **2–4**
LPs: 10/12-Inch 33rpm
ENTERPRISE: *70–72* **8–10**
Also see HAYES, Isaac & David Porter

PORTER, Nolan (N.F. Porter; Nolan)
Singles: 7-Inch
ABC: *73* **2–3**
LIZARD: *71* **2–4**
LPs: 10/12-Inch 33rpm
LIZARD: *71* **8–10**

Price Range   *Price Range*

PORTNOY, Gary
Singles: 7-Inch
APPLAUSE: 83. . . . . $1–3

POSEY, Sandy
Singles: 7-Inch
AUDIOGRAPH: 83. 1–3
COLUMBIA: 71–72 2–3
MGM: 66–67. 2–4
POLYDOR: 83 1–3
WARNER BROS: 78–79 1–3
Picture Sleeves
MGM: 66–67. 3–5
LPs: 10/12-Inch 33rpm
COLUMBIA: 72 8–10
51 WEST: 83 5–8
GUSTO 5–8
MGM: 66–70 10–12

POSEY, Sandy / Skeeter Davis
LPs: 10/12-Inch 33rpm
GUSTO 5–8
  Also see DAVIS, Skeeter
  Also see POSEY, Sandy

POST, Mike (The Mike Post Coalition)
Singles: 7-Inch
BELL: 71. 2–3
ELEKTRA: 81–82 1–3
EPIC: 77 1–3
MGM: 75. 1–3
MUSIC FACTORY: 68 2–3
REPRISE: 65–66. 2–4
WARNER BROS: 69 2–3
Picture Sleeves
ELEKTRA: 81–82 1–3
LPs: 10/12-Inch 33rpm
ELEKTRA: 82 5–8
MGM: 75. 5–10
WARNER BROS: 69. 8–12

POTLIQUOR
Singles: 7-Inch
CAPITOL: 79 2–3
JANUS: 72 2–4
LPs: 10/12-Inch 33rpm
CAPITOL: 79 5–8
JANUS: 70–73. 10–15

POURCEL, Franck (Franck Pourcel's French Fiddles)
Singles: 7-Inch
BLUE: 69. . . . . $1–3
CAPITOL: 59–64 2–4
IMPERIAL: 66–68. 1–3
PARAMOUNT: 71–73. 1–3
EPs: 7-Inch 33/45rpm
CAPITOL: 59 4–8
LPs: 10/12-Inch 33rpm
ATCO: 69 5–10
CAPITOL: 56–79 5–15
IMPERIAL: 66–68. 5–10
PARAMOUNT: 70–73. 5–8
WESTMINSTER: 54–55 10–20

POUSETTE-DART BAND, The (With Jon Pousette-Dart)
Singles: 7-Inch
CAPITOL: 76–79 2–3
LPs: 10/12-Inch 33rpm
CAPITOL: 76–80 5–10

POWELL, Adam Clayton
LPs: 10/12-Inch 33rpm
JUBILEE: 67. 5–15

POWELL, Bobby
Singles: 7-Inch
JEWEL: 67 3–5
WHIT: 65–71. 3–5
LPs: 10/12-Inch 33rpm
EXCELLO: 73. 8–10

POWELL, Cozy
Singles: 7-Inch
CHRYSALIS: 74. 2–3
  Also see BECK, Jeff

POWELL, Jane
Singles: 7-Inch
RANWOOD: 68 2–3
VERVE: 56 2–4
LPs: 10/12-Inch 33rpm
COLUMBIA: 55–57. 10–25
LION: 59 8–15
MGM: 55. 15–25
VERVE: 56 15–25

Price Range

Price Range

POWER STATION
Singles: 12-Inch 33/45rpm
CAPITOL: 85 .... $4–6
Singles: 7-Inch
CAPITOL: 85 1–3
LPs: 10/12-Inch 33rpm
CAPITOL: 85 5–8
Also see DURAN DURAN

POWERS, Joey (Joey Powers' Flower)
Singles: 7-Inch
AMY: 63–67 3–5
MGM: 65 3–5
RCA VICTOR (8000
series): 62 4–6
RCA VICTOR (9700
series): 69 2–4
LPs: 10/12-Inch 33rpm
AMY: 64 15–20
Also see ORBISON, Roy / Bobby Bare / Joey Powers

POWERS, Tom
Singles: 7-Inch
BIG TREE: 77 2–3

POZO-SECO SINGERS, The (Pozo Seco; Susan Taylor & The Pozo Seco Singers)
Singles: 7-Inch
CERTRON: 70 2–4
COLUMBIA: 65–70 2–5
LPs: 10/12-Inch 33rpm
CERTRON: 70 8–12
COLUMBIA: 66–68 12–15
Members: Don Williams; Susan Taylor; Lofton Kline.
Also see WILLIAMS, Don

PRADO, Perez, & His Orchestra
Singles: 7-Inch
RCA VICTOR: 50–64 2–4
UNITED ARTISTS: 64 2–3
Picture Sleeves
RCA VICTOR: 59 2–4
EPs: 7-Inch 33/45rpm
RCA VICTOR: 54–61 4–8
LPs: 10/12-Inch 33rpm
CAMDEN: 60 5–10
RCA VICTOR: 76 5–8

(With an "ANL1" prefix.)
RCA VICTOR: 54–72 .... $8–18
(With an "LPM," "LSP" or "VPS" prefix.)
SPRINGBOARD: 77 4–8
UNITED ARTISTS: 65–68 5–10
Also see CLOONEY, Rosemary, & Perez Prado
Also see HIRT, Al / Henry Mancini / Perez Prado

PRATT, Andy
Singles: 7-Inch
COLUMBIA: 73 2–4
NEMPEROR: 76–77 2–3

LPs: 10/12-Inch 33rpm
COLUMBIA: 73 8–10
NEMPEROR: 76–79 5–8
POLYDOR: 70 10–12
Also see SPRINGSTEEN, Bruce / Andy Pratt

PRATT-McCLAIN
Singles: 7-Inch
REPRISE: 76–77 2–3
LPs: 10/12-Inch 33rpm
DUNHILL: 73 8–10
REPRISE: 76 8–10
Members: Truett Pratt; Jerry McClain.

PRECISIONS, The
Singles: 7-Inch
ATCO: 69 2–4
D-TOWN: 65 4–6
DREW: 66–68 3–5
HEN-MAR: 73 2–4

PRELUDE
Singles: 7-Inch
ISLAND: 74 2–3
PYE: 75 2–3
LPs: 10/12-Inch 33rpm
ISLAND: 74 8–10
PYE: 76 8–10

PRELUDES FIVE, The
Singles: 7-Inch
PIK: 61 8–10

PREMIATA FORNEIRA
MARCONI: see P.F.M.

Price Range

PREMIERS, The
Singles: 7-Inch
FARO: *64–67.*................... $3–5
LEO: *64*......................... 3–5
WARNER BROS: *64*.............. 3–5

LPs: 10/12-Inch 33rpm
WARNER BROS: *64*............. 15–20

PRENTISS, Lee
Singles: 12-Inch 33/45rpm
MSB: *83*........................ 4–6

PREPARATIONS, The
Singles: 7-Inch
HEART & SOUL: *68*.............. 2–4

PRESIDENTS, The
Singles: 7-Inch
DELUXE: *69.*..................... 2–4
HOLLYWOOD: *68.*................ 3–5
SUSSEX: *70–71*................... 2–4

LPs: 10/12-Inch 33rpm
SUSSEX: *70*.................... 10–12

PRESLEY, Elvis
Singles: 78rpm (Commercial AND Promotional Issues)
RCA VICTOR (6357
   through 6383): *55* 70–80
RCA VICTOR (6420
   through 6604): *56* 45–55
RCA VICTOR (6420
   through 6604): *56* 175–200
   (White label. Promotional issues only.)
RCA VICTOR (6636
   through 6642): *56* 55–65
RCA VICTOR (6636
   through 6642): *56* 175–200
   (White label. Promotional issues only.)
RCA VICTOR (6643
   through 7150): *56–58* 45–55
RCA VICTOR (6643
   through 7150): *56–58* 175–200
   (White label. Promotional issues only. The highest number we've seen on white promo label is 7035, "Jailhouse Rock.")
RCA VICTOR (7240;
   "Wear My Ring Around
   Your Neck"): *58* 55–65

Price Range

RCA VICTOR (7280;
   "Hard Headed
   Woman"): *58*................. $70–80
RCA VICTOR (7410;
   "One Night"): *58.*............ 225–250
SUN (209; "That's All
   Right"): *54*................ 175–200
SUN (210; "Good Rockin'
   Tonight"): *54*................ 175–200
SUN (215; "You're A
   Heartbreaker"): *55.*........... 175–200
SUN (217; "Baby Let's
   Play House"): *55*............. 175–200
SUN (223; "Mystery
   Train"): *55*................. 150–175
   Notes: All of the Elvis 78s were simultaneously issued on 45rpm singles...Specific titles of any single can be found in the following section, which lists all singles individually...78rpm plastic soundsheets or flexi-discs are listed in a separate section...Sun singles, like RCA releases, can be found with label variations...Sun promotional singles were so indicated with "Sample" rubber stamped on the label.

Singles: 7-Inch (Commercial Issues)
COLLECTABLES: *86* 1–3
RCA VICTOR (0088;
   "Raised On Rock"): *73* 3–5
RCA VICTOR (0130;
   "How Great Thou Art"):
   69 15–20
RCA VICTOR (0196; "I've
   Got A Thing About You
   Baby"): *74* 3–5
RCA VICTOR (0280; "If
   You Talk In Your
   Sleep"): *74* 3–5
RCA VICTOR (0572;
   "Merry Christmas
   Baby"): *71* 12–15
RCA VICTOR (0619;
   "Until It's Time For
   You To Go"): *72*............... 3–5
RCA VICTOR (0651; "He
   Touched Me"): *72*............... 3–5
RCA VICTOR (0651; "He
   Touched Me"): *72*........... 80–100
   (With "He Touched Me" pressed at about 35rpm instead of 45rpm. These copies, the result of an error in production, were commercial issues.)

Price Range

RCA VICTOR (0672; "An
American Trilogy"): *72* **$10–12**

RCA VICTOR (0769;
"Burning Love"): *72*.............. **3–5**
(Orange label.)

RCA VICTOR (0769;
"Burning Love"): *72*........... **75–100**
(Gray label.)

RCA VICTOR (0815;
"Separate Ways"): *71* **3–5**

RCA VICTOR (0910;
"Steamroller Blues"): *73*........... **3–5**

RCA VICTOR (1017; "It's
Only Love"): *71*.................. **3–5**

RCA VICTOR (6357;
"Mystery Train"): *55* **40–60**
(With horizontal silver line.)

RCA VICTOR (6357;
"Mystery Train"): *55* **25–35**
(Without horizontal silver line.)

RCA VICTOR (6380;
"That's All Right"): *55* **40–60**
(With horizontal silver line.)

RCA VICTOR (6380;
"That's All Right"): *55* **25–35**
(Without horizontal silver line.)

RCA VICTOR (6381;
"Good Rockin'
Tonight"): *55*.................. **40–60**
(With horizontal silver line.)

RCA VICTOR (6381;
"Good Rockin'
Tonight"): *55*.................. **25–35**
(Without horizontal silver line.)

RCA VICTOR (6382;
"Milkcow Blues
Boogie"): *55*.................. **$40–60**
(With horizontal silver line.)

RCA VICTOR (6382;
"Milkcow Blues
Boogie"): *55*.................. **25–35**
(Without horizontal silver line.)

RCA VICTOR (6383;
"Baby, Let's Play
House"): *55* **40–60**
(With horizontal silver line.)

RCA VICTOR (6383;
"Baby, Let's Play
House"): *55* **25–35**
(Without horizontal silver line.)

RCA VICTOR (6420;
"Heartbreak Hotel"): *56*......... **25–30**
(With horizontal silver line.)

RCA VICTOR (6420;
"Heartbreak Hotel"): *56*......... **15–20**
(Without horizontal silver line.)

RCA VICTOR (6540; "I
Want You, I Need You,
I Love You"): *56*.............. **25–30**
(With horizontal silver line.)

RCA VICTOR (6540; "I
Want You, I Need You,
I Love You"): *56*.............. **15–20**
(Without horizontal silver line.)

RCA VICTOR (6604;
"Don't Be Cruel"): *56* **25–30**
(With horizontal silver line.)

RCA VICTOR (6604;
"Don't Be Cruel"): *56* **15–20**
(Without horizontal silver line.)

RCA VICTOR (6636;
"Blue Suede Shoes"): *56*......... **40–50**
(With horizontal silver line.)

RCA VICTOR (6636;
"Blue Suede Shoes"): *56*......... **20–30**
(Without horizontal silver line.)

RCA VICTOR (6637; "I
Got A Woman"): *56*............ **40–50**
(With horizontal silver line.)

RCA VICTOR (6637; "I
Got A Woman"): *56*............ **20–30**
(Without horizontal silver line.)

RCA VICTOR (6638; "I'm
Gonna Sit Right Down
And Cry"): *56* **40–50**
(With horizontal silver line.)

RCA VICTOR (6638; "I'm
Gonna Sit Right Down
And Cry"): *56* **$20–30**
(Without horizontal silver line.)

RCA VICTOR (6639;
"Tryin' To Get To
You"): *56* **40–50**
(With horizontal silver line.)

RCA VICTOR (6639;
"Tryin' To Get To
You"): *56* **20–30**
(Without horizontal silver line.)

RCA VICTOR (6640;
"Blue Moon"): *56* **40–50**
(With horizontal silver line.)

RCA VICTOR (6640;
"Blue Moon"): *56* **20–30**
(Without horizontal silver line.)

RCA VICTOR (6641;
"Money Honey"): *56* **40–50**
(With horizontal silver line.)

RCA VICTOR (6641;
"Money Honey"): *56* **20–30**
(Without horizontal silver line.)

RCA VICTOR (6642;
"Lawdy Miss Clawdy"):
56 . . . . **125–150**
(NO DOG on label.)

RCA VICTOR (6642;
"Lawdy Miss Clawdy"):
56 . . . . **40–50**
(With horizontal silver line.)

RCA VICTOR (6642;
"Lawdy Miss Clawdy"):
56 . . . . **20–30**
(Without horizontal silver line.)

RCA VICTOR (6643;
"Love Me Tender"): *56* **25–30**
(With horizontal silver line.)

RCA VICTOR (6643;
"Love Me Tender"): *56* **15–20**
(Without horizontal silver line.)

RCA VICTOR (6800;
"Too Much"): *57* **100–125**
(NO DOG on label.)

RCA VICTOR (6800;
"Too Much"): *57* **25–30**
(With horizontal silver line.)

RCA VICTOR (6800;
"Too Much"): *57* **15–20**
(Without horizontal silver line.)

RCA VICTOR (6870; "All
Shook Up"): *57* **$25–30**
(With horizontal silver line.)

RCA VICTOR (6870; "All
Shook Up"): *57* **15–20**
(Without horizontal silver line.)

RCA VICTOR (7000;
"Teddy Bear"): *57* **25–30**
(With horizontal silver line.)

RCA VICTOR (7000;
"Teddy Bear"): *57* **15–20**
(Without horizontal silver line.)

RCA VICTOR (7035;
"Jailhouse Rock"): *57* **35–40**
(With horizontal silver line. This was the last
silver line single.)

RCA VICTOR (7035;
"Jailhouse Rock"): *57* **15–20**
(Without horizontal silver line.)

RCA VICTOR (7150;
"Don't"): *58* **10–15**

RCA VICTOR (7240;
"Wear My Ring Around
Your Neck"): *58* **10–15**

RCA VICTOR (7280;
"Hard Headed
Woman"): *58* **10–15**

RCA VICTOR (7410;
"One Night"): *58* **10–15**

RCA VICTOR (7506; "A
Fool Such As I"): *59* **10–15**

RCA VICTOR (7600; "A
Big Hunk O' Love"): *59* **10–15**

RCA VICTOR (7740;
"Stuck On You"): *60* **8–10**

RCA VICTOR (7740;
"Stuck On You"): *60* **175–200**
(Living Stereo, numbered with a "61" prefix.)
Note: A slight premium, perhaps $2-$5, may be
placed on RCA's "Living Stereo" paper sleeves.
These were used for many RCA stereo singles,
by anyone on the label, and were not exclusively
an Elvis item.

RCA VICTOR (7777; "It's
Now Or Never"): *60* **8–10**

RCA VICTOR (7777; "It's
Now Or Never"): *60* **250–275**
(Living Stereo, numbered with a "61" prefix.)

RCA VICTOR (7810; "Are
You Lonesome
To-night"): *60* **8–10**

Price Range

Price Range

RCA VICTOR (7810; "Are
You Lonesome
To-night"): 60 .... **$250–275**
(Living Stereo, numbered with a "61" prefix.)
RCA VICTOR (7850;
"Surrender"): 61 .... **8–10**
RCA VICTOR (7850;
"Surrender"): 61 .... **250–275**
(Compact 33 Single, numbered with a "37" prefix.)
RCA VICTOR (7850;
"Surrender"): 61 .... **175–200**
(Living Stereo, numbered with a "61" prefix.)
RCA VICTOR (7850;
"Surrender"): 61 .... **900–1100**
(Stereo Compact 33 Single, numbered with a "68" prefix.)
RCA VICTOR (7880; "I
Feel So Bad"): 61 .... **8–10**
RCA VICTOR (7880; "I
Feel So Bad"): 61 .... **275–300**
(Compact 33 Single, numbered with a "37" prefix.)
RCA VICTOR (7908; "His
Latest Flame"): 61 .... **8–10**
RCA VICTOR (7908; "His
Latest Flame"): 61 .... **425–450**
(Compact 33 Single, numbered with a "37" prefix.)
RCA VICTOR (7968;
"Can't Help Falling In
Love"): 61 .... **8–10**
RCA VICTOR (7968;
"Can't Help Falling In
Love"): 61 .... **500–525**
(Compact 33 Single, numbered with a "37" prefix.)
RCA VICTOR (7992;
"Good Luck Charm"):
62 .... **8–10**
RCA VICTOR (7992;
"Good Luck Charm"):
62 .... **900–1000**
(Compact 33 Single, numbered with a "37" prefix. This disc and its sleeve, which is priced separately in the Picture Sleeve section, is the rarest and most valuable standard catalog Elvis release.)
RCA VICTOR (8041;
"She's Not You"): 62 .... **8–10**
RCA VICTOR (8100;
"Return To Sender"): 62 .... **8–10**

RCA VICTOR (8134;
"One Broken Heart For
Sale"): 63 .... **$8–10**
RCA VICTOR (8188;
"Devil In Disguise"): 63 .... **45–55**
(Flip side title incorrectly shown as "Please Don't Drag That String ALONG.")
RCA VICTOR (8188;
"Devil In Disguise"): 63 .... **5–8**
(Flip side title correctly shown as "Please Don't Drag That String AROUND.")
RCA VICTOR (8243;
"Bossa Nova Baby"): 63 .... **6–10**
RCA VICTOR (8307;
"Kissin' Cousins"): 64 .... **6–10**
RCA VICTOR (8360;
"Viva Las Vegas"): 64 .... **6–10**
RCA VICTOR (8400;
"Such A Night"): 64 .... **6–10**
RCA VICTOR (8440;
"Ask Me"): 64 .... **6–10**
RCA VICTOR (8500; "Do
The Clam"): 65 .... **5–10**
RCA VICTOR (8585; "It
Feels So Right"): 65 .... **5–8**
RCA VICTOR (8657; "I'm
Yours"): 65 .... **5–8**
RCA VICTOR (8740;
"Tell Me Why"): 65 .... **5–8**
RCA VICTOR (8780;
"Frankie & Johnny"): 66 .... **5–8**
RCA VICTOR (8870;
"Love Letters"): 66 .... **5–8**
RCA VICTOR (8941;
"Spinout"): 66 .... **5–8**
RCA VICTOR (9056;
"Indescribably Blue"): 67 .... **5–8**
RCA VICTOR (9115;
"Long Legged Girl"): 67 .... **5–8**
RCA VICTOR (9287;
"There's Always Me"):
67 .... **5–8**
RCA VICTOR (9341; "Big
Boss Man"): 67 .... **5–8**
RCA VICTOR (9425;
"Guitar Man"): 68 .... **5–8**
RCA VICTOR (9465;
"U.S. Male"): 68 .... **5–8**
RCA VICTOR (9547;
"Your Time Hasn't
Come Yet Baby"): 68 .... **5–8**

Price Range

Price Range

RCA VICTOR (9600;
"You'll Never Walk
Alone"): 68. . . . . $5–10
RCA VICTOR (9610;
"Almost In Love"): 68 5–8
RCA VICTOR (9670; "If I
Can Dream"): 68. 3–5
RCA VICTOR (9731;
"Memories"): 69 3–5
RCA VICTOR (9741; "In
The Ghetto"): 69. 3–5
RCA VICTOR (9747;
"Clean Up Your Own
Back Yard"): 69 3–5
RCA VICTOR (9764;
"Suspicious Minds"): 69. 3–5
RCA VICTOR (9768;
"Don't Cry Daddy"): 69 3–5
RCA VICTOR (9791;
"Kentucky Rain"): 70. 3–5
RCA VICTOR (9835;
"The Wonder Of You"):
70 3–5
RCA VICTOR (9873; "I've
Lost You"): 70. 3–5
RCA VICTOR (9916;
"You Don't Have To
Say You Love Me"): 70 3–5
RCA VICTOR (9960; "I
Really Don't Want To
Know"): 70 3–5
RCA VICTOR (9980;
"Where Did They Go
Lord"): 71 3–5
RCA VICTOR (9985;
"Life"): 71 3–5
RCA VICTOR (9998; "I'm
Leavin"): 71. 3–5
  Note: RCA numbers in the 10000-14000 series
  with a "GB" prefix are Gold Standard Series
  issues and are listed in a separate Gold Standard
  Singles section. Those in the regular release se-
  ries are listed below.
RCA VICTOR (10074;
"Promised Land"): 74. 3–5
  (Orange label.)
RCA VICTOR (10074;
"Promised Land"): 74. 20–25
  (Gray label.)
RCA VICTOR (10191;
"My Boy"): 75. 3–5

  (Orange label.)
RCA VICTOR (10191;
"My Boy"): 75. . . . . $8–10
  (Tan label.)
RCA VICTOR (10278;
"T-r-o-u-b-l-e"): 75 3–5
  (Orange label.)
RCA VICTOR (10278;
"T-r-o-u-b-l-e"): 75 8–10
  (Tan label.)
RCA VICTOR (10278;
"T-r-o-u-b-l-e"): 75 20–25
  (Gray label.)
RCA VICTOR (10401;
"Bringing It Back"): 75 45–55
  (Orange label.)
RCA VICTOR (10401;
"Bringing It Back"): 75 3–5
  (Tan label.)
RCA VICTOR (10601;
"Hurt"): 76 3–5
  (Tan label.)
RCA VICTOR (10601;
"Hurt"): 76 90–100
  (Black label.)
RCA VICTOR (10857;
"Moody Blue"): 76 3–5
  (Colored vinyl copies of "Moody Blue," were
  experimental and are listed in the Promotional
  Singles section that follows.)
RCA VICTOR (10998;
"Way Down"): 77. 3–5
RCA VICTOR (11099
through 11113): 77 2–4
  (Discs in this series were originally packaged in
  either 11301 and/or 11340, both of which were
  boxed sets of singles with sleeves.)
RCA VICTOR (11165;
"My Way"): 77. 3–5
  (With flip side title shown as "America.")
RCA VICTOR (11165;
"My Way"): 77 15–20
  (With flip side title shown as "America The
  Beautiful.")
RCA VICTOR (11212;
"Softly, As I Leave
You"): 78 3–5
RCA VICTOR (11301; "15
Golden Records"): 77. 40–50
  (Boxed set of 15 Elvis singles, each with a pic-
  ture sleeve.)
RCA VICTOR (11320;
"Teddy Bear"): 78. 3–5

Price Range

RCA VICTOR (11340; "20
  Golden Hits"): 77 . . . . **$65–75**
  (Boxed set of 10 Elvis singles, each with a picture sleeve.)
RCA VICTOR (11533;
  "Are You Sincere"): 79 . . . . **3–5**
RCA VICTOR (11679;
  "There's A Honky Tonk
  Angel"): 79. . . . . **12–15**
  (With production & backing credits shown on label.)
RCA VICTOR (11679;
  "There's A Honky Tonk
  Angel"): 79. . . . . **3–5**
  (With backing credits removed, leaving only production credits.)
RCA VICTOR (12158;
  "Guitar Man"): 81 . . . . **3–5**
RCA VICTOR (12205;
  "Lovin' Arms"): 81. . . . . **3–5**
RCA VICTOR (13058;
  "You'll Never Walk
  Alone"): 82. . . . . **3–5**
RCA VICTOR (13351;
  "The Elvis Medley"): 82 . . . . **3–5**
RCA VICTOR (13500; "I
  Was The One"): 83. . . . . **3–5**
RCA VICTOR (13547;
  "Little Sister"): 83. . . . . **3–5**
RCA VICTOR (13875;
  "Baby, Let's Play
  House"): 84 . . . . **5–8**
RCA VICTOR (13885
  through 13890): 84 . . . . **1–3**
  (Discs in this series were originally packaged in
  13897, "Golden Singles, Vol. I." Price includes
  sleeves.)
RCA VICTOR (13891
  through 13896): 84 . . . . **1–3**
  (Discs in this series were originally packaged in
  13898, "Golden Singles, Vol. II." Price includes
  sleeves.)
RCA VICTOR (13897;
  "Golden Singles, Vol.
  I"): 84. . . . . **10–15**
  (Package of six singles with sleeves.)
RCA VICTOR (13898;
  "Golden Singles, Vol.
  II"): 84. . . . . **10–15**
  (Package of six singles with sleeves.)
RCA VICTOR (13929;
  "Blue Suede Shoes"): 84. . . . . **5–8**

Price Range

  (With "Blue Suede Shoes" shown as stereo;
  "Promised Land" as mono.)
RCA VICTOR (13929;
  "Blue Suede Shoes"): 84. . . . . **$5–8**
  (With "Blue Suede Shoes" shown as mono;
  "Promised Land" as stereo.)
RCA VICTOR (14090;
  "Always On My Mind"):
  85 . . . . **2–4**
RCA VICTOR (14237;
  "Merry Christmas
  Baby"): 85 . . . . **5–8**
  (Black vinyl.)
RCA VICTOR (14237;
  "Merry Christmas
  Baby"): 85 . . . . **10–15**
  Notes: RCA numbers in the 10000-14000 series
  with a "GB" prefix are Gold Standard Series
  issues and are listed in a separate Gold Standard
  Singles section. Regular series issues are in the
  preceding section... Colored vinyl is not speci-
  fied on releases that were NOT also pressed on
  black vinyl and were not available in any form
  other than the colored vinyl...Plastic sound-
  sheets or flexi-discs are listed in a separate sec-
  tion.
SUN (209; "That's All
  Right"): 54. . . . . **375–400**
SUN (210; "Good Rockin'
  Tonight"): 54. . . . . **375–400**
SUN (215; "You're A
  Heartbreaker"): 55. . . . . **375–400**
SUN (217; "Baby Let's
  Play House"): 55. . . . . **350–400**
SUN (223; "Mystery
  Train"): 55. . . . . **225–275**

*Picture Sleeves: (Commercial AND
  Promotional Issues)*
RCA VICTOR (76;
  "Don't"/"Wear My Ring
  Around Your Neck"): 60 . . . . . **900–1000**
  (Promotional issue only.)
RCA VICTOR (0088;
  "Raised On Rock"): 73 . . . . **5–8**
RCA VICTOR (118;
  "King Of The Whole
  Wide World"): 62 . . . . **150–175**
  (Promotional issue only.)
RCA VICTOR (0130;
  "How Great Thou Art"):
  69 . . . . **70–80**

Price Range   *Price Range*

RCA VICTOR (162; "How
Great Thou Art"): *67* **$125–150**
(Promotional issue only.)

RCA VICTOR (0196; "I've
Got A Thing About You
Baby"): *74* **5–8**

RCA VICTOR (0280; "If
You Talk In Your
Sleep"): *74* **5–8**

RCA VICTOR (0572;
"Merry Christmas
Baby"): *71* **18–20**

RCA VICTOR (0619;
"Until It's Time For
You To Go"): *71* **5–8**

RCA VICTOR (0651; "He
Touched Me"): *71* **35–45**

RCA VICTOR (0672; "An
American Trilogy"): *72* **12–15**

RCA VICTOR (0769;
"Burning Love"): *72* **5–8**

RCA VICTOR (0815;
"Separate Ways"): *71* **5–8**

RCA VICTOR (0910;
"Steamroller Blues"): *73* **5–8**

RCA VICTOR (1017; "It's
Only Love"): *71* **5–8**

RCA VICTOR (6540; "I
Want You, I Need You,
I Love You"): *56* **300–350**
(Cartoon series "This Is His Life" sleeve. Pro-
motional issue only.)

RCA VICTOR (6604;
"Don't Be Cruel"): *56* **55–60**
(Showing "Don't Be Cruel" c/w "Hound
Dog.")

RCA VICTOR (6604;
"Hound Dog"): *56* **45–50**
(Showing "Hound Dog" c/w "Don't Be
Cruel.")

RCA VICTOR (6643;
"Love Me Tender"): *56* **100–125**
(Black & white sleeve.)

RCA VICTOR (6643;
"Love Me Tender"): *56* **50–60**
(Black & green sleeve.)

RCA VICTOR (6643;
"Love Me Tender"): *56* **35–40**
(Black & dark pink sleeve.)

RCA VICTOR (6643;
"Love Me Tender"): *56* **30–35**
(Black & light pink sleeve.)

RCA VICTOR (6800;
"Too Much"): *57* **$40–50**

RCA VICTOR (6870; "All
Shook Up"): *57* **40–50**

RCA VICTOR (7000;
"Teddy Bear"): *57* **40–50**

RCA VICTOR (7035;
"Jailhouse Rock"): *57* **40–50**

RCA VICTOR/MGM
"Jailhouse Rock" ticket/
sleeve): *57* **275–300**
(MGM "Jailhouse Rock" film preview invita-
tion ticket. Listed here because it was issued
wrapped around the standard 7035 disc &
sleeve and distributed promotionally to the
media.)

RCA VICTOR (7150;
"Don't"): *58* **30–40**

RCA VICTOR (7240;
"Wear My Ring Around
Your Neck"): *58* **30–40**

RCA VICTOR (7280;
"Hard Headed
Woman"): *58* **30–40**

RCA VICTOR (7410;
"One Night"): *58* **30–40**

RCA VICTOR (7506; "A
Fool Such As I"): *59* **125–150**
(With advertising for the "Elvis Sails" EP on
reverse side.)

RCA VICTOR (7506; "A
Fool Such As I"): *59* **25–30**
(With a listing of available Elvis EPs & 45s on
reverse side.)

RCA VICTOR (7600; "A
Big Hunk O' Love"): *59* **25–30**

RCA VICTOR (7740;
"Stuck On You"): *60* **15–20**

RCA VICTOR (7777; "It's
Now Or Never"): *60* **15–25**

RCA VICTOR (7810; "Are
You Lonesome
To-night"): *60* **15–25**

RCA VICTOR (7850;
"Surrender"): *61* **15–20**

RCA VICTOR (7850;
"Surrender"): *61* **200–225**
(Compact 33 Single sleeve, numbered with a
"37" prefix.)

RCA VICTOR (7880; "I
Feel So Bad"): *61* **15–20**

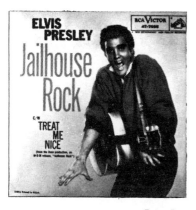

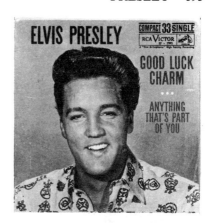

Price Range

Price Range

RCA VICTOR (7880; "I
Feel So Bad"): *61* **$275–300**
(Compact 33 Single sleeve, numbered with a
"37" prefix.)
RCA VICTOR (7908; "His
Latest Flame"): *61* **15–20**
RCA VICTOR (7908; "His
Latest Flame"): *61* **425–450**
(Compact 33 Single sleeve, numbered with a
"37" prefix.)
RCA VICTOR (7968;
"Can't Help Falling In
Love"): *61* **15–20**
RCA VICTOR (7968;
"Can't Help Falling In
Love"): *61* **500–525**
(Compact 33 Single sleeve, numbered with a
"37" prefix.)
RCA VICTOR (7992;
"Good Luck Charm"):
62 . . . . **15–20**
RCA VICTOR (7992;
"Good Luck Charm"):
62 . . . . **1200–1500**
(Compact 33 Single sleeve, numbered with a
"37" prefix. This sleeve and its disc, which is
priced separately in the Singles section, is the
rarest and most valuable standard catalog Elvis
release.)
RCA VICTOR (8041;
"She's Not You"): *62* **15–20**
RCA VICTOR (8100;
"Return To Sender"): *62* **15–20**

RCA VICTOR (8134;
"One Broken Heart For
Sale"): *63* **$15–20**
RCA VICTOR (8188;
"Devil In Disguise"): *63* **15–20**
RCA VICTOR (8243;
"Bossa Nova Baby"): *63* **15–20**
RCA VICTOR (8307;
"Kissin' Cousins"): *64* **15–20**
RCA VICTOR (8360;
"Viva Las Vegas"): *64* **15–20**
RCA VICTOR (8400;
"Such A Night"): *64* **15–20**
RCA VICTOR (8440;
"Ask Me"): *64* **15–20**
RCA VICTOR (8500; "Do
The Clam"): *65* **15–20**
RCA VICTOR (8585; "It
Feels So Right"): *65* **10–15**
RCA VICTOR (8657; "I'm
Yours"): *65.* **10–15**
RCA VICTOR (8740;
"Tell Me Why"): *65* **10–15**
RCA VICTOR (8780;
"Frankie & Johnny"): *66* **10–15**
RCA VICTOR (8870;
"Love Letters"): *66.* **10–15**
RCA VICTOR (8941;
"Spinout"): *66* **10–15**
RCA VICTOR (9056;
"Indescribably Blue"): *67.* **10–15**
RCA VICTOR (9115;
"Long Legged Girl"): *67* **10–15**

Price Range   *Price Range*

RCA VICTOR (9287;
"There's Always Me"):
67 . . . . **$10–15**

RCA VICTOR (9341; "Big
Boss Man"): 67 . . . . **10–15**

RCA VICTOR (9425;
"Guitar Man"): 68 . . . . **10–15**

RCA VICTOR (9465;
"U.S. Male"): 68 . . . . **10–15**

RCA VICTOR (9547;
"Your Time Hasn't
Come Yet Baby"): 68 . . . . **10–15**

RCA VICTOR (9600;
"You'll Never Walk
Alone"): 68. **35–45**

RCA VICTOR (9610;
"Almost In Love"): 68 . . . . **8–10**

RCA VICTOR (9670; "If I
Can Dream"): 68. . . . . **8–10**

RCA VICTOR (9731;
"Memories"): 69 . . . . **8–10**

RCA VICTOR (9741; "In
The Ghetto"): 69. . . . . **8–10**

RCA VICTOR (9747;
"Clean Up Your Own
Back Yard"): 69 . . . . **8–10**

RCA VICTOR (9764;
"Suspicious Minds"): 69. . . . . **8–10**

RCA VICTOR (9768;
"Don't Cry Daddy"): 69 . . . . **8–10**

RCA VICTOR (9791;
"Kentucky Rain"): 70. . . . . **8–10**

RCA VICTOR (9835;
"The Wonder Of You"):
70 . . . . **8–10**

RCA VICTOR (9873; "I've
Lost You"): 70. . . . . **8–10**

RCA VICTOR (9916;
"You Don't Have To
Say You Love Me"): 70 . . . . **8–10**

RCA VICTOR (9960; "I
Really Don't Want To
Know"): 70 . . . . **8–10**

RCA VICTOR (9980;
"Where Did They Go
Lord"): 71 . . . . **8–10**

RCA VICTOR (9985;
"Life"): 71 . . . . **8–10**

RCA VICTOR (9998; "I'm
Leavin"): 71. . . . . **8–10**

RCA VICTOR (10074;
"Promised Land"): 74. . . . . **$5–8**

RCA VICTOR (10191;
"My Boy"): 75. . . . . **5–8**

RCA VICTOR (10278;
"T-r-o-u-b-l-e"): 75 . . . . **5–8**

RCA VICTOR (10401;
"Bringing It Back"): 75 . . . . **5–8**

RCA VICTOR (10601;
"Hurt"): 76 . . . . **5–8**

RCA VICTOR (10857;
"Moody Blue"): 76. . . . . **5–8**

RCA VICTOR (10998;
"Way Down"): 77. . . . . **5–8**

RCA VICTOR (11099
through 11113): 77 . . . . **2–4**
(Sleeves in this series were originally packaged
in either RCA Victor 11301 and/or 11340, both
boxed sets of singles with sleeves.)

RCA VICTOR (11165;
"My Way"): 77. . . . . **5–8**
(With flip side title shown as "America.")

RCA VICTOR (11165;
"My Way"): 77. . . . . **15–20**
(With flip side title shown as "America The
Beautiful.")

RCA VICTOR (11212;
"Softly, As I Leave
You"): 78. . . . . **4–6**

RCA VICTOR (11320;
"Teddy Bear"): 78. . . . . **4–6**

RCA VICTOR (11533;
"Are You Sincere"): 79 . . . . **4–6**

RCA VICTOR (11679;
"There's A Honky Tonk
Angel"): 79. **4–6**

RCA VICTOR (12158;
"Guitar Man"): 81 . . . . **4–6**

RCA VICTOR (13058;
"You'll Never Walk
Alone"): 82. **4–6**

RCA VICTOR (13302;
"The Impossible
Dream"): 82. . . . . **75–100**
(Promotional issue only.)

RCA VICTOR (13351;
"The Elvis Medley"): 82 . . . . **4–6**

RCA VICTOR (13500; "I
Was The One"): 83 . . . . **4–6**

RCA VICTOR (13547;
"Little Sister"): 83. . . . . **4–6**

Price Range

RCA VICTOR (13875;
  "Baby, Let's Play
  House"): *84* **$5–8**
RCA VICTOR (13885
  through 13896): *84* **2–4**
  (Sleeves in this series were originally packaged
  in RCA Victor 13897 & 13898, "Golden Sin-
  gles." Price includes discs.)
RCA VICTOR (13929;
  "Blue Suede Shoes"): *85*. **5–8**
RCA VICTOR (14090;
  "Always On My Mind"):
  85 . . . . **5–8**
RCA VICTOR (14237;
  "Merry Christmas
  Baby"): *85* **8–10**
  Notes: Often, there may be a slight difference of
  value between one variation or another of a
  picture sleeve, such as a "Coming Soon" or
  "Ask For" sleeve. Likewise for variations in
  sleeve colors and paper stock used. Many times
  the difference is reflected by which one a collector needs to complete the set rather than one
  having an across-the-board value greater than
  the other. Regardless, sleeve variations that fall
  within the price range given do not require separate listings in this edition. If the value varies
  beyond the given range, a separate listing will
  definitely be used...Picture sleeves for the RCA
  "447" Gold Standard Series are listed in a separate section that follows the Gold Standard Singles...Since there are but six promo only sleeves,
  and considering they were rarely marked as
  promo issues, they are combined in the preceding section and identified as promotional issues
  only.

Gold Standard Singles with the 447 prefix:
  (Commercial Issues)
RCA VICTOR (0600
  through 0639): *59–64* **8–10**
  (Black label, dog on top.)
RCA VICTOR (0600
  through 0639): *65–66* **4–6**
  (Black label, dog on side.)
RCA VICTOR (0600
  through 0639): *68–69* **6–10**
  (Orange label.)
RCA VICTOR (0600
  through 0639): *70–74* **2–4**
  (Red label.)
RCA VICTOR (0600
  through 0639): *77* **2–3**
  (Black label, dog near top.)

Price Range

RCA VICTOR (0640
  through 0642): *64* **$20–25**
  (Black label, dog on top.)
RCA VICTOR (0640
  through 0642): *65–66* **4–6**
  (Black label, dog on side.)
RCA VICTOR (0640
  through 0642): *70–74* **2–4**
  (Red label.)
RCA VICTOR (0643;
  "Crying In The
  Chapel"): *65*. **5–8**
  (Black label, dog on side.)
RCA VICTOR (0643;
  "Crying In The
  Chapel"): *70–74*. **2–4**
  (Red label.)
RCA VICTOR (0643;
  "Crying In The
  Chapel"): *77*. **2–3**
  (Black label, dog near top.)
RCA VICTOR (0644
  through 0646): *65* **25–35**
  (Black label, dog on top.)
RCA VICTOR (0644
  through 0646): *65* **5–8**
  (Black label, dog on side.)
RCA VICTOR (0644
  through 0646): *68–69* **6–10**
  (Orange label.)
RCA VICTOR (0644
  through 0646): *70–74* **2–4**
  (Red label.)
RCA VICTOR (0644
  through 0646): *77* **2–3**
  (Black label, dog near top.)
RCA VICTOR (0647
  through 0650): *65* **5–8**
  (Black label, dog on side.)
RCA VICTOR (0647
  through 0650): *70–74* **2–4**
  (Red label.)
RCA VICTOR (0651 &
  0652): *66* **10–12**
  (Black label, dog on side.)
RCA VICTOR (0651 &
  0652): *70–74*. **2–4**
  (Red label.)
RCA VICTOR (0653
  through 0658): *66–68* **4–6**
  (Black label, dog on side.)

Price Range   *Price Range*

RCA VICTOR (0653
through 0658): *70–74* $2–4
(Red label.)
RCA VICTOR (0653
through 0658): *77* 2–3
(Black label, dog near top.)
RCA VICTOR (0659;
"Indescribably Blue"): *70* 10–15
(Red label.)
RCA VICTOR (0660;
"Long Legged Girl"): *70* 25–35
(Red label.)
RCA VICTOR (0661;
"Judy"): *70*. 10–15
(Red label.)
RCA VICTOR (0662; "Big
Boss Man"): *70* 8–10
(Red label.)
RCA VICTOR (0663
through 0685): *70–73* 2–4
(Red label.)
RCA VICTOR (0663
through 0685): *77* 2–3
(Black label, dog near top.)
RCA VICTOR (0720;
"Blue Christmas"): *64*. 10–15
(Black label, dog on top.)

Gold Standard Singles with the "GB" prefix
RCA VICTOR (10156
through 10489): *75–76* 2–4
(Red label.)
RCA VICTOR (10156
through 10489): *77* 2–3
(Black label, dog near top.)
RCA VICTOR (11326
through 13275): *77* 2–3
(Black label, dog near top.)
Note: Gold Standard promotional singles are in
numerical sequence in the section for Promo-
tional Singles.

Gold Standard Picture Sleeves
RCA VICTOR (0601
through 0618): *64* 50–60
RCA VICTOR (0639;
"Kiss Me Quick"): *64*. 20–25
RCA VICTOR (0643;
"Crying In The
Chapel"): *65*. 15–20
RCA VICTOR (0647;
"Blue Christmas"): *65*. 20–25
(Pictures Elvis on a Christmas card amidst
wrapped gifts.)

RCA VICTOR (0647;
"Blue Christmas"): *77*. $8–10
(Pictures Elvis in a circle amidst colored orna-
ments.)
RCA VICTOR (0650;
"Puppet On A String"):
65 20–25
RCA VICTOR (0651;
"Joshua Fit The Battle"):
66 50–75
RCA VICTOR (0652;
"Milky White Way"): *66* 50–75
RCA VICTOR (0720;
"Blue Christmas"): *64*. 30–35
Promotional Singles
CREATIVE RADIO
("Elvis 10th
Anniversary"): *87* 15–20
(Demonstration disc, promoting the syndicated
10th anniversary radio special.)
PARAMOUNT
PICTURES (2413;
"Roustabout"): *64*. 1000–1200
(Issued only to select theatres, designed for
lobby play.)
RCA VICTOR (15; "Old
Shep"): *56* 600–650
RCA VICTOR (76;
"Don't"/"Wear My Ring
Around Your Neck"): *60*. 500–550
(Issued with a special sleeve, which is listed in
the Picture Sleeve section.)
RCA VICTOR (0088;
"Raised On Rock"): *73* 8–10
(Yellow label.)
RCA VICTOR (118;
"King Of The Whole
Wide World"): *62* 200–225
(Issued with a special sleeve, which is listed in
the Picture Sleeve section.)
RCA VICTOR (0130;
"How Great Thou Art"):
69 25–30
(Yellow label.)
RCA VICTOR (139;
"Roustabout"): *64*. 175–200
RCA VICTOR (162; "How
Great Thou Art"): *67*. 100–125
(Issued with a special sleeve, which is listed in
the Picture Sleeve section.)

Price Range   *Price Range*

RCA VICTOR (0196; "I've
Got A Thing About You
Baby"): *74* **$8–10**
(Yellow label.)

RCA VICTOR (0280; "If
You Talk In Your
Sleep"): *74* **8–10**
(Yellow label.)

RCA VICTOR (0517;
"Little Sister"): *83*............ **100–125**
(12-Inch single.)

RCA VICTOR (0572;
"Merry Christmas
Baby"): *71* **12–15**
(Yellow label.)

RCA VICTOR (0601
through 0618): *64* **40–50**
(RCA 447 prefix Gold Standard Series. White
labels.)

RCA VICTOR (0619;
"Until It's Time For
You To Go"): *72*.............. **10–12**
(Yellow label.)

RCA VICTOR (0639;
"Kiss Me Quick"): *64*........... **20–25**
(RCA 447 prefix Gold Standard Series. White
label.)

RCA VICTOR (0643;
"Crying In The
Chapel"): *65*................... **15–20**
(RCA 447 prefix Gold Standard Series. White
label.)

RCA VICTOR (0647 &
0650): *65* **20–25**
(RCA 447 prefix Gold Standard Series. White
labels.)

RCA VICTOR (0651 &
0652): *66* **30–40**
(RCA 447 prefix Gold Standard Series. White
labels.)

RCA VICTOR (0651; "He
Touched Me"): *72*.............. **45–55**
(Yellow label.)

RCA VICTOR (0672; "An
American Trilogy"): *72* **12–15**
(Yellow label.)

RCA VICTOR (0720;
"Blue Christmas"): *64*........... **25–30**
(RCA 447 prefix Gold Standard Series. White
label.)

RCA VICTOR (0808;
"Blue Christmas"): *56*....... **1000–1200**

RCA VICTOR (0815;
"Separate Ways"): *72* **$8–10**
(Yellow label.)

RCA VICTOR (0910:
"Steamroller Blues"): *73*.......... **8–10**
(Yellow label.)

RCA VICTOR (6357;
"Mystery Train"): *55* **140–160**
(White label.)

RCA VICTOR (8360;
"Viva Las Vegas"): *64* **20–25**
(White label.)

RCA VICTOR (8400;
"Such A Night"): *64*.......... **500–525**
(White label.)

RCA VICTOR (8440;
"Ask Me"): *64*................. **20–25**
(White label.)

RCA VICTOR (8500; "Do
The Clam"): *65*................ **20–25**
(White label.)

RCA VICTOR (8585; "It
Feels So Right"): *65* **20–25**
(White label.)

RCA VICTOR (8657; "I'm
Yours"): *65*.................... **20–25**
(White label.)

RCA VICTOR (8740;
"Tell Me Why"): *65* **20–25**
(White label.)

RCA VICTOR (8780;
"Frankie & Johnny"): *66* **20–25**
(White label.)

RCA VICTOR (8870;
"Love Letters"): *66*............. **20–25**
(White label.)

RCA VICTOR (8941;
"Spinout"): *66* **20–25**
(White label.)

RCA VICTOR (9056;
"Indescribably Blue"): *67*........ **20–25**
(White label.)

RCA VICTOR (9115;
"Long Legged Girl"): *67* **20–25**
(White label.)

RCA VICTOR (9287;
"There's Always Me"):
67 .... **20–25**
(White label.)

RCA VICTOR (9341; "Big
Boss Man"): *67* **20–25**
(White label.)

Price Range

RCA VICTOR (9425;
"Guitar Man"): *68* **$15–20**
(Yellow label.)
RCA VICTOR (9465;
"U.S. Male"): *68* **15–20**
(Yellow label.)
RCA VICTOR (9547;
"Your Time Hasn't
Come Yet Baby"): *68* **15–20**
(Yellow label.)
RCA VICTOR (9600;
"You'll Never Walk
Alone"): *68*. **15–20**
(Yellow label.)
RCA VICTOR (9610;
"Almost In Love"): *68* **10–15**
(Yellow label.)
RCA VICTOR (9670; "If I
Can Dream"): *68*. **10–15**
(Yellow label.)
RCA VICTOR (9731;
"Memories"): *69* **10–15**
(Yellow label.)
RCA VICTOR (9741; "In
The Ghetto"): *69*. **10–15**
(Yellow label.)
RCA VICTOR (9747;
"Clean Up Your Own
Back Yard"): *69* **10–15**
(Yellow label.)
RCA VICTOR (9764;
"Suspicious Minds"): *69*. **10–15**
(Yellow label.)
RCA VICTOR (9768;
"Don't Cry Daddy"): *69* **10–15**
(Yellow label.)
RCA VICTOR (9791;
"Kentucky Rain"): *70*. **10–15**
(Yellow label.)
RCA VICTOR (9835;
"The Wonder Of You"):
70 .... **10–15**
(Yellow label.)
RCA VICTOR (9873; "I've
Lost You"): *70*. **10–15**
(Yellow label.)
RCA VICTOR (9916;
"You Don't Have To
Say You Love Me"): *70* **10–15**
(Yellow label.)

Price Range

RCA VICTOR (9960; "I
Really Don't Want To
Know"): *70* **$10–15**
(Yellow label.)
RCA VICTOR (9980;
"Where Did They Go
Lord"): *71* **10–15**
(Yellow label.)
RCA VICTOR (9985;
"Life"): *71* **10–15**
(Yellow label.)
RCA VICTOR (9998; "I'm
Leavin"): *71*. **10–15**
(Yellow label.)
RCA VICTOR (10074;
"Promised Land"): *74*. **8–10**
(Yellow label.)
RCA VICTOR (10191;
"My Boy"): *75*. **8–10**
(Yellow label.)
RCA VICTOR (10278;
"T-r-o-u-b-l-e"): *75* **8–10**
(Yellow label.)
RCA VICTOR (10401;
"Bringing It Back"): *75* **8–10**
(Yellow label.)
RCA VICTOR (10601;
"Hurt"): *76* **8–10**
(Yellow label.)
RCA VICTOR (10857;
"Moody Blue" - black
vinyl): *76* **6–10**
(Yellow label.)
RCA VICTOR (10857;
"Moody Blue" - colored
vinyl): *76* **900–1000**
(Experimental pressings only. Never issued nor
intended for distribution.)
RCA VICTOR (10951;
"Let Me Be There"): *77*. **100–125**
RCA VICTOR (10998;
"Way Down"): *77*. **125–150**
(White label.)
RCA VICTOR (10998;
"Way Down"): *77*. **6–10**
(Yellow label.)
RCA VICTOR (11165;
"My Way"): *77* **6–10**
(Yellow label.)
RCA VICTOR (11212;
"Softly, As I Leave
You"): *78* **6–10**
(Yellow label.)

Price Range

RCA VICTOR (11320;
"Teddy Bear"): *78* **$6–10**
(Yellow label.)
RCA VICTOR (11533;
"Are You Sincere"): *79* **6–10**
(Yellow label.)
RCA VICTOR (11679;
"There's A Honky Tonk
Angel"): *79.* **6–10**
(Yellow label.)
RCA VICTOR (12158;
"Guitar Man" - black
vinyl): *81* **6–10**
(Yellow label.)
RCA VICTOR (12158;
"Guitar Man" - colored
vinyl): *81* **225–250**
(Yellow label.)
RCA VICTOR (12205;
"Lovin' Arms" - black
vinyl): *81* **6–10**
(Yellow label.)
RCA VICTOR (12158;
"Lovin' Arms" - colored
vinyl): *81* **250–275**
(Bright yellow label.)
RCA VICTOR (13058;
"You'll Never Walk
Alone"): *82.* **6–10**
(Yellow label.)
RCA VICTOR (13302;
"The Impossible
Dream"): *82.* **75–100**
RCA VICTOR (13351;
"The Elvis Medley" -
black vinyl): *82* **6–10**
(Yellow label.)
RCA VICTOR (13351;
"The Elvis Medley" -
colored vinyl): *82.* **200–225**
(Gold label.)
RCA VICTOR (13500; "I
Was The One" - black
vinyl): *83* **6–10**
(Yellow label.)
RCA VICTOR (13500; "I
Was The One" - colored
vinyl): *83* **200–225**
(Bright yellow label.)

Price Range

RCA VICTOR (13547;
"Little Sister" - black
vinyl): *83* **$6–10**
(Yellow label.)
RCA VICTOR (13547;
"Little Sister" - colored
vinyl): *83* **175–200**
(Blue label.)
RCA VICTOR (13875;
"Baby, Let's Play
House" - colored vinyl):
84 . . . . **150–175**
(Gold label.)
RCA VICTOR (13929;
"Blue Suede Shoes" -
colored vinyl): *84.* **6–10**
(Gold label.)
RCA VICTOR (14090;
"Always On My Mind" -
colored vinyl): *85.* **6–10**
(Gold label.)
RCA VICTOR (14237;
"Merry Christmas
Baby"): *85* **6–10**
Note: Elvis 50th Anniversary singles, which
began with RCA Victor 13875, used the same
gold label for both commercial and promotional
issues. Promo singles have "Not For Sale"
printed on the label.)
UNITED STATES AIR
FORCE (125; "It's Now
Or Never"): *61.* **300–325**
(Add approximately 10%-15% if accompanied
by special mailing box. One side of this disc
features Jaye P. Morgan.)
UNITED STATES AIR
FORCE (159;
"Surrender"): *61* **300–325**
(Add approximately 10%-15% if accompanied
by special mailing box. One side of this disc
features Lawrence Welk.)
WHAT'S IT ALL ABOUT
(78; "Life"): *77* **45–55**
(One side of this disc features Helen Reddy.)
WHAT'S IT ALL ABOUT
(1840; "Elvis Presley"):
80 . . . . **70–75**
WHAT'S IT ALL ABOUT
(3025; "Elvis Presley"):
82 . . . . **50–60**

Price Range

Note: Plastic soundsheets or flexi-discs are listed in a separate section that follows...Promotional 78s are listed in the section of Singles: 78rpm.

Plastic Soundsheets/Flexi-discs

EVA-TONE (38713; "Elvis Speaks! The Truth About Me") **$30–40**
(Eva-Tone number is not on label but is etched in the trail-off.)

EVA-TONE (52578; "The King Is Dead Long Live The King"): *78* **90–100**

EVA-TONE (726771; "The Elvis Presley Story"): *77*. **8–10**

EVA-TONE (1037710; "Elvis Live"): *78* **30–40**
(Price for magazine, titled "Collector's Issue," with bound-in soundsheet.)

EVA-TONE (1037710; "Elvis Live"): *78* **15–20**
(Price for soundsheet only.)

EVA-TONE (1227785; "Thompson Vocal Eliminator"): *78*. **15–20**
(Contains segments of songs by three artists, including Elvis.)

EVA-TONE (10287733; "Elvis: Six Hour Special"): *77*. **15–20**

LYNCHBURG AUDIO ("The Truth About Me"): *56*. **125–150**
(Lynchburg Audio number is not on label but is etched in the trail-off.)

RAINBO ("Elvis Speaks-In Person"): *56*. **300–325**
(Price for magazine, "Elvis Answers Back," with 78rpm flexi-disc still attached to front cover.)

RAINBO ("Elvis Speaks-In Person"): *56*. **100–125**
(Price for flexi-disc only.)

RAINBO ("The Truth About Me"): *56*. **300–325**
(Price for magazine, "Elvis Answers Back," with 78rpm paper flexi-disc still attached to front cover.)

RAINBO ("The Truth About Me"): *56*. **100–125**
(Price for flexi-disc only.)

Price Range

Note: All soundsheets & flexi-discs were used for some type of promotional purpose.

EPs: 7-Inch 33/45rpm (Commercial AND Promotional Issues)

CREATIVE RADIO SHOWS ("Elvis Remembered"): *79*. **$40–45**
(Promotional demonstration EP. One side features Frank Sinatra & Nat King Cole. Issued to radio stations only.)

CREATIVE RADIO SHOWS ("The Elvis Hour"): *86* **25–35**
(Promotional demonstration EP. One side features Gary Owens' Supertracks. Issued to radio stations only.)

RCA VICTOR (2; "Dealers' Prevue"): *57* **700–750**
(Contains eight songs by four artists, including two by Elvis. Promotional issue only.)

RCA VICTOR (2; "Elvis Presley At His Greatest"): *57*. **350–400**
(Paper mailing envelope used with the preceding "Dealers' Prevue" EP. Number on the envelope is 7000, the same as the "Teddy Bear"/ "Loving You" single, rather than SDS-7-2.)

RCA VICTOR (7; "Love Me Tender"): *56* **125–140**
(Also shows the 45rpm number for "Love Me Tender," 6643. Not issued with a special sleeve or cover. One side of this EP is by Jean Chapel. Promotional issue only.)

RCA VICTOR (12; "Old Shep"): *56* **700–800**
(Contains 4 songs by 4 artists, including one by Elvis. Promotional issue only.)

RCA VICTOR (12; "WOHO Featuring RCA Victor"): *56* **700–800**
(Special paper sleeve custom made for WOHO radio, Toledo, Ohio, and used with the PRO-12 disc for some promotional purpose.)

RCA VICTOR (15; Extended Play Package): *56* **2500–3000**

Price Range

(Only one of the 10 EPs in this set is by Elvis. Thus far, despite all the publicity we've given this item, no discoveries of the box or package that this set came in are known. Since no sales have taken place, the value range given is based on offers that have been made as well as the sales of the similar, but slightly more common, SPD-19. Price estimate includes complete package which probably includes paper inserts, title strips, etc. Also, since the black label pressing of the individual Elvis EP, 9089, is much scarcer than the gray, a complete set on black should be more valuable than a gray set.)

RCA VICTOR (15; Elvis
disc 9089, black label):
56 . . . . **$700–800**

RCA VICTOR (15; Elvis
disc 9089, gray label): *56* **600–700**
(This is the Elvis EP from the SPD-15 set. The gray pressings were for jukebox operators and the black was probably a commercial release. The individual number on this disc is 9089.)

RCA VICTOR (19; "The
Sound Of Leadership"):
56 . . . . **1800–2000**
(An eight EP boxed set, with one EP containing one Elvis track. The number on the disc is 9113. Prepared as a souvenir for those attending a June 1956 convention. Price is for complete set including inserts.)

RCA VICTOR (19; "The
Sound Of Leadership"):
56 . . . . **750–800**
(Price for the EP from the SPD-19 set containing Elvis. This EP, numbered 9113, is actually untitled.)

RCA VICTOR (22; "Elvis
Presley"): *56*. **600–650**
(A two-EP bonus promotional item. Discs are numbered 9121 & 9122.)

RCA VICTOR (23; "Elvis
Presley"): *56*. **2000–2500**
(A three-EP bonus promotional item. Discs are numbered 9123, 9124 & 9125.)

RCA VICTOR (26; "Great
Country/Western Hits"):
56 . . . . **900–1000**
(A 10-EP boxed set containing one Elvis EP with the number 9141. Price is for the complete box set including paper inserts.)

RCA VICTOR (26; "Great
Country/Western Hits"):
56 . . . . **200–250**

| SPD-23

Price Range

(Price for the EP from the SPD-26 set containing Elvis. This EP, numbered 9141, is actually untitled.)

RCA VICTOR (27;
"Save-On Records"): *56* **$600–650**
(Price for EP & paper sleeve. A sampler of music by Elvis & other artists.)

RCA VICTOR (27;
"Save-On Records"): *56* **175–200**
(Price for EP only. A sampler of music by Elvis & other artists.)

RCA VICTOR (37;
"Perfect For Parties"):
56 . . . . **75–90**
(Without horizontal silver line. Offered through mail-order coupon ads. Contains six songs by different artists, including Elvis who is also the narrator on the disc.)

RCA VICTOR (37;
"Perfect For Parties"):
56 . . . . **60–75**
(With horizontal silver line. Promotional issue, reads "Not For Sale.")

RCA VICTOR (37;
"Perfect For Parties"):
56 . . . . **90–100**
(Paper sleeve for the "Perfect For Parties Highlight Album.")

RCA VICTOR (39;
"Dealers' Prevue"): *57* **600–650**
(Contains two songs each by six different artists, including Elvis. Promotional issue only.)

RCA VICTOR (39;
"Dealers' Prevue"
mailer): *57* **350–400**

Price Range

(Paper mailing envelope used with the promotional SDS-57-39 "Dealers' Prevue" EP.)

RCA VICTOR (56; "Too
Much"): *57.* **$125–140**
(Also shows the 45rpm number for "Too Much," 6800. Not issued with a special sleeve or cover. One side of this EP is by Dinah Shore. Promotional issue only.)

RCA VICTOR (61;
Extended Play Sampler):
57 . . . . **1000–1200**
(A sampling of 12 different RCA EPs, all by different artists, including "Jailhouse Rock" by Elvis. No sleeve or cover is known to exist for this disc. Promotional issue only.)

RCA VICTOR (121;
"RCA Family Record
Center"): *61* **1000–1200**
(Contains one song each by eight different artists including Elvis. In-store Promotional issue only.)

RCA VICTOR (128; "Elvis
By Request"): *61* **50–60**

RCA VICTOR (747; "Elvis
Presley"): *56.* **140–160**
(Black label, NO DOG.)

RCA VICTOR (747; "Elvis
Presley"): *56.* **70–80**
(Black label, dog on top. With horizontal silver line. With song title strip across the top of front cover.)

RCA VICTOR (747; "Elvis
Presley"): *56.* **55–65**
(Black label, dog on top. Without horizontal silver line. With song title strip across the top of front cover.)

RCA VICTOR (747; "Elvis
Presley"): *65.* **25–35**
(Black label, dog on side.)

RCA VICTOR (747; "Elvis
Presley"): *69.* **20–30**
(Orange label.)

RCA VICTOR (747; "Blue
Suede Shoes"): *56* **475–525**
(Temporary paper sleeve for 1956 issue of EPA-747. Price is for sleeve only.)

RCA VICTOR (0793: see
RCA VICTOR 1254)

RCA VICTOR (0794: see
RCA VICTOR 1254)

RCA VICTOR (821
through 994): *56* **140–160**
(Black label, NO DOG.)

Price Range

RCA VICTOR (821
through 994): *56* **$70–80**
(Black label, dog on top. With horizontal silver line. With song title strip across the top of front cover.)

RCA VICTOR (821
through 994): *56* **55–65**
(Black label, dog on top. Without horizontal silver line. With song title strip across the top of front cover.)

RCA VICTOR (821
through 994): *65* **25–35**
(Black label, dog on side.)

RCA VICTOR (821
through 994): *69* **20–30**
(Orange label.)
Notes: Not every EP in the 821-994 series was issued with ALL of the possible label variations...EPA-940 was the only EP from this period that was reissued in the Gold Standard Series, as EPA-5120.

RCA VICTOR (992 & 689;
"Elvis/Jaye P. Morgan"):
56 . . . . **900–1000**
(A 2-EP set, with 992 by Presley and 689 by Jaye P. Morgan coupled together in a promotional double pocket package. Since the discs were standard pressings at least 95% of the value here is represented by the custom EP cover.)

RCA VICTOR (1254;
"Elvis Presley"): *56.* **350–375**
(Black label, NO DOG. A two-EP set.)

RCA VICTOR (1254;
"Elvis Presley"): *56.* **300–325**
(Black label, dog on top. With horizontal silver line. A two-EP set.)

RCA VICTOR (1254;
"Elvis Presley"): *56.* **275–300**
(Black label, dog on top. Without horizontal silver line. A two-EP set.)

RCA VICTOR (1254;
"Most Talked-About
New Personality"): *56.* **1000–1100**
(Two EPs, also numbered 0793 & 0794, in a single pocket paper sleeve. Promotional issue only.)

RCA VICTOR (1254;
"Most Talked-About
New Personality"): *56.* **400–425**

Price Range

Price Range

(Price for the two EPs WITHOUT the sleeve. Either disc would be worth about half the amount shown for both. Discs, numbered 0793 & 0794, are actually untitled. Promotional issue only.)

RCA VICTOR (1515;
"Loving You"): *57* **$70–80**
(Black label, dog on top. With horizontal silver line. With song title strip across the top of front cover.)

RCA VICTOR (1515;
"Loving You"): *57* **55–65**
(Black label, dog on top. Without horizontal silver line. With song title strip across the top of front cover.)

RCA VICTOR (1515;
"Loving You"): *65* **25–35**
(Black label, dog on side.)

RCA VICTOR (1515;
"Loving You"): *69* **20–30**
(Orange label.)
Note: The above information applies to both 1-1515 & 2-1515, "Loving You" Volumes 1 & 2.

RCA VICTOR (2006;
"Aloha From Hawaii"):
74 . . . . **60–75**
(Price includes sheet of 10 title strips. Issued for jukebox operators as one of four "Little LPs." The other three in the campaign were by John Denver, Harry Nilsson & The Three Suns.)

RCA VICTOR (3736;
"Pop Transcribed 30 Sec.
Spot"): *58* **400–500**
(No release number given, 3736 being the matrix number on the Elvis side of this disc. Announcer Vaughn Monroe presents sales pitch and excerpts from four RCA LPs, including "Elvis' Golden Records.")

RCA VICTOR (4006;
"Love Me Tender"): *56* **140–160**
(Black label, NO DOG. With song title strip across the top of front cover.)

RCA VICTOR (4006;
"Love Me Tender"): *56* **75–80**
(Black label, dog on top. With horizontal silver line. With song title strip across the top of front cover.)

RCA VICTOR (4006;
"Love Me Tender"): *56* **55–65**
(Black label, dog on top. Without horizontal silver line. With EP title strip across the top of front cover.)

RCA VICTOR (4006;
"Love Me Tender"): *65* **$25–35**
(Black label, dog on side.)

RCA VICTOR (4006;
"Love Me Tender"): *69* **20–30**
(Orange label.)

RCA VICTOR (4041;
"Just For You"): *57* **140–160**
(Black label, NO DOG. With EP title strip across the top of front cover.)

RCA VICTOR (4041;
"Just For You"): *57* **75–80**
(Black label, dog on top. With horizontal silver line. With EP title strip across the top of front cover.)

RCA VICTOR (4041;
"Just For You"): *57* **55–65**
(Black label, dog on top. Without horizontal silver line. With EP title strip across the top of front cover.)

RCA VICTOR (4041;
"Just For You"): *65* **25–35**
(Black label, dog on side.)

RCA VICTOR (4041;
"Just For You"): *69* **20–30**
(Orange label.)

RCA VICTOR (4054;
"Peace In The Valley"):
57 . . . . **75–80**
(Black label, dog on top. With horizontal silver line. With EP title strip across the top of front cover.)

RCA VICTOR (4054;
"Peace In The Valley"):
57 . . . . **55–65**
(Black label, dog on top. Without horizontal silver line. With EP title strip across the top of front cover.)

RCA VICTOR (4054;
"Peace In The Valley"):
65 . . . . **25–35**
(Black label, dog on side.)

RCA VICTOR (4054;
"Peace In The Valley"):
69 . . . . **20–30**
(Orange label.) (Reissues of this EP were in the Gold Standard Series, numbered EPA-5121.)

RCA VICTOR (4108;
"Elvis Sings Christmas
Songs"): *57* **55–65**
(Black label, dog on top. With EP title strip across the top of front cover.)

Price Range

RCA VICTOR (4108;
  "Elvis Sings Christmas
  Songs"): *65* **$25–35**
  (Black label, dog on side.)
RCA VICTOR (4108;
  "Elvis Sings Christmas
  Songs"): *69* **20–30**
  (Orange label.)
RCA VICTOR (4114;
  "Jailhouse Rock"): *57* **55–65**
  (Black label, dog on top.)
RCA VICTOR (4114;
  "Jailhouse Rock"): *65* **25–35**
  (Black label, dog on side.)
RCA VICTOR (4114;
  "Jailhouse Rock"): *69* **20–30**
  (Orange label.)
RCA VICTOR (4319;
  "King Creole"): *58* **55–65**
  (Reissues of this EP were in the Gold Standard
  Series, numbered EPA-5122.)
RCA VICTOR (4321;
  "King Creole" Vol. 2):
  58 . . . . **55–65**
  (Black label, dog on top.)
RCA VICTOR (4321;
  "King Creole" Vol. 2):
  65 . . . . **25–35**
  (Black label, dog on side.)
RCA VICTOR (4321;
  "King Creole" Vol. 2):
  69 . . . . **20–30**
  (Orange label.)
RCA VICTOR (4325;
  "Elvis Sails"): *58* **70–80**
  (Reissues of this EP were in the Gold Standard
  Series, numbered EPA-5157.)
RCA VICTOR (4340;
  "Christmas With Elvis"):
  58 . . . . **75–85**
  (Black label, dog on top.)
RCA VICTOR (4340;
  "Christmas With Elvis"):
  65 . . . . **25–35**
  (Black label, dog on side.)
RCA VICTOR (4340;
  "Christmas With Elvis"):
  69 . . . . **20–30**
  (Orange label.)
RCA VICTOR (4368;
  "Follow That Dream"):
  62 . . . . **45–55**

Price Range

  (Black label, dog on top.)
RCA VICTOR (4368;
  "Follow That Dream"):
  62 . . . . **$125–150**
  (Special paper sleeve for this EP, issued to radio
  stations and jukebox operators. Promotional
  issue only. Price is for sleeve only, and would be
  about $25 higher with the disc which is identi-
  cal to store stock copies.)
RCA VICTOR (4368;
  "Follow That Dream"):
  65 . . . . **25–35**
  (Black label, dog on side.)
RCA VICTOR (4368;
  "Follow That Dream"):
  69 . . . . **20–30**
  (Orange label.)
RCA VICTOR (4371;
  "Kid Galahad"): *62* **45–55**
  (Black label, dog on top.)
RCA VICTOR (4371;
  "Kid Galahad"): *65* **25–35**
  (Black label, dog on side.)
RCA VICTOR (4371;
  "Kid Galahad"): *69* **20–30**
  (Orange label.)
RCA VICTOR (4382;
  "Viva Las Vegas"): *64* **45–55**
  (Black label, dog on top.)
RCA VICTOR (4382;
  "Viva Las Vegas"): *65* **25–35**
  (Black label, dog on side.)
RCA VICTOR (4382;
  "Viva Las Vegas"): *69* **20–30**
  (Orange label.)
RCA VICTOR (4383;
  "Tickle Me"): *65* **40–50**
  (Black label, dog on side.)
RCA VICTOR (4383;
  "Tickle Me"): *69* **20–30**
  (Orange label.)
RCA VICTOR (4387;
  "Easy Come, Easy Go"):
  67 . . . . **40–50**
  (Black label, dog on side.)
RCA VICTOR (4387;
  "Easy Come, Easy Go"):
  67 . . . . **75–90**
  (White label. Promotional Issue Only.)
RCA VICTOR (4387;
  "Easy Come, Easy Go"):
  69 . . . . **20–30**
  (Orange label.)

Price Range

Price Range

RCA VICTOR (5088; "A
Touch Of Gold" Vol. I):
59 .... **$250–300**
(Maroon label.)

RCA VICTOR (5088; "A
Touch Of Gold" Vol. I):
59 .... **75–85**
(Black label, dog on top.)

RCA VICTOR (5088; "A
Touch Of Gold" Vol. I):
65 .... **25–35**
(Black label, dog on side.)

RCA VICTOR (5088; "A
Touch Of Gold" Vol. I):
69 .... **20–30**
(Orange label.)

RCA VICTOR (5101; "A
Touch Of Gold" Vol.
II): *59* **250–300**
(Maroon label.)

RCA VICTOR (5101; "A
Touch Of Gold" Vol.
II): *59* **75–85**
(Black label, dog on top.)

RCA VICTOR (5101; "A
Touch Of Gold" Vol.
II): *65* **25–35**
(Black label, dog on side.)

RCA VICTOR (5101; "A
Touch Of Gold" Vol.
II): *69* **20–30**
(Orange label.)

RCA VICTOR (5120;
"The Real Elvis"): *59* **300–350**
(Maroon label. Reissue of EPA-940.)

RCA VICTOR (5120;
"The Real Elvis"): *59* **50–60**
(Black label, dog on top.)

RCA VICTOR (5120;
"The Real Elvis"): *65* **25–35**
(Black label, dog on side.)

RCA VICTOR (5120;
"The Real Elvis"): *69* **20–30**
(Orange label.)

RCA VICTOR (5121;
"Peace In The Valley):
59 .... **300–350**
(Maroon label. Reissue of EPA-4054.)

RCA VICTOR (5121;
"Peace In The Valley):
59 .... **50–60**
(Black label, dog on top.)

RCA VICTOR (5121;
"Peace In The Valley):
65 .... **$25–35**
(Black label, dog on side.)

RCA VICTOR (5121;
"Peace In The Valley):
69 .... **20–30**
(Orange label.)

RCA VICTOR (5122;
"King Creole"): *59* **300–350**
(Maroon label. Reissue of EPA-4319.)

RCA VICTOR (5122;
"King Creole"): *59* **50–60**
(Black label, dog on top.)

RCA VICTOR (5122;
"King Creole"): *65* **25–35**
(Black label, dog on side.)

RCA VICTOR (5122;
"King Creole"): *69* **20–30**
(Orange label.)

RCA VICTOR (5141; "A
Touch Of Gold" Vol. 3):
60 .... **250–300**
(Maroon label.)

RCA VICTOR (5141; "A
Touch Of Gold" Vol. 3):
60 .... **75–85**
(Black label, dog on top.)

RCA VICTOR (5141; "A
Touch Of Gold" Vol. 3):
65 .... **25–35**
(Black label, dog on side.)

RCA VICTOR (5141; "A
Touch Of Gold" Vol. 3):
69 .... **20–30**
(Orange label.)

RCA VICTOR (5157;
"Elvis Sails"): *65* **35–40**
(Black label, dog on top. Reissue of EPA-4325.)

RCA VICTOR (5157;
"Elvis Sails"): *65* **25–35**
(Black label, dog on side.)

RCA VICTOR (5157;
"Elvis Sails"): *69* **20–30**
(Orange label.)

RCA VICTOR (8705; "TV
Guide Presents Elvis"):
56 .... **950–1000**
(Price for disc without either insert sheet. No
sleeve or cover is known to exist for this disc.
Promotional issue only.)

Price Range

RCA VICTOR (8705; "TV
Guide Presents Elvis"):
56 .... **$200–250**
(Price for "Elvis Exclusively" gray insert.)
RCA VICTOR (8705; "TV
Guide Presents Elvis"):
56 .... **125–150**
(Price for "Elvis Exclusively" pink insert, with
suggested continuity.)
RCA VICTOR (9089: see
RCA VICTOR 15)
RCA VICTOR (9113: see
RCA VICTOR 19)
RCA VICTOR (9121: see
RCA VICTOR 22)
RCA VICTOR (9122: see
RCA VICTOR 22)
RCA VICTOR (9123: see
RCA VICTOR 23)
RCA VICTOR (9124: see
RCA VICTOR 23)
RCA VICTOR (9125: see
RCA VICTOR 23)
RCA VICTOR (9141: see
RCA VICTOR 26)
TUPPERWARE (11973;
"Tupperware's Hit
Parade"): *73* **50–60**
(Contains excerpts of songs by numerous art-
ists, including Elvis. A promotional sales tool
used by Tupperware representatives.)
Notes: Unless listed and priced separately, all
EP values include both disc and cover with ap-
proximately half of the total attached to each.
Some of the rarer pieces that are often traded
individually (disc or sleeve), as well as those
sleeves that have an exceptionally higher value
than their disc, are listed separately in this section...All EPs in the 5000 series are Gold Standard Series issues although not noted as such on
the labels, only on the covers...As noted earlier,
in the picture sleeve notes, EP label and cover
variations that do not require separate listing
and pricing are not detailed in this edition.

LPs: 10/12-Inch 33rpm (Commercial AND
Promotional Issues)

ABC RADIO (1003; "Elvis
Memories"): *78* **425–450**

Price Range

(A three-LP boxed set. Price includes a 16-page
programmer's booklet and four pages of additional information, which represents $40-$50 of
the value. Issued only to radio stations. A 7-
inch reel tape, with spots and promotional an-
nouncements, accompanied this set and would
be worth another $45-$50.)
Note: Highlights of this program were issued on
Michelob 810.
ATV (1; "In The
Beginning"): *80* **$50–75**
(Contains 20 songs by 15 artists, including one
by Elvis. Promotional issue only.)
ASSOCIATED
BROADCASTERS
(1001; "Legend Of A
King"): *80* **125–150**
(White label. Advance pressing.)
ASSOCIATED
BROADCASTERS
(1001; "Legend Of A
King"): *80* **25–30**
(Picture disc. First pressings were numbered
from 3000 through 6000. Number appears
under "Side One" on the disc itself. Cover is
standard, die-cut, picture disc cover. Several
spelling errors on back cover, including "idle"
for idol and "Jordinaires" instead of Jor-
danaires.)
ASSOCIATED
BROADCASTERS
(1001; "Legend Of A
King"): *80* **20–25**
(Picture disc. Second pressings were numbered
from 6001 through 9000. Most of the spelling
errors were corrected on this cover.)
ASSOCIATED
BROADCASTERS
(1001; "Legend Of A
King"): *80* **15–20**
(Picture disc. Third pressings were numbered
from 00001 through 02999 and 09001 through
15000. Cover errors have all been corrected.)
ASSOCIATED
BROADCASTERS
(1001; "Legend Of A
King"): *84* **10–12**
(Picture disc. Fourth pressings were also numbered from 3000 through 6000, but were packaged in a clear plastic sleeve instead of a conventional cover.)

Price Range

ASSOCIATED
BROADCASTERS
(1001; "Legend Of A
King"): *85* **$8–10**
(Picture disc. Discs are not numbered. Packaged in a plastic sleeve.)

ASSOCIATED
BROADCASTERS
("Legend Of A King"):
85 .... **200–250**
(A three hour, three-LP set. Not boxed. Price includes 6 pages of cue sheets. Available to radio stations only.)

ASSOCIATED
BROADCASTERS
("Legend Of A King"):
85 .... **300–350**
(Same as above, but packaged in a specially printed box.)

ASSOCIATED
BROADCASTERS
("Legend Of A King"):
86 .... **300–350**
(Three-LP boxed set, same as above except time on segment 1-B is increased from 14:25 to 15:15 in order to include a Johnny Bernero interview.)

ASSOCIATED PRESS
(1977; "The World In
Sound"): *77* **80–100**
(Contains news highlights of 1977, including coverage of Elvis' death.)

BEALE STREET
("Rebirth Of Beale
Street"): *84*. **200–225**
(A collection of songs by Memphis artists, including one by Elvis. A promotionally distributed LP by the city of Memphis. Price includes a photo booklet, which represents $20-$25 of the value.)

BILLBOARD ("Sound Of
77"): *77* **175–200**
(A 5-LP boxed set with various artists, including eight songs by Elvis. Price includes a five-page script, which represents about $5 of the value. Promotional issue only.)

BILLBOARD ("1979
Yearbook"): *79* **175–200**
(A 5-LP boxed set with various artists, including one song by Elvis. Price includes a 10-page script, which represents about $5 of the value. Promotional issue only.)

Price Range

BOXCAR ("Having Fun
With Elvis On Stage"):
74 .... **$100–125**
(Sold in conjunction with Elvis' concert appearances.)
Note: This LP was reissued as RCA Victor CPM1-0818.

CBS SONGS (101;
"Radio's Million
Performance Songs"): *84* **45–55**
(Contains 15 songs by 15 artists, including Elvis. Promotional issue only.)

CAEDMON (1572; "On
The Record"): *78*. **50–75**
(Contains news highlights of 1977, including coverage of Elvis' death.)

CAMDEN (2304;
"Flaming Star"): *69* **15–18**
Note: This LP was first issued as RCA Victor 279. It was reissued in 1975 as Pickwick 2304.

CAMDEN (2408; "Let's
Be Friends"): *70* **15–18**
Note: This LP was reissued in 1975 as Pickwick 2408.

CAMDEN (2428; "Elvis'
Christmas Album"): *70*. **15–18**
Note: Eight songs on this LP were first issued on LOC-1035. This package was reissued in 1975 as Pickwick 2428.

CAMDEN (2440; "Almost
In Love"): *70* **25–30**
(With the track "Stay Away Joe.")

CAMDEN (2440; "Almost
In Love"): *73*. **15–18**
(With the track "Stay Away" replacing "Stay Away Joe.")
Note: This LP was reissued in 1975 as Pickwick 2440.

CAMDEN (2472; "You'll
Never Walk Alone"): *71*. **15–18**
Note: This LP was reissued in 1975 as Pickwick 2472.

CAMDEN (2518; "C'mon
Everybody"): *71*. **15–18**
Note: This LP was reissued in 1975 as Pickwick 2518.

CAMDEN (2533; "I Got
Lucky"): *71* **15–18**
Note: This LP was reissued in 1975 as Pickwick 2533.

CAMDEN (2567; "Elvis
Sings Hits From His
Movies"): *72*. **15–18**

Price Range

Note: This LP was reissued in 1975 as Pickwick 2567.

CAMDEN (2595; "Burning
Love"): *72* **$20–25**
(Price includes a 7x9 Elvis photo, which represents $5-$7 of the value.)
Note: This LP was reissued in 1975 as Pickwick 2595.

CAMDEN (2611;
"Separate Ways"): *73* **15–18**
Note: This LP was reissued in 1975 as Pickwick 2611.

CENTURY 21
PRODUCTIONS ("Epic
Of The 70s"): *76* **175–200**
(A 6-LP program of various 70s songs, including one by Elvis. Promotional issue only. Not issued with a special cover.)

COLLECTOR'S EDITION
(505; "All-Time
Christmas Favorites"):
78 .... **250–275**
(A five-LP boxed set, including one side of one disc by Elvis.)

COUNTRY
CROSSROADS (32-83;
"Country Crossroads"):
83 .... **75–100**
(A Southern Baptist Radio-TV issue. Contains one track by Elvis.)

COUNTRY SESSIONS
U.S.A. (122; "Best Of
Country Sessions
U.S.A."): *83* **75-100**
(Contains various country artists, including two tracks by Elvis. Price includes cue sheets. Promotional issue only.)

COUNTRY SESSIONS
U.S.A. (126; "A Tribute
To Elvis"): *83* **225–250**
(Price includes cue sheets. Promotional issue only.)

CREATIVE RADIO
NETWORK ("Elvis 50th
Anniversary"): *85* **300–350**
(A six-LP set. Price includes 7 pages of programming instructions and cues. Packaged in a plain, unprinted, box. Issued to radio stations only. The Creative Radio Network was previously known as Creative Radio Shows.)

CREATIVE RADIO
SHOWS ("Elvis
Remembered"): *78* **275–300**

Price Range

(A three-LP set. Price includes six insert pages, which represent $25-$30 of the value. Issued to radio stations only. Advance copies of this set, which was not issued with a special cover or package, were with plain white, handwritten, labels. These copies may be valued at $300-$350.)

CURRENT AUDIO
MAGAZINE (1;
"Elvis-Press
Conference"): *72* **$35–45**
(Contains news & features on 13 topics, including Elvis.)

DIAMOND P.
PRODUCTIONS
("Reflections Of Elvis"):
77 .... **450–500**
(A three-LP set. Price includes cue sheets. Promotional issue only.)

DICK CLARK (402;
"Rock, Roll &
Remember"): *77*. **225–250**
(A six-LP set featuring various artists, including two songs and a phone interview from Elvis. Price includes a six-page script. Not issued with a special cover or package. Issued to radio stations only.)

DICK CLARK ("Rock,
Roll & Remember,
1982"): *82* **300–350**
(A four-LP boxed set, containing 48 songs by Elvis. Price includes four programming sheets.)

DRAKE-CHENAULT
("Elvis: A Three Hour
Special"): *77*. **300–350**
(A three-LP boxed set. Price includes three pages of cue sheets.)

DRAKE-CHENAULT
("Golden Years Of
Country"): *80*. **250–300**
(A 25-LP set with one LP for each year, 1955-1979. Includes eight songs by Elvis. Price includes 55-page operations manual, which represents $40-$50 of the value. Issued to radio stations only.)

EMR ENTERPRISES (8;
"The Age Of Rock"): *69* **100–125**
(Promotional issue only.)

EARTH NEWS (For
"August 29, 1977"): *77*. **300–350**
(Contains 14 five-minute programs, 12 of which are about Elvis. Issued to radio stations only. Not issued with a special cover.)

Price Range

ELEKTRA (60107;
"Diner"): *82* **$8–10**
(Contains 20 songs by 20 artists, including Elvis.)
**GOLDEN EDITIONS
LIMITED** (1; "The First
Year"): *79* **10–20**
(Print in upper corners on front cover is in white. Label is black. Includes 12-page booklet and one-page copy of a 1954 Elvis/Scotty Moore contract, which represents $5-$8 of the value.)
**GOLDEN EDITIONS
LIMITED** (101; "The
First Year"): *79* **15–30**
(Print in upper corners on front cover is in gold. Label is white. Includes 12-page booklet and one-page copy of a 1954 Elvis/Scotty Moore contract, which represents $5-$8 of the value.)
Note: Most of the material on this LP was previously issued on HALW 00001.
GREAT NORTHWEST
(4005; "The Elvis
Tapes"): *77* **10–15**
Note: These interviews were repackaged on Starday 995.
GREAT NORTHWEST
(4006; "The King
Speaks"): *77* **8–10**
Note: This press conference was first issued as Green Valley 2001.
GREEN VALLEY (2001;
"Elvis 1961 Press
Conference"): *77* **40–50**
(Cover is thin, soft, stock and does not have black bar on spine. Label does not have the catalog number on it.)
GREEN VALLEY (2001;
"Elvis 1961 Press
Conference"): *77* **12–15**
(Cover is standard stock and has black bar on spine. Label has the catalog number on it.)
Note: This LP was repackaged as one half of Green Valley 2001/2003. It was later repackaged as Great Northwest 4006.
GREEN VALLEY (2001/
2003; "Elvis Speaks To
You"): *78* **25–30**
Note: 2001 was first issued as a single LP.
HALW (00001; "The First
Years"): *78* **60–75**
(Embossed with a serial number on front cover.)

Price Range

HALW (00001; "The First
Years"): *78* **$35–45**
(No serial number on front cover.)
Note: This LP was repackaged in 1979 on Golden Editions 1.
**INTERNATIONAL
HOTEL PRESENTS
ELVIS**-1969 (Boxed set):
69 . . . . **900–1000**
(Custom gift box prepared by Col. Parker & RCA for International Hotel guests. Contained: RCA Victor LPM-4088 & LSP-4155, three 8x10 Elvis photos, RCA Elvis catalog, calendar & nine-page letter. Price is for complete set but box itself represents $800-$900 of value.)
**INTERNATIONAL
HOTEL PRESENTS
ELVIS**-1970 (Boxed set):
70 . . . . **900–1000**
(Custom gift box prepared by Col. Parker & RCA for International Hotel guests. Contained: RCA Victor LSP-6020 & 45-9791, one 8x10 Elvis photo, photo album, RCA Elvis catalog, calendar, menu & letter. Price is for complete set but box itself represents $800-$900 of value.)
K-TEL (9900; "Elvis Love
Songs"): *81* **15–20**
LOUISIANA HAYRIDE
(3061; "The Beginning
Years"): *84* **300–350**
(White label advance pressing from RCA, Indianapolis, where this LP was manufactured.)
LOUISIANA HAYRIDE
(3061; "The Beginning
Years"): *84* **10–15**
(Price includes 20-page "D.J. Fontana Remembers Elvis" booklet, a four-sheet copy of Elvis' Hayride contract and a 10x10 "Presleyana" flyer, all of which represent about $5 of the value.)
Note: Selections from this LP were also issued on The Music Works 3601 & 3602.
LOUISIANA HAYRIDE
(8454; "The Louisiana
Hayride"): *76* **600–650**
(Yellow label. A program of various artists, including one song by Elvis. Issued to radio stations only.)
LOUISIANA HAYRIDE
(8454; "The Louisiana
Hayride"): *81* **300–325**
(Gold label. A program of various artists, including one song by Elvis.)
MCA ("MCA Music") **40–60**

Price Range

Price Range

(No number shown on this 4-LP set, containing excerpts of 200 songs by various artists, including five Elvis songs.)

MFSL (059; "From Elvis
In Memphis"): *82* **$15–20**
Note: This LP was first issued as RCA Victor LSP-4155.

MARCH OF DIMES
(0653; "Discs For
Dimes"): *56* **1400–1600**
(Contains announcements by 20 artists, including one by Elvis. Price includes a 16-page packet for programmers, which represents $75-$100 of the value. Promotional issue only. The other side of this 16-inch LP is numbered 0654.)

MARCH OF DIMES
(0657; "Disc Jockey
Interviews"): *56* **1400–1600**
(Contains songs & interviews with six artists, including one by Elvis. Price includes an instruction packet for programmers, which represents $75-$100 of the value. Promotional issue only. The other side of this 16-inch LP is numbered 0658.)

MEDIA
ENTERTAINMENT
("The King's Gold"): *85* **50–75**
(Three reel-to-reel tapes, issued only to radio stations. Price includes cue sheets, which represent $4-$6 of the value. Not known to exist on disc.)

MICHELOB (810;
"Highlights Of Elvis
Memories"): *78* **175–200**
(A Michelob in-house promotional issue only.)
Note: "Elvis Memories" was first issued on ABC Radio 1003.

MORE MUSIC (333-72;
"A Chronology Of
American Music"): *72* **500–600**
(21 LPs of number one songs, including 16 Elvis songs. Issued to radio stations only. Not issued with any special box or package.)

MUTUAL BROADCAST
SYSTEM (4082; "The
Frantic Fifties"): *59* **175–200**
(Contains an excerpt of "Hound Dog." Promotional issue only.)

NEW WORLD (207;
"Country Music In The
Modern Era"): *77* **40–50**
(Contains 18 songs by 18 artists, including Elvis. Produced for use by libraries.)

ORIGINAL SOUND
RECORDINGS (11;
"Rock Rock Rock"): *72* **$40–50**
(Contains 14 songs by 14 artists, including one by Elvis. Title may also be shown as "All Star Rock, Vol. 11.")

PAIR (1010; "Double
Dynamite"): *82* **20–25**
Note: This LP was first issued as Pickwick 5001.

PAIR (1037;
"Remembering Elvis"):
83 . . . . **20–25**

PICKWICK (2304;
"Flaming Star"): *75* **8–10**
Note: This LP was first issued as RCA Victor 279.

PICKWICK (2408; "Let's
Be Friends"): *75* **8–10**
Note: This LP was first issued as Camden 2408.

PICKWICK (2428; "Elvis'
Christmas Album"): *75* **8–10**
Note: This package of songs was first issued as Camden 2428.

PICKWICK (2440;
"Almost In Love"): *75* **8–10**
Note: This LP was first issued as Camden 2440.

PICKWICK (2472; "You'll
Never Walk Alone"): *75* **8–10**
Note: This LP was first issued as Camden 2472.

PICKWICK (2518;
"C'mon Everybody"): *75* **8–10**
Note: This LP was first issued as Camden 2518.

PICKWICK (2533; "I Got
Lucky"): *75* **8–10**
Note: This LP was first issued as Camden 2533.

PICKWICK (2567; "Elvis
Sings Hits From His
Movies"): *75* **8–10**
Note: This LP was first issued as Camden 2567.

PICKWICK (2595;
"Burning Love"): *75* **8–10**
Note: This LP was first issued as Camden 2595.

PICKWICK (5001;
"Double Dynamite"): *75* **25–30**
Note: This LP was repackaged in 1982 as Pair 1010.

PICKWICK (7007;
"Frankie And Johnny"):
76 . . . . **8–10**
Note: This LP was first issued as RCA Victor LPM/LSP-3553.

Price Range

PICKWICK (7064;
"Mahalo From Elvis"):
78 .... **$15–20**
PLAYBOY (7473; "The
Playboy Music Hall Of
Fame Winners"): *78* **30–40**
(Contains 10 songs by 10 different artists, including Elvis. A mail-order LP offer from Playboy magazine.)
RCA VICTOR (EPC-1;
"Special Christmas
Program" Reel Tape): *67* **300–325**
(Price includes programming insert, which represents $25-$35 of the value. This program was never issued commercially on disc. 10-inch red vinyl LPs of this material, with the EPC-1 number, are unauthorized.)
RCA VICTOR (TB-1; "A
Collectors Edition"): *76* **90–100**
(A 5-disc boxed set. Price includes a 20-page booklet, which represents $10-$15 of the value. A TV mail-order LP offer.)
RCA VICTOR (0001;
"Robert W. Sarnoff"): *73* **600–750**
(Contains a diverse assortment of RCA product, including four songs by Elvis. An RCA in-house promotional item prepared as a tribute to Sarnoff's 25 years with the company.)
RCA VICTOR (4; Untitled
RCA Sampler): *56* **1000–150C**
(Contains 21 songs by 21 different artists, including Elvis. Promotional issue only.)
RCA VICTOR (10;
Untitled RCA Sampler):
58 .... **900–1000**
(Contains 14 songs by 14 different artists, including Elvis. Promotional issue only.)
RCA VICTOR (010;
"Elvis! His Greatest
Hits"): *79* **375–400**
(WHITE box edition. An eight-LP boxed set, sold mail-order by Reader's Digest.)
RCA VICTOR (010;
"Elvis! His Greatest
Hits"): *83* **40–60**
(YELLOW box edition. An eight-LP boxed set, sold mail-order by Reader's Digest.)
Note: See 181 for the bonus LP offered with this edition.
RCA VICTOR (016; "The
Grammy Award
Winners"): *85*. **50–75**

Price Range

(A 4-LP boxed set, one in a series of boxed sets available through the Franklin Mint by mail order. This set features eight different artists, one of which is Elvis, each heard on one full side of a disc. Includes six Elvis tracks. Issued on colored vinyl.)
RCA VICTOR (27;
"August 1959 Sampler"):
59 .... **$700–800**
(Contains 13 songs by 13 different artists, including Elvis. Promotional issue only.)
RCA VICTOR (0034;
"QSP Presents A Gift Of
Music"): *84* **50–75**
(QSP is a direct sales organization. This LP was a company promotional sampler, which contains 12 songs by 12 artists, including Elvis.)
RCA VICTOR (54;
"October Christmas
Sampler"): *59*. **600–700**
(Contains 13 songs by 13 different artists, including Elvis. Promotional issue only.)
RCA VICTOR (0056;
"Elvis"): *73* **40–50**
(Mustard color label. Cover shows "Brookville Records" in upper right. A mail-order LP offer.)
RCA VICTOR (0056;
"Elvis"): *73* **20–25**
(Blue label. Cover doesn't show "Brookville Records." A mail-order LP offer.)
Note: This LP was repackaged in 1978 and titled "Elvis Commemorative Album."
RCA VICTOR (0056;
"Elvis Commemorative
Album"): *78*. **75–80**
(Price includes a "Registered Certificate Of Ownership," which represents $4-$6 of the value. A mail-order LP offer.)
Note: This LP was first titled "Elvis," using the same catalog number.
RCA VICTOR (59;
"February Sampler"): *59* **600–700**
(Contains 8 songs by 8 different artists, including Elvis. Full number shown as SP-33-59-7. Has RCA Victor black label on one side and RCA Camden label on side 2, thus sampling tunes from LPs on both labels. Promotional issue only.)
RCA VICTOR (66;
"Christmas Programming
From RCA"): *59*. **500–550**
(Contains 12 songs by 12 different artists, including Elvis. Promotional issue only.)

Price Range

Price Range

RCA VICTOR (66;
"Christmas Programming
From RCA"): *59* **$550–600**
(Special paper sleeve for SP-33-66. Promotional issue only.)

RCA VICTOR (072; "Elvis
Presley, Great Hits Of
1956-57"): *87* **10–20**
(Offered as a bonus LP, by Reader's Digest, with the purchase of one of their boxed sets, which, for the record, contains no Elvis tracks.)

RCA VICTOR (0086;
"Brightest Stars Of
Christmas"): *74* **35–45**
(Contains 11 songs by 11 artists, including Elvis. Custom made for J.C. Penny's stores and sold only in their stores.)

RCA VICTOR (96;
"October 1960 Stereo
Sampler"): *60* **500–600**
(Contains 14 songs by 14 different artists, including Elvis. Promotional issue only.)

RCA VICTOR (0108;
"E-Z Country No. 2"):
55 . . . . **250–275**
(A 10-inch LP with 12 songs by 11 different artists, including two by Elvis. Promotional issue only. The other side of this LP is numbered 0109.)

RCA VICTOR (141;
"October '61 Pop
Sampler"): *61* **500–600**
(Contains 11 songs by 11 different artists, including Elvis. Promotional issue only.)

RCA VICTOR (0168;
"Elvis In Hollywood"):
76 . . . . **35–45**
(Price includes a 20-page photo booklet, which represents $10-$15 of the value.)

RCA VICTOR (181; "Elvis
Sings Inspirational
Favorites"): *83* **15–20**
(Special Products issue. A Reader's Digest mail-order bonus LP for buyers of the 1983 edition of RCA Victor 010. Price includes 24-page Reader's Digest Music catalog, which represents $1-$3 of the value.)

RCA VICTOR (191; RCA
Sampler): *62* **500–600**
(Promotional issue only. More information is needed about this LP.)

RCA VICTOR (191;
"Elvis, The Legend Lives
On"): *86* **$40–45**
(A seven-LP boxed set, sold mail-order by Reader's Digest. Includes booklet.)

RCA VICTOR (0197;
"E-Z Pop No. 6): *56* **250–275**
(A 10-inch LP with 12 songs by 12 different artists, including Elvis. Promotional issue only. The other side of this LP is numbered 0198.)

RCA VICTOR (0199;
"E-Z Country No. 3"):
56 . . . . **250–275**
(A 10-inch LP with 12 songs by nine different artists, including two by Elvis. Promotional issue only. The other side of this LP is numbered 0200.)

RCA VICTOR (215; "30
Years Of No. 1 Country
Hits"): *86* **40–45**
(A various artists seven-LP boxed set, containing 84 songs, including three by Elvis. Includes booklet.)

RCA VICTOR (219; RCA
Sampler): *63* **500–600**
(Promotional issue only. More information is needed about this LP.)

RCA VICTOR (242; "Elvis
Sings Country
Favorites"): *84* **20–30**
(Offered as a bonus LP, by Reader's Digest, with the purchase of their seven-disc boxed set, "The Great Country Entertainers.")

RCA VICTOR (247;
"December '63 Pop
Sampler"): *63* **500–600**
(Contains 11 songs by 10 different artists, including one by Elvis. Promotional issue only.)

RCA VICTOR (0263;
"The Elvis Presley
Story"): *77* **30–40**
(Special Products five-LP boxed set. A Candelite Music mail-order offer.)

RCA VICTOR (0264;
"Songs Of Inspiration"):
77 . . . . **10–12**
(Special Products issue. A Candelite Music mail-order bonus LP for buyers of RCA Victor 0263.)

RCA VICTOR (272;
"April '64 Pop
Sampler"): *64* **500–600**

(Contains 14 songs by 14 different artists, including Elvis. Promotional issue only.)

RCA VICTOR (279;
"Singer Presents Elvis"):
68 . . . . **$70–80**
Note: This LP was reissued in 1969 as Camden 2304 and in 1975 as Pickwick 2304.

RCA VICTOR (0283;
"Elvis-Including Fool"):
73 . . . . **50–60**

RCA VICTOR (331;
"April '65 Pop
Sampler"): *65* **500–600**
(Contains 14 songs by 14 different artists, including Elvis. Promotional issue only.)

RCA VICTOR (0341;
"Legendary Performer"
Vol. 1): *74* **20–25**
(With die-cut cover. Price includes "The Early Years" booklet, which represents $5-$8 of the value.)

RCA VICTOR (0341;
"Legendary Performer"
Vol. 1): *83* **5–8**
(With standard cover rather than die-cut.)

RCA VICTOR (0341;
"Legendary Performer"
Vol. 1): *78* **800–1000**
(Picture discs of the 0341 material but with pictures from any of about six different LP covers pressed on the disc. RCA Experimental in-house item.)

RCA VICTOR (347;
"August '65 Pop
Sampler"): *65* **500–600**
(Contains 12 songs by 12 different artists, including Elvis. Promotional issue only.)

RCA VICTOR (0347;
"Memories Of Elvis"):
78 . . . . **35–45**
(Special Products five-LP boxed set. A Candelite Music mail-order offer. Price includes a 16-page booklet and an Elvis print, which represent $8-$10 of the value. Apparently not all sets were issued with the print & booklet.)

RCA VICTOR (0348;
"Greatest Show On
Earth"): *78* **10–12**
(Special Products issue. A Candelite Music mail-order bonus LP for buyers of RCA Victor 0347.)

RCA VICTOR (0388;
"Raised On Rock"): *73* **15–20**

(Orange label.)

RCA VICTOR (0388;
"Raised On Rock"): *77* **$8–10**
(Black label.)

RCA VICTOR (403;
"April '66 Pop
Sampler"): *66*. **500–600**
(Contains 14 songs by 14 different artists, including Elvis. Promotional issue only.)

RCA VICTOR (0401;
RCA Radio Victrola
Division Spots"): *56* **600–800**
(One-sided disc, containing four 50-second radio commercials for RCA's Victrolas, as well as for the SPD-22 & SPD-23 EPs that were offered as a bonus. Elvis is the announcer on all of the spots, which include excerpts of some of his songs. Issued only to radio stations scheduling the spots.)

RCA VICTOR (0412;
"The Legendary
Recordings"): *79* **30–40**
(Special Products six-LP boxed set. A Candelite Music mail-order offer.)

RCA VICTOR (0413;
"Greatest Moments In
Music"): *80* **10–15**
(Special Products issue. A Candelite Music mail-order bonus LP for buyers of RCA Victor 0412.)

RCA VICTOR (0437;
"Rock 'N Roll
Forever"): *81* **10–15**
(A Candelite Music mail-order LP offer.)

RCA VICTOR (461;
"Special Palm Sunday
Programming"): *63* **500–600**
(Price includes programming packet, which represents $100-$125 of the value. Promotional issue only.)

RCA VICTOR (0461;
"The Legendary
Magic"): *80* **10–15**
(A Candelite Music mail-order LP offer.)

RCA VICTOR
(CPL1-0475; "Good
Times"): *74*. **15–20**

RCA VICTOR
(AFL1-0475; "Good
Times"): *77*. **8–10**

RCA VICTOR (0561;
"Country Gold"): *82*. **20–25**

Price Range

Price Range

(Contains 10 songs by 10 artists, including one by Elvis. Special Products LP.)

RCA VICTOR (571; "Madison Square Garden"): *72* **$250–275**
(A two-LP, double pocket, issue. Promotional issue only.)
Note: This LP was commercially issued as RCA Victor LSP-4776.

RCA VICTOR (DJL1-0606; "On Stage In Memphis"): *74* **250–275**
(Banded edition. Promotional issue only.)

RCA VICTOR (CPL1-0606; "On Stage In Memphis"): *74* **15–18**
(Orange label.)

RCA VICTOR (CPL1-0606; "On Stage In Memphis"): *76* **15–18**
(Tan label.)

RCA VICTOR (APD1-0606; "On Stage In Memphis"): *74* **120–130**
(Quadradisc. Orange label.)

RCA VICTOR (AFL1-0606; "On Stage In Memphis"): *77* **5–8**

RCA VICTOR (AQL1-0606; "On Stage In Memphis"): *79* **5–8**

RCA VICTOR (0608; "Happy Holidays" Vol. 18): *83* **8–10**
(Contains 10 songs by 10 artists, including Elvis. Sold only at True Value Hardware Stores.)

RCA VICTOR (0632; "The Elvis Presley Collection"): *84* **50–60**
(A Special Products three-LP boxed set, produced for Candlelite Music. A mail-order LP offer.)

RCA VICTOR (DPK1-0679; "Savage Young Elvis"): *84* **5–8**
(Cassette tape of a package that was never available on LP. Price is for tape still attached to 12x12 photo card.)

RCA VICTOR (0704; "Elvis-HBO Special"): *84* **25–35**
(Special Products issue for HBO cable TV subscribers.)

Note: This material was first issued as LPM-4088.

RCA VICTOR (0710; "Elvis: 50 Years-50 Hits"): *85* **$20–22**
(A five-LP set. Offered by TV mail-order and through the RCA Record Club.)

RCA VICTOR (0713; "Happy Holidays" Vol. 20): *85* **8–10**
(Contains 14 songs by 14 artists, including Elvis. Sold only at True Value Hardware Stores.)

RCA VICTOR (0716; "A Christmas Treasury From Avon"): *85*. **10–15**
(Contains 10 songs by 10 artists, including Elvis. Available only from Avon representatives as a Christmas bonus item. Packaged in a specially printed cardboard mailer which, at this point, is included in the price.)

RCA VICTOR (0728; "Elvis, His Songs Of Faith & Inspiration"): *86* **15–18**
(A two LP, mail-order, offer.)

RCA VICTOR (0751; "Avon Valentine Favorites"): *86*. **10–15**
(Contains 10 songs by 9 artists, including one by Elvis. Available only from Avon representatives as a bonus item. Packaged in a specially printed cardboard mailer which, at this point, is included in the price.)

RCA VICTOR (CPM1-0818; "Having Fun With Elvis On Stage"): *74* **15–18**
(Orange label.)

RCA VICTOR (CPM1-0818; "Having Fun With Elvis On Stage"): *76* **10–15**
(Tan label.)

RCA VICTOR (AFM1-0818; "Having Fun With Elvis On Stage"): *77* **8–10**
Note: This LP was first issued on Boxcar, without a catalog number.

RCA VICTOR (0835; "Elvis Presley Interview Record"): *84*. **75–100**
(Promotional issue only.)

RCA VICTOR
(APL1-0873; "Promised
Land"): *75* **$15–18**
(Orange label.)

RCA VICTOR
(APL1-0873; "Promised
Land"): *76* **10–15**
(Tan label.)

RCA VICTOR
(AFL1-0873; "Promised
Land"): *77* **5–8**

RCA VICTOR
(APD1-0873; "Promised
Land"): *75* **100–125**
(Quadradisc. Orange label.)

RCA VICTOR
(APD1-0873; "Promised
Land"): *77* **40–50**
(Quadradisc. Black label.)

RCA VICTOR
(ANL1-0971; "Pure
Gold"): *75* **15–18**
(Orange label.)

RCA VICTOR
(ANL1-0971; "Pure
Gold"): *76* **10–15**
(Yellow label.)

RCA VICTOR
(ANL1-0971; "Pure
Gold"): *77* **8–10**
(Black label.)
Note: This LP was reissued in 1980 as AYL1-
3732.

RCA VICTOR (1001;
"The Sun Collection"):
75 . . . . **20–25**
(Label does not have "Starcall" on it. Back
cover pictures other LPs.)

RCA VICTOR (1001;
"The Sun Collection"):
75 . . . . **15–20**
(Label has "Starcall" on it. Back cover with
liner notes.)
Note: This English import was distributed
throughout the U.S. It was repackaged in 1976
as RCA Victor APM1-1675.

RCA VICTOR (LOC-1035;
"Elvis' Christmas
Album"): *57* **450–500**
(With gold foil gift-giving sticker.)

RCA VICTOR (LOC-1035;
"Elvis' Christmas
Album"): *57* **$225–250**
(Without gold foil gift-giving sticker.)
Note: This LP was repackaged in 1958 as RCA
Victor LPM-1951, in 1970 as Camden 2428 and
in 1985 as RCA Victor AFM1-5486.

RCA VICTOR
(APL1-1039; "Today"):
75 . . . . **15–18**
(Orange label.)

RCA VICTOR
(APL1-1039; "Today"):
76 . . . . **10–15**
(Tan label.)

RCA VICTOR
(AFL1-1039; "Today"):
77 . . . . **8–10**

RCA VICTOR
(APD1-1039; "Today"):
75 . . . . **100–125**
(Quadradisc. Orange label.)

RCA VICTOR
(APD1-1039; "Today"):
77 . . . . **40–50**
(Quadradisc. Black label.)

RCA VICTOR
(LPM-1254; "Elvis
Presley"): *56* **100–125**
(Black label with "Long Play" at bottom. Cover
with catalog number in upper right corner.)

RCA VICTOR
(LPM-1254; "Elvis
Presley"): *63* **45–55**
(Black label with "Mono" at bottom. Cover
with catalog number on left.)

RCA VICTOR
(LPM-1254; "Elvis
Presley"): *64–65* **25–30**
(Black label with "Monaural" at bottom. Cover
with catalog number on left.)

RCA VICTOR
(LSP-1254e; "Elvis
Presley"): *62* **75–85**
(Black label, all print on label is silver.)

RCA VICTOR
(LSP-1254e; "Elvis
Presley"): *64* **25–30**
(Black label, RCA logo is white, other label
print is silver.)

Price Range

RCA VICTOR
(LSP-1254e; "Elvis
Presley"): *68–69* $10–15
(Orange label.)
RCA VICTOR
(LSP-1254e; "Elvis
Presley"): *76* 10–15
(Tan label.)
RCA VICTOR
(AFL1-1254e; "Elvis
Presley"): *77* 5–8
Note: A digitally remastered edition of this LP
was issued in 1984 on RCA Victor 5198.
RCA VICTOR
(ANL1-1319; "His Hand
In Mine"): *76* 8–10
(This LP was first issued as LPM/LSP-2328.)
RCA VICTOR (1349;
"Legendary Performer"
Vol. 2): *76* 45–55
(Pressed WITHOUT the studio out-takes. This
was a production error.)
RCA VICTOR (1349;
"Legendary Performer"
Vol. 2): *76* 20–25
(With die-cut cover. Price includes "The Early
Years...Continued" booklet, which represents
$5-$8 of the value.)
RCA VICTOR (1349;
"Legendary Performer"
Vol. 2): *83* 5–8
(With standard cover rather than die-cut.)
RCA VICTOR
(LPM-1382; "Elvis"): *56* 750–1000
(Black label with "Long Play" at bottom. Cover
with catalog number in upper right corner.
Contains the otherwise unreleased alternate
take of "Old Shep." This pressing has the desig-
nation "17S" following the matrix number
stamped in the vinyl trail-off. We've yet to learn
of any copies of this oddity with a number
OTHER than "17S.")
RCA VICTOR
(LPM-1382; "Elvis"): *56* 200–225
(Black label, selections numbered as "Band 1"
through "Band 6.")
RCA VICTOR
(LPM-1382; "Elvis"): *56* 100–125
(Black label with "Long Play" at bottom. Cover
with catalog number in upper right corner.)
RCA VICTOR
(LPM-1382; "Elvis"): *63* 45–55

Price Range

(Black label with "Mono" at bottom. Cover
with catalog number on left.)
RCA VICTOR
(LPM-1382; "Elvis"):
64–65 . . . . $25–30
(Black label with "Monaural" at bottom. Cover
with catalog number on left.)
RCA VICTOR
(LSP-1382e; "Elvis"): *62* 75–85
(Black label, all print on label is silver.)
RCA VICTOR
(LSP-1382e; "Elvis"): *64* 25–30
(Black label, RCA logo is white, other print on
label is silver.)
RCA VICTOR
(LSP-1382e; "Elvis"):
68–69 10–15
(Orange label.)
RCA VICTOR
(LSP-1382e; "Elvis"): *76* 10–15
(Tan label.)
RCA VICTOR
(AFL1-1382e; "Elvis"):
77 5–8
Note: A digitally remastered edition of this LP
was issued in 1984 on RCA Victor 5199.
RCA VICTOR
(APL1-1506; "From
Elvis Presley
Boulevard"): *76* 12–15
RCA VICTOR
(AFL1-1506; "From
Elvis Presley
Boulevard"): *77* 8–10
RCA VICTOR
(LPM-1515; "Loving
You"): *57* 100–125
(Black label with "Long Play" at bottom. Cover
with catalog number in upper right corner.)
RCA VICTOR
(LPM-1515; "Loving
You"): *63* 45–55
(Black label with "Mono" at bottom. Cover
with catalog number on left.)
RCA VICTOR
(LPM-1515; "Loving
You"): *64–65* 25–30
(Black label with "Monaural" at bottom. Cover
with catalog number on left.)
RCA VICTOR
(LSP-1515e; "Loving
You"): *62* 75–85
(Black label, all print on label is silver.)

RCA VICTOR
(LSP-1515e; "Loving
You"): *64* **$25–30**
(Black label, RCA logo is white, other label
print is silver.)

RCA VICTOR
(LSP-1515e; "Loving
You"): *68–69* **10–15**
(Orange label.)

RCA VICTOR
(LSP-1515e; "Loving
You"): *76* **10–15**
(Tan label.)

RCA VICTOR
(AFL1-1515e; "Loving
You"): *77* **5–8**

RCA VICTOR
(APM1-1675; "The Sun
Sessions"): *76* **12–15**

RCA VICTOR
(AFM1-1675; "The Sun
Sessions"): *77* **8–10**
Note: This LP was first issued as RCA Victor
HY-1001 and was reissued in 1981 as RCA
Victor AYM1-3893.

RCA VICTOR
(LPM-1707; "Elvis'
Golden Records"): *58* **100–125**
(Black label with "Long Play" at bottom. Cover
with catalog number in upper right corner and
LP title in light blue letters.)

RCA VICTOR
(LPM-1707; "Elvis'
Golden Records"): *63* **45–55**
(Black label with "Mono" at bottom. Cover
with catalog number on left and LP title in
white letters.)

RCA VICTOR
(LPM-1707; "Elvis'
Golden Records"): *64–65* **25–30**
(Black label with "Monaural" at bottom. Cover
with catalog number on left.)

RCA VICTOR
(LSP-1707e; "Elvis'
Golden Records"): *62* **75–85**
(Black label, all print on label is silver.)

RCA VICTOR
(LSP-1707e; "Elvis'
Golden Records"): *64* **25–30**
(Black label, RCA logo is white, other label
print is silver.)

RCA VICTOR
(LSP-1707e; "Elvis'
Golden Records"): *68–69* **$10–15**
(Orange label.)

RCA VICTOR
(LSP-1707e; "Elvis'
Golden Records"): *76* **10–15**
(Tan label.)

RCA VICTOR
(AFL1-1707e; "Elvis'
Golden Records"): *77* **8–10**

RCA VICTOR
(AQL1-1707e; "Elvis'
Golden Records"): *79* **5–8**
Note: A digitally remastered edition of this LP
was issued in 1984 on RCA Victor 5196.

RCA VICTOR (1785;
"WRCA Plays The
Hits"): *76* **300–350**
(Contains 16 songs by 16 artists, including
Elvis. Promotional issue only. Not issued with
a special cover.)

RCA VICTOR
(LPM-1884; "King
Creole"): *58* **100–125**
(Black label with "Long Play" at bottom. Cover
with catalog number in upper right corner. Add
$50-$100 if accompanied by the 8x10 black &
white bonus photo of Elvis in uniform.)

RCA VICTOR
(LPM-1884; "King
Creole"): *63* **45–55**
(Black label with "Mono" at bottom. Cover
with catalog number on left.)

RCA VICTOR
(LPM-1884; "King
Creole"): *64–65* **25–30**
(Black label with "Monaural" at bottom. Cover
with catalog number on left.)

RCA VICTOR
(LSP-1884e; "King
Creole"): *62* **75–85**
(Black label, all print on label is silver.)

RCA VICTOR
(LSP-1884e; "King
Creole"): *62* **25–30**
(Black label, RCA logo is white, other label
print is silver.)

RCA VICTOR
(LSP-1884e; "King
Creole"): *68–69* **10–15**
(Orange label.)

Price Range

RCA VICTOR
(LSP-1884e; "King
Creole"): 76 . . . . **$10–15**
(Tan label.)

RCA VICTOR
(AFL1-1884e; "King
Creole"): 77 . . . . **8–10**
Note: This LP was reissued in 1980 as RCA
Victor AYL1-3733.

RCA VICTOR
(ANL1-1936;
"Wonderful World Of
Christmas"): 77 . . . . **5–8**
Note: This LP was first issued as RCA Victor
LSP-4579.

RCA VICTOR
(LPM-1951; "Elvis'
Christmas Album"): 58 . . . . **90–100**
(Black label with "Long Play" at bottom. Cover
with catalog number in upper right corner.)

RCA VICTOR
(LPM-1951; "Elvis'
Christmas Album"): 63 . . . . **45–55**
(Black label with "Mono" at bottom. Cover
with catalog number on left.)

RCA VICTOR
(LPM-1951; "Elvis'
Christmas Album"): 64 . . . . **25–30**
(Black label with "Monaural" at bottom. Cover
with catalog number on left.)

RCA VICTOR
(LSP-1951e; "Elvis'
Christmas Album"): 64 . . . . **25–30**
(Black label, RCA logo is white, other label
print is silver.)

RCA VICTOR
(LSP-1951e; "Elvis'
Christmas Album"): 68 . . . . **10–15**
(Orange label.)
Note: This LP is a repackage of RCA Victor
LOC-1035. It was repackaged in 1970 as Cam-
den 2428 and again in 1985 as RCA Victor
AFM1-5486.

RCA VICTOR (1981;
"Felton Jarvis Talks
About Elvis"): 81 . . . . **150–200**
(Price includes three script sheets, which repre-
sent $5-$10 of the value. Price also includes
"Guitar Man" engraved Elvis belt buckle,
which represents $40-$50 of the value.)

RCA VICTOR
(LPM-1990; "For LP
Fans Only"): 59 . . . . **100–125**

Price Range

(Black label with "Long Play" at bottom. Cover
with catalog number in upper right corner.)

RCA VICTOR
(LPM-1990; "For LP
Fans Only"): 63 . . . . **$45–55**
(Black label with "Mono" at bottom. Cover
with catalog number on left.)

RCA VICTOR
(LPM-1990; "For LP
Fans Only"): 65 . . . . **25–30**
(Black label with "Monaural" at bottom. Cover
with catalog number on left.)

RCA VICTOR
(LSP-1990e; "For LP
Fans Only"): 65 . . . . **25–30**
(Black label, RCA logo is white, other label
print is silver.)

RCA VICTOR
(LSP-1990e; "For LP
Fans Only"): 68–69 . . . . **10–15**
(Orange label.)

RCA VICTOR
(LSP-1990e; "For LP
Fans Only"): 76 . . . . **10–15**
(Tan label.)

RCA VICTOR
(AFL1-1990e; "For LP
Fans Only"): 77 . . . . **8–10**

RCA VICTOR
(LPM-2011; "A Date
With Elvis"): 59 . . . . **200–225**
(Black label with "Long Play" at bottom. With
gatefold cover and 1960 calendar. WITH
"NEW GOLDEN AGE OF SOUND" wrap-
around banner.)

RCA VICTOR
(LPM-2011; "A Date
With Elvis"): 59 . . . . **150–175**
(Black label with "Long Play" at bottom. With
gatefold cover and 1960 calendar, but without
"NEW GOLDEN AGE OF SOUND" ban-
ner.)

RCA VICTOR
(LPM-2011; "A Date
With Elvis"): 65 . . . . **45–55**
(Black label with "Mono" at bottom. Cover
with catalog number on left.)

RCA VICTOR
(LPM-2011; "A Date
With Elvis"): 65 . . . . **25–30**
(Black label with "Monaural" at bottom. Cover
with catalog number on left.)

Price Range

Price Range

RCA VICTOR
(LSP-2011e; "A Date
With Elvis"): *65*. **$25–30**
(Black label, RCA logo is white, other label
print is silver.)
RCA VICTOR
(LSP-2011e; "A Date
With Elvis"): *68–69*. **10–15**
(Orange label.)
RCA VICTOR
(LSP-2011e; "A Date
With Elvis"): *76*. **10–15**
(Tan label.)
RCA VICTOR
(AFL1-2011e; "A Date
With Elvis"): *77*. **8–10**
RCA VICTOR
(LPM-2075; "Elvis'
Golden Records" Vol.
2): *59* **100–125**
(Black label with "Long Play" at bottom. Cover
with catalog number in upper right corner.)
RCA VICTOR
(LPM-2075; "Elvis'
Golden Records" Vol.
2): *63* **45–55**
(Black label with "Mono" at bottom. Cover
with catalog number on left.)
RCA VICTOR
(LPM-2075; "Elvis'
Golden Records" Vol.
2): *64–65* **25–30**
(Black label with "Monaural" at bottom. Cover
with catalog number on left.)
RCA VICTOR
(LSP-2075e; "Elvis'
Golden Records" Vol.
2): *62* **75–85**
(Black label, all print on label is silver.)
RCA VICTOR
(LSP-2075e; "Elvis'
Golden Records" Vol.
2): *64* **25–30**
(Black label, RCA logo is white, other label
print is silver.)
RCA VICTOR
(LSP-2075e; "Elvis'
Golden Records" Vol.
2): *68–69* **10–15**
(Orange label.)

RCA VICTOR
(LSP-2075e; "Elvis'
Golden Records" Vol.
2): *76* **$10–15**
(Tan label.)
RCA VICTOR
(AFL1-2075e; "Elvis'
Golden Records" Vol.
2): *77* **5–8**
Notes: This LP may also be shown as
"50,000,000 Elvis Presley Fans Can't Be
Wrong"...A digitally remastered edition of this
LP was issued in 1984 on RCA Victor 5197.
RCA VICTOR
(LPM-2231; "Elvis Is
Back"): *60* **100–125**
(Black label with "Long Play" at bottom. Cover
with a yellow sticker listing song titles.)
RCA VICTOR
(LPM-2231; "Elvis Is
Back"): *63* **45–55**
(Black label with "Mono" at bottom. Cover
with catalog number on left.)
RCA VICTOR
(LPM-2231; "Elvis Is
Back"): *64–65* **25–30**
(Black label with "Monaural" at bottom. Cover
with catalog number on left.)
RCA VICTOR (LSP-2231;
"Elvis Is Back"): *60* **125–150**
(Black label with "Living Stereo" at bottom.
Cover with a yellow sticker listing song titles.)
RCA VICTOR (LSP-2231;
"Elvis Is Back"): *64* **25–30**
(Black label, RCA logo is white, other label
print is silver.)
RCA VICTOR (LSP-2231;
"Elvis Is Back"): *68–69* **10–15**
(Orange label.)
RCA VICTOR (LSP-2231;
"Elvis Is Back"): *76* **10–15**
(Tan label.)
RCA VICTOR
(AFL1-2231; "Elvis Is
Back"): *77* **8–10**
RCA VICTOR
(LPM-2256; "G.I.
Blues"): *60* **100–125**
(Black label with "Long Play" at bottom. Price
includes "Elvis Is Back" inner sleeve, which
represents $15-$25 of the value.)

Price Range

Price Range

RCA VICTOR
(LPM-2256; "G.I.
Blues"): *63* **$45–55**
(Black label with "Mono" at bottom.)

RCA VICTOR
(LPM-2256; "G.I.
Blues"): *64–65* **25–30**
(Black label with "Monaural" at bottom.)

RCA VICTOR (LSP-2256;
"G.I. Blues"): *60* **100–125**
(Black label with "Living Stereo" at bottom.
Price includes "Elvis Is Back" inner sleeve,
which represents $15-$25 of the value.)

RCA VICTOR (LSP-2256;
"G.I. Blues"): *64* **25–30**
(Black label, RCA logo is white, other label
print is silver.)

RCA VICTOR (LSP-2256;
"G.I. Blues"): *68–69* **10–15**
(Orange label.)

RCA VICTOR (LSP-2256;
"G.I. Blues"): *76* **10–15**
(Tan label.)

RCA VICTOR
(AFL1-2256; "G.I.
Blues"): *77* **8–10**
Note: This LP was reissued in 1984 as RCA
Victor AYL1-3735.

RCA VICTOR
(APL1-2274; "Welcome
To My World"): *77* **10–15**

RCA VICTOR
(AFL1-2274; "Welcome
To My World"): *77* **8–10**

RCA VICTOR
(AQL1-2274; "Welcome
To My World"): *79* **5–8**

RCA VICTOR
(LPM-2328; "His Hand
In Mine"): *60* **75–90**
(Black label with "Long Play" at bottom.)

RCA VICTOR
(LPM-2328; "His Hand
In Mine"): *63* **40–50**
(Black label with "Mono" at bottom.)

RCA VICTOR
(LPM-2328; "His Hand
In Mine"): *64–65* **25–30**
(Black label with "Monaural" at bottom.)

RCA VICTOR (LSP-2328;
"His Hand In Mine"):
60 .... **90–100**

(Black label with "Living Stereo" at bottom.)

RCA VICTOR (LSP-2328;
"His Hand In Mine"):
64 .... **$25–30**
(Black label, RCA logo is white, other label
print is silver.)

RCA VICTOR (LSP-2328;
"His Hand In Mine"):
68–69 .... **10–15**
(Orange label.)

RCA VICTOR (LSP-2328;
"His Hand In Mine"):
76 .... **10–15**
(Tan label.)
Note: This LP was repackaged in 1976 as RCA
Victor ANL1-1319 and in 1981 as RCA Victor
AYM1-3935.

RCA VICTOR (2347;
"Elvis-Greatest Hits Vol.
One"): *81* **10–15**
(With embossed letters on front cover.)

RCA VICTOR (2347;
"Elvis-Greatest Hits Vol.
One"): *83* **5–8**
(Standard printed cover. No embossed letters.)

RCA VICTOR
(LPM-2370; "Something
For Everybody"): *61* **75–90**
(Black label with "Long Play" at bottom. Back
cover promotes Compact 33s.)

RCA VICTOR
(LPM-2370; "Something
For Everybody"): *63* **40–50**
(Black label with "Mono" at bottom.)

RCA VICTOR
(LPM-2370; "Something
For Everybody"): *64–65* **25–30**
(Black label with "Monaural" at bottom.)

RCA VICTOR (LSP-2370;
"Something For
Everybody"): *61* **90–100**
(Black label with "Living Stereo" at bottom.
Back cover promotes Compact 33s.)

RCA VICTOR (LSP-2370;
"Something For
Everybody"): *64* **25–30**
(Black label, RCA logo is white, other label
print is silver.)

RCA VICTOR (LSP-2370;
"Something For
Everybody"): *68–69* **10–15**
(Orange label.)

Price Range

Price Range

RCA VICTOR (LSP-2370;
"Something For
Everybody"): *76*. **$10–15**
(Tan label.)

RCA VICTOR
(AFL1-2370; "Something
For Everybody"): *77*. **8–10**
Note: This LP was reissued in 1981 as RCA
Victor AYM1-4116.

RCA VICTOR
(LPM-2426; "Blue
Hawaii"): *61*. **75–90**
(Black label with "Long Play" at bottom.)

RCA VICTOR
(LPM-2426; "Blue
Hawaii"): *63*. **40–50**
(Black label with "Mono" at bottom.)

RCA VICTOR
(LPM-2426; "Blue
Hawaii"): *64–65*. **25–30**
(Black label with "Monaural" at bottom.)

RCA VICTOR
"Blue Hawaii"): *61* **90–100**
(Black label with "Living Stereo" at bottom.)

RCA VICTOR (LSP-2426;
"Blue Hawaii"): *64* **25–30**
(Black label, RCA logo is white, other label
print is silver.)

RCA VICTOR (LSP-2426;
"Blue Hawaii"): *68–69* **10–15**
(Orange label.)

RCA VICTOR (LSP-2426;
"Blue Hawaii"): *76* **10–15**
(Tan label.)

RCA VICTOR
(AFL1-2426; "Blue
Hawaii"): *77*. **8–10**
Note: This LP was reissued in 1981 as RCA
Victor AYL1-3683.

RCA VICTOR
(AFL1-2428; "Moody
Blue"): *77*. **1000–1200**
(Colored vinyl, OTHER THAN blue. Experi-
mental production discs for RCA in-house use
only.)

RCA VICTOR
(AFL1-2428; "Moody
Blue"): *77*. **10–12**
(Blue vinyl.)

RCA VICTOR
(AFL1-2428; "Moody
Blue"): *77*. **125–150**

(Black vinyl.)

RCA VICTOR
(AQL1-2428; "Moody
Blue"): *79*. **$5–8**

RCA VICTOR
(LPM-2523; "Pot
Luck"): *62* **75–90**
(Black label with "Long Play" at bottom.)

RCA VICTOR
(LPM-2523; "Pot
Luck"): *63* **40–50**
(Black label with "Mono" at bottom.)

RCA VICTOR
(LPM-2523; "Pot
Luck"): *64–65* **25–30**
(Black label with "Monaural" at bottom.)

RCA VICTOR (LSP-2523;
"Pot Luck"): *62*. **90–100**
(Black label with "Living Stereo" at bottom.)

RCA VICTOR (LSP-2523;
"Pot Luck"): *64*. **25–30**
(Black label, RCA logo is white, other label
print is silver.)

RCA VICTOR (LSP-2523;
"Pot Luck"): *68–69*. **10–15**
(Orange label.)

RCA VICTOR (LSP-2523;
"Pot Luck"): *76*. **10–15**
(Tan label.)

RCA VICTOR
(AFL1-2523; "Pot
Luck"): *77* **8–10**

RCA VICTOR
(APL1-2558; "Harum
Scarum"): *77* **8–10**
Note: This LP was first issued as RCA Victor
LPM/LSP-3468. It was reissued in 1980 as
RCA Victor AYL1-3734.

RCA VICTOR
(APL1-2560; "Spinout"):
77 . . . . **8–10**
Note: This LP was first issued as RCA Victor
LPM/LSP-3702. It was reissued in 1980 as
RCA Victor AYL1-3684.

RCA VICTOR
(APL1-2564; "Double
Trouble"): *77*. **8–10**
Note: This LP was first issued as RCA Victor
LPM/LSP-3787.

RCA VICTOR
(APL1-2565;
"Clambake"): *77* **8–10**

Price Range

Price Range

Note: This LP was first issued as RCA Victor
LPM/LSP-3893.

RCA VICTOR
(APL1-2568; "It
Happened At The
World's Fair"): 77............. **$8–10**
Note: This LP was first issued as RCA Victor
LPM/LSP-2697.

RCA VICTOR
(APL2-2587; "Elvis In
Concert"): 77................. **15–20**
(Price includes insert flyer listing other Elvis
LPs, which represents $2-$3 of the value.)

RCA VICTOR
(CPL2-2587; "Elvis In
Concert"): 82................. **12–15**

RCA VICTOR
(LPM-2621; "Girls!
Girls! Girls!"): 62.............. **75–90**
(Black label with "Long Play" at bottom.)

RCA VICTOR
(LPM-2621; "Girls!
Girls! Girls!"): 63.............. **40–50**
(Black label with "Mono" at bottom.)

RCA VICTOR
(LPM-2621; "Girls!
Girls! Girls!"): 64–65............ **25–30**
(Black label with "Monaural" at bottom.)

RCA VICTOR (LSP-2621;
"Girls! Girls! Girls!"): 62....... **90–100**
(Black label with "Living Stereo" at bottom.)

RCA VICTOR (LSP-2621;
"Girls! Girls! Girls!"): 64....... **25–30**
(Black label, RCA logo is white, other label
print is silver.)

RCA VICTOR (LSP-2621;
"Girls! Girls! Girls!"):
68–69 .... **10–15**
(Orange label.)

RCA VICTOR (LSP-2621;
"Girls! Girls! Girls!"): 76........ **10–15**
(Tan label.)

RCA VICTOR
(AFL1-2621; "Girls!
Girls! Girls!"): 77.............. **8–10**

RCA VICTOR
(CPD2-2642; "Aloha
From Hawaii"): 75 .... **15–20**
(Orange label.)

RCA VICTOR
(CPD2-2642; "Aloha
From Hawaii"): 77 .... **10–12**

(Black label.)
Note: This LP was first issued as RCA Victor
VPSX-6089.

RCA VICTOR
(LPM-2697; "It
Happened At The
World's Fair"): 63.......... **$100–115**
(Black label with "Long Play" at bottom. Price
includes an 8x10 bonus color photo, which
represents $25-$35 of the value.)

RCA VICTOR
(LPM-2697; "It
Happened At The
World's Fair"): 63.............. **40–50**
(Black label with "Mono" at bottom.)

RCA VICTOR
(LPM-2697; "It
Happened At The
World's Fair"): 64–65.......... **25–30**
(Black label with "Monaural" at bottom.)

RCA VICTOR (LSP-2697;
"It Happened At The
World's Fair"): 63........... **115–125**
(Black label with "Living Stereo" at bottom.
Price includes an 8x10 bonus color photo,
which represents about $25-$35 of the value.)

RCA VICTOR (LSP-2697;
"It Happened At The
World's Fair"): 64.............. **25–30**
(Black label, RCA logo is white, other label
print is silver.)

RCA VICTOR (LSP-2697;
"It Happened At The
World's Fair"): 68–69.......... **10–15**
(Orange label.)

RCA VICTOR (LSP-2697;
"It Happened At The
World's Fair"): 76.............. **10–15**
(Tan label.)
Note: This LP was reissued in 1977 as RCA
Victor APL1-2568.

RCA VICTOR
(LPM-2756; "Fun In
Acapulco"): 63................. **60–70**
(Black label with "Mono" at bottom.)

RCA VICTOR
(LPM-2756; "Fun In
Acapulco"): 64–65.............. **25–30**
(Black label with "Monaural" at bottom.)

RCA VICTOR (LSP-2756;
"Fun In Acapulco"): 63........ **60–70**
(Black label, all print on label is silver.)

RCA VICTOR (LSP-2756;
"Fun In Acapulco"): *64* **$25–30**
(Black label, RCA logo is white, other label print is silver.)

RCA VICTOR (LSP-2756;
"Fun In Acapulco"):
68–69 . . . . **10–15**
(Orange label.)

RCA VICTOR (LSP-2756;
"Fun In Acapulco"): *76* **10–15**
(Tan label.)

RCA VICTOR
(AFL1-2756; "Fun In
Acapulco"): *77*. **8–10**

RCA VICTOR
(LPM-2765; "Elvis'
Golden Records" Vol.
3): *63* **90–100**
(Black label with "Mono" at bottom. Price includes bonus 8x10 photo booklet, which represents $30-$40 of the value.)

RCA VICTOR
(LPM-2765; "Elvis'
Golden Records" Vol.
3): *64–65* **25–30**
(Black label with "Monaural" at bottom.)

RCA VICTOR (LSP-2765;
"Elvis' Golden Records"
Vol. 3): *63* **90–100**
(Black label, all print on label is silver. Price includes bonus 8x10 photo booklet, which represents $30-$40 of the value.)

RCA VICTOR (LSP-2765;
"Elvis' Golden Records"
Vol. 3): *64* **25–30**
(Black label, RCA logo is white, other label print is silver.)

RCA VICTOR (LSP-2765;
"Elvis' Golden Records"
Vol. 3): *68–69* **10–15**
(Orange label.)

RCA VICTOR (LSP-2765;
"Elvis' Golden Records"
Vol. 3): *68–69* **10–15**
(Tan label.)

RCA VICTOR
(AFL1-2765; "Elvis'
Golden Records" Vol.
3): *77* **5–8**

RCA VICTOR
(AFL1-2772; "He Walks
Beside Me"): *77*. **8–10**

(Price includes a 20-page photo booklet, which represents $2-$3 of the value.)

RCA VICTOR
(LPM-2894; "Kissin'
Cousins"): *64* **$100–125**
(Black label with "Mono" at bottom. DOES NOT picture film cast in lower right corner photo on cover.)

RCA VICTOR
(LPM-2894; "Kissin'
Cousins"): *64* **60–70**
(Black label with "Mono" at bottom. DOES picture film cast in lower right corner photo on cover.)

RCA VICTOR
(LPM-2894; "Kissin'
Cousins"): *64–65* **25–30**
(Black label with "Monaural" at bottom.)

RCA VICTOR (LSP-2894;
"Kissin' Cousins"): *64* **100–125**
(Black label, all print on label is silver. DOES NOT picture film cast in lower right corner photo on cover.)

RCA VICTOR (LSP-2894;
"Kissin' Cousins"): *64* **60–70**
(Black label, all print on label is silver. DOES picture film cast in lower right corner photo on cover.

RCA VICTOR (LSP-2894;
"Kissin' Cousins"): *64* **25–30**
(Black label, RCA logo is white, other label print is silver.)

RCA VICTOR (LSP-2894;
"Kissin' Cousins"):
68–69 . . . . **10–15**
(Orange label.)

RCA VICTOR (LSP-2894;
"Kissin' Cousins"): *76* **10–15**
(Tan label.)

RCA VICTOR
(AFL1-2894; "Kissin'
Cousins"): *77*. **8–10**
Note: This LP was reissued in 1981 as RCA Victor AYM1-4115.

RCA VICTOR
(CPL1-2901; "Elvis Sings
For Children"): *78* **8–10**
(Price includes "Special Memories" greeting card, which represents $2-$4 of the value.)

RCA VICTOR
(LPM-2999;
"Roustabout"): *64* **60–70**
(Black label with "Mono" at bottom.)

Price Range   *Price Range*

RCA VICTOR
(LPM-2999;
"Roustabout"): *64–65* **$25–30**
(Black label with "Monaural" at bottom.)

RCA VICTOR (LSP-2999;
"Roustabout"): *64* **700–750**
(Black label, ALL PRINT, including RCA
logo, on label is silver.)

RCA VICTOR (LSP-2999;
"Roustabout"): *64* **25–30**
(Black label, RCA logo is white, other label
print is silver.)

RCA VICTOR (LSP-2999;
"Roustabout"): *68–69* **10–15**
(Orange label.)

RCA VICTOR (LSP-2999;
"Roustabout"): *76* **10–15**
(Tan label.)

RCA VICTOR
(AFL1-2999;
"Roustabout"): *77* **8–10**

RCA VICTOR (3078;
"Legendary Performer"
Vol. 3): *78* **25–30**
(Picture disc. Price includes "Yesterdays"
booklet, which represents $5-$8 of the value.
May be found with the actual disc pressed on
either blue or black vinyl.)
Note: This LP was also issued on standard
black vinyl as 3082.

RCA VICTOR (3082;
"Legendary Performer"
Vol. 3): *78* **8–10**
(Price includes "Yesterdays" booklet, which
represents $5-$8 of the value.)
Note: This LP was also issued on a picture disc,
as RCA Victor 3078.

RCA VICTOR (3279;
"Our Memories Of
Elvis"): *79* **8–10**

RCA VICTOR
(LPM-3338; "Girl
Happy"): *65* **35–45**

RCA VICTOR (LSP-3338;
"Girl Happy"): *65* **35–45**
(Black label.)

RCA VICTOR (LSP-3338;
"Girl Happy"): *68–69* **10–15**
(Orange label.)

RCA VICTOR (LSP-3338;
"Girl Happy"): *76* **10–15**
(Tan label.)

RCA VICTOR
(AFL1-3338; "Girl
Happy"): *77* **$5–8**

RCA VICTOR (3448;
"Our Memories Of
Elvis" Vol. 2): *79* **8–10**
Note: A sampling of tracks from this LP ap-
peared on RCA Victor 3455, "Pure Elvis."

RCA VICTOR
(LPM-3450; "Elvis For
Everyone"): *65* **35–45**

RCA VICTOR (LSP-3450;
"Elvis For Everyone"):
65 . . . . **35–45**
(Black label.)

RCA VICTOR (LSP-3450;
"Elvis For Everyone"):
68–69 . . . . **10–15**
(Orange label.)

RCA VICTOR (LSP-3450;
"Elvis For Everyone"):
76 . . . . **10–15**
(Tan label.)

RCA VICTOR
(AFL1-3450; "Elvis For
Everyone"): *77* **8–10**
Note: This LP was reissued in 1982 as RCA
Victor AYM1-4332.

RCA VICTOR (3455;
"Pure Elvis"): *79* **275–300**
(Cover reads "Pure Elvis," but label reads "Our
Memories Of Elvis - Vol. 2." Promotional issue
only.)

RCA VICTOR
(LPM-3468; "Harum
Scarum"): *65* **65–75**
(Price includes bonus 12x12 photo, which
represents about $30 of the value.)

RCA VICTOR (LSP-3468;
"Harum Scarum"): *65* **65–75**
(Price includes bonus 12x12 photo, which
represents about $30 of the value.)
Note: This LP was reissued in 1977 as RCA
Victor APL1-2558 and in 1980 as RCA Victor
AYL1-3734.

RCA VICTOR
(LPM-3553; "Frankie &
Johnny"): *66*. **65–75**
(Price includes bonus 12x12 photo, which
represents about $30 of the value.)

RCA VICTOR (LSP-3553;
"Frankie & Johnny"): *66* **65–75**

Price Range

Price Range

(Price includes bonus 12x12 photo, which represents about $30 of the value.)
Note: This LP was reissued in 1977 as RCA Victor APL1-2559. A repackage appeared in 1976 on Pickwick 7007.

RCA VICTOR
(LPM-3643; "Paradise
Hawaiian Style): *66* **$35–45**

RCA VICTOR (LSP-3643;
"Paradise Hawaiian
Style): *66* **35–45**
(Black label.)

RCA VICTOR (LSP-3643;
"Paradise Hawaiian
Style): *68–69.* **10–15**
(Orange label.)

RCA VICTOR (LSP-3643;
"Paradise Hawaiian
Style): *76* **10–15**
(Tan label.)

RCA VICTOR
(AFL1-3643; "Paradise
Hawaiian Style): *77*. **8–10**

RCA VICTOR
(AYL1-3683; "Blue
Hawaii"): *80*. **5–8**
Note: This LP was first issued as RCA Victor LPM/LSP-2426.

RCA VICTOR
(AYL1-3684; "Spinout"):
80 . . . . **5–8**
Note: This LP was first issued as RCA Victor LPM/LSP-3702, but was reissued in 1977 as RCA Victor APL1-2560.

RCA VICTOR
(CPL8-3699; "Elvis Aron
Presley"): *80*. **80–100**
(An eight-LP boxed set. Price includes a 20-page booklet, which represents $5-$8 of the value.)

RCA VICTOR
(CPL8-3699; "Elvis Aron
Presley"): *80*. **450–500**
(REVIEWER SERIES edition. Silver sticker on back also identifies the Reviewer Series copy as "NS-3699." Price includes a 20-page booklet, which represents $5-$8 of the value.)

RCA VICTOR
(CPK8-3699; "Elvis
Aron Presley"): *80* **80–100**
(A four-cassette boxed set. Price includes a 20-page booklet and eight 12x12 Elvis photos, which represent $10-$15 of the value.)

RCA VICTOR
(CPS8-3699; "Elvis Aron
Presley"): *80*. **$100–125**
(A four 8-track boxed set. Price includes a 20-page booklet and eight 12x12 Elvis photos, which represent $10-$15 of the value.)
Note: Excerpts of songs in this set appeared on RCA Victor 3729. Selections from this LP were issued on RCA Victor 3781. The tape sets of this issue contain some sought-after takes and variations of songs not heard on the LP editions.

RCA VICTOR (LSP-3702;
"Spinout"): *66* **65–75**
(Price includes bonus 12x12 photo, which represents about $30 of the value.)
Note: This LP was reissued in 1977 as APL1-2560.

RCA VICTOR (3729;
"Elvis Aron Presley" -
Excerpts): *80* **100–125**
(Contains 37 excerpts from RCA Victor 3699. Promotional issue only.)

RCA VICTOR
(AYL1-3732; "Pure
Gold"): *80* **5–8**
Note: This LP was first issued as RCA Victor ANL1-0971.

RCA VICTOR
(AYL1-3734; "Harum
Scarum"): *80* **5–8**
Note: This LP was first issued as RCA Victor LPM/LSP-3468.

RCA VICTOR
(AYL1-3735; "G.I.
Blues"): *80*. **5–8**
Note: This LP was first issued as RCA Victor LPM/LSP-2256.

RCA VICTOR
(LPM-3758; "How Great
Thou Art"): *67* **35–45**

RCA VICTOR (LSP-3758;
"How Great Thou Art"):
67 . . . . **30–40**
(Black label.)

RCA VICTOR (LSP-3758;
"How Great Thou Art"):
68–69 . . . . **10–15**
(Orange label.)

RCA VICTOR (LSP-3758;
"How Great Thou Art"):
76 . . . . **10–15**
(Tan label.)

Price Range

RCA VICTOR
(AFL1-3758; "How
Great Thou Art"): *77* **$5–8**
RCA VICTOR (3781;
"Elvis Aron Presley" -
Selections): *80* **100–125**
(Contains 12 selections from RCA Victor 3699.
Promotional issue only.)
RCA VICTOR
(LPM-3787; "Double
Trouble"): *67* **40–50**
(Front cover notes "Special Bonus Full Color
Photo." Price includes 7x9 photo, which repre-
sents about $5 of the value.)
RCA VICTOR (LSP-3787;
"Double Trouble"): *67* **30–40**
(Front cover notes "Special Bonus Full Color
Photo." Price includes 7x9 photo, which repre-
sents about $5 of the value. Black label.)
RCA VICTOR (LSP-3787;
"Double Trouble"):
68–69 . . . . **10–15**
(Orange label.)
RCA VICTOR (LSP-3787;
"Double Trouble"): *76* **10–15**
(Tan label.)
Note: This LP was reissued in 1977 as RCA
Victor APL1-2564.
RCA VICTOR
(AYL1-3892; "Elvis In
Person"): *81* **5–8**
Note: This LP was first issued as RCA Victor
LSP-4428.
RCA VICTOR
(LPM-3893;
"Clambake"): *67* **150–200**
(Price includes bonus 12x12 photo, which
represents about $30 of the value.)
RCA VICTOR (LSP-3893;
"Clambake"): *67* **60–70**
(Price includes bonus 12x12 photo, which
represents about $30 of the value. Black label.)
RCA VICTOR (LSP-3893;
"Clambake"): *68–69* **10–15**
(Orange label.)
RCA VICTOR (LSP-3893;
"Clambake"): *76* **10–15**
(Tan label.)
Note: This LP was reissued in 1977 as RCA
Victor APL1-2565.
RCA VICTOR
(AYM1-3893; "The Sun
Sessions"): *81* **5–8**

Price Range

Note: This LP was first issued as RCA Victor
APM1-1675.
RCA VICTOR
(AYM1-3894; "Elvis TV
Special"): *81* **$8–10**
Note: This LP was first issued as RCA Victor
LPM-4088.
RCA VICTOR (3917;
"Guitar Man"): *81* **8–12**
(Price includes a "This Is Elvis" flyer, which
represents $3-$4 of the value.)
Note: Producer Felton Jarvis talks about Elvis
and the making of this LP on RCA Victor 1981.
RCA VICTOR
(LPM-3921; "Elvis' Gold
Records" Vol. 4): *68* **450–500**
(Price includes a 7x9 Elvis photo, which repre-
sents $5-$10 of the value.)
RCA VICTOR (LSP-3921;
"Elvis' Gold Records"
Vol. 4): *68* **35–45**
(Black label. Price includes a 7x9 Elvis photo,
which represents $5-$10 of the value.)
RCA VICTOR (LSP-3921;
"Elvis' Gold Records"
Vol. 4): *68–69* **10–15**
(Orange label.)
RCA VICTOR (LSP-3921;
"Elvis' Gold Records"
Vol. 4): *76* **10–15**
(Tan label.)
RCA VICTOR
(AFL1-3921; "Elvis'
Gold Records" Vol. 4):
77 . . . . **5–8**
RCA VICTOR
(AYM1-3935; "His Hand
In Mine"): *81* **5–8**
Note: This LP was first issued as RCA Victor
LPM/LSP-2328.
RCA VICTOR
(AYL1-3956; "That's
The Way It Is"): *81* **5–8**
Note: This LP was first issued as RCA Victor
LSP-4460.
RCA VICTOR
(LPM-3989;
"Speedway"): *68* **800–900**
(Price includes an 8x10 Elvis photo, which
represents $5-$10 of the value.)
RCA VICTOR (LSP-3989;
"Speedway"): *68* **35–45**

RCA VICTOR
(AYM1-4115; "Kissin'
Cousins"): *81* **$5–8**
Note: This LP was first issued as RCA Victor
LPM/LSP-2894.
RCA VICTOR
(AYM1-4116;
"Something For
Everybody"): *81*................. **5–8**
Note: This LP was first issued as RCA Victor
LPM/LSP-2370.
RCA VICTOR (LSP-4155;
"From Elvis In
Memphis"): *69*................ **20–25**
(Orange label. Price includes an 8x10 Elvis
photo, which represents $5-$10 of the value.)
RCA VICTOR (LSP-4155;
"From Elvis In
Memphis"): *69*................ **10–15**
(Tan label.)
RCA VICTOR
(AFL1-4155; "From
Elvis In Memphis"): *77* **5–8**
Note: A half-speed mastered issue of this LP
was released in 1982 as MFSL 059.
RCA VICTOR
(AYM1-4332; "Elvis For
Everyone"): *82*................. **5–8**
Note: This LP was first issued as RCA Victor
LPM/LSP-3450.
RCA VICTOR (4351; "60
Years Of Country
Music"): *82* **8–10**
(Contains 24 songs by 24 artists, including
Elvis.)
RCA VICTOR (LSP-4362;
"On Stage"): *70*............... **15–18**
(Orange label.)
RCA VICTOR (LSP-4362;
"On Stage"): *76*................ **10–15**
(Tan label.)
RCA VICTOR
(AFL1-4362; "On
Stage"): *77*.................... **8–10**
RCA VICTOR
(AQL1-4362; "On
Stage"): *83* **5–8**
RCA VICTOR (4395;
"Memories Of
Christmas"): *82* **8–10**
(Price includes a 7x9 calendar, which represents
$2-$4 of the value.)

Price Range

(Black label. Price includes an 8x10 Elvis
photo, which represents $5-$10 of the value.)
RCA VICTOR (LSP-3989;
"Speedway"): *68–69* **$10–15**
(Orange label.)
RCA VICTOR (LSP-3989;
"Speedway"): *76* **10–15**
(Tan label.)
RCA VICTOR
(AFL1-3989;
"Speedway"): *77*................ **8–10**
RCA VICTOR (4031;
"This Is Elvis"): *80*............. **10–15**
RCA VICTOR
(LPM-4088; "Elvis TV
Special"): *68*................... **15–18**
(Orange label.)
RCA VICTOR
(LPM-4088; "Elvis TV
Special"): *76*................... **10–15**
(Tan label.)
RCA VICTOR
(AFM1-4088; "Elvis TV
Special"): *77*................... **8–10**
Note: This LP was reissued in 1981 as RCA
Victor AYM1-3894. It was repackaged for
HBO as RCA Victor 0704.
RCA VICTOR
(AYL1-4114; "That's
The Way It Is"): *81* **5–8**
Note: This LP was first issued as RCA Victor
LSP-4445.

Price Range

RCA VICTOR (LSP-4428;
"Elvis In Person"): 70 . . . . **$15–18**
(Orange label.)
RCA VICTOR (LSP-4428;
"Elvis In Person"): 76 . . . . **10–15**
(Tan label.)
RCA VICTOR
(AFL1-4428; "Elvis In
Person"): 77. . . . . **8–10**
Note: This LP, first released as half of RCA
Victor LSP-6020, was reissued in 1981 as RCA
Victor AYL1-3892.
RCA VICTOR (LSP-4429;
"Elvis Back In
Memphis"): 70. . . . . **15–18**
(Orange label.)
RCA VICTOR (LSP-4429;
"Elvis Back In
Memphis"): 76. . . . . **10–15**
(Tan label.)
RCA VICTOR
(AFL1-4429; "Elvis Back
In Memphis"): 77 . . . . **8–10**
Note: This LP was first issued as half of RCA
Victor LSP-6020.
RCA VICTOR (LSP-4445;
"That's The Way It Is"):
70 . . . . **15–18**
(Orange label.)
RCA VICTOR (LSP-4445;
"That's The Way It Is"):
76 . . . . **10–15**
(Tan label.)
RCA VICTOR (LSP-4445;
"That's The Way It Is"):
77 . . . . **8–10**
(Black label.)
RCA VICTOR
(AFL1-4445; "That's
The Way It Is"): 77 . . . . **8–10**
Note: This LP was reissued in 1981 as RCA
Victor AYL1-4114.
RCA VICTOR (LSP-4460;
"Elvis Country"): 71. . . . . **15–18**
(Orange label. Price includes a 7x9 Elvis photo,
which represents $5-$10 of the value.)
RCA VICTOR (LSP-4460;
"Elvis Country"): 76. . . . . **10–15**
(Tan label.)
RCA VICTOR
(AFL1-4460; "Elvis
Country"): 77. . . . . **8–10**

Price Range

Note: This LP was reissued in 1981 as RCA
Victor AYL1-3956.
RCA VICTOR (LSP-4530;
"Love Letters"): 71. . . . . **$30–40**
(Orange label. Full title, "Love Letters From
Elvis," on TWO lines on front cover.)
RCA VICTOR (LSP-4530;
"Love Letters"): 71. . . . . **15–18**
(Orange label. Full title, "Love Letters From
Elvis," on THREE lines on front cover.)
RCA VICTOR (LSP-4530;
"Love Letters"): 76. . . . . **10–15**
(Tan label.)
RCA VICTOR
(AFL1-4530; "Love
Letters"): 77. . . . . **8–10**
Note: This LP was reissued in 1981 as RCA
Victor AYL1-3956.
RCA VICTOR
(AHL1-4530; "The Elvis
Medley"): 82 . . . . **8–10**
RCA VICTOR (LSP-4579;
"Wonderful World Of
Christmas"): 71 . . . . **20–25**
(Price includes a 5x7 Elvis postcard, which
represents $4-$6 of the value.)
Note: This LP was reissued in 1977 as RCA
Victor ANL1-1936.
RCA VICTOR (LSP-4671;
"Elvis Now"): 72. . . . . **50–60**
(With white titles/times sticker on front cover.
Promotional issue only.)
RCA VICTOR (LSP-4671;
"Elvis Now"): 72. . . . . **15–18**
(Orange label.)
RCA VICTOR (LSP-4671;
"Elvis Now"): 76. . . . . **10–15**
(Tan label.)
RCA VICTOR
(AFL1-4671; "Elvis
Now"): 77 . . . . **8–10**
RCA VICTOR (LSP-4690;
"He Touched Me"): 72. . . . . **50–60**
(With white titles/times sticker on front cover.
Promotional issue only.)
RCA VICTOR (LSP-4690;
"He Touched Me"): 72. . . . . **15–18**
(Orange label.)
RCA VICTOR (LSP-4690;
"He Touched Me"): 76. . . . . **10–15**
(Tan label.)

Price Range

Price Range

RCA VICTOR
(AFL1-4690; "He
Touched Me"): *77* **$5–8**

RCA VICTOR (4678; "I
Was The One"): *83* **5–8**

RCA VICTOR (LSP-4776;
"Madison Square
Garden"): *72* **50–60**
(Orange label. With white programming stickers applied to front cover. Promotional issue only.)

RCA VICTOR (LSP-4776;
"Madison Square
Garden"): *72* **15–18**
(Orange label.)

RCA VICTOR (LSP-4776;
"Madison Square
Garden"): *76* **10–15**
(Tan label.)

RCA VICTOR
(AQL1-4776; "Madison
Square Garden"): *77*. **5–8**
Note: A two-record promotional version of this LP was issued as RCA Victor SPS-571.

RCA VICTOR (4809; "A
Country Christmas" Vol.
2): *83* **8–10**
(Contains eight songs by eight artists, including Elvis.)

RCA VICTOR (4848;
"Legendary Performer"
Vol. 4): *83* **8–10**
(Price includes a 12-page "Memories Of The King" booklet.)

RCA VICTOR (4941;
"Elvis' Gold Records"
Vol. 5): *84* **5–8**

RCA VICTOR (5172; "A
Golden Celebration"): *84* **40–50**
(A six-LP boxed set. Price includes an envelope containing an 8x10 Elvis photo and a 50th Anniversary flyer, which represents $4-$5 of the value.)

RCA VICTOR (5172; "A
Golden Celebration"): *84* **15–20**
(Special "Advance Cassette" sampler of the boxed set.)

RCA VICTOR (5182;
"Rockers"): *84*. **5–8**

RCA VICTOR (5196;
"Elvis' Golden
Records"): *84*. **5–8**

(Digitally remastered quality mono pressing. Price includes gold "The Definitive Rock Classic" banner.)
Note: This LP was first issued as RCA Victor LPM-1707.

RCA VICTOR (5197;
"Elvis' Gold Records"
Vol. 2): *84* **$5–8**
(Digitally remastered quality mono pressing. Price includes gold "The Definitive Rock Classic" banner.)
Note: This LP was first issued as RCA Victor LPM-2075.

RCA VICTOR (5198;
"Elvis Presley"): *84*. **5–8**
(Digitally remastered quality mono pressing. Price includes gold "The Definitive Rock Classic" banner.)
Note: This LP was first issued as RCA Victor LPM-1254.

RCA VICTOR (5199;
"Elvis"): *84* **5–8**
(Digitally remastered quality mono pressing. Price includes gold "The Definitive Rock Classic" banner.)
Note: This LP was first issued as RCA Victor LPM-1382.

RCA VICTOR (5353; "A
Valentine Gift For
You"): *84* **8–10**
(Colored vinyl.)

RCA VICTOR (5353; "A
Valentine Gift For
You"): *84*. **5–8**
(Black vinyl.)

RCA VICTOR (5418;
"Reconsider Baby"): *85* **5–8**

RCA VICTOR (5430;
"Always On My Mind"):
85 .... **5–8**

RCA VICTOR (5463;
"Rock And Roll-The
Early Days"): *85* **5–8**
(Contains 12 songs by 12 artists, including Elvis.)

RCA VICTOR (5486;
"Elvis Christmas
Album"): *85*. **5–8**
(Colored vinyl.)

RCA VICTOR (5486;
"Elvis Christmas
Album"): *85*. **25–50**

Price Range

(Black vinyl. Thus far, all black vinyl copies discovered were packaged with stickers reading "pressed on green vinyl.")

RCA VICTOR (5600;
"Elvis Return Of The
Rocker")...................... **$86**

RCA VICTOR (5697;
"Special Christmas
Programming"): *67* **800–900**
(Promotional issue only.)

RCA VICTOR (5800;
"Best Of The '50s"): *86* **10–15**
(Contains 10 songs by 10 artists, including Elvis.)

RCA VICTOR (5802;
"Best Of The '60s"): *86* **10–15**
(Contains 10 songs by 10 artists, including Elvis.)

RCA VICTOR (5837;
"Best Of The '70s"): *86* **10–15**
(Contains 10 songs by 10 artists, including Elvis.)

RCA VICTOR (5838;
"Best Of The '50s, '60s
& '70s"): *86* **10–15**
(Contains 10 songs by 10 artists, including Elvis.)

RCA VICTOR (LSP-6020;
"From Memphis To
Vegas"): *69*. **25–30**
(Orange label. Price includes two 8x10 Elvis photos, which represent $5-$10 of the value.)

RCA VICTOR (LSP-6020;
"From Memphis To
Vegas"): *76*. **15–20**
(Tan label.)

RCA VICTOR (LSP-6020;
"From Memphis To
Vegas"): *77*. **10–15**
Note: Each of the two LPs in this set was reissued individually, "Elvis In Person At The International Hotel" as LSP-4428 and "Elvis Back In Memphis" as LSP-4429, both in 1970.

RCA VICTOR
(VPSX-6089; "Aloha
From Hawaii"): *73* **1000–1500**
(With "Chicken Of The Sea," Quadradisc & contents stickers on cover. Promotional in-house issue by the Van Camps Company.)

RCA VICTOR
(VPSX-6089; "Aloha
From Hawaii"): *73* **200–225**

Price Range

(With white titles/times sticker on front cover. Promotional issue only.)

RCA VICTOR
(VPSX-6089; "Aloha
From Hawaii"): *73* **$75–90**
(With Quadradisc & contents stickers on cover. Red/orange label.)

RCA VICTOR
(VPSX-6089; "Aloha
From Hawaii"): *74* **25–30**
(With Quadradisc/RCA logo in lower right corner of front cover. Titles are printed on back cover. Orange label.)

RCA VICTOR
(VPSX-6089; "Aloha
From Hawaii"): *76* **25–30**
(Tan label.)
Note: This LP was issued through the RCA Record Club as RCA Victor 213736 and was later issued in 1977 as RCA Victor CPD2-2642.

RCA VICTOR
(LPM-6401; "Worldwide
50 Gold Hits" Vol. 1):
70 .... **60–75**
(Orange label. Price includes 20-page Elvis photo booklet, which represents $10-$20 of the value. This is a four-LP boxed set.)

RCA VICTOR
(LPM-6401; "Worldwide
50 Gold Hits" Vol. 1):
76 .... **30–40**
(Tan label.)

RCA VICTOR
(LPM-6401; "Worldwide
50 Gold Hits" Vol. 1):
77 .... **20–25**

Price Range

Price Range

(Black label.)

Note: Two of the LPs in this set were repackaged for the RCA Record Club in 1974 as RCA Victor 213690 and the other two in 1978 as RCA Victor 214657.

RCA VICTOR
(LPM-6402; "Worldwide
50 Gold Hits" Vol. 2):
71 . . . . **$60–75**
(Orange label. Price includes an Elvis print and envelope with piece of material, which represents $10-$20 of the value. This is a four-LP boxed set.)

RCA VICTOR
(LPM-6402; "Worldwide
50 Gold Hits" Vol. 2):
76 . . . . **30–40**
(Tan label. With bonus items shown as included.)

RCA VICTOR
(LPM-6402; "Worldwide
50 Gold Hits" Vol. 2):
76 . . . . **25–35**
(Tan label. No bonus items shown as being included.)

RCA VICTOR
(LPM-6402; "Worldwide
50 Gold Hits" Vol. 2):
77 . . . . **20–25**
(Black label.)

Note: Two of the LPs in this set were repackaged for the RCA Record Club in 1978 as RCA Victor 214567.

RCA VICTOR (7004; "14
#1 Country Hits"): *85* **10–12**
(Contains 14 songs by 14 artists, including Elvis.)

RCA VICTOR (7013;
"The Best Of
Christmas"): *85* **8–10**
(Contains eight songs by eight artists, including Elvis.)

RCA VICTOR (7031;
"Elvis Forever"): *74* **25–35**
(A TV mail-order LP offer.)

RCA VICTOR (9681;
"E-Z Pop No. 5): *56* **250–275**
(Contains 16 songs by 12 different artists, including two by Elvis. Promotional issue only. The other side of this LP is numbered 9682.)

RCA VICTOR (7065; "A
Canadian Tribute"): *78* **10–12**

(Price includes photo inner-sleeve, which represents $2-$3 of the value. Canadian issues of this LP had the same number but are clearly marked on back cover as Canadian.)

RCA VICTOR (213690;
"Worldwide 50 Gold
Hits" Parts 1&2): *74* **$75–100**
(Orange label. RCA Record Club issue only.)

RCA VICTOR (213690;
"Worldwide 50 Gold
Hits" Parts 1&2): *76* **25–30**
(Tan label. RCA Record Club issue only.)

RCA VICTOR (213690;
"Worldwide 50 Gold
Hits" Parts 1&2): *77* **12–15**
(Black label. RCA Record Club issue only.)
Note: The two discs in this set were first issued as half of RCA Victor LPM-6401.

RCA VICTOR (213736;
"Aloha From Hawaii"):
73 . . . . **45–55**
(Orange label.)

RCA VICTOR (213736;
"Aloha From Hawaii"):
76 . . . . **18–20**
(Tan label.)

RCA VICTOR (214657;
"Worldwide 50 Gold
Hits" Parts 3&4): *78* **12–15**
(RCA Record Club issue only.)
Note: The two discs in this set were first issued as half of RCA Victor LPM-6401.

RCA VICTOR (233299;
"Country Classics"): *80* **20–25**
(RCA Record Club issue only.)

RCA VICTOR (234340;
"From Elvis With
Love"): *78* **20–25**
(RCA Record Club issue only.)

RCA VICTOR (244047;
"Legendary Concert
Performances"): *78* **20–25**
(RCA Record Club issue only.)

RCA VICTOR (244069;
"Country Memories"):
78 . . . . **20–25**
(RCA Record Club issue only.)

REBIRTH OF BEALE
ST. (1; "Rebirth Of
Beale St."): *83* **125–175**

Price Range

(Limited edition, individually numbered, release by The City Of Memphis, containing 16 songs by 10 artists, including two by Elvis. Includes eight-page color booklet. Promotional issue only.)

RHINO (71103; "The Sun
  Story"): *86* **$8–12**
  (A two-LP set, containing 27 songs by 15 artists, including two by Elvis. Also includes booklet.)

SSS-SHELBY
SINGLETON MUSIC
  (1; "Songs For The
  Seventies"): *69* **300–325**
  (A two-LP set containing 48 songs by 34 artists, including one by Elvis. Price includes a 66-page songbook, which represents $50-$75 of the value. Promotional issue only.)

SCANA (27022; "White
  Christmas, Volume 1"):
  86 . . . . **10–15**
  (Contains 10 songs by six artists, including one by Elvis. A German import that was widely distributed in the U.S.)

SCANA (27023; "White
  Christmas, Volume 2"):
  86 . . . . **10–15**
  (Contains 10 songs by six artists, including one by Elvis. A German import that was widely distributed in the U.S.)

SILHOUETTE (10001/
  10002; "Personally
  Elvis"): *79* **18–20**

STARDAY (995;
  "Interviews With Elvis"):
  78 . . . . **40–50**
  (These interviews were previously issued on Great Northwest 4005.)

SUN (1001; "The Sun
  Years"): *77* **75–80**
  (Light yellow label with "Memphis" at bottom. Light yellow cover with light brown printing.)

SUN (1001; "The Sun
  Years"): *77* **15–20**
  (Darker yellow label with four target circles. Dark yellow cover with dark brown printing.)

SUN (1001; "The Sun
  Years"): *77* **25–30**
  (White cover with brown printing.) *

SUNRISE MEDIA: see
  PRESLEY, Elvis / Hank
  Williams

Price Range

THE GOODMAN
  GROUP (1: "Just Let
  Me Hear Some Of That
  Rock'N'Roll Music"): *79* **$100-150**
  (A two-LP set containing excerpts of 100 songs, including three by Elvis. Promotional issue only.)

THE LOWERY GROUP
  (1; "25 Golden Years"):
  80 . . . . **40–60**
  (A two-LP set containing 25 songs by 21 artists, including one by Elvis. Promotional issue only.)

THE MUSIC WORKS
  (3601; "The First Live
  Recordings"): *84* **8–10**
  Note: This material was first issued on Louisiana Hayride 3061.

THE MUSIC WORKS
  (3602; "The Hillbilly
  Cat"): *84* **8–10**
  Note: This material was first issued on Louisiana Hayride 3061.

THE UNITED
  STATIONS (April 8-12,
  1985; "Solid Gold
  Country"): *85* **20–25**
  (A five-LP boxed set, of which one LP, for April 10th, is devoted to Elvis. Price includes six pages of script & information and a "Proof Of Broadcasting" reply card. The Elvis LP is worth $15-$20 by itself.)

THE WELK MUSIC
  GROUP (3002; "Blue
  Christmas"): *84* **60–75**

Price Range

(Contains 15 versions of "Blue Christmas" by 15 artists, including Elvis. Also includes five other Christmas tunes, but none by Elvis. Promotional issue only.)

THE WORLD OF ELVIS
PRESLEY: *83* **$50–75**
(A one-hour weekly radio show, on discs numbered program 1 through program 30. The show ceased operation after 30 programs. Each disc was accompanied by a single cue sheet. Price is for any one of the discs.)

TIME-LIFE (106;
"Country Music"): *81* **35–45**

TIME-LIFE (106; "Elvis
Presley: 1954-1961"): *85* **15–18**
(A two-LP boxed set, part of the "Rock'N'Roll Era" series of sets available from Time-Life by mail-order. The other LPs in this series did not feature Elvis. Includes fold-open brochure.)

TIME-LIFE (107; "The
Time-Life Treasury Of
Christmas"): *85* **15–20**
(A two-LP boxed set containing 45 songs by 33 artists, including two by Elvis.)

UNITED
DISTRIBUTORS: see
PRESLEY, Elvis / The
Beatles

WATERMARK ("The
Elvis Presley Story,"
1975): *75* **800–900**
(A 13-LP set. White label with pink letters. Price includes a 48-page operations manual, which represents about $100 of the value. Promotional issue only. Not issued with a special cover or package.)

WATERMARK ("The
Elvis Presley Story,"
1977): *77* **700–800**
(A 13-LP set. White label with pink letters. Price includes a 48-page operations manual, which represents about $100 of the value. Promotional issue only. Not issued with a special cover or package.)

WESTWOOD ONE ("A
Golden Celebration"): *84* **200–250**
(A three-LP boxed set. Price includes instructions and cue sheets, which represent $10-$15 of the value. Issued to radio stations only.)

Price Range

Notes: Prefix letters or numbers are used on some LP listings in order to more quickly identify the variations available...You'll notice a slight price difference in some similar recent releases from the same period of time. This is because some titles are currently available whereas others have now been deleted...A few items that have no label name are listed by title, such as the International Hotel boxed sets...LPs that have a sticker applied over the catalog number should be considered as the same as those without the sticker...Beginning in 1961, many Elvis LPs had a separate sticker, applied to the wrap or directly on the cover, promoting such things as certain songs or bonus photos. When not listed separately in this edition, a premium of 10%-15% could be placed on LPs with these original stickers...Several LPs were pressed on the RCA "Dog Near Top" label using the older LSP prefix, prior to being switched to the AFL1 series. These are not listed separately since there seems to be no price difference between the two.

Also see AUDREY
Also see BLACK, Bill
Also see BLOSSOMS, The
Also see CRICKETS, The
Also see DONNER, Ral
Also see HARRIS, Emmylou
Also see KENNEDY, Jerry
Also see MOORE, Bob
Also see RANDOLPH, Boots
Also see REDDY, Helen
Also see SINATRA, Nancy
Also see SWEET INSPIRATIONS, The

PRESLEY, Elvis / The Beatles
LPs: 10/12-Inch 33rpm
UNITED
DISTRIBUTORS (2382;
"Lightning Strikes
Twice"): *81* **$25–50**
(Promotional issue only. Contains five songs by each artist.)
Also see BEATLES, The

PRESLEY, Elvis / Hank Williams
LPs: 10/12-Inch 33rpm
SUNRISE MEDIA (3011;
"History Of Country
Music"): *81* **10–15**
(Contains four songs by each artist.)
Also see PRESLEY, Elvis
Also see WILLIAMS, Hank

Price Range

Price Range

PRESLEY, Elvis
Singles: 7-Inch
ELVIS CLASSIC (5478;
"Tell Me Pretty Baby"):
78 .... **$2–4**
(Despite being labeled as a 1954 recording by
Elvis Presley, this track was nothing more than
a 1978 recording by a singer performing in an
Elvis style, and is listed separately here to elimi-
nate confusion. It definitely is NOT Elvis Pres-
ley!)

Picture Sleeves
ELVIS CLASSIC (5478;
"Tell Me Pretty Baby"):
78 .... **4–6**
(Sleeve pictures an artist's sketch of Elvis Pres-
ley.)

PRESSURE
Singles: 7-Inch
LAX: 79–80 .... **1–3**
LPs: 10/12-Inch 33rpm
LAX: 79 .... **5–8**

PRESSURE DROP
Singles: 12-Inch 33/45rpm
TOMMY BOY: 82 .... **4–6**
Singles: 7-Inch
TOMMY BOY: 82 .... **1–3**

PRESTON, Billy
Singles: 12-Inch 33/45rpm
MEGATONE: 84 .... **4–6**
MONTAGE: 84 .... **4–6**
Singles: 7-Inch
A&M: 72–78 .... **2–4**
APPLE: 69–72 .... **3–5**
CAPITOL: 66–69 .... **3–5**
CONTRACT: 61 .... **8–10**
MOTOWN: 79–82 .... **1–3**
VEE JAY: 65 .... **5–8**
Picture Sleeves
A&M: 73–75 .... **2–4**
APPLE: 69 .... **3–5**
LPs: 10/12-Inch 33rpm
A&M: 71–82 .... **6–10**
APPLE: 69–70 .... **10–15**
BUDDAH: 69 .... **10–12**
CAPITOL (ST series): 66 .... **10–15**
CAPITOL (SM series): 75 .... **6–10**
DERBY: 63 .... **40–50**

EXODUS: 65 .... **$12–15**
GNP/CRESCENDO: 73 .... **10–12**
MOTOWN: 79–82 .... **5–8**
MYRRH: 78 .... **5–8**
PEACOCK: 73 .... **8–10**
SPRINGBOARD: 78 .... **5–8**
TRIP: 73 .... **8–10**
VEE JAY: 65 .... **15–20**
Also see BEATLES, The
Also see MOTHERS OF INVENTION, The

PRESTON, Billy, & Syreeta
Singles: 7-Inch
MOTOWN: 79–81 .... **1–3**
TAMLA: 80 .... **1–3**

LPs: 10/12-Inch 33rpm
MOTOWN: 79–81 .... **5–8**
Also see PRESTON, Billy
Also see SYREETA

PRESTON, Johnny
Singles: 7-Inch
ABC: 68–73 .... **2–4**
HALL/HALL WAY:
64–66 .... **3–5**
IMPERIAL: 63 .... **3–5**
MERCURY: 59–62 .... **4–6**
TCF: 65 .... **3–5**

Picture Sleeves
MERCURY: 60–62 .... **4–8**

EPs: 7-Inch 33/45rpm
MERCURY: 60 .... **15–20**

LPs: 10/12-Inch 33rpm
MERCURY (Black label):
60–61 .... **40–50**
MERCURY (Chicago
"Skyline" label): 81 .... **5–8**
WING: 63 .... **15–20**
Also see BIG BOPPER, The

PRESTON, Mike
Singles: 7-Inch
LONDON: 58–63 .... **3–5**

PRESTON, Terry (Ferlin Husky)
Singles: 7-Inch
CAPITOL: 52–53 .... **5–10**
Also see HUSKY, Ferlin

Price Range

PRETENDERS, The (Featuring Chrissie Hynde)
Singles: 7-Inch
SIRE: *80–83* **$1–3**
Picture Sleeves
SIRE: *80–83* **1–3**
LPs: 10/12-Inch 33rpm
SIRE: *80–84* **5–8**
Also see UB40

PRETTY BOY (Don Covay; With Johnny Fuller's Band)
Singles: 7-Inch
ATLANTIC: *57* **25–30**
BIG: *57* **25–30**
Also see COVAY, Don

PRETTY POISON
Singles: 12-Inch 33/45rpm
MONTAGE: *84*. **4–6**
SVENGALI: *84*. **4–6**
Singles: 7-Inch
MONTAGE: *84*. **1–3**
SVENGALI: *84*. **1–3**

PRETTY THINGS, The
Singles: 7-Inch
FONTANA: *64–66*. **5–8**
LAURIE: *68* **3–5**
SWAN SONG: *75–76*. **2–3**
LPs: 10/12-Inch 33rpm
FONTANA: *66*. **25–30**
MOTOWN: *76*. **10–12**
RARE EARTH (506; "S.F. Sorrow"): *69*. **20–25**
RARE EARTH (515; "Parachute"): *70* **15–20**
SIRE: *76* **8–10**
SWAN SONG: *75–76*. **8–10**
WARNER BROS: *73–80* **8–10**
Also see GREEN, Jack

PRETTY TONY (Tony Butler)
Singles: 7-Inch
MUSIC: *84* **1–3**

PREVIN, Andre (Andre Previn & David Rose's Orchestra)
Singles: 7-Inch
COLUMBIA: *60–64*. **2–4**
DECCA: *61*. **2–4**

Price Range

MGM: *59*. **$2–4**
RCA VICTOR: *67* **2–3**
EPs: 7-Inch 33/45rpm
MGM: *59*. **4–8**
LPs: 10/12-Inch 33rpm
ALLEGIANCE: *84*. **5–8**
ANGEL: *80–81*. **5–8**
ASCOT (505; "Two For The Seesaw"): *64*. **15–25**
(Soundtrack.)
CAMDEN: *64*. **5–10**
COLUMBIA: *60–65* **10–20**
CONTEMPORARY: *57–60* **15–30**
DECCA (4000 series): *61–63* **8–15**
(Decca LP numbers in this series preceded by a "7" or a "DL-7" are stereo issues.)
DECCA (8000 series): *55–56* **20–40**
EVEREST: *70* **5–10**
HARMONY: *67* **5–10**
MGM: *59–64* **10–15**
METRO JAZZ: *59* **10–20**
MONARCH: *54* **20–40**
(10-Inch LPs.)
ODYSSEY: *68*. **8–12**
RCA VICTOR (1000 series): *75* **5–10**
(With an "ARL1" prefix.)
RCA VICTOR (1000 series): *54* **20–45**
(With an "LPM" prefix.)
RCA VICTOR (1300 series): *56* **20–30**
RCA VICTOR (2900 series): *67* **6–12**
RCA VICTOR (3000 series): *52* **30–60**
(10-Inch LPs.)
RCA VICTOR (3400 through 3800 series): *65–67* **6–12**
20TH CENTURY-FOX (165; "Goodbye Charlie"): *65* **25–30**
(Soundtrack.)
UNITED ARTISTS (103; "Two For The Seesaw"): *62* **25–35**
(Soundtrack.)

Price Range

UNITED ARTISTS (145;
"The Fortune Cookie"):
66 .... **$15–25**
(Soundtrack.)
UNITED ARTISTS (5200
series): 71 .... **5–10**
VERVE: 63 .... **10–15**
WARNER BROS. (1536;
"Dead Ringer"): 64 .... **25–35**
(Soundtrack.)
Also see DAY, Doris, & Andre Previn
Also see ROSE, David
Also see SHORE, Dinah, & Andre Previn

PREVIN, Andre, & Diahann Carroll
Singles: 7-Inch
UNITED ARTISTS: 60 .... **3–5**
LPs: 10/12-Inch 33rpm
UNITED ARTISTS: 60 .... **10–20**
Also see PREVIN, Andre

PREYER, Ron
Singles: 7-Inch
SHOCK: 78 .... **2–3**

PRICE, Alan (The Alan Price Set)
Singles: 7-Inch
COTILLION: 69 .... **3–5**
EPIC: 84 .... **1–3**
JET: 77–79 .... **2–3**
PARROT: 66–68 .... **4–6**
WARNER BROS: 72 .... **2–4**
LPs: 10/12-Inch 33rpm
ACCORD: 82 .... **5–8**
JET: 77–80 .... **8–10**
PARROT: 68 .... **15–20**
TOWNHOUSE: 81 .... **5–8**
WARNER BROS: 74 .... **8–10**
Also see ANIMALS, The

**PRICE, Lloyd (The Lloyd Price
Orchestra; Lloyd Price & The Dukes)**
Singles: 7-Inch
ABC: 67–73 .... **1–3**
ABC-PARAMOUNT
(Except stereo singles):
57–60 .... **4–6**
ABC-PARAMOUNT
(Stereo singles): 59 .... **10–12**
COLLECTABLES **1–3**
DOUBLE-L: 63–66 .... **3–5**
GSF: 72–73 .... **2–4**

Price Range

JAD: 68 .... **$2–4**
KRC (Except 587): 57–59 .... **5–8**
KRC (587; "Just
Because"): 57 .... **35–40**
LPG: 76 .... **2–3**
MCA **1–3**
MONUMENT: 64–65 .... **3–5**
PARAMOUNT: 72 .... **2–4**
REPRISE: 66 .... **3–5**
ROULETTE **1–3**
SCEPTER: 71 .... **2–4**
SPECIALTY (400 series):
52–54 .... **15–20**
(Black vinyl.)
SPECIALTY (400 series):
53–54 .... **30–35**
(Colored vinyl.)
SPECIALTY (500 series):
55–56 .... **10–15**
SPECIALTY (600 series):
59 .... **3–6**
TURNTABLE: 69 .... **2–4**
Picture Sleeves
DOUBLE-L: 64 .... **5–8**
EPs: 7-Inch 33/45rpm
ABC-PARAMOUNT:
59–60 .... **15–20**
LPs: 10/12-Inch 33rpm
ABC: 72–76 .... **8–10**
ABC-PARAMOUNT:
59–61 .... **25–35**
DOUBLE-L: 63 .... **20–25**
GRAND PRIX **10–12**
GUEST STAR **10–12**
JAD: 69 .... **10–12**
MCA: 82 .... **5–8**
MONUMENT: 65 .... **10–15**
SPECIALTY (2100 series):
59 .... **25–30**
(Specialty LP reissues, using original catalog
numbers, are currently available.)
TRIP: 76 .... **8–10**
TURNTABLE: 69 .... **8–10**
UPFRONT **8–10**
Also see COOKE, Sam / Lloyd Price / Larry
Williams
Also see DOMINO, Fats

PRICE, Priscilla
Singles: 7-Inch
BASF: 73 .... **2–4**

Price Range

PRICE, Ray (Ray Price & The Cherokee Cowboys)
Singles: 7-Inch
ABC: *75* $2–3
ABC/DOT: *75–77* 1–3
COLUMBIA (10000
    series): *74–77* 1–3
COLUMBIA (20000 &
    21000 series): *52–56* 4–8
COLUMBIA (40000
    through 43000 series):
    57–66 3–5
COLUMBIA (44000
    through 45000 series):
    67–73 2–4
DIMENSION: *81–82* 1–3
MONUMENT: *78–79* 1–3
MYRRH: *74–75* 1–3
STEP ONE: *85* 1–3
WARNER BROS: *82–83* 1–3
WORD: *78* 1–3
Picture Sleeves
COLUMBIA: *66* 2–5
EPs: 7-Inch 33/45rpm
COLUMBIA: *53–60* 10–18
LPs: 10/12-Inch 33rpm
ABC/DOT: *75–77* 6–10
COLUMBIA (28; "The
    World Of Ray Price"):
    70 8–12
COLUMBIA (1015; "Ray
    Price Sings Heart
    Songs"): *57* 30–40
COLUMBIA (1148; "Talk
    To Your Heart"): *58* 25–35
COLUMBIA (1400
    through 2600 series):
    60–67 10–25
    (Monaural issues.)
COLUMBIA (8200
    through 9400 series):
    60–67 10–25
    (Stereo issues.)
COLUMBIA (9700
    through 9900 series):
    68–70 8–12
COLUMBIA (10000
    series): *73* 5–10
COLUMBIA (30000
    through 37000 series):
    70–81 5–10

Price Range

DIMENSION: *81* $5–8
51 WEST: *84* 5–8
HARMONY: *66–71* 8–15
MONUMENT: *79* 5–8
MYRRH: *74* 5–8
RADIANT: *81* 5–8
WARNER BROS: *83* 5–8
WORD: *77* 5–8
    Also see ROBBINS, Marty / Johnny Cash /
    Ray Price

PRICE, Ray / Lefty Frizzell / Carl Smith
LPs: 10/12-Inch 33rpm
COLUMBIA (1200 series):
    59 15–25
COLUMBIA (8700 series):
    63 12–18
    Also see FRIZZELL, Lefty
    Also see SMITH, Carl

PRICE, Ray, & Willie Nelson
Singles: 7-Inch
COLUMBIA: *80* 1–3

LPs: 10/12-Inch 33rpm
COLUMBIA: *80* 5–8
    Also see NELSON, Willie
    Also see PRICE, Ray

PRIDE, Charley (Country Charley Pride; Charley Pride & The Pridesmen)
Singles: 7-Inch
RCA VICTOR (0100
    through 0500 series):
    66–69 2–4
RCA VICTOR (0600
    through 0900 series):
    72–73 1–3
RCA VICTOR (8700 &
    8800 series): *66* 3–5
RCA VICTOR (9000
    through 9900 series):
    66–71 2–4
RCA VICTOR (10000
    series): *74–85* 1–3

Picture Sleeves
RCA VICTOR: *71–74* 2–4

Price Range

Price Range

LPs: 10/12-Inch 33rpm
RCA VICTOR (Except
LPM/LSP 3700 through
4800 series): *74–84* $5–10
RCA VICTOR (3700
through 4800 series):
66–73 8–18
(With an "LPM" or "LSP" prefix.)
Also see DAVE & SUGAR
Also see MANCINI, Henry, & Charley Pride

PRIMA, Louis (Louis Prima & His Orchestra)
Singles: 7-Inch
ABC: *68–74* 1–3
BUENA VISTA: *66–74* 1–3
CAPITOL: *62* 2–4
COLUMBIA: *52–53* 3–5
DECCA: *54* 2–4
DOT: *59–62* 2–4
HBR: *66* 2–3
KAMA SUTRA: *66* 2–3
MERCURY: *50* 3–5
PRIMA: *63–64* 2–4
ROBIN HOOD: *50* 3–6
SAVOY: *53* 3–5
UNITED ARTISTS: *67* 1–3

EPs: 7-Inch 33/45rpm
CAPITOL: *56* 4–8
JUBILEE: *55* 5–8
VARSITY: *54* 5–10

LPs: 10/12-Inch 33rpm
BUENA VISTA: *65–74* 8–18
CAPITOL: *56–62* 8–18
DE-LITE: *68* 5–10
DOT: *60* 10–15
HBR: *66* 5–12
HAMILTON: *65* 5–10
MERCURY (25000 series):
53 15–30
(10-Inch LPs.)
PRIMA: *72–76* 5–8
RONDO/RONDOLETTE:
59 10–20
UNITED ARTISTS: *67* 5–10

PRIMA, Louis, & Keely Smith
Singles: 7-Inch
CAPITOL: *58–59* 2–4
DOT: *59–61* 2–4

Picture Sleeves
DOT: *59* $2–4
EPs: 7-Inch 33/45rpm
CAPITOL: *58* 4–8
DOT: *60* 3–6
LPs: 10/12-Inch 33rpm
CAPITOL: *75* 5–8
(With an "SM" prefix.)
CAPITOL: *58–61* 10–20
(With a "T" or "ST" prefix.)
DOT: *59–60* 10–20
Also see SMITH, Keely

PRIMETTES, The (The Supremes)
Singles: 7-Inch
LUPINE: *61* 200–225
Also see SUPREMES, The

PRINCE (Prince & The Revolution)
Singles: 12-Inch 33/45rpm
PAISLEY PARK: *85–86* 4–6
WARNER BROS: *78–85* 4–6
Promotional 12-Inch Singles
PAISLEY PARK: *85–86* 5–8
WARNER BROS (Black
vinyl): *78–85* 5–8
WARNER BROS (Colored
vinyl): *85* 10–15
Singles: 7-Inch
PAISLEY PARK: *85–86* 1–3
WARNER BROS: *78–85* 1–3
Picture Sleeves
PAISLEY PARK: *85–86* 1–3
WARNER BROS: *80–85* 1–3
LPs: 10/12-Inch 33rpm
PAISLEY PARK: *85–86* 5–8
WARNER BROS (Black
vinyl): *78–85* 5–8
WARNER BROS (Colored
vinyl): *84* 15–20
Also see E., Sheila

PRINCE BUSTER (Prince Buster & The Sea Busters)
Singles: 7-Inch
AMY: *64* 3–5
ATLANTIC: *64* 3–5
PHILIPS: *67* 3–5
RCA VICTOR: *67* 3–5
STELLAR: *64* 3–5

Price Range

Price Range

LPs: 10/12-Inch 33rpm
RCA VICTOR: 67 . . . . $10–15

PRINCE HAROLD
Singles: 7-Inch
MERCURY: 66 3–5
SPRING: 67 3–5
VERVE: 67 3–5

PRINCE LA LA
Singles: 7-Inch
AFO: 61–62 4–6

PRINCESS
Singles: 12-Inch 33/45rpm
NEXT PLATINUM: 85 4–6

PRINCIPLE, Jamie
Singles: 12-Inch 33/45rpm
PERSONA: 85 4–6

PRINE, John
Singles: 7-Inch
ASYLUM: 78 2–3
ATLANTIC: 71–75 2–4
LPs: 10/12-Inch 33rpm
ASYLUM: 78–80 5–8
ATLANTIC: 71–76 8–10

PRISCILLA: see
COOLIDGE-JONES, Priscilla

PRISM
Singles: 7-Inch
ARIOLA AMERICA:
  77–79 2–3
CAPITOL: 82 1–3
LPs: 10/12-Inch 33rpm
ARIOLA AMERICA:
  77–79 10–12
CAPITOL: 80–82 5–8
Promotional LPs
ARIOLA AMERICA
  (50034; "Live Tonite"):
  78 15–20

PROBY, P.J.
Singles: 7-Inch
IMPERIAL: 64 3–5
LIBERTY: 61–68 3–5

LONDON: 64 . . . . $3–5
SURFSIDE: 65 3–5
Picture Sleeves
LIBERTY: 67 3–5
LPs: 10/12-Inch 33rpm
LIBERTY: 65–68 15–20
Also see FOCUS & P.J. PROBY

PROCESS & THE DOO RAGS
Singles: 7-Inch
COLUMBIA: 85 1–3

PROCOL HARUM (With Gary
Brooker & Robin Trower)
Singles: 7-Inch
A&M: 67–72 3–5
CHRYSALIS: 74–77 2–4
DERAM: 67 3–5
Picture Sleeves
A&M: 72 3–5
LPs: 10/12-Inch 33rpm
A&M (Except 4294 &
  8053): 68–73 8–12
A&M (4294; "Broken
  Barricades"): 71 12–15
  (With die-cut gatefold cover.)
A&M (4294; "Broken
  Barricades"): 72 10–12
  (With standard cover.)
A&M (8053; "Procol
  Harum Lives") 15–25
CHRYSALIS: 73–77 8–10
DERAM: 67 25–30
Also see TROWER, Robin

PRODUCERS, The
Singles: 7-Inch
PORTRAIT: 81–82 1–3
LPs: 10/12-Inch 33rpm
PORTRAIT: 81–82 5–8

PROFESSOR FUNK & HIS
EIGHTH STREET FUNK BAND
Singles: 7-Inch
ROXBURY: 73 2–3

PROFESSOR MORRISON'S
LOLLIPOP: see MORRISON,
Professor

Price Range

PROFILES, The
Singles: 7-Inch
BAMBOO: 69 . . . . $2–4
DUO: 68 3–5

PROJECT FUTURE
Singles: 12-Inch 33/45rpm
CAPITOL: 83 4–6
Singles: 7-Inch
CAPITOL: 83 1–3

PROPHECY
Singles: 7-Inch
MAINSTREAM: 75 2–3

PROPHETS, Thee: see THEE PROPHETS

PROTHEROE, Brian
Singles: 7-Inch
CHRYSALIS: 75 2–3
LPs: 10/12-Inch 33rpm
CHRYSALIS: 75–76 8–10

PROVINE, Dorothy
Singles: 7-Inch
WARNER BROS: 61 2–4
LPs: 10/12-Inch 33rpm
WARNER BROS: 60–61 10–20

PROVINE, Dorothy, & Joe "Fingers" Carr
LPs: 10/12-Inch 33rpm
WARNER BROS: 60–62 10–20
Also see CARR, Joe "Fingers"
Also see PROVINE, Dorothy

PRUETT, Jeanne (Jean Pruett)
Singles: 7-Inch
AUDIOGRAPH: 83 1–3
DECCA: 68–72 2–3
IBC: 79–80 1–3
MCA: 73–77 1–3
MERCURY: 78 1–3
PAID: 81 1–3
RCA VICTOR: 63–64 2–4
LPs: 10/12-Inch 33rpm
ALLEGIANCE: 84 5–8
AUDIOGRAPH: 83 5–8
DECCA: 72 8–10

IBC: 79 . . . . $5–8
MCA: 73–75 4–8
OUT OF TOWN DIST: 82 5–8
Also see ROBBINS, Marty, & Jeanne Pruett

PRYOR, Richard
Singles: 7-Inch
LAFF: 80 1–3
WARNER BROS: 76–79 1–3
LPs: 10/12-Inch 33rpm
DOVE: 68 8–15
LAFF: 71–81 5–10
PARTEE: 74 5–10
REPRISE: 68–77 5–12
TIGER LILY: 77 5–10
WARNER BROS: 76–85 5–10

PRYSOCK, Arthur
Singles: 7-Inch
BETHLEHEM: 72 1–3
DECCA (25000 series): 65 2–5
DECCA (27000 through
  29000 series): 52–54 4–8
DECCA (31000 series):
  64–65 2–5
GUSTO: 79 1–3
KING: 69–71 2–4
MCA: 78 1–3
MERCURY: 54–55 4–6
OLD TOWN (100 series):
  73–76 1–3
OLD TOWN (1000 series):
  59–60 3–5
  (Light blue label.)
OLD TOWN (1000 series):
  76–77 1–3
  (Dark blue or black label.)
OLD TOWN (1100 series):
  61–66 2–5
VERVE: 66–69 2–4
LPs: 10/12-Inch 33rpm
DECCA: 64–65 10–20
KING: 69–71 8–12
MCA: 78 5–8
MGM: 70 2–3
OLD TOWN (100 series):
  60–62 20–30
OLD TOWN (2000 series):
  62–65 15–25
OLD TOWN (12000
  series): 73–77 6–10

Price Range   *Price Range*

POLYDOR: *77* **$5–8**
VERVE: *66–69* **10–18**
   Also see JOHNSON, Buddy

PRYSOCK, Arthur, & Count Basie
Singles: 7-Inch
VERVE: *66* **2–4**
LPs: 10/12-Inch 33rpm
VERVE: *66* **10–20**
   Also see BASIE, Count
   Also see PRYSOCK, Arthur

PSYCHEDELIC FURS
Singles: 12-Inch 33/45rpm
COLUMBIA: *84–85* **4–6**
Singles: 7-Inch
COLUMBIA: *80–85* **1–3**
LPs: 10/12-Inch 33rpm
COLUMBIA: *80–85* **5–8**
   Members: Tim Butler; Richard Butler; John
   Ashton; Mars Williams; Paul Garisto; Marty
   Williamson.

PUBLIC IMAGE LTD.
LPs: 10/12-Inch 33rpm
ISLAND: *80* **8–10**
WARNER BROS: *81* **8–10**
   Also see SEX PISTOLS, The

PUCKETT, Gary (Gary Puckett & The Union Gap; The Union Gap Featuring Gary Puckett)
Singles: 7-Inch
COLUMBIA: *67–72* **3–5**
Picture Sleeves
COLUMBIA: *67–69* **4–6**
LPs: 10/12-Inch 33rpm
BACK-TRAC: *85* **5–8**
COLUMBIA: *68–71* **10–15**
HARMONY: *72* **8–10**

PULLINS, Leroy
Singles: 7-Inch
KAPP: *66* **2–4**

PUMPKIN (Pumpkin & The Profile All-Stars)
Singles: 12-Inch 33/45rpm
PROFILE: *84* **4–6**
Singles: 7-Inch
PROFILE: *84* **1–3**

PUPPETS, The
Singles: 12-Inch 33/45rpm
QUALITY/RFC: *84* **$4–6**
Singles: 7-Inch
QUALITY/RFC: *84* **1–3**

PURDIE, Pretty (Bernard Purdie)
Singles: 7-Inch
COLUMBIA: *69* **2–4**
DATE: *67–68.* **3–5**
LPs: 10/12-Inch 33rpm
DATE: *67* **10–15**
FLYING DUTCHMAN:
73 . . . . **8–10**
PRESTIGE: *71* **8–10**

PURE ENERGY
Singles: 12-Inch 33/45rpm
PRISM: *80–84* **4–6**
Singles: 7-Inch
PRISM: *80–84* **1–3**

PURE LOVE & PLEASURE
Singles: 7-Inch
DUNHILL: *70.* **2–4**
LPs: 10/12-Inch 33rpm
DUNHILL: *70.* **10–12**

PURE PRAIRIE LEAGUE
Singles: 7-Inch
RCA VICTOR: *72–79* **2–3**
CASABLANCA: *80–81* **1–3**
EPIC: *77* **2–3**
LPs: 10/12-Inch 33rpm
CASABLANCA: *80–81* **5–8**
RCA VICTOR: *72–80* **8–10**
   Also see AMERICAN FLYER

PURIFY, James & Bobby
Singles: 7-Inch
BELL: *66–69* **3–5**
CASABLANCA: *74–75* **2–3**
MERCURY: *76–77.* **2–3**
LPs: 10/12-Inch 33rpm
BELL: *66–67* **12–15**
MERCURY: *77.* **8–10**
   Members: James Purify; Bobby Dickey.

PURIM, Flora
LPs: 10/12-Inch 33rpm
MILESTONE: *75–77* **5–10**

Price Range

WARNER BROS: *78* **$5–8**

PURPLE REIGN
Singles: 7-Inch
GO-RILLA: *75* **3–5**
PRIVATE STOCK: *75*. **2–4**

PURSELL, Bill
Singles: 7-Inch
COLUMBIA: *62–66* **2–3**
DOT: *69*. **1–3**
EPIC: *67* **1–3**
LPs: 10/12-Inch 33rpm
COLUMBIA: *63–65* **5–15**

PUSHE
Singles: 12-Inch 33/45rpm
PARTYTYME: *84* **4–6**

PYRAMIDS, The
Singles: 7-Inch
BEST: *63* **8–12**
(Label makes no mention of "Distributed By London.")
BEST: *63–64* **4–6**
(Label reads "Distributed By London.")
CEDWICKE: *64* **4–6**
Picture Sleeves
BEST: *63* **8–15**
LPs: 10/12-Inch 33rpm
BEST: *64* **50–60**
WHAT: *83*. **5–8**

PYTHON LEE JACKSON (With Rod Stewart)
Singles: 7-Inch
GNP/CRESCENDO: *72* **3–5**
LPs: 10/12-Inch 33rpm
GNP/CRESCENDO: *72* **10–15**
Also see SMALL FACES
Also see STEWART, Rod

Q

Q
Singles: 7-Inch
EPIC: *77* **2–3**
LPs: 10/12-Inch 33rpm
EPIC: *77* **8–10**
Members: Robert Peckman & Don Garvin.

Price Range

Also see JAGGERZ, The

QUADRANT SIX
Singles: 12-Inch 33/45rpm
ATLANTIC: *83* **$4–6**
Singles: 7-Inch
ATLANTIC: *83* **1–3**

QUAITE, Christine
Singles: 7-Inch
WORLD ARTISTS: *64* **3–5**

QUAKER CITY BOYS, The
Singles: 7-Inch
SWAN: *58–59* **4–6**

QUANDO QUANDO
Singles: 12-Inch 33/45rpm
FACTORY: *83* **4–6**

QUARTER NOTES, The
Singles: 7-Inch
DOT: *57*. **5–8**
GUYDEN: *63* **4–6**
IMPERIAL: *60*. **4–6**
RCA VICTOR: *58* **4–6**
WIZZ: *59*. **5–8**

QUARTERFLASH
Singles: 12-Inch 33/45rpm
GEFFEN: *81–82*. **4–6**
Singles: 7-Inch
GEFFEN: *81–85*. **1–3**
WARNER BROS: *82*. **1–3**
LPs: 10/12-Inch 33rpm
GEFFEN: *81–85*. **5–8**

QUARTERMAN, Joe, & Free Soul
Singles: 7-Inch
MERCURY: *74*. **2–4**

QUARTZ
Singles: 7-Inch
MARLIN: *78*. **2–3**
POLYDOR: *79* **1–3**
LPs: 10/12-Inch 33rpm
POLYDOR: *79* **5–8**

QUATEMAN, Bill
Singles: 7-Inch
COLUMBIA: *72–73* **2–4**

Price Range

RCA VICTOR: *77–78* $2–3
LPs: 10/12-Inch 33rpm
COLUMBIA: *73* 8–10
RCA VICTOR: *77–78* 5–8

QUATRO, Suzi (Susie Quatro)
Singles: 7-Inch
ARISTA: *75* 2–3
BELL: *73–74* 2–4
BIG TREE: *76* 2–3
DREAMLAND: *80–81* 1–3
RAK: *72–74* 2–4
RSO: *79* 1–3
Picture Sleeves
DREAMLAND: *80* .... INC
LPs: 10/12-Inch 33rpm
ARISTA: *75* 8–10
BELL: *74* 10–12
DREAMLAND: *80* 5–8
RSO: *79* 5–8

QUATRO, Suzi, & Chris Norman
Singles: 7-Inch
RSO: *79* 1–3
Also see QUATRO, Suzi
Also see SMOKIE

QUAZAR
Singles: 7-Inch
ARISTA: *78* 2–3
LPs: 10/12-Inch 33rpm
ARISTA: *78* 5–8

QUEEN
Singles: 12-Inch 33/45rpm
CAPITOL: *84–85* 4–6
Singles: 7-Inch
CAPITOL: *84–85* 1–3
ELEKTRA: *74–82* 2–4
Picture Sleeves
ELEKTRA: *77–82* 2–4
LPs: 10/12-Inch 33rpm
CAPITOL: *84* 5–8
ELEKTRA (Except 166):
73–82 6–10
ELEKTRA (166; "Jazz"):
78 40–50
(Picture disc. Promotional issue only.)
Members: Freddie Mercury; John Deacon;
Brian May; Roger Taylor.
Also see MAY, Brian

Price Range

Also see MERCURY, Freddie
Also see TAYLOR, Roger

QUEEN & DAVID BOWIE
Singles: 7-Inch
ELEKTRA: *81* $1–3
Picture Sleeves
ELEKTRA: *81* 2–3
Also see BOWIE, David
Also see QUEEN

QUEENSRYCHE
Singles: 7-Inch
EMI AMERICA: *83–84*............. 1–3
LPs: 10/12-Inch 33rpm
EMI AMERICA: *83–84*............. 5–8

? AND THE MYSTERIANS
(Question Mark & The Mysterians)
Singles: 7-Inch
ABKCO 1–3
CAMEO: *66–67*................... 4–6
CAPITOL: *68* 5–8
CHICORY: *67*.................... 12–15
LUV: *73*........................ 4–6
PA-GO-GO: *66*.................. 40–45
SUPER K: *69* 3–5
TANGERINE...................... 4–6
LPs: 10/12-Inch 33rpm
CAMEO: *66–67*.................. 25–30
Also see MYSTERIONS, The

QUICK
Singles: 12-Inch 33/45rpm
EPIC: *82* 4–6
PAVALION: *81* 4–6
Singles: 7-Inch
EPIC (37000 series): *82* 1–3
PAVALION: *81* 1–3
LPs: 10/12-Inch 33rpm
EPIC: *82* 5–8

QUICK, The (Featuring Eric Carmen)
Singles: 7-Inch
EPIC (10516; "Ain't
Nothin' Gonna Stop
Me"): *69*..................... 10–15
Also see CARMEN, Eric

QUICKEST WAY OUT
Singles: 7-Inch
WARNER BROS: *75–76*............ 2–4

Price Range

Price Range

QUICKSILVER (Quicksilver Messenger Service)
Singles: 7-Inch
CAPITOL: *68–76* $2–5

LPs: 10/12-Inch 33rpm
CAPITOL (288;
 "Quicksilver Messenger
 Service"): *69*. 25–35
CAPITOL (391 through
 819): *69–71*. 12–15
CAPITOL (2904;
 "Quicksilver Messenger
 Service"): *68*. 15–20
CAPITOL (11000 series):
 72–75 10–12
CAPITOL (16000 series):
 80 5–8
   Also see HOPKINS, Nicky
   Also see JEFFERSON AIRPLANE, The
   Also see MILLER, Steve / The Band / Quick-
   silver Messenger Service
   Also see VALENTI, Dino

QUIET RIOT
Singles: 12-Inch 33/45rpm
PASHA: *83–85* 4–6
Singles: 7-Inch
PASHA: *83–85* 1–3

LPs: 10/12-Inch 33rpm
PASHA (Except picture
 discs): *83–84*. 5–8
PASHA (Picture discs): *83* 10–12

QUINELLA
Singles: 7-Inch
BECKET: *81* 1–3

QUINN, Carmel
Singles: 7-Inch
COLUMBIA: *55–56* 2–4
DOT: *64* 2–3
HEADLINE: *59–62* 2–4
EPs: 7-Inch 33/45rpm
COLUMBIA: *55* 5–10
LPs: 10/12-Inch 33rpm
CAMDEN: *65* 5–10
COLUMBIA: *55–56* 10–20
DOT: *65* 5–12
HEADLINE: *59–62* 8–15

QUIN-TONES, The
Singles: 7-Inch
COLLECTABLES $1–3
HUNT: *58* 5–8
RED TOP: *58* 10–15

R

RCR
Singles: 7-Inch
RADIO: *80* 1–3
   Members: Donna Rhodes; Charles Chalmers;
   Sandy Rhodes.

R.E.M.
Singles: 7-Inch
I.R.S.: *82–84* 1–3
EPs: 7-Inch 33/45rpm
I.R.S.: *82* 3–5
LPs: 10/12-Inch 33rpm
I.R.S.: *82–83* 6–10
   Members: Michael Stipe; Bill Berry; Peter
   Buck; Mike Mills.

REO SPEEDWAGON
Singles: 7-Inch
EPIC (Except 10000 &
 11000 series): *75–85* 1–3
EPIC (10000 & 11000
 series): *72–74* 2–4
Picture Sleeves
EPIC: *80–85* .... INC
LPs: 10/12-Inch 33rpm
EPIC (Except 40000
 series): *71–84* 6–10
EPIC (40000 series): *81–82* 12–15
   (Half-speed mastered LPs.)
Promotional LPs
EPIC (643; "Nine Lives") 12–15
   Also see MAY, Brian

R.J.'S LATEST ARRIVAL (Ralph James)
Singles: 7-Inch
ARIOLA AMERICA: *79* 2–3
ATLANTIC: *85* 1–3
BUDDAH: *81* 1–3
LARC: *83* 1–3
QUALITY/RFC. 1–3
SUTRA: *81* 1–3

Price Range

ZOO YORK: *82* **$1–3**
    LPs: 10/12-Inch 33rpm
ARIOLA AMERICA: *79* **5–8**
ATLANTIC: *85* **5–8**

RABBITT, Eddie
Singles: 7-Inch
DATE: *68* **2–4**
ELEKTRA: *74–83* **1–3**
20TH CENTURY-FOX:
  64 .... **3–5**
WARNER BROS: *83–85* **1–3**
    Picture Sleeves
ELEKTRA: *81* .... **INC**
    LPs: 10/12-Inch 33rpm
ELEKTRA: *75–82* **5–10**
WARNER BROS: *84–85* **5–8**

RABBITT, Eddie, & Crystal Gayle
Singles: 7-Inch
ELEKTRA: *82* **1–3**
  Also see CRYSTAL GAYLE
  Also see RABBITT, Eddie

RABIN, Trevor
Singles: 7-Inch
CHRYSALIS: *78–80*. **1–3**
    LPs: 10/12-Inch 33rpm
CHRYSALIS: *78–80*. **5–8**

RACE
Singles: 7-Inch
OCEAN FRONT: *83* **1–3**

RACING CARS, The
Singles: 7-Inch
CHRYSALIS: *77–78*. **2–3**
    LPs: 10/12-Inch 33rpm
CHRYSALIS: *77–78*. **5–8**

RADIANCE (Radiance With Andrea Stone)
Singles: 12-Inch 33/45rpm
ARE 'N BE: *83*. **4–6**
    Singles: 7-Inch
WARNER BROS: *85*. **1–3**

RADIANTS, The (Featuring Maurice McAlister)
Singles: 7-Inch
CHESS: *62–69*. **3–5**

Price Range

ERIC **$1–3**
TWINIGHT: *71* **2–4**
  Also see McALISTER, Maurice, & The Radiants

RADICE, Mark
Singles: 7-Inch
UNITED ARTISTS: *76*. **2–4**
    LPs: 10/12-Inch 33rpm
ROADSHOW: *77*. **8–10**

RADNER, Gilda
Singles: 7-Inch
WARNER BROS: *79–80*. **1–3**
    LPs: 10/12-Inch 33rpm
WARNER BROS: *79*. **5–8**

RAE, Fonda (Fonda Raye)
Singles: 12-Inch 33/45rpm
POSSE: *83* **4–6**
VANGUARD: *82*. **4–6**
    Singles: 7-Inch
VANGUARD: *82*. **1–3**

RAE, Robbie
Singles: 7-Inch
QUALITY: *83*. **1–3**

RAELETTES, The (The Raeletts; The Raelets)
Singles: 7-Inch
TRC: *70*. **2–4**
TANGERINE: *67–73*. **2–4**
    LPs: 10/12-Inch 33rpm
TRC: *71–72* **8–10**
TANGERINE: *72*. **8–10**
  Also see CHARLES, Ray
  Also see TURNER, Ike & Tina

RAES, The
Singles: 7-Inch
A&M: *78* **2–3**
    LPs: 10/12-Inch 33rpm
A&M: *79* **5–8**

RAFFERTY, Gerry
Singles: 7-Inch
BLUE THUMB: *72* **2–4**
LIBERTY: *82* **1–3**
SIGNPOST: *72* **2–4**
UNITED ARTISTS: *77–80*. **1–3**

Price Range

Picture Sleeves
UNITED ARTISTS: *77–78* **$1–3**
  LPs: 10/12-Inch 33rpm
BLUE THUMB: *73–78* **8–10**
LIBERTY: *82* **5–8**
UNITED ARTISTS: *78–80* **8–10**
VISA: *78* **5–8**
  Also see STEALERS WHEEL

RAG DOLLS, The
  Singles: 7-Inch
MALA: *65* **4–6**

RAG DOLLS, The / The Caliente Combo
  Singles: 7-Inch
PARKWAY: *64* **3–5**
  Also see RAG DOLLS, The

RAIDERS, The, & Paul Revere: see REVERE, Paul, & The Raiders

RAIL
  Singles: 7-Inch
EMI AMERICA: *84* **1–3**
  LPs: 10/12-Inch 33rpm
EMI AMERICA: *84* **5–8**
PASSPORT **5–8**

RAINBOW (With Ritchie Blackmore)
  Singles: 7-Inch
MERCURY: *82–83* **1–3**
POLYDOR: *79* **2–3**
  LPs: 10/12-Inch 33rpm
MERCURY: *82* **5–8**
OYSTER: *77* **8–10**
POLYDOR: *78–81* **5–8**
  Also see ALCATRAZZ
  Also see BLACKMORE'S RAINBOW
  Also see CAREY, Tony
  Also see GLOVER, Roger

RAINDROPS, The
  Singles: 7-Inch
JUBILEE: *63–65* **4–6**
VIRGO: *73* **1–3**
  LPs: 10/12-Inch 33rpm
JUBILEE: *63* **30–35**
MURRAY HILL **5–8**
  Members: Jeff Barry; Ellie Greenwich.
  Also see GREENWICH, Ellie

Price Range

RAINES, Rita
  Singles: 7-Inch
DEED: *56* **$4–6**

RAINWATER, Marvin
  Singles: 7-Inch
BRAVE: *63–67* **2–4**
CORAL: *56* **5–8**
HILLTOP **5–8**
MGM (12000 & 12100
  series): *55* **4–8**
MGM (12200 series): *56* **15–25**
MGM (12300 series): *56* **8–15**
MGM (12400 through
  12800 series): *57–60* **4–8**
MGM (12900 series): *60* **3–5**
NU TRAYL: *76* **2–3**
UNITED ARTISTS: *65–66* **2–4**
WARNER BROS: *70* **2–3**
WARWICK: *61* **2–4**
  EPs: 7-Inch 33/45rpm
MGM: *57* **10–20**
  LPs: 10/12-Inch 33rpm
CROWN **10–15**
MGM (3500 & 3700
  series): *57–58* **50–75**
MGM (4000 series): *62* **40–50**
MOUNT VERNON **8–10**
SPINORAMA **8–10**

RAINWATER, Marvin, & Connie Francis
  Singles: 7-Inch
MGM: *57* **4–6**
  Also see FRANCIS, Connie
  Also see RAINWATER, Marvin

RAINY DAZE, The
  Singles: 7-Inch
CHICORY: *67* **6–10**
UNI: *67* **3–5**
WHITE WHALE: *68* **3–5**
  LPs: 10/12-Inch 33rpm
UNI: *67* **12–15**

RAITT, Bonnie
  Singles: 7-Inch
WARNER BROS: *72–82* **1–3**
  LPs: 10/12-Inch 33rpm
WARNER BROS: *71–82* **5–12**

RAITT, Bonnie / Gilley's "Urban Cowboy" Band
Singles: 7-Inch
FULL MOON/ASYLUM:
80 . . . . **$1–3**
Picture Sleeves
FULL MOON/ASYLUM:
80 . . . . **1–3**
Also see RAITT, Bonnie

RAKE
Singles: 7-Inch
PROFILE: 83 . . . . **1–3**

RALKE, Don (The Big Sound Of Don Ralke)
Singles: 7-Inch
CROWN: 55 . . . . **2–4**
DRUM BOY: 66. . . . . **2–3**
REAL: 56 . . . . **2–4**
WARNER BROS: 59–64 . . . . **2–4**
LPs: 10/12-Inch 33rpm
CROWN: 55 . . . . **8–15**
WARNER BROS: 59–60 . . . . **8–15**

RALPH, Sheryl Lee
Singles: 12-Inch 33/45rpm
NYM: 84–85 . . . . **4–6**
Singles: 7-Inch
NYM: 84–85 . . . . **1–3**

RAM JAM
Singles: 12-Inch 33/45rpm
EPIC: 77 . . . . **6–10**
Singles: 7-Inch
EPIC: 77–78 . . . . **2–3**
LPs: 10/12-Inch 33rpm
EPIC: 77–78 . . . . **6–10**
Also see LEMON PIPERS, The

RAMA
Singles: 12-Inch 33/45rpm
SUGARSCOOP: 84 . . . . **4–6**

RAMATAM
Singles: 7-Inch
ATLANTIC: 72–73 . . . . **2–4**
LPs: 10/12-Inch 33rpm
ATLANTIC: 72–73 . . . . **10–12**
Also see PINERA, Mike

RAMBEAU, Eddie
Singles: 7-Inch
BELL: 69 . . . . **$2–4**
DYNA VOICE: 65–66 . . . . **3–5**
SWAN: 61–62 . . . . **3–5**
20TH CENTURY-FOX:
64 . . . . **3–5**
VIRGO: 72 . . . . **1–3**
LPs: 10/12-Inch 33rpm
DYNO VOICE: 65 . . . . **15–20**
Also see MARCY JO & EDDIE RAMBEAU

RAMBLERS, The
Singles: 7-Inch
ADDIT: 60 . . . . **3–5**

RAMBLERS, The
Singles: 7-Inch
ALMONT: 64 . . . . **3–5**

RAMIN, Sid, & Orchestra
LPs: 10/12-Inch 33rpm
RCA VICTOR: 63 . . . . **5–10**

RAMONES, The
Singles: 7-Inch
SIRE: 76–79 . . . . **2–3**
Picture Sleeves
SIRE: 77 . . . . **2–3**
EPs: 7-Inch
SIRE: 79 . . . . **5–8**
(Promotional issues only.)
LPs: 10/12-Inch 33rpm
SIRE (Black vinyl): 76–83 . . . . **5–8**
SIRE (Colored vinyl): 78 . . . . **15–20**

RAMRODS, The
Singles: 7-Inch
AMY: 60–62 . . . . **4–6**
PLYMOUTH: 66 . . . . **3–5**
QUEEN: 62 . . . . **3–5**
R&H: 63. . . . . **4–6**

RAMRODS, The
Singles: 7-Inch
RAMPAGE: 72. . . . . **2–4**

Price Range   *Price Range*

RANDAZZO, Teddy (Teddy Randazzo & All 6)
Singles: 7-Inch
ABC-PARAMOUNT:
  59–62 .... $3–5
COLPIX: *62–63*. 3–5
DCP: *64–66* 3–5
MGM: *66* 2–4
VERVE/FOLKWAYS: *67* 2–4
VIK: *58* 3–6
LPs: 10/12-Inch 33rpm
ABC-PARAMOUNT:
  61–62 15–20
MGM: *66* 15–20
  Also see CHUCKLES, The
  Also see THREE CHUCKLES, The

RAN-DELLS, The
Singles: 7-Inch
R.S.V.P.: *64* 5–8
CHAIRMAN: *63–64* 4–8
Picture Sleeves
CHAIRMAN: *63* 10–15

RANDOLPH, Boots (Homer Randolph)
Singles: 7-Inch
MONUMENT: *61–83* 1–3
PALO ALTO. 1–3
RCA VICTOR: *59–61* 3–5
Picture Sleeves
MONUMENT: *64*. 1–3
LPs: 10/12-Inch 33rpm
CAMDEN: *64* 12–15
MONUMENT (Except
  8000 & 18000 series):
  71–82 5–12
MONUMENT (8000 &
  18000 series): *63–71* 8–18
PALO ALTO. 5–8
RCA VICTOR: *60* 15–25
  Also see HIRT, Al, & Boots Randolph
  Also see KNIGHTSBRIDGE STRINGS, The
  Also see PRESLEY, Elvis
  Also see RANDOLPH, Randy

RANDOLPH, Randy (Homer Randolph)
Singles: 7-Inch
RCA VICTOR: *58–59* 4–6
  Also see RANDOLPH, Boots

RANDY & THE RAINBOWS
Singles: 7-Inch
B.T. PUPPY: *67* $5–8
LAURIE 1–3
MIKE: *66* 5–8
RUST (Blue label): *63* 12–15
RUST (Rust & white
  label): *63*. 5–8
LPs: 10/12-Inch 33rpm
AMBIENT SOUND: *82* 8–10
MAGIC CARPET 8–10
  Members: Dominick "Randy" Safuto; Frank
  Safuto; Mike Zero; Sal Zero; Ken Arcipowski.

RANK & FILE
Singles: 7-Inch
SLASH: *83–84*. 1–3
LPs: 10/12-Inch 33rpm
SLASH: *83–84*. 5–8
  Also see SEATRAIN

RANKIN, Billy
Singles: 7-Inch
A&M: *84* 1–3
LPs: 10/12-Inch 33rpm
A&M: *84* 5–8

RANKIN, Kenny (Ken Rankin)
Singles: 7-Inch
ABC-PARAMOUNT: *61* 3–5
COLUMBIA: *63–65* 3–5
DECCA: *58–60* 4–6
LITTLE DAVID: *73–77* 2–3
MERCURY: *68–69*. 2–4
Picture Sleeves
MERCURY: *68*. 2–4
LPs: 10/12-Inch 33rpm
ATLANTIC: *80* 5–8
LITTLE DAVID: *72–75* 8–10
MERCURY: *67–69*. 10–15

RAPP, Captain: see CAPTAIN RAPP

RARE BIRD
Singles: 7-Inch
ABC: *72* 2–4
POLYDOR: *73–74* 2–4
PROBE: *70* 2–4
LPs: 10/12-Inch 33rpm
ABC: *72* 8–10

Price Range

	Price Range
POLYDOR: *73–74*	**$8–10**
PROBE: *70*	**10–12**

RARE EARTH
Singles: 7-Inch

MOTOWN: *81.*	**1–3**
PRODIGAL: *78*	**2–3**
RARE EARTH: *70–76*	**2–4**
VERVE: *68*	**3–5**

Picture Sleeves

RARE EARTH: *71–73*	**2–4**

LPs: 10/12-Inch 33rpm

MOTOWN: *81.*	**5–8**
PRODIGAL: *77–78*	**5–8**
RARE EARTH (Except 507): *70–76.*	**8–10**
RARE EARTH (507; "Get Ready"): *69*	**8–10**

(With an "S" prefix. Standard cover.)

RARE EARTH (507; "Get Ready"): *69*	**12–15**

(With an "RS" prefix. Round-top cover.)

VERVE: *68*	**12–15**

RARE ESSENCE
Singles: 12-Inch 33/45rpm

FANTASY: *82.*	**4–6**

RASCALS, The (The Young Rascals)
Singles: 7-Inch

ATLANTIC: *65–70*	**3–5**
COLUMBIA: *71–72*	**2–4**

LPs: 10/12-Inch 33rpm

ATLANTIC (137; "Freedom Suite"): *69*	**18–20**

(Promotional issue only.)

ATLANTIC (901; "Freedom Suite"): *69*	**12–15**
ATLANTIC (8123 through 8148): *66–67.*	**12–15**
ATLANTIC (8169 through 8276): *68–71.*	**10–12**
COLUMBIA: *71–72*	**8–10**
PAIR: *86*	**6–10**

Picture Sleeves

ATLANTIC: *66–70*	**4–8**

Also see BULLDOG
Also see CAVALIERE, Felix
Also see FOTOMAKER
Also see SWEET INSPIRATIONS, The

RASPBERRIES
Singles: 7-Inch

CAPITOL: *72–74*	**$3–5**

Picture Sleeves

CAPITOL: *72–73*	**5–10**

LPs: 10/12-Inch 33rpm

CAPITOL (11036 through 11329): *72–74.*	**15–20**
CAPITOL (11524; "Raspberries' Best"): *76*	**8–10**
CAPITOL (16095; "Raspberries' Best"): *80*	**5–8**

Members: Eric Carmen; Wally Bryson; Dave Smalley; Jim Bonfanti.
Also see CARMEN, Eric

RATCHELL
Singles: 7-Inch

DECCA: *72*	**2–4**

LPs: 10/12-Inch 33rpm

DECCA: *71–72*	**10–12**

RATIONALS, The
Singles: 7-Inch

A SQUARE: *66.*	**5–8**
CAMEO: *66–67.*	**3–5**
CAPITOL: *68*	**3–5**
CREWE: *69.*	**3–5**
GENESIS.	**4–6**

LPs: 10/12-Inch 33rpm

CREWE: *69.*	**15–20**

RATT
Singles: 7-Inch

ATLANTIC: *84–85*	**1–3**
TIME COAST: *83–84.*	**1–3**

LPs: 10/12-Inch 33rpm

ATLANTIC: *84–85*	**5–8**
TIME COAST: *83–84.*	**5–8**

RATTLES, The
Singles: 7-Inch

LONDON	**3–5**
MERCURY: *66.*	**4–6**
PROBE: *70*	**2–4**

LPs: 10/12-Inch 33rpm

MERCURY: *67.*	**15–20**

Also see SEARCHERS, The / The Rattles

Price Range

Price Range

RAVAN, Genya
Singles: 7-Inch
DE LITE: 75 . . . . $2–3
DUNHILL: 73 2–4
COLUMBIA: 71–72 2–4
20TH CENTURY-FOX:
  78–79 2–3
LPs: 10/12-Inch 33rpm
COLUMBIA: 72 8–10
DUNHILL: 73 8–10
20TH CENTURY-FOX:
  78–79 5–8
Also see TEN WHEEL DRIVE

RAVEN
Singles: 7-Inch
RAMPART 2–3
LPs: 10/12-Inch 33rpm
ATLANTIC: 85 5–8

RAVEN, Marcia
Singles: 12-Inch 33/45rpm
PROFILE: 83 4–6
Singles: 7-Inch
PROFILE: 83 1–3

RAVENS, The
Singles: 7-Inch
ARGO (5255; "Kneel &
  Pray"): 56 15–20
ARGO (5261; "A Simple
  Prayer"): 56 25–30
ARGO (5276; "That'll Be
  The Day"): 57 10–12
CHECKER: 57 5–8
COLUMBIA (1-903;
  "Time Takes Care Of
  Everything"): 50 225–250
  (Compact 33 Single.)
COLUMBIA (6-903;
  "Time Takes Care Of
  Everything"): 50 150–175
COLUMBIA (1-925; "My
  Baby's Gone"): 50 225–250
  (Compact 33 Single.)
COLUMBIA (6-925; "My
  Baby's Gone"): 50 150–175
COLUMBIA (39112; "You
  Don't Have To Drop A
  Heart To Break It"): 51 150-175

COLUMBIA (39194;
  "You're Always In My
  Dreams"): 51 . . . . $150–175
COLUMBIA (39408; "You
  Foolish Thing"): 51 425–450
JUBILEE: 55–56 10–15
MERCURY (5000 series,
  except 5764): 52 25–35
MERCURY (5764;
  "There's No Use
  Pretending"): 51 75–90
MERCURY (8000 series):
  51–52 20–30
MERCURY (70060;
  "Don't Mention My
  Name"): 52 40–50
MERCURY (70119
  through 70240): 53–54 25–35
MERCURY (70307
  through 70554): 54–55 35–45
NATIONAL: 50–51 400–450
OKEH (Except 6888): 51 250–275
OKEH (6888;
  "Mam'selle"): 52 100–125
SAVOY: 58 5–8
TOP RANK: 59 4–6
VIRGO: 72 1–3
EPs: 7-Inch 33/45rpm
KING: 55 175–200
RENDITION: 52 200–225
LPs: 10/12-Inch 33rpm
HARLEM HIT PARADE:
  75 10–12
REGENT (Green label) 25–30
REGENT (Red label) 15–20
SAVOY: 78 10–12
  Members: Ollie Jones; Joe Van Loan; Jimmy
  Ricks; Len Puzey; Warren Suttles; Louis Hey-
  ward; James Stewart; Lou Frazier; Tom Evans;
  James Van Loan; David Bowers; Paul Van
  Loan.
  Also see WASHINGTON, Dinah, & The Rav-
  ens

RAW SILK
Singles: 7-Inch
WEST END: 82 1–3

Price Range

Also see VEGA, Tata

RAWLS, Lou, & Les McCann Ltd.
Singles: 7-Inch
CAPITOL: 62 . . . . $3–5
LPs: 10/12-Inch 33rpm
CAPITOL: 75 5–8
(With an "SM" prefix.)
CAPITOL: 62 20–30
(With a "T" or "ST" prefix.)
Also see McCANN, Les
Also see RAWLS, Lou

RAY, Baby: see BABY RAY

RAY, Diane
Singles: 7-Inch
MERCURY: 63–64 3–5
Picture Sleeves
MERCURY: 63 5–8
LPs: 10/12-Inch 33rpm
MERCURY: 64 20–25

RAY, Don
Singles: 7-Inch
POLYDOR: 78 2–3
LPs: 10/12-Inch 33rpm
POLYDOR: 78 5–8

RAY, Harry
Singles: 7-Inch
SUGAR HILL: 82–83 1–3
LPs: 10/12-Inch 33rpm
SUGAR HILL: 83 5–8
Also see RAY, GOODMAN & BROWN

RAY, James
Singles: 7-Inch
CAPRICE: 61–62 3–5
CONGRESS: 63–64 3–5
DYNAMIC: 62 3–5
LPs: 10/12-Inch 33rpm
CAPRICE: 62 30–40
Also see GRANT, Janie

RAY, Johnnie (Johnnie Ray & The Four Lads)
Singles: 7-Inch
CADENCE: 60 2–4
COLUMBIA (39000 &
41000 series): 52–60 3–5
DECCA: 63–64 2–4

Price Range

RAWLS, Lou
Singles: 12-Inch 33/45rpm
PHILADELPHIA INT'L:
79 . . . . $4–6
Singles: 7-Inch
ARISTA: 75 2–3
BELL: 74 2–3
CANDIX: 60–61 3–5
CAPITOL: 61–70 2–5
EPIC: 82–83 1–3
MGM: 71–73 2–3
PHILADELPHIA INT'L:
76–81 1–3
SHAR-DEE: 60 4–6
Picture Sleeves
CAPITOL: 67 2–3
LPs: 10/12-Inch 33rpm
ALLEGIANCE: 84 5–8
BELL: 74 8–10
CAPITOL (Except 1700
through 2900 series):
69–77 5–12
CAPITOL (1700 through
2900 series): 63–68 10–25
EPIC: 82–83 5–8
MGM: 71–73 8–10
PHILADELPHIA INT'L:
76–80 5–8
POLYDOR: 76 8–10
Also see COOKE, Sam
Also see PHILADELPHIA INTERNATIONAL ALL STARS, The

YOU DON'T OWE ME A THING
LOOK HOMEWARD, ANGEL
COLUMBIA
JOHNNIE RAY

Price Range

GROOVE: *64*.	**$2–4**
LIBERTY: *62*	**2–4**
OKEH: *52*	**4–6**
UNITED ARTISTS: *61*	**2–4**

Picture Sleeves

COLUMBIA: *57*	**3–5**

EPs: 7-Inch 33/45rpm

COLUMBIA: *52–59*	**5–15**
EPIC: *52–54*	**10–20**

LPs: 10/12-Inch 33rpm

COLUMBIA (900 series):
57	**15–30**

COLUMBIA (1300 series):
59	**10–20**

COLUMBIA (2500 series):
54	**20–40**
(10-Inch LPs.)	

COLUMBIA (6000 series):
52	**25–50**
(10-Inch LPs.)	

COLUMBIA (8100 series):
59	**10–20**
EPIC: *54*	**20–40**
HARMONY: *71*	**6–10**
SUNSET: *66*	**8–12**

Also see DAY, Doris, & Johnnie Ray
Also see FOUR LADS, The

RAY, Johnnie, & Timi Yuro
Singles: 7-Inch

LIBERTY: *61*	**2–4**

Also see RAY, Johnnie
Also see YURO, Timi

Price Range

RAY, Ricardo
Singles: 7-Inch

ALEGRE: *68*	**$3–5**

RAY & BOB
Singles: 7-Inch

LEDO: *62*	**4–6**

Members: Ray Swayne; Bob Appleberry.

RAY, GOODMAN & BROWN
Singles: 7-Inch

PANORAMIC: *84*	**1–3**
POLYDOR: *80*	**1–3**

LPs: 10/12-Inch 33rpm

POLYDOR: *80*	**5–8**

Members: Harry Ray; Al Goodman; Bill Brown.
Also see MOMENTS, The
Also see RAY, Harry

RAYBURN, Margie
Singles: 7-Inch

ALMA: *54*	**4–6**
CAPITOL: *65*	**2–4**
CHALLENGE: *61*	**3–5**
DOT: *62–66*	**2–4**
LIBERTY: *56–62*	**3–5**
S&G: *54*	**4–6**

Picture Sleeves

LIBERTY: *57*	**3–5**

LPs: 10/12-Inch 33rpm

LIBERTY: *59*	**20–25**

RAYDIO (Featuring Ray Parker, Jr.)
Singles: 7-Inch

ARISTA: *78–79*	**2–3**

Picture Sleeves

ARISTA: *78–79*	**2–3**

LPs: 10/12-Inch 33rpm

ARISTA: *78–79*	**5–8**

Also see KNIGHT, Jerry
Also see PARKER, Ray, Jr.

RAYE, Fonda: see RAE, Fonda

RAYE, Susan
Singles: 7-Inch

CAPITOL: *69–76*	**2–4**
UNITED ARTISTS: *76–77*	**2–3**
WESTEXAS: *85*	**1–3**

Price Range

Picture Sleeves
CAPITOL: *71* $2–3
LPs: 10/12-Inch 33rpm
CAPITOL: *70–76* 8–12
UNITED ARTISTS: *77* 6–10
Also see OWENS, Buck, & Susan Raye

RAY-O-VACS, The (Featuring Lester Harris & Herb Milliner)
Singles: 7-Inch
ATCO: *57* 6–10
DECCA: *50–53* 10–15
JOSIE: *54* 10–15
JUBILEE: *52* 15–20
KAISER: *56* 10–15
SHARP: *60* 4–6

RAYS, The (Featuring Hal Miller)
Singles: 7-Inch
ABKCO 1–3
AMY: *64* 3–5
ARGO 3–5
CAMEO: *57* 5–8
CHESS: *55–57* 5–8
PERRI: *62* 8–10
XYZ (Except 100 & 102):
 58–61 5–8
XYZ (100 & 102): *57* 20–30
EPs: 7-Inch 33/45rpm
CHESS: *58* 25–30

RAZOR'S EDGE, The
Singles: 7-Inch
POW: *66* 3–5

RAZZY: see BAILEY, Razzy

REA, Chris
Singles: 7-Inch
COLUMBIA: *82* 1–3
RCA VICTOR: *84* 1–3
UNITED ARTISTS: *78–79* 2–3
Picture Sleeves
UNITED ARTISTS: *78* 2–3
LPs: 10/12-Inch 33rpm
COLUMBIA: *80–82* 5–8
RCA VICTOR: *84* 5–8
UNITED ARTISTS: *79* 5–8
Also see WILLIE & THE POOR BOYS

XYZ
Distributed by
UNART RECORDS
A Division of
UNITED ARTISTS RECORDS, INC.

Conley Music
BMI - 2:10

UR 2001
106E

ELEVATOR OPERATOR
(Frank C. Slay, Jr; Bob Crewe)
THE RAYS

Price Range

READ, John Dawson
Singles: 7-Inch
CHRYSALIS: *75* $2–4
LPs: 10/12-Inch 33rpm
CHRYSALIS: *75–76* 5–10

READY FOR THE WORLD
Singles: 12-Inch 33/45rpm
MCA: *84–86* 4–6
Singles: 7-Inch
MCA: *84–86* 1–3
LPs: 10/12-Inch 33rpm
MCA: *86* 5–8

REAL LIFE
Singles: 12-Inch 33/45rpm
CURB/MCA: *83–84* 4–6
Singles: 7-Inch
CURB/MCA: *83–84* 1–3
LPs: 10/12-Inch 33rpm
CURB/MCA: *83–84* 5–8

REAL ROXANNE (With Hitman Howie Tee)
Singles: 12-Inch 33/45rpm
SELECT: *85* 4–6

REAL THING, The
Singles: 12-Inch 33/45rpm
BELIEVE IN A DREAM:
 81 4–6
EPIC: *79* 4–6

Price Range

Singles: 7-Inch
BELIEVE IN A DREAM:
  81 .... **$1–3**
EPIC: *79* **1–3**
UNITED ARTISTS: *76–77*......... **2–3**
WHIZ: *69* **2–4**
  LPs: 10/12-Inch 33rpm
UNITED ARTISTS: *76*........... **5–10**

REAL TO REEL
  Singles: 12-Inch 33/45rpm
ARISTA: *83–84*.................. **4–6**
  Singles: 7-Inch
ARISTA: *83–84*.................. **1–3**
  LPs: 10/12-Inch 33rpm
ARISTA: *83* **5–8**

REAVES, Paulette
  Singles: 7-Inch
BLUE CANDLE: *77–78* **2–3**

REBELS, The
  Singles: 7-Inch
MAR-LEE (0094; "Wild
  Weekend"): *60*................ **10–12**
SWAN: *62–63* **3–5**
  Also see BUFFALO REBELS, The
  Also see ROCKIN' REBELS, The

REBENNACK, Mac
  Singles: 7-Inch
A.F.O.: *62* **5–8**
ACE: *61*........................ **8–10**
REX: *59*........................ **10–15**
  Also see DR. JOHN

RECORD, Eugene
  Singles: 12-Inch 33/45rpm
WARNER BROS: *79*.............. **4–6**
  Singles: 7-Inch
WARNER BROS: *77–79*........... **2–3**
  LPs: 10/12-Inch 33rpm
WARNER BROS: *77–79*........... **5–8**
  Also see CHI-LITES, The

RECORDS, The
  Singles: 7-Inch
VIRGIN: *79–81*................... **2–3**
  Picture Sleeves
VIRGIN: *79–81*................... **2–3**

Price Range

  EPs: 7-Inch 33/45rpm
VIRGIN: *79* **$3–5**
(Issued as a bonus with Virgin LP 13130, "The
Records.")
  LPs: 10/12-Inch 33rpm
VIRGIN: *79–82*.................. **8–10**

RED RIDER
  Singles: 7-Inch
CAPITOL: *80–84* **1–3**
  Picture Sleeves
CAPITOL: *80–84* .... **INC**
  LPs: 10/12-Inch 33rpm
CAPITOL: *80–83* **5–8**

RED RIVER DAVE (Dave McEnery)
  Singles: 7-Inch
COPYRIGHT: *61*................. **2–4**
SAVOY: *60–65* **2–4**
  EPs: 7-Inch 33/45rpm
VARSITY **5–10**
  LPs: 10/12-Inch 33rpm
BLUEBONNET **6–12**
CONTINENTAL: *62*............. **10–15**
PLACE.......................... **8–10**
SUTTON **5–8**

RED ROCKERS
  Singles: 12-Inch 33/45rpm
COLUMBIA: *84–85*.............. **4–6**
  Singles: 7-Inch
COLUMBIA: *84–85*.............. **1–3**
  LPs: 10/12-Inch 33rpm
COLUMBIA: *83* **5–8**

Price Range

Price Range

REDBONE
Singles: 7-Inch
EPIC: *71–74* **$2–4**
RCA VICTOR: *78* **2–3**
LPs: 10/12-Inch 33rpm
ACCORD: *82* **5–8**
EPIC: *70–75* **8–12**
RCA VICTOR: *77* **8–10**
Members: Pat Vegas; Lolly Vegas.

REDBONE, Leon
Singles: 7-Inch
EMERALD CITY: *81* **1–3**
WARNER BROS: *77–78* **2–3**
LPs: 10/12-Inch 33rpm
ACCORD: *82* **5–8**
EMERALD CITY: *81* **5–8**
WARNER BROS: *77–78* **5–10**

REDD, Sharon
Singles: 12-Inch 33/45rpm
PRELUDE: *81–83*. **4–6**
Singles: 7-Inch
COLUMBIA: *78* **2–3**
PRELUDE: *81–83*. **1–3**
VEEP: *67* **3–5**
LPs: 10/12-Inch 33rpm
COLUMBIA: *78* **5–10**
PRELUDE: *82*. **5–8**
Also see MIDLER, Bette

REDD HOT (Redd Hott)
Singles: 7-Inch
VENTURE: *81–82* **1–3**
Members: Kevin "Flash" Ferrell; Robert Parson; Daryl Simmons; Greg Russell; De Morris Smith.
Also see MANCHILD

REDDING, Gene
Singles: 7-Inch
HAVEN: *74*. **2–3**

REDDING, Otis (Otis Redding & The Pinetoppers; Otis Redding & The Pinetones)
Singles: 7-Inch
ATCO: *68–71*. **2–4**
BETHLEHEM: *64* **4–6**
CONFEDERATE: *62*. **6–10**
KING: *68* **2–4**

STAX: *68*. **$2–4**
VOLT: *62–68*. **3–5**
EPs: 7-Inch 33/45rpm
VOLT: *66*. **12–15**
LPs: 10/12-Inch 33rpm
ALSHIRE: *68* **6–10**
ATCO (161; "Pain In My
Heart"): *64*. **15–20**
ATCO (200 series): *68–69* **8–15**
ATCO (300 series): *70* **8–12**
ATCO (801; "Best Of Otis
Redding"): *72*. **10–20**
(Currently available, using the same catalog number.)
ATLANTIC: *82* **5–8**
SOMERSET: *68* **6–10**
VOLT: *65–68*. **12–18**
Also see BAR-KAYS, The
Also see OTIS & CARLA

REDDING, Otis / Jimi Hendrix
LPs: 10/12-Inch 33rpm
REPRISE: *70*. **8–12**
Also see HENDRIX, Jimi
Also see REDDING, Otis

REDDINGS, The
Singles: 12-Inch 33/45rpm
BELIEVE IN A DREAM:
83 . . . . **4–6**
Singles: 7-Inch
BELIEVE IN A DREAM:
80–83 . . . . **1–3**
POLYDOR: *85* **1–3**
LPs: 10/12-Inch 33rpm
BELIEVE IN A DREAM:
80–83 . . . . **5–8**
POLYDOR: *85* **5–8**
Members: Otis Redding III; Dexter Redding; Mark Locket.

REDDS & THE BOYS
Singles: 7-Inch
4TH & BROADWAY: *85* **1–3**

REDDY, Helen
Singles: 12-Inch 33/45rpm
CAPITOL: *79* **4–6**
Singles: 7-Inch
CAPITOL: *71–81* **1–3**
FONTANA: *68*. **3–5**

Price Range

MCA: *81–83* **$1–3**

LPs: 10/12-Inch 33rpm
CAPITOL: *71–81* **6–10**
MCA. **81–83**
Also see PRESLEY, Elvis

REDEYE
Singles: 7-Inch
PENTAGRAM: *70–71* **2–4**

LPs: 10/12-Inch 33rpm
PENTAGRAM: *70–71* **10–12**

REDJACKS, The
Singles: 7-Inch
APT: *58* **4–6**
OKLAHOMA: *58* **10–15**

REDNOW, Eivets (Stevie Wonder)
Singles: 7-Inch
GORDY: *68* **4–6**

LPs: 10/12-Inch 33rpm
GORDY: *68* **25–30**
Also see WONDER, Stevie

REDWAY, Michael (Mike Redway)
Singles: 7-Inch
LONDON: *64* **3–5**
PHILIPS: *73* **2–4**

REED, Clarence: see REID, Clarence

REED, Dean
Singles: 7-Inch
CAPITOL: *59–61* **4–6**
IMPERIAL: *61* **3–5**

REED, Denny
Singles: 7-Inch
ASPIRE: *77* **2–3**
DOT: *62* **3–5**
MCI: *60* **10–12**
TREY: *60–61* **4–6**
TOWER: *65* **3–5**
UNITED ARTISTS: *61* **4–6**

Jerry Reed, 10 charted singles (1962–82), seven charted LPs (1970–73).

Price Range

REED, Jerry (Jerry Reed & The Hully Girlies)
Singles: 7-Inch
CAPITOL: *55–56* **$6–10**
COLUMBIA: *61–63* **3–6**
NRC: *59* **4–6**
RCA VICTOR (Except
    8500 through 9700
    series): *69–85* **1–3**
RCA VICTOR (8500
    through 9700 series):
    65–69 . . . . **3–5**

Picture Sleeves
COLUMBIA: *61* **3–6**
RCA VICTOR: *72–85* **1–3**

LPs: 10/12-Inch 33rpm
CAMDEN: *72–74* **6–12**
HARMONY: *71* **8–10**
PICKWICK/HILLTOP. **6–10**
RCA VICTOR (Except
    LPM & LSP series):
    73–83 . . . . **5–10**
RCA VICTOR (LPM &
    LSP series): *67–73* **8–15**
Also see HART, Freddie / Sammi Smith /
Jerry Reed
Also see JENNINGS, Waylon, & Jerry Reed

Price Range

Price Range

REED, Jerry, & Chet Atkins
LPs: 10/12-Inch 33rpm
RCA VICTOR: 72 .... **$8–12**
  Also see ATKINS, Chet
  Also see REED, Jerry

REED, Jimmy
Singles: 7-Inch
ABC: 73 .... **1–3**
ABC-PARAMOUNT: 66 .... **2–4**
BLUESWAY: 67 .... **2–4**
CHANCE: 53 .... **60–75**
COLLECTABLES **1–3**
EXODUS: 66 .... **3–5**
VEE JAY (100; "High
  And Lonesome"): 53 .... **60–75**
  (Black vinyl.)
VEE JAY (100; "High
  And Lonesome"): 53 .... **100–125**
  (Colored vinyl.)
VEE JAY (105; "High
  And Lonesome"): 53 .... **15–20**
  (Black vinyl.)
VEE JAY (105; "High
  And Lonesome"): 53 .... **30–40**
  (Colored vinyl.)
VEE JAY (119 through
  298): 53–58 .... **5–8**
  (Black vinyl.)
VEE JAY (119 through
  298): 53–58 .... **12–15**
  (Colored vinyl. Not all numbers in this series
  were available on colored vinyl, but several
  were.)
VEE JAY (300 through
  700 series): 59–65 .... **3–5**

LPs: 10/12-Inch 33rpm
BLUES ON BLUES **8–10**
BLUESWAY: 67–73 .... **8–12**
BUDDAH: 69 .... **10–12**
CHARLY **5–8**
EVEREST: 69 .... **5–8**
EXODUS: 66 .... **10–12**
GNP/CRESCENDO: 74 .... **8–10**
KENT: 69–71 .... **8–10**
ROKER **8–10**
SUNSET: 68 .... **10–12**
TRADITION **5–8**
TRIP: 71–78 .... **8–10**
VEE JAY (Except 1004
  through 1035): 62–65 .... **15–20**

VEE JAY (1004 through
  1035): 58–61 .... **$20–30**
  Also see MAYFIELD, Curtis
  Also see UPCHURCH, Phil

REED, Lou (Lou Reed & The Velvet Underground)
Singles: 12-Inch 33/45rpm
RCA VICTOR: 84 .... **4–6**
Singles: 7-Inch
ARISTA: 76 .... **2–3**
RCA VICTOR: 73–86 .... **2–4**
LPs: 10/12-Inch 33rpm
ARISTA: 76–80 .... **5–8**
PRIDE: 73 .... **8–10**
RCA VICTOR (AFL1
  series): 80–83 .... **5–8**
RCA VICTOR (ANL1
  series): 77 .... **5–8**
RCA VICTOR (APL1
  series): 73–77 .... **8–12**
RCA VICTOR (AYL1
  series): 80–83 .... **5–8**
RCA VICTOR (CPL1
  series): 74 .... **8–10**
RCA VICTOR (LSP
  series): 72 .... **10–12**
  Also see VELVET UNDERGROUND, The

REED, Vivian
Singles: 7-Inch
ATCO: 73 .... **2–3**
EPIC: 68–69 .... **2–4**
UNITED ARTISTS: 78–79 .... **1–3**
LPs: 10/12-Inch 33rpm
EPIC: 69 .... **10–12**
UNITED ARTISTS: 78 .... **5–8**

REESE, Della (Della Reese & The Meditation Singers)
Singles: 7-Inch
ABC: 67–73 .... **1–3**
ABC-PARAMOUNT:
  65–66 .... **2–4**
AVCO EMBASSY: 69–72 .... **2–3**
CHI-SOUND: 77 .... **1–3**
JUBILEE: 57–59 .... **3–5**
LMI: 73 .... **1–3**
RCA VICTOR: 59–64 .... **2–5**
VIRGO: 72 .... **1–3**

Price Range

Price Range

Picture Sleeves
RCA VICTOR: *60–63* $2–5
LPs: 10/12-Inch 33rpm
ABC: *76* 5–8
ABC-PARAMOUNT:
  65–67 10–12
JUBILEE (1000 & 5000
  series): *57–63* 15–20
JUBILEE (6000 series): *69* 8–12
LMI: *73* 5–10
RCA VICTOR (2000
  through 4600 series):
  60–72 8–18
SUNSET: *71* 6–10
  Also see ANN-MARGRET / Kitty Kalen /
  Della Reese

REEVES, Del (Del Reeves & The Goodtime Charlies)
Singles: 7-Inch
CHART: *70* 2–3
COLUMBIA: *64* 2–4
DECCA: *61–62* 3–5
KOALA: *80–82* 1–3
LAS VEGAS: *59* 3–6
PEACH: *60* 3–5
REPRISE: *63* 2–5
UNITED ARTISTS
  (Except 800 & 900
  series): *66–78* 1–3
UNITED ARTISTS (800
  & 900 series): *66–76* 2–4
Picture Sleeves
KOALA: *80* .... INC
UNITED ARTISTS: *67* 2–4
LPs: 10/12-Inch 33rpm
KOALA: *79–80* 5–8
STARDAY 5–8
SUNSET: *69–70* 6–10
UNITED ARTISTS (200
  through 600 series):
  73–76 6–10
UNITED ARTISTS (3000
  & 6000 series): *65–71* 8–18

REEVES, Del, & Bobby Goldsboro
Singles: 7-Inch
UNITED ARTISTS: *65–71* 3–5
LPs: 10/12-Inch 33rpm
UNITED ARTISTS: *68* 10–15
  Also see GOLDSBORO, Bobby

REEVES, Del / Red Sovine
LPs: 10/12-Inch 33rpm
EXACT: *80* $5–8
  Also see SOVINE, Red

REEVES, Del, & Billie Jo Spears
Singles: 7-Inch
UNITED ARTISTS: *76* 2–3
LPs: 10/12-Inch 33rpm
LIBERTY: *82* 5–8
UNITED ARTISTS: *76* 6–10
  Also see REEVES, Del
  Also see SPEARS, Billie Jo

REEVES, Jim
Singles: 7-Inch
ABBOTT (100 series): *53* 5–10
FABOR: *54* 5–8
RCA VICTOR (0100
  through 0800 series):
  69–74 2–3
RCA VICTOR (6200
  through 7500 series):
  55–59 3–6
RCA VICTOR (7600
  through 9900 series):
  59–71 2–4
RCA VICTOR (10000
  through 13000 series):
  75–84 1–3
Picture Sleeves
RCA VICTOR: *60–65* 4–8
EPs: 7-Inch 33/45rpm
RCA VICTOR (Except
  1200 series): *56–61* 10–20
RCA VICTOR (1200
  series): *56* 20–30
LPs: 10/12-Inch 33rpm
ABBOTT: *56* 450–550
CAMDEN (Except 500 &
  600 series): *64–73* 5–15
CAMDEN (500 & 600
  series): *60–63* 10–20
GUEST STAR: *64* 10–15
HISTORY OF COUNTRY
  MUSIC: *72* 6–10
PAIR: *82* 8–12
PICKWICK: *72* 5–10
PICKWICK/HILLTOP:
  74 5–10

Price Range

Price Range

RCA VICTOR (0039
through 4800 series):
73–83 . . . . **$5–10**
(With an "AHL1," "ANL1," "APL1,"
"AYL1" or "CPL1" prefix.)
RCA VICTOR (0587;
"Golden Collection") **25–35**
(A Special Products 5-LP set.)
RCA VICTOR (1200
series): *56* **80–100**
(With an "LPM" prefix.)
RCA VICTOR (1400 &
1500 series): *57* **35–50**
(With an "LPM" prefix.)
RCA VICTOR (1600
through 1900 series): *58* **25–35**
(With an "LPM" prefix.)
RCA VICTOR (2000
through 2300 series):
59–61 . . . . **15–25**
(With an "LPM" or "LSP" prefix.)
RCA VICTOR (2400
through 3903): *62–67* **10–20**
(With an "LPM" or "LSP" prefix.)
RCA VICTOR (3987; "A
Touch Of Sadness"): *68* **40–50**
(With an "LPM" prefix. Monaural issue.)
RCA VICTOR (3987; "A
Touch Of Sadness"): *68* **10–12**
(With an "LSP" prefix. Stereo issue.)
RCA VICTOR (4000
through 4700): *68–72* **8–12**
(With an "LSP" prefix.)
READER'S DIGEST (210;
"Unforgetable Jim
Reeves"): *76* **40–50**
(A 6-LP set.)
Also see KERR, Anita

REEVES, Jim, & Patsy Cline
Singles: 7-Inch
MCA: *82* **1–3**
RCA VICTOR: *81* **1–3**
LPs: 10/12-Inch 33rpm
MCA: *82* **5–8**
RCA VICTOR: *81* **5–8**
Also see CLINE, Patsy

REEVES, Jim, & Dottie West
Singles: 7-Inch
RCA VICTOR: *64* **2–4**
Also see WEST, Dottie
Also see REEVES, Jim

REEVES, Martha
Singles: 12-Inch 33/45rpm
FANTASY: *78–79*. **$4–6**
Singles: 7-Inch
ARISTA: *75–77*. **2–3**
FANTASY: *78–80*. **1–3**
MCA: *74* **2–3**
LPs: 10/12-Inch 33rpm
ARISTA: *76* **8–10**
FANTASY: *78–79*. **5–8**
MCA: *74* **8–10**
PHONORAMA. **5–8**
Also see MARTHA & THE VANDELLAS

REFLECTIONS, The
Singles: 7-Inch
ABC-PARAMOUNT: *66*. **3–5**
ERIC **1–3**
GOLDEN WORLD: *64–65*. **3–5**
LPs: 10/12-Inch 33rpm
GOLDEN WORLD: *64*. **30–35**

REFLECTIONS, The
Singles: 7-Inch
CAPITOL: *75–76* **2–3**

RE-FLEX
Singles: 12-Inch 33/45rpm
CAPITOL: *83–84* **4–6**
Singles: 7-Inch
CAPITOL: *83–84* **1–3**
LPs: 10/12-Inch 33rpm
CAPITOL: *83* **5–8**

REGAL DEWY, The
Singles: 12-Inch 33/45rpm
MILLENNIUM: *77* **5–8**
Singles: 7-Inch
MILLENNIUM: *77* **2–4**

REGAN, Joan
Singles: 7-Inch
COLUMBIA: *66*. **2–3**
LONDON: *55* **2–4**
Picture Sleeves
COLUMBIA: *66*. **2–3**

REGENTS, The
Singles: 7-Inch
ABC: *73*. **1–3**
COUSINS: *61* **40–50**

Price Range

GEE: *61–62* **$6–10**
ROULETTE **1–3**
LPs: 10/12-Inch 33rpm
CAPITOL: *64* **20–25**
GEE: *61* **40–50**
MURRAY HILL **5–8**
Members: Guy Villari; Sal Cuomo; Chuck Fassert; Don Jacobucci; Tony Gravagna.

REID, Clarence (Clarence Reed)
Singles: 7-Inch
ALSTON: *68–74* **2–4**
DIAL: *64* **3–5**
PHIL-L.A. OF SOUL: *67* **3–5**
SELMA: *63* **4–6**
TAY-STER: *67* **3–5**
WAND: *65* **3–5**
LPs: 10/12-Inch 33rpm
ATCO: *69* **10–12**

REID, Terry
Singles: 7-Inch
EPIC: *69* **2–4**
LPs: 10/12-Inch 33rpm
ATLANTIC: *73* **8–10**
EPIC: *68–69* **10–15**

REILLY, Mike
Singles: 7-Inch
PARAMOUNT: *71* **2–4**

REINER, Carl, & Mel Brooks
LPs: 10/12-Inch 33rpm
CAPITOL (1600 series): *61* **15–25**
CAPITOL (2900 series): *68* **8–12**
WARNER BROS (2741;
"2000 & Thirteen"): *73* **5–10**
WARNER BROS (2744;
"2000 Years With Carl
Reiner & Mel Brooks"):
73 . . . . **15–25**
(A 3-LP set.)
WORLD PACIFIC: *60* **20–30**

REIRRUC, Det: see DET REIRRUC

REISMAN, Joe, & His Orchestra
Singles: 7-Inch
LANDA: *61* **2–4**
RCA VICTOR: *55–59* **2–4**
ROULETTE: *59–60* **2–3**

Price Range

EPs: 7-Inch 33/45rpm
RCA VICTOR: *56* **$4–8**
LPs: 10/12-Inch 33rpm
CAMDEN: *72* **5–10**
RCA VICTOR: *56* **8–18**
ROULETTE: *59–60* **5–15**

REJOICE
Singles: 7-Inch
DUNHILL: *68–69* **3–5**
LPs: 10/12-Inch 33rpm
DUNHILL: *69* **10–15**

RENAISSANCE
Singles: 7-Inch
CAPITOL: *72–73* **2–4**
SIRE: *76–78* **2–3**
LPs: 10/12-Inch 33rpm
CAPITOL: *72–78* **8–10**
ELEKTRA: *69* **10–12**
I.R.S.: *81–83* **5–8**
SIRE: *74–79* **8–10**
SINGCORD: *76–77* **8–10**
SOVEREIGN: *73* **8–10**
Also see ARMAGEDDON

RENAISSANCE
Singles: 7-Inch
RANWOOD: *71* **1–3**
LPs: 10/12-Inch 33rpm
RANWOOD: *70* **4–8**
Also see HASLAM, Annie

RENAY, Diane
Singles: 7-Inch
ATCO: *62–63* **3–5**
ERIC **1–3**
FONTANA: *69* **2–4**
MGM: *64* **3–5**
NEW VOICE: *65* **3–5**
20TH CENTURY-FOX:
64 . . . . **3–5**
UNITED ARTISTS: *66* **3–5**
LPs: 10/12-Inch 33rpm
20TH CENTURY-FOX:
64 . . . . **20–25**

RENDER, Rudy
Singles: 7-Inch
DOT: *60–61* **3–5**
EDISON INT'L: *59* **4–6**

Price Range

LONDON: *51* $6–10

RENE, Delia
Singles: 7-Inch
AIRWAVE: *81* 1–3

RENE, Googie (Googie Rene & His Combo)
Singles: 7-Inch
CLASS: *57–66* 2–5
KAPP: *62* 3–5
NEW BAG: *67* 2–4
REED: *60* 3–5
RENDEZVOUS: *60* 2–4
Picture Sleeves
RENDEZVOUS: *60* 2–4
LPs: 10/12-Inch 33rpm
CLASS: *59–63* 15–20

RENE, Henri, & His Orchestra
Singles: 7-Inch
DECCA: *62* 2–4
IMPERIAL: *59* 2–3
RCA VICTOR: *51–56* 2–4
STANDARD: *52–53* 2–4
EPs: 7-Inch 33/45rpm
CAMDEN: *54–57* 4–8
RCA VICTOR: *53–56* 4–8
LPs: 10/12-Inch 33rpm
CAMDEN: *54–57* 5–15
KAPP: *67* 5–10
RCA VICTOR (Except
3000 series): *56–61* 5–15
RCA VICTOR (3000
series): *53* 10–20
(10-Inch LPs.)
Also see BELL SISTERS, The

RENE & ANGELA
Singles: 12-Inch 33/45rpm
MERCURY: *85* 4–6
Singles: 7-Inch
CAPITOL: *80–83* 1–3
MERCURY: *85* 1–3
LPs: 10/12-Inch 33rpm
CAPITOL: *80–83* 5–8
MERCURY: *85* 5–8

RENE & RAY
Singles: 7-Inch
DONNA: *62* 4–6

Price Range

RENE & RENE
Singles: 7-Inch
ABC: *73* $1–3
ABC-PARAMOUNT: *65* 3–5
ARU: *64* 3–5
COBRA: *65* 3–5
COLUMBIA: *64* 3–5
EPIC: *69* 2–4
JOX: *64–66* 4–8
WHITE WHALE: *68–69* 2–4
Picture Sleeves
COLUMBIA: *64* 3–5
LPs: 10/12-Inch 33rpm
EPIC: *69* 10–12
WHITE WHALE: *68* 10–15

RENFRO, Anthony C., Orchestra
Singles: 7-Inch
RENFRO: *76* 2–3

RENO, Mike, & Ann Wilson
Singles: 7-Inch
COLUMBIA: *84* 1–3
Also see LOVERBOY
Also see WILSON, Ann, & The Daybreaks

REO, Diamond: see DIAMOND REO

REPARATA & THE DELRONS (Reparata)
Singles: 7-Inch
BIG TREE: *71* 2–4
KAPP: *69–70* 3–5
LAURIE: *72* 2–4
MALA: *67–68* 4–6
NAMI: *74* 2–4
POLYDOR: *75* 2–4
RCA VICTOR: *65–67* 4–6
WORLD ARTISTS: *64–65* 4–6
LPs: 10/12-Inch 33rpm
AVCO EMBASSY: *70* 10–12
WORLD ARTISTS: *65* 20–25

RESTIVO, Johnny
Singles: 7-Inch
EPIC: *62* 3–5
RCA VICTOR (7000
series): *59–60* 4–6
(With a "47" prefix. Monaural singles.)

Price Range

RCA VICTOR (7000
  series): *59–60* **$8–12**
  (With a "61" prefix. Stereo singles.)
20TH CENTURY-FOX:
  61 .... **4–8**

Picture Sleeves

RCA VICTOR: *60* **8–10**
20TH CENTURY-FOX:
  61 .... **4–8**

LPs: 10/12-Inch 33rpm

RCA VICTOR
  (LPM-2149; "Oh
  Johnny"): *59* **25–30**
  (Monaural issue.)
RCA VICTOR (LSP-2149;
  "Oh Johnny"): *59* **40–45**
  (Stereo issue.)

RETURN TO FOREVER
Singles: 7-Inch

COLUMBIA: *77–79* **2–3**
POLYDOR: *75* **2–4**

LPs: 10/12-Inch 33rpm

COLUMBIA: *76–79* **5–8**
ECM: *75*. **8–10**
POLYDOR: *73–75* **8–10**
  Members: Chick Corea; Lenny White; Stanley
  Clarke; Al DiMeola.
  Also see CLARKE, Stanley
  Also see COREA, Chick
  Also see DI MEOLA, Al
  Also see WHITE, Lenny

REUNION
Singles: 7-Inch

MR. G.: *68* **3–5**
RCA VICTOR: *74–75* **2–4**
  Also, see OHIO EXPRESS, The

REVELATION, The
Singles: 7-Inch

COMBINE: *67*. **4–6**
HANDSHAKE: *80–82*. **1–3**
MERCURY: *70*. **2–4**
MUSIC FACTORY: *68*. **3–5**
RCA VICTOR: *79* **1–3**
RSO: *76* **2–3**

LPs: 10/12-Inch 33rpm

HANDSHAKE: *82*. **5–8**
MERCURY: *70*. **8–10**
RCA VICTOR: *79* **5–8**

Price Range

REVELS, The
Singles: 7-Inch

NORGOLDE (103; "Dead
  Man's Stroll"): *59* **$10–15**
NORGOLDE (103;
  "Midnight Stroll"): *59* **4–6**
NORGOLDE (104; "Foo
  Man Choo"): *59* **5–8**

**REVERE, Paul, & The Raiders (Paul
Revere & The Raiders Featuring
Mark Lindsay; The Raiders)**
Singles: 7-Inch

COLUMBIA (10000
  series): *75* **3–5**
COLUMBIA (42814
  through 44970): *63–69* **4–6**
COLUMBIA (45082
  through 45898): *69–73* **3–5**
DRIVE: *76* **3–5**
GARDENA: *60–62*. **10–15**
JERDEN: *66*. **8–10**
SANDE: *63* **8–12**
20TH CENTURY-FOX:
  76 .... **3–5**

Picture Sleeves

COLUMBIA: *65–66* **5–8**

Promotional Singles

COLUMBIA (Colored
  vinyl). **66**

LPs: 10/12-Inch 33rpm

BACK-TRAC: *85* **5–8**

Price Range

COLUMBIA (12; "Two
Great Selling LPs"): *69* **$15–20**
COLUMBIA (462;
"Greatest Hits"): *67* **20–25**
COLUMBIA (2307
through 2721): *65–67* **20–25**
(Monaural issues.)
COLUMBIA (2755/9555;
"Christmas Present &
Past"): *67* **30–40**
(Monaural/stereo numbers.)
COLUMBIA (2805/9605;
"Goin' To Memphis"):
68 .... **20–25**
(Monaural/stereo numbers.)
COLUMBIA (9107
through 9521): *65–67* **20–25**
(Stereo issues.)
COLUMBIA (9665
through 9964): *68–70* **15–20**
COLUMBIA (30000
series): *71–76* **6–15**
HARMONY: *70–72* **10–15**
GARDENA: *61*. **125–150**
JERDEN: *66* **40–50**
PICKWICK **10–12**
SANDE: *63* **175–200**
SEARS **40–50**
(Special Products Sears promotional issue.)
Members: Mark Lindsay; Freddy Weller; Paul
Revere; Keith Allison; Joe Correro, Jr.
Also see BROTHERHOOD
Also see LINDSAY, Mark
Also see WELLER, Freddy

Price Range

REVERE, Paul, & The Raiders / The Cyrkle
Singles: 7-Inch
COLUMBIA: *66* **$8–10**
(Special Products Chevrolet promotional issue
only.)

Picture Sleeves
COLUMBIA: *66* **10–15**
Also see CYRKLE, The
Also see REVERE, Paul, & The Raiders

REX, T.: see T-REX

REYNOLDS, Burt
Singles: 7-Inch
MCA: *80* **1–3**
MERCURY: *73–74*. **2–4**
Picture Sleeves
MCA: *80* .... **INC**
LPs: 10/12-Inch 33rpm
MERCURY: *73*. **8–10**

REYNOLDS, Debbie
Singles: 7-Inch
ABC: *74*. **1–3**
ABC-PARAMOUNT: *65*. **2–4**
BEVERLY HILLS: *72*. **2–3**
CORAL: *57–58*. **3–6**
DOT: *59–63*. **3–5**
JANUS: *70* **2–3**
MCA. **2–3**
MGM (11000 & 12000
series): *55* **3–6**
MGM (13000 series):
63–66 .... **2–4**
PARAMOUNT: *73*. **1–3**
EPs: 7-Inch 33/45rpm
CORAL: *58* **8–10**
MGM: *55*. **10–12**
LPs: 10/12-Inch 33rpm
DOT: *59–63*. **15–20**
MGM: *60–66*. **10–25**
METRO: *65*. **10–15**
Also see CARPENTER, Carleton, & Debbie
Reynolds

REYNOLDS, Jeannie
Singles: 7-Inch
CASABLANCA: *75* **2–4**

Price Range

Price Range

REYNOLDS, Jody
Singles: 7-Inch
ABC: *73* $1–3
BRENT: *63* 3–5
COLLECTABLES 1–3
DEMON: *58–59* 5–8
PULSAR: *69* 2–4
SMASH: *63* 3–5
TITAN: *66.* 3–5
LPs: 10/12-Inch 33rpm
TRU-GEMS: *78* 8–10
Also see CASEY, Al

REYNOLDS, Jody, & Bobbie Gentry
Singles: 7-Inch
TITAN: *67.* 3–5
Also see GENTRY, Bobbie

REYNOLDS, Jody / The Olympics
Singles: 7-Inch
LIBERTY: *63* 2–4
TITAN: *62.* 3–5
Also see OLYMPICS, The
Also see REYNOLDS, Jody

REYNOLDS, L.J. (L.J. Reynolds & The Chocolate Syrup)
Singles: 12-Inch 33/45rpm
CAPITOL: *82* 4–6
Singles: 7-Inch
CAPITOL: *81–82* 1–3
FANTASY: *85.* 1–3
LAW-TON: *71–72* 2–4
MAINSTREAM: *69.* 2–4
MERCURY: *84.* 1–3
LPs: 10/12-Inch 33rpm
CAPITOL: *81–82* 5–8
MERCURY: *84.* 5–8

REYNOLDS, Lawrence
Singles: 7-Inch
COLUMBIA: *72* 2–3
WARNER BROS: *69–70* 2–4
LPs: 10/12-Inch 33rpm
WARNER BROS: *69* 8–10

RHEIMS, Robert
Singles: 7-Inch
RHEIMS: *59* 2–3
EPs: 7-Inch 33/45rpm
RHEIMS: *59* 3–6

LPs: 10/12-Inch 33rpm
MISTLETOE: *75.* $4–6
RHEIMS: *58–63* 5–10
UNITED ARTISTS: *72–74* 4–8

RHINOCEROS
Singles: 7-Inch
ELEKTRA: *69–70* 2–5
LPs: 10/12-Inch 33rpm
ELEKTRA: *68–70* 10–12

RHODES, Emitt
Singles: 7-Inch
DUNHILL: *70–73.* 2–4
LPs: 10/12-Inch 33rpm
A&M: *70* 10–12
DUNHILL: *70–73.* 8–10
Also see MERRY-GO-ROUND, The

RHODES, Todd
Singles: 7-Inch
KING (4469; "Gin Gin
Gin"): *51* 25–30
KING (4486; "Good
Man"): *51* 8–10
KING (4509; "Your
Daddy's Doggin'
Around"): *51* 15–20
(Black vinyl.)
KING (4509; "Your
Daddy's Doggin'
Around"): *51* 35–40
(Colored vinyl.)
KING (4528; "Rocket
69"): *52* 30–35
KING (4556 through
4601): *52–53.* 8–12
(LaVern Baker is the vocalist on one side of
each of the four King issues in the 4556-4601
series.)
KING (4648 through
4775): *53–54.* 5–8
EPs: 7-Inch 33/45rpm
KING 12–15
LPs: 10/12-Inch 33rpm
KING (88; "Todd Rhodes
Plays The Hits") 70–80
KING (658; "Dance
Music"): *60* 35–45
Also see BAKER, LaVern

Price Range

Price Range

RHYTHM HERITAGE
Singles: 12-Inch 33/45rpm
ABC: 78 . . . . $4–6
Singles: 7-Inch
ABC: 75–78 2–3
LPs: 10/12-Inch 33rpm
ABC: 76–77 5–10

RHYTHM MAKERS, The
Singles: 7-Inch
VIGOR: 76 2–3
LPs: 10/12-Inch 33rpm
VIGOR: 76 8–10

RHYZE
Singles: 7-Inch
20TH CENTURY-FOX:
  81 1–3
LPs: 10/12-Inch 33rpm
20TH CENTURY-FOX:
  81 5–8

RIBBONS, The
Singles: 7-Inch
ERA: 72 1–3
MARSH: 63 4–6
PARKWAY: 64 3–5

RICE, Mack (Sir Mack Rice)
Singles: 7-Inch
ATCO: 69 2–4
BLUE ROCK: 65 3–5
LUPINE: 64 3–5
MERCURY: 66 3–5
STAX: 67–78 2–4

RICH, Buddy (The Buddy Rich Band)
Singles: 7-Inch
ARGO: 61 2–4
CLEF: 54 3–5
EVEREST: 71 1–3
GROOVE MERCHANT:
  74 1–3
MCA: 81 1–3
NORGRAN: 55–56 3–5
PACIFIC JAZZ: 66–67 2–3
RCA VICTOR: 76 1–3
EPs: 7-Inch 33/45rpm
NORGRAN: 54–56 10–25

LPs: 10/12-Inch 33rpm
ARGO: 61 . . . . $15–25
CLEF: 56 50–75
EMARCY: 65–76 10–20
GREAT AMERICAN
  GRAMOPHONE: 78 5–8
GROOVE MERCHANT:
  74–75 5–10
GRYPHON: 79 5–8
LIBERTY: 70 8–12
MCA: 81 5–8
MERCURY: 59–60 20–40
  (Black label.)
MERCURY: 69 8–12
  (Red label.)
NORGRAN (26; "Buddy
  Rich Swingin"): 54 50–75
NORGRAN (1000 series):
  55–56 25–50
PACIFIC JAZZ (Except
  10000 series): 66–70 8–15
PACIFIC JAZZ (10000
  series): 81 5–8
PAUSA 5–8
RCA VICTOR: 72–77 5–10
ROOST: 66 10–20
TRIP: 76 5–8
VSP: 67 8–12
VERVE: 57–58 20–40
  (Reads "Verve Records, Inc." at bottom of
  label.)
VERVE: 61–69 10–25
  (Reads "MGM Records - A Division Of Metro-
  Goldwyn-Mayer, Inc." at bottom of label.)
VERVE: 73–84 5–10
  (Reads "Manufactured By MGM Record
  Corp.," or mentions either Polydor or Poly-
  gram at bottom of label.)
WHO'S WHO IN JAZZ:
  78 5–8
WING: 69 6–12
WORLD PACIFIC: 68 8–12
  Also see TORME, Mel

RICH, Buddy, & Max Roach
LPs: 10/12-Inch 33rpm
MERCURY: 81 5–8
  Also see RICH, Buddy

RICH, Charlie
Singles: 7-Inch
ARISTA: 80 1–3

Lonely Weekends with Charlie Rich

Price Range

	Price Range
COLUMBIA: *82*	$1–3
EPIC: *70–81*	1–3
ELEKTRA: *78–81*	1–3
GROOVE: *63–64.*	3–5
HI: *66–67.*	3–5
MERCURY: *73–74.*	2–3
PHILLIPS INT'L: *59–63*	6–10
RCA VICTOR (Except 8000 series): *74–77*	2–4
RCA VICTOR (8000 series): *64–65*	3–5
SSS/SUN	1–3
SMASH: *65–66*	3–5
UNITED ARTISTS: *78–80*	1–3

Picture Sleeves

GROOVE: *63.*	3–5

LPs: 10/12-Inch 33rpm

BUCKBOARD	8–10
CAMDEN: *70–74*	8–10
CHARLY	5–8
EPIC (Except 139): *68–78*	8–12
EPIC (139; "Everything You Wanted To Hear"): *76*	12–15
(Promotional issue only.)	
ELEKTRA: *80*	5–8
51 WEST	5–8
GROOVE: *64.*	20–25
HARMONY: *73*	8–10
HI (Except 32037): *74–77*	8–10
HI (32037; "Charlie Rich"): *67*	12–15
HILLTOP	8–10
MERCURY: *74.*	10–12
PHILLIPS INT'L: *60*	90–100
PHONORAMA	5–8
POWER PAK: *74.*	8–10
RCA VICTOR (Except 3000 series): *73–77*	8–10
RCA VICTOR (3000 series): *65–66*	15–20
SSS/SUN: *69–79*	5–8
SMASH: *65–66*	15–20
TRIP: *74*	8–10
UNITED ARTISTS: *78–79*	8–10
WING: *69*	10–12

Also see CASH, Johnny
Also see LEWIS, Jerry Lee, Carl Perkins & Charlie Rich
Also see SHERIDAN, Bobby

Price Range

RICHARD, Cliff (Cliff Richard & The Drifters; Cliff Richard & The Shadows)

Singles: 12-Inch 33/45rpm

EMI AMERICA: *83*	$4–6

Singles: 7-Inch

ABC-PARAMOUNT: *59–61*	6–10
BIG TOP: *62*	4–6
CAPITOL: *59*	8–10
DOT: *62*	3–5
EMI AMERICA: *79–84*	1–3
EPIC: *63–67*	3–5
MONUMENT: *70–72*	2–4
ROCKET: *76–79.*	2–3
SIRE: *73*	2–3
UNI: *68–69*	3–5
WARNER BROS: *69*	2–4

Picture Sleeves

EMI AMERICA: *80–81*	1–3
EPIC: *63–66*	4–8

LPs: 10/12-Inch 33rpm

ABC-PARAMOUNT: *60–61*	25–30
EMI AMERICA: *79–83*	5–8
EPIC: *63–65*	15–25
ROCKET: *76–78.*	8–10

Also see NEWTON-JOHN, Olivia, & Cliff Richard

RICHARD, Little: see LITTLE RICHARD

Price Range

RICHARDS, Diane
Singles: 7-Inch
ZOO YORK: 83 .... $1–3

RICHARDS, Turley
Singles: 7-Inch
ATLANTIC: 80 1–3
COLUMBIA: 66–67 3–5
EPIC: 76–78 2–3
KAPP: 68 2–4
MGM: 64 3–5
20TH CENTURY-FOX:
  65 3–5
WARNER BROS: 70 2–4
Picture Sleeves
COLUMBIA: 66 3–5
LPs: 10/12-Inch 33rpm
ATLANTIC: 80 5–8
EPIC: 76 5–8
20TH CENTURY-FOX:
  65 12–15
WARNER BROS: 70–71 10–12

RICHARDSON, Jape (Jape Richardson & His Japettes)
Singles: 7-Inch
MERCURY: 57–58 10–15
Also see BIG BOPPER, The

RICHIE, Lionel
Singles: 12-Inch 33/45rpm
MOTOWN: 83 4–6
Singles: 7-Inch
MOTOWN: 82–86 1–3
LPs: 10/12-Inch 33rpm
MOTOWN: 82–86 5–8
Also see COMMODORES, The
Also see ROSS, Diana, & Lionel Ritchie
Also see U.S.A. FOR AFRICA

RICHMOND EXTENSION
Singles: 7-Inch
SILVER BLUE: 74 2–4

RICK & THE KEENS
Singles: 7-Inch
AUSTIN: 61 15–20
JAMIE: 62 4–6
LE CAM: 61–64 8–12
SMASH: 61 3–5
TOLLIE: 64 3–5

Price Range

TROY $15–20

RIDDLE, Nelson, & His Orchestra
Singles: 7-Inch
CAPITOL: 53–62 2–4
LIBERTY: 67 2–3
REPRISE: 63–66 2–3
20TH CENTURY-FOX:
  66 2–3
VERVE: 59 2–4
Picture Sleeves
CAPITOL: 60 2–4
EPs: 7-Inch 33/45rpm
CAPITOL: 55–59 5–10
VERVE: 59 4–8
LPs: 10/12-Inch 33rpm
ALSHIRE: 70–71 4–8
CAPITOL: 55–78 5–15
DAYBREAK: 73 5–8
EPIC (114; "El Dorado"):
  67 45–55
  (Soundtrack.)
HARMONY: 69 5–8
LIBERTY: 67 5–10
MPS: 73 5–8
PICKWICK: 65 5–10
RCA VICTOR (2976;
  "The Rogues"): 64 15–25
  (Soundtrack.)
REPRISE: 63–65 5–15
SOLID STATE: 67 5–10
SUNSET: 68 5–10
UNITED ARTISTS: 68 5–10
VERVE: 59 5–15
WARNER BROS. (1599;
  "Harlow"): 65 20–30
  (Soundtrack.)
  Also see FITZGERALD, Ella
  Also see PETERSON, Oscar

RIGHT KIND, The
Singles: 7-Inch
GALAXY: 68 3–5

RIGHTEOUS BROTHERS, The
Singles: 7-Inch
HAVEN: 74–76 2–4
MGM: 78–79 2–3
MOONGLOW: 63–66 4–6
PHILLES: 64–66 4–6
POLYDOR 1–3

Price Range

Price Range

VERVE: 65–70 .... $3–5
Picture Sleeves
PHILLES: 65–66. 5–8
VERVE: 66–67 3–6
LPs: 10/12-Inch 33rpm
HAVEN: 74–75. 10–12
MGM: 70–73. 10–15
MOONGLOW: 63–66 20–25
PHILLES: 64–65. 20–25
VERVE: 66–69 15–20
Members: Bill Medley; Bobby Hatfield.
Also see HATFIELD, Bobby
Also see MEDLEY, Bill
Also see PARAMOURS, The
Also see SONNY & CHER

RILEY, Billy (Billy Lee Riley; Billy Riley & His Little Green Men)
Singles: 7-Inch
ATLANTIC: 68 2–4
BRUNSWICK: 58. 40–50
ENTRANCE: 72. 2–4
GNP/CRESCENDO: 66 3–5
HIP: 68 3–5
HOME OF THE BLUES:
  61 8–10
MERCURY: 64–65. 3–5
MOJO: 67 3–5
SUN (245; "Rock With Me
  Baby"): 56 25–30
SUN (260; "Flying Saucers
  Rock & Roll"): 57. 25–30
SUN (277; "Red Hot"): 57 10–12
SUN (289; "Wouldn't You
  Know"): 58 5–8
SUN (313; "No Name
  Girl"): 58 5–8
SUN (322; "Got The
  Water Boiling"): 59. 20–30
SSS/SUN: 69–70. 1–3
LPs: 10/12-Inch 33rpm
CROWN: 63 12–15
GNP/CRESCENDO: 66 12–15
MERCURY: 64–65. 12–15
MOJO. 15–20

RILEY, Jeannie C.
Singles: 7-Inch
CAPITOL: 69 2–4
CROSS COUNTRY: 79. 1–3
GARPAX: 80 1–3

GOD'S COUNTRY: 75 .... $1–3
MCA: 82 1–3
MGM: 71–74. 2–3
MERCURY: 74. 2–3
PLANTATION: 68–72. 2–4
WARNER BROS: 76 1–3
EPs: 7-Inch 33/45rpm
PLANTATION: 68. 5–10
LPs: 10/12-Inch 33rpm
ALBUM GLOBE 5–8
CAPITOL: 69 8–12
CROSS COUNTRY: 79. 5–10
HSRD/PLEASANT
  SOUNDS: 82. 5–8
HEARTWARMING: 79 4–6
LITTLE DARLIN': 68 10–15
MGM: 72–74. 6–10
OUT OF TOWN DIST: 82 5–8
PLANTATION: 68–82. 5–12
POWER PAK. 5–8
SONGBIRD: 81–83 4–8
TRIP: 74 8–12

RIMSHOTS, The
Singles: 7-Inch
STANG: 76–77 2–3
LPs: 10/12-Inch 33rpm
STANG: 76 5–8

RINGS, The
Singles: 7-Inch
MCA: 81 1–3
LPs: 10/12-Inch 33rpm
MCA: 81 5–8

RINKY-DINKS, The (Featuring Bobby Darin)
Singles: 7-Inch
ATCO: 58 15–20
Also see DARIN, Bobby

RIOS, Augie (Augie Rios & The Notations)
Singles: 7-Inch
MGM: 60–64. 3–5
METRO: 58–59. 4–6
SHELLY: 63–64 4–8

RIOS, Miguel
Singles: 7-Inch
A&M: 70 2–4

Price Range

Price Range

LPs: 10/12-Inch 33rpm
A&M: 70 . . . . **$8–12**

RIOT
Singles: 7-Inch
MOTOWN: 74. . . . . **2–3**

LPs: 10/12-Inch 33rpm
CAPITOL: 80–82 . . . . **5–8**
ELEKTRA: 81–82 . . . . **5–8**
FIRE-SIGN: 78. . . . . **10–15**
MOTOWN: 74. . . . . **8–10**
QUALITY/RFC: 84. . . . . **5–8**

RIP CHORDS, The
Singles: 7-Inch
COLUMBIA (3-42000
   series): 63 . . . . **5–10**
   (Compact 33 singles.)
COLUMBIA (4-42000 &
   43000 series): 62–65 . . . . **4–6**

Promotional Singles
COLUMBIA (Colored
   vinyl): 63–64. . . . . **10–15**

Picture Sleeves
COLUMBIA: 63 . . . . **12–15**
   (Promotional issue only.)

LPs: 10/12-Inch 33rpm
COLUMBIA: 64 . . . . **20–30**
   Members: Bruce Johnston; Terry Melcher.
   Also see BRUCE & TERRY

RIPERTON, Minnie
Singles: 12-Inch 33/45rpm
EPIC: 77 . . . . **4–6**

Singles: 7-Inch
CAPITOL: 79 . . . . **2–3**
EPIC: 74–77 . . . . **2–4**
GRT: 72. . . . . **2–4**
JANUS: 75–76. . . . . **2–4**

LPs: 10/12-Inch 33rpm
ACCORD: 82 . . . . **5–8**
CAPITOL: 79–81 . . . . **5–8**
EPIC: 74–77 . . . . **10–12**
51 WEST **5–8**
GRT: 70. . . . . **12–15**
JANUS: 74 . . . . **8–10**
   Also see JONES, Quincy
   Also see ROTARY CONNECTION, The

RIPPLE
Singles: 7-Inch
GRC: 73–75. . . . . **$2–4**
SALSOUL: 77–78 . . . . **1–3**

LPs: 10/12-Inch 33rpm
GRC: 74. . . . . **8–10**
SALSOUL: 77 . . . . **5–8**

RIPPLES & WAVES PLUS
MICHAEL, The (The Jackson Five)
Singles: 7-Inch
STEELTOWN (688; "Let
   Me Carry Your School
   Books"): 69 . . . . **45–55**
   (Mono pressing. "Steeltown" is in all upper case
   letters on label.)
STEELTOWN (688; "Let
   Me Carry Your School
   Books"): 69 . . . . **60–70**
   (Stereo pressing. "Steeltown" is in upper &
   lower case letters.)
   Also see JACKSON FIVE, The

RITCHARD, Cyril
LPs: 10/12-Inch 33rpm
CAEDMON: 69 . . . . **4–8**
RIVERSIDE: 60–62 . . . . **5–12**

RITCHIE FAMILY, The
Singles: 12-Inch 33/45rpm
MARLIN: 76. . . . . **4–6**
RCA VICTOR: 82 . . . . **4–6**

Singles: 7-Inch
CASABLANCA: 79–80 . . . . **1–3**
MARLIN: 76–78. . . . . **2–3**
RCA VICTOR: 82–83 . . . . **1–3**
20TH CENTURY-FOX:
   75 . . . . **2–3**

LPs: 10/12-Inch 33rpm
CASABLANCA: 79–80 . . . . **5–8**
MARLIN: 76–78. . . . . **5–8**
RCA VICTOR: 82 . . . . **5–8**
20TH CENTURY-FOX:
   75 . . . . **8–10**

RITCHIE'S ROOM 222 GANG
Singles: 7-Inch
SCEPTER: 71 . . . . **2–4**

CAPITOL (1100 through
   2800 series): *59–68* **$10–20**
   (With a "T" or "ST" prefix.)
CAPITOL (1200 series): *78* **4–6**
   (With an "SM" prefix.)
CAPITOL (1500 series): *61* **25–35**
   (With a "W" or "SW" prefix.)
CAPITOL (4000 series): *53* **25–40**
   (10-Inch LPs.)
CORONET **8–12**
HILLTOP **10–15**
LA BREA: *62* **15–25**
PICKWICK/HILLTOP:
   66–68 .... **6–12**
SHASTA **8–12**
SPIN-O-RAMA. **8–12**
   Also see KENTON, Stan

RIVERA, Hector
Singles: 7-Inch
BARRY: *66* **3–5**
LPs: 10/12-Inch 33rpm
EPIC: *61* **5–12**
WING: *60* **5–15**

RIVERS, Joan
LPs: 10/12-Inch 33rpm
BUDDAH: *69* **6–12**
GEFFEN: *83* **5–8**
WARNER BROS: *65* **8–15**

RIVERS, Johnny
Singles: 7-Inch
ATLANTIC: *74* **2–4**
BIG TREE: *77–78* **2–3**
CAPITOL: *62–64* **4–6**
CHANCELLOR: *61–62* **6–10**
CORAL: *64* **5–8**
CUB: *59–60* **8–10**
DEE DEE: *59* **10–12**
EPIC: *75–76* **2–4**
ERA: *61* **5–8**
GONE: *58* **15–20**
GUYDEN (2003; "Hole In
   The Ground"): *58* **10–12**
GUYDEN (2110; "Hole In
   The Ground"): *64* **4–6**
IMPERIAL: *64–70* **3–5**
MGM: *64* **4–6**
RSO: *80* **1–3**
RIVERAIRE: *59*. **10–12**

RITENOUR, Lee
Singles: 7-Inch
ELEKTRA: *81–82* **$1–3**
EPIC: *76–80* **2–3**
Picture Sleeves
ELEKTRA: *81* **1–3**
LPs: 10/12-Inch 33rpm
ELEKTRA: *78–82* **5–8**
EPIC: *76–80* **5–10**
JVC: *78* **5–8**
   Also see GRUSIN, Dave

RITTER, Tex
Singles: 7-Inch
CAPITOL (1100 through
   3900 series): *50–58* **3–5**
   (Purple labels.)
CAPITOL (2000 through
   4000 series): *68–76* **1–3**
   (Orange labels.)
CAPITOL (4000 through
   5900 series): *58–67* **2–4**
Picture Sleeves
CAPITOL: *68* **2–4**
EPs: 7-Inch 33/45rpm
CAPITOL: *53–60* **5–12**
LPs: 10/12-Inch 33rpm
ALBUM GLOBE **5–8**
BUCKBOARD **5–8**
CAPITOL (200 through
   400 series): *69–71* **8–12**

Price Range

Price Range

ROULETTE: *64* $5–8
SOUL CITY (Except 008):
76–77 2–3
SOUL CITY (008; "Slow
Dancing"): *77*. 3–5
UNITED ARTISTS
(Except 700 series):
71–73 2–4
UNITED ARTISTS (700
series): *64* 4–6

Picture Sleeves
IMPERIAL: *64–69* 3–6
UNITED ARTISTS: *71* 2–4

LPs: 10/12-Inch 33rpm
ATLANTIC: *74* 8–10
CAPITOL: *64* 20–25
CUSTOM. 10–12
EPIC: *75* 8–10
GUEST STAR. 10–12
IMPERIAL: *64–70*. 15–20
LIBERTY: *82* 5–8
PICKWICK 8–10
PRIORITY: *83* 5–8
RSO: *80* 5–8
SEARS. 20–25
(Special Products issue for Sears stores.)
SOUL CITY: *77* 8–10
SUNSET: *67–69* 10–12
UNITED ARTISTS
(Except UAL, UAS &
UXS series): *73–75* 6–10
UNITED ARTISTS
(UAL-3386; "Go Johnny
Go"): *64*. 20–25
(Monaural issue.)
UNITED ARTISTS
(UAS-6386; "Go Johnny
Go"): *64*. 20–30
(Stereo issue.)
UNITED ARTISTS
(UAS-5532;
"Homegrown"): *71* 10–12
UNITED ARTISTS
(UAS-5650; "L.A.
Reggae"): *72*. 10–12
UNITED ARTISTS
(UXS-93; "Johnny
Rivers"): *72* 12–15
Also see JONES, Tom / Freddie & The Dream-
ers / Johnny Rivers

**RIVERS, Johnny / Ricky Nelson /
Randy Sparks**
LPs: 10/12-Inch 33rpm
MGM: *64*. $20–25
Also see NELSON, Ricky
Also see RIVERS, Johnny

RIVIERAS, The
Singles: 7-Inch
COED (Except 592): *58–60* 8–10
COED (592; "Moonlight
Cocktails"): *64*. 3–5
(Reissue.)
COLLECTABLES 1–3
ERIC 1–3
LOST-NITE 1–3
LPs: 10/12-Inch 33rpm
POST 8–10
Members: Homer Dunn; Andy Jones; Charles
Allen; Ron Cook.

RIVIERAS, The
Singles: 7-Inch
RIVIERA: *63–65* 4–6
LPs: 10/12-Inch 33rpm
RIVIERA: *64* 35–45
USA: *64* 40–50

RIVINGTONS, The
Singles: 7-Inch
A.R.E. AMERICAN: *64* 5–8
BATON MASTER. 4–6
COLUMBIA: *66*. 4–6
J.D.: *76*. 2–5
LIBERTY (Except 55610):
62–64 4–6
LIBERTY (55610;
"Cherry"): *63*. 15–20
QUAN: *67* 3–5
RCA VICTOR: *69* 3–5
REPRISE: *64*. 4–6
VEE JAY: *64–65*. 4–6
WAND: *73* 2–4
Picture Sleeves
LIBERTY (Except 55610):
63 4–8
LPs: 10/12-Inch 33rpm
LIBERTY (3282/7282;
"Doin' The Bird"): *63* 30–40
LIBERTY (10184; "Papa-
Oom-Mow-Mow"): *82*. 5–8

Price Range

Price Range

Members: Carl White; Al Frazier; Sonny Harris; Turner Wilson; Darryl White.

RIX, Jerry
Singles: 7-Inch
A.V.I.: 77 . . . . $2–3

ROAD, The
Singles: 7-Inch
KAMA SUTRA: 68–71 2–4
LPs: 10/12-Inch 33rpm
KAMA SUTRA: 69–71 10–12
NATURAL RESOURCES:
72 10–12

ROAD APPLES, The
Singles: 7-Inch
POLYDOR: 75 2–3

Marty Robbins, 24 charted singles (1956–70), nine charted LPs (1959–83).

ROBBINS, Marty
Singles: 7-Inch
COLUMBIA (02000 &
03000 series): 81–83 1–3
COLUMBIA (10305
through 11425): 76–81 1–3
COLUMBIA (21022
through 21324): 53–54 8–10
COLUMBIA (21351;
"That's All Right"): 54 15–18
COLUMBIA (21352
through 21414): 54–55 5–8

COLUMBIA (21448;
"Maybellene"): 55 . . . . $15–18
COLUMBIA (21461;
"Pretty Mama"): 55 8–10
COLUMBIA (21477;
"Tennessee Toddy"): 56 15–20
COLUMBIA (21508;
"Singing The Blues"): 56 10–12
COLUMBIA (21545;
"Singing The Blues"): 56 5–8
COLUMBIA (30000
series): 60 8–15
(Compact 33 stereo singles.)
COLUMBIA (40679;
"Long Tall Sally"): 56 15–20
COLUMBIA (40706;
"Respectfully Miss
Brooks"): 56 10–15
COLUMBIA (40815
through 41408): 57–59 4–6
COLUMBIA (41511
through 43770): 59–66 3–5
COLUMBIA (43845
through 45775): 67–73 2–4
DECCA: 72–00 2–4
MCA: 73–75 1–3
Picture Sleeves
COLUMBIA (40815
through 41408): 57–59 6–10
COLUMBIA (41511
through 43770): 59–66 3–6
EPs: 7-Inch 33/45rpm
COLUMBIA (1785;
"Marty Robbins"): 56 15–25
COLUMBIA (2116;
"Singing The Blues"): 56 15–20
COLUMBIA (2134; "A
White Sport Coat"): 57 15–20
COLUMBIA (2153;
"Marty Robbins"): 56 15–20
COLUMBIA (2808;
"Marty Robbins"): 57 20–25
COLUMBIA (2814;
"Marty Robbins"): 58 8–12
COLUMBIA (9700 series):
57 15–20
COLUMBIA (10000
through 14000 series):
57–60 10–20
LPs: 10/12-Inch 33rpm
ARTCO: 73 30–40

Price Range

Price Range

CANDLELITE: 77 . . . . $8–12

COLUMBIA (15; "Marty's
Country"): 69 8–12

COLUMBIA (237; "Saddle
Tramp"): 66 25–30
(Columbia Record Club offer.)

COLUMBIA (445; "Bend
In The River"): 68 35–45
(Columbia Record Club offer.)

COLUMBIA (890; "Marty
Robbins Gold"): 75 8–10

COLUMBIA (976; "The
Song Of Robbins"): 57 25–30

COLUMBIA (1087; "Song
Of The Islands"): 57 25–30

COLUMBIA (1189;
"Marty Robbins"): 58 25–30

COLUMBIA (1256;
"Return Of The
Gunfighter"): 69 15–20
(Columbia "Country Star" series issue.)

COLUMBIA (1325;
"Marty's Greatest Hits"):
59 15–20

COLUMBIA (1349;
"Gunfighter Ballads &
Trail Songs"): 59 15–20

COLUMBIA (1481; "More
Gunfighter Ballads &
Trail Songs"): 60 15–20

COLUMBIA (1599;
"Marty's Greatest Hits"):
69 15–20
(Columbia "Country Star" series issue.)

COLUMBIA (1635; "More
Greatest Hits"): 61 15–20

COLUMBIA (1666; "Just
A Little Sentimental"):
61 15–20

COLUMBIA (1801;
"Marty After
Midnight"): 62 40–50

COLUMBIA (1855;
"Portrait Of Marty"): 62 25–35
(With bonus portrait of Marty.)

COLUMBIA (1855;
"Portrait Of Marty"): 62 15–25
(Without bonus portrait of Marty.)

COLUMBIA (1918; "Devil
Woman"): 62 15–20

COLUMBIA (2016; "The
Heart Of Marty
Robbins"): 69 . . . . $80–100
(Columbia "Country Star" series issue.)

COLUMBIA (2040;
"Hawaii's Calling Me"):
62 20–30

COLUMBIA (2072;
"Return Of The
Gunfighter"): 63 15–20

COLUMBIA (2167;
"Island Woman"): 64 35–40

COLUMBIA (2220;
"R.F.D."): 64 40–50

COLUMBIA (2304; "Turn
The Lights Down Low"):
65 15–25

COLUMBIA (2448; "What
God Has Done"): 65 15–20

COLUMBIA (2527; "The
Drifter"): 66 10–20

COLUMBIA (2563; "What
God Has Done"): 69 15–20
(Columbia "Country Star" series issue.)

COLUMBIA (2601;
"Rock'n Roll'n
Robbins"): 56 475–500
(10-Inch LP.)

COLUMBIA (2645; "My
Kind Of Country"): 67 15–20

COLUMBIA (2725;
"Tonight Carmen"): 67 10–20

COLUMBIA (2735;
"Christmas With Marty
Robbins"): 67 20–30

COLUMBIA (2762; "More
Gunfighter Ballads &
Trail Songs"): 69 15–20
(Columbia "Country Star" series issue.)

COLUMBIA (2817; "By
The Time I Get To
Phoenix"): 68 20–30

COLUMBIA (3557; "The
Drifter"): 69 15–20
(Columbia "Country Star" series issue.)

COLUMBIA (3867; "My
Kind Of Country"): 69 15–20
(Columbia "Country Star" series issue.)

COLUMBIA (5489;
"Tonight Carmen"): 69 15–20
(Columbia "Country Star" series issue.)

Price Range

COLUMBIA (5498;
"Christmas With Marty
Robbins"): *69*. $15–20
(Columbia "Country Star" series issue.)

COLUMBIA (5812;
"Marty"): *72* 20–40
(5-LP set. Columbia Special Products issue.)

COLUMBIA (6994; "I
Walk Alone"): *69* 15–20
(Columbia "Country Star" series issue.)

COLUMBIA (8158;
"Gunfighter Ballads &
Trail Songs"): *59*. 15–20
(With a "CS" prefix.)

COLUMBIA (8158;
"Gunfighter Ballads &
Trail Songs") 5–8
(With a "PC" prefix.)

COLUMBIA (8272; "More
Gunfighter Ballads &
Trail Songs"): *60*. 15–20
(With a "CS" prefix.)

COLUMBIA (8272; "More
Gunfighter Ballads &
Trail Songs") 5–8
(With a "PC" prefix.)

COLUMBIA (8435; "More
Greatest Hits"): *61* 15–20
(With a "CS" prefix.)

COLUMBIA (8435; "More
Greatest Hits") 5–8
(With a "PC" prefix.)

COLUMBIA (8466; "Just
A Little Sentimental"):
61 15–20

COLUMBIA (8601;
"Marty After
Midnight"): *62*. 40–50

COLUMBIA (8655;
"Portrait Of Marty"): *62* 25–35
(With bonus portrait of Marty.)

COLUMBIA (8655;
"Portrait Of Marty"): *62* 15–25
(Without bonus portrait of Marty.)

COLUMBIA (8718; "Devil
Woman"): *62*. 15–20

COLUMBIA (8840;
"Hawaii's Calling Me"):
62 20–30

COLUMBIA (8872;
"Return Of The
Gunfighter"): *63* 15–20

Price Range

COLUMBIA (8976;
"Island Woman"): *64* $35–40

COLUMBIA (9020;
"R.F.D."): *64*. 40–50
(With a "CS" prefix.)

COLUMBIA (9020;
"R.F.D."). 8–10
(With a "CSRP" prefix. Columbia Special
Products issue.)

COLUMBIA (9104; "Turn
The Lights Down Low"):
65 20–30

COLUMBIA (9248; "What
God Has Done"): *65*. 15–20
(With a "CS" prefix.)

COLUMBIA (9248; "What
God Has Done"). 5–8
(With an "ACS" prefix. Columbia Special
Products issue.)

COLUMBIA (9327; "The
Drifter"): *66*. 10–20

COLUMBIA (9421; "The
Song Of Robbins"): *67* 30–40

COLUMBIA (9445; "My
Kind Of Country"): *67*. 15–25

COLUMBIA (9525;
"Tonight Carmen"): *67*. 10–20

COLUMBIA (9535;
"Christmas With Marty
Robbins"): *67*. 10–20

COLUMBIA (9617; "By
The Time I Get To
Phoenix"): *68*. 8–12

COLUMBIA (9725; "I
Walk Alone"): *68* 8–15

COLUMBIA (9811; "It's
A Sin"): *69*. 20–30

COLUMBIA (9978; "My
Woman, My Woman,
My Wife"): *70*. 8–12

COLUMBIA (10022
through 10579): *73–75* 8–10
(Columbia's Limited Edition series, identified
with an "LE" prefix.)

COLUMBIA (10980;
"Christmas With Marty
Robbins"): *70*. 15–20
(Columbia Special Products issue.)

COLUMBIA (11222;
"Marty's Greatest Hits"):
75 5–8

Price Range

COLUMBIA (11311; "By
The Time I Get To
Phoenix"): *70*. **$6–10**
(Columbia Special Products issue.)
COLUMBIA (11513; "By
The Time I Get To
Phoenix"): *71*. **15–20**
(Columbia Special Products issue.)
COLUMBIA (12416;
"Marty Robbins' Own
Favorites"): *74*. **12–15**
(Special Products issue for Vaseline Hair
Tonic.)
COLUMBIA (13358;
"Christmas With Marty
Robbins"): *72*. **6–10**
(Columbia Special Products issue.)
COLUMBIA (14035;
"Legendary Music
Man"): *77* **8–12**
(Columbia Special Products issue.)
COLUMBIA (14613; "Best
Of Marty Robbins"): *78*. **5–8**
(Columbia Special Products issue.)
COLUMBIA (15594;
"Number One
Cowboy"): *81*. **5–8**
(Columbia Special Products issue.)
COLUMBIA (15812;
"Marty Robbins' Best"):
82 . . . . **5–8**
(Columbia Special Products issue.)
COLUMBIA (16561;
"Reflections"): *82* **5–8**
(Columbia Special Products issue.)
COLUMBIA (16578;
"Classics"): *83* **15–20**
(3-LP set. Columbia Special Products issue.)
COLUMBIA (16914;
"Country Classics"): *83* **5–8**
(Columbia Special Products issue.)
COLUMBIA (17120;
"Sincerely"): *83*. **5–8**
(Columbia Special Products issue.)
COLUMBIA (17136;
"Forever Yours"): *83* **5–8**
(Columbia Special Products issue.)
COLUMBIA (17137;
"That Country Feeling"):
83 . . . . **5–8**
(Columbia Special Products issue.)

Price Range

COLUMBIA (17138;
"Banquet Of Songs"): *83* **$5–8**
(Columbia Special Products issue.)
COLUMBIA (17159; "The
Great Marty Robbins"):
83 . . . . **5–8**
(Columbia Special Products issue.)
COLUMBIA (17206; "The
Legendary Marty
Robbins"): *83*. **5–8**
(Columbia Special Products issue.)
COLUMBIA (17209;
"Country Cowboy"): *83* **5–8**
(Columbia Special Products issue.)
COLUMBIA (17367;
"Song Of The Islands"):
83 . . . . **5–8**
(Columbia Special Products issue.)
COLUMBIA (30000
through 40000 series):
70–86 . . . . **5–12**
DECCA: *72*. **8–12**
GUSTO/COLUMBIA: *81* **8–10**
HARMONY (Except
31258): *69–72*. **8–15**
HARMONY (31258; "Song
Of The Islands"): *72*. **20–25**
K-TEL: *77*. **8–10**
MCA: *73–74* **5–12**
ORBIT: *84*. **8–10**
PICKWICK **5–10**
READER'S DIGEST (054;
"Greatest Hits"): *83* **20–30**
(5-LP set.)
SUNRISE MEDIA: *81*. **5–8**
TIME-LIFE: *81*. **5–8**
Note: When a Columbia LP title in the "1000"
or "2000" series is duplicated in the "8000" or
"9000" series, the lower number is a monaural
issue, the higher a stereo issue.

ROBBINS, Marty / Johnny Cash / Ray Price
LPs: 10/12-Inch 33rpm
COLUMBIA: *70*. **8–10**
Also see CASH, Johnny
Also see PRICE, Ray

ROBBINS, Marty, & Jeanne Pruett
Singles: 7-Inch
AUDIOGRAPH: *83*. **1–3**
Also see PRUETT, Jeanne

Price Range

ROBBINS, Marty / Carl Smith / Lefty Frizzell
LPs: 10/12-Inch 33rpm
COLUMBIA (2544; "Carl,
Lefty & Marty"): *56* **$80–120**
(10-Inch LP.)
Also see FRIZZELL, Lefty
Also see ROBBINS, Marty
Also see SMITH, Carl

ROBBINS, Rockie
Singles: 7-Inch
A&M: *79–81* **1–3**
MCA: *85* **1–3**
Picture Sleeves
A&M: *80* **1–3**
LPs: 10/12-Inch 33rpm
A&M: *80–81* **5–8**
MCA: *85* **5–8**

ROBBS, The
Singles: 7-Inch
ATLANTIC: *68* **3–5**
DUNHILL: *69–70*. **2–4**
MERCURY: *66–67*. **3–5**
Picture Sleeves
MERCURY: *67*. **3–5**
LPs: 10/12-Inch 33rpm
MERCURY: *67*. **20–25**

ROBERT & JOHNNY
Singles: 7-Inch
COLLECTABLES **1–3**

Price Range

OLD TOWN: *57–62* **$4–6**
Members: Robert Carr; Johnny Mitchell.

ROBERT & JOHNNY / The Fiestas
Singles: 7-Inch
ATCO. **1–3**
Also see FIESTAS, The
Also see ROBERT & JOHNNY

ROBERTA LEE: see LEE, Roberta

ROBERTINO (The Robertino Orchestra)
Singles: 7-Inch
4 CORNERS: *63* **2–4**
KAPP: *61–62*. **2–4**
LPs: 10/12-Inch 33rpm
KAPP: *61–66*. **5–15**
UNITED ARTISTS
INT'L: *67*. **5–10**

ROBERTS, Austin
Singles: 7-Inch
ARISTA: *78* **2–3**
CHELSEA: *72–75*. **2–4**
COLLECTABLES **1–3**
GUSTO **1–3**
PHILIPS: *68–71* **2–4**
PRIVATE STOCK: *75–76*. **2–3**
LPs: 10/12-Inch 33rpm
CHELSEA: *72–73*. **8–10**

ROBERTS, John
Singles: 7-Inch
DUKE: *67–69* **3–5**

ROBERTS, Lea
Singles: 7-Inch
UNITED ARTISTS: *74–75* **2–3**

ROBERTSON, Don
Singles: 7-Inch
CAPITOL: *56–59* **2–4**
MONUMENT: *66–76*. **1–3**
RCA VICTOR: *61–68* **2–4**
LPs: 10/12-Inch 33rpm
RCA VICTOR: *65* **8–12**

ROBEY
Singles: 12-Inch 33/45rpm
SILVER BLUE: *84–85* **4–6**

Price Range

Singles: 7-Inch
SILVER BLUE: *84–85*............ $1–3

ROBIC, Ivo
Singles: 7-Inch
LAURIE: *59–60* 2–5
PHILIPS: *62* 2–4

ROBIN, Cock: see COCK ROBIN

ROBIN, Tina
Singles: 7-Inch
CORAL: *57–59*.................... 5–8
MERCURY: *61–63*................. 3–5

ROBINS, The (The Robbins)
Singles: 7-Inch
ARVEE: *60* 4–6
ATCO (6059; "Smokey
Joe's Cafe"): *55* 5–8
CROWN: *54* 60–75
GONE: *61* 4–6
KNIGHT: *58*.................... 5–8
LAVENDER: *61*................. 8–10
PUSH 3–5
RCA VICTOR (5100 &
5200 series): *53* 70–80
RCA VICTOR (5400 &
5500 series): *53* 45–55
SPARK (103 through 110):
54–55 25–35
SPARK (113 through 116):
55 15–20
SPARK (122; "Smokey
Joe's Cafe"): *55* 40–45
WHIPPET: *56–58*................ 6–10
LPs: 10/12-Inch 33rpm
GNP/CRESCENDO: *75* 5–8
WHIPPET: *58*.................. 60–75
Members: Ty Terrell; Bobby Nunn; Carl Gard-
ner; Bill Richards; Grady Chapman; H.B. Bar-
num; Roy Richards; Richard Berry.
Also see BARNUM, H.B.
Also see COASTERS, The
Also see LITTLE ESTHER & THE ROBINS
Also see NUNN, Bobby

ROBINS, Jimmy
Singles: 7-Inch
KENT: *68* 3–5

SMOKEY JOE'S CAFE
(Leiber and Stoller)
THE ROBINS
122–45

Price Range

ROBINSON, Alvin
Singles: 7-Inch
ATCO: *68* $2–4
BLUE CAT: *65*................... 4–6
JOE JONES: *66*.................. 3–5
RED BIRD: *64*................... 4–6
TIGER: *64*...................... 4–6

ROBINSON, Ed
Singles: 7-Inch
COTILLION: *70*.................. 2–4

ROBINSON, Dutch
Singles: 7-Inch
CBS ASSOCIATED: *84–85*.......... 1–3

ROBINSON, Floyd
Singles: 7-Inch
DOT: *61–62*..................... 3–5
GROOVE: *64*.................... 3–5
JAMIE: *61*...................... 3–5
RCA VICTOR: *59–60* 4–6
UNITED ARTISTS: *63–66*.......... 4–6
EPs: 7-Inch 33/45rpm
RCA VICTOR: *59* 12–15
LPs: 10/12-Inch 33rpm
RCA VICTOR: *60* 20–30

ROBINSON, Freddy
Singles: 7-Inch
CHECKER: *66*.................... 3–5
LIBERTY: *70* 2–4

Price Range

LIMELIGHT. **$4–6**
PACIFIC JAZZ: *69–70* **2–4**
QUEEN: *61* **3–5**
WORLD PACIFIC: *70* **2–4**
    LPs: 10/12-Inch 33rpm
ENTERPRISE: *71* **6–10**
PACIFIC JAZZ: *69* **8–12**
   Also see LITTLE WALTER
   Also see HOWLING WOLF

ROBINSON, J.P.
Singles: 7-Inch
ALSTON: *68–69* **2–4**

ROBINSON, Jackie
Singles: 7-Inch
ARIOLA AMERICAN: *76* **2–3**

ROBINSON, Roscoe (Rosco Robinson)
Singles: 7-Inch
ATLANTIC: *69* **2–4**
FAME: *70* **2–4**
SOUND STAGE 7: *67–69* **3–5**
WAND: *66–67* **3–5**

ROBINSON, Smokey (William Robinson)
Singles: 7-Inch
TAMLA: *73–86* **1–3**
MOTOWN **1–3**
    LPs: 10/12-Inch 33rpm
MOTOWN: *82* **5–8**
TAMLA: *73–86* **6–10**
   Also see JAMES, Rick, & Smokey Robinson
   Also see MIRACLES, The
   Also see ROSS, Diana, Stevie Wonder, Marvin
   Gaye & Smokey Robinson
   Also see TEMPTATIONS, The
   Also see U.S.A. FOR AFRICA

ROBINSON, Smokey, & Barbara Mitchell
Singles: 7-Inch
TAMLA: *83* **1–3**
   Also see HIGH INERGY

ROBINSON, Stan
Singles: 7-Inch
AMY: *60–61* **3–5**
MONUMENT: *59* **3–5**

Price Range

ROBINSON, Tom, Band
Singles: 7-Inch
HARVEST: *78–79* **$2–3**
    LPs: 10/12-Inch 33rpm
HARVEST: *78* **8–10**
I.R.S.: *80* **5–8**

ROBINSON, Vicki Sue
Singles: 12-Inch 33/45rpm
PROFILE: *83–84* **4–6**
Singles: 7-Inch
PROFILE: *83–84* **1–3**
RCA VICTOR: *76–77* **2–3**
    LPs: 10/12-Inch 33rpm
PROFILE: *83* **5–8**
RCA VICTOR: *79–81* **5–8**

ROBINSON, Wanda
LPs: 10/12-Inch 33rpm
PERCEPTION: *71* **5–10**

ROBOTNICK, Alexander
Singles: 7-Inch
SIRE: *85* **1–3**

ROCCA, John
Singles: 12-Inch 33/45rpm
STREETWISE: *84* **4–6**
Singles: 7-Inch
STREETWISE: *84* **1–3**
   Also see FREEZ

ROCHELL
Singles: 12-Inch 33/45rpm
WARNER BROS: *85* **4–6**
Singles: 7-Inch
WARNER BROS: *85* **1–3**

ROCHELL & THE CANDLES
(With Rochell Henderson & Johnny Wyatt)
Singles: 7-Inch
CHALLENGE: *62–63* **5–8**
COLLECTABLES **1–3**
SWINGIN': *61* **8–10**

ROCHES, The
LPs: 10/12-Inch 33rpm
COLUMBIA: *75* **8–10**
WARNER BROS: *79–82* **5–8**

Price Range

Members: Suzzy Roche; Maggie Roche; Terre Roche.

ROCK & ROLL DOUBLE BUBBLE TRADING CARD CO. OF PHILADELPHIA, 19141, The
Singles: 7-Inch
BUDDAH: 68 .... $3–5

ROCK FLOWERS, The
Singles: 7-Inch
WHEEL: 71–73 2–4
LPs: 10/12-Inch 33rpm
WHEEL: 71–72 8–10

ROCK MASTER SCOTT & THE DYNAMIC THREE
Singles: 12-Inch 33/45rpm
REALITY: 84–85 4–6
Singles: 7-Inch
REALITY: 84–85 1–3

ROCK SQUAD, The
Singles: 12-Inch 33/45rpm
TOMMY BOY: 85 4–6

ROCK STEADY CREW, The
Singles: 12-Inch 33/45rpm
ATLANTIC: 83–84 4–6
Singles: 7-Inch
ATLANTIC: 83–84 1–3

ROCK-A-TEENS, The
Singles: 7-Inch
DORAN: 59 20–25
ROULETTE: 59–60 8–10
LPs: 10/12-Inch 33rpm
MURRAY HILL 5–8
ROULETTE: 60 75–80

ROCKER'S REVENGE
Singles: 12-Inch 33/45rpm
STREETWISE: 83–84 4–6
Singles: 7-Inch
STREETWISE: 82–84 1–3

ROCKET
Singles: 12-Inch 33/45
QUALITY/RFC: 83 4–6
LPs: 10/12-Inch 33rpm
QUALITY/RFC: 83 5–8

Price Range

ROCKETS, The
Singles: 7-Inch
RSO: 79 .... $1–3
TORTOISE INT'L: 77–78 2–3
LPs: 10/12-Inch 33rpm
RSO: 79–80 5–8
TORTOISE INT'L: 77 8–10
Also see DETROIT

ROCKIN' Rs, The
Singles: 7-Inch
STEPHENY: 60 4–6
TEMPUS: 59–60 6–10
VEE JAY: 60 4–6

ROCKIN' REBELS, The
Singles: 7-Inch
ABC: 73 1–3
ERIC 1–3
ITZY 5–8
STORK: 64 4–6
SWAN: 62–63 3–6
LPs: 10/12-Inch 33rpm
SWAN: 63 40–50
Members: Tom Gorman; Paul Balon; Mickey Kipler; Jim Kipler.
Also see BUFFALO REBELS, The
Also see HOT-TODDYS, The
Also see REBELS, The

ROCKINGHAM, David, Trio
Singles: 7-Inch
JOSIE: 63–64 3–5

Price Range

Price Range

ROCKPILE
Singles: 7-Inch
COLUMBIA: *80* $1–3
EPs: 7-Inch 33/45rpm
COLUMBIA (1219; "Nick
 Lowe & Dave
 Edmunds"): *80*. 2–4
 (Bonus EP, issued with the LP "Seconds Of
 Pleasure.")
LPs: 10/12-Inch 33rpm
COLUMBIA (36886;
 "Seconds Of Pleasure"):
 80 5–8
 (Includes the bonus EP, 1219, "Nick Lowe &
 Dave Edmunds.")
 Members: Nick Lowe; Dave Edmunds.
 Also see EDMUNDS, Dave
 Also see LOWE, Nick

ROCKWELL
Singles: 12-Inch 33/45rpm
MOTOWN: *84*. 4–6
Singles: 7-Inch
MOTOWN: *84–85*. 1–3
LPs: 10/12-Inch 33rpm
MOTOWN: *84*. 5–8
 Also see JACKSON, Michael

ROCKY FELLERS, The
Singles: 7-Inch
DONNA: *63* 4–6
PARKWAY: *62* 4–6
SCEPTER: *62–63* 4–6
WARNER BROS: *64–65* 4–6
LPs: 10/12-Inch 33rpm
SCEPTER: *63* 20–25

ROD
Singles: 7-Inch
PRELUDE: *80*. 1–3

RODGERS, Eileen
Singles: 7-Inch
COLUMBIA: *56–60* 3–5
KAPP: *61* 2–4
EPs: 7-Inch 33/45rpm
COLUMBIA: *58* 5–10
LPs: 10/12-Inch 33rpm
COLUMBIA: *58* 10–20
 Also see MITCHELL, Guy / Eileen Rodgers

RODGERS, Jimmie
Singles: 7-Inch
A&M: *67–70* $2–4
ABC: *73* 1–3
DOT: *62–67*. 2–4
EPIC: *71–72* 2–3
RCA VICTOR: *73–75* 2–3
ROULETTE: *57–61* 3–5
SCRIMSHAW: *78*. 1–3
Picture Sleeves
DOT: *62–64*. 3–5
ROULETTE: *57–61* 5–8
EPs: 7-Inch 33/45rpm
ROULETTE: *57–60* 8–10
LPs: 10/12-Inch 33rpm
A&M: *67–70* 8–12
DOT: *62–67*. 10–15
FORUM: *60* 12–15
HAMILTON: *64–65*. 10–12
RCA VICTOR: *73–75* 8–10
ROULETTE (25000
 series): *57–62* 15–20
ROULETTE (42000 series) 5–8
SCRIMSHAW: *78*. 5–8

RODGERS, Nile
Singles: 12-Inch 33/45rpm
WARNER BROS: *85* 4–6
Singles: 7-Inch
WARNER BROS: *85* 1–3
LPs: 10/12-Inch 33rpm
MIRAGE: *84*. 5–8
WARNER BROS: *85* 5–8
 Also see CHIC
 Also see HONEYDRIPPERS, The

RODGERS, Paul
Singles: 7-Inch
ATLANTIC: *83* 1–3
LPs: 10/12-Inch 33rpm
ATLANTIC: *83* 5–8
 Also see BAD COMPANY
 Also see FIRM, The
 Also see FREE

RODRIGUEZ, Johnny
Singles: 7-Inch
COLUMBIA: *80*. 1–3
EPIC: *79–84* 1–3
MERCURY: *72–79*. 2–3

Price Range

ROGERS, Julie
Singles: 7-Inch
MEGA: 72 .... $2–3
MERCURY: 64–66 3–5
Picture Sleeves
MERCURY: 65 3–5
LPs: 10/12-Inch 33rpm
MEGA: 72 5–10
MERCURY: 65 10–15

ROGERS, Kenny (Kenneth Rogers)
Singles: 7-Inch
CARLTON: 58 8–10
KEN-LEE 8–10
LIBERTY: 80–86 1–3
MERCURY: 66 3–5
RCA VICTOR: 84–86 1–3
UNITED ARTISTS: 76–80 1–3
Picture Sleeves
LIBERTY: 80–86 1–3
RCA VICTOR: 84–86 1–3
UNITED ARTISTS: 76–80 1–3
LPs: 10/12-Inch 33rpm
LIBERTY: 80–83 5–8
RCA VICTOR: 84–86 5–8
UNITED ARTISTS: 76–80 5–8
Promotional LPs
UNITED ARTISTS ("The
Gambler" - picture disc):
79 40–50
Also see EASTON, Sheena, & Kenny Rogers
Also see U.S.A. FOR AFRICA

ROGERS, Kenny, & Kim Carnes
Singles: 7-Inch
UNITED ARTISTS: 80 1–3
Picture Sleeves
UNITED ARTISTS: 80 .... INC
Also see CARNES, Kim

ROGERS, Kenny, & The First Edition
Singles: 7-Inch
JOLLY ROGER: 72–73 2–4
REPRISE: 68–72 3–5
LPs: 10/12-Inch 33rpm
JOLLY ROGERS: 72–73 8–12
REPRISE: 69–72 10–15
Members: Kenny Rogers; Mike Settle; Thelma
Lou Camacho; Terry Williams; Mickey Jones.
Also see FIRST EDITION, The

Price Range

ROGERS, Kenny, & Dolly Parton
Singles: 7-Inch
RCA VICTOR: 83–85 .... $1–3
Also see PARTON, Dolly

ROGERS, Kenny, & Dottie West
Singles: 7-Inch
UNITED ARTISTS: 78–79 1–3

LPs: 10/12-Inch 33rpm
UNITED ARTISTS: 78–79 5–8

LPs: 10/12-Inch 33rpm
Also see ROGERS, Kenny
Also see WEST, Dottie

ROGERS, Lee
Singles: 7-Inch
D-TOWN: 65 3–5

ROGERS, Roy (Roy Rogers & Dale Evans; Roy Rogers & The Sons Of The Pioneers)
Singles: 7-Inch
CAPITOL: 70–71 2–4
MCA: 80 1–3
NEW DISC: 56 2–5
RCA VICTOR: 51–52 2–5
20TH CENTURY-FOX:
74–75 2–3

EPs: 7-Inch 33/45rpm
BLUEBIRD 10–15
RCA VICTOR: 50–57 10–20

LPs: 10/12-Inch 33rpm
BLUEBIRD: 59 12–25
CAMDEN: 60–75 6–15
CAPITOL: 62–72 10–20
GOLDEN: 62 8–15
PICKWICK 5–10
RCA VICTOR (1400
series): 57 20–25
RCA VICTOR (3000
series): 52–54 25–35
(10-Inch LPs.)
20TH CENTURY-FOX:
75 5–10
WORD: 73–77 4–8

Price Range

Price Range

ROGERS, Timmie (Timmie "Oh Yeah" Rogers; Timmie Rogers & The Excelsior Hep Cats; Timmie Rogers & The Stomp Russell Trio; Timmy Rogers; Super Soul Brother Alias Clark Dark.)
Singles: 7-Inch
CADET: 71 . . . . $2–4
CAMEO: 57–58. 4–6
CAPITOL: 53 5–8
EPIC: 65–66 3–5
MERCURY: 54. 8–10
PARKWAY: 60 3–5
PARTEE: 73 2–4
PHILIPS: 62 3–5
SIGNATURE: 60 3–5
LPs: 10/12-Inch 33rpm
EPIC: 65 12–15
PARTEE: 73 8–10
PHILIPS: 63 12–15

ROLLE, Ralph
Singles: 12-Inch 33/45rpm
STREETWISE: 85 4–6
Singles: 7-Inch
STREETWISE: 85 1–3

ROLLERS, The
Singles: 7-Inch
BELLE STAR: 62. 4–6
LIBERTY: 61 4–6

ROLLERS, The
Singles: 7-Inch
ARISTA: 79 . . . . $1–3
LPs: 10/12-Inch 33rpm
ARISTA: 79 5–8
Also see BAY CITY ROLLERS, The

ROLLIN, Dana
Singles: 7-Inch
TOWER: 67. 3–5

ROLLING STONES, The
Singles: 12-Inch 33/45rpm
ATCO: 79 6–10
ROLLING STONES (70; "Hot Stuff"): 76. 35–45
(Promotional issue only.)
ROLLING STONES (119; "Miss You"): 78 15–20
(Promotional issue only.)
ROLLING STONES (253; "If I Was A Dancer"): 79 12–15
(Promotional issue only.)
ROLLING STONES (367; "Emotional Rescue"): 80 12–15
(Promotional issue only.)
ROLLING STONES (397; "Start Me Up"): 81. 12–15
(Promotional issue only. Price includes special cover.)
ROLLING STONES (4609; "Miss You"): 78 8–10
(Price includes special cover.)
ROLLING STONES (685: "Undercover Of The Night"): 83. 18–20
(White label. Promotional issue only.)
ROLLING STONES (685: "Undercover Of The Night"): 83. 12–15
(Yellow label. Promotional issue only.)
ROLLING STONES (574; "She Was Hot"): 84 12–15
(Promotional issue only.)
ROLLING STONES (96902; "Too Much Blood"): 85. 4–6
(Price includes special cover.)

Price Range

ROLLING STONES
(96978: "Undercover Of
The Night"): *83* **$8–10**
(Price includes special cover.)
ROLLING STONES (692;
"Too Much Blood"): *85* **12–15**
(Promotional issue only. Price includes special cover.)

Singles: 7-Inch

ABKCO: *75* **2–4**
LONDON (901 through
910): *66–69* **3–5**
LONDON (9657 through
9725): *64–65* **8–12**
(Purple & white labels.)
LONDON (9657 through
9725): *64–65* **3–5**
(Blue swirl label.)
LONDON (9741 through
9823): *65–66* **3–5**
ROLLING STONES:
71–85 . . . . **2–4**

Picture Sleeves

LONDON (901 through
904): *66–67* **10–15**
LONDON (905;
"Dandelion"): *67* **60–70**
LONDON (906; "She's A
Rainbow"): *67* **10–15**
LONDON (908; "Jumpin'
Jack Flash"): *68* **10–15**
LONDON (909; "Street
Fighting Man"): *68* **1500–2000**
LONDON (910; "Honky
Tonk Women"): *69* **8–10**
LONDON (9657; "Not
Fade Away"): *64* **45–55**
LONDON (9682; "Tell
Me"): *64* **20–25**
LONDON (9687 & 9708):
64 . . . . **15–20**
LONDON (9725; "Heart
Of Stone"): *65* **65–80**
LONDON (9741 & 9766):
65 . . . . **20–25**
LONDON (9823; "19th
Nervous Breakdown"):
66 . . . . **15–20**
ROLLING STONES
(Except 228, 316, &
19309): *78–85* **3–5**

Price Range

ROLLING STONES (228;
"Time Waits For No
One"): *76* **$15–20**
(Promotional issue only.)
ROLLING STONES (316;
"Before They Make Me
Run"): *78* **15–20**
(Promotional issue only.)
ROLLING STONES
(19309; "Beast Of
Burden"): *78* **200–250**

Promotional Singles: 7-Inch

ABKCO: *75* **5–8**
LONDON (901 through
910): *66–69* **10–12**
LONDON (9641;
"Stoned"): *64* **225–275**
LONDON (9657; "Not
Fade Away"): *64* **15–20**
LONDON (9682 through
9823): *64–65* **12–15**
ROLLING STONES (228;
"Time Waits For No
One"): *76* **12–15**
ROLLING STONES (316;
"Before They Make Me
Run"): *78* **10–12**
ROLLING STONES
(19000 through 21301):
71–82 . . . . **6–10**
ROLLING STONES
(90000 series): *82–85* **4–6**

EPs: 7-Inch 33/45rpm

ATLANTIC: *72–73* **25–35**
(Jukebox issues only.)
LONDON: *64–67* **75–100**
(Jukebox issues only.)

LPs: 10/12-Inch 33rpm

ABKCO (1;
"Metamorphosis"): *75* **12–15**
ABKCO (1; "Songs Of The
Rolling Stones"): *75* **75–100**
(Promotional issue only.)
ABKCO (0268; "Greatest
Hits") **20–25**
(A 2-LP TV mail-order offer.)
CRAWDADDY ("Rolling
Stones Tour Special"): *76* **150–175**
(Promotional issue to college radio stations only.)

Price Range

Price Range

D.I.R. (312 & 325; "King
Biscuit Flower Hour"):
80 . . . . **$150–200**
(Promotional issue only.)

INS RADIO: *65* **50–75**

LONDON (1; "Big Hits" -
mono): *66* **15–20**

LONDON (2; "Their
Satanic Majesties
Request" - mono): *67* **40–50**

LONDON (2; "Their
Satanic Majesties
Request" - stereo): *67* **20–25**
(With 3-D cover.)

LONDON (2; "Their
Satanic Majesties
Request" - stereo): *70* **8–10**
(With standard cover.)

LONDON (3 through 5):
69–70 . . . . **8–10**

LONDON (375 through
509): *64–67.* **8–10**
(Stereo issues. Mono releases of these LPs are in
the 3000 series.)

LONDON (539; "Beggers
Banquet"): *68.* **15–20**
(All songs are shown as written by Jagger &
Richard.)

LONDON (539; "Beggers
Banquet") **8–10**
("Prodigal Son" is shown as written by Rev.
Wilkins.)

LONDON (600 series): *72* **10–12**

LONDON (3375; "The
Rolling Stones" - mono):
64 . . . . **50–60**
(Price includes a 12x12 bonus photo, which
represents $10-$15 of the value. This issue also
has a printed promotional mention of the bonus
photo on the front cover.)

LONDON (3375; "The
Rolling Stones" - mono):
64 . . . . **15–25**
(This issue has neither the 12x12 photo nor the
printed promotional mention of it on the front
cover.)

LONDON (3375; "The
Rolling Stones" - mono):
64 . . . . **250–275**
(White label. Promotional issue only.)

LONDON (3402; "12 X 5"
- mono): *64.* **15–20**

LONDON (3420; "Rolling
Stones Now" - mono):
65 . . . . **$15–20**

LONDON (3429; "Out Of
Our Heads" - mono): *65* **15–20**

LONDON (3451;
"December's Children" -
mono): *65.* **15–20**

LONDON (3476;
"Aftermath" - mono): *66* **15–20**

LONDON (3493; "Got
Live If You Want It" -
mono): *66.* **15–20**

LONDON (3499; "Between
The Buttons" - mono):
67 . . . . **15–20**

LONDON (3509;
"Flowers" - mono): *67* **15–20**

MUTUAL
BROADCASTING
SYSTEM ("The Rolling
Stones: Past & Present"):
84 . . . . **800-1000**
(A 12-LP boxed set, issued only to radio sta-
tions. Price includes programming sheets.)

ROLLING STONES
(2900; "Exile On Main
St."): *72* **12–15**
(Price includes 12 bonus postcards, which represent $2-$3 of the value.)

ROLLING STONES (9000
series): *77.* **10–12**

ROLLING STONES
(16000 series): *81* **5–8**

ROLLING STONES
(39000 series, except
39108): *78–82.* **5–8**

ROLLING STONES
(39108; "Some Girls"):
78 . . . . **10–12**
(With all girls' faces shown.)

ROLLING STONES
(39108; "Some Girls"):
78 . . . . **5–8**
(Not all girls' faces shown. Cover is "Under
Construction.")

ROLLING STONES
(59100; "Sticky
Fingers"): *71* **8–10**
(Yellow label.)

out of
our heads
THE ROLLING
STONES

Price Range

ROLLING STONES
(59100; "Sticky
Fingers"): *71* $100–125
(White label. Promotional issue only.)
ROLLING STONES
(59101; "Goats Head
Soup"): *73* 8–10
ROLLING STONES
(79000 series): *73–76*............. 8–10
ROLLING STONES
(90000 series): *83–84*.............. 5–8
WESTWOOD ONE ("The
Rolling Stones Special"):
82 175–200
(Promotional issue only.)
Members: Mick Jagger; Keith Richards; Bill
Wyman; Brian Jones; Charlie Watts; Mick Tay-
lor; Ron Wood.
Also see BEACH BOYS, The
Also see FAITHFUL, Marianne
Also see HOPKINS, Nicky
Also see JAGGER, Mick
Also see JONES, Brian
Also see SIMON, Carly
Also see TOSH, Peter
Also see WILLIE & THE POOR BOYS
Also see WOOD, Ron
Also see WYMAN, Bill

ROMAN HOLIDAY
Singles: 7-Inch
JIVE: *83–85*...................... 1–3
LPs: 10/12-Inch 33rpm
JIVE: *83*........................ 5–8

Price Range

ROMANTICS, The
Singles: 12-Inch 33/45rpm
NEMPEROR: *83–85* $4–6
Singles: 7-Inch
BOMP: *78* 3–5
NEMPEROR: *80–85* 1–3
LPs: 10/12-Inch 33rpm
NEMPEROR: *80–83* 5–8

ROMEO & JULIET
Singles: 7-Inch
CAPITOL: *69* 2–3

ROMEO VOID
Singles: 12-Inch 33/45rpm
COLUMBIA: *82–84*............... 4–6
Singles: 7-Inch
COLUMBIA: *82–84*............... 1–3
LPs: 10/12-Inch 33rpm
COLUMBIA: *82–84*............... 5–8
415: *82*......................... 8–10

ROMEOS, The
Singles: 7-Inch
MARK II: *67* 3–5
LPs: 10/12-Inch 33rpm
MARK II: *67* 12–15

RON & BILL
Singles: 7-Inch
ARGO: *59*...................... 15–20
TAMLA: *60* 25–30
Members: Ron White; Bill "Smokey" Robin-
son.
Also see MIRACLES, The

RONALD & RUBY
Singles: 7-Inch
RCA VICTOR: *58* 4–6

**RONDELLS, The (The Ron-Dells;
The Rondels)**
Singles: 7-Inch
ABC-PARAMOUNT: *65*............ 3–5
DOT (16000 series): *63–64*.......... 4–6
DOT (17000 series): *70*............. 2–4
SHALIMAR: *63* 4–6
XPRESS......................... 3–5

Price Range

RONDELS, The
Singles: 7-Inch
AMY: *61–62* $3–5
NOTE: *61* 3–5

RONDO, Don
Singles: 7-Inch
ATLANTIC: *63* 2–4
CARLTON: *60–61* 2–4
DECCA: *55* 2–4
JUBILEE: *56–66* 2–5
ROULETTE: *59–60* 2–4
TUBA: *65* 2–4
UNITED ARTISTS: *66–67* 2–4
VIRGO: *72* 1–3
LPs: 10/12-Inch 33rpm
JUBILEE: *57–58* 10–20
VOCALION: *70* 5–10

RONETTES, The
Singles: 7-Inch
A&M: *69* 4–6
BUDDAH: *73–74* 3–5
COLPIX: *62* 15–20
DIMENSION: *64* 25–35
MAY: *63* 10–15
PAVILLION: *82.* 1–3
PHILLES: *63–66* 5–8
Picture Sleeves
PHILLES: *64–65* 10–15
LPs: 10/12-Inch 33rpm
COLPIX (486; "The
  Ronettes, Featuring
  Veronica"): *65* 40–50
  (Blue label. Monaural issue.)
COLPIX (486; "The
  Ronettes, Featuring
  Veronica"): *65* 50–60
  (Gold label. Monaural issue.)
COLPIX (486; "The
  Ronettes, Featuring
  Veronica"): *65* 60–75
  (Blue label. Stereo issue.)
COLPIX (486; "The
  Ronettes, Featuring
  Veronica"): *65* 75–100
  (White label. Promotional issue only.)
PHILLES (4006;
  "Presenting The
  Fabulous Ronettes"): *65* 100–125
  (Blue label. Monaural issue.)

Price Range

PHILLES (4006;
  "Presenting The
  Fabulous Ronettes"): *65* $75–100
  (Yellow label. Monaural issue.)
PHILLES (4006;
  "Presenting The
  Fabulous Ronettes"): *65* 200–225
  (Yellow label with red print. Stereo issue.)
PHILLES (4006;
  "Presenting The
  Fabulous Ronettes"): *65* 125–150
  (Yellow label with black print. Stereo issue
  through Capitol Record Club.)
MURRAY HILL: *86* 5–8
  Members: Veronica Bennett-Spector; Estelle
  Bennett; Nedra Talley-Ross.
  Also see RONNIE & THE RELATIVES
  Also see SPECTOR, Ronnie
  Also see VERONICA

RONETTES, The / The Crystals / Darlene Love
Singles: 7-Inch
PAVILLION (1354; "Phil
  Spector's Christmas
  Medley"): *81* 3–5
  (Promotional issue only.)

RONETTES, The / The Crystals / Darlene Love / Bob B. Soxx & The Blue Jeans
EPs: 7-Inch 33/45rpm
PHILLES ("Christmas
  EP"): *63* 20–40
LPs: 10/12-Inch 33rpm
APPLE (3400; "Phil
  Spector's Christmas
  Album"): *72.* 10–12
PASSPORT (3604; "Phil
  Spector's Christmas
  Album"): *85.* 5–8
PHILLES (4005; "A
  Christmas Gift For
  You"): *63* 50–60
  (Blue label.)
PHILLES (4005; "A
  Christmas Gift For
  You"): *63* 25–30
  (Yellow & red label.)
  Note: Phil Spector is heard speaking on this LP.
  The Apple & Passport LPs are reissues of the
  Philles album.

Also see BOB B. SOXX & THE BLUE JEANS
Also see CRYSTALS, The
Also see LOVE, Darlene
Also see RONETTES, The

RONNIE & THE HI-LITES
Singles: 7-Inch
ABC-PARAMOUNT: *65*............ **$3–5**
COLLECTABLES **1–3**
ERIC **1–3**
JOY: *62* **4–6**
RAVEN: *63*..................... **5–8**
WIN: *63*....................... **4–6**

RONNIE & THE RELATIVES (The Ronettes)
Singles: 7-Inch
COLPIX: *61* **20–25**
MAY: *62* **20–25**
Also see RONETTES, The

RONNY & THE DAYTONAS (Featuring Bucky Wilkin)
Singles: 7-Inch
MALA: *64–66* **4–6**
RCA VICTOR: *66–68* **3–5**
Picture Sleeves
RCA VICTOR: *66* **3–5**
LPs: 10/12-Inch 33rpm
MALA: *64–66* **20–25**

RONSON, Mick
LPs: 10/12-Inch 33rpm
RCA VICTOR: *74* **8–10**

RONSTADT, Linda (Linda Ronstadt & The Stone Poneys)
Singles: 7-Inch
ASYLUM: *73–85*................. **$1–3**
CAPITOL (2110 through
2438): *67–69*................... **4–6**
CAPITOL (5000 series): *67*.......... **4–6**
ELEKTRA: *75–78* **1–3**
SIDEWALK: *66*................. **15–20**
Picture Sleeves
ASYLUM: *73–85*................. **1–3**
CAPITOL: *68* **5–10**
LPs: 10/12-Inch 33rpm
ASYLUM (Except picture
discs): *73–85*................. **5–8**
ASYLUM (Picture discs):
78 .... **10–15**
CAPITOL (208 through
635): *69–72*................... **10–15**
CAPITOL (2000 series): *68*....... **12–15**
CAPITOL (11000 series):
74–75 .... **8–10**
CAPITOL (16000 series):
80 .... **5–8**
ELEKTRA: *80* **5–8**
Also see ALLAN, Davie
Also see CHRISTMAS SPIRIT
Also see EAGLES, The
Also see NEWMAN, Randy
Also see NITTY GRITTY DIRT BAND, The,
& Linda Ronstadt
Also see STONE PONEYS, The

RONSTADT, Linda, & Emmylou Harris
Singles: 7-Inch
ASYLUM: *75*..................... **2–3**
Also see HARRIS, Emmylou
Also see NITTY GRITTY DIRT BAND, The,
& Linda Ronstadt

ROOFTOP SINGERS, The
Singles: 7-Inch
ATCO: *67* **2–4**
VANGUARD: *62–65*............... **3–5**
Picture Sleeves
VANGUARD: *63*.................. **3–5**
LPs: 10/12-Inch 33rpm
VANGUARD: *63–65*............. **10–15**
Members: Erik Darling; Lynne Taylor; Bill
Svanoe.
Also see TARRIERS, The

Price Range

ROOMATES, The
Singles: 7-Inch
ADDIT: *60* $5–8
CAMEO: *62* 4–6
CANADIAN
  AMERICAN: *64*................. 4–6
COLLECTABLES 1–3
PHILIPS: *63–64* 4–6
PROMO: *60* 5–8
VALMOR: *61–62* 8–10
Also see CATHY JEAN & THE ROOMATES

ROS, Edmundo, & His Orchestra
Singles: 7-Inch
LONDON: *51–63* 1–3
EPs: 7-Inch 33/45rpm
CORAL: *54*....................... 3–6
LONDON: *52–59* 3–6
LPs: 10/12-Inch 33rpm
CORAL: *54* 5–15
LONDON: *52–78* 5–15

ROSCOE & MABLE
Singles: 7-Inch
CHOCOLATE CITY: *77*........... 2–3

ROSE, Andy (Andy Rose & The Thorns)
Singles: 7-Inch
AAMCO: *58* 4–6
CORAL: *59–62*.................... 3–5
EMBER: *64*...................... 3–5
GOLDEN CREST: *64* 3–5

ROSE, Biff
Singles: 7-Inch
BUDDAH: *71*..................... 2–4
TETRAGRAMMATON:
  68–70 2–4
LPs: 10/12-Inch 33rpm
BUDDAH: *71*.................... 8–10
TETRAGRAMMATON:
  68–69 10–12
UNITED ARTISTS: *73*........... 8–10

ROSE, David, & His Orchestra
Singles: 7-Inch
CAPITOL: *66–69* 1–3
MGM: *50–67*..................... 2–4
Picture Sleeves
MGM: *56–62*..................... 2–4

Price Range

EPs: 7-Inch 33/45rpm
KAPP: *59* $3–6
MGM: *51–58*..................... 3–8
LPs: 10/12-Inch 33rpm
CAPITOL: *66–69* 5–12
DINO: *72*....................... 5–10
KAPP: *59–61*.................... 5–10
LION: *59*....................... 5–10
MCA: *83* 5–8
MGM: *51–70*.................... 5–15
METRO: *65–66*.................. 5–10
Also see PREVIN, Andre

ROSE COLORED GLASS
Singles: 7-Inch
BANG: *71*....................... 2–4

ROSE GARDEN, The
Singles: 7-Inch
ATCO: *67–68*.................... 4–6
LPs: 10/12-Inch 33rpm
ATCO: *68* 12–15

ROSE ROYCE
Singles: 12-Inch 33/45rpm
MONTAGE: *84*................... 4–6
Singles: 7-Inch
C&R: *84*........................ 1–3
MCA: *76–77* 2–3
WHITFIELD: *77–82* 1–3
LPs: 10/12-Inch 33rpm
EPIC: *82* 5–8
WHITFIELD: *77–81* 5–8

ROSE TATOO
Singles: 7-Inch
MIRAGE: *80–82*.................. 1–3
LPs: 10/12-Inch 33rpm
MIRAGE: *80–82*.................. 5–8

ROSELLI, Jimmy
Singles: 7-Inch
RIC: *65* 3–5
UNITED ARTISTS: *65–69*......... 1–3
LPs: 10/12-Inch 33rpm
RIC: *65* 10–15
UNITED ARTISTS: *65–72*........ 5–12

ROSIE (Rosie & The Originals)
Singles: 7-Inch
ABC: *73*........................ 1–3

Price Range

HIGHLAND: *60–61*. **$4–6**
BRUNSWICK: *61*. **4–6**
　　　LPs: 10/12-Inch 33rpm
BRUNSWICK: *61*. **30–40**
　　Also see ROSIE & RON

ROSIE & RON
　　　Singles: 7-Inch
DONNA: *61* **4–6**
　　Members: Rosie Hamlin; Ron Holden.
　　Also see HOLDEN, Ron
　　Also see ROSIE

ROSS, Charlie
　　　Singles: 7-Inch
BIG TREE: *75–76* **2–3**

ROSS, Diana
　　　Singles: 12-Inch 33/45rpm
MOTOWN: *78–80*. **5–8**
　　　Singles: 7-Inch
MOTOWN: *70–81*. **1–3**
RCA VICTOR: *81–85* **1–3**
　　　Picture Sleeves
MOTOWN: *70–81*. **1–3**
　　　LPs: 10/12-Inch 33rpm
KORY: *77*. **8–10**
MOTOWN (100 series):
　81–83 . . . . **5–8**
MOTOWN (700 through
　900 series): *70–81* **8–12**
MOTOWN (5000 series):
　83 . . . . **5–8**
MOTOWN (6000 series):
　83 . . . . **8–12**
RCA VICTOR: *81–85* **5–8**
　　　Promotional LPs
MOTOWN (Colored vinyl):
　79 . . . . **10–15**
　　Also see GAYE, Marvin, & Diana Ross
　　Also see IGLESIAS, Julio, & Diana Ross
　　Also see SUPREMES, The
　　Also see TEMPTATIONS, The
　　Also see U.S.A. FOR AFRICA

ROSS, Diana, & Michael Jackson
　　　Singles: 7-Inch
MCA: *78* **1–3**
　　　Picture Sleeves
MCA: *78* **1–3**
　　Also see JACKSON, Michael

Price Range

ROSS, Diana, & Lionel Richie
　　　Singles: 7-Inch
MOTOWN: *81*. **$1–3**
　　Also see RICHIE, Lionel

ROSS, Diana, Stevie Wonder, Marvin Gaye & Smokey Robinson
　　　Singles: 7-Inch
MOTOWN: *79*. **1–3**
　　Also see GAYE, Marvin
　　Also see ROBINSON, Smokey
　　Also see ROSS, Diana
　　Also see WONDER, Stevie

ROSS, Jack
　　　Singles: 7-Inch
DOT: *61–63*. **3–5**
ROMAL: *61* **4–6**
　　　LPs: 10/12-Inch 33rpm
DOT: *62*. **15–20**

ROSS, Jackie
　　　Singles: 7-Inch
BRUNSWICK: *67–68*. **3–5**
CAPITOL: *76* **2–3**
CHESS: *64*. **3–5**
FOUNTAIN: *69* **2–4**
GSF: *72–73* **2–4**
MERCURY: *70–71*. **2–4**
SCEPTER: *72* **2–4**
　　　LPs: 10/12-Inch 33rpm
CHESS: *64*. **15–20**

ROSS, Jimmy
　　　Singles: 7-Inch
RFC: *81*. **1–3**

ROSS, Spencer
　　　Singles: 7-Inch
COLUMBIA: *59–60* **2–4**
　　　LPs: 10/12-Inch 33rpm
COLUMBIA: *60*. **5–12**

ROSSINGTON-COLLINS BAND
　　　Singles: 7-Inch
MCA: *80* **1–3**
　　　LPs: 10/12-Inch 33rpm
MCA: *80–81* **5–8**
　　Members: Gary Rossington; Al Collins.
　　Also see LYNYRD SKYNYRD

ROTA, Nino
Singles: 7-Inch
PARAMOUNT: 72 . . . . $1–3
UNITED ARTISTS: 72 1–3

**ROTARY CONNECTION, The
(Featuring Minnie Riperton)**
Singles: 7-Inch
CADET CONCEPT: 68–70 3–5
LPs: 10/12-Inch 33rpm
CADET CONCEPT: 68–70 12–15
   Also see NEW ROTARY CONNECTION,
   The
   Also see RIPPERTON, Minnie

ROTH, David Lee
Singles: 7-Inch
WARNER BROS: 85 1–3
LPs: 10/12-Inch 33rpm
WARNER BROS: 85 5–8
   Also see BEACH BOYS, The

ROUGH DIAMOND
Singles: 7-Inch
ISLAND: 77 2–3
LPs: 10/12-Inch 33rpm
ISLAND: 77 8–10
   Members: Byron Britton; Geoff Britton.
   Also see URIAH HEEP

ROUGH TRADE
Singles: 7-Inch
BOARDWALK: 82 1–3
LPs: 10/12-Inch 33rpm
UMBRELLA: 77 10–12

ROUND ROBIN
Singles: 7-Inch
CAPITOL: 67 3–5
DOMAIN: 63–65 3–5
LPs: 10/12-Inch 33rpm
CHALLENGE: 65 15–20
DOMAIN: 64 20–25

ROUNDTREE
Singles: 12-Inch 33/45rpm
ISLAND: 78 4–6
Singles: 7-Inch
ISLAND: 78 2–3

ROUNDTREE, Richard
Singles: 7-Inch
ARTISTS OF AMERICA:
   76 . . . . $2–3
MGM: 73 2–4
VERVE: 72–73 2–4
LPs: 10/12-Inch 33rpm
MGM: 72 8–12

ROUSSOS, Demis
Singles: 7-Inch
BIG TREE: 74–75 2–4
MGM: 73 2–4
MERCURY: 76–78 2–3
LPs: 10/12-Inch 33rpm
BIG TREE: 74–75 8–12
MGM: 72 10–15
MERCURY: 76–78 5–10

ROUTERS, The
Singles: 7-Inch
WARNER BROS: 62–64 3–5
LPs: 10/12-Inch 33rpm
MERCURY: 73 10–15
WARNER BROS: 63–65 15–20

ROUX, Le: see LE ROUX

**ROVER BOYS, The (Featuring Billy
Albert)**
Singles: 7-Inch
ABC: 73 1–3
ABC-PARAMOUNT: 56 4–6
CORAL: 54 4–6
RCA VICTOR: 59 3–5
UNITED ARTISTS: 61 3–5

ROVERS, The
Singles: 7-Inch
EPIC: 81 1–3
LPs: 10/12-Inch 33rpm
CLEVELAND INT'L:
   81–82 5–8
   Also see IRISH ROVERS, The

ROWANS, The
Singles: 7-Inch
ASYLUM: 75–76 2–3
COLUMBIA: 72–73 2–4

LPs: 10/12-Inch 33rpm
ASYLUM: *75–77*................. **$8–10**
COLUMBIA: *72*................. **10–12**
Members: Peter Rowan; Chris Rowan; Lorin Rowan.

ROWLES, John
Singles: 7-Inch
KAPP: *68–71*..................... **2–4**
UNI: *68*......................... **2–4**
LPs: 10/12-Inch 33rpm
KAPP: *69*..................... **10–12**

ROXANNE WITH UTFO
Singles: 12-Inch 33/45rpm
SELECT: *85*..................... **4–6**
Singles: 7-Inch
SELECT: *85*..................... **1–3**
Also see UTFO

ROXY MUSIC (Featuring Bryan Ferry)
Singles: 7-Inch
ATCO: *75–80*..................... **1–3**
WARNER BROS: *82–83*............ **1–3**
Picture Sleeves
WARNER BROS: *82–83*............ **1–3**
LPs: 10/12-Inch 33rpm
ATCO (Except 106): *75–80*........ **8–10**
ATCO (106; "Country
Life"): *75*..................... **12–15**
(Cover pictures two women in their underwear.)
ATCO (106; "Country
Life"): *75*..................... **8–10**
(With the women no longer pictured on cover.)
ATLANTIC: *74*.................. **8–10**
REPRISE: *72*.................... **8–10**
WARNER BROS (Except
2696): *82–83*.................... **5–8**
WARNER BROS (2696;
"For Your Pleasure"): *73*........ **12–15**
Also see ENO, Brian
Also see FERRY, Bryan
Also see MANZANERA, Phil

ROY, Barbara
Singles: 12-Inch 33/45rpm
ASCOT: *84*..................... **4–6**
Also see ECSTASY, PASSION & PAIN

ROY C.
Singles: 7-Inch
BLACK HAWK: *65–66*........... **$3–5**
MERCURY: *73–77*................ **2–4**
SHOUT: *66*..................... **3–5**
UPTOWN: *66*.................... **3–5**
LPs: 10/12-Inch 33rpm
MERCURY: *77*.................. **8–10**

ROYAL, Billy Joe
Singles: 7-Inch
ALL WOOD: *62*.................. **4–6**
ATLANTIC (2300 series):
66............................ **3–5**
ATLANTIC (89000 series):
85–86......................... **1–3**
COLUMBIA: *65–73*............... **3–5**
FAIRLANE: *61–62*.............. **5–8**
KAT FAMILY: *81*................. **1–3**
MGM/SOUTH: *73*................. **2–4**
MERCURY: *80*................... **1–3**
PLAYER'S: *65*.................. **4–6**
PRIVATE STOCK: *78*............. **2–3**
SCEPTER: *76*.................. **2–3**
TOLLIE: *64*.................... **4–6**
LPs: 10/12-Inch 33rpm
ATLANTIC AMERICA:
86............................ **5–8**
BRYLEN......................... **5–8**
COLUMBIA: *65–69*............. **12–15**
51 WEST: *83*................... **5–8**
KAT FAMILY: *81*................ **5–8**
MERCURY: *80*.................. **5–8**

ROYAL GUARDSMEN, The
Singles: 7-Inch
LAURIE: *66–69*................. **3–5**
LPs: 10/12-Inch 33rpm
LAURIE: *67–68*................ **12–15**
Members: Chris Nunley; Barry Winslow.

ROYAL JOKERS, The
Singles: 7-Inch
ATCO: *55–56*.................... **15–20**
FORTUNE (500 series): *63*........ **6–10**
FORTUNE (800 series): *58*........ **15–20**
HI-Q: *57*...................... **10–15**

Price Range

Price Range

ROYAL PHILHARMONIC ORCHESTRA, The (Conducted by Louis Clark)
Singles: 7-Inch
RCA VICTOR: *81–83* $1–3

LPs: 10/12-Inch 33rpm
RCA VICTOR: *81–83* 5–8

ROYAL SCOTS DRAGOON GUARDS, The
Singles: 7-Inch
RCA VICTOR: *72* 1–3

LPs: 10/12-Inch 33rpm
RCA VICTOR: *72* 5–8

ROYAL TEENS, The
Singles: 7-Inch
ABC: *73* 1–3
ABC-PARAMOUNT:
    57–58 5–8
ALLNEW: *62* 3–5
ASTRA 4–6
CAPITOL: *59–60* 5–8
JUBILEE: *62* 3–5
MCA 1–3
MIGHTY (Except 112):
    58–61 4–6
MIGHTY (112; "Cave
    Man"): *59* 8–10
MUSICOR: *69–70* 3–5
POWER: *57* 25–30
SWAN: *65* 5–8
TCF: *65* 3–5

LPs: 10/12-Inch 33rpm
DEMAND 10–15
MUSICOR: *70* 10–15
TRU-GEMS: *75* 8–10
    Members: Bob Gaudio, Al Kooper, Buddy
    Randell; Joey Villa; Billy Crandall; Tom Austin; Tony Grochowski.
    Also see FOUR SEASONS, The
    Also see KOOPER, Al

ROYALCASH
Singles: 12-Inch 33/45rpm
SUTRA: *83* 4–6

Singles: 7-Inch
SUTRA: *83* 1–3

ROYALETTES, The
Singles: 7-Inch
CHANCELLOR: *62–63* $4–6
MGM: *64–66* 3–5
ROULETTE: *67* 3–5
WARNER BROS: *64* 3–5

LPs: 10/12-Inch 33rpm
MGM: *65–66* 12–15

ROYALS, The
Singles: 7-Inch
FEDERAL (12064; "Every
    Beat Of My Heart"): *52* 200–225
    (Black vinyl.)
FEDERAL (12064; "Every
    Beat Of My Heart"): *52* 375–400
    (Colored vinyl.)
FEDERAL (12077;
    "Starting From
    Tonight"): *52* 325–350
FEDERAL (12088;
    "Moonrise"): *52* 250–275
FEDERAL (12098; "A
    Love In My Heart"): *52* 200–225
FEDERAL (12113; "Are
    You Forgetting"): *52* 175–200
FEDERAL (12121; "The
    Shrine Of St. Cecilia"):
    53 150–175
FEDERAL (12133; "Get
    It"): *53* 35–45
FEDERAL (12150; "Hey
    Miss Fine"): *53* 35–45
FEDERAL (12160; "That's
    It"): *54* 40–50
FEDERAL (12169; "Work
    With Me Annie"): *54* 35–45
GUSTO 1–3
    Members: Henry Booth; Hank Ballard; Charles
    Sutton; Lawson Smith; Alonzo Tucker; Sonny
    Woods.
    Also see BALLARD, Hank
    Also see MIDNIGHTERS, The

ROYALTONES, The
Singles: 7-Inch
ABC: *73* 1–3
GOLDISC: *60–61* 4–6
JUBILEE (Blue label):
    58–59 5–8
JUBILEE (Black label): *62* 3–5

Price Range

MALA: *63–64*	**$4–6**
PENTHOUSE: *59*	**15–20**
ROULETTE: *71*	**1–3**
VIRGO: *72*	**1–3**

RUBBER BAND
Singles: 7-Inch

ABC: *66*	**3–5**
COLUMBIA: *66–67*	**3–5**
REPRISE: *67*	**3–5**

RUBBER RODEO
Singles: 7-Inch

MERCURY: *84–85*	**1–3**

LPs: 10/12-Inch 33rpm

MERCURY: *85*	**5–8**

RUBEN & THE JETS (The Mothers Of Invention)
Singles: 7-Inch

VERVE: *68*	**10–12**

LPs: 10/12-Inch 33rpm

VERVE (5055; "Crusin'
With Ruben & The
Jets"): *68* **30–40**
(Price includes paper inserts, which represent
$10-$15 of the value.)
Also see MOTHERS OF INVENTION, The

RUBEN & THE JETS
Singles: 7-Inch

MERCURY: *73*	**2–4**

LPs: 10/12-Inch 33rpm

MERCURY: *73*	**10–12**

RUBETTES, The
Singles: 7-Inch

MCA: *76*	**2–3**
POLYDOR: *74–75*	**2–4**

LPs: 10/12-Inch 33rpm

MCA: *76*	**6–10**

RUBICON
Singles: 7-Inch

20TH CENTURY-FOX:
78–79 .... **2–3**

LPs: 10/12-Inch 33rpm

20TH CENTURY-FOX:
78–79 .... **5–8**
Also see SLY & THE FAMILY STONE

RUBINOOS, The (Featuring Jon Rubin)
Singles: 12-Inch 33/45rpm

WARNER BROS: *83*	**$4–6**

Singles: 7-Inch

BESERKLEY: *77–79*	**1–3**
WARNER BROS: *84*	**1–3**

Picture Sleeves

BESERKLEY: *77–79*	**1–3**

LPs: 10/12-Inch 33rpm

BESERKLEY: *77–79*	**5–8**

RUBY & THE PARTY GANG
Singles: 7-Inch

GAMBLE: *72*	**2–4**
SAW-TON: *71*	**2–4**

RUBY & THE ROMANTICS (Featuring Ruby Nash)
Singles: 7-Inch

A&M: *69*	**2–4**
ABC: *67–68*	**3–5**
KAPP: *62–67*	**3–5**
MCA	**1–3**

Picture Sleeves

KAPP: *63–64*	**3–6**

LPs: 10/12-Inch 33rpm

ABC: *68*	**10–15**
KAPP: *63–67*	**15–20**
MCA	**5–8**

RUFFIN, David
Singles: 7-Inch

CHECK MATE: *61–62*	**10–15**
MOTOWN: *69–76*	**2–4**
WARNER BROS: *79–80*	**1–3**

LPs: 10/12-Inch 33rpm

MOTOWN (100 & 200
series): *82* **5–8**
MOTOWN (600 series): *69* **10–15**
MOTOWN (700 & 800
series): *73–76* **8–10**
WARNER BROS: *77–80* **8–10**
Also see HALL, Daryl, & John Oates
Also see NIGHTINGALE, Maxine, & Jimmy
Ruffin
Also see TEMPTATIONS, The

Price Range

RUFFIN, David & Jimmy (The Ruffin Brothers)
Singles: 7-Inch
SOUL: 70 . . . . $2–4
LPs: 10/12-Inch 33rpm
MOTOWN: 80 5–8
SOUL: 70 10–12
Also see RUFFIN, David
Also see RUFFIN, Jimmy

RUFFIN, Jimmy
Singles: 12-Inch 33/45rpm
EPIC: 77 4–6
Singles: 7-Inch
EPIC: 77 2–3
MIRACLE: 61 20–25
MOTOWN 1–3
RSO: 80 1–3
SOUL: 64–71 3–5
LPs: 10/12-Inch 33rpm
RSO: 80 5–8
SOUL: 67–69 10–15
Also see RUFFIN, David & Jimmy

RUFUS (Rufus Featuring Chaka Khan)
Singles: 12-Inch 33/45rpm
WARNER BROS: 83–84 4–6
Singles: 7-Inch
ABC: 74–78 2–3
ATLANTIC: 74 2–3
BEARSVILLE: 75 2–3
EPIC: 70–71 2–4
MCA: 79–81 1–3
WARNER BROS: 83–84 1–3
LPs: 10/12-Inch 33rpm
ABC: 73–78 8–10
COMMAND: 74–75 8–10
MCA: 79–82 5–8
WARNER BROS: 83 5–8
Promotional LPs
ABC ("Street Player" -
picture disc): 78 20–25
Also see AMERICAN BREED, The
Also see KHAN, Chaka

RUFUS & CARLA
Singles: 7-Inch
STAX: 64–65 3–5
Members: Rufus Thomas; Carla Thomas.
Also see THOMAS, Carla

Price Range

Also see THOMAS, Rufus

RUGBYS, The
Singles: 7-Inch
AMAZON: 69–70 . . . . $3–5
SMASH: 65 4–6
TOP DOG 4–6
LPs: 10/12-Inch 33rpm
AMAZON: 70 10–15

RUMBLERS, The (With Adrian Lloyd; Little Johnny & The Rumblers)
Singles: 7-Inch
DOT: 63–64 4–6
DOWNEY: 63–65 6–10
LPs: 10/12-Inch 33rpm
DOT: 63 20–25
DOWNEY: 63 50–60

RUMOUR
Singles: 7-Inch
ARISTA: 79 1–3
MERCURY: 78 2–3
LPs: 10/12-Inch 33rpm
ARISTA: 79 5–8
MERCURY: 77 8–10
Also see PARKER, Graham

RUN D.M.C.
Singles: 12-Inch 33/45rpm
PROFILE: 83–85 4–6
QUALITY/RFC: 83 4–6
Singles: 7-Inch
PROFILE: 83–85 1–3
LPs: 10/12-Inch 33rpm
PROFILE: 84–85 5–8
Members: Joe "Run" Simmons; Daryll McDaniels.
Also see KRUSH GROVE ALL STARS, The

RUNAWAYS, The
Singles: 7-Inch
MERCURY: 76–77 3–5
LPs: 10/12-Inch 33rpm
MERCURY: 76–77 8–10
RHINO (Except picture
discs): 82 5–8
RHINO (Picture discs): 82 8–10
Members: Joan Jett; Cherie Currie; Lita Ford; Sandy West; Vicki Blue.
Also see FORD, Lita
Also see JETT, Joan, & The Blackhearts

Price Range   *Price Range*

RUNDGREN, Todd (Todd Rundgren's Utopia)
Singles: 7-Inch
BEARSVILLE (Black
  vinyl): *72–83.* **$2–4**
BEARSVILLE (Colored
  vinyl): *72* **10–15**

LPs: 10/12-Inch 33rpm
BEARSVILLE (2066;
  "Something/Anything"):
  72 . . . . **10–12**
BEARSVILLE (2133; "A
  Wizard/A True Star"):
  73 . . . . **5–8**
BEARSVILLE (3522;
  "Healing"): *81* **8–10**
  (Price includes the bonus single, "Time
  Heals.")
BEARSVILLE (6952;
  "Todd"): *74* **12–15**
  (Price includes bonus poster.)
BEARSVILLE (6957;
  "Initiation"): *75.* **8–10**
BEARSVILLE (6961;
  "Another Live"): *75* **10–12**
BEARSVILLE (6963;
  "Faithful"): *76.* **8–10**
BEARSVILLE (6965;
  "Ra"): *77.* **10–12**
BEARSVILLE (6970;
  "Oops, Wrong Planet"):
  77 . . . . **10–12**
BEARSVILLE (6981;
  "Hermit Of Mink
  Hollow"): *78* **5–8**
BEARSVILLE (6986;
  "Back To The Bars"): *78* **8–10**
BEARSVILLE (23732;
  "Ever Popular Tortured
  Artist Effect"): *83* **5–8**

Promotional LPs
BEARSVILLE (524;
  "Todd Rundgren Radio
  Show") **40–50**
BEARSVILLE (597;
  "Radio Interview"): *81* **120–130**
BEARSVILLE (788;
  "Todd Rundgren Radio
  Sampler"): *79.* **25–40**

BEARSVILLE (2066;
  "Something/Anything"):
  72 . . . . **$120–130**
  (Colored vinyl. Price includes lyrics insert.)
  Also see NAZZ
  Also see RUNT
  Also see UTOPIA

RUNNER
Singles: 7-Inch
ISLAND: *79* **2–3**
LPs: 10/12-Inch 33rpm
ISLAND: *79* **5–8**

RUNT (Featuring Todd Rundgren)
Singles: 7-Inch
AMPEX: *70.* **3–5**
BEARSVILLE: *71* **3–5**
LPs: 10/12-Inch 33rpm
AMPEX: *70–71.* **30–40**
  Also see RUNDGREN, Todd

RUSH
Singles: 7-Inch
MERCURY: *75–82.* **1–3**
Picture Sleeves
MERCURY: *81.* **1–3**
LPs: 10/12-Inch 33rpm
MERCURY (1000 through
  4000 series): *74–82* **5–8**
MERCURY (7000 series):
  76–81 . . . . **8–12**
MERCURY (9000 series):
  76–81 . . . . **10–15**
MERCURY (818000
  series): *84* **5–8**
  Members: Geddy Lee; Neil Peart; Alex Lifeson.

RUSH, Bobby
Singles: 7-Inch
ABC: *68.* **2–4**
CHECKER: *67.* **3–5**
GALAXY: *71* **2–4**
SALEM: *69* **2–4**
PHILADELPHIA INT'L:
  79 . . . . **1–3**
LPs: 10/12-Inch 33rpm
PHILADELPHIA INT'L:
  79 . . . . **5–8**

Price Range

RUSH, Merrilee (Merrilee Rush & The Turnabouts)
Singles: 7-Inch
AGP: *69–70* $2–4
BELL: *68* 2–4
GTP: *68* 2–4
MERRILIN 3–5
SCEPTER: *71* 2–4
UNITED ARTISTS: *77–78* 2–3
LPs: 10/12-Inch 33rpm
BELL: *68* 12–15
LIBERTY: *82* 5–8
UNITED ARTISTS: *77* 8–10

RUSH, Otis
Singles: 7-Inch
CHESS: *60* 4–6
COBRA: *56–59* 5–8
COTILLION: *69* 2–4
DUKE: *62* 3–5
LPs: 10/12-Inch 33rpm
BLUE HORIZON: *68–70* 10–12
BULLFROG: *77* 8–10
COTILLION: *69* 10–12
DELMARK: *75–79* 5–8
Also see KING, Albert, & Otis Rush

RUSH, Tom
Singles: 7-Inch
COLUMBIA: *72–74* 2–4
ELEKTRA: *66–70* 3–5
PRESTIGE: *64* 3–5
LPs: 10/12-Inch 33rpm
COLUMBIA: *70–76* 6–10
ELEKTRA: *65–70* 8–12
FANTASY: *72* 5–8
LY CORNU 15–20
PRESTIGE: *64–68* 10–15

RUSHEN, Patrice
Singles: 12-Inch 33/45rpm
ELEKTRA: *79–84* 4–6
Singles: 7-Inch
ELEKTRA: *80–84* 1–3
PRESTIGE: *76* 2–3
Picture Sleeves
ELEKTRA: *80* 1–3
LPs: 10/12-Inch 33rpm
ELEKTRA: *78–82* 5–8
PRESTIGE: *75–80* 5–10

Price Range

RUSHEN, Patrice, & D.J. Rogers
Singles: 7-Inch
ELEKTRA: *80* $1–3
Also see ROGERS, D.J.
Also see RUSHEN, Patrice

RUSS, Lonnie
Singles: 7-Inch
4J: *62* 3–5

RUSSELL, Bobby (Bobby Russell & The Beagles; Bobby & Sadie Russell)
Singles: 7-Inch
COLUMBIA: *73–74* 2–3
D: *60* 3–5
ELF: *68–69* 2–4
FELSTED: *59* 4–6
IMAGE: *61* 4–6
MONUMENT: *65–66* 3–5
NATIONAL GENERAL:
    70 2–3
RISING SONS: *67* 2–4
SPAR: *64* 4–6
UNITED ARTISTS: *71–72* 2–3
VISTA: *69* 2–4
LPs: 10/12-Inch 33rpm
BELL: *69* 8–10
ELF: *68* 10–15
UNITED ARTISTS: *71* 8–10

RUSSELL, Brenda
Singles: 7-Inch
A&M: *79–81* 1–3
HORIZON: *79* 2–3
LPs: 10/12-Inch 33rpm
A&M: *79* 5–8
HORIZON: *79* 5–8

RUSSELL, Lee (Leon Russell)
Singles: 7-Inch
BATON: *59* 5–8
ROULETTE: *58* 8–10
Also see RUSSELL, Leon

RUSSELL, Leon (Leon Russell & The Shelter People; Leon Russell & The New Grass Revival)
Singles: 7-Inch
A&M (700 series): *64* 4–6
A&M (1200 series): *71* 2–4
ABC: *78* 2–3

Price Range

Price Range

LPs: 10/12-Inch 33rpm
CAMEO (1006; "We Got
Love"): *59* **$25–30**
CAMEO (1007; "Bobby
Sings-Bobby Swings"): *60*....... **20–25**
CAMEO (1009; "Bobby's
Biggest Hits"): *61* **35–40**
(With gatefold cover and 12x12 photo insert.)
CAMEO (1009; "Bobby's
Biggest Hits"): *61* **30–35**
(With gatefold cover but without 12x12 photo
insert.)
CAMEO (1009; "Bobby's
Biggest Hits"): *62* **15–20**
(With standard cover.)
CAMEO (1010 through
1080): *61–64*................. **15–20**
CAMEO (2000 & 4000
series) **15–20**
CAPITOL: *65* **15–20**
P.I.P.: *76* **8–10**
SPINORAMA................... **10–15**
STRAND...................... **25–35**
Also see CHECKER, Chubby, & Bobby Rydell

RYDER, John & Anne
Singles: 7-Inch
DECCA: *69*..................... **2–4**
LPs: 10/12-Inch 33rpm
DECCA: *70*.................... **10–12**

**RYDER, Mitch (Mitch Ryder & The
Detroit Wheels)**
Singles: 7-Inch
ABC: *73*......................... **1–3**
AVCO EMBASSY: *70* **2–4**
DOT: *69*......................... **3–5**
DYNO VOICE: *67–68*............. **3–5**
ERIC **1–3**
NEW VOICE (Except
820): *65–68*................... **3–5**
NEW VOICE (820; "Sock
It To Me-Baby"): *67*............. **4–6**
(With "Feels like a punch" lyrics.)
NEW VOICE (820; "Sock
It To Me-Baby"): *67*............. **3–5**
(With "Hits me like a punch" lyrics.)
RIVA: *83*....................... **1–3**
VIRGO: *73* **1–3**
Picture Sleeves
NEW VOICE: *67* **3–6**

LPs: 10/12-Inch 33rpm
CREWE...................... **$12–15**
DOT: *69*........................ **12–15**
DYNO VOICE: *67*............... **12–15**
NEW VOICE: *66–68* **15–20**
RIVA: *83*........................ **5–8**
ROULETTE **5–8**
SEEDS & STEMS: *78–80* **5–8**
VIRGO: *73* **8–10**
Also see DETROIT
Also see LEE, Billy, & The Rivieras

RYLES, John Wesley
Singles: 7-Inch
ABC/DOT: *77*................... **1–3**
COLUMBIA: *68–70*............... **2–3**
GRT: *70*........................ **2–3**
MCA: *79–83* **1–3**
MUSIC MILL: *75–76*............. **1–3**
PLANTATION: *72–73*............. **2–3**
PRIMERO: *82*................... **1–3**
RCA VICTOR: *74* **2–3**
LPs: 10/12-Inch 33rpm
ABC: *78*........................ **6–10**
ABC/DOT: *77*................... **8–10**
COLUMBIA: *69*................. **8–12**
MCA: *79–83* **4–8**
PLANTATION: *77*................ **5–8**

S

S.O.S. BAND, The
Singles: 12-Inch 33/45rpm
TABU: *80–85*................... **4–6**
Singles: 7-Inch
TABU: *80–85*................... **1–3**
LPs: 10/12-Inch 33rpm
TABU: *80–85*................... **5–8**

S.O.U.L.
Singles: 7-Inch
MUSICOR: *71–74*............... **2–4**
LPs: 10/12-Inch 33rpm
MUSICOR: *72*.................. **8–10**

SRC (Scott Richardson Case)
Singles: 7-Inch
CAPITOL: *68–69* **2–5**

Price Range

LPs: 10/12-Inch 33rpm
CAPITOL (134;
"Milestones"): *69*............. **$20–25**
CAPITOL (273; "Travelers
Tale"): *69*.................... **12–15**
CAPITOL (2991; "SRC"):
68 .... **25–30**

S.S.O.
Singles: 7-Inch
SHADY BROOK: *75–76*........... **1–3**

SSQ
Singles: 12-Inch 33/45rpm
ENIGMA: *84*.................... **4–6**
Singles: 7-Inch
ENIGMA: *84*.................... **1–3**
LPs: 10/12-Inch 33rpm
ENIGMA: *84*.................... **5–8**
Also see ST. JAMES, Jon

SAAD, Sue, & The Next
Singles: 7-Inch
PLANET: *80*..................... **1–3**
LPs: 10/12-Inch 33rpm
PLANET: *80*..................... **5–8**

SACCO (Lou Christie)
Singles: 12-Inch 33/45rpm
LIFESONG: *78*................. **10–15**
Singles: 7-Inch
LIFESONG: *78*................... **2–4**
Also see CHRISTIE, Lou

SAD CAFE (Featuring Paul Young)
Singles: 7-Inch
A&M: *78–79* **2–3**
SWAN SONG: *81*................. **1–3**
Picture Sleeves
SWAN SONG: *81*.............. **INC**
LPs: 10/12-Inch 33rpm
A&M: *78–79* **6–10**
SWAN SONG: *81*................. **5–8**
Also see YOUNG, Paul

SADANE, Marc (Sadane)
Singles: 7-Inch
WARNER BROS: *81–82*........... **1–3**
Picture Sleeves
WARNER BROS: *81*.............. **INC**

LPs: 10/12-Inch 33rpm
WARNER BROS: *81*............. **$5–8**

SADE
Singles: 12-Inch 33/45rpm
PORTRAIT: *84–85*................ **4–6**
Singles: 7-Inch
PORTRAIT: *84–85*................ **1–3**
LPs: 10/12-Inch 33rpm
PORTRAIT: *85*................... **5–8**

SADLER, Barry (S/SGT. Barry Sadler)
Singles: 7-Inch
GAS: *78*........................ **1–3**
RCA VICTOR: *66–67* **2–5**
Picture Sleeves
RCA VICTOR: *66–67* **2–5**
LPs: 10/12-Inch 33rpm
RCA VICTOR: *66–67* **10–15**

SAFARIS, The (With The Phantom's Band; Featuring Jimmy Stephens)
Singles: 7-Inch
ELDO: *60–61*.................... **5–8**

SAGA
Singles: 7-Inch
POLYDOR: *79*................... **1–3**
PORTRAIT: *82–85*............... **1–3**
LPs: 10/12-Inch 33rpm
POLYDOR: *79*................... **5–8**
PORTRAIT: *82–85*............... **5–8**

SAGER, Carole Bayer (Carole Bayer)
Singles: 7-Inch
BOARDWALK: *81* **1–3**
ELEKTRA: *77–78* **1–3**
METROMEDIA: *72*............... **2–4**
Picture Sleeves
BOARDWALK: *81* .... **INC**
LPs: 10/12-Inch 33rpm
BOARDWALK: *81* **5–8**
ELEKTRA: *77–78* **6–10**

SAGITTARIUS
Singles: 7-Inch
COLUMBIA: *67–69*.............. **4–6**
TOGETHER: *68–69*.............. **4–6**

Price Range

LPs: 10/12-Inch 33rpm
BACK-TRAC: 85 .... $5–8
COLUMBIA: 68 15–20
TOGETHER: 69 20–25
Members: Gary Usher; Glen Campbell; Bruce
Johnston; Terry Melcher; Curt Boetcher
Also see BRUCE & TERRY
Also see CAMPBELL, Glen

SAHL, Mort
LPs: 10/12-Inch 33rpm
GNP/CRESCENDO: 73 5–10
MERCURY: 67 5–12
REPRISE: 61 10–15
VERVE: 59–64 10–20

SAHM, Doug (Doug Sahm & The Mex Trip; Doug Sahm & The Texas Tornados)
Singles: 7-Inch
ABC/DOT: 76 2–3
ATLANTIC: 73 8–10
HARLEM: 60 10–12
PERSONALITY: 59 15–20
RENNER: 61–62 10–12
SATIN 20–25
SOFT 8–10
SWINGIN': 60 10–15
TEXAS RECORD 8–10
WARNER BROS: 74 2–4
WARRIOR: 59 25–30
LPs: 10/12-Inch 33rpm
ATLANTIC: 73 8–10
HARLEM: 79 8–10
MERCURY: 73 8–10
TAKOMA: 80 5–8
WARNER BROS: 74 8–10
Also see BROMBERG, David
Also see DR. JOHN
Also see DYLAN, Bob
Also see SIR DOUGLAS QUINTET, The

SAHM, Doug, & Augie Meyers
Singles: 7-Inch
TEARDROP: 83 1–3
Also see SAHM, Doug

SAILCAT
Singles: 7-Inch
ELEKTRA: 72–73 2–4
LPs: 10/12-Inch 33rpm
ELEKTRA: 72 10–12

Price Range

SAIN, Oliver
Singles: 7-Inch
ABET: 71–77 .... $2–4
BOBBIN: 62 3–5
HCRC: 82 1–3
LPs: 10/12-Inch 33rpm
ABET (400 series): 71–73 8–10
ABET (8700 series): 77 5–8

ST. JAMES, Jon
Singles: 12-Inch 33/45rpm
EMI AMERICA: 84 4–6
Singles: 7-Inch
EMI AMERICA: 84 1–3
LPs: 10/12-Inch 33rpm
EMI AMERICA: 84 5–8
Also see SSQ

ST. PETERS, Crispian
Singles: 7-Inch
JAMIE: 66–68 3–5
LPs: 10/12-Inch 33rpm
JAMIE: 66 20–25

ST. ROMAIN, Kirby
Singles: 7-Inch
INETTE: 63–64 3–5
TEARDROP: 64 3–5

SAINT TROPEZ
Singles: 12-Inch 33/45rpm
BUTTERFLY: 77–79 4–6
DESTINY: 82 4–6
Singles: 7-Inch
BUTTERFLY: 77–79 2–3
DESTINY: 82 1–3
LPs: 10/12-Inch 33rpm
BUTTERFLY (Black
vinyl): 77–79 8–10
BUTTERFLY (Colored
vinyl): 77–79 10–15
DESTINY: 82 5–8

SAINTE-MARIE, Buffy
Singles: 7-Inch
ABC: 76 1–3
MCA: 74–75 1–3
VANGUARD: 65–72 2–5
LPs: 10/12-Inch 33rpm
ABC: 76 5–8
MCA: 74–75 5–10

Price Range

VANGUARD: *64–74* **$8–15**

SAKAMOTO, Kyu
Singles: 7-Inch
CAPITOL: *63–64* **3–5**
EMI: *75* **2–3**
LPs: 10/12-Inch 33rpm
CAPITOL: *63* **12–15**

Soupy Sales, one charted single (1965), two charted LPs (1965).

SALES, Soupy
Singles: 7-Inch
ABC-PARAMOUNT: *65* **3–5**
CAPITOL: *66* **3–5**
MOTOWN: *69*. **2–4**
REPRISE: *62*. **3–5**
Picture Sleeves
CAPITOL: *66* **3–5**
LPs: 10/12-Inch 33rpm
ABC-PARAMOUNT:
64–65 . . . . **15–20**
MOTOWN: *69*. **10–15**
REPRISE: *61–62*. **15–20**

SALSOUL ORCHESTRA, The
Singles: 12-Inch 33/45rpm
SALSOUL: *78–83* **4–6**
Singles: 7-Inch
SALSOUL: *75–83* **1–3**
LPs: 10/12-Inch 33rpm
SALSOUL: *75–83* **5–8**
Also see CHARO
Also see HOLLOWAY, Loleatta

Price Range

SALVAGE
Singles: 7-Inch
ODAX: *71* **$2–4**

SALVO, Sammy
Singles: 7-Inch
DOT: *60*. **3–5**
HICKORY: *61–63* **3–5**
IMPERIAL: *59–60*. **3–5**
MARK V. **4–6**
RCA VICTOR: *57–59* **4–6**

SAM, Butch, & The Station Band
Singles: 7-Inch
PRIVATE I: *85*. **1–3**

SAM & BILL
Singles: 7-Inch
DECCA: *67*. **3–5**
JODA: *65–66*. **3–5**
Members: Sam Gary; Bill Johnson.

SAM & DAVE
Singles: 7-Inch
ATLANTIC: *68–71* **2–4**
ROULETTE: *62–66* **3–5**
STAX: *65–68*. **3–5**
UNITED ARTISTS: *74* **2–4**
LPs: 10/12-Inch 33rpm
ATLANTIC (8205; "I
Thank You"): *68* **12–15**
ATLANTIC (8218; "Best
Of Sam & Dave"): *69*. **8–10**
GUSTO **5–8**
ROULETTE: *66* **12–15**
STAX: *66–67*. **12–15**
UNITED ARTISTS: *74–75* **8–10**
Members: Sam Moore; Dave Prater.
Also see STARS ON 45 (Featuring Sam & Dave)

SAM THE SHAM & THE PHARAOHS (The Sam The Sham Revue; Sam; Sam Samudio)
Singles: 7-Inch
DINGO: *64* **5–8**
MGM (13000 series):
64–69 . . . . **3–5**
MGM (14000 series): *73*. **2–4**
POLYDOR **1–3**
TUPELO: *63* **5–8**

Price Range

WARRIOR $20–30
XL: *64–65* **10–15**
Picture Sleeves
MGM: *65–67*..................... **4–6**
LPs: 10/12-Inch 33rpm
MGM: *65–68*.................. **12–15**

SAMI JO (Sami Jo Cole)
Singles: 7-Inch
FAME: *71* **2–4**
MGM: *74–75*.................... **2–3**
POLYDOR: *76* **1–3**
LPs: 10/12-Inch 33rpm
MGM: *74–75*................... **5–10**

SAMPLE, Joe
Singles: 7-Inch
ABC: *78–79*..................... **2–3**
MCA: *80–83* **1–3**
LPs: 10/12-Inch 33rpm
ABC: *78–79*..................... **5–10**
MCA: *81–83* **5–8**
Also see CRUSADERS, The

SAN REMO GOLDEN STRINGS, The
Singles: 7-Inch
GORDY: *67* **2–3**
RIC-TIC: *65–66.* **2–4**
LPs: 10/12-Inch 33rpm
GORDY: *67–68*.................. **8–12**
RIC-TIC: *66* **10–15**

SAN SEBASTIAN STRINGS, The (Rod McKuen With The San Sebastian Strings)
Singles: 7-Inch
WARNER BROS: *67–73* **1–3**
LPs: 10/12-Inch 33rpm
WARNER BROS (Except 2754): *67–75*.................. **5–15**
WARNER BROS (2754; "Spring-Summer-Winter-Autumn"): *73*................. **10–20**
(4-LP set.)
Also see McKUEN, Rod

SANBORN, David
Singles: 12-Inch 33/45rpm
WARNER BROS: *81–85* **4–6**

Price Range

Singles: 7-Inch
WARNER BROS: *76–85* $1–3
LPs: 10/12-Inch 33rpm
WARNER BROS: *81–85*........... **5–8**

SANDALS, The
Singles: 7-Inch
WORLD PACIFIC (400 series): *64* **4–6**
WORLD PACIFIC (77000 series): *65–67*.................... **3–5**
Members: John Blakely; Danny Brawner; John Gibson; Gaston Georis; Walter Georis.

SANDERS, Felicia
Singles: 7-Inch
COLUMBIA: *52–57*................ **2–5**
DECCA: *59–61*................... **2–4**
MGM: *65*........................ **2–3**
TIME: *60*........................ **2–3**
EPs: 7-Inch 33/45rpm
COLUMBIA: *55–56*............... **5–10**
LPs: 10/12-Inch 33rpm
COLUMBIA: *55–57*.............. **10–20**
SPECIAL EDITIONS: *67*.......... **5–10**
TIME: *60–64*................... **5–15**
Also see FAITH, Percy

SANDERS, Pharoah
Singles: 7-Inch
ARISTA: *78* **2–3**
LPs: 10/12-Inch 33rpm
ARISTA: *78* **5–8**
IMPULSE: *69–74* **8–12**
INDIA NAVIGATION: *77* **5–8**
NOVUS: *81* **5–8**
THERESA: *80–81*................ **5–12**
TRIP: *71* **5–10**

SANDLER, Tony, & Ralph Young (Sandler & Young)
Singles: 7-Inch
CAPITOL: *66–70* **2–4**
LPs: 10/12-Inch 33rpm
A.V.I.: *79*....................... **4–8**
CAPITOL: *66–78* **5–15**

SANDPEBBLES, The
Singles: 7-Inch
ABC: *73*......................... **1–3**

Price Range

CALLA: *67–69* **$3–5**

SANDPIPERS, The
Singles: 7-Inch

A&M: *66–72* **2–4**
KISMET: *66* **3–5**
TRU-GLOW-TOWN: *66* **3–5**
LPs: 10/12-Inch 33rpm
A&M: *66–73* **8–12**

SANDS, Evie
Singles: 7-Inch
ABC-PARAMOUNT:
  63–64 . . . . **3–5**
A&M: *68–70* **2–4**
BLUE CAT: *65* **4–6**
CAMEO: *66–68* **3–5**
GOLD: *64* **3–5**
HAVEN: *75–76* **2–3**
RCA VICTOR: *79* **1–3**
LPs: 10/12-Inch 33rpm
A&M: *69* **10–15**
HAVEN: *74* **8–10**
RCA VICTOR: *79* **5–8**

SANDS, Jodie
Singles: 7-Inch
ABC: *74* **1–3**
ABC-PARAMOUNT:
  62–63 . . . . **3–5**
BERNLO: *57* **4–6**
CHANCELLOR: *57–59* **4–6**
PARIS: *60–61* **3–5**
SIGNATURE: *59* **4–6**
TEEN: *55* **5–8**
THOR: *59* **4–6**

SANDS, Tommy (Tommy Sands & The Raiders)
Singles: 7-Inch
ABC-PARAMOUNT:
  63–64 . . . . **3–5**
CAPITOL (3639 through
  4082): *57–58* **5–8**
CAPITOL (4160 through
  4580): *59–61* **4–6**
IMPERIAL: *66–67* **3–5**
LIBERTY: *65* **3–5**
RCA VICTOR: *54–56* **5–8**
SUPERSCOPE: *69* **2–4**

Price Range

Picture Sleeves
CAPITOL: *58–59* **$5–8**
EPs: 7-Inch 33/45 rpm
CAPITOL: *57–59* **15–20**
LPs: 10/12-Inch 33rpm
BRUNSWICK: *78* **8–10**
CAPITOL (848 through
  1239): *57–59* **25–30**
CAPITOL (1300 & 1400
  series): *60* **20–25**
Also see ANNETTE & TOMMY SANDS

SANDS OF TIME, The (The Tokens)
Singles: 7-Inch
KIRSHNER: *76* **3–5**
Also see TOKENS, The

SANFORD-TOWNSEND BAND, The
Singles: 7-Inch
WARNER BROS: *77–79* **2–3**
LPs: 10/12-Inch 33rpm
WARNER BROS: *78–79* **5–8**
Members: Ed Sanford; John Townsend.

SANG, Samantha
Singles: 7-Inch
ATCO: *69* **3–5**
PRIVATE STOCK: *77–78* **2–3**
UNITED ARTISTS: *79* **1–3**
LPs: 10/12-Inch 33rpm
PRIVATE STOCK: *77–78* **5–8**
UNITED ARTISTS: *79* **5–8**
Also see BEE GEES, The

SANS, Billie
Singles: 7-Inch
INVICTUS: *71* **2–4**

SANTA ESMERALDA: see ESMERALDA, Santa

SANTAMARIA, Mongo (Mongo Santamaria & His Afro-Latin Group)
Singles: 12-Inch 33/45rpm
TAPPAN ZEE: *79* **4–6**
Singles: 7-Inch
ATLANTIC: *69–72* **2–4**
BATTLE: *63* **2–5**
COLLECTABLES **1–3**
COLUMBIA: *64–69* **2–4**

Price Range   *Price Range*

FANTASY: *61–62.* $2–4
RIVERSIDE: *62–66* 2–4
TAPPAN ZEE: *79* 1–3
VAYA: *73* 2–3
   LPs: 10/12-Inch 33rpm
ATLANTIC: *70* 8–10
BATTLE: *63* 12–15
COLUMBIA: *65–79* 5–12
FANTASY: *59–62.* 5–15
  (Many Fantasy LPs are still available, using
  original catalog numbers in the 8000 series.
  Fantasy 3000 series numbers were mono and
  obviously out of print.)
MILESTONE: *73–76* 5–12
PRESTIGE: *72* 6–12
RIVERSIDE: *62–66* 8–15
VAYA: *73–74* 5–10

SANTANA
   Singles: 12-Inch 33/45rpm
COLUMBIA: *85* 4–6
   Singles: 7-Inch
COLUMBIA: *69–82* 1–3
   Picture Sleeves
COLUMBIA: *70–82* 1–3
   LPs: 10/12-Inch 33rpm
COLUMBIA: *69–82* 6–12
  Members: Devadip Carlos Santana; Armando
  Peraza; Graham Lear; David Margen; Richard
  Baker; Alex Ligertwood; Orestes Vilato; Raul
  Rekow.
  Also see BOOKER T. & THE MGs
  Also see COLTRANE, Alice, & Carlos Santana
  Also see ESCOVEDO, Coke
  Also see FABULOUS THUNDERBIRDS, The
  Also see FRANKLIN, Aretha
  Also see HAGAR, SCHON, AARONSON, SHRIEVE
  Also see HANCOCK, Herbie
  Also see NOVO COMBO

SANTANA, Carlos, & Buddy Miles
   Singles: 7-Inch
COLUMBIA: *72* 2–4
   LPs: 10/12-Inch 33rpm
COLUMBIA: *72* 6–10
  Also see MILES, Buddy
  Also see SANTANA

SANTANA, Jorge
   Singles: 7-Inch
TOMATO: *78–79* 2–3

  Also see MALO

SANTIAGO
   Singles: 7-Inch
AMHERST: *76* $2–3

SANTO & JOHNNY
   Singles: 7-Inch
CANADIAN
  AMERICAN: *59–66* 3–5
ERIC 1–3
IMPERIAL: *67–68* 2–4
ERIC 1–3
UNITED ARTISTS: *66* 3–5
   Picture Sleeves
CANADIAN
  AMERICAN: *60–64* 4–6
   LPs: 10/12-Inch 33rpm
CANADIAN
  AMERICAN: *59–64* 15–20
IMPERIAL: *67–69* 10–12
  Members: Santo Farina; Johnny Farina.

SANTOS, Larry
   Singles: 7-Inch
CASABLANCA: *76–77* 2–3
   LPs: 10/12-Inch 33rpm
CASABLANCA: *77* 8–10
  Also see 4 SEASONS, The

SAPPHIRES, The
   Singles: 7-Inch
ABC: *73* 2–3
ABC-PARAMOUNT:
  64–66 3–5
COLLECTABLES 1–3
ERIC 1–3
SWAN: *63–64* 4–6
   LPs: 10/12-Inch 33rpm
SWAN: *64* 30–40

SARDUCCI, Father Guido
   Singles: 7-Inch
A&M: *74* 2–3
WARNER BROS: *80* 1–3
   LPs: 10/12-Inch 33rpm
WARNER BROS: *80* 5–8

SARIDIS, Saverio
   Singles: 7-Inch
UNITED ARTISTS: *66* 1–3

Price Range

WARNER BROS: *61–62* **$2–4**
Picture Sleeves
WARNER BROS: *61* **2–4**
LPs: 10/12-Inch 33rpm
WARNER BROS: *62* **5–10**

SARSTEDT, Peter
Singles: 7-Inch
SIRE: *78* **2–3**
UNITED ARTISTS: *72* **2–4**
WORLD PACIFIC: *69* **2–4**
LPs: 10/12-Inch 33rpm
UNITED ARTISTS: *71* **8–10**
WORLD PACIFIC: *69* **10–12**

SASS
Singles: 7-Inch
20TH CENTURY-FOX:
77 . . . . **2–3**

SATELLITE, Billy: see BILLY SATELLITE

SATISFACTIONS, The
Singles: 7-Inch
CHESAPEAKE: *63* **4–6**
IMPERIAL: *66* **3–5**
LIONEL: *70–71* **2–4**
1-2-3: *69* **2–4**
SMASH: *66–67* **3–5**

SATTERFIELD, Esther
LPs: 10/12-Inch 33rpm
A&M: *76* **5–10**

SATURDAY NIGHT BAND, The
Singles: 7-Inch
PRELUDE: *78* **2–3**
LPs: 10/12-Inch 33rpm
PRELUDE: *78* **5–8**

SAULSBERRY, Rodney
Singles: 7-Inch
ALLEGIANCE: *84–85* **1–3**

SAUNDERS, Merl
Singles: 7-Inch
FANTASY: *64–69* **3–5**
LPs: 10/12-Inch 33rpm
FANTASY: *68–73* **10–15**

Price Range

Also see FOGERTY, Tom
Also see GARCIA, Jerry

SAUNDERS, Red (Featuring Delores Hawkins)
Singles: 7-Inch
OKEH (6000 series): *52–53* **$5–8**
OKEH (7000 series): *63* **3–5**
Picture Sleeves
OKEH (7000 series): *63* **3–5**

SAVAGE GRACE
Singles: 7-Inch
REPRISE: *70–71* **2–4**
LPs: 10/12-Inch 33rpm
REPRISE: *70–71* **10–12**

SAVALAS, Telly
Singles: 7-Inch
MCA: *74–75* **2–3**
LPs: 10/12-Inch 33rpm
AUDIO FIDELITY: *75* **5–10**
MCA: *74–76* **5–10**

SAVOY, Ronnie
Singles: 7-Inch
CANDELO: *59* **4–6**
EPIC: *63–64* **3–5**
GONE: *59* **4–6**
MGM: *60–61* **3–5**
PHILIPS: *62–63* **3–5**
WING GATE: *65* **3–5**

SAVOY BROWN (The Savoy Brown Blues Band)
Singles: 7-Inch
LONDON: *74–75* **2–4**
PARROT: *69–73* **3–5**
TOWN HOUSE: *81* **1–3**
LPs: 10/12-Inch 33rpm
LONDON (600 & 700
series): *74–77* **8–10**
LONDON (50000; "Best
Of Savoy Brown"): *77* **5–8**
PARROT: *68–73* **10–15**
(Many Parrot LPs are currently available, using original catalog numbers.)
TOWN HOUSE: *81* **5–8**
Also see FOGHAT

SAWYER, Ray
Singles: 7-Inch
CAPITOL: 76–79 . . . . $2–3
SANDY: 60–62 10–15
LPs: 10/12-Inch 33rpm
CAPITOL: 76 6–10
Also see DR. HOOK

SAWYER BROWN
Singles: 7-Inch
CAPITOL/CURB: 84–86 1–3
LPs: 10/12-Inch 33rpm
CAPITOL/CURB: 85 5–8

SAXON
Singles: 7-Inch
CARRERE: 83–84 1–3
Also see MOTORHEAD

SAYER, Leo
Singles: 7-Inch
WARNER BROS: 73–84 1–3
LPs: 10/12-Inch 33rpm
WARNER BROS: 75–84 6–10

SCAFFOLD, The (Featuring Mike McGear)
Singles: 7-Inch
BELL: 68 4–6
WARNER BROS: 74 3–5
LPs: 10/12-Inch 33rpm
BELL: 68 25–30

SCAGGS, Boz
Singles: 7-Inch
ATLANTIC: 69 3–5
COLUMBIA: 71–81 1–3
FULL MOON: 81 1–3
Picture Sleeves
COLUMBIA: 76–81 1–3
EPs: 7-Inch 33/45rpm
COLUMBIA: 76 5–8
LPs: 10/12-Inch 33rpm
ATLANTIC (8239; "Boz Scaggs"): 69 8–12
ATLANTIC (19166; "Boz Scaggs"): 78 5–8
COLUMBIA (Except 40000 series): 71–80 6–10
COLUMBIA (40000 series): 80 12–15

(Half-speed mastered LPs.)
Promotional LPs
COLUMBIA (203; "The Boz Scaggs Sampler"):
76 . . . . $10–15
Also see MILLER, Steve, Band

SCALES, Harvey (Harvey Scales & The Seven Sounds)
Singles: 7-Inch
CHESS: 70 2–4
MAGIC TOUCH: 67–68 3–5
MERCURY: 69 2–4
LPs: 10/12-Inch 33rpm
CASABLANCA: 79 5–8

SCANDAL (Scandal Featuring Patty Smyth)
Singles: 12-Inch 33/45rpm
COLUMBIA (Except picture discs): 82–85 4–6
COLUMBIA (Picture discs): 82 5–8
Singles: 7-Inch
COLUMBIA: 82–85 1–3
LPs: 10/12-Inch 33rpm
COLUMBIA: 82–85 5–8

SCARBURY, Joey
Singles: 7-Inch
BELL: 71–73 2–4
BIG TREE: 73 2–4
COLUMBIA: 77–79 2–3
ELEKTRA: 81 1–3
LIONEL: 71 2–4
PLAYBOY: 74 2–3
RCA VICTOR: 84 1–3
REENA: 68 3–5
Picture Sleeves
ELEKTRA: 81 . . . . INC
LPs: 10/12-Inch 33rpm
ELEKTRA: 81 5–8

SCHAFER, Kermit
Singles: 7-Inch
JUBILEE (5258; "Rock Around The Blooper"):
56 10–15
LPs: 10/12-Inch 33rpm
AUDIO FIDELITY: 69 6–12
JUBILEE: 58–63 8–15

Price Range

KAPP: *68–70*. $5–10
MCA: *74–77* 5–8

SCHENKER, Michael, Group
Singles: 7-Inch
CHRYSALIS: *80–83*. 1–3
LPs: 10/12-Inch 33rpm
CHRYSALIS: *80–83*. 5–8
Also see ALCATRAZZ
Also see UFO

SCHIFRIN, Lalo
Singles: 12-Inch 33/45rpm
TABU: *78–79*. 4–6
Singles: 7-Inch
A&M: *75* 1–3
CTI: *76–77*. 1–3
DOT: *67*. 2–4
MCA: *77–83* 1–3
MGM: *63–70*. 2–3
PABLO: *77* 1–3
PARAMOUNT: *69*. 2–3
TABU: *78–79*. 1–3
TETRAGRAMMATON:
69 2–3
20TH CENTURY-FOX:
74–75 1–3
UNITED ARTISTS: *70*. 1–3
VERVE: *63–71* 2–3
WARNER BROS: *68–69*. 2–3
LPs: 10/12-Inch 33rpm
AUDIO FIDELITY: *62–68*. 5–15
CTI: *76–77*. 5–8
COLGEMS (5003;
"Murderer's Row"): *66*. 25–40
(Soundtrack.)
DOT (831; "Mission
Impossible"): *67*. 12–20
(Soundtrack. Dot monaural issues are preceded
by a "3," stereo by a "25.")
DOT (833; "Cool Hand
Luke"): *68* 20–30
(Soundtrack. Dot monaural issues are preceded
by a "3," stereo by a "25.")
DOT (25852; "There's A
Whole Lalo Schifrin
Goin' On"): *68*. 5–12
MCA (2284;
"Rollercoaster"): *77* 8–12
(Soundtrack.)
MCA (2374; "Nunzio"): *78* 8–12
(Soundtrack.)

Price Range

MCA (5000 series): *81* $5–10
MGM: *63–70*. 5–15
PARAMOUNT (5002;
"More Mission
Impossible"): *69*. 10–15
(Soundtrack.)
PARAMOUNT (5004;
"Mannix"): *69* 15–20
(Soundtrack.)
ROULETTE: *62* 8–15
TABU: *79* 5–8
TETRAGRAMMATON
(5006; "Che"): *69* 20–30
(Soundtrack.)
TICO: *60* 8–15
VERVE (Except 8624):
63–69 8–15
VERVE (8624; "Music
From 'Once A Thief' &
Other Themes"): *65*. 20–35
(Soundtrack.)
WARNER BROS. (1738;
"The Fox"): *68* 30–35
(Soundtrack.)
WARNER BROS. (2727;
"Enter The Dragon"): *73* 10–15
(Soundtrack.)

SCHILLING, Nina
Singles: 12-Inch 33/45rpm
MOBY DICK: *84* 4–6

SCHILLING, Peter
Singles: 12-Inch 33/45rpm
ELEKTRA: *83* 4–6
Singles: 7-Inch
ELEKTRA: *83* 1–3
LPs: 10/12-Inch 33rpm
ELEKTRA: *83* 5–8

SCHMIT, Timothy B.
Singles: 7-Inch
FULL MOON: *82*. 1–3
LPs: 10/12-Inch 33rpm
ASYLUM: *84*. 5–8
Also see EAGLES, The
Also see POCO

SCHNEIDER, Fred, & The Shake Society
Singles: 12-Inch 33/45rpm
WARNER BROS: *84* 4–6

Price Range   *Price Range*

Singles: 7-Inch
WARNER BROS: *84* $1–3

SCHNEIDER, John
Singles: 7-Inch
MCA: *84–86* 1–3
SCOTTI BROS: *81–83* 1–3
Picture Sleeves
MCA: *84–86* . . . . INC
SCOTTI BROS: *81–83* 1–3
LPs: 10/12-Inch 33rpm
MCA: *84–86* 5–8
SCOTTI BROS: *81–83* 5–8

SCHNEIDER, John, & Jill Michaels
Singles: 7-Inch
SCOTTI BROS: *83* 1–3
Also see SCHNEIDER, John

SCHON, Neal, & Jan Hammer
LPs: 10/12-Inch 33rpm
COLUMBIA: *81–83* 5–8
Also see HAGAR, SCHON, AARONSON,
SHRIEVE
Also see HAMMER, Jan
Also see JOURNEY

SCHOOLBOYS, The
Singles: 7-Inch
JUANITA: *58* 5–8
OKEH: *57* 8–10
Members: Les Martin; Jim Edwards; Roger
Hayes; Jim McKay; Renaldo Gamble.
Also see CADILLACS, The

SCHORY, Dick (Dick Schory's Percussion Pops Orchestra)
LPs: 10/12-Inch 33rpm
RCA VICTOR: *59–63* 5–15

SCHUMANN, Walter (The Voices Of Walter Schumann)
Singles: 7-Inch
CAPITOL: *52* 2–4
RCA VICTOR: *53–56* 2–4
EPs: 7-Inch 33/45rpm
CAPITOL: *52* 4–8
RCA VICTOR: *53–56* 4–8
LPs: 10/12-Inch 33rpm
CAPITOL: *52* 5–15
RCA VICTOR: *53–56* 5–15

SCHWARTZ, Eddie
Singles: 7-Inch
ATCO: *81–82* $1–3
LPs: 10/12-Inch 33rpm
ATCO: *82* 5–8

SCORPIONS, The
Singles: 7-Inch
MERCURY: *79–85* 1–3
RCA VICTOR: *74–80* 2–4
LPs: 10/12-Inch 33rpm
MERCURY: *79–85* 5–8
RCA VICTOR: *74–80* 6–10

SCOTT, Billy
Singles: 7-Inch
CAMEO: *57–58* 4–6
EVEREST: *59* 5–8

SCOTT, Bobby
Singles: 7-Inch
ABC: *73* 1–3
ABC-PARAMOUNT: *56* 4–6

SCOTT, Christopher (Sir Christopher Scott)
LPs: 10/12-Inch 33rpm
DECCA: *69–70* 5–10
MCA: *73* 4–8

SCOTT, Freddie (Freddy Scott)
Singles: 7-Inch
ABC: *74* 1–3
COLPIX: *63–64* 3–5
COLUMBIA: *64–65* 3–5
ERIC: *68* 1–3
JOY: *61–63* 3–5
P.I.P.: *72* 2–4
PROBE: *70* 2–4
SHOUT: *66–71* 3–5
SOLID GOLD: *73* 2–4
VANGUARD: *71* 2–3
LPs: 10/12-Inch 33rpm
COLPIX (Gold label): *64* 15–20
COLPIX (Blue label): *65* 12–15
COLUMBIA: *64–67* 10–15
PROBE: *70* 8–12
SHOUT: *67* 10–15

Price Range　　　　　　　　　　　　　　*Price Range*

SCOTT, Gloria
Singles: 7-Inch
CASABLANCA: 75 .... $2–4

Jack Scott, 19 charted singles (1958–61), no charted LPs.

SCOTT, Jack (Jack Scott & The Chantones)
Singles: 7-Inch
ABC: 66 4–6
ABC-PARAMOUNT: 57 30–35
CAPITOL: 61–63 6–10
CARLTON (Except stereo
　singles): 58–59 6–10
CARLTON (Stereo
　singles): 59 12–15
COLLECTABLES 1–3
DOT: 73 2–4
ERIC 1–3
GRT: 70 2–4
GROOVE (0027; "There's
　Trouble Brewin' "): 63 8–10
GROOVE (0031; "I Knew
　You First"): 64 4–6
GROOVE (0037; "Wiggle
　On Out"): 64 8–10
GROOVE (0042; "Thou
　Shalt Not Steal"): 64 4–6
GROOVE (0049; "Flakey
　John"): 64 8–10
GUARANTEED (209;
　"What Am I Living
　For"): 60 4–6

GUARANTEED (211;
　"Go Wild Little Sadie"):
　60 .... $10–12
JUBILEE: 67 4–6
RCA VICTOR: 65 4–6
TOP RANK: 60–61 4–6
Picture Sleeves
CAPITOL: 61–62 10–15
CARLTON: 58–59 10–15
TOP RANK: 60–61 10–15
EPs: 7-Inch 33/45rpm
CARLTON: 58–60 35–45
TOP RANK: 60 30–40
LPs: 10/12-Inch 33rpm
CAPITOL: 64 60–75
CARLTON: 58–60 75–85
JADE 8–10
PONIE: 74 8–10
TOP RANK: 60–61 75–85

SCOTT, Jay & Tommy
Singles: 7-Inch
FIDELITY: 63 3–5

SCOTT, Judy
Singles: 7-Inch
CAPITOL: 60 3–5
DECCA: 57–59 4–6
EMBER: 64 3–5
TOP RANK: 59 3–5

SCOTT, Linda
Singles: 7-Inch
CANADIAN
　AMERICAN: 61–62 4–6
CONGRESS: 62–64 3–5
ERIC 1–3
KAPP: 64–66 3–5
RCA VICTOR: 68 3–5
EPs: 7-Inch 33/45rpm
CONGRESS (3001; "Linda
　Scott"): 62 15–20
(Promotional issue only. Issued with picture insert, but not with cover.)
LPs: 10/12-Inch 33rpm
CANADIAN
　AMERICAN: 61–62 35–40
CONGRESS: 62 25–35
KAPP: 65 20–25

Price Range

SCOTT, Marilyn
Singles: 7-Inch
BIG TREE: 77 . . . . $2–3
MERCURY: 83–85 1–3
LPs: 10/12-Inch 33rpm
ATCO: 79 5–8
MERCURY: 83 5–8

SCOTT, Neal (Neal Scott & The Concords; Neil Scott; Neil Bogart)
Singles: 7-Inch
CAMEO: 67 3–5
CLOWN: 60 4–6
COMET 5–8
HERALD: 63 8–10
PORTRAIT: 61–62 5–8
Also see BECK, BOGART & APPICE

SCOTT, Peggy, & Jo Jo Benson
Singles: 7-Inch
SSS INT'L: 68–69 2–4
SUN 1–3
LPs: 10/12-Inch 33rpm
AVI: 84 5–8
SSS INT'L: 69 5–8

SCOTT, Rena
Singles: 7-Inch
BUDDAH: 79 2–3
EPIC: 72–74 2–4

SCOTT, Tom (Tom Scott & The L.A. Express; Tom Scott & The California Dreamers)
Singles: 12-Inch 33/45rpm
SIRE: 83 4–6
Singles: 7-Inch
A&M: 72 2–4
ATLANTIC: 83 1–3
COLUMBIA: 79 1–3
IMPULSE: 68 3–5
ODE: 74–79 2–4
SIRE: 83 1–3
LPs: 10/12-Inch 33rpm
COLUMBIA: 78–81 5–8
EPIC/ODE: 84 5–8
IMPULSE: 68 10–12
ODE: 74–77 8–10
MUSICIAN: 82 5–8
RCA VICTOR: 81 5–8

Price Range

Also see CLAYTON, Merry
Also see HARRISON, George

SCOTT-HERON, Gil
Singles: 7-Inch
ARISTA: 75–84 . . . . $1–3
LPs: 10/12-Inch 33rpm
ARISTA: 75–84 5–12
FLYING DUTCHMAN
(100 through 0600
series): 71–74 8–15
FLYING DUTCHMAN
(3800 series): 80 5–8

SCOTT-HERON, Gil, & Brian Jackson
Singles: 7-Inch
ARISTA: 75–80 1–3
LPs: 10/12-Inch 33rpm
ARISTA: 75–80 5–12
STRATA-EAST: 74 8–15
Also see SCOTT-HERON, Gil

SCRITTI POLITTI
Singles: 12-Inch 33/45rpm
WARNER BROS: 84–85 4–6
Singles: 7-Inch
WARNER BROS: 84–85 1–3
LPs: 10/12-Inch 33rpm
WARNER BROS: 84–85 5–8

SCRUGGS, Earl (The Earl Scruggs Revue)
Singles: 7-Inch
COLUMBIA: 70–83 1–3
LPs: 10/12-Inch 33rpm
COLUMBIA: 73–83 5–10
Also see FLATT, Lester, & Earl Scruggs
Also see HALL, Tom T., & Earl Scruggs

SEA, Johnny (Johnny Seay)
Singles: 7-Inch
CAPITOL: 61 2–4
COLUMBIA: 67–69 2–4
NRC: 59–60 3–5
PHILIPS: 64–65 3–5
VIKING: 70–71 2–3
WARNER BROS: 66–67 2–4
Picture Sleeves
COLUMBIA: 68 2–4

Price Range

LPs: 10/12-Inch 33rpm
GUEST STAR.................... **$5–10**
PHILIPS: *64–65* **10–15**
PICKWICK/HILLTOP:
    65 .... **6–12**
WARNER BROS: *66*............. **10–15**

SEA LEVEL
Singles: 7-Inch
ARISTA: *80* **1–3**
CAPRICORN: *77–79*.............. **2–3**
    LPs: 10/12-Inch 33rpm
ARISTA: *80* **5–8**
CAPRICORN: *77–80*............. **8–10**
    Also see ALLMAN BROTHERS BAND, The

SEALS, Dan (England Dan Seals)
Singles: 7-Inch
ATLANTIC: *80–82* **1–3**
EMI AMERICA: *84–86*............. **1–3**
LIBERTY: *83–84* **1–3**
    LPs: 10/12-Inch 33rpm
ATLANTIC: *80–82* **8–10**
EMI AMERICA: *84–86*............. **5–8**
LIBERTY: *83* **5–8**
    Also see ENGLAND DAN & JOHN FORD
    COLEY

SEALS, Dan, & Marie Osmond
Singles: 7-Inch
CAPITOL: *85* **1–3**
    Also see OSMOND, Marie
    Also see SEALS, Dan

SEALS & CROFTS
Singles: 7-Inch
T.A.: *69–71* **3–5**
WARNER BROS: *71–80*............ **1–3**
    LPs: 10/12-Inch 33rpm
T.A.: *69–70* **20–25**
WARNER BROS (Except
    2809): *71–80*................... **6–10**
WARNER BROS (2809;
    "Seals & Crofts I & II"):
    74 .... **10–12**
    Members: Jimmy Seals; Dash Crofts.
    Also see CHAMPS, The
    Also see SEALS, Jimmy

SEARCHERS, The
Singles: 7-Inch
ERIC **1–3**

Price Range

KAPP: *64–67*..................... **$4–6**
LIBERTY (55646; "Sugar
    & Spice"): *63* **5–8**
LIBERTY (55689; "Sugar
    & Spice"): *63* **3–6**
MERCURY: *63*..................... **5–8**
RCA VICTOR: *71–72* **3–5**
SIRE: *80–81* **2–3**
    Picture Sleeves
KAPP: *64* **8–12**
    LPs: 10/12-Inch 33rpm
KAPP: *64–66*.................... **20–30**
MERCURY: *64*................... **25–30**
PYE: *76*......................... **10–12**
SIRE: *80–81* **8–10**
    Promotional LPs
MERCURY: *64*.................... **50–60**
    (White label.)

SEARCHERS, The / The Rattles
LPs: 10/12-Inch 33rpm
MERCURY: *65*................... **35–45**
    Promotional LPs
MERCURY: *64*................... **50–60**
    (White label.)
    Also see RATTLES, The
    Also see SEARCHERS, The

SEATRAIN
Singles: 7-Inch
A&M: *68* **4–6**
CAPITOL: *71–72* **3–5**
WARNER BROS: *73*............... **2–4**
    LPs: 10/12-Inch 33rpm
A&M: *69* **10–12**
CAPITOL (600 series): *71* **8–10**
CAPITOL (16000 series):
    80 .... **5–8**
WARNER BROS: *73*.............. **8–10**
    Also see BLUES PROJECT, The
    Also see RANK & FILE

SEAWIND
Singles: 7-Inch
A&M: *80–82* **1–3**
CTI: *77–78*....................... **2–3**
HORIZON: *79*..................... **2–3**
    LPs: 10/12-Inch 33rpm
A&M: *80–82* **5–8**
CTI: *77–78*...................... **8–10**
HORIZON: *79*.................... **8–10**

Price Range

SEAY, Johnny: see SEA, Johnny

SEBASTIAN, John
Singles: 7-Inch
KAMA SUTRA: *68–70* $3–5
MGM: *68–70* 3–5
REPRISE: *70–77* 2–4
Picture Sleeves
KAMA SUTRA: *69* 3–5
LPs: 10/12-Inch 33rpm
KAMA SUTRA: *70* 10–12
MGM: *69–70* 12–15
REPRISE: *70–76* 8–10
Also see LOVIN' SPOONFUL, The

SECO, Pozo, Singers: see POZO SECO SINGERS, The

SECOND VERSE
Singles: 7-Inch
IX CHAINS: *74* 2–4

SECRET WEAPON
Singles: 7-Inch
PRELUDE: *82–83* 1–3

SECRETS, The
Singles: 7-Inch
DCP: *65* 3–5
OMEN: *66* 3–5
PHILIPS: *63–64* 3–5
Picture Sleeves
PHILIPS: *64* 4–8

SEDAKA, Neil (Neil Sedaka & The Marvels)
Singles: 7-Inch
DECCA: *58* 15–20
ELEKTRA: *77–80* 1–3
GUYDEN: *58* 15–20
KIRSHNER: *72–80* 1–3
LEGION: *58* 25–30
MCA: *75–84* 1–3
MGM: *73* 2–4
PYRAMID: *62* 8–10
RCA VICTOR (7000
   series): *58–61* 4–6
   (With a "47" prefix.)
RCA VICTOR (7000
   series): *59–60* 10–12

Price Range

(With a "61" prefix. Stereo singles.)
RCA VICTOR (7000 &
   8000 series): *60–62* $12–15
   (With a "37" prefix. Compact 33 Singles.)
RCA VICTOR (8000 &
   9000 series): *62–67* 3–5
   (With a "47" prefix.)
ROCKET: *74–76* 2–4
S.G.C.: *68–69* 3–5
Promotional Singles
RCA VICTOR (7408;
   "The Diary"): *58* 8–10
   (White label, with photo of Neil.)
Picture Sleeves
RCA VICTOR: *60–65* 4–8
EPs: 7-Inch 33/45rpm
RCA VICTOR (EPA
   series): *59* 20–25
RCA VICTOR (LPC
   series): *61* 15–20
   (Compact 33 Doubles.)
LPs: 10/12-Inch 33rpm
ACCORD: *81* 5–8
CAMDEN 8–10
ELEKTRA: *77–81* 5–8
51 WEST 5–8
INTERMEDIA: *85* 5–8
KIRSHNER: *71–72* 12–15
MCA: *84* 5–8
RCA VICTOR (AFL1 &
   APL1 series): *75–78* 8–10
RCA VICTOR (ANL1
   series): *75–79* 5–8
RCA VICTOR (LPM/LSP
   2035; "Neil Sedaka"): *59* 25–35
RCA VICTOR (LPM/LPS
   2317 through 2627):
   61–62 20–30
RCA VICTOR
   (LPM-10181; "Smile"):
   66 12–15
RCA VICTOR (VPL1
   series): *76* 10–12
ROCKET: *74–77* 8–10
Also see ANKA, Paul / Sam Cooke / Neil
   Sedaka
Also see COOKE, Sam / Rod Lauren / Neil
   Sedaka / The Browns
Also see JOHN, Elton
Also see 10CC
Also see WILLOWS, The

Price Range   *Price Range*

SEDAKA, Neil & Dara
Singles: 7-Inch
ELEKTRA: *80* **$1–3**
MCA: *84* **1–3**

SEDAKA, Neil, & The Tokens
LPs: 10/12-Inch 33rpm
GUEST STAR.................. **10–15**
VERNON **10–15**

SEDAKA, Neil, & The Tokens / The Coins
LPs: 10/12-Inch 33rpm
CROWN: *63* **10–15**
  Also see SEDAKA, Neil
  Also see TOKENS, The

SEEDS, The (Featuring Sky Saxon)
Singles: 7-Inch
GNP/CRESCENDO (354;
  "Can't Seem To Make
  You Mine"/"Daisy
  Mae"): *65*..................... **5–8**
GNP/CRESCENDO (354;
  "Can't Seem To Make
  You Mine"/"I Tell
  Myself"): *67*................... **4–6**
GNP/CRESCENDO (364;
  "You're Pushing Too
  Hard"): *65* **8–10**
  (Reissued on 372, titled "Pushing Too Hard"
  and with a different flip side, "Try To Under-
  stand.")
GNP/CRESCENDO (370;
  "The Other Place"): *65*........... **5–8**
GNP/CRESCENDO (372
  through 422): *66–69* **4–6**
MGM: *69–70*.................... **4–6**
Picture Sleeves
GNP/CRESCENDO: *67* **10–15**
LPs: 10/12-Inch 33rpm
GNP/CRESCENDO (2023
  through 2043): *66–67* **20–30**
  (All Seeds LPs, except 2043, "Raw & Alive,"
  are shown as currently available from GNP/
  Crescendo, using the original catalog numbers.
  Original issue 1960s LPs have the logo, "GNP
  /Crescendo," on a horizontal line. Reissues
  have the label name in a circular manner on the
  label.)
GNP/CRESCENDO (2100
  series): *77*..................... **5–8**

SEEGER, Pete
Singles: 7-Inch
COLUMBIA: *63–67*.............. **$3–5**
FOLKWAYS: *59*.................. **3–5**
PIONEER: *60*.................... **3–5**
LPs: 10/12-Inch 33rpm
ARAVEL: *63–64*.................. **8–18**
ARCHIVE OF FOLK
  MUSIC: *65*.................... **8–15**
BROADSIDE: *63* **8–18**
CAPITOL: *64–67* **8–15**
COLUMBIA: *63–72*.............. **8–18**
DISC: *64* **8–15**
FOLKWAYS: *59–75*.............. **8–18**
HARMONY: *68–70* **5–10**
ODYSSEY: *68*................... **5–12**
OLYMPIC: *73*................... **5–10**
PHILIPS: *63* **8–15**
STINSON: *70* **5–10**
TRADITION: *73* **5–10**
VANGUARD: *78*................. **6–12**
VERVE/FOLKWAYS: *65*......... **8–15**
WARNER BROS: *79*.............. **5–8**
  Also see SEEGERS, The
  Also see WEAVERS, The

SEEGER, Pete, & Arlo Guthrie
LPs: 10/12-Inch 33rpm
REPRISE: *75*.................... **8–12**
WARNER BROS: *81*.............. **6–10**
  Also see GUTHRIE, Arlo

SEEGER, Pete, & Pacific Gas & Electric
LPs: 10/12-Inch 33rpm
COLUMBIA (3540; "Tell
  Me That You Love Me,
  Junie Moon"): *70*.............. **8–15**
  (Soundtrack.)
  Also see PACIFIC GAS & ELECTRIC

SEEGERS, The
LPs: 10/12-Inch 33rpm
PRESTIGE: *65* **8–15**
  Members: Pete Seeger; Peggy Seeger; Mike See-
  ger; Barbara Seeger; Penny Seeger.
  Also see SEEGER, Pete

SEEKERS, The (Featuring Judy Durham)
Singles: 7-Inch
ATMOS: *65*...................... **3–5**

Price Range

CAPITOL: 65–68 .... **$3–5**
MARVEL: 65 .... **3–5**
Picture Sleeves
CAPITOL: 65 .... **4–6**
LPs: 10/12-Inch 33rpm
CAPITOL (100 series): 69 .... **10–12**
CAPITOL (2000 series):
  65–67 .... **10–15**
CAPITOL (16000 series):
  80 .... **5–8**
MARVEL: 65 .... **12–15**
  Also see NEW SEEKERS, The

SEELY, Jeannie
Singles: 7-Inch
CHALLENGE: 64–65 .... **3–5**
COLUMBIA: 77–78 .... **1–3**
DECCA: 69–73 .... **2–4**
MCA: 73–75 .... **1–3**
MONUMENT: 66–68. .... **2–4**
LPs: 10/12-Inch 33rpm
DECCA: 69–70 .... **8–12**
HARMONY: 72 .... **5–10**
MCA: 73 .... **5–8**
MONUMENT: 66–77. .... **6–12**
  Also see GREENE, Jack, & Jeannie Seely

SEGAL, George (George Segal & The Imperial Jazzband)
Singles: 7-Inch
FLYING DUTCHMAN:
  74 .... **1–3**
PHILIPS: 67 .... **2–4**
LPs: 10/12-Inch 33rpm
PHILIPS: 67 .... **8–15**
SIGNATURE: 74 .... **5–10**

SEGER, Bob (Bob Seger & The Last Heard; The Bob Seger System; Bob Seger & The Silver Bullet Band)
Singles: 7-Inch
ABKCO: 72–75 .... **2–4**
CAMEO: 66–67. .... **8–12**
CAPITOL (Except 2000
  series): 71–84 .... **1–3**
CAPITOL (2000 series):
  68–70 .... **3–5**
HIDEOUT: 68. .... **8–10**
PALLADIUM: 71–74. .... **2–4**
REPRISE: 72. .... **2–4**

Price Range

Promotional Singles
CAPITOL (Colored vinyl):
  78 .... **$4–6**
CAPITOL (9878; "Shame
  On The Moon"): 82 .... **3–5**
  (This was an edited version, at 4:22, and not the
  promo single of 5187, which ran 4:55.)
Picture Sleeves
CAPITOL: 78–84 .... **1–3**
LPs: 10/12-Inch 33rpm
CAPITOL (SM-172;
  "Ramblin' Gamblin'
  Man"): 75 .... **8–10**
CAPITOL (ST-172;
  "Ramblin' Gamblin'
  Man"): 69 .... **12–15**
CAPITOL (ST-236;
  "Noah"): 69. .... **15–20**
CAPITOL (SKAO-499;
  "Mongrel"): 70 .... **12–15**
CAPITOL (SM-499;
  "Mongrel"): 75 .... **8–10**
CAPITOL (ST-731;
  "Brand New Morning"):
  71 .... **10–15**
CAPITOL (11000 series,
  except picture discs):
  75–77 .... **8–12**
CAPITOL (11904;
  "Stranger In Town" -
  picture disc): 79. .... **15–20**
CAPITOL (12000 series):
  80–83 .... **6–10**
CAPITOL (16000 series):
  80 .... **5–8**
PALLADIUM: 72–74. .... **10–15**
Promotional LPs
CAPITOL ("Night Moves"
  - picture disc): 78 .... **30–40**
CAPITOL (8433; "Live
  Bullet-Consensus Cuts"):
  75 .... **15–20**
  Also see BEACH BUMS, The
  Also see NEWMAN, Randy

SELECTOR
Singles: 7-Inch
CHRYSALIS: 79–81. .... **1–3**
LPs: 10/12-Inch 33rpm
CHRYSALIS: 79–81. .... **5–8**

Price Range

SELF, Ronnie
Singles: 7-Inch
ABC-PARAMOUNT: *56* **$40–50**
AMY: *68* **3–5**
COLUMBIA (Except
  41241): *57–58* **10–15**
COLUMBIA (41241;
  "Petrified"): *58* **35–45**
DECCA: *59–62* **4–6**
KAPP: *63* **3–5**
EPs: 7-Inch 33/45rpm
COLUMBIA: *57* **50–60**

SELLARS, Marilyn
Singles: 7-Inch
MEGA: *74–77* **2–3**
ZODIAC: *76–77* **1–3**
LPs: 10/12-Inch 33rpm
MEGA: *74–77* **5–10**
ZODIAC: *77* **5–8**

SEMBELLO, Michael
Singles: 12-Inch 33/45rpm
CASABLANCA: *83* **4–6**
WARNER BROS: *83–84* **4–6**
Singles: 7-Inch
CASABLANCA: *83* **1–3**
GEFFEN: *85* **1–3**
WARNER BROS: *83–84* **1–3**
LPs: 10/12-Inch 33rpm
MCA: *85* **5–8**
WARNER BROS: *83* **5–8**

SENATOR BOBBY
Singles: 7-Inch
RCA VICTOR: *67* **3–5**
Also see HARDLY WORTHIT PLAYERS,
The

SENATOR McKINLEY: see
HARDLY WORTHIT PLAYERS,
The

SENAY, Eddy
Singles: 7-Inch
SUSSEX: *72–73* **2–4**
LPs: 10/12-Inch 33rpm
SUSSEX: *72* **8–10**

Price Range

SENECA, Joe
Singles: 7-Inch
EVEREST: *59–60* **$3–5**

SEÑOR SOUL
Singles: 7-Inch
DOUBLE SHOT: *67–68* **3–5**
WHIZ: *69–70* **2–4**
LPs: 10/12-Inch 33rpm
DOUBLE SHOT: *68–69* **10–12**

SENSATIONS, The (Yvonne Baker & The Sensations)
Singles: 7-Inch
ARGO: *61–62* **3–5**
ATCO: *55* **8–10**
CHESS: *73* **1–3**
JUNIOR: *62–64* **4–6**
TOLLIE: *64* **3–5**
LPs: 10/12-Inch 33rpm
ARGO: *63* **25–35**
Also see MILLS, Yvonne, & The Sensations

SEQUENCE
Singles: 7-Inch
SUGAR HILL: *80–82* **1–3**
LPs: 10/12-Inch 33rpm
SUGAR HILL: *81* **5–8**

SEQUINS, The
Singles: 7-Inch
GOLD STAR: *70* **2–4**

SERENDIPITY SINGERS, The
Singles: 7-Inch
PHILIPS: *64–66* **3–5**
UNITED ARTISTS: *67–69* **2–4**
Picture Sleeves
PHILIPS: *64–66* **3–5**
LPs: 10/12-Inch 33rpm
PHILIPS: *64–65* **10–15**
WING: *68* **8–12**

SERIOUS INTENTION
Singles: 12-Inch 33/45rpm
EASY STREET: *84* **4–6**

SESAME STREET KIDS: see
ERNIE

Price Range

707
Singles: 7-Inch
BOARDWALK: *82* **$1–3**
CASABLANCA: *80* **1–3**
LPs: 10/12-Inch 33rpm
BOARDWALK: *82* **5–8**
CASABLANCA: *80* **5–8**

SEVEN SEAS, The
Singles: 7-Inch
GLADES: *75* **2–4**

SEVENTH WONDER, The (The 7th Wonder)
Singles: 12-Inch 33/45rpm
CASABLANCA: *80* **4–6**
PARACHUTE: *79* **4–6**
Singles: 7-Inch
ABET: *73* **2–4**
CASABLANCA: *80* **1–3**
CHOCOLATE CITY: *80* **1–3**
PARACHUTE: *78–79* **2–3**
LPs: 10/12-Inch 33rpm
CHOCOLATE CITY: *80* **5–8**
PARACHUTE: *78–79* **5–8**

SEVERINSEN, Doc, Orchestra (Doc Severinsen & The Dodge City Boys)
Singles: 7-Inch
COMMAND: *65–70* **1–3**
EPIC: *59–76* **1–3**
FRONTLINE: *80* **1–3**
RCA VICTOR: *72–73* **1–3**
Picture Sleeves
COMMAND: *70* **1–3**
LPs: 10/12-Inch 33rpm
ABC: *71–73* **5–10**
COMMAND: *61–73* **5–15**
EPIC: *76–81* **5–8**
EVEREST: *78* **5–8**
JUNO: *70–79* **5–8**
MCA: *82* **4–8**
RCA VICTOR: *71* **5–10**
Also see MANCINI, Henry, & Doc Severinsen

SEVILLE, David (Ross Bagdasarian)
Singles: 7-Inch
LIBERTY: *56–61* **4–6**
Picture Sleeves
LIBERTY: *57* **6–10**

Price Range

EPs: 7-Inch 33/45rpm
LIBERTY: *57* **$20–25**
LPs: 10/12-Inch 33rpm
LIBERTY (3073; "The
   Music Of David
   Seville"): *57* **25–35**
LIBERTY (3092; "The
   Witch Doctor"): *58* **35–45**
Also see CHIPMUNKS, The

SEVILLES, The
Singles: 7-Inch
CAL-GOLD: *62* **3–5**
GALAXY: *64* **3–5**
J.C.: *61* **4–6**

SEX PISTOLS, The
Singles: 7-Inch
WARNER BROS: *78* **2–3**
LPs: 10/12-Inch 33rpm
WARNER BROS: *77* **5–8**
Also see PUBLIC IMAGE LTD.
Also see SIOUXSIE & THE BANSHEES

SEXTON, Ann
Singles: 7-Inch
MONUMENT: *77* **2–3**
SEVENTY SEVEN: *72–74* **2–4**
SOUND STAGE: *77* **2–3**

SEYMOUR, Phil
Singles: 7-Inch
BOARDWALK: *81* **1–3**
LPs: 10/12-Inch 33rpm
BOARDWALK: *81* **5–8**
Also see TEXTONES, The
Also see TWILLEY, Dwight, Band

SHA NA NA
Singles: 7-Inch
KAMA SUTRA: *70–75* **2–4**
SUTRA: *74* **2–3**
LPs: 10/12-Inch 33rpm
ACCORD: *81–83* **5–8**
BUDDAH: *77* **5–8**
CSP: *78* **8–10**
EMUS: *78* **8–10**
K-TEL: *81* **8–10**
KAMA SUTRA: *69–76* **10–15**
NASHVILLE: *80* **8–10**
Also see GROSS, Henry
Also see SIMON, Screamin' Scott
Also see TRAVOLTA, John / Sha Na Na

Price Range

SHACK
Singles: 7-Inch
VOLT: 71 .... $2–4

SHACKLEFORDS, The
Singles: 7-Inch
CAPITOL: 66 2–4
LHI: 67–68 2–4
MERCURY: 63 3–5
LPs: 10/12-Inch 33rpm
CAPITOL: 66 10–15
MERCURY: 63 15–20
 Members: Lee Hazelwood; Marty Cooper; Al
 Stone; Garcia Nitzsche.
 Also see HAZELWOOD, Lee
 Also see MOMENTS, The

SHADES OF BLUE, The
Singles: 7-Inch
COLLECTABLES 1–3
IMPACT: 66–67 3–5
LPs: 10/12-Inch 33rpm
IMPACT: 66 20–25

SHADES OF LOVE
Singles: 7-Inch
VENTURE: 82 1–3

SHADOW
Singles: 7-Inch
ELEKTRA: 79–81 1–3
LPs: 10/12-Inch 33rpm
ELEKTRA: 79–81 5–8

SHADOWFAX
Singles: 7-Inch
WINDHAM HILL: 82 1–3
LPs: 10/12-Inch 33rpm
PASSPORT: 76 8–10
WINDHAM HILL: 82–84 5–8

SHADOWS OF KNIGHT, The
Singles: 7-Inch
ATCO: 69 4–6
DUNWICH: 66–67 5–8
SUPER K: 69 4–6
TEAM: 68 4–6
Picture Sleeves
DUNWICH: 66 5–10

Price Range

LPs: 10/12-Inch 33rpm
DUNWICH (666;
 "Gloria"): 66 .... $40–50
DUNWICH (667; "Back
 Door Men"): 66 30–40
SUPER K: 69 10–15

SHAFTO, Bobby
Singles: 7-Inch
RUST: 64–65 4–6

SHAKATAK
Singles: 12-Inch 33/45rpm
POLYDOR: 82–84 4–6
Singles: 7-Inch
POLYDOR: 82–84 1–3
LPs: 10/12-Inch 33rpm
POLYDOR: 82 5–8

SHALAMAR
Singles: 12-Inch 33/45rpm
COLUMBIA: 84–85 4–6
SOLAR: 79–85 4–6
Singles: 7-Inch
COLUMBIA: 84–85 1–3
MCA: 84 1–3
SOLAR: 78–85 1–3
SOUL TRAIN: 77 2–3
LPs: 10/12-Inch 33rpm
SOLAR: 78–85 5–8
SOUL TRAIN: 77 8–10
 Members: Howard Hewett; Jody Watley; Jef-
 frey Daniel.

SHANGO
Singles: 12-Inch 33/45rpm
CELLULOID: 83 4–6
Singles: 7-Inch
A&M: 69 2–4
CELLULOID: 83 1–3
GNP/CRESCENDO: 69 2–4
LPs: 10/12-Inch 33rpm
A&M: 69 10–12
DUNHILL: 70 8–10
 Also see AFRIKA BAMBAATAA & THE
 SOUL SONIC FORCE

SHANGRI-LAS, The (The Shangra-Las)
Singles: 7-Inch
COLLECTABLES 1–3

Price Range

ERIC	$1–3
MERCURY: *66–67.*	4–6
RED BIRD: *64–66*	5–8
SSS INT'L	1–3
SCEPTER: *65*	4–6
SMASH: *63*	5–8
SPOKANE: *64*	5–8
TRIP.	1–3

LPs: 10/12-Inch 33rpm

BACK-TRAC: *85*	5–8
CHARLY	5–8
COLLECTABLES	5–8
MERCURY: *66.*	15–20
POST	10–12
RED BIRD (101; "Leader Of The Pack"): *65*	25–30
RED BIRD (104; "Shangri-Las '65"): *65*	30–35
RED BIRD (104; "I Can Never Go Home Amymore"): *65*	20–25

SHANK, Bud
Singles: 7-Inch

GOOD TIME JAZZ: *54*	3–5
PACIFIC JAZZ: *61–70*	2–4
WORLD PACIFIC: *64–68*	2–4

EPs: 7-Inch 33/45rpm

NOCTURNE: *53.*	20–40
PACIFIC JAZZ: *54–58*	15–30

LPs: 10/12-Inch 33rpm

CONCORD JAZZ: *76*	5–8
CROWN: *63*	10–20
KIMBERLY: *63*	10–20
LIBERTY: *56*	20–40
NOCTURNE: *53.*	75–125
(10-Inch LPs.)	
PACIFIC JAZZ (14 through 20): *54–55*	40–60
(10-Inch LPs.)	
PACIFIC JAZZ (4 through 89): *60–65*	10–20
(12-Inch LPs.)	
PACIFIC JAZZ (400 series): *57*	15–30
PACIFIC JAZZ (1200 series): *55–57*	20–40
PACIFIC JAZZ (10000 & 20000 series): *66–81*	5–15
SUNSET: *66*	5–12

Price Range

WORLD PACIFIC (1000 through 1200 series): *58–60*	$15–30
WORLD PACIFIC (1400 series): *61–63*	10–20
WORLD PACIFIC (1800 series): *64–67*	5–15
WORLD PACIFIC (21000 series): *68*	5–12

Also see FOLKSWINGERS, The
Also see LONDON, Julie, & The Bud Shank Quintet

SHANKAR, Ravi
Singles: 7-Inch

APPLE: *71*	2–4
DARK HORSE: *75*	2–3
WORLD PACIFIC: *59–68*	2–4

LPs: 10/12-Inch 33rpm

ANGEL: *67.*	8–15
APPLE: *71–73.*	8–15
CAPITOL: *67–72*	5–12
COLUMBIA: *66–68*	5–15
DARK HORSE: *74–76*	5–10
FANTASY: *73.*	8–12
PRESTIGE: *68*	5–12
SPARK: *73*	5–10
WORLD PACIFIC: *59–69*	5–15

SHANNON (Marty Wilde)
Singles: 7-Inch

EPIC/MAGNET: *75*	2–3
HERITAGE: *69*	2–4

Also see WILDE, Marty

SHANNON (Shannon Greene)
Singles: 12-Inch 33/45rpm

EMERGENCY: *83–84*	4–6
MIRAGE: *84–85.*	4–6

Singles: 7-Inch

EMERGENCY: *83–84*	1–3
MIRAGE: *84–85.*	1–3

LPs: 10/12-Inch 33rpm

MIRAGE: *84–85.*	5–8

SHANNON, Del
Singles: 7-Inch

AMY: *64–65*	4–6
BERLEE: *63–64*	5–8
BIG TOP: *61–63.*	6–10
COLLECTABLES	1–3

Price Range

DUNHILL: *69*. **$3–5**
ERIC **1–3**
ISLAND: *75* **2–4**
LANA **1–3**
LIBERTY: *66–68* **3–5**
NETWORK: *81–82*. **2–3**
WARNER BROS: *85* **1–3**
Picture Sleeves
LIBERTY: *68* **4–6**
LPs: 10/12-Inch 33rpm
AMY: *64–65* **25–30**
BIG TOP (1303;
    "Runaway"): *61*. **40–50**
    (Monaural issue.)
BIG TOP (1303;
    "Runaway"): *61*. **225–250**
    (Stereo issue.)
BIG TOP (1308; "Little
    Town Flirt"): *63* **35–45**
BUG: *85*. **5–8**
DOT: *67*. **15–20**
LIBERTY: *66–68* **15–20**
NETWORK/ELEKTRA:
    81 . . . . **5–8**
PICKWICK **8–10**
POST **10–12**
SIRE: *75* **10–12**
SUNSET: *70* **10–12**
UNITED ARTISTS: *73*. **10–12**

SHANNON, Jackie (Jackie Shannon & The Cajuns; Jackie DeShannon)
Singles: 7-Inch
DOT: *59*. **10–12**
FRATERNITY: *59*. **10–15**
P.J.: *59* **25–30**
SAGE: *59*. **20–25**
SAND: *59* **15–20**
    Also see DE SHANNON, Jackie

SHANTE, Roxanne
Singles: 7-Inch
POP ART: *85* **4–6**
Singles: 7-Inch
POP ART: *85* **1–3**
LPs: 10/12-Inch 33rpm
POP ART: *85* **5–8**

SHANTELLE
Singles: 7-Inch
PANDISC: *85*. **4–6**

Price Range

SHAPIRO, Helen
Singles: 7-Inch
CAPITOL: *61–62* **$2–5**
EPIC: *62–63* **2–4**
JANUS: *70* **1–3**
MUSICOR: *65*. **2–3**
TOWER: *67*. **2–3**
Picture Sleeves
EPIC: *62* **2–4**
LPs: 10/12-Inch 33rpm
EPIC: *63* **5–15**

SHA-RAE, Billy (Sha-Rae)
Singles: 7-Inch
BAY-UKE: *61–62*. **4–6**
LAURIE **2–3**
SPECTRUM: *71* **2–4**

SHARKS, The
Singles: 7-Inch
MCA: *73–74* **2–4**
LPs: 10/12-Inch 33rpm
MCA: *73–74* **8–12**

SHARP, Dee Dee (Dee Dee Sharp Gamble)
Singles: 7-Inch
ABKCO: *83–84*. **1–3**
ATCO: *66–68*. **3–5**
CAMEO: *62–66*. **3–5**
FAIRMOUNT: *66* **3–5**
GAMBLE: *68* **2–4**
PHILADELPHIA INT'L:
    77–81 . . . . **1–3**
TSOP: *76* **2–3**
Picture Sleeves
CAMEO: *62–65*. **4–8**
LPs: 10/12-Inch 33rpm
CAMEO: *62–63*. **15–20**
PHILADELPHIA INT'L:
    75–81 . . . . **8–10**
    Also see CHECKER, Chubby, & Dee Dee Sharp
    Also see KING, Ben E., & Dee Dee Sharp
    Also see PHILADELPHIA INTERNA-TIONAL ALL STARS, The

SHARPE, Mike
Singles: 7-Inch
LIBERTY: *66–69* **3–5**

Price Range

LPs: 10/12-Inch 33rpm
LIBERTY: *67–69* **$10–15**

SHARPE, Ray (Ray Sharpe & The Blues Whalers; Ray Sharpe & The Soul Set)
Singles: 7-Inch
A&M: *71* **2–4**
ATCO: *66* **3–5**
DOT: *59*........................ **4–6**
FLYING HIGH **2–4**
GAREX: *63*...................... **3–5**
GREGMARK: *62*................. **3–5**
HAMILTON: *59*................. **8–10**
JAMIE (Except 1128):
58–60 .... **4–6**
JAMIE (1128; "Linda
Lu"/"Monkey's Uncle"):
59 .... **8–10**
JAMIE (1128; "Linda
Lu"/"Red Sails In The
Sunset"): *59* **5–8**
LHI............................. **3–5**
MONUMENT: *65*................. **3–5**
PARK AVE **3–5**
SOCK & SOUL.................... **3–5**
TREY: *61* **4–6**
LPs: 10/12-Inch 33rpm
AWARD **15–20**
Also see KING CURTIS

SHARPEES, The
Singles: 7-Inch
ONE-DERFUL: *65–66*.............. **3–5**

SHARPLES, Bob (Bob Sharples' Living Strings)
Singles: 7-Inch
LONDON: *56–61* **2–4**
LPs: 10/12-Inch 33rpm
CAMDEN: *60*.................... **5–10**
LONDON: *61–64* **5–15**
METRO: *65*...................... **5–10**

SHAW, Georgie
Singles: 7-Inch
DECCA: *53–56* **2–4**
EPs: 7-Inch 33/45rpm
DECCA: *56*....................... **4–8**

Price Range

LPs: 10/12-Inch 33rpm
DECCA: *53–56*.................. **$8–15**

SHAW, Marlena
Singles: 12-Inch 33/45rpm
COLUMBIA: *79*................... **4–6**
SOUTH BAY: *83* **4–6**
Singles: 7-Inch
BLUE NOTE: *72–76* **2–3**
CADET: *66–69*................... **2–5**
COLUMBIA: *77–79*............... **2–3**
SOUTH BAY: *83* **1–3**
Picture Sleeves
CADET: *67*...................... **2–5**
LPs: 10/12-Inch 33rpm
BLUE NOTE: *72–75* **6–12**
CADET: *68–69*.................. **8–15**
COLUMBIA: *77–79*............... **5–8**

SHAW, Robert, Chorale
Singles: 7-Inch
RCA VICTOR: *50–62* **2–4**
EPs: 7-Inch 33/45rpm
RCA VICTOR: *54–56* **4–8**
LPs: 10/12-Inch 33rpm
ALMANAC: *66* **4–8**
CAMDEN: *64*.................... **4–8**
RCA VICTOR: *50–70* **5–15**
VICTROLA: *70*................... **4–8**

SHAW, Roland, Orchestra
Singles: 7-Inch
LONDON: *56–67*.................. **2–4**
LPs: 10/12-Inch 33rpm
LONDON: *64–78* **5–15**

SHAW, Sandie
Singles: 7-Inch
MERCURY: *64*.................... **3–5**
RCA VICTOR: *68–70* **2–4**
REPRISE: *64–67*.................. **3–5**
LPs: 10/12-Inch 33rpm
REPRISE: *65–66*................. **15–20**

SHAW, Timmy
Singles: 7-Inch
JAMIE: *61–62*.................... **3–5**
SCEPTER: *73* **1–3**
WAND: *63–64*.................... **3–5**

Price Range

SHAW, Tommy
Singles: 7-Inch
A&M: *84–85* $1–3
LPs: 10/12-Inch 33rpm
A&M: *84* 5–8
Also see STYX

SHAWN, Damon
Singles: 7-Inch
WESTBOUND: *73* 2–4

SH-BOOMS, The (The Chords)
Singles: 7-Inch
ATCO: *61* 3–5
ATLANTIC: *60* 10–15
CAT: *55* 8–10
VIK: *57* 8–10
Also see CHORDS, The

SHEAR, Jules
Singles: 12-Inch 33/45rpm
EMI AMERICA: *84–85*............. 4–6
Singles: 7-Inch
EMI AMERICA: *84–85*............. 1–3

SHEARING, George, Quintet
Singles: 7-Inch
CAPITOL: *55–67* 2–4
LONDON: *63* 2–3
MGM: *50–56* 2–5
SHEBA: *71* 1–3
EPs: 7-Inch 33/45rpm
CAPITOL: *55–60* 4–8
MGM: *51–55*...................... 5–15
LPs: 10/12-Inch 33rpm
ARCHIVE OF FOLK
    MUSIC: *68*.................... 5–10
BASF: *73* 5–8
CAPITOL: *55–77* 5–15
CONCORD JAZZ: *80–82* 4–8
DISCOVERY: *50* 15–30
    (10-Inch LPs.)
EVEREST: *69*..................... 4–8
LION: *59* 5–10
MGM (90 through 252):
    51–53 15–30
    (10-Inch LPs.)
MGM (100 series): *70*.............. 5–8
    (12-Inch LPs.)
MGM (3000 series): *55–60*.......... 8–18
MGM (4000 series): *62–63*.......... 6–12

Price Range

MPS: *74–75* $5–8
METRO: *65*...................... 5–10
PAUSA: *79–82* 5–8
SAVOY (15000 series): *50* 15–30
SHEBA: *71–76*................... 5–10
VSP: *66–67* 5–10
Also see COLE, Nat "King," & George Shearing
Also see LEE, Peggy, & George Shearing

SHEARING, George, & The Montgomery Brothers
Singles: 7-Inch
JAZZLAND: *62* 2–4
LPs: 10/12-Inch 33rpm
JAZZLAND (55; "George
Shearing And The
Montgomery Brothers"):
    61 20–35
    (Cover pictures Shearing with the three brothers.)
JAZZLAND (55; "George
Shearing And The
Montgomery Brothers"):
    62 10–20
    (Cover pictures a lady.)
RIVERSIDE: *82* 5–8
Also see MONTGOMERY BROTHERS, The
Also see SHEARING, George, Quintet
Also see WILSON, Nancy, & George Shearing

SHEEN, Bobby
Singles: 7-Inch
CAPITOL: *66–69* 3–5
CHELSEA: *75*..................... 2–4
DIMENSION: *65* 4–6
LIBERTY: *62* 5–8
WARNER BROS: *72*............... 2–4
Also see BOB B. SOXX & THE BLUE JEANS

SHEEP
Singles: 7-Inch
BOOM: *66*...................... 10–15
Also see STRANGELOVES, The

SHEILA (Sheila & B. Devotion)
Singles: 7-Inch
CARRERE: *80–81* 1–3
CASABLANCA: *78* 2–3
Picture Sleeves
CARRERE: *80–81* .... INC

Price Range

Price Range

Promotional Singles
CARRERE (37675; "Little
Darlin' "): *81* $3–5
(Price includes special sleeve.)

LPs: 10/12-Inch 33rpm
CARRERE: *80* 5–8
CASABLANCA: *78* 5–8

SHELIA E: see E., Shelia

SHELLEY, Pete (Peter Shelley)
Singles: 12-Inch 33/45rpm
ARISTA: *82–83* 4–6
Singles: 7-Inch
ARISTA: *82–83* 1–3
BELL: *74* 2–4
LPs: 10/12-Inch 33rpm
ARISTA: *82* 5–8
Also see BUZZCOCKS, The

SHELLS, The
Singles: 7-Inch
ABC: *75* 1–3
COLLECTABLES 1–3
END: *58* 40–50
GONE: *61* 8–10
JOHNSON (099; "My
Cherie"): *72* 3–5
JOHNSON (104; "Baby
Oh Baby"/"Angel
Eyes"): *57* 15–20
JOHNSON (104; "Baby
Oh Baby"/"What's In
An Angel Eyes"): *60* 5–8
(The 1960 issue label has two parallel lines with
one thinner than the other. On the 1957 issue,
these lines are both the same thickness. MOST
1957 issues have the shorter flip side title, but
ALL 1960 issues have the longer title.)
JOHNSON (106; "Pleading
No More"): *58* 45–55
JOHNSON (107 through
127): *61–63* 8–12
JOHNSON (300 series): *61* 5–8
JOSIE: *63* 4–6
ROULETTE: *59* 8–10
SELSOM: *65* 3–5
LPs: 10/12-Inch 33rpm
CANDLELITE 10–12
JUBILEE 10–15

Members: Nat Boucknight; Shade Alston;
Bobby Nurse; Danny Small; Gus Geter; Roy
Jones.
Also see DUBS, The / The Shells

SHELTO, Steve
Singles: 12-Inch 33/45rpm
SAM: *83* $4–6

SHELTON, Anne
Singles: 7-Inch
COLUMBIA: *56* 3–5
EPIC: *59* 2–4

SHELTON, Roscoe
Singles: 7-Inch
BATTLE: *62–63* 3–5
EXCELLO: *59–61* 4–6
SIMS: *64–65* 3–5
SOUND STAGE 7: *65–68* 3–5
LPs: 10/12-Inch 33rpm
EXCELLO: *61* 20–30
SOUND STAGE 7: *66* 12–15

**SHEP & THE LIMELITES
(Featuring James Sheppard)**
Singles: 7-Inch
ABC: *73* 1–3
HULL: *61–65* 6–10
ROULETTE: *73* 1–3
LPs: 10/12-Inch 33rpm
HULL: *62* 100–125
ROULETTE: *67* 35–40
Also see HEARTBEATS, The
Also see HEARTBEATS, The / Shep & The
Limelites

SHEPARD, Jean
Singles: 7-Inch
CAPITOL: *53–61* 3–6
(Purple labels.)
CAPITOL: *61–72* 2–4
(Orange or orange/yellow labels.)
MERCURY: *72* 2–3
SCORPION: *78* 1–3
UNITED ARTISTS: *73–77* 1–3
EPs: 7-Inch 33/45rpm
CAPITOL: *56–61* 5–10
LPs: 10/12-Inch 33rpm
CAPITOL (100 through
800 series): *69–71* 5–10

Price Range

CAPITOL (700 through
  1200 series): *56–59* **$15–20**
  (With a "T" prefix.)
CAPITOL (1500 through
  2900 series): *61–68* **8–15**
CAPITOL (11000 series):
  72–79 .... **5–8**
MERCURY: *71*.................. **5–10**
PICKWICK/HILLTOP:
  67–68 .... **6–12**
POWER PAK.................... **5–8**
UNITED ARTISTS: *73–76*........ **5–10**

SHEPARD, Jean, & Ferlin Huskey
Singles: 7-Inch
CAPITOL: *53* **4–6**
  Also see HUSKY, Ferlin
  Also see SHEPARD, Jean

SHEPHERD SISTERS, The (The Sheppard Sisters; The Shepard Sisters; The Shephard Sisters)
Singles: 7-Inch
ABC: *73*........................ **1–3**
ATLANTIC: *63* ....∴ **3–5**
COLLECTABLES **1–3**
LANCE: *57*...................... **4–6**
MGM: *59*....................... **3–5**
MELBA: *56*..................... **4–6**
MERCURY: *57*................... **4–6**
20TH CENTURY-FOX:
  64 .... **3–5**
UNITED ARTISTS: *61*............. **3–5**
WARWICK: *59–60*............... **3–5**
YORK: *65*...................... **3–5**

SHEPPARD, T.G.
Singles: 7-Inch
COLUMBIA: *85*.................. **1–3**
HITSVILLE: *76* **2–3**
MELODYLAND: *74–75* **2–3**
WARNER BROS: *77–85*........... **1–3**

LPs: 10/12-Inch 33rpm
COLUMBIA: *85*.................. **5–8**
CURB: *84* **5–8**
HITSVILLE: *76* **5–10**
MELODYLAND: *75–76* **8–10**
WARNER BROS: *78–83*........... **1–3**
  Also see COLLINS, Judy, & T.G. Sheppard
  Also see EASTWOOD, Clint, & T.G. Sheppard

Price Range

SHERBET (The Sherbs)
Singles: 7-Inch
ATCO: *81* **$1–3**
MCA: *76–77* **2–3**

LPs: 10/12-Inch 33rpm
ATCO: *80–82*.................... **5–8**
MCA: *76–77* **8–10**

SHERIDAN, Bobby (Charlie Rich)
Singles: 7-Inch
SUN: *61*........................ **5–8**
  Also see RICH, Charlie

SHERIDAN, Tony & The Beat Brothers: see BEATLES, The

SHERIFF
Singles: 7-Inch
CAPITOL: *83* **1–3**

SHERMAN, Allan
Singles: 7-Inch
RCA VICTOR: *68* **2–3**
WARNER BROS: *63–66*........... **3–5**

Picture Sleeves
WARNER BROS: *63–64*........... **3–5**

LPs: 10/12-Inch 33rpm
RCA VICTOR: *64* **10–15**
RHINO: *85–86* **5–8**
WARNER BROS: *62–65*.......... **10–15**

Price Range

SHERMAN, Bobby
Singles: 7-Inch
CAMEO: *66* **$3–5**
CONDOR: *69* **3–5**
DECCA: *64–65* **4–6**
DOT: *63* **4–6**
EPIC: *67* **3–5**
GRT: *76* **1–3**
JANUS: *75* **2–3**
METROMEDIA: *69–73* **2–4**
PARKWAY: *65* **4–6**
STARCREST: *62* **5–8**
Picture Sleeves
DECCA: *65* **5–8**
METROMEDIA: *69–72* **2–4**
LPs: 10/12-Inch 33rpm
METROMEDIA: *69–73* **10–12**

SHERMAN, Joe, & His Orchestra
(Joe Sherman & The Arena Brass)
Singles: 7-Inch
EPIC: *65–66* **2–3**
KAPP: *56–61* **2–4**
WORLD ARTISTS: *63–65* **2–4**
LPs: 10/12-Inch 33rpm
COLUMBIA: *68* **5–10**
EPIC: *66* **5–10**
RCA VICTOR: *67* **5–10**
WORLD ARTISTS: *63–64* **5–12**

SHERRYS, The
Singles: 7-Inch
GUYDEN: *62–63* **4–6**
MERCURY: *64* **3–5**
ROBERTS **3–5**
LPs: 10/12-Inch 33rpm
GUYDEN: *62* **40–50**

SHERWOOD, Roberta
Singles: 7-Inch
DECCA: *56–64* **2–4**
DUNHILL: *68* **2–3**
HAPPY TIGER: *69* **1–3**
HARMON: *62–63* **2–3**
KING: *71–72* **1–3**
MCA: *73* **1–3**
OLEN: *65* **2–3**
EPs: 7-Inch 33/45rpm
DECCA: *56–59* **5–10**

Price Range

LPs: 10/12-Inch 33rpm
ABC-PARAMOUNT:
  63–64 . . . . **$5–10**
DECCA: *56–65* **5–15**
HARMON: *63* **5–10**
KING: *70* **5–8**
VOCALION: *66–68* **5–8**

SHIELDS, The (Featuring Frankie Ervin)
Singles: 7-Inch
DOT (Except 15805):
  58–59 . . . . **10–12**
DOT (15805; "You
  Cheated"): *58* **5–8**
TENDER: *58–59* **12–15**
  (Label reads "Dist. By Dot.")
TENDER: *58* **25–35**
  (Label does NOT read "Dist. By Dot.")
TRANSCONTINENTAL **15–20**
LPs: 10/12-Inch 33rpm
BRYLEN **5–8**
  Also see WRIGHT, Charles

SHIELDS, Billy (Tony Orlando)
Singles: 7-Inch
HARBOUR: *69* **5–8**
  Also see ORLANDO, Tony

SHINDOGS, The (With Delaney & Bonnie Bramlett)
Singles: 7-Inch
VIVA: *66* **4–6**
WARNER BROS: *65* **4–6**
  Also see DELANEY & BONNIE

SHIRELLES, The
Singles: 7-Inch
COLLECTABLES **1–3**
BLUE ROCK: *68* **3–5**
DECCA: *58–61* **5–8**
ERIC **1–3**
GUSTO **1–3**
RCA VICTOR: *71–73* **2–4**
SCEPTER (White label):
  59–60 . . . . **8–10**
SCEPTER (Red label):
  60–68 . . . . **3–5**
TIARA: *57–58* **75–90**
UNITED ARTISTS: *70–71* **2–4**

Picture Sleeves
SCEPTER: *63* **$5–8**
LPs: 10/12-Inch 33rpm
BACK-TRAC: *85* **5–8**
EVEREST: *81* **5–8**
GUSTO **5–8**
PRICEWISE **15–20**
RCA VICTOR: *71–72* **10–15**
RHINO: *85* **5–8**
SCEPTER (501; "Tonight's
The Night"): *61* **30–35**
SCEPTER (502 through
562): *61–67* **20–30**
SCEPTER (599;
"Remember When"): *72* **15–20**
SPRINGBOARD: *72* **8–10**
UNITED ARTISTS: *71–75* **10–12**
> Members: Shirley Alston; Beverly Lee; Doris
> Jackson; Micki Harris.
> Also see 4 SEASONS, The / The Shirelles
> Also see SHIRLEY & THE SHIRELLES

SHIRELLES, The, & King Curtis
LPs: 10/12-Inch 33rpm
SCEPTER: *62* **25–30**
> Also see KING CURTIS
> Also see SHIRELLES, The

SHIRLEY, Donald (The Don Shirley Trio)
Singles: 7-Inch
BARNABY: *76* **1–3**
CADENCE: *60–64* **2–4**
COLUMBIA: *68–69* **1–3**
LPs: 10/12-Inch 33rpm
ATLANTIC: *72* **5–12**
AUDIO FIDELITY: *59* **10–25**
CADENCE: *55–63* **10–20**
COLUMBIA: *65–69* **8–12**

SHIRLEY AND COMPANY
(Shirley Goodman)
Singles: 7-Inch
VIBRATION: *75–76* **2–4**
LPs: 10/12-Inch 33rpm
VIBRATION: *75* **8–10**
> Also see SHIRLEY & LEE

SHIRLEY & LEE
Singles: 7-Inch
ABC: *73* **1–3**

ALADDIN (3152 through
3205): *52–53* **$40–50**
ALADDIN (3222 & 3244):
54 . . . . **20–25**
ALADDIN (3258; "Comin'
Over"): *54* **15–20**
ALADDIN (3289 through
3455): *55–59* **6–10**
IMPERIAL: *62–63* **3–5**
LIBERTY **1–3**
UNITED ARTISTS: *73* **2–4**
WARWICK: *60–61* **4–6**
LPs: 10/12-Inch 33rpm
ALADDIN: *56* **125–150**
IMPERIAL: *62* **20–30**
SCORE: *57* **60–75**
UNITED ARTISTS: *73–74* **20–25**
WARWICK: *61* **50–60**
> Members: Shirley Goodman; Leonard Lee.
> Also see SHIRLEY AND COMPANY

SHIRLEY & THE SHIRELLES
(Featuring Shirley Alston)
Singles: 7-Inch
BELL: *69* **3–5**
> Also see SHIRELLES, The

SHIRLEY & SQUIRRELY
Singles: 7-Inch
GRT: *76* **2–4**
LPs: 10/12-Inch 33rpm
GRT: *76* **5–8**

SHIRLEY, SQUIRRELY & MELVIN
Singles: 7-Inch
EXCELSIOR: *81* **1–3**
Picture Sleeves
EXCELSIOR: *81* . . . . **INC**
LPs: 10/12-Inch 33rpm
EXCELSIOR: *81* **5–8**
> Also see SHIRLEY & SQUIRRELY

SHOCK
Singles: 12-Inch 33/45rpm
FANTASY: *81–83* **4–6**
Singles: 7-Inch
DOWNTOWN: *78* **2–4**
FANTASY: *81–83* **1–3**
Picture Sleeves
DOWNTOWN: *78* **2–4**

Price Range

EPs: 7-Inch 33/45rpm

IMPACT: *78* $8–10
(Issued with a paper sleeve.)
LPs: 10/12-Inch 33rpm
FANTASY: *81–82*. 5–8
Members: Paul Lesperance; Steve Reiner; Kip
Brown; Gaylord.

SHOCKING BLUE, The
Singles: 7-Inch
BUDDAH: *71* 2–4
COLOSSUS: *69–71* 3–5
MGM: *72–73* 2–4
Picture Sleeves
COLOSSUS: *69–70* 3–5
LPs: 10/12-Inch 33rpm
COLOSSUS: *70* 12–15

SHOES, The
Singles: 7-Inch
BOMP: *78* 2–3
ELEKTRA: *79* 1–3
Picture Sleeves
ELEKTRA: *79* 1–3
LPs: 10/12-Inch 33rpm
BLACK VINYL 10–12
ELEKTRA: *77–82* 5–8
PVC: *78* 5–8

SHONDELL, Troy (Troy Shondel; Troy Shundell)
Singles: 7-Inch
BRITE STAR: *73–74* 2–4
COLLECTABLES 1–3
COMMERCIAL: *78* 2–3
DECCA: *64* 3–5
EVEREST: *62–64* 3–5
GAYE: *61* 15–20
GOLDCREAST: *61* 10–15
GOLDCREST: *61* 8–10
LIBERTY: *61–62* 4–6
LUCKY: *75* 2–4
MASTER 10–15
RIC: *65* 3–5
SUNSHINE: *76* 2–4
TRX: *67–69* 2–4

Price Range

TELESONIC: *80–81* $1–3
3 RIVERS 4–6
WRITERS & ARTISTS:
61 15–20
LPs: 10/12-Inch 33rpm
EVEREST: *63* 20–25
STAR-FOX 10–12
SUNSET: *67* 12–15

SHONDELLS, The / Rod Bernard / Warren Storm / Skip Stewart
LPs: 10/12-Inch 33rpm
LA LOUISIANNE: *64* 35–40
Also see BERNARD, Rod
Also see STORM, Warren

SHONDELLS, The (Featuring Tommy James)
Singles: 7-Inch
RED FOX: *66* 10–15
SELSOM: *65* 8–10
SNAP: *65* 10–15
Also see JAMES, Tommy

SHO-NUFF
Singles: 12-Inch 33/45rpm
MALACO: *81–84* 4–6
Singles: 7-Inch
MALACO: *81–84* 1–3
STAX: *78–79* 2–3
LPs: 10/12-Inch 33rpm
STAX: *78* 5–8

SHOOTING STAR
Singles: 7-Inch
EPIC: *82* 1–3
VIRGIN: *80* 1–3
Picture Sleeves
VIRGIN: *80* . . . . INC
LPs: 10/12-Inch 33rpm
EPIC: *82* 5–8
VIRGIN: *80–82* 5–8

Dinah Shore, 25 charted singles (1950–57), no charted LPs.

Price Range

SHORE, Dinah
Singles: 7-Inch
CAPITOL: *60–62* $2–4
DECCA: *69* 1–3
MERCURY: *74* 1–3
PROJECT 3: *67–68* 2–3
RCA VICTOR: *50–57* 3–6

Picture Sleeves
RCA VICTOR: *53* 5–10

EPs: 7-Inch 33/45rpm
CAMDEN: *56* 5–10
CAPITOL: *59* 4–8
COLUMBIA: *59* 4–8
RCA VICTOR: *51–57* 5–15

LPs: 10/12-Inch 33rpm
BAINBRIDGE: *82* 4–8
CAMDEN: *59–60* 5–10
CAPITOL (1200 series):
  59–60 10–20
CAPITOL (1354; "Dinah
  Sings Some Blues With
  Red Norvo"): *60* 15–30

Price Range

CAPITOL (1600 & 1700
  series): *62* $8–15
COLUMBIA (6000 series):
  50–51 15–30
  (10-Inch LPs.)
COLUMBIA (34000
  series): *77* 5–8
DECCA: *69* 5–10
HARMONY: *59–60* 5–10
PROJECT 3: *68* 5–10
RCA VICTOR (11;
  "Tangos"): *51* 15–30
RCA VICTOR (1100 &
  1200 series): *55–56* 10–20
RCA VICTOR (3000
  series): *53–54* 12–25
  (10-Inch LPs.)
REPRISE: *65* 6–15

SHORE, Dinah, & Andre Previn
LPs: 10/12-Inch 33rpm
CAPITOL: *60* 10–20
  Also see PREVIN, Andre
  Also see SHORE, Dinah

SHORR, Mickey, & The Cutups
Singles: 7-Inch
TUBA: *62* 4–6

SHORROCK, Glenn
Singles: 7-Inch
CAPITOL: *83* 1–3
  Also see LITTLE RIVER BAND, The

SHORT, Bobby
LPs: 10/12-Inch 33rpm
ATLANTIC: *59–74* 8–18

SHORTER, Wayne
LPs: 10/12-Inch 33rpm
BLUE NOTE: *62* 15–25
  (Label reads "Blue Note Records Inc. - New
  York, USA.")
BLUE NOTE: *66* 10–20
  (Label shows Blue Note Records as a division
  of either Liberty or United Artists.)
COLUMBIA: *75* 5–10
VEE JAY (Maroon label):
  60 20–35
VEE JAY (Black label):
  61–62 15–25
  Also see WEATHER REPORT

Price Range

SHOT IN THE DARK
Singles: 7-Inch
RSO: *81* $1–3
LPs: 10/12-Inch 33rpm
RSO: *81* 5–8
Also see STEWART, Al

SHOTGUN
Singles: 12-Inch 33/45rpm
MONTAGE: *82.* 4–6
Singles: 7-Inch
ABC: *77–79* 2–3
MCA: *80* 1–3
MONTAGE: *82.* 1–3
LPs: 10/12-Inch 33rpm
ABC: *77–79* 5–8
MCA: *80* 5–8
MONTAGE: *82.* 5–8

SHOW STOPPERS, The
Singles: 7-Inch
AMBER: *63.* 4–6
COLLECTABLES 1–3
COLUMBIA: *66–67* 3–5
HERITAGE: *68* 3–5
SHOWTIME: *67.* 4–6
LPs: 10/12-Inch 33rpm
COLLECTABLES 5–8

SHOWMEN, The (Featuring General Johnson)
Singles: 7-Inch
BB: *67* 3–5
IMPERIAL: *64.* 3–5
LIBERTY: *70–81* 1–3
MINIT: *61–63.* 6–10
SWAN: *65–66* 4–6
Also see JOHNSON, General

SHOWDOWN
Singles: 7-Inch
HONEY BEE: *77* 2–3

SHRIEKBACK
Singles: 12-Inch 33/45rpm
ARISTA: *84* 4–6
WARNER BROS: *83.* 4–6
Singles: 7-Inch
WARNER BROS: *83.* 1–3
LPs: 10/12-Inch 33rpm
WARNER BROS: *83.* 5–8

Also see GANG OF FOUR, The
Also see XTC

SIDE EFFECT
Singles: 12-Inch 33/45rpm
FANTASY: *78–81.* $4–6
Singles: 7-Inch
ELEKTRA: *80–82* 1–3
FANTASY: *75–81.* 1–3
LPs: 10/12-Inch 33rpm
ELEKTRA: *80–82* 5–8
FANTASY: *75–81.* 5–8

SIDEKICKS, The
Singles: 7-Inch
RCA VICTOR: *66–67* 3–5
LPs: 10/12-Inch 33rpm
RCA VICTOR: *66* 12–15

SIEGAL-SCHWALL BAND, The
Singles: 7-Inch
DEUTSCHE
  GRAMMOPHON: *73* 2–4
WOODEN NICKEL:
  72–74 2–4
LPs: 10/12-Inch 33rpm
VANGUARD: *66–70* 20–25
WOODEN NICKEL:
  72–74 15–20
Members: Corky Siegel; Jim Schwall.

SIGLER, Bunny (Mr. Emotions)
Singles: 12-Inch 33/45rpm
SALSOUL: *80* 4–6
Singles: 7-Inch
BEE: *59* 4–6
CRAIG: *61* 3–5
DECCA: *65–67* 2–4
GOLD MINE: *78* 2–3
PARKWAY: *67–69* 2–4
PHILADELPHIA INT'L:
  71–76 2–3
SALSOUL: *80.* 1–3
LPs: 10/12-Inch 33rpm
PARKWAY: *67* 10–12
SALSOUL: *80.* 5–8
Also see HOLLOWAY, Loleatta, & Bunny Sigler
Also see MASON, Barbara, & Bunny Sigler

Price Range

SILAS, Alfie (Alfie)
Singles: 7-Inch
MOTOWN: 85. . . . . $1–3
RCA VICTOR: 82–84 1–3
LPs: 10/12-Inch 33rpm
MOTOWN: 85. 5–8
RCA VICTOR: 82–84 4–8
Also see KING, Bobby

SILENCERS, The
Singles: 7-Inch
PRECISION: 80 1–3
LPs: 10/12-Inch 33rpm
PRECISION: 80–81 5–8

SILENT UNDERDOG
Singles: 12-Inch 33/45rpm
PROFILE: 85 4–6

SILHOUETTES, The
Singles: 7-Inch
ABC: 73. 1–3
ACE: 58. 8–10
COLLECTABLES 1–3
EMBER (Except 1037):
  57–58 8–10
EMBER (1037; "Bing
  Bong"): 58 30–35
FLASHBACK: 65. 1–3
IMPERIAL: 62. 4–6
JUNIOR (391; "Get A
  Job"): 57. 40–50
JUNIOR (396 & 400):
  58–59 10–15
JUNIOR (993; "Your
  Love"): 63 5–8
LPs: 10/12-Inch 33rpm
GOODWAY 40–50

SILK (With Michael Stanley)
Singles: 7-Inch
ABC: 69. 2–4
DECCA: 71. 2–4
LPs: 10/12-Inch 33rpm
ABC: 69. 10–15
Also see STANLEY, Michael, Band

SILK (With Debra Henry)
Singles: 12-Inch 33/45rpm
PHILADELPHIA INT'L:
  79–80 4–6

Price Range

Singles: 7-Inch
PHILADELPHIA INT'L:
  79–80 . . . . $1–3
PRELUDE: 77. 2–3
PYE: 76 2–3
LPs: 10/12-Inch 33rpm
ARISTA: 77 5–8
PHILADELPHIA INT'L:
  79 5–8
Also see BUTLER, Jerry, & Debra Henry

SILK, J.M.
Singles: 12-Inch 33/45rpm
D.J. INT'L: 85. 4–6

SILKIE, The
Singles: 7-Inch
FONTANA: 65–66. 3–5
LPs: 10/12-Inch 33rpm
FONTANA: 65. 20–25

SILVA-TONES, The
Singles: 7-Inch
ARGO: 57. 8–10
MONARCH (Yellow
  label): 57. 20–25
MONARCH (Black label):
  57 8–10

SILVER (With John Batdorf)
Singles: 7-Inch
ARISTA: 76–77. 2–4
LPs: 10/12-Inch 33rpm
ARISTA: 76 6–10
Also see BATDORF & RODNEY

SILVER, Horace, Quintet
Singles: 7-Inch
BLUE NOTE (300 through
  1000 series): 73–77 1–3
BLUE NOTE (1600 &
  1700 series): 54–61 3–5
BLUE NOTE (1800 &
  1900 series): 61–59 2–4
LPs: 10/12-Inch 33rpm
BLUE NOTE: 56–59 20–50
(Label gives New York street address for Blue
Note Records.)
BLUE NOTE: 59–65 15–25
(Label reads "Blue Note Records Inc. - New
York, USA.")

Price Range

BLUE NOTE: *66–80* **$8–18**
  (Label shows Blue Note Records as a division
  of either Liberty or United Artists.)
BLUE NOTE (5000 series):
  53–55 . . . . **50–80**
  (10-Inch LPs.)
EPIC (3300 series): *56* **25–50**
EPIC (16000 series): *56* **20–40**

SILVER, Horace, Quintet, & Stanley Turrentine
  LPs: 10/12-Inch 33rpm
BLUE NOTE: *68* **8–12**
  Also see SILVER, Horace, Quintet
  Also see TURRENTINE, Stanley

SILVER APPLES, The
  Singles: 7-Inch
KAPP: *68–69*. **2–4**
  LPs: 10/12-Inch 33rpm
KAPP: *68–69*. **10–15**

SILVER CONDOR
  Singles: 7-Inch
COLUMBIA: *81* **1–3**
  Picture Sleeves
COLUMBIA: *81* . . . . **INC**
  LPs: 10/12-Inch 33rpm
COLUMBIA: *81* **5–8**
  Members: Joe Cerisano; Earl Slick; John Corey;
  Claude Pepper; Jay Davis.

SILVER CONVENTION, The
  Singles: 7-Inch
MIDLAND INT'L: *75–78*. **1–3**
  Picture Sleeves
MIDLAND INT'L: *76*. **1–3**
  LPs: 10/12-Inch 33rpm
MIDSONG INT'L: *75–78* **8–10**

SILVER PLATINUM
  Singles: 7-Inch
SRI: *81*. **1–3**
SPECTOR: *81* **1–3**
  LPs: 10/12-Inch 33rpm
SPECTOR: *81* **5–8**

SILVER, PLATINUM & GOLD
  Singles: 7-Inch
FARR: *76–77*. **2–3**
WARNER BROS: *74–75*. **2–4**

Price Range

  LPs: 10/12-Inch 33rpm
NEPTUNE: *82* **$5–8**

SILVERADO
  Singles: 7-Inch
PAVILLION: *81*. **1–3**
RCA VICTOR: *77* **2–3**
  LPs: 10/12-Inch 33rpm
PAVILLION: *81*. **5–8**
RCA VICTOR: *77* **6–10**

SILVERSPOON, Dooley
  Singles: 7-Inch
COTTON: *74–75*. **2–4**

SILVERSTEIN, Shel
  Singles: 7-Inch
COLUMBIA: *71–75* **2–4**
ELEKTRA: *60* **3–6**
RCA VICTOR: *69–70* **2–4**
  LPs: 10/12-Inch 33rpm
ATLANTIC (8000 series):
  63 . . . . **15–20**
ATLANTIC (8200 series):
  70 . . . . **8–15**
CADET: *65–66* **12–20**
COLUMBIA: *72–84* **5–12**
CRESTVIEW: *63* **12–20**
ELEKTRA: *59* **20–30**
FLYING FISH: *80*. **5–8**
JANUS: *73* **8–10**
PARACHUTE: *78* **5–8**
RCA VICTOR: *69* **10–15**
  Promotional LPs
PARACHUTE (20512;
  "Selected Cuts From
  Songs & Stories"): *78* **12–15**

Price Range

SILVETTI
Singles: 7-Inch
SALSOUL: 77................... $2–3

LPs: 10/12-Inch 33rpm
SALSOUL: 77.................... 5–8

SIMEONE, Harry, Chorale
Singles: 7-Inch
COLUMBIA: 66–67............... 1–3
KAPP: 64–68..................... 1–3
MERCURY: 62–64................ 1–3
MISTLETOE: 74.................. 1–3
20TH CENTURY-FOX:
    58–79 1–3

Picture Sleeves
MERCURY: 62.................... 1–3
20TH CENTURY-FOX:
    58–63 1–3

LPs: 10/12-Inch 33rpm
DECCA: 62–64................... 5–10
KAPP: 65 5–10
MERCURY: 63–64............... 5–10
MISTLETOE: 73.................. 4–8
MOVIETONE: 67.................. 4–8
20TH CENTURY-FOX:
    58–79 5–15
WING: 69 4–8

SIMMONS, Gene (Jumpin' Gene Simmons; Morris Gene Simmons)
Singles: 7-Inch
AGP.............................. 3–5
CHECKER: 60 5–8
EPIC: 70 2–4
DELTUNE: 78 2–3
HI: 61–67....................... 4–6
HURSHEY: 73 2–4
MALA: 68....................... 3–5
SANDY.......................... 4–6
SUN: 58......................... 10–12
TUPELO 3–5

LPs: 10/12-Inch 33rpm
HI: 64.......................... 20–25

SIMMONS, Gene
Singles: 7-Inch
CASABLANCA: 78–79 2–3

LPs: 10/12-Inch 33rpm
CASABLANCA (Except
    picture discs): 78–79 .... $5–8
CASABLANCA (Picture
    discs): 79 10–15
Also see KISS

SIMMONS, Patrick
Singles: 12-Inch 33/45rpm
ELEKTRA: 83 4–6
Singles: 7-Inch
ELEKTRA: 83 1–3
LPs: 10/12-Inch 33rpm
ELEKTRA: 83 5–8
Also see DOOBIE BROTHERS, The
Also see EAGLES, The

SIMMONS, Simtec
Singles: 7-Inch
INNOCATION: 75................ 2–4

SIMMS, John & Arthur
Singles: 7-Inch
CASABLANCA: 80............... 1–3
LPs: 10/12-Inch 33rpm
CASABLANCA: 80............... 5–8

SIMMS TWINS, The: see SIMS TWINS, The

SIMON, Carly
Singles: 7-Inch
COLUMBIA: 73................... 2–4
ELEKTRA: 71–79 2–3
EPIC: 85–86 1–3
MIRAGE: 82...................... 1–3
WARNER BROS: 80–83............ 1–3
Picture Sleeves
ELEKTRA: 75–79 2–3
WARNER BROS: 80–83............ 1–3
LPs: 10/12-Inch 33rpm
ELEKTRA: 71–79 6–10
EPIC: 85–86 5–8
WARNER BROS: 80–83............ 5–8
Also see ROLLING STONES, The
Also see SIMON SISTERS, The

SIMON, Carly, & James Taylor
Singles: 7-Inch
ELEKTRA: 74–78 2–3
Also see SIMON, Carly
Also see TAYLOR, James

Price Range

SIMON, Joe (Joe Simon & The Checkmates; Joe Simon & The Mainstreeters)

Singles: 7-Inch
COMPLEAT $2–3
DOT: *64* 3–5
HUSH: *60–62.* 5–8
MONUMENT: *70–72.* 2–3
IRRAL: *63* 4–6
POSSE: *81–82* 1–3
SOUND STAGE 7: *66–72* 3–5
SPRING: *69–75.* 2–4
VEE JAY: *64–65.* 3–5

Picture Sleeves
SPRING: *71–73.* 2–4

LPs: 10/12-Inch 33rpm
BUDDAH: *69* 10–15
POSSE: *81–82* 5–8
SOUND STAGE 7: *67–75* 10–15
SPRING: *71–78.* 8–10

SIMON, Lowrell
Singles: 12-Inch 33/45rpm
ZOO YORK: *81* 4–6
Singles: 7-Inch
ZOO YORK: *81* 1–3

SIMON, Paul
Singles: 7-Inch
COLUMBIA: *72–77* 2–4
WARNER BROS: *80–83* 1–3

Picture Sleeves
COLUMBIA: *73* 2–4
WARNER BROS: *80* 1–3

LPs: 10/12-Inch 33rpm
COLUMBIA (Except C5X
   & 40000 series): *72–77* 6–10
COLUMBIA (C5X series):
   81 20–30
COLUMBIA (40000
   series): *81* 12–15
   (Half-speed mastered LPs.)
DMG: *75* 12–15
   (Promotional issue only.)
WARNER BROS: *80–83* 5–8
   Also see KANE, Paul
   Also see LANDIS, Jerry
   Also see NEWMAN, Randy, & Paul Simon
   Also see SIMON & GARFUNKEL

Price Range

Also see TAYLOR, True
Also see TICO & THE TRIUMPHS
Also see U.S.A. FOR AFRICA
Also see VALERY, Dana

SIMON, Paul, & Phoebe Snow (With The Jessy Dixon Singers)
Singles: 7-Inch
COLUMBIA: *75* $2–3
Also see SNOW, Phoebe

SIMON & GARFUNKEL
Singles: 7-Inch
ABC-PARAMOUNT: *66* 8–12
COLUMBIA (10000
   series): *75* 2–4
COLUMBIA (11000
   series): *66* 5–8
COLUMBIA (43000
   through 45000 series):
   65–72 3–5
WARNER BROS: *82* 1–3
Promotional Singles
COLUMBIA (43396; "The
   Sounds Of Silence"): *65* 25–30
   (Colored vinyl.)
COLUMBIA (43617; "I
   Am A Rock"): *66* 15–20
   (Colored vinyl.)
Picture Sleeves
COLUMBIA: *66–75* 3–6
EP: 7-Inch 33/45rpm
COLUMBIA: *68–69* 10–15
   (Jukebox issues only.)
LPs: 10/12-Inch 33rpm
COLUMBIA (C5X series):
   81 25–30
COLUMBIA (CL-2000
   series): *64–68* 10–15
COLUMBIA (CS-9000
   series): *64–70* 10–15
COLUMBIA (CQ series):
   71 10–15
COLUMBIA (JS series): *68* 10–12
COLUMBIA (OS series):
   68 12–15
COLUMBIA (40000
   series): *80–81* 12–15
   (Half-speed mastered LPs.)
OFFSHORE 10–15
PICKWICK: *66* 30–35
SEARS 20–25

Price Range

WARNER BROS: *82* **$5–8**
Members: Paul Simon; Art Garfunkel.
Also see GARFUNKEL, Art
Also see SIMON, Paul
Also see TOM & JERRY

SIMON SAID
Singles: 7-Inch
ATCO: *75–76* **2–4**
ROULETTE: *75* **2–4**

SIMON SISTERS, The
Singles: 7-Inch
COLUMBIA (02600
series): *82* **1–3**
COLUMBIA (45000
series): *73* **2–4**
KAPP: *64–65* **3–5**
LPs: 10/12-Inch 33rpm
COLUMBIA (21525;
"Lobster Quadrille"): *69* **12–15**
COLUMBIA (21539;
"Simon Sisters Sing For
Children"): *73* **10–12**
COLUMBIA (24506;
"Lobster Quadrille"): *69* **15–20**
COLUMBIA (37000
series): *82* **5–8**
KAPP: *64* **15–20**
WARNER BROS: *80* **5–8**
Members: Carly Simon; Lucy Simon.
Also see DOOBIE BROTHERS, The / Kate
Taylor & The Simon-Taylor Family
Also see SIMON, Carly

SIMONE, Nina
Singles: 7-Inch
BETHLEHEM: *59–70* **2–4**
CTI: *78* **1–3**
COLPIX: *59–63* **2–4**
PHILIPS: *64–66* **2–4**
RCA VICTOR: *67–71* **2–4**
TRIP: *72* **1–3**
EPs: 7-Inch 33/45rpm
BETHLEHEM: *59* **4–8**
LPs: 10/12-Inch 33rpm
ACCORD: *80* **4–8**
BETHLEHEM: *59* **15–25**
CTI: *78–79* **5–8**
COLPIX: *59–66* **10–20**
PHILIPS: *64–69* **10–20**
QUINTESSENCE: *80* **4–8**

Price Range

RCA VICTOR: *67–76* **$6–12**
STROUD: *73* **5–10**
UPFRONT: *72* **5–10**
TRIP: *72–77* **5–10**

SIMONE, Nina, Chris Connor & Carmen McRae
LPs: 10/12-Inch 33rpm
BETHLEHEM: *60* **15–25**
Also see CONNOR, Chris
Also see McRAE, Carmen
Also see SIMONE, Nina

SIMPLE MINDS, The
Singles: 12-Inch 33/45rpm
A&M: *82–85* **4–6**
Singles: 7-Inch
A&M: *82–85* **1–3**
LPs: 10/12-Inch 33rpm
A&M: *82–84* **5–8**
PVC: *79* **8–10**
Members: John Giblin; Charles Burchill; Jim
Kerr; Michael MacNeil; Mel Gaynor.

SIMPLY RED
Singles: 12-Inch 33/45rpm
ELEKTRA: *85* **4–6**
Singles: 7-Inch
ELEKTRA: *85* **1–3**

SIMPSON, Paul (The Paul Simpson Connection)
Singles: 12-Inch 33/45rpm
EASY STREET: *85* **4–6**
STREETWISE: *83* **4–6**
Singles: 7-Inch
STREETWISE: *83* **1–3**

Price Range

SIMPSON, Valerie
Singles: 7-Inch
TAMLA: *71–72* **$2–4**
LPs: 10/12-Inch 33rpm
TAMLA: *71–77* **8–10**
Also see ASHFORD & SIMPSON

SIMS, Marvin L.
Singles: 7-Inch
KAREN: *69* **2–4**
MELLOW: *66–67* **3–5**
REVUE: *68–69* **3–5**

SIMS TWINS, The (The Simms Twins)
Singles: 7-Inch
ABKCO **1–3**
CROSSOVER: *74* **2–3**
KENT: *71* **2–4**
PARKWAY: *68* **3–5**
SAR: *61–62* **4–6**
SPECIALTY **2–3**

SIMTEC & WYLIE
Singles: 7-Inch
MISTER CHAND: *70–72* **2–4**
SHAMA: *69–70* **2–4**
LPs: 10/12-Inch 33rpm
MISTER CHAND: *71–72* **8–10**

SINATRA, Frank (Frank Sinatra & Ray Anthony)
Singles: 7-Inch
CAPITOL (2700 through
  4800 series): *54–62* **3–6**
COLUMBIA (100 through
  900 series): *50–52* **8–15**
  (Microgroove 33 single series.)
COLUMBIA (38000 &
  39000 series): *50–51* **5–10**
REPRISE (45; "Gunga
  Din"): *66* **25–35**
  (Promotional issue only.)
REPRISE (0249 through
  1335): *64–75* **2–5**
REPRISE (20001 through
  20151): *61–63* **3–6**
REPRISE (20157;
  "California"): *63* **20–30**
REPRISE (29000 series):
  82 . . . . **1–3**

Price Range

REPRISE (49000 series):
  80–83 . . . . **$1–3**
Picture Sleeves
REPRISE (0249 through
  1300 series): *64–76* **2–5**
REPRISE (20001 through
  20151): *61–63* **4–8**
SINATRA: *75* **2–3**
EPs: 7-Inch 33/45rpm
CAPITOL: *54–61* **5–12**
COLUMBIA: *50–59* **5–15**
RCA VICTOR (3000
  series): *52* **10–20**
RCA VICTOR (5000
  series): *60* **5–10**
LPs: 10/12-Inch 33rpm
CAMDEN: *72–73* **5–10**
CAPITOL (200 & 300
  series): *69* **8–15**
CAPITOL (400 through
  1100 series): *54–59* **15–30**
  (With a "T" prefix.)
CAPITOL (500 through
  1600 series): *61–78* **5–15**
  (With a "DT," "DW," "SM," "STBB," "SW,"
  or "W" prefix.)
CAPITOL (1200 through
  1600 series): *59–62* **10–20**
  (With a "T" or "ST" prefix.)
CAPITOL (1729; "Love &
  Things"): *62* **10–20**
CAPITOL (1762; "Great
  Years"): *62* **20–30**
  (3-LP set.)
CAPITOL (1800 through
  2700 series): *62–67* **10–20**
CAPITOL (2814; "Frank
  Sinatra Deluxe Set"): *67* **35–50**
  (6-LP set.)
CAPITOL (11000 & 12000
  series): *74–80* **5–10**
CAPITOL (16000 series):
  80–82 . . . . **5–8**
COLUMBIA (6; "The
  Frank Sinatra Story"):
  58 . . . . **10–20**
COLUMBIA (42;
  "Essential Frank
  Sinatra"): *67* **15–30**
COLUMBIA (606 through
  803): *55–57* **15–25**

FRANK SINATRA
sings for
only
the
lonely

Orchestra conducted by NELSON RIDDLE

Price Range

COLUMBIA (842;
"Essential Frank
Sinatra"): 67................. **$15–30**
COLUMBIA (855 through
1400 series): 57–59 .... **12–25**
COLUMBIA (2400 & 2500
series): 66..................... **8–15**
(12-Inch LPs.)
COLUMBIA (2500 series):
55 .... **15–30**
(10-Inch LPs.)
COLUMBIA (2900 series):
69 .... **5–10**
COLUMBIA (6000 series):
50–54 .... **25–50**
(10-Inch LPs. Some LPs in this series have
paper sleeves.)
COLUMBIA (9200 & 9300
series): 66................... **8–15**
COLUMBIA (10000
series): 73.................... **5–10**
COLUMBIA (31000
series): 72.................... **5–10**
HARMONY: 66–71 .... **5–12**
ODYSSEY: 68.................... **8–15**
QWEST: 84 .... **5–8**
RCA VICTOR (400
through 1500 series):
72–76 .... **5–10**
RCA VICTOR (3000
series): 52.................... **20–40**
(10-Inch LP.)

Price Range

RCA VICTOR (4300
series): 82 .... **$8–12**
RCA VICTOR (4700
series): 83 .... **4–8**
REPRISE (1001 through
1024): 61–68.................. **10–20**
REPRISE (1025 through
1034): 68–72.................. **8–12**
REPRISE (2020 through
2275): 64–77.................. **5–15**
REPRISE (2300;
"Trilogy"): 80 .... **15–25**
(3-LP set.)
REPRISE (6000 series): 65 .... **10–15**
SINATRA: 75.................... **5–10**
Also see ANTHONY, Ray, Orchestra
Also see CROSBY, Bing, & Frank Sinatra
Also see DAY, Doris & Frank Sinatra
Also see DORSEY, Tommy
Also see JAMES, Harry

SINATRA, Frank, & Count Basie
LPs: 10/12-Inch 33rpm
REPRISE: 63–66................. **10–20**
Also see BASIE, Count

SINATRA, Frank, & Duke Ellington
Singles: 7-Inch
REPRISE: 68..................... **2–3**
LPs: 10/12-Inch 33rpm
REPRISE: 68..................... **8–15**
Also see ELLINGTON, Duke

SINATRA, Frank, & Antonio Carlos Jobim
LPs: 10/12-Inch 33rpm
REPRISE: 69–71................. **8–12**
Also see JOBIM, Antonio Carlos

SINATRA, Frank, & Keely Smith
Singles: 7-Inch
CAPITOL: 58 .... **3–5**
Also see SMITH, Keely

SINATRA, Frank, & Sammy Davis, Jr. / Dean Martin & Sammy Davis, Jr.
Singles: 7-Inch
REPRISE: 62..................... **3–5**
Picture Sleeves
REPRISE: 62..................... **5–8**
Also see DAVIS, Sammy, Jr.

Price Range

Also see MARTIN, Dean

SINATRA, Frank & Nancy (The Sinatra Family)
Singles: 7-Inch
REPRISE: *66–71* $2–4
LPs: 10/12-Inch 33rpm
REPRISE: *69* 8–15
Members: The Sinatra Family included Frank
Sinatra, Frank Jr., Nancy & Tina.
Also see SINATRA, Nancy

SINATRA, Nancy
Singles: 7-Inch
ELEKTRA: *80* 1–3
PRIVATE STOCK: *75–77* 2–3
RCA VICTOR: *72–73* 2–4
REPRISE: *61–71* 3–5
Picture Sleeves
REPRISE: *62–67* 3–5
EPs: 7-Inch 33/45rpm
REPRISE: *66* 10–12
(Jukebox issue only.)
LPs: 10/12-Inch 33rpm
RCA VICTOR: *72* 8–10
REPRISE: *66–72* 10–15
Also see BARRY, John
Also see MARTIN, Dean
Also see PRESLEY, Elvis
Also see SINATRA, Frank & Nancy

SINATRA, Nancy, & Lee Hazelwood
Singles: 7-Inch
PRIVATE STOCK: *76* 2–3
RCA VICTOR: *72* 2–3
REPRISE: *67–68* 3–5
LPs: 10/12-Inch 33rpm
RCA VICTOR: *72* 8–10
REPRISE: *68* 10–15
Also see HAZELWOOD, Lee
Also see SINATRA, Nancy

SINCLAIR, Gordon
Singles: 7-Inch
AVCO: *74* 2–4

SINFIELD, Pete
Singles: 7-Inch
MANTICORE: *73* 2–4
LPs: 10/12-Inch 33rpm
MANTICORE: *73* 8–10

Price Range

SINGING BELLS, The
Singles: 7-Inch
MADISON: *60* $4–6

SINGING DOGS, The (Don Charles Presents The Singing Dogs)
Singles: 7-Inch
RCA VICTOR: *55–72* 2–4
Picture Sleeves
RCA VICTOR: *55–56* 3–5

SINGING NUN, The (Soeur Sourire)
Singles: 7-Inch
PHILIPS: *63–64* 2–4
Picture Sleeves
PHILIPS: *63–64* 2–4
LPs: 10/12-Inch 33rpm
PHILIPS: *63–69* 6–15

SINGLE BULLET THEORY
Singles: 7-Inch
NEMPEROR: *83* 1–3
LPs: 10/12-Inch 33rpm
NEMPEROR: *83* 5–8

SINGLETON, Charlie
Singles: 7-Inch
ARISTA: *85* 1–3
LPs: 10/12-Inch 33rpm
ARISTA: *85* 5–8
Also see CAMEO
Also see COBHAM, Billy

Price Range

SINNAMON
Singles: 12-Inch 33/45rpm
BECKET: *82–83* $4–6
JIVE: *84* 4–6
Singles: 7-Inch
BECKET: *82–83* 1–3

SIOUXSIE & THE BANSHEES
Singles: 12-Inch 33/45rpm
PVC: *80–82* 4–6
Singles: 7-Inch
GEFFEN: *84* 1–3
PVC: *80–82* 1–3
POLYDOR: *79* 1–3
LPs: 10/12-Inch 33rpm
GEFFEN: *84* 5–8
PVC: *80–82* 6–10
POLYDOR: *79* 8–10
Also see SEX PISTOLS, The

SIR CHAUNCEY (Ernie Freeman)
Singles: 7-Inch
PATTERN: *60.* 3–6
WARNER BROS: *60* 2–4
Also see FREEMAN, Ernie

SIR DOUGLAS QUINTET, The (Featuring Doug Sahm; The Sir Douglas Band)
Singles: 7-Inch
ATLANTIC: *73* 5–8
CASABLANCA: *74–75* 2–4
MERCURY: *71*.................... 2–4
PHILIPS: *70–71* 2–4
SMASH: *68–70* 3–5
TRIBE: *65–67* 4–6
LPs: 10/12-Inch 33rpm
ACCORD: *82* 5–8
ATLANTIC: *73* 10–15
MERCURY: *72*.................... 10–12
PHILIPS: *70–71* 10–15
SMASH: *68–70* 15–20
TAKOMA: *80–83*.................. 5–8
TRIBE: *66* 20–25
Also see SAHM, Doug

SIR LORD BALTIMORE
Singles: 7-Inch
MERCURY: *70–71* 2–4
LPs: 10/12-Inch 33rpm
MERCURY: *70–71*................ 8–10

Price Range

SIREN
Singles: 7-Inch
MIDSONG INT'L: *79* $2–3

SIRENNE, Gianni
Singles: 12-Inch 33/45rpm
ATLANTIC: *84* 4–6
Singles: 7-Inch
ATLANTIC: *84* 1–3

SISTER & BROTHERS
Singles: 7-Inch
CALLA: *71*....................... 2–4
UNI: *70* 2–4

SISTER SLEDGE
Singles: 12-Inch 33/45rpm
ATLANTIC: *85* 4–6
COTILLION: *79–83*............... 4–6
Singles: 7-Inch
ATCO: *73–75*..................... 2–4
ATLANTIC: *85* 1–3
COTILLION: *76–83*............... 1–3
LPs: 10/12-Inch 33rpm
ATCO: *75* 8–10
ATLANTIC: *85* 5–8
COTILLION: *76–83*............... 5–8

SISTERS LOVE
Singles: 7-Inch
A&M: *69–71* 2–4

SIX TEENS, The
Singles: 7-Inch
FLIP: *56–60* **$5–8**
Members: Trudy Williams; Ed Wells; Bev
Pecot; Ken Sinclair; Louise Williams; Darrell
Lewis.

SKA KINGS, The
Singles: 7-Inch
ATLANTIC: *64* **3–5**

SKAGGS, Ricky
Singles: 7-Inch
EPIC: *81–85* **1–3**
ROUNDER: *80*................... **1–3**
SUGAR HILL: *80* **2–3**
LPs: 10/12-Inch 33rpm
EPIC: *81–85* **5–8**
ROUNDER: *82*................... **5–8**
SUGAR HILL: *79–80* **5–8**
WEL DUN: *78* **5–8**

SKELLERN, Peter
Singles: 7-Inch
LONDON: *72*.................... **2–4**
PRIVATE STOCK: *75*............. **2–3**
LPs: 10/12-Inch 33rpm
LONDON: *76*................... **6–10**

SKELTON, Red
Singles: 7-Inch
COLUMBIA: *69*.................. **2–4**
LPs: 10/12-Inch 33rpm
LIBERTY: *65–66* **5–15**

SKHY, A.B.: see A.B. SKHY

SKIP & FLIP
Singles: 7-Inch
BRENT: *59–62* **4–6**
CALIFORNIA: *63* **3–5**
COLLECTABLES **1–3**
ERIC **1–3**
TIME: *61*...................... **8–10**
Members: Clyde Batton; Gary Paxton.
Also see HOLLYWOOD ARGYLES, The

SKIP & THE CASUALS
Singles: 7-Inch
D.C. INT'L: *74*.................. **2–4**

SKIPWORTH & TURNER
Singles: 12-Inch 33/45rpm
4TH & BROADWAY: *85*.......... **$4–6**
Singles: 7-Inch
4TH & BROADWAY: *85*.......... **1–3**
Members: Rodney Skipworth; Philip Turner.

SKOOL BOYZ
Singles: 12-Inch 33/45rpm
COLUMBIA: *84–85*.............. **4–6**
Singles: 7-Inch
COLUMBIA: *84–85*.............. **1–3**
DESTINY: *81–82* **1–3**
LPs: 10/12-Inch 33rpm
DESTINY: *81* **5–8**
Also see TRIPLE "S" CONNECTION

SKRATCH
Singles: 12-Inch 33/45rpm
PASSION: *85*.................... **4–6**

SKY
Singles: 7-Inch
RCA VICTOR: *71–72* **2–4**
LPs: 10/12-Inch 33rpm
RCA VICTOR: *70–71* **10–12**

SKY (With Doug Fieger)
Singles: 7-Inch
ARISTA: *81* **1–3**
LPs: 10/12-Inch 33rpm
ARISTA: *81* **8–10**
Also see KNACK, The

SKYLARK (With Donny Gerrard & Carl Graves)
Singles: 7-Inch
CAPITOL: *72–73* **2–4**
LPs: 10/12-Inch 33rpm
CAPITOL: *72–74* **8–10**
Also see GERRARD, Donny

SKYLINERS, The (Featuring Jimmy Beaumont)
Singles: 7-Inch
ATCO: *63* **4–6**
CALICO: *59–60* **5–8**
CAMEO: *62* **4–6**
CAPITOL: *75* **2–4**
COLPIX: *61* **4–6**
JUBILEE: *65–66*................. **4–6**

Price Range

ORIGINAL SOUND **$1–3**
TORTOISE INT'L: *78* **2–3**
VIRGO: *73* **1–3**
VISCOUNT: *62* **4–6**
LPs: 10/12-Inch 33rpm
CALICO: *59* **70–80**
KAMA SUTRA: *71* **10–15**
ORIGINAL SOUND: *63* **15–20**
TORTOISE INT'L: *78* **8–10**
Also see BEAUMONT, Jimmy

SKYNYRD, Lynyrd: see LYNYRD SKYNYRD

SKYY
Singles: 12-Inch 33/45rpm
SALSOUL: *79–85* **4–6**
Singles: 7-Inch
SALSOUL: *79–85* **1–3**
LPs: 10/12-Inch 33rpm
SALSOUL: *79–82* **5–8**

SLADE
Singles: 7-Inch
CBS ASSOCIATED: *84–85* **1–3**
COTILLION: *71–72* **2–4**
POLYDOR: *72–73* **2–4**
REPRISE: *73* **2–4**
WARNER BROS: *73–76* **2–3**
LPs: 10/12-Inch 33rpm
CBS ASSOCIATED: *84* **5–8**
COTILLION: *70* **10–15**
POLYDOR: *72–73* **8–10**
REPRISE: *73* **10–12**
WARNER BROS: *74–76* **8–10**

SLADES, The
Singles: 7-Inch
DOMINO: *58–61* **8–10**
LIBERTY: *58* **5–8**
Also see SPADES, The

SLATKIN, Felix, Orchestra
Singles: 7-Inch
LIBERTY: *60–62* **2–4**
LPs: 10/12-Inch 33rpm
ANGEL: *72* **5–8**
CAPITOL: *59* **5–15**
LIBERTY: *60–64* **5–15**
SUNSET: *66–68* **5–10**
UNITED ARTISTS: *71* **5–10**

Price Range

SLAVE
Singles: 12-Inch 33/45rpm
COTILLION: *83* **$4–6**
Singles: 7-Inch
COTILLION: *77–84* **1–3**
LPs: 10/12-Inch 33rpm
COTILLION: *77–84* **5–8**
Also see ARRINGTON, Steve

SLAY, Emitt (The Emitt Slay Trio; Emitt Slay's Slayriders With Sweetie Dolores)
Singles: 7-Inch
CHECKER: *58* **5–8**
J.V.B.: *59* **4–6**
SAVOY: *52–53* **8–10**

SLAY, Frank, & His Orchestra
Singles: 7-Inch
SCA: *63* **2–4**
SWAN: *61* **2–4**

SLEDGE, Percy
Singles: 7-Inch
ATLANTIC: *66–72* **3–5**
CAPRICORN: *74–76* **2–4**
MONUMENT: *83* **1–3**
LPs: 10/12-Inch 33rpm
ATLANTIC: *66–69* **10–15**
CAPRICORN: *74–75* **8–10**
MONUMENT: *83* **5–8**

SLEDGE, Sister: see SISTER SLEDGE

SLEEPY KING
Singles: 7-Inch
JOY: *61* **3–5**

SLICK
Singles: 12-Inch 33/45rpm
FANTASY: *80* **4–6**
Singles: 7-Inch
FANTASY: *80* **1–3**
LPs: 10/12-Inch 33rpm
FANTASY: *80* **5–8**
WMOT: *79* **5–8**

SLICK, Grace (Grace Slick & The Great Society)
Singles: 7-Inch
GRUNT: *72–74*.................. **$2–4**
RCA VICTOR: *80–81* **1–3**
Picture Sleeves
RCA VICTOR: *80* .... **INC**
LPs: 10/12-Inch 33rpm
COLUMBIA (CS-9624;
"Conspicuous Only"): *68* **10–12**
COLUMBIA (PC-9624;
"Conspicuous Only") **5–8**
COLUMBIA (CS-9702;
"How It Was"): *68*............. **12–15**
COLUMBIA (30459;
"Collector's Item"): *71* **10–12**
GRUNT: *74*.................... **8–10**
HARMONY: *71* **10–12**
RCA VICTOR: *80–83* **5–8**
Promotional LPs
RCA VICTOR (3923;
"Special Radio Series"):
81 .... **10–15**
Also see CROSBY, David
Also see GREAT!! SOCIETY!!, The
Also see JEFFERSON AIRPLANE, The
Also see JEFFERSON STARSHIP, The
Also see KANTNER, Paul, & Grace Slick

SLIM, Guitar: see GUITAR SLIM

SLIM, Tarheel: see TARHEEL SLIM

SLIM & ANN: see TARHEEL SLIM & LITTLE ANN

SLIM HARPO: see HARPO, Slim

SLINGSHOT
Singles: 12-Inch 33/45rpm
QUALITY/RFC: *83*............... **4–6**
Singles: 7-Inch
QUALITY/RFC: *83*............... **1–3**

SLOAN, P.F. (Phil Sloan)
Singles: 7-Inch
ATCO: *69* **2–4**
DUNHILL: *65–67*................. **3–5**
MART: *60*...................... **8–10**

MUMS: *72*...................... **$2–4**
LPs: 10/12-Inch 33rpm
ATCO: *68* **10–12**
DUNHILL: *65–66*............... **12–15**
MUMS: *72*...................... **8–10**

SLY (Sly Stone)
Singles: 7-Inch
AUTUMN: *65*.................... **4–6**
Also see SLY & THE FAMILY STONE

SLY & THE FAMILY STONE (Featuring Sly Stone)
Singles: 12-Inch 33/45rpm
EPIC: *79* **4–6**
Singles: 7-Inch
EPIC: *67–75* **2–5**
WARNER BROS: *79–85*............ **1–3**
Picture Sleeves
EPIC: *68–70* **2–5**
LPs: 10/12-Inch 33rpm
EPIC (264; "Everything
You Always Wanted To
Hear"): *76* **10–15**
(Promotional issue only.)
EPIC (26000 series): *67–69* **10–12**
EPIC (30325; "Greatest
Hits"): *70*.................... **8–10**
(With a "KE" prefix.)
EPIC (30325; "Greatest
Hits") **5–8**
(With a "PE" prefix.)
EPIC (30325; "Greatest
Hits"): *73*.................... **20–25**
(With an "EQ" prefix. Quad issue. Contains
some true stereo tracks that were only available
in rechanneled stereo on the "KE" & "PE"
30325 issues.)
EPIC (30335 through
37071): *70–81*................. **6–10**
WARNER BROS: *79–83*............ **5–8**
Also see BANKS, Rose
Also see GRAHAM, Larry
Also see RUBICON
Also see SLY
Also see STONE, Sly

SMALL, Karen
Singles: 7-Inch
VENUS: *66* **3–5**

SMALL, Millie (The Blue Beat Girl)
Singles: 7-Inch
ATCO: *65* **$3–5**
ATLANTIC: *64* **3–5**
BRIT: *65* **4–6**
SMASH: *64* **3–5**
LPs: 10/12-Inch 33rpm
SMASH: *64* **15–20**

SMALL FACES (With Steve Marriott)
Singles: 7-Inch
IMMEDIATE: *67–68* **4–6**
PRESS: *65–68* **6–10**
RCA VICTOR: *66* **8–10**
WARNER BROS: *70* **3–5**
LPs: 10/12-Inch 33rpm
ACCORD: *82* **5–8**
ATLANTIC: *77–78* **8–10**
COMPLEAT: *86* **5–8**
IMMEDIATE (002;
　"There Are But Four
　Small Faces"): *68* **20–25**
IMMEDIATE (008;
　"Ogden's Nut Gone
　Flake"): *68* **20–25**
IMMEDIATE (4225;
　"Ogden's Nut Gone
　Flake"): *73* **10–12**
MGM: *74* **10–15**
PRIDE: *72–73* **10–15**
SIRE **10–15**
WARNER BROS: *70* **12–15**
　Also see FACES
　Also see HUMBLE PIE
　Also see McLAGAN, Ian

SMITH (Featuring Gayle McCormack)
Singles: 7-Inch
DUNHILL: *69–70* **2–4**
ROULETTE **1–3**
Picture Sleeves
DUNHILL: *69* **2–4**
LPs: 10/12-Inch 33rpm
DUNHILL: *69–70* **10–15**
　Also see McCORMACK, Gayle

SMITH, Betty, Group
Singles: 7-Inch
LONDON: *58* **4–6**

SMITH, Bro
Singles: 7-Inch
BIG TREE: *76* **$2–3**

SMITH, Cal
Singles: 7-Inch
DECCA: *70–73* **2–3**
KAPP: *66–70* **2–4**
PLAID: *60* **3–5**
MCA: *73–79* **1–3**
SOUNDWAVES: *82* **1–3**
LPs: 10/12-Inch 33rpm
CORAL: *73* **4–8**
DECCA: *72* **8–10**
KAPP: *66–70* **8–12**
MCA: *73–77* **4–8**

SMITH, Carl (Carl Smith & The Tunesmiths)
Singles: 7-Inch
ABC/HICKORY: *76–78* **1–3**
COLUMBIA (20000 &
　21000 series): *51–56* **3–6**
COLUMBIA (40000
　through 45000 series):
　56–72 .... **2–4**
HICKORY: *74–76* **1–3**
Picture Sleeves
COLUMBIA: *59* **3–5**
EPs: 7-Inch 33/45rpm
COLUMBIA: *57–58* **6–12**
LPs: 10/12-Inch 33rpm
ABC/HICKORY: *77–78* **5–8**
COLUMBIA (31;
　"Anniversary Album"):
　70 .... **8–12**
COLUMBIA (900 through
　1100 series): *57–58* **15–25**
COLUMBIA (1500
　through 2600 series):
　60–67 .... **10–20**
COLUMBIA (2500 series):
　56 .... **20–35**
　(10-Inch LPs.)
COLUMBIA (8300
　through 9800 series):
　60–72 .... **10–20**
　(12-Inch LPs.)
COLUMBIA (9000 series):
　54 .... **20–35**
　(10-Inch LPs.)

Price Range

COLUMBIA (10000
series): *73* $5–10
COLUMBIA (30000
series): *70–84* 5–10
GUSTO: *80* 5–8
HICKORY: *75* 5–10
HARMONY: *64–72* 5–15
LAKE SHORE 5–8
    Also see PRICE, Ray / Lefty Frizzell / Carl
    Smith
    Also see ROBBINS, Marty / Carl Smith /
    Lefty Frizzell

SMITH, Connie
Singles: 7-Inch
COLUMBIA: *73–77* 1–3
MONUMENT: *77–83* 1–3
RCA VICTOR: *64–74* 2–4
Picture Sleeves
RCA VICTOR: *67* 2–4
LPs: 10/12-Inch 33rpm
CAMDEN: *67–72* 5–10
COLUMBIA: *73–77* 5–10
MONUMENT: *77–78* 5–8
RCA VICTOR (0100 series
through 1200 series):
73–75 5–10
RCA VICTOR (3300 series
through 4800 series):
65–73 8–15

SMITH, Dawson
Singles: 7-Inch
ROADSHOW/SCEPTER:
75 2–4

SMITH, Effie
Singles: 7-Inch
ALADDIN (3200 series):
53 10–15
DUO DISC: *64–65* 3–5
EEE CEE: *68* 2–4
SPOT: *59* 4–6
VITA: *56* 8–10
LPs: 10/12-Inch 33rpm
JUBILEE: *66* 15–20

SMITH, Frankie
Singles: 7-Inch
WMOT: *81* 1–3

Price Range

LPs: 10/12-Inch 33rpm
WMOT: *81* $5–8

SMITH, Helene
Singles: 7-Inch
PHIL-L.A. OF SOUL:
67–69 3–5

SMITH, Huey (Huey Smith & His Band; Huey "Piano" Smith & His Clowns; Huey Smith & The Pitter Pats)
Singles: 7-Inch
ABC: *73* 2–3
ACE (521 through 571):
56–59 8–12
ACE (584 through 672):
60–65 4–6
COLLECTABLES 1–3
CONSTELLATION: *63* 3–5
COTILLION: *72* 2–4
IMPERIAL: *61* 4–6
INSTANT: *68–69* 3–5
SAVOY: *54* 30–35
VIN: *60* 4–6
EPs: 7-Inch 33/45rpm
ACE: *59* 20–25
LPs: 10/12-Inch 33rpm
ACE (1000 series): *59–62* 40–50
ACE (2000 series): *74* 25–35
GRAND PRIX 10–15
    Also see CRAWFORD, James
    Also see FORD, Frankie
    Also see KING, Earl
    Also see MARCHAN, Bobby, & The Clowns

SMITH, Hurricane
Singles: 7-Inch
CAPITOL: *72–73* 2–4
EMI: *74* 2–4
LPs: 10/12-Inch 33rpm
CAPITOL: *72* 8–10

SMITH, Jerry (Jerry Smith & His Pianos)
Singles: 7-Inch
ABC: *69* 2–3
AD: *59–61* 2–5
CHART: *67* 2–3
DECCA: *70–72* 1–3
RANWOOD: *73–78* 1–3

Price Range

RICE: *67* **$2–3**
SOUND STAGE 7: *65* **2–4**
LPs: 10/12-Inch 33rpm
ABC: *69* **5–10**
DECCA: *70–72* **5–10**
RANWOOD: *73–75* **5–8**
  Also see DIXIEBELLES, The
  Also see MAGIC ORGAN, The

SMITH, Jimmy
Singles: 7-Inch
BLUE NOTE: *56–63* **2–5**
MGM: *78* **1–3**
MERCURY: *77.* **1–3**
PRIDE: *74* **1–3**
VERVE: *62–73* **2–4**
LPs: 10/12-Inch 33rpm
BLUE NOTE: *56–60* **25–50**
  (Label gives New York street address for Blue
  Note Records.)
BLUE NOTE: *61–63* **15–25**
  (Label reads "Blue Note Records Inc. - New
  York, USA.")
BLUE NOTE: *66–73* **10–20**
  (Label shows Blue Note Records as a division
  of either Liberty or United Artists.)
COBBLESTONE: *72* **6–12**
ELEKTRA: *82–83* **5–8**
INNER CITY: *81* **5–8**
MGM: *70* **8–12**
MERCURY: *77–78* **5–10**
METRO: *67* **8–15**
MOJO: *75* **5–10**
PRIDE: *74* **5–10**
SUNSET: *70* **5–10**
VERVE: *63–72* **10–25**
  (Reads "MGM Records - A Division Of Metro-
  Goldwyn-Mayer, Inc." at bottom of label.)
VERVE: *73–84* **5–10**
  (Reads "Manufactured By MGM Record
  Corp.," or mentions either Polydor or Poly-
  gram at bottom of label.)

SMITH, Jimmy, & Wes Montgomery
LPs: 10/12-Inch 33rpm
VERVE: *66–69* **10–20**
  Also see MONTGOMERY, Wes
  Also see SMITH, Jimmy

SMITH, Kate
Singles: 7-Inch
ATLANTIC: *74* **1–3**
MGM: *78* **1–3**

Price Range

RCA VICTOR: *63–68* **$1–3**
TOPS: *60* **2–3**
Picture Sleeves
RCA VICTOR: *63–64* **2–3**
EPs: 7-Inch 33/45rpm
MGM: *52–57* **4–8**
RCA VICTOR: *59* **4–8**
LPs: 10/12-Inch 33rpm
CAMDEN: *70–73* **4–8**
CAPITOL: *54–57* **5–15**
COLUMBIA (6000 series):
  50 .... **10–20**
  (10-Inch LPs.)
HARMONY: *57* **5–12**
KAPP: *58* **5–15**
LION: *57–60* **5–12**
MGM: *52–66* **5–15**
METRO: *67* **5–10**
RCA VICTOR: *63–80* **5–12**

SMITH, Keely
Singles: 7-Inch
ATLANTIC: *67* **1–3**
CAPITOL: *56–58* **2–4**
DOLTON: *64.* **2–3**
DOT: *59–62* **2–3**
RCA VICTOR: *66–71* **1–3**
REPRISE: *63–66.* **1–3**
Picture Sleeves
DOT: *60* **2–3**
EPs: 7-Inch 33/45rpm
CAPITOL: *58–59* **4–8**
DOT: *60* **4–8**
LPs: 10/12-Inch 33rpm
CAPITOL: *58–75* **5–15**
DOT: *59–62* **5–15**
HARMONY: *69* **5–10**
REPRISE: *63–65.* **5–10**
  Also see PRIMA, Louis, & Keely Smith
  Also see SINATRA, Frank, & Keely Smith

SMITH, Leslie, & Merry Clayton
Singles: 7-Inch
ELEKTRA: *82* **1–3**
  Also see CLAYTON, Merry

SMITH, Lonnie
Singles: 7-Inch
BLUE NOTE: *69–70* **1–3**
GROOVE MERCHANT:
  75 .... **2–3**

Price Range

LRC: *78–79* **$1–3**

LPs: 10/12-Inch 33rpm
BLUE NOTE: *68–70* **8–15**
COLUMBIA: *67* **10–15**
GROOVE MERCHANT:
  75–76 . . . . **5–10**
KUDU: *71* **5–10**
LRC: *78* **5–8**

SMITH, Lonnie Liston (Lonnie Liston Smith & The Cosmic Echoes)
Singles: 12-Inch 33/45rpm
COLUMBIA: *79* **4–6**

Singles: 7-Inch
COLUMBIA: *78–80* **1–3**
DOCTOR JAZZ: *83* **1–3**
FLYING DUTCHMAN:
  75–76 . . . . **2–3**
RCA VICTOR: *77* **1–3**

LPs: 10/12-Inch 33rpm
COLUMBIA: *78–79* **5–8**
DOCTOR JAZZ: *83* **5–8**
FLYING DUTCHMAN:
  73–76 . . . . **8–12**
RCA VICTOR: *76–77* **5–10**

SMITH, O.C. (Ocie Smith)
Singles: 7-Inch
BIG TOP: *60* **3–5**
CARIBOU: *76–77* **2–3**
CITATION: *59* **3–5**
COLUMBIA: *66–74* **2–4**
FAMILY: *80* **1–3**
GORDY: *82* **1–3**
MGM: *56* **4–6**
MOTOWN: *82* **1–3**
SHADYBROOK: *78* **2–3**
SOUL WEST: *72* **2–4**
SOUTH BAY: *82* **1–3**

Picture Sleeves
COLUMBIA: *69* **2–4**

LPs: 10/12-Inch 33rpm
CARIBOU: *79* **5–8**
COLUMBIA: *67–74* **8–12**
HARMONY: *71* **8–10**
MGM: *72* **8–10**
MOTOWN: *82* **5–8**
SOUTH BAY: *82* **5–8**

Price Range

SMITH, Patti (The Patti Smith Group)
Singles: 7-Inch
ARISTA: *76–79* **$2–3**
MER (601; "Hey Joe"): *74* **30–35**
SIRE: *77* **2–3**

Picture Sleeves
ARISTA: *78* **2–3**

LPs: 10/12-Inch 33rpm
ARISTA: *75–79* **8–10**

Promotional LPs
ARISTA ("Easter" picture
  disc): *79* **15–20**

SMITH, Ray
Singles: 7-Inch
ABC: *73* **1–3**
CELEBRITY CIRCLE: *64* **3–5**
CINNAMON: *73–74* **2–4**
COLLECTABLES **1–3**
CORONA: *76–77* **2–3**
DIAMOND: *65* **3–5**
HEART **60–75**
INFINITY: *61* **3–5**
JUDD: *59–61* **5–8**
NU-TONE: *64* **3–5**
SMASH: *62* **3–5**
SSS INT'L **1–3**
SSS/SUN **1–3**
SUN (298; "Right Behind
  You Baby"): *58* **10–15**
SUN (308; "Why Why
  Why"): *59* **5–8**
SUN (319 through 375):
  59–62 . . . . **4–6**
TOLLIE: *64* **8–10**
TOPPA: *62* **3–5**
VEE JAY: *64* **3–5**
WARNER BROS: *63* **3–5**
WIX: *78* **2–3**

LPs: 10/12-Inch 33rpm
BOOT: *78* **5–8**
COLUMBIA: *63* **20–25**
CROWN: *63* **12–15**
JUDD: *60* **100–125**
T **10–12**
WIX **10–12**
  Also see DONNER, Ral / Ray Smith / Bobby
  Dale

Price Range

SMITH, Rex
Singles: 7-Inch
COLUMBIA: 76–81 .... $1–3
Picture Sleeves
COLUMBIA: 79–80 1–3
LPs: 10/12-Inch 33rpm
COLUMBIA: 76–81 5–8
Also see REX

SMITH, Rex, & Rachel Sweet
Singles: 7-Inch
COLUMBIA: 81 1–3
Picture Sleeves
COLUMBIA: 81 1–3
Also see SMITH, Rex
Also see SWEET, Rachel

SMITH, Richard Jon
Singles: 12-Inch 33/45rpm
JIVE: 83 4–6
Singles: 7-Inch
JIVE: 83 1–3
LPs: 10/12-Inch 33rpm
JIVE: 83 5–8

SMITH, Roger
Singles: 7-Inch
JEROME: 61 3–5
WARNER BROS: 59 3–6
Picture Sleeves
WARNER BROS: 59 3–6
LPs: 10/12-Inch 33rpm
WARNER BROS: 59 20–25

SMITH, Sammi
Singles: 7-Inch
COLUMBIA: 67–69 2–4
CYCLONE: 79 1–3
ELEKTRA: 75–78 1–3
MEGA: 70–76 1–3
SOUND FACTORY:
80–82 1–3
TRIP: 74 1–3
ZODIAC: 76 1–3
Picture Sleeves
MEGA: 70 2–3
LPs: 10/12-Inch 33rpm
CYCLONE: 79 5–8
ELEKTRA: 76–78 5–8
HARMONY: 71 5–10
MEGA: 70–75 5–10

Price Range

TRIP: 74 .... $5–8
UNITED ARTISTS: 75 5–8
ZODIAC: 76 5–8
Also see HART, Freddie / Sammi Smith /
Jerry Reed

SMITH, Somethin,' & The Redheads
Singles: 7-Inch
EPIC: 54–59 2–4
MGM: 61 2–3
Picture Sleeves
EPIC: 58 2–5
LPs: 10/12-Inch 33rpm
EPIC: 59 8–15
MGM: 61 5–15

SMITH, Tab (Tab Smith & His Band)
Singles: 7-Inch
ARGO: 58–59 4–6
ATLANTIC: 52 10–12
B&F: 61 3–5
CHECKER: 59 4–6
CHESS: 52 8–10
KING (5000 series): 60–61 3–5
UNITED (Black vinyl):
51–57 5–8
UNITED (Colored vinyl):
51 10–15
EPs: 7-Inch 33/45rpm
KING 10–15
LPs: 10/12-Inch 33rpm
CHECKER: 59 15–20
UNITED (001; "Music
Styled By Tab Smith") 30–35
UNITED (003; "Red Hot
& Cool Blue Moods") 20–25

SMITH, Verdelle
Singles: 7-Inch
CAPITOL: 66–67 3–5
COLUMBIA: 65 3–5
JANUS: 75 2–4
Picture Sleeves
COLUMBIA: 65 3–5
LPs: 10/12-Inch 33rpm
CAPITOL: 66 12–15
JANUS: 75 8–10

Price Range

SMITH, Warren
Singles: 7-Inch
LIBERTY: *60–64* **$3–5**
MERCURY: *68*. **2–4**
SUN (239; "Rock 'N' Roll
  Ruby"): *56* **20–25**
SUN (250; "Ubangi
  Stomp"): *56* **10–15**
SUN (268 through 314):
  57–59 .... **5–8**
SSS/SUN: *80* **1–3**
WARNER BROS: *59* **4–6**
LPs: 10/12-Inch 33rpm
LIBERTY: *61* **30–40**

SMITH, Whistling Jack
Singles: 7-Inch
DERAM: *67–69* **2–4**
LPs: 10/12-Inch 33rpm
DERAM: *67* **10–12**

SMITH CONNECTION, The
Singles: 7-Inch
MUSIC MERCHANT: *73* **2–4**

SMITHS, The
Singles: 12-Inch 33/45rpm
SIRE: *84–85* **4–6**
Singles: 7-Inch
SIRE: *84–85* **1–3**
LPs: 10/12-Inch 33rpm
SIRE: *84–85* **5–8**

SMOKE CITY
Singles: 7-Inch
EPIC: *84–85* **1–3**

SMOKE RING
Singles: 7-Inch
BUDDAH: *69* **2–4**
DOT: *66* **3–5**

SMOKESTACK LIGHTNIN'
Singles: 7-Inch
BELL: *68–70* **3–5**
WHITE WHALE: *67* **4–6**
LPs: 10/12-Inch 33rpm
BELL: *69* **10–15**

Price Range

SMOKIE (Featuring Chris Norman; Smokey)
Singles: 7-Inch
MCA: *75* **$2–4**
RSO: *76–79* **2–3**
LPs: 10/12-Inch 33rpm
MCA: *75* **8–10**
RSO: *76–79* **5–8**
Also see QUATRO, Suzi, & Chris Norman

SMOTHERS BROTHERS, The
Singles: 7-Inch
MERCURY: *62–66* **2–5**
Picture Sleeves
MERCURY: *64–65* **2–5**
LPs: 10/12-Inch 33rpm
MERCURY (20000 &
  60000 series): *61–68* **10–20**
Members: Dick Smothers; Tom Smothers.

SNAIL
Singles: 7-Inch
CREAM: *78–79* **2–3**
LPs: 10/12-Inch 33rpm
CREAM: *78–79* **5–8**

SNEAKER
Singles: 7-Inch
HANDSHAKE: *81–82* **1–3**
LPs: 10/12-Inch 33rpm
HANDSHAKE: *81* **5–8**

SNEED, Lois
Singles: 7-Inch
CAPITOL: *73* **2–4**

SNELL, Annette
Singles: 7-Inch
DIAL: *73–74* **2–4**
EPIC: *77* **2–3**

SNIFF 'N' THE TEARS
Singles: 7-Inch
ATLANTIC: *79–80* **1–3**
MCA: *81* **1–3**
LPs: 10/12-Inch 33rpm
ATCO: *79* **5–8**
ATLANTIC: *80* **5–8**
MCA: *81* **5–8**
Also see NETTO, Loz

Price Range   *Price Range*

SNOW, Hank
Singles: 7-Inch
RCA VICTOR (0100 &
  0900 series): *69–74* **$2–4**
  (Orange labels.)
RCA VICTOR (0300 &
  0400 series): *50–51* **5–10**
  (Gray labels.)
RCA VICTOR (4300
  through 7700 series):
  52–60 .... **4–8**
RCA VICTOR (7800
  through 9900 series):
  61–70 .... **2–5**
RCA VICTOR (10000 &
  11000 series): *74–80* **1–3**
Picture Sleeves
RCA VICTOR: *63* **3–5**
EPs: 7-Inch 33/45rpm
RCA VICTOR (295
  through 1113): *54–56* **10–25**
RCA VICTOR (1156; "Old
  Doc Brown"): *55*............... **30–40**
RCA VICTOR (1200
  series): *55*.................... **15–20**
RCA VICTOR (1400
  series): *57*.................... **8–12**
RCA VICTOR (4000
  series): *58*.................... **8–12**
RCA VICTOR (5000
  series): *58–60*................. **8–12**
RCA VICTOR (3000 &
  3100 series): *52–53* **35–45**
LPs: 10/12-Inch 33rpm
CAMDEN: *59–74*................. **8–15**
HANK SNOW SCHOOL
OF MUSIC (1149/50;
  "The Guitar"): *58* **175–225**
  (Special issue from the Hank Snow School Of
  Music. Includes guitar instruction booklet.)
PICKWICK: *75–76* **5–10**
RCA VICTOR (0134;
  "The Living Legend"):
  78 .... **100–125**
  (RCA Special Products issue.)
RCA VICTOR (0162
  through 0900 series):
  73–75 .... **5–10**
RCA VICTOR (1004; "I'm
  Movin' On"): *82* **15–20**
  (RCA Special Products issue.)

RCA VICTOR (1052
  through 3500 series):
  75–79 .... **$5–10**
  (With an "AHL1, "ANL1" or "APL1" prefix.)
RCA VICTOR (1113;
  "Just Keep A-Movin' "):
  55 .... **25–35**
  (With an "LPM" prefix.)
RCA VICTOR (1156; "Old
  Doc Brown"): *55*............ **125–175**
RCA VICTOR (1200
  through 1800 series):
  55–58 .... **25–40**
RCA VICTOR (2000
  through 4700 series):
  60–72 .... **10–25**
RCA VICTOR (3000 &
  3100 series): *52–54* **40–60**
  (10-Inch LPs.)
RCA VICTOR (6014;
  "This Is My Story"): *66*........ **20–30**
READER'S DIGEST (216;
  "I'm Movin' On")........... **125–150**
  (6-LP set.)

SNOW, Hank, & Chet Atkins
Singles: 7-Inch
RCA VICTOR (5900
  series): *55*..................... **3–5**
LPs: 10/12-Inch 33rpm
RCA VICTOR (2900
  through 4200 series):
  64–70 .... **20–25**
  Also see ATKINS, Chet

**SNOW, Hank / Hank Locklin /
Porter Wagoner**
LPs: 10/12-Inch 33rpm
RCA VICTOR: *63* **10–20**
  Also see LOCKLIN, Hank
  Also see SNOW, Hank
  Also see WAGONER, Porter

SNOW, Phoebe
Singles: 7-Inch
COLUMBIA: *76–78*............... **2–3**
MIRAGE: *81*...................... **1–3**
SHELTER: *74–75*.................. **2–4**
LPs: 10/12-Inch 33rpm
COLUMBIA: *76–81*............... **5–8**
MCA: *79* **5–8**
MIRAGE: *81*.................... **5–8**

Price Range

SHELTER: *74* **$8–10**
 Also see GOODMAN, Steve, & Phoebe Snow
 Also see SIMON, Paul, & Phoebe Snow

SNUFF
  Singles: 7-Inch
WARNER BROS./CURB:
 83 . . . . **1–3**

SOBER, Errol
  Singles: 7-Inch
ABC: *74* **2–3**
ABNAK: *70* **2–4**
BELL: *72* **2–4**
CAPITOL: *76* **2–3**
NUMBER ONE: *79* **1–3**

SOCCIO, Gino
  Singles: 12-Inch 33/45rpm
ATLANTIC: *80–84* **4–6**
WARNER BROS/RFC:
 79–80 . . . . **4–6**
  Singles: 7-Inch
ATLANTIC: *80–84* **1–3**
WARNER BROS/RFC:
 79–82 . . . . **1–3**
  LPs: 10/12-Inch 33rpm
ATLANTIC: *80–84* **5–8**
WARNER BROS/RFC:
 79–80 . . . . **5–8**

SOFFICI, Piero
  Singles: 7-Inch
JUBILEE: *61* **3–5**
KIP: *61* **3–5**

SOFT CELL
  Singles: 12-Inch 33/45rpm
SIRE: *82* **4–6**
  Singles: 7-Inch
SIRE: *82* **1–3**
  LPs: 10/12-Inch 33rpm
ACCORD: *82* **5–8**
SIRE: *82–83* **5–10**
 Members: Marc Almond; David Ball.

SOFT MACHINE, The
  Singles: 7-Inch
PROBE: *69* **3–5**
  LPs: 10/12-Inch 33rpm
ACCORD: *82* **5–8**

Price Range

CHARLY **$5–8**
COLUMBIA: *70–73* **8–10**
COMMAND: *73* **12–15**
PROBE (4500; "The Soft
 Machine"): *68* **20–25**
 (With movable parts cover.)
PROBE (4500; "The Soft
 Machine"): *69* **15–20**
 (With standard cover.)
PROBE (4505; "The Soft
 Machine, Vol. 2"): *69* **15–20**

SOFTONES, The (The Soft Tones)
  Singles: 7-Inch
AVCO: *73–75* **2–4**
H&L: *77* **2–3**
  Picture Sleeves
H&L: *77* **2–3**

SOLARIS
  Singles: 7-Inch
DANA: *80* **1–3**
  LPs: 10/12-Inch 33rpm
DANA: *80* **5–8**

SOLO
  Singles: 12-Inch 33/45rpm
NEXT PLATINUM: *84* **4–6**

**SOME, Belouis: see BELOUIS
SOME**

SOMMER, Bert
  Singles: 7-Inch
BUDDAH: *71* **2–4**
CAPITOL: *77–78* **2–3**
ELEUTHERA: *70* **2–4**
  LPs: 10/12-Inch 33rpm
BUDDAH: *71* **8–12**
CAPITOL: *77* **8–10**

SOMMERS, Joanie
  Singles: 7-Inch
ABC: *78* **1–3**
CAPITOL: *67* **2–4**
COLUMBIA: *66* **2–4**
HAPPY TIGER: *70* **2–3**
WARNER BROS (5000
 series): *60–65* **3–5**
WARNER BROS (7000
 series): *68* **2–4**

Price Range

LPs: 10/12-Inch 33rpm

COLUMBIA: *66* **$10–15**
DISCOVERY: *83* **5–8**
WARNER BROS: *59–62* **15–20**
    Also see BYRNES, Edd "Kookie," With Joanie
    Sommers & The Mary Kaye Trio
    Also see NELSON, Rick / Joanie Sommers /
    Dona Jean Young

SOMMERS, Joanie, & Laurindo Almeida

LPs: 10/12-Inch 33rpm

WARNER BROS: *64* **10–20**
    Also see ALMEIDA, Laurindo
    Also see SOMMERS, Joanie

SOMMERS, Ronny (Sonny Bono)

Singles: 7-Inch

SWAMI: *61* **5–8**
    Also see SONNY

SONNY (Sonny Bono)

Singles: 7-Inch

ATCO: *65–67* **3–5**
HIGHLAND: *63* **5–8**
MCA: *72–74* **2–4**
SPECIALTY: *65–72* **2–5**

LPs: 10/12-Inch 33rpm

ATCO: *67* **12–15**
    Also see CHRISTY, Don
    Also see JACKSON, Roddy
    Also see SOMMERS, Ronny
    Also see SONNY & CHER

SONNY & CHER

Singles: 7-Inch

ATCO: *65–70* **3–5**
KAPP: *71–72* **2–4**
MCA: *73–74* **2–4**
REPRISE: *64–65* **5–8**
VAULT (916; "The
    Letter"): *65* **8–10**
WARNER BROS: *77* **2–4**

Picture Sleeves

VAULT: *65* **8–12**

EPs: 7-Inch 33/45rpm

ATCO: *65* **5–10**
    (Jukebox issues only.)
REPRISE: *65* **15–20**

HIGHLAND RECORDS
45 RPM   45 RPM
1160-B
Time 2:55
Dist. by MALYNN ENTERPRISES, INC.
PROMOTIONAL COPY   NOT FOR SALE
TRY IT OUT ON ME
(S. Christy)
SONNY

Price Range

LPs: 10/12-Inch 33rpm

ATCO: *65–72* **$12–15**
KAPP: *71–72* **10–12**
MCA: *73–74* **8–12**
REPRISE (6177; "Baby
    Don't Go"): *65* **20–30**
    (Shown as by "Sonny & Cher & Friends." In-
    cludes tunes by The Righteous Brothers & The
    Lettermen.)
    Members: Salvatore Bono; Cher LaPiere.
    Also see CAESAR & CLEO
    Also see CHER
    Also see LETTERMEN, The
    Also see RIGHTEOUS BROTHERS, The
    Also see SONNY

SONS OF CHAMPLIN, The (The Sons)

Singles: 7-Inch

ARIOLA AMERICA:
    75–77 .... **2–3**
CAPITOL: *69–70* **4–6**
COLUMBIA: *73* **2–4**
GOLDMINE **3–5**
VERVE: *67* **5–8**

LPs: 10/12-Inch 33rpm

ARIOLA AMERICA:
    75–76 .... **8–10**
CAPITOL: *69* **10–15**
COLUMBIA: *73* **10–12**
    Also see CHAMPLIN, Bill

Price Range

SOPHISTICATED LADIES
Singles: 7-Inch
MAYHEW: 77. . . . . $2–3

SOPWITH CAMEL, The
Singles: 7-Inch
KAMA SUTRA: 66–67 3–5
REPRISE: 73. 2–4
Picture Sleeves
KAMA SUTRA: 67 4–8
LPs: 10/12-Inch 33rpm
KAMA SUTRA: 67–73 15–20
REPRISE: 73. 15–20

SOUL: see S.O.U.L.

SOUL, David
Singles: 7-Inch
MGM: 66–67. 3–5
PARAMOUNT: 70. 2–4
PRIVATE STOCK: 77. 2–3
LPs: 10/12-Inch 33rpm
PRIVATE STOCK: 77. 8–10

SOUL, Jimmy (Jimmy Soul & The Chants)
Singles: 7-Inch
S.P.Q.R.: 62–65 4–6
20TH CENTURY-FOX:
　63 3–5
Picture Sleeves
S.P.Q.R.: 62–63 5–10
LPs: 10/12-Inch 33rpm
S.P.Q.R.: 63 30–40

SOUL, Jimmy / The Belmonts
LPs: 10/12-Inch 33rpm
SPINORAMA: 63. 20–25
　Also see BELMONTS, The
　Also see SOUL, Jimmy

SOUL BROTHERS SIX, The
Singles: 7-Inch
ATLANTIC: 67–69 3–5
PHIL-L.A. OF SOUL:
　72–74 2–4

Price Range

SOUL CHILDREN, The
Singles 12-Inch 33/45rpm
STAX: 78–79. . . . . $4–6
Singles: 7-Inch
EPIC: 75–76 2–3
STAX: 69–74. 2–4
LPs: 10/12-Inch 33rpm
EPIC: 76 8–10
STAX: 69–79. 8–10

SOUL CLAN, The
Singles: 7-Inch
ATLANTIC: 68 2–5
Picture Sleeves
ATLANTIC: 68 2–5
　Members: Solomon Burke; Arthur Conley;
　Don Covay; Ben E. King; Joe Tex.
　Also see BURKE, Solomon
　Also see CONLEY, Arthur
　Also see COVAY, Don
　Also see KING, Ben E.
　Also see TEX, Joe

SOUL DOG
Singles: 7-Inch
AMHERST: 76 2–4
LPs: 10/12-Inch 33rpm
AMHERST: 77 8–10

SOUL GENTS, The (The Soul Generation)
Singles: 7-Inch
EBONY SOUNDS: 72–74 2–4
FROS RAY: 68–71 2–5
LPs: 10/12-Inch 33rpm
EBONY SOUNDS: 72 8–10

SOUL RUNNERS, The
Singles: 7-Inch
MO SOUL: 66–67. 3–5

SOUL SEARCHERS, The
Singles: 7-Inch
POLYDOR: 75 2–4
SUSSEX: 72–74. 2–4
LPs: 10/12-Inch 33rpm
SUSSEX: 73–74. 8–10

SOUL SISTERS, The
Singles: 7-Inch
GUYDEN: 62 3–5

Price Range

KAYO: *63* **$3–5**
SUE: *64–65* **3–5**
VEEP: *68* **3–5**
LPs: 10/12-Inch 33rpm
SUE: *64* **20–25**

SOUL SURVIVORS, The
Singles: 7-Inch
ATCO: *68–69.* 3–5
CRIMSON: *67–68.* 3–5
DECCA: *67* **4–6**
PHILADELPHIA INT'L:
76 . . . . **2–3**
TSOP: *74–75* **2–4**
LPs: 10/12-Inch 33rpm
ATCO: *69* **12–15**
CRIMSON: *67.* **15–20**
TSOP: *75* **8–10**

SOUL TORNADOS, The
Singles: 7-Inch
BURT: *69* **2–4**

SOUL TRAIN GANG, The
Singles: 7-Inch
SOUL TRAIN: *75–77* **2–3**
LPs: 10/12-Inch 33rpm
SOUL TRAIN: *76* **8–10**

**SOULE, George (George Soule &
Ava Aldridge)**
Singles: 7-Inch
LA LOUISIANNE: *65.* **3–5**
FAME: *73* **2–4**
MCA: *78* **1–3**
TETRAGRAMMATION:
69 . . . . **2–4**

SOULFUL STRINGS, The
Singles: 7-Inch
CADET: *66–73* **2–4**
LPs: 10/12-Inch 33rpm
CADET: *67–73* **8–10**

SOUND EXPERIENCE
Singles: 7-Inch
SOULVILLE: *74.* **2–4**

SOUNDS OF SUNSHINE, The
Singles: 7-Inch
P.I.P.: *76* **1–3**

Price Range

RANWOOD: *71–73* **$1–3**
LPs: 10/12-Inch 33rpm
P.I.P.: *76* **4–8**
RANWOOD: *71–72* **4–8**

SOUNDS ORCHESTRAL
Singles: 7-Inch
PARKWAY: *65–66* **2–4**
LPs: 10/12-Inch 33rpm
PARKWAY: *65–67* **6–15**

SOUPY SALES: see SALES, Soupy

**SOURIRE, Soeur: see SINGING
NUN, The**

**SOUTH, Joe (Joe South & The
Believers)**
Singles: 7-Inch
A&M: *68* **2–4**
ALL WOOD: *62.* **4–6**
APT: *65* **4–6**
CAPITOL: *67–75* **3–5**
COLUMBIA: *67.* **3–5**
FAIRLANE: *61–62* **4–6**
ISLAND: *75* **2–3**
MGM: *63–64.* **4–6**
NRC (Except 002): *58–60* **6–10**
NRC (002; "I'm Snowed"):
58 . . . . **15–20**
LPs: 10/12-Inch 33rpm
ACCORD: *81* **5–8**
CAPITOL: *68–72* **8–12**
ISLAND: *70* **10–12**
MINE: *70* **10–12**

SOUTH, Joe / The Dells
LPs: 10/12-Inch 33rpm
APPLE: *71* **15–20**
Also see DELLS, The
Also see SOUTH, Joe

**SOUTH SHORE COMMISSION,
The**
Singles: 7-Inch
WAND: *75–76.* **2–4**

SOUTHCOTE
Singles: 7-Inch
BUDDAH: *74.* **2–4**

Price Range

Price Range

SOUTHER, J.D. (John David Souther)
Singles: 7-Inch
ASYLUM: *74–76.* **$2–4**
COLUMBIA: *79* **2–3**
WARNER BROS: *85* **1–3**
LPs: 10/12-Inch 33rpm
ASYLUM: *72–76.* **8–10**
COLUMBIA: *79* **5–8**
WARNER BROS: *85* **5–8**
  Also see TAYLOR, James, & J.D. Souther
  Also see TILLOTSON, Johnny, & J.D. Souther

SOUTHER-HILLMAN-FURAY BAND, The
Singles: 7-Inch
ASYLUM: *74–75.* **2–4**
LPs: 10/12-Inch 33rpm
ASYLUM: *74–75.* **8–10**
  Members: J. D. Souther; Chris Hillman; Richie Furay.
  Also see FURAY, Richie
  Also see HILLMAN, Chris
  Also see SOUTHER, J.D.

SOUTHERN, Jeri
Singles: 7-Inch
CAPITOL: *59* **2–4**
DECCA: *51–58* **2–4**
EPs: 7-Inch 33/45rpm
DECCA: *55–56* **4–8**
LPs: 10/12-Inch 33rpm
CAPITOL: *59* **8–15**
DECCA: *55–58* **10–20**
ROULETTE: *57–59* **8–15**

SOUTHERN BELL SINGERS, The
Singles: 7-Inch
VEE JAY: *63.* **3–5**

SOUTHERN COMFORT
Singles: 7-Inch
CAPITOL: *71–72* **2–4**
COTILLION: *69.* **3–5**
LPs: 10/12-Inch 33rpm
BRYLEN. **5–8**
CAPITOL: *71* **10–12**
COLUMBIA: *70* **10–12**
SIRE: *69* **12–15**
  Also see MATTHEWS' SOUTHERN COMFORT

SOUTHERN COOKIN'
Singles: 7-Inch
POLYDOR: *79* **$1–3**
LPs: 10/12-Inch 33rpm
POLYDOR: *79* **5–8**

SOUTHROAD CONNECTION
Singles: 12-Inch 33/45rpm
UNITED ARTISTS: *79–80* **4–6**
Singles: 7-Inch
LIBERTY: *80* **1–3**
MAHOGANY: *78.* **2–3**
UNITED ARTISTS: *79–80* **1–3**
LPs: 10/12-Inch 33rpm
UNITED ARTISTS: *80* **5–8**

SOUTHSIDE JOHNNY & THE ASBURY JUKES (The Jukes)
Singles: 7-Inch
EPIC: *77–78* **2–4**
MERCURY: *79.* **2–3**
MIRAGE: *83–84.* **1–3**
LPs: 10/12-Inch 33rpm
EPIC: *76–79* **8–10**
MERCURY: *79–81* **5–8**
MIRAGE: *83–84.* **5–8**
  Also see FIVE SATINS

SOUTHSIDE MOVEMENT
Singles: 7-Inch
20TH CENTURY-FOX:
  74–75 . . . . **2–3**
WAND: *73* **2–4**
LPs: 10/12-Inch 33rpm
20TH CENTURY-FOX:
  75 . . . . **6–10**
WAND: *73* **8–10**

SOUTHWEST F.O.B.
Singles: 7-Inch
GPC: *68.* **3–5**
HIP: *68–69* **3–5**
LPs: 10/12-Inch 33rpm
HIP: *69* **20–25**
  Members: Dan Seals; John Ford Coley.
  Also see ENGLAND DAN & JOHN FORD COLEY

Price Range

SOVINE, Red
Singles: 7-Inch
CHART: *71–75* **$1–3**
DECCA: *54–66* **2–5**
GUSTO: *79–80* **1–3**
MGM: *50–53* **3–5**
RCA VICTOR: *62* **2–4**
RIC: *64–65* **2–4**
STARDAY (Except 500
   through 800 series):
   70–78 . . . . **1–3**
STARDAY (500 through
   800 series): *60–70* **2–4**

EPs: 7-Inch 33/45rpm
MGM: *57* **8–15**

LPs: 10/12-Inch 33rpm
CMI: *77* **5–8**
CHART: *72–74* **6–10**
DECCA (4400 series): *64* **15–25**
DECCA (4700 series): *66* **10–15**
GUSTO **4–8**
LAKE SHORE **8–12**
MGM (3465; "Red
   Sovine"): *57* **30–40**
METRO: *67* **8–15**
NASHVILLE: *70* **6–12**
POWER PAK **4–8**
RIC: *65* **10–15**
SOMERSET: *63* **8–12**
STARDAY (Except 100
   series): *65–70* **5–15**
STARDAY (100 series):
   61–62 . . . . **15–25**
STEREO FIDELITY: *63* **8–12**
VOCALION: *68* **8–12**
   Also see FELTS, Narvel / Red Sovine / Mel
   Tillis
   Also see REEVES, Del / Red Sovine

SOX, Bob B.; see BOB B. SOXX & THE BLUE JEANS

SPACE
Singles: 12-Inch 33/45rpm
CASABLANCA: *79–80* **4–6**

Price Range

Singles: 7-Inch
CASABLANCA: *79–80* **$1–3**
UNITED ARTISTS: *77* **2–3**

LPs: 10/12-Inch 33rpm
CASABLANCA: *78–79* **5–8**
UNITED ARTISTS: *77* **8–10**

SPACEMEN, The (The Space Men)
Singles: 7-Inch
ALTON: *59–60* **4–6**
FELSTED: *59* **4–6**
JAMECO: *65* **4–6**
JUBILEE: *59* **4–6**
MARKEY: *62* **3–5**

LPs: 10/12-Inch 33rpm
ROULETTE: *64–66* **15–20**

SPADES, The (The Slades)
Singles: 7-Inch
LIBERTY: *58* **10–15**
   Also see SLADES, The

SPADES, The (Thirteenth Floor Elevators)
Singles: 7-Inch
ZERO: *66* **100–125**
   Also see THIRTEENTH FLOOR ELEVA-
   TORS

SPAIN, Joanne
Singles: 7-Inch
CASINO: *77* **2–3**

SPANDAU BALLET
Singles: 12-Inch
CHRYSALIS: *84–85* **4–6**

Singles: 7-Inch
CHRYSALIS: *84–85* **1–3**

LPs: 10/12-Inch 33rpm
CHRYSALIS: *84–85* **5–8**
   Also see BAND AID

Spaniels, six charted singles (1953–70), no charted LPs.

Price Range

SPANIELS, The
Singles: 7-Inch
BUDDAH: *69* **$3–5**
CALLA: *70* **2–4**
CANTERBURY: *74* **2–4**
CHANCE (Black vinyl): *53* **150–175**
CHANCE (Colored vinyl):
   53 . . . . **225–250**
COLLECTABLES **1–3**
ERIC **1–3**
NORTH AMERICAN: *70* **2–4**
VEE JAY (101; "Baby, It's
   You" - black vinyl): *53* **275–300**
VEE JAY (101; "Baby, It's
   You" - colored vinyl): *53* **400–425**
VEE JAY (103; "The Bells
   Ring Out" - black vinyl):
   53 . . . . **60–75**
VEE JAY (103; "The Bells
   Ring Out" - colored
   vinyl): *53* **250–300**
VEE JAY (107; "Goodnite
   Sweetheart, Goodnite" -
   black vinyl): *53* **30–40**
VEE JAY (107; "Goodnite
   Sweetheart, Goodnite" -
   colored vinyl): *53* **100–125**
VEE JAY (116; "Play It
   Cool" - black vinyl): *54* **40–50**

Price Range

VEE JAY (116; "Play It
   Cool" - colored vinyl):
   54 . . . . **$200–225**
VEE JAY (131; "Don'cha
   Go"): *55* **20–25**
VEE JAY (154; "You
   Painted Pictures"): *55* **12–15**
VEE JAY (154; "Painted
   Picture"): *55*. **15–20**
   (Shown on this pressing as by The Spanials.)
VEE JAY (178; "False
   Love"): *56* **25–30**
VEE JAY (189; "Dear
   Heart"): *56*. **25–30**
VEE JAY (202; "Since I
   Fell For You"): *56* **20–25**
VEE JAY (229 through
   301): *56–58*. **12–15**
VEE JAY (310 through
   350): *59–60*. **8–12**
LPs: 10/12-Inch 33rpm
LOST-NITE (19; "The
   Spaniels"): *81* **5–8**
LOST-NITE (137; "The
   Spaniels") **10–15**
VEE JAY (1002;
   "Goodnite, It's Time To
   Go"): *59* **125–150**
   (Maroon label.)
VEE JAY (1002;
   "Goodnite, It's Time To
   Go"): *61*. **50–60**
   (Black label.)
VEE JAY (1024; "The
   Spaniels"): *60*. **60–75**
UPFRONT **10–15**
   Members: Pookie Hudson; Jerry Gregory; Er-
   nest Warren; Willie Jackson; Opal Courtney;
   James Cochran; Carl Rainge; Don Porter;
   Andy Magruder; Bill Carey.
   Also see HUDSON, Pookie

**SPANKY & OUR GANG (Featuring
Spanky McFarlane)**
Singles: 7-Inch
EPIC: *75–76* **2–4**
MERCURY: *67–69*. **3–5**
Picture Sleeves
MERCURY: *67–68*. **3–6**
LPs: 10/12-Inch 33rpm
EPIC: *75* **8–10**

Price Range

MERCURY: *67–71* **$10–15**

**SPARKLETONES, The, With Joe
Bennett: see BENNETT, Joe, & The
Sparkletones**

SPARKS, The
Singles: 12-Inch 33/45rpm
ATLANTIC: *84* **4–6**
Singles: 7-Inch
ATLANTIC: *82–84* **1–3**
BEARSVILLE: *72* **3–5**
COLUMBIA: *78* **2–3**
ELEKTRA: *79* **2–3**
ISLAND: *73–76* **2–4**
RCA VICTOR: *81* **1–3**
LPs: 10/12-Inch 33rpm
ATLANTIC: *82–84* **5–8**
BEARSVILLE: *72–73* **12–15**
COLUMBIA (Black vinyl):
  77 . . . . **8–10**
COLUMBIA (Colored
  vinyl): *77* **12–15**
ELEKTRA: *79* **8–10**
ISLAND: *74–76* **8–10**
RCA VICTOR: *81* **5–8**
  Members: Ron Mael; Russell Mael.

SPARKS & JANE WIEDLIN, The
Singles: 12-Inch 33/45rpm
ATLANTIC: *83* **4–6**
Singles: 7-Inch
ATLANTIC: *83* **1–3**
  Also see SPARKS, The
  Also see WIEDLIN, Jane

SPARQUE
Singles: 12-Inch 33/45rpm
WEST END: *84* **4–6**

SPARKY D
Singles: 12-Inch 33/45rpm
NIA: *85* **4–6**

**SPATS, The (Featuring Dick
Johnson)**
Singles: 7-Inch
ABC-PARAMOUNT:
  64–66 . . . . **3–5**
ENITH: *64* **5–8**
JANO: *67* **3–5**

Price Range

LPs: 10/12-Inch 33rpm
ABC-PARAMOUNT: *65* **$20–25**

SPEARS, Billie Jo
Singles: 7-Inch
CAPITOL: *68–71* **2–4**
LIBERTY: *81* **1–3**
PARLIAMENT: *84* **1–3**
UNITED ARTISTS
(Except 50000 series):
  74–80 . . . . **1–3**
UNITED ARTISTS (50000
  series): *66–67* **2–5**
LPs: 10/12-Inch 33rpm
CAPITOL: *68–79* **5–15**
LIBERTY: *81* **4–8**
PICKWICK/HILLTOP **5–8**
UNITED ARTISTS: *75–80* **5–10**
  Also see REEVES, Del, & Billie Jo Spears

SPECIAL AKA
Singles: 12-Inch 33/45rpm
CHRYSALIS: *84* **4–6**
Singles: 7-Inch
CHRYSALIS: *84* **1–3**
LPs: 10/12-Inch 33rpm
CHRYSALIS: *84* **5–8**
  Also see SPECIALS, The

**SPECIAL DELIVERY (Featuring
Terry Huff)**
Singles: 7-Inch
MAINSTREAM: *75–76* **2–4**
SHIELD: *77–78* **2–3**

SPECIALS, The
Singles: 7-Inch
CHRYSALIS: *80* **1–3**
LPs: 10/12-Inch 33rpm
CHRYSALIS: *80* **5–8**
  Also see FUN BOY THREE, The
  Also see SPECIALS AKA

**SPECTOR, Ronnie (Ronnie Spector
& The Ronettes; Ronnie Spector &
The E Street Band)**
Singles: 7-Inch
ALSTON: *78* **2–4**
APPLE: *70–71* **3–5**
BUDDAH: *74* **3–5**

Price Range

EPIC/CLEVELAND
   INT'L: *77*. **$2–4**
POLISH: *80*. **1–3**
TOM CAT (Black vinyl):
   75–76 . . . . **2–4**
TOM CAT (Colored vinyl):
   75 . . . . **4–6**
   (Promotional issues only.)
WARNER BROS./
   SPECTOR: *76*. **2–4**

Picture Sleeves

APPLE: *71* **4–6**
EPIC/CLEVELAND
   INT'L: *77*. **4–6**

LPs: 10/12-Inch 33rpm

POLISH: *80*. **8–10**
   Also see RONETTES, The
   Also see RONNIE & THE RELATIVES

SPEEDO & THE CADILLACS
Singles: 7-Inch
JOSIE: *60*. **4–6**
   Also see CADILLACS, The

SPELLBINDERS, The
Singles: 7-Inch
COLUMBIA: *65–66*. **3–5**
DATE: *67* **3–5**

LPs: 10/12-Inch 33rpm
COLUMBIA: *66*. **12–15**

SPELLBOUND
Singles: 7-Inch
EMI AMERICA: *78*. **2–3**

LPs: 10/12-Inch 33rpm
EMI AMERICA: *78*. **5–8**

SPELLMAN, Benny
Singles: 7-Inch
ALON: *66* **3–5**
ATLANTIC: *65* **3–5**
MINIT: *62*. **4–6**
SANSU: *67* **3–5**
WATCH: *64* **3–5**
   Also see K-DOE, Ernie

SPENCER, Sonny
Singles: 7-Inch
MEMO: *59*. **4–6**
MUSIC HALL **4–6**

Price Range

SPENCER & SPENCER
Singles: 7-Inch
ARGO: *59* **$5–8**
GONE: *59* **8–10**

SPERRY, Steve
Singles: 7-Inch
MERCURY: *77*. **2–3**

SPHEERIS, Jimmie
Singles: 7-Inch
COLUMBIA: *72*. **2–4**
EPIC: *75* **2–3**
LPs: 10/12-Inch 33rpm
EPIC: *75* **8–10**

SPIDER
Singles: 7-Inch
CAPITOL: *72* **2–4**
DREAMLAND: *80–81* **1–3**
Picture Sleeves
DREAMLAND: *80* **1–3**
LPs: 10/12-Inch 33rpm
CAPITOL: *72* **8–10**
DREAMLAND: *80* **5–8**

SPIDERS, The (Featuring Chuck Carbo)
Singles: 7-Inch
IMPERIAL (5265 through
   5344): *54–55*. **20–30**
IMPERIAL (5354; "Bells
   In My Heart"): *55*. **30–35**
IMPERIAL (5366 through
   5423): *55–56*. **8–12**
IMPERIAL (5618 through
   5739): *59–61*. **5–8**
LPs: 10/12-Inch 33rpm
IMPERIAL: *61*. **100–125**

SPIDERS, The (Alice Cooper)
Singles: 7-Inch
NASCOT: *65*. **100–125**
SANTA CRUZ: *66*. **80–100**
   Also see COOPER, Alice

SPIDERS FROM MARS, The
Singles: 7-Inch
PYE: *76* **2–4**
LPs: 10/12-Inch 33rpm
PYE: *76* **8–10**
   Also see BOWIE, David

Price Range

SPIN
Singles: 7-Inch
ARIOLA AMERICA: *76* $2–3
LPs: 10/12-Inch 33rpm
ARIOLA AMERICA: *76* 8–10

SPINAL TAP
Singles: 7-Inch
POLYDOR: *84* 1–3
LPs: 10/12-Inch 33rpm
POLYDOR: *84* 5–8

SPINNERS, The
Singles: 7-Inch
ATLANTIC: *72–85* 2–4
MOTOWN (1000 & 1100
　series): *64–68* 3–5
MOTOWN (1200 series):
　73 2–4
TRI-PHI: *61–62* 5–8
V.I.P.: *70* 3–5
LPs: 10/12-Inch 33rpm
ATLANTIC: *73–84* 6–10
MOTOWN (Except 639):
　73–82 6–10
MOTOWN (639; "The
　Original Spinners"): *67* 12–15
PICKWICK: *76* 8–10
TIME: *63* 30–35
V.I.P.: *70* 10–15
　Also see ABBA / The Spinners / Firefall /
　England Dan & John Ford Coley
　Also see GAYE, Marvin
　Also see WARWICK, Dionne, & The Spinners

SPIRAL STARECASE, The
(Featuring Pat Upton)
Singles: 7-Inch
COLUMBIA: *69–70* 3–5
LPs: 10/12-Inch 33rpm
COLUMBIA: *69* 15–20

SPIRIT
Singles: 12-Inch 33/45rpm
MERCURY: *84* 4–6
Singles: 7-Inch
EPIC: *70–73* 3–5
MERCURY: *75–76* 2–4
ODE: *68–70* 4–6

Price Range

POTATO: *78* $2–3
RHINO: *81* 2–3
ROULETTE: *67* 5–8
Picture Sleeves
POTATO: *78* 2–3
LPs: 10/12-Inch 33rpm
EPIC: *70–73* 8–12
MERCURY (Except
　818514): *75–77* 10–15
MERCURY (818514;
　"Spirit Of '84"): *84* 5–8
ODE (44003; "Spirit"): *68* 15–20
　(Monaural issue.)
ODE (44004; "Spirit"): *68* 12–15
　(Stereo issue.)
ODE (44014; "The Family
　That Plays Together"):
　68 10–15
ODE (44016; "Clear"): *69* 10–12
POTATO 10–12
RHINO: *81* 5–8
　Members: Jay Ferguson; Randy California;
　Mark Andes; Ed Cassidy; John Locke; John
　Arliss.
　Also see FERGUSON, Jay
　Also see YELLOW BALLOON, The

SPLINTER
Singles: 7-Inch
DARK HORSE: *74–77* 3–5
LPs: 10/12-Inch 33rpm
DARK HORSE: *74–77* 8–10
　Members: Bill Elliott; Bob Purvis.

SPLIT ENZ
Singles: 7-Inch
A&M: *80–81* 1–3
Picture Sleeves
A&M: *81* .... INC
LPs: 10/12-Inch 33rpm
A&M (Except picture
　discs): *80–82*. 5–8
A&M (Picture discs): *81*. 20–25
　(Promotional issue only.)
CHRYSALIS: *77*. 8–10
　Members: Tim Finn; Neil Finn.
　Also see FINN, Tim

SPOKESMEN, The
Singles: 7-Inch
DECCA: *65–66* 4–6
WINCHESTER: *67* 3–5

Price Range

LPs: 10/12-Inch 33rpm
DECCA: *65* **$25–30**
Members: Johnny Madara; David White.

SPOOKY TOOTH
Singles: 7-Inch
A&M: *69* **3–5**
MALA: *68* **4–6**
ISLAND: *72* **2–4**
LPs: 10/12-Inch 33rpm
A&M: *69–73* **10–12**
ACCORD: *82* **5–8**
BELL: *68* **15–20**
CHARLY **5–8**
ISLAND: *73–74* **8–10**
Also see WRIGHT, Gary

SPOONBREAD
Singles: 7-Inch
STANG: *72* **2–4**

SPOONIE GEE
Singles: 12-Inch 33/45
CBS ASSOCIATED: *83* **4–6**
Singles: 7-Inch
CBS ASSOCIATED: *83* **1–3**
TUFF CITY: *83* **1–3**

SPORTS, The
Singles: 7-Inch
ARISTA: *79* **1–3**
LPs: 10/12-Inch 33rpm
ARISTA: *79–80* **5–8**

SPRING
Singles: 7-Inch
IX CHAINS: *73* **2–4**

SPRING, McKendree:
see McKENDREE SPRING

SPRINGERS, The
Singles: 7-Inch
WAY OUT: *65* **5–8**

SPRINGFIELD, Dusty
Singles: 7-Inch
ATLANTIC: *68–71* **2–4**
CASABLANCA: *82* **1–3**
DUNHILL: *73* **2–4**
PHILIPS: *63–68* **3–5**

Price Range

20TH CENTURY-FOX:
  80 . . . . **$1–3**
UNITED ARTISTS: *77–79* **2–3**
Picture Sleeves
PHILIPS: *64–67* **3–6**
ATLANTIC: *68* **2–4**
LPs: 10/12-Inch 33rpm
ATLANTIC: *69–70* **10–15**
CASABLANCA: *82* **5–8**
DUNHILL: *73* **8–10**
PHILIPS: *64–67* **12–15**
UNITED ARTISTS: *78–79* **5–8**
WING: *68* **10–12**
Also see SPRINGFIELDS, The

SPRINGFIELD, Rick
Singles: 12-Inch 33/45rpm
RCA VICTOR: *83–84* **4–6**
Singles: 7-Inch
CAPITOL: *72–73* **3–5**
CHELSEA: *76–77* **2–4**
COLUMBIA: *74* **3–5**
MERCURY: *84–85* **1–3**
RCA VICTOR: *81–85* **1–3**
Picture Sleeves
CAPITOL: *72* **3–5**
RCA VICTOR: *81–85* **1–3**
LPs: 10/12-Inch 33rpm
CAPITOL (11000 series):
  72–73 . . . . **15–20**
CAPITOL (16000 series):
  81 . . . . **5–8**
CHELSEA: *76* **8–12**
COLUMBIA (32000
  series): *73* **8–12**
  (With a "KC" prefix.)
COLUMBIA (32000 series) **5–8**
  (With a "PC" prefix.)
MERCURY: *84* **5–8**
RCA VICTOR: *80–85* **5–8**

SPRINGFIELD, Rick, & Randy Crawford
Singles: 7-Inch
RCA VICTOR: *84* **1–3**
  Also see CRAWFORD, Randy
  Also see SPRINGFIELD, Rick

SPRINGFIELDS, The
Singles: 7-Inch
PHILIPS: *62–63* **3–5**

Price Range   *Price Range*

LPs: 10/12-Inch 33rpm

PHILIPS: *62–63* **$15–20**
Members: Dusty Springfield; Tom Springfield.
Also see SPRINGFIELD, Dusty

SPRINGSTEEN, Bruce (Bruce Springsteen & The E Street Band)

Singles: 12-Inch 33/45rpm

COLUMBIA (1332; "Santa
Claus Is Comin' To
Town"): *81* **30–40**
(White label. Promotional issue only.)

COLUMBIA (2007; "I'm
On Fire"): *85* **20–25**
(Red label. Black & white cover. Promotional
issue only.)

COLUMBIA (2082;
"Glory Days"): *85* **20–25**
(Red label. Black & white cover. Promotional
issue only.)

COLUMBIA (2174; "I'm
Goin' Down"): *85* **20–25**
(Red label. Black & white cover. Promotional
issue only.)

COLUMBIA (2233; "My
Hometown"): *85* **20–25**
(Red label. Black & white cover. Promotional
issue only.)

COLUMBIA (05028;
"Dancing In The
Dark"): *84* **5–8**

COLUMBIA (05028;
"Dancing In The
Dark"): *84* **20–30**
(With black & white cover. Promotional issue
only.)

COLUMBIA (05028;
"Dancing In The
Dark"): *84* **15–20**
(Promotional issue with color cover and gold
promo stamp.)

COLUMBIA (05087;
"Cover Me"): *84* **5–8**

COLUMBIA (05147;
"Born In The U.S.A."):
84 .... **4–6**

COLUMBIA (05147;
"Born In The U.S.A."):
84 .... **15–20**

(White label. Promotional issue only.)

Singles: 7-Inch

COLUMBIA (03243;
"Hungry Heart"): *84*. **$2–3**

COLUMBIA (04463;
"Dancing In The
Dark"): *84* **2–3**

COLUMBIA (04561;
"Cover Me"): *84* **2–3**

COLUMBIA (04680;
"Born In The U.S.A."):
84 .... **2–3**

COLUMBIA (04772; "I'm
On Fire"): *85* **2–3**

COLUMBIA (04924;
"Glory Days"): *85*. **2–3**

COLUMBIA (05606; "I'm
Goin' Down"): *85* **2–3**

COLUMBIA (05728; "My
Hometown"): *85* **2–3**

COLUMBIA (10209;
"Born To Run"): *75* **4–6**

COLUMBIA (10274;
"Tenth Avenue
Freeze-Out"): *75* **4–6**

COLUMBIA (10763;
"Prove It All Night"):
78 .... **2–4**

COLUMBIA (10801;
"Badlands"): *78*. **2–4**

COLUMBIA (11391;
"Hungry Heart"): *80*. **2–4**

COLUMBIA (11431;
"Fade Away"/"To Be
True"): *81* **30–40**

COLUMBIA (11431;
"Fade Away"/"Be
True"): *81* **2–4**

COLUMBIA (33323;
"Born To Run"): *76*. **2–3**

COLUMBIA (45805;
"Blinded By The
Light"): *73* **75–90**

COLUMBIA (45864;
"Sprit In The Night"):
73 .... **100–125**

Promotional Singles: 7-Inch

COLUMBIA (1332; "Santa
Claus Is Comin' To
Town"): *81*. **10–15**

Price Range

Price Range

COLUMBIA (04463;
"Dancing In The
Dark"): *84* $6–10

COLUMBIA (04561;
"Cover Me"): *84* 6–10

COLUMBIA (04680;
"Born In The U.S.A."):
84 6–10

COLUMBIA (04772; "I'm
On Fire"): *85* 6–10

COLUMBIA (04924;
"Glory Days"): *85* 6–10

COLUMBIA (05606; "I'm
Goin' Down"): *85* 6–10

COLUMBIA (05728; "My
Hometown"): *85* 6–10

COLUMBIA (10209;
"Born To Run"): *75* 15–20

COLUMBIA (10274;
"Tenth Avenue
Freeze-Out"): *75* 15–20

COLUMBIA (10763;
"Prove It All Night"):
78 15–20

COLUMBIA (10801;
"Badlands"): *78* 15–20

COLUMBIA (11391;
"Hungry Heart"): *80* 15–20

COLUMBIA (11431;
"Fade Away"): *81* 10–15

COLUMBIA (45805;
"Blinded By The
Light"): *73* 45–55

COLUMBIA (45864;
"Sprit In The Night"):
73 35–45

Picture Sleeves

COLUMBIA (1332; "Santa
Claus Is Comin' To
Town"): *81* 15–20
(Promotional issue only.)

COLUMBIA (03243;
"Hungry Heart"): *84* 2–3

COLUMBIA (11431;
"Fade Away"): *81* 3–5

COLUMBIA (45805;
"Blinded By The
Light"): *73* 100–125

LPs: 10/12-Inch 33rpm

COLUMBIA (KC-31903;
"Greetings From Asbury
Park"): *73* $15–20

COLUMBIA (PC-31903;
"Greetings From Asbury
Park"): *75* 8–12

COLUMBIA (JC-31903;
"Greetings From Asbury
Park"): *78* 5–8

COLUMBIA (KC-32432;
"The Wild, The Innocent
& The E Street Shuffle"):
73 15-18

COLUMBIA (PC-32432;
"The Wild, The Innocent
& The E Street Shuffle"):
73 10-15

COLUMBIA (JC-32432;
"The Wild, The Innocent
& The E Street Shuffle"):
78 5-8

COLUMBIA (PC-33795;
"Born To Run"): *75* 25–30
(With credits showing Jon as 'John.')

COLUMBIA (PC-33795;
"Born To Run"): *75* 15–20
(With correction strip applied to cover.)

COLUMBIA (PC-33795;
"Born To Run"): *75* 8–12
(With correction to 'Jon' printed on cover.)

COLUMBIA (JC-33795;
"Born To Run"): *78* 5–8

COLUMBIA (JC-35318;
"Darkness On The Edge
Of Town"): *78* 5–8

COLUMBIA (PC2-36854;
"The River"): *80* 10–15

COLUMBIA (QC-38358;
"Nebraska"): *82* 5–8

COLUMBIA (QC-38653;
"Born In The U.S.A."):
84 5–8

COLUMBIA (HC-43795;
"Born To Run"): *80* 12–15
(Half-speed mastered.)

COLUMBIA (HC-45318;
"Darkness On The Edge
Of Town"): *81* 12–15
(Half-speed mastered.)

Price Range

Promotional LPs

COLUMBIA (978; "Bruce
Springsteen As
Requested Around The
World"): *81* **$30-40**

COLUMBIA (1957; "Born
In The U.S.A."): *84* **15–20**

COLUMBIA (KC-31903;
"Greetings From Asbury
Park"): *73* **25–30**
(White label.)

COLUMBIA (KC-32432;
"The Wild, The Innocent
& The E Street Shuffle"):
73 .... **30-35**
(White label.)

COLUMBIA (PC-33795;
"Born To Run"): *75* **225–250**
(With special "script" cover.)

COLUMBIA (PC-33795;
"Born To Run"): *75* **40–50**
(White label.)

COLUMBIA (JC-35318;
"Darkness On The Edge
Of Town"): *78* **30–40**
(White label.)

COLUMBIA (PAL-35318;
"Darkness On The Edge
Of Town"): *78* **75–100**
(Picture disc.)

COLUMBIA (PC2-36854;
"The River"): *80* **25–35**
(White label.)

COLUMBIA (QC-38358;
"Nebraska"): *82* **15–20**
(White label.)

COLUMBIA (QC-38653;
"Born In The U.S.A."):
84 .... **12–15**
(White label.)
Also see BONDS, Gary "U.S."
Also see CLEMMONS, Clarence, & The Red
Bank Rockers
Also see LITTLE STEVEN & THE DISCI-
PLES OF SOUL
Also see PARKER, Graham
Also see THOMPSON, Robbin, Band
Also see U.S.A. FOR AFRICA

Price Range

SPRINGSTEEN, Bruce / Andy Pratt
Singles: 7-Inch
COLUMBIA/
PLAYBACK: *73* **$35–45**
Picture Sleeves
COLUMBIA/
PLAYBACK: *73* **10–15**
Also see PRATT, Andy

**SPRINGSTEEN, Bruce / Albert
Hammond / Loudon Wainwright, III
/ Taj Mahal**
Singles: 7-Inch
COLUMBIA/
PLAYBACK: *73* **50–75**
Picture Sleeves
COLUMBIA/
PLAYBACK: *73* **10–15**
Also see HAMMOND, Albert
Also see TAJ MAHAL
Also see WAINWRIGHT, Loudon, III

**SPRINGSTEEN, Bruce / Johnny
Winter / The Hollies**
Singles: 7-Inch
COLUMBIA/
PLAYBACK: *73* **35–45**
Picture Sleeves
COLUMBIA/
PLAYBACK: *73* **10–15**
Also see HOLLIES, The
Also see SPRINGSTEEN, Bruce
Also see WINTER, Johnny

SPRINGWELL
Singles: 7-Inch
PARROT: *71* **2–4**

SPUNK
Singles: 7-Inch
GOLD COAST: *81* **1–3**
LPs: 10/12-Inch 33rpm
GOLD COAST: *81* **5–8**

SPYDER-D (Spyder-D & D.J. Divine
Singles: 12-Inch 33/45rpm
PROFILE: *84–85* **4–6**

SPYRO GYRA
Singles: 7-Inch
AMHERST: *78* **2–3**

Price Range

INFINITY: *79*. **$2–3**
MCA: *80–85* **1–3**
Picture Sleeves
INFINITY: *79*. **2–3**
LPs: 10/12-Inch 33rpm
AMHERST: *78*. **5–8**
INFINITY: *79*. **5–8**
MCA (5000 series): *80–85* **5–8**
MCA (6000 series): *84* **8–10**
Members: Chet Catallo; Jay Beckenstein.

SPYS
Singles: 7-Inch
EMI AMERICA: *82*. **1–3**
LPs: 10/12-Inch 33rpm
EMI AMERICA: *82*. **5–8**
Also see FOREIGNER

SQUEEZE (U.K. Squeeze)
Singles: 7-Inch
A&M: *79–81* **1–3**
Picture Sleeves
A&M: *80* . . . . **INC**
LPs: 10/12-Inch 33rpm
A&M: *72–85* **5–10**
(Black vinyl.)
A&M: *78* **8–12**
(Colored vinyl.)
Also see CARRACK, Paul
Also see DIFFORD & TILBROOK

SQUIER, Billy
Singles: 7-Inch
CAPITOL: *80–86* **1–3**
Picture Sleeves
CAPITOL: *80–86* . . . . **INC**
LPs: 10/12-Inch 33rpm
CAPITOL: *80–85* **5–8**

SQUIRE, Chris
Singles: 7-Inch
ATLANTIC: *76* **2–3**
LPs: 10/12-Inch 33rpm
ATLANTIC: *76* **8–10**
Also see YES

STACKRIDGE (Featuring Mutter Slater)
Singles: 7-Inch
DECCA: *71–72*. **2–4**
MCA: *73* **2–4**
ROCKET: *76*. **2–3**

Price Range

SIRE: *74–75* **$2–4**
LPs: 10/12-Inch 33rpm
DECCA: *71*. **10–12**
MCA: *73* **8–10**
ROCKET: *76*. **5–8**
SIRE: *74–75* **8–10**

STACY, Clyde (Clyde Stacy & The Nitecaps)
Singles: 7-Inch
ARGYLE: *59*. **5–8**
BULLSEYE (Except 1008):
58 . . . . **5–8**
BULLSEYE (1008; "Sure
Do Love You Baby"): *58*. **15–20**
CANDLELIGHT: *57*. **30–35**
G&H: *58* **10–12**
LEN: *61*. **8–10**

STAEKHOUSE, Ruby (Ruby Andrews)
Singles: 7-Inch
KELLMAC: *65*. **3–5**
Also see ANDREWS, Ruby

STAFFORD, Jim
Singles: 7-Inch
COLUMBIA: *84*. **1–3**
ELEKTRA: *80–81* **1–3**
ISLAND: *74* **2–4**
MGM: *73–75*. **2–4**
POLYDOR: *75–78* **1–3**
TOWNHOUSE: *82*. **1–3**
WARNER BROS: *76–80*. **1–3**
LPs: 10/12-Inch 33rpm
MGM: *74–75*. **8–10**
POLYDOR: *76* **5–8**

STAFFORD, Jo
Singles: 7-Inch
COLPIX: *62* **2–4**
COLUMBIA: *50–60*. **2–5**
DECCA: *68*. **2–3**
DOT: *65*. **2–3**
REPRISE: *63*. **2–4**
EPs: 7-Inch 33/45rpm
CAPITOL: *50–57* **5–15**
COLUMBIA: *50–59* **5–15**
LPs: 10/12-Inch 33rpm
BAINBRIDGE: *82*. **5–8**

Price Range

CAPITOL (75 through
   435): *50–53* **$20–35**
   (10-Inch LPs.)
CAPITOL (400 through
   1600 series): *55–62* **10–20**
   (12-Inch LPs.)
CAPITOL (1900 through
   2100 series): *63–64* **8–15**
CAPITOL (9000 series): *54* **15–25**
   (10-Inch LPs.)
CAPITOL (11000 series):
   79 .... **5–8**
COLUMBIA (600 through
   1300 series): *55–59* **10–25**
COLUMBIA (1561; "Jo
   Plus Jazz"): *60* **25–50**
   (Monaural issue.)
COLUMBIA (2500 series):
   55 .... **15–30**
   (10-Inch LPs.)
COLUMBIA (6000 series):
   50–54 .... **20–35**
   (10-Inch LPs.)
COLUMBIA (8361; "Jo
   Plus Jazz"): *60* **30–60**
   (Stereo issue.)
DECCA: *68* **5–15**
DOT: *66* **5–15**
TRIBUTE: *71* **5–10**
VOCALION: *68–69* **5–10**
   Also see LAINE, Frankie, & Jo Stafford
   Also see MacRAE, Gordon, & Jo Stafford
   Also see WESTON, Paul

STAFFORD, Terry
Singles: 7-Inch
ATLANTIC: *73–74* **2–4**
COLLECTABLES **1–3**
CRUSADER: *64* **4–6**
ERIC **1–3**
FIRSTLINE: *81* **1–3**
MGM: *71* **2–4**
MELODYLAND: *75* **2–4**
MERCURY: *66* **3–5**
SIDEWALK: *66–67* **3–5**
WARNER BROS: *69* **2–4**

LPs: 10/12-Inch 33rpm
ATLANTIC: *73* **8–10**
CRUSADER: *64* **30–40**
   Also see ALLAN, Davie

Price Range

STAIRSTEPS, The
Singles: 7-Inch
BUDDAH: *71–72* **$2–4**
DARK HORSE: *75–76* **2–4**
   Also see FIVE STAIRSTEPS, The

STALLION
Singles: 7-Inch
CASABLANCA: *77–78* **2–3**
LPs: 10/12-Inch 33rpm
CASABLANCA: *77–78* **5–8**

STALLONE, Frank
Singles: 12-Inch 33/45rpm
RSO: *83* **4–6**
Singles: 7-Inch
POLYDOR: *84–85* **1–3**
SCOTTI BROS: *80* **1–3**
LPs: 10/12-Inch 33rpm
POLYDOR: *84* **5–8**

STAMPEDERS, The
Singles: 7-Inch
BELL: *71* **2–4**
CAPITOL: *73* **2–4**
FLASHBACK: *74* **1–3**
MGM: *68* **3–5**
QUALITY: *76* **2–4**
LPs: 10/12-Inch 33rpm
BELL: *71* **10–12**
CAPITOL: *73–74* **8–10**
PRIVATE STOCK/
   QUALITY: *76* **8–10**
   Also see WOLFMAN JACK

STAMPLEY, Joe
Singles: 7-Inch
ABC: *77* **1–3**
ABC/DOT: *75–76* **2–3**
CHESS: *63* **4–6**
COLUMBIA: *81–84* **1–3**
DOT: *70–74* **2–4**
EPIC: *75–83* **1–3**
IMPERIAL: *59* **5–8**
PARAMOUNT: *70* **2–4**
PAULA: *74* **2–3**
LPs: 10/12-Inch 33rpm
ABC: *77* **10–12**
ABC/DOT: *74–76* **8–10**
ACCORD: *82* **5–8**
COLUMBIA: *82–84* **5–8**

Price Range

EPIC: *75–83* **$6–10**
PHONORAMA.................... **5–8**

STANDELLS, The
Singles: 7-Inch
COLLECTABLES **1–3**
LIBERTY: *64* **10–15**
MGM: *65*...................... **10–15**
SUNSET: *66* **10–12**
TOWER: *66–68*.................. **5–8**
VEE JAY: *65*.................... **8–10**
Picture Sleeves
TOWER: *67*..................... **8–15**
VEE JAY: *65*................... **10–20**
LPs: 10/12-Inch 33rpm
LIBERTY: *64* **40–50**
RHINO **5–8**
SUNSET: *66* **15–20**
TOWER: *66–67*.................. **30–40**
Members: Dick Dodd; Larry Tamblyn; Gary
Lane; Tony Valentino; Dave Burke.

STANDLEY, Johnny
Singles: 7-Inch
CAPITOL: *52–56* **2–5**
MAGNOLIA: *60*. **15–20**

STANKY-BROWN GROUP, The
Singles: 7-Inch
SIRE: *76–78* **2–3**
LPs: 10/12-Inch 33rpm
SIRE: *76–78* **8–10**

STANLEY, Michael, Band
Singles: 7-Inch
ARISTA: *78–79*.................. **2–3**
EMI AMERICA: *80–82*............ **1–3**
EPIC: *77* **2–3**
TUMBLEWEED: *72–73* **2–4**
LPs: 10/12-Inch 33rpm
ARISTA: *78–79*.................. **5–8**
EMI AMERICA: *80–82*............ **5–8**
EPIC: *75–76* **8–10**
MCA: *73* **10–12**
TUMBLEWEED: *73* **8–12**
Also see SILK

STANLEY, Pamala
Singles: 12-Inch 33/45rpm
KOMANDER: *83*.................. **4–6**
MIRAGE: *84–85*.................. **4–6**

Price Range

TSR: *84* **$4–6**
Singles: 7-Inch
EMI AMERICA: *79*............... **2–3**
MIRAGE: *84–85*.................. **1–3**
LPs: 10/12-Inch 33rpm
EMI AMERICA: *79*............... **5–8**

STANLEY, Paul
Singles: 7-Inch
CASABLANCA: *78* **2–3**
LPs: 10/12-Inch 33rpm
CASABLANCA (Except
  picture discs): *78* **5–8**
CASABLANCA (Picture
  discs): *79* **10–15**
Also see KISS

STAPLE SINGERS, The (The Staples)
Singles: 7-Inch
ABC: *73*....................... **2–3**
CURTOM: *75–77*................. **2–3**
EPIC: *64–71* **2–4**
RIVERSIDE: *62–63* **2–4**
SHARP: *60* **3–5**
STAX: *68–74*.................... **2–4**
20TH CENTURY-FOX:
  81 .... **1–3**
VEE JAY: *59–62*................. **3–5**
WARNER BROS: *76–80*........... **1–3**
LPs: 10/12-Inch 33rpm
BUDDAH: *69*................... **6–10**
CREED: *73* **5–10**
CURTOM: *76* **5–10**
EPIC: *65–71* **10–12**
EVEREST: *68–69* **8–12**
FANTASY: *73*. **5–10**
51 WEST **5–8**
GOSPEL: *59* **5–15**
HARMONY: *72* **5–10**
MILESTONE: *75* **5–10**
PRIVATE I: *84*. **5–8**
RIVERSIDE: *62–65* **10–15**
STAX: *68–81*................... **5–10**
20TH CENTURY-FOX:
  81 .... **5–8**
TRIP: *71–77* **5–10**
VEE JAY (5000 through
  5030): *59–63*................. **10–15**
WARNER BROS: *77–78*........... **5–8**
Also see STAPLES, Mavis

Price Range   *Price Range*

STAPLES, Mavis
Singles: 7-Inch
CURTOM: 77 .... $2–3
PHONO: 84 1–3
VOLT: 70–72 2–4
WARNER BROS: 79 1–3
LPs: 10/12-Inch 33rpm
VOLT: 69–70 8–12
Also see BELL, William, & Mavis Staples
Also see FLOYD, Eddie, & Mavis Staples
Also see STAPLE SINGERS, The

STAPLETON, Cyril, & His Orchestra
Singles: 7-Inch
DECCA: 67 1–3
LONDON: 51–63 2–4
MGM: 55–56 2–4
STAGE: 62 1–3
EPs: 7-Inch 33/45rpm
LONDON: 55–57 4–8
MGM: 55–56 4–8
LPs: 10/12-Inch 33rpm
IMPERIAL: 61 5–10
LONDON: 55–59 5–15
MGM: 55–56 5–15
RICHMOND: 59–61 5–15

STAR WARS INTERGALACTIC DROID CHOIR & CHORALE, The
Singles: 7-Inch
RSO: 80 1–3
Also see MECO

STARBUCK
Singles: 7-Inch
A.V.I.: 84 1–3
ATCO: 73 2–4
ELEKTRA: 71 2–4
PRIVATE STOCK: 76–77 2–4
VALIANT: 66 3–5
UNITED ARTISTS: 78–79 2–3
LPs: 10/12-Inch 33rpm
PHONORAMA 5–8
PRIVATE STOCK: 77 8–10
UNITED ARTISTS: 78 8–10

STARCASTLE
Singles: 7-Inch
EPIC: 76–78 2–4

LPs: 10/12-Inch 33rpm
EPIC (Except "Citadel" picture disc): 76–79 .... $8–10
EPIC ("Citadel" - picture disc): 79 50–60
(Promotional issue only.)

STARCHER, Buddy
Singles: 7-Inch
BOONE: 66 2–4
DECCA: 66 2–4
HEARTWARMING: 67 2–3
STARDAY: 59–66 2–4
EPs: 7-Inch 33/45rpm
FOUR STAR 4–8
STARDAY: 61 4–8
LPs: 10/12-Inch 33rpm
BLUEBONNET 8–12
DECCA: 66 8–15
HEARTWARMING: 68 5–10
STARDAY: 62–66 8–15

STARGARD
Singles: 12-Inch 33/45rpm
WARNER BROS: 79–81 4–6
Singles: 7-Inch
MCA: 77–78 2–3
WARNER BROS: 79–81 1–3
LPs: 10/12-Inch 33rpm
MCA: 82 5–8
WARNER BROS: 79–81 5–8

STARGAZE
Singles: 12-Inch 33/45rpm
T.N.T.: 83 4–6

STARK & McBRIEN
Singles: 7-Inch
RCA VICTOR: 74–76 2–4
LPs: 10/12-Inch 33rpm
RCA VICTOR: 75 8–10
Members: Fred Stark; Rod McBrien.

STARLAND VOCAL BAND, The
Singles: 7-Inch
WINDSONG: 76–80 2–4
LPs: 10/12-Inch 33rpm
WINDSONG: 76–80 8–10
Members: Bill Danoff; Taffy Danoff.
Also see BILL & TAFFY

Price Range

STARLETS, The
Singles: 7-Inch
CHESS: *67–68* **$3–5**
LUTE: *60*. **4–6**
PAM: *61* **4–6**
TOWER: *65*. **4–6**

STARPOINT
Singles: 12-Inch 33/45rpm
BOARDWALK: *83* **4–6**
CHOCOLATE CITY:
  80–82 . . . . **4–6**
ELEKTRA: *83–85* **4–6**
Singles: 7-Inch
BOARDWALK: *83* **1–3**
CHOCOLATE CITY:
  80–82 . . . . **1–3**
ELEKTRA: *83–85* **1–3**
LPs: 10/12-Inch 33rpm
CHOCOLATE CITY:
  80–82 . . . . **5–8**
ELEKTRA: *83–85* **5–8**
Also see DAWSON, Cliff, & Renee Diggs

STARR, Brenda K.
Singles: 12-Inch 33/45rpm
MIRAGE: *85*. **4–6**
Singles: 7-Inch
MIRAGE: *85*. **1–3**

STARR, Edwin
Singles: 12-Inch 33/45rpm
20TH CENTURY-FOX:
  77–80 . . . . **4–6**
Singles: 7-Inch
CASABLANCA: *84* **1–3**
GRANITE: *75–76*. **2–4**
GORDY: *67–71*. **2–4**
MONTAGE: *82*. **1–3**
MOTOWN: *73–74*. **2–4**
RIC-TIC: *65–66*. **3–5**
SOUL: *72–73* **2–4**
20TH CENTURY-FOX:
  77–84 . . . . **1–3**
LPs: 10/12-Inch 33rpm
GORDY: *69–71*. **10–12**
GRANITE: *75*. **8–10**
MOTOWN: *73–82*. **8–10**
20TH CENTURY-FOX:
  77–81 . . . . **8–10**

Price Range

STARR, Edwin, & Blinky
Singles: 7-Inch
GORDY: *69* **$2–4**
LPs: 10/12-Inch 33rpm
GORDY: *69* **10–12**
Also see STARR, Edwin

STARR, Kay
Singles: 7-Inch
ABC: *67–68* **2–3**
CAPITOL (900 through
  2800 series): *50–54* **3–6**
CAPITOL (4000 & 5000
  series): *58–64* **2–4**
DOT: *68*. **2–3**
GNP/CRESCENDO:
  74–75 . . . . **1–3**
HAPPY TIGER: *70*. **1–3**
RCA VICTOR (0100
  series): *73* **1–3**
RCA VICTOR (6000 &
  7000 series): *55–59* **2–5**
Picture Sleeves
CAPITOL: *62* **2–4**
EPs: 7-Inch 33/45rpm
CAPITOL: *50–61* **5–15**
RCA VICTOR: *55–58* **5–10**
LPs: 10/12-Inch 33rpm
ABC: *68* **5–15**
CAMDEN: *60–61*. **5–15**
CAPITOL (211; "Songs By
  Kay Starr"): *50* **40–60**
  (10-Inch LP. With an "H" prefix.)
CAPITOL (211; "Songs By
  Kay Starr"): *55* **20–40**
  (With a "T" prefix.)
CAPITOL (415; "The Hits
  Of Kay Starr"): *53* **20–35**
  (10-Inch LP. With an "H" prefix.)
CAPITOL (400 through
  1200 series): *53–59* **15–30**
  (With a "T" or "ST" prefix.)
CAPITOL (400 through
  900 series): *63–75* **5–15**
  (With a "DT" or "SM" prefix.)
CAPITOL (1300 series): *60* **10–20**
CAPITOL (1438; "Kay
  Starr, Jazz Singer"): *60*. **20–35**
CAPITOL (1468 through
  2100 series): *61–64* **8–15**

Price Range

CAPITOL (11000 series):
74–79 . . . . $5–8
CORONET: 63 10–20
GNP/CRESCENDO:
74–75 5–10
LIBERTY (3200 series): 63 10–20
LIBERTY (9000 series): 56 20–40
RCA VICTOR (1100
through 1700 series):
55–57 15–25
RONDO-LETTE: 58 15–35

STARR, Kay, & Count Basie
LPs: 10/12-Inch 33rpm
MCA: 83 5–8
PARAMOUNT: 69. 8–15
Also see BASIE, Count

STARR, Kay, & Tennessee Ernie Ford
Singles: 7-Inch
CAPITOL: 50–56 3–6

EPs: 7-Inch 33/45rpm
CAPITOL: 56 5–15
Also see FORD, Tennessee Ernie

STARR, Kay / Erroll Garner
LPs: 10/12-Inch 33rpm
CROWN: 57 15–30
MODERN: 56. 20–45
Also see GARNER, Erroll
Also see STARR, Kay

STARR, Kenny
Singles: 7-Inch
MCA: 73–78 2–3
S.S. TITANIC: 81. 1–3

LPs: 10/12-Inch 33rpm
MCA: 75 5–8

STARR, Lucille
Singles: 7-Inch
A&M: 66 2–4
ALMO: 64–65 3–5
EPIC: 67–69 2–4

LPs: 10/12-Inch 33rpm
EPIC: 69 8–10

Randy Starr, one charted single (1957), no charted LPs.

Price Range

STARR, Randy
Singles: 7-Inch
DALE: 57–59. $4–6
MAYFLOWER: 59. 3–5
Also see ISLANDERS, The

STARR, Randy, & Frank Metis
LPs: 10/12-Inch 33rpm
MAYFLOWER: 59. 15–20
Also see STARR, Randy

STARR, Ringo
Singles: 12-Inch 33/45rpm
ATLANTIC: 77 18–20
(Promotional issues only.)
Singles: 7-Inch
APPLE (1831; "It Don't
Come Easy"): 71 2–4
APPLE. (1849; "Back Off
Boogaloo"): 72. 5–8
(With a blue apple on the label.)
APPLE (1849; "Back Off
Boogaloo"): 73. 2–4
(With a green apple on the label.)
APPLE (1865;
"Photograph"): 73. 2–4
APPLE (1880; "No No
Song"): 75 2–4
APPLE (1872; "Oh My
My"): 74. 2–4

Price Range

APPLE (1870; "You're
  Sixteen"): *73*. $2–4
APPLE (1876; "Only
  You"): *74*. 2–4
APPLE (1882; "Goodnight
  Vienna"): *75*. 2–4
APPLE (2969; "Beaucoups
  Of Blues"): *70* 3–5
CAPITOL (Orange label). 2–4
CAPITOL (Purple label) 2–3
ATLANTIC: *76–77* 2–4
BOARDWALK: *81–82* 2–3
PORTRAIT: *78*. 2–3

Picture Sleeves

APPLE (1826; "Beaucoups
  Of Blues"): *70* 12–15
  (With the 2969 catalog number mistakenly
  shown as Apple 1826.)
APPLE (1831; "It Don't
  Come Easy"): *71* 8–10
APPLE (1849; "Back Off
  Boogaloo"): *72*. 8–10
APPLE (1865;
  "Photograph"): *73*. 5–8
APPLE (1870; "You're
  Sixteen"): *73*. 5–8
APPLE (1876; "Only
  You"): *74*. 5–8
APPLE (1882; "Goodnight
  Vienna"): *75*. 5–8
APPLE (2969; "Beaucoups
  Of Blues"): *70* 10–12
  (With the catalog number correctly shown.)

Promotional Singles

APPLE (1831; "It Don't
  Come Easy"): *71* 12–15
APPLE (1849; "Back Off
  Boogaloo"): *72*. 12–15
APPLE (1865;
  "Photograph"): *73*. 10–12
APPLE (1870; "You're
  Sixteen"): *73*. 10–12
APPLE (1872; "Oh My
  My"): *74*. 10–12
APPLE (1876; "Only
  You"): *74*. 10–12
APPLE (1880; "No No
  Song"): *75* 10–12
APPLE (1882; "Goodnight
  Vienna"/"Goodnight
  Vienna"): *75*. 10–12

Price Range

APPLE (1882;
  "Oo-Wee"/"Oo-Wee"):
  75 . . . . $18–20
APPLE (2969; "Beaucoups
  Of Blues"): *70* 12–15
ATLANTIC: *76–77* 5–8
BOARDWALK: *81–82* 5–8
PORTRAIT: *78*. 5–8

LPs: 10/12-Inch 33rpm

APPLE (Except 3413):
  70–75 10–15
APPLE (3413; "Ringo"):
  73 50–60
  (Price here applies ONLY to promo copies that
  contain the 5:26 version of "Six O'Clock."
  Some copies list the track at 5:26, when it actu-
  ally runs only 4:05. Play and time the tune to
  be sure.)
APPLE (3413; "Ringo"):
  73 10–15
  (With the 4:05 version of "Six O'Clock.")
ATLANTIC: *75–77* 8–10
BOARDWALK: *81* 8–10
CAPITOL: *80–81* 5–8
PORTRAIT: *78*. 8–10
  Also see BEATLES, The
  Also see CLAPTON, Eric
  Also see FRAMPTON, Peter
  Also see JOHN, Elton
  Also see LOMAX, Jackie
  Also see NILSSON

STARS ON (Stars On 45; Stars On Long Play)

Singles: 12-Inch 33/45rpm
RADIO: *81–82* 5–8
  Singles: 7-Inch
RADIO: *81–82* 1–3
TWENTY-ONE: *83* 1–3
  LPs: 10/12-Inch 33rpm
RADIO: *81–82* 8–10
TWENTY-ONE: *83* 5–8

STARS ON 45 (Featuring Sam & Dave)

Singles: 7-Inch
TWENTY-ONE: *85* 1–3
  Also see SAM & DAVE

STARSHINE

Singles: 12-Inch 33/45rpm
PRELUDE: *83*. 4–6

Price Range

Price Range

Singles: 7-Inch
PRELUDE: *83.* **$1–3**

STARSHIP (Jefferson Starship)
Singles: 7-Inch
GRUNT: *85–86.* **1–3**
LPs: 10/12-Inch 33rpm
GRUNT: *85–86.* **5–8**
Also see JEFFERSON STARSHIP

STARSKI, Love Bug
Singles: 7-Inch
ATLANTIC: *85* **1–3**

STARZ
Singles: 7-Inch
CAPITOL: *76–79* **2–3**
Picture Sleeves
CAPITOL: *76–79* **2–3**
LPs: 10/12-Inch 33rpm
CAPITOL (Black vinyl):
76–78 . . . . **8–10**
CAPITOL (Colored vinyl):
77 . . . . **12–15**

STATE OF GRACE
Singles: 12-Inch 33/45rpm
PROFILE: *83* **4–6**
Singles: 7-Inch
PROFILE: *83* **1–3**

STATLER BROTHERS, The
Singles: 7-Inch
COLUMBIA: *64–69* **2–5**
MERCURY: *70–84.* **2–3**
LPs: 10/12-Inch 33rpm
COLUMBIA (2000 series):
66–67 . . . . **15–25**
COLUMBIA (9000 series):
66–69 . . . . **12–25**
(With a "CS" prefix.)
COLUMBIA (9000 series) **5–8**
(With a "PC" prefix.)
COLUMBIA (31000 series) **5–10**
51 WEST **5–8**
HARMONY: *71–73* **6–12**
MERCURY: *71–84.* **5–12**
PRIORITY: *82* **5–8**
TIME-LIFE: *81.* **5–8**
Members: Harold Reid; Don Reid; Lew De-
Witt; Phil Balsley; Jimmy Fortune.

STATON, Candi
Singles: 7-Inch
FAME: *69–73* **$2–4**
L.A.: *81* **1–3**
SUGAR HILL: *82* **1–3**
WARNER BROS: *74–80* **1–3**
LPs: 10/12-Inch 33rpm
FAME: *70–72* **10–12**
SUGAR HILL: *82* **5–8**
WARNER BROS: *74–80* **8–10**

STATON, Dakota
Singles: 7-Inch
CAPITOL: *55–63* **2–5**
GROOVE MERCHANT:
72 . . . . **1–3**
EPs: 7-Inch 33/45rpm
CAPITOL: *58–60* **5–15**
LPs: 10/12-Inch 33rpm
CAPITOL (800 through
1600 series): *58–63* **15–35**
HALF MOON: *83* **5–8**
LONDON: *67* **10–15**
UNITED ARTISTS: *63–64* **10–20**
VERVE: *71* **8–12**

STATUES, The (Featuring Garry Miles)
Singles: 7-Inch
LIBERTY: *60* **5–8**
Also see MILES, Gary

STATUS VI
Singles: 12-Inch 33/45rpm
RADAR: *83* **4–6**

STATUS QUO, The
Singles: 7-Inch
A&M: *73–74* **2–4**
CADET/CONCEPT:
68–69 . . . . **3–5**
CAPITOL: *75–77* **2–3**
JANUS: *72* **2–4**
PYE: *75* **2–4**
RIVA: *80* **1–3**
LPs: 10/12-Inch 33rpm
A&M: *73–74* **8–10**
CADET CONCEPT: *68.* **10–15**
CAPITOL: *74–79* **8–10**
JANUS: *71* **10–12**
PYE: *72* **10–12**
Also see BAND AID

Price Range

STEALERS WHEEL
Singles: 7-Inch
A&M: *73–78* $2–4

Picture Sleeves
A&M: *73* 2–4

LPs: 10/12-Inch 33rpm
A&M: *73–78* 6–10
Members: Gerry Rafferty; Joe Egan.
Also see RAFFERTY, Gerry

STEAM
Singles: 7-Inch
FONTANA: *69* 2–4
MERCURY: *70–76*................ 2–4

Picture Sleeves
MERCURY (30160; "Na
Na Hey Hey Kiss Him
Goodbye"): *76* 8–10
(Promotional Chicago White Sox sleeve.)

LPs: 10/12-Inch 33rpm
MERCURY: *69*................. 12–15

STEEL, Jake & Jeff
Singles: 7-Inch
PEACH/MINT: *74*................ 2–4

STEEL BREEZE
Singles: 7-Inch
RCA VICTOR: *82–83* 1–3

LPs: 10/12-Inch 33rpm
RCA VICTOR: *82* 5–8

STEEL PULSE
Singles: 7-Inch
ELEKTRA: *82* 1–3

LPs: 10/12-Inch 33rpm
ELEKTRA: *82* 5–8
MANGO: *80* 5–8

STEELE, Ben, & His Bare Hands
Singles: 12-Inch 33/45rpm
VANITY: *83* 4–6

STEELERS, The
Singles: 7-Inch
DATE: *69* 2–4
EPIC: *71* 2–4

Price Range

STEELEYE SPAN
Singles: 7-Inch
CHRYSALIS: *72–78*.............. $2–4

LPs: 10/12-Inch 33rpm
BIG TREE: *71* 12–15
CHRYSALIS: *72–78*.............. 8–12
MFSL: *78*...................... 12–15
TAKOMA: *81*................... 8–10

STEELY DAN
Singles: 7-Inch
ABC: *72–78* 2–4
MCA: *78–81* 1–3

EPs: 7-Inch 33/45rpm
ABC: *73–77*..................... 8–10
(Jukebox issues only.)

LPs: 10/12-Inch 33rpm
ABC: *72–78* 6–10
COMMAND: *74*.................. 8–10
MCA: *79–82* 5–8
MFSL: *78*...................... 10–15
Members: Donald Fagen; Walter Beckers.
Also see FAGEN, Donald
Also see McDONALD, Michael

STEIN, Lou
Singles: 7-Inch
BRUNSWICK: *52–53*.............. 2–4
EPIC: *55–56* 2–4
JUBILEE: *54*..................... 2–4
MURBO: *69* 1–3
RKO UNIQUE: *57*................ 2–4

EPs: 7-Inch 33/45rpm
EPIC: *55–56* 4–8
JUBILEE: *54*..................... 4–8

LPs: 10/12-Inch 33rpm
CHIAROSCURO: *76–81* 4–8
CORAL: *53*..................... 5–15
EPIC: *55–56* 5–15
EVEREST: *60* 5–12
JUBILEE: *54*................... 5–15
MERCURY: *55–60*.............. 5–15
MUSICOR: *67–68*............... 5–10
OLD TOWN: *61*................. 5–15
WING: *62* 5–10
WORLD JAZZ: *81*................ 4–8

STEINBERG, David
Singles: 7-Inch
COLUMBIA: *74*.................. 2–3

Price Range

LPs: 10/12-Inch 33rpm
COLUMBIA: 74–75 . . . . **$5–10**
ELEKTRA: 70 . . . . **5–10**
UNI: 68 . . . . **8–15**

STEINMAN, Jim
Singles: 7-Inch
EPIC/CLEVELAND
  INT'L: 81 . . . . **1–3**
LPs: 10/12-Inch 33rpm
EPIC/CLEVELAND
  INT'L: 81 . . . . **5–8**

STEPHENS, Tennyson (Tennyson Stephens)
Singles: 7-Inch
ARIES: 69 . . . . **2–4**
CHESS: 69 . . . . **2–4**
BACK BEAT: 61 . . . . **3–5**
  Also see UPCHURCH, Phil, & Tennyson
  Stephens

STEPHENS, Tennyson, & Rheta Hughes
LPs: 10/12-Inch 33rpm
COLUMBIA: 65 . . . . **10–15**
  Also see STEPHENS, Tennyson

STEPHENSON, Van
Singles: 7-Inch
HANDSHAKE: 81 . . . . **1–3**
MCA: 84 . . . . **1–3**
LPs: 10/12-Inch 33rpm
HANDSHAKE: 81 . . . . **5–8**
MCA: 84 . . . . **5–8**

STEPPENWOLF (Featuring John Kay)
Singles: 7-Inch
ABC: 70 . . . . **2–4**
DUNHILL: 67–71 . . . . **3–5**
IMMEDIATE: 67 . . . . **4–6**
MUMS: 74–75 . . . . **2–4**
ROULETTE **1–3**
Picture Sleeves
DUNHILL: 71 . . . . **3–5**
MUMS: 74 . . . . **2–4**
EPs: 7-Inch 33/45rpm
DUNHILL: 68 . . . . **4–8**

Price Range

(Jukebox issues only.)
LPs: 10/12-Inch 33rpm
ABC: 75–76 . . . . **$8–10**
ALLEGIANCE **5–8**
DUNHILL: 68–73 . . . . **10–12**
EPIC: 75–76 . . . . **6–10**
MCA: 79 . . . . **5–8**
MUMS: 74 . . . . **8–10**
  Also see KAY, John

STEPTOE
Singles: 12-Inch 33/45rpm
FANTASY: 82 . . . . **4–6**
Singles: 7-Inch
FANTASY: 82 . . . . **1–3**

STEREO FUN INC.
Singles: 12-Inch 33/45rpm
MOBY DICK: 83 . . . . **4–6**

STEREOS, The
Singles: 7-Inch
MINK (22; "Memory
  Lane"): 59 . . . . **10–15**
  ("Memory Lane" was reissued, still in 1959,
  showing the group as The Tams. The same
  track was again issued in 1963, shown as by The
  Tams and then by The Hippies.)
  Also see HIPPIES, The / Reggie Harrison
  Also see TAMS, The

STEREOS, The
Singles: 7-Inch
CADET: 67–68 . . . . **3–5**
CUB: 61–62 . . . . **4–6**
GIBRALTAR: 59 . . . . **5–8**
WORLD ARTISTS: 63 . . . . **3–5**

STERLING, Michael
Singles: 7-Inch
SUCCESS: 83 . . . . **1–3**

STEVE & EYDIE: see LAWRENCE, Steve, & Eydie Gorme

STEVENS, April
Singles: 7-Inch
A&M: 72 . . . . **2–3**
ATCO: 65 . . . . **2–4**
CONTRACT: 61 . . . . **3–5**
IMPERIAL: 59–65 . . . . **2–5**

Price Range

KING: *64* $2–5
MGM: *67*......................... 2–4
RCA VICTOR: *51–52* 3–6
VERVE: *71* 2–3
LPs: 10/12-Inch 33rpm
IMPERIAL: *61–64*............... 15–20
LIBERTY: *83* 5–8
Also see TEMPO, Nino, & April Stevens

STEVENS, April / Marg Phelan
LPs: 10/12-Inch 33rpm
AUDIO LAB: *59* 15–20
Also see STEVENS, April

STEVENS, Cat
Singles: 12-Inch 33/45rpm
A&M: *77* 5–8
Singles: 7-Inch
A&M: *70–79* 1–3
DERAM: *66–72* 3–5
Picture Sleeves
A&M: *71–78* 2–3
LPs: 10/12-Inch 33rpm
A&M: *70* 8–10
(Jukebox issue only.)
LPs: 10/12-Inch 33rpm
A&M: *69–84* 6–10
DERAM: *67–72* 10–15
LONDON: *78* 5–8

STEVENS, Connie
Singles: 7-Inch
BELL: *70–72*..................... 2–4
MGM: *68*......................... 2–4
WARNER BROS: *59–66*............. 3–5
Picture Sleeves
WARNER BROS: *60*............... 5–8
LPs: 10/12-Inch 33rpm
HARMONY: *69* 10–12
WARNER BROS: *58–62*.......... 20–25
Also see BYRNES, Edward

STEVENS, Dodie
Singles: 7-Inch
CRYSTALETTE: *59* 4–6
DOLTON: *63*...................... 3–5
DOT: *59–62*...................... 3–5
IMPERIAL: *63*.................... 3–5
Picture Sleeves
CRYSTALETTE: *59* 15–20

Price Range

LPs: 10/12-Inch 33rpm
DOT: *60–61*................... $20–25

STEVENS, Ray (Ray Stevens & The Merry Melody Singers)
Singles: 7-Inch
BARNABY: *70–76*................. 2–4
CAPITOL: *58–59*................. 8–10
MCA: *85–86* 1–3
MERCURY (71000 &
72000 series): *61–68* 4–6
MERCURY (810000
series): *83*...................... 1–3
MONUMENT: *65–69*............... 3–5
NRC: *59–60*...................... 5–8
PREP: *57*........................ 8–10
PRIORITY 1–3
RCA VICTOR: *81–82* 1–3
WARNER/AHAB: *76–79*........... 2–3
Picture Sleeves
BARNABY: *70* 2–4
MERCURY: *61–64*................. 5–10
WARNER/AHAB: *79*.............. 2–3
Promotional Singles
MERCURY (66; "Butch
Barbarian"): *64* 5–8
EPs: 7-Inch 33/45rpm
MERCURY (85; "Ray
Stevens"): *62* 10–15
(Promotional issue only. Not issued with special sleeve.)
LPs: 10/12-Inch 33rpm
BARNABY: *70–78*............... 8–10
CROWN: *63* 12–15
MCA: *85* 5–8
MERCURY (0732; "1,837
Seconds Of Humor"): *62* 30–40
MERCURY (0732; "Ahab
The Arab"): *62* 20–25
MERCURY (0828; "This
Is Ray Stevens"): *63* 20–25
MERCURY (61272; "The
Best Of Ray Stevens"):
70 10–12
MERCURY (810000
series): *83* 5–8
MONUMENT: *66–69*............. 10–12
PRIORITY: *82* 5–8
RCA VICTOR: *80–82* 5–8
WARNER BROS: *76–79*.......... 8–10
WING: *68* 10–12

Singles: 7-Inch
WARNER BROS: *83* $1–3

STEWART, Dave, & Barbara Gaskin
Singles: 7-Inch
PLATINUM: *81* 1–3

STEWART, Gary
Singles: 7-Inch
CORY 8–12
DECCA: *71* 2–3
KAPP: *68–70.* 2–4
MCA: *75* 2–3
RCA VICTOR: *73–83* 1–3
Picture Sleeves
RCA VICTOR: *82* 1–3
LPs: 10/12-Inch 33rpm
MCA: *75* 4–8
RCA VICTOR: *75–83* 5–10

STEWART, Jermaine
Singles: 12-Inch 33/45rpm
ARISTA: *84–85.* 4–6
Singles: 7-Inch
ARISTA: *84–85.* 1–3

STEWART, John
Singles: 7-Inch
ALLEGIANCE. 1–3
CAPITOL: *69* 2–4
RCA VICTOR: *73* 2–4
RSO: *79* 1–3
WARNER BROS: *71* 2–4
LPs: 10/12-Inch 33rpm
ALLEGIANCE. 5–8
CAPITOL: *69–70* 10–12
RCA VICTOR: *73* 8–10
RSO: *79* 5–8
WARNER BROS: *71* 8–10
Also see BUCKINGHAM, Lindsey
Also see KINGSTON TRIO, The
Also see NICKS, Stevie

STEWART, John, & Buffy Ford
LPs: 10/12-Inch 33rpm
CAPITOL: *68* 10–12

STEWART, John, & Nick Reynolds
LPs: 10/12-Inch 33rpm
TAKOMA 5–8
Also see KINGSTON TRIO, The

Also see STEWART, John

STEWART, Mel
Singles: 12-Inch 33/45rpm
MERCURY: *83* $4–6
Singles: 7-Inch
MERCURY: *83* 1–3

STEWART, Rod (Rod Stewart & The Faces)
Singles: 12-Inch 33/45rpm
WARNER BROS: *78–82* 5–8
Singles: 7-Inch
GNP/CRESCENDO: *73* 3–5
MERCURY: *70–76.* 3–5
PRESS: *65* 10–12
PRIVATE STOCK: *76.* 2–4
WARNER BROS: *75–86* 1–3
Picture Sleeves
MERCURY: *72–73.* 4–6
WARNER BROS: *75–86* 1–3
LPs: 10/12-Inch 33rpm
ACCORD: *81* 5–8
MERCURY (Except 61000
  series): *71–76* 8–12
MERCURY (61000 series):
  69–70 10–15
PRIVATE STOCK: *77.* 8–10
SPRINGBOARD: *72* 8–10
TRIP: *77* 8–10
WARNER BROS (Except
  picture discs): *75–85* 6–10
WARNER BROS (Picture
  discs): *79* 10–15
  Also see BECK, Jeff, & Rod Stewart
  Also see FACES
  Also see PYTHON LEE JACKSON

STEWART, Sandy
Singles: 7-Inch
ATCO: *59* 2–4
COLPIX: *62–63.* 2–4
DCP: *64* 2–4
EPIC: *54* 2–5
OKEH: *53* 2–5
20TH CENTURY: *54.* 2–5
UNITED ARTISTS: *60–61* 2–4
X: *55.* 2–5
Picture Sleeves
COLPIX: *62* 2–4

Price Range

LPs: 10/12-Inch 33rpm
COLPIX: 63 .... **$10–20**

STEWART, Wynn (Wynn Stewart & The Tourists)
Singles: 7-Inch
ATLANTIC: 74 .... **2–3**
CAPITOL (2000 series):
  67–71 .... **2–4**
CAPITOL (3000 series):
  56–57 .... **3–6**
CAPITOL (5000 series):
  62–67 .... **2–4**
CHALLENGE: 59–64 .... **2–5**
4 STAR: 80..................... **1–3**
JACKPOT: 59.................. **10–15**
PLAYBOY: 75–76 .... **2–3**
PRETTY WORLD: 85............. **1–3**
RCA VICTOR: 72–73 .... **2–3**
WINS: 79....................... **1–3**
Picture Sleeves
CAPITOL: 67–69 .... **2–4**
LPs: 10/12-Inch 33rpm
CAPITOL: 67–75 .... **5–12**
PICKWICK/HILLTOP:
  67 .... **6–12**
PLAYBOY: 76 .... **6–10**
STARDAY: 68 .... **8–12**
WRANGLER: 62............... **15–25**
Also see PIERCE, Webb / Wynn Stewart

STILLS, Stephen (Stephen Stills & Manassas)
Singles: 7-Inch
ATLANTIC: 70–73 .... **2–4**
COLUMBIA: 75–78 .... **1–3**
Picture Sleeves
ATLANTIC: 71 .... **2–4**
LPs: 10/12-Inch 33rpm
ATLANTIC: 70–84 .... **6–10**
COLUMBIA: 75–78 .... **5–10**
Also see BLOOMFIELD, Mike, Al Kooper & Steve Stills
Also see BUFFALO SPRINGFIELD
Also see CROSBY, STILLS & NASH
Also see STILLS-YOUNG BAND, The

STILLS-YOUNG BAND, The
Singles: 7-Inch
REPRISE: 77..................... **2–3**

Price Range

LPs: 10/12-Inch 33rpm
REPRISE: 76.................... **$5–8**
Members: Stephen Stills; Neil Young.
Also see STILLS, Stephen
Also see YOUNG, Neil

STILLWATER
Singles: 7-Inch
CAPRICORN: 77–78............... **2–3**
LPs: 10/12-Inch 33rpm
CAPRICORN: 78–79............... **5–8**

STING (Gordon Sumner)
Singles: 7-Inch
A&M: 85 .... **1–3**
ABC: 78.......................... **2–3**
LPs: 10/12-Inch 33rpm
A&M: 85 .... **5–8**
ABC: 78 .... **6–10**
Also see BAND AID
Also see POLICE, The

STIRLING SILVER
Singles: 7-Inch
COLUMBIA: 76................... **2–3**

STITES, Gary
Singles: 7-Inch
CARLTON: 59–60 .... **5–8**
EPIC: 66 .... **3–5**
MADISON: 60–61 .... **5–8**
MR. PEEKE: 62.................. **4–6**
LPs: 10/12-Inch 33rpm
CARLTON: 60 .... **40–50**

STITT, Sonny
Singles: 7-Inch
ARGO: 58–65 .... **2–4**
ATLANTIC: 63 .... **2–4**
CADET: 74....................... **1–3**
CATALYST: 77 .... **1–3**
ENTERPRISE: 69 .... **2–3**
IMPULSE: 64 .... **2–4**
PRESTIGE: 63–69 .... **2–4**
ROULETTE: 65–67 .... **2–3**
WINGATE: 65 .... **2–4**
WORLD PACIFIC: 63 .... **2–4**
EPs: 7-Inch 33/45rpm
PRESTIGE: 53 .... **10–25**
LPs: 10/12-Inch 33rpm
ARGO: 58–65 .... **15–30**

Price Range

ATLANTIC: *62–64* **$15–25**
CADET: *65–74* **8–18**
CATALYST: *76–77* **5–10**
CHESS: *76* **8–12**
COLPIX: *66* **10–20**
EVEREST: *82* **5–8**
FLYING DUTCHMAN:
  75–76 .... **5–10**
IMPULSE: *63–64* **15–25**
JAMAL: *71* **8–12**
JAZZLAND: *62* **20–35**
JAZZTONE: *56*. **20–40**
MUSE: *73–82*. **5–12**
PACIFIC JAZZ: *63* **15–25**
PAULA: *74* **5–10**
PRESTIGE (060;
  "Kaleidoscope"): *83* **5–8**
PRESTIGE (100 series):
  51–53 .... **50–75**
  (10-Inch LPs.)
PRESTIGE (7000 series):
  56–64 .... **20–45**
  (Yellow labels.)
PRESTIGE (7000 series):
  65–70 .... **10–20**
  (Blue labels.)
PRESTIGE (10000 series):
  71–74 .... **8–12**
PRESTIGE (20000 series):
  74 .... **8–15**
ROOST (400 series): *52* **75–150**
  (10-Inch LPs.)
ROOST (1200 series): *56* **20–40**
ROOST (2200 series):
  57–66 .... **10–30**
ROULETTE: *65–70* **10–25**
SAVOY (9000 series): *53* **40–60**
  (10-Inch LPs.)
SOLID STATE: *69*. **8–15**
TRIP: *73* **6–12**
UPFRONT: *77* **5–8**
VERVE: *57–59* **20–40**
  (Reads "Verve Records, Inc." at bottom of
  label.)
VERVE: *62–72* **10–20**
  (Reads "MGM Records - A Division Of Metro-
  Goldwyn-Mayer, Inc." at bottom of label.)
VERVE: *73–84* **5–10**
  (Reads "Manufactured By MGM Record
  Corp.," or mentions either Polydor or Poly-
  gram at bottom of label.)
  Also see AMMONS, Gene, & Sonny Stitt

Price Range

Also see PETERSON, Oscar, & Sonny Stitt

STOKES, Simon T. (Simon Stokes & The Nighthawks)
Singles: 7-Inch
CASABLANCA: *74* **$2–4**
ELEKTRA: *69–70* **2–4**
IN SOUND: *68* **3–5**
LPs: 10/12-Inch 33rpm
MGM: *70*. **10–12**
SPINDIZZY: *73* **8–10**
UNITED ARTISTS: *77*. **8–10**

STOLOFF, Morris (Morris Stoloff Conducts The Columbia Studio Orchestra)
Singles: 7-Inch
COLPIX: *59* **2–4**
DECCA: *56*. **2–4**
MERCURY: *54*. **2–4**
REPRISE: *65*. **2–3**
LPs: 10/12-Inch 33rpm
DECCA: *56* **5–15**
WARNER BROS. (1416;
  "Fanny"): *61* **25–35**
  (Soundtrack.)

STOMPERS, The
Singles: 7-Inch
GONE: *61* **5–8**
LANDA: *62* **4–6**
MERCURY (72000 series):
  63 .... **4–6**

STOMPERS, The
Singles: 7-Inch
BOARDWALK: *83* **1–3**

STONE
Singles: 7-Inch
WEST END: *82* **1–3**

STONE, Cliffie (The Cliffie Stone Singers)
Singles: 7-Inch
CAPITOL: *50–69* **2–5**
TOWER: *67*. **2–3**
LPs: 10/12-Inch 33rpm
CAPITOL (100 through
  300 series): *68–69* **5–10**

Price Range

CAPITOL (1000 through
  1600 series): *58–62* **$15–30**
CAPITOL (2100 series): *64* **5–15**
TOWER: *67*. **8–12**

STONE, Kirby, Four (The Kirby Stone Quartet)
Singles: 7-Inch
COLUMBIA: *57–65* **2–4**
MGM: *67*. **2–3**
WARNER BROS: *63–64* **2–4**
LPs: 10/12-Inch 33rpm
COLUMBIA: *58–62* **8–15**
WARNER BROS: *63–64* **5–12**
  Members: Kirby Stone; Edward Hall; Michael
  Gardner; Larry Foster.

STONE, Sly (Sylvester Stewart)
Singles: 12-Inch 33/45rpm
EPIC: *80* **4–6**
Singles: 7-Inch
EPIC: *75–79* **2–4**
LPs: 10/12-Inch 33rpm
EPIC: *79* **5–8**
  Also see SLY & THE FAMILY STONE

STONE CITY BAND, The
Singles: 7-Inch
GORDY: *80–83*. **1–3**
LPs: 10/12-Inch 33rpm
GORDY: *80–83*. **5–8**
  Also see JAMES, Rick

STONE FURY
Singles: 7-Inch
MCA: *84* **1–3**
LPs: 10/12-Inch 33rpm
MCA: *84* **5–8**

STONE PONEYS, The (Featuring Linda Ronstadt)
Singles: 7-Inch
CAPITOL: *67* **5–8**
LPs: 10/12-Inch 33rpm
CAPITOL (2600 & 2700
  series): *67*. **15–20**
  Also see RONSTADT, Linda

STONEBOLT
Singles: 7-Inch
PARACHUTE: *78–79* **2–3**

Price Range

RCA VICTOR: *80* **$1–3**
LPs: 10/12-Inch 33rpm
PARACHUTE: *78* **8–10**
RCA VICTOR: *80* **5–8**

STONEY & MEAT LOAF
Singles: 7-Inch
RARE EARTH: *71* **2–4**
LPs: 10/12-Inch 33rpm
PRODIGAL: *78* **5–8**
RARE EARTH: *71* **10–15**
  Also see MEAT LOAF

STOOGES, The (Featuring Iggy Pop)
Singles: 7-Inch
ELEKTRA: *69–70* **3–5**
LPs: 10/12-Inch 33rpm
ELEKTRA: *69–70* **12–15**
  Also see POP, Iggy

STOOKEY, Paul
Singles: 7-Inch
ERIC **1–3**
WARNER BROS: *71–72* **2–4**
LPs: 10/12-Inch 33rpm
NEWPAX **5–8**
WARNER BROS: *71* **8–10**
  Also see PETER, PAUL & MARY

STOREY SISTERS, The
Singles: 7-Inch
BATON: *58* **5–8**
CAMEO: *58* **5–8**
MERCURY: *59*. **4–6**

STORIES, The
Singles: 7-Inch
ERIC **1–3**
KAMA SUTRA: *72–74* **2–4**
RADIOACTIVE GOLD:
  74 . . . . **2–4**
LPs: 10/12-Inch 33rpm
KAMA SUTRA: *72–73* **8–10**
  Members: Ian Lloyd; Michael Brown.
  Also see BROWN, Michael
  Also see LLOYD, Ian

STORM
Singles: 7-Inch
PHI KAPPA: *74*. **2–3**

Price Range

STORM, Billy (Billy Storm & The Valiants)
Singles: 7-Inch
ATLANTIC: *60–61* $3–5
BUENA VISTA: *63* 3–5
COLUMBIA: *59* 4–6
ENSIGN: *59* 4–6
GREGMARK: *61* 3–5
HBR: *66* 3–5
INFINITY: *62–63* 3–5
LOMA: *64–65* 3–5
ODE: *69* 2–4
Picture Sleeves
HBR: *66* 3–5
LPs: 10/12-Inch 33rpm
BUENA VISTA: *63* 15–20
FAMOUS: *69* 15–20
Also see VALIANTS, The

STORM, Gale
Singles: 7-Inch
DOT (Maroon label):
55–56 4–6
DOT (Black label): *57–60* 3–5
Picture Sleeves
DOT: *58* 4–6
EPs: 7-Inch 33/45rpm
DOT: *55–56* 10–15
LPs: 10/12-Inch 33rpm
DOT: *56–59* 20–25
HAMILTON: *66* 8–10
MCA: *82* 5–8

STORM, Warren
Singles: 7-Inch
ATCO: *68* 2–4
DOT: *61* 4–6
KINGFISH 4–6
NASCO: *58–60* 4–6
SOUTH STAR: *83* 1–3
STARFLITE: *79* 2–3
Also see SHONDELLS, The / Rod Bernard /
Warren Storm / Skip Stewart

STOTT, Lally
Singles: 7-Inch
PHILIPS: *71* 2–4

STRAIT, George
Singles: 7-Inch
MCA: *81–85* 1–3

Price Range

LPs: 10/12-Inch 33rpm
MCA: *81–85* $5–8

STRAKER, Nick, Band
Singles: 7-Inch
PRELUDE: *82* 1–3
LPs: 10/12-Inch 33rpm
PRELUDE: *82* 5–8

STRANGE, Billy (Billy Strange & The Telstars; Billy Strange & The Transients)
Singles: 7-Inch
BUENA VISTA: *62–63* 2–5
CAPITOL: *54–55* 3–6
COLISEUM: *63* 2–5
DECCA: *55* 4–6
GNP/CRESCENDO:
64–65 3–5
LIBERTY: *61–62* 2–5
TOWER: *69* 2–4
LPs: 10/12-Inch 33rpm
COLISEUM: *62* 10–15
GNP/CRESCENDO:
63–75 6–10
HORIZON: *63* 10–15
SUNSET: *68* 8–10
SURREY: *65* 10–15
TRADITION: *68* 6–10
Also see CAMPBELL, Glen, & Billy Strange

STRANGELOVES, The
Singles: 7-Inch
BANG: *65–67* 4–6
SIRE: *68* 3–5
SWAN: *64* 5–8
LPs: 10/12-Inch 33rpm
BANG: *65* 30–35
Members: Bob Feldman; Jerry Goldstein;
Richie Gottehrer.
Also see SHEEP

STRANGERS, The (With Joel Hill)
Singles: 7-Inch
TITAN: *59–60* 5–8

STRAWBERRY ALARM CLOCK, The
Singles: 7-Inch
ALL AMERICAN: *67* 5–8
MCA 1–3

Price Range

UNI: *67–70* **$3–5**
   LPs: 10/12-Inch 33rpm
BACK-TRAC: *85* **5–8**
UNI: *67–70* **20–30**
VOCALION: *71* **12–15**
   Also see THEE SIXPENCE
   Also see WHO, The / The Strawberry Alarm
   Clock

STRAWBS, The
Singles: 7-Inch
A&M: *68–75* **2–4**
ARISTA: *78* **1–3**
OYSTER: *76–77* **2–4**
   LPs: 10/12-Inch 33rpm
A&M: *71–78* **8–12**
ARISTA: *78* **5–8**
OYSTER: *76–77* **8–10**
   Also see WAKEMAN, Rick

STRAY CATS (Featuring Brian Setzer)
Singles: 7-Inch
EMI AMERICA: *82–84* **1–3**
   Picture Sleeves
EMI AMERICA: *82–84* **1–3**
   LPs: 10/12-Inch 33rpm
EMI AMERICA: *82–83* **5–8**

STREEK
Singles: 7-Inch
COLUMBIA: *81* **1–3**
   LPs: 10/12-Inch 33rpm
COLUMBIA: *81* **5–8**

STREET, Janey
Singles: 7-Inch
ARISTA: *84* **1–3**
   LPs: 10/12-Inch 33rpm
ARISTA: *84–85* **5–8**

STREET CHRISTIANS, The
Singles: 7-Inch
P.I.P.: *73* **2–3**

STREET PEOPLE, The
Singles: 7-Inch
MUSICOR: *69–70* **2–4**
VIGOR: *75–77* **2–3**
   LPs: 10/12-Inch 33rpm
MUSICOR: *70* **12–15**

Price Range

PICKWICK: *72* **$8–10**
   Also see HOLMES, Rupert

STREET PLAYERS, The
Singles: 7-Inch
ARIOLA AMERICA: *79* **1–3**
   LPs: 10/12-Inch 33rpm
ARIOLA AMERICA: *79* **5–8**

STREETS, The (With Steve Walsh)
Singles: 7-Inch
ATLANTIC: *83–84* **1–3**
   LPs: 10/12-Inch 33rpm
ATLANTIC: *83–84* **5–8**
   Also see KANSAS

STREISAND, Barbra
Singles: 12-Inch 33/45rpm
COLUMBIA (White
  labels): *79–85* **12–25**
   (Promotional issue only.)
   Singles: 7-Inch
COLUMBIA (04000 &
  05000 series): *83–86* **1–3**
COLUMBIA (10000 &
  11000 series): *76–80* **1–3**
COLUMBIA (3-42648;
  "My Coloring Book"):
  62 .... **20–25**
   (Compact 33 Single.)
COLUMBIA (4-42648;
  "My Coloring Book"):
  62 .... **8–10**
COLUMBIA (42631;
  "Happy Days Are Here
  Again"): *63* **5–8**
COLUMBIA (42965
  through 43469): *64–65* **3–5**
COLUMBIA (43518
  through 46024): *66–74* **2–4**
   Picture Sleeves
COLUMBIA (Except
  43000 series): *73–84* **1–3**
COLUMBIA (43000
  series): *66* **3–5**
   LPs: 10/12-Inch 33rpm
COLUMBIA (1779; "The
  Legend Of Barbra
  Streisand"): *83* **20–40**
   (Promotional issue only. A one-hour interview
   program.)

Price Range

DONNA SUMMER & BARBRA STREISAND

33 1/3 RPM
STEREO
NBD 20199 DJ
PROMOTIONAL COPY
(NBD 20199 AS)
NOT FOR SALE
73256
1. NO MORE TEARS (Enough Is Enough) 11:40
(Paul Jabara-Bruce Roberts)
Olga Music/Fedora Music (BMI)
PRODUCED BY GARY KLEIN for The Entertainment Company
and GIORGIO MORODER
Executive Producer: Charles Koppelman
Arranged by Greg Mathieson & Harold Faltermeyer
Mixdown by Harold Faltermeyer & Giorgio Moroder
From the DONNA SUMMER album "ON THE RADIO -
GREATEST HITS VOL. I & II" NBLP-2-7191 and
the BARBRA STREISAND album
"WET" FC 36258
℗ 1979 Casablanca Record
& FilmWorks, Inc.

Price Range

COLUMBIA (2007
through 2682): *63–67* $15–25
(With a "CL" prefix.)
COLUMBIA (8807
through 9482): *63–67* 15–25
(With a "CS" prefix.)
COLUMBIA (9710
through 9968): *68–70* 10–15
COLUMBIA (8000 & 9000
series) 5–8
(With a "PC" prefix.)
COLUMBIA (9000 series) 5–8
(With a "JC" prefix.)
COLUMBIA (30086
through 40000 series):
70–86 6–15
Also see ARLEN, Harold, With "Friend"
(Barbra Streisand)

STREISAND, Barbra, & Kim Carnes
Singles: 7-Inch
COLUMBIA: *84* 1–3
Also see CARNES, Kim

**STREISAND, Barbra, & Neil
Diamond**
Singles: 7-Inch
COLUMBIA: *78* 2–3
Also see DIAMOND, Neil

STEISAND, Barbra, & Barry Gibb
Singles: 7-Inch
COLUMBIA: *80–81* 1–3
Also see GIBB, Barry

**STREISAND, Barbra, & Donna
Summer**
Singles: 12-Inch 33/45rpm
COLUMBIA/
CASABLANCA: *79* $8–10
(Promotional issue only. Issued with special
cover.)
Singles: 7-Inch
COLUMBIA: *79* 1–3
Picture Sleeves
COLUMBIA: *79* 2–3
Also see STREISAND, Barbra
Also see SUMMER, Donna

STRIKERS, The
Singles: 7-Inch
PRELUDE: *81*. 1–3
LPs: 10/12-Inch 33rpm
PRELUDE: *81*. 5–8

STRING-A-LONGS, The
Singles: 7-Inch
ATCO: *69* 2–4
DOT: *62–65*. 3–5
WARWICK (Except 603 &
606): *61–62*. 4–6
WARWICK (603;
"Wheels"/"Tell The
World"): *60* 10–15
WARWICK (603;
"Wheels"/"Am I Asking
Too Much"): *61*. 4–6
WARWICK (606; "Tell
The World"): *61* 8–10
LPs: 10/12-Inch 33rpm
ATCO: *68* 10–15
DOT: *62–66*. 15–20
WARWICK: *61*. 30–40

STROKE
Singles: 12-Inch 33/45rpm
OMNI: *85* 4–6

STROLLERS, The
Singles: 7-Inch
CARLTON: *61* 5–8

STRONG, Barrett
Singles: 7-Inch
ANNA: *60*. 8–10
ATCO: *62* 3–5

Price Range

CAPITOL: *75* $2–4
EPIC: *73* 2–4
MOTOWN. 1–3
TAMLA (54027;
  "Money"): *60*. 25–30
  (With horizontal lines on label.)
TAMLA (54027;
  "Money"): *60*. 10–12
  (With Tamla globe logo on label.)
TAMLA (54029;
  "Money"): *60*. 50–60
  (With horizontal lines on label.)
TAMLA (54033;
  "Whirlwind"): *60*. 4–6
TAMLA (54035; "Money
  And Me"): *61* 5–8
TAMLA (54043;
  "Misery"): *61*. 20–25
Picture Sleeves
EPIC: *73* 2–4
LPs: 10/12-Inch 33rpm
CAPITOL: *74* 8–10

STRUNK, Jud (Jud Strunk & The Coplin Kitchen Band)
Singles: 7-Inch
CAPITOL: *74* 2–4
COBURT: *71*. 2–4
COLUMBIA: *70* 2–4
MCA: *77* 2–3
MGM: *72–73*. 2–4
MELODYLAND: *75–76* 2–4
LPs: 10/12-Inch 33rpm
COLUMBIA: *70* 8–12
HARMONY: *73* 5–10
MCA: *77* 5–8
MGM: *71–73* 6–10

STUDENTS, The (Featuring Leroy King)
Singles: 7-Inch
ARGO: *61* 4–6
CHECKER: *58–62* 6–10
CHESS: *73*. 1–3
COLLECTABLES 1–3
NOTE: *58* 80–90
RED TOP: *58* 40–45

STUFF
Singles: 7-Inch
WARNER BROS: *76–80* 1–3

Price Range

  LPs: 10/12-Inch 33rpm
WARNER BROS: *76–80* $5–8

STUFF 'N' RAMJETT
Singles: 7-Inch
CHELSEA: *76*. 2–3

STYLE COUNCIL, The
Singles: 7-Inch
GEFFEN: *84*. 1–3
POLYDOR: *83* 1–3
LPs: 10/12-Inch 33rpm
GEFFEN: *84*. 5–8
POLYDOR: *83* 5–8
  Also see BAND AID
  Also see JAM, The

STYLERS, The
Singles: 7-Inch
GOLDEN CREST: *57–58* 5–8
JUBILEE: *55–57*. 5–8
KICKS: *54*. 75–85

STYLISTICS, The (Featuring Russell Tompkins, Jr.)
Singles: 7-Inch
AMHERST: *85* 1–3
AVCO: *70–76*. 2–4
H&L: *76–79*. 2–3
MERCURY: *79*. 2–3
PHILADELPHIA INT'L:
  82 1–3
STREETWISE: *84–85* 1–3
TSOP: *80–84* 1–3
Picture Sleeves
AVCO: *76* 2–4
LPs: 10/12-Inch 33rpm
AVCO: *71–75*. 8–10
H&L: *78–79* 5–8
MERCURY: *78–79*. 5–8
PHILADELPHIA INT'L:
  82 5–8
STREETWISE: *84–85* 5–8
TSOP: *80–81* 5–8

STYX
Singles: 7-Inch
A&M: *76–84* 1–3
ONYX 2–4
PARAMOUNT: *71–72*. 2–4
RCA VICTOR: *76* 2–3

Price Range

Price Range

WOODEN NICKEL:
72–78 .... $2–4
Picture Sleeves
A&M: 77–84 1–3
LPs: 10/12-Inch 33rpm
A&M (Except picture
discs): 75–84. 5–8
A&M (Picture discs): 79. 10–15
MFSL: 78. 12–15
RCA VICTOR: 72–82 5–8
WOODEN NICKEL:
72–77 8–10
Promotional LPs
A&M (8431; "Styx Radio
Special"): 77. 15–20
A&M (17053; "Styx Radio
Special"): 78. 35–40
Members: Dennis DeYoung; James Young;
Tommy Shaw; John Panozzo; Chuck Panozzo.
Also see DE YOUNG, Dennis
Also see SHAW, Tommy

SUE ANN
Singles: 7-Inch
WARNER BROS: 81 1–3
LPs: 10/12-Inch 33rpm
WARNER BROS: 81 5–8

SUGAR BEARS, The
Singles: 7-Inch
BIG TREE: 72 2–4
LPs: 10/12-Inch 33rpm
BIG TREE: 71 10–12

SUGAR BILLY
Singles: 7-Inch
FAST TRACK: 75 2–3

SUGAR DADDY
Singles: 12-Inch 33/45rpm
BC: 81 4–6
Singles: 7-Inch
BC: 81 1–3

SUGAR PIE & HANK
Singles: 7-Inch
FEDERAL: 55 10–15
Member: Hank Ballard.
Also see BALLARD, Hank

SUGARHILL GANG, The
Singles: 12-Inch 33/45rpm
SUGAR HILL: 79–85 .... $4–6
Singles: 7-Inch
SUGAR HILL: 79–85 1–3
LPs: 10/12-Inch 33rpm
SUGAR HILL: 80–85 5–8
Also see FURIOUS FIVE & THE SUGAR-
HILL GANG, The

SUGARLOAF (Featuring Jerry Corbetta)
Singles: 7-Inch
BRUT: 73–74. 2–4
CLARIDGE: 74–76 2–3
LIBERTY: 70–71 2–4
UNITED ARTISTS: 71 2–4
Picture Sleeves
LIBERTY: 71 2–4
LPs: 10/12-Inch 33rpm
BRUT: 73 8–10
CLARIDGE: 75 8–10
LIBERTY: 70–71 12–15

SULTON, Kasim
Singles: 7-Inch
EMI AMERICA: 82. 1–3
LPs: 10/12-Inch 33rpm
EMI AMERICA: 82. 5–8

SUMMER, Donna
Singles: 12-Inch 33/45rpm
CASABLANCA: 78–80 5–8
GEFFEN: 80–84. 4–6
MERCURY: 83. 4–6
OASIS: 75–76 5–8
Singles: 7-Inch
CASABLANCA: 75–80 1–3
GEFFEN: 80–84. 1–3
OASIS: 75–76 2–4
Picture Sleeves
GEFFEN: 80–84. 1–3
OASIS: 76 1–3
LPs: 10/12-Inch 33rpm
CASABLANCA (Except
20110): 75–80. 5–8
CASABLANCA (20110;
"Once Upon A Time"):
77 12–15
(Promotional issue only.)
GEFFEN: 80–82. 5–8

MERCURY: *83*.................. **$5–8**
OASIS: *75–76* **8–10**
    Also see BROOKLYN DREAMS
    Also see MORODER, Giorgio
    Also see STREISAND, Barbra, & Donna Summer

**SUMMERS, Andy, & Robert Fripp:
see FRIPP, Robert, & Andy Summers**

**SUMMERS, Bill (Bill Summers &
Summers Heat)**
    Singles: 12-Inch 33/45rpm
MCA: *81–84* **4–6**
    Singles: 7-Inch
MCA: *81–84* **1–3**
PRESTIGE: *77–80* **1–3**
    LPs: 10/12-Inch 33rpm
MCA: *81* **5–8**
    Also see HANCOCK, Herbie

SUN
    Singles: 7-Inch
AIR CITY: *84*.................... **1–3**
CAPITOL: *76–82* **1–3**
    Picture Sleeves
CAPITOL: *76–82* **1–3**
    LPs: 10/12-Inch 33rpm
CAPITOL: *77–82* **5–8**

SUN, Joe
    Singles: 7-Inch
A.M.I.: *85* **1–3**
ELEKTRA: *82–83* **1–3**
OVATION: *78–80*................. **1–3**
    LPs: 10/12-Inch 33rpm
ELEKTRA: *82–83* **5–8**
OVATION: *78–80*................. **5–8**

SUNBEAR
    Singles: 7-Inch
SOUL TRAIN: *77* **1–3**
    LPs: 10/12-Inch 33rpm
SOUL TRAIN: *77* **5–8**

SUNDOWN COMPANY, The
    Singles: 7-Inch
POLYDOR: *76* **2–3**

SUNFIRE
    Singles: 12-Inch 33/45rpm
WARNER BROS: *82*.............. **$4–6**
    Singles: 7-Inch
WARNER BROS: *82*.............. **1–3**
    LPs: 10/12-Inch 33rpm
WARNER BROS: *82*.............. **5–8**

**SUNGLOWS, The (Sunny & The
Sunglows; Sunny & The Sunliners;
Sunny Ozuna & The Sunliners)**
    Singles: 7-Inch
DISCO GRANDE: *65* **4–6**
KEY LOC: *66*.................... **3–5**
OKEH: *61* **4–6**
RPR: *69*........................ **2–4**
SUNGLOW: *62–66*................ **3–5**
TEAR DROP: *63–64* **3–5**
    LPs: 10/12-Inch 33rpm
KEY LOC: *66*................... **10–15**
SUNGLOW: *65*.................. **15–20**
TEAR DROP: *63* **20–25**

**SUNNY & THE SUNGLOWS: see
SUNGLOWS, The**

**SUNNY & THE SUNLINERS: see
SUNGLOWS, The**

SUNNYSIDERS, The
    Singles: 7-Inch
KAPP: *55–60*.................... **2–4**
MARQUEE: *55–56*................ **2–4**
NRC: *60*........................ **2–4**
ZENITH: *60* **2–4**
    EPs: 7-Inch 33/45rpm
KAPP: *56* **4–8**
    LPs: 10/12-Inch 33rpm
KAPP: *56* **5–15**

SUNRAYS, The
    Singles: 7-Inch
TOWER: *64–67*................... **5–8**
WARNER BROS: *62*.............. **5–8**
    Picture Sleeves
TOWER: *67*..................... **5–10**
    LPs: 10/12-Inch 33rpm
TOWER: *66*.................... **35–40**
    Member: Rick Henn.

Price Range

SUNRIZE
Singles: 7-Inch
BOARDWALK: *82* **$1–3**

SUNSHINE BAND, The: see KC & THE SUNSHINE BAND

SUNSHINE COMPANY, The
Singles: 7-Inch
IMPERIAL: *67–68* **3–5**
LPs: 10/12-Inch 33rpm
IMPERIAL: *67–68* **10–15**

SUPER MAX
Singles: 7-Inch
VOYAGE: *79* **1–3**

SUPER NATURE
Singles: 12-Inch 33/45rpm
POP ART: *85* **4–6**

SUPERBS, The
Singles: 7-Inch
COLLECTABLES **1–3**
DORE: *64–67* **3–5**
HERITAGE: *61* **4–6**

SUPERIOR MOVEMENT
Singles: 7-Inch
CHYCAGO INT'L: *81–82* **1–3**
LPs: 10/12-Inch 33rpm
CHYCAGO INT'L: *82* **5–8**

SUPERLATIVES, The
Singles: 7-Inch
UPTITE: *66*...................... **3–5**
WESTBOUND: *69* **2–4**

SUPERSAX
LPs: 10/12-Inch 33rpm
CAPITOL: *73–74* **5–10**

SUPERTRAMP
Singles: 12-Inch 33/45rpm
A&M: *82–85* **4–6**
Singles: 7-Inch
A&M: *71–85* **1–3**
Picture Sleeves
A&M: *77–85* **1–3**

Price Range

LPs: 10/12-Inch 33rpm
A&M: *70–85* **$8–12**
MFSL: *78*...................... **12–15**
Members: Rick Davies; Roger Hodgson; Doug Thomson; Bob Benberg; John Helliwell.
Also see HODGSON, Roger

SUPREMES, The
Singles: 12-Inch 33/45rpm
MOTOWN: *81*................... **6–10**
Singles: 7-Inch
GEORGE ALEXANDER
INC. (1079; "The Only
Time I'm Happy"): *65* **20–30**
(Special premium record, contains a Supremes interview on the flip side.)
MOTOWN (400 series) **1–3**
MOTOWN (1027; "Your
Heart Belongs To Me"):
62 .... **10–15**
MOTOWN (1034; "Let Me
Go The Right Way"): *62* **8–10**
MOTOWN (1040; "My
Heart Can't Take It No
More"): *63* **20–25**
MOTOWN (1044; "A
Breath Taking, First
Sight Soul Shaking, One
Night Love Love
Making, Next Day Heart
Breaking Guy"): *63*............ **20-25**
MOTOWN (1044; "A
Breath Taking Guy"): *63* **4–6**
(Reissue, using the shorter title.)
MOTOWN (1051; "When
The Lovelight Starts
Shining Through His
Eyes"): *63* **4-6**
MOTOWN (1054; "Run,
Run, Run): *64* **4–6**
MOTOWN (1060 through
1156): *64–69*.................... **3–5**
TAMLA (54038; "I Want
A Guy"): *61*................... **60–75**
TAMLA (54045; "Buttered
Popcorn"): *61*................ **35–45**
Picture Sleeves
MOTOWN (1027; "Your
Heart Belongs To Me"):
62 .... **25–35**

Price Range

MOTOWN (1074 through
  1156): *64–69* **$4–6**
  (Not ALL of the numbers in this series were
  issued with picture sleeves.)

Promotional Singles

MOTOWN (1027 through
  1054): *62–64* **10–15**
MOTOWN (1060 through
  1156): *64–69* **5–8**

EPs: 7-Inch 33/45rpm

MOTOWN: *64* **20–25**

LPs: 10/12-Inch 33rpm

MOTOWN (100 & 200
  series): *80–82* **5–8**
MOTOWN (606; "Meet
  The Supremes"): *63* **100–125**
  (Front cover pictures each member sitting on a
  chair.)
MOTOWN (606; "Meet
  The Supremes"): *63* **30–35**
  (Front cover pictures the head of each group
  member.)
MOTOWN (621 through
  638): *64–65* **20–25**
MOTOWN (643 through
  708): *66–70* **15–20**
MOTOWN (794;
  "Anthology"): *74* **12–15**
MOTOWN (900 series): *75* **6–10**
MOTOWN (5000 series):
  83–84 .... **6–10**
NATURAL RESOURCES:
  78 .... **6–10**
   Members: Diana Ross; Mary Wilson; Florence
   Ballard; Cindy Birdsong.
   Also see PRIMETTES, The
   Also see ROSS, Diana
   Also see WILSON, Mary

SUPREMES, The

Singles: 7-Inch

MOTOWN (400 series) **1–3**
MOTOWN (1162 through
  1415): *70–77* **2–4**

LPs: 10/12-Inch 33rpm

MOTOWN (102;
  "Touch"): *71* **15–20**
  (An open-end interview LP. Price includes
  script. Promotional issue only.)
MOTOWN (700 & 800
  series): *70–78* **8–12**

Price Range

Members: Jean Terrell; Mary Wilson; Cindy
Birdsong.
Also see PAYNE, Scherrie
Also see TERRELL, Jean

SUPREMES, The, & The Four Tops

Singles: 7-Inch

MOTOWN (400 series) **$1–3**
MOTOWN (1100 series):
  70–71 .... **2–4**

LPs: 10/12-Inch 33rpm

MOTOWN (100 series): *82* **5–8**
MOTOWN (700 series):
  70–71 .... **10–12**
  Also see FOUR TOPS, The

SUPREMES, The, & The
Temptations

Singles: 7-Inch

MOTOWN (400 series) **1–3**
MOTOWN (1100 series):
  68–69 .... **3–5**

Picture Sleeves

MOTOWN: *68* **3–5**

LPs: 10/12-Inch 33rpm

MOTOWN (100 series): *82* **5–8**
MOTOWN (600 series):
  68–69 .... **10–12**
  Also see SUPREMES, The
  Also see TEMPTATIONS, The

SURFACE

Singles: 12-Inch 33/45rpm

SALSOUL: *83* **4–6**

Price Range

Singles: 7-Inch
SALSOUL: *83* **$1–3**

SURFARIS, The
Singles: 7-Inch
ABC: *74* **1–3**
CHANCELLOR: *63* **5–8**
DFS: *63* **50–75**
DECCA: *63–66* **5–8**
DEL-FI: *63* **5–8**
DOT (Except 144 &
  16479): *65–67* **5–8**
DOT (144; "Wipe Out"):
  66 . . . . **3–5**
DOT (16479; "Wipe Out"):
  63 . . . . **4–6**
FELSTED: *64* **5–8**
MCA **1–3**
PRINCESS: *63* **20–25**
REGANO: *63* **5–8**
Promotional Singles
DOT (144; "Wipe Out" -
  colored vinyl): *66* **25–30**
LPs: 10/12-Inch 33rpm
DECCA: *63–65* **25–30**
DOT (535; "Wipe Out"):
  63 . . . . **30–35**
  (Front cover simply reads "Wipe Out & Surfer
  Joe.")
DOT (535; "Wipe Out"):
  63 . . . . **25–30**
  (Front cover reads "Wipe Out & Surfer Joe
  And Other Popular selections By Other Instru-
  mental Groups." The Surfaris are heard only on
  "Wipe Out" & "Surfer Joe." Other tracks on
  this LP are by The Challengers.)
DIPLOMAT **12–15**
PICKWICK: *78* **8–10**
  Also see BEACH BOYS, The

SURFARIS, The / The Biscaynes
Singles: 7-Inch
NORTHRIDGE: *63* **8–10**
REPRISE: *63* **4–6**

SURRETT, Alfonzo
Singles: 7-Inch
MCA: *80* **1–3**

SURVIVOR
Singles: 12-Inch 33/45rpm
SCOTTI BROS: *79–85* **4–6**

Price Range

Singles: 7-Inch
CASABLANCA: *84* **$1–3**
SCOTTI BROS: *80–85* **1–3**
LPs: 10/12-Inch 33rpm
SCOTTI BROS: *79–84* **5–8**
Promotional LPs
SCOTTI BROS (362;
  "Rebel Girl"): *80* **10–12**
  Members: Jim Peterik & Jim Jameson.
  Also see IDES OF MARCH, The

SURVIVORS, The
Singles: 7-Inch
CAPITOL: *64* **90–100**
  Members: Brian Wilson; Dave Nowlen; Bob
  Norberg; Rich Peterson.
  Also see BEACH BOYS, The

SUSAN
Singles: 7-Inch
RCA VICTOR: *79* **1–3**
SCEPTER: *70* **2–4**
LPs: 10/12-Inch 33rpm
RCA VICTOR: *79* **5–8**

SUTCH, Lord: see LORD SUTCH

SUTHERLAND BROTHERS, The
(The Sutherland Brothers & Quiver)
Singles: 7-Inch
COLUMBIA: *75–79* **2–3**
ISLAND: *72–73* **2–4**
LPs: 10/12-Inch 33rpm
COLUMBIA: *76* **8–10**
ISLAND: *72–74* **8–10**

SUTTON, Glenn
Singles: 7-Inch
ABC: *73* **2–3**
EPIC: *67* **2–4**
MGM: *64–65* **3–5**
MERCURY: *78–82* **1–3**
LPs: 10/12-Inch 33rpm
MERCURY: *79* **5–8**
  Also see KELLUM, Murray / Glenn Sutton

SUTTON, Mike & Brenda
Singles: 7-Inch
SAM: *81–82* **1–3**

Price Range   *Price Range*

SUTTONS, The
Singles: 7-Inch
ROCSHIRE: *84* **$1–3**
LPs: 10/12-Inch 33rpm
ROCSHIRE: *84* **5–8**

SUZY & THE RED STRIPES (Linda McCartney & Wings)
Singles: 12-Inch 33/45rpm
EPIC: *77* **25–30**
(Promotional issue only.)
Singles: 7-Inch
EPIC (Black vinyl): *77* **3–5**
EPIC (Colored vinyl): *77* **20–25**
(Promotional issue only.)
Also see McCARTNEY, Paul

SUZY Q
Singles: 7-Inch
ATLANTIC: *81* **1–3**

SWALLOWS, The
Singles: 7-Inch
AFTER HOURS: *54* **225–250**
GUSTO **1–3**
KING (4458; "Will You
Be Mine"): *51* **300–325**
KING (4466; "Since
You've Been Away"): *51* **375–400**
KING (4501; "Eternally" -
black vinyl): *51* **200–225**
KING (4501; "Eternally" -
colored vinyl): *51* **275–300**
KING (4515; "Tell Me
Why"): *51* **200–225**
(Based on other King numbers that have been
found on colored vinyl, this issue should have
been pressed on colored as well as black, but we
can't yet confirm their existence.)
KING (4525; "Beside
You"): *52* **90–100**
KING (4533; "I Only
Have Eyes For You"):
52 .... **150–175**
KING (4579; "Where Do I
Go From Here"): *52* **125–150**
KING (4612; "Laugh"): *53* **75–90**
KING (4632; "Nobody's
Lovin' Me"): *53* **75–90**
KING (4656; "Trust Me"):
53 .... **75–90**

KING (4676; "I'll Be
Waiting"): *53* **$100–125**
Members: Junior Denby; Ed Rich; Earl Hurley;
Fred Johnson; Norris Mack; Dee Bailey; Buddy
Bailey; Irving Turner; Al France; Cal Kollette.

SWALLOWS, The
Singles: 7-Inch
FEDERAL: *58* **6–10**

SWAMP DOGG (Swamp Dogg With The Riders Of The New Funk)
Singles: 7-Inch
CANYON: *70* **2–4**
CREAM: *73* **2–4**
MUSICOR: *77* **2–3**
SWAMP DOGG: *72* **2–4**
LPs: 10/12-Inch 33rpm
CANYON: *70* **10–15**
CHARLY **5–8**
CREAM: *72* **8–10**
ELEKTRA: *71* **8–10**
ISLAND: *73* **8–10**
MUSICOR: *77* **5–8**
TAKOMA: *81* **5–8**
WIZARD: *78* **5–8**

SWAN, Billy
Singles: 7-Inch
A&M: *78–79* **2–3**
COLUMBIA: *76–77* **2–3**
EPIC: *81–83* **1–3**
MGM: *68* **2–4**
MONUMENT: *66–76* **2–4**
RISING SONS: *67* **2–4**
LPs: 10/12-Inch 33rpm
A&M: *78* **5–8**
COLUMBIA/
MONUMENT: *77* **5–8**
EPIC: *81* **5–8**
MONUMENT: *74–78* **6–10**

SWANN, Bettye
Singles: 7-Inch
A-BET: *72–74* **2–4**
ATLANTIC: *72–76* **2–4**
BIG TREE **2–3**
CAPITOL: *68–70* **2–4**
FAME: *71* **2–4**
MONEY: *65–67* **3–5**

Price Range

Picture Sleeves
CAPITOL: *69* $2–4
LPs: 10/12-Inch 33rpm
A-BET: *72* 8–10
ATLANTIC: *72–75* 8–10
CAPITOL: *69* 10–12
MONEY: *67* 10–15
Also see DEES, Sam, & Bettye Swann

SWANS, The
Singles: 7-Inch
CAMEO: *64* 10–15
SWAN: *63* 4–6

SWANSON, Brad, & His Whispering Organ
LPs: 10/12-Inch 33rpm
THUNDERBIRD: *69.* 5–10

SWEAT BAND, The
Singles: 7-Inch
UNCLE JAM: *80* 1–3
LPs: 10/12-Inch 33rpm
UNCLE JAM: *80* 5–8
Also see BOOTSY'S RUBBER BAND

SWEATHOG
Singles: 7-Inch
COLUMBIA: *71* 2–4
LPs: 10/12-Inch 33rpm
COLUMBIA: *71–72* 8–10

SWEENEY, Jimmy
Singles: 7-Inch
BUCKLEY: *62* 3–5
COLUMBIA: *59* 3–5

SWEENY TODD (Featuring Bryan Guy Adams)
Singles: 7-Inch
LONDON: *76* 2–4
Also see GILDER, Nick

SWEET
Singles: 7-Inch
BELL: *71–74* 2–4
CAPITOL: *75–79* 2–3
LPs: 10/12-Inch 33rpm
BELL: *73* 10–12
CAPITOL (Except 16000
series): *75–79* 8–10

CAPITOL (16000 series):
80–82 . . . . $5–8
KORY: *77* 8–10
Promotional LPs
CAPITOL (8849; "Short &
Sweet"): *78.* 20–25
CAPITOL (11129; "Cut
Above The Rest"): *79.* 40–50
(Boxed set, containing the LP, 8-track & cassette issues of "Cut Above The Rest," plus a group photo & biography.)

SWEET, Rachel
Singles: 12-Inch 33/45rpm
STIFF/COLUMBIA: *79* 10–15
(Promotional issue only.)
Singles: 7-Inch
COLUMBIA: *81–83* 1–3
DERRICK: *76–78.* 2–4
STIFF/COLUMBIA:
79–80 1–3
LPs: 10/12-Inch 33rpm
COLUMBIA: *81–82* 5–8
STIFF/COLUMBIA:
79–80 5–8
Also see SMITH, Rex, & Rachel Sweet

SWEET CREAM
Singles: 12-Inch 33/45rpm
SHADYBROOK: *78.* 4–6
Singles: 7-Inch
SHADYBROOK: *78.* 2–3

SWEET DREAMS
Singles: 7-Inch
ABC: *74.* 2–4

SWEET G.
Singles: 12-Inch 33/45rpm
FEVER: *83* 4–6

SWEET INSPIRATIONS, The
Singles: 12-Inch 33/45rpm
RSO: *79* 4–6
Singles: 7-Inch
ATLANTIC: *67–71* 2–4
CARIBOU: *77.* 2–3
RSO: *79* 2–3
STAX: *73–74.* 2–4
LPs: 10/12-Inch 33rpm
ATLANTIC: *68–70* 10–12

Price Range

RSO: *79* **$5–8**
STAX: *73* **8–10**
   Members: Cissy Houston; Sylvia Shemwell;
   Myrna Smith; Estelle Brown.
   Also see FRANKLIN, Aretha
   Also see HOUSTON, Cissy
   Also see PRESLEY, Elvis
   Also see RASCALS, The

SWEET MUSIC
Singles: 7-Inch
WAND: *76* **2–3**

SWEET SENSATION
Singles: 7-Inch
PYE: *74–75* **2–3**
LPs: 10/12-Inch 33rpm
PYE: *75* **6–10**

SWEET THUNDER
Singles: 7-Inch
FANTASY: *79* **1–3**
WMOT: *79* **1–3**
LPs: 10/12-Inch 33rpm
WMOT: *79* **5–8**

SWEETWATER
Singles: 7-Inch
REPRISE: *68–71* **3–5**
LPs: 10/12-Inch 33rpm
REPRISE: *68–71* **10–15**

SWINGIN' MEDALLIONS, The
Singles: 7-Inch
CAPITOL: *68* **3–5**
COLLECTABLES **1–3**
DOT: *65* **5–8**
4 SALE: *66* **12–15**
1-2-3: *70* **2–4**
SMASH: *66–67* **4–6**
LPs: 10/12-Inch 33rpm
SMASH: *66* **25–30**
   Also see PIECES OF EIGHT, The

SWINGING BLUE JEANS, The
Singles: 7-Inch
IMPERIAL: *64–67* **5–8**
LPs: 10/12-Inch 33rpm
IMPERIAL: *64* **25–35**
LIBERTY: *82* **5–8**

Price Range

SWINGLE SINGERS, The
LPs: 10/12-Inch 33rpm
COLUMBIA: *76* **$4–6**
PHILIPS: *63–72* **4–10**

SWISS MOVEMENT
Singles: 7-Inch
CASABLANCA: *74* **2–4**
RCA VICTOR: *73* **2–4**
LPs: 10/12-Inch 33rpm
RCA VICTOR: *73* **8–12**

SWITCH
Singles: 7-Inch
GORDY: *78–82* **1–3**
TOTAL EXPERIENCE:
  82–84 .... **1–3**
LPs: 10/12-Inch 33rpm
GORDY: *78–81* **5–8**
TOTAL EXPERIENCE:
  82–84 .... **5–8**

SYKES, Keith
Singles: 7-Inch
BACKSTREET: *80* **1–3**
LPs: 10/12-Inch 33rpm
BACKSTREET: *80* **5–8**
MIDLAND INT'L: *77* **8–10**
VANGUARD: *70–71* **10–12**

SYLVAIN SYLVAIN
Singles: 7-Inch
RCA VICTOR: *79* **2–3**
LPs: 10/12-Inch 33rpm
RCA VICTOR: *79* **5–8**
   Also see NEW YORK DOLLS, The

SYLVERS, The
Singles: 12-Inch 33/45rpm
CASABLANCA: *79* **4–6**
GEFFEN: *84–85* **4–6**
SOLAR: *81–82* **4–6**
Singles: 7-Inch
CAPITOL: *75–78* **2–3**
CASABLANCA: *78–79* **1–3**
GEFFEN: *84–85* **1–3**
MGM: *72–74* **2–3**
PRIDE: *72–73* **2–4**
SOLAR: *81–82* **1–3**
VERVE: *71* **2–4**

Price Range

LPs: 10/12-Inch 33rpm
CAPITOL: 75–78 .... $5–8
CASABLANCA: 78–79 5–8
CONCEPT: 81 5–8
GEFFEN: 84 5–8
MGM: 72–74 8–10
PRIDE: 72–73 8–10
SOLAR: 81 5–8
Members: Foster Sylvers; Pay Sylvers; Edmund Sylvers; Angie Sylvers.

SYLVERS, Edmund
Singles: 7-Inch
CASABLANCA: 80 1–3
LPs: 10/12-Inch 33rpm
CASABLANCA: 80 5–8
Also see SYLVERS, The

SYLVERS, Foster
Singles: 7-Inch
MGM: 73 2–3
PRIDE: 73 2–4
LPs: 10/12-Inch 33rpm
MGM: 74 6–10
PRIDE: 73 8–10
Also see SYLVERS, The

SYLVESTER (Sylvester James)
Singles: 12-Inch 33/45rpm
FANTASY: 78–79 4–6
MEGATONE: 83–85 4–6
Singles: 7-Inch
FANTASY: 78–79 1–3
HONEY: 80–81 1–3
MEGATONE: 83–85 1–3
LPs: 10/12-Inch 33rpm
FANTASY: 78–81 5–8
HONEY: 80–81 5–8
MEGATONE: 83–84 5–8

SLYLVESTER, Tony, & The New Ingredient
Singles: 7-Inch
MERCURY: 76 2–3

SYLVIA (Sylvia Vanderpool; Sylvia Robinson)
Singles: 12-Inch 33/45rpm
SUGARHILL: 82 4–6
VIBRATION: 77 4–6

Singles: 7-Inch
ALL PLATINUM: 74 .... $2–4
STANG: 70 2–4
SUGARHILL: 81 1–3
VIBRATION: 73–78 2–4
LPs: 10/12-Inch 33rpm
SUGARHILL: 81 5–8
VIBRATION: 73–78 6–10
Also see LITTLE SYLVIA
Also see MICKEY & SYLVIA
Also see SYLVIA & THE MOMENTS
Also see SYLVIA & RALFI PAGAN
Also see TURNER, Ike & Tina

SYLVIA (Sylvia Kirby Allen)
Singles: 7-Inch
RCA VICTOR: 81–85 1–3
Picture Sleeves
RCA VICTOR: 81–85 .... INC
LPs: 10/12-Inch 33rpm
RCA VICTOR: 81–85 5–8

SYLVIA & THE MOMENTS
Singles: 7-Inch
ALL PLATINUM: 74 2–4
Also see MOMENTS, The
Also see SYLVIA (Sylvia Vanderpool; Sylvia Robinson)

SYLVIA & RALFI PAGAN
Singles: 7-Inch
VIBRATION: 73 2–4
Also see SYLVIA (Sylvia Vanderpool; Sylvia Robinson)

SYMBA
Singles: 7-Inch
VENTURE: 80 1–3

SYMBOL 8
Singles: 7-Inch
SHOCK: 77–78 2–3

SYMS, Sylvia
Singles: 7-Inch
ATLANTIC: 52–53 3–6
COLUMBIA: 59–65 2–4
DECCA: 56–64 2–5
PRESTIGE: 67 2–3
RORI: 62 2–4
EPs: 7-Inch 33/45rpm
ATLANTIC: 56 5–15

Price Range

DECCA: *55* **$5–15**

LPs: 10/12-Inch 33rpm
A&M: *78* **5–8**
ATLANTIC (137; "Songs
By Sylvia Syms"): *53* **50–75**
(10-Inch LPs.)
ATLANTIC (1243; "Songs
By Sylvia Syms"): *56* **20–40**
(With Atlantic logo at top of label.)
ATLANTIC (1243; "Songs
By Sylvia Syms"): *60* **15–25**
(With Atlantic logo on side of label.)
ATLANTIC (18000 series):
76 . . . . **5–8**
COLUMBIA: *60* **15–25**
DECCA: *55* **20–40**
KAPP: *61* **10–20**
MOVIETONE: *67.* **10–15**
PRESTIGE: *65–67* **10–25**
REPRISE: *82.* **5–8**
20TH CENTURY-FOX:
64 . . . . **10–20**
VERSION: *54* **20–40**
(10-Inch LPs.)

SYNDICATE OF SOUND, The
Singles: 7-Inch
BELL: *66–67.* **3–5**
BUDDAH: *70* **2–4**
CAPITOL: *69* **2–4**
DEL-FI: *66* **4–6**
HUSH: *66* **8–10**
SCARLET: *66.* **8–10**

LPs: 10/12-Inch 33rpm
BELL: *66* **25–30**

SYNERGY
Singles: 7-Inch
PASSPORT: *76.* **2–3**

LPs: 10/12-Inch 33rpm
PASSPORT (Black vinyl):
75–84 . . . . **5–8**
PASSPORT (Clear vinyl):
78 . . . . **8–10**

SYREETA (Syreeta Wright)
Singles: 7-Inch
MOTOWN: *74–80.* **1–3**
MOWEST: *72* **2–4**
TAMLA: *80–83.* **2–3**

Price Range

LPs: 10/12-Inch 33rpm
MOTOWN: *74–77.* **$8–10**
TAMLA: *77–81.* **5–8**
Also see PRESTON, Billy, & Syreeta

SYSTEM, The
Singles: 12-Inch 33/45rpm
MIRAGE: *83–85.* **4–6**

Singles: 7-Inch
MIRAGE: *83–85.* **1–3**

LPs: 10/12-Inch 33rpm
MIRAGE: *83–85.* **5–8**

SZABO, Gabor
Singles: 7-Inch
BLUE THUMB: *70* **2–3**
BUDDAH: *70* **2–3**
CTI: *73.* **1–3**
IMPULSE: *66–68* **2–4**
MERCURY: *76–77.* **1–3**
REPRISE: *73.* **1–3**
SKYE: *68–70.* **2–3**

LPs: 10/12-Inch 33rpm
BLUE THUMB: *70* **8–12**
BUDDAH: *70* **8–12**
CTI: *73–74.* **8–12**
IMPULSE: *66–70* **10–20**
MCA: *82* **5–8**
MERCURY: *76.* **5–10**
SALVATION: *75* **5–10**
SKYE: *68–70.* **8–12**
Also see HORNE, Lena, & Gabor Szabo
Also see WOMACK, Bobby, & Gabor Szabo

T

TFO
Singles: 7-Inch
VENTURE: *80–81* **1–3**

T.H.P. ORCHESTRA, The
Singles: 7-Inch
ATLANTIC: *79* **1–3**
BUTTERFLY: *77–78* **2–3**

LPs: 10/12-Inch 33rpm
ATLANTIC: *79* **5–8**
BUTTERFLY: *77.* **8–10**

Price Range

TKO
Singles: 7-Inch
INFINITY: 79.................... $2–3
LPs: 10/12-Inch 33rpm
INFINITY: 79.................... 5–8

T.M.G.
Singles: 7-Inch
ATCO: 79 2–3
LPs: 10/12-Inch 33rpm
ATCO: 79 5–8

TNT BAND, The
Singles: 7-Inch
COTIQUE: 69.................... 2–5

T.S.U. TORONADOS, The
Singles: 7-Inch
ATLANTIC: 68–69 2–4
VOLT: 69–70.................... 2–4

TTF (Today, Tomorrow, Forever)
Singles: 7-Inch
CURTOM: 80.................... 1–3
GOLD COAST: 81................ 1–3
RSO: 80 1–3
LPs: 10/12-Inch 33rpm
GOLD COAST: 81................ 5–8

T.Z.
Singles: 12-Inch 33/45rpm
STREET SOUND: 83.............. 4–6

TA MARA & THE SEEN
Singles: 12-Inch 33/45rpm
A&M: 85 4–6
Singles: 7-Inch
A&M: 85 1–3
LPs: 10/12-Inch 33rpm
A&M: 85 5–8

TA'BOO
Singles: 12-Inch 33/45rpm
ACME: 84 4–6

TACO (Taco Ockerse)
Singles: 12-Inch 33/45rpm
RCA VICTOR: 83–84 4–6
Singles: 7-Inch
RCA VICTOR: 83–84 1–3

Price Range

LPs: 10/12-Inch 33rpm
RCA VICTOR: 83–84 .... $5–8

TAJ MAHAL
Singles: 7-Inch
COLUMBIA (10000
  series): 75..................... 2–3
COLUMBIA (44000
  series): 67–69.................. 3–5
COLUMBIA (45000
  series): 69–74.................. 2–4
Picture Sleeves
COLUMBIA: 67.................. 3–5
LPs: 10/12-Inch 33rpm
COLUMBIA: 68–81............... 6–12
WARNER BROS: 77.............. 5–10
Also see SPRINGSTEEN, Bruce / Albert
Hammond / Loudon Wainwright, III /
Taj Mahal

TAKA BOOM: see BOOM, Taka

TALK TALK
Singles: 12-Inch 33/45rpm
EMI AMERICA: 82–84............. 4–6
Singles: 7-Inch
EMI AMERICA: 82–84............. 1–3
LPs: 10/12-Inch 33rpm
EMI AMERICA: 82–84............. 5–8

TALKING HEADS, The (Featuring David Byrne)
Singles: 12-Inch 33/45rpm
SIRE: 79–85 4–6
Singles: 7-Inch
SIRE: 77–85 1–3
Picture Sleeves
SIRE: 78–85 1–3
LPs: 10/12-Inch 33rpm
SIRE: 77–85 5–8
WARNER BROS (104;
  "Live On Tour"): 79............ 10–15
(Promotional issue only.)
Also see BYRNE, David

TAMPA RED (Hudson Whittaker)
Singles: 7-Inch
RCA VICTOR (47-4000 &
  47-5000 series): 51–54.......... 15–20
RCA VICTOR (50-0000
  series): 49–51.................. 20–30

Price Range

LPs: 10/12-Inch 33rpm
BLUEBIRD: *75*.................. **$10–15**
BLUES CLASSICS.................. **5–8**
PRESTIGE
   BLUESVILLE: *61–62*.......... **20–25**
   YAZOO **10–12**

TAMS, The
Singles: 7-Inch
MINK (22; "Memory
   Lane"): *59* **8–10**
   ("Memory Lane" was first issued, in 1959,
   showing the group as The Stereos. The same
   track was again issued in 1963, shown as by The
   Tams and then by The Hippies.)
PARKWAY (863;
   "Memory Lane"): *63*............. **4–8**
   Also see HIPPIES, The / Reggie Harrison
   Also see STEREOS, The

TAMS, The
Singles: 7-Inch
ABC: *68–73*...................... **2–4**
ABC-PARAMOUNT:
   63–64 .... **3–5**
APT: *72* **2–4**
ARLEN: *62–63* **4–6**
CAPITOL: *71* **2–4**
COLLECTABLES **1–3**
COMPLEAT: *83*................... **1–3**
DUNHILL: *71*.................... **2–4**
GENERAL AMERICAN:
   62 .... **5–8**
GUSTO: *80* **1–3**
KING: *65* **3–5**
MCA............................ **1–3**
ROULETTE **1–3**
SOUTH: *73* **2–4**
SWAN: *60* **5–8**
LPs: 10/12-Inch 33rpm
ABC: *67–69*.................... **10–12**
ABC-PARAMOUNT: *64*......... **15–20**
BRYLEN: *84*..................... **5–8**
CAPITOL: *79* **5–8**
COMPLEAT: *83*.................. **5–8**
1-2-3: *70*....................... **8–10**
SOUNDS SOUTH: *77* **8–10**

TANEGA, Norma
Singles: 7-Inch
ABC: *73*......................... **2–4**

Price Range

ERIC **$1–3**
NEW VOICE: *66–67* **3–5**
VIRGO: *73* **1–3**
LPs: 10/12-Inch 33rpm
NEW VOICE: *66* **15–20**

TANGERINE DREAM
Singles: 7-Inch
EMI AMERICA: *84*............... **1–3**
VIRGIN: *75–77*................... **2–3**
LPs: 10/12-Inch 33rpm
EMI AMERICA: *84*............... **5–8**
ELEKTRA: *81* **5–8**
MCA: *77* **5–8**
VIRGIN: *74–77*................. **8–12**
   Members: Peter Baumann; Chris Franks; Ed
   Froese.
   Also see BAUMANN, Peter

TANNER, Gary
Singles: 7-Inch
20TH CENTURY-FOX:
   78 .... **2–3**

TANNER, Marc, Band
Singles: 7-Inch
ELEKTRA: *79* **1–3**
PRIVATE I....................... **2–3**
LPs: 10/12-Inch 33rpm
ELEKTRA: *78–80* **5–8**
PRIVATE I....................... **5–8**

TANTRUM
Singles: 7-Inch
OVATION: *79*.................... **1–3**
LPs: 10/12-Inch 33rpm
OVATION: *79*.................... **5–8**

TARHEEL SLIM (Alden Bunn)
Singles: 7-Inch
FIRE: *59–60* **8–10**
FURY: *59* **10–15**
   Also see BUNN, Allen
   Also see LOVERS, The

TARHEEL SLIM & LITTLE ANN
(Slim & Ann; Slim & Little Ann;
Tarheel Slim & Lil' Annie)
Singles: 7-Inch
ATCO: *63* **4–6**
FIRE: *59–62* **8–10**

PORT: 65. . . . . **$3–5**
Also see TARHEEL SLIM

TARNEY-SPENCER BAND, The
Singles: 7-Inch
A&M: 78–81 . . . . **1–3**
PRIVATE STOCK: 76. . . . . **2–3**
LPs: 10/12-Inch 33rpm
A&M: 79 . . . . **5–8**
Members: Alan Tarney; Trevor Spencer.

TARRIERS, The
Singles: 7-Inch
DECCA: 63–64. . . . . **2–4**
GLORY: 56. . . . . **3–6**
UNITED ARTISTS: 59. . . . . **2–5**
LPs: 10/12-Inch 33rpm
ATLANTIC: 60 . . . . **15–20**
DECCA: 62–64. . . . . **10–15**
GLORY: 57. **25–35**
KAPP: 63 . . . . **10–15**
UNITED ARTISTS: 59. . . . . **15–20**
Members: Erik Darling; Alan Arkin; Bob
Carey.
Also see MARTIN, Vince
Also see ROOFTOP SINGERS, The

TASSELS, The
Singles: 7-Inch
AMY: 66 . . . . **3–5**
MADISON: 59 . . . . **4–6**

TASTE (With Rory Gallagher)
Singles: 7-Inch
ATCO: 69–70. **2–4**
LPs: 10/12-Inch 33rpm
ATCO: 69–70. . . . . **10–15**
Also see GALLAGHER, Rory

TASTE OF HONEY, A
Singles: 12-Inch 33/45rpm
CAPITOL (Except 9572):
78–79 . . . . **4–6**
CAPITOL (9572;
"Sukiyaki"): 80 . . . . **8–10**
(Fan shaped disc. Promotional issue only.)
MCA: 84 . . . . **4–6**
Singles: 7-Inch
CAPITOL: 78–82 . . . . **1–3**
MCA: 84 . . . . **1–3**
Picture Sleeves
CAPITOL: 78–82 . . . . **INC**

LPs: 10/12-Inch 33rpm
CAPITOL: 78–82 . . . . **$5–8**
Members: Janice Johnson; Hazel Payne.

TATE, Howard
Singles: 7-Inch
TURNTABLE: 69–70. . . . . **2–4**
VERVE: 66–68 . . . . **3–5**
LPs: 10/12-Inch 33rpm
ATLANTIC: 69 . . . . **10–15**
TURNTABLE. **8–10**
VERVE: 67–68 . . . . **10–15**

TATE, Tommy
Singles: 7-Inch
KOKO: 72–76. **2–4**
OKEH: 66 . . . . **3–5**

TAVARES
Singles: 12-Inch 33/45rpm
CAPITOL: 77–79 . . . . **4–6**
RCA VICTOR: 82–84 . . . . **4–6**
Singles: 7-Inch
CAPITOL: 73–80 . . . . **1–3**
RCA VICTOR: 82–84 . . . . **1–3**
LPs: 10/12-Inch 33rpm
CAPITOL: 73–81 . . . . **8–10**
RCA VICTOR: 82–83 . . . . **5–8**

TAXXI
Singles: 7-Inch
FANTASY: 82. **1–3**
LPs: 10/12-Inch 33rpm
FANTASY: 82. **5–8**
MCA: 85 . . . . **5–8**

TAYLOR, Alex
Singles: 7-Inch
BANG: 78–79 . . . . **1–3**
CAPRICORN: 71. . . . . **2–4**
DUNHILL: 74. **2–4**
LPs: 10/12-Inch 33rpm
CAPRICORN: 71. . . . . **8–10**
DUNHILL: 74. . . . . **8–10**

TAYLOR, Austin
Singles: 7-Inch
LAURIE: 60–61 . . . . **4–6**

Price Range

TAYLOR, B.E.
Singles: 12-Inch 33/45rpm
EPIC: *84* **$4–6**
Singles: 7-Inch
EPIC: *84* **1–3**
MCA: *83–84* **1–3**
LPs: 10/12-Inch 33rpm
MCA: *83* **5–8**

TAYLOR, Bobby (Bobby Taylor & The Vancouvers)
Singles: 7-Inch
BUDDAH: *72* **2–4**
GORDY: *68–69* **3–5**
INTEGRA: *68* **3–5**
PLAYBOY: *75* **2-4**
SUNFLOWER: *72* **2–4**
TOMMY: *73* **2–4**
LPs: 10/12-Inch 33rpm
GORDY: *68–69* **10–15**

TAYLOR, Debbie
Singles: 7-Inch
ARISTA: *75–76* **2–3**
DECCA: *68* **2–4**
GWP: *69* **2–4**
POLYDOR: *74* **2–4**
TODAY: *72* **2–4**
LPs: 10/12-Inch 33rpm
TODAY: *72* **6–10**

TAYLOR, Felice
Singles: 7-Inch
KENT: *68* **3–5**
MUSTANG: *67* **3–5**

TAYLOR, Gloria
Singles: 7-Inch
COLUMBIA: *74* **2–4**
GLO-WHIZ: *69* **3–5**
SILVER FOX: *69* **2–4**

TAYLOR, James (James Taylor & The Original Flying Machine)
Singles: 7-Inch
APPLE: *69–70* **2–4**
CAPITOL: *76* **2–3**
COLUMBIA: *77–85* **1–3**
EUPHORIA: *71* **2–4**
WARNER BROS: *70–76* **2–4**

Price Range

LPs: 10/12-Inch 33rpm
APPLE: *69* **$10–15**
COLUMBIA: *77* **8–10**
EUPHORIA: *71* **12–15**
TRI: *73* **8–10**
WARNER BROS: *70–77* **8–10**
　　Also see DOOBIE BROTHERS, The, James Hall & James Taylor
　　Also see DOOBIE BROTHERS, The / Kate Taylor & The Simon-Taylor Family
　　Also see FLYING MACHINE, The
　　Also see GARFUNKEL, Art
　　Also see HALL, James, & James Taylor
　　Also see SIMON, Carly, & James Taylor

TAYLOR, James, & J.D. Souther
Singles: 7-Inch
COLUMBIA: *81* **1–3**
　　Also see SOUTHER, J.D.
　　Also see TAYLOR, James

TAYLOR, Johnnie (Johnny Taylor)
Singles: 7-Inch
BEVERLY GLEN: *82* **1–3**
COLUMBIA: *76–80* **1–3**
DERBY: *63–64* **3–5**
MALACO: *83–85* **1–3**
RCA VICTOR: *77* **2–3**
SAR: *61–65* **3–5**
STAX: *66–77* **2–4**
LPs: 10/12-Inch 33rpm
BEVERLY GLEN: *82* **5–8**
COLUMBIA: *76–81* **6–10**
MALACO: *83* **5–8**
RCA VICTOR: *77* **8–10**
STAX: *67–83* **6–10**

TAYLOR, Johnnie, & Carla Thomas
Singles: 7-Inch
STAX: *69* **2–4**
　　Also see TAYLOR, Johnnie
　　Also see THOMAS, Carla

TAYLOR, Kate
Singles: 7-Inch
COLUMBIA: *77–79* **2–3**
COTILLION: *71* **2–4**
LPs: 10/12-Inch 33rpm
COLUMBIA: *78–79* **5–8**
COTILLION: *71* **8–10**
　　Also see DOOBIE BROTHERS, The / Kate Taylor & The Simon-Taylor Family

TAYLOR, Koko (Cocoa Taylor)
Singles: 7-Inch
CHECKER: *66–68* **$3–5**
U.S.A.: *63* **5–8**
LPs: 10/12-Inch 33rpm
ALLIGATOR: *76–81*.............. **5–8**
CHESS: *69–72*.................. **10–12**

TAYLOR, Little Johnny
Singles: 7-Inch
GALAXY: *63–64* **3–5**
RONN: *71–79*.................... **2–4**
LPs: 10/12-Inch 33rpm
GALAXY: *63* **15–20**
RONN: *72–79*................... **6–10**

TAYLOR, Little Johnny, & Ted Taylor
LPs: 10/12-Inch 33rpm
RONN: *73*...................... **8–10**
Also see TAYLOR, Little Johnny
Also see TAYLOR, Ted

TAYLOR, Livingston
Singles: 7-Inch
CAPRICORN: *71–73*.............. **2–4**
EPIC: *78–80* **2–3**
LPs: 10/12-Inch 33rpm
CAPRICORN: *79*................. **5–8**
EPIC: *78* **5–8**
Also see DOOBIE BROTHERS, The / Kate Taylor & The Simon-Taylor Family

TAYLOR, Mick
Singles: 7-Inch
COLUMBIA: *79*.................. **2–3**
LPs: 10/12-Inch 33rpm
COLUMBIA: *79*.................. **5–8**
Also see MAYALL, John
Also see ROLLING STONES, The

TAYLOR, R. Dean
Singles: 7-Inch
FARR: *76* **2–4**
JANE: *77*........................ **2–3**
MALA: *62*....................... **4–6**
MOTOWN........................ **1–3**
RAGAMUFFIN: *79*............... **1–3**
RARE EARTH: *70–72* **2–4**
20TH CENTURY-FOX:
  81 .... **1–3**

V.I.P.: *65–68* **$3–5**
Picture Sleeves
RARE EARTH: *71* **2–4**
LPs: 10/12-Inch 33rpm
RARE EARTH: *70* **10–12**

TAYLOR, Roger
Singles: 7-Inch
CAPITOL: *84* **1–3**
ELEKTRA: *81* **1–3**
LPs: 10/12-Inch 33rpm
CAPITOL: *84* **5–8**
ELEKTRA: *81* **5–8**
Also see ARCADIA
Also see QUEEN

TAYLOR, Ted
Singles: 7-Inch
ALARM: *76* **2–4**
APT: *62* **3–5**
ATCO: *65–66*.................... **3–5**
DADE: *63* **3–5**
DUKE: *59*....................... **4–6**
EPIC: *66* **3–5**
GOLD EAGLE: *61* **4–6**
JEWEL: *66–67*................... **3–5**
OKEH: *62–65* **3–5**
RONN: *67–72*.................... **2–4**
SONCRAFT: *61* **3–5**
TOP RANK: *60–61* **4–6**
WARWICK: *61*................... **3–5**
LPs: 10/12-Inch 33rpm
OKEH: *63–66* **15–20**
MCA: *78* **5–8**
RONN: *69–72*................... **8–10**
Also see CADETS, The
Also see REED, Bob
Also see TAYLOR, Little Johnny & Ted Taylor

TAYLOR, True (Paul Simon)
Singles: 7-Inch
BIG: *58* **15–20**
Also see SIMON, Paul

T-BONES, The
Singles: 7-Inch
LIBERTY: *64–66* **3–6**
EPs: 7-Inch 33/45rpm
LIBERTY: *65* **4–8**
(Jukebox issues only.)

Price Range

LPs: 10/12-Inch 33rpm
LIBERTY: 64–66 .... **$15–20**
SUNSET: 66 .... **10–12**
Also see HAMILTON, JOE FRANK & REY-
NOLDS

TCHAIKOVSKY, Bram
Singles: 7-Inch
ARISTA: 81 .... **1–3**
POLYDOR: 79 .... **1–3**

LPs: 10/12-Inch 33rpm
ARISTA: 81 .... **5–8**
POLYDOR: 79–80 .... **5–8**
Also see MOTORS, The

T-CONNECTION, The
Singles: 12-Inch 33/45rpm
CAPITOL: 81–84 .... **4–6**

Singles: 7-Inch
CAPITOL: 81–84 .... **1–3**
DASH: 77–79. .... **2–3**

LPs: 10/12-Inch 33rpm
CAPITOL: 81–84 .... **5–8**
DASH: 77–79. .... **5–8**

TEARDROP EXPLODES
Singles: 7-Inch
MERCURY: 81–82. .... **1–3**

LPs: 10/12-Inch 33rpm
MERCURY: 81–81. .... **5–8**

TEARS FOR FEARS
Singles: 12-Inch 33/45rpm
MERCURY: 83–85. .... **4–6**

Singles: 7-Inch
MERCURY: 83–85. .... **1–3**

LPs: 10/12-Inch 33rpm
MERCURY: 83–85. .... **5–8**

TECHNIQUE
Singles: 12-Inch 33/45rpm
ARIAL: 83 .... **4–6**

*Techniques, one charted single (1957), no
charted LPs.*

Price Range

TECHNIQUES, The
Singles: 7-Inch
ROULETTE: 57–58 .... **$4–6**
STARS: 57. .... **8–10**

TEDDY & THE TWILIGHTS
Singles: 7-Inch
SWAN: 62 .... **3–5**

TEDDY BEARS, The
Singles: 7-Inch
COLLECTABLES **1–3**
DORE: 58–59 .... **5–8**
IMPERIAL: 58–59 .... **8–10**
LPs: 10/12-Inch 33rpm
IMPERIAL (12010; "The
Teddy Bears Sing"): 59 .... **90–100**
(Monaural issue.)
IMPERIAL (9067; "The
Teddy Bears Sing"): 59 .... **225–250**
(Stereo issue.)
Members: Phil Spector; Annette Klienbard;
Marshall Leib.
Also see NELSON, Sandy

TEE, Willie
Singles: 7-Inch
A.F.O.: 62 .... **4–6**
ATLANTIC: 65 .... **3–5**
CAPITOL: 68–69 .... **2–4**

Price Range

NOLA: 65 . . . . $5–8
UNITED ARTISTS: 76 2–3
LPs: 10/12-Inch 33rpm
CAPITOL: 69 10–12
UNITED ARTISTS: 76 5–10

TEE SET, The
Singles: 7-Inch
COLLECTABLES 1–3
COLOSSUS: 70–71 2–4
Picture Sleeves
COLOSSUS: 70 2–4
LPs: 10/12-Inch 33rpm
COLOSSUS: 70 10–12

TEEGARDEN & VAN WINKLE
Singles: 7-Inch
ATCO: 68 3–5
PLUMM: 70 3–6
WESTBOUND: 69–72 2–4
Picture Sleeves
WESTBOUND: 70 2–4
LPs: 10/12-Inch 33rpm
ATCO: 68 10–15
WESTBOUND: 69–72 10–12
Members: David Teegarden; Skip Knape.

TEEN KINGS, The (Featuring Roy Orbison)
Singles: 7-Inch
JE-WEL: 56 225–250
Also see ORBISON, Roy

TEEN QUEENS, The
Singles: 7-Inch
ANTLER: 60–61 4–6
COLLECTABLES 1–3
KENT: 61 3–5
RCA VICTOR: 58 4–6
RPM: 56–57 6–10
LPs: 10/12-Inch 33rpm
CROWN (5022; "Eddie
   My Love"): 56 35–40
CROWN (5373; "The Teen
   Queens"): 63 15–20
Members: Rose Collins; Betty Collins.

TEENA MARIE: see MARIE, Teena

Price Range

TEENAGERS, The
Singles: 7-Inch
END: 60 . . . . $8–12
GEE (1046; "Flip-Flop"):
   57 5–8
Also see CLIFFORD, Buzz
Also see LYMON, Frankie

TEMPER
Singles: 12-Inch 33/45rpm
MCA: 84 4–6
Singles: 7-Inch
MCA: 84 1–3

TEMPO, Nino (Nino Tempo & 5th Ave. Sax)
Singles: 7-Inch
A&M: 73–74 2–4
RCA VICTOR: 59–60 3–5
TOWER: 67 2–4
UNITED ARTISTS: 60 3–5
LPs: 10/12-Inch 33rpm
A&M: 74 8–10
ATCO: 66 10–12

TEMPO, Nino, & April Stevens
Singles: 7-Inch
A&M: 72–75 2–4
ABC: 73 1–3
ATCO: 62–66 2–5
BELL: 69 2–4

Price Range

CHELSEA: *76*. **$2–3**
MARINA: *72* **2–4**
WHITE WHALE: *66–68*. **2–5**
LPs: 10/12-Inch 33rpm
ATCO: *63–66*. **10–15**
CAMDEN: *64*. **10–15**
WHITE WHALE: *69*. **10–15**
Also see STEVENS, April
Also see TEMPO, Nino

TEMPOS, The
Singles: 7-Inch
CLIMAX: *59*. **5–8**
KAPP: *57–58*. **5–8**
PARIS: *59*. **4–6**
ROULETTE **1–3**

TEMPREES, The
Singles: 7-Inch
EPIC: *76* **2–4**
STAX: *84*. **1–3**
WE PRODUCE: *72–74* **2–4**
LPs: 10/12-Inch 33rpm
STAX: *84*. **5–8**
WE PRODUCE: *72–74* **8–10**

TEMPTATIONS, The
Singles: 7-Inch
GOLDISC (Multi-color
label): *60*. **8–10**
GOLDISC (Black label):
60 . . . . **5–8**
ROULETTE: *71* **1–3**

TEMPTATIONS, The
Singles: 7-Inch
ATLANTIC: *77–78* **1–3**
GORDY (1600 & 1700
series): *82–85*. **1–3**
GORDY (7001; "Dream
Come True"): *62*. **12–15**
GORDY (7010;
"Paradise"): *62* **8–12**
GORDY (7015; "I Want A
Love I Can See"): *63* **6–10**
GORDY (7020; "May I
Have This Dance"): *63*. **6–10**
GORDY (7028 through
7074): *64–68*. **3–5**
GORDY (7081 through
7213): *68–81*. **2–4**

Price Range

MIRACLE (5; "Oh
Mother Of Mine"): *61* **$60–75**
MIRACLE (12; "Check
Yourself"): *62* **15–20**
MOTOWN. **1–3**
Picture Sleeves
GORDY: *65–70*. **3–5**
LPs: 10/12-Inch 33rpm
ATLANTIC: *77–78* **8–10**
GORDY (911 through
927): *64–68*. **15–20**
GORDY (938 through
1006): *68–80*. **10–15**
GORDY (6000 series):
82–84 . . . . **5–8**
KORY: *77* **8–10**
MOTOWN (100 & 200
series): *81–82* **5–8**
MOTOWN (782;
"Anthology"): *73*. **12–15**
NATURAL RESOURCES:
78 . . . . **5–8**
Promotional LPs
MOTOWN (998; "Give
Love At Christmas"): *80* **12–15**
Members: David Ruffin; Eddie Kendricks;
Melvin Franklin; Otis Williams; Paul Williams;
Damon Harris; Dennis Edwards.
Also see EDWARDS, Dennis
Also see FOUR TOPS, The / The Temptations
Also see KENDRICKS, Eddie
Also see LANDS, Liz, & The Temptations
Also see PIRATES, The
Also see ROBINSON, Smokey
Also see ROSS, Diana
Also see RUFFIN, David
Also see SUPREMES, The, & The Temptations

TEMPTATIONS, The, & Rick James
Singles: 12-Inch 33/45rpm
GORDY: *82* **4–6**
Singles: 7-Inch
GORDY: *82* **1–3**
Also see JAMES, Rick

**TEMPTATIONS, The / Stevie
Wonder**
LPs: 10/12-Inch 33rpm
TAMLA (101; "The Sky's
The Limit"): *71*. **18–20**
(Promotional issue only.)
Also see TEMPTATIONS, The
Also see WONDER, Stevie

Price Range

Price Range

10CC
Singles: 7-Inch
MERCURY: 75–77 . . . . $2–4
POLYDOR: 78 2–4
UK: 72–74 3–5

Picture Sleeves
MERCURY: 75–77 5–8

LPs: 10/12-Inch 33rpm
MERCURY: 75–77 10–15
POLYDOR: 78–79 5–8
UK: 73–75 10–15
WARNER BROS: 80 8–10
    Also see GODLEY, Kevin, & Lol Creme
    Also see HOTLEGS
    Also see KASENETZ-KATZ SINGING OR-
    CHESTRAL CIRCUS, The
    Also see OHIO EXPRESS, The
    Also see SEDAKA, Neil
    Also see WAX

TEN WHEEL DRIVE (With Genya Ravan)
Singles: 7-Inch
CAPITOL: 73 2–4
POLYDOR: 69–71 2–4

LPs: 10/12-Inch 33rpm
CAPITOL: 73 8–10
POLYDOR: 69–71 10–12
    Also see RAVAN, Genya
    Also see ZAGER, Michael, Band

TEN YEARS AFTER (With Alvin Lee)
Singles: 7-Inch
COLUMBIA: 71–73 2–4
DERAM: 68–70 3–5

LPs: 10/12-Inch 33rpm
CHRYSALIS: 83 5–8
COLUMBIA: 71–76 8–12
DERAM: 68–75 8–12
LONDON: 77 5–8
    Also see LEE, Alvin

10-SPEED
Singles: 12-Inch 33/45rpm
QUALITY/RFC: 83 4–6

Singles: 7-Inch
QUALITY/RFC: 83 1–3

TENDER SLIM
Singles: 7-Inch
GREY CLIFF: 59 . . . . $4–6
HERALD: 62 4–6

TENNANT, Jimmy (Jimmy Velvet; Jimmy Tenant)
Singles: 7-Inch
AMP: 59 4–6
WARWICK: 60 8–10
    Also see VELVET, Jimmy

TENNESSEE ERNIE: see FORD, "Tennessee" Ernie

TENNILLE, Toni
Singles: 7-Inch
MIRAGE: 84 1–3
LPs: 10/12-Inch 33rpm
MIRAGE: 84 5–8
    Also see CAPTAIN & TENNILLE, The

TERRELL, Jean
Singles: 7-Inch
A&M: 78 2–3
LPs: 10/12-Inch 33rpm
A&M: 78 8–10
    Also see SUPREMES, The

TERRELL, Tammi
Singles: 7-Inch
MOTOWN: 65–69 3–5
LPs: 10/12-Inch 33rpm
MOTOWN (200 series): 82 5–8
MOTOWN (600 series): 67 12–15
    Also see GAYE, Marvin, & Tammi Terrell
    Also see JACKSON, Chuck, & Tammi Terrell

TERRY, Sonny (Sonny "Hootin" Terry & His Night Owls; Sonny Terry & His Buckshot Five)
Singles: 7-Inch
CAPITOL (900 series): 50 25–30
CHOICE: 61 3–5
GOTHAM: 51 12–15
GRAMERCY (Black
   vinyl): 52 10–15
GRAMERCY (Colored
   vinyl): 52 20–25
GROOVE: 54–55 10–15
HARLEM: 52 20–25

Price Range

JACKSON (Colored vinyl):
52 .... **$35–40**
JAX (Colored vinyl) **30–35**
JOSIE: *56*........................ **5–8**
OLD TOWN: *56*................. **8–10**
RCA VICTOR: *53* **12–15**
RED ROBIN: *53* **40–50**

LPs: 10/12-Inch 33rpm
ARCHIVE OF FOLK
   MUSIC: *65*................... **12–15**
EVEREST **5–8**
PRESTIGE
   BLUESVILLE: *61–63*.......... **20–25**
   WASHINGTON: *61*.............. **20–25**
     Note: Most of the Sonny Terry sessions included Brownie McGhee on guitar.
     Also see BAGBY, Doc
     Also see HOPKINS, Lightnin', & Sonny Terry
     Also see McGHEE, Brownie, & Sonny Terry

TEX, Joe (Joe Tex & The Class Mates)
Singles: 12-Inch 33/45rpm
EPIC: *77* **4–6**

Singles: 7-Inch
ACE: *58–60*..................... **6–10**
ANNA: *60–61*.................... **5–8**
ATLANTIC: *72* **2–4**
CHECKER: *63* **3–5**
DIAL (1000 series): *71–76*...... **2–4**
DIAL (2800 series): *78*.......... **2–3**
DIAL (3000 series): *61–64*....... **4–6**
DIAL (4000 series): *64–69*....... **3–5**
EPIC: *77–79* **2–3**
HANDSHAKE: *81*................. **1–3**
JALYNNE: *61*.................... **4–6**
KING: *55–57*.................... **6–10**

LPs: 10/12-Inch 33rpm
ACCORD: *82* **5–8**
ATLANTIC: *65–72* **10–15**
CHECKER: *64* **12–15**
DIAL: *72–79* **8–10**
EPIC: *77–78* **8–10**
KING: *65* **12–15**
LONDON: *79*.................... **5–8**
PARROT: *65*.................... **12–15**
PRIDE: *73*...................... **8–10**
     Also see KELLY, Paul
     Also see SOUL CLAN, The

Price Range

TEXANS, The
Singles: 7-Inch
GOTHIC: *61*.................... **$5–8**
INFINITY: *61*................... **5–8**
JOX: *64* **5–8**
VEE JAY: *65*.................... **3–5**
     Members: Dorsey Burnette; Johnny Burnette.
     Also see BURNETTE, Dorsey
     Also see BURNETTE, Johnny

TEXAS GUITAR SLIM (Johnny Winter)
Singles: 7-Inch
MOON-LITE: *60* **40–50**
     Also see WINTER, Johnny

TEXTONES, The
Singles: 7-Inch
GOLD MOUNTAIN: *84*........... **1–3**
I.R.S./FAULTY
   PRODUCTS: *80* **1–3**

LPs: 10/12-Inch 33rpm
GOLD MOUNTAIN: *84*........... **5–8**
     Members: Carla Olson; Mark Cuff; Kathy Valentine; David Provost; George Callins; Phil Seymour; Tom Morgan; Joe Read.
     Also see DREAM SYNDICATE, The
     Also see GO-GOs, The
     Also see SEYMOUR, Phil

THE, The
Singles: 12-Inch 33/45rpm
EPIC: *84–85* **4–6**
SIRE: *84* **4–6**

Singles: 7-Inch
EPIC: *84–85* **1–3**

LPs: 10/12-Inch 33rpm
EPIC: *84* **5–8**

THEE MIDNITERS
Singles: 7-Inch
CHATTAHOOCHEE:
   65–66 .... **4–6**
UNI: *69* **2–4**
WHITTIER: *66–68*................ **3–5**

LPs: 10/12-Inch 33rpm
CHATTAHOOCHEE: *65* **20–25**
RHINO: *83* **5–8**
WHITTIER: *66–67*.............. **15–20**

THEE PROPHETS
Singles: 7-Inch
KAPP: 69 . . . . $3–5

LPs: 10/12-Inch 33rpm
KAPP: 69 15–20

THEE SIXPENCE (The Strawberry Alarm Clock)
Singles: 7-Inch
DOT: 66 8–10
Also see STRAWBERRY ALARM CLOCK

THELONIOUS MONK: see MONK, Thelonious

THEM (Featuring Van Morrison)
Singles: 7-Inch
HAPPY TIGER: 69–70 3–5
KING: 65 8–10
LOMA: 66 5–8
LONDON 1–3
PARROT (Except 365):
  64–66 6–10
PARROT (365; "Gloria"):
  65 10–15
  (Copies with later copyright dates are, of course, reissues.)
RUFF: 67 6–10
SULLY 15–20
TOWER: 67–69 4–6

LPs: 10/12-Inch 33rpm
HAPPY TIGER: 69–71 10–15
LONDON 77
PARROT (71005;
  "Them"): 65 30–35
PARROT (71008; "Them
  Again"): 66 25–30
PARROT (71053; "Them
  Featuring Van
  Morrison"): 72 12–15
TOWER: 68 20–25
Also see MORRISON, Van

THEO VANESS
Singles: 7-Inch
PRELUDE: 79 1–3

LPs: 10/12-Inch 33rpm
PRELUDE: 79 5–8

THEODORE, Mike, Orchestra
Singles: 7-Inch
WESTBOUND: 77–79 . . . . $2–3

LPs: 10/12-Inch 33rpm
WESTBOUND: 77–79 5–8

THIN LIZZY
Singles: 12-Inch 33/45rpm
WARNER BROS: 78 4–8
(Promotional issue only.)
Singles: 7-Inch
LONDON: 73 2–4
MERCURY: 76–77 2–3
VERTIGO: 75 2–4
WARNER BROS: 78–79 2–3
Picture Sleeves
VERTIGO 1–3

LPs: 10/12-Inch 33rpm
LONDON (500 & 600
  series): 71 10–15
LONDON (50000 series):
  77 5–8
MERCURY: 76–77 8–12
VERTIGO: 74–75 10–12
WARNER BROS: 78–82 5–8
Members: Philip Lynott; Gary Moore; Brian Robertson.
Also see MOORE, Gary

THINK (Featuring Lou Stallman)
Singles: 7-Inch
BIG TREE: 74 2–4
COLUMBIA: 68–69 3–5
LAURIE: 71 2–4
LPs: 10/12-Inch 33rpm
LAURIE: 72 8–10

THIRD POWER, The
Singles: 7-Inch
VANGUARD: 70 2–4
LPs: 10/12-Inch 33rpm
VANGUARD: 70 10–15

THIRD RAIL, The
Singles: 7-Inch
CAMEO: 66 4–6
EPIC: 67–69 3–5
LPs: 10/12-Inch 33rpm
EPIC: 67 20–25

Price Range

THIRD WORLD
Singles: 12-Inch 33/45rpm
COLUMBIA: *81–82* **$4–6**
ISLAND: *78–80* **4–6**
Singles: 7-Inch
COLUMBIA: *81–82* **1–3**
ISLAND: *79* **2–3**
LPs: 10/12-Inch 33rpm
COLUMBIA: *81–82* **5–8**
ISLAND: *76–80* **6–9**
Also see WONDER, Stevie

THIRTEENTH FLOOR ELEVATORS (Featuring Roky Erickson)
Singles: 7-Inch
CONTACT: *66* **25–35**
HBR: *66* **40–50**
INTERNATIONAL
  ARTISTS: *66–68* **10–15**
LPs: 10/12-Inch 33rpm
INTERNATIONAL
  ARTISTS (Except 1):
  67–68 . . . . **40–50**
  (Does NOT have "Masterfonics" stamped in
  the vinyl trail-off.)
INTERNATIONAL
  ARTISTS (1;
  "Psychedelic Sounds"):
  67 . . . . **50–60**
  (Does NOT have "Masterfonics" stamped in
  the vinyl trail-off.)
INTERNATIONAL
  ARTISTS (White label):
  67–68 . . . . **90–100**
  (Promotional issues only.)
INTERNATIONAL
  ARTISTS **10–15**
  (Reissues, with "Masterfonics" stamped in the
  vinyl trail-off.)
  Also see SPADES, The

.38 SPECIAL (With Dave Van Zandt)
Singles: 7-Inch
A&M: *77–83* **1–3**
CAPITOL: *84* **1–3**
Picture Sleeves
A&M: *80–83* **1–3**
LPs: 10/12-Inch 33rpm
A&M: *77–83* **5–8**
CAPITOL: *84* **5–8**

*B.J. Thomas, 25 charted singles (1966–78),
10 charted LPs (1969–83).*

Price Range

THOMAS, B.J. (B.J. Thomas & The Triumphs)
Singles: 7-Inch
ABC: *75* **$2–4**
CLEVELAND INT'L: *83* **1–3**
COLLECTABLES **1–3**
COLUMBIA: *83* **1–3**
HICKORY: *66* **3–5**
MCA: *77–82* **1–3**
MYRRH: *77–81* **1–3**
PACEMAKER: *66* **10–15**
PARAMOUNT: *73–74* **2–4**
SCEPTER (12100 series):
  66–67 . . . . **3–5**
SCEPTER (12200 & 12300
  series): *68–72* **2–4**
SCEPTER (21000 series):
  73–74 . . . . **2–3**
Picture Sleeves
MCA: *79* **1–3**
LPs: 10/12-Inch 33rpm
ABC: *74–77* **8–10**
ACCORD: *81–82* **5–8**
CLEVELAND INT'L: *83* **5–8**
EXACT: *80* **5–8**
EVEREST: *81* **5–8**
HICKORY: *66* **35–45**
MCA: *80–82* **5–8**
MYRRH: *78–83* **5–8**

Price Range

PACEMAKER: *66* **$40–50**
PARAMOUNT: *73.* **8–10**
PRIORITY: *83* **5–8**
SCEPTER: *69–73* **8–12**
SONGBIRD: *80* **5–8**
SPRINGBOARD: *73–79* **6–10**
TRIP: *76* **8–10**
UNITED ARTISTS: *74* **8–10**
    Also see EDDY, Duane

THOMAS, B.J., & Ray Charles
Singles: 7-Inch
COLUMBIA: *85* **1–3**
    Also see CHARLES, Ray
    Also see THOMAS, B.J.

THOMAS, Carla
Singles: 7-Inch
ATLANTIC: *60–65* **3–5**
STAX: *65–72* **2–4**
Picture Sleeves
STAX: *67.* **2–4**
EPs: 7-Inch 33/45rpm
STAX: *66* **10–15**
    (Jukebox issues only.)
LPs: 10/12-Inch 33rpm
ATLANTIC (8057; "Gee
  Whiz"): *61* **20–30**
ATLANTIC (8232; "Best
  Of Carla Thomas"): *69.* **10–15**
STAX: *66–71* **10–15**
    Also see BELL, William, & Carla Thomas
    Also see OTIS & CARLA
    Also see RUFUS & CARLA
    Also see TAYLOR, Johnnie

THOMAS, Evelyn
Singles: 12-Inch 33/45rpm
TSR: *84* **4–6**
Singles: 7-Inch
CASABLANCA: *78* **2–3**
TSR: *84* **1–3**
VANGUARD: *85* **1–3**
LPs: 10/12-Inch 33rpm
A.V.I.: *79* **5–8**
CASABLANCA: *78* **5–8**

THOMAS, Gene
Singles: 7-Inch
HICKORY: *71* **2–4**
TRX: *69.* **2–4**
UNITED ARTISTS: *61–65* **3–5**

Price Range

VENUS: *61–62* **$5–8**
    Also see GENE & DEBBE

THOMAS, Ian
Singles: 7-Inch
ATLANTIC: *78* **2–3**
CHRYSALIS: *75.* **2–3**
JANUS: *73–74.* **2–4**
MERCURY: *84.* **1–3**

LPs: 10/12-Inch 33rpm
ATLANTIC: *78* **5–8**
JANUS: *73* **8–10**
MERCURY: *84.* **5–8**

THOMAS, Irma
Singles: 7-Inch
CANYON: *70* **2–4**
CHESS: *68.* **2–4**
COTILLION: *71–72.* **2–4**
FUNGUS: *73.* **2–4**
IMPERIAL: *64–66.* **3–5**
MINIT: *61–63* **3–5**
RCS: *79–81* **2–3**
ROKER: *71.* **2–4**
RON: *59–60.* **4–6**

LPs: 10/12-Inch 33rpm
FUNGUS: *73.* **8–10**
IMPERIAL (266; "Wish
  Someone Would Care"):
  64 .... **15–20**
IMPERIAL (302; "Take A
  Look"): *66* **12–15**
RCS: *80* **5–8**
    Also see BROWN, Maxine / Irma Thomas

THOMAS, Jamo, & The Party Brothers
Singles: 7-Inch
CHESS: *66.* **3–5**
DECCA: *68.* **2–4**
SOUND STAGE 7: *67.* **3–5**
THOMAS: *66* **4–6**

THOMAS, Joe
Singles: 7-Inch
KING (Black vinyl): *51* **8–10**
KING (Colored vinyl): *51* **25–30**

Price Range　　　　　　　　　　　　　　*Price Range*

THOMAS, Joe
Singles: 7-Inch
GROOVE MERCHANT:
　76 .... $2–4
LRC: 77–79 2–3
SUE: 64 3–5
LPs: 10/12-Inch 33rpm
LRC: 77–78 5–8
TODAY: 72 8–10

THOMAS, Joe, & Bill Elliott
LPs: 10/12-Inch 33rpm
SUE: 64 10–20
　Also see THOMAS, Joe

THOMAS, Jon (John Thomas)
Singles: 7-Inch
ABC-PARAMOUNT:
　60–61 4–6
CHECKER: 55 5–8
JUNIOR: 64 3–5
VEEP: 67–68 3–5
LPs: 10/12-Inch 33rpm
ABC-PARAMOUNT: 60 20–30
MERCURY: 63 15–20

THOMAS, Leone
Singles: 7-Inch
DON: 76 2–4

THOMAS, Lillo
Singles: 12-Inch 33/45rpm
CAPITOL: 83–85 4–6
Singles: 7-Inch
CAPITOL: 83–85 1–3
LPs: 10/12-Inch 33rpm
CAPITOL: 83–85 5–8

THOMAS, Lillo, & Melba Moore
Singles: 7-Inch
CAPITOL: 84 1–3
　Also see MOORE, Melba
　Also see THOMAS, Lillo

THOMAS, Nolan
Singles: 12-Inch 33/45rpm
EMERGENCY: 84–85 4–6
Singles: 7-Inch
MIRAGE: 84–85 1–3

THOMAS, Pat
Singles: 7-Inch
MGM: 62–63 .... $2–4
VERVE: 62–64 2–4
Picture Sleeves
MGM: 62 2–4
LPs: 10/12-Inch 33rpm
MGM: 62–64 10–20
STRAND: 61 10–20

THOMAS, Ray
Singles: 7-Inch
THRESHOLD: 75–76 2–4
LPs: 10/12-Inch 33rpm
THRESHOLD (Except
　102): 75–76 8–10
THRESHOLD (102; "Ray
　Thomas Discusses 'From
　Mighty Oaks' "): 75 12–15
　(Promotional issue only.)
　Also see MOODY BLUES, The

THOMAS, Rufus
Singles: 12-Inch 33/45rpm
A.V.I.: 78 4–6
Singles: 7-Inch
A.V.I.: 77–78 2–3
ARTISTS OF AMERICA:
　76 2–3
HI: 78 2–3
METEOR: 56 35–40
STAX (100 & 200 series):
　62–68 3–5
STAX (0010 through
　0236): 68–75 2–4
SUN (181; "Bearcat"): 53 60–75
SUN (188; "Tiger Man"):
　53 75–90
LPs: 10/12-Inch 33rpm
A.V.I.: 77–78 5–8
ARTISTS OF AMERICA:
　76 8–10
GUSTO: 80 5–8
STAX (Except 704): 70–79 6–10
STAX (704; "Walking The
　Dog"): 63 15–20
　Also see RUFUS & CARLA

THOMAS, Tasha
Singles: 7-Inch
ATLANTIC: 78–79 2–3

Price Range

THOMAS, Timmy
Singles: 12-Inch 33/45rpm
GOLD MOUNTAIN: *84* $4–6
SPECTOR: *83* 4–6
Singles: 7-Inch
GLADES: *72–77* 2–4
GOLD MOUNTAIN:
  84–85 1–3
GOLDWAX: *67* 3–5
MARLIN: *80–81* 2–3
SPECTOR: *83* 1–3
TM: *78* 2–3
LPs: 10/12-Inch 33rpm
GLADES: *72–76* 8–10
GOLD MOUNTAIN: *84* 5–8

THOMPSON, Chris, & Night
Singles: 7-Inch
PLANET: *79* 2–3
Also see NIGHT

THOMPSON, Hank (Hank Thompson & The Brazos Valley Boys)
Singles: 7-Inch
ABC: *75–79* 1–3
ABC/DOT: *74–77* 2–3
CAPITOL (1000 through
  3000 series): *50–58* 4–6
CAPITOL (4000 & 5000
  series): *58–66* 2–5
CHURCHILL: *83* 1–3
DOT: *68–74* 2–3
MCA: *79–80* 1–3
WARNER BROS: *66–67* 2–4
Picture Sleeves
CAPITOL: *61* 3–5
EPs: 7-Inch 33/45rpm
CAPITOL: *53–59* 8–18
LPs: 10/12-Inch 33rpm
ABC: *78* 5–8
ABC/DOT: *74–77* 5–10
CAPITOL (400 series): *53* 40–60
  (With an "H" prefix. 10-Inch LPs.)
CAPITOL (400 series): *55* 25–40
  (With a "T" prefix.)
CAPITOL (600 series): *55* 35–50
  (With an "H" prefix. 10-Inch LPs.)
CAPITOL (600 series): *55* 25–40
  (With a "T" prefix.)
CAPITOL (700 series): *56* 30–45

Price Range

CAPITOL (800 & 900
  series): *57–58* $20–30
CAPITOL (1100 through
  2100 series): *59–64* 15–25
CAPITOL (2000 series): *75* 5–8
  (With an "SM" prefix.)
CAPITOL (2200 through
  2800 series): *65–67* 10–20
  (With a "T" or "ST" prefix.)
CAPITOL (9000 series): *53* 40–60
  (10-Inch LPs.)
CAPITOL (11000 series):
  79 5–8
CHURCHILL: *84* 5–8
DOT: *68–74* 6–15
GUSTO: *80* 5–8
PICKWICK/HILLTOP:
  67–68 6–15
TOWER: *68* 8–15
WACO 8–10

THOMPSON, Kay
Singles: 7-Inch
CADENCE: *56* 2–4
MGM: *54–55* 2–4

THOMPSON, Richard
Singles: 7-Inch
HANNIBAL: *83* 1–3
POLYDOR: *85* 1–3
REPRISE: *72* 2–4

Price Range

LPs: 10/12-Inch 33rpm
HANNIBAL: *83* **$5–8**
POLYDOR: *85* **5–8**
REPRISE: *72*. **8–10**
Also see FAIRPORT CONVENTION

THOMPSON, Richard & Linda
Singles: 7-Inch
CHRYSALIS: *78*. **2–3**
ISLAND: *74–75* **2–4**
LPs: 10/12-Inch 33rpm
CHRYSALIS: *78*. **5–8**
ISLAND: *74–75* **8–10**
Also see THOMPSON, Richard

THOMPSON, Robbin, Band
Singles: 7-Inch
NEMPEROR: *76–77* **2–3**
OVATION: *80*. **1–3**
LPs: 10/12-Inch 33rpm
NEMPEROR: *76* **8–10**
OVATION: *80*. **5–8**
Also see SPRINGSTEEN, Bruce

THOMPSON, Roy
Singles: 7-Inch
OKEH: *66–67* **3–5**

THOMPSON, Sonny
Singles: 7-Inch
KING (4500 through 5300
  series): *52–60* **5–8**
KNIGHT: *61*. **3–5**
EPs: 7-Inch 33/45rpm
KING. **15–20**
LPs: 10/12-Inch 33rpm
KING (500 series): *56* **30–40**
KING (600 series): *59* **20–25**
Also see KING, Freddie / Lulu / Sonny
Thompson

*Sue Thompson, seven charted singles
(1961–65), one charted LP (1965).*

Price Range

THOMPSON, Sue
Singles: 7-Inch
GUSTO **$1–3**
HICKORY (Except 1100
  & 1200 series): *66–76* **2–4**
HICKORY (1100 & 1200
  series): *61–65* **3–5**

Picture Sleeves
HICKORY: *64* **4–6**

LPs: 10/12-Inch 33rpm
HICKORY (Except 104
  through 121): *69–74* **8–12**
HICKORY (104 through
  121): *62–65*. **15–20**
WING: *66* **8–15**
Also see GIBSON, Don, & Sue Thompson
Also see LUMAN, Bob, & Sue Thompson

THOMPSON TWINS, The
Singles: 12-Inch 33/45rpm
ARISTA: *83–86*. **4–6**

Singles: 7-Inch
ARISTA: *82–86*. **1–3**

LPs: 10/12-Inch 33rpm
ARISTA: *82–86*. **5–8**
Members: Tom Bailey; Alannah Currie; Joe
Leeway.

Price Range

THOMSON, Ali
Singles: 7-Inch
A&M: 80–81 . . . . $1–3

LPs: 10/12-Inch 33rpm
A&M: 80 5–8

THORNE, David (David Throne)
Singles: 7-Inch
ADMIRAL: 64–65 3–5
CHOICE: 60 4–6
RIVERSIDE: 62 3–5
SAVOY: 59 3–5

THORNTON, Fonzi
Singles: 12-Inch 33/45rpm
RCA VICTOR: 83 4–6

Singles: 7-Inch
RCA VICTOR: 83 1–3

LPs: 10/12-Inch 33rpm
RCA VICTOR: 83 5–8

THORNTON, Willie Mae (Big Mama Thornton)
Singles: 7-Inch
ABC: 73 2–3
ARHOOLIE: 68 2–4
BAY TONE: 61 8–10
GALAXY: 66 3–5
KENT: 65 4–6
MERCURY: 69 2–4
PEACOCK (Maroon
  label): 52 10–15
PEACOCK (Red label):
  53–55 8–12
PEACOCK (White label):
  56–57 5–8
(White label numbers below 1676 are reissues, which Peacock continued carrying in their catalog through the seventies.)
SOTOPLAY: 65 6–10

LPs: 10/12-Inch 33rpm
ARHOOLIE: 66–67 10–15
BACK BEAT: 70 20–25
MERCURY: 69–70 10–15
PENTAGRAM: 71 10–12
ROULETTE: 70 10–12
VANGUARD: 74–75 8–10

THOROGOOD, George, & The Destroyers
Singles: 12-Inch 33/45rpm
EMI AMERICA: 83–85 . . . . $4–6
Singles: 7-Inch
EMI AMERICA: 82–85 1–3
MCA: 79 1–3
ROUNDER: 78–80 1–3
LPs: 10/12-Inch 33rpm
EMI AMERICA: 82–84 5–8
MCA: 79 5–8
ROUNDER: 77–80 5–8

THORPE, Billy
Singles: 7-Inch
CAPRICORN: 79 2–5
POLYDOR: 79 2–3
LPs: 10/12-Inch 33rpm
CAPRICORN: 79 25–35
ELEKTRA: 80 5–8

THREE CHUCKLES, The (Featuring Teddy Randazzo)
Singles: 7-Inch
BOULEVARD: 53 25–35
CLOUD: 66 3–5
VIK: 56 5–8
X: 54–56 5–10
EPs: 7-Inch 33/45rpm
RCA VICTOR: 55 10–15
VIK (4; "The Three
  Chuckles"): 57 10–15
(Promotional issue only. Not issued with cover.)
LPs: 10/12-Inch 33rpm
VIK: 55 35–45
Also see CHUCKLES, The
Also see RANDAZZO, Teddy

THREE DEGREES, The
Singles: 7-Inch
ARIOLA AMERICA:
  78–80 1–3
EPIC: 76 2–3
METROMEDIA: 69 2–4
NEPTUNE: 70 2–4
PHILADELPHIA INT'L:
  73–76 2–4
ROULETTE: 70–73 2–4
SWAN: 64–66 3–5
WARNER BROS: 68 2–4

Price Range

LPs: 10/12-Inch 33rpm
ARIOLA AMERICA:
78–81 .... **$5–8**
EPIC: 77 .... **8–10**
PHILADELPHIA INT'L:
74–76 .... **8–10**
ROULETTE: 70–75 .... **10–15**
Also see MFSB

THREE DOG NIGHT (3 Dog Night)
Singles: 7-Inch
ABC: 70–76 .... **2–4**
DUNHILL (Except 4168):
69–75 .... **2–4**
DUNHILL (4168;
"Nobody"): 68 .... **4–6**
PASSPORT: 83 .... **1–3**
Promotional Singles
DUNHILL (4168;
"Nobody"): 68 .... **5–8**
(White label.)
Picture Sleeves
DUNHILL (Except 4168):
70 .... **2–4**
DUNHILL (4168;
"Nobody"): 68 .... **8–10**
LPs: 10/12-Inch 33rpm
ABC: 75–76 .... **8–12**
COMMAND: 74–75 .... **10–15**
DUNHILL (50048 through
50068): 68–69 .... **10–15**
DUNHILL (50078; "It
Ain't Easy"): 70 .... **15–20**
(Cover pictures nude people.)
DUNHILL (50078; "It
Ain't Easy"): 70 .... **10–12**
(Cover doesn't show nudes.)
DUNHILL (50088 through
50158): 70–73 .... **10–15**
DUNHILL (50168; "Hard
Labor"): 74 .... **15–18**
(With baby delivery cover.)
DUNHILL (50168; "Hard
Labor"): 74 .... **10–12**
(With Band-Aid cover.)
DUNHILL (50178; "Joy
To The World"): 74 .... **8–10**
MCA: 82 .... **5–8**
PASSPORT: 83 .... **5–8**
Members: Danny Hutton; Cory Wells; Chuck
Negron.
Also see HUTTON, Danny

3 FRIENDS, The
Singles: 7-Inch
CAL-GOLD: 61 .... **$4–6**
IMPERIAL: 61 .... **4–6**

THREE Gs, The
Singles: 7-Inch
COLUMBIA: 58–61 .... **3–5**

THREE MILLION
Singles: 12-Inch 33/45rpm
COTILLION: 84–84 .... **4–6**
Singles: 7-Inch
COTILLION: 83–84 .... **1–3**

3 OUNCES OF LOVE
Singles: 7-Inch
MOTOWN: 78 .... **2–3**
LPs: 10/12-Inch 33rpm
MOTOWN: 78 .... **5–8**

THREE PLAYMATES, The
Singles: 7-Inch
SAVOY: 58 .... **4–6**

THREE SUNS, The
Singles: 7-Inch
RCA VICTOR: 50–64 .... **2–4**
EPs: 7-Inch 33/45rpm
RCA VICTOR: 50–61 .... **4–8**
LPs: 10/12-Inch 33rpm
CAMDEN: 60–64 .... **5–10**
MUSICOR: 66 .... **5–10**
RCA VICTOR: 50–76 .... **5–15**
RONDO: 59 .... **5–12**
Members: Al Nevins; Morty Nevins; Art Dunn.

THRILLS
Singles: 7-Inch
G&P: 80 .... **1–3**
LPs: 10/12-Inch 33rpm
G&P: 80 .... **5–8**

THUNDER, Johnny
Singles: 7-Inch
ABC: 74 .... **1–3**
CALLA: 69 .... **2–4**
DIAMOND: 62–68 .... **3–5**
EPIC: 59 .... **5–8**
UNITED ARTISTS: 70 .... **2–4**

Price Range

Picture Sleeves
DIAMOND: *63*.................... **$5–8**
LPs: 10/12-Inch 33rpm
DIAMOND: *63*.................. **20–30**
REAL RECORDS **10–12**

THUNDER, Johnny, & Ruby Winters
Singles: 7-Inch
DIAMOND: *67–68*................ **3–5**
Also see THUNDER, Johnny
Also see WINTERS, Ruby

THUNDER, Margo
Singles: 7-Inch
HAVEN: *74*..................... **2–4**

THUNDERCLAP NEWMAN: see NEWMAN, Thunderclap

THUNDERFLASH
Singles: 7-Inch
JAMPOWER: *83*................. **1–3**

THUNDERKLOUD, Billy, & The Chieftones
Singles: 7-Inch
POLYDOR: *76–77*.............. **2–3**
20TH CENTURY-FOX:
74–75 .... **2–4**
LPs: 10/12-Inch 33rpm
SUPERIOR: *74*.................. **8–12**
20TH CENTURY-FOX:
74–75 .... **6–10**

THURSTON, Bobby
Singles: 7-Inch
PRELUDE: *80*................... **1–3**

TICO & THE TRIUMPHS (Featuring Paul Simon)
Singles: 7-Inch
AMY (Except 876): *61–62*.......... **6–10**
AMY (876; "Cards Of
Love"): *62* **15–20**
MADISON: *62* **15–20**
Also see SIMON, Paul

TICTOC
Singles: 12-Inch 33/45rpm
RCA VICTOR: *84* **4–6**

Price Range

Singles: 7-Inch
RCA VICTOR: *84* **$1–3**
LPs: 10/12-Inch 33rpm
RCA VICTOR: *84* **5–8**

TIERRA
Singles: 7-Inch
ASI: *80*........................ **1–3**
BOARDWALK: *80–82* **1–3**
SALSOUL: *81*................... **1–3**
MCA: *79* **1–3**
TODY **2–4**
LPs: 10/12-Inch 33rpm
ASI: *80*........................ **5–8**
BOARDWALK: *80* **5–8**
SALSOUL: *81*................... **5–8**
Also see EL CHICANO

TIGGI CLAY
Singles: 7-Inch
MOROCCO: *84*.................. **1–3**
LPs: 10/12-Inch 33rpm
MOROCCO: *84*.................. **5–8**

TIGHT FIT
Singles: 7-Inch
ARISTA: *81* **1–3**

TIJUANA BRASS, The: see ALPERT, Herb

TIL, Sonny (Sonny Til & The Orioles)
Singles: 7-Inch
JUBILEE (Blue label): *53* **20–30**
JUBILEE (Black label):
59–60 .... **4–6**
RCA VICTOR: *69–72* **2–4**
ROULETTE: *58* **4–6**
LPs: 10/12-Inch 33rpm
DOBRE: *78*..................... **5–8**
RCA VICTOR: *70–71* **10–15**
Also see McGRIFF, Edna, & Sonny Til
Also see ORIOLES, The

TIL TUESDAY
Singles: 7-Inch
EPIC: *85* **1–3**
LPs: 10/12-Inch 33rpm
EPIC: *85* **5–8**

Price Range

Price Range

Members: Aimee Mann; Michael Hausman; Robert Holmes; Joey Pesce.

TILLMAN, Bertha
Singles: 7-Inch
BRENT: 62 .... $3–5

TILLOTSON, Johnny
Singles: 7-Inch
AMOS: 69–70 2–4
BARNABY: 76 2–3
BUDDAH: 71–73 2–4
CADENCE (1300 series):
  58–61 4–6
CADENCE (1400 series):
  61–63 3–5
COLUMBIA: 73–75 2–4
ERIC 1–3
MGM: 63–68 3–5
REWARD: 82–84 1–3
UNITED ARTISTS: 76–77 2–3
Picture Sleeves
CADENCE: 60 5–10
MGM: 63–66 4–6
EPs: 7-Inch 33/45rpm
CADENCE: 60–61 15–20
LPs: 10/12-Inch 33rpm
ACCORD: 82 5–8
AMOS: 69 10–15
BARNABY: 77 8–10
BUDDAH: 72 10–12
CADENCE: 61–63 30–40
EVEREST: 82 5–8
METRO: 66 10–15
MGM: 66–71 12–15
UNITED ARTISTS: 77 8–10
Also see IVAN / Johnny Tillotson

TILLOTSON, Johnny / J.D. Souther
Singles: 7-Inch
BUDDAH: 71 2–4
Also see SOUTHER, J.D.
Also see TILLOTSON, Johnny

TIM TAM & THE TURN-ONS
Singles: 7-Inch
PALMER (5002; "Wait A
  Minute"): 66 4–6
PALMER (5003; "Cheryl
  Ann"): 66 10–12

PALMER (5006;
  "Kimberly"): 66 .... $15–20
PALMER (5014; "Don't
  Say Hi"): 67 4–6

TIME, The
Singles: 12-Inch 33/45rpm
WARNER BROS: 82–84 4–6
Singles: 7-Inch
WARNER BROS: 81–84 1–3
LPs: 10/12-Inch 33rpm
WARNER BROS: 81–84 5–8
Members: Morris Day; Jesse Johnson; Jimmy Jam; Monte Moir; Jellybean Johnson; Stacy Adams; Terry Lewis.
Also see DAY, Morris
Also see JOHNSON, Jesse
Also see VANITY 6

TIME BANDITS
Singles: 12-Inch 33/45rpm
COLUMBIA: 85 4–6

TIME ZONE
Singles: 12-Inch 33/45rpm
CELLULOID: 84 4–6

TIMETONES, The (With Slim Rose)
Singles: 7-Inch
ATCO: 61 8–10
TIMES SQUARE (Except
  421): 64 3–5
TIMES SQUARE (421;
  "Here In My Heart"): 61 4–6
TIMES SQUARE (421;
  "In My Heart"): 61 3–5

TIN TIN (Steve Kipner; Steve Groves)
Singles: 12-Inch 33/45rpm
SIRE: 81–83 4–6
Singles: 7-Inch
ATCO: 71 2–4
LPs: 10/12-Inch 33rpm
ATCO: 70–71 12–15

TINA B.
Singles: 12-Inch 33/45rpm
ATLANTIC: 82 4–6
ELEKTRA: 83 4–6

Singles: 7-Inch
ATLANTIC: *82* **$1–3**
ELEKTRA: *83* **1–3**
LPs: 10/12-Inch 33rpm
ATLANTIC: *82* **2–3**
ELEKTRA: *83* **5–8**

TINDLEY, George (George Tindley & The Modern Red Caps; George Tinley)
Singles: 7-Inch
EMBER: *60*..................... **4–6**
HERALD: *61* **4–6**
ROWAX **4–6**
PARKWAY: *62* **3–5**
SMASH: *62* **3–5**
WAND: *69–70*................... **2–4**

TINY TIM (Herbert Khaury)
Singles: 7-Inch
REPRISE: *68–71*................. **3–5**
ROULETTE **1–3**
VIC TIM: *71*.................... **2–4**
LPs: 10/12-Inch 33rpm
REPRISE: *68*................... **12–15**

TINY TIM & MISS VICKI
Singles: 7-Inch
REPRISE: *71*.................... **2–4**

TINY TIM / Michelle Ramos / Bruce Haack
LPs: 10/12-Inch 33rpm
RA-JO INT'L: *86*................ **5–8**
Also see TINY TIM

TJADER, Cal
Singles: 7-Inch
FANTASY: *54–71*................. **2–5**
SAVOY: *53–54* **3–5**
SKYE: *68*....................... **2–3**
VERVE: *61–66* **2–4**
EPs: 7-Inch 33/45rpm
FANTASY: *54–55*............... **10–20**
SAVOY: *54* **10–20**
LPs: 10/12-Inch 33rpm
BUDDAH: *70*................... **8–12**
CLASSIC JAZZ: *80*.............. **5–8**
CONCORD JAZZ: *80–82* **5–8**

FANTASY (3-9 through
3-17 series): *54*.............. **$30–60**
(10-Inch LPs.)
FANTASY (200 series):
54–56 .... **10–25**
FANTASY (3200 series):
55–60 .... **20–45**
FANTASY (3300 series):
60–65 .... **15–30**
FANTASY (8000 & 8100
series): *58–61*................. **20–45**
FANTASY (8300 series):
65 .... **15–30**
FANTASY (8400 series):
71–72 .... **8–12**
FANTASY (9000 series):
72–77 .... **6–12**
GALAXY: *78–79* **5–8**
METRO: *67*.................... **8–15**
PRESTIGE: *73* **6–10**
SAVOY (9000 series): *54* **25–50**
(10-Inch LPs.)
SAVOY (12000 series): *56* **20–40**
SKYE: *68–69*................... **8–12**
VERVE: *61–69* **10–20**
(Reads "MGM Records - A Division Of Metro-
Goldwyn-Mayer, Inc." at bottom of label.)
VERVE: *73–84* **5–12**
(Reads "Manufactured By MGM Record
Corp.," or mentions either Polydor or Poly-
gram at bottom of label.)
Also see BRUBECK, Dave
Also see O'DAY, Anita, & Cal Tjader

TJADER, Cal, & Stan Getz
LPs: 10/12-Inch 33rpm
FANTASY (3200 series):
58 .... **20–40**
FANTASY (3300 series):
65 .... **10–20**
FANTASY (8000 series):
58 .... **20–40**
FANTASY (8300 series):
65 .... **10–20**
Also see GETZ, Stan
Also see TJADER, Cal

TOBY BEAU
Singles: 7-Inch
RCA VICTOR: *78–80* **1–3**
LPs: 10/12-Inch 33rpm
RCA VICTOR: *81* **5–8**

Price Range

TODAY'S PEOPLE
Singles: 7-Inch
20TH CENTURY-FOX:
73 .... **$2–4**

TODD, Art & Dotty
Singles: 7-Inch
CAPITOL: 62 .... **3–5**
COLLECTABLES **1–3**
DAKAR: 63 .... **3–5**
DART: 59–67 .... **3–5**
DECCA: 61 .... **3–5**
DOT: 66 .... **2–4**
ERA: 58–59 .... **4–6**
M.O.L.: 68 .... **2–4**
SIGNET: 65 .... **2–4**
LPs: 10/12-Inch 33rpm
BEVERLY HILLS: 73 .... **8–10**
DART: 60 .... **15–20**
DOT: 66 .... **10–15**
REPRISE: 65 .... **10–15**

TODD, Nick
Singles: 7-Inch
DOT: 57–60 .... **4–6**

TOKENS, The
Singles: 7-Inch
ABC: 73 .... **1–3**
ATCO: 74 .... **2–4**
B.T. PUPPY: 64–69 .... **4–6**
BELL: 72 .... **2–4**
BUDDAH: 69–70 .... **3–5**
LAURIE: 63 .... **5–8**
MELBA: 56 .... **20–25**
RCA VICTOR (7000 &
8000 series): 61–65 .... **4–6**
(With a "47" prefix.)
RCA VICTOR (7000 &
8000 series): 61–62 .... **10–20**
(With a "37" prefix. Compact 33 Singles.)
WARNER BROS: 67–69 .... **3–5**
WARWICK: 61 .... **5–8**
Picture Sleeves
B.T. PUPPY: 66 .... **5–8**
RCA VICTOR: 61–63 .... **5–10**
WARNER BROS: 67 .... **3–5**
LPs: 10/12-Inch 33rpm
B.T. PUPPY: 66–78 .... **15–20**
BUDDAH: 70 .... **15–20**
RCA VICTOR: 61–66 .... **20–30**

Price Range

WARNER BROS: 67 .... **$20–25**
Members: Jay Siegal; Mitchell Margo; Philip
Margo; Henry Medress.
Also see CROSS COUNTRY
Also see SEDAKA, Neil, & The Tokens
Also see SANDS OF TIME, The

TOKENS, The / The Happenings
LPs: 10/12-Inch 33rpm
B.T. PUPPY: 67 .... **15–20**
Also see HAPPENINGS, The
Also see TOKENS, The

TOLBERT, Israel "Popper Stopper"
Singles: 7-Inch
WARREN: 70–71 .... **2–4**

LPs: 10/12-Inch 33rpm
WARREN: 71 .... **8–10**

TOM & JERRIO
Singles: 7-Inch
ABC-PARAMOUNT: 65 .... **3–5**
Members: Eddie Thomas; Jerry Murray.

TOM & JERRY
Singles: 7-Inch
ABC-PARAMOUNT
(10363; "Surrender,
Please Surrender"): 62 .... **15–20**
ABC-PARAMOUNT
(10788; "This Is My
Story"): 66 .... **8–10**
BIG (613; "Hey,
Schoolgirl"): 57 .... **10–20**
BIG (616; "Two
Teenagers"): 58 .... **20–25**
BIG (618; "Don't Say
Goodbye"): 58 .... **15–20**
BIG (621; "Baby Talk"):
58 .... **35–40**
EMBER (1094; "I'm
Lonesome"): 59 .... **25–30**
HUNT (319; "Don't Say
Goodbye"): 58 .... **20–25**
KING (5167; "Hey,
Schoolgirl"): 58 .... **25–40**
Members: Paul Simon; Art Garfunkel.
Also see SIMON & GARFUNKEL

Price Range   *Price Range*

TOM & JERRY / Ronnie Lawrence
Singles: 7-Inch
BELL (120; "Baby Talk"):
71 .... $20–25
Also see TOM & JERRY

TOM TOM CLUB
Singles: 12-Inch 33/45rpm
SIRE: 81–83 4–6
Singles: 7-Inch
SIRE: 81–83 1–3
LPs: 10/12-Inch 33rpm
SIRE: 81–83 5–8
Also see TALKING HEADS

TOMLIN, Lily
Singles: 7-Inch
POLYDOR: 73–75 1–3
LPs: 10/12-Inch 33rpm
ARISTA: 77 5–8
POLYDOR: 71–75 5–10

TOMMY TUTONE
Singles: 7-Inch
COLUMBIA: 80–82 1–3
LPs: 10/12-Inch 33rpm
COLUMBIA (Except
1461): 80–82 5–8
COLUMBIA (1461; "Alive
& Almost Dangerous"):
82 10–12
(Promotional issue only.)

TOMPALL & THE GLASER BROTHERS (Tompall & The Glasers; Tompall Glaser)
Singles: 7-Inch
DECCA: 59–65 2–5
ELEKTRA: 80–81 1–3
MGM: 66–71 2–4
RICH: 61 5–8
ROBBINS: 57 10–12
LPs: 10/12-Inch 33rpm
ABC: 77 8–10
DECCA: 60 30–45
ELEKTRA: 81 5–8
MGM: 67–75 8–15
UNITED ARTISTS: 66 25–30
VOCALION: 67 8–12

TOMORROW'S EDITION
Singles: 7-Inch
ATLANTIC: 82 .... $1–3
GANG: 75 2–4

TOMORROW'S PROMISE
Singles: 7-Inch
CAPITOL: 73–74 2–4
MERCURY: 75 2–3

TOMS, Gary (Gary Toms' Empire)
Singles: 12-Inch 33/45rpm
MCA: 77 4–6
Singles: 7-Inch
MCA: 77 2–3
MERCURY: 78 2–3
P.I.P.: 75–76 2–4
LPs: 10/12-Inch 33rpm
MCA: 77 5–10
MERCURY: 78 5–8
P.I.P.: 75 8–10

TONES, The
Singles: 7-Inch
CRIMINAL: 83 1–3

TONEY, Oscar, Jr.
Singles: 7-Inch
BELL: 67–69 3–5
KING: 64 3–5
LPs: 10/12-Inch 33rpm
BELL: 67 12–15

TONEY LEE: see LEE, Toney

TONY & CAROL
Singles: 7-Inch
ROULETTE: 72 2–4

TONY & JOE
Singles: 7-Inch
DORE: 61–62 3–5
ERA: 58 4–6
FLYTE: 59 4–6
GARDENA: 60 4–6
Members: Tony Savonne; Joe Saraceno.
Also see BEACH BOYS, The / Tony & Joe

TONY, BOB & JIMMY
Singles: 7-Inch
CAPITOL: 62 3–5

Price Range

Members: Tony Butala; Bob Engemann; Jim Pike
Also see LETTERMEN, The

TOOTS & THE MAYTALS
Singles: 12-Inch 33/45rpm
MANGO: 82 . . . . $4–6
Singles: 7-Inch
MANGO: 76–82 1–3
LPs: 10/12-Inch 33rpm
MANGO: 76–82 5–8

TOP SHELF
Singles: 7-Inch
LO LO: 69–70 2–4
SOUND TOWN: 80 1–3

TORCH
Singles: 12-Inch 33/45rpm
PACIFIC: 83 4–6

TORCHSONG
Singles: 12-Inch 33/45rpm
I.R.S.: 83–84 4–6
Singles: 7-Inch
I.R.S.: 83–84 1–3
LPs: 10/12-Inch 33rpm
I.R.S.: 83 5–8

TORME, Mel (Mel Torme & The Meltones)
Singles: 7-Inch
ATLANTIC: 62–64 2–4
BETHLEHEM: 56–58 2–5
CAPITOL (1000 & 2000
  series): 50–53 3–6
  (Purple labels.)
CAPITOL (2000 series):
  69–70 2–3
  (Orange labels.)
COLUMBIA: 64–67 2–4
CORAL: 53–56 2–5
LIBERTY: 68 2–4
VERVE: 59–61 2–4
EPs: 7-Inch 33/45rpm
CAPITOL: 50 5–15
LPs: 10/12-Inch 33rpm
ATLANTIC (8000 series):
  62–64 10–25
ATLANTIC (18000 series):
  75 5–8

Price Range

ATLANTIC (80000 series):
  83 . . . . $5–8
BETHLEHEM (34 through
  52): 55–56 20–35
BETHLEHEM (4000
  series): 65 10–20
BETHLEHEM (6000
  series): 58–60 15–35
  (Maroon labels.)
BETHLEHEM (6000
  series): 77–78 5–10
  (Gray labels.)
CAPITOL (200 series): 50 15–30
  (10-Inch LPs.)
CAPITOL (300 & 400
  series): 69–70 8–12
COLUMBIA (2000 series):
  64–66 10–20
  (Monaural issues.)
COLUMBIA (9000 series):
  64–66 10–20
  (Stereo issues.)
CONCORD JAZZ: 82 5–8
CORAL (57000 series):
  54–55 25–50
EVEREST: 76 5–8
GLENDALE: 78–79 5–8
GRYPHON: 79 5–8
LIBERTY: 68 8–15
MGM (500 series): 52 30–60
  (10-Inch LPs.)
MAYFAIR: 58 20–30
METRO: 65 10–20
MUSICRAFT: 83 5–8
STRAND: 60 12–25
VERVE: 58–60 15–30
  (Reads "Verve Records, Inc." at bottom of
  label.)
VERVE: 61–72 10–20
  (Reads "MGM Records - A Division Of Metro-
  Goldwyn-Mayer, Inc." at bottom of label.)
VERVE: 73–84 5–10
  (Reads "Manufactured By MGM Record
  Corp.," or mentions either Polydor or Poly-
  gram at bottom of label.)
VOCALION: 70 5–10
  Also see RICH, Buddy
  Also see WHITING, Margaret

TORNADER
Singles: 7-Inch
POLYDOR: 77 2–3

Price Range

TORNADOES, The
Singles: 7-Inch
LONDON: *62–63* $3–5
TOWER: *65* 3–5
LPs: 10/12-Inch 33rpm
LONDON: *62–63* 20–30

TOROK, Mitchell (Mitchell Torok & The Louisiana Hayride Band; Mitchell Torok & The Matches)
Singles: 7-Inch
ABBOTT: *53–54* 5–10
CAPITOL: *62–63* 3–5
DECCA: *57–59* 4–6
GUYDEN: *59–60* 4–6
INETTE: *63* 3–5
MERCURY: *61* 3–5
RCA VICTOR: *65* 3–5
REPRISE: *66–67* 2–4
Picture Sleeves
GUYDEN: *59–60* 8–12
LPs: 10/12-Inch 33rpm
GUYDEN: *60* 25–35
REPRISE: *66* 10–15

TORONTO
Singles: 7-Inch
NETWORK: *82* 1–3
SOLID GOLD 1–3
LPs: 10/12-Inch 33rpm
A&M: *80–81* 5–8
SOLID GOLD 5–8

TORRANCE, George (George Torrance & The Naturals; Georgie Torrance & The Dippers)
Singles: 7-Inch
DUO DISC: *66* 3–5
EPIC: *61* 5–8
KING: *60* 4–6
SHOUT: *68* 3–5

TORRANCE, Richard (Richard Torrance & Eureka)
Singles: 7-Inch
CAPITOL: *77–79* 2–3
SHELTER: *75* 2–4
LPs: 10/12-Inch 33rpm
CAPITOL: *77* 5–8
SHELTER: *74–75* 8–10

Price Range

TOSH, Peter
Singles: 12-Inch 33/45rpm
EMI AMERICA: *83* $4–6
Singles: 7-Inch
COLUMBIA: *77* 2–3
EMI AMERICA: *81–84* 1–3
ROLLING STONES:
78–79 2–3
Picture Sleeves
ROLLING STONES: *78* 2–3
EPs: 7-Inch 33/45rpm
COLUMBIA: *76* 4–6
(Promotional issue only.)
LPs: 10/12-Inch 33rpm
COLUMBIA: *77* 5–8
EMI AMERICA: *81–84* 5–8
ROLLING STONES: *79* 5–8

TOSH, Peter, & Mick Jagger
Singles: 7-Inch
ROLLING STONES
(19308; "Don't Look
Back"): *78* 3–5
(With "Rolling Stones" at top of label.)
ROLLING STONES
(19308; "Don't Look
Back"): *78* 2–3
(Without "Rolling Stones" at top of label.)
Promotional Singles
ROLLING STONES (130;
"Don't Look Back"): *78* 12–15
ROLLING STONES
(7500; "Don't Look
Back"): *78* 5–8
LPs: 10/12-Inch 33rpm
ROLLING STONES: *78* 5–8
Also see JAGGER, Mick
Also see MARLEY, Bob, & The Wailers

TOTAL COELO
Singles: 12-Inch 33/45rpm
CHRYSALIS: *83* 4–6
Singles: 7-Inch
CHRYSALIS: *83* 1–3

TOTAL CONTRAST
Singles: 12-Inch 33/45rpm
LONDON: *85* 4–6
Singles: 7-Inch
LONDON: *85* 1–3

Price Range

TOTO
Singles: 12-Inch 33/45rpm
COLUMBIA: *79–85* **$4–6**
Singles: 7-Inch
COLUMBIA: *78–85* **1–3**
LPs: 10/12-Inch 33rpm
COLUMBIA ("Isolation"):
  84 .... **8–12**
  (Picture disc.)
COLUMBIA ("Toto"): *79* **30–40**
  (Picture disc. Promotional issue only.)
COLUMBIA (30000
  series): *78–84* **5–10**
COLUMBIA (40000
  series): *83* **10–15**
  (Half-speed mastered.)
POLYDOR: *84* **5–8**
  Also see VOICES OF AMERICA, The /
  U.S.A. For Africa

TOUCH, The (With Don Gallucci)
Singles: 7-Inch
ATCO: *80–81*..................... **1–3**
BRUNSWICK: *77*................. **2–3**
COLISEUM: *69*.................. **4–6**
LECASVER: *69*.................. **5–8**
LPs: 10/12-Inch 33rpm
ATCO: *80* **5–8**
COLISEUM: *68*................. **15–20**
  Also see DON & THE GOODTIMES

TOUCH OF CLASS
Singles: 12-Inch 33/45rpm
NEXT PLATINUM: *84*............ **4–6**
Singles: 7-Inch
ATLANTIC: *82* **1–3**
MIDLAND INT'L: *75–77*.......... **2–4**
ROADSHOW: *79–84* **1–3**
LPs: 10/12-Inch 33rpm
MIDLAND INT'L: *76*............. **5–10**
ROADSHOW: *79* **5–8**

TOURISTS, The
Singles: 7-Inch
EPIC: *80* **2–3**
LPs: 10/12-Inch 33rpm
EPIC: *81* **6–10**
  Members: Annie Lennox; David Stewart.
  Also see EURYTHMICS, The

Price Range

TOWER OF POWER
Singles: 7-Inch
COLUMBIA: *76–78* **$2–3**
SAN FRANCISCO: *64–73* **4–6**
WARNER BROS: *72–75*........... **2–4**
LPs: 10/12-Inch 33rpm
COLUMBIA: *78–79* **5–8**
SAN FRANCISCO: *71* **10–15**
WARNER BROS: *72–76*.......... **8–10**
  Also see WILLIAMS, Lenny

TOWNES, Carol Lynn
Singles: 12-Inch 33/45rpm
POLYDOR: *84–85* **4–6**
Singles: 7-Inch
POLYDOR: *84–85* **1–3**
LPs: 10/12-Inch 33rpm
POLYDOR: *84* **5–8**

TOWNSEND, Ed
Singles: 7-Inch
CAPITOL: *58–59* **4–6**
CHALLENGE: *61–62* **3–5**
DYNASTY: *60* **3–5**
GLO-TOWN: *66*................. **2–4**
LIBERTY: *62–63* **3–5**
MGM: *67*....................... **2–4**
MAXX: *64*...................... **3–5**
POLYDOR: *70* **2–4**
WARNER BROS: *60–61*.......... **3–5**
EPs: 7-Inch 33/45rpm
CAPITOL: *58* **10–15**
LPs: 10/12-Inch 33rpm
CAPITOL: *59* **15–20**
CURTOM: *76* **8–12**

TOWNSHEND, Pete
Singles: 7-Inch
ATCO: *80–83*.................... **1–3**
LPs: 10/12-Inch 33rpm
ATCO: *80–83*.................... **5–8**
DECCA: *72*..................... **10–12**
  Also see WHO, The

TOWNSHEND, Pete, & Ronnie Lane
Singles: 7-Inch
MCA: *77–78* **2–3**
LPs: 10/12-Inch 33rpm
MCA: *77* **8–10**
  Also see CLAPTON, Eric
  Also see ENTWISTLE, John
  Also see TOWNSHEND, Pete

Price Range

TOWNSHEND, Simon
Singles: 7-Inch
21: *83* **$1–3**
LPs: 10/12-Inch 33rpm
21: *83* **5–8**

TOY DOLLS, The
Singles: 7-Inch
ERA: *62* **3–5**

TOYS, The
Singles: 7-Inch
ABC: *73* **1–3**
DYNO VOICE: *65–66* **3–5**
ERIC **1–3**
GUSTO **1–3**
MUSICOR: *68* **3–5**
PHILIPS: *67* **3–5**
VIRGO: *72* **1–3**
LPs: 10/12-Inch 33rpm
DYNO VOICE: *66* **25–30**
SECTET: *81* **5–8**

TRACY, Jeanie (Jeanne Tracy)
Singles: 12-Inch 33/45rpm
MEGATONE: *84–85* **4–6**
Singles: 7-Inch
FANTASY: *83* **1–3**
SMOGSVILLE: *67* **3–5**

TRADE WINDS, The
Singles: 7-Inch
ERIC **1–3**
KAMA SUTRA: *66–67* **3–5**
RED BIRD: *65* **5–8**
LPs: 10/12-Inch 33rpm
KAMA SUTRA: *67* **20–30**
Members: Pete Anders; Vinnie Poncia.
Also see INNOCENCE, The
Also see VIDELS, The

TRADEWINDS, The
Singles: 7-Inch
RCA VICTOR: *59* **4–6**

TRAFFIC
Singles: 7-Inch
ASYLUM: *74* **2–4**
ISLAND: *72–73* **2–4**

Price Range

UNITED ARTISTS: *67–72* **$3–5**
Picture Sleeves
UNITED ARTISTS: *67* **3–5**
LPs: 10/12-Inch 33rpm
ASYLUM: *74* **8–10**
ISLAND (9000 series):
71–75 .... **8–10**
ISLAND (90000 series): *83* **5–8**
UNITED ARTISTS: *68–75* **10–20**
Members: Jim Capaldi; Dave Mason; Steve
Winwood; Chris Wood.
Also see CAN
Also see CAPALDI, Jim
Also see MASON, Dave
Also see WINWOOD, Steve

TRAITS, The (With Roy Head)
Singles: 7-Inch
ASCOT: *62* **8–10**
PACEMAKER: *67* **5–8**
RENNER: *62* **10–12**
SCEPTER: *66* **3–5**
TNT: *59–60* **10–15**
LPs: 10/12-Inch 33rpm
TNT: *65* **100–150**
Also see HEAD, Roy

TRAITS, The (With Johnny Winter)
Singles: 7-Inch
UNIVERSAL: *66* **20–25**
Also see WINTER, Johnny

TRAMAINE (Tramaine Hawkins)
Singles: 12-Inch 33/45rpm
A&M: *85* **4–6**
Singles: 7-Inch
A&M: *85* **1–3**

TRAMMPS, The
Singles: 7-Inch
ATLANTIC: *75–80* **1–3**
BUDDAH: *72–76* **2–4**
ERIC: *78* **1–3**
GOLDEN FLEECE: *73–75* **2–4**
VENTURE: *83* **1–3**
Picture Sleeves
ATLANTIC: *77* .... **INC**
LPs: 10/12-Inch 33rpm
ATLANTIC: *76–80* **6–10**
BUDDAH: *75* **8–10**
GOLDEN FLEECE: *75* **8–10**

Price Range

PHILADELPHIA INT'L:
77 . . . . **$8–10**

TRAPEZE
Singles: 7-Inch
PAID: *81* **1–3**
THRESHOLD: *72.* **2–4**
WARNER BROS: *74–75* **2–4**
LPs: 10/12-Inch 33rpm
PAID: *81* **5–8**
SHARK **8–10**
THRESHOLD: *70–74.* **10–15**
WARNER BROS: *74–75* **8–10**
Also see DEEP PURPLE

TRASHMEN, The
Singles: 7-Inch
ARGO: *66* **5–8**
ERA: *72.* **1–3**
ERIC **1–3**
GARRETT: *63–64* **5–8**
METROBEAT: *68* **4–6**
TRIBE: *66.* **5–8**
Picture Sleeves
GARRETT: *64* **5–10**
LPs: 10/12-Inch 33rpm
GARRETT: *64* **35–45**

TRAVERS, Mary
Singles: 7-Inch
CHRYSALIS: *78–79.* **1–3**
WARNER BROS: *71–73.* **2–3**
LPs: 10/12-Inch 33rpm
CHRYSALIS: *78.* **5–8**
WARNER BROS: *71–74* **8–10**
Also see PETER, PAUL & MARY

TRAVERS, Pat (The Pat Travers Band; Pat Travers' Black Pearl)
Singles: 7-Inch
POLYDOR: *77–80* **1–3**
LPs: 10/12-Inch 33rpm
POLYDOR: *76–84* **5–8**

TRAVIS, McKinley
Singles: 7-Inch
PRIDE: *70.* **2–4**

TRAVIS & BOB
Singles: 7-Inch
BIG TOP: *60.* **3–5**

Price Range

MERCURY: *61.* **$3–5**
SANDY: *59.* **4–6**
(Reads "Distributed By Dot" on label.)
SANDY: *59.* **5–8**
(Does not read "Distributed By Dot" on label.)
Members: Travis Pritchett; Bob Weaver.

TRAVOLTA, Joey
Singles: 7-Inch
CASABLANCA: *78–79* **2–3**
MILLENNIUM: *78* **2–3**
Picture Sleeves
MILLENNIUM: *78* **2–3**
LPs: 10/12-Inch 33rpm
CASABLANCA: *78–79* **5–8**
MILLENNIUM: *78* **5–8**

John Travolta, six charted singles (1976–78), three charted LPs (1976–78). (Includes issues shown as by Olivia Newton-John & John Travolta.)

TRAVOLTA, John
Singles: 7-Inch
MIDLAND INT'L: *76–80.* **1–3**
RCA VICTOR: *77* **2–3**
RSO: *78–79* **1–3**
Picture Sleeves
MIDLAND INT'L: *76–80.* **2–3**
RCA VICTOR: *77* **2–3**
RSO: *78–79* **1–3**
LPs: 10/12-Inch 33rpm
MIDLAND INT'L: *76–77.* **8–10**
MIDSONG INT'L: *78* **8–10**

Also see NEWTON-JOHN, Olivia, & John Travolta

TRAVOLTA, John / Sha Na Na
Singles: 7-Inch
RSO: 78 . . . . $2–3
Also see SHA NA NA
Also see TRAVOLTA, John

TREASURES, The
Singles: 7-Inch
EPIC: 77 2–3
MERCURY: 76. 2–4
LPs: 10/12-Inch 33rpm
EPIC: 77 5–8

TREE SWINGERS, The
Singles: 7-Inch
GUYDEN: 60 4–6

TREMELOES, The
Singles: 7-Inch
DJM: 74–75 2–4
EPIC (Except 10075):
  67–70 3–5
EPIC (10075; "Good Day
  Sunshine"): 66 4–6
Picture Sleeves
EPIC: 67 3–5
LPs: 10/12-Inch 33rpm
DJM: 74 8–10
EPIC: 67–68 15–20
Also see POOLE, Brian

T-REX (Tyrannosaurus Rex; Featuring Marc Bolan)
Singles: 7-Inch
A&M: 68 5–8
BLUE THUMB: 71–72 4–6
CASABLANCA: 75 2–4
REPRISE: 71–74. 3–5
LPs: 10/12-Inch 33rpm
A&M (3000 series): 72 10–15
A&M (4000 series): 68 15–20
BLUE THUMB: 71–72 10–15
CASABLANCA: 74 8–10
REPRISE: 71–73. 8–12
Also see BOLAN, Marc
Also see GREEN, Jack

TRIBE
Singles: 7-Inch
ABC: 73–74 . . . . $2–4
C & CT: 71 2–4
LPs: 10/12-Inch 33rpm
ABC: 73–74 8–10
FARR: 77 8–10

TRINERE
Singles: 7-Inch
JAMPACKED: 85 1–3

TRIO+: see LEWIS, Jerry Lee, Carl Perkins & Charlie Rich

TRIPLE "S" CONNECTION, The
Singles: 12-Inch 33/45rpm
20TH CENTURY-FOX:
  79–80 4–6
Singles: 7-Inch
20TH CENTURY-FOX:
  79–80 1–3
LPs: 10/12-Inch 33rpm
20TH CENTURY-FOX:
  79 5–8
Also see SKOOL BOYZ, The

TRIUMPH
Singles: 7-Inch
MCA: 85 1–3
RCA VICTOR: 78–84 1–3
LPs: 10/12-Inch 33rpm
MCA: 85 5–8
RCA VICTOR: 78–84 5–8
Members: Mike Levine; Gil Moore; Rik Emmett.

TRIUMVIRAT
Singles: 7-Inch
CAPITOL: 79 1–3
LPs: 10/12-Inch 33rpm
CAPITOL: 74–80 6–10
HARVEST: 74. 10–12

TROGGS, The
Singles: 7-Inch
ATCO: 66–67. 5–8
BELL: 73 3–5
FONTANA: 66–69. 4–6
PAGE ONE: 69–70 3–5
PRIVATE STOCK: 77. 2–4

Price Range

PYE: *75–76* **$2–4**

LPs: 10/12-Inch 33rpm
ATCO: *66* **35–45**
FONTANA: *66–68* **20–30**
LIBERTY: *66* **20–30**
MKC: *80* **8–10**
PRIVATE STOCK: *76* **10–15**
PYE: *75* **10–15**
SIRE: *76* **12–15**

TROLLS, The
Singles: 7-Inch
ABC: *66–67* **3–5**
U.S.A.: *68* **3–5**
WARRIOR **4–6**
LPs: 10/12-Inch 33rpm
SMASH: *69* **10–15**

TROOPER
Singles: 7-Inch
LEGEND: *75–77* **2–4**
MCA: *77–78* **2–3**
LPs: 10/12-Inch 33rpm
LEGEND: *75–76* **8–10**
MCA: *78–80* **5–8**
RCA VICTOR: *82* **5–8**

TROPEA
Singles: 7-Inch
MARLIN: *76–77* **2–3**
LPs: 10/12-Inch 33rpm
MARLIN: *76–77* **8–10**

TROUBADOURS DU ROI BAUDOUIN
LPs: 10/12-Inch 33rpm
PHILIPS: *63–69* **4–10**

TROUBLE
Singles: 7-Inch
AL & THE KIDD: *80* **1–3**
UNITED ARTISTS: *77* **2–3**
LPs: 10/12-Inch 33rpm
UNITED ARTISTS: *77* **8–10**

TROUBLE FUNK
Singles: 12-Inch 33/45rpm
SUGAR HILL: *82* **4–6**
Singles: 7-Inch
D.E.T.T.: *83* **1–3**

Price Range

ISLAND: *85* **$1–3**
LPs: 10/12-Inch 33rpm
SUGAR HILL: *82* **5–8**

TROUTMAN, Tony
Singles: 7-Inch
GRAM-O-PHONE: *75* **2–4**
T. MAIN: *82–83* **1–3**

TROWER, Robin
Singles: 7-Inch
CHRYSALIS: *72–78* **2–3**
LPs: 10/12-Inch 33rpm
CHRYSALIS: *73–82* **6–10**
Also see BRUCE, Jack, & Robin Trower
Also see PROCOL HARUM

TROY, Benny (Benny Troy & Maze)
Singles: 7-Inch
DE-LITE: *75* **2–4**
20TH CENTURY-FOX **1–3**

TROY, Doris
Singles: 7-Inch
APPLE: *70* **2–4**
ATLANTIC: *63–65* **3–5**
CALLA: *66* **3–5**
CAPITOL: *67* **2–4**
MIDLAND INT'L: *76* **2–3**
LPs: 10/12-Inch 33rpm
APPLE: *70* **15–20**
ATLANTIC: *64* **20–25**

TROYER, Eric
Singles: 7-Inch
CHRYSALIS: *80* **1–3**
LPs: 10/12-Inch 33rpm
CHRYSALIS: *80* **5–8**

Andrea True, four charted singles (1976–78), one charted LP (1976).

Price Range

TRUE, Andrea (The Andrea True Connection)
Singles: 7-Inch
BUDDAH: *76–78* $2–4
ERIC: *78* 1–3

LPs: 10/12-Inch 33rpm
BUDDAH: *76–78* 5–8

TRUMPETEERS, The (With Billy Mure)
Singles: 7-Inch
SPLASH: *59* 2–4
Also see MURE, Billy

TRUSSELL
Singles: 7-Inch
ELEKTRA: *80* 1–3

LPs: 10/12-Inch 33rpm
ELEKTRA: *80* 5–8

TRUTH
Singles: 7-Inch
DEVAKI: *80–81* 1–3
ROULETTE: *74–75* 2–3

LPs: 10/12-Inch 33rpm
PARAGON: *78* 5–8
ROULETTE: *75* 8–10

Price Range

TRYTHALL, Gil
Singles: 7-Inch
ATHENA: *69–70* $1–3
LPs: 10/12-Inch 33rpm
ATHENA: *69–70* 5–8
PANDORA: *81* 5–8

TUBES, The (Featuring Fee Waybill)
Singles: 12-Inch 33/45rpm
CAPITOL: *83* 4–6
Singles: 7-Inch
A&M: *75–79* 2–4
CAPITOL: *81–85* 1–3
Picture Sleeves
CAPITOL: *81* . . . . INC
LPs: 10/12-Inch 33rpm
A&M: *75–81* 6–10
CAPITOL: *81–85* 5–8
Also see WAYBILL, Fee

TUCKER, Junior
Singles: 7-Inch
GEFFEN: *83* 1–3
LPs: 10/12-Inch 33rpm
GEFFEN: *83* 5–8

TUCKER, Louis
Singles: 7-Inch
ARISTA: *83* 1–3
LPs: 10/12-Inch 33rpm
ARISTA: *83* 4–8

TUCKER, Marshall: see MARSHALL TUCKER BAND, The

TUCKER, Tanya
Singles: 7-Inch
ARISTA: *82–84* 1–3
COLUMBIA: *72–77* 2–4
MCA: *75–81* 1–3
Picture Sleeves
COLUMBIA: *72–75* 3–5
MCA: *75–81* 1–3
LPs: 10/12-Inch 33rpm
ARISTA: *82–84* 5–8
COLUMBIA (KC series):
72–75 8–10
COLUMBIA (PC series):
77 5–8
MCA: *75–81* 5–8

Price Range

Also see CAMPBELL, Glen, & Tanya Tucker
Also see HARRIS, Emmylou

TUCKER, Tommy
Singles: 7-Inch
CHECKER: *64–67* **$3–5**
FESTIVAL: *66* **3–5**
HI: *59–60* **4–6**
RCA VICTOR (37-7800
   series): *61* **5–8**
   (Compact 33 Single.)
RCA VICTOR (47-7800
   series): *61* **3–5**
RCA VICTOR (68-7800
   series): *61* **10–15**
   (Stereo Compact 33 Single.)
SUNBEAM: *59* **4–6**
XL: *66* **3–5**
LPs: 10/12-Inch 33rpm
CHECKER: *64* **15–20**
Also see DUSTERS, The

TUFANO & GIAMMARESE
Singles: 7-Inch
ODE: *73–76* **2–4**
LPs: 10/12-Inch 33rpm
EPIC/ODE: *76–77* **8–10**
ODE: *73–74* **10–12**
Members: Dennis Tufano; Carl Giammarese.
Also see BUCKINGHAMS, The

TUFF DARTS, The
Singles: 7-Inch
SIRE: *78* **2–4**
LPs: 10/12-Inch 33rpm
SIRE: *78* **5–8**

TULL, Jethro: see JETHRO TULL

TUNE ROCKERS, The
Singles: 7-Inch
PET: *58* **5–8**
UNITED ARTISTS: *58* **4–6**

TUNE WEAVERS, The
Singles: 7-Inch
CASA GRANDE (Except
   4037): *57–60* **8–12**
CASA GRANDE (4037;
   "Happy, Happy Birthday
   Baby"): *57* **25–30**
CHECKER: *57–62* **5–8**

Price Range

CHESS: *73* **$1–3**
ERIC **1–3**
LPs: 10/12-Inch 33rpm
CASA GRANDE **10–15**
Members: Margo Sylvia; Charlotte Davis; Gil
Lopez; John Sylvia.

TUNETOPPERS, The: see BROWN, Al, & His Tunetoppers

TUNNELL, Jimi
Singles: 12-Inch 33/45rpm
MCA: *84* **4–6**
Singles: 7-Inch
MCA: *84* **1–3**

TURBANS, The
Singles: 7-Inch
ABC: *73* **1–3**
COLLECTABLES **1–3**
FLASHBACK: *65* **1–3**
HERALD: *55–57* **10–12**
HI-OLDIES **1–3**
IMPERIAL: *61–62* **4–6**
MONEY: *55* **15–20**
PARKWAY: *61* **5–8**
RED TOP: *60* **8–10**
ROULETTE: *60–61* **5–8**
LPs: 10/12-Inch 33rpm
COLLECTABLES **5–8**
LOST-NITE: *81* **5–8**
RELIC **10–12**
Members: Al Banks; Matt Platt; Andrew Jones;
Charles Williams.

TURBANS, The / The Turks
Singles: 7-Inch
MONEY: *55* **15–20**
Also see TURBANS, The
Also see TURKS, The

TURNER, Ike & Tina (Ike & Tina Turner & The Ikettes; Ike & Tina Turner & Home Grown Funk)
Singles: 7-Inch
A&M: *69* **2–4**
BLUE THUMB: *69–71* **2–4**
COLLECTABLES **1–3**
FANTASY **2–3**
INNIS: *68–71* **3–5**
KENT (400 series): *64* **3–5**

Price Range

KENT (4500 series): *70*	**$2–4**
LIBERTY: *70–71*	**2–4**
LOMA: *65*	**3–5**
MINIT: *69–70*	**2–4**
MODERN: *65*	**3–5**
PHILLES: *66*	**5–8**
POMPEII: *68–70*	**3–5**
SONJA: *63–64*	**3–5**
SUE (100 series): *65–66*	**3–5**
SUE (700 series): *60–63*	**4–6**
TRC: *71*	**2–4**
TANGERINE: *66*	**3–5**
UNITED ARTISTS: *71–75*	**2–4**
WARNER BROS: *64*	**3–5**

Picture Sleeves

WARNER BROS: *64*	**3–5**

LPs: 10/12-Inch 33rpm

A&M (3000 series): *82*	**5–8**
A&M (4000 series): *69*	**10–15**
ABC	**8–10**
ACCORD: *81*	**5–8**
BLUE THUMB: *69–73*	**8–12**
CAPITOL (500 series): *75*	**5–8**
(With an "SM" prefix.)	
CAPITOL (500 series): *69*	**10–12**
(With an "ST" prefix.)	
CENCO	**15–20**
FANTASY: *80*	**5–8**
HARMONY (11000 series): *69*	**10–12**
HARMONY (30000 series): *71*	**8–10**
KENT: *61–64*	**15–20**
LIBERTY (7000 series): *70*	**10–12**
LIBERTY (51000 series): *85*	**5–8**
LOMA: *66*	**12–15**
MINIT: *70*	**10–12**
PHILLES: *66*	**35–45**
PICKWICK	**6–10**
POMPEII: *68–69*	**10–12**
SUE: *61–65*	**20–30**
SUNSET: *69–70*	**8–10**
UNART	**5–10**
UNITED ARTISTS: *71–78*	**8–12**
UNITED SUPERIOR	**8–10**
WARNER BROS: *65–69*	**12–15**

Also see BLAND, Bobby, & Ike Turner
Also see IKETTES, The
Also see RAELETTES, The
Also see SYLVIA

Price Range

Also see TURNER, Tina

TURNER, Jesse Lee
Singles: 7-Inch

CARLTON: *59*	**$4–6**
FRATERNITY: *59*	**4–6**
GENE NORMAN PRESENTS (184; "All You Gotta Do"): *62*	**3–5**
GENE NORMAN PRESENTS (188; "Shotgun Boogie"): *62*	**10–15**
IMPERIAL: *60*	**5–8**
SUDDEN	**3–5**
TOP RANK: *60*	**3–5**

Picture Sleeves

CARLTON: *59*	**5–10**
FRATERNITY: *59*	**8–12**

TURNER, Joe (Big Joe Turner; Joe Turner & His Blues Kings; Joe Turner With Pete Johnson & His Orchestra)
Singles: 7-Inch

ATLANTIC (939; "Chains Of Love"): *51*	**35–40**
ATLANTIC (949; "Bump Miss Susie"): *51*	**30–35**
ATLANTIC (960; "Sweet Sixteen"): *52*	**30–35**
ATLANTIC (970; "Don't You Cry"): *52*	**25–30**
ATLANTIC (982; "Don't You Cry"): *52*	**20–25**
ATLANTIC (1001; "Honey Hush"): *53*	**12–15**
ATLANTIC (1016; "TV Mama"): *53*	**20–25**
ATLANTIC (1026 through 1184): *54–58*	**6–10**
ATLANTIC (2000 series): *59–60*	**4–6**
BAYOU: *53*	**40–50**
BLUESWAY: *67*	**3–5**
CORAL (62000 series): *64*	**3–5**
DECCA (29000 series): *55–56*	**10–15**
KENT: *69–71*	**2–4**
RPM: *51*	**50–75**
RONN: *69*	**2–4**

Price Range　　　　　　　　　　　　*Price Range*

EPs: 7-Inch 33/45rpm
ATLANTIC: *55–57* $20–30
EMARCY: *56* 20–30

LPs: 10/12-Inch 33rpm
ARHOOLIE: *62* 15–20
ATCO: *71* 8–10
ATLANTIC (1234; "Boss
　Of The Blues"): *58* 30–40
ATLANTIC (1332; "Big
　Joe Rides Again"): *60*.......... 25–30
ATLANTIC (8005; "Joe
　Turner" - black label):
　57 35–45
ATLANTIC (8005; "Joe
　Turner" - red label): *59* 20–25
ATLANTIC (8023;
　"Rockin' The Blues" -
　black label): *58*. 30–40
ATLANTIC (8023;
　"Rockin' The Blues" -
　red label): *59* 20–25
ATLANTIC (8033; "Big
　Joe Is Here" - black
　label): *59*..................... 30–40
ATLANTIC (8033; "Big
　Joe Is Here" - red label):
　59 20–25
ATLANTIC (8081; "Best
　Of Joe Turner"): *63* 15–20
ATLANTIC (8812; "Boss
　Of The Blues"): *81* 5–8
BIG TOWN: *78*. 5–8
BLUES SPECTRUM 10–12
BLUESWAY: *67–73*............... 8–12
CHIARDSCURO: *76*.............. 8–10
CLASSIC JAZZ: *79* 5–8
EMARCY: *56* 35–45
INTERMEDIA: *83–84*............. 5–8
LMI: *74* 8–10
MCA: *80* 5–8
PABLO: *76–83* 5–8
SAVOY: *77* 5–8
UNITED 8–10
　Also see BIG VERNON
　Also see WILLIAMS, Dootsie

TURNER, Joe / Jimmy Nelson
LPs: 10/12-Inch 33rpm
CROWN: *62* 10–20
　Also see NELSON, Jimmy
　Also see TURNER, Joe

**TURNER, Sammy (Sammy Turner &
The Twisters)**
Singles: 7-Inch
BIG TOP (3007 & 3016):
　59 .... $4–6
BIG TOP (3029;
　"Always"): *59* 4–6
BIG TOP (3029;
　"Always"): *59* 8–10
　(Stereo single.)
BIG TOP (3032 through
　3070): *60–61*.................... 3–5
BIG TOP (3089;
　"Falling"): *61*.................. 8–10
ERIC 1–3
MILLENNIUM: *78* 2–3
MOTOWN: *64*. 10–15
PACIFIC: *59*.................... 15–20
20TH CENTURY-FOX:
　65 3–5
VERVE: *66* 3–5
LPs: 10/12-Inch 33rpm
BIG TOP: *60*.................... 20–30

TURNER, Spyder
Singles: 7-Inch
MGM: *66–71*...................... 3–5
POLYDOR: *84* 1–3
WHITFIELD: *78–79* 2–3
LPs: 10/12-Inch 33rpm
MGM: *67*....................... 15–20
WHITFIELD: *78–79* 5–8
　Also see BRISTOL, Johnny, & Spyder Turner

TURNER, Tina
Singles: 12-Inch 33/45rpm
CAPITOL: *84–85* 4–6
Singles: 7-Inch
CAPITOL: *84–85* 1–3
POMPEII: *68*. 3–5
UNITED ARTISTS: *75–78* 2–4
WAGNER: *79*..................... 2–3
LPs: 10/12-Inch 33rpm
CAPITOL: *84–85* 5–8
FANTASY 5–8
SPRINGBOARD: *72* 8–10
UNITED ARTISTS
　(Except 200): *75–78*. 8–10
UNITED ARTISTS (200;
　"Tina Turner Turns The
　Country On"): *67* 10–15

WAGNER: *79*.................... **$5–8**
  Also see BOWIE, David
  Also see JOHN, Elton / Tina Turner
  Also see TURNER, Ike & Tina
  Also see U.S.A. FOR AFRICA

TURNER, Titus
Singles: 7-Inch
ATCO: *64* **3–5**
ATLANTIC: *57* **5–8**
COLUMBIA: *63* **3–5**
ENJOY: *62–63*................... **3–5**
GLOVER (Except 302):
  59–60 .... **4–6**
GLOVER (302; "When
  The Sergeant Comes
  Marching Home"): *60*.......... **10–15**
GUARANTEED: *61–62* **3–5**
JAMIE: *61*...................... **3–5**
JOSIE: *68–69*.................... **2–4**
KING (Except stereo
  singles): *57–61* **4–6**
KING (Stereo singles): *59* **5–8**
MURBO: *65* **3–5**
OKEH (6844 through
  7038): *52–54*.................. **10–12**
OKEH (7200 series): *66*............. **3–5**
PHILIPS: *67* **3–5**
WING: *55* **8–10**
LPs: 10/12-Inch 33rpm
JAMIE: *61*...................... **20–25**
  Also see BAKER, Mickey

TURRENTINE, Stanley
Singles: 7-Inch
BLUE NOTE: *61–69* **2–4**
CTI: *72*........................ **1–3**
ELEKTRA: *79–81* **1–3**
FANTASY: *74–78*................. **1–3**
IMPULSE: *67*.................... **2–4**
LPs: 10/12-Inch 33rpm
BAINBRIDGE: *81*................ **5–8**
BLUE NOTE: *60–61* **25–50**
  (Label gives New York street address for Blue
  Note Records.)
BLUE NOTE: *62–65* **15–25**
  (Label reads "Blue Note Records Inc. - New
  York, USA.")
BLUE NOTE: *66–85* **8–18**
  (Label shows Blue Note Records as a division
  of either Liberty or United Artists.)
CTI: *71–75*...................... **8–12**

ELEKTRA: *79–81* **$5–8**
FPM: *75*........................ **5–8**
FANTASY: *74–78*................ **6–12**
IMPULSE: *67–78* **8–15**
MAINSTREAM: *65*.............. **12–25**
PRESTIGE: *70–71* **5–10**
SUNSET **69**
TIME: *62–63*.................... **25–50**
UPFRONT: *72* **6–10**
  Also see BYRD, Donald, & Stanley Turrentine
  Also see GILBERTO, Astrud, & Stanley Tur-
  rentine
  Also see HUBBARD, Freddie, & Stanley Tur-
  rentine
  Also see SILVER, Horace, Quintet, & Stanley
  Turrentine

TURTLES, The
Singles: 7-Inch
COLLECTABLES **1–3**
WHITE WHALE: *65–70*........... **3–5**
Picture Sleeves
WHITE WHALE: *66–69*........... **3–6**
LPs: 10/12-Inch 33rpm
RHINO (Except picture
  discs): *82–86*.................... **5–8**
RHINO (Picture discs): *83* **8–10**
SIRE: *74* **10–15**
WHITE WHALE: *65–71*.......... **20–25**
  Members: Mark Volman; Howard Kaylan.
  Also see CHRISTMAS SPIRIT
  Also see CROSSFIRES, The
  Also see FLO & EDDIE

TURZY, Jane
Singles: 7-Inch
DECCA: *51–54*................... **2–4**

TUXEDO JUNCTION
Singles: 12-Inch 33/45rpm
BUTTERFLY: *78–80*..............
Singles: 7-Inch
BUTTERFLY: *78–80*.......
LPs: 10/12-Inch 33
BUTTERFLY (Black
  vinyl): *77–79*..........
BUTTERFLY (Colored
  vinyl): *77* ....
  (Promotional issues only

Price Range   *Price Range*

TWENNYNINE (Featuring Lenny White)
Singles: 7-Inch
ELEKTRA: *79–81* $1–3
LPs: 10/12-Inch 33rpm
ELEKTRA: *79–81* 5–8
  Also see RETURN TO FOREVER
  Also see WHITE, Lenny

20-20
Singles: 7-Inch
PORTRAIT: *79*................... 1–3
LPs: 10/12-Inch 33rpm
ENIGMA: *83*..................... 5–8
PORTRAIT: *79–81*................ 5–8

21ST CENTURY
Singles: 7-Inch
RCA VICTOR: *75* 2–4

TWILIGHT 22
Singles: 12-Inch 33/45rpm
VANGUARD: *83–84*.............. 4–6
Singles: 7-Inch
VANGUARD: *83–84*.............. 1–3
LPs: 10/12-Inch 33rpm
VANGUARD: *84*................. 5–8

TWILLEY, Dwight, Band
Singles: 7-Inch
ARISTA: *77–79*.................. 2–3
EMI AMERICA: *82–84*........... 1–3
SHELTER: *75–76*................ 2–4
Picture Sleeves
SHELTER: *75–76*................ 2–4
LPs: 10/12-Inch 33rpm
ARISTA: *77–79*.................. 5–8
EMI AMERICA: *82–84*........... 5–8
SHELTER: *75–76*................ 8–10
  Also see SEYMOUR, Phil

TWIN IMAGE
Singles: 12-Inch 33/45rpm
PITOL: *84–85* 4–6
Singles: 7-Inch
OL: *84–85* 1–3
LPs: 10/12-Inch 33rpm
ᵀᴸ: *84* 5–8

TWINS
Singles: 12-Inch 33/45rpm
QUALITY/RFC: *83*.............. $4–6

TWISTED SISTER (Featuring Dee Snider)
Singles: 7-Inch
ATLANTIC: *83–84* 1–3
LPs: 10/12-Inch 33rpm
ATLANTIC: *83–84* 5–8

TWITTY, Conway (Conway Twitty & Loretta Lynn)
Singles: 7-Inch
ABC-PARAMOUNT
  (10507; "Go On &
  Cry"): *63* 5–8
ABC-PARAMOUNT
  (10550; "My Baby Left
  Me"): *64*.................... 8–12
DECCA: *65–72*.................. 2–4
ELEKTRA: *82–83* 1–3
MCA: *73–82* 1–3
MGM (500 series): *78*.......... 1–3
MGM (12000 & 13000
  series): *58–62*............... 4–6
MGM (14000 series):
  71–72 2–4
MGM (50000 series):
  58–59 15–25
  (Stereo singles.)
MERCURY: *57–58*.............. 15–20
POLYDOR 1–3
WARNER BROS: *83–84*........... 1–3
Picture Sleeves
ELEKTRA: *82* .... INC
MGM: *58–62*................... 6–10
EPs: 7-Inch 33/45rpm
MGM: *58–59*.................. 15–20
LPs: 10/12-Inch 33rpm
ACCORD: *82* 5–8
ALLEGIANCE: *84*............... 5–8
CANDLELITE.................. 10–12
CORAL: *73* 4–8
DECCA: *66–72*................. 8–15
DEMAND: *72*.................. 8–12
ELEKTRA: *82–83* 5–8
MCA: *73–85* 5–12
MGM (110; "Conway
  Twitty"): *70*................ 10–15

Price Range

MGM (3744; "Conway
Twitty Sings"): *59* $30–40
MGM (3786; "Saturday
Night With Conway
Twitty"): *59* 30–40
MGM (3818; "Lonely Blue
Boy"): *60* 20–30
MGM (3849; "Conway
Twitty's Greatest Hits"):
60 30–40
(Black label. With gatefold cover & poster.)
MGM (3849; "Conway
Twitty's Greatest Hits"):
68 10–12
(Blue & yellow label. With standard cover.)
MGM (3907; "The Rock &
Roll Story"): *61* 30–40
MGM (3943; "The Conway
Twitty Touch"): *61* 20–30
MGM (4019 through
4217): *62–64* 20–30
MGM (4650 through
4884): *69–73* 10–15
METRO: *65* 15–20
OPRYLAND (12636;
"Conway Twitty, Then
& Now") 60–80
(6-LP set. Promotional issue only.)
PICKWICK: *72* 10–12
TROLLY CAR 5–8
WARNER BROS: *83–84* 5–8
Also see LYNN, Loretta

2 OF CLUBS, The
Singles: 7-Inch
FRATERNITY: *66–67* 3–5

TWO SISTERS
Singles: 12-Inch 33/45rpm
SUGARSCOOP: *83* 4–6

TWO TONS O' FUN (Two Tons)
Singles: 12-Inch 33/45rpm
FANTASY: *80* 4–6
Singles: 7-Inch
FANTASY: *80* 1–3
HONEY: *80–81* 1–3
LPs: 10/12-Inch 33rpm
FANTASY: *80* 5–8
HONEY: *80* 5–8
Members: Martha Wash; Izora Armstead.

Price Range

Also see WEATHER GIRLS, The

TYCOON
Singles: 7-Inch
ARISTA: *79* $1–3
LPs: 10/12-Inch 33rpm
ARISTA: *78–81* 5–8

TYLER, Bonnie
Singles: 7-Inch
CHRYSALIS: *77* 2–4
COLUMBIA: *83–85* 1–3
RCA VICTOR: *78–79* 2–3
LPs: 10/12-Inch 33rpm
CHRYSALIS: *77* 10–12
COLUMBIA: *83–85* 5–8
RCA VICTOR: *78–81* 5–8

TYLER, Frankie (Frankie Valli)
Singles: 7-Inch
OKEH (7103; "I Go
Ape"): *58* 45–55
Promotional Singles
OKEH (7103; "I Go
Ape"): *58* 25–35
Also see VALLI, Frankie

TYMES, The
Singles: 7-Inch
ABKCO 1–3
COLUMBIA: *68–70* 2–4
MGM: *66* 3–5
PARKWAY (Except 871):
63–64 3–5
PARKWAY (871; "So In
Love"): *63* 5–8
PARKWAY (871; "So
Much In Love"): *63* 3–5
RCA VICTOR: *74–77* 2–4
WINCHESTER: *67* 3–5
Picture Sleeves
PARKWAY: *63–64* 4–8
LPs: 10/12-Inch 33rpm
ABKCO: *74* 5–8
COLUMBIA: *69* 10–15
PARKWAY: *63–64* 15–20
RCA VICTOR: *74–77* 8–10
Also see WILLIAMS, George, & The Tymes

Price Range

TYNER, McCoy (The McCoy Tyner Trio)
Singles: 7-Inch
COLUMBIA: 82 . . . . $1–3
IMPULSE: 65 2–4
LPs: 10/12-Inch 33rpm
BLUE NOTE: 66–76 8–15
COLUMBIA: 82 5–8
FPM: 75 5–8
IMPULSE: 62–78 10–20
MCA: 81 5–8
MILESTONE: 72–82 6–12
PAUSA: 82 5–8

TYRANNOSAURUS REX: see T-REX

TYZIK (Jeff Tyzik)
Singles: 12-Inch 33/45rpm
POLYDOR: 84 4–6
Singles: 7-Inch
CAPITOL: 82 1–3
POLYDOR: 84 1–3
LPs: 10/12-Inch 33rpm
CAPITOL: 82 5–8
POLYDOR: 84 5–8

U

UB40 (UB40 With Chrissie Hynde)
Singles: 12-Inch 33/45rpm
A&M: 83–85 4–6
Singles: 7-Inch
A&M: 83–85 1–3
LPs: 10/12-Inch 33rpm
A&M: 83–85 5–8
Also see PRETENDERS, The

U.F.O.
Singles: 7-Inch
CHRYSALIS: 73–78 2–3
LPs: 10/12-Inch 33rpm
CHRYSALIS: 74–82 8–12
RARE EARTH: 71 10–15
Also see SCHENKER, Michael, Group

U.K.
Singles: 7-Inch
POLYDOR: 78–79 2–3

Price Range

LPs: 10/12-Inch 33rpm
POLYDOR: 78–79 . . . . $5–8
Members: John Wetton; Eddie Jobson; Terry Bozzio; Bill Bruford; Allan Holdsworth.

U.K. SQUEEZE: see SQUEEZE

U.S.A. EUROPEAN CONNECTION, The
Singles: 7-Inch
MARLIN: 78–79 2–3
LPs: 10/12-Inch 33rpm
MARLIN: 78–79 5–8

U.S.A. FOR AFRICA
Singles: 12-Inch 33/45rpm
COLUMBIA: 85 4–6
Singles: 7-Inch
COLUMBIA: 85 1–3
LPs: 10/12-Inch 33rpm
COLUMBIA: 85 5–8
(This is actually a various artists LP, but is included here because the section seems incomplete without it...so what the heck.)
Note: U.S.A. For Africa was a 46-member all-star assemblage which included, among others, the following cross-referenced performers:
Also see CARNES, Kim
Also see CHARLES, Ray
Also see DYLAN, Bob
Also see HALL, Daryl
Also see INGRAM, James
Also see JACKSON, Michael
Also see JARRE, Jean-Michael
Also see JARREAU, Al
Also see JENNINGS, Waylon
Also see JOEL, Billy
Also see JONES, Quincy
Also see LAUPER, Cyndi
Also see LEWIS, Huey, & The News
Also see LOGGINS, Kenny
Also see MIDLER, Bette
Also see PERRY, Steve
Also see RITCHIE, Lionel
Also see ROBINSON, Smokey
Also see ROGERS, Kenny
Also see ROSS, Diana
Also see SIMON, Paul
Also see SPRINGSTEEN, Bruce
Also see TURNER, Tina
Also see VOICES OF AMERICA / U.S.A. FOR AFRICA
Also see WARWICK, Dionne
Also see WONDER, Stevie

Price Range

Price Range

U.S. BONDS: see BONDS, Gary "U.S."

U.S. 1
Singles: 7-Inch
PRIVATE STOCK: 75. . . . . $2–4

UTFO
Singles: 12-Inch 33/45rpm
SELECT: 85 4–6
Singles: 7-Inch
SELECT: 85 1–3
LPs: 10/12-Inch 33rpm
SELECT: 85 5–8
Also see ROXANNE WITH UTFO

U2
Singles: 12-Inch 33/45rpm
ISLAND: 83 4–6
Singles: 7-Inch
ISLAND: 81–84 1–3
Picture Sleeves
ISLAND: 81–84 . . . . INC
LPs: 10/12-Inch 33rpm
ISLAND: 81–84 5–8
Members: Paul "Bono" Hewson; David "The Edge" Evan; Adam Clayton; Larry Mullen.
Also see BAND AID

UBIQUITY
Singles: 7-Inch
ELEKTRA: 78 2–3
LPs: 10/12-Inch 33rpm
ELEKTRA: 78 2–3
Also see AYERS, Roy

UGGAMS, Leslie
Singles: 7-Inch
ATLANTIC: 65–70 2–3
COLUMBIA: 59–64 2–4
GORDY: 76 1–3
MGM: 54–55 2–5
SONDAY: 71. 1–3
EPs: 7-Inch 33/45rpm
MGM: 54 5–10
LPs: 10/12-Inch 33rpm
ATLANTIC: 66–69 5–10
COLUMBIA: 59–63 5–15
MOTOWN: 75. 5–10
SONDAY: 72. 5–10

ULLMAN, Tracey
Singles: 7-Inch
MCA: 84–85 . . . . $1–3
LPs: 10/12-Inch 33rpm
MCA: 84 5–8

ULLANDA
Singles: 7-Inch
OCEAN: 79. 2–3

ULTIMATE
Singles: 7-Inch
CASABLANCA: 78–80 1–3
LPs: 10/12-Inch 33rpm
CASABLANCA: 78–80 5–8

ULTIMATE SPINACH, The
Singles: 7-Inch
MGM: 68–69. 3–5
LPs: 10/12-Inch 33rpm
MGM: 68–69. 15–20

ULTRAVOX
Singles: 12-Inch 33/45rpm
CHRYSALIS: 83. 4–6
Singles: 7-Inch
ANTILLES: 78–80 1–3
CHRYSALIS: 80–83. 1–3
ISLAND: 77 8–10
LPs: 10/12-Inch 33rpm
ANTILLES: 78–80 5–8
CHRYSALIS: 80–83. 5–8
ISLAND: 77 8–10
Also see BAND AID

UMILANI, Piero
Singles: 7-Inch
ARIEL: 69. 2–3
LPs: 10/12-Inch 33rpm
ARIEL: 69. 8–12

UNCLE DOG
Singles: 7-Inch
MCA: 73 2–3
LPs: 10/12-Inch 33rpm
MCA: 73 8–10

UNCLE LOUIE
Singles: 7-Inch
MARLIN: 79. 2–3

Price Range

LPs: 10/12-Inch 33rpm
MARLIN: 78.................... **$5–8**

UNDERGROUND SUNSHINE, The
Singles: 7-Inch
INTREPID: 69................... **3–6**
LPs: 10/12-Inch 33rpm
INTREPID: 69................ **10–15**

UNDERTONES, The
Singles: 7-Inch
CAPITOL: 84.................... **1–3**
HARVEST: 81................... **1–3**
SIRE: 80 .... **1–3**
LPs: 10/12-Inch 33rpm
CAPITOL: 84.................... **5–8**
HARVEST: 81.................. **8–10**
SIRE: 80 .... **5–8**

UNDERWOOD, Veronica
Singles: 7-Inch
PHILLY WORLD: 85............. **1–3**

UNDISPUTED TRUTH, The
Singles: 12-Inch 33/45rpm
WHITFIELD: 77–79 .... **4–6**
Singles: 7-Inch
GORDY: 71–75................... **2–4**
MOTOWN....................... **1–3**
WHITFIELD: 76–79 .... **2–3**
LPs: 10/12-Inch 33rpm
GORDY: 71–75.................. **8–10**
WHITFIELD: 77–79 .... **5–8**

UNICORN
Singles: 7-Inch
CAPITOL: 74–77 .... **2–3**
LPs: 10/12-Inch 33rpm
CAPITOL: 74–77 .... **8–10**

UNIFICS, The
Singles: 7-Inch
FOUNTAIN: 71 .... **2–4**
KAPP: 68–69..................... **3–5**
MCA............................ **1–3**
Picture Sleeves
KAPP: 68–69..................... **3–5**
LPs: 10/12-Inch 33rpm
KAPP: 68 .... **10–15**

Price Range

UNION GAP, The: see PUCKETT, Gary

UNIPOP
Singles: 7-Inch
KAT FAMILY: 82............... **$1–3**
LPs: 10/12-Inch 33rpm
KAT FAMILY: 82................ **5–8**

UNIQUE
Singles: 12-Inch 33/45rpm
PRELUDE: 83.................... **4–6**
Singles: 7-Inch
PRELUDE: 83.................... **1–3**

UNIQUES, The
Singles: 7-Inch
PARAMOUNT: 70–72............. **2–4**
PAULA: 65–70................... **3–5**
LPs: 10/12-Inch 33rpm
PAULA: 66–70................. **15–20**
(Paula LPs are currently in print, using original catalog numbers.)
Members: Joe Stampley; Bobby Stampley; Jim Woodfield; Mike Love; Ray Mills; Bobby Sims; Ronnie Weiss.
Also see STAMPLEY, Joe

UNIT 4+2, The (With Russ Ballard)
Singles: 7-Inch
LONDON: 65–66 .... **3–5**
LPs: 10/12-Inch 33rpm
LONDON: 65 .... **20–25**
Also see BALLARD, Russ

UNITED STATES AIR FORCE BAND, The
LPs: 10/12-Inch 33rpm
RCA VICTOR: 63 .... **5–10**

UNITED STATES MARINE BAND, The
LPs: 10/12-Inch 33rpm
RCA VICTOR: 63 .... **5–10**

UNITED STATES NAVY BAND, The
LPs: 10/12-Inch 33rpm
RCA VICTOR: 63 .... **5–10**

Price Range   *Price Range*

UNITED STATES OF AMERICA, The
LPs: 10/12-Inch 33rpm
COLUMBIA: 68 .... $10–15

UNITS, The
Singles: 12-Inch 33/45rpm
EPIC: 84 4–6
UPROAR: 83 4–6
Singles: 7-Inch
EPIC: 84 1–3
LPs: 10/12-Inch 33rpm
EPIC: 84 5–8

UNIVERSAL ROBOT BAND, The
Singles: 7-Inch
RED GREG: 77 2–3
LPs: 10/12-Inch 33rpm
RED GREG: 77 5–8

UNKNOWNS, The (With Keith Allison)
Singles: 7-Inch
MARLIN: 67 3–5
PARROT: 66 4–6
SHIELD 4–6
LPs: 10/12-Inch 33rpm
SIRE: 81 5–8
Also see ALLISON, Keith

UNLIMITED TOUCH
Singles: 12-Inch 33/45rpm
PRELUDE: 81–84 4–6
Singles: 7-Inch
PRELUDE: 81–84 1–3
LPs: 10/12-Inch 33rpm
PRELUDE: 81–84 5–8
Also see LORBER, Jeff

UP WITH PEOPLE
LPs: 10/12-Inch 33rpm
PACE: 66–70 4–8

UPBEATS, The
Singles: 7-Inch
JOY: 58–59 4–6
PREP: 57–58 4–6
SWAN: 58 4–6

UPCHURCH, Phil (The Phil Upchurch Combo)
Singles: 7-Inch
BOYD: 61 .... $4–6
GOLDEN FLEECE: 74 2–3
MARLIN: 79 1–3
UNITED ARTISTS: 61–62 3–5
LPs: 10/12-Inch 33rpm
BLUE THUMB: 73 8–10
BOYD: 61 20–25
CADET: 69 8–10
MILESTINE 5–8
UNITED ARTISTS: 61–62 15–20
Also see REED, Jimmy

UPCHURCH, Phil, & Tennyson Stephens
LPs: 10/12-Inch 33rpm
KUDU: 75 8–10
Also see STEPHENS, Tennyson
Also see UPCHURCH, Phil

UPFRONT
Singles: 12-Inch 33/45rpm
SILVER CLOUD: 83 4–6

URGENT
Singles: 7-Inch
MANHATTAN: 85 1–3

URIAH HEEP
Singles: 7-Inch
CHRYSALIS: 78 2–3
MERCURY: 70–73 2–4
WARNER BROS: 73–78 2–4
LPs: 10/12-Inch 33rpm
CHRYSALIS: 78–79 5–8
MERCURY: 70–82 6–10
WARNER BROS: 73–81 8–10
Also see HENSLEY, Ken
Also see ROUGH DIAMOND

UTOPIA
Singles: 7-Inch
BEARSVILLE: 76–80 2–4
NETWORK: 82 1–3
PASSPORT: 84–85 1–3
LPs: 10/12-Inch 33rpm
BEARSVILLE: 80–82 5–8
KENT: 73 10–15
NETWORK: 82 8–10

Price Range

PASSPORT: *84–85* **$5–8**
    Members: Todd Rundgren; Willie Wilcox;
    Roger Powell; Kasim Sulton.
    Also see CASSIDY, Shaun
    Also see RUNDGREN, Todd

V

V.S.O.P.
LPs: 10/12-Inch 33rpm
COLUMBIA: *77* **5–8**
    Members: Herbie Hancock; Wayne Shorter;
    Freddie Hubbard; Tony Williams.

VACELS, The
Singles: 7-Inch
KAMA SUTRA: *65* **4–6**
    Also see RICKY & THE VACELS

VALADIERS, The
Singles: 7-Inch
GORDY: *62–63* **25–30**
MIRACLE: *61* **20–25**

VALE, Jerry
Singles: 7-Inch
BUDDAH: *78* **1–3**
COLUMBIA: *51–74* **2–5**
Picture Sleeves
COLUMBIA: *64–65* **2–4**
EPs: 7-Inch 33/45rpm
COLUMBIA: *56–59* **5–10**
LPs: 10/12-Inch 33rpm
COLUMBIA: *58–75* **5–15**
HARMONY: *69–74* **5–10**

VALE, Jerry, Peggy King & Felicia Sanders
LPs: 10/12-Inch 33rpm
COLUMBIA: *56* **10–15**
    Also see KING, Peggy
    Also see SANDERS, Felicia
    Also see VALE, Jerry

VALENS, Ritchie
Singles: 12-Inch 33/45rpm
DEL-FI **8–10**
Singles: 7-Inch
ABC: *74* **1–3**
DEL-FI: *58* **12–15**
    (Solid green label with black print.)

Price Range

DEL-FI: *58–60* **$6–10**
    (With rows of circles on label.)
ERIC **1–3**
GOODIES **1–3**
KASEY **5–8**
LANA **1–3**
Picture Sleeves
DEL-FI: *59–60* **10–20**
EPs: 7-Inch 33/45rpm
DEL-FI: *60* **35–45**
LPs: 10/12-Inch 33rpm
DEL-FI (Except 1214):
    59–65 .... **45–60**
DEL-FI (1214; "Ritchie
    Valens In Concert"): *61* **60–70**
GUEST STAR: *63* **15–20**
MGM: *70* **10–15**
RHINO (Except 2798): *81* **5–8**
RHINO (2798; "History Of
    Ritchie Valens"): *81* **20–25**
    Also see ALLENS, Arvee

VALENS, Ritchie / Jerry Kole
LPs: 10/12-Inch 33rpm
CROWN: *63* **15–20**
    Also see COLE, Jerry

VALENTE, Dino
Singles: 7-Inch
ELEKTRA: *64* **5–8**
LPs: 10/12-Inch 33rpm
EPIC: *68* **15–20**
    Also see QUICKSILVER MESSENGER
    SERVICE

VALENTE, Catrina
Singles: 7-Inch
DECCA: *54–59* **2–5**
LONDON: *60–68* **2–4**
RCA VICTOR: *59* **2–4**
TELEFUNKEN: *59* **2–4**
EPs: 7-Inch 33/45rpm
DECCA: *55* **5–10**
LPs: 10/12-Inch 33rpm
DECCA: *55–64* **5–15**
LONDON: *59–72* **5–15**
RCA VICTOR: *61* **5–15**

VALENTI, John
Singles: 7-Inch
ARIOLA AMERICA:
76–77 .... $2–3

VALENTIN, Dave
Singles: 7-Inch
GRP: 80–81 1–3
LPs: 10/12-Inch 33rpm
GRP: 80–81 5–8

VALENTINE, Lezli
Singles: 7-Inch
ALL PLATINUM: 68 2–4

VALENTINE BROTHERS, The
Singles: 12-Inch 33/45rpm
SOURCE: 78 4–6
Singles: 7-Inch
A&M: 84 1–3
BRIDGE: 82 1–3
SOURCE: 79 1–3
LPs: 10/12-Inch 33rpm
A&M: 84 5–8
BRIDGE: 82 5–8
SOURCE: 79 5–8

VALENTINO, Danny
Singles: 7-Inch
CONTRAST: 67 3–5
MGM: 59–60 4–6

VALENTINO, Mark
Singles: 7-Inch
SWAN: 62–63 4–6
Note: May be erroneously shown as Mark
Valentinon on some pressings.
LPs: 10/12-Inch 33rpm
SWAN: 63 25–30

VALENTINOS, The
Singles: 7-Inch
ABKCO 1–3
CHESS: 66 3–5
CLEAN: 73 2–4
JUBILEE: 68–69 2–4
SAR: 62–64 4–6
Members: Bobby Womack; Curtis Womack.
Also see WOMACK, Bobby
Also see WOMACK BROTHERS, The

VALERIE & NICK
Singles: 7-Inch
GLOVER: 64 .... $5–8
Members: Valerie Simpson; Nick Ashford.
Also see ASHFORD & SIMPSON

VALERY, Dana
Singles: 7-Inch
ABC: 68–69 3–5
COLUMBIA: 67 8–10
PHANTOM: 75 2–4
SCOTTI BROS: 79 2–3
Picture Sleeves
PHANTOM: 75 2–4
Also see SIMON, Paul

VALIANTS, The (Featuring Billy Storm)
Singles: 7-Inch
KEEN: 57–58 10–15
SHAR-DEE: 59 8–10
Also see STORM, Billy

VALINO, Joe
Singles: 7-Inch
BANDBOX: 61 2–4
CROSLEY: 59–60 2–4
DEBUT: 67–68 2–4
RCA VICTOR: 59 2–4
UNITED ARTISTS: 57 3–5
VIK: 56 3–5
Picture Sleeves
UNITED ARTISTS: 57 3–5
LPs: 10/12-Inch 33rpm
DEBUT: 67 8–12

VALJEAN (Valjean Johns)
Singles: 7-Inch
CARLTON: 62–63 2–4
Picture Sleeves
CARLTON: 62 3–5
LPs: 10/12-Inch 33rpm
CARLTON: 62–63 10–20

VALLEY, Frankie: see VALLI, Frankie

Frankie Valli, 14 charted singles (1966–80), six charted LPs (1967–78).

Price Range

VALLI, Frankie (Frankie Valley & The Travelers; Frankie Valle; Frankie Vally; Frankie Vallie & The Romans)
Singles: 10/12-Inch 33/45rpm
MOTOWN: 73................... $15–20
PRIVATE STOCK: 77............ 10–15

Singles: 7-Inch
CINDY: 59 75–90
COLLECTABLES 1–3
CORONA: 53 200–225
DECCA (30994; "Please
   Take A Chance"): 59 50–75
MERCURY (Maroon
   label): 54..................... 75–90
MERCURY (Black label):
   55 35–45
MOTOWN: 73.................... 8–10
MOWEST: 72 5–8
PHILIPS (40407 through
   45098): 66–70.................. 4–6
PHILIPS (40661 & 40680):
   69–70 10–12
PRIVATE STOCK: 74–78........... 2–4
RSO: 78 2–4
SMASH: 65–66 5–8
WARNER/CURB: 78–80 2–4

Price Range

Promotional Singles
BOB CREWE PRESENTS
   (1; "The Girl I'll Never
   Know"): 69 .... $25–30
DECCA (30994; "Please
   Take A Chance"): 59 30–40
MERCURY: 55.................. 50–60
MOWEST (5025; "The
   Night"): 71.................. 12–15
PHILIPS (40407 through
   45098): 66–70.................. 5–8
PHILIPS (40661 & 40680):
   69–70 8–10
PRIVATE STOCK: 74–78.......... 6–10
SMASH: 65–66 8–10
Picture Sleeves
PHILIPS: 66–69 8–12
LPs: 10/12-Inch 33rpm
MOTOWN (100 series): 81 5–8
MOTOWN (800 series): 75 8–12
MCA: 79–80 5–8
PHILLIPS (200000 series):
   67 35–40
PHILLIPS (600000 series):
   67–68 20–25
PRIVATE STOCK: 75–78.......... 8–10
WARNER BROS: 78............. 8–10
   Also see FOUR LOVERS, The
   Also see 4 SEASONS, The
   Also see HARTFORD, Ken
   Also see LEE, Larry
   Also see NOLAN, Frankie
   Also see REID, Matthew
   Also see TYLER, Frankie

VALLI, Frankie, & Chris Forde
Singles: 7-Inch
MCA: 80 3–5

VALLI, Frankie, & Cheryl Ladd
Singles: 7-Inch
CAPITOL: 82 2–3
   Also see LADD, Cheryl
   Also see VALLI, Frankie

VALLI, June
Singles: 7-Inch
ABC-PARAMOUNT: 63............ 2–4
DCP: 64........................ 2–4
MERCURY: 58–61................. 2–4
RCA VICTOR: 52–56 2–5
UNITED ARTISTS: 62............. 2–4

Price Range

Price Range

Picture Sleeves
MERCURY: *61*. $2–4
EPs: 7-Inch 33/45rpm
RCA VICTOR: *55–56* 5–10
LPs: 10/12-Inch 33rpm
AUDIO FIDELITY: *69*. 5–10
MERCURY: *60*. 8–15
RCA VICTOR: *55–56* 8–18
Also see ZABACH, Florian

VALLIE, Frankie: see VALLI, Frankie

VALLY, Frankie: see VALLI, Frankie

VAN & TITUS
Singles: 7-Inch
ELF: *68* 3–5

VANCE, Paul
Singles: 7-Inch
ROULETTE: *62* 3–5
SCEPTER: *66* 3–5
LPs: 10/12-Inch 33rpm
SCEPTER: *66* 10–15
Also see LEE & PAUL

VANDENBERG (Adrian Vandenberg)
Singles: 7-Inch
ATCO: *83–84*. 1–3
LPs: 10/12-Inch 33rpm
ATCO: *83–84*. 5–8

VANDROSS, Luther
Singles: 12-Inch 33/45rpm
EPIC: *82–85* 4–6
Singles: 7-Inch
COTILLION: *76*. 2–4
EPIC: *81–85* 1–3
LPs: 10/12-Inch 33rpm
EPIC: *81–85* 5–8
Also see BOWIE, David
Also see LYNN, Cheryl, & Luther Vandross
Also see WARWICK, Dionne, & Luther Vandross

VAN DYKE, Leroy
Singles: 7-Inch
ABC: *74–75*. 1–3
ABC/DOT: *75–77*. 1–3

DECCA: *70–72*. $2–3
DOT (15000 series, except
  15698): *56–57*. 4–6
DOT (15698; "Leather
  Jacket"): *57* 20–30
KAPP: *68–70*. 2–3
MCA: *73* 2–3
MERCURY: *61–64*. 3–5
PLANTATION: *78*. 1–3
SUN: *79*. 1–3
WARNER BROS: *65–67*. 2–4
Picture Sleeves
MERCURY: *64*. 3–5
LPs: 10/12-Inch 33rpm
DECCA: *72*. 8–10
HARMONY: *69* 8–12
KAPP: *68–69*. 8–12
MCA: *73* 5–10
MERCURY: *62–64*. 10–20
PLANTATION: *77–79*. 5–8
SUN: *74*. 5–8
WARNER BROS: *65–66*. 10–15
WING: *65–66* 8–12

VAN DYKES, The
Singles: 7-Inch
DELUXE: *61*. 5–8
KING: *58* 25–30

VAN DYKES, The
Singles: 7-Inch
DONNA: *60* 5–8
FELSTED: *59*. 5–8
SPRING: *60* 10–12

VAN DYKES, The
Singles: 7-Inch
MALA: *65–67*. 3–5
LPs: 10/12-Inch 33rpm
BELL: *67*. 12–15

VANGELIS
Singles: 7-Inch
POLYDOR: *81* 1–3
RCA VICTOR: *78* 1–3
Picture Sleeves
POLYDOR: *81* . . . . INC
LPs: 10/12-Inch 33rpm
POLYDOR: *81–85* 5–8
RCA VICTOR: *78–82* 5–8

Price Range

VANGUARDS, The
Singles: 7-Inch
LAMP: 70 .... $2–4
WHIZ: 69 2–4

VAN HALEN
Singles: 12-Inch 33/45rpm
WARNER BROS: 83–84 4–6
Singles: 7-Inch
WARNER BROS: 78–84 1–3
Picture Sleeves
WARNER BROS: 78–84 .... INC
LPs: 10/12-Inch 33rpm
WARNER BROS: 78–84 5–8
Members: David Lee Roth; Eddie Van Halen;
Alex Van Halen; Michael Anthony.
Also see MAY, Brian
Also see ROTH, David Lee

VANILLA FUDGE
Singles: 7-Inch
ATCO: 67–70 3–5
LPs: 10/12-Inch 33rpm
ATCO (200 & 300 series):
67–69 15–20
ATCO (90000 series): 82 5–8
Also see BECK, BOGERT & APPICE

VANITY (Denise Matthews)
Singles: 12-Inch 33/45rpm
MOTOWN: 84–85 4–6
Singles: 7-Inch
MOTOWN: 84–85 1–3
LPs: 10/12-Inch 33rpm
MOTOWN: 84 5–8
Also see VANITY 6

VANITY FARE
Singles: 7-Inch
BRENT: 67 3–5
DJM: 75 2–4
PAGE ONE: 68–70 2–4
20TH CENTURY-FOX:
73 2–4
LPs: 10/12-Inch 33rpm
PAGE ONE: 70 10–15
Also see VANITY 6

VANITY 6 (Featuring Denise Matthews)
Singles: 12-Inch 33/45rpm
WARNER BROS: 82–83 4–6

Price Range

Singles: 7-Inch
WARNER BROS: 82–83 .... $1–3
LPs: 10/12-Inch 33rpm
WARNER BROS: 82 5–8
Also see APOLLONIA 6
Also see TIL TUESDAY
Also see VANITY

VANN, Teddy
Singles: 7-Inch
CAPITOL: 67 2–4
COLUMBIA: 61 4–6
END: 59 5–8
JUBILEE: 62 3–5
ROULETTE: 60 4–6
TRIPLE-X: 60 5–8
Also see DIXIE DRIFTER
Also see WHEELS, The

VANNELLI, Gino
Singles: 12-Inch 33/45rpm
HME: 85 4–6
Singles: 7-Inch
A&M: 74–79 2–3
ARISTA: 81–82 1–3
CBS ASSOCIATES: 85 1–3
HME: 85 1–3
Picture Sleeves
A&M: 76–79 2–3
ARISTA: 81–82 .... INC
LPs: 10/12-Inch 33rpm
A&M (3000 series): 81 5–8
A&M (4000 series): 74–78 8–10
ARISTA: 81–82 5–8
HME: 85 5–8

VAN TIEGHEM, David
Singles: 12-Inch 33/45rpm
WARNER BROS: 84 4–6
Singles: 7-Inch
WARNER BROS: 84 1–3
LPs: 10/12-Inch 33rpm
WARNER BROS: 84 5–8

VANWARMER, Randy
Singles: 7-Inch
BEARSVILLE: 79 2–3
LPs: 10/12-Inch 33rpm
BEARSVILLE: 79–83 5–8

VAN ZANDT, Johnny, Band
Singles: 7-Inch
POLYDOR: *80–82* $1–3
LPs: 10/12-Inch 33rpm
POLYDOR: *80–82* 5–8

VAPORS, The
Singles: 7-Inch
LIBERTY: *81* 1–3
UNITED ARTISTS: *80*............ 1–3
LPs: 10/12-Inch 33rpm
LIBERTY: *81* 5–8
UNITED ARTISTS: *80*............ 5–8

VASEL, Marianne, & Erich Storz
Singles: 7-Inch
MERCURY: *58*.................... 2–4
LPs: 10/12-Inch 33rpm
DANA: *59*....................... 8–15

VAUGHAN, Frankie
Singles: 7-Inch
COLUMBIA: *59*.................. 2–4
EPIC: *58* 3–5
PHILIPS: *62–66* 2–4
LPs: 10/12-Inch 33rpm
COLUMBIA: *60*................. 8–15
PHILIPS: *62* 5–15

VAUGHAN, Sarah
Singles: 7-Inch
ATLANTIC: *81* 1–3
COLUMBIA (38000 &
  39000 series): *51–53* 3–5
MGM (10000 & 11000
  series): *50–51* 4–8
MAINSTREAM: *71–74*........... 2–3
MERCURY (70000 series):
  53–66 2–5
ROULETTE: *60–64* 2–4
WARNER BROS: *81*............. 1–3
Picture Sleeves
MERCURY: *65*................... 2–4
EPs: 7-Inch 33/45rpm
ATLANTIC: *55* 8–15
COLUMBIA: *50–56*............. 8–18
EMARCY: *54–56* 8–18
MGM: *52–55*................... 5–15
MERCURY: *53–59*.............. 5–15

LPs: 10/12-Inch 33rpm
ATLANTIC: *81* $5–8
COLUMBIA (600 & 700
  series): *55–56*................. 20–40
COLUMBIA (900 series):
  57 15–25
COLUMBIA (6000 series):
  50 50–80
  (10-Inch LPs.)
COLUMBIA (37000
  series): *82*..................... 5–8
CONCORD: *56*................. 15–25
EMARCY (400 series): *77*......... 8–12
EMARCY (1000 series): *81*......... 5–8
EMARCY (26000 series):
  54 30–60
  (10-Inch LPs.)
EMARCY (36000 series):
  54–57 20–40
EVEREST: *70–76*............... 5–10
HARMONY: *59–69* 5–12
MGM (100 through 500
  series): *52–54*................. 40–60
  (10-Inch LPs.)
MGM (3200 series): *55*.......... 25–50
MAINSTREAM: *71–75*.......... 6–12
MERCURY (100 series):
  57 15–25
MERCURY (1000 series):
  82 5–8
MERCURY (20000 series):
  58–64 15–25
MERCURY (21000 series):
  65–67 10–20
  (Monaural issues.)
MERCURY (25000 series):
  53 30–60
  (10-Inch LPs.)
MERCURY (60000 series):
  59–64 15–25
MERCURY (61000 series):
  65–67 10–20
  (Stereo issues.)
METRO: *65*..................... 8–15
MUSICRAFT: *83–84*............. 5–8
PABLO: *78–82*.................. 5–8
REMINGTON (1024;
  "Hot Jazz"): *53*............... 50–75
  (10-Inch LPs)
RIVERSIDE: *55* 20–40
RONDO: *59* 20–40

Price Range

RONDOLETTE: *59* $20–40
ROULETTE (100 series):
  71 8–15
ROULETTE (52000
  series): *60–67* 10–25
SCEPTER: *74* 5–10
TRIP: *74–76* 5–10
WING: *63–68* 5–15
  Also see BASIE, Count, & Sarah Vaughan
  Also see ECKSTINE, Billy, & Sarah Vaughan
  Also see LEGRAND, Michel
  Also see WASHINGTON, Dinah, & Sarah
  Vaughan

VAUGHAN, Sara, & Quincy Jones
  LPs: 10/12-Inch 33rpm
MERCURY: *59*. 15–25
  Also see JONES, Quincy
  Also see VAUGHAN, Sarah

VAUGHN, Billy, Orchestra
  Singles: 7-Inch
ABC: *74* 1–3
DOT: *54–70* 2–4
PARAMOUNT: *70–72* 1–3
  Picture Sleeves
DOT: *58–67* 2–4
  EPs: 7-Inch 33/45rpm
DOT: *55–59* 4–8
  LPs: 10/12-Inch 33rpm
ABC: *74* 4–8
DOT: *55–70* 5–15
HAMILTON: *65–66* 5–10
MCA: *83* 4–8
MISTLETOE: *76* 4–8
MUSICOR: *77* 4–8
PARAMOUNT: *70–74* 4–8
RANWOOD: *83* 4–8
  Also see HILLTOPPERS, The

VAUGHN, Denny
  Singles: 7-Inch
KAPP: *56* 2–5

**VAUGHN, Stevie Ray (Stevie Ray
Vaughn & Double Trouble)**
  Singles: 7-Inch
EPIC: *85* 1–3
  LPs: 10/12-Inch 33rpm
EPIC (Except picture
  discs): *84* 5–8
EPIC (Picture discs): *84* 8–10

*Bobby Vee, 38 charted singles (1959–70), 12
charted LPs (1961–68).*

Price Range

**VEE, Bobby (Bobby Vee & The
Shadows; Bobby Vee & The Eligibles;
Bobby Vee & The Strangers; Bobby
Vee & The Johnny Mann Singers;
Robert Thomas Velline)**
  Singles: 7-Inch
LIBERTY (3300 series): *61* $10–12
  (Stereo Compact 33 Single.)
LIBERTY (55208; "Suzie
  Baby"): *59* 10–12
LIBERTY (55234 through
  55325): *60–61* 4–6
LIBERTY (55234 through
  56208): *61–70* 3–5
SHADYBROOK: *75–77* 2–4
SOMA: *59* 25–30
UNITED ARTISTS: *71–78* 2–3

  Picture Sleeves
LIBERTY: *60–68* 5–10

  EPs: 7-Inch 33/45rpm
LIBERTY: *60–62* 15–20
UNITED ARTISTS: *72* 10–12

  LPs: 10/12-Inch 33rpm
LIBERTY (181 through
  385): *61–64* 20–25
LIBERTY (448 through
  612): *66–69* 15–20

Price Range

(Liberty 181 through 534 numbers were preceeded by a "3" for mono issues. Numbers 181 through 612 were preceeded by a "7" for stereo LPs.)

LIBERTY (10000 series):
84 .... **$5–8**
SUNSET: 66–67 .... **12–15**
UNITED ARTISTS (300
series): 73 .... **8–10**
UNITED ARTISTS (1000
series): 80 .... **5–8**

VEE, Bobby / Johnny Burnette / The Ventures / The Fleetwoods
LPs: 10/12-Inch 33rpm
LIBERTY (5503;
"Teensville"): 61 .... **15–20**
Also see BURNETTE, Johnny
Also see FLEETWOODS, The

VEE, Bobby, & The Crickets
Singles: 7-Inch
LIBERTY: 62 .... **4–6**
Picture Sleeves
LIBERTY: 60–63 .... **8–12**
LPs: 10/12-Inch 33rpm
LIBERTY: 62 .... **20–25**
Also see CRICKETS, The

VEE, Bobby, & The Ventures
LPs: 10/12-Inch 33rpm
LIBERTY: 63 .... **20–25**
Also see VEE, Bobby
Also see VENTURES, The

VEGA, Tata
Singles: 12-Inch 33/45rpm
TAMLA: 79 .... **4–6**
Singles: 7-Inch
TAMLA: 76–80 .... **1–3**
LPs: 10/12-Inch 33rpm
TAMLA: 76–80 .... **5–8**
Also see RAWLS, Lou

VEJTABLES, The
Singles: 7-Inch
AUTUMN: 65–66 .... **5–8**
UPTOWN: 67 .... **4–6**

VELAIRES, The
Singles: 7-Inch
HI-MAR: 65 .... **4–6**

Price Range

JAMIE: 61–62 .... **$5–8**

VELEZ, Martha
Singles: 7-Inch
MCA: 80 .... **1–3**
POLYDOR: 73 .... **2–4**
SIRE: 69–76 .... **2–4**
LPs: 10/12-Inch 33rpm
SIRE (7000 series): 74–76 .... **8–10**
SIRE (97000 series): 69 .... **10–12**

VELLINE, Robert Thomas: see VEE, Bobby

VELOURS, The
Singles: 7-Inch
CUB: 58–59 .... **8–10**
END: 61 .... **8–10**
GOLDISC: 60 .... **5–8**
GONE: 60 .... **8–10**
ONYX (501; "My Love
Come Back"): 56 .... **30–40**
ONYX (508; "Romeo"): 57 ...... **125–150**
ONYX (512; "Can I Come
Over Tonight"): 57 .... **25–35**
ONYX (515; "This Could
Be The Night"): 57 .... **20–30**
ONYX (520;
"Remember"): 58 .... **15–20**
ORBIT: 58 .... **8–10**
ROULETTE **1–3**
STUDIO: 59 .... **6–10**
Members: Jerry Ramos; Pete Winston; John Pearson; Don Heywood; John Cheetom; Charles Moffett; Keith Williams; Troyce Key.

VELS, The
Singles: 12-Inch 33/45rpm
MERCURY: 84–85 .... **4–6**
Singles: 7-Inch
MERCURY: 84–85 .... **1–3**
LPs: 10/12-Inch 33rpm
MERCURY: 84 .... **5–8**

VELVELETTES, The
Singles: 7-Inch
I.P.G.: 63 .... **4–6**
SOUL: 66 .... **3–5**
V.I.P.: 64–65 .... **3–5**

Price Range

VELVET, Jimmy (The Jimmy Velvet Five; James Velvet; Jimmy Velvit)
Singles: 7-Inch
ABC-PARAMOUNT:
 63–64 .... **$3–5**
BELL: *67* **3–5**
CAMEO: *67* **3–5**
CUB: *61–62* **4–6**
DIVISION: *61* **5–8**
PHILIPS: *65* **3–5**
ROYAL AMERICAN: *69* **2–4**
TOLLIE: *64* **3–5**
UNITED ARTISTS: *68* **3–5**
VELVET: *61* **5–8**
VELVET TONE (Except
 102): *67* **3–5**
VELVET TONE (102;
 "It's Almost
 Tomorrow"): *65* **4–6**
  LPs: 10/12-Inch 33rpm
VELVET TONE: *67* **12–15**
 Also see TENNANT, Jimmy

VELVET UNDERGROUND, The
Singles: 7-Inch
COTILLION: *71* **3–5**
MGM: *69* **4–6**
VERVE: *67* **4–6**
  LPs: 10/12-Inch 33rpm
COTILLION: *70–72* **10–15**
MGM (100 series): *71* **8–10**
MGM (4000 series): *69–74* **10–15**
MERCURY: *72* **12–15**
PRIDE: *73* **10–15**
VERVE (5046; "White
 Light/White Heat"): *67* **20–30**
VERVE (800000 series): *84* **5–8**
 Members: Lou Reed; John Cale; Sterling Morrison; Maureen Tucker; Doug Yule.
 Also see AMERICAN FLYER
 Also see CALE, John
 Also see REED, Lou

VELVET UNDERGROUND, The, & Nico
Singles: 7-Inch
VERVE: *66–67* **5–8**
  LPs: 10/12-Inch 33rpm
VERVE (5008; "Velvet
 Underground & Nico"):
 67 .... **30–35**

(With banana sticker on front cover.)
VERVE (5008; "Velvet
 Underground & Nico"):
 67 .... **$20–25**
(Without banana sticker on front cover.)
VERVE (800000 series): *84* **5–8**
 Also see VELVET UNDERGROUND, The

VELVETS, The (Featuring Virgil Johnson)
Singles: 7-Inch
MONUMENT (400 series):
 61–62 .... **6–10**
MONUMENT (800 & 900
 series): *63–66* **3–5**
PLAID: *59* **5–8**
20TH CENTURY-FOX:
 59 .... **5–8**

VENTURES, The
Singles: 7-Inch
BLUE HORIZON: *60* **6–10**
DOLTON: *61–66* **3–5**
LIBERTY (54000 series):
 62 .... **3–5**
LIBERTY (56000 series):
 67–70 .... **2–4**
TRIDEX: *81* **2–3**
UNITED ARTISTS: *71–78* **2–4**
  Picture Sleeves
DOLTON: *60–66* **5–10**
  EPs: 7-Inch 33/45rpm
DOLTON: *60* **20–25**
  LPs: 10/12-Inch 33rpm
DOLTON (003; "Walk
 Don't Run"): *60* **25–35**
 (With light blue label.)
DOLTON (003; "Walk
 Don't Run"): *61* **20–25**
 (With dark blue label.)
DOLTON (004 through
 035): *61–65* **20–25**
DOLTON (037 through
 050): *65–67* **15–20**
DOLTON (17000 series):
 65–66 .... **15–20**
LIBERTY (052 through
 060): *67–70* **10–15**
 (Liberty & Dolton numbers, under 100, that are preceded by a "2" are mono. Stereo LPs in this series were preceded by an "8.")

Price Range

Price Range

LIBERTY (10000 series):
  81–84 .... **$5–8**
LIBERTY (35000 series):
  70 .... **12–15**
SUNSET: *66–71* **10–15**
TRIDEX: *81–83* **5–8**
UNITED ARTISTS: *71–77* **10–15**
  Members: Don Wilson; Bob Bogle; Mel Taylor;
  Nokie Edwards; Jerry McGee.
  Also see VEE, Bobby, & The Ventures

VENUS, Vic
  Singles: 7-Inch
BUDDAH: *69* **3–5**

VERA, Billy (Billy Vera & The Contrasts; Billy Vera & Blue Eyed Soul)
  Singles: 7-Inch
ATLANTIC: *68–69* **3–5**
RUST: *62* **4–6**
  LPs: 10/12-Inch 33rpm
ALFA: *82* **5–8**
ATLANTIC: *68* **10–15**
MIDSONG INT'L: *77* **8–10**
  Also see BILLY & THE BEATERS

VERA, Billy & Judy Clay
  Singles: 7-Inch
ATLANTIC: *67–68* **3–5**
  LPs: 10/12-Inch 33rpm
ATLANTIC: *68* **10–15**
  Also see CLAY, Judy

VERA LYNN: see LYNN, Vera

VERLAINE, Tom
  Singles: 7-Inch
ELEKTRA: *80* **1–3**
WARNER BROS: *83–84* **1–3**
  LPs: 10/12-Inch 33rpm
ELEKTRA: *80* **5–8**
WARNER BROS: *83–84* **5–8**

VERNE, Larry
  Singles: 7-Inch
COLLECTABLES **1–3**
ERA: *60–64* **3–5**
  Picture Sleeves
ERA: *60* **5–8**

  LPs: 10/12-Inch 33rpm
ERA: *60* **$25–30**

VERONICA (Veronica "Ronnie" Spector)
  Singles: 7-Inch
PHIL SPECTOR: *64* **10–15**
  Also see RONETTES, The

VIA AFRIKA
  Singles: 12-Inch 33/45rpm
EMI AMERICA: *84* **4–6**
  Singles: 7-Inch
EMI AMERICA: *84* **1–3**
  LPs: 10/12-Inch 33rpm
EMI AMERICA: *84* **5–8**

VIBRATIONS, The
  Singles: 7-Inch
ABC: *74* **1–3**
ATLANTIC: *63–64* **3–5**
BET: *60* **8–10**
CHECKER: *60–63* **3–5**
CHESS: *74* **2–4**
EPIC: *68* **2–4**
MANDALA: *72* **2–4**
NEPTUNE: *69–70* **2–4**
OKEH: *64–68* **3–5**
  LPs: 10/12-Inch 33rpm
CHECKER: *61* **20–30**
MANDALA: *72* **12–15**
OKEH: *65–69* **20–30**
  Also see JAYHAWKS, The
  Also see MARATHONS, The

VICKY D
  Singles: 7-Inch
SAM: *82* **1–3**

VIDAL, Maria
  Singles: 12-Inch 33/45rpm
EMI AMERICA: *84* **4–6**
  Singles: 7-Inch
EMI AMERICA: *84* **1–3**
  Also see CHILD, Desmond, & Rouge

VIDEEO
  Singles: 7-Inch
H.C.R.C.: *82* **1–3**

Price Range

VIDELS, The
Singles: 7-Inch
COLLECTABLES $1–3
DUSTY DISC.................... 5–8
JDS: *60*......................... 5–8
KAPP: *61* 8–10
MEDIEVAL: *59* 4–6
MUSICNOTE: *63* 8–10
RHODY: *59* 10–12
Members: Pete Anders; Vinnie Poncia.
Also see INNOCENCE, The
Also see TRADE WINDS, The

VIGRASS & OSBORNE
Singles: 7-Inch
EPIC: *74* 2–3
UNI: *72* 2–4
LPs: 10/12-Inch 33rpm
EPIC: *74* 8–10
UNI: *71* 10–15
Members: Paul Vigrass; Gary Osborne.

VILLAGE PEOPLE, The
Singles: 12-Inch 33/45rpm
CASABLANCA: *78–79* 4–6
Singles: 7-Inch
CASABLANCA: *78–79* 1–3
RCA VICTOR: *81* 1–3
Picture Sleeves
CASABLANCA: *78–79* 1–3
RCA VICTOR: *81* .... INC
LPs: 10/12-Inch 33rpm
CASABLANCA (Except
picture discs): *77–79* 5–8
CASABLANCA (Picture
discs): *78* 10–15
RCA VICTOR: *81* 5–8

VILLAGE SOUL CHOIR, The
Singles: 7-Inch
ABBOTT: *69–70*.................. 2–4

VILLAGE STOMPERS, The
Singles: 7-Inch
EPIC: *63–67* 2–4
Picture Sleeves
EPIC: *63–65* 2–4
LPs: 10/12-Inch 33rpm
EPIC: *63–67* 10–15
Also see VINTON, Bobby, & The Village
Stompers

Price Range

**VINCENT, Gene (Gene Vincent &
His Blue Caps)**
Singles: 7-Inch
CAPITOL (3450 through
3617): *56–57*.................. $8–10
CAPITOL (3678; "B-I-
Bickey-Bi-Bo-Bo-Go"):
57 10–15
CAPITOL (3763 through
4665): *57–61*.................... 6–10
CHALLENGE: *6–67* 4–6
FOREVER: *69–70*.................. 3–5
KAMA SUTRA: *70–73* 2–4
PLAYGROUND: *68* 60–75
Picture Sleeves
CAPITOL (4237; "Right
Now"): *60* 40–55
Promotional Singles
CAPITOL: *56–61* 12–20
(White label.)
EPs: 7-Inch 33/45rpm
CAPITOL (Except 985):
57–59 40–50
CAPITOL (985; "Hot Rod
Gang"): *58*................. 100–125
LPs: 10/12-Inch 33rpm
CAPITOL (DKAO-380;
"Gene Vincent's
Greatest"): *69*................. 10–15
CAPITOL (SM-380; "Gene
Vincent's Greatest"): *78* 5–8
CAPITOL (764; "Bluejean
Bop"): *57* 100–125
CAPITOL (811; "Gene
Vincent & His Blue
Caps"): *57* 100–125
CAPITOL (970; "Gene
Vincent Rocks"): *58* 100–125
CAPITOL (1059; "Gene
Vincent Record Date"):
58 100–125
CAPITOL (1207; "Sounds
Like Gene Vincent"): *59* 100–125
CAPITOL (1342; "Crazy
Times"): *60*................. 85–100
CAPITOL (11000 series):
74 8–10
CAPITOL (16000 series):
81 5–8
DANDELION: *70* 10–15

Price Range

KAMA SUTRA: *70–71* **$10–15**
ROLLIN' ROCK: *80–81* **5–8**

VINTON, Bobby (The Bobby Vinton Orchestra)
Singles: 7-Inch
ABC: *74–77* **1–3**
ALPINE: *59* **4–6**
DIAMOND: *62* **3–5**
ELEKTRA: *78* **1–3**
EPIC (9000 series): *60–66* **3–5**
EPIC (10000 series): *66–75* **2–4**
LARC: *83* **1–3**
TAPESTRY: *79–82* **1–3**
Picture Sleeves
EPIC: *62–72* **2–5**
TAPESTRY: *80* . . . . **INC**
EPs: 7-Inch 33/45rpm
EPIC: *63–64* **8–12**
LPs: 10/12-Inch 33rpm
ABC: *74–77* **8–10**
COLUMBIA: *73* **8–10**
EPIC (500 series): *60* **20–25**
EPIC (3000 series): *60* **15–20**
EPIC (20000 series): *62–70* **8–15**
EPIC (30000 series): *72–79* **5–10**
HARMONY: *70* **6–10**
TAPESTRY: *80* **5–8**

VINTON, Bobby, & The Village Stompers
LPs: 10/12-Inch 33rpm
EPIC: *66* **10–15**
Also see VILLAGE STOMPERS, The
Also see VINTON, Bobby

VIRTUES, The (Frank Virtue & The Virtues)
Singles: 7-Inch
ABC: *73* **1–3**
ABC-PARAMOUNT: *59* **3–5**
FAYETTE: *64* **3–5**
HIGHLAND: *60* **3–5**
HUNT: *59* **4–6**
SURE (500 series): *59* **8–10**
SURE (1700 series): *62* **3–5**
VIRNON: *60* **4–6**
VIRTUE: *66–69* **2–4**
WYNNE: *60* **3–5**
LPs: 10/12-Inch 33rpm
STRAND: *60* **20–25**

Price Range

WYNNE: *60* **$25–30**

VISAGE
Singles: 12-Inch 33/45rpm
POLYDOR: *80–82* **4–6**
Singles: 7-Inch
POLYDOR: *81* **1–3**
LPs: 10/12-Inch 33rpm
POLYDOR: *80–82* **5–8**

VISCOUNTS, The (The Vicounts)
Singles: 7-Inch
AMY: *65–66* **3–5**
CORAL: *66–67* **3–5**
MADISON: *59–61* **4–6**
MR. PEACOCK: *61* **3–5**
MR. PEEKE: *63* **3–5**
LPs: 10/12-Inch 33rpm
AMY: *65* **20–25**
MADISON: *60* **30–40**

VISUAL
Singles: 12-Inch 33/45rpm
PRELUDE: *83–84* **4–6**
Singles: 7-Inch
PRELUDE: *83–84* **1–3**

VITALE, Joe
Singles: 7-Inch
ASYLUM: *82* **1–3**
ATLANTIC: *74* **2–4**
LPs: 10/12-Inch 33rpm
ASYLUM: *82* **5–8**

Price Range

ATLANTIC: *74* **$8–10**
   Also see EAGLES, The
   Also see WALSH, Joe

VITAMIN E
Singles: 7-Inch
BUDDAH: *77* **2–3**

VITAMIN Z
Singles: 12-Inch 33/45rpm
GEFFEN: *85* **4–6**
Singles: 7-Inch
GEFFEN: *85* **1–3**
LPs: 10/12-Inch 33rpm
GEFFEN: *85* **5–8**

VITO & THE SALUTATIONS
(Featuring Vito Balsamo)
Singles: 7-Inch
APT: *65* **5–8**
BOOM: *66* **5–8**
CRYSTAL BALL: *78.* **2–3**
HAROLD: *62* **10–15**
HERALD: *63–64* **5–8**
KRAM: *62.* **20–25**
RAYNA: *62* **10–15**
RED BOY: *66* **3–5**
REGINA: *64* **5–8**
RUST: *66.* **4–6**
SANDBAG: *68* **3–5**
WELLS (Black vinyl): *64* **8–10**
WELLS (Colored vinyl): *64* **20–25**
LPs: 10/12-Inch 33rpm
RED BOY: *81* **10–15**
   Also see MAGIC TOUCH, The

VOCALEERS, The
Singles: 7-Inch
OLD TOWN: *60.* **5–8**
OLDIES 45: *65* **2–4**
PARADISE: *59.* **8–10**
RED ROBIN: *52–54* **50–75**
TWISTIME: *62* **3–5**
VEST: *60* **8–10**
   Members: Joe Duncan; Curtis Dunham; Ted
   Williams; Mel Walton; Bill Walker; Lamarr
   Cooper; Joe Powell; Richard Blandon; Leo Ful-
   ler; Curtis Blandon; Caesar Williams.

VOGUES, The
Singles: 7-Inch
ABC: *73* **1–3**

Price Range

ABC-PARAMOUNT: *65* **$3–5**
ASTRA: *73* **2–4**
BELL: *71* **2–4**
BLUE STAR: *65.* **8–10**
CASCADE: *59* **4–6**
CO & CE: *65–67.* **3–5**
DOT: *58–59.* **5–8**
GUSTO **1–3**
MGM: *67.* **3–5**
MAINSTREAM: *72.* **2–4**
REPRISE: *68–71.* **2–4**
SUN: *79* **1–3**
20TH CENTURY-FOX:
   73 .... **2–4**

LPs: 10/12-Inch 33rpm
CO & CE: *65–66.* **25–30**
51 WEST **5–8**
PICKWICK: *71* **8–10**
REPRISE: *68–70.* **10–15**
SSS INT'L: *77.* **5–8**
   Also see VAL-AIRES, The

VOICE MASTERS, The
Singles: 7-Inch
ANNA (100 series): *59.* **15–20**
ANNA (1100 series): *60.* **8–10**
BAMBOO: *68* **3–5**
   Also see HUNTER, Ty

VOICES OF AMERICA, The /
U.S.A. For Africa
Singles: 7-Inch
EMI: *86* **1–3**
   Also see TOTO
   Also see U.S.A. FOR AFRICA

VOICES OF EAST HARLEM, The
Singles: 7-Inch
ELEKTRA: *70–72* **2–4**
JUST SUNSHINE: *73–74* **2–4**

LPs: 10/12-Inch 33rpm
ELEKTRA: *70* **8–10**
JUST SUNSHINE: *73–74* **5–10**

VOLCANOS, The
Singles: 7-Inch
ARCTIC: *65–67* **3–5**
VIRTUE: *70* **2–4**

VOLLENWEIDER, Andreas
LPs: 10/12-Inch 33rpm
CBS: *84* $5–8
FM/CBS: *85* 5–8

VOLUMES, The
Singles: 7-Inch
ABC: *73* 1–3
AMERICAN ARTS:
  64–65 4–6
CHEX: *62* 5–8
IMPACT: *66* 3–5
INFERNO: *67–68* 3–5
OLD TOWN: *64* 3–5
JUBILEE: *63* 5–8
VIRGO: *73* 1–3
LPs: 10/12-Inch 33rpm
RELIC: *85* 5–8
  Also see NUTMEGS, The / The Volumes

VOLUMES, The
Singles: 7-Inch
JAGUAR: *54* 60–75

VONTASTICS, The
Singles: 7-Inch
CHESS: *67* 3–5
ST. LAWRENCE: *65–66* 3–5
SATELLITE: *65* 4–6

VOUDOURIS, Roger
Singles: 7-Inch
WARNER BROS: *78–79* 2–3
LPs: 10/12-Inch 33rpm
WARNER BROS: *79* 5–8

VOXPOPPERS, The
Singles: 7-Inch
AMP 3: *58* 8–10
MERCURY: *58* 4–6
POPLAR: *58* 5–8
VERSAILLES: *59* 5–8

VOYAGE
Singles: 7-Inch
ATLANTIC: *82* 1–3
MARLIN: *78–79* 2–3
LPs: 10/12-Inch 33rpm
ATLANTIC: *82* 5–8
MARLIN: *78* 5–8

VOYEUR
Singles: 7-Inch
MCA: *85* $1–3

W

W.A.G.B.
Singles: 7-Inch
STREET SOUNDS: *82* 1–3

W.A.S.P.
Singles: 7-Inch
CAPITOL: *84–85* 1–3
LPs: 10/12-Inch 33rpm
CAPITOL: *84–85* 5–8
  Members: Blackie Lawless; Randy Piper; Chris
  Holmes; Steve Riley.
  Also see NEW YORK DOLLS, The

WACKERS, The
Singles: 7-Inch
ELEKTRA: *71–73* 2–4
LPs: 10/12-Inch 33rpm
ELEKTRA: *71–72* 8–10

WADE, Adam
Singles: 7-Inch
COED: *59–61* 3–5
EPIC: *62–66* 2–4
KIRSHNER: *77* 2–3
REMEMBER: *69* 2–4
WARNER BROS: *67–68* 2–4
Picture Sleeves
COED: *60–61* 3–6
EPIC: *62–63* 2–4
LPs: 10/12-Inch 33rpm
COED: *60* 20–25
EPIC: *62* 15–20
KIRSHNER: *77* 5–10

WADSWORTH MANSION
Singles: 7-Inch
SUSSEX: *70* 2–4
LPs: 10/12-Inch 33rpm
SUSSEX: *71* 12–15
  Note: Some Sussex issues showed the group as
  "Wadsworth Manison."

Price Range

WAGNER, Jack
Singles: 7-Inch
QWEST: *84–85* **$1–3**
LPs: 10/12-Inch 33rpm
QWEST: *84* **5–8**

WAGONER, Porter
Singles: 7-Inch
ACCORD: *82* **5–8**
H.S.R.D.: *81* **5–10**
RCA VICTOR (0013
through 1000 series):
69–73 .... **1–3**
RCA VICTOR (5600
through 6500 series):
56–56 .... **4–8**
RCA VICTOR (6600
through 9900 series):
56–71 .... **2–5**
RCA VICTOR (10000
through 11000 series):
74–79 .... **1–3**
WARNER BROS: *82–83* **1–3**
EPs: 7-Inch 33/45rpm
RCA VICTOR: *56* **8–12**
LPs: 10/12-Inch 33rpm
CAMDEN: *63–73* **5–15**
PICKWICK: *75–77* **5–10**
RCA VICTOR (Except
1300 through 2900
series): *66–79* **5–15**
RCA VICTOR (1300
series): *56* **30–40**
RCA VICTOR (2700
through 2900 series):
63–65 .... **15–25**
(With an "LPM" or "LSP" prefix.)
TUDOR: *84* **5–8**
WARNER BROS: *83* **5–8**
Also see SNOW, Hank / Hank Locklin / Porter Wagoner

WAGONER, Porter, & Skeeter Davis
LPs: 10/12-Inch 33rpm
RCA VICTOR: *62* **10–15**
Also see DAVIS, Skeeter

WAGONER, Porter, & Dolly Parton
Singles: 7-Inch
RCA VICTOR: *67–71* **2–5**

Price Range

LPs: 10/12-Inch 33rpm
RCA VICTOR: *68–80* **$5–15**
Also see PARTON, Dolly
Also see WAGONER, Porter

WAIKIKIS, The
Singles: 7-Inch
KAPP: *64–68* **2–4**
PALETTE: *62–63* **2–5**
LPs: 10/12-Inch 33rpm
BOOT: *78* **4–8**
KAPP: *64–69* **8–12**
MCA **5–8**

WAILERS, The
Singles: 7-Inch
BELL: *67* **3–5**
ETIQUETTE: *63–66* **4–6**
GOLDEN CREST: *59* **4–6**
(Label pictures the group.)
GOLDEN CREST: *60–64* **3–5**
(Label does not picture group.)
IMPERIAL: *64* **3–5**
VIVA: *67* **2–5**
UNITED ARTISTS: *67* **2–5**
LPs: 10/12-Inch 33rpm
BELL: *68* **10–15**
ETIQUETTE: *66* **50–60**
GOLDEN CREST (3075;
"The Fabulous
Wailers"): *60* **20–30**
GOLDEN CREST (3075;
"The Wailers Wail") **15–20**
IMPERIAL: *64* **15–20**
UNITED ARTISTS: *67* **10–15**

WAINWRIGHT, Loudon, III
Singles: 7-Inch
ARISTA: *76–78* **2–3**
COLUMBIA: *73* **2–4**
LPs: 10/12-Inch 33rpm
ARISTA: *76–78* **5–8**
ATLANTIC: *70–71* **12–15**
COLUMBIA (KC series):
72–73 .... **10–15**
COLUMBIA (PC series):
75 .... **5–10**
ROUNDER: *80–83* **5–8**
Also see SPRINGSTEEN, Bruce / Albert Hammond / Loudon Wainwright, III / Taj Mahal

WAITE, John
Singles: 12-Inch 33/45rpm
EMI AMERICA: *84*. **$4–6**
Singles: 7-Inch
CHRYSALIS: *82–85*. **1–3**
EMI AMERICA: *84–85*. **1–3**
LPs: 10/12-Inch 33rpm
CHRYSALIS: *82*. **5–8**
EMI AMERICA: *84*. **5–8**
Also see BABYS, The

WAITRESSES, The
Singles: 7-Inch
ANTILLES: *80*. **2–5**
POLYDOR: *82*. **1–3**
LPs: 10/12-Inch 33rpm
POLYDOR: *82–83* **5–8**

WAITS, Tom
Singles: 7-Inch
ASYLUM: *74*. **2–3**
ELEKTRA: *83* **1–3**
ISLAND: *83* **1–3**
LPs: 10/12-Inch 33rpm
ASYLUM: *73–80*. **6–10**
ELEKTRA: *83* **5–8**
ISLAND: *83* **5–8**
Also see CRYSTAL GAYLE & TOM WAITS

WAKELY, Jimmy
Singles: 7-Inch
ARTCO: *74*. **1–3**
CAPITOL (1300 through
2100 series): *50–52* **4–6**
CORAL: *53–55*. **3–6**
DECCA: *55–70*. **2–5**
DOT: *66*. **2–4**
SHASTA (100 series):
58–67 . . . . **2–5**
SHASTA (200 series): *71* **2–3**
Picture Sleeves
SHASTA: *58* **4–8**
EPs: 7-Inch 33/45rpm
CAPITOL: *50–53* **8–15**
CORAL: *54*. **8–15**
DECCA: *58*. **6–12**
LPs: 10/12-Inch 33rpm
ALBUM GLOBE: *81* **5–8**
CAPITOL: *50–53* **20–30**
CORAL: *73*. **4–6**
DANNY **8–10**

DECCA (8400 through
8600 series): *56–57* **$20–30**
DECCA (75000 through
78000 series): *67–70* **8–15**
DOT: *66*. **8–12**
MCA. **4–6**
MCR: *74* **6–10**
SHASTA: *58–75* **5–15**
TOPS **8–15**
VOCALION: *68–70* **5–10**
Also see CHANDLER, Karen, & Jimmy
Wakely
Also see WHITING, Margaret, & Jimmy
Wakely

WAKELIN, Johnny, & The Kinshasa Band
Singles: 7-Inch
PYE: *75* **2–4**

WAKEMAN, Rick (Rick Wakeman With The London Symphony Orchestra & English Chamber Choir; Rick Wakeman & The English Rock Ensemble)
Singles: 7-Inch
A&M: *73* **2–4**
LPs: 10/12-Inch 33rpm
A&M (3000 series): *74* **5–8**
A&M (4000 series): *73–77* **8–10**
A&M (6000 series): *79* **10–12**
Also see DALTREY, Roger, & Rick Wakeman
Also see STRAWBS, The
Also see YES

WALDEN, Narada Michael
Singles: 12-Inch 33/45rpm
ATLANTIC: *82–83* **4–6**
WARNER BROS: *85*. **4–6**
Singles: 7-Inch
ATLANTIC: *77–83* **1–3**
WARNER BROS: *85*. **1–3**
LPs: 10/12-Inch 33rpm
ATLANTIC: *79–83* **5–8**

WALDMAN, Wendy
Singles: 7-Inch
EPIC: *82–83* **1–3**
WARNER BROS: *77–78* **2–3**
LPs: 10/12-Inch 33rpm
EPIC: *82–83* **5–8**

Price Range

WARNER BROS: *78* **$5–8**

WALDO
Singles: 7-Inch
COLUMBIA: *82* **1–3**
LPs: 10/12-Inch 33rpm
COLUMBIA: *82* **5–8**

WALKER, Billy
Singles: 7-Inch
CAPRICE: *79* **1–3**
COLUMBIA (21000
series): *54–56* **4–6**
COLUMBIA (40000
series): *56–60* **3–5**
COLUMBIA (42000 &
43000 series): *61–65* **2–4**
DIMENSION: *83* **1–3**
MCA: *77* **1–3**
MGM: *70–74* **2–3**
MRC: *78* **1–3**
MONUMENT: *66–70* **2–4**
RCA VICTOR: *75–76* **2–3**
SCORPION: *78* **1–3**
TALL TEXAN: *83* **1–3**
Picture Sleeves
COLUMBIA: *63–67* **2–5**
LPs: 10/12-Inch 33rpm
COLUMBIA: *63–69* **8–18**
GUSTO **5–8**
H.S.R.D.: *84* **5–8**
HARMONY: *64–70* **8–15**
MGM: *70–74* **8–12**
MONUMENT: *66–72* **8–15**
RCA VICTOR: *75–76* **5–8**

WALKER, Billy, & Barbara Fairchild
Singles: 7-Inch
PAID: *81* **1–3**
LPs: 10/12-Inch 33rpm
PAID: *81* **5–8**
Also see FAIRCHILD, Barbara

WALKER, Bobbi
Singles: 7-Inch
CASABLANCA: *80* **1–3**

WALKER, Boots
Singles: 7-Inch
RUST: *67–68* **3–5**

Price Range

WALKER, David T.
Singles: 7-Inch
ODE: *73–76* **$2–4**
REVUE: *69–69* **2–5**
ZEA: *70* **2–4**
LPs: 10/12-Inch 33rpm
ODE: *74–76* **8–10**
REVUE: *68–69* **10–15**

WALKER, Gloria (Gloria Walker & The Chevelles)
Singles: 7-Inch
FLAMING ARROW:
68–69 .... **3–5**

WALKER, Jay (Jay Walker & The Pedestrians)
Singles: 7-Inch
AMY: *62* **3–5**
VEE JAY: *61* **3–5**

WALKER, Jerry Jeff
Singles: 7-Inch
ATCO: *68–70* **2–5**
MCA: *73–80* **1–3**
LPs: 10/12-Inch 33rpm
ATCO (Except 297): *68–70* **15–20**
ATCO (297; "Five Years
Gone"): *69* **40–50**
DECCA: *72* **10–12**
ELEKTRA **8–10**
MCA: *73–80* **6–10**
SOUTH COAST: *81* **5–8**
VANGUARD: *69* **10–12**

WALKER, Jimmy
Singles: 7-Inch
BUDDAH: *75* **2–4**
LPs: 10/12-Inch 33rpm
BUDDAH: *75* **8–10**

WALKER, Junior (Junior Walker & The All Stars; Junior Walker & All The Stars)
Singles: 12-Inch 33/45rpm
WHITFIELD: *79* **4–6**
Singles: 7-Inch
HARVEY: *62–64* **5–8**
MOTOWN: *83* **1–3**

Price Range

SOUL (Except 35003):
65–76 . . . . **$2–5**
(Motown subsidiary collectors may value Soul labels with a black band at the bottom of the label higher than standard Soul issues, but we don't have any specifics for this edition. The band was printed over the erroneous "Distributed By Bell Records" that originally appeared on some Soul labels.)
SOUL (35003; "Monkey
Jump"): *64* **4–6**
WHITFIELD: *79* **2–3**

Picture Sleeves
SOUL: *65–66* **2–5**

LPs: 10/12-Inch 33rpm
MOTOWN (Except 700
series): *80–83* **5–8**
MOTOWN (700 series): *74* **8–12**
SOUL (701 through 721):
65–70 . . . . **10–15**
SOUL (725 through 750):
70–78 . . . . **8–10**
WHITFIELD: *79* **5–8**

WALKER BROTHERS, The
Singles: 7-Inch
SMASH: *64–66* **4–6**

Picture Sleeves
SMASH: *65–66* **5–10**

LPs: 10/12-Inch 33rpm
SMASH: *66–67* **20–25**
Members: Scott Engel; John Maus; Gary Leeds.

WALL OF VOODO (Featuring Stanard Ridgway)
Singles: 12-Inch 33/45rpm
I.R.S.: *83* **4–6**

Singles: 7-Inch
I.R.S.: *81–83* **1–3**

LPs: 10/12-Inch 33rpm
I.R.S.: *81–83* **5–8**
Also see COPELAND, Stewart, & Stanard Ridgway

Jerry Wallace, 13 charted singles (1958–72), two charted LPs (1964–73).

Price Range

WALLACE, Jerry (Jerry Wallace & The Jewels)
Singles: 7-Inch
ALLIED: *54* **$5–8**
BMA: *77–78* **2–3**
CHALLENGE (1000
series): *57* **8–12**
CHALLENGE (9100
series): *61–63* **3–5**
CHALLENGE (59013
through 59098): *58–60* **5–10**
CHALLENGE (59200
series): *63–65* **3–5**
CLASS: *53* **5–8**
DECCA: *71–72* **2–4**
DOOR KNOB: *80* **1–3**
ERIC **1–3**
4-STAR: *78–79* **1–3**
GLENOLDEN: *68* **2–4**
GUSTO **1–3**
LIBERTY: *67–70* **2–4**
MCA: *73–74* **2–3**
MGM: *75* **2–3**
MERCURY (Except 72000
series): *55–56* **3–6**
MERCURY (72000 series):
64–66 . . . . **2–5**
TOPS: *53* **4–6**
UNITED ARTISTS: *72–75* **2–4**

Price Range

VOGUE: *52* **$8–10**
WING: *56* **4–6**
Picture Sleeves
CHALLENGE: *58–64* **4–8**
EPs: 7-Inch 33/45rpm
CHALLENGE: *60* **15–20**
LPs: 10/12-Inch 33rpm
BMA: *77* **8–10**
CHALLENGE (606; "Just
Jerry"): *59* **30–35**
CHALLENGE (612;
"There She Goes"): *61* **20–25**
CHALLENGE (616;
"Shutters & Boards"): *63* **15–20**
CHALLENGE (619; "In
The Misty Moonlight"):
64 . . . . **15–20**
CHALLENGE (2002;
"Greatest Hits"): *69* **10–15**
DECCA: *71* **8–12**
4-STAR: *83* **5–8**
LIBERTY: *68* **10–12**
MCA: *73–74* **8–10**
MGM: *75* **8–10**
MERCURY: *66* **10–15**
UNITED ARTISTS: *72–75* **8–12**
WING: *68* **10–12**
Also see BARE, Bobby / Donna Fargo / Jerry
Wallace

WALLACE BROTHERS, The
Singles: 7-Inch
JEWEL: *68–69* **2–4**
SIMS: *63–67* **3–5**
LPs: 10/12-Inch 33rpm
SIMS: *65* **15–20**

WALSH, James, Gypsy Band
Singles: 7-Inch
RCA VICTOR: *78–79* **2–3**
LPs: 10/12-Inch 33rpm
RCA VICTOR: *79* **5–8**
Also see GYPSY

WALSH, Joe
Singles: 7-Inch
ABC: *75–78* **2–3**
ASYLUM: *78–81* **1–3**
DUNHILL: *73–75* **2–4**
FULL MOON: *80* **1–3**
MCA: *79* **1–3**

Price Range

LPs: 10/12-Inch 33rpm
ABC: *76–78* **$8–10**
ASYLUM: *78–81* **5–8**
COMMAND: *74–75* **8–12**
DUNHILL: *72–74* **8–10**
MCA: *79* **5–8**
WARNER BROS: *83* **5–8**
Also see EAGLES, The
Also see JAMES GANG, The
Also see VITALE, Joe

WALSH, Steve
Singles: 7-Inch
KIRSHNER: *80* **1–3**
LPs: 10/12-Inch 33rpm
KIRSHNER: *80* **5–8**

WAMMACK, Travis
Singles: 7-Inch
ARA: *64–65* **3–5**
ATLANTIC: *66* **3–5**
CAPRICORN: *75* **2–3**
FAME: *72–73* **2–4**
FRATERNITY: *58* **25–35**
LPs: 10/12-Inch 33rpm
CAPRICORN: *75* **8–10**
FAME: *72* **8–12**
PHONORAMA **5–8**

WANDERERS, The
Singles: 7-Inch
CUB: *58–62* **5–8**
MGM: *62* **4–6**
ONYX: *57* **20–25**
ORBIT: *58* **10–12**
SAVOY: *53* **75–100**
UNITED ARTISTS: *62* **3–5**
Members: Ray Pollard; Bob Yarborough; Shep-
pard Grant; Frank Joyner.

WANDERLEY, Walter
Singles: 7-Inch
A&M: *69* **1–3**
GNP/CRESCENDO: *81* **1–3**
TOWER: *66–67* **2–4**
VERVE: *66–68* **2–4**
WORLD PACIFIC: *66* **2–4**
LPs: 10/12-Inch 33rpm
A&M: *69* **6–10**
CAPITOL: *63* **8–15**
GNP/CRESCENDO: *81* **5–8**

Price Range

Price Range

PHILIPS: *67* **$8–12**
TOWER: *66–67*.................. **8–15**
VERVE: *66–68* **8–15**
WORLD PACIFIC: *66–67* **8–15**
   Also see GILBERTO, Astrud

WANG CHUNG (Huang Chung)
Singles: 12-Inch 33/45rpm
GEFFEN: *84*..................... **4–6**
Singles: 7-Inch
GEFFEN: *84*..................... **1–3**
LPs: 10/12-Inch 33rpm
ARISTA: *83* **5–8**
GEFFEN: *85*.................... **5–8**

WANSEL, Dexter
Singles: 12-Inch 33/45rpm
PHILADELPHIA INT'L:
   79 .... **4–6**
Singles: 7-Inch
PHILADELPHIA INT'L:
   76–79 .... **1–3**
LPs: 10/12-Inch 33rpm
PHILADELPHIA INT'L:
   76–79 .... **5–8**

WAR
Singles: 12-Inch 33/45rpm
MCA: *78–79* **4–6**
Singles: 7-Inch
BLUE NOTE: *77* **2–3**
LAX: *81*........................ **1–3**
MCA: *77–82* **1–3**
RCA VICTOR: *82–83* **1–3**
UNITED ARTISTS: *71–78* **2–4**
WAR: *77*....................... **2–3**
Picture Sleeves
MCA: *77* **1–3**
UNITED ARTISTS: *71–75* **2–4**
LPs: 10/12-Inch 33rpm
BLUE NOTE: *76* **8–10**
MCA: *77–82* **5–8**
RCA VICTOR: *82–83* **5–8**
UNITED ARTISTS
   (Except 103): *71–76*............ **8–10**
UNITED ARTISTS (103;
   "Radio Free War"): *74*......... **12–15**
   (Promotional issue only.)
   Also see BURDON, Eric, & War
   Also see JORDAN, Lonnie
   Also see OSKAR, Lee

WARD, Anita
Singles: 7-Inch
JUANA: *79* **$2–3**
LPs: 10/12-Inch 33rpm
JUANA: *79* **5–8**

Billy Ward & The Dominoes, eight charted singles (1952–58), no charted LPs.

WARD, Billy, & The Dominoes
Singles: 7-Inch
ABC-PARAMOUNT: *60*........... **4–6**
DECCA: *56–57*.................. **6–10**
FEDERAL (12105; "I'd Be
   Satisfied"): *52*................ **25–35**
FEDERAL (12106; "Yours
   Forever"): *52*................. **25–35**
FEDERAL (12114; "Pedal
   Pushin' Papa"): *52* **60–75**
FEDERAL (12129; "These
   Foolish Things"): *53*............ **60–75**
FEDERAL (12139 through
   12218): *53–55*.................. **15–20**
FEDERAL (12163 through
   12380): *56–57*.................. **8–12**
GUSTO **1–3**
JUBILEE: *54–55*................. **8–10**
KING (1000 series, except
   1281): *53–55*.................. **15–20**
KING (1281; "Christmas
   In Heaven"): *53*............... **30–40**
KING (5000 series): *60–61* **4–6**
KING (6000 series): *65* **3–5**
LIBERTY (54000 series):
   57–59 .... **4–6**
LIBERTY (55000 series):
   62 .... **3–5**
RO-ZAN: *62* **3–5**

Price Range

Picture Sleeves
LIBERTY: *57* **$15–20**
EPs: 7-Inch 33/45rpm
DECCA: *58* **35–45**
FEDERAL (Silver Top
label): *54–56* **45–55**
FEDERAL (Green label):
57 . . . . **25–35**
LIBERTY: *59* **15–25**
LPs: 10/12-Inch 33rpm
DECCA: *58* **60–75**
FEDERAL (94; "Billy
Ward & His
Dominoes"): *54* **400–450**
(10-Inch LP.)
FEDERAL (548; "Billy
Ward & His
Dominoes"): *56* **150–175**
FEDERAL (559; "Clyde
McPhatter With Billy
Ward & His
Dominoes"): *57* **125-150**
KING (548; "Billy Ward
& His Dominoes"): *58* **45–55**
KING (559; "Clyde
McPhatter With Billy
Ward & His
Dominoes"): *61* **40-50**
KING (733; "Billy Ward
& His Dominoes
Featuring Clyde
McPhatter & Jackie
Wilson"): *61* **45-55**
KING (952; "24 Songs"):
66 . . . . **20–30**
KING/GUSTO **5–8**
LIBERTY: *59* **25–35**
Members: Clyde McPhatter; Jackie Wilson;
Billy Ward; Gene Mumford; Milton Merle;
Milton Grayson; William Lamont; Cliff Giv-
ens.
Also see DOMINOES, The
Also see WILSON, Jackie

WARD, Dale
Singles: 7-Inch
BIG WAY **3–5**
BOYD: *62–65* **3–5**
DOT (16000 series): *63–65* **3–5**
DOT (17000 series): *71–72* **2–4**
MONUMENT: *66–69* **3–5**

Price Range

PARAMOUNT: *69–70* **$2–4**
Also see CRESCENDOS, The
Also see WARD, Robin

WARD, Joe
Singles: 7-Inch
KING: *55–56* **6–10**

WARD, Robin
Singles: 7-Inch
DOT: *63–64* **3–5**
SONGS UNLIMITED: *63* **3–5**
Picture Sleeves
SONGS UNLIMITED: *63* **3–5**
LPs: 10/12-Inch 33rpm
DOT: *63* **25–35**
Also see MARTINDALE, Wink, & Robin
Ward
Also see WARD, Dale

WARD, Singin' Sammy
Singles: 7-Inch
SOUL: *64* **3–5**
TAMLA (54030; "What
Makes You Love Him"):
61 . . . . **25–30**
(With horizontal lines.)
TAMLA (54030; "What
Makes You Love Him"):
61 . . . . **15–20**
(With Tamla globe logo.)
TAMLA (54049; "What
Makes You Love Him"):
62 . . . . **15–20**
TAMLA (54057;
"Everybody Knows It"):
62 . . . . **30–35**
TAMLA (54071; "Part
Time Love"): *62* **5–8**

WARE, Leon
Singles: 7-Inch
ELEKTRA: *81* **1–3**
FABULOUS: *79* **1–3**
UNITED ARTISTS: *72* **2–4**
LPs: 10/12-Inch 33rpm
FABULOUS: *79* **5–8**
GORDY: *76* **6–10**
UNITED ARTISTS: *72* **8–12**

Price Range

WARING, Fred (Fred Waring & The Pennsylvanians)

Singles: 7-Inch
CAPITOL: 57–59 . . . . $2–4
DECCA: 50–68 2–4
REPRISE: 64 1–3

EPs: 7-Inch 33/45rpm
CAPITOL: 57–58 3–6
DECCA: 50–59 3–8

LPs: 10/12-Inch 33rpm
CAPITOL: 57–69 5–12
DECCA: 50–68 5–15
HARMONY: 69 4–8
MCA: 77 4–8
MEGA: 71 4–8
REPRISE: 64–65 4–8
RCA VICTOR: 68 4–8

WARNES, Jennifer (Jennifer Warren)

Singles: 12-Inch 33/45rpm
20TH CENTURY-FOX
(379; "It Goes Like It
Goes"): 79 5–8
(Shown as by Jennifer Warren.)
20TH CENTURY-FOX
("It Goes Like It
Goes"): 79 4–6
(Shown as by Jennifer Warnes. This release was
not numbered. Both of these 12-Inch singles
were promotional issues of the Oscar winning
theme from "Norma Rae.")

Singles: 7-Inch
ARISTA: 77–81 1–3
PARROT: 68 3–5
WARNER BROS: 83 1–3

LPs: 10/12-Inch 33rpm
ARISTA: 76–79 5–8
REPRISE: 72 8–10
Also see COCKER, Joe, & Jennifer Warnes
Also see JENNIFER

WARP 9

Singles: 12-Inch 33/45rpm
PRISM: 83–84 4–6

Singles: 7-Inch
PRISM: 83–84 1–3

RUSTY WARREN IN ORBIT

Price Range

WARREN, Rusty

LPs: 10/12-Inch 33rpm
GNP/CRESCENDO:
74–77 . . . . $5–12
JUBILEE: 60–68 10–20

WARRIOR, Jade: see JADE WARRIOR

WARWICK, Dee Dee (Dee Dee Warwick & The Dixie Flyers)

Singles: 7-Inch
ATCO: 70–71 2–4
BLUE ROCK: 65 3–5
HURT: 66 3–5
JUBILEE: 63 3–5
MERCURY: 66–69 3–5
PRIVATE STOCK: 75 2–3
SUTRA 2–3
TIGER: 64 3–5

LPs: 10/12-Inch 33rpm
ATCO: 70 8–10
HERITAGE SOUND: 83 5–8
MERCURY: 67–69 10–15

WARWICK, Dionne (Dionne Warwicke)

Singles: 12-Inch 33/45rpm
ARISTA: 84 4–6
Singles: 7-Inch
ARISTA: 79–86 1–3
COLLECTABLES 1–3

Price Range

MERCURY (70046
through 70968): *52–56* **$5–8**
MERCURY (71000 &
72000 series): *57–63* **2–5**
ROULETTE: *62–63* **2–4**
Picture Sleeves
MERCURY: *61–62*................ **2–5**
EPs: 7-Inch 33/45rpm
EMARCY: *54–56* **10–20**
MERCURY (3000 through
3200 series): *51–57* **15–20**
MERCURY (3300 series):
60 .... **10–15**
MERCURY (4000 series):
61 .... **8–12**
LPs: 10/12-Inch 33rpm
EMARCY (400 series): *76* **8–12**
EMARCY (26000 series):
54 .... **40–50**
(10-Inch LPs.)
EMARCY (36000 series):
54–58 .... **25–35**
EVEREST: *75* **8–10**
MERCURY (103; "This Is
My Story"): *63*................ **20–25**
MERCURY (121;
"Original Queen Of
Soul"): *69*................... **12–15**
MERCURY (603; "This Is
My Story"): *63*................ **20–25**
MERCURY (20100 &
20200 series): *55–58* **30–40**
MERCURY (20400
through 20900 series):
59–63 .... **15–20**
MERCURY (21100 series):
67 .... **10–12**
MERCURY (25000 series):
50–51 .... **50–60**
(10-Inch LPs.)
MERCURY (60100
through 60900 series):
59–63 .... **15–25**
MERCURY (61100 series):
67 .... **10–12**
ROSETTA: *84*................... **5–8**
ROULETTE (100 series):
71–72 .... **10–12**
ROULETTE (25000
series): *62–65*................. **12–15**
TRIP: *73–78* **8–10**

Price Range

WING: *59–64* **$15–20**
Also see BENTON, Brook, & Dinah Washington
Also see HAMPTON, Lionel
Also see JONES, Quincy

WASHINGTON, Dinah, & The Ravens
Singles: 7-Inch
MERCURY: *51*................. **40–50**
Also see RAVENS, The

WASHINGTON, Dinah / Joe Williams / Sarah Vaughan
LPs: 10/12-Inch 33rpm
ROULETTE: *64* **15–20**
Also see VAUGHAN, Sarah
Also see WASHINGTON, Dinah
Also see WILLIAMS, Joe

WASHINGTON, Donna
Singles: 7-Inch
CAPITOL: *81* **1–3**
LPs: 10/12-Inch 33rpm
CAPITOL: *81* **5–8**

WASHINGTON, Ella
Singles: 7-Inch
ATLANTIC: *67* **3–5**
SOUND STAGE: *67–69* **2–4**
LPs: 10/12-Inch 33rpm
SOUND STAGE: *69* **10–12**

WASHINGTON, Grover, Jr.
Singles: 7-Inch
ELEKTRA: *79–84* **1–3**
KUDU: *71–78*.................... **2–3**
MOTOWN: *78–83*................. **1–3**
Picture Sleeves
ELEKTRA: *80* **1–3**
LPs: 10/12-Inch 33rpm
ELEKTRA: *79–84* **5–8**
KUDO: *71–77*................... **8–12**
MOTOWN: *78–83*................ **6–10**
Also see LABELLE, Patti, & Grover Washington, Jr.
Also see MATTHEWS, David
Also see WITHERS, Bill

WASHINGTON, Jeanette: see WASHINGTON, Baby

Price Range

WASHINGTON, Jerry
Singles: 7-Inch
EXCELLO: 73................... $2–4

WATERS, Freddie
Singles: 7-Inch
KARI: 81........................ 1–3
OCTOBER: 77................... 2–3

WATERS, Muddy
Singles: 7-Inch
CHESS (1509 through
1542): 52–53.................. 25–35
CHESS (1550 through
1571): 53–54.................. 15–20
CHESS (1579 through
1596): 54–55................... 8–12
CHESS (1600 series):
55–59 5–8
CHESS (1700 series):
59–61 4–6
CHESS (1800 & 1900
series): 62–66.................. 3–5
CHESS (2000 series):
67–73 2–4
LPs: 10/12-Inch 33rpm
BLUE SKY: 77–81................ 5–8
CADET CONCEPT: 68–69....... 10–12
CHESS (1427; "The Best
Of Muddy Waters"): 57......... 35–45
CHESS (1444; "Muddy
Waters Sings Big Bill"):
60 25–35
CHESS (1449; "Muddy
Waters At Newport"):
64 20–25
CHESS (1483; "Folk
Singer"): 64 15–20
CHESS (1500 series):
66–71 10–15
CHESS (50012 through
50023): 72–73.................. 6–10
CHESS (50033; "Fathers &
Sons"): 75..................... 15–20
CHESS (60006; "McKinley
Morganfield"): 71 10–12
CHESS (60013 through
60035): 72–75.................. 6–10
DOUGLAS: 68 10–12
MUSE: 73 5–8

Price Range

TESTAMENT.................. $10–12
Also see ROGERS, Jimmy
Also see WELLS, Junior
Also see WINTER, Johnny

WATERS, Muddy, & Howlin' Wolf
LPs: 10/12-Inch 33rpm
CHESS: 74...................... 8–10
Also see DIDDLEY, Bo, Howlin' Wolf &
Muddy Waters
Also see HOWLIN' WOLF
Also see WATERS, Muddy

WATERS, Patty
LPs: 10/12-Inch 33rpm
ESP: 66........................ 12–15

**WATERS, Roger (With Madeline
Bell, Katie Kissoon, Eric Clapton &
Doreen Chanter)**
Singles: 12-inch
COLUMBIA: 84.................. 4–6
Singles: 7-Inch
COLUMBIA: 84.................. 1–3
LPs: 10/12-Inch 33rpm
COLUMBIA: 84.................. 5–8
Also see BELL, Madeline
Also see CLAPTON, Eric
Also see KISSOON, Mac & Katie
Also see PINK FLOYD

WATKINS, Tip
Singles: 7-Inch
H&L: 77........................ 2–4

WATSON, Doc
Singles: 7-Inch
POPPY: 72–74................... 2–3
UNITED ARTISTS: 75–79......... 1–3
LPs: 10/12-Inch 33rpm
FLYING FISH: 81................ 5–8
FOLKWAYS: 63–69.............. 8–18
LIBERTY: 83 5–8
POPPY: 72 6–12
UNITED ARTISTS: 75–76........ 8–15
VANGUARD: 64–77.............. 8–18
VERVE/FOLKWAYS: 66......... 10–15
Also see ATKINS, Chet, & Doc Watson
Also see FLATT, Lester, Earl Scruggs & Doc
Watson

WATSON, Johnny (Johnny Guitar Watson; Young John Watson; The Johnny Watson Trio)
Singles: 7-Inch
ALL STAR: 58 . . . . $5–8
ARVEE: 60 4–6
CLASS: 59 4–6
DJM: 77 2–3
ESCORT 4–6
FANTASY: 73–75 2–3
FEDERAL: 53–54 30–40
GOTH: 60 4–6
KEEN: 57 8–10
KENT: 60 3–5
KING: 61–64 3–5
OKEH: 66–67 3–5
RPM: 55–56 10–15
VALLEY VUE: 84 1–3

LPs: 10/12-Inch 33rpm
A&M: 81 5–8
BIG TOWN: 77 8–10
CADET: 67 10–15
CHESS: 64 15–20
DJM: 76–81 5–8
FANTASY: 73–81 5–8
KING: 63 40–50
OKEH: 67 10–15
MCA: 81 5–8
Also see BLAND, Bobby, & Johnny Guitar Watson
Also see OTIS, Johnny
Also see WATSONIAN INSTITUTE, The
Also see WILLIAMS, Larry, & Johnny Watson

WATSONIAN INSTITUTE, The
Singles: 7-Inch
DJM: 78 2–3

LPs: 10/12-Inch 33rpm
DJM: 78 5–8
Also see WATSON, Johnny

WATTS, Ernie
Singles: 7-Inch
QWEST: 82 1–2

LPs: 10/12-Inch 33rpm
QWEST: 82 5–8

WATTS, Noble (Noble "Thin Man" Watts & His Rhythm Sparks; The Noble Watts Quintet; Noble Watts & June Bateman)
Singles: 7-Inch
BATON: 57 . . . . $4–6
BRUNSWICK: 68 3–5
CLAMIKE: 63–64 3–5
CUB: 60 3–5
DELUXE: 54 5–8
ENJOY: 63 3–5

WATTS 103RD ST. RHYTHM BAND, The (Featuring Charles Wright)
Singles: 7-Inch
KEYMEN: 67 3–5
WARNER BROS: 68–69 3–5
LPs: 10/12-Inch 33rpm
WARNER BROS: 68–69 10–15
Also see WRIGHT, Charles

WAX
Singles: 12-Inch 33/45rpm
RCA VICTOR: 86 4–6
Singles: 7-Inch
RCA VICTOR: 81–86 1–3
LPs: 10/12-Inch 33rpm
COTILLION: 80 5–8
RCA VICTOR: 81–86 5–8
Members: Graham Gouldman; Andrew Gold.
Also see GOLD, Andrew
Also see 10CC

WAYBILL, Fee
Singles: 7-Inch
CAPITOL: 84 1–3
LPs: 10/12-Inch 33rpm
CAPITOL: 84 5–8
Also see TUBES, The

WAYLON & WILLIE: see JENNINGS, Waylon, & Willie Nelson

WAYNE, Bobby
Singles: 7-Inch
MERCURY: 51–54 3–6
EPs: 7-Inch 33/45rpm
MERCURY: 53 5–10

Price Range

WAYNE, James (James Waynes; Wee Willie Wayne)
Singles: 7-Inch
ANGELTONE: *60* $5–8
ALADDIN: *54* 15–20
IMPERIAL (5200 series):
53 20–25
IMPERIAL (5300 series):
55 8–12
IMPERIAL (5600 & 5700
series): *60–61* 3–5
MILLION: *54* 10–15
PEACOCK: *57* 5–8

LPs: 10/12-Inch 33rpm
IMPERIAL: *61* 40–50

WAYNE, John
Singles: 7-Inch
CASABLANCA: *79* 1–3
RCA VICTOR: *73* 2–3

LPs: 10/12-Inch 33rpm
RCA VICTOR (3000
series): *79–81* 4–8
RCA VICTOR (4800
series): *73* 8–15

WAYNE, Thomas (Thomas Wayne & The DeLons)
Singles: 7-Inch
CAPEHART: *61* 3–5
CHALET: *69* 2–4
COLLECTABLES 1–3
ERIC 1–3
FERNWOOD (Except
106): *59–60* 4–6
FERNWOOD (106;
"You're The One That
Done It"): *58* 35–40
MERCURY (71287;
"You're The One That
Done It"): *58* 25–35
MERCURY (71454;
"You're The One That
Done It"): *59* 20–25
OLDIES 45: *64* 1–3
PHILLIPS INT'L: *62* 3–5
RACER: *65* 3–5
SANTO: *62* 3–5

Price Range

WE FIVE
Singles: 7-Inch
A&M: *65–69* $3–5
MGM: *73* 2–4
VAULT: *67* 3–5
VERVE: *68–73* 2–4
LPs: 10/12-Inch 33rpm
A&M: *65–69* 10–15
A.V.I.: *77* 5–8
VAULT: *70* 10–12

WE THE PEOPLE
Singles: 7-Inch
CHALLENGE: *66–67* 8–10
DAVEL: *75* 2–3
IMPERIAL: *69* 2–4
LION: *72–74* 2–4
MAP CITY: *69* 2–4
RCA VICTOR: *67* 4–6
REENA: *68* 2–4
VERVE: *71* 2–4

WEAPONS OF PEACE
Singles: 7-Inch
PLAYBOY: *76–77* 2–3
LPs: 10/12-Inch 33rpm
PLAYBOY: *77* 5–8

WEATHER GIRLS, The
Singles: 12-Inch 33/45rpm
COLUMBIA: *83–85* 4–6
Singles: 7-Inch
COLUMBIA: *83–85* 1–3
LPs: 10/12-Inch 33rpm
COLUMBIA: *84* 5–8
Also see TWO TONS O' FUN

WEATHER REPORT
Singles: 7-Inch
COLUMBIA: *73–84* 2–3
LPs: 10/12-Inch 33rpm
ARC/COLUMBIA: *78–82* 5–10
COLUMBIA: *71–84* 5–10
Also see PASTORIUS, Jaco
Also see SHORTER, Wayne

WEATHERLY, Jim
Singles: 7-Inch
ABC: *76–77* 2–3
BUDDAH: *74–75* 2–4
ELEKTRA: *79–80* 1–3

Price Range

ERIC: *78* $1–3
RCA VICTOR: *72–74* 2–4
20TH CENTURY-FOX:
  65 3–5
Picture Sleeves
BUDDAH: *74* 2–4
LPs: 10/12-Inch 33rpm
ABC: *77* 5–8
BUDDAH: *74–75* 8–10
RCA VICTOR: *72* 8–10

WEATHERS, Carl
Singles: 7-Inch
MIRAGE: *81* 1–3

WEATHERS, Oscar
Singles: 7-Inch
BLUE CANDLE: *73* 2–4
TOP & BOTTOM: *69–72* 2–4

WEAVER, Dennis (Dennis Weaver & The Good Time People)
Singles: 7-Inch
CASCADE: *59* 5–8
CENTURY CITY: *69* 2–4
EVA: *63* 4–6
IM'PRESS: *72* 2–4
OVATION: *75* 2–3
WARNER BROS: *63* 3–5
LPs: 10/12-Inch 33rpm
IM'PRESS: *72* 8–10
OVATION: *75* 5–10

WEAVERS, The (The Weavers With Gordon Jenkins' Orchestra)
Singles: 7-Inch
DECCA (27000 through
  29000 series): *50–55* 4–8
DECCA (31000 series): *62* 2–4
NSD: *82* 1–3
VANGUARD: *60–62* 3–5
EPs: 7-Inch 33/45rpm
DECCA: *51–52* 5–15
LPs: 10/12-Inch 33rpm
DECCA (Except 5000
  series): *58–70* 8–18
DECCA (5000 series):
  51–52 15–30
  (10-Inch LPs.)

Price Range

VANGUARD (15-16;
  "Greatest Hits"): *71* $8–12
VANGUARD (2000
  series): *59–63* 10–20
VANGUARD (3000
  through 6000 series):
  67–70 8–15
VANGUARD (9000
  series): *56–63* 12–25
VANGUARD (9100
  series): *65* 10–20
  Members: Pete Seeger; Lee Hays; Fred Heller-
  man; Ronnie Gilbert.
  Also see JENKINS, Gordon, & His Orchestra
  Also see SEEGER, Pete

WEB, Ebony: see EBONEE WEBB

WEBB, Jack, & Jazz Combo
EPs: 7-Inch 33/45rpm
RCA VICTOR (1126;
  "Pete Kelly's Blues"): *55* 15–25
LPs: 10/12-Inch 33rpm
RCA VICTOR (1126;
  "Pete Kelly's Blues"): *55* 20–35
RCA VICTOR (2040;
  "Pete Kelly's Blues"): *59* 15–25
  Members: Jack Webb; Matty Matlock; Dick
  Cathcart; Nick Fatool; Elmer "Moe"
  Schneider; George Van Eps; Ray Sherman; Jud
  DeNaut.

WEBB, Paula
Singles: 7-Inch
WESTBOUND: *75* 2–3

WEBER, Joan
Singles: 7-Inch
COLUMBIA: *54–56* 3–5
CROSLEY: *63* 2–4
MAPLE: *61* 2–4
EPs: 7-Inch 33/45rpm
COLUMBIA: *55* 5–10

WEBS, The
Singles: 7-Inch
GUYDEN: *63* 4–6
HEART: *61–62* 3–5
MGM: *66* 3–5
POPSIDE: *67–68* 3–5
VERVE: *68* 3–5

Price Range   *Price Range*

WEDNESDAY
Singles: 7-Inch
CELEBRATION: 76 .... $2–3
SKY: 76 2–3
SUSSEX: 73–74 2–4

LPs: 10/12-Inch 33rpm
SUSSEX: 74 8–10

WEE GEE
Singles: 7-Inch
COTILLION: 80 1–3
JUNEY: 78 2–3

WEEKS & CO.
Singles: 12-Inch 33/45rpm
SALSOUL: 83 4–6
Singles: 7-Inch
SALSOUL: 83 1–3
LPs: 10/12-Inch 33rpm
SALSOUL: 83 5–8

WEIR, Bob
Singles: 7-Inch
ARISTA: 78 2–3
WARNER BROS: 72 3–5

LPs: 10/12-Inch 33rpm
ARISTA: 81 5–8
WARNER BROS: 72 8–12
Also see BOBBY & THE MIDNITES
Also see GRATEFUL DEAD, The
Also see KINGFISH

WEIR, Frank, Orchestra
Singles: 7-Inch
CAPITOL: 56 2–4
COLUMBIA: 57 2–4
LONDON: 54–63 2–4

EPs: 7-Inch 33/45rpm
LONDON: 54–55 4–8

LPs: 10/12-Inch 33rpm
COLUMBIA: 57 8–15
LONDON: 54 8–15

WEISBERG, Tim
Singles: 7-Inch
A&M: 71–79 2–3
MCA: 79 1–3
UNITED ARTISTS: 77–80 1–3

LPs: 10/12-Inch 33rpm
A&M: 73–79 .... $5–10
MCA: 79–80 5–8
NAUTILUS: 80 5–8
UNITED ARTISTS: 77–78 5–10
Also see FOGELBERG, Dan, & Tim Weisberg

WEISSBERG, Eric (Eric Weissberg & Steve Mandell; Eric Weissberg & Marshall Brickman)
Singles: 7-Inch
WARNER BROS: 72–73 2–3

LPs: 10/12-Inch 33rpm
ELEKTRA: 63 10–20
WARNER BROS: 73 5–10

WELCH, Bob
Singles: 7-Inch
CAPITOL: 77–81 1–3
RCA VICTOR: 81–83 1–3

Picture Sleeves
CAPITOL: 81 1–3

LPs: 10/12-Inch 33rpm
CAPITOL (Except 16000
  series): 77–80 8–10
CAPITOL (16000 series):
  80–82 5–8
RCA VICTOR: 81–83 5–8

Promotional LPs
CAPITOL ("French Kiss"
  - picture disc): 79 25–30
Also see FLEETWOOD MAC
Also see PARIS

WELCH, Honey
Singles: 7-Inch
CHEVELL: 65 3–5

WELCH, Lenny
Singles: 7-Inch
ATCO: 72 2–4
BARNABY: 76 1–3
BIG TREE: 78–83 1–3
CADENCE (Except 1422):
  59–64 3–5
CADENCE (1422;
  "Congratulations Baby"):
  62 5–8
COLUMBIA: 67 2–4

Price Range

COMMONWEALTH
  UNITED: *69* **$2–4**
  DECCA: *59* **3–5**
  KAPP: *65–67.* **2–4**
  MAINSTREAM: *73–74* **2–4**
  MERCURY: *68.* **2–4**
  ROULETTE: *71* **2–3**

  LPs: 10/12-Inch 33rpm
  CADENCE: *64* **15–20**
  COLUMBIA: *65* **10–15**
  KAPP: *66–67.* **10–15**

WELK, Lawrence, & His Orchestra
Singles: 7-Inch
CORAL: *50–66* **2–4**
DOT: *59–67.* **1–3**
MERCURY: *50–55.* **2–4**
RANWOOD: *68–77* **1–3**

EPs: 7-Inch 33/45rpm
CORAL: *50–58* **3–8**
DOT: *59–60.* **3–6**

LPs: 10/12-Inch 33rpm
CORAL: *50–65* **5–15**
DECCA: *72* **5–10**
DOT: *59–67.* **4–12**
HAMILTON: *64–66.* **4–8**
HARMONY: *68–70* **4–8**
MCA: *74–76* **4–8**
RANWOOD: *68–85* **4–8**
SUNNYVALE: *79* **4–6**
TRADITION: *75* **4–8**
VOCALION: *59–70* **4–8**
WING: *60–62* **4–8**
  Also see HODGES, Johnny, & Lawrence Welk
  Also see HUDSON, Emperor Bob, & Lawrence
  Welk
  Also see LENNON SISTERS, The

WELLER, Freddy
Singles: 7-Inch
ABC/DOT: *75.* **2–3**
APT: *65* **4–6**
COLUMBIA: *69–80* **1–3**
DORE: *61* **5–8**

Price Range

  LPs: 10/12-Inch 33rpm
COLUMBIA: *69–80* **$6–10**
EPIC: *74* **8–10**
51 WEST **5–8**
  Also see REVERE, Paul, & The Raiders

WELLES, Orson
LPs: 10/12-Inch 33rpm
MEDIARTS: *70* **8–12**
  Also see CROSBY, Bing, & Orson Welles

WELLS, Brandi
Singles: 7-Inch
WMOT: *81–82.* **1–3**

WELLS, Jean
Singles: 7-Inch
ABC-PARAMOUNT: *65* **3–5**
CALLA: *67–68* **3–5**
VOLARE: *69.* **2–4**

WELLS, Junior (Junior Wells & His Eagle Rockers; Junior Wells' Chicago Blues Band)
Singles: 7-Inch
BLUE ROCK: *68–69* **3–5**
BRIGHT STAR: *66–67* **3–5**
CHIEF: *57–62.* **8–10**
PROFILE: *59–60* **4–6**
SHAD: *59* **5–8**
STATES (Colored vinyl):
  52–54 . . . . **45–55**
U.S.A.: *63–64.* **4–6**
VANGUARD: *67.* **3–5**

  LPs: 10/12-Inch 33rpm
BLUE ROCK: *68* **10–12**
DELMARK: *66–69.* **10–15**
VANGUARD: *66–68* **10–15**
  Also see WATERS, Muddy

WELLS, Junior, & Buddy Guy
LPs: 10/12-Inch 33rpm
BLIND PIG: *82* **5–8**
INTERMEDIA **5–8**
  Also see GUY, Buddy
  Also see WELLS, Junior

Kitty Wells, one charted single (1958), no charted LPs.

Price Range

WELLS, Kitty
Singles: 7-Inch
CAPRICORN: *74–76* **$2–3**
DECCA (28000 & 29000
  series): *52–56* **4–8**
DECCA (30000 through
  32000 series): *56–71* **2–5**
MCA: *73* **1–3**
RUBOCA: *79–80.* **1–3**
  Picture Sleeves
DECCA: *69* **2–4**
  EPs: 7-Inch 33/45rpm
DECCA: *55–65* **6–15**
  LPs: 10/12-Inch 33rpm
CAPRICORN: *74* **6–10**
DECCA (Except 8800
  series): *61–72* **12–25**
DECCA (8800 series):
  56–59 .... **30–40**
EXACT: *80* **5–8**
IMPERIAL HOUSE: *80* **5–10**
KOALA: *79.* **5–8**
MCA: *73–83* **4–8**
MISTLETOE. **5–8**
PICKWICK/HILLTOP. **6–12**
ROUNDER: *82.* **5–8**
RUBOCA: *79.* **8–12**

Price Range

SUFFOLK
  MARKETING: *80* **$5–10**
VOCALION: *66–69* **8–15**
  Also see PARTON, Dolly / Kitty Wells
  Also see PIERCE, Webb, & Kitty Wells

WELLS, Kitty, & Red Foley
Singles: 7-Inch
DECCA: *54–69* **2–5**
  EPs: 7-Inch 33/45rpm
DECCA: *59* **8–12**
  LPs: 10/12-Inch 33rpm
DECCA: *61–67* **15–20**
  Also see FOLEY, Red

WELLS, Kitty, & Roy Drusky
Singles: 7-Inch
DECCA: *60* **2–4**
  Also see DRUSKY, Roy
  Also see WELLS, Kitty

WELLS, Mary
Singles: 12-Inch 33/45rpm
EPIC: *82* **4–6**
  Singles: 7-Inch
ATCO: *66–67.* **3–5**
EPIC: *82* **1–3**
JUBILEE: *68–71.* **2–4**
MOTOWN (1003; "Bye
  Bye Baby"): *60* **6–10**
  (Pink label.)
MOTOWN (1011; "I Don't
  Want To Take A
  Chance"): *61* **10–15**
  (Pink label.)
MOTOWN (1011; "I Don't
  Want To Take A
  Chance"): *61* **5–8**
  (Blue label.)
MOTOWN (1024 through
  1056): *62–64.* **4–6**
REPRISE: *71–74.* **2–4**
20TH CENTURY-FOX:
  64–66 .... **3–5**
  Picture Sleeves
MOTOWN: *61–62.* **8–15**
20TH CENTURY-FOX:
  65 .... **3–5**
  LPs: 10/12-Inch 33rpm
ALLEGIANCE: *84.* **5–8**
ATCO: *66* **15–20**
EPIC: *81* **5–8**

51 WEST: *83* $5–8
JUBILEE: *68* **10–15**
MOTOWN (100 & 200
 series): *82* **5–8**
MOTOWN (600; "Mary
 Wells"): *61* **50–60**
MOTOWN (605; "The One
 Who Really Loves
 You"): *62* **35–45**
MOTOWN (607 through
 653): *63–66* **20–30**
MOVIETONE: *66* **15–20**
POWER PAK **5–8**
20TH CENTURY-FOX:
 65 . . . . **20–25**
 Also see GAYE, Marvin, & Mary Wells

WELLS, Terri
Singles: 12-Inch 33/45rpm
PHILLY WORLD: *84* **4–6**
Singles: 7-Inch
PHILLY WORLD: *84* **1–3**

WERNER, David
Singles: 7-Inch
EPIC: *79* **2–3**
RCA VICTOR: *74–76* **2–4**
LPs: 10/12-Inch 33rpm
RCA VICTOR: *75* **8–10**

WERNER, Max
Singles: 7-Inch
RADIO: *81* **1–3**
 Also see KAYAK

WESLEY, Fred (Fred Wesley & The Horny Horns; Fred Wesley & The J.B.s)
Singles: 7-Inch
ATLANTIC: *77* **2–3**
PEOPLE: *72–74* **2–4**
RSO: *80* **1–3**
LPs: 10/12-Inch 33rpm
ATLANTIC: *77* **8–10**
 Also see BROWN, James, Band

WEST, Belinda
Singles: 7-Inch
PANORAMA: *80* **1–3**

WEST, Dr.: see DR. WEST'S MEDICINE SHOW & JUNK BAND

WEST, Dottie
Singles: 7-Inch
ATLANTIC: *62* $3–5
LIBERTY: *80–82* **1–3**
RCA VICTOR (Except
 8000 series): *66–81* **1–3**
RCA VICTOR (8000
 series): *63–66* **2–5**
STARDAY (500 series):
 60–61 . . . . **4–6**
STARDAY (700 series): *65* **2–5**
UNITED ARTISTS: *76–80* **1–3**
Picture Sleeves
LIBERTY: *80–81* . . . . INC
LPs: 10/12-Inch 33rpm
CAMDEN: *71–73* **6–10**
COLUMBIA: *80* **5–8**
LIBERTY: *81–82* **5–8**
NASHVILLE **8–12**
PICKWICK: *75* **5–10**
RCA VICTOR: *65–75* **5–15**
STARDAY: *64–65* **10–20**
UNITED ARTISTS: *73–80* **5–10**
 Also see DEAN, Jimmy, & Dottie West
 Also see GIBSON, Don, & Dottie West
 Also see REEVES, Jim, & Dottie West
 Also see ROGERS, Kenny, & Dottie West

WEST, Dottie / Melba Montgomery
LPs: 10/12-Inch 33rpm
STARDAY: *65* **10–15**
 Also see MONTGOMERY, Melba
 Also see WEST, Dottie

WEST, Leslie (The Leslie West Band)
Singles: 7-Inch
PHANTOM: *75–76* **2–4**
LPs: 10/12-Inch 33rpm
PHANTOM: *75–76* **8–10**
WINDFALL: *69* **10–15**
 Also see JAGGER, Mick
 Also see MOUNTAIN
 Also see WEST, BRUCE & LAING

WEST, Mae
Singles: 7-Inch
MGM: *73* **2–4**

Price Range

RADIO CINEMA: *79* $1–3
UNITED ARTISTS: *69* 2–4
Picture Sleeves
KAPP: *67* 2–5
LPs: 10/12-Inch 33rpm
AVALANCHE: *73* 8–10
FLYING FISH: *79* 5–8
KAPP: *64–68* 10–18
MONITOR: *61–62* 15–25
RCA VICTOR: *71* 8–10
UNITED ARTISTS: *69* 8–12

WHIRLWIND
Singles: 12-Inch 33/45rpm
ROULETTE: *77* 4–6
Singles: 7-Inch
ROULETTE: *76* 2–3

WHISPERS, The
Singles: 12-Inch 33/45rpm
SOLAR: *80–84* 4–6
Singles: 7-Inch
COLLECTABLES 1–3
DORE: *65–66* 3–5
FONTANA: *66* 3–5
JANUS: *70–75* 2–4
SOLAR: *79–84* 1–3
SOUL CLOCK: *69–70* 2–4
SOUL TRAIN: *75–77* 2–3
LPs: 10/12-Inch 33rpm
ACCORD: *81* 5–8
ALLEGIANCE: *84* 5–8
DORE: *80* 5–8
JANUS: *72–75* 8–10
SOLAR: *78–84* 5–8
SOUL TRAIN: *76–77* 8–10
Also see LUCAS, Carrie, & The Whispers

WHITCOMB, Ian (Ian Whitcomb & Bluesville; Ian Whitcomb & Somebody's Chyldren)
Singles: 7-Inch
TOWER: *65–68* 3–5
UNITED ARTISTS: *73* 2–4
Picture Sleeves
TOWER: *66* 4–6
LPs: 10/12-Inch 33rpm
FIRST AMERICAN:
78–82 5–8
SIERRA: *80* 5–8
TOWER: *65–68* 15–20

Price Range

UNITED ARTISTS: *72* $8–10

WHITE, Artie "Blues Boy"
Singles: 7-Inch
ALTEE: *77* 2–3
RONN 2–3

WHITE, Barry (Barry White With Love Unlimited & The Love Unlimited Orchestra; Barry White & Glodean)
Singles: 12-Inch 33/45rpm
20TH CENTURY-FOX:
73–78 4–6
UNLIMITED GOLD: *83* 4–6
Singles: 7-Inch
BRONCO: *67* 3–5
CASABLANCA 1–3
20TH CENTURY-FOX:
73–78 1–3
UNLIMITED GOLD:
79–83 1–3
LPs: 10/12-Inch 33rpm
20TH CENTURY-FOX
(Except 1): *73–81* 6–10
20TH CENTURY-FOX (1;
"Barry White Radio
Special") 10–15
(Promotional issue only.)
UNLIMITED GOLD:
79–81 6–10
Also see BOB & EARL
Also see LOVE UNLIMITED

WHITE, Barry, & The Atlantics / The Atlantics
Singles: 7-Inch
FARO: *63* 5–8
Also see WHITE, Barry

WHITE, Danny
Singles: 7-Inch
ABC-PARAMOUNT: *64* 3–5
ATLAS: *66* 3–5
DECCA: *66–67* 2–5
DOT: *61* 3–5
FRISCO: *62* 3–5
KING: *58* 8–10
ROCKY COAST: *77* 2–3
SSS INT'L: *69* 2–4

Price Range

Price Range

WHITE, Kitty
Singles: 7-Inch
CLOVER: 66 .... **$2–4**
DECCA: 51 .... **3–6**
DOT: 60 .... **2–4**
GNP/CRESCENDO: 59 .... **2–4**
MERCURY: 55–56 .... **3–6**

EPs: 7-Inch 33/45rpm
EMARCY: 54 .... **5–15**
PACIFIC JAZZ: 54 .... **5–15**

LPs: 10/12-Inch 33rpm
EMARCY: 54 .... **20–40**
CLOVER: 66 .... **6–12**
MERCURY: 55 .... **15–36**
PACIFIC JAZZ: 54–55 .... **20–40**

WHITE, Lenny
Singles: 7-Inch
ELEKTRA: 78–83 .... **1–3**
NEMPEROR: 76 .... **2–4**

LPs: 10/12-Inch 33rpm
ELEKTRA: 78–83 .... **5–8**
NEMPEROR: 75–77 .... **8–10**
Also see RETURN TO FOREVER
Also see TWENNYNINE

WHITE, Maurice
Singles: 7-Inch
COLUMBIA: 85 .... **1–3**
GOLD: 59 .... **8–10**
PRIDE: 60 .... **5–8**

LPs: 10/12-Inch 33rpm
COLUMBIA: 85 .... **5–8**

WHITE, Tony Joe
Singles: 7-Inch
ARISTA: 79 .... **1–3**
CASABLANCA: 80 .... **1–3**
COLUMBIA: 83–85 .... **1–3**
MONUMENT: 67–70 .... **3–5**
20TH CENTURY-FOX:
   76 .... **2–3**

LPs: 10/12-Inch 33rpm
CASABLANCA: 80 .... **5–8**
COLUMBIA: 83 .... **5–8**
MONUMENT: 69–70 .... **8–12**
20TH CENTURY-FOX:
   77 .... **5–8**
WARNER BROS: 71–73 .... **8–10**

WHITE PLAINS
Singles: 7-Inch
DERAM: 70–71 .... **$2–4**
LONDON **1–3**
LPs: 10/12-Inch 33rpm
DERAM: 70 .... **10–15**
Also see DAVID & JONATHAN

WHITE WOLF
Singles: 7-Inch
RCA VICTOR: 85 .... **1–3**
LPs: 10/12-Inch 33rpm
RCA VICTOR: 85 .... **5–8**

WHITEHEAD, Charles (Charlie Whitehead & The Swamp Dogg Band)
Singles: 7-Inch
ISLAND: 75 .... **2–4**
LPs: 10/12-Inch 33rpm
FUNGUS **10–15**
WIZARD: 78 .... **5–10**

WHITEMAN, Paul, Orchestra
Singles: 7-Inch
CORAL: 50–56 .... **2–4**
EPs: 7-Inch 33/45rpm
CORAL: 50–56 .... **3–8**
LPs: 10/12-Inch 33rpm
CAPITOL: 62 .... **5–10**
CORAL: 50–56 .... **5–15**
GRAND AWARD: 56–59 .... **5–15**
RCA VICTOR: 68–69 .... **4–8**
WESTMINSTER: 74 .... **4–8**

WHITESNAKE
Singles: 7-Inch
GEFFEN: 82 .... **1–3**
MIRAGE: 80 .... **1–3**
UNITED ARTISTS: 79 .... **2–3**
Picture Sleeves
MIRAGE: 80 .... **1–3**
LPs: 10/12-Inch 33rpm
GEFFEN: 82 .... **5–8**
MIRAGE: 80–81 .... **5–8**
UNITED ARTISTS: 79 .... **6–10**
Members: David Coverdale; Jon Lord
Also see DEEP PURPLE

WHITFIELD, David
Singles: 7-Inch
LONDON: 53–63 .... **2–4**

Price Range

EPs: 7-Inch 33/45rpm
LONDON: *54* **$4–8**
LPs: 10/12-Inch 33rpm
LONDON: *54–66* **5–15**

WHITING, Margaret
Singles: 7-Inch
CAPITOL: *50–56* **2–5**
DOT: *57–59* **2–4**
LONDON: *66–70* **2–4**
VERVE: *60* **2–4**
EPs: 7-Inch 33/45rpm
CAPITOL: *50–56* **4–8**
LPs: 10/12-Inch 33rpm
CAPITOL: *50–56* **8–18**
DOT: *57–67* **5–15**
HAMILTON: *59–65* **5–12**
LONDON: *67–68* **6–12**
VERVE: *60* **5–15**
Also see TORME, Mel

WHITING, Margaret, & Jimmy Wakely
Singles: 7-Inch
CAPITOL: *50* **3–5**
EPs: 7-Inch 33/45rpm
CAPITOL: *53* **8–12**
LPs: 10/12-Inch 33rpm
PICKWICK: *67* **8–12**
Also see WHITING, Margaret
Also see WAKELY, Jimmy

WHITLOCK, Bobby
Singles: 7-Inch
DUNHILL: *72* **2–4**
LPs: 10/12-Inch 33rpm
CAPRICORN: *76* **8–10**
DUNHILL: *72* **10–12**
Also see BELL, Maggie, & Bobby Whitlock
Also see DELANEY & BONNIE
Also see DEREK & THE DOMINOES

WHITMAN, Slim
Singles: 7-Inch
CLEVELAND INT'L:
80–82 . . . . **1–3**
EPIC: *84* **1–3**
IMPERIAL (5000 series):
61–63 . . . . **3–5**
IMPERIAL (8000 through
8200 series): *52–58* **5–10**

Price Range

IMPERIAL (8300 series):
59–60 . . . . **$3–6**
IMPERIAL (50000 series):
70–71 . . . . **2–3**
IMPERIAL (65000 &
66000 series): *61–69* **2–5**
UNITED ARTISTS: *70–77* **2–3**

EPs: 7-Inch 33/45rpm
IMPERIAL: *54–65* **30–50**
RCA VICTOR (3217;
"Slim Whitman Sings &
Yodels"): *54* **90–125**

LPs: 10/12-Inch 33rpm
CAMDEN: *66* **8–12**
CLEVELAND INT'L:
80–81 . . . . **5–8**
EPIC: *84* **5–8**
IMPERIAL (3004;
"America's Favorite Folk
Artist"): *54* **400–450**
(10-Inch LP.)
IMPERIAL (9000 series):
56–60 . . . . **25–40**
(Maroon labels, or black with "Imperial" name
at top.)
IMPERIAL (9000 series):
66 . . . . **8–12**
(Black labels with "Imperial" name on left
side.)
IMPERIAL (9100 series):
60–62 . . . . **15–30**
(Black labels with "Imperial" name at top.)
IMPERIAL (9100 series):
66 . . . . **8–12**
(Black labels with "Imperial" name on left
side.)
IMPERIAL (9200 & 9300
series): *63–67* **10–25**
IMPERIAL (12100 series):
62 . . . . **15–25**
(Black labels with "Imperial" name at top.)
IMPERIAL (12100 series):
66 . . . . **8–12**
(Black labels with "Imperial" name on left
side.)
IMPERIAL (12200 &
12300 series): *65–68* **10–25**
IMPERIAL (12400 series):
68–69 . . . . **8–12**
LIBERTY: *80–82* **5–8**
PICKWICK **5–10**

Price Range

RCA VICTOR (3217;
  "Slim Whitman Sings &
  Yodels"): *54* **$250–300**
RCA VICTOR (3700
  series): *80* **5–8**
SUFFOLK
  MARKETING: *79–82* **8–12**
SUNSET: *66–70* **8–12**
UNITED ARTISTS: *70–80* **6–12**
  Also see WILLIAMS, Hank / Slim Whitman

WHITNEY, Marva (Marva Whitney
& Ellie Taylor)
Singles: 7-Inch
EXCELLO: *72* **2–4**
KING: *67–69* **2–4**
T-NECK: *70* **2–4**
LPs: 10/12-Inch 33rpm
KING: *69* **8–12**
  Also see BROWN, James, & Marva Whitney

WHITTAKER, Roger
Singles: 7-Inch
MAIN STREET: *84* **1–3**
RCA VICTOR: *70–84* **1–3**
Picture Sleeves
RCA VICTOR: *80* . . . . **INC**
LPs: 10/12-Inch 33rpm
MAIN STREET: *84* **5–8**
RCA VICTOR: *70–84* **5–12**

WHO, The
Singles: 7-Inch
ATCO (6409;
  "Substitute"): *67* **15–20**
ATCO (6509;
  "Substitute"): *67* **12–20**
DECCA (31725; "I Can't
  Explain"): *64* **12–15**
DECCA (31801; "Anyway
  Anyhow Aywhere"): *65* **15–20**
DECCA (31877; "My
  Generation"): *65* **10–15**
DECCA (31988; "The
  Kids Are Alright"): *66* **15–20**
DECCA (32058; "I'm A
  Boy"): *66* **12–15**
DECCA (32114; "Happy
  Jack"): *67* **8–10**
DECCA (32156; "Pictures
  Of Lily"): *67* **8–10**

Price Range

DECCA (32206; "I Can
  See For Miles"): *67* **$4–6**
DECCA (32288; "Call Me
  Lightning"): *68* **8–10**
DECCA (32362; "Magic
  Bus"): *68* **4–6**
DECCA (32465; "Pinball
  Wizard"): *69* **4–6**
DECCA (32519; "I'm
  Free"): *69* **4–6**
DECCA (32670; "The
  Seeker"): *70* **5–8**
DECCA (32708;
  "Summertime Blues"):
  70 . . . . **4–6**
DECCA (32729; "See Me,
  Feel Me"): *70* **4–6**
DECCA (32737; "Young
  Man Blues"): *70* **10–15**
DECCA (32846; "Won't
  Get Fooled Again"): *71* **4–6**
DECCA (32888; "Behind
  Blue Eyes"): *71* **5–8**
DECCA (32983; "Join
  Together"): *72* **4–6**
DECCA (33041; "The
  Relay"): *72* **4–6**
  Note: some Decca singles numbers in the 30000
  series may be preceded by the number "7."
MCA: *74–79* **2–4**
POLYDOR: *75–79* **2–4**
TRACK: *72–74* **3–5**
WARNER BROS: *81–83* **1–3**

Picture Sleeves
DECCA: *67–70* **5–10**
WARNER BROS: *81–83* **1–3**

LPs: 10/12-Inch 33rpm
DECCA (DL-4664; "My
  Generation" - mono): *66* **40–50**
DECCA (DL7-4664; "My
  Generation" - stereo): *66* **30–40**
DECCA (DL-4892;
  "Happy Jack" - mono):
  67 . . . . **30–40**
DECCA (DL7-4892;
  "Happy Jack" - stereo):
  67 . . . . **20–30**
DECCA (DL-4950; "The
  Who Sell Out" - mono):
  67 . . . . **30–40**

Price Range

DECCA (DL7-4950; "The
Who Sell Out" - stereo):
67 . . . . **$20–30**
DECCA (7205; "Tommy"):
69 . . . . **20–25**
(Price includes bonus booklet.)
DECCA (75064; "Magic
Bus"): 68 . . . . **25–30**
DECCA (79175; "Live At
Leeds"): 70. . . . . **15–20**
DECCA (79182; "Who's
Next"): 71 . . . . **15–20**
DECCA (79184; "Meaty
Beaty Big & Bouncy"):
71 . . . . **15–20**
MCA (2126; "Odds &
Sods"): 74. . . . . **8–10**
MCA (2161; "The Who By
Numbers"): 75 . . . . **8–10**
MCA (3050; "Who Are
You" - black vinyl): 78 . . . . **8–10**
MCA (3050; "Who Are
You" - colored vinyl): 78 . . . . **15–20**
MCA (4000 series): 74 . . . . **10–12**
MCA (5000 series): 83–85 . . . . **5–8**
MCA (6000 series): 74 . . . . **10–12**
MCA (8000 series): 84 . . . . **10–12**
MCA (10004;
"Quadrophenia"): 79. . . . . **10–15**
MCA (11005; "The Kids
Are Alright"): 79. . . . . **10–12**
MCA (12001;
"Hooligans"): 81 . . . . **10–12**
MCA (14950; "Who Are
You" - picture disc): 79 . . . . **12–15**
MCA (37000 series): 79 . . . . **5–8**
MFSL: 84. . . . . **12–15**
TRACK: 74. **10–15**
WARNER BROS: 81–82. . . . . **5–8**

Promotional LPs

DWJ: 78. . . . . **30–40**
DECCA (7205; "Tommy"):
69 . . . . **50–75**
(White label.)
MCA (1987; "Who Are
You"): 78 . . . . **15–20**
Members: Roger Daltrey; Pete Townshend;
John Entwistle; Keith Moon; Kenny Jones.
Also see DALTREY, Roger
Also see ENTWISTLE, John
Also see MOON, Keith

Price Range

Also see TOWNSHEND, Pete

WHO, The / The Strawberry Alarm Clock
LPs: 10/12-Inch 33rpm
DECCA: 69 . . . . **$45–55**
(Philco-Ford Special Products promotional
issue.)
Also see STRAWBERRY ALARM CLOCK,
The
Also see WHO, The

WHODINI
Singles: 12-Inch 33/45rpm
JIVE: 84–85. . . . . **4–6**
Singles: 7-Inch
JIVE: 84–85. . . . . **1–3**
LPs: 10/12-Inch 33rpm
JIVE: 84. . . . . **5–8**

WHOLE DARN FAMILY, The
Singles: 7-Inch
SOUL INT'L: 76–77. . . . . **2–4**
LPs: 10/12-Inch 33rpm
SOUL INT'L: 76. . . . . **8–10**

WHOLE OATS
Singles: 7-Inch
ATLANTIC: 72 . . . . **4–6**
Members: Daryl Hall; John Oates.
Also see HALL, Daryl, & John Oates

WICHITA TRAIN WHISTLE, The
Singles: 7-Inch
DOT: 68. . . . . **4–6**
LPs: 10/12-Inch 33rpm
DOT: 68. . . . . **15–20**

WIDE BOY AWAKE
Singles: 12-Inch 33/45rpm
RCA VICTOR: 83 . . . . **4–6**
Singles: 7-Inch
RCA VICTOR: 83 . . . . **1–3**
LPs: 10/12-Inch 33rpm
RCA VICTOR: 83 . . . . **5–8**

WIDOWMAKER
Singles: 7-Inch
JET: 76–77. . . . . **2–3**
LPs: 10/12-Inch 33rpm
UNITED ARTISTS: 76–77. . . . . **8–10**
Members: John Butler; Aerial Bender.

Price Range

Price Range

WIEDLIN, Jane
Singles: 7-Inch
I.R.S.: 85 . . . . $1–3
LPs: 10/12-Inch 33rpm
I.R.S.: 85 5–8
Also see GO-GOs, The
Also see SPARKS, The, & Jane Wiedlin

WIER, Rusty
Singles: 7-Inch
ABC: 74 2–4
COLUMBIA: 76 2–3
COMPLEAT: 83–84 1–3
20TH CENTURY-FOX:
75–76 2–4
LPs: 10/12-Inch 33rpm
ABC: 74 8–12
COLUMBIA: 76 8–10
20TH CENTURY-FOX:
75 8–10

WIGGINS, Spencer
Singles: 7-Inch
FAME: 69–70 2–4
GOLDWAX: 66–69 3–5

WILCOX, Eddie, Orchestra
(Featuring Sunny Gale)
Singles: 7-Inch
DERBY (Colored vinyl):
52 8–10
Also see GALE, Sunny

WILCOX, Harlow (Harlow Wilcox &
The Oakies)
Singles: 7-Inch
PLANTATION: 69 2–4
SSS INT'L 1–3
LPs: 10/12-Inch 33rpm
PLANTATION: 70–71 5–8

WILD, Jack
Singles: 7-Inch
BUDDAH: 71 2–4
CAPITOL: 70 2–4
Picture Sleeves
CAPITOL: 70 2–4

WILD CHERRY
Singles: 12-Inch 33/45rpm
EPIC: 76–79 4–6

Singles: 7-Inch
A&M: 75 . . . . $2–3
BROWN BAG: 72–73 2–4
EPIC: 76–79 1–3
LPs: 10/12-Inch 33rpm
EPIC: 76–79 6–10

WILD MAGNOLIAS, The
Singles: 7-Inch
POLYDOR: 74 2–4
LPs: 10/12-Inch 33rpm
POLYDOR: 74 8–10

WILD MAN STEVE (Steve Gallon)
LPs: 10/12-Inch 33rpm
RAW: 69–70 6–12

WILD ONES, The
Singles: 7-Inch
MAINLINE: 65 3–5
MALA: 67 4–6
S.P.Q.R.: 64 4–6
SEARS 3–5
UNITED ARTISTS: 65–66 4–6
LPs: 10/12-Inch 33rpm
UNITED ARTISTS: 65 15–20
Also see ANTELL, Peter

WILD TURKEY
Singles: 7-Inch
CHRYSALIS: 72–73 2–4
REPRISE: 72 2–4
LPs: 10/12-Inch 33rpm
CHRYSALIS: 72–73 8–10
REPRISE: 72 10–12
Also see JETHRO TULL

WILD-CATS, The
Singles: 7-Inch
UNITED ARTISTS (154;
"Gazachstahagen"): 58 5–8
UNITED ARTISTS (169;
"King Size Guitar"): 59 5–8
UNITED ARTISTS (1154;
"Gazachstahagen"): 58 10–12
Also see MURE, Billy

WILDE, Eugene
Singles: 7-Inch
PHILLY WORLD: 84–85 1–3

Price Range

Price Range

LPs: 10/12-Inch 33rpm
PHILLY WORLD: *84* **$5–8**

WILDE, Kim
Singles: 12-Inch 33/45rpm
MCA: *85* **4–6**
Singles: 7-Inch
EMI AMERICA: *82.* **1–3**
MCA: *85* **1–3**
LPs: 10/12-Inch 33rpm
EMI AMERICA: *82.* **5–8**
MCA: *85* **5–8**

WILDE, Marty
Singles: 7-Inch
BELL: *74.* **2–4**
EPIC: *58–60* **4–6**
LPs: 10/12-Inch 33rpm
EPIC: *60* **25–30**
Also see SHANNON

WILDER, Matthew
Singles: 12-Inch 33/45rpm
PRIVATE I: *83–85.* **4–6**
Singles: 7-Inch
PRIVATE I: *83–85.* **1–3**
LPs: 10/12-Inch 33rpm
PRIVATE I: *83–85.* **5–8**

WILDFIRE
Singles: 7-Inch
CASABLANCA: *77.* **2–3**

WILDWEEDS
Singles: 7-Inch
CADET: *67–68* **4–6**
CADET CONCEPT: *68.* **4–6**
VANGUARD: *71.* **2–4**
LPs: 10/12-Inch 33rpm
VANGUARD: *70.* **10–15**

WILEY, Ed
Singles: 7-Inch
ATLANTIC: *51* **45–55**
SITTIN' IN WITH (545;
   "Cry, Cry Baby"): *50* **45–55**
   Members: Teddy Reynolds; King Tut.

WILEY, Michelle
Singles: 7-Inch
20TH CENTURY-FOX:
   77 . . . . **2–3**

WILLESDEN-DODGERS
Singles: 12-Inch 33/45rpm
JIVE: *83.* **$4–6**
Singles: 7-Inch
JIVE: *83.* **1–3**

**WILLIAMS, Andre (Andre Williams
& The Don Juans; Andre Williams &
The Five Dollars; Andre Wiliams &
Diablos; Andre "Bacon Fat" Williams
With The Inspirations; Andre "Mr.
Rhythm" Williams; Andre Williams &
Gino Parks)**
Singles: 7-Inch
AVIN: *66.* **3–5**
CHECKER: *68–69* **2–4**
EPIC: *57* **5–8**
FORTUNE: *55–60* **5–10**
SPORT: *67.* **3–5**
WINGATE: *66* **3–5**
LPs: 10/12-Inch 33rpm
FORTUNE: *86* **5–8**

WILLIAMS, Andy
Singles: 12-Inch 33/45rpm
COLUMBIA: *79.* **4–6**
Singles: 7-Inch
CADENCE: *56–64* **2–5**
COLUMBIA: *61–79* **1–3**
Picture Sleeves
CADENCE: *59* **2–4**
COLUMBIA: *61–76* **1–3**
EPs: 7-Inch
CADENCE: *57–59* **8–15**
LPs: 10/12-Inch 33rpm
CADENCE: *58–62* **15–25**
COLUMBIA: *62–77* **5–15**

WILLIAMS, Andy & David
Singles: 7-Inch
BARNABY: *74–75* **1–3**
KAPP: *72–73.* **2–3**
LPs: 10/12-Inch 33rpm
KAPP: *72* **5–10**

WILLIAMS, Anson
Singles: 7-Inch
CHELSEA: *77.* **2–4**

Price Range

Picture Sleeves
CHELSEA: 77. . . . . $2–4

WILLIAMS, Billy (The Billy Williams Quartet)
Singles: 7-Inch
CORAL (61200 through
  61800 series): 54–57 4–6
CORAL (61900 through
  65500 series): 58–64 3–5
MCA. 1–3
MGM (10000 & 11000
  series): 50–52 5–10
MGM (12000 series): 57. 4–6
MERCURY: 52–54. 5–8
EPs: 7-Inch 33/45rpm
CORAL: 57. 10–15
MGM: 57. 10–15
MERCURY: 53–55. 15–20
LPs: 10/12-Inch 33rpm
CORAL: 57–60 20–25
MGM: 57. 20–25
MERCURY: 58. 20–25
WING: 59 15–20
  Members: Billy Williams; Claude Reddick;
  John Bell; Gene Dixon.

WILLIAMS, Bobby Earl
Singles: 7-Inch
IV CHAINS: 74 2–4

WILLIAMS, Carol
Singles: 7-Inch
SALSOUL: 76. 2–4

WILLIAMS, Danny
Singles: 7-Inch
PILOT: 62 3–5
UNITED ARTISTS: 61–66 3–5
LPs: 10/12-Inch 33rpm
UNITED ARTISTS: 63–66 15–20

WILLIAMS, Denice
Singles: 12-Inch 33/45rpm
COLUMBIA: 77–85 4–6
Singles: 7-Inch
ARC: 79–82. 1–3
COLUMBIA: 76–85 1–3
LPs: 10/12-Inch 33rpm
COLUMBIA: 76–84 5–8

Price Range

Also see MATHIS, Johnny, & Denice Williams
Also see WONDER, Stevie

WILLIAMS, Diana
Singles: 7-Inch
CAPITOL: 76 . . . . $2–3
LITTLE GEM: 77 2–4

WILLIAMS, Don
Singles: 7-Inch
ABC: 75–78. 1–3
ABC/DOT: 74–77. 2–3
DOT: 74. 2–3
JMI: 72–74. 2–4
MCA: 79–85 1–3
LPs: 10/12-Inch 33rpm
ABC (Except 28): 77–78. 5–10
ABC (28; "Don
  Williams"): 77 10–15
  (Promotional issue only.) 5-10 74-77
ABC/DOT: 74–77. 8–10
JMI: 73–74. 15–20
MCA (Except 44): 75–85 4–8
MCA (44; "Expressions"):
  78 12–18
  (Picture disc.)
  Also see POZO SECO SINGERS, The

WILLIAMS, Esther
Singles: 7-Inch
FRIENDS & CO.: 76–78. 2–4

WILLIAMS, Hank (Hank Williams & The Drifting Cowboys; Hank Williams as "Luke The Drifter"; Hank & Audrey Williams)
Singles: 7-Inch
MGM (10000 & 11000
  series): 50–55 5–15
MGM (12000 series):
  55–59 4–8
MGM (13000 series):
  64–67 2–5
EPs: 7-Inch 33/45rpm
ARHOOLIE: 83 4–6
  (Not issued with cover.)
MGM (100 & 200 series):
  52–54 20–30
MGM (1000 through 1600
  series): 55–60 10–20

Price Range

LPs: 10/12-Inch 33rpm
BLAINE HOUSE: *72*............ **$15–20**
BOLL WEEVIL: *76*.............. **8–12**
COLUMBIA (5616; "Hank
Williams Treasury") **35–45**
(Offered only through Columbia House record
club. A 4-LP set.)
GOLDEN COUNTRY.............. **5–8**
MGM (2; "36 Of Hank
Williams Greatest Hits"):
57...................... **80–100**
(A 3-LP set.)
MGM (4; "36 More Of
Hank Williams Greatest
Hits"): *58*................... **80–100**
(A 3-LP set.)
MGM (100 & 200 series):
52–54 .... **40–50**
(10-Inch LPs.)
MGM (240-2; "24 Karat
Hits Hank Williams").............. **68**
MGM (1000 series): *76*............ **8–10**
(Special Products issue.)
MGM (3200 through 3900
series): *55–61*................. **20–40**
(With an "E" prefix.)
MGM (3200 through 3900
series): *63–70*................. **10–20**
(With an "SE" prefix.)
MGM (4000 through 4700
series, except 4267):
63–71 .... **10–20**
MGM (4267; "The Hank
Williams Story"): *66*............ **35–45**
(A 4-LP set.)
MGM (4900 through 5400
series): *75–77*................. **5–10**
METRO: *65–67*................. **10–15**
POLYDOR: *83–84* **6–12**
SUNRISE MEDIA: *81*............ **8–10**
TIME-LIFE: *82*................... **5–8**
Also see PRESLEY, Elvis / Hank Williams

WILLIAMS, Hank / Slim Whitman
LPs: 10/12-Inch 33rpm
SUNRISE MEDIA: *81*............ **8–10**
Also see WHITMAN, Slim

**WILLIAMS, Hank, & Hank
Williams, Jr.**
LPs: 10/12-Inch 33rpm
MGM (4200 series): *65*........... **15–25**

Price Range

MGM (4300 through 4900
series): *66–74*................. **$10–15**
Also see WILLIAMS, Hank, Jr.

**WILLIAMS, Hank, Jr. (Hank
Williams, Jr. & The Cheatin' Hearts)**
Singles: 7-Inch
ELEKTRA: *79–83*................. **1–3**
MGM (13000 series):
64–68 .... **3–5**
MGM (14000 series):
68–73 .... **2–4**

Picture Sleeves
MGM (13000 series):
64–68 .... **4–8**

LPs: 10/12-Inch 33rpm
CURB: *83–84*.................... **1–3**
ELEKTRA: *79–82* **5–8**
MGM (Except 5009):
63–76 .... **8–18**
MGM (5009; "Hank
Williams, Jr. &
Friends"): *76* **40–60**
WARNER BROS: *77–86*........... **5–10**
Also see CHARLES, Ray, & Hank Williams,
Jr.
Also see FRANCIS, Connie, & Hank Williams,
Jr.
Also see WILLIAMS, Hank, & Hank Wil-
liams, Jr.

WILLIAMS, Jeanette
Singles: 7-Inch
BACK BEAT: *66–69* **3–5**

WILLIAMS, John, Orchestra
Singles: 7-Inch
ARISTA: *77–80*.................. **1–3**
COLUMBIA: *83*.................. **1–3**
MCA: *74–76* **1–3**
RCA VICTOR: *79* **1–3**
20TH CENTURY-FOX:
77–78 .... **1–3**
WARNER BROS: *79*.............. **1–3**

Picture Sleeves
ARISTA: *77* **1–3**
20TH CENTURY-FOX:
78 .... **1–3**
WARNER BROS: *79*.............. **1–3**

Price Range

LPs: 10/12-Inch 33rpm

ARISTA (9500; "Close
Encounters Of The Third
Kind"): *78* **$8–10**
(Soundtrack.)
CAPITOL: *71* **5–10**
COLUMBIA (3510; "The
Reivers"): *70* **15–20**
(Soundtrack.)
COLUMBIA (31091;
"Changes"): *71*................. **5–10**
COLUMBIA (37000
series): *81*..................... **5–8**
DISCOVERY: *84* **4–8**
MCA (2087; "Jaws"): *75* **8–10**
(Soundtrack.)
MCA (2088; "The Eiger
Sanction"): *75* **8–10**
(Soundtrack.)
MCA (3045; "Jaws 2"): *78* **8–10**
(Soundtrack.)
RCA VICTOR: *77* **5–8**
UNITED ARTISTS (623;
"Missouri Breaks"): *76*........... **8–10**
(Soundtrack.)
Also see BOSTON POPS ORCHESTRA, The

WILLIAMS, Johnny
Singles: 7-Inch
CUB: *68*......................... **2–4**
PHILADELPHIA INT'L:
73 .... **2–4**

WILLIAMS, L.C. (The L.C. Williams Orchestra; L.C. Williams With Conney's Combo)
Singles: 7-Inch
BAYOU: *53*.................... **30–35**

WILLIAMS, Larry
Singles: 7-Inch
CHESS: *59–60*.................... **4–6**
MERCURY: *63*.................... **3–5**
OKEH: *66–67* **3–5**
SMASH: *66* **3–5**
SPECIALTY (608 through
658): *57–59*.................... **5–8**
SPECIALTY (665 through
682): *59–60*..................... **4–6**
VENTURE: *68* **3–5**

Price Range

Picture Sleeves
SPECIALTY: *58*................ **$10–15**
LPs: 10/12-Inch 33rpm
OKEH: *67*...................... **10–15**
SPECIALTY: *59*................ **40–50**
(Specialty LP reissues, using original catalog
numbers, are currently available.)
Also see COOKE, Sam / Lloyd Price / Larry
Williams

WILLIAMS, Larry, & Johnny Watson
Singles: 7-Inch
OKEH: *67*....................... **3–5**
LPs: 10/12-Inch 33rpm
OKEH: *67*...................... **10–15**
Also see WATSON, Johnny
Also see WILLIAMS, Larry

WILLIAMS, Lee (Lee Williams & The Moonrays; Lee Williams & The Cymbals; Lee "Shot" Williams)
Singles: 7-Inch
CARNIVAL: *66–69* **3–5**
FEDERAL: *63–64* **3–5**
KING: *60* **8–10**
SHAMA: *69* **2–4**

WILLIAMS, Lenny
Singles: 12-Inch 33/45rpm
ABC: *78*......................... **4–6**
ROCSHIRE: *83–84*................ **4–6**
Singles: 7-Inch
ABC: *77–78* **2–3**
MCA: *79–81* **1–3**
MOTOWN: *75*.................... **2–3**
ROCSHIRE: *83–84*................ **1–3**
LPs: 10/12-Inch 33rpm
ABC: *77–78*..................... **8–10**
MOTOWN: *75*................... **8–10**
ROCSHIRE: *83–84*................ **5–8**
WARNER BROS: *74*............. **8–12**
Also see TOWER OF POWER

WILLIAMS, Linda
Singles: 7-Inch
ARISTA: *79* **1–3**

WILLIAMS, Little Jerry
Singles: 7-Inch
ACADEMY: *64*................... **3–5**

Price Range

CALLA: *65–66* **$3–5**
LOMA: *64* **3–5**
SOUTHERN SOUND: *64* **4–6**

WILLIAMS, Mason
Singles: 7-Inch
WARNER BROS: *68–71* **2–4**

LPs: 10/12-Inch 33rpm
EVEREST: *69* **6–12**
FLYING FISH: *78* **5–8**
VEE JAY: *64* **10–20**
WARNER BROS: *68–71* **6–12**

WILLIAMS, Maurice (Maurice Williams & The Zodiacs)
Singles: 7-Inch
ATLANTIC: *70* **2–4**
COLLECTABLES **1–3**
DEESU: *67* **3–5**
ERIC **1–3**
FLASHBACK: *65* **1–3**
HERALD: *60–62* **4–6**
SEA HORN: *64* **3–5**
SPHERE SOUND: *65* **3–5**
VEEP: *69* **2–4**

LPs: 10/12-Inch 33rpm
COLLECTABLES **5–8**
HERALD: *61* **50–60**
RELIC **10–12**
SNYDER **25–30**
SPHERE SOUND: *66* **15–20**

WILLIAMS, Mike
Singles: 7-Inch
ATLANTIC: *65–66* **3–5**
KING: *66* **3–5**

WILLIAMS, Otis (Otis Williams & The Midnight Cowboys)
Singles: 7-Inch
DELUXE (6100 series): *59* **4–6**
KING: *60–64* **3–5**
OKEH: *66* **3–5**
STOP: *71* **2–3**

LPs: 10/12-Inch 33rpm
POWER PAK: *74* **8–10**
STOP: *71* **8–12**
Also see CHARMS, The

Price Range

WILLIAMS, Paul (Paul Williams & His Orchestra)
Singles: 7-Inch
ASCOT: *62* **$3–5**
CAPITOL: *55* **6–10**
GROOVE: *54* **10–12**
JAX (Colored vinyl): *54* **25–30**
JOSIE: *56* **6–10**
RAMA (167;
"Ring-A-Ling"): *55* **40–50**
(The vocal on this release is believed to be by Little Willie John, though no credit is given the vocalist on the label.)
SAVOY (1100 series):
54–59 .... **4–6**
VEE JAY: *57* **4–6**
Also see JOHN, Little Willie
Also see McNEELY, Big Jay / Paul Williams
Also see McPHERSON, Wyatt "Earp," & Paul Williams

WILLIAMS, Paul
Singles: 7-Inch
A&M: *72–77* **2–3**
PAID: *81* **1–3**
PORTRAIT: *79* **1–3**
REPRISE: *70* **2–4**

LPs: 10/12-Inch 33rpm
A&M: *71–77* **6–10**
PAID: *81* **5–8**
PORTRAIT: *79* **5–8**
REPRISE: *70* **8–12**

WILLIAMS, Robin
Singles: 12-Inch 33/45rpm
CASABLANCA: *79* **4–6**
Singles: 7-Inch
BOARDWALK: *80* **1–3**
Picture Sleeves
BOARDWALK: *80* **1–3**
LPs: 10/12-Inch 33rpm
CASABLANCA: *79–83* **5–8**

WILLIAMS, Roger
Singles: 7-Inch
KAPP: *55–72* **2–4**
MCA: *73–78* **1–3**
WARNER BROS: *80* **1–3**
Picture Sleeves
KAPP: *55–66* **2–4**

Price Range

EPs: 7-Inch 33/45rpm
KAPP: 55–58.................... $3–6

LPs: 10/12-Inch 33rpm
KAPP: 55–72.................... 5–15
MCA: 73–83 4–8
VOCALION: 71 4–8

WILLIAMS, Roger, & Jane Morgan
Singles: 7-Inch
KAPP: 56 2–4
Also see MORGAN, Jane
Also see WILLIAMS, Roger

WILLIAMSON, Sonny Boy (John Lee Williamson)
Singles: 7-Inch
RCA VICTOR (50-0000
series): 49.................... 25–35

WILLIAMSON, Sonny Boy (Aleck "Rice" Miller)
Singles: 7-Inch
ACE: 54....................... 25–30
CHECKER (800 series):
55–58 10–15
CHECKER (900 series):
58–62 5–8
CHECKER (1000 & 1100
series): 62–66.................. 3–5
TRUMPET (100 series):
51–52 20–30
TRUMPET (200 series):
53–54 15–20

LPs: 10/12-Inch 33rpm
ARHOOLIE 8–12
BLUES CLASSICS: 64........... 15–20
CHESS (200 series): 76........... 10–12
CHESS (1400 series): 60.......... 30–40
CHESS (1500 series):
66–69 10–15
CHESS (50000 series): 72......... 10–12
STORYVILLE: 80 5–8
Also see MEMPHIS SLIM

WILLIAMSON, Sonny Boy, & Big Joe Williams
LPs: 10/12-Inch 33rpm
BLUES CLASSICS................. 5–8
Also see WILLIAMS, Big Joe
Also see WILLIAMSON, Sonny Boy (Aleck 'Rice' Miller)

Price Range

WILLIAMSON, Sonny Boy, & The Yardbirds
LPs: 10/12-Inch 33rpm
MERCURY: 66................. $15–20
Also see PAGE, Jimmy, & Sonny Boy Williamson
Also see WILLIAMSON, Sonny Boy (Aleck 'Rice' Miller)
Also see YARDBIRDS, The

WILLIAMSON, Sonny Boy
Singles: 7-Inch
RAM: 61 10–15
Note: This Sonny Boy Williamson, as well as the first one listed, on RCA Victor, are included to enable you to separate their records from the above Sonny Boy, the only one of the three to chart.

WILLIE, Wet: see WET WILLIE

WILLIE & THE POOR BOYS
LPs: 10/12-Inch 33rpm
PASSPORT: 85.................... 5–8
Note: This gathering of recording artists included, but was not limited to, the following cross-referenced performers:
Also see FAIRWEATHER-LOW, Andy
Also see PAGE, Jimmy
Also see REA, Chris
Also see ROLLING STONES, The

WILLIS, Chuck (Chuck Willis & The Royals; Chuck Willis & The Sandmen)
Singles: 7-Inch
ATLANTIC (1100 series):
56–59 5–8
COLUMBIA (30238;
"Can't You See"): 51 25–30
OKEH (6000 series, except
6985): 51–53................... 8–12
OKEH (6985; "Don't
Deceive Me"): 53............... 15–20
OKEH (7000 series): 53–56......... 6–10
EPs: 7-Inch 33/45rpm
ATLANTIC: 57–58 25–30
EPIC: 56 35–40
LPs: 10/12-Inch 33rpm
ATCO: 71 10–12
ATLANTIC (8018; "King
Of The Stroll"): 58 40–50
(Black label.)

Price Range

ATLANTIC (8018; "King
Of The Stroll"): *59* $20–30
(Red label.)
ATLANTIC (8079; "I
Remember Chuck
Willis"): *63* 30–35
COLUMBIA: *80* 5–8
EPIC: *58–60* 80–100

WILLIS, M-D-L-T
Singles: 7-Inch
IVORY TOWER: *74* 2–4

WILLIS, Timmy
Singles: 7-Inch
JUBILEE: *69* 2–4
VEEP: *68* 3–5

WILLIS "THE GUARD" & VIGORISH
Singles: 7-Inch
HANDSHAKE: *80* 2–4
Members: Jerry Buckner; Gary Garcia.
Also see BUCKNER & GARCIA

WILL-O-BEES, The
Singles: 7-Inch
DATE: *67* 3–5
SGC: *68–69* 3–5

WILLOWS, The
Singles: 7-Inch
ABC: *73* 1–3
COLLECTABLES 1–3
MELBA (Except 102):
56–57 15–20
MELBA (102; "Church
Bells Are Ringing"): *56* 50–60
MELBA (102; "Church
Bells May Ring): *56* 10–15
Members: Tony Middleton; Richard Davis;
Ralph Martin; Joe Martin; John Steele; Richard
Simon; Dotty Martin.
Also see MIDDLETON, Tony
Also see SEDAKA, Neil

WILMER & THE DUKES
Singles: 7-Inch
APHRODISIAC: *69* 2–4
LPs: 10/12-Inch 33rpm
APHRODISIAC: *69* 10–15

Price Range

WILSON, Al
Singles: 7-Inch
BELL: *70* $2–4
BELL GOLD. 1–3
CAROUSEL: *71* 2–4
PLAYBOY: *76* 2–4
ROADSHOW: *79* 2–3
ROCKY ROAD: *72–75* 2–4
SOUL CITY: *67–69* 3–5
LPs: 10/12-Inch 33rpm
PLAYBOY: *76* 8–10
ROADSHOW: *79* 5–8
ROCKY ROAD: *73–74* 8–10
SOUL CITY: *69* 10–15
Also see JEWELS, The
Also see ROLLERS, The

WILSON, Ann, & The Daybreaks
Singles: 7-Inch
TOPAZ: *67* 5–8
Also see HEART
Also see RENO, Mike, & Ann Wilson

WILSON, Bobby
Singles: 7-Inch
BUDDAH: *75* 2–4
CHAIN: *73* 2–4

WILSON, Brian (Brian Wilson & Mike Love)
Singles: 7-Inch
BROTHER: *67* 12–15
CAPITOL: *66* 12–15

Price Range

Also see BEACH BOYS, The
Also see BERRY, Jan
Also see HONDELLS, The
Also see CAMPBELL, Glen
Also see TIMERS, The

WILSON, Carl
Singles: 7-Inch
CARIBOU: *81–83* $2–3
LPs: 10/12-Inch 33rpm
CARIBOU: *81–82* 5–8
Also see BEACH BOYS, The
Also see NEWTON-JOHN, Olivia

WILSON, Dennis
Singles: 7-Inch
CARIBOU: *77* 4–6
LPs: 10/12-Inch 33rpm
CARIBOU: *77* 10–15
Also see BEACH BOYS, The

WILSON, Flip
Singles: 7-Inch
LITTLE DAVID: *72–75* 2–3
LPs: 10/12-Inch 33rpm
ATLANTIC: *67–68* 8–15
IMPERIAL: *61* 10–20
LITTLE DAVID: *70–72* 5–10
MINIT: *68* 8–15
SUNSET: *70* 8–10

WILSON, Hank (Leon Russell)
Singles: 7-Inch
SHELTER: *73–74* 2–4
LPs: 10/12-Inch 33rpm
SHELTER: *73* 8–10
Also see RUSSELL, Leon

WILSON, J. Frank, (J. Frank Wilson & The Cavaliers)
Singles: 7-Inch
ABC: *73* 1–3
APRIL 3–5
CHARAY: *69* 3–5
COLLECTABLES 1–3
ERIC 1–3
JOSIE: *64–65* 3–5
LE CAM (500 series): *81* 2–3
LE CAM (722; "Last
Kiss"): *64* 10–15
LE CAM (1000 series): *65* 3–5
LE CAM (12000 series) 2–3

Price Range

SOLLY: *66* $3–5
TAMARA: *64* 8–10
VIRGO: *72* 1–3
LPs: 10/12-Inch 33rpm
DILL PICKEL: *71* 8–10
JOSIE: *64* 40–50

WILSON, Jackie
Singles: 7-Inch
BRUNSWICK (55024
through 55086): *57–58* 8–12
BRUNSWICK (55105
through 55165): *58–59* 5–8
BRUNSWICK (55166
through 55236): *60–62* 4–6
BRUNSWICK (55238
through 55504): *63–73* 2–5
ERIC: *83* 1–3
GUSTO 1–3
Picture Sleeves
BRUNSWICK (55166
through 55236): *60–62* 6–10
BRUNSWICK (55238
through 55467): *63–72* 4–6
EPs: 7-Inch 33/45rpm
BRUNSWICK: *59–63* 15–25
LPs: 10/12-Inch 33rpm
BRUNSWICK (54045;
"Lonely Teardrops"): *59* 35–45
BRUNSWICK (54042;
"He's So Fine"): *59* 35–40
BRUNSWICK (54050; "So
Much"): *60* 30–35
BRUNSWICK (54055;
"Jackie Sings The
Blues"): *60* 30–35
BRUNSWICK (54058;
"My Golden Favorites"):
60 30–35
BRUNSWICK (54059; "A
Woman, A Lover, A
Friend"): *60* 30–35
BRUNSWICK (54100;
"You Ain't Heard
Nothin' Yet"): *61* 25–30
BRUNSWICK (54101; "By
Request"): *61* 25–30
BRUNSWICK (54105;
"Body & Soul"): *62* 25–30
BRUNSWICK (54108; "At
The Copa"): *62* 25–30

Price Range

Price Range

BRUNSWICK (54110
through 54130): *63–67* **$20–25**
(Beginning with 54050, Brunswick indicated
stereo LPs with a "7" preceeding the catalog
number. Numbers after 54130 were available as
stereo issues only, and are shown here as the
75000 series.)
BRUNSWICK (754138
through 754167): *68–71* **15–20**
BRUNSWICK (754185
through 754212): *72–77* **10–15**
DISCOVERY: *78* **8–10**
EPIC: *83* **10–12**
Also see WARD, Billy, & The Dominoes

WILSON, Jackie, & LaVern Baker
Singles: 7-Inch
BRUNSWICK: *65*. **3–5**
Also see BAKER, LaVern

WILSON, Jackie, & Count Basie
Singles: 7-Inch
BRUNSWICK: *68*. **3–5**
LPs: 10/12-Inch 33rpm
BRUNSWICK: *68*. **15–20**
Also see BASIE, Count

WILSON, Jackie, & The Chi-Lites
Singles: 7-Inch
BRUNSWICK: *75*. **2–4**
Also see CHI-LITES, The

WILSON, Jackie, & Linda Hopkins
Singles: 7-Inch
BRUNSWICK: *62–65*. **3–5**
EPs: 7-Inch 33/45rpm
BRUNSWICK: *63*. **15–20**
LPs: 10/12-Inch 33rpm
BRUNSWICK: *68*. **25–35**
Also see WILSON, Jackie

WILSON, Mary
Singles: 7-Inch
MOTOWN: *79*. **2–3**
LPs: 10/12-Inch 33rpm
MOTOWN: *79*. **5–8**
Also see SUPREMES, The

WILSON, Meri
Singles: 7-Inch
GRT: *77*. **2–3**

WILSON, Murray
Singles: 7-Inch
CAPITOL: *67* **$8–10**
LPs: 10/12-Inch 33rpm
CAPITOL: *67* **25–30**

WILSON, Nancy
Singles: 12-Inch 33/45rpm
CAPITOL: *79* **4–6**
Singles: 7-Inch
CAPITOL (Except 4000 &
5000 series): *68–79* **1–3**
CAPITOL (4000 & 5000
series): *59–67* **2–5**
(Includes orange/yellow and '50s and '60s pur-
ple labels, not to be confused with the late '70s
purple label.)
Picture Sleeves
CAPITOL: *65* **2–4**
LPs: 10/12-Inch 33rpm
ASI: *81*. **5–8**
CAPITOL (100 through
800 series): *69–71* **5–12**
CAPITOL (1300 through
1700 series): *59–62* **15–30**
CAPITOL (1800 through
2900 series): *63–68* **8–18**
(With a "T" or "ST" prefix.)
CAPITOL (1800 through
2900 series): *78* **5–8**
(With an "SM" prefix.)
CAPITOL (11000 & 12000
series): *74–80* **5–10**
CAPITOL (16000 series):
80 .... **5–8**
COLUMBIA: *84* **5–8**
Also see LEWIS, Ramsey

WILSON, Nancy, & Julian "Cannonball" Adderley
Singles: 7-Inch
CAPITOL: *62* **2–5**
LPs: 10/12-Inch 33rpm
CAPITOL (1657; "Nancy
Wilson & Cannonball
Adderley"): *62*. **15–25**
(With a "T" or "ST" prefix.)
CAPITOL (1657; "Nancy
Wilson & Cannonball
Adderley"): *75*. **5–8**
(With an "SM" prefix.)

Price Range

CAPITOL (16000 series):
81 .... **$4–8**
  Also see ADDERLEY, Cannonball

WILSON, Nancy, & George Shearing
Singles: 7-Inch
CAPITOL: 61 .... **2–5**
LPs: 10/12-Inch 33rpm
CAPITOL (1524;
"Swingin's Mutual"): 61 .... **15–25**
  (With a "T" or "ST" prefix.)
CAPITOL (1524;
"Swingin's Mutual"): 75 .... **5–8**
  (With an "SM" prefix.)
  Also see SHEARING, George
  Also see WILSON, Nancy

WILSON, Phill
Singles: 7-Inch
HURON: 61 .... **3–5**

WILSON, Timothy
Singles: 7-Inch
BLUE ROCK: 69 .... **2–4**
BUDDAH: 67–68 .... **3–5**
VEEP: 65 .... **3–5**

WILSON BROTHERS, The
Singles: 7-Inch
ATCO: 79 .... **2–3**
LPs: 10/12-Inch 33rpm
ATCO: 79 .... **5–8**

WILTON PLACE STREET BAND
Singles: 7-Inch
ISLAND: 77 .... **2–3**

WINCHESTER, Jesse
Singles: 7-Inch
AMPEX: 70 .... **2–4**
BEARSVILLE: 76–81 .... **1–3**
LPs: 10/12-Inch 33rpm
BEARSVILLE/AMPEX:
70 .... **15–20**
BEARSVILLE: 71–81 .... **6–10**
Promotional LPs
BEARSVILLE (692; "Live
At The Bijou"): 75 .... **20–25**
BEARSVILLE (693; "Live
At The Bijou/Live
Interview"): 75 .... **30–40**

Price Range

  Also see HARRIS, Emmylou
  Also see LARSON, Nicolette
  Also see MURRAY, Anne

WIND (Featuring Tony Orlando)
Singles: 7-Inch
LIFE: 69 .... **$4–6**
LPs: 10/12-Inch 33rpm
LIFE: 69 .... **15–20**
  Also see COOL HEAT
  Also see ORLANDO, Tony

WIND IN THE WILLOWS, The
Singles: 7-Inch
CAPITOL: 68 .... **4–6**
LPs: 10/12-Inch 33rpm
CAPITOL: 68 .... **25–35**
  Members: Deborah Harry; Paul Klein; Peter
  Brittain; Anton Carysforth; Steve DePhillips.
  Also see BLONDIE
  Also see HARRY, Debbie

WINDING, Kai, & His Orchestra
(Kai Winding & J.J. Johnson)
Singles: 7-Inch
BETHLEHEM: 60 .... **2–4**
COLUMBIA: 56–59 .... **2–5**
IMPULSE: 61 .... **2–4**
MGM: 78 .... **1–3**
VERVE: 62–67 .... **2–4**
EPs: 7-Inch 33/45rpm
COLUMBIA: 58–59 .... **5–15**
SAVOY: 53 .... **10–20**
LPs: 10/12-Inch 33rpm
A&M: 68 .... **8–12**
COLUMBIA (900 through
1300 series): 56–59 .... **15–30**
COLUMBIA (8100 series):
59 .... **15–25**
GLENDALE: 76–77 .... **5–8**
IMPULSE: 61 .... **15–25**
JAZZTONE: 56 .... **20–35**
PICKWICK: 65–70 .... **5–10**
ROOST (400 series): 52 .... **60–80**
  (10-Inch LPs.)
SAVOY (9000 series): 53 .... **50–75**
  (10-Inch LPs.)
VERVE: 61–67 .... **10–25**
  (Reads "MGM Records - A Division Of Metro-
  Goldwyn-Mayer, Inc." at bottom of label.)
VERVE: 73–84 .... **5–10**

Price Range

(Reads "Manufactured By MGM Record Corp.," or mentions either Polydor or Polygram at bottom of label.)
WHO'S WHO IN JAZZ:
78 .... **$5–8**

WINE, April: see APRIL WINE

WINDJAMMER
Singles: 7-Inch
MCA: 83–85 .... **1–3**
LPs: 10/12-Inch 33rpm
MCA: 83 .... **5–8**

WINDSTORM
Singles: 7-Inch
POLYDOR: 80 .... **1–3**

WINDY CITY
Singles: 7-Inch
CHI-SOUND: 77 .... **2–3**
KELLI-ARTS: 80 .... **1–3**

WING & A PRAYER FIFE & DRUM CORPS., The
Singles: 7-Inch
WING & A PRAYER:
75–77 .... **2–3**
LPs: 10/12-Inch 33rpm
WING & A PRAYER:
76–77 .... **5–8**

WINGFIELD, Pete
Singles: 7-Inch
ISLAND: 75–77 .... **2–3**
LPs: 10/12-Inch 33rpm
ISLAND: 75 .... **5–8**

WINGS: see McCARTNEY, Paul

WINNERS, The
Singles: 7-Inch
ARIOLA-AMERICA: 78 .... **2–3**
LPs: 10/12-Inch 33rpm
ARIOLA-AMERICA: 78 .... **5–8**
ROADSHOW: 78 .... **5–10**

WINSTON, George
LPs: 10/12-Inch 33rpm
WINDHAM HILL: 83–84 .... **5–8**

Price Range

WINSTONS, The
Singles: 7-Inch
METROMEDIA: 69 .... **$2–4**
LPs: 10/12-Inch 33rpm
METROMEDIA: 69 .... **8–12**

WINTER, Edgar (The Edgar Winter Group; Edgar Winter's White Trash)
Singles: 12-Inch 33/45rpm
BLUE SKY: 80 .... **4–6**
BODY ROCK: 83 .... **4–6**
Singles: 7-Inch
BLUE SKY: 75–81 .... **1–3**
EPIC: 70–75 .... **2–4**
LPs: 10/12-Inch 33rpm
BACK-TRAC: 85 .... **5–8**
BLUE SKY: 75–81 .... **6–10**
EPIC: 70–75 .... **10–15**
Also see DERRINGER, Rick
Also see HARTMAN, Dan
Also see MONTROSE, Ronnie
Also see WINTER, Johnny & Edgar

WINTER, Jimmy: see WINTER, Johnny

WINTER, Johnny (Johnny Winter & The Crystaliers; Jimmy Winter)
Singles: 7-Inch
ATLANTIC: 64 .... **5–8**
BLUE SKY: 75 .... **2–4**
COLUMBIA: 69–74 .... **2–4**
FROLIC **20–25**
GRT: 69 .... **3–5**
IMPERIAL: 69 .... **3–5**
KRCO: 61 .... **50–75**
MGM: 65 .... **4–6**
SONOBEAT: 68 .... **5–8**
TODD: 63 .... **8–10**
Picture Sleeves
SONOBEAT: 68 .... **20–40**
(Some sleeves picture the Vulcan Gas Co., an Austin nightclub, and those are at the high end of the price range given. Sleeves that do not picture the club are priced at the lower end.)
LPs: 10/12-Inch 33rpm
ACCORD: 81 .... **5–8**
ALLIGATOR: 85 .... **5–8**
BLUE SKY: 74–80 .... **6–10**
BUDDAH: 69 .... **10–15**
CBS ASSOCIATED **5–8**

Price Range

COLUMBIA (9800 & 9900
  series): *69* $15–20
COLUMBIA (30000
  through 33000 series):
  70–75 . . . . **10–15**
GRT: *69* **10–12**
IMPERIAL: *69* **15–20**
JANUS: *69–70* **10–12**
SONOBEAT ("Progressive
  Blues Experiment"): *68* **100–125**
  (Limited edition, autographed issue.)
SONOBEAT ("Progressive
  Blues Experiment"): *68* **75–100**
  (Limited edition, NOT autographed.)
UNITED ARTISTS: *73–74* **8–10**
  Also see JOHNNY & THE JAMMERS
  Also see GREAT BELIEVERS, The
  Also see GUITAR SLIM
  Also see SPRINGSTEEN, Bruce / Johnny
  Winter / The Hollies
  Also see TEXAS GUITAR SLIM
  Also see TRAITS, The
  Also see WATERS, Muddy

WINTER, Johnny & Edgar
Singles: 7-Inch
BLUE SKY: *76* **2–4**
CASCADE: *64* **35–45**

LPs: 10/12-Inch 33rpm
BLUE SKY (Except 242):
  76 . . . . **5–8**
BLUE SKY (242; "Johnny
  & Edgar Winter Discuss
  'Together' "): *76* **10–20**
  (Promotional issue only.)
  Also see WINTER, Edgar
  Also see WINTER, Johnny

WINTER, Paul (Paul Winter & Winter Consort; The Paul Winter Sextet)
Singles: 7-Inch
A&M: *69–77* **2–4**
COLUMBIA: *62* **2–4**
EPIC: *72–73* **2–4**

LPs: 10/12-Inch 33rpm
A&M: *69–78* **8–12**
COLUMBIA: *62–65* **10–20**
EPIC: *72* **8–10**
LIVING MUSIC: *83* **5–8**
  Also see WINTER CONSORT

Price Range

WINTER, Ruby: see WINTERS, Ruby

WINTER CONSORT: see WINTER, Paul

WINTERHALTER, Hugo, & His Orchestra
Singles: 7-Inch
ABC-PARAMOUNT: *63* $1–3
COLUMBIA: *50* **2–4**
KAPP: *64–65* **1–3**
MUSICOR: *68–70* **1–3**
RCA VICTOR: *50–63* **2–4**
EPs: 7-Inch 33/45rpm
RCA VICTOR: *50–59* **3–6**
LPs: 10/12-Inch 33rpm
ABC-PARAMOUNT: *63* **4–8**
CAMDEN: *69–72* **4–8**
KAPP: *65* **4–8**
MUSIC DISC: *69* **4–8**
MUSICOR: *68–71* **5–10**
RCA VICTOR: *50–77* **5–15**
TRIP: *76* **4–8**
  Also see HEYWOOD, Eddie

WINTERS, Jonathan
LPs: 10/12-Inch 33rpm
COLUMBIA: *68–73* **8–15**
VERVE: *59–60* **15–30**
  (Reads "Verve Records, Inc." at bottom of
  label.)
VERVE: *61–67* **10–20**
  (Reads "MGM Records - A Division Of Metro-
  Goldwyn-Mayer, Inc." at bottom of label.)
VERVE: *73–84* **5–10**
  (Reads "Manufactured By MGM Record
  Corp.," or mentions either Polydor or Poly-
  gram at bottom of label.)

WINTERS, Robert, & Fall
Singles: 7-Inch
BUDDAH: *80–81* **1–3**
CASABLANCA: *82–84* **1–3**
LPs: 10/12-Inch 33rpm
CASABLANCA: *82–83* **5–8**

WINTERS, Ruby (Ruby Winter)
Singles: 7-Inch
CERTRON: *71* **2–4**
DIAMOND: *66–69* **3–5**

Price Range

MILLENNIUM: *78* $2–3
POLYDOR: *73–75* 2–4
    LPs: 10/12-Inch 33rpm
MILLENNIUM: *78* 5–8
    Also see THUNDER, Johnny, & Ruby Winters

WINWOOD, Steve
    Singles: 7-Inch
ISLAND: *77–84* 1–3
UNITED ARTISTS: *71* 2–4
    Picture Sleeves
ISLAND: *80–84* .... INC
    LPs: 10/12-Inch 33rpm
ISLAND: *77–84* 5–8
UNITED ARTISTS: *71* 10–12
    Also see BAKER, Ginger
    Also see BLIND FAITH
    Also see DAVIS, Spencer
    Also see TRAFFIC
    Also see YAMASHTA, Stomu

WIRE TRAIN
    Singles: 12-Inch 33/45rpm
COLUMBIA: *84* 4–6
    Singles: 7-Inch
COLUMBIA: *84* 1–3
    LPs: 10/12-Inch 33rpm
COLUMBIA: *84* 5–8

WISH (Featuring Fonda Rae)
    Singles: 12-Inch 33/45rpm
KN: *84* 4–6
    Singles: 7-Inch
PERSONAL: *84–85* 1–3

WISHBONE ASH
    Singles: 7-Inch
ATLANTIC: *77* 2–3
DECCA: *71–72* 2–4
MCA: *73–77* 2–3
    LPs: 10/12-Inch 33rpm
ATLANTIC: *76* 6–10
DECCA (Except 1922):
    71–72 10–15
DECCA (1922; "Live
    From Memphis"): *72* 15–20
    (Promotional issue only.)
MCA: *73–82* 5–8
    Also see FOGHAT

Price Range

WITCH QUEEN
    Singles: 7-Inch
ROADSHOW: *79* $2–3
    LPs: 10/12-Inch 33rpm
ROADSHOW: *79* 5–8

WITHERS, Bill
    Singles: 12-Inch 33/45rpm
COLUMBIA: *79* 4–6
    Singles: 7-Inch
COLUMBIA: *75–85* 1–3
SUSSEX: *71–75* 2–4
    Picture Sleeves
SUSSEX: *72* 2–4
    LPs: 10/12-Inch 33rpm
COLUMBIA: *75–81* 5–8
SUSSEX: *71–75* 8–12
    Also see WASHINGTON, Grover, Jr.
    Also see WOMACK, Bobby, & Bill Withers

WITHERSPOON, Jimmy (Jimmy Witherspoon & Groove Holmes; Jimmy Witherspoon With Jay McShann & His Band; Jimmy Witherspoon & Ben Webster; Jimmy Witherspoon With Panama Francis & The Savoy Sultans)
    Singles: 7-Inch
ABC: *71* 2–4
BLUE NOTE: *75* 2–3
BLUESWAY: *69* 2–4
CAPITOL: *74* 2–3
CHECKER: *54–55* 10–15
FEDERAL: *52–53* 15–20
GNP/CRESCENDO: *59* 4–6
HI FI: *60* 4–6
KENT: *71* 2–4
KING: *65* 3–5
MODERN (857 through
    903): *52–53* 15–20
PACIFIC JAZZ: *62* 3–5
PRESTIGE: *63–65* 3–5
RCA VICTOR: *57* 5–8
REPRISE: *61–64* 3–5
RIP: *58* 5–8
VEE JAY: *59* 4–6
VERVE: *66–67* 3–5
WORLD PACIFIC: *59* 4–6
    LPs: 10/12-Inch 33rpm
ABC: *70* 8–10

Price Range

BLUE NOTE: *75* **$8–10**
BLUESWAY: *69–73* **8–10**
CAPITOL: *74* **8–10**
CONSTELLATION: *64* **15–20**
CROWN: *61* **15–20**
FANTASY: *72.* **10–12**
HI FI: *59* **20–30**
INNER CITY: *81* **5–8**
MCA: *83* **5–8**
MUSE: *83* **5–8**
OLYMPIC: *73.* **8–10**
PRESTIGE: *64–69* **10–15**
(Many Prestige LPs remain currently available, using original catalog numbers.)
RCA VICTOR (1048;
"Goin' To Kansas City
Blues"): *75* **6–10**
RCA VICTOR (1639;
"Goin' To Kansas City
Blues"): *58* **30–40**
REPRISE: *61–62.* **20–30**
SURREY: *65* **12–15**
UNITED **8–10**
VERVE (5000 series):
66–68 . . . . **12–15**
VERVE (8000 series): *74* **8–10**
VERVE/FOLKWAYS
(3011; "Blues Box"): *66* **25–30**
WORLD PACIFIC: *59–61* **20–30**
Also see BURDON, Eric, & Jimmy Witherspoon
Also see FREEMAN, Ernie
Also see HOLMES, Richard "Groove"
Also see McSHANN, Jay

WITHERSPOON, Jimmy, & The Lamplighters
Singles: 7-Inch
FEDERAL: *52* **20–30**

WITHERSPOON, Jimmy, & The Quintones
Singles: 7-Inch
ATCO: *57* **10–12**
Also see WITHERSPOON, Jimmy

WITT, Joachim
Singles: 12-Inch 33/45rpm
W.E.A.
INTERNATIONAL: *84.* **4–6**

Price Range

WITTER, Jimmy
Singles: 7-Inch
ELVIS **$125–150**
NEPTUNE: *61* **20–30**
UNITED ARTISTS: *61* **8–10**

WOLCOTT, Charles, Orchestra
Singles: 7-Inch
MGM: *60.* **2–4**

WOLF (Bill Wolfer)
Singles: 7-Inch
CONSTELLATION: *81–83* **1–3**
LPs: 10/12-Inch 33rpm
CONSTELLATION: *83* **5–8**

WOLF, Peter
Singles: 12-Inch 33/45rpm
EMI AMERICA: *84–85* **4–6**
Singles: 7-Inch
EMI AMERICA: *84–85.* **1–3**
LPs: 10/12-Inch 33rpm
EMI AMERICA: *84–85.* **5–8**
Also see FRANKLIN, Aretha
Also see GEILS, J., Band

WOLFMAN JACK (Bob Smith; Wolfman Jack & The Wolf Pack)
Singles: 7-Inch
BREAD **4–6**
WOODEN NICKEL:
72–73 . . . . **2–4**
LPs: 10/12-Inch 33rpm
BREAD **15–20**
COLUMBIA: *75* **8–10**
WOODEN NICKEL:
72–73 . . . . **8–10**
Also see FLASH CADILLAC & THE CONTINENTAL KIDS
Also see GUESS WHO, The
Also see STAMPEDERS, The

WOMACK, Bobby (Bobby Womack & Brotherhood; Bobby Womack & Peace)
Singles: 12-Inch 33/45rpm
ELEKTRA/WOMACK:
83 . . . . **4–6**
Singles: 7-Inch
ARISTA: *79* **2–3**
ATLANTIC: *67* **3–5**

Price Range

BEVERLY GLEN: *81–84* **$1–3**
CHECKER: *65* **3–5**
COLUMBIA: *76–78* **2–3**
COLUMBIA/
  BROTHERHOOD:
  76–77 .... **2–3**
ELEKTRA/WOMACK:
  83 .... **1–3**
LIBERTY: *70* **2–4**
MINIT: *67–70* **2–4**
UNITED ARTISTS: *71–76* **2–4**
    EPs: 7-Inch 33/45rpm
UNITED ARTISTS: *72* **10–12**
  (Promotional issue only.)
    LPs: 10/12-Inch 33rpm
ARISTA: *79* **5–8**
BEVERLY GLEN: *81–84* **5–8**
COLUMBIA: *75–78* **8–10**
COLUMBIA/
  BROTHERHOOD: *76* **8–10**
ELEKTRA/WOMACK:
  83 .... **5–8**
LIBERTY (7600 series): *70* **8–10**
LIBERTY (10000 series) **5–8**
MINIT: *68–70* **10–12**
UNITED ARTISTS: *71–76* **8–10**
  Also see BROTHERHOOD
  Also see FELDER, Wilton, & Bobby Womack
  Also see VALENTINOS, The
  Also see WOMACK BROTHERS, The

WOMACK, Bobby, & Patti Labelle
  Singles: 7-Inch
BEVERLY GLEN: *84* **1–3**
  Also see LABELLE, Patti
  Also see WOMACK, Bobby

WOMACK, Bobby, & Bill Withers
  Singles: 7-Inch
UNITED ARTISTS: *75* **2–4**
  Also see WITHERS, Bill

WOMACK & WOMACK
  Singles: 7-Inch
ELEKTRA: *84–85* **1–3**
    LPs: 10/12-Inch 33rpm
ELEKTRA: *84–85* **5–8**
  Members: Linda Womack; Cecil Womack.

WOMACK BROTHERS, The
  Singles: 7-Inch
SAR: *61* **4–6**

Price Range

  Also see VALENTINOS, The
  Also see WOMACK, Bobby

WOMBLES, The (Featuring Mike Batt)
  Singles: 7-Inch
COLUMBIA: *74–75* **$2–4**
    LPs: 10/12-Inch 33rpm
COLUMBIA: *74* **8–10**

WOMENFOLK, The
  Singles: 7-Inch
RCA VICTOR: *64–66* **2–4**
    LPs: 10/12-Inch 33rpm
RCA VICTOR: *63–66* **10–15**

WONDER, Stevie (Little Stevie Wonder)
  Singles: 12-Inch 33/45rpm
MOTOWN **4–6**
TAMLA **4–6**
    Singles: 7-Inch
TAMLA (1600 & 1700
  series): *82–86* **1–3**
TAMLA (54061; "I Call It
  Pretty Music"): *62* **8–10**
TAMLA (54074; "Contract
  On Love"): *63* **5–8**
TAMLA (54080;
  "Fingertips"): *63* **3–5**
TAMLA (54086; "Workout
  Stevie, Workout"): *63* **3–5**
TAMLA (54090; "Castles
  In The Sand"): *64* **4–6**
TAMLA (54096; "Hey
  Harmonica Man"): *64* **3–5**
TAMLA (54103; "Happy
  Street"): *64* **8–10**
TAMLA (54119 through
  54139): *65–66* **3–5**
TAMLA (54142; "Someday
  At Christmas"): *66* **6–10**
TAMLA (54147 through
  54323): *67–81* **2–4**
MOTOWN: *82* **1–3**
    Picture Sleeves
TAMLA (54061; "I Call It
  Pretty Music"): *62* **10–15**
TAMLA (54080 through
  54096): *63–64* **4–6**

Price Range

TAMLA (54136 through
54317): *66–80.* **$2–5**

EPs: 7-Inch 33/45rpm

TAMLA (340; "Something
Extra For Songs In The
Key Of Life"): *76* **10–15**

LPs: 10/12-Inch 33rpm

MOTOWN (100 & 200
series): *82* **5–8**
MOTOWN (800 series): *77* **12–15**
TAMLA (232; "Tribute To
Uncle Ray"): *63.* **50–65**
TAMLA (233; "The Jazz
Soul Of Stevie Wonder"):
63 . . . . **50–65**
TAMLA (240; "Little
Stevie Wonder"): *63* **40–50**
TAMLA (232 through
255): *63–64.* **30–40**
TAMLA (268 through
279): *66–67.* **15–20**
TAMLA (281; "Someday
At Christmas"): *67* **30–40**
TAMLA (282 through
371): *68–79.* **10–15**
TAMLA (373; "Hotter
Than July"): *80.* **5–8**
TAMLA (6000 series): *82* **10–12**

Promotional LPs

MOTOWN (77; "Hotter
Than July"): *80.* **10–15**
TAMLA (61; "Stevie
Wonder"): *79.* **10–15**

    Also see CHARLENE & STEVIE WONDER
    Also see DIONNE & FRIENDS
    Also see JACKSONS, The
    Also see McCARTNEY, Paul, & Stevie Wonder
    Also see REDNOW, Eivets
    Also see ROSS, Diana, Stevie Wonder, Marvin Gaye & Smokey Robinson
    Also see TEMPTATIONS, The / Stevie Wonder
    Also see THIRD WORLD
    Also see U.S.A. FOR AFRICA
    Also see WILLIAMS, Deniece

WONDER, Stevie, & Clarence Paul (Little Stevie Wonder & Clarence Paul)

Singles: 7-Inch

TAMLA: *62* **25–35**

Price Range

WONDER, Stevie / Dionne Warwick

LPs: 10/12-Inch 33rpm

MOTOWN: *84.* **$5–8**

    Also see WARWICK, Dionne
    Also see WONDER, Stevie

WONDER BAND, The

Singles: 7-Inch

ATCO: *79* **2–3**

LPs: 10/12-Inch 33rpm

ATCO: *79* **5–8**

WONDER WHO?, The (The 4 Seasons)

Singles: 7-Inch

COLLECTABLES **1–3**
PHILIPS: *65–67* **3–5**
VEE JAY: *64.* **12–15**

Picture Sleeves

PHILIPS: *65–67* **10–15**

    Also see 4 SEASONS, The

WONDER-LAND, Alice: see ALICE WONDER-LAND

WOOD, Bobby

Singles: 7-Inch

CHALLENGE: *62* **3–5**
CINNAMON: *74* **2–3**
JOY: *63–65* **3–5**
LUCKY ELEVEN: *73* **2–3**
MALA: *66.* **3–5**
MGM: *67–69.* **2–4**
SUN: *63* **3–5**

LPs: 10/12-Inch 33rpm

JOY: *64* **10–15**

WOOD, Brenton

Singles: 7-Inch

BRENT: *66* **3–5**
CREAM: *76–78.* **2–3**
DOUBLE SHOT: *67–71.* **2–4**
MR. WOOD: *72–73* **2–4**
PRESIDENT: *60.* **4–6**
PROPHESY: *73* **2–4**
WARNER BROS: *75.* **2–3**

LPs: 10/12-Inch 33rpm

CREAM: *77* **5–8**
DOUBLE SHOT: *67.* **12–15**

WOOD, Del
Singles: 7-Inch
CHART: *71–72* $1–3
DECCA: *53–54* 3–5
MERCURY: *62–64* 2–4
RCA VICTOR: *55–59* 2–5
REPUBLIC: *51–54* 3–8
TENNESSEE: *51* 5–10

EPs: 7-Inch 33/45rpm
RCA VICTOR: *55–60* 5–12
REPUBLIC: *54–57* 4–10

LPs: 10/12-Inch 33rpm
CAMDEN: *62–64* 5–12
COLUMBIA: *66* 8–12
MERCURY: *62–64* 5–12
RCA VICTOR: *55–60* 5–15
REPUBLIC: *54–57* 5–15
VOCALION 5–10

WOOD, Lauren
Singles: 7-Inch
WARNER BROS: *79–81* 1–3

Picture Sleeves
WARNER BROS: *81* 1–3

LPs: 10/12-Inch 33rpm
WARNER BROS: *81* 5–8
Also see McDONALD, Michael

WOOD, Ron
Singles: 7-Inch
COLUMBIA: *79* 2–3
WARNER BROS: *75–76* 2–4

LPs: 10/12-Inch 33rpm
COLUMBIA: *79–81* 5–8
WARNER BROS: *74* 8–10
Also see BECK, Jeff
Also see FACES
Also see ROLLING STONES, The

WOOD, Roy (Roy Wood's Wizard; Roy Wood Wizzo Band)
Singles: 7-Inch
UNITED ARTISTS: *73–76* 2–4

LPs: 10/12-Inch 33rpm
UNITED ARTISTS: *73–74* 8–10
WARNER BROS: *79* 5–8
Also see ELECTRIC LIGHT ORCHESTRA
Also see MOVE, The

WOODBURY, Woody
LPs: 10/12-Inch 33rpm
STEREODDITIES: *59–63* $10–20

WOODS, Ren
Singles: 7-Inch
ARC: *79* 2–3
ELEKTRA: *82* 1–3

WOODS, Maceo (Rev. Maceo & The Christian Tabernacle Choir)
Singles: 7-Inch
ABC: *73* 1–3
VOLT: *69* 2–4

LPs: 10/12-Inch 33rpm
GOSPEL TRUTH: *72–74* 4–8
SAVOY: *76–83* 4–8
STAX: *78* 4–8
TRIP: *73* 4–8
VEE JAY: *60–65* 5–15
VOLT: *69* 5–12

WOODS, Stevie
Singles: 7-Inch
COTILLION: *81–83* 1–3
LPs: 10/12-Inch 33rpm
COTILLION: *81–82* 5–8

WOODS EMPIRE
Singles: 12-Inch 33/45rpm
TABU: *81* 4–6
Singles: 7-Inch
TABU: *81* 1–3
LPs: 10/12-Inch 33rpm
TABU: *81* 5–8

WOOLEY, Sheb
Singles: 7-Inch
MGM (12000 series):
   55–61 4–6
MGM (13000 series):
   61–68 3–5
MGM (14000 series):
   68–75 2–4
POLYDOR 1–3
Picture Sleeves
MGM: *59–62* 3–6
EPs: 7-Inch 33/45rpm
MGM: *56–58* 10–15

LPs: 10/12-Inch 33rpm
MGM (3299; "Sheb
Wooley"): *56* **$20–25**
MGM (4136 through
4026): *61–62* **15–20**
MGM (4275 through
4615): *65–69* **8–15**
Also see COLDER, Ben

WOOLIES, The
Singles: 7-Inch
DUNHILL: *66–67* **3–5**
SPIRIT: *66* **5–8**
LPs: 10/12-Inch 33rpm
SPIRIT: *66* **20–30**

WOOLLEY, Bruce, & The Camera Club
Singles: 7-Inch
COLUMBIA: *80* **1–3**
Picture Sleeves
COLUMBIA: *80* **1–3**
LPs: 10/12-Inch 33rpm
COLUMBIA: *80* **5–8**

WORD OF MOUTH (Featuring D.J. Cheese)
Singles: 12-Inch 33/45rpm
BEAUTY & THE BEAST:
85 .... **4–6**

WORLD PREMIER
Singles: 12-Inch 33/45rpm
CAPITOL: *84* **4–6**
Singles: 7-Inch
CAPITOL: *84* **1–3**

WORLD'S FAMOUS SUPREME TEAM, The
Singles: 12-Inch 33/45rpm
ISLAND: *84* **4–6**
Singles: 7-Inch
ISLAND: *84* **1–3**

WORRELL, Bernie
Singles: 7-Inch
ARISTA: *79* **1–3**
LPs: 10/12-Inch 33rpm
ARISTA: *79* **5–8**
Also see McLAREN, Malcom

WORTH, Marion
Singles: 7-Inch
CHEROKEE: *59*. **$3–5**
COLUMBIA: *60–67* **2–4**
DECCA: *67–70* **2–3**
GUYDEN: *59–60* **3–5**
Picture Sleeves
COLUMBIA: *61–62* **2–5**
LPs: 10/12-Inch 33rpm
COLUMBIA: *63–64* **10–18**
DECCA: *67* **8–12**

WRABIT
Singles: 7-Inch
MCA: *82* **1–3**
LPs: 10/12-Inch 33rpm
MCA: *82* **5–8**

WRAY, Bill
Singles: 7-Inch
ABC: *79* **2–3**

WRAY, Link (Link Wray & His Ray Men; Link Wray & His Wray Men; Link Ray)
Singles: 7-Inch
ATLAS: *62* **4–6**
BARNABY: *76* **1–3**
CADENCE: *58* **5–8**
EPIC: *59–61* **5–8**
HEAVY: *68*. **3–5**
KAY. **45–55**
MR. G: *69* **3–5**
OKEH: *67* **3–5**
POLYDOR: *70–74* **2–4**
RUMBLE: *61* **15–20**
SWAN (4137; "Jack The
Ripper"): *63* **6–10**
SWAN (4154; "Week
End"): *63* **5–8**
SWAN (4163 through
4187): *63–64*. **4–6**
SWAN (4201; "Good
Rockin' Tonight"): *65* **10–15**
SWAN (4211 through
4232): *65* **4–6**
SWAN (4239; "Ace Of
Spades"): *65*. **10–12**
SWAN (4244; "The
Batman Theme"): *66*. **5–8**

POPPIN' POPEYE

Link Wray

Price Range

SWAN (4261; "Ace Of Spades"): *66*	$8–10
SWAN (4273 through 4282): *66–67*	3–5
Picture Sleeves	
EPIC: *59*	20–30
LPs: 10/12-Inch 33rpm	
CHARLY	5–8
EPIC: *60*	40–50
POLYDOR: *71–74*	8–10
RECORD FACTORY	20–25
SWAN: *63*	50–60
VERMILLION	20–25
VISA: *79–80*	5–8

Also see GORDON, Robert
Also see DUDLEY, Dave / Link Wray
Also see WRAY, Lucky
Also see WRAY, Vernon
Also see WRAY BROTHERS, The

WRAY, Link / Red Saunders
Singles: 7-Inch

OKEH (7100 series): *63*	4–6
OKEH (7200 series): *67*	3–5

WRAY, Lucky (Link Wray)
Singles: 7-Inch

STARDAY (500 series): *56*	20–25
STARDAY (600 series): *57*	40–50

WRAY, Vernon (With Link Wray)
LPs: 10/12-Inch 33rpm

VERMILLION	20–25

Also see WRAY BROTHERS, The

WRAY BROTHERS, The (The Wray Family)
Singles: 7-Inch

INFINITY: *62*	$6–10
LAWN: *63*	6–10

Members: Link Wray; Doug Wray; Vernon Wray.
Also see WRAY, Doug
Also see WRAY, Link

WRECKING CREW
Singles: 12-Inch 33/45rpm

ERECT: *83*	4–6
Singles: 7-Inch	
ERECT: *83*	1–3
SOUND OF FLORIDA: *83*	1–3

WRIGHT, Bernard
Singles: 12-Inch 33/45rpm

ARISTA: *83*	4–6
Singles: 7-Inch	
ARISTA: *83–84*	1–3
GRP: *81–82*	1–3
LPs: 10/12-Inch 33rpm	
ARISTA: *83*	5–8
GRP: *81*	5–8

WRIGHT, Betty
Singles: 12-Inch 33/45rpm

EPIC: *81*	4–6
JAMAICA: *84–85*	4–6
Singles: 7-Inch	
ALSTON: *68–79*	2–4
ATCO: *83*	1–3
EPIC: *81–83*	1–3
JAMAICA: *84–85*	1–3
LPs: 10/12-Inch 33rpm	
ALSTON: *72–79*	6–10
ATCO: *68*	10–15
EPIC: *81–83*	5–8

Also see ALAIMO, Steve, & Betty Wright
Also see BROWN, Peter, & Betty Wright
Also see KC & THE SUNSHINE BAND

WRIGHT, Billy
Singles: 7-Inch

CARROLLTON: *59*	4–6
SAVOY (776; "Mean Old Wine"): *51*	15–20

Price Range

SAVOY (827; "Drinkin' &
Thinkin' "): *52* **$8–12**

WRIGHT, Charles, & The Watts 103rd Street Rhythm Band
Singles: 7-Inch
ABC: *75* **2–4**
DUNHILL: *73–74.* **2–4**
WARNER BROS: *70–71* **2–4**

LPs: 10/12-Inch 33rpm
ABC: *75* **6–10**
DUNHILL: *73–74.* **6–10**
WARNER BROS: *70–72* **8–12**
Also see SHIELDS, The
Also see WATTS 103RD STREET RHYTHM
BAND, The

WRIGHT, Dale (Dale Wright & The Rock-Its; Dale Wright With The Wright Guys & The Dons)
Singles: 7-Inch
ALCAR: *60* **4–6**
FRATERNITY: *58–59* **5–8**

WRIGHT, Duke
Singles: 7-Inch
MOOLA: *60* **4–6**

WRIGHT, Gary (Gary Wright & Spooky Tooth)
Singles: 7-Inch
A&M: *70–72* **2–4**
WARNER BROS: *75–81* **1–3**

LPs: 10/12-Inch 33rpm
A&M: *70–76* **8–12**
WARNER BROS: *75–79* **5–8**
Also see SPOOKY TOOTH

WRIGHT, O.V.
Singles: 7-Inch
ABC: *75–76* **2–4**
BACK BEAT: *65–74* **2–5**
GOLDWAX: *64* **4–6**
HI: *76–79* **2–3**

LPs: 10/12-Inch 33rpm
BACK BEAT: *65–72* **10–15**
HI: *78–79* **5–8**

Price Range

WRIGHT, Priscilla
Singles: 7-Inch
20TH CENTURY-FOX:
59 .... **$4–6**
UNIQUE: *55* **5–8**

WRIGHT, Ruben
Singles: 7-Inch
CAPITOL: *64–67* **3–5**
WYNNE: *60* **3–5**

WRIGHT, Ruby
Singles: 7-Inch
FRATERNITY: *57.* **4–6**
KING (Except stereo
singles): *59* **3–5**
KING (Stereo singles): *59* **4–8**

WRIGHT, Ruby, & Dick Pike
Singles: 7-Inch
KING (5192; "Three
Stars"): *59* **8–10**
Also see WRIGHT, Ruby

WRITERS, The
Singles: 12-Inch 33/45rpm
COLUMBIA: *79* **4–6**
Singles: 7-Inch
COLUMBIA: *78–79* **2–3**
LPs: 10/12-Inch 33rpm
COLUMBIA: *79* **5–8**

WUF TICKET
Singles: 12-Inch 33/45rpm
PRELUDE: *81.* **4–6**
Singles: 7-Inch
PRELUDE: *81.* **1–3**

WYCOFF, Michael
Singles: 12-Inch 33/45rpm
RCA VICTOR: *83* **4–6**
Singles: 7-Inch
RCA VICTOR: *80–84* **1–3**
LPs: 10/12-Inch 33rpm
RCA VICTOR: *83* **5–8**
Also see CLAYTON, Merry

WYLIE, Richard (Richard "Popcorn" Wylie)
Singles: 7-Inch
ABC: *75* **2–4**

Price Range

XAVIER (Xavier Smith)
Singles: 12-Inch 33/45rpm
LIBERTY: 82 . . . . **$4–6**
Singles: 7-Inch
LIBERTY: 82 . . . . **1–3**
LPs: 10/12-Inch 33rpm
LIBERTY: 82 . . . . **5–8**

XAVION
Singles: 7-Inch
ASYLUM: 84–85. . . . . **1–3**
LPs: 10/12-Inch 33rpm
ASYLUM: 84. **5–8**

XENA
Singles: 12-Inch 33/45rpm
EMERGENCY: 83 . . . . **4–6**

X-25 BAND, The
Singles: 7-Inch
H.C.R.C.: 82 . . . . **1–3**

Y

Y&T (Yesterday & Today)
Singles: 7-Inch
A&M: 81–85 . . . . **1–3**
LPs: 10/12-Inch 33rpm
A&M: 81–85 . . . . **5–8**
LONDON: 78 . . . . **8–10**

YACHTS, The
Singles: 7-Inch
POLYDOR: 79 . . . . **2–3**
LPs: 10/12-Inch 33rpm
POLYDOR: 79–80 . . . . **5–8**
RADAR. **6–10**

YAMBU
Singles: 7-Inch
MONTUNO GRINGO: 75 . . . . **2–4**

YAMASHTA, Stomu
LPs: 10/12-Inch 33rpm
ARISTA: 77 . . . . **5–8**
ISLAND: 76–78 . . . . **5–8**
VANGUARD: 71–74. . . . . **8–10**

Price Range

Also see WINWOOD, Steve

YANKOVIC, "Weird Al"
Singles: 12-Inch 33/4rpm
ROCK 'N' ROLL: 84. . . . . **$4–6**
Singles: 7-Inch
CAPITOL: 79 . . . . **2–4**
ROCK 'N' ROLL: 83–85. . . . . **1–3**
TK: 81 . . . . **2–3**
LPs: 10/12-Inch 33rpm
ROCK 'N' ROLL: 83–85. . . . . **5–8**

YARBROUGH, Glenn
Singles: 7-Inch
PRIDE: 72. . . . . **2–3**
RCA VICTOR: 64–68 . . . . **2–4**
STAX: 73–74. . . . . **2–3**
WARNER BROS: 68–71. . . . . **2–3**
Picture Sleeves
RCA VICTOR: 65 . . . . **3–5**
LPs: 10/12-Inch 33rpm
FIRST AMERICAN: 81 . . . . **5–8**
IM'PRESS: 71 . . . . **8–10**
RCA VICTOR: 64–69 . . . . **8–18**
STAX: 74. . . . . **8–10**
TRADITION: 67–70 . . . . **8–15**
WARNER BROS: 68–71. . . . . **8–12**
Also see LIMELITERS, The

YARBROUGH & PEOPLES
Singles: 12-Inch 33/45rpm
TOTAL EXPERIENCE:
  82–84 . . . . **4–6**
Singles: 7-Inch
MERCURY: 80–81. . . . . **1–3**
TOTAL EXPERIENCE:
  82–84 . . . . **1–3**
LPs: 10/12-Inch 33rpm
MERCURY: 80. . . . . **5–8**
TOTAL EXPERIENCE:
  82–84 . . . . **5–8**
Members: Calvin Yarbrough; Alisa Peoples.

YARDBIRDS, The
Singles: 7-Inch
EPIC (9709; "I Wish You
  Could"): 64. . . . . **15–20**
EPIC (9790 through
  10204): 65–67. . . . . **5–8**
EPIC (10248; "Ten Little
  Indians"): 67 . . . . **10–15**

Price Range

EPIC (10303; "Goodnight
Sweet Josephine"): *68* **$15–20**

Picture Sleeves
EPIC (Except 9709): *65–66* **10–15**
EPIC (9709; "I Wish You
Could"): *64.* **75–100**

LPs: 10/12-Inch 33rpm
ACCORD: *81–83* **5–8**
CHARLY **6–10**
COLUMBIA (11311; "Live
Yardbirds"): *72* **25–35**
(Columbia Special Products issue.)
COMPLEAT: *86.* **8–12**
EPIC (24167; "For Your
Love" - mono): *65.* **60–70**
EPIC (24177; "Having A
Rave Up" - mono): *65* **40–50**
EPIC (24210; "Over Under
Sideways Down" -
mono): *66.* **40–50**
EPIC (24246; "Yardbirds'
Greatest Hits" - mono):
66 . . . . **30–40**
EPIC (24313; "Little
Games" - mono): *67* **40–50**
EPIC (26167; "For Your
Love" - stereo): *65* **30–35**
EPIC (26177; "Having A
Rave Up" - stereo): *65* **30–35**
EPIC (26210; "Over Under
Sideways Down" -
stereo): *66.* **30–40**
EPIC (26246; "Yardbirds'
Greatest Hits" - stereo):
66 . . . . **30–35**
EPIC (26313; "Little
Games" - stereo): *67* **35–45**
EPIC (30135; "The
Yardbirds Featuring
Performances By Jeff
Beck, Eric Clapton,
Jimmy Page"): *70* **50–75**
EPIC (30615; "Live
Yardbirds"): *71* **45–55**
EPIC (34490; "Yardbirds
Favorites"): *77.* **8–10**
EPIC (34491; "Yardbirds'
Great Hits"): *77.* **8–10**
EPIC (38455; "The
Yardbirds"): *83* **5–8**

Price Range

EPIC (48455; "The
Yardbirds"): *83* **$12–15**
(Half-speed mastered.)
RHINO: *82–86* **6–10**
SPRINGBOARD: *72* **8–10**
Members: Eric Clapton; Jeff Beck; Keith Relf;
Jimmy Page; Jim McCarty; Chris Dreja.
Also see ARMAGEDDON
Also see BECK, Jeff
Also see BOX OF FROGS
Also see CACTUS
Also see CLAPTON, Eric
Also see PAGE, Jimmy
Also see WILLIAMSON, Sonny Boy, & The
Yardbirds

YARROW, Peter
Singles: 7-Inch
WARNER BROS: *68–75* **2–4**

LPs: 10/12-Inch 33rpm
WARNER BROS: *72–75* **8–10**
Also see PETER, PAUL & MARY

YAZ (Yazoo)
Singles: 12-Inch 33/45rpm
SIRE: *82–84* **4–6**

Singles: 7-Inch
SIRE: *82–84* **1–3**

LPs: 10/12-Inch 33rpm
SIRE: *82–83* **5–8**
Members: Alison Moyet; Vince Clarke.
Also see MOYET, Alison

Price Range *Price Range*

YELLO
Singles: 12-Inch 33/45rpm
ELEKTRA: *83–85* **$4–6**
RALPH: *81* **4–6**
Singles: 7-Inch
ELEKTRA: *83–85* **1–3**
RALPH: *81* **1–3**
LPs: 10/12-Inch 33rpm
ELEKTRA: *83–85* **5–8**
RALPH: *81* **5–8**

YELLOW BALLOON, The
(Featuring Don Grady)
Singles: 7-Inch
CANTERBURY: *67–68* **4–6**
LPs: 10/12-Inch 33rpm
CANTERBURY: *67* **15–20**
Also see GRADY, Don
Also see SPIRIT

YELLOW JACKETS, The
Singles: 7-Inch
SMASH: *68* **3–5**

YELLOW MAGIC ORCHESTRA, The
Singles: 12-Inch 33/45rpm
A&M: *80* **4–6**
Singles: 7-Inch
A&M: *80* **1–3**
HORIZON: *80* **1–3**
LPs: 10/12-Inch 33rpm
A&M: *80–81* **5–8**

YELLOWMAN
Singles: 12-Inch 33/45rpm
COLUMBIA: *84* **4–6**
Singles: 7-Inch
COLUMBIA: *84* **1–3**
LPs: 10/12-Inch 33rpm
COLUMBIA: *84* **5–8**

YES
Singles: 7-Inch
ATCO: *83–84* **1–3**
ATLANTIC (Black vinyl):
70–78 .... **2–4**
ATLANTIC (Colored
vinyl): *70–78* **4–8**
LPs: 10/12-Inch 33rpm
ATCO: *83* **5–8**

ATLANTIC (100 series):
73 .... **$12–15**
ATLANTIC (500 series):
80 .... **8–12**
ATLANTIC (900 series):
74 .... **12–15**
ATLANTIC (7000 series):
71 .... **10–12**
ATLANTIC (8000 series):
69–71 .... **10–15**
ATLANTIC (16000 series):
80 .... **5–8**
ATLANTIC (19000 series):
77–82 .... **5–8**
Members: Jon Anderson; Rick Wakeman; Steve Howe; Chris Squire; Tony Kaye; Alan White; Bill Bruford; Patrick Moraz; Geoff Downes; Trevor Horn.
Also see ANDERSON, Jon
Also see BANKS, Peter
Also see BUGGLES, The
Also see MORAZ, Patrick
Also see SQUIRE, Chris
Also see WAKEMAN, Rick

YIPES
Singles: 7-Inch
MILLENNIUM: *79–80* **1–3**
LPs: 10/12-Inch 33rpm
MILLENNIUM: *79–80* **5–8**

YORK, Dave, & The Beachcombers
Singles: 7-Inch
P.K.M.: *62* **4–6**

YORK, Rusty
Singles: 7-Inch
CHESS: *59* **5–8**
GAYLORD: *63* **3–5**
KING (5100 series): *58* **5–8**
KING (5500 series): *61–62* **4–6**
NOTE: *59* **10–15**
P.J.: *59* **10–15**
SAGE: *60* **8–10**
Also see MACK, Lonnie, & Rusty York

YOST, Dennis
Singles: 7-Inch
MGM: *75* **2–4**
ROBOX: *81* **1–3**
LPs: 10/12-Inch 33rpm
ACCORD: *81* **5–8**

Price Range

ROBOX: *82* **$5–8**
Also see CLASSICS IV, The

YOU KNOW WHO GROUP, The
Singles: 7-Inch
CASUAL: *65* **4–6**
4 CORNERS: *64* **4–6**
LPs: 10/12-Inch 33rpm
INTERNATIONAL
ALLIED: *65* **15–20**

YOUNG, Barry
Singles: 7-Inch
COLUMBIA: *66* **2–4**
DOT: *65–66* **2–4**
EVA: *63* **3–5**
HOOKS BROTHERS: *66* **2–4**
Picture Sleeves
COLUMBIA: *66* **2–4**
LPs: 10/12-Inch 33rpm
DOT: *65* **10–12**

YOUNG, Faron
Singles: 7-Inch
CAPITOL (2200 through
3900 series): *53–58* **4–8**
CAPITOL (4000 through
4800 series): *58–62* **3–5**
MCA: *79–80* **1–3**
MERCURY: *63–78* **2–4**
Picture Sleeves
CAPITOL: *61* **3–5**
MERCURY: *68* **2–4**
EPs: 7-Inch 33/45rpm
CAPITOL: *54–61* **8–15**
LPs: 10/12-Inch 33rpm
ALBUM GLOBE: *81* **5–8**
ALLEGIANCE: *84* **5–8**
CAPITOL (700 series): *57* **30–40**
CAPITOL (1000 series):
58–59 . . . . **20–25**
CAPITOL (1100 series): *59* **30–40**
CAPITOL (1400 through
2500 series): *60–66* **12–25**
(With a "T," "DT" or "ST" prefix.)
CAPITOL (1500 series): *75* **5–8**
(With an "SM" prefix.)
CASTLE **5–8**
EXACT: *80* **5–8**
FARON YOUNG **15–20**
MCA: *79–83* **4–8**

FARON YOUNG
XCLUSIVE MANAGEMENT HUBERT LONG 66 Exchange Bldg.

Price Range

MARY CARTER
PAINTS (1000; "Faron
Young Sings On Stage") **$35–45**
(Promotional issue only.)
MERCURY: *63–77* **5–15**
PICKWICK/HILLTOP:
66–68 . . . . **8–12**
SEARS **8–12**
TOWER: *66–68* **12–15**
WING: *68* **8–12**
Also see ATKINS, Chet / Faron Young
Also see NELSON, Willie / Faron Young
Also see OWENS, Buck / Faron Young / Fer-
lin Husky

YOUNG, Faron / Carl Perkins / Claude King
LPs: 10/12-Inch 33rpm
PICKWICK/HILLTOP:
65 . . . . **8–15**
Also see KING, Claude
Also see PERKINS, Carl

YOUNG, Georgie (Georgie Young & The Rockin' Bocs; George Young)
Singles: 7-Inch
CAMEO: *58–59* **4–6**
CHANCELLOR: *61* **3–5**
FORTUNE: *57* **5–8**
MERCURY (71259; "Can't
Stop Me"): *58* **30–40**

SWAN: *60* **$4–6**

YOUNG, Jesse Colin (Jesse Colin Young With The Youngbloods)
Singles: 7-Inch
ELEKTRA: *78* **2–3**
REPRISE: *73*. **2–4**
WARNER BROS: *70–77*. **2–4**
LPs: 10/12-Inch 33rpm
CAPITOL (2000 series): *64* **20–25**
CAPITOL (11000 series):
 74 . . . . **8–10**
CAPITOL (16000 series):
 80 . . . . **5–8**
ELEKTRA: *78* **5–8**
MERCURY (61005;
 "Young Blood"): *65* **20–25**
MERCURY (61273; "Two
 Trips"): *70* **10–15**
WARNER BROS: *72–75*. **8–10**
Also see YOUNGBLOODS, The

YOUNG, John Paul
Singles: 7-Inch
ARIOLA AMERICA:
 75–76 . . . . **2–3**
SCOTTI BROTHERS: *78* **2–3**
LPs: 10/12-Inch 33rpm
SCOTTI BROTHERS: *78* **5–8**

YOUNG, Karen
Singles: 7-Inch
WEST END: *78* **2–3**

YOUNG, Kathy (Kathy Young & The Innocents)
Singles: 7-Inch
COLLECTABLES **1–3**
ERA: *72*. **1–3**
ERIC **1–3**
INDIGO: *60–62* **5–8**
MONOGRAM: *62* **4–6**
STARFIRE: *79*. **2–4**
VIRGO: *72* **1–3**
Picture Sleeves
INDIGO: *60–61* **6–12**
LPs: 10/12-Inch 33rpm
INDIGO: *61* **40–45**
Also see INNOCENTS, The
Also see CHRIS & KATHY

YOUNG, Neil (Neil Young & Crazy Horse; Neil & The Shocking Pinks)
Singles: 7-Inch
GEFFEN: *83*. **$1–3**
REPRISE (0785 through
 0898): *68–70*. **3–5**
REPRISE (0911 through
 1396): *70–79*. **2–3**
REPRISE (49000 series):
 79–81 . . . . **1–3**

Picture Sleeves
REPRISE: *80–81*. **1–3**

EPs: 7-Inch 33/45rpm
REPRISE: *72*. **10–15**
 (Jukebox issue only.)

LPs: 10/12-Inch 33rpm
GEFFEN: *83*. **5–8**
REPRISE (2000 series,
 except 2257 & 2296):
 72–81 . . . . **5–8**
REPRISE (2257;
 "Decade"): *77* **12–15**
REPRISE (2296; "Live
 Rust"): *79* **10–12**
REPRISE (6317; "Neil
 Young"): *68*. **40–50**
 (Front cover does NOT have Neil Young's
 name on it.)
REPRISE (6317; "Neil
 Young"): *68*. **8–12**
 (Front cover has Neil Young's name on it.)
REPRISE (6349;
 "Everybody Knows This
 Is Nowhere"): *69*. **10–12**
REPRISE (6383; "After
 The Gold Rush"): *70* **10–12**
REPRISE (6480; "Journey
 Through The Past"): *72* **12–15**
WARNER BROS (Except
 358): *79* **5–8**
WARNER BROS (358;
 "The Big Ball"): *79*. **12–15**
 (Promotional issue only.)
 Also see BUFFALO SPRINGFIELD
 Also see CASCADES, The
 Also see CRAZY HORSE
 Also see CROSBY, STILLS, NASH & YOUNG
 Also see HARRIS, Emmylou
 Also see LARSON, Nicolette

Price Range

Price Range

YOUNG, Neil, & Jim Messina
Singles: 7-Inch
REPRISE: 70. **$3–5**
Also see MESSINA, Jim

YOUNG, Neil, & Graham Nash
Singles: 7-Inch
REPRISE: 72. **2–4**
Also see NASH, Graham
Also see STILLS-YOUNG BAND, The
Also see YOUNG, Neil

YOUNG, Paul
Singles: 12-Inch 33/45rpm
COLUMBIA: 83–85 . . . . **4–6**
Singles: 7-Inch
COLUMBIA: 83–85 . . . . **1–3**
EPIC: 74 . . . . **2–4**
LPs: 10/12-Inch 33rpm
COLUMBIA: 84–85 . . . . **5–8**
Also see BAND AID
Also see SAD CAFE

YOUNG, Retta
Singles: 7-Inch
ALL PLATINUM: 75 . . . . **2–4**

YOUNG, Tommie
Singles: 7-Inch
MCA: 78 . . . . **2–3**
SOUL POWER: 73–75. . . . . **2–4**
LPs: 10/12-Inch 33rpm
MCA: 78 . . . . **5–8**

YOUNG, Val
Singles: 12-Inch 33/45rpm
GORDY: 85 . . . . **4–6**
Singles: 7-Inch
GORDY: 85 . . . . **1–3**
LPs: 10/12-Inch 33rpm
GORDY: 85 . . . . **5–8**

YOUNG, Victor
Singles: 7-Inch
DECCA: 50–57. . . . . **2–4**
EPs: 7-Inch 33/45rpm
DECCA: 50–57. . . . . **3–6**
LPs: 10/12-Inch 33rpm
DECCA: 50–59 . . . . **5–15**
Also see CROSBY, Bing
Also see GARLAND, Judy

YOUNG AMERICANS, The
LPs: 10/12-Inch 33rpm
ABC: 69. . . . . **$5–10**

YOUNG & COMPANY
Singles: 7-Inch
BRUNSWICK: 81. . . . . **1–3**
RCA VICTOR: 69 . . . . **2–4**
LPs: 10/12-Inch 33rpm
BRUNSWICK: 81. . . . . **5–8**

YOUNG HEARTS, The
Singles: 7-Inch
AVCO EMBASSY: 70 . . . . **2–4**
MINIT: 68–69. . . . . **3–5**
LPs: 10/12-Inch 33rpm
MINIT: 69. **10–12**

YOUNG-HOLT UNLIMITED (The Young-Holt Trio)
Singles: 7-Inch
BRUNSWICK: 66–69. . . . . **2–4**
COTILLION: 70–71. . . . . **2–3**
ERIC: 83 . . . . **1–3**
PAULA: 73 . . . . **2–3**
LPs: 10/12-Inch 33rpm
ATLANTIC: 73 . . . . **8–10**
BRUNSWICK: 67–69. . . . . **10–15**
COTILLION: 70–71. . . . . **8–10**
PAULA: 73 . . . . **5–8**
Members: Eldee Young; Isaac Holt.
Also see LEWIS, Ramsey

YOUNG RASCALS, The: see RASCALS, The

YOUNG VANDALS, The
Singles: 7-Inch
T-NECK: 70 . . . . **2–4**

YOUNGBLOOD, Lonnie
Singles: 7-Inch
FAIRMOUNT: 67 . . . . **3–5**
LOMA: 67–68 . . . . **3–5**
RADIO: 81 . . . . **1–3**
SHAKAT: 74. . . . . **2–4**
TURBO: 71–73 . . . . **2–4**
LPs: 10/12-Inch 33rpm
RADIO: 81 . . . . **5–8**
TURBO: 71 . . . . **8–10**

Price Range

Price Range

Also see HENDRIX, Jimi, & Lonnie Young-blood

YOUNGBLOODS, The (Featuring Jesse Colin Young)
Singles: 7-Inch
MERCURY: 66–69............... $5–8
RCA VICTOR: 66–71 4–6
WARNER/RACCOON:
  70–72 2–4
Picture Sleeves
RCA VICTOR: 66 4–6
LPs: 10/12-Inch 33rpm
RCA VICTOR (3000
  series): 80..................... 5–8
  (With an "ALY1" prefix.)
RCA VICTOR (3000
  series): 67.................... 12–15
  (With an "LPM" or "LSP" prefix.)
RCA VICTOR (4000
  series): 70–71 10–15
  (With an "LPM" or "LSP" prefix.)
RCA VICTOR (6000
  series): 72.................... 12–15
WARNER BROS./
  RACOON: 70–72 10–12
  Also see BOWIE, David / Joe Cocker / The
  Youngbloods
  Also see YOUNG, Jesse Colin

YOUNGHEARTS, The
Singles: 7-Inch
ABC: 77......................... 2–3
CANTERBURY: 67................. 3–5
20TH CENTURY-FOX:
  73–76 2–4
LPs: 10/12-Inch 33rpm
ABC: 77......................... 5–8
20TH CENTURY-FOX:
  73–74 8–10

YURO, Timi
Singles: 7-Inch
LIBERTY (55000 series):
  61–64 3–5
LIBERTY (56000 series):
  68 2–4
MERCURY: 64–67................. 2–4
PLAYBOY: 75 2–4
EPs: 7-Inch 33/45rpm
LIBERTY: 61 8–10

(Jukebox issues only.)
LPs: 10/12-Inch 33rpm
COLGEMS: 68 .... $8–10
LIBERTY (Except 7500
  series): 61–63 15–20
LIBERTY (7500 series): 68 8–10
SUNSET: 66–70 6–12
UNITED ARTISTS: 75–76 5–8
WING: 68 8–10
  Also see RAY, Johnnie, & Timi Yuro

YUTAKA
Singles: 7-Inch
ALFA: 81 1–3
Picture Sleeves
ALFA: 81 .... INC
LPs: 10/12-Inch 33rpm
ALFA: 81 5–8
  Also see AUSTIN, Patti

Z

ZZ TOP
Singles: 12-Inch 33/45rpm
WARNER BROS: 84............... 4–6
Singles: 7-Inch
LONDON: 70–77 2–4
SCAT 5–8
WARNER BROS: 80–85............ 1–3
Picture Sleeves
LONDON: 75 2–4
LPs: 10/12-Inch 33rpm
LONDON (Except 1001):
  71–77 8–12
LONDON (1001; "World
  Wide Texas Tour"): 76.......... 12–15
  (Promotional issue only.)
WARNER BROS: 79–85............ 5–8
  Members: Bill Gibbons; Frank Beard; Dusty
  Hill.

ZABACH, Florian
Singles: 7-Inch
CADENCE: 61 2–3
DECCA: 51–54................... 2–4
MERCURY: 56–58................. 2–4
EPs: 7-Inch 33/45rpm
DECCA: 51–54................... 3–8
MERCURY: 56–58................. 3–6

Price Range

LPs: 10/12-Inch 33rpm
DECCA: 51–65 .... **$5–15**
MERCURY: 56–60 .... **5–15**
VOCALION: 63–66 .... **4–8**
WING: 63 .... **4–8**
Also see VALLI, June

ZACHARIAS, Helmut (Helmut Zacharias' Magic Violins)
Singles: 7-Inch
CAPITOL: 69 .... **1–3**
DECCA: 56–64 .... **2–3**
EPs: 7-Inch 33/45rpm
DECCA: 56–58 .... **3–6**
LPs: 10/12-Inch 33rpm
CAPITOL: 69 .... **4–8**
DECCA: 56–61 .... **5–15**
PHILIPS: 62 .... **4–8**
RCA VICTOR: 66 .... **4–8**

ZACHERLEY, John (Zacherley; The "Cool Ghoul")
Singles: 7-Inch
ABKCO **1–3**
CAMEO: 58 .... **5–8**
COLPIX: 64 .... **4–6**
ELEKTRA: 60 .... **4–6**
PARKWAY: 62 .... **3–5**
LPs: 10/12-Inch 33rpm
CRESTVIEW: 63 .... **25–35**
ELEKTRA: 60 .... **25–35**
PARKWAY: 62–63 .... **25–35**

ZADORA, Pia (Pia Zadora & The London Symphony Orchestra)
Singles: 12-Inch 33/45rpm
MCA: 83 .... **4–6**
Singles: 7-Inch
CURB: 83 .... **1–3**
ELEKTRA: 82–83 .... **1–3**
MCA: 83–84 .... **1–3**
WARNER BROS: 78 .... **2–3**
LPs: 10/12-Inch 33rpm
CBS ASSOCIATED: 86 .... **5–8**
ELEKTRA: 82 .... **5–8**
Also see JACKSON, Jermaine, & Pia Zadora

ZAGER, Michael, Band
Singles: 12-Inch 33/45rpm
CBS ASSOCIATED: 84 .... **4–6**
COLUMBIA: 79 .... **4–6**

Price Range

Singles: 7-Inch
BANG: 78 .... **$2–3**
CBS ASSOCIATED: 84 .... **1–3**
PRIVATE STOCK: 78 .... **2–3**
LPs: 10/12-Inch 33rpm
COLUMBIA: 79 .... **5–8**
PRIVATE STOCK: 78 .... **5–8**
Also see TEN WHEEL DRIVE

ZAGER, Michael, Moon Band, & Peabo Bryson
Singles: 7-Inch
BANG: 76 .... **2–3**
Also see BRYSON, Peabo
Also see ZAGER, Michael, Band

ZAGER & EVANS
Singles: 7-Inch
RCA VICTOR: 69–70 .... **3–5**
TRUTH: 69 .... **8–12**
VANGUARD: 71 .... **2–4**
LPs: 10/12-Inch 33rpm
RCA VICTOR (1000
series): 75 .... **8–10**
RCA VICTOR (4000
series): 69–70 .... **12–15**
VANGUARD: 71 .... **10–12**
WHITE WHALE: 69 .... **12–15**
Members: Denny Zager; Rick Evans.

ZAHND, Ricky, & The Blue Jeaners
Singles: 7-Inch
COLUMBIA: 55–56 .... **3–5**

ZAPP (With Roger Troutman)
Singles: 7-Inch
WARNER BROS: 80–85 .... **1–3**
LPs: 10/12-Inch 33rpm
WARNER BROS: 80–85 .... **5–8**
Also see BOOTSY'S RUBBER BAND
Also see ROGER

ZAPPA, Frank (Frank Zappa & The Mothers; Francis Vincent Zappa)
Singles: 12-Inch 33/45rpm
BARKING PUMPKIN
(1114; "Goblin Girl"): 79 .... **15–20**
(Picture disc.)
Singles: 12-Inch 33/45rpm
ZAPPA: 80 .... **4–6**

Price Range

Price Range

Singles: 7-Inch
BARKING PUMPKIN:
82 .... $2–3
BIZARRE/REPRISE
(0800 series): 69–70. 10–15
BIZARRE/REPRISE
(0900 series): 70. 6–10
DISCREET: 73–74 3–5
UNITED ARTISTS: 71 5–8
VERVE: 66–68 8–12
WARNER BROS: 76–77 4–6
ZAPPA: 79–80 2–4
Promotional Singles
DISCREET (586; "Cosmik
Debris"): 74 10–12
EPs: 7-Inch 33/45rpm
REPRISE (336; "Hot
Rats"): 72 35–40
(Promotional issue only.)
UNITED ARTISTS ("200
Motels"): 71 35–40
(Promotional issue only.)
Picture Sleeves
ZAPPA: 80 1–3
LPs: 10/12-Inch 33rpm
BARKING PUMPKIN
(37000 series): 81 10–15
BARKING PUMPKIN
(38000 series): 82–83 5–8
BARKING PUMPKIN
(74000 series): 84 5–8
BIZARRE: 69–72 10–15
DISCREET (2100 series):
74 10–15
DISCREET (2200 series):
74–79 10–12
VERVE (8741; "Lumpy
Gravy"): 68 25–30
UNITED ARTISTS: 71 15–20
ZAPPA (1500 series): 79 12–15
ZAPPA (1600 series): 79 8–12
Promotional LPs
BARKING PUMPKIN
(1111; "Shut Up 'N'
Play Yer Guitar"): 81 12–15
(A mail-order LP offer.)
BARKING PUMPKIN
(1112; "Shut Up 'N'
Play Yer Guitar Some
More"): 81 12-15
(A mail-order LP offer.)

BARKING PUMPKIN
(1113; "Return Of Shut
Up 'N' Play Yer
Guitar"): 81 .... $12-15
(A mail-order LP offer.)
BIZARRE (368;
"Zapped"): 69 20–25
(With cartoon cover.)
WARNER BROS. (368;
"Zapped"): 69 12–15
(Cover pictures Frank Zappa.)
ZAPPA (78; "Sheik
Yerbouti, Clean Cuts"):
79 18–20
ZAPPA (129; "Joe's
Garage, Acts I, II &
III"): 79 18–20
Also see BABY RAY & THE FERNS
Also see GUY, Bob
Also see MOTHERS OF INVENTION, The

ZAPPA, Frank & Moon
Singles: 12-Inch 33/45rpm
BARKING PUMPKIN
(03069; "Valley Girl"):
82 5–8

Singles: 7-Inch
BARKING PUMPKIN
(02972; "Valley Girl"):
82 2–3

Promotional Singles:
BARKING PUMPKIN
(1490; "Valley Girl"): 82 4–6
Also see ZAPPA, Frank

ZAVARONI, Lena
Singles: 7-Inch
STAX: 74 2–4

ZEBRA
Singles: 7-Inch
ATLANTIC: 83–84 1–3

LPs: 10/12-Inch 33rpm
ATLANTIC: 83–84 5–8

ZELLA, Danny, & His Zell Rocks
Singles: 7-Inch
FOX: 59 5–8

ZENTNER, Si, & His Orchestra (Si Zentner's Orchestra & The Johnny Mann Singers)
Singles: 7-Inch
BEL CANTO: *59* $2–4
LIBERTY: *59–67* 2–4
RCA VICTOR: *64–66* 1–3
Picture Sleeves
LIBERTY: *62* 2–4
LPs: 10/12-Inch 33rpm
BEL CANTO: *59* 8–15
LIBERTY: *59–67* 5–15
RCA VICTOR: *65–66* 5–10
SUNSET: *66* 5–10
  Also see DENNY, Martin
  Also see MANN, Johnny, Singers

ZEPHYR
Singles: 7-Inch
PROBE: *70* 5–8
WARNER BROS: *70* 2–4
LPs: 10/12-Inch 33rpm
PROBE: *69* 30–35
WARNER BROS: *71–72* 25–30
  Members: Candy Givens; Tommy Bolin.
  Also see BOLIN, Tommy

ZEPPELIN, Led: see LED ZEPPELIN

ZEVON, Warren (Zevon)
Singles: 7-Inch
ASYLUM: *77–80* 1–3
LPs: 10/12-Inch 33rpm
ASYLUM: *78–82* 5–8
IMPERIAL: *70* 10–12

ZILL, Pat
Singles: 7-Inch
BIG C: *62* 3–5
ERA: *63* 3–5
INDIGO: *61* 3–5
SAND: *61* 5–8

ZINGARA
Singles: 7-Inch
WHEEL: *80–81* 1–3
LPs: 10/12-Inch 33rpm
WHEEL: *81* 5–8

ZINO
Singles: 12-Inch 33/45rpm
PACIFIC 6: *84* $4–6

ZION BAPTIST CHURCH CHOIR, The
Singles: 7-Inch
MYRRH: *73* 1–3

ZOMBIES, The
Singles: 7-Inch
DATE: *68–69* 3–5
EPIC: *74* 2–4
ERIC: *83* 1–3
LONDON 1–3
PARROT: *64–66* 4–6
Picture Sleeves
PARROT: *65* 10–20
LPs: 10/12-Inch 33rpm
BACK-TRAC: *85* 5–8
DATE (4013; "Odyssey & Oracle"): *68* 20–25
  (No promotional mention of "Time Of The Season" on front cover.)
DATE (4013; "Odyssey & Oracle"): *68* 15–20
  (With promo for "Time Of The Season" on front cover.)
EPIC: *74* 10–12
LONDON: *69* 10–15
PARROT: *65* 30–35
RHINO 5–8
  Members: Colin Blunstone; Rod Argent.
  Also see ARGENT, Rod

ZOOM
Singles: 7-Inch
MCA: *83* 1–3
POLYDOR: *81–82* 1–3
LPs: 10/12-Inch 33rpm
A&M: *74* 8–10
MCA: *83* 5–8
POLYDOR: *81* 5–8

ZULEMA (Zulema Cusseaux)
Singles: 7-Inch
LE JOINT: *78–79* 2–3
RCA VICTOR: *74–76* 2–4
SUSSEX: *72–73* 2–4
LPs: 10/12-Inch 33rpm
LE JOINT: *78* 5–8

Price Range

Price Range

RCA VICTOR: 75–76 . . . . $5–8
SUSSEX: 72–74 8–10

ZWOL (Walter Zwol)
Singles: 7-Inch
EMI AMERICA: 78–79 2–3
LPs: 10/12-Inch 33rpm
EMI AMERICA: 78–79 5–8

ABOUT THE AUTHOR

Jerry Osborne's name and background are certainly well known to those in the business and hobby of collectible records. However, to those recently captivated by this fascinating pastime, or soon to be, a bit about Jerry:

Osborne has been authoring record price guides and reference books, full-time, since 1975. His published works on music now number about 30 and counting, as he continues on a several-books-a-year schedule.

In related ventures, Jerry publishes the monthly news and new release newsletter, "The Osborne Report." He writes a weekly newspaper column, titled "Mr. Music," that answers readers' questions on music and records. The column is nationally syndicated by World Features Syndicate. He also is the voice of the syndicated "Mr. Music's History of Rock & Roll Trivia" contest, heard on radio stations in many parts of the country. Jerry is a frequent guest on radio and TV talk shows, as well as a popular subject for newspapers and magazines. He was previously a technical advisor and consultant for the acclaimed ABC-TV nostalgic news-magazine program, "Our World."

With every conceivable accreditation and qualification necessary for the job, Jerry Osborne was clearly our choice to author the House of Collectibles record price guide series. His name offers unparalleled assurance to the reader.

The HOUSE OF COLLECTIBLES Series

☐ Please send me the following price guides—
☐ I would like the most current edition of the books listed below.

THE OFFICIAL PRICE GUIDES TO:

☐ 199-3	**American Silver & Silver Plate** 5th Ed.	$11.95
☐ 513-1	**Antique Clocks** 3rd Ed.	10.95
☐ 283-3	**Antique & Modern Dolls** 3rd Ed.	10.95
☐ 287-6	**Antique & Modern Firearms** 6th Ed.	11.95
☐ 738-X	**Antiques & Collectibles** 8th Ed.	10.95
☐ 289-2	**Antique Jewelry** 5th Ed.	11.95
☐ 539-5	**Beer Cans & Collectibles** 4th Ed.	7.95
☐ 521-2	**Bottles Old & New** 10th Ed.	10.95
☐ 532-8	**Carnival Glass** 2nd Ed.	10.95
☐ 295-7	**Collectible Cameras** 2nd Ed.	10.95
☐ 548-4	**Collectibles of the '50s & '60s** 1st Ed.	9.95
☐ 740-1	**Collectible Toys** 4th Ed.	10.95
☐ 531-X	**Collector Cars** 7th Ed.	12.95
☐ 538-7	**Collector Handguns** 4th Ed.	14.95
☐ 748-7	**Collector Knives** 9th Ed.	12.95
☐ 361-9	**Collector Plates** 5th Ed.	11.95
☐ 296-5	**Collector Prints** 7th Ed.	12.95
☐ 001-6	**Depression Glass** 2nd Ed.	9.95
☐ 589-1	**Fine Art** 1st Ed.	19.95
☐ 311-2	**Glassware** 3rd Ed.	10.95
☐ 243-4	**Hummel Figurines & Plates** 6th Ed.	10.95
☐ 523-9	**Kitchen Collectibles** 2nd Ed.	10.95
☐ 291-4	**Military Collectibles** 5th Ed.	11.95
☐ 525-5	**Music Collectibles** 5th Ed.	11.95
☐ 313-9	**Old Books & Autographs** 7th Ed.	11.95
☐ 298-1	**Oriental Collectibles** 3rd Ed.	11.95
☐ 746-0	**Overstreet Comic Book** 17th Ed.	11.95
☐ 522-0	**Paperbacks & Magazines** 1st Ed.	10.95
☐ 297-3	**Paper Collectibles** 5th Ed.	10.95
☐ 744-4	**Political Memorabilia** 1st Ed.	10.95
☐ 529-8	**Pottery & Porcelain** 6th Ed.	11.95
☐ 524-7	**Radio, TV & Movie Memorabilia** 3rd Ed.	11.95
☐ 288-4	**Records** 7th Ed.	10.95
☐ 247-7	**Royal Doulton** 5th Ed.	11.95
☐ 280-9	**Science Fiction & Fantasy Collectibles** 2nd Ed.	10.95
☐ 747-9	**Sewing Collectibles** 1st Ed.	8.95
☐ 358-9	**Star Trek/Star Wars Collectibles** 2nd Ed.	8.95
☐ 086-5	**Watches** 8th Ed.	12.95
☐ 248-5	**Wicker** 3rd Ed.	10.95

THE OFFICIAL:

☐ 445-3	**Collector's Journal** 1st Ed.	4.95
☐ 549-2	**Directory to U.S. Flea Markets** 1st Ed.	4.95
☐ 365-1	**Encyclopedia of Antiques** 1st Ed.	9.95
☐ 369-4	**Guide to Buying and Selling Antiques** 1st Ed.	9.95
☐ 414-3	**Identification Guide to Early American Furniture** 1st Ed.	9.95
☐ 413-5	**Identification Guide to Glassware** 1st Ed.	9.95
☐ 448-8	**Identification Guide to Gunmarks** 2nd Ed.	9.95

☐ 412-7	**Identification Guide to Pottery & Porcelain** 1st Ed.	$9.95
☐ 415-1	**Identification Guide to Victorian Furniture** 1st Ed.	9.95

THE OFFICIAL (SMALL SIZE) PRICE GUIDES TO:

☐ 309-0	**Antiques & Flea Markets** 4th Ed.	4.95
☐ 269-8	**Antique Jewelry** 3rd Ed.	4.95
☐ 085-7	**Baseball Cards** 8th Ed.	4.95
☐ 647-2	**Bottles** 3rd Ed.	4.95
☐ 544-1	**Cars & Trucks** 3rd Ed.	5.95
☐ 519-0	**Collectible Americana** 2nd Ed.	4.95
☐ 294-9	**Collectible Records** 3rd Ed.	4.95
☐ 306-6	**Dolls** 4th Ed.	4.95
☐ 359-7	**Football Cards** 7th Ed.	4.95
☐ 540-9	**Glassware** 3rd Ed.	4.95
☐ 526-3	**Hummels** 4th Ed.	4.95
☐ 279-5	**Military Collectibles** 3rd Ed.	4.95
☐ 745-2	**Overstreet Comic Book Companion** 1st Ed.	4.95
☐ 278-7	**Pocket Knives** 3rd Ed.	4.95
☐ 527-1	**Scouting Collectibles** 4th Ed.	4.95
☐ 494-1	**Star Trek/Star Wars Collectibles** 3rd Ed.	3.95
☐ 307-4	**Toys** 4th Ed.	4.95

THE OFFICIAL BLACKBOOK PRICE GUIDES OF:

☐ 743-6	**U.S. Coins** 26th Ed.	3.95
☐ 742-8	**U.S. Paper Money** 20th Ed.	3.95
☐ 741-X	**U.S. Postage Stamps** 10th Ed.	3.95

THE OFFICIAL INVESTORS GUIDE TO BUYING & SELLING:

☐ 534-4	**Gold, Silver & Diamonds** 2nd Ed.	12.95
☐ 535-2	**Gold Coins** 2nd Ed.	12.95
☐ 536-0	**Silver Coins** 2nd Ed.	12.95
☐ 537-9	**Silver Dollars** 2nd Ed.	12.95

THE OFFICIAL NUMISMATIC GUIDE SERIES:

☐ 254-X	**The Official Guide to Detecting Counterfeit Money** 2nd Ed.	7.95
☐ 257-4	**The Official Guide to Mint Errors** 4th Ed.	7.95

SPECIAL INTEREST SERIES:

☐ 506-9	**From Hearth to Cookstove** 3rd Ed.	17.95
☐ 530-1	**Lucky Number Lottery Guide** 1st Ed.	4.95
☐ 504-2	**On Method Acting** 8th Printing	6.95

	TOTAL		

SEE REVERSE SIDE FOR ORDERING INSTRUCTIONS